GRUNDIG
THE DIGITAL REVOLUTION
YB 500

A REVOLUTION IN DIGITAL DESIGN

Grundig Yacht Boy 500 World Receiver – Listening to the world has never been easier, with direct digital tuning, 40 programmable memory positions and 90 factory preprogrammed frequencies for world-wide reception. Features Include:

- PLL Tuning
- Dual Clocks
- Programmable Timers with Sleep Timer
- Upper/Lower Side Band
- Audio Power Booster
- Alphanumeric Memory Labelling
- Carrying Case
- Grundig Shortwave Listening Guide

GRUNDIG
P.O. Box 2307
Menlo Park
CA 94026

Local 415 361-1611
US 1 800 872-2228
Canada 1 800 637-1648

P9-DVJ-187

1994 Passport To

Page 27

World Band Radio

Page 53

Page 143

10 YEARS!

1984: It all started with a modest 64-page
book called *Radio Database International*.
Now, *Passport to World Band Radio*, the title
adopted in 1988, has grown into one of the
best-selling annual books worldwide.

ISSN 0897-0157

 **International Broadcasting Services, Ltd.**

Passport To World Band Radio™

1994

Our reader is the most important person in the world!

EDITORIAL

Editor-in-Chief	Lawrence Magne
Editor	Tony Jones
Contributing Editors	Jock Elliott • Craig Tyson
Consulting Editors	John Campbell • Don Jensen
Editorial Contributors	James Conrad (U.S.) • Gordon Darling (Papua New Guinea) • Antonio Ribeiro da Motta (Brazil) • Anatoly Klepov (Russia) • Marie Lamb (U.S.) • *Número Uno*/John Herkimer (U.S.) • Toshimichi Ohtake (Japan) • *Radio Nuevo Mundo*/Tetsuya Hirahara (Japan) • Jairo Salazar (Venezuela) • Don Swampo (Uruguay) • David Walcutt (U.S.)
WorldScan™ Software	Richard Mayell
Laboratory	Sherwood Engineering Inc.
Graphic Arts	Mike Wright, CCI
Cover Artwork	Gahan Wilson

ADMINISTRATION & OPERATIONS

Publisher	Lawrence Magne
Associate Publisher	Jane Brinker
Advertising & Production	Mary Kroszner, MWK
Order Fulfillment	Konrad Kroszner • Mary Kroszner, MWK
Media Communications	Jock Elliott, Consultech Communications, Inc. • Tel +1 (518) 283-8444 • Fax +1 (518) 283 0830

OFFICES

IBS - North America	Box 300, Penn's Park PA 18943 USA • Advertising & Distribution: Tel +1 (215) 794-3396; Fax +1 (215) 794 3410 • Editorial: Fax +1 (215) 598 3794
IBS - Latin America	Casilla 1844, Asunción, Paraguay • Fax +595 (21) 446 373
IBS - Australia	Box 2145, Malaga WA 6062 • Fax +61 (9) 342 9158
IBS - Japan	5-31-6 Tamanawa, Kamakura 247 • Fax +81 (467) 43 2167

Library of Congress Cataloging-in-Publication Data

Passport to World Band Radio.
   1.   Radio Stations, Short wave—Directories.
I. Magne, Lawrence
TK9956.P27   1993   384.54'5   93-22739
ISBN 0-914941-30-5

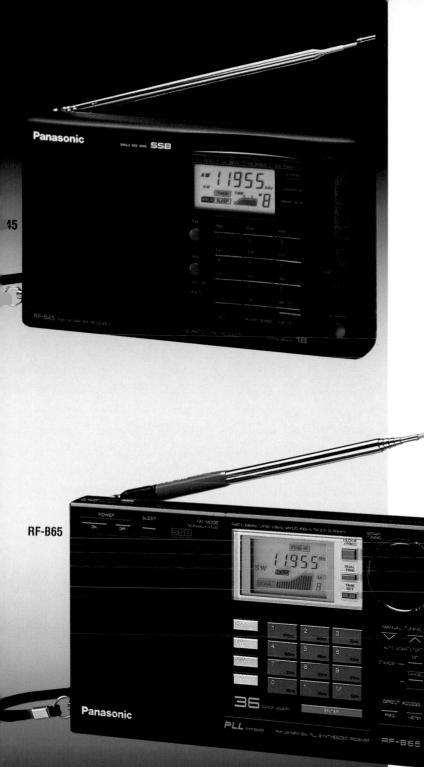

Panasonic presents compact portable multi-band radios.

You don't have to travel the world to see it. With a Panasonic portable multi-band radio you can see it like never before . . . with your ears.

So if you're just going as far as the beach, you can still hear what's going on in the gulf. That's because Panasonic's compact multi-band radios are engineered to be small in size, but they're loaded with features for outstanding performance.

RF-B45 — PLL Quartz synthesized tuner with macro computer control.
- Receives Single Side Band
- Up-conversion double super-hetrodyne system
- 6-way multi-tuning system
- DX/local sensitivity selector
- Frequency step (9kHz/10kHz) selectable
- 18-station preset memory
- LCD multi-information readout
- Quartz clock/timer with sleep/standby function
- 10-key direct time setting
- Feather Touch electronic controls
- Power switch light

RF-B65 — Receives Single Side Band
- PLL quartz synthesized tuner with MCC
- FM/MW/LW/SW, Single Side Band
- SSB fine tuning
- 1kHz-step fine tuning for LW/MW/SW
- 36-station preset memory
- Built-in dual clock/timer keeps time in two zones
- Sleep/standby function
- Multi-function LCD readout with signal strength indicator

So with a Panasonic compact multi-band radio, when it's tea time, you can take the time to tune in the BBC.

SEE THE WORLD THROUGH YOUR EARS

Panasonic®
just slightly ahead of our time.®

THE WORLD
OF WORLD BAND RADIO

WORLD TIME EXAMPLE: 1300 World Time is 7AM (−6 hours) in Chicago. For more, see **Addresses** PLUS section.

+11	+12	−11	−10	−9	−8	−7	−6	−5	−4	−3	−2

Anchor Point, Alaska, USA

Calgary AB, Canada
Salmon Arm BC, Canada

Petropavlovsk-Kamchatskiy, Russia
Magadan, Russia

Vancouver BC, Canada

Sapporo, Japan

Salt Lake City UT, USA
Boulder CO, USA
San Francisco CA, USA
Redwood City CA, USA
Delano CA, USA
Los Angeles CA, USA
Mesquite NM, USA
Dallas TX, USA
Hermosillo, Mexico
Linares, Mexico
Mérida, Mexico
México City, Mexico
Veracruz, Mexico
Belize City, Belize
Guatemala City, Guatemala
San Salvador, El Salvador
Puerto Cabezas, Nicaragua
Managua, Nicaragua
Maracaibo, Venezuela
Mérida, Venezuela
Santa Fé de Bogotá, Colombia
Villavicencio, Colombia
Florencia, Colombia

Tokyo, Japan

Osaka, Japan

Hiroshima, Japan

Kekaha, Kauai Island, Hawai'i, USA
Naalehu, "Big Island," Hawai'i, USA

Saipan, Northern Mariana Islands
Guam

Palau

Biak, Indonesia
Wewak, Papua New Guinea
Madang, Papua New Guinea
Rabaul, Papua New Guinea
Mendí, Papua New Guinea
Honiara, Solomon Islands
Morobe, Papua New Guinea
Port Moresby, Papua New Guinea

Tarawa, Kiribati

Tahiti, French Polynesia

Quito, Ecuador
Iquitos, Perú
Cajamarca, Perú
Pucallpa, Perú
Cobija, Bolivia
Lima, Perú
Guayaramerín, Bolivia
Cusco, Perú
Arequipa, Perú
La Paz, Bolivia
Santa Cruz, Bolivia
Sucre, Bolivia

Port-Vila, Vanuatu

Brandon, Australia

Nuku'alofa, Tonga

Brisbane, Australia

Canberra, Australia

Shepparton, Australia

Melbourne, Australia

Rangitaiki, New Zealand

Levin, New Zealand

Asunción, Paraguay
Encarnación, Paraguay

Santiago, Chile

Malargüé, Argentina
Temuco, Chile

Coyhaique, Chile

Toronto ON, Canada
Montréal PQ, Canada
Scotts Corners ME, USA
St. John's NF, Canada
Sackville NB, Canada
Halifax NS, Canada
Noblesville IN, USA
Bethel PA, USA
Red Lion PA, USA
Cincinnati OH, USA
Upton KY, USA
Nashville TN, USA
Greenville NC, USA
Cypress Creek SC, USA
Birmingham AL, USA
New Orleans LA, USA
Okeechobee FL, USA
Miami FL, USA
Havana, Cuba
Cap-Haïtien, Haiti
Santo Domingo, Dominican Republic
Antigua

Tegucigalpa, Honduras
San José, Costa Rica

Bonaire, Netherlands Antilles
Caracas, Venezuela
Maturín, Venezuela
Georgetown, Guyana
Paramaribo, Surinam
Cayenne, French Guiana

Montsinéry, French Guiana
Belem, Brazil
Manaus, Brazil
Pôrto Velho, Brazil
Recife, Brazil
Salvador, Brazil
Cuiabá, Brazil
Brasília, Brazil
Goiânia, Brazil

Belo Horizonte, Brazil
Rio de Janeiro, Brazil
São Paulo, Brazil
Curitiba, Brazil
Foz do Iguaçú, Brazil
Florianópolis, Brazil
Pôrto Alegre, Brazil
Artigas, Uruguay

Montevideo, Uruguay
Buenos Aires, Argentina

Base Esperanza, Antarctica (−3)

McMurdo, Antarctica (+13)

+11	+12	−11	−10	−9	−8	−7	−6	−5	−4	−3	−2

TO HEAR THE NEWS FASTER, YOU'D HAVE TO BE THERE.

Imagine traveling from London to Moscow to Tokyo, all in the time it takes to touch a button. With Sony's World Band Receiver™ radio, the preprogrammed Station Name Tuning lets you change stations as easily as time zones. For more information, call 1-800-548-SONY. And get your current events while they're still current.

Ten of the Best: Top News Shows for 1994

Click on the TV, see a war. Filmed by one of a handful of outfits that provides the world's nets with nearly all their overseas video. A typical piece opens in a village, with spattered babies and wailing moms. They're Groatlims. We see a lot of the "Groatlims" on the screen these days. The story closes by zooming in on a broken crucifix in a bombed-out church.

Public opinion, once against this war, rallies to the Groatlims. Hardly ever are they told that Groatlims aren't the only victims. At least not by TV, where the availability of pictures drives the story. It's the Bad Guys *vs.* the Kindly Folk. Where the hell is John Wayne, anyway?

TV "newscasts" are little more than uptown soaps.

Reality check: Groatlims do unto their enemies pretty much as they do unto them, but those who control the world's video don't show this. Perhaps they can't get the footage. Perhaps they don't want to.

A century ago, William Randolph Hearst used newspapers to do the same thing, because he wanted to. Spaniards were depicted as beasts violating innocent Cuba. The public got the message, Americans got a war. Hearst sold lots of papers.

Another reality check: TV "newscasts" are little more than uptown soaps, news operas reflecting the views of interested parties. Only rarely is television airtime given over to reporting the various sides to a conflict, or even the real issues. Much is made of the "human factor"—brave little Igor who loses an eye gets more air time than do any of the causes of the conflict—but where is the "why" and "wherefore" of each story? Where are the opposing points of view?

Radio news is news, video news is entertainment.

This is one reason why world band radio is catching on. Its reporters and editors aren't blessed with any special talents or standards. It's just that the environment they work in leads to results that are different from what you get on TV.

It's radio, not video, for one. Radio news is news, video news is entertainment. Old timers, remember "news" at the movies?

Then there are the number and quality of sources. Because so much is on world band from so many perspectives, you wind up being your own editor. Nowhere else can you hear as much news from so many different places.

There are no third-party "gatekeepers,"

The best newscast from North America—on radio or TV—is *Monitor Radio*. Shown: Skip Thurman.

Newshour reaches out from downtown London to every corner of the planet. Its listenership is estimated to be well over 100 million.

either. This means the program isn't edited, tossed, ignored or censored by some unknown hand. Compare this to a network show where a mountain of news is distilled into twenty-odd minutes that are pretty much the same as all the other networks' twenty-odd minutes. TV networks, old-boy networks.

It all adds up to an electronic *Elephant's Parable*. With ordinary news, the elephant is a tree or hose or whatever the editorial elite decides it should be. With world band, the elephant can be the whole elephant. *You* decide.

TV will probably always carry the numbers, even though those numbers continue to slip. It's what more people want.

World band, though, reaches those who are concerned, tired of being handled like intellectual serfs. These are doers, people who aren't going to lie down and take it any more. They make things happen.

World band stations know this. That's why they are on the air, why their audience is up. It's also why you should be listening.

There are millions of stories in the Global Village. Here are where you can find some of the best . . .

"Newshour"
BBC World Service

While CBS News spends $4 million a year to pay one individual, Dan Rather, the BBC World Service doles out a like amount for its entire army of first-rate correspondents to report the news on-the-spot, as it happens. The result is predictable: real news, hard news—not the cutsie-poo, blow-dry-hairdo stuff that passes for news on the Tube.

"Newshour" is almost certainly the best way to get up-to-the-moment news over the air. It not only covers all types of news, including sports and finance, it makes heavy use of those expert correspondents scattered worldwide.

> CBS pays Dan Rather what the BBC pays it entire army of correspondents.

"Newshour" goes out three times a day, which is its only real shortcoming. The times chosen are unhandy for some parts of the world, such as eastern *North America*. For

IF YOU LISTEN TO BBC WORLD SERVICE, YOU SHOULD READ THIS.

The BBC World Service Magazine
– including full Radio and TV Guide

BBC WORLDWIDE

Wherever you are in the world, and whether you are travelling or resident abroad, BBC World Service will keep you informed and entertained.

Broadcasting 24 hours a day, seven days a week, it provides not only the highest standards of news and current affairs, but also many hours a week of top quality sport, drama, science and business features, comedy, and music ranging from Handel to hip-hop.

A subscription to new BBC Worldwide, BBC World Service's own magazine, will make sure you don't miss a thing.

Published monthly in full colour, it contains within its 100 pages comprehensive details of all BBC World Service TV and radio programmes broadcast in English – together with a lively and well written blend of in-depth previews and special features, reflecting all the many facets of the BBC's world.

And if you take out a subscription now, at just £24 or $40 per annum, you'll also pick up a free BBC World Service World Time alarm clock, showing the time in 22 different countries around the world.

To take advantage of this very special offer, which will only last for a limited period, please complete the coupon now.

BBC WORLD SERVICE

that continent, the 1300 morning transmission is heard well on 15220 kHz, plus 9515 kHz for eastern parts, and 9740 and 11820 kHz for areas farther west. The 2100 late-afternoon broadcast is audible in eastern North America on 5975 and 9590 kHz, while the entire continent can tune in evenings at 0500 on 5975 kHz.

If you're in *Europe*, you have access to all three editions. At 0500 there's 3955, 6180, 6195 and 9410 kHz. Incredibly, only 9410 kHz is available for the full hour throughout the year, as in summer the other channels carry separate programming from 0530 onwards!

There's no such awkwardness at 1300, when you can choose from 9410, 9660, 9760, 12095, 15070, 17640 and 17705 kHz. The third and final broadcast goes out at 2100 on 6180, 6195, 7325, 9410 and either 3955 or 12095 kHz.

In the *Middle East*, you have just two shots: 0500 and 1300 on 11760, 15575 and 21470 kHz. The year-round channel of 9410 kHz is also available until 0530 (sigh), and there is an additional summer frequency of 15070 kHz at 1300-1400.

East Asia, like Europe, is served by all three editions; 0500 on 15280, 17830 and 21715 kHz; 1300 on 7180, 9740 and 11820 kHz; and 2100 on 7180 and one or more channels from 9570, 11955 and 15370 kHz. For Australia and the Pacific, there's 1300 on 9740 kHz, and 2100 on 11955 and 15340 kHz.

"The World at Six"
"As It Happens"
Radio Canada International
(Canadian Broadcasting
Corporation)

Although aired by Radio Canada International, both these excellent newscasts emanate from the domestic-service Canadian Broadcasting Corporation. Up-to-the-minute news predominates with the half-hour "The World at Six," while "As It Happens" takes a deeper, longer-term view.

Although much is devoted to Canada and Canadians, there are still plenty of international stories. "As It Happens" also emphasizes people and personal experiences, and if you want to let them know what you think, there's their "Talkback Machine." Here, listeners leave their comments on just about anything they've heard, ranging from

bananas to bigots. Dial +1 (416) 205-3331; all callers are welcome.

"The World at Six" goes out live at 2300-2330, followed on the same frequencies by "As It Happens" (2330-0100). Both are one hour earlier in summer.

In *North America*, listen on 5960 and 9755 kHz. In *Europe*, if you're still awake, tune to 5995 and (summer) 7195 or (winter) 7250 kHz. Additionally, "The World at Six" is beamed to the Caribbean: winters on 9535, 11845 and 11940 kHz; and summers on 11730, 11875, 13670 and 15305 kHz. Many of these are audible in North America. A condensed version of "As It Happens" is also included in the 1300 (1200 summer) weekday broadcast to North America on 11855 and 17820 kHz.

"European Journal"
Deutsche Welle

If you want to know what's going in Europe, this show's for you. Germany is not only the most influential member of the European Community, it also has close ties to several members of the former Warsaw Pact in Europe. So it's no surprise that "European Journal" does a thoroughly professional job of reporting, analyzing and explaining European events and policies from the Atlantic, on one side, to the Urals on the other. Reporters and analysts are articulate and knowledgeable, while production and presentation are of the highest quality.

Although nominally Monday through Friday only, the first edition of the week goes out at 2100 Sunday, with the final one at 0500 Saturday, World Dates. There's also a television version that is shown on local stations and cable-TV systems in parts of North America and elsewhere.

In *North America*, you can hear "European Journal" Tuesday through Saturday (one day earlier, local days) at 0100, 0300 and 0500. The first transmission can be heard winters on 6040, 6085, 6120, 6145, 9515, 9565, 9610, 9700, 9770 and 11865 kHz; summers on 6040, 6085, 6145, 9565, 9700, 9765, 11810, 11865, 13610, 13770 and 15105 kHz.

At 0300, winter channels are 6045, 6055, 6085, 6120, 9535, 9545, 9640, 9705 and 9770 kHz; summers, try 6085, 6145, 9700, 11810, 11890, 13610, 13770, 13790 and 15205 kHz. The third and final broadcast goes out at 0500, winters on 5960, 6045,

It's a small, small world.

Sangean Portables. Get away from it all and still stay in touch

Whether traveling around the world or across town, Sangean portables keep you informed. Tune into international broadcasters or wake up to your favorite morning DJ wherever you are. There's no need to leave it all behind, because Sangean goes where you go… and further.

Multiple Band. Multiple Choice

From the full featured ATS-818CS Digital Receiver with pro-gram-mable built-in  cassette recorder to the world's most advanced ultra compact digital receiver, our  highly acclaimed ATS-606 with Automatic Tuning System which automatical-ly sets up your memory presets at the push of a button, Sangean's complete line of full fea-tured analog and digital receivers offer the utmost in reliability and performance at a price just right for your budget.

To Fully Understand The Difference Between Us And Them… Just Listen

Only Sangean offers you the features and  advanced technology of a high priced communica-tion receiver at a portable price.

Features like Automatic Preset Tuning Systems, PLL Tuning for rock steady short-wave listening, tuneable BFO for single side-band reception, dual displayed time sys-tems, up to 45 presets, AM/FM/FM Stereo in addition to all shortwave bands,  continuously tuneable receivers offering reception of all shortwave bands and any-thing and everything in between, snooze/sleep timers, auto-scan and manual tuning, as well as a host of additional fea-tures making Sangean the most popular choice of shortwave enthusiasts.

All models carry the standard Sangean one year warranty of quality and workmanship: the signature of a  company recognized throughout the world as a pioneer and leader in the design and development of multi-band portable radios. Sangean portables, somehow with them the world seems a wee bit smaller.

Call or write for more information.

SANGEAN
A M E R I C A ,   I N C .
2651 Troy Ave. • S. El Monte, CA 91733 • (818) 579-1600 • FAX (818) 579-6806

A WORLD OF LISTENING

6120, 6130, 9535, 9670 and 9690 kHz; summers on 5960, 6130, 9515, 9605, 9670, 11705 and 13610 kHz. This last slot is best for western North America.

Surprisingly, there is no specific Deutsche Welle broadcast in English to *Europe*, but "European Journal" can still be heard there. In the United Kingdom, reception of the 0500 broadcast to *North America* is usually excellent on 6120 kHz (winters), 9515 kHz (summers) and 11705 kHz (year-round). Also, at 0600 try 11765, 13610, 13790 or 15185 kHz.

In *Asia and Australasia*, listen at 2100 Sunday through Thursday on 6185 (or 13690), 9670, 9765 and 11785 kHz.

"Monitor Radio" World Service of the Christian Science Monitor

The only real competition to the BBC World Service's "Newshour" is "Monitor Radio." It provides that rare combination of excellent and in-depth news reporting coupled with calm presentation.

The BBC is tops in sheer scope of news coverage, but "Monitor Radio" has the juice when it comes to reporting on North America. Yet, it is not restricted just to hard news. There are many lighter items tossed in, including cultural and business reports, ecological news—even the reasons for President Clinton's faulty grammar!

> **"Monitor Radio" is the only real competition to the BBC's "Newshour."**

There is also a "Listener Line" if you want to comment on what you've heard on the program. These recorded opinions are sometimes used in later broadcasts. Just call +1 (617) 450-7777.

The only rub is that over the weekend the station becomes heavily oriented towards

What's going on in the European Community and former Warsaw Pact nations? Tune in Deutsche Welle's *European Journal,* prepared by Dan Karpenchuk, Charles Ashton, Deborah Piroch, Cameron Morell and Willy Mauhs. Especially if you live outside Europe, this is the best way to keep up with events throughout the Continent. A variation, also called "European Journal," is seen on television in some parts of the world.

Ed Thomas and Dave Casanave prepare *Monitor Radio*, heard weekdays over the World Service of the Christian Science Monitor.

Bill Grant

religious matters, with news reduced to barebones bulletins. Come Monday, though, everything returns to normal.

In eastern *North America*, you can hear "Monitor Radio" Monday through Friday at 1000 and 1200 on 9495 kHz; 1800 on 15665 or 17510 kHz; 2000 on any two channels from 7510, 13770, 15665 and 17510 kHz; and 2200 on 9465 kHz. An additional broadcast is scheduled for 0000 Tuesday through Saturday (Monday through Friday, local date) on 5850 kHz.

Farther west, you can listen at 0200 and 0400 Tuesday through Friday and 0600 Monday through Friday on 5850 or 9455 kHz; and again at 1400 Monday through Friday on 13760 kHz. Although beamed elsewhere, 13760 kHz also provides good reception in much of North America at 0000-0555 Tuesday through Friday.

Europe? Try Monday through Friday at 0600 on 5850, 9840 or 9870 kHz; 0800 on 9840 or 11705 kHz; 1400 on 15665 or 17510 kHz; 1800 on 15665 and 9355 or 17510 kHz; 2000 on any two channels from 7510, 13770, 15665 and 17510 kHz; and

2200 on 7510, 13770 or 15665 kHz. The *Middle East* is best served at 1800 on 9355 or 15665 kHz; 2000 on 7510, 13770 or 15665 kHz; and summers at 0200 on 9350 kHz. The 1800 and 2000 broadcasts are heard Monday through Friday; 0200 is Tuesday through Friday only.

East Asia is the most fortunate of all, with virtually sixteen hours daily. All transmissions are Monday through Friday. Choose from 0400 and 0600 on 17780 kHz, 0800 and 1000 on 17555 kHz, 1400 on 9530 kHz, 1600 on 11580 kHz, 2000 on 9455 kHz, and 2200 on 15405 kHz. Listeners in *Australasia* can tune in at 0800 on 13615 and 15665 kHz, 1000 on 13625 kHz, 1200 on 9425 or 15665 kHz, 1800 and 2000 on 9430, 13625 or 13840 kHz, and 2200 on 13625 kHz.

"Dateline"
Swiss Radio International

For a while, people wondered what strange things were stirring within the walls of Swiss Radio International. There was serious talk

THE GRUNDIG SATELLIT 700

World Receiver

FEATURES

- FM, AM (MW), LW and "gapless" (continuous) SW range from 1.6 – 30 MHz. FM stereo operation via headphones or additional external speaker.
- ROM table: 12 or 15 AM stations with 120 frequencies can be tuned from internal memory.
- 64 memories with 8 alternate frequencies.
- Illuminated multifunction display with indication of frequency, wave band, memory position, m-band, stereo, field strength, battery check, station name (8 digits), RDS, USB/LSB, bandwidth, MGC, LOC, ext.ant., ROM table, automatic memory, synchronis detector, clock time, timer setting, time zone, "sleep".
- Alphanumeric indication of station name by programmable letter/digits, for RDS stations automatically.

- Store compare function with indication of station number and station name in the display.
- Ferrite aerial for AM (MW)/LW, multi-match telescopic aerial for FM/SW reception, switchable.
- Direct frequency input. Direct input of SW-bands.
- RDS (Radio Data System): For FM, staion names (PS code) and alternative frequencies can be tuned and memorized (PI/AF code).
- AM: Genuine double superset with band with selector, gain control and preselection tuning. Built-in SSB/BFO section (switchable to USB/LSB) for receiving single-sideband and unmodulated telegraph transmitters.

- 2 x 3 watts peak power. Powerful wideband speaker. Individual bass and treble control.
- Timer: The built-in 24-hour quartz clock timer can be used to pre-program 2 switch-on and switch-off times per day. 2 time zones. Switch-on automatically.
- Connections: Outdoor/external aerial (75Ω coaxial socket for all bands), Line-out (CINCH), external loudspeaker, stereo headphones (3.5 mm jack plug), external power supply 9 – 12 V.
- PLL frequency synthesizer.

Automatic or manual search.
- 3 additional memory elements with a total of 2048 frequencies can be built-in.
- Accu/mains operation.
- Battery operation.
- Dimensions: approx. 30.4 x 17.8 x 6.6 cm (12 x 7 1/2 x 3").
- Weight: approx. 1.8 kg (without batteries).
- Finish: black metallic.

RDS | BFO ∎SSB | SW RANGE 1.6 - 30.0 MHz

◀▮▶ | TIMER

Awards won 1993

1993	PASSPORT TO WORLD BAND RADIO "Best Portable Introduced this Year, Editors Choice"
1993	ELECTRONIC INDUSTRY ASSOCIATION "Innovations Design & Engineering Award."
1993	BBC WORLDSERVICE, "Editors Choice, Five Stars"
1993	AMERICAN SURVIVAL GUIDE "Best Portable World Band Radio Available"

Satellit® 700

The new definition of top class.
The Satellit® 700 is a modern
world receiver which also sets
standards for FM reception.

Radio Data System for FM

First class reception convenience with
RDS for FM, e.g. the station names are
displayed. Connection possibility for
stereo headphones and external loud-
speakers.

Series-equipped with 512 memories

64 memories on 8 frequencies extend
the memory capacity to 512 memory
positions. Digits and letters can be
recalled.

3 further chips ensure up to 2048 memory possibilities

3 easy to build-in chips (not included in deliv-
ery) extend the memory possibilities to 256 stations with 8 alternative frequencies. Overall,
you have then up to 2048 memory positions.

SATELLIT 700 GRUNDIG
ROM table

Code	Station	Display
0.1	Deutsche Welle	DW.....D
0.2	Deutsche Welle	DW.....D
0.3	Radio Austria International	ROEI . AUT
0.4	Swiss Radio International	SRI .. SUI
0.5	Radio Nederland	RNED. HOL
0.6	Radio France International	R F I .... F
0.7	Radio Televisione Italiana	RAI I
0.8	BBC / London	BBC .WS. G
0.9	BBC / London	BBC .WS. G
0.10	Radio Moscow World Service	RMWS.URS
0.11	Radio Moscow World Service	RMWS.URS
0.12	Radio Japan	NHK .... J

Easy operation with the ROM table for SW

12 of the worldwide most important stations
with 96 frequencies can be recalled via
code from the internal memory.

GRUNDIG

P.O. Box 2307, Menlo Park, CA 94026
Local   415 361-1611
US   1 800 872-2228
Canada   1 800 637-1648

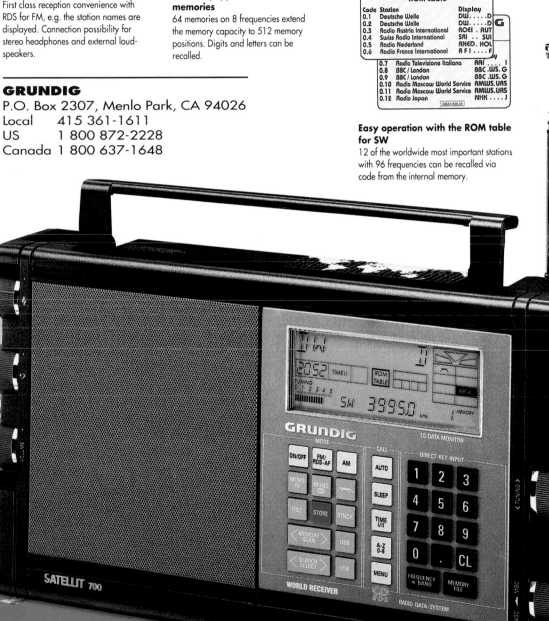

Eduard Rieben

Swiss Radio International's *Dateline* staff includes (from left front) Bob Zanotti, Bob Thomann, Lori Hieber, Devra Pitt and Imogen Foulkes. Just behind: Mike Morris, Gillian Zbinden and Richard Dawson. Back row: James Nason, Paul Sufrin, Julie Hunt, Marion Canute, Peter Capella, Paul English and Mark Butcher.

of dropping world band, where listeners are, and moving to satellite/cable radio, where they aren't.

Insiders at SRI finger the cause as effective lobbying by those with ties to the satellite and cable industries. However, healthy doses of reality have brought about a stage of rethinking to avoid a fiasco. Not only is SRI's world band operation likely to continue, they are planning to establish, along with the French, a major new short-wave relay facility in French Guiana!

One of the best reasons to cheer this is their flagship news program, "Dateline." Currently one of the most news-oriented stations on the international airwaves, SRI takes full advantage of its close proximity to Geneva-based United Nations agencies. It is also near the headquarters of the International Committee of the Red Cross, with which it cooperates.

"Dateline" is a slick half-hour program. It consists of a five-minute bulletin of news, followed by a series of concise, professionally produced interviews and reports. Although one of the best sources of information about war-torn countries, "Dateline" covers a wide array of other topics from biodiversity to European financial affairs. There is also Swiss news, especially on Friday.

"Dateline" is shortened weekends, so tuning in during the week is best. As we go to press, there is talk of including more "cultural" content in SRI's programs. Whether this will affect "Dateline" remains to be seen.

If you're in *North America*, tune in at 0000 on 6135, 9650, 9885, 12035 and 17730 kHz; 0200 on 6135, 9650, 9885 and 12035 kHz; and again at 0400 on 6135, 9860, 9885 and 12035 kHz.

In *Europe*, listen at 0500 weekdays on 3985, 6165 and 9535 kHz; and at 1100 daily on 6165 and 9535 kHz. Both are one hour earlier summers.

Best bets for *Asia and Australasia* are 0900 on 9885, 13685, 17670 and 21820 kHz; plus 1100 and 1300 on 13635, 15505, 17670 and 21820 kHz. There is also a relay via the facilities of China Radio International at 1300 on 7480 and 11690 kHz. A further broadcast (also available to the *Middle East*) can be heard at 1500 on 13635, 15505, 17670 and 21820 kHz; with a repeat at 1700 on 9985, 13635, 15430 and 17635 kHz. For the *Middle East* there is also a broadcast at 2000 on 9885, 12035, 13635 and 15505 kHz.

"International Report"
Radio Australia

Some years back, the Australian Broadcasting Commission decided to have Radio Australia broadcast only to Asia and the Pacific. Since then, listeners in other parts of the world have found themselves struggling to rely on signals beamed outside their area.

That's the bad news. The good news only gradually became apparent: Radio Australia, because it is restricted to broadcasting to Asia and the Pacific, has become the best source for news about that region.

Radio Australia broadcasts news hourly throughout the day, on the hour. News alternates between a straightforward 13-minute bulletin, on one hand, and the half-hour "International Report," which is aired at even-numbered hours.

The actual news content of both programs varies slightly, to coincide with prime-time listening in the intended target areas. In addition, "International Report" sometimes includes regional "specials" devoted to a particular country or region. No surprise that there's even a weekly "Australian edition."

Although Radio Australia does not officially broadcast to *North America*, reception there is still reasonable, even on the East Coast. Conditions vary considerably from season to season, but the best bets are 9580 kHz early mornings year-round, as well as 21740 and 17795 kHz summer evenings. For more choices, here is a broader guide to where and when you are most likely to hear "International Report": 2200 and 0000 on 15320 and 15365 kHz, best in the winter. 0200 and 0400 on 15240, 15320 and 15365 kHz, best in the winter; also, 17795 and 21740 kHz, best in the summer (15240 and 21740 kHz are Sunday through Friday only). Ditto 0600, except for 17795 kHz. 0800 and 1000 on 9580 kHz (5995 kHz can be tried, too). 1200 on 9580 kHz (5995 and 6020 kHz can be tried, too). On the West Coast, you can also try 1400, 1600, 1800 and 2200 on 9580 kHz (plus 11800 kHz at 1400 and 1600).

In *Europe and the Middle East*, you can eavesdrop at 1000 and 1200 on 21725 or 21745 kHz; 1600 on 9510 and 13755 kHz; and 1800 and 2000 on 5880 (or 6000) and 7260 kHz.

East Asia is targeted at 0000 on 15510 or 17715 kHz; 0200 on 21525 kHz; 0400 on 17670 or 17840 kHz; 0600 on 21525 kHz;

0800 on 17750 and 25750 kHz; 1200 on 6080 and 9710 kHz; 1800 on 6080 kHz; 2000 on 6080 and 11855 kHz; and 2200 on 9540 (or 15320), 9645 and 11855 kHz.

"Report from Austria"
Radio Austria International

Most stations lack the resources to compete with the major international broadcasters, although some try. Most content themselves to carve out a niche as invaluable sources of regional news in areas not regularly covered by the larger international stations.

Such is Radio Austria International. Its "Report from Austria" is a valuable source of information not only about national affairs, but also about events in other Central and East European countries—notably Hungary, Romania and the former Yugoslavia.

But this isn't a daily regimen. Some days events warrant such news, other days the program may cover totally different topics. Yet, by listening regularly, you can build up an exceptional picture of what is really happening throughout that important region.

"Report from Austria" is approximately 25 minutes long, and is beamed to *North America* at 0130 (daily) and 0330 (Tuesday-Saturday) on 6015 and 9880 kHz (9870 kHz, beamed elsewhere, also offers reasonable reception in eastern areas); 0530 (daily) and 0630 (Tuesday-Sunday) on 6015 kHz; and 1230 (Monday-Saturday, and one hour earlier in summer) on 13730 kHz.

In *Europe*, tune in at 0530 (winter), 0730 (summer), 0830 (winter), 1030 (Monday-Saturday, winter), 1130 (Monday-Saturday, summer), 1230 (Monday-Saturday, winter), 1430 (summer) and 1530 (winter); all on 6155 and 13730 kHz. There are further airings at 1830 (summer), 1930 (winter) and 2130 (Monday-Saturday, summer) on 5945 and 6155 kHz.

In the *Middle East*, try 0530 winter and 0730 summer on 15410 and 17870 kHz; and 1830 summer and 1930 winter on 9880 kHz.

In *East Asia*, tune in at 1230 (Monday-Saturday, winter), 1330 (Monday-Saturday) and 1430 (summer) on 15450 kHz; while those in the southeast of the continent can listen at 1530 (year-round) and 1630 winter on 11780 kHz.

(continued on page 118)

JRC NRD-535D

"Best Communications Receiver"
World Radio TV Handbook 1992

"Unsurpassed DX Performance"
Passport to World Band Radio 1992

Setting the industry standard once again for shortwave receivers, the NRD-535D is the most advanced HF communications receiver ever designed for the serious DXer and shortwave listener. Its unparalleled performance in all modes makes it the ultimate receiver for diversified monitoring applications.

Designed for DXers by DXers! The NRD-535D (shown above with optional NVA-319 speaker) strikes the perfect balance between form and function with its professional-grade design and critically acclaimed ergonomics. The NRD-535D is the recipient of the prestigious World Radio TV Handbook Industry Award for "Best Communications Receiver."

- Phase-lock ECSS system for selectable-sideband AM reception.
- Maximum IF bandwidth flexibility! The Variable Bandwidth Control (BWC) adjusts the wide and intermediate IF filter bandwidths from 5.5 to 2.0 kHz and 2.0 to 0.5 kHz—continuously.
- Stock fixed-width IF filters include a 5.5 kHz (wide), a 2.0 kHz (intermediate), and a 1.0 kHz (narrow). Optional JRC filters include 2.4 kHz, 300 Hz, and 500 Hz crystal type.
- All mode 100 kHz – 30 MHz coverage. Tuning accuracy to 1 Hz, using JRC's advanced Direct Digital Synthesis (DDS) PLL system and a high-precision magnetic rotary encoder. The tuning is so smooth you will swear it's analog! An optional high-stability crystal oscillator kit is also available for ±0.5 ppm stability.
- A superior front-end variable double tuning circuit is continuously controlled by the CPU to vary with the receive frequency automatically. The result: Outstanding 106 dB Dynamic Range and +20 dBm Third-Order Intercept Point.
- Memory capacity of 200 channels, each storing frequency, mode, filter, AGC and ATT settings. Scan and sweep functions built in. All memory channels are tunable, making "MEM to VFO" switching unnecessary.
- A state-of-the-art RS-232C computer interface is built into every NRD-535D receiver.
- Fully modular design, featuring plug-in circuit boards and high-quality surface-mount components. No other manufacturer can offer such professional-quality design and construction at so affordable a price.

JRC *Japan Radio Co., Ltd.*

Japan Radio Company, Ltd., New York Branch Office – 430 Park Avenue (2nd Floor), New York, NY 10022, USA Tel: (212) 355-1180 / Fax: (212) 319-5227

Japan Radio Company, Ltd. – Akasaka Twin Tower (Main), 17-22, Akasaka 2-chome, Minato-ku, Tokyo 107, JAPAN Tel: (03) 3584-8836 / Fax: (03) 3584-8878

Ten of the Best: 1994's Top Entertainment

World band radio offers more shows than ice cream has flavors. To help scoop out what you want from this Häagen-Dazs of the air, here are ten entertainment classics. They have the quality, diversity and originality to set them apart from the pack, to add sparkle to your day.

These are among the very best of world band's offerings. Yet, there are many other juicy offerings, detailed in "What's On Tonight?" farther on in this edition. That "TV Guide" type section leads you through the ceiling-to-floor choices of what's on in English around the clock.

"Play of the Week"
BBC World Service

Here is just what you'd expect from the BBC, and more. Drama at this level is hard to find even in most theaters, never mind on everyday radio or TV. Its list of authors reads like a Who's Who of world literature throughout the ages: Euripides, Shakespeare, Sterne, Cervantes, Ibsen, Greene, Shaw, García Lorca, Pinter, Stoppard, and so on.

Here's the kicker, and why this show beats the predictable "Laura Ashley" classics on BBC-TV: Some of its most moving plays aren't from any titans of the marquee, at all. Instead, they're written by amateurs—BBC listeners, ordinary people—in places like India and Nigeria and Sri Lanka. That's the real secret behind this show's electric success, and why it is "must" listening for any lover of good drama.

> **Beats the predictable "Laura Ashley" classics on BBC-TV.**

Another is acting. Scofield, Dench, Matthau, "Gandhi" Kingsley. Ditto production, direction.

Just as the roster of authors and playwrights is endless, so, too, are the types of plays: Greek tragedies, period comedies, sci-fi, whodunits, political thrillers—the full range of human experience and imagination.

Length varies, too. In order to minimize "tyranny of the clock," which can frustrate creative energies, each play runs anywhere from 30 to 180 minutes. A half hour? You get two plays for the price of one. With the Big 180, you've got to tap your fingers for a week until the conclusion. Most times, though, it is a full hour or 90 minutes straight through.

"Play of the Week" curtsies three times each Sunday so you can hear it at a convenient time. North Americans have their first shot at 0101 World Time (Saturday evening local date) on 5975, 6175, 7325, 9590 and

---

Jorge Zambrano, of *Música del Ecuador*, plays on the *charango*, a Latin stringed instrument.

Russia's musical heritage is among the world's most finest. You can hear it over Radio Moscow International's *Folk Box*, presented by Olga Shapovalova (seated), Olga Nesterova and host Kate Starkova.

9915 kHz; with a repeat twelve hours later, at 1201, on 6195, 9740 and 15220 kHz. For *Europe* it's heard at 1201 on 9410, 9750, 9760, 12095, 15070 and 17640 kHz; with a second chance later in the day, at 1901, on 3955 (winter), 6195 and 9410 kHz, plus the summer frequencies of 12095 and 15070 kHz.

Listeners in the *Middle East* have the same opportunities as those in Europe. Try at 1201 on 11760, 15575, 17640 and 21470 kHz; and again at 1901 on 7160, 9410, 9740, 12095 and 15070 kHz. In *East Asia*, listen at 0101 on 15280, 17790 and 21715 kHz; or at 1201 on 9740 kHz, also available for *Australia and the Pacific*. If you're "down under," you can also tune in at 1901 on 11955 kHz.

When "Play of the Week" runs 90 minutes, it starts a half hour early.

"Folk Box"
Radio Moscow International

Eclectic, exotic, informative, entertaining, original, enjoyable: a treasure-chest of ethnic music. And not just music. Where else can you discover the rites and rituals of some 300 million of the most ethnically and culturally diverse people around?

Step right up to the Greatest Folk Music Show on Earth! Thrill to the rousing sounds of balalaikas! Marvel at the pentatonic acrobatics of Tatars and Bashkirs! Be seduced by chang and Kashgar rubabs!

With so much succulent raw material at its disposal, "Folk Box" airs everything from sublime songs of the Siberian steppe to the guttural gymnastics of Central Asia. Its authenticity and originality, when added to the friendly presentation by host Kate Starkova and friends, makes for 25 minutes of uncommon listening pleasure.

Seduced by chang and Kashgar rubabs!

The program is broadcast several times a week, so you can hear it anywhere in the world. It's available to all continents, with most editions being aired one hour earlier in summer.

In *North America* during the winter, try 0031 World Time Monday and Saturday (Tuesday and Sunday evenings, local time)

VOA's Leo Sarkisian, writer and producer of the popular weekly program *Music Time in Africa*, and Rita Rochelle interview Ko Nimo in Kumasi, Ghana.

on 6045, 7105, 9750, 9870, 12050, 15425 and 21480 kHz. In summer, one hour earlier, best reception is likely to be found on the western side of the continent on channels like 12050, 15410 and 15425 kHz. Listeners in eastern North America should try dialing around between 9750 and 9890 kHz, with 11790 kHz a secondary bet.

There is another chance on these same channels at 0231 Tuesday (0131 during summer), but reception can be iffy.

The final opportunity for North America is at 0530 Thursday on 7150, 7165, 7180 and 9870 kHz; summers at 0330 on 9530, 9765 and 11790 kHz. If you can't hear anything on these channels, try other nearby frequencies—RMI channel usage often resembles an aerial game of musical chairs.

Europeans can tune in at 0931 Wednesday and Saturday, 1231 Tuesday and 1531 Monday (one hour earlier in summer) on (among others) 13650, 15345 and 15540 kHz. For other frequencies, dial around the 11 and 15 MHz segments, except for 1531 winters, when 7 and 9 MHz channels will yield better results.

Europe has two further opportunities, 1831 Friday and 2131 Thursday, with fre-

quencies in the 7 and 9 MHz segments being reasonable bets. Best summer reception (at 1731 Friday and 1931 Thursday) can generally be found in the 9 and 11 MHz segments—tune around to find a suitable channel.

In *East Asia*, at 0031 Monday and Saturday (an hour earlier in summer), dial around the 7, 9 and 11 MHz segments, where a number of frequencies should provide reasonable reception. At 0531 Thursday (0331 during summer) the principal Asian targets are in the south and southeast of the continent. Fortunately, many of these channels are also widely heard in other parts of Asia. Good workhorse channels include 21690 and 21790 kHz, but 15 and 17 MHz frequencies should also provide good reception.

For the 0931 Wednesday and Saturday broadcasts (one hour earlier in summer), try the same channels as at 0531 Thursday, although listeners in the northeast of the continent would probably do better within the 7 and 9 MHz segments during the winter months.

Most of the 15 and 17 MHz channels are still available for the 1231 Tuesday

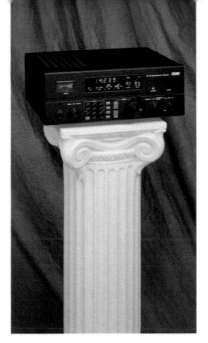

Innovation, Ingenuity, Intelligence.

Seeker 500E™ Wideband Receiver

SASI engineering innovation enabled the production of the Seeker 500E™— an ultra-miniaturized wideband receiver with frequency coverage from 2-950 MHz. It represents the cutting edge in advanced receiver technology with stealth-style portability. Contact SASI for more information on the Seeker 500E™.

Remote Control Scanning System

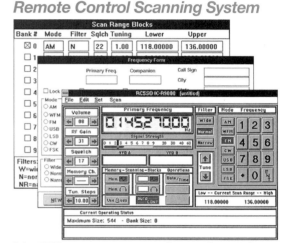

SASI's RCSS™ provides computer control over Seeker 500E™ and ICOM™ models R7000, R7100, R71 and R9000 receivers. RCSS™ simplifies receiver operation while providing feature-rich, enhanced control over all receiver functions. Contact SASI for more information on RCSS™. Both PC and Mac versions available.

■ ■

You only find the innovation and ingenuity required to produce intelligent products like the Seeker 500E™ and RCSS™ in a small engineering firm where the engineers are encouraged to explore the unexplored and push the envelope of technology. Systems and Software International developed these and other advanced products by making quality paramount and encouraging individual thinking.

Fundamental to SASI's mission is the commitment to develop and produce real products that meet real needs and to support these products over their full life cycle. This philosophy has enabled SASI to create products such as the stealth-like Seeker 500E™ ultra-miniaturized wideband receiver and the RCSS™ remote control scanning system.

SASI doesn't rest on todays accomplishments, however. To gain the advantage over tomorrows technologies SASI aggressively pursues projects identified by its customers in the fields of communications engineering, computer and software engineering, and systems engineering. SASI offers a variety of services including requirements analysis, system design, system installation, and "special projects".

SASI's clients include private industry, government organizations, military groups, and entrepreneurs. The one thing they all have in common is a belief in SASI's dedication to quality and commitment to excellence.

For more information on SASI, RCSS™ or the Seeker 500E™, contact SASI by calling **(703) 680-3559**.

Systems & Software International is a small business and manufactures all equipment in the USA. Please contact us at:
4639 Timber Ridge Drive, Dumfries, Virginia, 22026-1059, USA; (703) 680-3559; Fax (703) 878-1460; Compuserve 74065,1140

YOU EXPECT THE WORLD FROM ICOM RECEIVERS

ICOM's IC-R71A and IC-R7000 are the professional's choice for receiving international broadcasts, aircraft, marine, business, emergency services, television, and government bands. These people demand the finest in communications and so do you. ICOM puts the world at your fingertips with the IC-R7000 25-2000MHz* and IC-R71A 0.1-30MHz commercial quality scanning receivers.

Incomparable Frequency Control.
Both the IC-R71A and IC-R7000 feature **direct frequency access** via their front keypad, main tuning dial, optional infrared remote control and/or computer interface adapter. **Incredible Flexibility!**

Full Coverage, Maximum Performance.
The superb IC-R71A is your key to worldwide SSB, CW, RTTY, AM and FM (optional) communications plus foreign broadcasts in the 100kHz to 30MHz range. It features IF Notch, low noise mixer circuits and a 100db dynamic range. The pacesetting **IC-R7000** receives today's hot areas of interest, including aircraft, marine, public services, amateur, and satellite transmissions in the 25MHz

to 2000MHz* range. It includes **all mode operation** low noise circuits plus outstanding sensitivity and selectivity. The IC-R71A/R7000 combination is your window to the world!

The IC-R71A is a shortwave listener's delight. Its **32 tunable memories** store frequency and mode information, and they are single-button reprogrammable **independent of VFO A or VFO B's operations!** Dual width, an adjustable noise blanker, panel selectable RF preamp, and selectable AGC combined with **four scan modes** and all-mode squelch further enhance the IC-R71A's HF reception!

The IC-R7000 features 99 tunable memories and **six scanning modes**. It even scans a band and loads memories 80 to 99 with active frequencies without

operator assistance! Additional features include selectable scan speed pause delays, wide/narrow FM reception and high frequency stability.

Options. IC-R7000: RC-12 remote control, EX-310 voice synthesizer, CK-70 DC adapter, MB-12 mobile bracket. IC-R71A: RC-11 remote control, EX-310 voice synthesizer, CK-70 DC adapter, MB-12 mobile bracket, FL-32A 500Hz, FL-63A 250Hz and FL-44A filters.

See these quality ICOM receivers at your local authorized ICOM dealer today or call 1-206-450-6088.

*Specifications of the IC-R7000 guaranteed from 25-1000MHz and 1260-1300MHz. No coverage from 1000-1025MHz.

ICOM America, Inc., 2380-116th Ave. N.E., Bellevue, WA 98004
Customer Service Hotline (206) 454-7619
CUSTOMER SERVICE CENTERS:
18102 Skypark South, Ste. 52-B, Irvine, CA 92714
1777 Phoenix Parkway, Suite 201, Atlanta, GA 30349
ICOM CANADA, A Division of ICOM America, Inc.,
3071 - #5 Road, Unit 9, Richmond, B.C. V6X 2T4 Canada

All stated specifications are subject to change without notice or obligation. All ICOM radios significantly exceed FCC regulations limiting spurious emissions. Receivers493

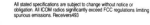

ICOM
First in Communications

version but, again, listeners in the northeast should try the lower frequencies. In winter, dial around the 6, 7 and 9 MHz segments, while 11 and 15 MHz should be better at 1131 in summer.

Finally, there is another edition at 2131 winter Thursdays on 7 and 9 MHz channels; and 1931 summers on an ample choice of frequencies in the range between 15350 and 15600 kHz.

In *Australia and the South Pacific*, try 0031 Monday and Saturday (one hour earlier in summer) and 0531 Thursday (0331 during summer) on 15420, 21690 and 21790 kHz, plus frequencies between 17550 and 17720 kHz. Several of these channels are still available for the repeats at 1231 Tuesday, and 0931 Thursday and Saturday (both one hour earlier in summer). The other opportunity is at 2131 Thursday (1931 summer) on channels in the 9690-9890 and 15390-15590 kHz ranges.

"Discovery"
"Science in Action"
BBC World Service

These two sister programs are arguably the world's best for keeping up with science and technology. They respect your intelligence, yet present findings that even techno-dummies can enjoy. Add to this that they stuff the equivalent of two pounds of knowledge into a one-pound bag, and you have a winning formula.

> The BBC's two science offerings are enjoyable whether you have a Ph.D in particle physics or are a science tortoise.

"Discovery" emphasizes the latest in scientific activity. Topics range from genetic engineering to global temperature mapping and human resonance. (A lowering of temperature in the tropics can affect human resonance in Brooklyn, New York.)

"Science in Action" spreads its wings a little broader, covering both science and technology. The scope of the program is at least as extensive as that of "Discovery," with subjects ranging from the sublime to the bizarre.

Try this: the study of worms, several yards or meters long, two miles below the sea . . . computer technology advancing medicine . . . possible new cures for multiple sclerosis and rheumatoid arthritis . . . simultaneous multiple-language translation by computers . . . cheaper and cleaner energy sources . . . instruments for astronauts. All this, and it's enjoyable whether you have a Ph.D in particle physics or are a science tortoise.

Both shows air three times a week. "Discovery" is targeted to *Europe* at 1001 Tuesday on 9750, 9760, 12095 and 15070 kHz; and later the same day at 1830 on 6195, 7325 (winter), 12095 (summer) and 9410 kHz. It is also available to the *Middle East* at these same times, at 1001 on 11760, 15575, 17640 and 21470 kHz; and at 1830 on 9410, 9740, 12095 and 15070 kHz. There is an additional repeat at 0330 Wednesday on 9410, 11760 and 11955 kHz.

In *North American*, there's just one opportunity: 0330 Wednesday (Tuesday evening local date), winters on 5975, 7325 and 9915 kHz; and summers on 5975 and 12095 kHz.

In *East Asia*, you also get only one shot, 1001 Tuesday on 9740, 17830 and 21715 kHz; while in *Australia and the Pacific* you can choose between this same slot and later the same day at 1830, both on 11955 kHz.

Broadcasts of "Science in Action" follow a somewhat similar pattern, with *North America* again receiving only a small slice of the cake. Best bet is 1615 Friday on 9515 and 15260 kHz, although easterners should be able to hear the repeat at 2030, later the same day, on 5975 and 15260 kHz.

In *East Asia* there's only one weekly slot, 1001 Sunday on 17830 and 21715 kHz. This is also available for *Australia and the Pacific* on 11750 and 17830 kHz, should listeners there have missed the 2030 Friday edition on 11955 and 15340 kHz.

For *Europe* there's 1615 Friday on 6195, 9410 and 12095 kHz; with a repeat at 2030 the same day, winters on 7325 and 9410 kHz, and summers on 6180, 6195, 7325, 9410 and 12095 kHz. The third, and final, broadcast goes out at 1001 Sunday on 9750, 9760, 12095 and 15070 kHz. It is also available to the Middle East at 1615 Friday on 9410, 9740, 12095 and 15070 kHz; and at 1001 Sunday on 11760, 15575, 17640 and 21470 kHz.

Both shows take a short break around midsummer, just like the rest of us.

Blues, Rags and All That Jazz, hosted each Sunday by Britain's Bill Rapley over Ecuadorian station HCJB. The best in classic jazz and blues.

"Music from China"
China Radio International

If you believe that China is populated exclusively by Chinese of Han descent, here's a surprise. The ethnic makeup of the world's most populous country is a patchwork of diverse peoples and cultures. They don't all look alike, and they don't all sound alike, either.

This diversity is reflected in China Radio International's "Music from China." Ancient Tibetan chants, rarely heard before by Western ears; lusty ballads by Mongolian tribesmen; traditional Chinese opera ("Gong with the Wind"); ehru, zheng and horse-bone fiddling—all these and more are featured at one time or another.

"Music from China" is heard Saturday in each listening area during the final third of each 55-minute transmission. In *Europe*,

listen in around 2035 or 2135 on 6950 (winter), 11500 (summer) and 9920 kHz; and again at 2235 winters on 7170 kHz, summers on 9880 kHz.

In eastern *North America*, try 1235 on 9655 (winter) or 15210 kHz. For listeners farther west there are two morning broadcasts, 1435 and 1535 winters on 7405 kHz, and 1335 and 1435 summers on 11855 kHz. Repeat broadcasts are available to the North American audience at 0035 on 9770 and 11715 kHz; 0335 on 9690, 9770 and 11715 kHz; 0435 summers on 11840 kHz, year-round on 11680 kHz; and 0535 winters on 11840 kHz.

In *Southeast Asia* (there is no transmission for East Asia), tune to 9715 and 11660 kHz for the 1235 and 1335 editions; while in *Australia and the Pacific* you'll find it at 0935 and 1035 on 11775, 15440 and 17710 kHz. Failing this, there are two more opportunities, at 1235 on 11795 and 15440 kHz, and 1335 on 15440 kHz.

"Blues, Rags and All That Jazz"
HCJB—Voice of the Andes
FEBC International

Far from being just for jazz buffs, "Blues, Rags and All That Jazz" appeals across the board to folks who normally avoid jazz like castor oil. It's where you can relax to the haunting sounds of Sidney Bechet or kick up your heels in the company of the Red Hot Peppers, Kid Ory, Jelly Roll Morton and Johnny Dodds.

Included are classic performances from some of New Orleans' greatest names, plus more recent recordings from European artists like Chris Barber, Terry Lightfoot, Monty Sunshine and Alex Welsh—masters who reached the height of their popularity in pre-Beatles England.

"Blues, Rags and All That Jazz" is available in HCJB's *European* service at 2130 Sunday on 15270 (or 21480) and 17790 kHz, plus 17490 and 21455 kHz in the in the upper-sideband mode. For *North America*, it's on Saturday at 0630 on 11925 kHz, plus 17490 and 21455 kHz upper sideband. Alas, most world band radios are ill-equipped to receive such signals. That's the bad news. The good news is that the program is now also carried via FEBC International in the Philippines, which is widely heard in *East and South East Asia*. Listeners in these areas can tune in at 1000 Thursday on 11690 kHz.

R.L. Drake R-8 Receiver with 5 built-in Filters. Features: • Good dynamic range • Excellent stability, synchronous detection • A notch filter • Passband tuning • Covers 110 kHz to 30 MHz • 100 memory channels.

SONY ICF-SW55 MINIFICENT OBSESSION. A miracle of miniaturization. You'll love sensitivity/selectivity. Features: • 25 page (5 freq's per page) memory • Super lite-weight.

PHILIPS DC-777 AM/FM/ Shortwave for your car! Finally a good shortwave radio/ cassette deck to put into your car. Features: • PLL Quartz synthesis Digital Tuner • Integral Amplifier (2x25 Watts RMS) • Low distortion output. • Optional retractable anti-theft cage.

BEST UHF/VHF reciever - Icom IC-R7100 Features: • 25-1999 MHz continuous. • SSB, AM, FM (Triple-conversion superheterodyne), WFM (Double-conversion superheterodyne) • 900 memories.

DRESSLER ARA-1500: Compact (20" tall, 4" round) and powerful with 11-16 dB gain • Better than discone and takes less space • Mount indoors or outdoors • Comes with 12 VDC adaptor, 25" coax cable with "N" type connectors and mounting brackets.

WHAT ARE YOU MISSING?

To know everything that's happening on the HF bands, you need a listing of the hundreds of stations other than international broadcasts. You need the CONFIDENTIAL FREQUENCY LIST. Popular Communications Magazine says: "Can't imagine anyone attempting to listen to HF voice or CW/RTTY/FAX communications without a handy copy." Recognized worldwide as the indisputable leader and most comprehensive list of utilities from 1605 kHz to 28 MHz giving world-wide coverage. Call sign, country, time and pertinent notes listed for aeronautical, marine, embassy, weather, press, feeders, INTERPOL, time signals, channel markers and more. Includes 544 pages with 35,000 stations listed by frequency, maps of NAVAREAS, World Time Charts and full explanation of abbreviations.

**Book cost is only $22.95.
Add $4.00 in USA
and Canada. $15.00 overseas.**

*Easy ride from anywhere in the tri-state area,
exit 172 off of Garden State Parkway.*

JRC NRD-535D BEST SHORTWAVE RECEIVER ON THE MARKET. Features: • Synchronous detection • Variable AM bandwidth • ECSS • All modes • .1-30 MHz • NVA-319 matching speaker.

YAESU FRG-100 Features: • Coverage 50 kHz - 30 MHz • Microprocessor control of major functions. • Tuning steps 10 Hz, 100 Hz, 1 kHz • 50 tunable memory channels • Modifications: Let GILFER modify this excellent receiver to tighter the skirts on both the wide and narrow settings. For a reasonable price, you can get excellent selectivity improvement. Call (201) 391-7887 for specs and prices.

DATONG Active antennas. Enjoy the fine quality of the imported English AD-270 (indoor) or the AD-370 (outdoor, shown above).

DRESSLER ARA-60: Best selling indoor/ outdoor model: • Only 37" tall • 10 dB gain from 200 kHz to 30 MHz (with limited performance up to 100MHz). • Includes 18 VDC adapter, cable and brackets.

Yleisradio

Tired of English? Here's a different "best" . . . the best in *Latin* from Radio Finland, presented each week by Reijo Pitkäranta and Virpi Seppälä-Pekkanen.

"Concert Hall"
"International Recital"
"From the Proms"
BBC World Service

"Concert Hall," "International Recital" and "From the Proms": three variations on classical music at its very best. Virtually all styles and periods of recordings are featured, from medieval madrigals to twentieth-century masterpieces.

Although "Concert Hall" runs for several months at a clip, the series is periodically interrupted by "International Recital," a series of performances by some of the world's finest musicians. These are aired live on Sundays, and repeated twice the following Tuesday. Full information can be obtained from International Recital, BBC World Service, Bush House, P.O. Box 76, London WC2B 4PH, United Kingdom.

As with "Concert Hall," quality and variety abound. One week there's gypsy music from the Swiss-Hungarian I Salonisti, the following week the nimble fingers of Brazilian guitarist Christina Azuma.

The high point of the year, though, is the annual orgy of world-class Promenade Concerts, "the Proms." From mid-July to roughly mid-September, "From the Proms" features a feast of almost thirty concerts, most live, from London's Royal Albert Hall.

European fans can tune in at 1515 Sunday on 6195, 9410, 9750, 9760, 12095 and 15070 kHz; and again at 0815 Tuesday on 7325, 9410, 12095, 15070 and 17640 kHz. These times are also available for the *Middle East*: 1515 Sunday on 12095, 15070 and 21470 kHz (plus 9410 kHz in winter); and 0815 Tuesday on 12095 or 17640 kHz.

In *North America*, try 1515 Sunday on 9515, 15260 and 17840 kHz; and 2315 Tuesday on 5975, 6175 and 9590 kHz. An additional winter frequency of 7325 kHz is replaced by 12095 and 15070 kHz during the summer months.

In *East Asia* there is a chance to hear all three transmissions; 1515 Sunday on 7180 and 9740 kHz; 0815 Tuesday on 15280, 15360, 17830 and 21715 kHz; and 15 hours later, at 2315, on 11945, 11955 and 15280 kHz. In *Australasia*, listeners can choose between 1515 Sunday on 9740 kHz and 0815 Tuesday on 11955 and 17830 kHz.

Note, however, that when there are live "Prom" broadcasts, these start at 1830, irrespective of the date. They are available for *Europe* on 6180, 6195, 9410, 12095 and 15070 kHz; to the *Middle East* on 9410, 9740, 12095 and 15070 kHz; and in *Australia and the Pacific* on 11955 kHz. Listeners in *East Asia and North America* miss out, but can still hear the repeats at the usual times.

"Music Time in Africa"
Voice of America

African music has influenced modern sounds not only in North America and the Caribbean, but also in places as far afield as Europe and South America. Much music the world over owes its very existence to this influence. Yet, what is happening in the musical motherland of Africa?

Lots, and it's exciting. To find out, tune in "Music Time in Africa," the Voice of

(continued on page 124)

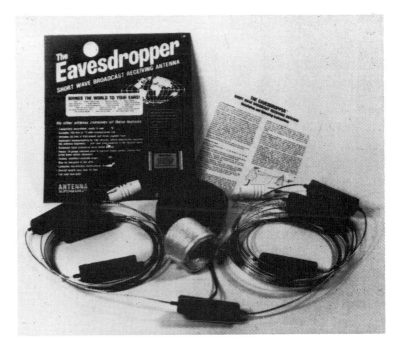

Compleat Idiot's Guide to Getting Started

Welcome to World Band Radio, your direct connection to what's going on, anywhere. Tuning into world band, you pick and choose from your own international wire service. The world's facts and perspectives appear *before* they can be filtered and molded by editorial arbiters. It's news you want to hear, not just what you're supposed to know.

That, plus remarkable entertainment, is what you can expect. Here's how to go about getting them . . .

"Must" #1: Set Clock for World Time

Research has shown that world band listeners who try to wing it without *Passport* have about a 50–50 chance of dropping out within their first year of listening. Yet, less than one person in 20 who uses *Passport* gives up. That's mainly because *Passport's* schedule details take away the "hit-and-miss" of shortwave.

However, these schedules use the *World Time* standard. That's because world band radio is global, with nations broadcasting around-the-clock from virtually every time zone. Imagine the chaos if each broadcaster used its own local time for scheduling. In England, 9 PM is different from nine in the evening in Japan or Canada. How could anybody know when to tune in?

To eliminate confusion, international broadcasters use World Time, or UTC, as a standard reference. Formerly and in some circles still known as Greenwich Mean Time (GMT), it is keyed to the Greenwich meridian in England and is announced in 24-hour format, like military time. So 2 PM, say, is 1400 ("fourteen hundred") hours.

There are three easy ways to know World Time. First, you can tune in one of the standard time stations, such as WWV in Colorado and WWVH in Hawaii in the United States. These are on 5000, 10000 and 15000 kHz around-the-clock, with WWV also on 2500 and 20000 kHz. There, you will hear time "pips" every second, followed just before the beginning of each minute by an announcement of the exact World Time. Boring, yes, but very handy when you need it.

Second, you can tune in one of the major international broadcasters, such as Britain's BBC World Service or the Voice of America. Most announce World Time at the top of the hour.

Third, here's a quick calculation. If you live on the East Coast of the United States, *add* five hours winter (four hours summer) to your local time to get World Time. So, if it is 8 PM EST (the 20th hour of the day) in New York, it is 0100 hours World Time. On the U.S. West Coast, add eight hours winter (seven hours summer).

In Britain, it's easy—World Time (oops,

See, it really works!

For listening to a few superpower stations, even a simple radio will do. Here, southern Africans tune in to Trans World Radio's powerful signal from Swaziland.

Greenwich Mean Time) is the same as local winter time. However, there you have to subtract one hour from local summer time to get World Time. Elsewhere in the European Community, subtract one hour winter (two hours summer) from local time. In *Passport's* "Addresses PLUS" section you will find information for calculating World Time wherever you are in the world. This is handy not only in determining World Time, but also to know the local time in any country you are listening to.

First Taste: *Passport's* Five-Minute Start

In a hurry? Here's how to get off and running, chop-chop:

1. Wait until evening, preferably before midnight. If you live in a concrete-and-steel building, place the radio alongside a window.

2. Ensure your radio is plugged in or has fresh batteries. Extend the telescopic antenna fully and straight up. The DX/local switch (if there is one) should be set to "DX." Leave the other controls the way they came from the factory.

3. Turn on your radio. Set it to 5950 kHz and begin tuning slowly toward 6200 kHz. You will now begin to encounter a number of stations from around the world. Adjust the volume to a level that is comfortable for you. Voilà! You are now an initiate of world band radio.

Other times? Read this article. It tells you where to tune day and night.

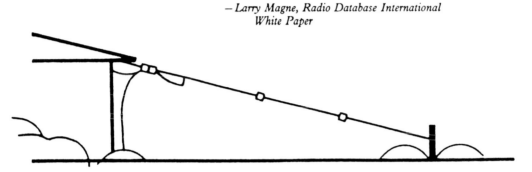

MONITOR <u>MORE</u> WITH ADVANCED EQUIPMENT FROM UNIVERSAL!

COMMUNICATIONS RECEIVERS

The **Drake R-8** is an American made receiver for the 90's. Five bandwidths, synchronous tuning, 100 memories, RS232 and much more. Rated five stars & *Editor's Choice* in *Passport '93*.

KENWOOD

The **Kenwood R-5000** is a powerful receiver for the serious DX'er. Keypad, notch, IF shift, 100 memories, 10 Hz display, dual VFOs. An exceptional value.

The **Japan Radio NRD-535D** is for the communications connoisseur. Rated 5 stars & *Editor's Choice* in *Passport '93*. The "D" deluxe version includes BWC, ECSS and three filters. Universal also carries the affordable "standard" **Japan Radio NRD-535**.

YAESU

Don't let the compact size and affordable price tag fool you. The **Yaesu FRG-100** is a full featured, high performance receiver. Please see our half-page ad elsewhere in this publication.

The **Icom R-9000** is *the* ultimate receiver! Covers .1 to 1999.8 MHz. Built-in CRT displays: VFO status, incoming data, video, TV, memory contents, timer settings and spectrum analysis. Rated 5 stars & *Editor's Choice* in *Passport '93*. The pro's choice. Under $5000.

The **Lowe HF-150** performs like a full-sized communications receiver but is only 8"x3"x6.5" Please see our half-page ad on this unique British import elsewhere in this publication.

DIGITAL PORTABLE RECEIVERS

■ Sony ICF-SW55
Sony's newest radio is receiving rave reviews. Compact, yet with solid performance and full features. One of our favorites. **$369.95** (+$5)

■ Sangean ATS-803A
A proven performer and an unbeatable value. *Editor's Choice* in *Passport '93*. Keypad, nine memories, BFO, clock, etc. Great SSB. With AC adapter & record-out jack. **$169.95** (+$5)

■ Sangean ATS-818CS
Finally; a quality digital receiver with a built-in cassette recorder. Full coverage of LW, MW, SW and FM. **$249.95** (+$7)

■ Sony ICF-SW77
Sophisticated performance and features that rival a communications receiver. Spec. sheet available on request. **$479.95** (+$5)

■ Sony ICF-SW1S
At less than 3" by 5", this is the ultimate digital travel radio. With case, active antenna, AC, headphones, more. **$279.95** (+$6)

■ Panasonic RFB-45
Affordable performance in a compact and stylish package. With 18 memories, SSB and fine-tuning. **$169.95** (+$5)

■ Grundig Satellit 700
Beautiful fidelity, features, style. 512 memories expandable to 2048. Selected *Editor's Choice* in *Passport '93*. Incredible sound. Please see our ad elsewhere in this publication. **$479.95** (+$6)

■ Magnavox AE3625
An affordable digital with 20 memories. Has 1 kHz display resolution. This is our favorite "under $100" portable. **$99.95** (+$5)
Note: Many other models available. Please see catalog.

ANTENNAS
Universal is pleased to offer an excellent selection of antennas by manufacturers such as Alpha-Delta, Barker & Williamson, Antenna Supermarket, RF Systems, Diamond, MFJ, McKay Dymek Sony and Palomar. Please request our free catalog.

USED SHORTWAVE EQUIPMENT
Universal offers a wide selection of used shortwave receivers and radioteletype receiving equipment. All items have been tested by our service center and are protected by a thirty day limited warranty. Our computerized used list is published twice a month. Please send one or more self-addressed stamped envelopes to receive this free list. Universal also buys used radio equipment.

HUGE FREE CATALOG
Universal offers a huge **100 page** catalog covering all types of shortwave, amateur and scanner equipment. An unbeatable selection of antennas, books, parts and accessories is also featured. Radioteletype and facsimile decoders are fully explained. This informative publication covers absolutely everything for the radio enthusiast. With prices, photos and full descriptions.

★ **FREE by fourth class mail in the USA.**
★ **$1 by first class mail in USA/Canada.**
★ **5 IRC's outside of North America.**

Universal Radio, Inc.
6830 Americana Pkwy.
Reynoldsburg, OH 43068
➤ 800 431-3939 Orders
➤ 614 866-4267 Information
➤ 614 866-2339 Fax

♦ **Universal is happy to ship worldwide.**
♦ **Serving radio enthusiasts since 1942.**
♦ **Visa, Mastercard and Discover accepted.**
♦ **Written dealer inquiries welcomed.**
♦ **Prices and specifications are subject to change.**
♦ **Visit our fully operational showroom.**
♦ **Used equipment list available.**

universal radio inc.

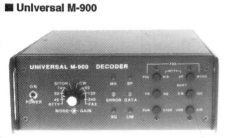

Chen Lifang answers listener correspondence for the English Department of Radio Beijing.

R. Beijing

Once you find the correct World Time, set your radio's clock so you'll have World Time handy whenever you want to listen. No 24-hour clock? Pick up the phone and order one. World band specialty firms sell them for as little as $10 (see box, page 48).

"Must" #2: Understand World Day

There's a trick to World Time that can occasionally catch even the most experienced listener. What happens at midnight? A new day, *World Day*, arrives as well.

Don't forget to "wind your calendar."

Remember: Midnight World Time means a new day, too. So if it is 9 PM EST Wednesday in New York, it is 0200 hours World Time *Thursday*. Don't forget to "wind your calendar."

"Must" #3: Know How to Find Stations

You can find world band broadcasters by looking them up in *Passport's* by-country or "What's On Tonight" sections. Or you can flip through *Passport's* vast Blue Pages to cruise within the several *segments*, or "bands"—neighborhoods within the short-wave spectrum where stations are found.

Incidentally, frequencies may be given in kilohertz, kHz, or Megahertz, MHz. The only difference is three decimal places, so 6175 kHz is the same as 6.175 MHz. But forget all the technobabble. All you need to know is that 6175, with or without decimals, refers to a certain spot on your radio's dial.

Here are the main "neighborhoods" where you'll find world band broadcasters and when they're most active. Except for the 4700-5100 kHz segment, which has mainly low-powered Latin American and African stations, you'll discover a huge variety of stations on these bands.

4700 -5100 kHz	Night and twilight, mainly during winter
5850 -6250 kHz	Night and twilight
7100 -7600 kHz	Night and twilight
9300 -10000 kHz	Night, early morning and late afternoon
11500 -12160 kHz	Night and day, especially twilight
13600 -13900 kHz	Day and, to some degree, night
15000 -15700 kHz	Day and, to some degree, night
17500 -17900 kHz	Day and, to a slight degree, night
21450 -21850 kHz	Day and, to a very slight degree, night

If you have never before experienced world band radio, you will be accustomed to hearing local stations at the same place on the dial day and night. Things are very different when you roam the international airwaves.

> ## Stations try to outshout each other, like merchants in a bazaar.

World band radio is like a global bazaar where merchants come and go at different times. Stations enter and leave the same spot on the dial throughout the day and night. Where you once tuned in a British station, hours later you will find a Russian or Chinese broadcaster roosting on that same spot.

Or on a nearby perch. If you suddenly

IF YOU TURN THIS PAGE, YOU GET SOMETHING FREE

Seiko's World Time Touch Sensor, which includes World Day and date, is the best clock for world band listening.

hear interference from a station on an adjacent channel, it doesn't mean something is wrong with your radio; it means another station has begun broadcasting on a nearby frequency. There are more stations on the air than there is space for them, so sometimes they try to outshout each other, like merchants in a bazaar: "Come over here! Listen to me!"

The best way to cope with this is to purchase a radio with superior adjacent-channel rejection, also known as selectivity. Read the "*Passport* Buyer's Guide" to find out what's what in this regard.

Daytime is best above 11500 kHz; night, below 10000 kHz.

One of the most enjoyable things about world band radio is cruising up and down the airwaves. Daytime, you'll get best results above 11500 kHz; night, below 10000 kHz.

Tune slowly, savor the sound of foreign tongues cuddled alongside the regular English shows. Enjoy the music, weigh the opinions of other peoples.

If a station disappears, there is prob-

World Time Clocks: Which Are Best?

Bargains

Each of the following simple small clocks contains identical "mechanisms" . . .

★★★ **MFJ-24-107B**, $9.95. Despite its paucity of features, this "Volksclock" is highly recommended if you're watching your kopeks.

★★★ **NI8F LCD**, $14.95. Same as the MFJ, above, but with a handsome walnut frame instead of aluminum. It is less likely than MFJ models to scratch surfaces. From Universal Radio.

★★★ **MFJ-108**, $19.95. For those who also want local time. Two LCD clocks—24-hour format for World Time, separate 12-hour display for local time—side-by-side.

Performers

Seiko for features, others for split-second accuracy . . .

★★★★½ **Seiko World Time Touch Sensor**, $110.00. At last, a digital clock that shows not only time and day, but also date! This is the best choice among any of the clocks tested—and gives some local times worldwide, to boot. Runner-up in the Seiko stable: ★★★★ **Seiko World Time Clock**, pricey at $295.00. *Caution:* These models, which use London Time for World Time, don't give the correct World Time if the "summer" feature is used. Yet, if that feature isn't used, some displayed local times will be one hour off during the summer.

★★★★ **Heath GCW-1000-H**, $399.95. For use in North and Central America, the Caribbean and the central Pacific only. Controlled by signals from WWV or WWVH (see story), this is the most accurate clock tested. Potentially as good in Europe is the **Jünghans** line of 24-hour radio-controlled clocks. (Thus far, Jünghans clocks sold in North America are only in the 12-hour format.)

ably nothing wrong with your radio. The atmosphere's *ionosphere*, which reflects world band signals, changes constantly. The result is that broadcasters operate in different parts of the world band spectrum, depending on the time of day and season of the year. *Passport*'s schedules show you where to tune and retune. On advanced radios, you can store these favorite channels on presets for immediate call-up, day-after-day.

That same changeability can also work in your favor. Sometimes stations from exotic locales—places you would not ordinarily hear—arrive at your radio, thanks to the shifting characteristics of the ionosphere. After all, world band radio, unlike other media, sometimes allows stations to be heard thousands of miles beyond where they are beamed.

"Must" #4: Obtain a Radio That Works Properly

If you haven't yet purchased a world band radio, here's some good news: Although cheap radios should be avoided—they suffer from one or more major defects—you don't need an expensive set to enjoy exploring the world's airwaves. With one of the better-rated portables, about the price of an ordinary VCR, you'll be able to hear much of what world band has to offer.

You won't need an outside antenna, either, unless you're using a tabletop model. All portables are designed to work off the built-in telescopic antenna. Try, though, to purchase a radio with digital frequency display. Its accuracy will make tuning around the bands far easier than with outmoded slide-rule tuning.

In the *"Passport* Buyers Guide," you'll find much more information about radios: independent laboratory and hands-on tests of nearly all radios currently available, as well as solid recommendations for a best starter radio. It's all there to help you make an informed, cost-effective choice.

> Avoid cheap radios, but you don't need an expensive set.

Radio in hand, read the owner's manual. You'll find that, despite a few unfamiliar controls, your new world band receiver isn't all that much different from radios you have used all your life. Experiment with the con-

First Tries: 10 Easy Catches

Hundreds of stations worldwide are on the air, but many take some doing to flush out. Here are some easy catches, all in English and in World Time . . .

EUROPE
France

Radio France Internationale airs not only France's language, but also its culture. Yet, RFI's English service, although relatively small, produces programs that are right up there with the very best.

North America: 1230-1300 on 15365 and 17575 (or 21645) kHz. 1600-1700 on 11705, 15530, 17620, 17795 and 17850 kHz.

Europe: 1230-1300 on 9805, 11670, 15155 and 15195 kHz. 1600-1700 on 6175 kHz.

Middle East: 1400-1500 on 17650 kHz.

Asia: 1400-1500 on 11910 and 15405 (or 17695) kHz.

Germany

Deutsche Welle is arguably the most professional of all world band stations. Technically excellent, with programming to match, its outlook is similar to that of the BBC World Service: to reach an ever-increasing number of listeners, regardless of cultural or national boundaries.

North and Central America: 0100-0150 winters on 6040, 6085, 6120, 6145, 9515, 9565, 9610, 9700, 9770 and 11865 kHz; summers on 6040, 6085, 6145, 9565, 9700, 9765, 11810, 11865, 13610, 13770 and 15105 kHz. The first repeat is at 0300-0350 winters on 6045, 6055, 6085, 6120, 9535, 9545, 9640, 9705 and 9770 kHz; summers on 6085, 6145, 9700, 11810, 11890, 13610, 13770, 13790 and 15205 kHz. The third and final broadcast goes out at 0500-0550 winters on 5960, 6045, 6120, 6130, 9535, 9670 and 9690 kHz; summers on 5960, 6130, 9515, 9605, 9670, 11705 and 13610 kHz. This last slot is best for western North America.

Europe: Surprisingly, there is no specific broadcast in English to Europe, but Deutsche Welle can still be heard 0500-0550 on 6120 kHz (winters), 9515 kHz (summers) and 11705 kHz (year-round). 0600-0650, try 11765, 13610, 13790 or 15185 kHz. 1900-1950, winters on 9765, 11765 and 13790 kHz; summers on 11810, 13790, 15350 and 15390 kHz.

Middle East: 1900-1950 winters on 11905 kHz, summers on 13690 kHz.

Asia and the Pacific: 0900-0950 on 6160, 11715, 17780, 17820, 21465, 21650 and 21680 kHz. 2100-2150 on 6185 (or 13690), 9670, 9765 and 11785 kHz.

Holland

Radio Nederland, which announces in English as Radio Netherlands, introduced changes to its English language programming in 1993.

North America: The station is now well heard throughout much of North America at 2330-0125 on 6020 and 6165 kHz, with the final 55 minutes also available on 11835 kHz. Also, 0330-0425 on 6165 and 9590 kHz. Broadcasts for Africa at 1730-1925 on 21515 and 21590 kHz, and 1930-2025 on 17605 and 21590 kHz are also well heard in many parts of North America. These broadcasts contain some shows which are different from the others.

(continued on page 134)

A good portable is all you need. A favorite among connoisseurs is Sony's advanced ICF-2010.

trols so you'll become comfortable with them. You can't harm your radio by twiddling switches and knobs.

"Must" #5: Refer to *Passport*

Throughout *Passport*, you'll find the full wealth of information you need to make the best use of your listening moments. It's designed to carry you through everything— opportunities and problems, alike—you can be expected to encounter when experiencing world band. Now, and in the times to come.

———————————

Prepared by Jock Elliott, Tony Jones and Lawrence Magne.

Love it or hate it: Sony pulls out virtually all the technology stops with the ICF-SW77, improved for 1994.

1994 Buyer's Guide to World Band Radio

Overleaf: Grundig's Yacht Boy 500, to be introduced in early 1994.

How to Choose a World Band Radio

Buy a TV, you get a TV. Differences among models aren't all that great. Not so world band receivers, which vary greatly from model to model. As usual, money talks—but even that's a fickle barometer. Some models use old technology, or misuse new technology, and barely function. Others, more advanced, perform superbly.

World band radio is a jungle: 1,100 channels, stations scrunched cheek-by-jowl. This crowding is much greater than on FM or mediumwave AM, and to make matters worse, the international voyage makes signals weak and quivery. To cope, a radio has to perform some tough electronic gymnastics. Some succeed, others don't.

This is why the *Passport* Buyer's Guide was created. Since 1977 we've tested hundreds of world band products. These evaluations, free from any extraneous influence, include rigorous hands-on use by veteran listeners and newcomers alike, plus specialized lab tests. These form the basis of this Buyer's Guide, and are detailed even more fully in the various Radio Database International™ White Paper™ reports.

Checklist: What to Consider

But before you get into the specifics of which radio does what, here's a basic checklist to help you decide on a course of action.

What to spend? Don't be fooled by the word "radio"—able world band radios are surprisingly sophisticated devices. Yet, for all they do, they cost only about as much as a basic VCR.

It's best not to be guided solely by price, even within a given brand. Take Radio Shack, whose offerings, like those of other firms, don't necessarily perform in concert with price (five stars is best):

$59.95	Realistic DX-350	★½
$69.95	Realistic DX-342	★½
$99.95	Realistic SW-100	★
$119.95	Realistic DX-370	★★½
$179.95	Realistic DX-380	★★★
$239.95	Realistic DX-390	★★½

What kind of stations do you want to hear? Just the main stations? Or do you also hanker for softer voices from exotic lands? Determine what you feel is the minimum performance you want, then choose a model that surpasses that by a notch or so. This helps ensure against disappointment without wasting money.

For hearing all but the tough catches, that "sweet spot" is $150-250, or £100-200, in a compact or mid-sized portable. This is where you should start and where most veteran listeners stay. On the other hand, to ferret out as much as possible, think four stars—perhaps five—in a $650 (£400)-or-more tabletop or portatop.

Two-figure deals? Research shows that once the novelty wears off, most people quit using cheap radios, especially those under $100 or £70. They sound terrible on many stations and are clumsy to tune.

Where are you located? Signals are strongest in and around Europe, different but almost as good in Eastern North America. If you live in either place, you might get by with any of a number of models. However, elsewhere in North America, or in Australasia, choose with more care. You'll need a receiver that's unusually sensitive to weak signals—some sort of extra antenna might help, too.

What features make sense to you? Separate these into those that affect performance and those that don't (see box). Don't rely on performance features alone, though. As our Buyer's Guide tests show, much more besides features goes into performance.

Where to buy? Unlike TVs and ordinary radios, world band sets don't test well in stores other than specialty showrooms with outdoor antennas. Even so, given the fluctuations in world band reception, long-term satisfaction is hard to gauge from a spot test.

Exceptions are audio quality and ergonomics. Even if a radio can't pick up world band stations in the store, you can get a thumbnail idea of fidelity by catching some mediumwave AM stations. By playing with the radio, you can also get a feel for handiness of operation.

If you're not familiar with a particular store, a good way to judge it is to bring along or mention your *Passport*. Reputable dealers—reader feedback suggests most are—welcome it as a sign you are serious and knowledgeable. The rest react accordingly.

Otherwise, whether you buy in the mall or through the mail makes little difference. Use the same horse sense you would for any other appliance.

Are repairs important? Judging from our experience and reports from *Passport* readers, the quality or availability of repairs tends to correlate with price. At one extreme, some off-brand portables from China are essentially unserviceable, although most outlets will replace a defective unit within warranty. Better portables are almost always serviced properly or replaced within warranty. Yet, after warranty expiration, virtually all factory-authorized service departments except Grundig's tend to fall short.

On the other hand, for high-priced tabletop models, factory-authorized service is usually available to keep them purring for many years to come. Drake is legendary in

---

Favorite Radios

If there were one best car, the roads would be filled with identical wheeled boxes. That's not the way it is with autos, nor with world band radios.

When push comes to shove, we have to make buying decisions just like anybody else. "I'll take this one," and that's that. We aren't you; yet, we're frequently asked which current models we use ourselves.

Now that you are forewarned, here are the answers, which include purchases made and planned.

Portables: Most of us use the mid-sized *Sony ICF-2010*, sold throughout North America. Elsewhere, where it was sold as the *ICF-2001D*, it is apparently no longer available, according to dealers. We've worn out a number of these over the years, and keep coming back for more.

The smaller new *Grundig Yacht Boy 400*, which nearly everybody likes, is a close runner-up and lots cheaper. Most want no part of the new *Sony ICF-SW77*, but those who do like it take to it with a passion usually reserved for the Chicago Bulls.

Tabletops: The *Drake R8* is a delight for listening and nearly all DXing. The *Japan Radio NRD-535D*'s ergonomics are preferred, especially for channel monitoring to prepare station schedules for *Passport*.

Portatops: In this interesting new category, the tough little *Lowe HF-150* is sometimes used for *Passport* monitoring where electricity is not available. Most are keeping a hopeful eye out for the forthcoming *Drake SWL8*, as well.

Gifts for Newcomers: For that very special person or occasion, the *Grundig Yacht Boy 400*. One notch down the price ladder are the *Panasonic RF-B45* and *Sangean ATS-808*, also sold as the *Realistic DX-380* (watch for sales at Radio Shack) and under other designations. All are hassle-free and do the job well. The cheapest-of-the-cheap *Apex 2138*, more a toy than a real radio, makes a nice stocking stuffer for youngsters and outdoorsmen.

this regard within North America, with Lowe building up a similar reputation in Europe. Their service is first-rate, just as it is at a number of other firms, such as Japan Radio, Kenwood and Yaesu. But, in addition, they tend to maintain a healthy parts inventory, even for older models.

Of course, nothing quite equals service at the factory itself. So if repair is especially important to you, bend a little toward the home team: Drake in the United States, Grundig in Germany, Lowe in the United Kingdom, and so on.

Features to Look for on Better Models

You can't tell by looking at a world band radio in a store whether it will work better than another model, or how long it will hold up. That's why junkers sell well to the uninitiated. But features are another story. Salespeople love features: If the customer's attention can be focused on "bells and whistles," then performance and reliability usually slide to the back burner.

Performance Features

Still, certain performance features can be genuinely useful. For example, *multiple conversion* (also called "double conversion," "up conversion," "dual conversion," "two IFs") is essential to rejecting spurious signals—unwanted growls, whistles, dih-dah sounds and the like. Few models under $100 or £70 have it; most over $150 or £100 do. A power lock also borders on a "must" if you travel frequently with your radio.

Also look for two or more *bandwidths* for superior rejection of stations on adjacent channels; properly functioning *synchronous detection* for yet greater adjacent-channel rejection, and also to reduce fading; and *continuously tuned bass and treble* tone controls. For world band reception, *single-sideband* (SSB) reception capability is unimportant, but it is essential if you want to tune in shortwave utility or "ham" signals.

On heavy-hitting tabletop models, designed to flush out virtually the most stubborn signal, you pay more so you expect more. Look for a tunable *notch filter* to zap howls; *passband offset*, also known as *IF shift*, for superior adjacent-channel rejection and audio contouring; and multiple *AGC* rates with selectable *AGC off*.

A *noise blanker* sounds like a better idea than it really is, given the technology world band manufacturers use. Noises that are equal to or lower in strength than the received signal aren't chopped out by a noise blanker until they become stronger than the signal. Innovative circuits by such firms as RCA and Motorola exist in the laboratory and even as chips (e.g., MC13027, which apparently can be configured to blank off the IF, rather than the received frequency, and thus operate independent of the received carrier level). But this sort of noise-reduction technology is, as yet, nowhere to be found on world band radios.

Operating Features

Desirable operating, or nonperformance, features for any world band radio include *digital frequency readout*, a virtual "must"; a 24-hour *World Time clock*, especially one that always shows; direct-access tuning via *keypad* and *presets* ("memories"); and any combination of *"signal-seek" scanning*, a *tuning knob* or up/down *slewing controls* to "fish around" for stations.

Useful, but less important, are *on/off timing*, especially if it can control a tape recorder; *illuminated display*; *single-keystroke callup* (a separate button for each preset), rather than having to use the keypad (multiple-keystroke callup); *numerically displayed seconds* on the 24-hour clock; and a good *signal-strength indicator*.

Outdoor Antennas: Do You Need One?

If you're wondering what antenna you'll need for your new radio, the answer for portables and portatops is simple: none. All come with built-in telescopic antennas.

Indeed, for evening use in Eastern North America or Europe, nearly all portables perform *less* well with sophisticated outboard antennas than with their built-in ones. But if you listen during the day, or live in such places as the North American Midwest or West, your portable may need more oomph.

The best solution in the United States is also the cheapest: $8.49 for Radio Shack's 75-foot (23-meter) "SW Antenna Kit" (#278-758), which comes with insulators and other goodies, plus $1.99 for a claw clip (Radio Shack #270-349 or #270-345). The antenna itself may be a bit too long for your circumstances, but you can always trim it. Alternatively, many electronics and world band specialty firms sell the necessary parts and wire for you to make your own. An appendix in *Passport's* publication, the RDI™ White Paper™ *Popular Outdoor Antennas*, gives minutely detailed step-by-step instructions on making and erecting such an antenna.

Basically, you attach the claw clip onto your radio's rod antenna (*not* the set's external antenna input socket, which may have a desensitizing circuit) and run it out of your window, as high as is safe and practical, to something like a tree. *Keep it clear of any hazardous wiring—the electrical service to your house, in particular—and respect heights.* If you live in an apartment, run it to your balcony or window—as close to the fresh outdoors as possible.

This "volksantenna"—best disconnected when thunder, snow or sand storms are nearby—will probably help with most signals. But if it occasionally makes a station sound worse, disconnect the claw clip.

It's a different story with tabletop receivers. They require an external antenna, either electrically amplified (so-called "active") or passive. Although portatop models don't require an outboard antenna, they may work better with one.

Amplified antennas use small wire or rod elements that aren't very efficient, but make up for it with electronic circuitry. For apartment dwellers, they're a godsend—provided they work right. Choosing a suitable amplified antenna for your tabletop or portatop receiver takes some care. Certain models—notably, California's McKay Dymek DA100D and Britain's Datong AD 370—are designed better than others and sell for under $200 or £125.

If you have space, a passive outdoor wire antenna is better, especially when it's designed for world band frequencies. Besides not needing problematic electronic circuits, good passive antennas also tend to reduce interference from the likes of fluorescent lights and electric shavers—noises which amplified antennas amplify, right along with the signal. As the cognoscenti put it, the "signal-to-noise ratio" with passive antennas tends to be better.

With any outdoor antenna, especially if it is high out in the open, disconnect it and affix it to something like an outdoor ground rod if there is lightning nearby. Handier, and equally effective except for a direct strike, is a modestly priced "gas-pill" lightning protector, such as is made by Alpha Delta. Or, if you can afford it, the $295 Ten-Tec Model 100 protector, which automatically shuts out your antenna and power cord when lightning appears nearby. Otherwise, sooner or later, odds are you will be facing a very expensive repair bill.

Many firms—some large, some tiny—offer world band antennas. Among the best passive models—all under $100 or £60—are those made by Antenna Supermarket and Alpha Delta Communications. A detailed report on these is available as the Radio Database International™ White Paper™ *Evaluation of Popular Outdoor Antennas*.

Digital Portables for 1994

Portable or Tabletop?
If you eat, breathe and dream world band radio, stop right now and go to the tabletop section of this *Passport* Buyer's Guide. That's where you'll find the ultimate performers, the Ferraris and Mercedes of world band.

Otherwise, this section on digitally tuned portables is the place to start. The best-rated of these radios almost certainly will meet your needs—especially if you listen evenings, when signals are strongest.

Analog or Digital?

Analog, or slide-rule, tuning goes back to the earliest days of radio. It's fading from the marketplace, with few tears being shed by listeners. With analog, finding the one station you want from the hundreds on the air is a hit-and-miss proposition that chews up time and patience. With digital models costing little more, there's hardly any reason to go any other route. Aside from low battery consumption, analog portables have no real virtues over digital units.

Accordingly, starting this year, analog portables have their own separate category within the *Passport* Buyer's Guide.

Nearly All Available Models Included

Here are the results of this year's hands-on and laboratory testing. We've evaluated nearly every digital portable currently produced, or at least reasonably available, which meets minimum performance standards. This is why we have excluded such models as the Icom IC-R1 and Kenwood RZ-1

that lack bandwidths narrow enough to qualify for acceptable world band reception.

Longwave Useful Only for Some

The longwave band is used for some domestic broadcasts in Europe, North Africa and Russia. If you live in or travel to these parts of the world, longwave coverage is a slight plus. Otherwise, forget it.

Keep in mind, though, that when a model is available with longwave, it may be included at the expense of some world band coverage.

Quality of Chinese Models Improving

In the past few years, Chinese manufacturers have flooded the marketplace with inexpensive digital and analog world band portables. Some perform reasonably for the price—this year's Yorx AS-908 is an excellent example—but they have usually been shoddily constructed.

Fortunately, this is now showing signs of improving as the Chinese make products of more competitive quality. Indeed, one major Western expert considers production quality at the very best Chinese radio plants to be better than that of plants in some of the other Asian "tiger" countries.

That's good news, indeed, as China is likely to become the chief source for world band radios later in the decade.

Shelling Out

For the United States, suggested retail ("list") prices are given. Discounts for most models are common, although those sold under the "Realistic" brand name are usually discounted only during special Radio Shack or Tandy sales. Elsewhere, observed selling prices (including VAT) are usually given.

Duty-free shopping? For the time being, in some parts of the European Community it may save you ten percent or more, *provided* you don't have to declare the radio at your destination. Check on warranty coverage, though. In the United States, where prices are already among the world's lowest, you're better off buying from shortwave specialty outlets and regular stores. Canada, also, and to an increasing extent the United Kingdom and Germany.

Naturally, all prices are as we go to press and may fluctuate. Some will probably have changed before the ink dries.

We try to stick to plain English, but some specialized terms have to be used. If you come across something that's not clear, check it out in the Glossary at the back of the book.

What *Passport's* Ratings Mean

Star ratings: ★ ★ ★ ★ ★ is best. Stars are awarded solely for overall performance and meaningful features, both with portable and tabletop model reviews. The same star-rating standard applies regardless of price, size or whathaveyou. A star is a star, so you can cross-compare any radio—little or big, portable or tabletop, analog or digital—with any other radio evaluated in this edition of *Passport.*

A rating of three stars or more should please most day-to-day listeners. However, for occasional use on trips, a small portable with as little as one-and-a-half stars may suffice.

Editor's Choice models are our test team's personal picks of the litter—what we would prefer to buy ourselves.

¢: denotes a price-for-performance bargain. It may or may not be a great set, but gives uncommon value for your money.

Models in **(parentheses)** have not been tested by us, but appear to be essentially identical to model(s) tested.

How Models Are Listed

Models are listed by size; and, within size, in order of world band listening suitability. Unless otherwise indicated:

- Each radio covers the usual 87.5-108 MHz FM band.
- AM band (mediumwave) coverage includes the forthcoming 1605-1705 kHz segment for the Americas.

MINI-PORTABLES

Great for Travel, Poor for Home

Mini-portables weigh under a pound, or half-kilogram, and are somewhere between the size of an audio cassette box and one of the larger hand-held calculators. They operate off two to four ordinary small "AA" (UM-3 penlite) batteries. These diminutive models do one job well: provide news and entertainment when you're traveling, especially abroad.

Listening to tiny speakers can be downright tiring, so most minis don't provide pleasant hour-after-hour listening. Accordingly, they don't make the best choices for day-to-day listening, except through good headphones—not an attractive prospect, given that none has the full array of Walkman-type features, such as a hidden antenna.

Best bet? Sangean's relatively affordable new ATS 606p and ATS 606, also available as the Siemens RK 659. Among the largest of the minis, its more generous speaker size results in relatively pleasant sound quality. If smallness is more important than speaker quality, check out the Sony ICF-SW1S and ICF-SW1E.

Don't forget to look over the large selection of compact models, just after the minis in this *Passport* Buyer's Guide. They're not much larger than minis, but usually have more sizable speakers and so tend to sound better.

New for 1994
★ ★ ★   *Editor's Choice*

| Sangean ATS 606p |
| Sangean ATS 606 |
| (Siemens RK 659) |

Price: *ATS 606p:* $269.00 in the United States and Continental European Community. *ATS 606:* $249.00 in the United States and Continental European Community. AUS$249.00 in Australia.

Advantages: Superior overall world band performance for size. Exceptional simplicity of

Sangean's ATS-606, new for 1994, is the best mini around.

operation for technology class. Speaker audio quality superior for size class, improves with (usually supplied) earpieces. Various helpful tuning features. Weak-signal sensitivity at least average for size. Keypad has exceptional feel and tactile response. Longwave. World Time clock, displayed separately from frequency, and local clock. Alarm/sleep features. Travel power lock. Clear warning when batteries weak. Stereo FM via earpieces. Superior FM reception. *ATS 606p:* Reel-in passive wire antenna. Self-regulating AC adaptor, with American and European plugs, adjusts automatically to most local voltages worldwide.

Disadvantages: No tuning knob. Tunes only in coarse 5 kHz increments. World Time clock readable only when radio is switched off. Display not illuminated. Keypad not in telephone format. No meaningful signal-strength indicator. No carrying strap or handle. Supplied earpieces inferior to comparable foam-padded headphones. *ATS 606:* AC adaptor extra.

Comment: Although the many Sangean world band radios we have tested have held up unusually well over years of hard use, our particular '606 ceased operating in the longwave, mediumwave AM and world bands two months after our tests were completed.

Bottom Line: Here's good news for 1994: This new model is not only the best mini around, it's fairly priced, to boot. If the regular "606" Sangean version seems Spartan, there's the "606p" version, complete with handy goodies. It's well worth the small extra price.

Evaluation of New Model: Sangean's new ATS 606, also available with an AC adaptor and outboard antenna as the ATS 606p, is one of the larger minis. This generous size allows for

a speaker which delivers reasonable audio quality for world band, even if it's mediocre for FM.

The '606, which has no tuning knob, selects frequencies by up/down slewing buttons, frequency scanning, 45 presets (19 for world band) and direct-frequency entry via keypad. There is also handy scanning of presets for the longwave, mediumwave AM and FM bands, but not those for world band. Keys have the usual excellent feel characteristic of Sangean digital models, even though the zero is below the "7," rather than the "8" as on telephones.

The '606 virtually covers it all: longwave from 153-513 kHz; mediumwave AM from 520-1710 kHz; world band from 1715-29995 kHz; and FM, which is in stereo through earpieces, from 87.5-108 MHz. Only the 66-73 MHz OIRT FM band, already being phased back in most parts of Eastern Europe where it was once the standard, and the 76.1-87.3 MHz portion of the Japanese FM band are not covered.

Tuning is in 9 kHz steps on longwave; switchable 10 kHz (Americas) and 9 kHz (elsewhere) steps on AM; 5 kHz steps on world band; and 50 kHz steps on FM. Our new '606 came with mediumwave AM set to the wrong tuning-steps position from the factory, so be sure to check this when you unpack the radio.

Add to this the travel power lock and the '606p's self-setting, multi-plug 110-230 VAC adaptor, and you have a receiver that's just about ideal for globetrotting.

The '606 has two 24-hour clocks. Unfortunately, neither is displayed when the received station's frequency is shown. There are also handy timer and sleep-off functions for use at home or in lonely hotels.

There's only a single-LED "glow light" for a signal-strength indicator and no carrying strap or handle. Yet, there is an excellent battery-strength indicator that's coupled to other prompts to let you know, unmistakably, when batteries are starting to peter out. You can take up to three minutes to change those batteries without causing the memory circuitry to erase, another plus.

The telescopic antenna rotates and swivels, plus the '606p comes with a reel-in-type passive wire antenna to improve reception at home or on the road. There's also a fold-out panel on the back so the radio can be operated at a comfortable angle.

The '606 comes with only one bandwidth. Yet, it's tight enough to keep at bay most adjacent-channel interference without being so narrow as to muffle the audio. The radio doesn't demodulate single-sideband signals, a disadvantage for some radiophiles, but an advantage to most others in that it makes operation more foolproof.

The radio's 5 kHz tuning steps make reception of off-channel stations—those not on the usual 5 kHz channels—difficult. However, as the Blue Pages show, relatively few stations operate a kilohertz or more off channel.

Performance is above average for a portable and clearly superior for a mini. Weak-signal sensitivity is better than most, and overloading is not a significant problem so long as the supplied antennas are used.

There are larger models that are better and smaller models that are cheaper. Yet, Sangean's new ATS 606, especially in the "p" version, is the best available choice for traveling ultra-light—providing you don't wish to tune utility or ham stations.

Sony's ICF-SW1S comes with an outstanding array of useful accessories.

★ ★ ★   *Editor's Choice*

Sony ICF-SW1S

Price: $349.95 in the United States. CAN$450 in Canada. Under £250 in the United Kingdom. $370-480 elsewhere in the European Community. AUS$599.00 in Australia.

Advantages: Superior overall world band performance for size. High-quality audio when earpieces (supplied) are used. Various helpful tuning features. Unusually straightforward to operate for advanced-tech model. World Time clock. Alarm/sleep features. Travel power lock also disables alarm and display illumination. FM stereo through earpieces. Receives longwave and Japanese FM bands. Amplified outboard antenna (supplied), in addition to usual built-in antenna, enhances weak-signal reception below about 15 MHz. Self-regulating AC adaptor, with American and European plugs, adjusts automatically to all local voltages worldwide. Rugged travel case for radio and accessories.

Disadvantages: Tiny speaker with mediocre sound. No tuning knob. Tunes only in coarse 5 kHz increments. World Time clock readable only when radio is switched off. Volume control at rear, vulnerable to accidental change. For price class, substandard rejection of certain spurious signals ("images"). No meaningful signal-strength indicator. Earpieces less comfortable than foam-padded headphones. Amplified antenna does not switch on and off with radio.

Bottom Line: Although pricey with mediocre speaker sound, the itsy Sony ICF-SW1S, a generally superior performer, is the closest thing available to a "world band Walkman."

Tips for Globetrotting

Customs and airport security people are used to world band portables, which are now a staple among world travelers. Yet, a few simple practices will help in avoiding hassles:
- Stow your radio in a carry-on bag, not checked luggage.
- Take along batteries so you can demonstrate that the radio actually works, as gutted radios can be used to carry illegal material.
- Travel outside Europe, North America, the Caribbean, Pacific islands and Australasia with nothing larger than a compact model.
- Avoid models with built-in tape recorders.
- If asked what the radio is for, state that it is for your personal use.
- If traveling in war zones or off the beaten path in East Africa, take along a radio you can afford to lose.

Finally, remember that radios, cameras, binoculars and the like are almost always stolen to be resold. The grungier it looks—affixing worn stickers helps—the less likely it is to be "confiscated" by corrupt inspectors or stolen by thieves.

The Sony ICF-SW1E competes well with Sangean's ATS-606, but is not sold in North America.

★ ★ ★   *Editor's Choice*

Sony ICF-SW1E

Price: £179.99 in the United Kingdom. $260-340 elsewhere in the European Community. AUS$499.00 in Australia.

Bottom Line: Identical to Sony ICF-SW1S, except lacks a carrying case and most accessories. Not available in North America.

COMPACT PORTABLES

Good for Travel, Fair for Home

Compacts tip in at 1.0-1.5 pounds, or 0.5-0.7 kg, and are typically sized 8 × 5 × 1.5", or 20 × 13 × 4 cm. Like minis, they feed off "AA" (UM-3 penlite) batteries—but more of them. They travel almost as well as minis, but sound better and usually receive better, too. For some travelers, they also suffice as home sets—something minis can't really do. However, if you don't travel abroad often, you will probably find better value and performance in a mid-sized portable.

Which stand out? This year, there's a clear winner, sort of: Grundig's new Yacht Boy 400. "Sort of," assuming that what comes off the production line by the time you read this equals what we have already tested from their late pre-production batch.

Otherwise, any of the remaining

Editor's Choice models performs well, with the main differences being in what you have to do to operate them.

New for 1994
★ ★ ★ ½   *Editor's Choice*

Grundig Yacht Boy 400

Note: The unit tested, shortly before we went to press, was created just before production at the regular plants was to begin. It is not our custom to reproduce our findings concerning units other than those from regular production. However, the results from these tests were interesting enough for us to make this exception.

Price: $249.95 in the United States. CAN$299.95 in Canada. Prices elsewhere not yet established as of press time.

Advantages: Best performance for price/size category, and among the choicest portables of any size, at any price. Audio quality tops in size category. Superior weak-signal sensitivity in tested unit. Two bandwidths, both excellent. Easy to operate for advanced-technology radio. A number of helpful tuning features, including keypad, up/down slewing, 40 presets, frequency scanning and scanning of presets. Signal-strength indicator. World Time clock with second time zone, any one of which displayed at all times. Clock displays seconds, if only when radio is off. Illuminated display. Alarm/sleep features. Demodulates single-sideband signals, used by hams and utility stations, with unusual precision for a portable. Superior FM performance. FM in stereo through headphones (not supplied). Longwave. Microprocessor reset control.

Surprise of the year: Grundig's Yacht Boy 400, the lowest-priced portable with such a high rating.

Disadvantages: No tuning knob. Some break-through of local FM stations may cause distortion on higher world band frequencies in certain locations. The only portable ranked this high that lacks fidelity-enhancing synchronous detection. Keypad not in telephone format. AC adaptor extra. No LSB/USB switch.

Bottom Line: Subject to the condition that what comes off the assembly lines is equal to what we have tested, the Grundig Yacht Boy 400 is as good a portable as currently available as we have come across at any price, in any size class. When it came to choosing any one portable for their own use, price and size be damned, *Passport* panelists were largely split between the '400 (favored by regular program listeners) and the larger Sony ICF-2010 (favored by radio enthusiasts), heretofore the clear favorite.

Evaluation of New Model: Grundig's new Yacht Boy 400 is the surprise of the year!

Reasonably priced, yet among the very best of portables, it covers longwave and mediumwave AM to 1710 kHz, FM in stereo through headphones, and shortwave continuously from 1711-30000 kHz. There's no tuning knob, but world band tunes in user-selectable 1 or 5 kHz increments by up/down slewing buttons.

Tuning either up or down by "signal-seek" scanning works unusually well. Individual world band segments can also be chosen, which helps make bandscanning easier. For going directly to a favorite station, there's an excellent keypad, as well as 40 presets. Not only can each preset be accessed directly, you also can scan through the active presets by using the radio's *second* set of up/down slewing buttons.

There's also a dual-zone 24-hour clock for World Time and a second time zone. The clock displays even when the radio is on, and seconds are shown numerically, albeit only when the radio is off. The clock, along with the rest of the LCD, is nicely illuminated, too.

When the batteries start to go, the LCD flags "BATTERY CHECK." That LCD also has a digital signal-strength indicator with five gradations.

Microprocessors occasionally can "hang up," disrupting operation. Unlike other radios, the '400 actually has a control to reset it if this happens. It's a welcomed improvement over calling a repairman, although it also means that the presets and clocks need to be reloaded.

The '400 receives single-sideband signals unusually well, but lacks an LSB/USB switch. Although the analog-potentiometer technology used is somewhat stale, it does allow for the precise fine tuning needed for natural-sounding voices and music.

The '400 comes with two bandwidths, rather than the one found on most portables. Both are excellent and, taken together, allow you to make a sensible tradeoff between audio "highs" and rejection of adjacent-channel interference. Result: The oddball sounds for which world band is notorious are encountered less on the '400 than on nearly any other portable. It's a major plus, even though it is not accompanied by fidelity-enhancing synchronous detection.

Still, good reception means little if you can't pick up a station in the first place. In some parts of the world, such as central and western North America and Australasia, signals tend to be weak, so superior weak-signal sensitivity is a "must."

Here, the '400—at least the sample we tested—is clearly superior to other portables in its price and size class when operated with its built-in telescopic antenna. Finally, here is a serious portable which doesn't require a stethoscope or extra gadget to hear interesting stations!

Keep in mind, though, that while many factors tend to remain constant both in pre-production and production samples, experience shows that weak-signal sensitivity can

South Korea Lifts Ban on World Band Radios

Why hasn't enterprising South Korea been producing world band radios? After all, many high-quality consumer electronic products emanate from that country.

One explanation may be that from 1950 until 1993, South Koreans were not allowed to own shortwave radios. The ban was imposed to keep out North Korean propaganda, but official distrust went further: Those with world band radios were suspected to be spies or Communist subversives.

With the world band ban now lifted, it is possible that South Korean manufacturers may emerge to compete with China, Taiwan, Indonesia and Malaysia in the lucrative world band radio market. However, the price advantage for Chinese-made products is such that Korea could well find it increasingly hard to compete.

vary, depending on how production goes. If you live where signals are weak, you may wish to purchase the '400 on a money-back basis to ensure its performance meets your expectations.

Rejection of spurious signals is generally good. However, depending on your local FM situation, there may be some breakthrough of FM stations distorting within the higher reaches of the world band spectrum. The level of synthesizer chugging during tuning is acceptable.

The '400's FM performance is right up there with the very best among world band radios. It has a superior capture ratio and worthy adjacent-channel rejection. There's also an almost complete absence of "flyback," which if present would cause stations to repeat at weaker levels alongside their proper channels.

Even though there is only an elementary high-low tone control, the '400 more than lives up to Grundig's reputation for audio quality. In no way does this handheld box put out what could be called "high fidelity." Yet, it's the best-sounding audio we have come across in a compact portable: good enough to be used not only on the occasional trip, but also for everyday listening at home. Panelists particularly commented that listening, especially to voices, is less of a "strain" with the '400 than with virtually any other model tested.

The Grundig Yacht Boy 400—assuming production units perform as nicely as ours did—is, hands down, the best-performing, best-sounding compact world band portable we have tested.

★ ★ ★   *Editor's Choice*

Sony ICF-SW55

Price: $429.95 in the United States. CAN$599.00 in Canada. £279.99 in the United Kingdom. AUS$699.00 in Australia.

Advantages: Among the best-performing compact portables. Although sound emerges through a small port, rather than the usual speaker grille, audio quality is among the best in its size class. Dual bandwidths. Tunes in precise 0.1 kHz increments (displays only in 1 kHz increments). Controls neatly and logically laid out. Innovative tuning system, including factory pre-stored presets and displayed alphabetic identifiers for groups ("pages") of stations. Good single-sideband reception, although reader reports suggest some BFO "pulling" (not found in our unit). Comes complete with carrying case containing reel-in wire antenna, AC adaptor, DC power cord and in-the-ear earpieces. Signal/battery

Sony's ICF-SW55 compact works well, but is relatively complicated to operate.

strength indicator. Local and World Time clocks, either (but not both) of which is displayed separately from frequency. Summer time adjustment for local time clock. Sleep/alarm features. Five-event (daily only) timer nominally can automatically turn on/off many models of voice-activated cassette recorders, such as the Realistic CTR-67—a major plus for VCR-type multiple-event recording. Illuminated display. Receives longwave and Japanese FM bands.

Disadvantages: Tuning system unusually difficult for many people to grasp. Operation sometimes unnecessarily complicated by any yardstick, but especially for listeners in the Americas. Spurious-signal rejection, notably in higher world band segments, not fully commensurate with price class. Wide bandwidth somewhat broad for world band reception. Display illumination dim and uneven. Costly to operate from batteries. Cabinet keeps antenna from swiveling fully, a slight disadvantage for reception of some FM signals.

Note for North Americans Traveling Abroad: In North America, the Sony ICF-SW55's AC adaptor is for 120V only. However, some printed specifications of the '55 indicate that it is supposed to come with a worldwide multivoltage AC adaptor. Possible solution: *Passport* reader Keith Hook received a multi-voltage adaptor after he complained to Sony's Customer Service Department (Sony Drive, Park Ridge NJ 07656 USA) that it was promoted as having such an adaptor.

Bottom Line: If the ICF-SW55's operating scheme meets with your approval—say, you are comfortable utilizing the more sophisticated features of a typical VCR or computer—

and you're looking for a small portable with good audio, this radio is a superior performer in its size class. It also can tape like a VCR, provided you have a suitable recorder to connect to it.

★ ★ ★ *Editor's Choice*

Panasonic RF-B65
(Panasonic RF-B65D)
(Panasonic RF-B65L)
(National B65)

Price: *RF-B65:* $269.95-279.95 in the United States. CAN$399 in Canada. AUS$499.00 in Australia. *RF-B65 and RF-B65D:* £169.95 in the United Kingdom. $290-450 elsewhere in the European Community. *RP-65 120V AC adaptor:* $6.95 in the United States. *RP-38 120/220V AC worldwide adaptor:* $14.95 in the United States. (Adaptor prices are as provided by Panasonic; actual selling prices in stores are higher.)

Advantages: Superior overall world band performance for size. Very easy to operate for advanced-technology radio. Pleasant audio. Various helpful tuning features. Signal-strength indicator. World Time clock, plus second time-zone clock. Alarm/sleep features. Demodulates single-sideband signals, used by hams and utility stations. Longwave. Travel power lock. AC adaptor included (outside North America).

Disadvantages: Cumbersome tuning knob inhibits speed. With built-in antenna, weak-signal sensitivity slightly low. Adjacent-channel rejection (selectivity) slightly broad. Clocks not displayed separately from frequency. Display not illuminated. Keypad not in telephone format. AC adaptor extra (North America).

Bottom Line: A very nice, easy-to-use portable, especially if you live in Europe or eastern North America, where world band signals are relatively strong.

Sony's ICF-SW7600 is the latest version of the world band radio George Bush uses.

★ ★ ★ *Editor's Choice*

Sony ICF-SW7600

Price: $249.95 in the United States. CAN$399 in Canada. £179.99 in the United Kingdom. $250-400 elsewhere in the European Community. AUS$399.00 in Australia.

Advantages: Superior overall for size. High-quality audio with supplied earpieces. Easy to operate for level of technology. Helpful tuning features. World Time clock with timer that controls certain tape recorders. Alarm/sleep features. Demodulates single sideband, used by hams and utility stations. Illuminated display. Travel power lock. Comes with reel-in portable wire antenna. Stereo FM, through earpieces, also covers Japanese FM band. Longwave. Comes with AC adaptor.

Disadvantages: No tuning knob. No meaningful signal-strength indicator. Earpieces less comfortable than foam-padded headphones.

Bottom Line: Excellent all-around performer for globetrotting.

★ ★ ★ *Editor's Choice*

Panasonic RF-B45
(Panasonic RF-B45DL)
(National B45)

Price: *RF-B45:* $189.95-199.95 in the United States. CAN$299 in Canada. AUS$329.00 in Australia. *RF-B45DL:* £129.95 in the United Kingdom. $220-320 in the European Community. *RP-65 120V AC adaptor:* $6.95 in the United States. *RP-38 120/220V AC worldwide adaptor:* $14.95 in the United States.

Advantages: Superior performance for price category. Easy to operate for advanced-technology radio. A number of helpful tuning

Panasonic's RF-B65 combines pleasant performance with ease of use.

One of the nicest radios for beginners is Panasonic's RF-B45. Well made, too.

High tech doesn't come much more easy to operate than in the Sangean ATS-808, also sold under Realistic and other names.

features. Signal-strength indicator. World Time clock. Alarm/sleep features. Demodulates single-sideband signals, used by hams and utility stations. Longwave.

Disadvantages: No tuning knob. Weak-signal sensitivity a bit lacking. Adjacent-channel rejection (selectivity) a bit broad. Clock not displayed separately from frequency. No display illumination. AC adaptor extra.

Bottom Line: The best buy in a compact portable under $200.

★ ★ ★   *Editor's Choice*

Sangean ATS-808
Aiwa WR-D1000
(Realistic DX-380)
(Roberts R808)
(Siemens RK 661)

Price: *Sangean:* $259.00 in the United States. CAN$279.95 in Canada. AUS$299.00 in Australia. *Aiwa:* $259.95 in the United States. *Realistic:* $179.95 in the United States. CAN$299.95 in Canada. AUS$299.95 in Australia. *Siemens:* 399.00 DM in Germany. *Roberts:* £119.99 in the United Kingdom. *ADP-808 120V AC adaptor:* $9.95 in the United States. CAN$14.95 in Canada.

Advantages: Attractively priced in some versions (*see* Comments, below). Exceptional simplicity of operation for technology class. Dual bandwidths, unusual in this size radio (*see* Disadvantages). Various helpful tuning features. Weak-signal sensitivity at least average for size. Keypad has exceptional feel and tactile response. Longwave. World Time clock, displayed separately from frequency, and local clock. Alarm/sleep features. Signal strength indicator. Travel power lock. Stereo FM via earpieces. Superior FM reception. *Realistic:* 30-day money-back trial period.

Disadvantages: Fast tuning mutes receiver when tuning knob is turned quickly. Narrow bandwidth performance only fair. Spurious-signal ("image") rejection very slightly sub-standard for class. Display not illuminated. Keypad not in telephone format. No carrying strap or handle. Supplied earpieces inferior to comparable foam-padded headphones. AC adaptor extra.

Comments: ¢ applies to Realistic and Roberts versions only. This is the only *Editor's Choice* compact that doesn't demodulate single-sideband signals—a disadvantage for some radiophiles, but an advantage for world band listening in that it makes operation less confusing. *Aiwa:* Cabinet styled differently from the other versions of this model.

Bottom Line: Exceptional simplicity of operation, worthy overall performance and reasonable price all make this a sensible choice among compact models. However, mediocre for bandscanning.

New for 1994   ¢
★ ★ ½

Sony ICF-SW33

Price: $199.95 in the United States.

Advantages: Superior reception quality, with excellent adjacent-channel rejection (selectivity) and spurious-signal rejection. Weak-signal sensitivity a bit above average. Easy to operate for advanced-technology radio. Some helpful tuning controls. Unusual clock gives World Time and local time with local city name displayed. Illuminated display. Audio, although lacking in bass, unusually intelligible. Alarm/ sleep features. Travel power lock. FM stereo through headphones (not supplied). Battery-life indicator. Receives Japanese FM band.

Disadvantages: No keypad or tuning knob. Synthesizer chugging and pokey slewing

Sony's ICF-SW33 has many worthwhile features, but mediocre tuning.

degrade bandscanning. Few (seven) world band presets. Does not cover two minor world band segments (2 and 3 MHz), the new 19 MHz segment and a scattering of other world band channels. Clock not displayed independent of frequency. Fragile 12/24-hour selector. Clock displays London time and World Time as one and the same, which is true for only part of the year. Radio suddenly goes dead when batteries get weak. No longwave. AC adaptor extra.

Bottom Line: Worthy performance and attention to detail, but lacking in tuning convenience. The Sony ICF-SW33 is an obvious choice for those wanting superior reception of a number of favorite stations.

Evaluation of New Model: By the usual standard of Sony digital portables, the ICF-SW33 looks, well, like a Plain Jane. In reality, it is . . . and isn't.

For the "is," take tuning. There's a single-speed up/down slewing control, only seven shortwave presets (ten more for other bands), "signal-seek" scanning and a meter-band carousel. No keypad, no tuning knob. No single-sideband, either.

Accessories? Only a tape-measure-type external antenna and a cloth carrying pouch. No AC power supply, even though the radio costs around 25-30 cents, 15-20 pence, an hour to operate off batteries. No earpieces, either, even though they usually improve sound quality.

The normal version of the radio tunes the regular and Japanese FM bands; medium-wave AM all the way through 1710 kHz; and world band from 3700-4200, 4650-5150, 5800-6300, 6950-7450, 9375-10000, 11525-

12150, 13375-14000, 14975-15600, 17475-18100, 21320-21950 and 25475-26100 kHz. (Versions for Saudi Arabia and much of Europe cover less.) That's pretty complete coverage, but some listeners will miss the 7455-7600, 9020-9080, 9250-9375, 11500-11525, 12150-12160, 15600-15800 and 18900-19020 kHz ranges that are increasingly used by world band broadcasters. A few will miss longwave.

None of this may inspire, but there's another and more interesting facet: the '33 excels in the helpful little touches, such as its unusual two-time-zone clock and an illuminated LCD. Its battery-life indicator is also sophisticated, even if the radio's habit of suddenly shutting down the radio when batteries are low can be disconcerting. (You have three minutes to change batteries without erasing the memory, an improvement over the otherwise-excellent and more costly Sony ICF-2010.)

Also nice are a travel power lock and reception of FM stereo through headphones, not supplied. For bedtime use, there's a sleep-off control, and the radio can be set to turn on at any one given time to function as an alarm, or simply to switch on a favorite program. Also for travel there's a key lock to prevent switching out the station by accident if you're listening on the move.

The telescopic antenna rotates and swivels, plus there's a flip-out elevation panel. Taken together, these allow the radio to be operated at a comfortable angle.

The '33's clock is particularly interesting, even though it doesn't show seconds numerically or appear independent of the displayed frequency. To clear away much of the fog newcomers encounter with World Time, the clock automatically sets World Time relative to your local time. It even includes a manual Daylight Savings Time adjustment for the local-time display. Although the operating guide's clock-setting instructions are not the best, the end result is nigh foolproof.

The clock displays the name of a major city in your chosen time zone, at least if you live in one of the "right" parts of the world. For example, for the North American East Coast, the LCD shows not only local Eastern Time, but also "NEW YORK."

World Time? "LONDON" is displayed in large letters alongside "World" in small letters. That's fine in the winter, when World Time and London time are one and the same. But in the summer London is one hour ahead of World Time, so the displayed location of "London" is wrong for roughly half the year.

Another small bugaboo is that the little 12/24-hour clock selector button, secreted above the battery compartment, is fragile. In North

America, the '33's clock comes factory-preset to the 12-hour standard. If you're trying to change over from that to the 24-hour norm and it doesn't work—the selectors seemed to have minds of their own on both our units—forget it and try again later on, when it may be more cooperative. If you persist and press down hard on this tiny switch, it may break, as did one of ours.

With so little flexibility in the way of operating controls, tuning the '33 can be downright frustrating. The lack of a keypad, the inability to select more than a single pokey slew rate, the paucity of presets: these all conspire to make tuning pretty marginal. The same is true trying to bandscan by slewing the synthesizer, which chugs such that it covers up much of what you're trying to hear.

Performance fares much better. Unlike many competing simpler portables with digital readout, the '33 has excellent rejection of spurious signals, worthy selectivity to keep adjacent-channel interference at bay, and good weak-signal sensitivity. Its through-the-speaker audio, while hardly high-fidelity, is unusually intelligible. Fading is hardly noticeable, and virtually banished are the 5 kHz howls that otherwise usually curse world band reception.

Overall, the '33 is something of a rarity: a reasonably priced, good performer that's not confusing to operate. It is clearly not an "enthusiast's radio," but it is honest, affordable and free from the characteristic aural annoyances of world band. For many, that's just the ticket.

The world's only radio to be tuned by "credit cards" is the Sony ICF-SW800.

★ ★ ½   ¢

Sony ICF-SW800 (Sony ICF-SW700)

Price: *ICF-SW800:* $149.95 in the United States. *ICF-SW700:* ¥13,000 (around $100) in Japan. *AC-D3M 120V AC/4.5V DC adaptor:* $12.95 in the United States.

Advantages: Attractively priced for level of technology provided. Innovative card-type tuning system helps newcomers get started. Also incorporates a number of other helpful tuning features. Refreshingly obvious to operate for level of technology. World Time clock. Alarm facility. Highly effective travel power lock. Comes with reel-in portable wire antenna.

Disadvantages: No tuning knob. Slightly limited world band coverage, including omission of important 21 MHz segment. No longwave. Adjacent-channel rejection (selectivity) only fair. Tunes only in coarse 5 kHz increments. Keypad uses unorthodox two-row configuration and offers no tactile feedback. Clock not

displayed separately from frequency. No display illumination. No signal-strength indicator. AC adaptor extra. Not widely distributed outside Japan. *ICF-SW800:* No mediumwave AM. *ICF-SW700:* No FM.

Bottom Line: Innovative tuning that's a snap to grasp, plus respectable performance at a low price. Yet, once you become familiar with world band, the ICF-SW800's tuning innovation tends to fade into novelty.

★ ★ ½   ¢

Sangean ATS 800 Realistic DX-370 (Roberts R801) (Siemens RP 647G4)

Price: *Sangean:* $139.00 in the United States. CAN$149.95 in Canada. *ADP-808 120V AC adaptor:* $7.99 in the United States. CAN$14.95 in Canada. *Realistic:* $119.95 in the United States. AUS$199.95 in Australia. *Roberts:* £79.99 in the United Kingdom. *Siemens:* About $90 in the European Community.

Advantages: Not expensive for model with digital frequency display and presets. Already-pleasant speaker audio improves with headphones. Five preset buttons retrieve up to ten world band and ten AM/FM stations. Reasonable adjacent-channel rejection (selectivity) for price class. Relatively sensitive to weak signals, a plus for listeners in central and western North America, as well as Australia and New Zealand. Simple to operate for radio at this technology level. World Time clock. Timer/sleep/alarm features. Travel power lock. Low-battery indicator, unusual in price class.

Sangean ATS 800: Okay performance at a popular price. Also sold under the Realistic and Siemens names.

Stereo FM via earpieces (supplied in Sangean version). *Realistic:* 30-day money-back trial period.

Disadvantages: Mediocre spurious-signal ("image") rejection. Inferior dynamic range, a drawback for listeners in Europe, North Africa and the Near East. Does not tune such important world band ranges as 7305-7600, 9300-9495 and 21755-21850 kHz. Tunes world band only in coarse 5 kHz steps. No tuning knob; tunes only via multi-speed up/down slewing buttons. No longwave. Signal-strength indicator nigh useless. No display illumination. Clock not displayed separately from frequency. No carrying strap or handle. AC adaptor extra. *Sangean:* Supplied earpieces inferior to comparable foam-padded earphones. *Realistic:* No earpieces. *Sangean and Realistic:* FM and mediumwave AM tuning steps do not conform to channel spacing in much of the world outside the Americas. *Siemens:* Mediumwave AM tuning steps do not conform to channel spacing within the Americas. *Sangean and Siemens:* Do not receive 1635-1705 kHz portion of forthcoming expanded AM band in Americas, although this could change.

Comment: Strong signals within the 7305-7595 kHz range can be tuned via the "image" signal 900 kHz down; e.g., 7435 kHz may be heard on 6535 kHz.

Bottom Line: A popular starter set that's okay for the price.

★ ★   ¢

(SEG SED ECL88)

Price: Y271 in China.
Advantages: Least costly portable tested with digital frequency display and presets (ten for world band, ten for AM/FM). Slightly more selective than usual for price category. Relatively simple to operate for technology class.

World Time clock. Alarm/sleep timer. Illuminated display. FM stereo via optional headphones. AC adaptor and stereo earphones included.

Disadvantages: Relatively lacking in weak-signal sensitivity. No tuning knob; tunes only via presets and multi-speed up/down slewing. Tunes world band only in coarse 5 kHz steps. Even-numbered frequencies displayed with final zero omitted; e.g., 5.75 rather than conventional 5.750. Poor spurious-signal ("image") rejection. Mediocre dynamic range. Does not tune relatively unimportant 6200-7100 and 25600-26100 kHz world band segments. Does not receive longwave or 1615-1705 kHz portion of forthcoming expanded AM band in the Americas. No signal-strength indicator. No travel power lock switch. No AC adaptor. Reportedly prone to malfunction; flimsy antenna, especially swivel, prone to breakage. Antenna swivels, but does not rotate. Mediumwave AM tuning steps do not conform to channel spacing within the Americas.

Bottom Line: Audi cockpit, moped engine.

New for 1994   ¢
★ ★

Lowe SRX-50
(Amsonic AS-908)
(Morphy Richards R191)
(Yorx AS-908)

Price: *Lowe:* £39.95 in the United Kingdom. *Morphy Richards:* £37.00 in the United Kingdom. *Yorx:* CAN$24.99 in Canada (may be available shortly in other countries).
Advantages: Inexpensive, dramatically so in the Yorx version, for a model with digital frequency display and 20 presets (five for world band, plus five each for longwave, mediumwave AM and FM). Relatively simple to operate for technology class. Illuminated display. Alarm/sleep timer with World Time clock. FM stereo via headphones. Longwave. *Yorx:* AC adaptor and stereo headphones come standard. *Lowe:* Headphones come standard.
Disadvantages: No tuning knob; tunes only via presets and multi-speed up/down slewing/scanning. Tunes world band only in coarse 5 kHz steps. Even-numbered frequencies displayed with final zero omitted; e.g., 5.75 rather than conventional 5.750 or 5750. Poor spurious-signal ("image") rejection. Mediocre selectivity. Does not receive 1605-1705 kHz portion of forthcoming expanded AM band in the Americas. No signal-strength indicator. No travel power lock. Quality of construction appears to be below average. Clock not displayed independent of frequency display. Mediumwave AM tuning increments not

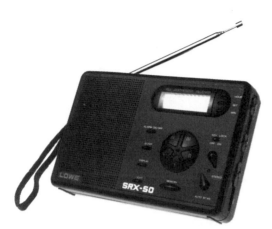

Popular as a "starter radio" in the U.K. is Lowe's SRX-50.

switchable, which may make for inexact tuning in some parts of the world other than where the radio was purchased. Power switch has no position labeled "off," although "auto radio" power-switch position performs a comparable role. *Except Yorx:* Does not tune important 5800-5895, 17500-17900 and 21750-21850 kHz segments; 15505-15695 kHz tunable only to limited extent. No AC adaptor. *Yorx:* Does not receive 7300-9499 and 21750-21850 kHz portions of the world band spectrum. Clock in 12-hour format.

Comment: Strong signals within the 15505-15800 kHz range can be tuned via the "image" signal 900 kHz down; e.g., 15685 kHz may be heard on 14785 kHz.

Bottom Line: An okay low-cost starter radio that's well suited to use on trips.

Evaluation of New Model: This Chinese-made radio has just two means for tuning: five presets for shortwave, plus a pair of multi-speed up/down slew/scan buttons. There's no keypad or tuning knob, yet tuning is much better than it is on analog models.

Sold mainly in Europe, this radio tunes longwave, plus the usual mediumwave AM and FM bands, each with its own five presets. World band coverage is typically only 5900-15500 kHz, but to some extent this can be extended slightly (*see* Comment, above).

Mediumwave AM channel spacing is permanently fixed at 10 or 9 kHz, depending upon the part of the world in which the radio is sold. If you travel where the spacing standard is different, you'll be able to receive only some of the stations on that important band. The set also omits the 1605-1705 kHz portion of the forthcoming expanded mediumwave AM band in the Americas.

Longwave and mediumwave AM performance are at least average for a low-cost portable. However, stereo FM reception, through headphones, is pedestrian.

The clock/frequency LCD is brightly illu-minated for nighttime use. Yet, instead of displaying frequency in the customary XXXXX kHz frequency layout, it reads as XX.XX or XX.XX5 MHz.

Ergonomics are reasonable, and the antenna rotates on its swivel. This is a real plus over most other cheap models, as it allows the set to be operated while laid on its back—the handiest position. There's also a lock switch for the keypad, but this doesn't serve as a power lock to prevent the radio or its dial light from coming on accidentally in transit, running down the batteries.

Performance is a mixed bag. Adjacent-channel rejection (selectivity), mediocre, is typical for its class. Audio quality, while tinny, is okay except on FM, where it becomes tiring. Single-conversion IF circuitry, one of the great remaining curses of cheap radios, means you hear annoying repeats—"images"—of radio signals that actually operate 900 kHz away.

Sensitivity to weak world band signals is quite reasonable for its class. Dynamic range, while hardly inspiring, is also better than we've come to expect from cheap Chinese digital portables.

In all, this radio offers few surprises, good or bad. It's a decent little performer for very little money, and should make a suitable budget starter or a low-cost radio to take on trips. If it's stolen or lost, who cares, and in some countries it would make a distinctive gift for that special host who made your stay so enjoyable.

★ ★

Rodelsonic Digital World Band
Rodelvox Digital World Band
(Amsonic AS-138)
(Dick Smith A-4338)
(Scotcade 65B 119 UCY Digital World Band)
(Shimasu PLL Digital)

Price: *Rodelvox and Rodelsonic:* $99.95 plus $6.95 shipping in United States. *Amsonic:* Y265 (about US$48) in China. *Scotcade:* £29.99 plus shipping in the United Kingdom. *Dick Smith:* AUS$99.95 in Australia.

Advantages: Relatively inexpensive for a model with digital frequency display and 20 presets (ten for world band, ten for mediumwave AM and FM). Relatively simple to operate for technology class. Alarm/sleep timer with World Time clock. Illuminated display. FM stereo via optional headphones.

Disadvantages: Modest weak-signal sensitivity. No tuning knob; tunes only via presets and multi-speed up/down slewing/scanning. Tunes world band only in coarse 5 kHz steps. Even-numbered frequencies displayed with

Many bags, same tea. The Rodelvox is sold under a wide variety of brand names.

final zero omitted; e.g., 5.75 rather than conventional 5.750. Poor spurious-signal ("image") rejection. Mediocre dynamic range. Does not receive 1635-1705 kHz portion of forthcoming expanded AM band in the Americas. No signal-strength indicator. Clock in 12-hour format, not displayed independent of frequency display. No travel power lock. No AC adaptor. Quality of construction appears to be below average. Mediumwave AM tuning increments not switchable, which may make for inexact tuning in some parts of the world other than where the radio was purchased. *Except Scotcade:* Does not tune important 7305-9495 and 21755-21850 kHz segments. No longwave.

Note: The Amsonic is available in at least five versions: AS-138 for China, AS-138-0 for Europe, AS-138-3 for USA/Canada, AS-138-4 for Japan, and AS-138-6 for other countries and Europe. Each version has FM and mediumwave AM ranges and channel spacing appropriate to the market region, plus the Japanese version replaces coverage of the 21 MHz band with TV audio.

Comment: Strong signals within the 7305-7595 kHz range can be tuned via the "image" signal 900 kHz down; e.g., 7435 kHz may be heard on 6535 kHz.

Bottom Line: No bargain in the United States, but more attractively priced elsewhere.

★ ★

(Pulser)

Comment: Not tested, but reportedly very similar to the above groups of low-cost digital models from China.

Price: CAN$59.99 in Canada.

★ ★

DAK DMR-3000 Global Interceptor

Price: $69.90 plus $6.00 shipping in the United States.

Advantages: Least costly portable tested with digital frequency display, keypad and presets (18 for world band, 18 for FM and mediumwave AM). Up/down slew tuning with "signal-seek" scanning. Slightly better adjacent-channel rejection (selectivity) than usual for price category. Relatively simple to operate for technology class. World Time and local clocks. Alarm/sleep timer. Illuminated display. Available on 30-day money-back basis. FM stereo via optional headphones. Selectable 9/10 kHz mediumwave AM increments, uncommon in price class.

Disadvantages: Insensitive to weak—or even moderate—signals on 9 and 11 MHz segments of the world band spectrum, and DAK's optional "Station Stalker" active antenna doesn't help much. Mediocre sensitivity to weak signals in other parts of the world band spectrum. No tuning knob. Tunes world band only in coarse 5 kHz steps. Inferior dynamic range and spurious-signal rejection. Does not tune important 9350-9495, 13600-13800 and 15000-15095 kHz portions of world band spectrum, along with some others. No longwave. No signal-strength indicator. No travel power lock, but power switch not easy to turn on accidentally. No AC adaptor. Clocks do not display independent of frequency.

Bottom Line: Excellent features, many carefully thought out and heretofore unheard of at this price. Yet, on some world band segments stations hardly come in. Were it not for this failing, the DMR-3000 would rank at the top of the two-star category.

The DAK DMR-3000 has many features, but is a limp performer.

The Jäger PL-440 is neatly laid out, but performs poorly.

★ ★

Jäger PL-440 (Omega)

Price: *Jäger:* $79.95 plus $6.00 shipping in the United States. *Omega:* 1,500 francs in Belgium.

Advantages: Not costly for a model with digital frequency display. Tuning aids include up/down slewing buttons with "signal-seek" scanning, and 20 presets (five each for world band, FM, longwave and mediumwave AM). Relatively simple to operate for technology class. World Time clock. Sleep/timer features. Longwave. Antenna rotates and swivels, unusual in price class. Travel power lock.

Disadvantages: Limited coverage of world band spectrum omits important 5800-5945, 15605-15695, 17500-17900 and 21450-21850 kHz ranges, among others. No tuning knob; tunes only via presets and multi-speed up/down slewing/scanning. Tunes world band only in coarse 5 kHz steps. Tortoise-slow band-to-band tuning, remediable by using presets as band selectors. Slow one-channel-at-a-time slewing is the only means for bandscanning between world band segments. Slightly insensitive to weak signals. Poor adjacent-channel rejection (selectivity). Apparently mediocre quality control. Even-numbered frequencies displayed with final zero omitted; e.g., 5.75 rather than conventional 5.750 or 5750. No signal-strength indicator. Clock not displayed independent of frequency display. Display not illuminated. Not offered with AC adaptor. Does not receive 1605-1705 kHz portion of forthcoming expanded AM band in the Americas. Lacks selector for 9/10 kHz mediumwave AM steps.

Bottom Line: This seeming improvement on the Giros has reasonable audio and nice features for the money, with presets and digital readout to make tuning easier than with analog models.

The Giros R918 has little but size to commend it.

★ ½

Giros R918

Price: CAN$64.50 plus shipping in Canada. Almost certainly available in parts of Asia and Europe.

Advantages: Inexpensive for a model with digital frequency display. Unusually small size for a compact—close to a mini, thus useful for travels. Tuning aids include up/down slewing buttons with "signal-seek" scanning, and 20 presets (five each for world band, FM, longwave and mediumwave AM). Relatively simple to operate for technology class. World Time clock. Sleep/timer features. Battery strength indicator. Longwave. Antenna rotates and swivels, unusual in price class. Selector for 9/10 kHz mediumwave AM steps, uncommon among cheap digital radios.

Disadvantages: Limited coverage of world band spectrum omits important 15605-15695, 17500-17900 and 21450-21850 kHz ranges, among others. Insensitive to weak signals. Audio quality mediocre, tinny and distorted. Poor adjacent-channel rejection (selectivity). Slow tuning with no tuning knob; tunes only via presets and multi-speed up/down slewing/scanning. Apparently mediocre quality control. Even-numbered frequencies displayed with final zero omitted; e.g., 5.75 rather than conventional 5.750 or 5750. Clock not displayed independent of frequency display. No signal-strength indicator. No travel power lock. Display not illuminated. Hums badly if an AC adaptor used. Not offered with AC adaptor. Does not receive 1605-1705 kHz portion of forthcoming expanded AM band in the Americas.

Bottom Line: Marginal performer.

(Digitor Portable A-4336)

Price: AUS$79.95 in Australia. Not tested, but appears to be similar to the Giros R918, preceding.

New for 1994

★½

Casio PR100

Price: $54.50, including shipping, in the United States.

Advantages: Inexpensive for a model with digital frequency display. Unusually small size for a compact—close to a mini, thus useful for travels. Tuning aids include up/down slewing buttons with "signal-seek" scanning, and 20 presets (10 for world band, plus five each for FM and mediumwave AM). Relatively simple to operate for technology class. World Time clock (some versions). Sleep/timer features. Battery strength indicator. Antenna rotates and swivels, unusual in price class. Selector for 9/10 kHz mediumwave AM steps, uncommon among cheap digital radios.

Disadvantages: Unusually insensitive to weak signals. Audio quality mediocre, tinny and distorted. Poor adjacent-channel rejection (selectivity). No tuning knob; tunes only via presets and multi-speed up/down slewing/scanning. Tunes world band slowly and only in coarse 5 kHz steps. Clock in inappropriate 12-hour format (some versions). Clock not displayed independent of frequency display. Does not receive 1605-1705 kHz portion of forthcoming expanded AM band in the Americas. No longwave. No signal-strength indicator. No travel power lock. No AC adaptor. Apparently mediocre quality control. Even-numbered frequencies displayed with final zero omitted; e.g., 5.75 rather than conventional 5.750 or 5750. Display not illuminated. Hums badly if AC adaptor used.

Bottom Line: Hardly the sort of performance you might expect from a firm with Casio's reputation.

Evaluation of New Model: High among the world's most respected names for clocks is Casio, so it comes as something of a surprise to find that the clock in one North American version of Casio's first world band radio uses the "AM/PM" 12-hour format, not the 24-hour format used for World Time. Obviously, the 24-hour version is much to be preferred.

The PR100 covers 2.3-6.2 and 7.1-21.85 MHz, excellent for this price class. However, tuning options are minimal. You have to make do with a pair of up/down/"signal seek" slew buttons and 20 presets: five each for mediumwave AM, FM, SW_1 (to 6200 kHz) and SW_2 (from 7100 kHz). There's also a 9/10 kHz switch to control mediumwave AM channel spacing (10 kHz for the Americas, 9 kHz elsewhere), a useful feature for globetrotters—even if our new radio came with that control incorrectly set.

Other features include a one-event-per-day timer, sleep control, large snooze button, earpiece jack and low-battery indicator. The telescopic antenna both swivels and rotates—uncommon in this price class. There's also a jack for an outboard AC adaptor (not supplied), but when we used one that works well on other radios it generated annoying hum.

Even-numbered world band channels appear in XX.XX MHz format (e.g., 6170 kHz appears as 6.17 MHz), whereas odd-numbered shortwave channels are in XX.XX5 format (e.g., 6175 kHz appears as 6.175 MHz). It's an odd custom found only on some Chinese portables.

Tuning with the slew buttons outside Casio's designated world band segments can be done only one channel per button-push. Press the button longer to activate faster tuning, and the radio's tuning system suddenly leaps to the nearest designated segment. For example, if you're tuning within the 9350-9495 kHz range that's chockablock with broadcasts, press the "down" button long enough to activate fast tuning and the radio leaps to 7300 kHz. Press the "up" button like that, and the radio leaps to 9500 kHz. This can be a valuable time saver if you're tuning strictly within the designated segments, but

Watchmaker Casio now sells a radio under its own brand name.

outside those segments tuning becomes even more of a chore than usual.

Performance disappoints. Even by the dismal standard of most other cheap Chinese-made digital portables, this Casio offering is unusually insensitive to weak shortwave signals. Adjacent-channel rejection (selectivity) is poor, image rejection mediocre and audio quality harsh.

Casio's PR100, mediocre by any standard, is a disappointment.

New for 1994

★ ½

Panda 2006

The Panda 2006 is hard to bear.

Price: Y185 (about $32) in China. To be established elsewhere; probably around the equivalent of $50-100 in most countries.

Advantages: Weak-signal sensitivity at least average for class. Tuning aids include up/down slewing buttons, "signal-seek" scanning and 20 presets (five for world band, plus five each for FM, mediumwave AM and longwave). Relatively simple to operate for technology class. Longwave. World Time clock with sleep/timer features.

Disadvantages: Poor adjacent-channel rejection (selectivity). FM signals, distorted, break through radio's circuitry to disrupt world band reception. Mediocre spurious signal rejection. Audio quality mediocre, tinny and distorted. No tuning knob; tunes only via five presets and single-speed up/down slewing/scanning. Tunes world band only in coarse 5 kHz steps. Slow band-to-band tuning, partially remediable by using presets as band selectors or by using scan function. Does not receive the 2, 3, 4, 5, 17, 19, 21 or 25 MHz world band segments, nor small portions of the 6 and 15 MHz segments. Clock not displayed independent of frequency display. Antenna swivels, but does not rotate. Does not receive 1605-1705 kHz portion of forthcoming expanded AM band in the Americas. No selector for 9/10 kHz mediumwave AM steps. No signal-strength indicator. No travel power lock. No battery indicator. Display not illuminated. No AC adaptor. Even-numbered frequencies displayed with final zero omitted; e.g., 5.75 rather than conventional 5.750. Quality of construction appears to be below average.

Bottom Line: A panda that's hard to bear.

Evaluation of New Model: The Panda 2006 is another and, in many ways, typical Chinese compact portable. World band is covered continuously from 5950-15600 kHz, which is reasonable but omits no less than eight segments between 2300-5100 and 17480-26100 kHz, as well as the 5800-5945 and 15605-15800 kHz portions of 49 and 19 meters.

The Panda comes with a World Time clock, useful even if it can't be read while the frequency is being displayed. Although the radio receives longwave, still active in Europe, its mediumwave AM band stops short of the forthcoming 1605-1705 kHz range for the Americas.

Mediumwave AM channel spacing is permanently fixed at 10 or 9 kHz, depending upon the part of the world in which the radio is sold. If you travel where the spacing standard is different, you'll be able to receive only some of the stations on that important band.

As with many of its inexpensive Chinese-made counterparts, the Panda's telescopic antenna swivels, but does not rotate. This makes world band and FM listening unhandy, unless the radio is rested on its tipsy bottom.

Yet, these shortcomings are niggling relative to the radio's two chief faults: slow tuning and mediocre performance.

Tuning is slow because there is neither a keypad nor a tuning knob. Instead, there are a mere five presets, pokey single-speed up/down slewing and "signal-seek" (up-frequency only) scanning.

What this means is that tuning the Panda requires great patience. With the slew buttons, the radio creeps, one channel at a time, through each and every frequency in the shortwave spectrum between where the radio was originally tuned and where you wish it to be tuned. This electronic pilgrimage can take minutes!

Fortunately, the scanner skips out-of-band

regions, making tuning faster—but only if you're tuning upward. It's a one-way carousel, with only the "down" slew button to fall back upon if you wish to tune downward.

A partial solution is to use the presets as "band buttons." With five presets and the radio's coverage limited to only six world band segments, at least some of the pokiness of tuning can be alleviated.

Performance? Even though the Panda's sensitivity to weak mediumwave AM signals is poor, its sensitivity to weak world band signals is fairly good. To some extent, this means more stations can be received. That's the good news.

However, adjacent-channel rejection—selectivity—is poor. As if that weren't enough,

grossly distorted spurious signals from local FM (87.5-108 MHz) broadcasts intrude while the radio is tuned to world band (5.9-15.6 MHz). How much this will affect your listening depends on the FM situation in your area. Topping off this dismal roster of noisemaking characteristics is that spurious signals, resulting from mediocre image rejection, also intrude to disrupt reception even further.

Audio quality? Tinny, but adequate for occasional world band listening, such as on trips. On FM, it's hard to endure.

Look to China to make some interesting world band radios in the not-too-distant future. They are catching on, but you'd never know it from the Panda 2006.

Record Programs While You're Away!

Millions do it daily: record television programs on VCRs so they can be enjoyed at a more convenient time. You'd think that with world band radio sales rising for several years now, history would repeat itself, and there would be a number of world band cassette recorders—radios with built-in tape recorders—from which to choose.

Not so—there's only one worth considering, the Sangean ATS-818CS, $329.00 in the United States, CAN$429.95 in Canada and AUS$399.00 in Australia. It's one-event, so you can't record more than one time bloc automatically, and even then it can be programmed for only one day. Too, while you can set the recording "on" time, it shuts off automatically only when the tape runs out.

The '818CS is the same as the two-and-a-half-star ATS-818—for performance details, see the review of the '818 elsewhere in this section—but with a cassette deck added and a smaller speaker cavity. Recording features are bare-bones (no level indicator, no counter, no stereo) but there is a condenser microphone. The fast-forward and rewind controls are inverted from the customary positions, so the indicator arrows are backwards—fast forward points left, rewind points right. Still, recording quality is acceptable, and the limited timing facility works as it should.

Sangean's ATS-818CS is clearly the finest radio available with built-in recording facilities.

Sangean's ATS-818CS is no high-tech wonder, but it is, hands down, the best device of its type on the market. It's also available for £199.99 in the United Kingdom as the Roberts RC818, and in Germany with factory preprogrammed stations as the Siemens RK 670. The RK 670 has also been found for sale every now and then on the gray market in New York for under $130.

That's it? Not really. A number of newer models, identified in this section, can be programmed to switch not only themselves on and off, but also a cassette recorder. While it's less handy than the Sangean offering, the results—if you use a well-rated radio—can be even better.

MID-SIZED PORTABLES

Good for Home, Fair for Travel

If you're looking for a home set, yet also one that can be taken out in the backyard and on the occasional trip, a mid-sized portable is probably your best bet. These are large enough to perform well and can sound pretty good, yet are compact enough to tote in your suitcase now and then. Most take 3-4 "D" (UM-1) cells, plus a couple of "AA" (UM-3) cells for their fancy computer circuits.

How large? Typically just under a foot wide—that's 30 cm—and weighing in around 3-4 pounds, or 1.3-1.8 kg. For air travel, that's okay if you are a dedicated listener, but a bit much otherwise. Too, larger sets with snazzy controls occasionally attract unwanted attention from suspicious customs and airport-security personnel in some parts of the world.

Three stand out for most listeners: the high-tech Sony ICF-2010, also sold as the ICF-2001D; Grundig's sleek Satellit 700; and the cheaper Sangean ATS-803A, also sold under other names. The mid-priced Sony is the obvious choice for radio enthusiasts, whereas the Grundig should appeal to the larger body of regular listeners to world band, FM and mediumwave AM stations. The Sangean ATS-803A is a good buy if you feel the others are outside your financial bounds.

The revised Sony ICF-SW77, like opera, is not for everybody. With this high-tech wonder, it's either love or hate—little between.

Still the best portable at any price is Sony's ICF-2010, an all-time classic.

★ ★ ★ ½   *Editor's Choice*

Sony ICF-2010
Sony ICF-2001D
(Sony ICF-2001DS)

Price: *ICF-2010:* $429.95 in the United States. CAN$499 in Canada. *ICF-2001D and ICF-2001DS:* £279.95 in the United Kingdom. $500-950 elsewhere in the European Community. AUS$899.00 in Australia.

Advantages: Lowest-priced radio having high-tech synchronous detection with selectable sideband; it performs very well, reducing adjacent-channel interference and fading distortion on world band, longwave and mediumwave AM signals; it also provides superior reception of reduced-carrier single-sideband

signals. Use of 32 separate preset buttons in rows and columns is ergonomically the best to be found on any model, portable or tabletop, at any price; simply pushing one button one time brings in your station, a major convenience. Numerous other helpful tuning features. Two bandwidths offer superior tradeoff between audio fidelity and adjacent-channel rejection (selectivity). Tunes and displays in precise 0.1 kHz increments. Separately displayed World Time clock. Alarm/sleep features, with four-event timer. Illuminated LCD. Travel power lock. Signal-strength indicator. Covers longwave and the Japanese FM band. Some reception of air band signals (most versions). Comes with AC adaptor. In the European Community, available in a special "ICF-2001DS" or "kit" version supplied with Sony AN-1 amplified antenna; elsewhere, that antenna may be purchased separately for around $90.

Disadvantages: Audio quality only average, with mediocre tone control. Controls and high-tech features, although exceptionally handy once you get the hang of them, initially may intimidate or confuse. Presets and clock/timer features immediately erase whenever computer batteries are replaced, and also sometimes erase when set is jostled. Wide bandwidth quite broad for world band reception. First RF transistor (Q-303) reportedly prone to damage by static electricity, as from nearby lightning strikes, when used with external wire antenna (such antennas should be disconnected with the approach of snow, sand, dry-wind or thunder storms); or when amplified (active) antennas other than Sony AN-1 are used. "Signal-seek" scanning works poorly. Telescopic antenna swivel gets slack with use, as do those of a number of other portable models, requiring periodic adjustment of tension screw. Synchronous detector does not switch off during tuning. Lacks up/down slewing.

Keypad not in telephone format. LCD clearly readable only when radio viewed from below. Chugs slightly when tuned. Non-synchronous single-sideband reception can be mistuned by up to 50 Hz. Uninspiring FM performance.

Bottom Line: Incredibly, after all these years, this radio is still the Big Enchilada for radiophiles, and fairly priced for all it does so well. Except for pedestrian audio quality and FM, plus the learning curve, Sony's high-tech offering remains, for many, the best performing travel-weight portable. Its use of separate pushbuttons for each preset makes station call-up easier than with virtually any other radio tested. Its synchronous detection, which works as it should, not only reduces distortion but also, as one reader puts it, offers the adjacent-channel rejection (selectivity) of a narrow filter with the fidelity of a wide filter.

 An *RDI WHITE PAPER* is available for this model.

★ ★ ★ ½   *Editor's Choice*

Grundig Satellit 700

Price: $499.00 in the United States. CAN$599.00 in Canada. £349.99 in the United Kingdom.
Advantages: Superior audio quality, aided by separate continuous bass and treble controls. High-tech synchronous detector circuit with selectable sideband reduces adjacent-channel interference and fading distortion on world band, longwave and mediumwave AM signals (*see* Disadvantages); it also provides superior reception of reduced-carrier single-sideband signals. Two bandwidths offer superior tradeoff between audio fidelity and adjacent-channel rejection (selectivity). 512 presets standard; up to 2048 presets optionally available. Schedules for 22 stations stored by factory in memory. Stored station names appear on LCD. Numerous other helpful tuning features. Tunes and displays in precise 0.1 kHz increments in synchronous and single-sideband modes; this, along with a fine-tuning clarifier, produce the best tuning configuration for single sideband in a conventional travel-weight portable. Separately displayed World Time clock. Alarm/sleep features with superior timer that, in principle, can also control a recorder. Superior FM reception. Stereo FM through headphones. Superior mediumwave AM reception. Illuminated LCD, which is clearly visible from a variety of angles. Travel power lock. Heavy-duty telescopic antenna. Screw mounts for mobile or maritime operation. Runs off AC power worldwide. Comes with built-in NiCd battery charger. RDS circuitry for European FM station selection—eventually North America, too—by program format. Excellent operator's manuals.

Disadvantages: Chugs when tuned slowly by knob; worse, mutes completely when tuned quickly, making bandscanning unnecessarily difficult. Using presets relatively complex. Synchronous detection circuit produces minor background rumble and has relatively little sideband separation. Some overall distortion except in AM mode. Wide bandwidth a touch broad for world band reception. Keypad lacks feel and is not in telephone format. Antenna keels over in certain settings. Location of tuning controls and volume control on separate sides of case tend to make listening a two-handed affair.

Bottom Line: Right up there with the very best in portables, and for many regular program listeners simply the very best. Withal, notably for bandscanning, not all it could be.

For 1994, Grundig has reduced the price of its well-rated Satellit 700.

New Version for 1994
★ ★ ★ ½

Sony ICF-SW77
Sony ICF-SW77E

Price: $624.95 in the United States. CAN$750 in Canada. £399.99 in the United Kingdom. AUS$999 in Australia.
Advantages: A rich variety of tuning features, including numerous innovative techniques not found in other world band radios. Synchronous detection, which performs as it should and is exceptionally handy to operate, reduces fading distortion and adjacent-channel interference on world band, longwave and mediumwave AM signals; it also provides superior reception of reduced-carrier single-sideband

signals. Two well-chosen bandwidths provide superior adjacent-channel rejection. Tunes in very precise 50 Hz increments; displays in precise 100 Hz increments. Two illuminated multi-function liquid crystal displays. Pre-set world band segments. Keypad tuning. Tuning "knob" with two speeds. 162 presets, including 96 frequencies stored by country or station name. "Signal-seek" scanning. Separately displayed World Time and local time clocks. Station name appears on LCD when presets used. Signal-strength indicator. Flip-up chart for calculating time differences. VCR-type five-event timer controls radio and recorder alike. Continuous bass and treble tone controls. Superior FM audio quality. Stereo FM through headphones. Receives longwave and Japanese FM. Comes with AC adaptor.

Disadvantages: Excruciatingly complex for many, but not all, to operate. Synthesizer chugging, as bad as we've encountered in our tests, degrades the quality of tuning by knob. Dynamic range only fair. Presets can't be accessed simply, as they can on most models. Flimsy telescopic antenna. Display illumination does not stay on with AC power. Relatively insensitive on mediumwave AM band.

Bottom Line: The Sony ICF-SW77, a superior performer, uses innovative high technology in an attempt to make listening easier. Results, however, are a mixed bag: What is gained in convenience in some areas is lost in others. The upshot is that whether using the '77 is enjoyable or a hair-pulling exercise comes down to personal taste. In our survey some relish it, most don't.

Note: We tested the latest version, which the manufacturer advises is "it." An earlier version or versions, now long gone from dealer shelves, had problems largely cleared up in the current, nominally final, version.

Evaluation of Current Version: For more than a decade, now, digital technology, as much as anything else, has accounted for the growth in sales of world band radios. Thanks to this, you can now find the station you want right off—and more quickly identify a strange signal. So, it's hardly surprising that some clever person might figure that if a little technology can do that much good, imagine what lots would be like!

Imagine no more. Sony has pulled out virtually all the technological stops in its innovative ICF-SW77. The result is as much a computer as a radio, and therein lies its ledger of pluses and minuses.

The version of the '77 sold in most countries covers longwave, mediumwave AM and world band from 150 kHz-30.0 MHz. Elsewhere? In Saudi Arabia, it's 150-285 kHz and 531-26100 kHz; Italy, 150-285 kHz, 531-1602 kHz and

The most advanced world band radio operating system is found in Sony's ICF-SW77, revised for 1994.

3850-26100 kHz. Reception modes are AM, LSB, USB and synchronous (lower and upper).

In addition, the regular version receives FM—stereo through earphones, mono through the speaker—from 76-108 MHz, which includes the Japanese FM band. Those versions for Saudi Arabia and Italy, as well as special versions for Austria, Germany and Scandinavia, omit the Japanese FM band, but still cover the usual 87.5-108 MHz band.

Many folks use world band portables as much off the wall plug as they do off batteries. So, with some other models, notably the little ICF-SW1S, Sony has included a "smart" AC adaptor. This senses the exact line voltage anywhere in the world and adjusts accordingly. It's ideal for globetrotting, and downright foolproof. Plug it in anywhere, and it automatically does all the rest.

Not so the costlier '77. It comes standard with an external AC adaptor, too, but smart it ain't. The U.S. version is for 120 VAC only, which for a pricey international portable is disappointing. The United Kingdom version is for 240 VAC only, whereas all other versions are equipped, as at a minimum they should be wherever the law allows, for 110-120/220-240 VAC.

The '77 is tricked out with a number of features to make listening easier and more pleasant: synchronous detection to fight fading distortion and adjacent-channel interference; 162 presets, including 96 frequencies factory-stored by name for 27 different stations and countries; World Time and local time clocks; flip-up chart for figuring time differences; five-event VCR-type timer; two bandwidths; two tuning speeds; direct entry keypad; two illuminated multi-function liquid crystal displays; digital frequency readout to 100 Hz increments; accessible pre-set world band segments; and automatic station scanner.

Particularly commendable are the separate, continuously tunable, bass and treble tone controls. With the "I can do almost anything if you'll let me try" '77, you can also tape programs, as with a VCR, with the recorder being switched on and off automatically by the radio.

The '77 offers two manually selectable tuning speeds: "fast," the receiver displays and tunes in 1 kHz increments; "slow," it displays in 100 Hz increments, but tunes in itsy *50 Hz* steps. This means single-sideband reception can be off by no more than 25 Hz, which although not ideal is usually adequate.

The radio has 162 presets, each of which stores station name, frequency, detection mode (wide/narrow, synchronous, and so on), and program starting and ending times. Just getting started? Ninety-six of these presets come pre-programmed from the factory with frequencies and active times from 27 different stations and countries.

As soon as a preset is selected, it is immediately brought into the main tuning circuit and thus becomes immediately tunable. Unless you decide to change the preset, it will return to its original status the next time you access it.

However, this means there is no way to return to a frequency you may have been tuning before you accessed the preset. To get back to a previous frequency, you must use the keypad, tuning "knob," or a preset in which you had stored the desired frequency.

Two well-chosen bandwidths come standard. These provide the flexibility to choose the bandwidth you want for best reception at any given moment.

Most will need nearly every one of the operating manual's 34 pages in English. Although three of our panelists found the '77 to be remarkably intuitive right out of the box, others made vigorous use of the manual to execute sophisticated functions. Fortunately, the manual is fairly clear, even though it contains a number of errors.

Yet, in many respects the '77 is easy to use. The tone controls and (annoyingly stiff) volume slider are tucked handily into the side of the receiver. Little-used controls, such as the pointless LCD contrast adjustment and more-useful clock-setting controls, are tucked away under a flap. All 39 pushbuttons are well-spaced and have a crisp, positive feel.

However, the tuning "knob" isn't a knob at all; it's a plastic disk that barely protrudes above its surrounding surface. It works adequately, but would have been much improved with a finger hole.

The tuning disk saw relatively little use

during our evaluation because of another and more serious problem: the synthesizer chugs, or pops, annoyingly between tuning steps. It's among the worst examples of this we have come across. The only way around the problem, besides avoiding the tuning knob altogether, is to tune glacially slowly—at, say, roughly the same rate that continents drift. From a practical standpoint, bandscanning by spinning the tuning knob is a flop.

Fortunately, direct frequency entry is a piece of cake. The '77 has a flip-down panel that props the receiver at a handy 30-degree angle for tabletop use. The three-over-three-plus-one keypad is configured as it should be: like a telephone keypad. The "1" is at the upper left, with the zero centered under the "8" at the bottom. If you want the BBC World Service on 6175, press 6, 1, 7, 5, EXE, and there it is. If you make a mistake, hit the ERASE button and start over. Short of Lowe Electronics' standard-setting outboard keypad, this is among the easiest-to-use keypads around.

There is also a "signal-seek" scan function that allows you to avoid the tuning knob. It works well, provided you're not trying to unearth weak stations.

One of the '77's two LCDs has an interesting 24-hour World Time line that indicates when some of the factory pre-programmed memory channels are expected to be active. So, if you select the #1 Sweden memory preset, the display darkens to show that 9695 kHz is expected to be active with Swedish programming from 2300 to 0600 hours.

The most unusual ergonomic feature of the '77 is the computer-oriented Windows™-type interface that you must use to store and retrieve presets. As each new "page" appears in the display, the names of pre-stored stations or countries—for example, Israel, Japan, Korea—appear above five function keys—labeled S1, S2, and so forth—at the bottom of the display. Abbreviated stations show, too. To select the station or country you want, press the function key immediately below your choice.

As soon as a function key below a station or country name is pressed, the '77 immediately checks its clock for World Time. The receiver then checks the frequencies stored under that station or country name—there may be as many as ten or as few as one—to see if any have been programmed as being active at that time. If so, the '77 activates the frequency that is listed as being active. If not, it activates the frequency last accessed under that station name.

Alternatively, you can activate a feature called AUTO TUNE. It automatically steps through the frequencies pre-programmed for a station or country, checks the signal strength of each, then activates the frequency with the strongest signal. Once activated, AUTO TUNE continues to function whenever you press the function key below that station or country—unless, of course, you deliberately turn it off.

This ingenious operating scheme allows the casual listener to browse through countries by name to find the one that interests him, then lets the receiver do the rest of the work.

Nice idea, so long as you keep in mind that world band stations may come and go on the same frequency at different times of day, like merchants in a Calcutta bazaar. This means that you don't always get what you think you're going to get when you access the frequencies pre-stored under a particular country name. Even if times are included and there's not another station dominating the channel, these variables often change with the seasons of the year. Such is the nature of world band.

More to the nature of the radio itself, the '77 provides no method to access a favorite preset directly. If the BBC is in, say, memory 10, you can't simply "punch it up." Instead, you must wade sequentially through the memory pages until you unearth the one you need, select the station you want, and only then access the desired frequency.

Compare this with the Sony ICF-2010, which has 32 buttons that allow you to access any preset instantly with one push of one button. It doesn't come any easier than that!

In sum, the '77's operating scheme can be useful, but for many it is too complicated and pokey. Whether it's viewed as a delight or a pain comes down to personal preference. For this reason, you may wish to purchase this model on a returnable basis so you can decide for yourself whether this is your particular cup of tea.

How well does the radio actually perform? Overall, it's top-of-the-line, although dynamic range is only fair.

Sensitivity to weak world band signals is right up there with many tabletop supersets, if you go by standard lab measurements. However, with the telescopic antenna, which is what most of us use, sensitivity is okay but unspectacular. (Reeling out a hank of external antenna wire helps.) The two bandwidths—5.5 kHz wide, 3.2 kHz narrow—both have excellent shape factors and superb ultimate rejection.

The '77 has minimal distortion, too. On FM, which sounds quite good, you will really appreciate this, especially as the radio has fully tunable separate bass and treble tone controls—a major plus. Yet, on world band and mediumwave AM, our ears told us that the '77's audio quality, while more mellow and

easier to shape than that of the excellent Sony ICF-2010, is not quite equal to that of some other portables, such as the Grundig Yacht Boy 400.

The radio's limited dynamic range means that in some parts of the world, such as Europe, the '77 may "overload" on some world band segments at certain times of the day. You'll know this if the receiver works fine with its built-in antenna, but with an external antenna sounds like murmuring in a TV courtroom scene.

Most listeners run world band portables off their telescopic antennas, so for them this is less of an issue. A cautionary note: the last segments of the telescoping antenna are exceptionally thin and bend easily.

One of the best ideas to hit world band receivers is called "synchronous detection." Although it adds slightly to the complexity of operation, it provides audible benefits: reduction of distortion that results from fading, plus less racket from adjacent-channel stations. Depending on what's being received, synchronous detection can make no real difference or produce a dramatic improvement. Few models have synchronous detection, and no other manufacturer of portables does it better than Sony. It's a real plus, although in North America it can also be obtained for less money on the Sony ICF-2010.

In many ways, the '77 is a superb world band portable, offering superior performance. Unfortunately, it is also seriously marred by synthesizer chugging. More subjectively, the convenience of its high-tech operating system is open to real question. For example, if you wish to scan the bands manually or want straightforward access to presets, you almost certainly won't be happy with the '77.

That's most people, but by no means all—and those who like the '77 aren't necessarily just computer types, either. One of our collaborators who gave the radio a "thumbs up" is the editor of a news magazine; another, a technical monitor in the Middle East. Yet another, a professional inventor of puzzle games, simply fell in love with the radio's operating system. All are computer literate, but none qualifies as a computer freak.

Chugging aside, this is a fascinating, innovative receiver for those who enjoy the '77's novel operating environment. If that's you, go for it. Otherwise, consider Sony's cheaper ICF-2010, if you can find it. (Outside North America, the '2010, sold as the ICF-2001D, appears to have been taken off the market, although Sony won't confirm this.) The '2010 has its share of warts, too, but they're decidedly different from those on the ICF-SW77.

One of Sangean's top models is the mid-sized ATS-803A.

Editor's Choice

Sangean ATS-803A
(Clairtone PR-291)
(TMR 7602 Hitech Tatung)
(Matsui MR-4099)
(Eska RX 33)
(Siemens RK 651)
(Quelle Universum)

Price: *Sangean:* $249.00 in the United States. CAN$299.95 in Canada. £119.95 in the United Kingdom. $150-330 in the European Community. AUS$269.00 in Australia. *Clairtone:* CAN$229.95 in Canada. *Tatung:* under £110 in the United Kingdom. *Matsui:* $160-220 in the European Community. *Eska:* Dkr. 1995 (about $315) in Denmark. *Siemens:* $180-250 in the European Community and the United States. *Quelle Universum:* $180-250 in the European Community.

Advantages: Superior overall world band performance. Numerous tuning features. Two bandwidths for good fidelity/interference tradeoff. Superior spurious-signal ("image") rejection. Illuminated display. Signal-strength indicator. World Time clock. Alarm/sleep/timer. Travel power lock. Separate bass and treble controls. Worthy reception of utility and ham signals for price class. Good reception of FM signals. FM stereo through headphones (supplied in Sangean ATS-803A and most other versions). Longwave. Sangean ATS-803A and many other versions supplied with AC adaptor.

Disadvantages: Synthesizer chugs a little. Clock not displayed separately from frequency, disables keypad when displayed. Keypad not in telephone format.

Bottom Line: An excellent model for getting started, provided all the features don't intimi-

date. Once without equal in its price class, it is now beginning to feel the effects of heads-up competition.

Sangean ATS-818
Realistic DX-390
Roberts R817

Price: *Sangean:* $299.00 in the United States. CAN$399.95 in Canada. *Realistic:* $239.95 plus #273-1454 AC adaptor at Radio Shack stores in the United States. CAN$299.95 plus #273-1454 AC adaptor in Canada. AUS$399.95 plus #273-1454 AC adaptor in Australia. *Roberts:* £169.99 in the United Kingdom.

Advantages: Superior overall world band performance. Numerous tuning features, including 18 world band presets. Two bandwidths for good fidelity/interference tradeoff. Superior spurious-signal ("image") rejection. Illuminated display. Signal-strength indicator. Two 24-hour clocks, one for World Time, with either displayed separately from frequency. Alarm/sleep/timer. Travel power lock. FM stereo through headphones. Longwave. Sangean version supplied with AC adaptor. *Realistic:* 30-day money-back trial period.

Disadvantages: Mutes when tuning knob turned quickly, making bandscanning difficult. Wide bandwidth a bit broad for world band reception. Keypad not in telephone format. For single-sideband reception, relies on a touchy variable control instead of separate LSB/USB switch positions. Does not come with tape-recorder jack. *Realistic:* AC adaptor extra.

Bottom Line: A decent, predictable radio—performance and features, alike—but mediocre for bandscanning, which is better on the sibling Sangean ATS-803A.

The Sangean ATS-818, also sold under the Realistic and Roberts labels, is an unexciting performer for the price.

Oldies, Some Goodies

The following digital models reportedly have been discontinued for some time, yet may still be available new at a limited number of retail outlets. Cited are typical recent sale prices in the United States ($) and United Kingdom (£). Prices elsewhere may differ.

★★★½ **Grundig Satellit 650** *Editor's Choice*

World band audio just doesn't get any better than that found on this full-sized, feature-laden model. Great FM and mediumwave AM, too. Rarely found, typically for under $1,000 or £460.

★★★½ **Grundig Satellit 500** *Editor's Choice*

Superior audio quality, FM and mediumwave AM, along with a host of advanced-tuning features, make this a pleasant mid-sized set for listening hour after hour. Sometimes still found for under $400, £300 or its equivalent in North America and Europe.

★★★½ **Sony CRF-V21** *Editor's Choice*

A fax-oriented "portable" with more ornaments than a Christmas tree. On world band, however, in most respects it doesn't equal some tabletops costing a fifth as much, and only modestly exceeds the performance of certain portables that are cheaper yet. Under $5,000 or £2,700.

★★★ **Magnavox D2999**
Philips D2999 *Editor's Choice*

A fine-sounding receiver—a classic, really, that is still the model most used by one of our editors who is awash in radios. Virtually impossible to find, but a delightful portatop with superior audio quality, FM and world band performance, among other virtues. About once a year we hear from a delighted reader of a new unit turning up in some weird place. Under $400 or £300.

★★★ **Sony ICF-PRO80**
(Sony ICF-PRO70)

Great for puzzle lovers. Otherwise, of value mainly to weak-signal chasers who need a small world band portable with a VHF scanner. Under $400 or £310.

★★½ **Magnavox AE 3805**
(Philips AE 3805) ¢

Very similar to the current Sangean ATS 800 (*see*). Under $100, around £80.

★★ **Sony ICF-7700**
(Sony ICF-7600DA)

In today's marketplace of rich choices, there's no longer any reason to put up with this overpriced model's utter lack of adjacent-channel rejection. Only model featuring digital frequency display complemented by unusual digitalized "analog" tuning scale. Under $150 or £130.

FULL-SIZED PORTABLES

Very Good for Home, Poor for Travel

Think of big portables as tabletop-type models that run off batteries—usually several "D" (UM-1) cells, plus some "AA" (UM-3) cells for their computer circuitry. Genuine tabletop models, though, have the advantage of lying flat, and so are better-suited for everyday home use. Real tabletop models also provide more performance for the money.

Some full-sized portables weigh as much as a stuffed suitcase, and are almost as large. Take one on a worldwide air excursion and you should have your head examined. The first customs or security inspector that sees your radio will probably do it for you.

The only full-sized digital portable still made is the dismal Marc II NR-108F1, also sold as the Pan Crusader.

★½

Marc II NR-108F1 (Pan Crusader)

Price: $300-550 worldwide.

Advantages: Unusually broad coverage, from 150 kHz longwave to 520 MHz UHF, plus 850-910 MHz UHF (North American/Japanese version). Many helpful tuning features. World Time clock, displayed separately from frequency. Sleep/timer. Signal-strength indicator. Illuminated display.

Disadvantages: Marginal overall performance within certain portions of world band, including hissing, buzzing, and serious overloading. Poor adjacent-channel rejection (selectivity). Poor spurious-signal ("image") rejection. Poorly performing preselector tuning compli-

cates operation. Excessive battery drain. Mediocre construction quality, including casual alignment. Not widely available.

Bottom Line: Timex watch at an Omega price.

The Passport *portable-radio review team, for digital and analog models alike, includes Lawrence Magne, along with Jock Elliott and Tony Jones, with laboratory measurements by Robert Sherwood. Additional research this year by Lars Rydén, Harlan Seyfer and Craig Tyson, with a tip of the hat to Avery Comarow, David Crystal, Michael Evans, Alan Hausner, Keith Hook, Marie Lamb, James McCool, Chris Norton, Mike Schuster and Julian Smith/ODXA.*

Analog Portables
for 1994

With digitally tuned portables now commonplace and affordable, there's precious little reason to purchase an analog, or slide-rule tuned, model. You can hardly tell which frequency the radio is on, so with hundreds of stations on the air, it's like trying to navigate through Mexico City without a map.

Yet, analog radios, like black-and-white televisions, haven't fully disappeared from the marketplace. In principle, they can be quieter than the digital variety, as they lack "synthesizer noise." However, this is rarely a problem with ordinary portables. Most of what is referred to as "synthesizer noise" is actually hiss from other circuits—noise that would be present whether the radio were digital or analog.

Adequate as Throwaways on Trips

Analog models have traditionally been less costly than digital variety. Yet, even this price advantage is being eclipsed. The digital Yorx AS-908, for example, is already being offered in some countries for the equivalent of $20. As limbo dancers say, how low can you go?

Yet, there are still some truly cheap analog radios that suffice for taking on trips where you won't be twiddling often with the dial. Best bet is to search out the bargains among decent compact models.

Battery Consumption Lower

A genuine plus with analog models is that, relative to their digital counterparts, they have lower battery consumption. This can be useful for long treks into the wilderness, in emergency shelters, and for those living away from electricity.

Buying It

Analog radios have all but disappeared from the shelves of world band specialty outlets, as people familiar with world band usually want no part of them.

Where they do proliferate is as novelties in catchall catalogs, Sunday newspaper supplements and the like, sometimes accompanied by outrageously inflated claims and even falsehoods. Even respectable retailers and catalog houses have been known to carry them, attracted by the high markups these dirt-cheap-to-manufacture models tend to offer.

In this section, suggested retail ("list") prices are given for the United States. Discounts for most models are common, although those sold under the "Realistic" brand name are usually discounted only during special Radio Shack or Tandy sales. Elsewhere, observed selling prices (including VAT) are usually given. Prices are as of when we go to press and may fluctuate.

What *Passport's* Ratings Mean

Star ratings: ★ ★ ★ ★ ★ is best. Stars are awarded solely for overall performance and meaningful features, with portable, portatop and tabletop model reviews. The same star-rating standard applies regardless of price, size or whathaveyou. A star is a star, so you can cross-compare any radio—little or big, portable or portatop or tabletop, analog or digital—with any other radio evaluated in this edition of *Passport*.

    ¢: denotes a price-for-performance bargain. It won't be a great set, but it will give uncommon value for your money.

    Models in **(parentheses)** have not been tested by us, but appear to be essentially identical, except for styling, to model(s) tested.

How Models Are Listed

Of course, all models lack digital frequency display, arguably the most important characteristic of a world band radio. Too, none demodulates single sideband signals or has a meaningful signal-strength indicator. All cover FM and mediumwave AM and most, but not all, of the world band spectrum.

    Models are listed by size; within size, they are in order of world band listening suitability.

MINI ANALOG PORTABLES

These weigh under a pound, or half-kilogram, and are rarely much larger than a hand-held calculator. They use two to four ordinary small "AA" (UM-3 penlite) batteries and are suitable for traveling, little else.

    Many analog minis sound unpleasant, are overpriced or both. Better for traveling are compact models. They're not much larger than minis, but usually have bigger speakers and sound better. Sometimes cheaper, too.

★ ★

Sony ICF-SW15

Price: $99.95 in the United States. CAN$149 in Canada. Around £70 in the United Kingdom. $110-150 elsewhere in the European Community. AUS$169.00 in Australia.

Small, Sony and so-so: the ICF-SW15 is nonetheless the best analog mini around.

Advantages: Superior adjacent-channel rejection (selectivity) and spurious-signal rejection for size. Travel power lock.

Disadvantages: Limited world band spectrum coverage. Tiny speaker, mediocre audio. No longwave. Dial not illuminated. No AC adaptor.

Bottom Line: Circuit design as stale as last year's bread, but partially redeemed by ability to keep away unwanted sounds.

New for 1994
★½

Grundig Yacht Boy 205

Price: $49.95 in the United States.

Advantages: Superior audio quality for genre. Longwave. Telescopic antenna swivels, as well as rotates.

Disadvantages: Poorly aligned frequency read-out on unit tested. Mediocre spurious-signal ("image") rejection. Adjacent-channel rejection (selectivity) and weak-signal sensitivity both only fair. Dial not illuminated. No AC adaptor.

Bottom Line: Distinguished by superior audio quality for price and size class.

Evaluation of New Model: Grundig's new Yacht Boy 205, made in China, covers world band roughly 3800-4050, 5850-6230, 7050-7550, 9450-9950, 11550-12100, 13450-13950, 15070-15640, 17430-17940 and 21350-21900 kHz. Our unit misreads by as much as 70 kHz, so these ranges should be regarded only as approximations of what you might find on a sample with (hopefully) better alignment.

    The '205 also covers mediumwave AM to about 1620 kHz, shy of the forthcoming 1705 kHz upper limit in the Americas. FM is the usual 87.5-108 MHz, mono only, plus there's longwave.

Grundig's Yacht Boy 205 wins no prizes, but is inexpensive and has reasonable audio quality.

The radio's case has a flip-down rear panel, and the telescopic antenna swivels, as well as rotates. Taken together, these allow the set to be operated comfortably and properly when it's laid down. It doesn't come with headphones, travel power lock or AC adaptor, and its single-LED tuning indicator is nigh useless.

Performance offers few surprises. Weak-signal sensitivity is fair. Ditto selectivity, which is rather broad. Spurious-signal rejection is mediocre.

What does stand out is audio quality: This is not the squawk box most such radios are. Add to this the '205's FM performance, which is quite respectable for a radio of this sort, and the upshot is one of the more pleasant analog offerings in the mini-size class.

★½

Sangean MS-103
(Sangean MS-103L)

Price: $75-150 in the European Community. No longer sold in the United States.

Advantages: Better world band coverage than otherwise-identical MS-101. Travel power lock. FM stereo through headphones. *MS-103L:* Longwave.

Disadvantages: Mediocre adjacent-channel rejection (selectivity) and spurious-signal ("image") rejection. Inferior audio. Dial not illuminated. No AC adaptor. *MS-103:* No longwave. *MS-103L:* Lacks coverage of world band from 2.3-5.2 MHz.

Bottom Line: Preferable to the cheaper MS-101. Also sold under other names, including Goodmans and Siemens.

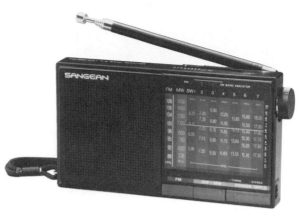

Similar to the MS-103, but with reduced world band coverage, is Sangean's MS-101.

★½

Sangean MS-101
Aiwa WR-A100
(Realistic DX-342)
(Roberts R101)

Price: *Sangean:* $85.95 in the United States. CAN$99.95 in Canada. $65-125 in the European Community. AUS$99.95 in Australia. *Aiwa:* $109.95 in the United States. *Realistic:* $69.95 in the United States. CAN$99.95 in Canada. *Roberts:* £49.99 in the United Kingdom.

Advantages: Travel power lock. FM stereo through headphones. *Realistic:* 30-day money-back trial period.

Disadvantages: Limited world band coverage. Mediocre adjacent-channel rejection (selectivity) and spurious-signal ("image") rejection. Inferior audio. Dial not illuminated. No AC adaptor.

Bottom Line: Low-priced, plain-vanilla. Also sold under other names, including Curry's, Dixons, Goodmans and Siemens.

Sangean's mediocre MS-103 is still sold in many countries, but not the United States.

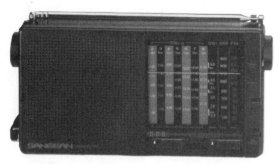

Cheap, but not cheap enough: the Sangean SG-789.

★½

Sangean SG-789
(Sangean SG-789L)

Price: *SG-789:* CAN$149.95 in Canada. AUS$79.95 in Australia. *SG-789L:* $60-95 in the European Community. No longer sold in the United States.

Advantages: FM stereo through headphones. *SG-789L:* Longwave.

Disadvantages: Limited coverage, omits important 13 MHz band. Mediocre adjacent-channel rejection (selectivity) and spurious-signal ("image") rejection. Inferior audio. Dial not illuminated. No AC adaptor. *SG-789:* No longwave. *SG-789L:* Lacks 2.3-5.2 MHz world band coverage.

Bottom Line: Similar to the Sangean MS-101, but with less complete coverage. Not cheap enough? Try the Sangean SG-796, $59.95 in the United States—same play, fewer acts.

COMPACT ANALOG PORTABLES

These run 1.0-1.5 pounds, or 0.5-0.7 kg, and are typically 8 × 5 × 1.5", or 20 × 13 × 4 cm. They use "AA" (UM-3 penlite) batteries, but more of them than minis. They travel almost as well as minis, but sound better and usually receive better, too.

The real virtue of these models is price, so look for a bargain among those rated with one-and-a-half stars.

★★

Sony ICF-7601*
*To be discontinued in 1994

Digital Replacement Model: With analog radios increasingly unable to compete with digital models, Sony is about to replace the aging ICF-7601 with the ICF-SW30. This will be a

A worthy performer in its time, the Sony ICF-7601 is finally being put out to graze.

digital model covering most world band segments. It will feature dual conversion, 15 presets, "signal-seek" tuning and a World Time clock. The price is expected to be unchanged. This bears watching, mainly because the 'SW30's dual conversion should result in better rejection of spurious signals than other digital models in its price class.

Price: $129.95 in the United States. CAN$199 in Canada. $125-170 in the European Community. AUS$199.00 in Australia.

Advantages: Superior weak-signal sensitivity. Travel power lock. Covers Japanese FM band.

Disadvantages: Dial not illuminated. Adjacent-channel rejection (selectivity) only fair. Some crosstalk among adjacent world band segments. No longwave. No AC adaptor.

Bottom Line: Honest, basic performance—for years, it was a favorite among international newsmen—but by now its technology has become dated. *Adios* to a deserving veteran!

★½

Sangean SG-700L
Realistic DX-350

Price: *Sangean:* $69.95 in the United States. CAN$79.95 in Canada. **Realistic:** $59.95 in the United States. AUS$99.95 in Australia. Realistic #273-1454 120V AC/6V DC adaptor $7.95.

Advantages: Longwave. *Realistic:* 30-day money-back trial period.

Disadvantages: Mediocre spurious-signal ("image") rejection. Adjacent-channel rejection (selectivity) only fair. Modest weak-signal sensitivity. Mediocre audio quality. Antenna swivels, but does not rotate. Dial not illuminated. AC adaptor optional.

Bottom Line: Adequate.

The Sangean SG-700L, also sold as the Realistic DX-350, is a dubious performer.

Grundig's Yacht Boy 230: Nice clock, blah radio.

★½

Panasonic RF-B20L
(Panasonic RF-B20)
(National B20)

Price: CAN$189.95 in Canada. Around £70 in the United Kingdom. $120-195 elsewhere. No longer offered in the United States.

Advantages: Above-average audio for size, with continuous tone control. Weak-signal sensitivity slightly above average.

Disadvantages: Limited world band coverage, omits important 13 and 21 MHz segments. Mediocre adjacent-channel rejection (selectivity). No AC adaptor.

Bottom Line: Lacks coverage and ability to sort out stations well.

★½

Grundig Yacht Boy 230
(Amsonic AS-912)
(Panopus Yacht Boy 230)

Price: *Grundig Yacht Boy 230:* $179.95 in the United States. CAN$199.95 in Canada. £79.00 in the United Kingdom. AUS$139.00 in Australia. *Panopus Yacht Boy 230:* AUS$169.00 in Australia.

Advantages: World Time and worldwide multi-country clock/alarm/sleep timer with electronic map. Illuminated dial. Longwave. Stereo FM through earphones.

Disadvantages: Mediocre spurious-signal ("image") and adjacent-channel rejection (selectivity). Tricky on-off switch. Pushbutton volume control increases or decreases sound in overly large bites. Tuning backlash. No AC adaptor.

Bottom Line: An undistinguished and, in North America, woefully overpriced radio of interest mainly for its clock.

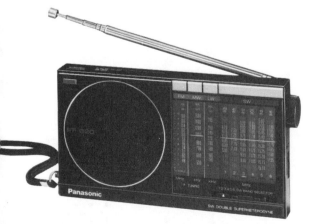

Fading from Panasonic's line is the overpriced RF-B20.

★½

Sangean SG 621
(Sangean SG 631)
(Siemens RK 710)
(Roberts R621)

Price: *SG 621:* $119.00 in the United States. Not available in Canada. *SG 631:* $139.00 in the United States. Not available in Canada. *RK 710:* DM149.00 in Germany. *R621:* £59.99 in the United Kingdom.

Advantages: World Time clock, plus second time-zone clock. Alarm/sleep features. Self-extinguishing clock light. Stereo FM through earpieces (supplied). Superior FM capture

Too much for too little: Sangean's SG 621.

ratio helps in selecting desired station. Smaller than most models in compact category. *SG 631:* Clock programmed with local time and date for 260 different cities around the world.

Disadvantages: Frequency dial not illuminated. Limited world band coverage. Mediocre spurious-signal ("image") rejection and adjacent-channel rejection (selectivity). Antenna swivels, but does not rotate. FM reception sometimes compromised by SCA interference. No longwave. No AC adaptor.

Bottom Line: No surprises, except perhaps the clock. Overpriced.

★½   ¢

International AC 100

Price: $34.95, including shipping, in the United States. £29.95, including shipping, in the United Kingdom.

Advantages: Weak-signal sensitivity at least average. Audio quality slightly above average for class. Longwave.

Disadvantages: Adjacent-channel rejection (selectivity) poor. Mediocre spurious-signal ("image") rejection. Limited world band coverage, omits important 13 MHz segment and

12000-12095 kHz portion of 11 MHz segment. Tested sample also lacks coverage of 2.3-5.1 MHz tropical stations; however, other versions may receive 2.3-5.1 MHz in lieu of longwave. Antenna swivels, but does not rotate. Dial not illuminated. Mediumwave AM coverage stops at roughly 1650 kHz. Tuning knob "mushy."

Bottom Line: Performs similarly to the Apex, below, but with greater frequency coverage and a clearer dial.

★½   ¢

Pomtrex 120-00300 (TEC 235TR) (MCE-7760) (Pace)

Price: *Pomtrex:* $29.95 plus shipping in the United States.

Advantages: Weak-signal sensitivity at least average. Audio quality slightly above average for class. Longwave (tested version).

Disadvantages: Adjacent-channel rejection (selectivity) poor. Mediocre spurious-signal ("image") rejection. Limited world band coverage, omits important 13 and 21 MHz segments and 11970-12095 kHz portion of 11 MHz segment. Lacks coverage of 2.3-5.1 MHz tropical stations; however, some other versions reportedly receive 2.3-5.1 MHz in lieu of longwave. Antenna swivels, but does not rotate. Dial not illuminated. Some dial numbering difficult to read. Mediumwave AM coverage stops before roughly 1650 kHz, five or more channels shy of American AM band's forthcoming upper limit. No AC adaptor.

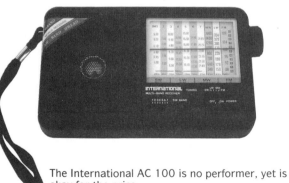

The International AC 100 is no performer, yet is okay for the price.

Sold under such names as Pomtrex is this basic, but cheap, offering from China.

Pomtrex warranty only 90 days, and even that is written up such that it is next to useless.

Bottom Line: Not noted for sale under the Pomtrex label for quite some time.

★½ ¢

SEG Precision World SED 110 (Kchibo KK-168)

Price: $33.50, including shipping, in the United States. Y142, about $26, in China.

Advantages: Unusually small for a compact. Longwave. Comes with twin earpieces.

Disadvantages: Limited coverage of world band spectrum. Mediocre weak-signal sensitivity, adjacent-channel rejection (selectivity) and spurious-signal ("image") rejection. Coarse frequency readout. Lacks power lock. No dial illumination. No AC adaptor. Antenna swivels, but does not rotate.

Bottom Line: Attractive size for traveling.

★½ ¢

(Precision World)

Price: Y138, about $25, in China.

Comment: Not tested, but appears to be essentially identical to the tested SEG Precision World SED 110, except that it lacks coverage of 13 MHz segment and longwave. This model has no designation on the box or radio itself other than "Precision World," so don't confuse it with other products sold under that name.

The SEG Precision World SED 110 has only small size in its favor.

Junk: the Panashiba FX-928.

★

Panashiba FX-928 (Shiba Electronics FX-928)

Price: $29.95-39.95 plus around $5.00 shipping when it was available in the United States.

Advantages: Longwave.

Disadvantages: Adjacent-channel rejection (selectivity) poor. Mediocre spurious-signal ("image") rejection. Lackluster weak-signal sensitivity. Limited world band coverage, omits important 13 MHz segment and 12010-12095 kHz portion of 11 MHz segment. Mediocre automatic-gain control (AGC) causes wide disparity in volume from signal to signal. Volume slider control touchy. Antenna swivels, but does not rotate. Dial not illuminated. Dial calibration off as much as 85 kHz. Medium-wave AM coverage stops at roughly 1620 kHz, eight channels shy of American AM band's forthcoming upper limit. No AC adaptor.

Bottom Line: You probably won't find it and surely won't want it. Possibly available under other brand designations; use photo as guide.

★

Cougar H-88 (Cougar RC210) (Precision World SED 901)

Price: *Cougar H-88:* $49.95 or less in the United States. $40-70 in the European Community. *Cougar RC210:* $49.95 in the United States. *Precision World:* Y140 (about $25) in China.

Advantages: Longwave. *Cougar RC210:* Comes with built-in cassette recorder.

Disadvantages: Frequency display (analog) grossly inaccurate in some samples. Limited

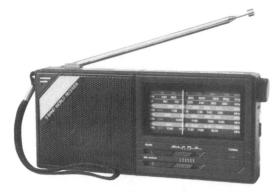

The Cougar H-88 is anything but the cat's whiskers.

The Windsor 2138, when sold under the Apex label, is so cheap that it's almost possible to overlook its dismal performance.

world band coverage. Mediocre adjacent-channel rejection (selectivity) and spurious-signal ("image") rejection. Modest weak-signal sensitivity. Tuning knob somewhat stiff. Power switch easily activated by accident, as when radio packed on trips. No dial illumination. No AC adaptor.

Bottom Line: A toy that also may be available under other brand designations.

★

Opal OP-35
(Grundig Traveller II)
(Siemens RK 702)

Price: *Opal and Grundig:* $99.95 in the United States, $99.95 in Canada. CAN$99.95 in Canada. *Siemens:* $75-160 in the European Community.

Advantages: Includes novel World Time and worldwide multi-country clock/timer ("World Time Handy Humane Wake System"). *Grundig:* Comes with stereo earpieces, even though radio is not stereo.

Disadvantages: World band coverage limited to 6, 7, 9, 11 and 15 MHz segments. Inferior adjacent-channel rejection (selectivity). Poor spurious-signal ("image") rejection in both world band and mediumwave AM band. Modest weak-signal sensitivity. Can drift off frequency when held. No longwave. No AC adaptor.

Bottom Line: Clock to tick you off.

★ ¢

Windsor 2138
(Apex 2138)
(Garrard Shortwave Radio 217)
(Silver International MT-798)

Price: *Windsor:* $34.99, including shipping, in the United States. *Apex:* $19.95 in the United States. *Garrard:* $49.95, plus shipping, in the United States. *Silver:* SIN$19-22 (about $11.50-13.50) in Singapore.

Advantages: *Apex:* Cheapest analog model tested.

Disadvantages: Distorted and tinny audio. Awful adjacent-channel rejection (selectivity). Poor rejection of spurious signals ("images"). Mediocre weak-signal sensitivity. Limited coverage of world band spectrum. Warranty on Apex box says one year, but in owner's booklet it turns out to be only 90 days.

Bottom Line: Not easy on the ears, but price may make it worth considering.

The Grundig Traveller II is all clock, no performance.

FULL-SIZED ANALOG PORTABLES

Bigger is better? Sure. When these large models fall over, they make an authoritative "thud." You may fall over, too, when you realize how you've wasted your money.

★

Venturer Multiband
(Alconic Series 2959)
(Dick Smith D-2832)
(Rhapsody Multiband)
(Shimasu Multiband)
(Steepletone MRB7)

Price: *Basic model:* $79.95-99.95 in the United States. £76.40 in the United Kingdom. AUS$129.00 in Australia. *With cassette player:* $129.95 in the United States. *With cassette player, stereo audio and digital clock:* $159.00 in the United States.

Advantages: Covers VHF-TV channels and air/weather bands. Audio at least average. Built-in cassette player (two versions only). Stereo audio (one version only). Digital clock (one version only), displayed separately from frequency. Useful signal-strength indicator. Rotating ferrite-bar direction finder for mediumwave AM. Built-in AC adaptor.

Disadvantages: No acceptable frequency display, so finding a station is a hit-and-miss exercise. World band coverage omits the 2, 3, 13, 15, 17, 21 and 26 MHz segments. Performance inferior in nearly every respect. No longwave.

Bottom Line: All glitz, no guts. Sold widely throughout North America, the European Community and beyond under various names—or even no advertised name.

★

(Realistic SW-100)

Price: $99.95 in the United States.
Bottom Line: Similar to basic Venturer model, above, but with 30-day money-back trial period.

★

Electro Brand 2971

Price: $149.95, including cassette player, stereo audio, NiCd battery charger, and digital clock/calendar in the United States.
Bottom Line: Big box that can't punch. Essentially identical in performance and features to cassette-player Venturer, above, except for appearance.

Another radio for the gullible: the Electro Brand 2971.

The dreadful Venturer Multiband reportedly sells well because it looks impressive.

Oldies, But No Goodies

The following analog models reportedly have been discontinued for some time, yet may still be available new at a limited number of retail outlets. Cited are typical recent sale prices in the United States ($) and United Kingdom (£). Prices elsewhere may differ.

★ ★   **Sony ICF-SW20**
Sony ICF-4920
(Sony ICF-4900II)
(Sony ICF-5100)

Virtually the same in all but styling to the current mini Sony ICF-SW15 (*see*). Under $80 or £60.

★½   **Magnavox OD1875BK**   ¢
(Philips OD1875BK)
Magnavox D1835
(Philips D1835)

Still available occasionally in the United States for as little as $30, in the United Kingdom for £49.95, but not in Canada. Industry rumors suggest Magnavox and Philips are turning over world band production to Grundig, which is 24.5% owned by Philips.

★½   **Magnavox AE 3205 GY**
(Philips AE 3205 GY)

Small, but not a competitive choice for the price. Under $60 or £40.

★   **Panasonic RF-B10**
(National B10)

Mini with third-rate performance and no 13 MHz coverage. Around $70 or £60.

★   **Grundig Explorer II**

A world band radio, cassette player, FM, mediumwave AM . . . and flashlight and howling siren. You'll howl, too, if you buy one: It has virtually no frequency readout, with performance to match. Under $50 in the United States; not known to have been sold elsewhere.

World Band Car Stereo for 1994

What a great idea: a first-class world band radio for your car, truck or boat! So the huge Dutch firm of Philips went out and designed just such a thing, the DC777 car stereo.

It works great, looks great, and reviews have been terrific. Even *Playboy* featured it. But there's been one problem: It's been a bust. Most are still sitting in warehouses, orphaned, like Annie.

> ## If you want world band in your car, now is the time to act.

Nobody is quite sure why people flock to world band portables, but not car radios. Yet, the bottom line is that if you want first-rate world band in your car, now is the time to act. In the United States, the distributor (800/544-0618) says there appears to be enough inventory to cover dealer and direct orders through 1994. There's still some stock in Europe, too.

Here's some even better news: In order to get rid of them, prices have been dropped. Although the list price continues to be $499 plus installation, the current street price is far lower.

Long-Distance Reception

World band, being long-distance, blankets large portions of land mass. This means it can offer hour upon hour of quality programs as you cover long distances. It just doesn't fade out the way ordinary radio signals do. Whether you're listening to Russia or Rush Limbaugh, the sound keeps coming through, mile after mile.

The '777, designed for in-dash installation, offers mediumwave AM, FM stereo, longwave, auto-reverse cassette and 50 watts

You're not likely to see the likes of this again! The Philips DC777 is easily the best world band car radio ever made . . . or likely to be offered anytime soon. But it probably won't be available after 1994.

of power to drive four speakers. It displays the frequency digitally and covers shortwave from 3170 to 21910 kHz continuously. That's virtually the whole world band spectrum.

> ## Whether you're listening to Russia or Rush Limbaugh, the sound doesn't fade out like ordinary radio.

There is no tuning knob, but a pair of slewing buttons allows you to cruise the airwaves in 1 kHz increments. Another button causes a small drawer to slide out at a 45-degree angle, revealing a six-over-six keypad for direct-frequency entry. Although the keypad layout is weird, it's straightforward enough to operate properly. If you want, say, the BBC World Service on 6175 kHz, press 6, 1, 7, 5, Enter, and there it is.

Handy Operation

Where the '777 really shines is in its ease of use for folks on the move. Press the SW button, and you can step through the world band spectrum—90 meters, 75 meters, right on up through 13 meters.

Poke the up or down SEARCH button, and the '777 mutes itself, scans your selected segment in 5 kHz steps, finds the next powerful station, then un-mutes so you can hear it. If you want a different station, press SEARCH again and the '777 trots off on its quest. If you wish to return to a station previously uncovered in the search process, just press the opposite SEARCH button to reverse the search. It's handy and works well.

> ## The Philips DC777 really shines for folks on the move.

The '777 has 20 presets for world band stations. One button allows you to step through these presets, carousel-style. This, too, works well, and allows you to punch up world band favorites while keeping your eyes where they should be—on the road.

Sounds Great

The '777 is reasonably sensitive to weak stations, but is not for chasing faint signals. The radio isn't up to it; ignition noise limits reception; and, in any event, DX band-scanning diverts a driver's attention from the road. Indeed, the limitation on what you can hear has more to do with your car's level of ignition, wiper and related electrical noises than with the radio's quality of performance.

> ## It sounds just great!

With everyday signals, though, the DC777 sounds great—just what you'd expect from a first-class car stereo.

The Passport *car stereo review team: Jock Elliott, along with Lawrence Magne.*

Portatop Receivers for 1994

Most people buy only one world band radio. It has to function not in just one room, but all over the house—perhaps outdoors, too. That's why portables sell so well.

But this results in some disturbing compromises: Portables, even the very best, don't sound as good as tabletop supersets. Nor can they cut the mustard with really tough signals.

First Digital Portatop Created by Philips

Some years back, Philips came up with an ingenious solution: combine the most desirable characteristics of portables and tabletops into one single receiver. The resulting creation, the "portatop" D2999, was also sold under the Magnavox label. This classic of its period was fully self-contained, with a telescopic antenna, a handle that also elevated the radio to a comfortable angle, a built-in multi-voltage AC power supply; and a cavity for batteries. With two speakers— woofer and tweeter—it sounded first-rate on both world band and FM. Street price: $400, equal to around $500 today.

Because of problems at the Philips plant where the D2999 was manufactured, it was discontinued before it could become really established in the marketplace. Yet, the precedent did not go unnoticed.

Lowe Offering Has Exceptional Sound

In England, Lowe Electronics eventually came up with its own idea of a portatop, the HF-150 (*see* below), which has exceptional "listenability." Quite distinct from that produced by Philips, the '150, lacking FM, is aimed at the dedicated world band, longwave and mediumwave AM listener. It is now available both in Europe and North America.

Looking Ahead: Sometime in 1994, another portatop will join the scene: Drake's SWL8. With FM and a combination carrying handle/elevation rod, it should have much in common with the earlier Philips offering. Yet, Drake's track record suggests that its world band performance could be interesting. We'll see when we test it for the next edition of *Passport.* In the interim, we hope to have a *Passport* RDI White Paper on the Drake SWL8 issued by around Spring of 1994. Should you be interested, check elsewhere in the book to see how these reports may be obtained.

What *Passport's* Rating Symbols Mean

Star ratings: ★ ★ ★ ★ ★ is best. Stars are awarded solely for overall performance and meaningful features, for portable, portatop and tabletop models, alike. The same star-rating standard applies regardless of price, size or whathaveyou. A star is a star, so you can cross-compare any radio of any type with any other radio evaluated in this edition of *Passport.*

Editor's Choice models are our test team's personal picks of the litter—what we would prefer to buy ourselves.

★ ★ ★ ★   *Editor's Choice*

Lowe HF-150

Price (including AC adaptor and optional mouse keypad): Around $700 in the United States. CAN$1,014.95 in Canada. £368.95 in the United Kingdom. AUS$995.00 in Australia. *AK-150 accessory kit:* $99.95 in the United States. CAN$119.95 in Canada. £39.99 in the United Kingdom. *XLS1 monitor speaker:* £59.95 in the United Kingdom. *IF-150 computer interface:* £39.00 in the United Kingdom.

Advantages: With AK-150 option, portatop design combines virtual tabletop performance with much of the convenience of a portable. Unsurpassed world band and mediumwave AM audio quality—a treat for the ears—provided a good external speaker or simple headphones are used. High-tech synchronous detection reduces adjacent-channel interference and fading distortion on world band, longwave and mediumwave AM signals. Synchronous detection also allows for either selectable-sideband or double-sideband reception—the only receiver tested, regardless of type or price, that does this. Synchronous detector switches out automatically during tuning, which aids in bandscanning. Exceptionally rugged cast-aluminum housing of a class normally associated with professional-grade equipment. Mouse keypad, virtually foolproof and a *de rigeur* option, performs superbly for tuning and presets. 60 presets store frequency and mode. Tunes, but does not display, in exacting 8 Hz increments, the most precise found in any model with portable characteristics. Single-sideband reception well above the portable norm. Small footprint saves space and adds to portability. Optional accessory kit, necessary for real portability, provides telescopic antenna, rechargeable nickel-cadmium batteries (four hours per charge) and shoulder strap with built-in antenna. High sensitivity to weak signals with accessory antenna helps make for exceptional portable performance and obviates the need for a large outdoor antenna. Excellent operating manual. Available with IF-150 optional computer interface.

Disadvantages: Inferior front-end selectivity can result in creation of spurious signals if the radio is connected to a significant external antenna or used near mediumwave AM transmitters. Lacks FM broadcast reception, normally found on portables. Built-in speaker produces only okay audio quality as compared to simple earphones or a good external speaker. No tone control. Frequency displays no finer than 1 kHz resolution. Lacks lock indicator or similar aid (e.g., finer frequency-display resolution) for proper use of synchro-

Lowe's HF-150 proves that good things can come in small packages.

nous detector, which can result in less-than-optimum detector performance. Bereft of certain features—among them notch filter, adjustable noise blanker and passband tuning—found on premium-priced tabletop models. Lacks signal-strength indicator. Operation of some front-panel button functions tends to be confusing until you get the hang of it. Light weight allows radio to slide on table during operation more than do heavier models. Lacks much-needed elevation feet. Erratic contact on outboard-speaker socket. Display not illuminated. AC power supply via a separate outboard adaptor, rather than inboard (*see* Note, below). AC adaptor, which comes as standard in Europe, is usually an extra-cost option with dealers outside Europe. *Portable operation:* Telescopic antenna swivels properly, but is clumsy to rotate. Comes with no convenient way to attach keypad to cabinet (remediable by affixing sticky-backed Velcro). This—plus the use of an outboard AC adaptor, the need for an outboard speaker or headphones for proper fidelity, and no dial illumination—all conspire to make this model less handy to tote around than a conventional portable.

Note: 120 VAC adaptors used thus far in North America have tended to generate at least some audible hum. According to dealer Universal Radio, a new adaptor, grounded to eliminate hum, is scheduled to be provided by Lowe to its American dealers by the time you read this.

Bottom Line: How sweet it sounds! This tough little radio provides superb fidelity on world band, longwave and mediumwave AM—provided a suitable outboard speaker or headphones are used. On shortwave, it also provides respectable tough-signal ("DX") performance, especially with the telescopic antenna that comes as part of the AK-150 option package. With that package, the Lowe HF-150 sets the current standard in combining full-fidelity tabletop performance with at least reasonable portability. For some, this makes it unnecessary to own two receivers, or to have to choose between a portable and a tabletop.

An *RDI WHITE PAPER* is available for this model.

Tabletop Receivers for 1994

For most, a good portable is more than adequate to enjoy the offerings found on world band radio. Others, though, aspire to something better. That "better" is a tabletop receiver. Many models excel at flushing out the really tough game—faint stations, or those swamped by interference from competing signals. The very best now also provide enhanced-fidelity reception, welcome relief from the aural gremlins of shortwave. Still, world band is far from a high-fidelity medium, even with the best of radios. International stations beam over great distances, and you can tell it with your ears.

Especially Helpful in American West

Tabletop models can be especially useful if you live in a part of the world, such as central and western North America, where signals tend to be weak and choppy—a common problem when world band signals have to follow "high-latitude" paths, those close to or over the geomagnetic North Pole. To get an idea how much this phenomenon might affect your listening, place a string on a globe (an ordinary map won't do) between where you live and where various signals you like come from. If the string passes near or above latitude 60° N, beware.

Daytime Signals Come in Better

Tabletop radios also excel for daytime listening, when signals tend to be weaker, and for listening to stations not beamed to your part of the world. Thanks to the scattering properties of shortwave, you can eavesdrop on some "off-beam" signals. But it's harder, so a better radio helps.

A good tabletop won't guarantee hearing a favorite daytime or off-beam station, but it will almost certainly improve the odds. Tabletops also do unusually well with nonbroadcasting signals, such as ham and utility stations—many of which use single-sideband and other specialized transmission modes.

Easily Found in Certain Countries

Tabletop models are easily found in certain countries, such as the United States, Canada, the United Kingdom, Germany and Japan, and almost as easily in places like Australia. At the other extreme, a few countries, such as Saudi Arabia and Singapore, frown upon the importation of tabletop models. That's because tabletops often look like transceivers, which can be used by terrorists and spies. However, when tabletop models are brought in as part of a household's goods, problems are less likely to arise.

Most tabletop models, unlike portables, are available only from electronics and world band specialty outlets. Firms that sell, distribute or manufacture world band tabletops usually support them with service that is incomparably superior to that for portables, and often continues well after the model has been discontinued. Drake and Lowe—as well as Kenwood, Japan Radio and Yaesu—have particularly good track records in this regard.

Higher Price, But No FM

For the most part, tabletop receivers are pricier than portables. For that extra money you tend to get not only better performance, but also a better-made device. However, what you rarely find in a tabletop is reception of the everyday 87.5-108 MHz FM band, much less FM stereo. That's because most tabletop manufacturers specialize in telecommunications equipment for hams and professionals. They don't have much experience in the consumer market, and thus tend not to realize the importance of FM to that market.

External Antenna Required

Most tabletop models also require, and should have, an outboard antenna. Indeed, tabletop performance is substantially determined by antenna quality and placement. A first-rate world band outdoor wire antenna, such as the various models manufactured by Antenna Supermarket and Alpha Delta, usually runs from $60 to $80 in the United States—a bit more elsewhere. These wire antennas are best, and should be used if at all possible. Check with the Radio Database International White Paper, *Passport Evaluation of Popular Outdoor Antennas*, for full details on performance and installation.

If not, a short amplified antenna suitable for indoors, and sometimes outdoors when space is at a premium, is the next-best choice. Leading models, such as those made by California's Stoner/McKay Dymek and Britain's Datong, go for $130-180 Stateside.

Virtually Every Model Tested

Models new for 1994 are covered at length in this year's *Passport* Buyer's Guide. Every receiver, regardless of its introduction year, has been put through the various testing hurdles we established and have honed since 1977, when our firm first started evaluating world band equipment.

Virtually every model available is thoroughly tested in the laboratory, using criteria developed especially for the strenuous requirements of world band reception. The receiver then undergoes hands-on evaluation, usually for months, before we begin preparing our internal report. That report, in turn, forms the basis for our findings, summarized in this *Passport* Buyer's Guide.

Unabridged Reports Available

Our unabridged laboratory and hands-on test results are far too exhaustive to reproduce here. However, for many tabletop models they are available as *Passport's* Radio Database International White Papers—details on price and availability are elsewhere in this book.

Tips for Using this Section

With tabletop receivers, "list" prices are sometimes quoted by manufacturers, sometimes not. In any event, the spread between "list" and actual selling prices is almost always small. Thus, prices given in this section reflect the higher end of actual selling prices. World band tabletop models are virtually unavailable at duty-free shops.

Receivers are listed in order of suitability for listening to difficult-to-hear world band radio broadcasts, with important secondary consideration being given to audio fidelity and ergonomics. Prices are as of when we go to press and are subject to fluctuation.

Unless otherwise stated, all tabletop models have:
• digital frequency synthesis and illuminated display;
• a wide variety of helpful tuning features;
• meaningful signal-strength indication;
• the ability to properly demodulate single-sideband and CW (Morse code); also, with suitable ancillary devices, radio-teletype and radiofax; and
• full coverage of at least the 155-29999 kHz (155-26099 kHz within Central Europe for some models) longwave, mediumwave AM and shortwave spectra—including all world band segments.

Unless otherwise stated, all tabletop models do *not*:
• tune the FM broadcast band (87.5-108 MHz); and
• come equipped with synchronous detection.

What *Passport's* Rating Symbols Mean

Star ratings: ★ ★ ★ ★ ★ is best. We award stars solely for overall performance and meaningful features; price, appearance and the like are not taken into account. To facilitate comparison, the same rating system is used for portable models, reviewed elsewhere in this *Passport*. Whether a radio is portable, a portatop or a tabletop model, a given rating—three stars, say—means essentially the same thing. A star is a star.

Editor's Choice models are our test team's personal picks of the litter—what we would buy ourselves.

¢: Denotes a model that costs appreciably less than usual for the level of performance provided.

Models in **(parentheses)** have not been tested by us, but appear to be essentially identical to the model(s) tested.

PROFESSIONAL MONITOR RECEIVERS

Professional receivers are made, of course, for professional applications, which usually have only some things in common with the needs of world band listening. Realistically, for world band listening there is precious little difference—sometimes none of import—between these pricey receivers and regular tabletop models costing a fraction as much.

Nevertheless, if money is no object, you may wish at least to consider these models, along with regular tabletop models, when weighing a purchase decision.

Looking Ahead: Not long back, the American firm of Watkins-Johnson tested the world band market by advertising one of its existing professional-grade models in the $5,000 price class. The results reportedly were favorable, so in 1994 they hope to release a new model having features more in keeping with the specialized needs of world band listeners. Watkins-Johnson provides the various branches of the American government with much of its shortwave receiving equipment, typically of excellent quality.

See and hear signals with the exceptional Icom IC-R9000.

used with suitable outboard speaker. Three AM-mode bandwidths. Tunes and displays frequency in precise 0.01 kHz increments. Video display of radio spectrum occupancy. Sophisticated scanner/timer. Extraordinarily broad coverage of radio spectrum. Exceptional assortment of flexible operating controls and sockets. Good ergonomics. Superb reception of utility and ham signals. Two 24-hour clocks.

Disadvantages: Very expensive. Power supply runs hot. Both AM-mode bandwidths too broad for most world band applications. Both single-sideband bandwidths almost identical. Dynamic range merely adequate. Reliability, especially when roughly handled, may be wanting. Front-panel controls of only average construction quality.

Bottom Line: The Icom IC-R9000, with at least one changed AM-mode bandwidth filter—available from world band specialty firms—is right up there with the best-performing models for DX reception of faint, tough signals. Nevertheless, other models offer virtually the same level of construction and performance, plus synchronous detection, lacking on the 'R9000, for far less money.

An *RDI WHITE PAPER* is available for this model.

★ ★ ★ ★ ★   *Editor's Choice*

Japan Radio NRD-93

Price: $6,850.00 in the United States. $6,000 to $10,000 elsewhere.

Advantages: Professional-quality construction with legendary durability to survive around-the-clock use in punishing environments. Uncommonly easy to repair on the spot. Unusually appropriate for hour-after-hour world band listening. Superb all-around performance. Excellent ergonomics and unsurpassed control feel. Above-average audio. Sophisticated optional scanner, tested. Superb reception of utility and ham signals.

★ ★ ★ ★ ★   *Editor's Choice*

Icom IC-R9000

Price: $6,265.00 in the United States. CAN$7,095.00 in Canada. £4,080.00 in the United Kingdom. AUS$6,399 in Australia.

Advantages: Unusually appropriate for hour-after-hour world band listening. Exceptional tough-signal performance. Flexible, above-average audio for a tabletop model, when

Tough enough to take on Hulk Hogan, the Japan Radio NRD-93 is a *real* radio!

Disadvantages: Very expensive. Designed several years ago, so lacks some advanced-technology tuning aids and synchronous detection. Distribution limited to Japan Radio offices and a few specialty organizations, such as shipyards.

Bottom Line: Crafted like a watch, but tough as a tank, the Japan Radio NRD-93, although technologically stale, is a breed apart. It is a pleasure to operate for bandscanning hour after hour, but its overall performance is not appreciably different from that of some cheaper tabletop models.

An *RDI WHITE PAPER* is available for this model.

★ ★ ★ ★

Lowe HF-235/R
(Lowe HF-235/F)
(Lowe HF-235/H)
(Lowe HF-235)

Editor's Note: As the Lowe HF-235 in its various configurations is based on, and in most performance respects is very similar to, the Lowe HF-225 (see), the following summarizes how the '235 differs from the '225.

Price: Up to $2,700.00 in the United States, depending on configuration. CAN$2,995.00 in Canada in some configurations. £1,116.00-1,509.95, depending on configuration, in the United Kingdom.

Advantages over HF-225: Physically and electrically more rugged, including enhanced capability to handle high-voltage signal input. AGC may be switched off. Rack mounting, preferred for most professional applications. Power supply inboard and dual-voltage (110/220V). IF gain. *HF-235/R:* Scan/search and other remote control via personal computer using RS-232C interface. Allows for computer display of receiver data. *HF-235/F:* Fax capability. *HF-235/H:* Enhanced stability.

Disadvantages over HF-225: Larger footprint. Lacks tone control and optional mouse-type remote keypad. Built-in AC power supply nominally not suited to voltages in 120-129V range commonly found in the United States (in practice, however, this may not be a problem). *HF-235/F:* Does not receive lower-sideband signals.

Bottom Line: This radio is essentially the Lowe HF-225 reconfigured for selected professional applications. For this reason, it offers features some professionals require, but lacks certain niceties for home use and bandscanning. World band listeners and manual-band-scanning professionals are better served by the cheaper Lowe HF-225 and its portatop HF-150 sibling (see).

An *RDI WHITE PAPER* is available for the Lowe HF-225/HF-235.

TABLETOP RECEIVERS

If you want a top performer, here is where your money stretches farthest. Five-star models should satisfy even the fussiest, and four-star models are no slouches, either.

The best tabletop models are the Ferraris and Mercedes of the radio world. As with their automotive counterparts, like-ranked receivers may come out of the curve at the same speed, though how they do it can differ greatly from model to model. So, if you're thinking of choosing from the top end, study each contender in detail.

Looking Ahead: The Drake R8's price and performance have led it to dominate the tabletop market. Yet, the R8 doesn't begin to

Lowe Electronics also produces for professionals. Here, the rack-mounted HF-235.

approach the ergonomic excellence of the Japan Radio NRD-535 series. This has left a hole in the market which wannabes are scrambling to try to fill.

The first of these is expected to be the Japanese firm of AOR, which has a strong background in scanners. Also warming up in the bullpen is the British firm of Lowe Electronics, already a world band major leaguer. Both indicate that their offerings are due out sometime in 1994.

★ ★ ★ ★ ★   *Editor's Choice*

Drake R8 (Drake R8E)

Price: $979.00 in the United States. CAN$1,199.00 in Canada. £1195.00 in the United Kingdom. AUS$2,400 in Australia.

Advantages: Unparalleled all-round performance for sophisticated listening to world band programs. Superior audio quality, especially with suitable outboard speaker. High-tech synchronous detection, with selectable sideband, performs exceptionally well—it reduces adjacent-channel interference and fading distortion on world band, longwave and mediumwave AM signals; and also provides superior reception of reduced-carrier single-sideband signals. Five bandwidths, four suitable for world band—among the best configurations of any model tested. Highly flexible operating controls, including 100 superb presets, variable (albeit AF) notch filter and excellent passband offset. Superior reception of utility, ham and mediumwave AM signals. Tunes in precise 0.01 kHz increments. Displays frequency for some modes in those same 0.01 kHz increments. Superior blocking performance. Slow/fast/off AGC. Sophisticated scan functions. Can access all presets quickly via tuning knob and slew buttons. Built-in preamplifier. Accepts two antennas. Two 24-hour clocks, with seconds displayed numerically, and timer features.

Reigning heavyweight champ of world band, the Drake R8.

Disadvantages: Ergonomics mediocre. Notch filter extremely fussy to adjust. Most push-buttons rock on their centers. XX.XXXXX MHz frequency display format lacks decimal for integers finer than kHz, annoying to read. Neither clock displays for more than three seconds when radio on. Individual presets not tunable. Flimsy front feet. Matching optional MS8 outboard speaker not equal to receiver's fidelity potential.

Bottom Line: First-rate performance, third-rate ergonomics. Unsurpassed for pleasant listening to news, music and entertainment from afar. Superb for DX reception of faint, tough signals, too. A good small outboard hi-fi speaker is needed for the R8 to really shine—but don't bother with Drake's mediocre MS8 offering.

An *RDI WHITE PAPER* is available for this model.

★ ★ ★ ★ ★   *Editor's Choice*

Japan Radio NRD-535D

Price: $2,029.00 in the United States. CAN$2,599.00 in Canada. AUS$3,499.00 in Australia.

Evaluation: See below.

★ ★ ★ ★ ½   *Editor's Choice*

Japan Radio NRD-535

Price: $1,429.00 in the United States. CAN$2,249.00 in Canada. £1,195.00 in the United Kingdom, plus £229.00 for CMF-78 synchronous detector ("ECSS"), £359.00 for CFL-243 variable bandwidth and £117.50 (£193.87 after purchase) for Lowe performance upgrade. AUS$2,499.00 in Australia.

Advantages: One of the best and quietest DX receivers ever tested. Very good ergonomics, including non-fatiguing display. Construction quality slightly above average, likely to be unusually reliable. Computer-type modular plug-in circuit boards ease repair. Highly flexible operating controls, including 200 superb presets, tunable notch filter and passband offset. Superior reception of utility and ham signals. The only receiver tested that tunes frequency in exacting 0.001 kHz increments. Displays frequency in precise 0.01 kHz increments. Slow/fast/off AGC. Superior front-end selectivity. Sophisticated scan functions. World Time clock with timer features; displays seconds, albeit only if a wire inside the receiver is cut. Excellent optional NVA-319 outboard speaker. *NRD-535D:* Synchro-

Japan Radio's NRD-535 comes in two flavors from the factory, plus a new modified version.

nous detection with selectable sideband for reduced fading and easier rejection of interference. Continuously variable bandwidth in single-sideband (narrow bandwidth) and AM (wide bandwidth) modes.

Disadvantages: Audio quality, although improved over some earlier Japan Radio offerings, still somewhat muddy. Dynamic range and blocking performance adequate, but not fully equal to price class. Excessive beats and birdies. AGC sometimes causes "pop" sounds. Clock shares readout with frequency display. Clock not visible when receiver off. Front feet do not tilt receiver upwards. *NRD-535D:* Synchronous detection circuit locking performance suboptimal, notably with passband offset in use. Variable bandwidth comes at the expense of deep-skirt selectivity.

Bottom Line: An exceptional receiver, especially in the "D" version, with the best ergonomics in a tabletop model. Yet, performance is a touch shy of what it could have been. Outstanding reception of faint DX signals, plus superior quality of construction.

An *RDI WHITE PAPER* is available that covers both versions of this model.

Japan Radio "NRD-535SE"

The Japan Radio NRD-535D is clearly one of the best receivers ever made. Yet, its synchronous detector loses lock easily, particularly when the passband shift is used; audio quality tends to be "muddy"; and the variable bandwidth system doesn't have the deep-skirt selectivity found with fixed-bandwidth filters.

Colorado's Sherwood Engineering, one of the small tribe of Japan Radio dealers in North America, put its energies to work and came up with its own version, the so-called "NRD-535SE." The regular '535, which lacks variable bandwidth or synchronous detection, is used as the platform, inasmuch as the extra features on the costlier "D" version would have been scrapped, anyway, as part of the upgrade. This approach allows Sherwood to sell this extra-high-performance version at the same price as the list price for the high-performance "D" version. Of course, the '535D's list price is higher than its street price, so the Sherwood version actually sells at a premium equal to the '535D's discount.

The regular '535 comes standard with 2.2 kHz and 5.7 kHz voice bandwidths, to which Sherwood has added 4.0 kHz and 8.0 kHz filters. The end result comes only a little closer to the flexibility of the "D" version, but has much better deep-skirt selectivity.

However, the *pièce de résistance* is a special version of the newly redesigned Sherwood SE-3 synchronous detector, an outboard fidelity-enhancing device that attaches through an IF port Sherwood installs in the back of the cabinet. The SE-3 has been available for a number of years for various receivers, including Japan Radio models, and enjoys a small but enthusiastic following.

Following are my findings with the "NRD-535SE." I was asked to analyze this receiver completely independently of the usual *Passport* team effort, as Sherwood Engineering—although not involved in the analysis and conclusions in this Buyer's Guide—is contracted by *Passport* to perform laboratory measurements. However, to keep things simple, I have prepared my findings more or less in the traditional Buyer's Guide format.

Price: $1,995.00 in the United States.

★ ★ ★ ★ ½ *Editor's Choice*

Kenwood R-5000

Price: $1,149.95 in the United States. CAN$1,299.00 in Canada. £999.95 in the United Kingdom. $1,200-1,800 elsewhere in Europe. AUS$1,500.00 in Australia.

Advantages: Commendable all-round performance. Good audio for a tabletop, provided a suitable outboard speaker is used. Exceptionally flexible operating controls, including tunable notch filter and passband offset. Tunes and displays frequency in precise 0.01 kHz increments. Excellent reception of utility and ham signals. Superior frequency-of-repair record.

Disadvantages: Ergonomics only fair—especially keypad, which uses an offbeat horizontal format. Mediocre wide bandwidth filter supplied with set; replacement with high-quality YK-88A-1 substitute adds $88.95 to cost. Audio significantly distorted at tape-recording output.

Bottom Line: The Kenwood R-5000's combination of superior tough-signal performance and good audio quality makes it an excellent choice for those who need a receiver for

Kenwood's top-of-the-line R-5000 has above-average audio quality.

tough-signal DXing, as well as reasonable fidelity for listening to world band programs.

 An *RDI WHITE PAPER* is available that covers both versions of this model.

★ ★ ★ ★

Icom IC-R71A
(Icom IC-R71E)
(Icom IC-R71D)

Price: *IC-R71A:* $1,279.00 in the United States. CAN$1,439.00 in Canada. AUS$1,599.00 in Australia. *IC-R71E:* £875.00 in the United Kingdom. *IC-R71E and IC-R71D:* $1,000-1,800 in continental Europe.

Advantages: The SE-3 synchronous detector outperforms the one available from Japan Radio by leaps and bounds. It is well-nigh unshakable, hanging on with bulldog tenacity to stations even during really deep fades. In addition, it becomes far easier to escape adjacent-channel interference, as the SE-3 allows the '535 to be detuned by more than 3 kHz with virtually no distortion. (Detuning like this usually increases distortion appreciably, even intolerably.) Deep-skirt selectivity is of the DX caliber it should be, thanks to properly selected fixed-bandwidth filters. And because the SE-3 replaces virtually *all* the '535's audio circuitry, the radio sounds much better; indeed, my ears vote it to sound as good as any other model available, notably the Drake R8 and Lowe HF-150.

Disadvantages: All these improvements diminish one of the '535's chief virtues: ergonomic excellence. The SE-3—with its own volume knob, headphone jack and speaker jack—is far more complicated to operate than the '535's standard synchronous detector. One other SE-3 control puts the detector into synchronous mode, while yet another pulls it exactly onto the right frequency or adjusts the offset from center frequency. There are yet two more controls: one to reduce flutter and "thump" in trans-polar transmissions, the second to boost or attenuate high audio frequencies. Ergonomics aside, the various fixed-bandwidth filters offer less flexibility than the innovative variable-bandwidth scheme on the "D" version.

Bottom Line: Rocky Mountain shogun with stick shift. Hardly the La-Z-Boy of receivers, but performance is virtually unbeatable. If you don't mind the big bucks and diminished ergonomics, the "NRD-535SE" offers improved rejection of unwanted signals and outstanding audio quality, as compared with the standard offerings from Japan Radio. A solid five stars for performance, but lop off a star for ergonomics.

— Jock Elliott

The Icom IC-R71 has outstanding narrow-bandwidth performance.

Advantages: Variable bandwidth. Superb reception of weak, hard-to-hear signals. Reception of faint signals alongside powerful competing ones aided by superb ultimate selectivity, as well as excellent dynamic range. Flexible operating controls, including tunable notch filter. Excellent reception of utility and ham signals. Tunes in precise 0.01 kHz increments (but displays in 0.1 kHz increments).

Disadvantages: Mediocre audio. Diminutive controls, and otherwise generally substandard ergonomics. Should backup battery die, operating system software erases, requiring reprogramming by Icom service center (expected battery life is in excess of 10 years).

Bottom Line: The venerable Icom IC-R71 was formerly a favorite among those chasing faint, hard-to-hear signals. Indeed, until 1991 it was still being procured by a quality-conscious official agency seeking compact, low-cost radio surveillance gear. Nonetheless, the 'R71 is no longer competitive with some other tabletop models for hour-on-hour program listening, nor is it equal to today's best models for chasing faint DX signals. According to Icom, although the 'R71 is costly to produce, so long as the set continues to sell well, it will be kept in production.

 An *RDI WHITE PAPER* is available for this model.

★ ★ ★ ★   *Editor's Choice*

Lowe HF-225

Note: In Europe and Canada only, this model is also available in a special "Europa" version (not tested) for £699 of CAN$1,369.00, including keypad and synchronous detector. Changes over the regular HF-225 include more powerful audio; changed AGC time constants; bandwidth improvements; and a quieter, more precise and more stable frequency synthesizer.

Price (including optional keypad): $839.90 in the United States; CAN$999.00 in Canada, £468.95 in the United Kingdom, AUS$1,425.00

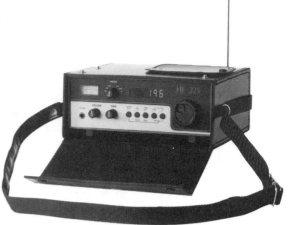

Lowe's HF-225 comes in two tabletop versions that can be configured for portable use.

in Australia. Synchronous detector and other accessories additional.

Advantages: Well-suited for listening to world band programs hour after hour. Superior audio with outboard speaker. Straightforward to operate. Generally excellent ergonomics, especially with keypad. Four bandwidths. Tunes in precise 8 Hz increments. Physically rugged. Optional synchronous detector, tested, reduces distortion. Optional field-portable configuration, tested. Small footprint. Attractively priced.

Disadvantages: Limited operational flexibility, including AGC. Two of four bandwidths too wide for most world band applications. Frequency displays in relatively coarse 1 kHz increments. Optional synchronous detector works only in double sideband, not selectable sideband. Front-end selectivity only fair. In tabletop use, less sensitive to weak signals than top-rated models. Optional portable configuration relatively insensitive to weak signals. Uses AC adaptor instead of built-in power supply.

Bottom Line: A hardy, easy-to-operate set with superior audio quality.

 An *RDI WHITE PAPER* is available for this model and the Lowe HF-235.

★ ★ ★ ½

Icom IC-R72
(Icom IC-R72E)

Price: $1,145.00 in the United States. CAN$1,289.00 in Canada. £859.00 in United Kingdom. AUS$1,199.00 in Australia.

Advantages: Pleasant audio with outboard

speaker or headphones. Generally superior ergonomics. Tunes and displays frequency in precise 0.01 kHz increments. World clock/ timer. Operates for about one hour off built-in rechargeable battery—useful during power failure. Novel center-tuning LED for world band and certain other signals. Superb image and IF rejection. Small footprint. Smoothly operating tuning knob. Preamplifier.

Disadvantages: Wide bandwidth too broad. Dreadful audio from built-in speaker. Noisy synthesizer. Noise blanker reduces dynamic range. Relatively few features, compared to better models. In our unit, poor low-frequency audio reproduction in upper-sideband.

Bottom Line: Nice, but nothing special—especially considering the price. A number of other models offer much better value.

The Icom IC-R72 is overpriced for what it does.

Full Static Protection: Antenna, Power and Phone Line

If your radio is hooked up to either an outdoor antenna or a wall plug, you need some sort of lightning protection.

Actually, "lightning protection" is a misnomer. Nothing—repeat, nothing!—will protect your receiver in the event of a direct strike. However, antenna lightning protection systems and power surge devices will protect from nearby strikes, which generate powerful *inductive* charges. These charges are picked up by your radio's outdoor antenna and, through the electrical wiring, the radio's plug. These don't put out enough juice to turn your house into Waco II, but they can zap your receiver's electronic innards to a fare-thee-well.

Most protection systems shunt inductive lightning energy harmlessly to ground. If you prefer, you can simply disconnect your antenna, toss the lead-in outside, and unplug the radio whenever an electrical storm approaches.

But if your pockets are deep and your standards high, here's something better yet: the ILD/P Model 100 Equipment Protection System. Manufactured by Rabun Labs, Inc., and marketed in the United States by Ten-Tec, this diminutive box connects to your outdoor antenna and wall socket. You then connect your receiver's power plug and antenna input to the '100.

A little separate antenna (not supplied—Radio Shack P/N 21-921 with adaptor P/N 278-120 is recommended) is attached to the back of the '100. Through that little antenna, the '100 detects oncoming electrical storms and automatically disconnects your receiver from both the radio's antenna and the house current before a lightning strike can do any real damage. (It is also supposed to be able to protect a telephone line, though the high impedance of a phone line automatically provides much protection.) Everything stays shut down for 20 minutes. Then if the storm is still around, the process repeats itself.

As our real-life "Ben Franklin" tests showed during the summer storm season, it works. Thunder rumbles, '100 activates, radio stays safe.

Ten-Tec (800/833-7373) offers the Model 100 with a 30-day, money-back guarantee for $295. If this is too steep, seriously consider the Alpha Delta device for your antenna, supplemented by a surge protector for the power line. Cheap ones are usually good enough, but if you have $149 to spare, the innovative 120 VAC Zero Surge Eliminator (103 Claremont Rd., Bernardsville NJ 07924 USA) performs exceptionally.

Or buy a kite and key.

Yaesu's new FRG-100 falls short of its potential.

New for 1994 ¢
★ ★ ★ ½

Yaesu FRG-100

Price: $639.00 in the United States. CAN$779.00 in Canada. £599.00 in the United Kingdom. AUS$999.00 in Australia. Filter modifications $40-200.

Advantages: Excellent performance in many respects. Lowest price of any tabletop model tested. Covers 50 Hz to 30 MHz in the LSB, USB, AM and CW modes. Includes three bandwidths, a noise blanker, selectable AGC, two attenuators, the ability to select 16 pre-programmed world band segments, two clocks, on-off timers, 52 tunable presets that store frequency and mode data, a variety of scanning schemes and an all-mode squelch. A communications-FM module, 500 Hz CW bandwidth and high-stability crystal are optional.

Disadvantages: Dreadful AM narrow and wide bandwidths (remediable, see story). No keypad for direct frequency entry (may eventually be remediable, see story). No fade/distortion-fighting synchronous detection. Lacks features found in "top-gun" receivers: passband offset, notch filter, adjustable RF gain. Simple controls and display, combined with complex functions, can make certain operations confusing. Dynamic range only fair.

Bottom Line: The Yaesu FRG-100 attempts to break some interesting new ground in the price/performance ratio of world band receivers. While this relatively small receiver is sometimes light on features often found in tabletop models, in certain respects it succeeds in delivering commendable performance. Yet, at the same time, performance is compromised by appalling AM bandwidths and the lack of a keypad for direct frequency entry. Independent firms offer, and plan to offer, interesting modifications, at extra cost, to remedy the main shortcomings.

Evaluation of New Model: Attention K-Mart shoppers! On sale now in our World Band aisle is the new Yaesu FRG-100 for only $639. Little enough for mobile use, with a price tag to match!

Yes, price really does count. A recent independent survey shows that most people want absolutely no part of a world band radio selling for more than $500. This means that the appearance of the '100 is no trivial development. Although it breaks the $500 barrier, it opens up the possibility of at least some tabletop models' eventually becoming part of the larger world band market.

The multi-voltage '100, unlike most tabletop models, operates off an external plug-in wall transformer, or adaptor. In addition to the jack for the adaptor, there are connectors for high- and low-impedance antennas, a switch for choosing between them, a jack for remote control of a tape recorder, and connectors for an external speaker, tape recorder and computer control of the receiver.

Absent, however, are controls radio aficionados have come to cherish for nurturing faint signals into intelligibility: passband offset, notch filter, RF gain control. Worse for aurally fastidious listeners is that there is no synchronous detector. Even worse . . . well, we'll get to *that* omission in a moment.

The '100 has 50 fully tunable presets that store frequency, mode and narrow filter settings for the CW and AM modes. In addition, there are two additional tunable presets, "Lo" and "Hi," that can be used for special scanning purposes. Any of these presets can be used, in effect, as a second VFO.

The '100 offers a variety of scanning techniques and modes to suit almost any need. Scanning of presets allows the listener to check automatically on activity within all or selected presets (empty presets are ignored). The default mode of scanning is carrier delay—the receiver automatically stops on any preset with a signal strong enough to break the squelch and stays there until the signal drops below the squelch threshold. Scanning then resumes until the next strong signal is encountered.

An alternative mode of operation is time-delay, in which scanning automatically proceeds to the next preset after a five-second delay. Another, Scan Stop, allows you to direct the '100 to stop scanning altogether and remain on a preset, once activity has been detected. Scanning will not resume until you press the SCAN button again.

Scanning with the '100 isn't restricted to presets; it can also scan a segment of frequencies that is defined by those special Lo and Hi presets. The '100 will cruise the segment you have selected, stopping at signals that are strong enough to penetrate the squelch threshold. As with presets scanning, you can choose between the carrier-delay and time-delay modes.

Another technique, Selectable Group

Scanning, allows you to arrange your 50 presets into five groups of ten presets each for more convenient scanning. Priority Scans allows the listener to listen to one frequency while keeping watch on another. This is a neat idea, particularly for antsy "A" types who like to do two things at once.

The '100 comes standard with three bandwidths—nominally 6, 4 and 2.4 kHz—of which two may be used for world-band listening. (A software option allows you to select which two you want.) On paper, this combination of bandwidths is nigh perfect: 6 kHz would provide relatively good fidelity with reasonable rejection of adjacent-channel signals; 4 kHz would yield better rejection of interference, yet offer moderate sound quality. 2.4 kHz would offer good selectivity in the single-sideband (SSB) mode, and also in a pinch for world band listening when the need for audio quality has to take a back seat to the need for rejection of massive interference.

The nominal 2.4 kHz ultra-narrow filter measures 2.6 kHz at -6 dB, with a superb shape factor. For single-sideband reception, that's good news, indeed.

Unfortunately, the other two bandwidths have about as much in common with reality as do politicians' promises. The "6 kHz" filter actually measures 7.6 kHz at -6 dB, about 26% over specification. Although its shape factor is good, this translates into a whopping 17.9 kHz at –60 db. Heterodynes from adjacent stations, like werewolves baying at the moon, sneak in to spoil the listening experience.

But there's the narrower 4 kHz filter, right? Think again—Yaesu has a nasty surprise in store for you. This "narrow" filter measures not 4, or 5, or even 6 kHz; but nearly *7 kHz*. Yes, 6.9 kHz—*72%* broader than Yaesu claims—at –6 dB. (At -60 dB, it's a barn-wide 17.2 kHz.)

Holy howling heterodynes! You can hardly hear the difference between the AM wide and AM narrow filters. Both are too broad for scanning the various world band segments or for listening to stations that are not out in the clear. Checks using other samples, plus a test by Yaesu itself after we informed them of our findings, confirmed our disappointing measurements.

Thankfully, the nominal 2.4 kHz filter performs admirably, and the receiver's software allows you to change the default filter for any mode. So, the AM narrow bandwidth can be easily changed from 6.9 kHz to 2.6 kHz.

This helps, even if the gap between the resulting two bandwidths is clearly excessive. The 2.6 kHz filter produces muffled audio, but if you detune the receiver 1.5 kHz or so, things improve, albeit at the price of some increase in distortion.

Solutions? According to informed sources

within Yaesu, the manufacturer has no intention of undoing this mess. It seems that the '100 was designated "best communications receiver" by a European organization; so Yaesu, beaming with pride, sees no way that the "best" can be made better!

However, others, at least in the United States, are trying to make things right. Electronic Equipment Bank, for example, offers a turnkey retrofit of the '100's bandwidths for about $200. The resulting revised AM narrow bandwidth measures 5.9 kHz; the narrow, 3.9 kHz. Both have excellent shape factors.

Universal Radio, also in the United States, plans to offer a replacement "narrow" filter for under $80, perhaps considerably less, installed. Gilfer Shortwave is also to offer a sophisticated filter modification for $150 with its new radios, $175 for retrofits.

Kiwa Electronics offers a replacement true 4 kHz (or other bandwidth) AM-narrow filter, installed, for around $70 (proficient do-it-yourselfers can install the kit themselves for $40); also, a switching module with two filters for $116 plus installation. Other specialty firms have indicated they may eventually follow suit. Who knows? Perhaps even Yaesu will see fit to revamp its latest offering.

Outwardly, the '100 is both attractive and simple-looking: there are only four knobs and 24 buttons, most of which serve a single purpose. Yet, this outward simplicity is deceiving. Many of the '100's operating parameters can be altered in ways that are not readily apparent by eyeballing the front panel.

Fortunately, the '100 is accompanied by well-written, easy-to-follow documentation. This is one radio where it really pays to read the manual first. Even better, once you have familiarized yourself with all the '100 can do, you can use the laminated plastic Handy Reference Guide that also comes with the radio.

The '100 is fitted with a six-pin DIN socket for computer control of frequency, mode, VFO, presets and other settings, when used with the optional FIF Interface and software. Fully five pages in the Operating Manual are devoted to computer control of the receiver.

Ergonomically, the '100 is a mixed bag. Except for the memory backup and antenna selection switches, both tucked away on the back panel, all controls are appropriately sized, well spaced and easy to handle. Each has a crisp, positive feel. A rubber-covered metal rod can be flipped down to cock the receiver at a jaunty angle for tabletop operation.

That's commendable, but this isn't: The '100 has *no keypad whatsoever* for direct frequency access! Not as standard, not as an option. In a 1993 survey of American world band listeners, the tuning control most desired turned out to be . . . yep, the keypad (see box).

Keypads are on some ordinary portables that sell for under $100, but not on this model costing several times more.

This is an incredible omission. If you habitually cruise the airwaves with the tuning knob, you'll miss a keypad less than will most listeners. Otherwise, while you're waiting for your receiver to limp from point "A" to point "B," you can scratch your head and wonder how any manufacturer can manage to get it so wrong.

Again, non-Yaesu sources may be coming up with solutions. At least one American firm, Electronic Equipment Bank, is looking into the possibility of offering an outboard keypad, à la the Lowe HF-150. Nothing has been said as yet about price, but something in the vicinity of $100 would seem to be appropriate.

In partial redemption, the '100 can be navigated through 16 pre-stored (factory-defined) world band segments. These can be scanned for activity using one of the '100's helpful scanning techniques.

However, using this feature isn't always straightforward. If you engage any one of these segments, tune to a different frequency, jump to another segment, then return later, you'll discover that you have returned not to the segment's lower edge but, rather, to whatever frequency you were at when you left the segment. This could prove handy for checking for parallel frequencies from the same broadcaster, but there is an additional thickening of the plot.

What if you want to use the segment presets as a convenient way to access the lower edge of each segment quickly, then scan each segment in turn? Disengage the segment preset mode? Turn the radio off? Unplug the power supply? Forget it, nothing works. When you re-engage the segment preset mode, it still returns not to the segment edges, but to the last-tuned frequencies.

Otherwise, ergonomic intricacies with the '100 tend to occur when its relatively simple controls and uncomplicated display run afoul of this receiver's extensive capabilities. The operating manual, while written in a far more readable style than most, does not go far enough to warn the listener of the often-invisible pitfalls of operation.

In almost every criterion of performance, save dynamic range and the ill-chosen bandwidths, the '100 is a real performer. It has excellent-to-superb sensitivity in the shortwave spectrum, and good-to-excellent sensitivity in the mediumwave AM and longwave portions.

In this regard, the performance of the '100 is right up there with top-gun receivers. Equally important, the circuitry of the '100 is quiet—you don't hear circuit hiss, and you don't hear digital hash, both of which can interfere with hearing a faint signal.

The '100 sounds good to the ear, too, and our lab tests confirm better-than-average audio. However, if you want the best audio the radio has to offer, its small, top-mounted speaker is inadequate. Headphones or a good outboard speaker are better.

The '100's dynamic range could not be measured properly at 20 kHz spacing because of synthesizer noise—a failing sometimes found on models costing much more. However, when measured at the more critical

---

Listener Survey . . .

Favorite Way to Tune: By Keypad

In 1993, a private survey of American world band listeners—not enthusiasts—was undertaken by a nonprofit institute. Among its findings are that the tuning control of choice is the keypad. Survey results for tuning devices (100, as in school, being the most important):

Favorite
Keypad	83.5

Next Favorite
Presets	80.1
Ability to Scan	79.6

Least Favorite
Up/Down Slewing	76.4
Tuning Knob	76.1

None of these, however, holds a candle to that ultimate aid in tuning world band, a digital frequency display. Score: 89.8.

5 kHz spacing, which relates to the actual 5 kHz channel norm of world band radio, it is only fair.

This limits to some extent the ability to flush out faint signals by coupling the receiver to a high-caliber external antenna and/or antenna amplifier. This is especially true in Europe, North Africa and the Near East within such congested world band segments as 6, 7 and 9 MHz at night. However, for listening within the Americas and Australasia the, '100's dynamic range is largely adequate.

Overall, color this receiver apteryx: a potentially excellent performer that, without decent bandwidths, can't fly; an ergonomic pleasure that can't be tuned properly.

But let's also tip our hats to those who are solving these problems. Properly modified, to the extent modifications have been available for us to test, the '100 is a much-improved piece of gear. For some, the additional expense is worth it. For others, the portatop Lowe HF-150, the '100's closest competitor, remains a better choice.

An *RDI WHITE PAPER* is available for this model.

★ ★ ★

Kenwood R-2000

Price: $829.95 in the United States. No longer available in Canada. £549.00 in the United Kingdom. $750-1,250 elsewhere in Europe.

Advantages: Straightforward to operate, with reasonable ergonomics. Audio pleasant for tabletop model. High sensitivity to weak signals makes model relevant to needs of listeners in such places as western North America and Australasia, where world band signals tend to be relatively weak. Two 24-hour clocks.

Disadvantages: Dismal dynamic range materially compromises performance by allowing overloading to take place in many parts of the world, such as Europe and even eastern North America—especially with high-gain antennas. "Wide" bandwidth too broad for most world band applications. Keypad uses nonstandard, unhandy layout.

The veteran Kenwood R-2000 pales against recent offerings.

Bottom Line: This model, which came on the market years ago, can be pleasant for listening to the major world band stations—especially if you live in western North America or Australasia. But for other, more demanding applications, it is in need of tighter selectivity and better dynamic range. Why bother, when almost any other tabletop model is better?

New for 1994
★ ★ ½

American Electrola DXC-100 World Access Radio 8A

Note: We have tested the initial and the revised versions, both released within a few months of each other. The initial version sold out immediately, so this report is confined to our findings with the revised version, which can be distinguished by the presence of a screw-adjusted attenuator on the rear panel.

Further revisions are planned that should be in place early in 1994.

Price: $319.95 plus shipping in the United States. Not yet sold in other countries.

Advantages: Among the lowest-priced tabletop models available. Receives FM broadcasts. Overall FM performance good, especially through headphones. Straightforward to operate. Tuning via knob, presets, keypad, scanning of presets and "signal-seek" scanning. Tuning knob, like scanner, not only tunes frequencies, but also presets. Powerful audio. Built-in telescopic antenna. World Time clock displays seconds numerically, along with the day of the week (1-7). Sophisticated 12-event timer for hands-off listening; nominally also turns recorder on and off. Sleep function. Clock, timer and other stored data protected against lengthy power failure. Large, bright LED display for frequency and preset information is unusually easy to read. Design has modest-sized footprint, yet allows the set to be handy to operate. Styled to be attractive in a typical home. Longwave has fairly good front-end selectivity. Comes with outboard mediumwave AM antenna which may be peaked, aimed and tilted to improve reception. Computer interface via DIN port. Optional IBM PC interface software. Comes with technical manual to explain radio and computer-interface details. Optional braille faceplate and owner's manual.

Disadvantages: Membrane keypad, especially power "key," extremely annoying and tiring to operate. In many locations, spurious FM broadcasting signals (from 87.5-108 MHz) penetrate excessively into shortwave spectrum, causing distorted interference. Considerable hiss in audio. Excessive whine from digital circuitry. Only one bandwidth, so bandwidth

New for 1994, the American Electrola DXC-100, also sold as the World Access Radio 8A, has some excellent concepts. Needs more engineering spit and polish, though.

can't be tailored to characteristics of received signal. Sensitivity to weak world band signals varies greatly from segment-to-segment. Mediocre dynamic range. Spurious "image" signal rejection (from signals 910 kHz higher up) only fair. "Signal-seek" scanner sometimes stops off frequency. Clock does not display when frequency being shown. Lacks signal-strength indicator. Uses AC adaptor, rather than built-in power supply. FM audio and adjacent-channel rejection (selectivity) only fair. *According to the manufacturer, the following disadvantage will be remedied in all future production:* Adjacent-channel rejection (selectivity) mediocre (apparently remediable, see story).

Bottom Line: Lots of outstanding features in a refreshingly practical radio for the general public. Although improvements have been made in the second version ("Production Revision 1"), performance needs a healthy additional dose of engineering spit and polish, and the membrane keypad urgently needs to be replaced by one with conventional keys. According to the manufacturer, at least one of these changes—selectivity—is about to take place, whereas other potential improvements are being investigated.

Evaluation of New Model: It's about time: an affordable world band radio designed for the way most normal people listen. Not a portable—most world band listening is done at home, not on the road—and not a techy DX tabletop model that's evolved from ham gear. This radio even looks like something you'd expect to find in a real home instead of an electronics lab.

All this came about because of an American populist radio program, "For The People." They reasoned that since the United States has the fastest-growing world band audience, it made little sense that there was not a single American firm manufacturing a world band radio on the sunny side of $900. So they commissioned the EDSI Co. of Pittsburgh,

Pennsylvania to solve the problem. Result: the American Electrola.

The Electrola was so well received that EDSI gave it a different name, World Access Radio, so it could be sold to regular electronic dealers. While they were at it, they even gave their company a separate distribution subsidiary for these "non-For The People" sales: Quality U.S. Technologies.

No matter what it is called, the radio is straightforward to operate. Absent altogether are the sophisticated controls DX radio enthusiasts cherish, but most people find confusing. However, present is something that, astonishingly, most manufacturers overlook: FM. Yes, everyday FM, which is all that many people ever tune to when they're not enjoying world band. And, except for adjacent-channel rejection, this radio's FM performance is reasonably good—even if, as we'll see in a moment, it creates some problems.

Something else tabletop manufacturers usually overlook: In the real world, most people don't want to go out and buy a separate external antenna, much less install it. This radio solves this by coming complete with a telescopic antenna for world band and FM, plus a nice little outboard antenna for mediumwave AM.

Even the price attracts. Not $1,000 or $800 or even $600, but around $300. Made in China or Indonesia? No, even at that price it's not only designed in the United States, it's made there, too. The manufacturer doesn't let you forget it, either: "USA 1" beams out at you in bright red letters as the factory default setting for the display.

It takes some getting used to—imagine "JAPAN 1" flashing on your Sony radio or TV!—but otherwise that display is a honey. Absent altogether are the gray-on-gray characters that most manufacturers foist on listeners' strained eyes. This is one radio that doesn't require the eyesight of a carrot-munching teenager to operate.

When the tuned frequency is no longer of interest, a button can be pressed to show World Time. This is no ordinary clock. It not only displays time, but also shows seconds numerically, as well as the day of the week ("1" for Sunday, "2" for Monday, and so forth).

This allows for hands-off listening via the radio's outstanding 12-event timer. With it, you not only choose the time and station, but also whatever day or combination of days of the week when you want to hear that station. This system is no easier to operate than the timer on a typical VCR, but it is more versatile than most VCR timers in that it not only has more events, but also it allows for more sophisticated selection of desired days. With the $14.95 Remote Recorder Interface accessory, which should be available by the time you read this, the radio will nominally also be able to turn a recorder on and off via a DIN port.

Obviously, many of the basic concepts of this radio are simply top drawer. Yet, there are some dandy goofs, earmarks that this is EDSI's first time at bat with a world band radio.

Take tuning. The radio tunes, in appropriate increments, the entire longwave, medium-wave AM and shortwave spectra, plus the usual FM band. Sixty presets are used to call up stations chop-chop.

There's also the usual tuning knob, plus a scanner. These not only tune frequency, but also can be used to tune through the bank of presets—a nice touch. However, in its "signal-seek" mode the scanner tends to stop somewhat off frequency, limiting its usefulness. So far, so good.

Yet, the most popular way to tune is with a keypad (see box elsewhere in this section), and most listeners poke at the keys quite often. Yet, this radio's keypad is of the membrane variety typically found on washing machines and microwave ovens—relatively large, heavy appliances that are typically operated far less often than radio controls. This radio's squishy "keys" don't depress easily and are utterly lacking in feel; indeed, the power "key" is so stiff it would help to have a thimble!

Our panelists were unanimous that even if the radio were otherwise pretty much all they desired—and in many respects it is—they wouldn't buy it simply because of the keypad. TV and VCR manufacturers, seasoned in the ways of the marketplace, know this. That's why nearly all clickers use real buttons instead of membranes.

Yet, there are listeners who don't use key-pads often. For them, the key issue isn't keys, but performance. Here, too, the report card is mixed.

The original version was exceptionally sensitive to weak signals. However, presumably in order to correct other problems, sensitivity was reduced, sort of, in the revised version tested. "Sort of," because within some world band segments, such as 6 MHz, sensitivity continues to be quite good. On higher segments, sensitivity varies a bit, but is generally more than adequate. Yet, on some other bands, such as 5 and 7 MHz—even with the attenuator off—sensitivity is far below what it should be. Ironically, "For The People" is aired evenings over WHRI on 7 MHz.

Although the radio has no signal-strength indicator, your ears spot the problem right off: noise. Sensitivity is not just how much a signal moves a signal-strength indicator; it's also how much that signal overcomes noise inherent in receiver circuitry. On this radio, that noise—hiss—is considerable and obtrusive.

Also obtrusive are distorted sounds from FM broadcasts penetrating into the shortwave spectrum, disturbing world band signals. How badly this will affect your actual listening depends on where you tune the radio and the FM situation in your locality.

Unrelated to your locality, but a problem nonetheless, is digital "whine" that comes through to mix with the station you're listening to. Again, this is a design shortcoming, and it's worse on this model than on any other we've tested in recent years.

One of the most important variables in a world band radio's performance is its adjacent-channel rejection, also known as selectivity. That's because most world band stations are crammed so closely together on the dial that they can cause interference to each other if selectivity is inadequate.

It's the bandwidth filter that chiefly determines the quality of adjacent-channel rejection. Because of an overly broad 12 kHz bandwidth filter (there's only one, which in itself is a drawback), adjacent-channel rejection on both units tested was woefully inadequate; strong stations could be heard fully two channels away. That's the bad news.

The good news is that by the time you read this the radio will be manufactured with a 4 kHz bandwidth. This development took place just as we were going to press, so we weren't able to include it in our tests. Yet, it has to represent a major improvement. If you already have a radio with the older filter, EDSI states that they will retrofit it with the newer filter for $15.

Image rejection, another important measure of keeping unwanted racket at bay, is adequate for the receiver's price class. Yet, it is not fully up to the standard of most other tabletop models.

As this model was designed for the American market, it lacks certain characteristics that would make it suitable elsewhere. For example, its dynamic range is mediocre, which would be a real problem in Europe, North Africa or the Near East. Yet, the radio receives longwave, which is not used for broadcasting in the Western Hemisphere. Front-end selectivity is important in this band, and here the radio does reasonably well.

Although outboard AC adaptors are less desirable than built-in power supplies—well-meaning rules of Underwriters Laboratories and its Canadian counterpart encourage this sort of foolishness—one advantage is that if Americans decide to take this radio abroad, they can simply purchase an adaptor suited to the local current.

Audio quality, once the forgotten stepchild of world band radios, has improved greatly in recent years. Here, the EDSI offering does well, even if not outstandingly. Its audio stage and speaker are more than adequate, pumping out gobs of room-filling audio. Yet, the various shortcomings that occur earlier in the radio's circuitry conspire to make listening something less than an exhilarating aural experience.

Overall, this is a radio that's basically on the right track. When Britain's Lowe Electronics first went into the business of manufacturing shortwave radios, the result left something to be desired, and we said so. Yet, they built on that basic design, improving at each step. Now, they're busy building a new plant to keep up with the orders.

Whether EDSI will evolve similarly remains to be seen. However, this radio's basic design and the manufacturer's seeming eagerness to make continuing improvements suggests it is on the right track.

No amount of nostalgia or Art Deco can rescue this Tunemaster turkey. Give it the axe!

Reintroduced for 1994
★

Tunemaster Shortwave Radio

Price: $99.95 plus $8.00 shipping in the United States.
Advantages: Eye-catching appearance; styled after a French art-deco radio originally built in the 1940s. Also covers VHF from 110-137 and 144-164 MHz. Audio quality at least average. Very inexpensive for a tabletop model.
Disadvantages: You virtually cannot tell where the radio is tuned: 1) it lacks digital frequency display or synthesized tuning circuitry; 2) its coarse analog readout provides virtually no indication of what channel is being tuned; and 3) portions of even that horrible readout are

misaligned or mislabeled. Lacks any tuning facilities except spongy tuning knob and a fine-tuning knob secreted on the back of the set. Mediocre adjacent-channel selectivity. Poor rejection of certain spurious signals ("images"). Mediocre dynamic range results in significant overloading when connected to outdoor antenna (comes with no built-in antenna or attenuator). Relatively unstable, making for marginal reception of single-sideband signals. Does not receive longwave broadcasts.
Bottom Line: Sold by Sharper Image, but performance is more like sharper images. Two years ago, it appeared this receiver had been discontinued. No such luck—it's resurfaced to reclaim its ranking as the worst tabletop we've ever tested.

The Passport tabletop-model review team: Lawrence Magne, along with Jock Elliott and Tony Jones, with laboratory measurements by Robert Sherwood.

Two Oldies

The following models have been discontinued, yet may still be available new at some retail outlets.

★ ★ ★ ★ ½   **Japan Radio NRD-525U**   *Editor's Choice*
(Japan Radio NRD-525E)
(Japan Radio NRD-525J)
(Japan Radio NRD-525G)

An excellent performer that's well put together, but lacks audio fidelity, the '525 has been replaced by the NRD-535 (*see*). Priced at under: $1,000 in the United States, CAN$1,400 in Canada, £800 in the United Kingdom and AUS$2,000 in Australia.

★ ★ ★ ½   **Yaesu FRG-8800**

A touch better than the newer Kenwood R-100, yet still well past its technological prime. Under $700 or £600.

Where to Find It:

Index to Radios Tested for 1994

Passport tests nearly every model on the market, and here's where each review can be found. In addition, summary comments and ratings are given on pages 83 and 94 for recently discontinued models: Grundig Satellit 500 and 650; Japan Radio NRD-525; Magnavox/Philips AE 3805 and D2999; Sony CRF-V21, ICF-PRO80/70 and ICF-7700/ICF-7600DA; and Yaesu FRG-8800.

Not enough? For premium receivers and antennas there are comprehensive *Passport* Radio Database International White Papers™. These usually run 15–30 pages in length, with one report thoroughly covering a single model or topic. Each RDI White Paper™—$5.95 in North America, $7.95 airmail in most other regions—contains virtually all our panel's findings and comments during hands-on testing, as well as laboratory measurements and what these mean to you. They're available from key world band dealers; also, write us or call our 24-hour automated order line (+1 215/794-8252), or write Passport RDI White Papers, Box 300, Penn's Park, PA 18943 USA.

Choosing a Premium Receiver?

Get premium advice before you buy!

If you could, you'd spend weeks with each receiver, learning its charms and foibles. Seeing for yourself how it handles—*before* you spend.

Now, you can do the next best thing—better, some readers insist. Radio Database International White Papers™, from the *Passport to World Band Radio*™ library of in-depth test reports, put the facts right into your hands.

We test run each receiver for you. We put it through comprehensive laboratory and bench tests to find out where it shines. And where it doesn't.

Then our panel takes over: DXers, professional monitors, program listeners—experts all. They're mean, grumpy, hypercritical ... and take lots of notes. They spend weeks with each receiver, checking ergonomics and long-run listening quality with all kinds of stations. Living with it day and night.

With *Passport*'s RDI White Papers, these findings—the good, the bad and the ugly—are yours, along with valuable tips on how to operate your radio to best advantage. Each receiver report covers one model in depth, and is $5.95 postpaid in the United States; CAN$7.95 in Canada; US$7.95 airmail in the European Community, Scandinavia, Australia, New Zealand and Japan; US$12.35 registered air elsewhere.

Separate reports are available for each of the following premium radios:

Drake R8/R8E
Icom IC-R71
Icom IC-R9000
Japan Radio NRD-93
Japan Radio NRD-535/NRD-535D
Kenwood R-5000
Lowe HF-150
Lowe HF-225 and HF-235
Sony ICF-2010/ICF-2001D
Yaesu FRG-100 (available from 12/93)
Yaesu FRG-8800

Other *Passport* RDI White Papers available:

How to Interpret Receiver Specifications
and Lab Tests
Popular Outdoor Antennas

Available from world band radio dealers or direct. For VISA/MasterCard orders, call our 24-hour automated order line: +1 (215) 794-8252. Or send your check or money order (Pennsylvania add 6%), specifying which report or reports you want, to:

Passport RDI White Papers
Box 300
Penn's Park, PA 18943 USA

- **U.S.:** DX Radio, EEB, Universal
- **Canada:** Sheldon Harvey (Radio Books)
- **U.K.:** Lowe • **Japan:** IBS-Japan
- **Latin America:** IBS-Latin America

"We strongly recommend the *Passport* RDI White Papers before purchasing any receiver over $100. The *Consumer Reports* of shortwave radio."

—What's New, *Monitoring Times*

Top News Shows for 1994

(continued from page 24)

For *Australasia*, there's 0830 daily and 1030 Monday through Saturday on 15450 and 21490 kHz.

"Commonwealth Update"
Radio Moscow International

Despite the fact that Radio Moscow International has lost some of its best journalistic talent to domestic competition, "Commonwealth Update" remains a prime source of information about events in the former Soviet Union.

Each 15-minute broadcast starts with a review of the latest Russian newspapers. This is followed by reports and commentary on recent happenings in Russia and the Commonwealth of Independent States.

"Commonwealth Update" is aired six times a day, five days a week, though listeners in certain areas, because of their location, can tune in on a sixth day. The program can be heard Monday through Friday at 1911 and 2311, and Tuesday through Saturday at

0211, 0511, 0811 and 1111. All transmissions are one hour earlier in summer.

Winters in *North America*, try 2311 on 6045, 7105, 9750, 9870, 12050, 15425 and 21480 kHz. In summer, best reception is likely to be found on the western side of the continent on channels like 12050, 15410 and 15425 kHz. Listeners in eastern North America should try dialing around between 9750 and 9890 kHz, with 11790 kHz also a reasonable bet.

There is another opportunity on these same channels at 0211, but reception may be chancy.

The final opportunity for North America is at 0511 on 7150, 7165, 7180 and 9870 kHz; summers on 9530, 9765 and 11790 kHz. If you cannot hear anything on these channels, try nearby—RMI is inclined to move its frequencies around on monthly or bimonthly basis.

If you're in *Europe*, at 0511 winters you can choose from the likes of 5905, 5950, 7150, 7165, 7180, 7330 and 7390 kHz. Later, at 0811 and 1111, they can try the likes of 12020, 12070, 13650, 13705, 15345 and 15540 kHz. For other frequencies, dial

Report from Austria is particularly valuable for news about Hungary, Romania and the former Yugoslavia. English staffers include (left) Patricia Maadi, Murray Hall, David Ward, Eugene Hartzell, Ann Dubsky, David Hermges and Elizabeth Blane.

around the 11 and 15 MHz bands, which is where you will also find most of the channels used in summer. Finally, the 1911 edition can be heard most of the year on frequencies in the 7 and 9 MHz bands. Dial around, and find the channel that best suits your location.

In the *Middle East*, tune in at 0211, 0511, 0811 and 1111. This is RMI's best served target area, so tune around the bands to find a decent signal—it shouldn't take you long.

In *East Asia* the broadcasts at 2311 and 0211 can best be heard winters in the 7 and 9 MHz bands, and on 11 and 15 MHz frequencies in summer. At 0511, the 17 and 21 MHz bands provide reliable all-year reception, as they also do at 0811 and 1111 in summer. During winter, try 15 and 17 MHz channels at 0811, and 9 MHz frequencies for the later slot. The 1911 broadcast can best be heard in the 7 and 9 MHz bands in winter, and on 9, 11 and 15 MHz channels in summer.

For *Australia and the South Pacific*, the 1911 and 2311 editions are best heard on frequencies in the 9 MHz band, with 15 MHz a better bet in summer. At 0211, 0511 and 0811, there should be good year-round reception on 17 and 21 MHz frequencies.

"Ukraine Today"
Radio Ukraine International

If world band news were to be classified into "national," "regional," and "international," "Ukraine Today" would probably fall into the first category, although there is some additional coverage of Russian and other stories.

There is arguably no other program on the international airwaves which provides such comprehensive coverage of a country's domestic political, economic and cultural affairs. It is also to the credit of all concerned that as much information is served up in so digestible a manner. Unfortunately for news buffs, most of the weekend programming is given over to a listener-response show or Ukrainian music, also good stuff.

If you're in *Europe*, you can hear "Ukraine Today" at 2200 winters on 4825, 6010, 6020, 7195, 7240, 9710 and 15385 kHz; and 2100 summers on 4825, 6090, 7150, 7240, 7285, 9600, 9640, 9685, 15135, 15195 and 17725 kHz. Some of these channels are also audible in eastern *North America*

A repeat broadcast for eastern *North America* and *European* night owls goes out at 0100 winters on 4825, 6010, 6020, 6070, 6080, 6145, 7180, 7195, 7240, 9710, 9750 and 9860 kHz; and 0000 summers on 6010, 6090, 7150, 7195, 7240, 9500, 9550, 9560, 9600, 9640, 9685, 9860, 11720 and 15195 kHz. This transmission can also be heard in Western North America, winters on 17605 and 17690 kHz, and summers on 15180 and 15580 kHz.

"World Business Report"
"World Business Review"
BBC World Service

These two outstanding BBC programs provide up-to-the-minute news from the world's major markets in such a way that it interests lay people as much as it does financial pros.

"World Business Report" airs nine minutes of the latest in news from markets in the Far East, Europe and the United States. This is supplemented by information and comment on market reaction to world political events. Also covered are current bond and treasury prices, commodity trends, movement in the world currency markets and, most important to most of us, how all this is likely to affect our daily lives.

"World Business Report" is heard at 0905 Monday through Saturday and 1705 and 2305 Monday through Friday. It is replaced Sundays, at the same times, by "World Business Review"—a look back at the previous week's business and a peek at upcoming events.

For *North America* there's 1705 on 9515 and 15260 kHz, and 2305 on 5975, 6175, 7325 (winter), 9590, 9915 (winter), 12095 (summer) and 15070 (summer) kHz.

In *Europe*? Tune in at 0905 on 7325, 9410, 9750, 9760, 12095, 15070 and 17640 kHz; 1705 on 6180, 6195, 9410, 12095 and (summer) 15070 kHz; and 2305 on 3955 (winter) and 6195 kHz. In the *Middle East*, try 0905 on 11760, 15575 and 21470 kHz; and 1705 on 9410, 9740, 12095 and 15070 kHz.

Best bets in *East Asia* are 0905 on 15280, 15360, 17830 and 21715 kHz; and 2305 on 11945, 11955, 15280 and 15370 kHz. In *Australia*, tune in at these same times, but at 0905 dial 11750, 11955 and 17830 kHz; and 2305 go to 11955 (winter) and 15340 kHz.

Total Coverage Radios

AOR AR1000XLT
AM Broadcast to Microwave
1000 Channels

500KHz to 1300MHz coverage in a programmable hand held. Ten scan banks, ten search banks. Lockout on search and scan. AM plus narrow and broadcast FM. Priority, hold, delay and selectable search increment of 5 to 995 KHz. Permanent memory. 4 AA ni-cads and wall plus cig charger included along with belt clip, case, ant. & earphone. Size: 6 7/8 x 1 3/4 x 2 1/2. Wt 12 oz. Fax fact # 205

AR2500
2016 Channels
1 to 1300MHz
Computer Control

62 Scan Banks, 16 Search Banks, 35 Channels per second. Patented Computer control for logging and spectrum display. AM, NFM, WFM, & BFO for CW/SSB. Priority bank, delay/hold and selectable search increments. Permanent memory. DC or AC with adaptors. Mtng Brkt & Antenna included. Size: 2 1/4H x 5 5/8W x 6 1/2D. Wt. 1lb. #305

AR3000
400 Channels
100KHz to 2036MHz
Patented Computer Control

Patented computer control, top rated receiver in its class, offers AM, NFM Wide FM, LSB, USB, CW modes. RS232 control. 4 priority channels. 4 banks of 100 channels each plus 4 search memory banks. Programmable attenuation by memory channel with 15 band pass filters to eliminate image interference. Alarm or sleep timing control modes with VFO for tuning. 2.8KHz filter for CW and SSB. Delay & Hold & Freescan. AC/DC pwr and whip ant. Size: 3 1/7H x 5 2/5W x 7 7/8D.Wt 2lbs., 10oz. Fax fact doc. #105

AOR AR1500
Full Coverage with BFO control and 1000 Channels.

500KHz to 1300MHz. Ten scan banks, ten search banks. Search lock and store. BFO. 2 Antennas. AM/NFM/WFM. Selectable increments. Tons of features, small size: 5 7/8 x 1 1/2 x 2. Wt 14 oz. Fax fact document # 250

YUPITERU MVT7100
530KHz to 1650MHz
50Hz Tuning with LSB & USB Mode Select.

530KHz to 1650MHz coverage in a programmable hand held. Ten scan banks, ten search banks. Lockout on search and scan. AM plus narrow and broadcast FM. Priority, hold, delay and selectable search increments and search lockout. Permanent memory. Also features VFO, attenuator, signal strength meter, and standby mode. 4 AA ni-cads and wall plus cig charger included along with belt clip, case, ant. & earphone. Size: 6 7/8 x 1 3/4 x 2 1/2. Wt 12 oz. Fax fact # 290

YUPITERU
MVT8000 & MVT7000
100KHz to 1300MHz Mobile and Hand Held Units.

Top rated receivers from Japan now available in the USA. Tune down to 100KHz. Sensitivity guaranteed from 8MHz up. 200 scan channels. AM/NFM/WFM. No gaps, no cut-outs. Mobile is super slim line. AC/DC. Order MVT8000, includes antenna, mbl mnt. Order MVT7000 for the hand held. Complete with Ni-Cads, Charger, antenna & earphone. Fax fact document #275

NEW Receivers

AR3300/330X

HF Receiver with *Direct Digital Synthesis, Microprocessor Control, Keyboard Input and Digital Display. A compact yet full featured receiver. Call or use our fax fact service for more information on this exciting new receiver!*

Sangean Receivers

ATS-818CS 16 Band digital receiver with programmable cassette recorder, BFO for SSB, AM/FM Stereo, 45 preset memories LCD display with dual time. Signal & Batt. strength indicator. Sleep timer & tone control. Fast Fax #505

ATS-818 Same as 818CS but w/o cassette. Fax Fact #506

ATS-803A The perennial best buy receiver. 16 band

digital receiver with AM/FM/FM Stereo modes. 9 memory presets. Auto/Manual and Scan modes. BFO RF Gain and Dual Filter controls. Complete with adaptors and headphones. Fax Fact #507

ATS-808 Compact size, great performance in a 16 band digital receiver.

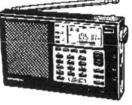

AM/FM/Stereo with 45 memory presets. LCD display with dual time clock. Complete with adaptors and head phones. Fax fact #508

ATS-606 16 band ultra compact digital receiver with auto tuning and scan system. 45 memory presets cover AM/FM/Stereo. Dual time display, alarm timer, adjustable sleep timer. Fax Fact #509.

SG-621 Compact 10 band receiver with AM/FM/Stereo. Analog tuning with a digital display. Fax Fact #513.

ATS-800 13 band digital receiver with AM/FM/Stereo and 20 memory presets. Auto/Manual, scan clock and sleep timer. Fax fact #510.

SG-631 10 band analog tuning with digital display which shows time and day for 260 cities throughout the world. Fax fact #511.

SG-789 10 band analog tuning super compact and very economical. Fax fact #512.

SG-621 Compact 10 band receiver with AM/FM/Stereo. Analog tuning with a digital display. Fax Fact #513.

SG-700L 12 band AM/FM compact portage analog receiver Fax Fact #514

Bearcat Receivers

New models of 30 MHz and above receivers now offer continuous coverage and enhanced digital tuning. Call us for details. And if you have an old American made Regency or Bearcat scanning receiver call us. Between the ex-Regency and ex-Bearcat factory people here, we have over 70 years combined experience in scanning receiver design and manufacturing . So in addition to being able to give you the straight scoop on our tool free help line, we can probably do a job in restoring your old radios.

1994's Top Entertainment

(continued from page 38)

America's two-part weekly window on popular African music. Produced by artist and musicologist genius Leo Sarkisian, and hosted by the popular and delightful Rita Rochelle, this is "must" listening for lovers of the genre. Although there is a relative dearth of music from places like Somalia, Ethiopia and Sudan, there is ample compensation in the contagious rhythms of such countries as the Congo, Zaïre and Tanzania.

> ### Much music owes its existence to this influence.

Both parts of the program go out on Sunday: the first at 1733, the second two hours later. Some listeners may prefer the second segment because of the extra musical content, but those who have an interest in the African musical scene will also wish to hear the earlier broadcast. Like an African *Rolling Stone*, it includes reports and interviews from and about African musicians.

Although beamed to Africa, this show can be heard in many parts of the world well beyond the intended target area, including North America. At 1733, tune to 11920, 11995, 13710, 15320 or 15445 kHz; for the 1933 edition, try 11920, 11995, 13710, 15320, 15410, 15495, 15580, 17800 and 21485 kHz.

"Focus on Faith"
BBC World Service

Here's a breath of fresh air—a religious program that's not out to convert you to anything or plead for your money!

"Focus on Faith" covers news about religion, *all* religions, worldwide. Dispassionate, yet hard-hitting, nothing is above being covered to the usual standards of the BBC. Whether it be a governmental takeover of Egyptian mosques or criticism of the Anglican church's attitude over the return of Hong Kong to China, there are no sacred cows.

Topics such as the relationship between religion and politics, or violations of human rights, are dealt with in the same spirit,

GRUNDIG
SATELLIT 700
The Ultimate AM/FM/Shortwave Radio

Journey to the furthest corners of the globe. The sky's the limit with a world band radio. You can listen in on events around the world. Discover hourly newscasts from the BBC, enjoy the latest music from West Africa, listen in on weather reports from Australia. It's the perfect tool for keeping in touch with the world, excellent for travellers away from home who want to keep posted on the news.

- **World Class Reception**

- **Unparalleled Sensitivity and Selectivity**

- **Superior Sideband Performance**

- **512 Alphanumeric Memory Positions**

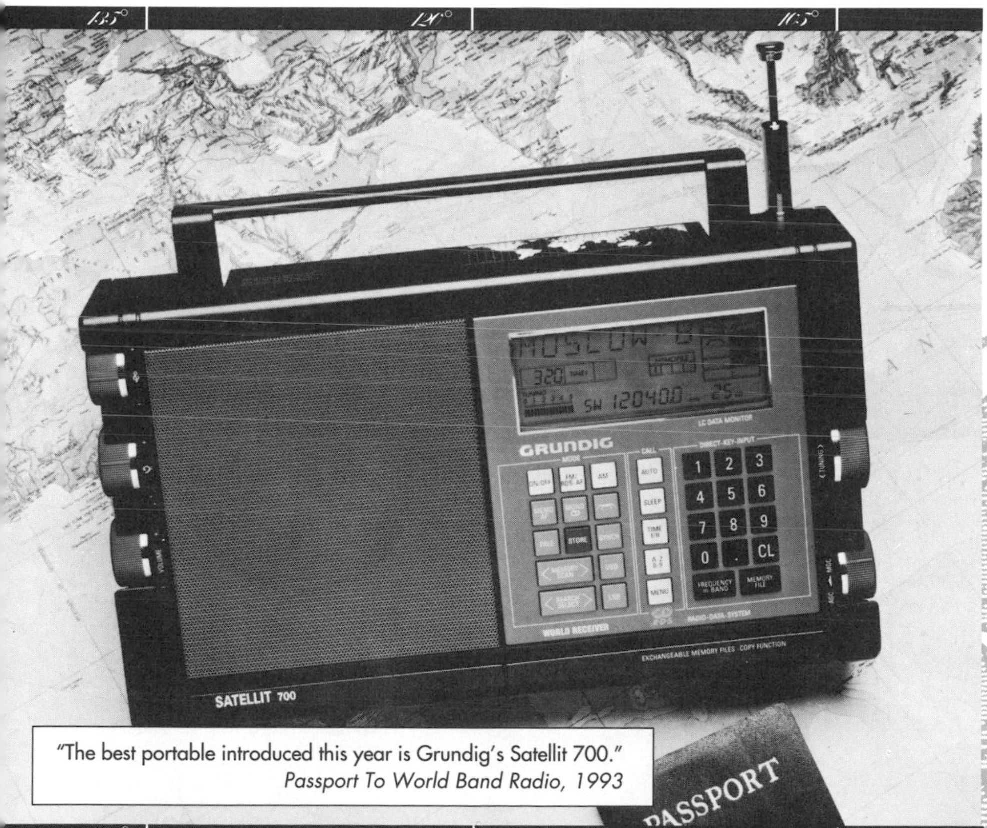

"The best portable introduced this year is Grundig's Satellit 700."
Passport To World Band Radio, 1993

C. CRANE COMPANY

558 10th Street
Fortuna, CA 95540-2350
1-800-522-TUNE (8863)
1-707-725-9000
Fax: 1-707-725-9060

MFJ ACCESSORIES

Here's an economical desktop tuned active antenna with performance that rivals or exceeds outside long wires hundreds of feet long!

MFJ-1020A
$79⁹⁵

Receive strong clear signals from all over the world with this indoor tuned active antenna that rivals the reception of long wires hundreds of feet long!

"World Radio TV Handbook" says MFJ-1020 is a "fine value…fair price…performs very well indeed! " Set it on your desktop and listen to the world!

No need to go through the hassle of putting up an outside antenna you have to disconnect when it storms.

Covers 300 kHz to 30 MHz so you can pick up all of your favorite stations. And discover new ones you couldn't get before. Tuned circuitry minimizes intermodulation, improves selectivity and reduces noise from phantom signals, images and out-of-band signals.

Adjustable telescoping whip gives you maximum signal with minimum noise. Full set of controls for tuning, band selection, gain and On-Off/Bypass.

Also, functions as preselector with external antenna connected to MFJ-1020A.

Measures a compact 5" x 2" x 6". Use 9 volt battery (not included) 9-18 VDC or 110 VAC with MFJ-1312, $12.95. Get yours today.

MFJ Antenna Matcher

MFJ-959B
$89⁹⁵

Don't miss rare DX because of signal power loss between receiver and antenna!

The MFJ-959B provides proper impedance matching so you transfer maximum signal from antenna to receiver.

Covers 1.6-30 MHz. 20 dB preamp with gain control boosts weak stations. 20 dB attenuator prevents overload. Select from 2 antennas, 2 receivers (SO-239 connectors). Measures 9" x 2" x 6". Use 9-18 VDC or 110 VAC with MFJ-1312, $12.95.

MFJ LW/MW/SW Preselector/ Tuner

MFJ-956
$39⁹⁵

MFJ-956

lets you boost your favorite stations while rejecting images, intermod and other phantom signals. It improves reception from 150 KHz to 30 MHz with most dramatic results below 2 MHz. Has tuner bypass and ground receiver postition. Measures 2" x 3" x 4".

Outdoor Active Antenna

"World Radio TV Handbook" says MFJ-1024 is a "first rate easy-to-operate…quiet…excellent dynamic range…good gain…low noise …broad coverage…excellent choice."

Mount it outdoors away from electrical noise for maximum signal, minimum noise. Covers 0.5-30 MHz.

Receives strong, clear signals from all over the world. 20 dB attenuator, gain control. On LED. Switch two receivers and aux. or active antenna. 6x3x5in. Remote unit has 54 inch whip, 50 ft. coax and connector. 3x2x4 in.

MFJ-1024 **$129⁹⁵**

Use 12-VDC or 110 VAC with MFJ-1312, $12.95.

MFJ DXers' World Map Clock

MFJ-112 **$24⁹⁵**

This new MFJ-112 DXers' World Map Clock, $24.95, not only shows you the time at any QTH throughout the world--it also gives you an attractive world map so you can *see the place where your contact is!* Also shows day of the week, month, date and year. Time displays hour/minute/second. User selectable for 12 or 24 hour display format. Has day-light-savings-time feature.

Easy push-buttons let you move east and west on the map diplay to a QTH in every time zone. Attractive gold color, brown trims. Great gift or use as logging clock. Measures 4.5"W x 3³/₈"H x2¹/₄"D.

SWL's Guide for Apartment/ Condo Dwellers

Even if you're in an apartment in the middle of a crowded city and you can't pick anything up, world renowned SWL expert Ed Noll's newest book gives you the key to hearing news as it's happening, concerts from Vienna and soccer games from Germany!

MFJ-36 **$9⁹⁵**

You learn what shortwave bands to listen to, the best times to tune in, how to DX and successfully QSL. This antenna guide shows you how to make the most of a small space. Much more.

MFJ-1278B Multimode

MFJ-1278B
$279⁹⁵

MFJ's famous top-of-the-line computer interface lets you receive FAX, RTTY, PACTOR, Amtor, Morse code, Packet, Navtex, Color SSTV and ASCII on your computer screen. Zillions of features … Automatic Signal Analysis™ analyzes RTTY, ASCII, AMTOR and HF Packet. Optional starter packet **MFJ-1289** $59.95, for IBM; **MFJ-1282B**, $39.95, C64; **MFJ-1287B**, $59.95, for Macintosh; **MFJ-1290** $59.95, for Amiga. Gives you multi-gray news photos, weather maps and SSTV.

MFJ Dual Tunable Filter

MFJ-752C
$99⁹⁵

This all mode **dual** tunable filter lets you zero in and pull-out your favorite stations and notch out interference at the same time. Two independently tunable filters letyou peak, notch, low or high pass signals to eliminate heterodynes and interference-- even on the most crowded shortwave bands. Tune both filters from 300 Hz to 3000 Hz. Vary bandwidth from 40 Hz to flat. Notch depth to 70 dB.

Headphone and speaker jacks with 2 watts audio provided let you monitor stations through filter. Inputs for 2 radios (switch selectable). Switchable noise limiter from impulse noise through clipper removes background noise. OFF bypasses filter. Use 9-18 VDC or 110 VAC with MFJ-1312B, $12.95. 10" x 2" x 6".

All Band Transceiver/ Preselector

MFJ-1040B
$99⁹⁵

Lets you copy weak signals. Rejects out-of-band signals, images. Covers 1.8 to 54 MHz. Up to 20 dB gain. Gain control. Dual gate MOSFET, bipolar transistors for low noise, high gain. 20 dB at tenuator. Connect 2 antennas, 2 receivers. Coax and phone jacks. Automatic bypass when transmitting to 350 watts. Delay. Jack for PTT. Use 9-18 VDC or 110 VAC with MFJ-1312, $12.95.

MFJ-1045B, $69.95. Like MFJ-1040B without attenuator, auto transceiver bypass, delay control or PTT.

Receive *color* fax news photos

Receive color fax news photos on your computer screen using your shortwave receiver and the new MFJ-1214 computer interface ... you'll pick up wire service photos, high resolution weather maps, RTTY, ASCII and Morse Code ...

High Resolutions weather map recieved off short-wave with the MFJ-1214

You can pick up Wire Service News Photos with the MFJ-1214

MFJ-1214PC or MFJ-1214AM $149⁹⁵

See amazing full color news photos as they appear on your computer. Watch them as they're transmitted by shortwave FAX around the world.

Read tomorrow morning's newspaper copy as it is transmitted to newspapers by radioteletype (RTTY).

Is it going to rain? See for yourself when you receive highly detailed weather maps that even show you cloud densities.

Have you ever wondered what hams are doing on their digital modes like RTTY, ASCII and CW? Now you can eavesdrop -- the MFJ-1214 will decipher them for you.

You ain't heard nothing yet. You'll also copy military RTTY, ship-to-shore, coast guard CW, distress and safety, dipomatic and embassy communications, telex, Interpol, utilities, Tass .

What do you need to receive these fascinating digital modes? Your shortwave receiver, your 286/386/486 computer with VGA monitor and the MFJ-1214PC package -- that's all. (MFJ-1214AM for Amiga).

Everything is included--multimode, computer interface, software, cables and power supply. All you do is plug it all in, run the friendly software and tune in a station. Then sit back and watch digital transmissions come to life on your computer .

Easy-Up Antennas Book

MFJ-38 $16⁹⁵

SWL expert Ed Noll, W3FQJ, shows you how to build and put up inexpensive, fully tested wire antennas using readily available parts that'll bring signals in like you've never heard before.

Covers receiving antennas from 100 KHz to almost 1000 MHz. Includes antennas for long, medium and shortwave broadcast, utility, marine and VHF/UHF services.

.3-200 MHz Antenna

MFJ-1022 $39⁹⁵

This tiny 3¹/₃x1¹/₄x4 inch *active* antenna lets you hear signals from all over the world from 300 KHz to 200 MHz including low, medium, shortwave and VHF bands.

A J-310 FET handles strong signals and a new *noiseless feedback* circuit gives you excellent low noise reception. A 4.5 GHz MRF-901 transistor lets you receive weak signals well into VHF. Uses 9V bat., 12 VDC or 110 VAC with MFJ-1312B, $12.95.

MFJ Antenna Switches

MFJ-1704 $59⁹⁵

MFJ-1702B $21⁹⁵

MFJ-1704 heavy duty antenna switch lets you select 4 antennas or ground them for static and lightning protection. Unused antennas automatically grounded. Replaceable lightning surge protection device. Good to over 500 MHz. 60 db isolation at 30 MHz.

MFJ-1702B, $21.95, for 2 antennas.

Super Hi-Q Loop™ Antenna

MFJ-1786 $249⁹⁵

The MFJ *Super Loop*™ is a professional quality remotely tuned 10-30 MHz high-Q antenna. It has a very narrow bandwidth that reduces receiver over-loading and out-of-band interference.

It's a very quiet receiving antenna because it responds to magnetic fields and not electric fields -- you'll hardly

notice electrical noises or even static crashes during a storm.

Gray Line DX Advantage

MFJ-1286 $29⁹⁵

The Gray Line is the day /night divider line where the most amazing DX happens. Now, you'll know exactly when to take advantage of it.

The MFJ-1286 Gray Line DX Advantage is a DXing program for IBM compatible computers. It predicts DX propagation by showing you the moving Gray Line.

Regenerative Receiver Kit

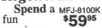

Spend a fun evening putting this simple high quality kit together and marvel at what the shortwave listener of yesteryear heard with a simple *regenerative* receiver.

MFJ-8100K $59⁹⁵

This baby performs. An RF stage really picks up weak signals. Stations all over the world will come in loud and clear with just a 10 foot wire antenna.

Listen to international shortwave AM broadcasts, hams on SSB and CW, WWV, RTTY, packet and much more. Covers all or part of 75/80, 49, 40, 30, 31, 20, 25, 22, 19, 17, 16, 15 and 13 Meters in five bands.

It has smooth vernier reduction tuning. Use Walkman style earphones or plug-in speakers and 9 volt battery.

MFJ-8100K, $59.95 kit;
MFJ-8100W, $79.95 wired/tested.

2 Meter Receiver Kit

Enjoy a fun evening building this high quality tunable 2 Meter receiver kit and have fun listening to interesting ham conversations on 2 Meter repeaters all around your area.

MFJ-8400K $69⁹⁵

Super sensitive dual conversion superhet receiver with low noise RF preamp and sharp ceramic filters.

Tune, squelch, volume, speaker.
MFJ-8400K, $69.95 kit;
MFJ-8400W, $89.95 wired/tested.

12/24 Hour Clocks

MFJ-107B $9⁹⁵
MFJ-108B $19⁹⁵
MFJ-105B $19⁹⁵

MFJ-108B, $19.95, dual clock displays 24 UTC and 12 hour local time *simultaneously*

MFJ-107B, $9.95, single clock shows you 24 hour UTC time.

Both have easy-to-see 5/8 inch LCD digits in brushed aluminum frame.

MFJ-105B, $19.95, is an accurate 24 hour UTC quartz wall clock with analog dial. Large 10 inch diameter face is easy-to-read across room.

QuickStudy™ License Guide

MFJ-3212 $14⁹⁵

Get your No Code Tech ham radio license on your very first try without learning Morse code!

MFJ No Code Tech *QuickStudy*™ License Guide has all the *exact* questions on the exam and *only the correct* answer for each question.

When you take the exam, *the correct answer jumps out at you* -- there's no confusion, nothing to clutter your mind. Plus, you have a lot less material to study so you're ready for the exam faster.

Code Practice Oscillator

MFJ-557 $24⁹⁵

Use this MFJ-557 Deluxe Code Practice Oscillator to practice sending Morse code.

Features Morse code key mounted on a heavy steel base, built-in speaker, tone, volume controls. Uses 9V battery, 12 VDC or 110 VAC with MFJ-1305B, $12.95.

Call or write for FREE catalog
Nearest Dealer/Orders: 800-647-1800
Technical Help: 800-647-TECH (8324)
• 1 year *unconditional* guarantee • 30 day money back guarantee (less s/h) on orders from MFJ • Free catalog

MFJ ENTERPRISES, INC.
Box 494, Miss. State, MS 39762
(601) 323-5869; FAX: (601) 323-6551
Add $6 s/h. © 1993 MFJ Enterprises, Inc.
8:00 - 4:30 CST, Mon.-Fri.

MFJ ... making quality affordable

Prices and Specifications subject to change without notice.

HCJB's *Música del Ecuador* brings delightful sounds to the living rooms of the world.

regardless of where they occur. Kashmir gets the same coverage as Northern Ireland, if the situation warrants it.

Producing and presenting a program of this nature is akin to walking through a minefield with horseshoes on, but "Focus on Faith" gets away with it. Beyond the serious stuff, the program also has lighter moments. Do you know what the best-dressed clergyman will be wearing in the mid-nineties? You don't? Well, you would if you were a regular listener to the program.

In *Europe,* tune in at 1830 Thursday on 6180, 6195, 9410, 12095 or 15070 kHz; and at 1001 Friday on 9750, 9760, 12095 or 15070 kHz. The program is available to the *Middle East* at 1830 Friday on 9410, 9740, 12095 and 15070 kHz; 0330 Friday on 9410, 11760 and 11955 kHz; and 1001 Friday on 11760, 15575, 17640 and 21470 kHz.

East Asia gets two Friday slots. The first is at 0330 on 15280 and 21715 kHz, with the other at 1001 on 17830 and 21715 kHz. For *Australasia* there is 1830 Thursday on 11955 kHz, repeated 1001 Friday on 11955 and 17830 kHz.

In *North America,* there's just one opportunity: 0330 Friday (Thursday evening local date), winters on 5975, 7325 and 9915 kHz; and summers on 5975 and 12095 kHz.

"Música del Ecuador" HCJB—Voice of the Andes

There are lots of good shows, but how many would you call "nice"? Not nice as in simple-minded, but old-fashioned, neighborly niceness. Agreeable music, friendly presentation, with no gimmicks, jingles, PSAs, Preparation H ads or other annoyances. It's the way broadcasting—and people—used to be.

If this sounds tempting, listen to the friendly voice of Jorge Zambrano and his "Música del Ecuador." It comes from the granddaddy of South American world band broadcasters, religious station HCJB, "The Voice of the Andes," in Quito, Ecuador.

Yes, Ecuador. The Andes is home to some of the most enjoyable music on earth. There are sounds of the *roncador* ("snorer") and other folk instruments, along with lively Andean rhythms and plaintive Ecuadorian songs. Each has its own particular *encanto,* charm. Titles are given in both Spanish and English—Zambrano is thoroughly bilingual—along with other snippets of helpful information.

> ## It's the way broadcasting—and people—used to be.

Surprisingly, this would seem to be the only regularly scheduled program of South American music which can be heard worldwide. Stations like Radio Habana Cuba and Radio Nacional do Brasil carry fair amounts of local music in their broadcasts. Yet, such offerings are used more as a filler than as a fixed part of the programming, and the range of their signals is limited.

The first edition of the show goes out at 0800 Friday, to *Europe* on 6205 (or 9600) and 11835 kHz, and to *Australasia* on 9745 and 11955 kHz. *Europeans* have a second chance later in the day, at 1930, on 15270 (or 21480) and 17790 kHz. There are three opportunities for *North America*: 0100 and 0330 Saturday (Friday night local date) on 9745 and 15155 kHz, and again at 0530 on 11925 kHz. *Outside these areas,* there is also 17490 and 21455 kHz in the upper-sideband mode, assuming your radio is equipped to receive such signals, as many better world band radios are.

"Music at Your Request" Radio Moscow International

Imagine yourself in a concert hall somewhat past its prime, decor faded, and acoustics which never were great. In these uninspiring surroundings you have come to listen to

Tune into Com-West

A t Com-West Radio Systems Ltd. our only business is radio. We eat, sleep, and breathe radio so we are always up to date on the latest models, techniques and breakthroughs.

Our knowledgable staff can help you with that critical receiver purchase to ensure you get the maximum effectiveness for your dollar. Or if you are having trouble with your antenna or radio operation, we are ready to help. We want you to get the most out of your radio.

Naturally, we stock many brands of radio equipment, accessories, antenna systems, and publications. And if we don't have it in stock, we'll get it for you, pronto, and ship it anywhere in the world to you.

Just remember us as the one-stop source for all of your radio needs, whether Short Wave, Ham, Commercial, or Marine.

Call or write us today for our new catalog for '92.

AEA AOR ALINCO ASTRON BEARCAT BUTTERNUT B&W CONNECTSYSTEMS CUSHCRAFT DAIWA DELHI DIAMOND DIGIMAX GRUNDIG HEIL HUSTLER ICOM JRC KANTRONICS KENWOOD LARSEN MFJ MOTOROLA NYEVIKING PALOMAR RFCONCEPTS SANGEAN SONY TELEXHYGAIN UNADILLA VANGORDEN VIBROPLEX WINTENNA YAESU

C W Com-West Radio Systems Ltd.

8179 Main Street
Vancouver, B.C.   CANADA V5X 3L2
(604) 321-1833   Fax (604) 321-6560

Canada's Specialty Radio Store

Luciano Pavarotti accompanied by the Vienna Philharmonic. The orchestra strikes up, Pavarotti's voice and presence fill the hall, and all of a sudden the faded curtains and so-so acoustics don't seem to matter any more.

So it is with "Music at Your Request," Radio Moscow International's showplace of Russian songs and classical music. As any seasoned world band listener will tell you, RMI's audio quality never has been any prize. But when your radio pours forth the sounds of a great Russian pianist playing Rachmaninoff, or the voice of the great Feodor Chaliapin, inferior audio hardly counts.

This is not a request show in the traditional sense. It is more a case of listeners writing in to let the program's producers know which artists, composers or styles of music they would like to hear. As a result, we are spared the embarrassment of having

to listen to little Johnny Windgassen being wished a happy birthday in the interval between two songs from *Boris Godunov*.

"Music at Your Request" is broadcast at the same times as "Folk Box," cited earlier in this article, but on different days of the week. Look at that writeup for details of frequencies beamed to where you live. The first slot of the week is at 1230 Monday, followed by 0930 Tuesday, 0530 and 2130 Wednesday, 0030 and 1830 Thursday, 0230 and 1530 Friday, and 1230 Saturday. All times move back one hour in summer, with the exception of 0530 and 2130 Wednesday, both of which move back two hours to 0330 and 1930, respectively.

_____

Prepared by the staff of Passport to World Band Radio.

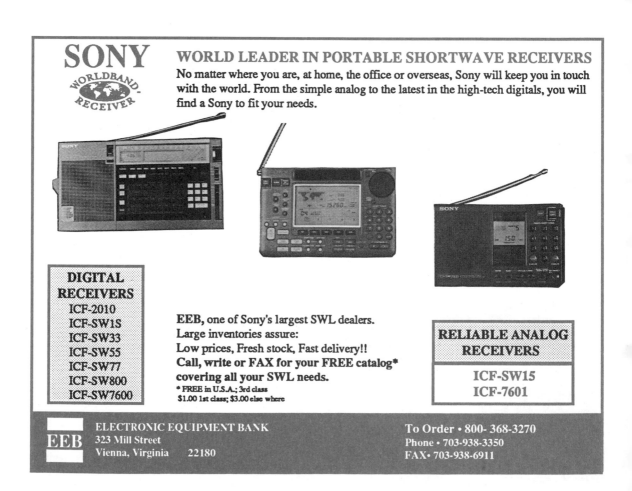

GRUNDIG
Satellit® 700
The Ultimate in Digital Technology

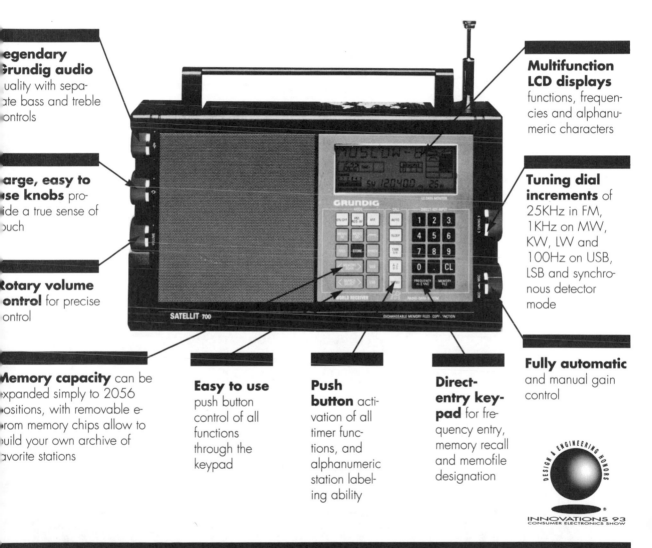

Legendary Grundig audio quality with separate bass and treble controls

Large, easy to use knobs provide a true sense of touch

Rotary volume control for precise control

Memory capacity can be expanded simply to 2056 positions, with removable e-rom memory chips allow to build your own archive of favorite stations

Easy to use push button control of all functions through the keypad

Push button activation of all timer functions, and alphanumeric station labeling ability

Direct-entry keypad for frequency entry, memory recall and memofile designation

Multifunction LCD displays functions, frequencies and alphanumeric characters

Tuning dial increments of 25KHz in FM, 1KHz on MW, KW, LW and 100Hz on USB, LSB and synchronous detector mode

Fully automatic and manual gain control

DESIGN & ENGINEERING HONORS

INNOVATIONS 93
CONSUMER ELECTRONICS SHOW

Universal Radio, Inc.

6830 Americana Pkwy.
Reynoldsburg, Ohio
43068 U.S.A.

800 431-3939 Orders
614 866-4267 Info.
614 866-2339 Fax

universal radio inc.

Canada's Best Stocked S.W.L. Store

ALLOWS YOU TO EXPERIENCE 49 YEARS OF LEGENDARY GERMAN ENGINEERING !

GRUNDIG Yacht Boy 400 *New!*

Now available from Grundig, a small Digital Shortwave Radio with all the latest high quality features. The YB-400 is a compact general converage shortwave receiver measuring 7 3/4 x 4 5/8 x 1 1/4". Coverage includes 1.6 to 30 MHz AM and Single Side Band (SSB), FM Broadcast band in stereo, the AM broadcast band (MW), and Long Wave (LW). 31 randomly programmable memory positions allow for quick access to favourite stations. The memory "FREE" feature automatically shows which memories are unoccupied and ready to program.

The multi-function LCD readout simultaneosly shows time, frequency, band, automatic turn-on and a sleep timer. An external antenna can be connected via the built-in receptacle to boost reception. The YB-400 comes with an owner's manual, warranty card, operating instructions, carrying case and shortwave guide. 6 "AA batteries are required.

GRUNDIG Satellit 700

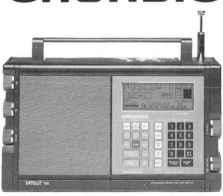

Atlantic Ham Radio improves on the Grundig version. We give you an extra memory chip which increases your memories from 512 to 1024 and more importantly we fill over 300 of them with frequencies from countries all around the world. These frequencies are good in Eastern North America, unlike the preprogrammed ones which are mainly European. No other dealer can match our shortwave expertise. 1993 Passport to World Band Radio says *"The best new portable introduced this year"*. Grundig shortwave radios give you excellent audio fidelity, as well as stereo FM through headphones or external speakers.

We ship this extra value Satellit 700 anywhere in Canada or the U.S.A.

ATLANTIC HAM RADIO LTD

Monday - Friday 10 am - 6 pm	**368 Wilson Ave**
Saturdays 10 am - 2 pm	**Downsview, Ontario**
after 7 pm call (416) 222-2506	**Canada M3H 1S9**
to place an order . . . **(24 Hour Fax 416-631-0747)**	**(416) 636-3636**

First Tries: 10 Easy Catches, Continued

Europe: 1130-1325 on 5955 and 9650 (or 9855/9860) kHz.

Middle East and South Asia: 1330-1625 on 9890, 13700, 15150 and 17610 kHz. To South Asia, but widely heard elsewhere, is 0030-0325 on 9860, 11655 and 13700 kHz.

East Asia: 0930-1125 on 12065 and 15470 kHz.

Australia and the Pacific: 0730-0825 on 9630 kHz, 0730-1025 on 11895 kHz and 0930-1025 on 9720 kHz.

Russia

Radio Moscow International's 24-hour World Service is a major feature of the world band spectrum. Precariously funded and with a high staff turnover, it produces several outstanding programs, veritable gems by any standard. It also provides a valuable insight into the volatile world of domestic Russian politics. RMI's frequency usage changes often and is virtually impossible to predict. Yet, historically we know they are likely to broadcast within certain spectrum segments at given times.

Eastern North America: Reception quality varies, but best is late afternoon and evening. Winter, try 7100-7180 and 9680-9890 kHz, with 11 and 15 MHz channels a better bet in summer.

Western North America: Better service, with 12050, 15425 and 17690 kHz being reasonable bets. If there's nothing on these frequencies, try other nearby channels, since Moscow often makes adjustments to its schedule.

Europe: Winter, 0400-2300. Early morning and late afternoon/evening, dial around the 6, 7 and 9 MHz segments; daylight, 13 and 15 MHz, plus 11980-12070 kHz 0800-1400 (try 11980, 12010, 12020, 12070, 13650 and 13705 kHz). Summer, 0300-2200, is usually good daytime within the 11, 13 and 15 MHz segments, but go for the 9 and 11 MHz channels evenings.

Middle East: 0100-1700, heard within virtually all world band segments, from 4940 kHz at the low end to 21845 kHz at the top end. Just dial around—there are plenty of channels from which to choose.

East Asia: 24-hour coverage! 2000 onwards, best winter bets are within the 7 and 9 MHz segments; summer, try 11 and 15 MHz channels. During daylight hours, dial around the 15, 17 and 21 MHz segments for best results. For evening and nighttime winter listening, frequencies in the 7 and 9 MHz segments will probably give best results; summer, look for channels in the 11 and 15 MHz segments.

Southeast Asia and Australasia: Best channels are in the 15, 17 and 21 MHz segments, with several being year-round frequencies.

Switzerland

More news-oriented than most world band stations, **Swiss Radio International** is in an excellent position to report and analyze events in war-torn countries, thanks to a program cooperation agreement with the International Committee of the Red Cross and its close proximity to the numerous United Nations agencies located in Geneva. Broadcasts are 30 minutes for all areas except Europe, where duration varies according to when it is broadcast.

First Tries: 10 Easy Catches, Continued

There are plans afoot to increase the proportion of cultural content in SRI's programs, but it remains to be seen how much of this will actually come about.

North America: 0000 on 6135, 9650, 9885, 12035 and 17730 kHz; 0200 on 6135, 9650, 9885 and 12035 kHz; and again at 0400 on 6135, 9860, 9885 and 12035 kHz.

Europe: (everything one hour earlier summer) 0500-0530 and 0600-0615 weekdays, plus 0700-0715 daily, on 3985, 6165 and 9535 kHz. 1100-1145 on 6165 and 9535 kHz.

Asia and Australasia: 0900 on 9885, 13685, 17670 and 21820 kHz; plus 1100 and 1300 on 13635, 15505, 17670 and 21820 kHz (1300 also via China on 7480 and 11690 kHz). A further broadcast, also for the Middle East, is at 1500 on 13635, 15505, 17670 and 21820 kHz; with a repeat at 1700 on 9985, 13635, 15430 and 17635 kHz.

Middle East and Africa: 2000 on 9885, 12035, 13635 and 15505 kHz.

United Kingdom

Supposedly, it's impossible to be all things to all people, but the **BBC World Service** comes close. The most popular station on the international airwaves, "the Beeb" is synonymous with much of what is best about world band radio. You'll hear all kinds of shows, from news to comedy to music and sports—all prepared to a fare-thee-well.

North America: Mornings to eastern North America at 1100-1400 on 5965 (winters), 9515 and 15220 kHz; at 1400-1615 on 9515 and 17840 kHz; and at 1615-1745 on 9515 kHz. In western North America, try 1100-1400 on 15220 kHz, 1200-1400 and 1500-1515 (1200-1515 Saturday and Sunday) on 9740 kHz, and 1400-1745 on 15260 kHz. Listeners in or near the Caribbean can tune in at 1100-1400 on 15220 kHz, 1100-1430 on 6195 kHz, and 1400-1615 on 17840 kHz.

Early evenings in eastern North America, 2000-2200 is heard on a wealth of frequencies, including 5975 or 15260 kHz. An additional plum is "Caribbean Report," aired at 2115-2130 (Monday through Friday only) on 6110, 15390 and 17715 kHz, and repeated three and a half hours later on 9590 kHz—one of the few ways you can get regular news about that part of the Western Hemisphere.

Throughout the evening, North Americans can listen in at 2200-0730 on a number of frequencies. Best bets are 5975 kHz (to 0730), 6175 kHz (to 0330 or 0430), 7325 and 9915 kHz (0000-0330, summers; 2200-0430, winters) and 9640 kHz (0500-0730).

Europe: A powerhouse 0300-2315 on 3955, 7325, 9410, 12095 and 15070 kHz; also, 6195, 9570 and 9760 kHz (times vary on each channel).

Middle East: 0200-0330 on 6195 and 7135 kHz; 0230-0430 on 11955 kHz; 0300-0530 on 9410 (or 12095) kHz; 0300-0815 and 0900-1400 on 11760 kHz; 0400-0730 and 0900-1500 (0400-1500, weekends) on 15575 kHz; 0800-1515 on 17640 kHz; 0430-0730 and 0900-1615 (0430-1615, weekends) on 21470 kHz; and on 7160, 9410, 9740, 12095 or 15070 kHz thereafter (until 2030).

East Asia: 0100-0330 on 17790 kHz; 0330-0915 (also 0100-0300, weekends) on 15280 and 21715 kHz; 0500-0915 on 15360 and 17830 kHz; and 0915-1030 on 17830 and 21715 kHz; 1000-1400 on 9740 kHz; 1300-1400 on 7180 and 11820 kHz; 1500-1600 on 7180 and 9740 kHz; 2100-2200 on 7180 and 11955 kHz; 2200-2300 on 9570 and 11955 kHz; and 2300-0030 on 11945, 11955 and 15370 kHz.

Australia and New Zealand: 0600-0815 on 7150, 9640, 11955 and 17830 kHz; 0815-0915 on 11955 and 17830 kHz; 0915-1030 on 11750 and 17830 kHz; 1030-

SANGEAN
A WORLD OF LISTENING

THE WORLD'S MOST POPULAR SHORTWAVE RECEIVERS

MS-101
One of Sangean's ultra-compact shortwave receivers

ATS-818CS

WORLD'S ONLY PORTABLE SHORTWAVE RECEIVER WITH BUILT-IN PROGRAMMABLE CASSETTE RECORDER

- PLL Synthesized Receiver
- All SW Bands from 120m to 11m
- Radio/Buzzer Clock Alarm
- BFO for Single Side Band & CW
- Continuous AM Coverage from 150-29999kHz plus FM

- 45 Memory Presets
- Dual Conversion Receiver
- AM Wide/Narrow Filter
- Dual Time Display
- Adjustable Sleep Timer
- Five Tuning Methods
- RF Gain Control

TOTALLY DIGITAL, ULTRA-COMPACT WORLD BAND RECEIVER WITH PRESET AUTO-TUNE SYSTEM

- Auto-Tune (ATS) scans and automatically presets all memory by signal strength
- All SW Bands from 120m to 11m
- Dual Time Display
- Dual Alarm for Radio/Buzzer
- 5 Tuning Methods

- Continuous AM coverage from 150-29999kHz plus FM
- 45 Memory Presets
- DX/Local Switch
- Count Down Timer
- Sleep Timer

ATS-606
ATS-606P: Attractively boxed ATS-606 Shortwave Receiver with ANT-60 Portable Shortwave Antenna and Multi-Voltage Power Adapter

ATS-800

ATS-803A

ATS-808

WE CARRY A COMPLETE STOCK OF ALL SANGEAN DIGITAL & ANALOG WORLD BAND RECEIVERS

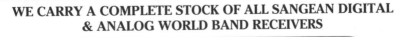

C. CRANE COMPANY

558 Tenth Street • Fortuna, California 95540
(707) 725-9000 FAX (707) 725-9060 (800) 522-8863

1400 and 1500-1615 (1030-1615, weekends) on 9740 kHz; 1800-2000 on 11955 kHz; and 2000-2300/2315 on 11955 and 15340 kHz.

ASIA
Japan

For those who wish to keep up with what's happening in the Far East, **Radio Japan** is a good place to start. The news bulletins are updated regularly, and coverage of regional events is more than adequate. Each broadcast normally lasts an hour, but this can vary.

Eastern North America: The General Service is at 1100 on 6120 kHz, and again at 0300 (0100 summers) on 5960 kHz.

Western North America: Via Radio Canada International's Sackville site at 0500 on 9725 kHz and 1400 on 11735 kHz; and direct from Tokyo at 0300 on 15230 kHz; 0500 on 11725 and 15230 kHz; and 1400, 1700 and 1900 on 9535 or 11865 kHz. There is a separate broadcast to the Americas at 0300 on 11725, 15325 and 21610 kHz.

Europe: 0500 on 6085 and 7230 kHz; 0700 on 5970 (or 7230), 6025 (or 6050) and 21575 kHz; 2100 on 11925 kHz; and 2300 on 6050 (or 6060) and 6125 kHz.

Middle East: 0700 on 21575 kHz, and 1700 on 15210 (or 17775) kHz.

Asia: Transmissions to Asia are also often heard elsewhere. 0100 on 11815 (or 17810), 11840, 11860, 15195, 17775 and 17845 kHz. 0300 on 11815 (or 17810) and 15210 kHz. 0500 on 11740, 15410 and 17810 kHz. 0600 on 11860 and 21610 kHz. 0700 on 11740, 15410, 17810 and 21610 kHz. 0900 on 9750, 11740, 11815, 11890 (or 11915) and 15190 kHz. 1100 on 11915 and 15240 kHz. 1400 on 9535, 9750 and 11815 kHz. 1500 on 9750 and 11815 kHz. 1700 and 1900 on 9750 (or 7140) and 11815 kHz. 2100 on 6035, 7140 (and/or 9750), 11815 and 15430 kHz. Finally, 2300 on 7140, 11815 (or 17810) and 15430 kHz.

Australasia: 0700 on 17860 kHz, 0900 on 15270 and/or 17860 kHz, 1900 on 9640 and/or 11875 kHz, and 2100 on 9640 or 15280/17890 kHz.

NORTH AMERICA
Canada

Radio Canada International still has some way to go to return to its pre-1991 level, before it was reduced to relaying programs from the domestic Canadian Broadcasting Corporation (CBC). Yet, even with additional belt-tightening, things are moving in the right direction.

More shows now originate at RCI. These appeal to the general listener, rather than just to Canadians resident abroad. However, listeners to RCI would be foolish to restrict their listening just to RCI programs; the best of news and current affairs output is still produced in the CBC studios. News programs like "The World at Six" and "As It Happens" are class acts by any standard.

North America: Reception is much better in eastern North America than farther west, but the station can still be heard in most of the United States. Try Monday through Friday at 1300-1400 on 11855 and 17820 kHz; 1400-1700 Sunday on 11955 and 17820 kHz; and 2300-0100 daily on 5960 and 9755 kHz (all one hour earlier in summer). There is a year-round broadcast at 0200-0300, plus an additional transmission at 0100-0200, summers only, on 6120 and 9755 kHz. Finally, at 0300-0400 winters, tune to 6010, 9725 and 9755 kHz.

THE GRUNDIG DIFFERENCE

Tuning In to the World, via Shortwave

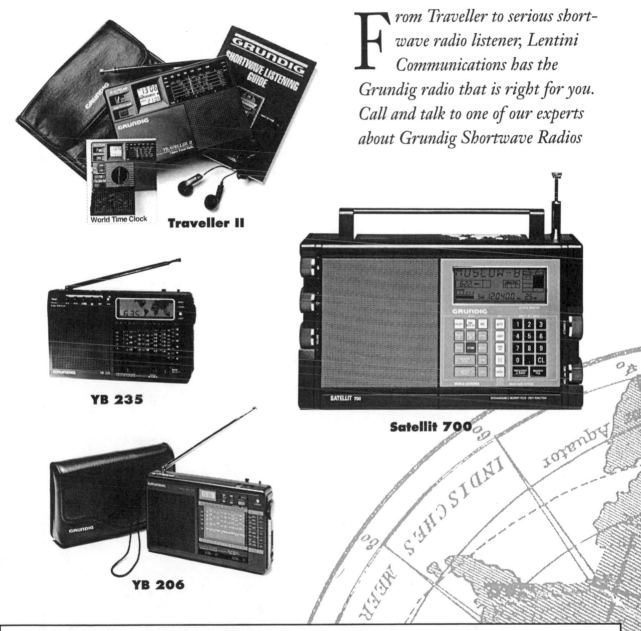

From Traveller to serious short-wave radio listener, Lentini Communications has the Grundig radio that is right for you. Call and talk to one of our experts about Grundig Shortwave Radios

World Time Clock

Traveller II

YB 235

Satellit 700

YB 206

First Tries: 10 Easy Catches, Continued

The afternoon transmission to Africa, heard fairly well in parts of North America, can be heard at 2130-2230 (one hour earlier in summer) on 13670, 15140 (or 17850) and 17820 kHz.

Europe: 1430-1500 on 9555 and 11915 (replaced by 21455 and 21710 in summer), 11935, 15315, 15325 and 17820 kHz; 2130-2230 on 5995, 7260 (or 7235), 11945 (or 17875), 13650 and 15325 kHz; and 2300-0100 on 5995 and 7250 (or 7195) kHz. All broadcasts are one hour earlier in summer.

Europe, Middle East and Africa: There is a special program for Canadian peace-keeping forces which is broadcast winter weekdays at 0600-0630 on 6050, 6150, 7155, 9740, 9760 and 11905 kHz. Summers, it goes out one hour earlier on 6050, 6150, 7295, 15430 and 17840 kHz.

Middle East: 0400-0430 (year-round), winters on 6150, 9505 and 9670 kHz, and summers on 9650, 11905, 11925 and 15275 kHz.

Asia: To East Asia 1230-1300 on 6150 and 11730 kHz (winters) or 9660 and 15195 kHz (summers), and 1330-1400 on 6150 (summers on 11795) and 9535 kHz. To Southeast Asia at 2200-2230 on 11705 kHz.

United States

When Congress set up the **Voice of America** in the emerging Cold War days before C-Span, it mandated that the VOA could not broadcast to Americans. This was to prevent American innocents from being reduced to Orwellian bloboids by government-prepared propaganda. To elevate this reasoning to outright idiocy, the Federal Communications Commission followed up by decreeing that if the VOA couldn't broadcast to Americans, then neither could any other American world band stations— *even though they weren't government owned or operated!*

"The Voice," with its long record of accomplishment, deserves better than to be classified by its own government as Unsuitable for Listening. So, too, do many of the private American world band stations.

But there's good news: Americans can and do tune into these "forbidden" U.S. world band broadcasters, anyway—no matter how much the stations are forced to aim their transmissions in other directions. Nature has seen to that by scattering world band signals hither and yon, regardless of the dictates of Man or Govern-Man. (And, no, it's not against the law to listen.)

The Voice of America is one of the oldest and best-known of all international broadcasters, with much to offer. Particularly noteworthy are the regional variations of mainstream programming, especially the African and Pacific services.

North America: The two best times to sneak in a listen are at 0000-0200 (to 0230, Tuesday through Saturday) on 5995, 6130, 7405, 9455, 9775, 11580, 15120 and 15205 kHz; and 1000-1200 on 9590, 11915 and 15120 kHz. This is when the VOA broadcasts to South America and the Caribbean. The African Service is also audible in North America—try 0300-0700 on 6035, 7405 and 9575 kHz; at 1600-1800 on 13710, 15445 and 17895 kHz; and 1800-2200 on 13710, 15410, 15495, 15580, 17800 and 21485 kHz.

Europe: 0400-0700 on 5995, 6040, 6140, 7170 and 11965 kHz; 0400-0600 on 7200 and 15205 kHz; 1500-1800 on 15255 kHz; and 1700-2200 on 6040, 9760 and 15205 kHz.

Middle East: 0800-1000 on 11740, 15160, 15195, 21455 and 21570 kHz; 1500-1700 on 9700 and 15205 kHz; and 1700-2200 on 9700 kHz.

COMMUNICATIONS ELECTRONICS™

SATELLIT 700
World's Most Advanced Shortwave Portable

German shortwave technology in its most advanced form. For serious listening to international broadcasts and long distance two-way communications. More flexibility than any other shortwave portable.

Digital/Alphanumeric display with PLL tuning, general coverage shortwave receiver, with SSB and advanced synchronous detector. Dual clocks and turn on/off timers. Sleep timer. Eight character memory page labeling. 512 memories standard; 2048 possible with optional memofiles. Multi-voltage adapter. Built-in Ni-cad charger.

Continuous shortwave tuning from 1.6 to 30 megahertz covers all shortwave bands, plus FM-stereo, AM and LW. Single sideband (SSB) circuitry allows for reception of two-way amateur, military and commercial communications, including maritime and aeronautical. 120 factory pre-programmed frequencies for world-wide reception. Dual conversion superheterodyne receiver design.

Memory presets: 512 user-programmable memory positions. Capable of 2048 memories with 3 user-programmable 512 memory EEPROMS (not supplied).

Multifunction liquid crystal display: The LCD shows time, frequency band, alphanumeric memory labels, automatic turn on/off, sleep timer, bandwidth select position, synchronous detector status and USB/LSB status.

Clock, alarm and timer: Dual, independently programmable quartz clocks, each with its own programmable turn on/off timer. Both timers programmable to access any memory. LCD shows time and clock /timer modes. Dual clocks show time in 24 hour format. Sleep timer programmable in 10 minute increments to 60 minutes.

Synchronous detector: Selectable sideband synchronous detector helps to eliminate interference from adjacent stations and annoying heterodyne tones.

Power: Four "D" batteries, not included. 110/220 volt, user-switchable AC adapter included. Built-in nickel cadmium battery charger.

Other important features: Selectable upper/lower sideband. User selectable wide/narrow bandwidth filter. Fully automatic preselector tuner, with manual override feature. Separate, fully adjustable bass and treble control. Automatic gain control, user switchable to full range manual control. WEIGHT: 4 lbs.; 12-1/4"L x 7-1/4"W x 3"H.

Shipped with owner's manual, Grundig Shortwave Listening Guide, warranty card, dual voltage AC adapter and antenna connector.

COMMUNICATIONS ELECTRONICS INC.

Emergency Operations Center
P.O. 1045 □ Ann Arbor, Michigan 48106-1045 U.S.A.
For orders call 313-996-8888 or FAX 313-663-8888

For credit card orders call
1-800-USA-SCAN

Powerhouse Radio France Internationale provides exceptional coverage of African news and culture.

First Tries: 10 Easy Catches, Continued

Australasia: 1000-1200 on 5985, 11720 and 15425 kHz; 1200-1330 on 11715 and 15425 kHz, 1330-1500 on 15425 kHz; 1900-2000 on 9525, 11870 and 15180 kHz; 2100-2200 on 11870, 15185 and 17735 kHz; and 2200-0100 on 15185 and 17735 kHz.

East Asia: 1100-1400 on 9760 and 15155 kHz; 1400-1500 on 9760 and 15160 kHz; 2200-2400 on 15290, 15305, 17735 and 17820 kHz; and 0000-0100 on 15290, 17735 and 17820 kHz.

The **World Service of the Christian Science Monitor** is arguably the only station to rival the BBC World Service's in-depth news coverage. A hundred minutes of each two-hour weekday broadcast are heavily slanted in favor of news-related fare, with the remainder being devoted to listener-response and religious features. On weekends the format is inverted, with most of the broadcast being given over to religious programming.

North America: In eastern North America, try tuning in at 0000 on 5850 kHz; 1000 and 1200 on 9495 kHz; 1800 on 15665 or 17510 kHz; 2000 on any two channels from 7510, 13770, 15665 and 17510 kHz; and 2200 on 9465 kHz. Farther west, you can listen at 0200, 0400 and 0600 on 5850 or 9455 kHz; and again at 1400 on 13760 kHz. Although beamed elsewhere, 13760 kHz also provides good reception within much of North America at 0000-0555. Note that Friday through Monday some of these channels carry a certain amount of Spanish programming.

Europe: 0600 on 5850, 9840 or 9870 kHz; 0800 on 9840 or 11705 kHz; 1400 on 15665 or 17510 kHz, 1800 on 15665 and 9355 or 17510 kHz; 2000 on any two channels from 7510, 13770, 15665 and 17510 kHz; and 2200 on 7510, 13770 or 15665 kHz.

Middle East: 1800 on 9355 or 15665 kHz; 2000 on 7510, 13770 or 15665 kHz; and summers at 0200 on 9350 kHz.

East Asia: Virtually sixteen hours a day! Choose from 0400 and 0600 on 17780 kHz; 0800 and 1000 on 17555 kHz, 1400 on 9530 kHz, 1600 on 11580 kHz, 2000 on 9455 kHz, and 2200 on 15405 kHz.

Australasia: 0800 on 13615 and 15665 kHz, 1000 on 13625 kHz; 1200 on 9425 or 15665 kHz, 1800 and 2000 on 9430, 13625 or 13840 kHz; and 2200 on 13625 kHz.

BCC

Small country, strong voice: The Voice of Free China's English Service comes to listeners not only direct from Taiwan, but also via the robust transmitters of Family Radio in Okeechobee, Florida.

WorldScan™

What's On Tonight?

Passport's Hour-by-Hour Guide to World Band Shows

World band provides unequalled news output, plus heaps of music and other juicy entertainment. Yet, there is so much on the air that it's nigh impossible to keep track of it all.

Passport is here to help. We keep track of thousands of shows all year long so you'll know precisely where and when to tune. Even then, that's a lot to wade through; so, to get straight to the good stuff, look for these symbols:

■ station with superior overall merit
● program of special merit
▲ program with curiosity value, although not necessarily of high quality

Times are given in World Time, days as World Day, both explained in the Glossary and "Compleat Idiot's Guide to Getting Started." Tip: Many stations announce World Time at the beginning of each broadcast or on the hour.

Schedules include not only observed activity, but also that which we have creatively opined will take place throughout 1994. This latter information is original from Passport, and since world band radio is a dynamic medium, this material will not be so exact as real-time factual information. Key frequencies are given for North America, Western Europe, East Asia and Australasia, plus general coverage of the Mideast. Information on secondary and seasonal channels, as well as channels for other parts of the world, are in "Worldwide Broadcasts in English" and the Blue Pages.

"Summer" and "winter"? These refer to seasons in the Northern Hemisphere. Exceptions to this, such as shows from Argentina, are stated clearly for your convenience.

Many stations supplement their programs with newsletters, tourist brochures, magazines, books and other goodies—often free. See the "Addresses PLUS" section for full details

High technical standards are but one of the reasons Swiss Radio International is a big hit among world band listeners.

00:00

■ **BBC World Service.** The best. There's nothing else like it on world band, or anywhere else for that matter. At this hour there's the 30-minute ●*Newsdesk*, which includes both international and British news. This is followed by any one of a wide variety of programs, including *The Ken Bruce Show* (Sunday), *From the Weeklies* and *Recording of the Week* (Saturday) and ● *Omnibus* (Wednesday). On other days you can hear such offerings as *In Praise of God* (Monday) or music programs (Tuesday and Friday). Continuous to North America on 5975, 6175, 7325, 9590 and 9915 kHz (12095 kHz is also available during summer); to East Asia until 0030 on 11945, 11955, 15280, and 15370 kHz; and to Australasia (winters only) until 0030 on 11955 kHz.

World Service of the Christian Science Monitor, USA. North America's number one station for news and in-depth analysis. *News,* then ● *Monitor Radio*—news analysis and news-related features with emphasis on international developments. The first part of a two-hour cyclical broadcast repeated throughout the day to different parts of the globe. To eastern North America and the Caribbean Tuesday through Saturday (Monday through Friday, local American day) on 5850 kHz, and heard throughout much of North America on 13760 kHz although targeted elsewhere. Also to Southeast Asia Monday through Friday on 17555 kHz. On other days, the broadcasts feature Herald of Christian Science and Christian Science Sentinel religious programming (all of it not necessarily in English) or transmissions of the Sunday Service from the Mother Church in Boston.

Radio Bulgaria. Winters only, the final quarter-hour of a 90-minute broadcast (see 2245). To North America on 7225, 9700 and 11720 kHz. For a separate summer service, see the next item.

Radio Bulgaria. Summers only, a 60-minute potpourri of news, commentary, interviews and features, liberally sprinkled with lively Bulgarian rhythms. One of the few stations from Eastern Europe which still has reasonable amounts of ethnic music. To North America on 11720 and 15330 kHz. One hour later during winter.

Spanish Foreign Radio. *News,* followed most days by *Panorama,* which features commentary, a review of the Spanish press, weather and foreign press comment on matters affecting Spain. The remainder of the program is a mixture of literature, science, music and general programming. Each day's programming has a special emphasis; for instance, the arts on Friday. On weekends the format is varied somewhat, including *Who's Visiting Spain?* and *Radio Club.* Sixty minutes to eastern North America on 9530 kHz.

Radio Norway International. Monday only. *Norway Now.* Repeat of the 2300 transmission. Thirty minutes of friendly programming to North and Central America, year-round on 9675 kHz, plus summers on 15165 kHz.

Radio Prague, Czech Republic. *News,* then features, including *Sports Roundup* (Tuesday), *Mailbag* (Thursday), *Ecology* (Friday) and *Tip for a Trip* (Saturday). Monday (Sunday evening local American day) features the popular *Scrapbook.* Thirty minutes to North America on 7345, 9485 and 11990 kHz.

Radio Canada International. Winters only at this time. On weekdays, relays the final hour of the CBC domestic service *news* program ● *As It Happens,* which features international stories, Canadian news and general human interest features. Weekends, it's *The Inside Track* (sports) and the cultural *Open House,* both from the CBC's domestic output. To North America on 5960 and 9755 kHz, and to Europe on 5995 kHz. One hour earlier in winter.

Radio Sweden. Thirty minutes of *news* and features, concentrating heavily on Scandinavian topics. To South America, also audible in eastern North America, on 9695 kHz.

Radio Moscow World Service. Beamed to various parts of the world at this hour. Winter programming is aimed at a general audience, with *news* and comment taking up the first 30 minutes, and some excellent musical fare during the second half hour. Monday and Saturday (Sunday and Friday evenings local American days), there's the incomparable ● *Folk Box;* Thursday brings ● *Music at your Request;* and Wednesday and Friday feature jazz. Summers, it's *News,* followed Tuesday through Saturday by *Focus on Asia and the Pacific,* a summary of developments in the CIS, and a music program. On the remaining days there's a listener-response program and ● *Audio Book Club* (Sunday) or *Russian by Radio* (Monday). Available on more than 20 channels, so tune around. Listeners in North America are best served winters by such frequencies as 6045, 7105, 9750, 9870, 12050, 15425 and 21480 kHz. In summer, Easterners can try the segments between 9750 and 9890, and 11750 and 11850 kHz. Farther west, 12050,

15410 and 15425 kHz should be best. Listeners in East Asia should look to outlets in the 7 and 9 MHz segments in winter, and 11 and 15 MHz in summer (though 9480 kHz should be a good all-year channel). For Southeast Asia and Australasia, try year-round frequencies in the 17 and 21 MHz segments; frequencies such as 21690 and 21790 kHz are established favorites. If you cannot hear the station on any of these, tune around nearby—Moscow is not renowned for sticking to its frequencies.

Radio Prague, Czech Republic. *News,* followed by a lively magazine-style program covering a variety of topics. A half-hour to North America on 5930, 7345, 9485, 9810 and 11990 kHz.

Radio Vilnius, Lithuania. Winters only at this time. *News* about events in Lithuania, plus short features about the country's history and culture. Thirty minutes to eastern North America on 7150 kHz. One hour earlier in summer. As we go to press, Radio Vilnius only broadcasts at this hour Tuesday through Saturday (local weekday evenings in North America), due to the country's unfavorable economic situation. Should conditions take an upturn, there is a possibility of resuming daily broadcasts.

Swiss Radio International. Tuesday through Saturday, it's ● *Dateline*, a thoroughly workmanlike compilation of news and background reports on world and Swiss events. On the remaining days there's less news and more general programming, with Sunday featuring *The Grapevine* and *Swiss Shortwave Merry-Go-Round*, which answers technical questions sent in by listeners. Monday's broadcast includes *Supplement*, *Roundabout Switzerland*, *Rhythmmakers* or *The Name Game*—features which alternate on a regular basis. A half-hour to North America on 6135, 9650, 9885, 12035 and 17730 kHz.

Croatian Radio. A special relay via religious station WHRI in Noblesville, Indiana. Mostly in Croatian, but with five or more minutes of English *news* and (sometimes) commentary, usually during the first quarter-hour of the broadcast. To North America on 7315 kHz.

Radio Pyongyang, North Korea. See 1100 for program details. Fifty minutes of old-fashioned communist propaganda to the Americas on 11335, 13760 and 15130 kHz.

Radio Ukraine International. Summers only at this time. An hour's ample coverage of just about everything Ukrainian, including news, sports, politics and culture. Not to be missed is the feast of Ukrainian music which fills most of the Monday (Sunday evening in the Americas) broadcast. Sixty minutes to Europe and North America on 6010, 6090, 7150, 7195, 7240, 9500, 9550, 9560, 9600, 9640, 9685, 9860, 11720,

15180, 15195 and 15580 kHz. 15180 and 15580 kHz are best for western North America. One hour later in winter.

Voice of America. First hour of the VOA's two-hour broadcasts to the Caribbean and Latin America. *News*, followed by split programming Tuesday through Saturday (Monday through Friday evenings in the Americas). Listeners in the Caribbean can tune in to ● *Report to the Caribbean*, followed by *Music USA*. For Latin America there is *Newsline* and Special English news and features. On Sunday this service carries ● *On the Line* and the Special English feature ● *American Stories*, while *Agriculture Today* and *Weekend Magazine* are targeted at the Caribbean. Monday's programming consists of *Newsline* (Caribbean) or ● *Encounter* (Latin America), with the second half-hour's ● *Spotlight* being common to both services. An excellent way to keep in touch with events in the Western Hemisphere. The service to the Caribbean is on 6130, 9455 and 11695 kHz; and the one to the Americas is on 5995, 7405, 9775, 11580, 15120 and 15205 kHz. The final hour of a separate service to East and Southeast Asia and Australasia (see 2200) can be heard on 9770, 11760, 15185, 15290, 17735 and 17820 kHz.

China Radio International. *News*, then *News About China* and *Current Affairs*. These are followed by various feature programs, such as *Culture in China* (Friday), *Listeners' Letterbox* (Monday and Wednesday), *Cooking Show*, *Travel Talk* and ● *Music from China* (Sunday). The interesting *Music Album* is aired Monday (local Saturday evening in the Americas). One hour to eastern North America on 9770 and 11715 kHz.

Radio Habana Cuba. The start of a two-hour cyclical broadcast to North America on 6010 kHz. *News*, followed by feature programs, such as *Newsbreak*, *Spotlight on Latin America*, *DXers Unlimited*, *Dateline Havana* and ● *The Jazz Place*, interspersed with some good Cuban music. With Cuba's future clouded in uncertainty, this station's programs are likely to produce some interesting listening in the time to come. Also available on 9815 kHz upper sideband, though not all radios, unfortunately, can process such signals.

Radio New Zealand International. Sunday through Friday only at this time. *News*, then features, music and—later in the broadcast—special programs for the South Sea Islands. Part of a much longer broadcast for the South Pacific, but also heard in parts of North America on 15120 kHz.

WJCR, Upton, Kentucky. Twenty-four hours of gospel music targeted at North America on 7490 and 13595 kHz. Also heard elsewhere, mainly during darkness hours. For more religious broadcasting at this hour, try **WYFR-Family Radio** (summers only) on 6085 kHz, **KTBN** on 7510 kHz, **WINB** on 15145 kHz, and **KVOH-**

Voice of Hope Tuesday through Saturday (Monday through Friday, local American day) on 17775 kHz. For something a little more controversial, tune to Dr. Gene Scott's University Network, via **WWCR** on 13845 kHz.

00:30

Radio Nederland. *News*, followed Tuesday through Sunday by *Newsline*, a current affairs program. Then there's a different feature each day, including the well-produced ● *Research File* (science, Tuesday); *Mirror Images* (arts in Holland, Wednesday); *Towards 2000* (social affairs, Saturday); the communications program *Media Network* (Friday); and a feature documentary (Thursday). Monday (Sunday evening local time in North America) is devoted to *The Happy Station*, a program of chat, music and greetings now only a shadow of the uniquely successful show it used to be. Fifty-five minutes to North America on 6020, 6165 and 11835 kHz, and a full hour to South Asia (also widely heard in other parts of the continent, as well as Australasia) on 7305 (9825 in summer), 9860, 11655 and (summers) 13700 kHz.

Radio Vlaanderen International, Belgium. Winters only at this time; see 1900 for program details, although they're one day later, World Day. Twenty-five minutes to eastern North America on 7370 kHz; also audible on 9930 kHz, though beamed elsewhere. One hour earlier in summer.

Radio Yugoslavia. Summers only at this time. *News*, followed by short features (see 0130). A reasoned and reasoning voice from a region where violence and destruction have almost become a way of life. Thirty minutes to eastern North America on 9580 kHz.

Voice of the Islamic Republic of Iran. One hour of *news*, commentary and features with a strong Islamic slant. Targeted at North America on 9022, 11790 and 15260 kHz. May be broadcast one hour earlier in summer.

HCJB—Voice of the Andes, Ecuador. *Studio 9*, featuring eight minutes of world and Latin American *news*, followed Tuesday through Saturday (Monday through Friday, local American day) by 20 minutes of in-depth reporting on Latin America. The final portion of *Studio 9* is given over to one of a variety of 30-minute features—including *Introspect* (Tuesday), *Happiness Is* (Wednesday), *Ham Radio Today* (Thursday), *What's Cooking in the Andes* (Friday), and the unique ● *Música del Ecuador* (Saturday). On Sunday (Saturday evening in the Americas), news is followed by *DX Partyline*, which in turn is replaced Monday by *Saludos Amigos*—HCJB's international friendship program. To North America on 9745 and 15155 kHz, also available to many parts of the world on 17490 and 21455 kHz, upper sideband.

■ **BBC World Service.** Tuesday through Saturday (weekday evenings in North America) it's *News*, followed by *Outlook*, a program of news and human-interest stories. This is succeeded by a variety of features, including ● *Health Matters* (Tuesday), *Waveguide*, *Book Choice* and *The Farming World* (Thursday), ● *Global Concerns* (Friday), and *Seeing Stars* and ● *Short Story* (Saturday). There are also 15-minute jazz, folk or country music programs on several of these days. On Sunday and Monday, weekends in North America, look for a summary of *news* and longer drama and classical music programs, including Sunday's not-to-be-missed ● *Play of the Week*. Continuous to North America on 5975, 6175, 9590 (except 0145-0200 local weekdays), 9915 and 7325 or 12095 kHz; and to East Asia on 17790 kHz, plus—weekends only—15280 and 21715 kHz.

World Service of the Christian Science Monitor, USA. The second half of the 0000 broadcast to eastern North America and the Caribbean. *News* and continuation of ● *Monitor Radio*. The final 15 minutes consist of a listener-response program and a religious article from the *Christian Science Monitor* newspaper. Tuesday through Saturday (Monday through Friday, local American day) on 5850 kHz, and heard throughout much of North America on 13760 kHz although targeted elsewhere. Also to Southeast Asia Monday through Friday on 17555 kHz. On other days, the broadcasts feature Herald of Christian Science and Christian Science Sentinel religious programming (all of it not necessarily in English) or transmissions of the Sunday Service from the Mother Church in Boston.

Radio Canada International. Summers only. *News*, followed weekdays (Tuesday through Saturday World Day) by *Spectrum*, which in turn is replaced Sunday by *Innovation Canada* (science) and *Earth Watch*. On Monday (Sunday evening in North America) there's *Arts in Canada* and a listener-response program. Sixty minutes to eastern North America on 9755 kHz, and to western parts on 6120 kHz. One hour later in winter.

Radio Slovakia International. One of the new kids on the block. A 30-minute window on life and events in Slovakia. To North America on 5930, 7310 and 9810 kHz.

Radio Australia. Part of a 24-hour service to Asia and the Pacific, but which can also be heard at this time throughout much of North America. Begins with world and regional *news*,

then music or features. Targeted at Southeast Asia and the Pacific on about ten channels, and heard in North America (best during summer) on 15240, 17795 and 21740 kHz.

Radio Norway International. Monday only. *Norway Now*. Repeat of the 2300 broadcast. Thirty minutes of *news* and chat from and about Norway. To North America on 9560 or 9565 kHz.

Radio Argentina al Exterior—R.A.E. Tuesday through Saturday only. Lots of minifeatures dealing with aspects of life in Argentina, interspersed with samples of the country's various musical styles, from tango to zamba. Fifty-five minutes to North America on 11710 kHz. Broadcast an hour later during winter in Argentina (summer in the Northern Hemisphere).

Radio Prague, Czech Republic. *News*, followed most days by a variety of short features. Thirty minutes of pleasant listening to North America on 7345, 9485 and 11990 kHz.

Radio Sweden. *News* and features of mainly Scandinavian content, sometimes touching on subjects considered unsavory or taboo in many other countries. Thirty minutes to Asia and Australasia on 9695 and 11820 kHz.

Radio Bulgaria. Winters only at this time; see 0000 for more specifics. Sixty minutes to North America on 7225, 9700 and 11720 kHz. One hour earlier in summer.

Radio Japan. One hour to eastern North America summers only on 5960 kHz via the powerful relay facilities of Radio Canada International in Sackville, New Brunswick. See 0300 for program details, except that all programs are one day later, and *Hello From Tokyo* replaces *Media Roundup* and the Japanese language lesson local Sunday evening in North America. As we go to press, Radio Japan is implementing a number of changes to both its program and transmission schedules, so be prepared for some adjustments.

Spanish Foreign Radio. Repeat of the 0000 transmission. To eastern North America on 9530 kHz.

Radio For Peace International, Costa Rica. One of the few remaining places where you can still find the peace and "peoplehood" ideals of the Sixties. This hour is the start of English programming—the initial hour being in Spanish. *FIRE* (Feminist International Radio Endeavor) is one of the better offerings from the mélange of programs that make up RFPI's eight-hour cyclical blocks of predominantly counterculture and New Wave programming. Sixty minutes audible, with strength varying from hopeless to fair and with telephone-like audio quality, in Europe and throughout the Americas on 7375, 7385, 13630 and 15030 kHz. Some transmissions are in the single-sideband mode, which can be processed properly only on certain radios.

Radio Korea, South Korea. See 0600 for specifics, although programs are a day later, World Day. Sixty minutes to eastern North America on 15575 kHz, and for European night owls on 7550 kHz.

Radio Moscow World Service. *News*, features and music on a multitude of frequencies. Tuesday through Saturday, winters, it's *Focus on Asia and the Pacific*, replaced summers by ● *Commonwealth Update* (Tuesday through Saturday only). The second half-hour contains mainly musical fare. In summer, look for ● *Folk Box* (Tuesday), ● *Music at your Request* (Friday), jazz (Thursday and Saturday), and ● *Music and Musicians* (from 0111, Sunday and Monday). Pick of the winter fare is Sunday's ● *Audio Book Club*. Where to tune? Best bet is to try the same channels as at 0000.

Radio Habana Cuba. See 0000 for program details. Continues to North America on 6010 kHz. Also available on 9815 kHz upper sideband.

Radio Roma, Italy. A strong candidate for the title of the most soporific broadcast on world band. Approximately fifteen minutes of *news* read by a sleep-inducing announcer, then five minutes of music. Well, actually, you're lucky if you get the full five minutes, since the soporific announcer sometimes has an almost instantaneous effect, with the person in the studio either forgetting or being unable to change the disc. Twenty minutes to North America on 9575 and 15245 kHz. Worth a try, if only to see whether you can last the course.

HCJB—Voice of the Andes, Ecuador. The second part of *Studio 9* (different programs at the weekend—see 0030), followed Tuesday through Saturday by *Focus on the Family* (replaced weekends by syndicated religious features). To North America on 9745 and 15155 kHz; also available to many parts of the world on 17490 and 21455 kHz upper sideband.

Voice of America. *News*, then *Report to the Americas*, a series of news features about the United States and other countries in the Americas. This is replaced Sunday by *Communications World* and ● *Press Conference U.S.A.*, and Monday by the science program ● *New Horizons* and ● *Issues in the News*. To the Americas on 5995, 6130, 7405, 9455, 9775, 11580, 15120 and 15205 kHz.

Radio Ukraine International. Winters only at this time; see 0000 for program details. Sixty minutes of informative programming targeted at North America and European night owls. Try 4825, 6020, 6070, 6080, 6145, 7180, 7195, 7240, 9710, 9750, 9860, 17605 and 17690 kHz. The last two frequencies are for western North America.

Radio Tashkent, Uzbekistan. *News* and features reflecting local and regional issues. Thirty minutes to South Asia, occasionally heard in North America; winters on 5930, 5955, 7190,

7265 and 9715 kHz; summers on 7190, 7250, 9715 and 9740 kHz.

■ **Deutsche Welle,** Germany. *News*, followed Tuesday through Saturday by the comprehensive ● *European Journal*, which includes commentary, interviews, background reports and analysis. The Saturday edition is followed by *Through German Eyes*, while Sunday (Saturday night in North America) is given over to *Commentary*, *Mailbag* (or *Nickelodeon*) and *German by Radio*. Monday brings *Living in Germany* and the popular ● *Larry's Random Selection*. Fifty minutes of very good reception in North America on 6040, 6085, 6145, 9565, 9700 and 11865 kHz; plus seasonal channels of 6120, 9515, 9610 and 9770 kHz (winter); and 9765, 11810, 13610, 13770 and 15105 kHz (summer).

"National Vanguard Radio," WRNO. This time summers only. Neo-Nazi skinhead program. Thirty minutes Sunday (Saturday local day) on 7355 kHz; try four hours later on 7395 kHz if preempted by live sports. Targeted at North America, but reaches beyond.

WJCR, Upton, Kentucky. Continues with gospel music to North America on 7490 and 13595 kHz. Also with religious programs to North America at this hour are **WYFR-Family Radio** on 6065, 9505 and 15440 kHz, **WWCR** on 13845 kHz, **KTBN** on 7510 kHz, **WINB** on 15145 kHz, and Tuesday through Saturday, **KVOH-Voice of Hope** on 17775 kHz.

01:30

Radio Austria International. ● *Report from Austria*, which includes a brief bulletin of *news*, followed by a series of current events and human interest stories. Ample coverage of national and regional issues, and an excellent source for news of Central and Eastern Europe. Thirty minutes to North America on 6015 and 9875 kHz; also audible on 9870 kHz, which is targeted farther south.

RDP International—Radio Portugal. Summers only at this time. *News*, which usually takes up at least half the broadcast, followed by features: *Notebook on Portugal* (Tuesday), *Musical Kaleidoscope* (Wednesday), *Challenge of the 90's* (Thursday), *Spotlight on Portugal* (Friday), and either *Mailbag* or *DX Program* and *Collector's Corner* (Saturday). For some mysterious reason, there are no broadcasts on Sunday or Monday (Saturday and Sunday evenings local North American days). Only fair reception in eastern North America—worse to the west—on 9570 and 9705 kHz. One hour later in winter.

Radio Tirana, Albania. Just about the only way to keep up with what is happening in Europe's most obscure backwater, with some pleasantly enjoyable music, to boot. Twenty-five minutes to North America on 9580 and 11840 kHz.

Radio Nederland. *News*, followed Tuesday through Saturday by *Newsline*, a current affairs

program. Then there's a different feature each day, including *No Boundaries* (Tuesday); ● *Encore* (Wednesday); *Media Network* (communications, Thursday); ● *Research File* (science, Friday) and a documentary (Saturday). Sunday's *The Happy Station* and Monday's offbeat *East of Edam* complete the week. One hour to South Asia (also widely heard in other parts of the continent, as well as Australasia) on 9860, 11655, 12025 and (summers) 13700 kHz.

Voice of Greece. Preceded and followed by lots of delightful Greek music, plus news and features in Greek. There's a ten-minute English bulletin of *news* more or less at 0130, heard daily except Sunday (Saturday evening local North American day). To eastern North America on 9380 (or 9395), 9420 kHz and 11645 (or 7450) kHz.

Radio Yugoslavia. *News*, reports and short features, dealing almost exclusively with local and regional topics. A half hour to North America on 9580 kHz.

01:45

■ **BBC World Service for the Caribbean.** *Caribbean Report*, although intended for listeners in the area, can also be clearly heard throughout much of North America. This brief, 15-minute program provides comprehensive coverage of Caribbean economic and political affairs, both within and outside the region. Tuesday through Saturday (local weekday evenings in the Americas) on 9590 kHz.

■ **BBC World Service for South Asia.** *South Asia Report*, 15 minutes of in-depth analysis of political and other developments in the region. Also audible in parts of North America and Australasia. Monday through Saturday only, on 9580 (or 15310) and 11955 kHz.

Radio Finland. Summers only at this time. Monday through Saturday it's *Compass North*, while Sunday (Saturday evening in North America) features *Focus* and *Nuntii Latini*, a bulletin of news in Latin. This curiosity of the airwaves has been sufficiently popular that it is now also available as a book. For those interested in learning yet another language, there is Saturday's *Starting Finnish*. Thirty minutes to North America on 11755 and 15185 kHz, and one hour later in winter.

02:00

■ **BBC World Service.** Thirty minutes of ● *Newsdesk*, followed on different days of the week by a variety of features, including a documentary (Sunday), *Composer of the Month* (Monday), ● *People and Politics* (Saturday), ● drama (Friday), a quiz (Tuesday) and *Sports International* (Thursday). Continuous to North America

on 5975, 6175, 9590 (to 0230), 9915, and 7325 or 12095 kHz; and to East and Southeast Asia on 17790 kHz. For East Asia there are two additional Sunday frequencies—15280 and 21715 kHz. Also available to the Mideast on 6195 and 7135 kHz.

World Service of the Christian Science Monitor, USA. See 0000 for program details. To the Mideast Monday through Friday on 9350 kHz, and to western North America Tuesday through Friday (Monday through Thursday, local American days) on 5850 or 9455 kHz. Also audible throughout much of North America on 13760 kHz, although not beamed there. Programming on the remaining days relates to the teachings and experiences of the Christian Science Church.

Radio Cairo, Egypt. The first hour of a 90-minute potpourri of exotic Arab music and features reflecting Egyptian life and culture, with *news* and commentary about events in Egypt and the Arab world. There are also quizzes, mailbag shows, and answers to listeners' questions. Fair reception and mediocre audio quality to North America on 9475 and 11600 kHz.

Voice of America. *News*, then ● *Focus—* an examination of the major issues of the day. Thirty minutes to the Americas, Tuesday through Saturday, on 5995, 7405, 9775, 11580, 15120 and 15205 kHz.

Radio Argentina al Exterior—R.A.E. Broadcast at this time only during the Argentinian winter (summer in the Northern Hemisphere). See 0100 for program details. To North America Tuesday through Saturday (Monday through Friday, local American days) on 11710 kHz.

Radio Budapest, Hungary. This time summers only. Repeat of the 2100 transmission, but all features are one day later World Day. Sixty minutes to North America on 5970 (or 6110), 9835, 11910 and 15220 kHz. One hour later in winter.

Radio Canada International. Starts off with *News*, then winter weekdays (Tuesday through Saturday World Day) it's *Spectrum*. Sunday (Saturday evening in North America), there's *Innovation Canada* and *Earth Watch*, replaced Monday by *Arts in Canada* and a listener-response program. Summers, *News* is followed by features taken from the Canadian Broadcasting Corporation's domestic output. Tuesday through Saturday, there's the *Best of Morningside*, Sunday features *The Inside Track* (sports), and Monday has the cultural *Open House*. One hour to eastern North America on 9755 kHz, and to western parts on 6120 kHz.

Radio Norway International. Monday only. *Norway Now*. Repeat of the 2300 transmission. *News* and features from one of the friendliest stations on the international airwaves. Thirty minutes to North America; year-round on 9560 (or 9565) kHz, plus 11925 kHz in summer.

HCJB—Voice of the Andes, Ecuador. Predominantly religious programming. If you're looking for something a little more on the secular side, try *HCJB Today* (0200 Monday) or *Musical Mailbag* (0230 Sunday). To North America on 9745 and 15155 kHz; also widely available on 17490 and 21455 kHz upper sideband.

Voice of Free China, Taiwan. *News,* followed by three different features. The last is *Lets Learn Chinese,* which has a series of segments for beginning, intermediate and advanced learners. Other features include *Focus, Jade Bells and Bamboo Pipes, Journey into Chinese Culture* and *Kaleidoscope*—a potpourri of business, science, interviews and just about anything else. One hour to North and Central America on 5950, 9680 and 11740 kHz; to East Asia on 15345 kHz; and to Australasia on 9765 kHz.

Radio Sweden. Repeat of the 1500 transmission. Thirty minutes to North America on 9695 and 11705 kHz.

Radio Moscow World Service. Continuous to Asia, Australasia and North America. *News,* features and music to suit all tastes. Winter fare includes ● *Commonwealth Update* (Tuesday through Saturday), ● *Music and Musicians* (Sunday and Monday), and after 0230, ● *Folk Box* (Tuesday), ● *Music at your Request* (Friday), and jazz on Thursday and Saturday. Best in summer is ● *Audio Book Club* at 0231 Tuesday, Thursday and Saturday; though some listeners may prefer *Science and Engineering* (0211 Wednesday) or

the business-oriented *Newmarket* (same time, Tuesday). Winters in eastern North America, try channels in the 6 and 7 MHz bands; farther west, dial around the 9, 11, 15 and 17 MHz segments. Best summer opportunities are to be found on 11, 15 and 17 MHz channels, depending on your location. Optimum winter frequencies for East Asia can be found in the 9 and 11 MHz segments; try 15 MHz and higher in summer. Listeners in Southeast Asia and Australasia have several year-round frequencies in the 15, 17 and 21 MHz bands, the best of which are usually 21690 and 21790 kHz.

Radio Australia. Begins with the 30-minute ● *International Report,* then music or a feature. Targeted at Asia and the Pacific on about ten channels, and heard in North America (best during summer) on 15240, 17795 and 21740 kHz. For East Asia, try 21525 kHz.

Radio Habana Cuba. Repeat of the 0000 transmission. To North America on 6010 and 9655 or 13660 kHz.

Swiss Radio International. Repeat of the 0000 broadcast to North America. Thirty minutes on 6135, 9650, 9885 and 12035 kHz.

Radio For Peace International, Costa Rica. Part of an eight-hour cyclical block of counterculture and New Wave programming audible in Europe and the Americas on 7375, 7385, 13630 and 15030 kHz. Some transmissions

are in the single-sideband mode, which can be properly processed on only some radios.

Radio Romania International. *News,* commentary, press review and features on Romania. Regular spots include *Romanian Musicians* (Thursday), *Youth Club* (Wednesday), *Friendship and Cooperation* (Thursday), ● *Skylark* (Romanian folk music, Friday) and *Cultural Survey* (Saturday). To North America on 5990, 6155, 9510, 9570, 11830 and 11940 kHz.

WJCR, Upton, Kentucky. Continues with gospel music to North America on 7490 and 13595 kHz. Also with religious programs to North America at this hour are **WYFR-Family Radio** on 6065, 9505 and 15440 kHz, **WWCR** on 5935 (or 5920) kHz, **KTBN** on 7510 kHz, **WINB** on 15145 kHz, and Tuesday through Saturday, **KVOH-Voice of Hope** on 17775 kHz.

"For the People," WHRI, Noblesville, Indiana. Repeat of the 1800 broadcast. Summers, the show begins at this time, but winters it doesn't start until 0300. Populism is currently a significant topic in the United States, and here is the most celebrated program on the air that promotes classic populism—an American political tradition going back to 1891. Suspicious of concentrated wealth and power, *For the People* promotes economic nationalism ("buying foreign amounts to treason"), little-reported health concepts and a sharply progressive income tax, while opposing the "New World Order" and international banking. This two-hour talk show, hosted by former deejay Chuck Harder, can be heard Tuesday-Saturday (Monday through Friday local days) on 7315 kHz. Targeted at North America, but heard far beyond.

"National Vanguard Radio," WRNO. Only winter Sundays (Saturday evenings, local American day) at this time. See 0100 for program details. Thirty tiresome minutes to North America and beyond on 7355 kHz; try four hours later on 7395 kHz if preempted by live sports.

"Radio Free America," WWCR, Nashville, Tennessee. This time summers only, see 0300 for details. Two hours to North America and beyond on 5810 or 7435 kHz.

02:30

Radio Yugoslavia. Winters only at this time. See 0130 for specifics. Thirty minutes to North America on 9580 kHz.

Radyo Pilipinas, Philippines. Unlike most other stations, this one opens with features and closes with *news.* Monday's themes are business and authentic Filipino music; sports are featured Tuesday and Thursday; Friday fare includes *Listeners and Friends* and *Welcome to the Philippines;* Saturday airs *The Week that Passed;* and Sunday there's *Issues and Opinions.* Approximately one hour to South and East Asia on 17760, 17840 and 21580 kHz.

Radio Nederland. Repeat of the 0030 broadcast. Fifty-five minutes to South Asia, but heard well beyond, on 9860, 11655, 12025 and (summers) 13700 kHz.

Radio Tirana, Albania. Approximately 10 minutes of *news* about one of Europe's least known countries. To North America on 9580 and 11840 kHz.

RDP International—Radio Portugal. Winters only at this time. See 0130 for details. Thirty minutes Tuesday through Saturday (weekday evenings local North American days). Only fair reception in eastern North America—worse to the west—on 9570 and 9705 kHz. One hour earlier in summer.

02:45

Radio Yerevan, Armenia. Summers only at this time. Fifteen minutes of mostly *news* about Armenia, although Mondays (Sunday evenings in North America) are given over to Armenian culture. Mainly of interest to Armenians abroad. To North America on 11790, 15180 and 15580 kHz.

Radio Finland. Winters only at this time. See 0145 for program details. Thirty minutes to North America on any two channels from 9560, 11755 and 15185 kHz. One hour earlier in summer.

02:50

Vatican Radio. While concentrating mainly on issues affecting Catholics around the world, this station also airs some secularly oriented items, including some interesting ecological features. Weekend programming is of a less secular nature. Twenty minutes to eastern North America, winters on 6095 and 7305 kHz, and summers on 9605 and 11620 kHz.

03:00

■ **BBC World Service.** International and British *news,* followed by *Sports Roundup.* On Monday, Tuesday and Saturday the next half-hour is taken up by music programs, while on the remaining days there's ● *Discovery* (Wednesday), ● *Assignment* (Thursday), ● *Focus on Faith* (Friday), and *From Our Own Correspondent* (Sunday). Continuous to North America on 5975, 6175 and 9915 kHz; also available to early risers in parts of Europe on 6195, 9410 and 3955 or 12095 kHz; to the Mideast on 9410 (or 12095) and 11955 kHz; and to East Asia on 17790 kHz until 0330, when 15280 and 21715 kHz take over.

World Service of the Christian Science Monitor, USA. See 0100 for program details. Continuation of transmission to the Mideast Monday through Friday on 9350 kHz; and to western North America, Tuesday through Friday (Monday through Thursday, local American days) on 5850 or 9455 kHz. Also audible in much of North America on 13760 kHz, despite being targeted elsewhere. Programs on other days are religious in nature.

Voice of Free China, Taiwan. Similar to the 0200 transmission, but with the same programs broadcast on different days of the week. To North and Central America on 5950 and 9680 kHz; to East Asia on 15345 kHz; and to Australasia on 9765 kHz.

China Radio International. Repeat of the 0000 transmission. One hour to North America on 9690, 9770 and 11715 kHz.

■ **Deutsche Welle,** Germany. Repeat of the 0100 broadcast. Fifty minutes to North America and the Caribbean, winters on 6045, 6055, 6085, 6120, 9535, 9545, 9640, 9705 and 9770 kHz; and summers on 6085, 6145, 9700, 11810, 11890, 13610, 13770, 13790 and 15205 kHz.

Radio Budapest, Hungary. Winters only at this time; see 2100 for program details, with all features being one day later World Day. Sixty minutes to North America on 5970 (or 6110), 9835 and 11910 kHz. One hour earlier in summer.

Voice of America. Four hours of continuous programming aimed at an African audience. Opens with *News,* followed Monday through Friday by the informative and entertaining ● *Daybreak Africa.* Weekends, there's *VOA Morning,* a mixed bag of sports, science, business and other features. Although beamed to Africa, this service is widely heard elsewhere, including many parts of the United States. Try 6035, 7265, 7280, 7405, 9575 and 9885 kHz.

Radio Moscow World Service. Continuous to North America, the Mideast, Asia and Australasia. Worthy options include ● *Audio Book Club* (0331 winters on Tuesday, Thursday, Saturday); *Jazz Show* (0331 summer Mondays) and ● *Folk Box* (same time, summer Thursdays). On more than 60 channels, so tune around and find it, though listeners in eastern North America might have to look a little harder than those in other parts. Generally speaking, check the lower bands in winter, and the higher ones in summer. For the Mideast, Asia and Australasia, the 15, 17 and 21 MHz bands offer the best opportunities.

Radio Canada International. Winters only at this time. *News,* followed by programs from the Canadian Broadcasting Corporation's domestic output. Tuesday through Saturday, it's the *Best of Morningside,* replaced Sunday (Saturday evening in North America) by *Inside Track* (sports), while Monday is given over to culture in *Open House.* Sixty minutes to North America on 6010, 9725 and 9755 kHz. One hour earlier in summer.

Radio Moscow North American Service. Summers only at this time. The first of four hours of separate programming for the West Coast, consisting of programs heard on the World Service at other times. To western North America and Hawai'i on 12050, 15180, 15410, 15425 and 17605 kHz. One hour later during winter.

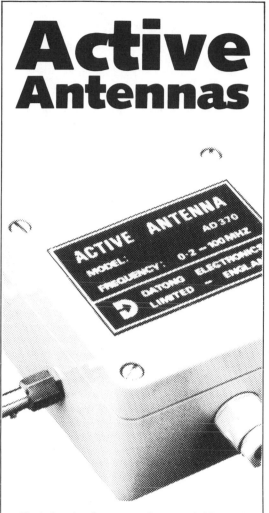

Active
Antennas

Satisfaction for you and your neighbours! Highly unobtrusive yet ideal for DX reception, Datong actives feature a dipole (not a monopole) for optimum rejection of local interference.

Our full catalogue plus further details of any product are available free on request. Dealers in most countries, please send for list. Credit cards accepted.

Datong Electronics Ltd.,
Clayton Wood Close,
West Park, Leeds LS16 6QE,
England.

Radio Bulgaria. Summers only at this time; see 0400 for more specifics. A 60-minute early-morning package for European listeners, also audible in North America, on 9850 and 11765 kHz.

Radio Australia. Begins with world and regional *news*, then music or features. Targeted at Asia and the Pacific on about ten channels, and heard in North America (best during summer) on 15240, 17795 and 21740 kHz. In East Asia, try 21525 kHz. A popular choice with many listeners.

Radio Habana Cuba. Repeat of the 0100 transmission; see 0000 for program details. To North America on 6010 and 9655 or 13660 kHz.

HCJB—Voice of the Andes, Ecuador. Tuesday through Saturday, it's *Studio 9* (see 0030 for program details). On the remaining days there's *News*, then *DX Partyline* (Sunday) or Monday's international friendship program *Saludos Amigos*. To the United States and Canada on 9745 and 15155 kHz; also available to many parts of the world on 17490 and 21455 kHz upper sideband.

Radio Cairo, Egypt. The final half-hour of a 90-minute broadcast to North America on 9475 and 11600 kHz.

Radio Japan. On most days, *News*, followed by *Radio Japan Magazine Hour*, an umbrella for features like *Asian Hotline* (Tuesday), *Business Today* (Thursday) and *A Glimpse of Japan* (Friday). Saturday, it's an hour of *This Week*, with *Let's Learn Japanese*, *Media Roundup* and *Viewpoint* on Sunday. One hour winters to eastern North America on 5960 kHz. There is also a separate year-round broadcast to the Americas, consisting of *News* followed by *Let's Learn Japanese* or a feature program. Thirty minutes on 11725, 15325 and 21610 kHz. As we go to press, Radio Japan is implementing a number of changes to both its program and transmission schedules, so be prepared for some adjustments.

Voice of Turkey. Summers only at this time. Repeat of the 2200 broadcast. *News*, followed by *Review of the Turkish Press* and features (some of them arcane) with a strong local flavor. Selections of Turkish popular and classical music complete the program. Fifty minutes to eastern North America on 9445 kHz. One hour later in winter.

Radio Prague, Czech Republic. *News* and features. An informative and entertaining half hour to North America, year-round on 5930, 7345 and 9485 kHz; and summers on 9810 and 11990 kHz.

WJCR, Upton, Kentucky. Continues with gospel music to North America on 7490 and 13595 kHz. Also with religious programs to North America at this hour are **WYFR-Family Radio** on 6065 and 9505 kHz, **WWCR** on 5935 (or 5920) kHz, **WINB** on 15145 kHz, **KTBN** on 7510 kHz, and **KVOH-Voice of Hope**, Tuesday through Saturday winters on 17775 kHz and daily summers on 9785 kHz.

"For the People," WHRI, Noblesville, Indiana. Starts at this time winters only; is halfway through its two-hour broadcast summers. See 0000 for specifics. Targeted weeknights to North America on 7315 kHz, but also heard elsewhere.

Radio For Peace International, Costa Rica. Continues with counterculture and New Wave programming. Audible in Europe and the Americas on 7375, 7385, 13630 and 15030 kHz. Some transmissions are in the single-sideband mode, which can be properly processed on only some radios.

"Radio Free America," WWCR, Nashville, Tennessee. Winters, starts at this time; summers, it is already at its halfway point. Sponsored by the Liberty Lobby, this live call-in show's populist features focus on what it perceives as conspiracies by the American medical establishment, as well as the Bilderberg meetings (which it tries to infiltrate), Trilateral Commission and similar internationalist organizations otherwise seldom reported upon. This program, unlike most other current populist agendas, is hostile towards Israel and conservative Arab states, and sympathetic to radical Arab governments. More illuminating are its continuing investigations of seldom-reported events surrounding the Waco calamity, as well as the shooting of the Randy Weaver family by Federal agents. When other, similar, incidents take place, Radio Free America often carries extended and unusual coverage, sometimes including gripping live interviews with the parties under siege. Hosted by Tom Valentine for two hours Tuesday through Saturday (Monday through Friday local days). Well heard in North America and beyond via the Sun Radio Network and WWCR on 5810 or 7435 kHz.

03:15

■ **BBC World Service for South Asia.** *South Asia Report*, 15 minutes of in-depth analysis of political and other developments in the region, also heard elsewhere. Sunday only, on 9580 (winters), 11955 and 15310 kHz.

03:30

United Arab Emirates Radio, Dubai. *News*, then a feature devoted to Arab and Islamic history or culture. Twenty-five minutes to North America on 11945, 13675, 15400 and 21485 (or 17890) kHz; heard best during the warm-weather months.

Radio Nederland. Repeat of the 0030 transmission. Fifty-five minutes to North America on 6165 and 9590 kHz.

■ **BBC World Service for Africa** provides separate programs for and about that continent, which otherwise tends to be inadequately covered by the international media. Although this special service is beamed only to Africa, it can often be heard in other parts of the world as well. There is a daily three-minute bulletin of African *news*, followed Monday through Friday by *Network Africa*, a fast-moving breakfast show. On Saturday it's *Quiz of the Week* or *This Week And Africa*, replaced Sunday by *Postmark Africa*. If you are interested in what's going on in the African continent, tune in to 3255, 6005, 6190, 7105, 9600, 9610, 11730, 15400 or 15420 kHz—you won't be disappointed!

Radio Austria International. Repeat of the 0130 broadcast except Monday (Sunday evening local American day) when ● *Report from Austria* is replaced by the entertainment program *Austrian Coffeetable*. A half hour to North and Central America on 6015 and 9870 kHz.

Voice of Greece. Repeat of the 0130 transmission. Ten minutes of English, surrounded by long periods of Greek music and programming. To North America, except Sunday (Saturday evening local American day), on 9380 (or 9395), 9420, and 11645 (or 7450) kHz.

03:45

Radio Yerevan, Armenia. Winters only at this time; see 0245 for specifics. Mainly of interest to Armenians abroad. To North America on 9870, 17605 and 17690 kHz.

04:00

■ **BBC World Service.** *News*, followed on the quarter-hour by one or more short features. Pick of the bunch is Tuesday's ● *Health Matters*. At 0430, Monday through Friday, it's ● *Off the Shelf*, readings from the best of world literature. Weekends are mostly devoted to music, with Saturday featuring the enjoyable *Jazz Now and Then*. The final quarter-hour features a variety of offerings, including ● *Andy Kershaw's World of Music* (Monday), *Country Style* (Wednesday), and ● *Folk Routes* (Friday). Continuous to North America on 5975 kHz; to Europe on 3955, 6180, 6195, 9410 and (summers) 12095 kHz; to the Mideast on 9410 (or 12095), 11760, 11955 (till 0430) and 15575 kHz; and to East Asia on 15280 and 21715 kHz.

World Service of the Christian Science Monitor, USA. See 0000 for program details. Monday through Friday to Africa (but also heard in parts of Europe and North America) on 9840 kHz, and to East Asia on 17780 kHz. Tuesday through Friday, the broadcast is also targeted at western North America on 5850 or 9455 kHz, with 9870 kHz (winter) or 13760 kHz (summer) also available to parts of the United States. Programming on the remaining days relates to the beliefs and teachings of the Christian Science Church.

Radio Habana Cuba. Repeat of the 0000 broadcast. To North America and the Caribbean on 6010, 6180 and (till 0430) 9655 or 13660 kHz.

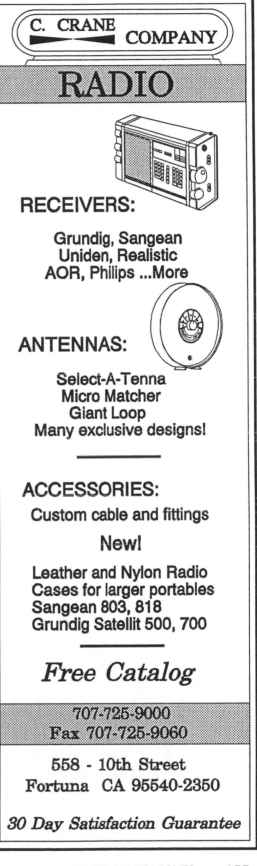

Swiss Radio International. Repeat of the 0000 broadcast to North America on 6135, 9885, 12035 and 13635 kHz. There is also a separate transmission to Europe, summer weekdays only, on 3985, 6165 and 9535 kHz—see 0500 for specifics.

Radio Prague, Czech Republic. *News* and a variety of short features wrapped in a friendly package. An entertaining half hour to North America, the Mideast and beyond on 5930 (winter), 7345, 9485, 9810, 11990, 13715 and (summers) 17535 kHz.

■ **BBC World Service for Africa.** Continuation of the 0330 broadcast. Monday through Friday, there's 15 minutes of *World News* and the second part of *Network Africa.* At 0450 Tuesday through Friday it's *African News* and *World Business Report for Africa.* Weekend programming consists of a half-hour feature at 0415; Saturdays, it's *TalkAbout Africa,* replaced Sunday by *African Perspective.* Targeted at African listeners, but also heard elsewhere, on 3255, 6005, 6190, 7105, 9600, 9610, 11730, 15400 and 15420 kHz.

Radio Norway International. Monday only. *Norway Now.* Repeat of the 2300 transmission. A half hour of *news* and human-interest stories targeted at North America on 9560 and 9565 (or 11865) kHz, and to the Mideast and South Asia on 11730 or 15175 kHz.

HCJB—Voice of the Andes, Ecuador. Thirty minutes of religious programming to North America on 9745 and 15155 kHz; also heard elsewhere on 17490 and 21455 kHz upper sideband.

Radio Australia. Begins with the 30-minute ● *International Report,* then music or a feature. Targeted at Asia and the Pacific on about ten channels, and heard in North America (best during summer) on 15240, 17795 and 21740 kHz.

Radio Bulgaria. Winters only at this time. A distinctly Bulgarian mix of news, commentary, interviews and features, plus a fair amount of music. Targeted at European early risers, but

With communism now dead, Radio Bulgaria, which recently changed its name from Radio Sofia, concentrates on presenting the Bulgarian people and their culture to the world.

also audible in North America, on 7290, 9700 and 11720 kHz. One hour earlier in summer.

■ **Deutsche Welle,** Germany. *News,* followed Monday through Friday by the informative and in-depth ● *European Journal* and the equally good ● *Africa Report* (replaced Monday by *Africa in the German Press.* Saturday features *Commentary, Panorama* and ● *Man and Environment;* substituted Sunday by *Sports Report* (or *Commentary*), *International Talking Point* and *People and Places.* A 50-minute broadcast aimed primarily at Africa on (amongst others) 6130, 7150, 7225, 9565, 9765 and 11765 kHz; but also available to the Mideast on 13770 kHz.

Radio Canada International. *News,* followed Tuesday through Saturday by *Spectrum.* This is replaced Sunday by the science feature *Innovation Canada,* and Monday by a listener-response program. Thirty minutes to the Mideast, winters on 6150, 9505 and 9670 kHz; summers on 9650, 11905, 11925 and 15275 kHz.

China Radio International. Repeat of the 0000 transmission. To North America on 11680 kHz; also on 11840 kHz during summer.

Voice of America. Directed to Europe, North Africa and the Mideast 0400-0700, but widely heard elsewhere. *News,* followed Monday through Friday by *Newsline* and *VOA Morning* (weekends it's all the latter)—a conglomeration of popular music, interviews, human interest stories, science digest, sports news, and so on, with news summaries on the half-hour. On 5995, 6040, 6140, 7170 and 7200 kHz. In the meantime, the popular African service also carries the same programs on 6035, 7265, 7280, 7405 and 9575 kHz. Reception of some of these channels is also good in North America.

Radio Romania International. An abbreviated version of the 0200 transmission, beginning with national and international *news* and commentary, then the feature program from the first half-hour of the 0200 broadcast. To North America on 5990, 6155, 9510, 9570, 11830 and 11940 kHz.

Voice of Turkey. Winters only at this time. Repeat of the 2300 broadcast; see 0300 for specifics. Fifty minutes to eastern North America on 9445 kHz. One hour earlier in summer.

WJCR, Upton, Kentucky. Continues with gospel music to North America on 7490 and 13595 kHz. Also with religious programs to North America at this hour are **WYFR-Family Radio** on 6065 and 9505 kHz, **WWCR** on 5935 (or 5920) kHz, **KTBN** on 7510 kHz, and **KVOH-Voice of Hope** on 9785 kHz.

Kol Israel. Summers only at this time. *News* for 15 minutes from Israel Radio's domestic network. To Europe and North America on 9435 kHz.

Radio For Peace International, Costa Rica. Part of an eight-hour cyclical block of counterculture and New Wave programming audible in Europe and the Americas on 7375, 7385, 13630 and 15030 kHz. Some transmissions are in the single-sideband mode, which can be properly processed on only some radios.

Radio Moscow World Service. Continuous to the Mideast, Asia and Australasia on scads of frequencies. Winters, it's *News and Views*, replaced Tuesday through Saturday summers by the timely ● *Commonwealth Update*. The final half hour is given over to paid programming from the Japanese *Aum Shinrikyo* religious movement. Listeners in the Mideast can chose from a wide variety of channels—just dial around; if you live in Asia or Australasia, try the 15, 17 and 21 MHz segments.

"For the People," WHRI, Noblesville, Indiana. Winters only at this time; see 0000 for specifics. The second half of a two-hour broadcast targeted weeknights to North America on 7315 kHz, and heard well beyond.

Radio Moscow North American Service. The only separate regional service still produced by Radio Moscow International, and a rehash of World Service features broadcast at other times. Beamed to the West Coast on several channels, including year-round 12050 kHz. Additional winter frequencies include 7270 and 9825 kHz; summers, try 15180, 15410, 15425 and 17605 kHz.

"Radio Free America," WWCR, Nashville, Tennessee. This time winters only. See 0300 for details. The second half of a broadcast targeted at North America on 5810 or 7435 kHz, but which is also heard well beyond.

04:30

■ **BBC World Service for Europe.** Monday through Saturday, summers only at this time. *Europe Today*, 30 minutes of the latest news, comment and analysis. To Europe on 15235 kHz.

Radio Finland. Summers only at this time. Monday through Saturday there's *Compass North*, replaced Sunday by *Focus*. Normally 20 minutes, but Sunday's broadcast is extended to include *Nuntii Latini*, a bulletin of news in Latin. To the Mideast on 11755 and 15440 kHz; also available Sundays to Europe on 6120 and 9665 kHz. One hour later in winter.

05:00

■ **BBC World Service.** ● *Newshour*—just about the most comprehensive and up-to-date news program to be heard anywhere. Sixty minutes of excellence, heard in North America on 5975 and 9640 kHz; in Europe on 3955, 6180, 6195 and 9410 kHz (though only 9410 kHz is available summer for the second half-hour); in the Mideast on 9410 or 12095 (till 0530), 11760 and 15575 kHz; and in East Asia on 15280, 15360, 17830 and 21715 kHz.

World Service of the Christian Science Monitor, USA. See 0100 for program details.

Monday through Friday to Africa (also heard in parts of Europe and North America) on 9840 kHz, and to East Asia on 17780 kHz. Tuesday through Friday, the broadcast is targeted at western North America on 5850 or 9455 kHz, with 9870 or 13760 kHz being additionally available to parts of the United States. On other days, programs are of a religious nature.

■ **Deutsche Welle,** Germany. Repeat of the 50-minute 0100 transmission to North America, winters on 5960, 6045, 6120, 6130, 9535, 9670 and 9690 kHz; and summers on 5960, 6130, 9515, 9605, 9670, 11705 and 13610 13790 kHz. This slot is by far the best for western North America.

Spanish Foreign Radio. Repeat of the 0000 and 0100 transmissions to North America, on 9530 kHz.

Croatian Radio. See 0000 for specifics. A special relay via religious station WHRI in Noblesville, Indiana. To North America on 7315 and 9495 kHz.

Swiss Radio International. Monday through Friday, winters, there's thirty minutes of *Dateline*, a well-produced résumé of world and Swiss events. This is replaced summers by a daily 15-minute relay of SRI's satellite service. To Europe on 3985, 6165 and 9535 kHz. One hour earlier in summer.

Radio Canada International. Summer weekdays only. See 0600 for program details. To Europe, Africa and the Mideast on 6050, 6150, 7295, 15430 and 17840 kHz. One hour later during winter.

China Radio International. This time winters only. Repeat of the 0000 broadcast; to North America on 11840 kHz.

HCJB—Voice of the Andes, Ecuador. Repeat of 0030 transmission. To North America on 11925 kHz; also audible in many areas on 17490 and 21455 kHz upper sideband.

Voice of America. Continues with the morning broadcast to Europe and the Mideast on the same frequencies as at 0400. This segment includes the *VOA Business Report* at 0510 Monday through Friday. The same programming is beamed to Africa on 6035, 7405, 9575 and 15600 kHz, with several of these channels providing good reception in North America.

Voice of Nigeria. Targeted at West Africa, but also audible in parts of Europe and North America, especially during winter. Monday through Friday, opens with *Morning Flight* followed by *VON Scope*, a half-hour of *news* and press comment. Pick of the weekend programs is *African Safari*, a musical journey around the African continent, which can be heard Saturdays at 0500. The first 60 minutes of a daily two-hour broadcast on 7255 kHz.

Radio Moscow North American Service. Continuation of the transmission beamed to western North America (see 0400); winters on 5905, 7270, 7345, 9825 and 12050 kHz; summers on 12050, 15180, 15410, 15425 and 17605 kHz.

Radio Australia. Begins with world and regional *news*, then music or features. Targeted at Asia and the Pacific on about ten channels, and heard in North America (best during summer) on 15240, 17795 and 21740 kHz.

Radio Moscow World Service. Continues to many parts of the world on more than 50 channels. Tuesday through Saturday, winters, the first half-hour features *News* and ● *Commonwealth Update*, the latter replaced summers by *Focus on Asia and the Pacific*. At 0531 winters, look for some interesting musical shows, including ● *Music at your Request* (Wednesday), ● *Folk Box* (Thursday), and Monday's jazz feature. Summers, this slot is given over to *Africa as we See It*. Best heard in Europe on various and changing frequencies within the 7, 9 or 11 MHz segments; with 15, 17 and 21 MHz more appropriate for Asia and Australasia. Dial around and take your pick.

WJCR, Upton, Kentucky. Continues with gospel music to North America on 7490 and 13595 kHz. Also with religious programs at this hour are **WYFR-Family Radio** on 5985 kHz, **WWCR** on 5935 (or 5920) kHz, **KTBN** on 7510 kHz, and **KVOH-Voice of Hope** on 9785 kHz.

Radio For Peace International, Costa Rica. Continues with a mixture of United Nations, counterculture and New Wave programming, including *Sound Currents of the Earth* (Monday) and *Outlaw for Peace* (Willie Nelson and Friends, 0530 Saturday). Audible in Europe and North America on 7375, 7385, 13630 and 15030 kHz. Some transmissions are in the single-sideband mode, which can be properly processed on only some radios.

Kol Israel. Winters only at this time. *News* for 15 minutes from Israel Radio's domestic network. To Western Europe and North America on 9435 kHz.

05:30

■ **BBC World Service for Europe.** Monday through Saturday, summers only at this time. See 0430 for program details. Thirty minutes on 3955, 3975, 6180, 6195 and 15360 kHz.

Radio Austria International. ● *Report from Austria*; see 0130 for more details. Year-round to North America on 6015 kHz, and winters only to Europe and the Mideast on 6155, 13730, 15410 and 17870 kHz.

Radio Finland. Winters only at this time; see 0430 for specifics. Twenty minutes to the Mideast on 9635 and 11755 kHz, and Sundays only to Europe on 6120 kHz. One hour earlier in summer.

United Arab Emirates Radio, Dubai. See 0330 for program details. To East Asia and Australasia on 15435, 17830 and 21700 kHz.

Australasia & East Asia—Evening Prime Time
Western North America—Late Evening
Europe & Mideast—Morning and Midday

06:00

■ **BBC World Service.** *News*, *News about Britain* and (Tuesday through Saturday) ● *The World Today* (replaced Sunday by ● *Letter from America* and Monday by *Recording of the Week)*. The second half-hour includes offerings such as *Meridian*, an arts show (Wednesday, Friday and Saturday); *Jazz for the Asking* (Sunday); and *Sports International* (Thursday). Continuous to North America on 5975 and 9640 kHz; to Europe on 3955, 6195, 9410, 12095 and 15575 kHz (some of which are only available till 0630); to the Mideast on 11760, 15575 and 21570 kHz; to East Asia on 15280, 15360, 17830 and 21715 kHz; and to Australasia on 7150, 9640, 11955 and 17830 kHz.

World Service of the Christian Science Monitor, USA. See 0000 for program details. Monday through Friday to Europe on 5850 or 9840 kHz, to western North America on 7395 or 9455 kHz, to East Asia on 17780 kHz, and to Southeast Asia on 17755 kHz. Weekend programs deal with various aspects of the Christian Science faith.

Radio Habana Cuba. Repeat of the 0000 transmission. To western North America on 6000 or 9510 kHz.

Croatian Radio. Monday through Saturday, summers only at this time; actually starts at 0603. Ten minutes of on-the-spot *news* from one of Europe's most troubled areas. Intended mainly for Europe at this hour, but also heard elsewhere. Frequencies vary, but try 5920, 9830 and 13830 kHz. Although not available at this time Sunday, there is a short summary of news at 0703 for those who have an interest in the region. One hour later during winter.

Swiss Radio International. Monday through Friday, it's ● *Dateline*, a thoroughly workmanlike compilation of Swiss and international *news*. Weekends see less news and more features. Saturday's menu includes *The Grapevine* and *Swiss Shortwave Merry-Go-Round* (which answers technical questions sent in by listeners), while Monday's broadcast includes *Supplement*, *Roundabout Switzerland*, *Rhythm-makers* or *The Name Game*—features which alternate on a regular basis. Thirty minutes to the Mideast and Africa on 13635, 15430 and 17565 kHz. For Europe there is a separate 15-minute relay of SRI's satellite service—weekdays during winter, but daily in summer—on 3985, 6165 and 9535 kHz.

Radio Canada International. Winter weekdays only. Thirty minutes of programming targeted at Canadians overseas. *News*, then *Info Canada*. To Europe, Africa and the Mideast on 6050, 6150, 7155, 9740, 9760 and 11905 kHz. One hour earlier in summer.

■ **BBC World Service for Africa.** Monday through Friday, it's a combination of *news* and the breakfast show *Network Africa*. Saturdays, there's *Quiz of the Week* (or *This Week and Africa*) and *Spice Taxi*, replaced Sunday by *Postmark Africa* and *African Perspective*. One hour to Africa (and heard well beyond) on 6190, 9600, 11940, 15400, 15420 and 17885 kHz.

Voice of America. Final hour of the transmission to Europe, North Africa and the Mideast. See 0400 for program details. On 6040, 6060, 7170, 7325 and 15205 kHz. Meanwhile, the mainstream program for the African continent continues with *News* and ● *Daybreak Africa* (replaced weekends by *VOA Morning*). Good reception in regions other than the target area (including North America) on 6035, 7405, 9530, 9575 and 15600 kHz.

Voice of Nigeria. The second (and final) hour of a daily broadcast intended for listeners in West Africa, but also heard in parts of Europe and North America (especially during winter). Features vary from day to day, but are predominantly concerned with Nigerian and West African affairs. There is a listener-response program at 0600 Friday and 0615 Sunday, and musicologists might try *Musical Heritage* at 0615 Saturday. There is a daily 25-minute program of *news* and commentary on the half-hour. To 0657 on 7255 kHz.

Radio Moscow World Service. Continuous and varied programming targeted at virtually everywhere except the Americas (though still sometimes heard there). *News*, followed winters by *Focus on Asia and the Pacific* (Tuesday through Saturday), *Science and Engineering* (Sunday), and *Mailbag* (Monday). The second half-hour is given over to *Africa as we See It*. In summer, the news is followed by *Science and Engineering* (Monday and Friday), *Culture and the Arts* (Saturday), the business-oriented *Newmarket* (Thursday), or a listener-response program. During the second half-hour it's mostly music, replaced Sunday and Monday by *Russian by Radio*. Look around for frequencies—they change often—within the 15, 17 and 21 MHz segments, although 7 and 9 MHz channels tend to be best for Europe during winter.

Radio For Peace International, Costa Rica. Continues with counterculture and New Wave programming ranging from *Sound Currents of the Earth* (Thursday) to *World Goodwill Forum* (Monday). Audible in Europe and the Americas on 7375, 7385, 13630 and 15030 kHz. Some transmissions are in the single-sideband mode, which can be properly processed only on some radios.

Radio Moscow North American Service. Another hour of programming to western North America (see 4000). Available on a variety of frequencies—winters, try 5905, 7175, 7270, 7345, 9825 and 12050 kHz; summers, on 12050, 15180, 15410, 15425 and 17605 kHz.

Radio Prague, Czech Republic. Summers only at this time. *News* and features with a distinct Central European flavor. Thirty minutes to Europe on 6055, 7345, 9505 and 11990 kHz. One hour later in winter.

■ **Deutsche Welle,** Germany. Repeat of the 0400 broadcast. Targeted at Africa, but one of the better opportunities for listeners in Western Europe. Fifty minutes on 11765 (11780, summers), 13610, 13790, 15185, 15435 (15205, summers) and 17875 kHz.

Radio Korea, South Korea. The hour-long broadcast opens with *News*, then commentary (except Sunday), followed Monday through Thursday by *Seoul Calling*. Weekly features include *Echoes of Korean Music* and *Shortwave Feedback* (Sunday), *Tales from Korea's Past*

(Monday), *Korean Cultural Trail* (Tuesday), *Let's Learn Korean* (Friday), and Sunday's listener-response program, *From Us To You*. To North America on 11945 and 15155 kHz, and to East Asia on 7275 kHz.

WJCR, Upton, Kentucky. Continues with gospel music to North America on 7490 and 13595 kHz. Also with religious programs for North American listeners at this hour are **WYFR-Family Radio** on 5985 kHz, **WWCR** on 5935 (or 5920) and 7435 kHz, **KTBN** on 7510 kHz, **WHRI-World Harvest Radio** on 7315 and 9495 kHz, and **KVOH-Voice of Hope** on 9785 kHz.

Voice of Malaysia. Actually starts at 0555 with opening announcements and program summary, followed by *News*. Then comes *This is the Voice of Malaysia*, a potpourri of news, interviews, reports and music. The hour is rounded off with *Personality Column*. Part of a 150-minute broadcast to Southeast Asia and Australia on 6175, 9750 and 15295 kHz.

HCJB—Voice of the Andes, Ecuador. An hour of predominantly religious programming. Popular features include *Musical Mailbag* (0200 Sunday), *HCJB Today* (same time Monday), and Bill Rapley's musical treasure trove, ● *Blues, Rags and All That Jazz* (0630 Saturday). To North America on 11925 kHz, and widely available elsewhere on 17490 and 21455 kHz upper sideband.

06:30

Radio Austria International. Tuesday through Sunday it's ● *Report from Austria* (see 0130), replaced Monday by the entertainment program *Austrian Coffeetable*. A half hour via the Canadian relay, aimed primarily at western North America on 6015 kHz.

■ **BBC World Service for Europe.** Monday through Saturday, winters only at this time. See 0430 for program details. Thirty minutes on 3955, 3975, 6180 and 6195 kHz.

Radio Vlaanderen International, Belgium. Summers only at this time. Weekdays, there's *News* and *Press Review*, followed Tuesday through Friday by *Belgium Today* (various topics) and features like *Focus on Europe* (Tuesday), *Around the Arts* (Wednesday), *Living in Belgium* and *Green Society* (Thursday), and *North-South* (Friday). Weekend features include *Radio World* and *Tourism* (Saturday), plus Sunday's *P.O. Box 26* (a listener-response program) and *Music from Flanders*, both of which are repeated Monday. Twenty-five minutes to Europe on 5910 and 9925 kHz; and to Australasia on 9925 kHz. One hour later in winter.

06:45

Radio Finland. Summers only at this time. See 0745 winter transmission for program details. Fifteen minutes to Europe on 6120, 9560 and 11755 kHz.

Radio Romania International. *News*, commentary, press review and a short feature, with interludes of lively Romanian folk music. A half-hour to Australasia on 11810, 11940, 15335, 17720, 17805 and 21665 kHz.

Ghana Broadcasting Corporation. Intended for listeners in neighboring countries, so reception is marginal outside the target area—especially during the summer months. The broadcast starts with West African music, followed by *news*, then a further serving of music to loosen up your limbs. On 6130 kHz.

07:00

■ **BBC World Service.** ● *Newsdesk*, followed by something of a mixed bag, depending on the day of the week. Of the regular year-round programs, try *From Our Own Correspondent* (Sunday), *Development 93* (Wednesday) or Thursday's *Network UK*, a valuable insight into the British way of life. Continuous to North America (till 0730) on 5975 and 9640 kHz; and for the full hour to Europe on 7325, 9410, 12095 and 15070 kHz; to the Mideast on 11760, 15575, 17640 and 21470 kHz (15575 and 21470 kHz are available only till 0730 from Monday through Friday, and for the full hour on weekends); to

East Asia on 15280, 15360, 17830 and 21715 kHz; and to Australasia on 7150, 9640, 11955 and 17830 kHz.

World Service of the Christian Science Monitor, USA. See 0100 for program details. Monday through Friday to Europe (and parts of North America) on 5850 or 9840 kHz, to western North America on 7395 or 9455 kHz, to East Asia on 17780 kHz, and to Southeast Asia on 17555 kHz. Weekends are given over to nonsecular programming, mainly of interest to members of, and others interested in, the Christian Science Church.

Voice of Malaysia. First, there is a daily feature with a Malaysian theme (except for Thursday, when *Talk on Islam* is aired), then comes a half-hour of *This is the Voice of Malaysia* (see 0600), followed by 15 minutes of *Beautiful Malaysia*. Not much doubt about where the broadcast originates! Continuous to Southeast Asia and Australia on 6175, 9750 and 15295 kHz.

Swiss Radio International. Winters only at this time. Fifteen minutes from SRI's satellite service. To Europe on 3985, 6165 and 9535 kHz. One hour earlier in summer.

Radio Prague, Czech Republic. This time winters only. Thirty minutes of *news* and features, with a strong emphasis on all things Czech and some things Slovak. A good way to start the European day. Available on 6055, 7345, 9505 and 11990 kHz. One hour earlier in summer.

Radio For Peace International, Costa Rica. Part of an eight-hour cyclical block of counterculture and New Wave programming audible in Europe and the Americas on 7375, 7385, 13630 and 15030 kHz. Some transmissions are in the single-sideband mode, which can be properly processed only on some radios.

Radio Moscow North American Service. Winters only at this time. The final hour of separate programming for West Coast North America (see 0400). Try 5905, 7175, 7270, 7345 and 9825 kHz.

Radio Moscow World Service. Continuous programming beamed to most parts of the world. *News*, followed Tuesday through Saturday, summers, by the informative ● *Commonwealth Update*. Then comes ● *Audio Book Club* (Tuesday, Thursday and Saturday) or *Russian by Radio* (Wednesday and Friday). At 0711 Saturday, lend an ear to ● *Music and Musicians*. Winter's offerings are a mixed bag, with *Science and Engineering* (0711 Monday and Friday) and *Culture and the Arts* (same time, Saturday) probably the most interesting. There is also a listener-response program at this time Sunday, Tuesday and Wednesday. For Europe winters, dial about for frequencies in the 9, 11, 13 and 15 MHz segments; at other times and in other areas tune around 15, 17 and 21 MHz. There are over 50 channels from which to choose.

WJCR, Upton, Kentucky. Continues with

gospel music to North America on 7490 and 13595 kHz. Also with religious programs to North America at this hour are **WWCR** on 5935 (or 5920) and 7435 kHz, **KTBN** on 7510 kHz, **WHRI-World Harvest Radio** on 7315 and 9495 kHz, and **KVOH-Voice of Hope** (winters only) on 9785 kHz.

Radio Pyongyang, North Korea. See 1100 for program details. Fifty minutes of curiosity value (and little else). May be worth a listen if the "Great Leader" finally makes it to the celestial fatherland. Until then, best given a miss except to experience that old-time communist propaganda. To East and Southeast Asia on 15340 kHz.

Croatian Radio. Monday through Saturday, winters only at this time; actually starts at 0703 (Sunday, there is a brief summary at 0803). Ten minutes of English *news* from one of Croatian Radio's domestic networks. In times of crisis, one of the few sources of up-to-date news on what is actually happening in the region. On at least three frequencies from 5020, 5085, 5920, 6145, 6210, 9830 and 13830 kHz. One hour earlier in summer.

Voice of Free China, Taiwan. Repeat of the 0200 transmission. Targeted at Central America, but audible in southern and western parts of the United States on 5950 kHz.

HCJB—Voice of the Andes, Ecuador. Opens with 30 minutes of religious programming—except for Saturday, when *Musical Mailbag* is on the air. Then comes *Studio 9* (see 0030 for more details, except that all features are one day earlier), replaced Saturday by *DX Partyline*. Sunday is given over to *Saludos Amigos*—the HCJB international friendship program. To Europe winters on 6205 and 9600 kHz; summers on any two channels from 9585, 11835 and 15270 kHz; and to Australasia (from 0715) on 9745 and 11925 kHz. Also widely available on 17490 and 21455 kHz upper sideband.

07:30

Radio Prague, Czech Republic. *News,* generally followed by short and varied features. Thirty minutes to Europe, Asia and Australasia on 6055, 11990, 13600, 17535, 17725 and 21705 kHz.

Radio Nederland. See 0030 for specifics, except that all features are one day earlier. To Australasia on 9630 and 11895 kHz, and worth a listen.

■ **BBC World Service for Africa.** See 0330 for details, the only difference being on Sunday, when the broadcast is taken up by ● *The Jive Zone*—a program of contemporary African and other music. Thirty minutes targeted at Africa (but also heard elsewhere) on 11860, 11940, 15105 and 17885 kHz.

Radio Austria International. Summers only at this time. ● *Report from Austria,* which includes a short bulletin of *news* followed by a

series of current events and human interest stories. Ample coverage of national and regional issues, and a valuable source of news from Central and Eastern Europe. Thirty minutes to Europe on 6155 and 13730 kHz, and to the Mideast on 15410 and 17870 kHz.

Radio Vlaanderen International, Belgium. Winters only at this time. See 0630 for program details. To Europe on 5900 (or 5910), 9905 and 11695 kHz; and to Australasia on 11695 kHz. One hour earlier in summer.

07:45

Radio Finland. Winters only at this time. Monday through Saturday it's *Compass North,* with Sunday's broadcast consisting of a Finnish language lesson. Fifteen minutes targeted at Europe on 6120, 9560 and 11755 kHz. One hour earlier in summer.

08:00

■ **BBC World Service.** *News,* then the religious *Words of Faith,* followed by a wide variety of programming, depending on the day of the week. Choice programs include ● *Concert Hall* (alternating periodically with ● *International Recital* or ● *From the Proms*) (Tuesday), ● *Health Matters* and ● *Anything Goes* (Monday), *Good Books* and *John Peel* (Thursday), and classical music on Friday and Sunday. Continuous to Europe on 7325, 9410, 12095 and 15070 kHz; to the Mideast on 17640 kHz (plus 15575 and 21470 kHz on weekends); to East Asia on 15280, 15360, 17830 and 21715 kHz; and to Australasia on 11955 and 17830 kHz.

World Service of the Christian Science Monitor, USA. See 0000 for program details. Monday through Friday to Europe and parts of North America on 9840 or 11705 kHz, with 9455 kHz available to the Americas. Listeners in East Asia can tune to 17555 kHz, while those in Australasia can choose from 13615 and 15665 kHz. Weekend programs are devoted to the teachings and beliefs of the Christian Science Church.

HCJB—Voice of the Andes, Ecuador. Continuous programming to Europe and Australasia. The final half-hour of *Studio 9* (or weekend variations), followed (for Australasia, only) by 30 minutes of religious fare. To Europe (until 0830), winters on 6205 and 9600 kHz; summers on any two channels from 9585, 11835 and 15270 kHz; and to Australasia on 9745 and 11925 kHz. Listeners in other areas, whose receivers are capable of receiving signals in the single-sideband mode, can try tuning 17490 and 21455 kHz.

Voice of Malaysia. *News* and commentary, followed Monday through Friday by *Instrumen-*

talia, which is replaced weekends by *This is the Voice of Malaysia* (see 0600). The final 25 minutes of a much longer transmission targeted at Southeast Asia and Australia on 6175, 9750 and 15295 kHz.

Croatian Radio. Monday through Saturday, summers only at this time; actually starts at 0803. Ten minutes of English *news* from one of the domestic networks (replaced Sunday by a brief summary at 0903). A good way to keep abreast of events in one of Europe's most unstable regions. Frequency usage varies, but try 5020, 5085, 5920, 6145, 6210, 9830 or 13830 kHz. One hour later in winter.

Radio Pakistan. Opens with a brief bulletin of *news* followed by recitations from the Koran (with English translation). This in turn is followed by a press review and a ten-minute interlude of Pakistani music. On the half-hour there's a feature on Pakistan or Islam, which then gives way to extracts from Pakistani concert recordings. Fifty minutes to Europe on 17900 and 21520 kHz.

Radio Australia. Part of a 24-hour service to Asia and the Pacific, but which can also be heard at this time throughout much of North America. Begins with ● *International Report*, followed Monday through Friday by *Stock Exchange Report*, then the daily *Sports Report*. Not very original titles, but the program content makes up for it. To southern parts of Asia and the Pacific on a variety of channels, and audible year-round in North America on 5995 and 9580 kHz.

WJCR, Upton, Kentucky. Continues with gospel music to North America on 7490 and 13595 kHz. Other U.S. religious broadcasters operating at this hour include **WWCR** on 5935 (or 5920) and 7435 kHz, **KTBN** on 7510 kHz, and **WHRI-World Harvest Radio** on 7315 and 7355 kHz.

Radio Finland. Summers only at this time; see 0900 for program details. To Southeast Asia and Australasia on 17800 and 21550 kHz.

Radio Moscow World Service. *News*, then Tuesday through Saturday, winters, it's ● *Commonwealth Update* followed by ● *Audio Book Club* or *Russian by Radio*. Pick of the remaining days is Sunday's ● *Music and Musicians*, which follows the news. In summer, the *news* is followed Tuesday through Saturday by *Focus on Asia and the Pacific*. This in turn gives way, on the half-hour, to some entertaining musical fare—● *Folk Box* (Wednesday and Saturday), *Yours for the Asking* (Monday), ● *Music at your Request* (Tuesday), and Friday's *Jazz Show*. Listeners in Europe and the Mideast can try dialing around the bands from 9 MHz upwards. These segments are also suitable for East Asia, while listeners in Southeast Asia and Australasia have year-round channels at their disposal in the 15, 17 and 21 MHz segments of the spectrum.

Trans World Radio transmits throughout southern Africa from a site in Swaziland's bush country.

KTWR-Trans World Radio, Guam. Actually starts at 0755. Eighty minutes of evangelical programming targeted at East Asia on 15200 kHz.

Radio New Zealand International. *News,* then features, music or special programs for the South Sea Islands, all with a distinctly Pacific flavor. Weekend programming features *Saturday Scrapbook* and relays from the domestic National Radio. Part of a much longer broadcast for the South Pacific, but well heard in North America on 9700 (or 9730) kHz.

Radio Korea, South Korea. See 0600 for program details. Sixty minutes to Europe on 7550 and 13670 kHz, and to the Mideast and Africa on 15575 kHz.

08:30

Radio Austria International. The comprehensive ● *Report from Austria;* see 0130 for more details. To Australia and the Pacific (year-round) on 15450 and 21490 kHz, and to Europe (winters only) on 6155 and 13730 kHz.

Radio Slovakia International. *News* and features with a heavy accent on Slovak life and culture. Thirty minutes to Australasia (and widely heard elsewhere) on 11990, 15605, 17535 and 21705 kHz.

Radio Nederland. The second of three hours aimed at Australasia. *News,* followed Monday through Saturday by *Newsline,* then a feature program. Best pickings are probably ● *Encore* (Wednesday), ● *Research File* (Thursday) and Sundays's offbeat *East of Edam.* On other days,

try *No Boundaries* (Tuesday), *Airtime Africa* (Saturday), and Friday's documentary. Monday through Saturday, there is also a daily *Press Review.* On 11895 kHz.

09:00

■ **BBC World Service.** Starts with *News* and business information, and ends with *Sports Roundup.* The remaining time is taken up by a series of short features, the pick of which are ● *Short Story* and ● *Folk Routes* (Sunday), ● *Andy Kershaw's World of Music* (Monday), *The Farming World* (Thursday), and ● *Global Concerns* (Friday). To Europe on 9750, 9760, 12095, 15070 and 17640 kHz; to the Mideast on 11760, 15575 and 21470 kHz; to East Asia on 17830 and 21715 kHz, and to Australasia on 11955 (replaced by 11750 at 0915) and 17830 kHz.

World Service of the Christian Science Monitor, USA. See 0100 for program details. Monday through Friday to Europe on 9840 or 11705 kHz, to East Asia on 17555 kHz, and to Australasia on 13615 and 15665 kHz. Also audible in parts of North America on 9455 and 9840 kHz. Weekend programs are of a religious nature and are mainly of interest to members of, and others interested in, the Christian Science faith.

■ **Deutsche Welle,** Germany. *News,* followed Monday through Friday by ● *Newsline Cologne* and a feature: *Science and Technology* (Monday), ● *Man and Environment* (Tuesday), *Insight* (Wednesday), *Living in Germany* (Thursday) and *Spotlight on Sport* (Friday). These are replaced Saturday by *International Talking Point*, *Development Forum* and *Religion and Society*; and Sunday by *Arts on the Air* and *German by Radio*. Fifty minutes to Asia and Australasia on 6160, 11715, 17780, 17820, 21465, 21650 and 21680 kHz.

Radio New Zealand International. Mostly relays programs from the domestic National Radio at this time, but some days has special programming for the islands of the South Pacific, where the broadcasts are targeted. Continuous on 9700 (or 9730) kHz, and audible in much of North America.

Radio Vlaanderen International, Belgium. Monday through Saturday, summers only at this time. See 0630 for program details. Twenty-five minutes to Europe on 5910, 9905 and 13675 kHz. One hour later in winter.

Croatian Radio. Monday through Saturday, winters only at this time; actually starts at 0903 (Sunday, there is only a brief summary at 1003). Ten minutes of on-the-spot *news* from the Balkan cauldron. Frequencies vary, but try 5020, 5085, 5920, 6145, 6210, 9830 and 13830 kHz. One hour earlier during summer.

HCJB—Voice of the Andes, Sixty minutes of religious programming to Australasia on 9745 and 11925 kHz, also available on 17490 and 21455 kHz, upper sideband.

China Radio International. *News* and various features—see 0000 for specifics, although programs are one day earlier. To Australasia on 11755, 15440 and 17710 kHz.

Swiss Radio International. Repeat of the 0600 transmission. Thirty minutes to East Asia and Australasia on 9885 (or 9560), 13685, 17670 and 21820 kHz. For Europe, summers only, there is a separate 45-minute relay of SRI's satellite service (one hour later in winter) on 6165 and 9535 kHz.

Radio Moscow World Service. Tuesday through Saturday, winters, *News* is followed by *Focus on Asia and the Pacific*. This is replaced summers by a variety of features—Wednesday's offering is the business-oriented *Newmarket*, Thursday features *Science and Engineering*, and there's a listener-response program on Tuesday, Friday and Saturday. Weekend programming is something of a mixed bag. Year-round, the second half-hour predominantly features music, with the main summer attractions being ● *Folk Box* (Wednesday and Saturday) and Monday's ● *Music at your Request*. Sixty minutes of continuous programming beamed just about everywhere. Dial around from 9 to 21 MHz and choose a frequency—with more than sixty available channels, there should be at least one for your location.

Radio Australia. World and Australian *news*, followed most days by music and information. Then, on the half-hour, comes any one of a wide variety of features. These change on a

seasonal basis (sometimes more often). Hardly the best way to keep the listeners happy, but to a certain extent this is made up for with some interesting program content. Heard well in North America on 5995 and 9580 kHz, in Europe and the Mideast on 21745 (or 21725) kHz, and in East Asia on 13605 and 15170 kHz.

Radio For Peace International, Costa Rica. *FIRE* (Feminist International Radio Endeavor). Repeat of the 0100 broadcast. Audible in Europe and the Americas on 7375, 7385 and 13630 kHz. Some of the transmissions are in the single-side-band mode, which can only be received on superior world band radios.

KTWR-Trans World Radio, Guam. Actually starts at 0855. Forty-five minutes of evangelical programming to Australasia on 11805 kHz.

WJCR, Upton, Kentucky. Continues with gospel music to North America on 7490 and 13595 kHz. Other U.S. religious broadcasters operating at this hour include **WWCR** on 5935 (or 5920) and 7435 kHz, **KTBN** on 7510 kHz, and **WHRI-World Harvest Radio** on 7315 and 7355 kHz.

Radio Finland. Winters only at this time. Monday through Saturday it's *Compass North*, a potpourri of items dealing with Finnish and other Nordic themes. The Saturday broadcast also includes *Starting Finnish* (a series of language lessons for beginners), while Sunday features *Focus* and the highly unusual *Nuntii Latini*, news in Latin. Thirty minutes to Southeast Asia and Australasia on 15330 and 17800 kHz. One hour earlier in summer.

09:30

Radio Nederland. Repeat of the 0730 broadcast. Fifty-five minutes to Australasia on 9720 and 11895 kHz; and a full hour to East and Southeast Asia, winters on 7260 and 9860 kHz, summers on 12065 and 15470 kHz.

10:00

■ **BBC World Service.** *News Summary*, followed by a variety of features, 15 or 30 minutes long (some of which start at 1030 or 1045). The list includes *Jazz Now and Then*, ● *Letter from America* and *From the Weeklies* (Saturday), ● *Science in Action* (Sunday), *The Vintage Chart Show* (Monday), ● *Discovery* (Tuesday), ● *Omnibus* and *Jazz for the Asking* (Wednesday), ● *Assignment* (Thursday), and ● *Focus on Faith* (Friday). Tune in any day of the week for some high-quality programming. Continuous to Western Europe on 9750, 9760, 12095, 15070 and 17640 kHz; to the Mideast on 11760, 15575 and 21470 kHz; and to East Asia and Australasia on 17830 kHz. 11750 kHz (for Australia) and 21715 kHz (for East Asia) are also available until 1030.

World Service of the Christian Science Monitor, USA. See 0000 for program details. Monday through Friday to eastern North America on 9495 kHz (also audible farther west on 9455 kHz). Listeners in East Asia can tune to 17555 kHz, while those in the south-east of the continent can try 13625 kHz. Weekend programming is nonsecular, and is devoted to the teachings and beliefs of the Christian Science Church.

Radio Australia. ● *International Report,* followed Monday through Friday by *Stock Exchange Report,* then one of several feature programs, some of which are subject to seasonal rescheduling. Heard well in North America on 5995 and 9580 kHz, and in Europe and the Mideast on 21745 (or 21725) kHz.

Radio New Zealand International. A mixed bag of Pacific regional *news,* features, and relays of the domestic National Radio network. Continuous to the Pacific on 9700 (or 9730) kHz, and easily audible in much of North America.

Voice of Vietnam. Much better heard in Europe than in North America. Begins with *news,* then political commentary, interviews, short features, and some pleasant Vietnamese music. Heard extensively on 9840 and (winters) 12019 or (summers) 15009 kHz. Repeats of this transmission can be heard on the same frequencies at 1230, 1330, 1600, 1800, 1900, 2030 and 2330 World Time.

Radio Vlaanderen International, Belgium. Monday through Saturday, winters only at this time. See 0630 for program details. Twenty-five minutes to Europe on 5900 (or 5910) and 9905 kHz. One hour earlier in summer.

Kol Israel. Summers only at this time. *News* from Israel Radio's domestic network, followed by various features: *Israel Mosaic* (a variety of topics, Monday), *Letter from Jerusalem* and *Thank Goodness It's Friday* (yes, Friday), *Talking Point* (discussion, Tuesday), *Studio Three* (arts in Israel, Thursday), *This Land* (travel show, Wednesday), and *Spotlight* (issues in the news, Saturday). A half-hour to Europe—occasionally audible in eastern North America—on 17545 kHz. One hour later during winter.

Voice of America. The start of VOA's daily broadcasts to the Caribbean. *News, Newsline* (weekdays only) and *VOA Morning*—a compendium of sports, science, business and features—on 9590, 11915 and 6030 or 15120 kHz. For a separate service to Australasia, see the next item.

Voice of America. *News,* followed Monday through Friday by *Newsline* and *Magazine Show.* On the remaining days there are features such as *Weekend Magazine* (1030 Saturday) and *Critic's Choice* (1010 Sunday). To Australasia on 5985, 11720, and 15425 kHz.

Radio For Peace International, Costa Rica. Another hour of counterculture programming, audible in Europe and the Americas on 7375, 7385 and 13630 kHz. Some transmissions are in the single-sideband mode, which can be properly processed only on some radios.

China Radio International. *News* and various features—see 0000 for specifics, although programs are one day earlier. To Australasia on 11755, 15440 and 17710 kHz.

All India Radio. *News,* then a composite program of commentary, press review and features, interspersed with ample servings of enjoyable Indian music. Just the thing to curry favor. To East Asia on 15050, 17895 and 21735 kHz; and to Australasia on 15050 and 17387 kHz.

WJCR, Upton, Kentucky. Continues with gospel music to North America on 7490 and 13595 kHz. Other U.S. religious broadcasters operating at this hour include **WWCR** on 5935 (or 5920) and 7435 kHz, **KTBN** on 7510 kHz, **WYFR-Family Radio** on 5950 kHz, and **WHRI-World Harvest Radio** on 7315 kHz.

Radio Moscow World Service. *News,* followed winters by a variety of features. Sunday and Wednesday it's business in *Newmarket,* Monday features *Culture and the Arts,* Thursday has *Science and Engineering,* and there's a listener-response program on the remaining days. The second half-hour consists of a summary of events in the CIS, followed by music (Tuesday through Friday); Saturday's potpourri, *Kaleidoscope;* and Monday's ● *Audio Book Club*—a unique window on Russian literature. In summers, the news is followed Tuesday through Saturday by the timely ● *Commonwealth Update,* replaced Sunday by *Culture and the Arts* and Monday by *Science and Engineering.* These, in turn, are followed by ● *Audio Book Club* (Sunday, Wednesday and Friday), *Russian by Radio* (Tuesday and Thursday) or music. A truly worldwide broadcast, beamed to all continents at this time. Dial around above 9 MHz and find yourself a channel.

HCJB—Voice of the Andes, Ecuador. Monday through Friday it's *Studio 9.* As 0030, but one day earlier. Saturdays feature *DX Partyline,* while Sundays are given over to *Saludos Amigos.* To Australasia on 9745 and 11925 kHz; also broadcast on 17490 and 21455 kHz upper sideband.

10:30

Radio Korea, South Korea. Summers only at this time. Monday through Saturday, starts off with *News,* replaced Sunday by *Weekly News in Review.* The remainder of the 30-minute broadcast is taken up by one or more features, including *Shortwave Feedback* (a listener-response program, Sunday), *Seoul Calling* (Monday and Tuesday), *Pulse of Korea* (Thursday), *Let's Sing Together* (Friday) and *From Us To You* (Saturday). On 11715 kHz via Canadian relay, so this is the best chance for North Americans to hear the station. One hour later in winter.

Radio Prague, Czech Republic. This time summers only. A pleasant mix of *news* and features from a genuinely friendly station. A half-hour to Europe, the Mideast and Africa on 6055, 7345, 13600, 15605 and 17535 kHz. One hour later in winter.

Radio Bulgaria. Summers only at this time. The first half hour of a 90-minute program of *news*, interviews, reports and entertainment. Targeted at the Mideast on 13670, 17660 and 17830 kHz. One hour later during winter.

Radio Nederland. Repeat of the 0830 broadcast, except for the press review. Fifty-five minutes to East and Southeast Asia, winters on 7260 and 9860 kHz, summers on 12065 and 15470 kHz.

Radio Austria International. Monday through Saturday it's ● *Report from Austria* (see 0730), replaced Sunday by 30 minutes of entertainment in *Austrian Coffeetable*. Year-round to Australasia on 15450 and 21490 kHz, and winters only to Europe on 6155 and 13730 kHz.

United Arab Emirates Radio, Dubai. *News*, then a feature dealing with one or more aspects of Arab life and culture. Weekends, there are replies to listeners' letters. To Europe on 13675, 15320, 15395 and 21605 kHz.

11:00

■ **BBC World Service.** ● *Newsdesk*, followed 30 minutes later by the arts program *Meridian* (Wednesday, Friday and Saturday), *The Ken Bruce Show* (Sunday), *Composer of the Month* (Monday), *Megamix* (Tuesday), and ● drama (Thursday). Continuous to North America on 5965, 6195, 9515 and 15220 kHz; to Western Europe on 9750, 9760, 12095, 15070 and 17640 kHz; to the Mideast on 11760, 15575 and 21470 kHz; and to East Asia and Australasia on 9740 kHz.

World Service of the Christian Science Monitor, USA. See 0100 for program details. Audible Monday through Friday in North America on 9455 and 9495 kHz, in East Asia on 17555 kHz, and in Southeast Asia on 13625 kHz. Weekends are given over to programming of a religious nature.

Voice of Asia, Taiwan. One of the few stations to open with a feature: *Asian Culture* (Monday), *Touring Asia* (Tuesday), *World of Science* (Wednesday), *World Economy* (Thursday), and music on the remaining days. There is also a listener-response program on Saturday. After the feature there's a bulletin of news, and no matter what comes next, the broadcast always ends with *Let's Learn Chinese*. One hour to Southeast Asia on 7445 kHz.

Radio Australia. World and Australian *news*, then music, followed on the half-hour by a 30-minute feature. A popular choice with many listeners. Heard clearly in North America on 5995 and 9580 kHz; in East Asia on 6080, 9710, 13605

and 15170 kHz; and also audible in Europe and the Mideast on 21745 (or 21725) kHz.

Voice of Vietnam. Repeat of the 1000 transmission. To Asia on 7420 and 9730 kHz.

HCJB—Voice of the Andes, Ecuador. Twenty-five minutes of religious programming to Australasia on 9745 and 11925 kHz; also available on 17490 and 21455 kHz upper sideband.

Voice of America. The second, and final, hour of the morning broadcast to the Caribbean. *News*, followed Monday through Friday by ● *Focus* and *VOA Morning*. On Saturday there's *Agriculture Today* and *Music U.S.A.*, while Sunday features *Critic's Choice* and *Studio One*. On 6030 (or 15120), 9590 and 11915 kHz. For a separate service to Asia and Australasia, see the next item.

Voice of America. These programs are, in the main, different from those to the Caribbean. *News*, then Saturday it's *Agriculture Today* and ● *Press Conference U.S.A.*; Sunday there's ● *New Horizons* and ● *Issues in the News*; and weekdays have special features and *Music U.S.A.* To East Asia on 6110, 9760 and 15155 kHz, and to Australasia on 5985, 11720 and 15425 kHz.

Kol Israel. Winters only at this time. *News* from Israel Radio's domestic network, followed by various features (see 1000). A half-hour to Europe—sometimes heard in eastern North America—on 17545 kHz.

Radio Bulgaria. Summers only at this time. The final hour of a 90-minute compendium of *news* and entertainment, including some highly enjoyable Bulgarian folk tunes. To the Mideast on 13670, 17660 and 17830 kHz. Winters, does not start until 1130, when it can be heard on 11720, 13670, 17780 (or 17660) and 17825 (or 17830) kHz.

Radio Moscow World Service. Continuous programming to virtually all parts of the globe. Starts off with *News*, then Tuesday through Saturday, winters, it's the informative ● *Commonwealth Update*, replaced Sunday by *Culture and the Arts*, and Monday by *Science and Engineering*. Summers at this time, there's *News and Views*, with the second half-hour mostly given over to a variety of musical styles, including the top-rated ● *Folk Box* (Tuesday) and ● *Music at your Request* (Monday and Saturday). Winters at 1131, it's the literary ● *Audio Book Club* (alternating with *Russian by Radio* or a music program). Forty available channels (most of them from 11675 kHz onwards)—just tune around until you find one.

Swiss Radio International. See 0600 for specifics. Thirty minutes to Asia and Australasia on 13635, 15505, 17670 and 21820 kHz. For Europe, winters only, there is a separate 45-minute relay of SRI's satellite service (one hour earlier in summer) on 6165 and 9535 kHz.

Radio Japan. On weekdays, opens with *Radio Japan News-Round*, with news oriented to Japanese and Asian affairs. This is followed by *Radio Japan Magazine Hour*, which includes features like *Crosscurrents* (Monday), *Environment Update* (Tuesday) and *A Glimpse of Japan* (Friday). *Commentary* and *News* round off the hour. On Saturday, there's *This Week*, and Sunday features *News*, *Hello from Tokyo*, and *Viewpoint*. One hour to North America on 6120 kHz, and to East Asia on any two channels from 11815, 11840, 11910 and 15240 kHz. As we go to press, Radio Japan is implementing a number of changes to both its program and transmission schedules, so be prepared for some adjustments.

Radio For Peace International, Costa Rica. Part of an eight-hour cyclical block of counterculture and New Wave programming audible in North America on 7375, 7385 and 13630 kHz. Some transmissions are in the single-sideband mode, which can be properly processed only on some radios.

Radio Pyongyang, North Korea. Lots of propaganda in defense of the indefensible combined with patriotic songs by children's choirs puts this station in the basement of the world band quality ratings. However, when Kim Il has finally sung his last, there may be some interesting programs in store. Starts with *News*, then praises to "The Happiness of Living under a Great Leader," with suitable choral accompaniment (in Korean, thankfully). Currently a curiosity item, but may bear watching. Fifty minutes to North America on 6576, 9977 and 11335 kHz.

WJCR, Upton, Kentucky. Continues with gospel music to North America on 7490 and 13595 kHz. Other U.S. religious broadcasters operating at this hour include **WWCR** on 5935 (or 5920) and 7435 (or 15685) kHz, **KTBN** on 7510 kHz, **WYFR-Family Radio** on 5950 and 7355 (or 11830) kHz, and **WHRI-World Harvest Radio** on 7315 kHz.

11:30

Radio Finland. Monday through Friday, summers only at this time. *Compass North*, a half hour of features dealing almost exclusively with Nordic culture and events. To North America on 11900 and 15400 kHz.

Radio Korea, South Korea. Winters only at this time. See 1030 for program details. A half hour on 9700 kHz via their Canadian relay, so a good chance for North Americans to hear the station.

Radio Vlaanderen International, Belgium. Summer Sundays only at this time. *News*, followed by *P.O. Box 26* (a mailbag program) and *Music from Flanders*. Twenty-five minutes to North America on 15540 kHz, and to Southeast Asia on 17540 kHz. One hour later in winter.

Radio Nederland. Repeat of the 0730 broadcast, except that an additional *Press Review* is included. One hour to Europe on 5955 and 9650 (or 9860) kHz.

Radio Austria International. Summers only at this time. Monday through Saturday features ● *Report from Austria* (see 0730 for further details), replaced Sunday by *Austrian Coffeetable*, which consists of light chat and musical entertainment. Thirty minutes to Europe on 6155 and 13730 kHz, and to North America on 13730 kHz.

Radio Prague, Czech Republic. Winters only at this time. A potpourri of *news* and entertainment targeted at Europe, the Mideast and Africa on 6055, 7345, 9505, 11990 and 15355 kHz. One hour earlier in summer.

HCJB—Voice of the Andes, Ecuador. First 30 minutes of a four-and-a-half-hour block of religious programming to North America on 11925, 15115 and 17890 kHz; also widely heard on 17490 and 21455 kHz, upper sideband.

Radio Thailand. Starts off with *World News in Brief*. This is followed Monday through Friday by *Mail Box*, replaced weekends by *Happy Holiday*. At 1200 there is a major *newscast*. One hour targeted at Asian listeners, but also heard in parts of Australasia and North America on 4830 and 9655 kHz.

Voice of the Islamic Republic of Iran. Sixty minutes of *news*, commentary and features, much of it reflecting the Islamic point of view. Targeted at the Mideast and Asia on 9525, 9685 (winter), 11715 (summer), 11745 (winter), 11790, 11910 and 11930 kHz. May be broadcast one hour earlier in summer.

1200-1759
Western Australia & East Asia—Evening Prime Time
North America—Morning
Europe & Mideast—Afternoon and Early Evening

12:00

■ **BBC World Service.** Except for Sunday, the hour starts with *News* and the religious *Words of Faith*, then *Multitrack* (Tuesday, Thursday, Saturday), a quiz, or a special feature. *Sports Roundup* follows at 45 minutes past the hour. This time Sunday there's a *news summary* followed by
● *Play of the Week*—the best in radio theater. Continuous to North America on 5965 (winters), 6195, 9515, 9740 and 15220 kHz; to Europe on 9410 (winters), 9750, 9760, 12095, 15070, and 17640 kHz; to the Mideast on 11760, 15575 and 21470 kHz; and to East Asia and Australasia on 9740 kHz.

World Service of the Christian Science Monitor, USA. See 0000 for program details. Monday through Friday to North America on 9495 and 13760 kHz, to Australasia on 9425 or 15665 kHz, and audible in Southeast Asia on 13625 kHz. Weekends, the news-oriented fare gives way to religious programming.

Radio Canada International. Summers only at this time; see 1300 for program details. Monday through Friday to North America and the Caribbean on 11855 and 17820 kHz. One hour later in winter.

Radio Tashkent, Uzbekistan. *News* and commentary, followed by features such as *Life in the Village* (Wednesday), a listeners' request program (Monday), and local music (Thursday). Heard better in Asia, Australasia and Europe than in North America. Thirty minutes winters on 5945, 9540, 15470 and 17745 kHz; and summers on 7285, 9640, 9715, 15295 and 17815 kHz.

Polish Radio Warsaw, Poland. This time summers only. Fifty-five minutes of *news*, commentary, features and music—all with a Polish accent. To Europe on 6135, 7145, 9525 and 11815 kHz. One hour later in winter.

Radio Australia. ● *International Report*, followed 30 minutes later, Sunday through Thursday, by *Soundabout*—a program of contemporary popular music. On the remaining days, there is a special feature program. Although targeted elsewhere, is well heard in North America on 5995 and 9580 kHz, and often audible in Europe and the Mideast on 21745 (or 21725) kHz.

Croatian Radio. Summers only at this time; actually starts at 1203. Ten minutes of English *news* from one of the domestic networks. A valuable source of up-to-the-minute information from a region renowned for its volatility. Heard best in Europe at this hour. Channel usage varies, but try 5920, 9830 and 13830 kHz. One hour later in winter.

Radio Korea, South Korea. Repeat of the 0600 broadcast. Sixty minutes to East Asia on 9640 kHz.

HCJB—Voice of the Andes, Ecuador. Continuous religious programming to North America on 11925, 15115 and 17890 kHz, also heard on 17490 and 21455 kHz, upper sideband.

Radio Norway International. Sunday only. *Norway Now*, a well-packaged half hour of *news* and features targeted at Asia and Australasia on any two channels from 17740, 17860 and 21705 kHz.

Voice of America. *News*, followed Monday through Friday by *Newsline* and *Magazine Show*. End-of-week programming consists of features like Saturday's *Weekend Magazine* or Sunday's ● *Encounter* and *Studio One*. To East Asia on 6110, 9760 and 15155 kHz; and to Australasia on 15425 kHz.

China Radio International. *News* and various features—see 0000 for specifics, although programs are one day earlier. To eastern North America winters on 9655 kHz, and summers on 15210 kHz; to East Asia on 9715 and 11660 kHz; and to Australasia on 11795 and 15440 kHz.

Radio Bulgaria. Winters only at this time. See 1100 for specifics. The final hour of a 90-minute broadcast to the Mideast on 11720, 13670, 17780 (or 17660) and 17825 (or 17830) kHz. One hour later during summer.

Radio Nacional do Brasil (Radiobras), Brazil. Monday through Saturday, you can hear *Life in Brazil* or *Brazilian Panorama*, a potpourri of news, facts and figures about this South American giant, interspersed with examples of the country's various unique musical styles. The *Sunday Special*, on the other hand, is devoted to one particular theme, and often contains lots of exotic Brazilian music. Eighty minutes to North America on 15445 kHz.

Radio For Peace International, Costa Rica. Part of an eight-hour cyclical block of counter-culture and New Wave programming audible in North America on 7375 and 13630 kHz. Some transmissions are in the single-sideband mode, which can be properly processed only on some radios.

Radio Moscow International. Winters, it's *News and Views*, then twenty-five minutes of entertainment. Monday's ● *Music at your Request* and Tuesday's and Saturday's ● *Folk Box* alternate with *Kaleidoscope* (Sunday), *Jazz Show* (Thursday) and music on the remaining days. Tuesday through Saturday, summers, there's *Focus on Asia and the Pacific* followed by a summary of developments in the CIS and music of various styles. Best of the rest is ● *Music and Musicians* at 1311 Sunday. Continuous programming worldwide. Tune around from 11 MHz upwards and choose a channel, although the 7 and 9 MHz segments are likely to be best for East Asia during winter.

WJCR, Upton, Kentucky. Continues with gospel music to North America on 7490 and 13595 kHz. Other U.S. religious broadcasters operating at this hour include **WWCR** on 5935 (or 5920) and 15685 kHz, **KTBN** on 7510 kHz, **WYFR-Family Radio** on 5950, 6015 (or 7355) and 11830 kHz, and **WHRI-World Harvest Radio** on 7315 kHz.

12:15

Radio Cairo, Egypt. The start of a 75-minute package of news, religion, culture and entertainment. The initial quarter-hour consists of virtually anything, from quizzes to Islamic religious talks, then there's *news* and commentary, which in turn give way to political and cultural items. To Asia on 17595 kHz.

12:30

Radio France Internationale. *News*, which gives ample coverage of French politics and international events, usually followed by one or more short features such as *French Weeklies* and the weekend's sports results (Monday), *Land of France* (Tuesday), *Books* (Wednesday), *Arts in France* (Thursday), or *Science* (Saturday). A half hour to North America, usually received with a so-so signal on 15365 and 17575 (or 21645) kHz; and to Europe on 9805, 11670, 15155 and 15195 kHz.

Radio Bangladesh. *News*, followed by Islamic and general interest features, not to mention some very pleasant Bengali music. Thirty minutes to Europe (sometimes heard in North America) on 11708 (variable) and 13620 kHz.

Radio Canada International. *News*, followed Monday through Friday by *Spectrum*. *Innovation Canada* is on Saturday, and a listener-response program occupies Sunday's slot. Thirty minutes to East and Southeast Asia, winters on 6150 and 11730 kHz, and summers on 9660 and 15195 kHz.

Radio Nederland. Repeat of the 0830 broadcast, except for the press review. Fifty-five minutes to Europe on 5955 and 9650 (or 9860) kHz.

Radio Finland. Monday through Friday, although summer Saturdays there is a program in "Special Finnish" targeted at listeners who are learning the language. Apart from this exception, it's *Compass North*, a half hour of predominantly Nordic fare. Targeted at North America on 11735 (winter), 11900 (summer) and 15400 kHz.

Radio Austria International. Winters only at this time. Monday through Saturday features ● *Report from Austria* (see 0730 for further details), replaced Sunday by *Austrian Coffeetable*, which consists of light chat and musical entertainment. Thirty minutes to Europe on 6155 and 13730 kHz, to North America on 13730 kHz, and to East Asia on 15450 kHz.

Voice of Turkey. This time summers only. Thirty minutes of *news*, features and Turkish music targeted at the Mideast and Southwest Asia on 9675 kHz. One hour later in winter.

Radio Sweden. Summers only at this time. See 1500 for program details. To Asia and Australasia on 15240 and 21500 kHz. One hour later in winter.

Radio Vlaanderen International. Belgium. Winter Sundays only at this time. See 1130 for program details. Twenty-five minutes to North America on 15540 (or 21810) kHz, and to Southeast Asia on 17540 (or 17550) kHz. One hour earlier in summer.

13:00

■ **BBC World Service.** ● *Newshour*—60 minutes of incomparable news and in-depth analysis. To North America on 5965 (winters), 6195, 9515, 9740 or 15220 kHz. Continuous to Europe on 9410 (winters), 9750, 9760, 12095, 15070 and 17640 kHz; to the Mideast on 11760, 15575 and 21470 kHz; to East Asia on 7180, 9740 and 11820 kHz; and to Australasia on 9740 kHz.

World Service of the Christian Science Monitor, USA. See 0100 for program details. Monday through Friday to North America on 9495 and 13760 kHz, to Australasia on 9425 or 15665 kHz, and audible in Southeast Asia on 13625 kHz. Weekends are given over to religious offerings from and about the Christian Science Church.

Radio Canada International. Winter weekdays only. A shortened version of the Canadian Broadcasting Corporation's domestic *news* program ● *As It Happens*. Sixty minutes to North America and the Caribbean on 11855 and 17820 kHz. One hour earlier in summer. For an additional service, see next item.

Radio Canada International. Summers only at this time; see 1400 for program details. Sunday only to North America and the Caribbean on 11955 and 17820 kHz.

Radio Pyongyang, North Korea. Repeat of the 1100 transmission. To Europe on 9345 and 11740 kHz; and to North America and Asia on 9640 and 15230 kHz.

Swiss Radio International. See 0600 for specifics. Thirty minutes to Asia and Australasia on 7480, 11690, 13635, 15505, 17670 and 21820 kHz.

Radio Norway International. Sunday only. Repeat of the 1200 transmission. A half hour of *news* and features targeted at Europe on 9590 and 15230 (or 25730) kHz.

Radio Nacional do Brasil (Radiobras), Brazil. The final 20 minutes of the broadcast beamed to North America on 15445 kHz.

Radio Vlaanderen International, Belgium. Summers only at this time, Monday through Saturday. See 0630 for program details. Twenty-five minutes to North America on 15540 kHz, and to Southeast Asia on 17540 kHz. One hour later in winter.

China Radio International. See 0000 for program details, but one day earlier at this hour. To western North America summers on 11855 kHz, year-round to East Asia on 9715 and 11660 kHz, and to Australasia on 15440 kHz.

Polish Radio Warsaw, Poland. This time winters only. *News* and commentary, followed by a variety of features. Fifty-five minutes to Europe on 6135, 7145, 9525 and 11815 kHz. One hour earlier during summer.

Radio Cairo, Egypt. The final half-hour of the 1215 broadcast, consisting of listener participation programs, Arabic language lessons and a summary of the latest news. To Asia on 17595 kHz.

Radio Finland. Sunday, summers only at this time. Thirty minutes of *Good Morning* to North America on 11900 and 15400 kHz. One hour later in winter.

Radio Korea, South Korea. Repeat of the 0600 broadcast. Sixty minutes to Southeast Asia (also audible in Australia) on 9570 and 13670 kHz.

Radio Romania International. First daily broadcast for European listeners. *News*, commentary, press review and features about Romanian life and culture. Choose from 9590, 11940, 15365, 17720 and 17850 kHz.

Croatian Radio. Winters only at this time; actually starts at 1303. Ten minutes of on-the-spot *news* from one of Europe's political volcanoes. Best heard in Europe at this hour; frequency usage varies, but try 5020, 5085, 5920, 6145, 6210, 9830 or 13830 kHz. One hour earlier during summer.

Radio Australia. World and Australian *news*, followed by *Sports Report* and a half-hour of music. Beamed elsewhere, but tends to be easily audible in much of North America on 5995 and 9580 kHz.

Radio For Peace International, Costa Rica. Most days, starts off with United Nations features, with the remainder of the time being given over to counterculture or New Wave programming. Audible in North America on 7375 and 13630 kHz. Some transmissions are in the single-sideband mode, which can be properly processed only on some radios.

Kol Israel. Sunday through Thursday, summers only at this time. World and Israeli *news*, then one or more features —*Israel Sound* (Sunday), *Calling All Listeners* and *DX Corner* (Monday), *Israel Mosaic* and *New from Israel* (Tuesday), *This Land*, *Environment and Ecology*, and *New from Israel* (Wednesday), and *Jewish News Review* (Thursday). Twenty-five minutes targeted at Europe and eastern North America on 11587, 11605, 15640 and 17575 kHz; and to Southeast Asia and Australasia on 15650 kHz.

WJCR, Upton, Kentucky. Continues with gospel music to North America on 7490 and 13595 kHz. Other U.S. religious broadcasters operating at this hour include **WWCR** on 13845 and 15685 kHz, **KTBN** 7510 kHz, **WYFR-Family Radio** on 5950, 6015 (or 9705) and 11830 kHz, and **WHRI-World Harvest Radio** on 9465 and 11790 kHz.

Radio Moscow World Service. *News*, then very much a mixed bag, depending on the day and season. Winter programming includes *Focus on Asia and the Pacific* (Tuesday through Saturday) and Sunday's ● *Music and Musicians*, both of which start at 1311. At the same time summer there's the business feature *Newmarket* (Tuesday and Saturday), *Culture and the Arts* (Thursday), *Science and Engineering* (Sunday), and a listener-response program on the remaining days. ● *Audio Book Club* (Monday, Thursday and Saturday) is the obvious choice from 1330 onwards. Continuous to virtually everywhere, though eastern North America may be something of a black spot, especially in winter (try the 15 and 17 MHz bands in summer). Tune around and find a channel that suits you. Listeners in East Asia should try the 7 and 9 MHz segments

during winter, otherwise the best place to look is in the 11, 13, 15, 17 and 21 MHz segments of the spectrum.

HCJB—Voice of the Andes, Ecuador. Sixty minutes of religious broadcasting. Continuous to North America on 11925, 15115 and 17890 kHz; plus 17490 and 21455 kHz, upper sideband.

Voice of America. *News*, followed by ● *Focus* (weekdays), ● *On the Line* (Saturday) and *Critic's Choice* (Sunday). The second half-hour has features in Special English. To East Asia on 9760 and 15155 kHz; and to Australasia on 15425 kHz.

13:30

United Arab Emirates Radio, Dubai. *News*, then a feature devoted to Arab and Islamic history and culture. Twenty-five minutes to Europe on 13675, 15320, 15395, and 21605 kHz.

Radio Austria International. Monday through Saturday features ● *Report from Austria* (see 0730 for more details). This is replaced Sunday by *Austrian Coffeetable*, a half hour of music and light chat. To East Asia on 15450 kHz.

Voice of Turkey. This time winters only. A reduced version of the normal 50-minute broadcast (see 2000). A half-hour of *news* and features targeted at the Mideast and Southwest Asia on 9675 kHz. One hour earlier in summer.

Radio Finland. Monday through Friday, winters; daily in summer. Most days it's *Compass North*, a half hour potpourri of Finnish and other Nordic topics, except for summer Sundays, when you can hear *Focus* and *Nuntii Latini*, a news bulletin in Latin. To North America on 11900 (17740, winter) and 15400 kHz.

Radio Canada International. *News*, followed Monday through Friday by *Spectrum*, Saturday by *Innovation Canada*, and Sunday by *Arts in Canada*. Targeted at East Asia, winters on 6150 kHz, and summers on 11795 kHz. Also to Europe, summers only, on 11935, 15315, 15325, 17895, 21455 and 21710 kHz. The frequencies of 17820, 17895 and 21710 kHz are not available on Sunday.

Radio Nederland. Basically a repeat of the 0730 broadcast, except that *No Boundaries* replaces Tuesday's *Mirror Images*. Beamed to South Asia (and heard well beyond) on 9890 (or 9895), 13700 (or 13770) and 17610 kHz.

Radio Sweden. Winters only at this time; see 1500 for program details. To Asia and Australasia on 15240 and 21500 (or 21625) kHz. One hour earlier in summer.

Radio Tashkent, Uzbekistan. *News* and commentary, then features. Look for an information and music program on Tuesdays, with more music on Sundays. Apart from Wednesday's *Business Club*, most other features are broadcast on a non-weekly basis. Heard in Asia, Australasia, Europe and occasionally in North America; winters on 5945, 9540, 15470 and 17745 kHz; and summers on 7285, 9640, 9715, 15295 and 17815 kHz.

13:45

Vatican Radio. Twenty minutes of religious and secular programming to Asia and Australasia on 15090 and 17525 kHz.

14:00

■ **BBC World Service.** Weekdays, it's *News*, followed by *Outlook*. On the half-hour you can hear ● *Off the Shelf*, readings from some of the best of world literature. The final 15 minutes are mainly devoted to cultural themes. Saturday features *Sportsworld* (winters from 1430), and Sunday is given over to a documentary or phone-in program, followed by ● *Anything Goes*. Continuous to North America on 6195 (till 1430), 9515, 15260 and 17840 kHz; to Europe on 9410 (winters), 9750, 9760, 12095, 15070 and 17640 kHz; and to the Mideast on 15575 and 21470 kHz.

■ **BBC World Service for East Asia.** Monday through Friday, the BBC World Service airs a special program for the eastern part of that continent—the highly informative *Dateline East Asia*. Thirty minutes on 7180, 9740 and 11820 kHz, with 9740 also audible in Australasia and western North America.

World Service of the Christian Science Monitor, USA. See 0000 for program details. Monday through Friday to Europe on 15665 or 17510 kHz, to western North America on 13760 kHz, and to East and Southeast Asia on 9530 and 13625 kHz. All weekend programs are nonsecular.

Radio Japan. *News* and various features. See 0300 for details. One hour to western North America on 9535 (or 11865) and 11735 kHz, and to East Asia on 9750 and 11815 kHz. As we go to press, this station is implementing a number of changes to both its program and transmission schedules, so be prepared for some adjustments.

Radio France Internationale. *News*, press review and a variety of short features, including *Club 9516* (Sunday), *North/South* or *Look East* (Monday), *Land of France* (Tuesday), *Press on Asia* (Thursday) and *Made in France* (Friday). Fifty-five minutes to Southeast Asia and Australasia on 11910, 17650 and 15405 (or 17695) kHz.

Radio Moscow World Service. Winters, it's *News* and a variety of features (see 1300 summer programs), followed on the half-hour by ● *Audio Book Club* (Monday, Thursday and Saturday), *Russian by Radio* or a music program. Summer offerings include the daily *News and Views* followed by some of Radio Moscow's better entertainment features. Check out Monday's ● *Folk Box* and Friday's ● *Music at your Request*, both of which should please. For different tastes, there's also *Jazz Show* (Wednesday), *Yours for the Asking* (Thursday) and *Kaleidoscope* (Saturday). Continuous worldwide. Best channels are in the 11, 13, 15 and 17 MHz segments of the spectrum, except for East Asia winters, when 7 and 9 MHz frequencies are likely to be more suitable.

Radio Korea, South Korea. Repeat of the 0600 broadcast. Sixty minutes to East Asia on 5975 and 6135 kHz.

Radio Finland. Winter Sundays only at this time; thirty minutes of *Good Morning*. Targeted at North America on 15400 and 17740 kHz. One hour earlier in summer.

Radio Australia. ● *International Report*, followed Monday through Friday by *Stock Exchange Report* and, on the half-hour, special feature programs. Audible in much of North America on 5995 and 9580 kHz, despite being targeted elsewhere.

China Radio International. See 0000 for program details, but one day earlier at this hour. To western North America winters on 7405 kHz, and summers on 11855 kHz.

Radio Vlaanderen International, Belgium. Monday through Saturday, winters only, at this time. See 0630 for program details, including *News* and *Press Review*, followed by features such as *Belgium Today*, *Focus on Europe* and *Around the Arts*. Twenty-five minutes to North America on 15540 (or 21810) kHz, and to Southeast Asia on 17540 (or 17550) kHz.

Radio Canada International. *News* and the Canadian Broadcasting Corporation's popular ● *Sunday Morning*. A three-hour broadcast starting at 1400 winters, and 1300 summers. Sunday only to North America and the Caribbean on 11955 and 17820 kHz.

HCJB—Voice of the Andes, Ecuador. Another hour of religious fare to North America on 11925, 15115 (till 1430) and 17890 kHz. Also available in the upper sideband mode on 17490 and 21455 kHz.

Kol Israel. Sunday through Thursday, winters only at this time; see 1300 for specifics. Twenty-five minutes to Europe and eastern North America on 11587, 11605, 15640 and 17575 kHz; and to Southeast Asia and Australia on 15650 kHz.

Radio For Peace International, Costa Rica. Continues with counterculture programming to North America on 7375 and 13630 kHz. Some transmissions are in the single-sideband mode, which can be properly processed on only some radios.

Voice of America. *News*, followed weekdays by *Asia Report*. On Saturday there's jazz, and Sunday is given over to classical music. At 1455, there's a daily editorial. To East Asia on 9760 and 15160 kHz; and to Australasia on 15425 kHz.

WJCR, Upton, Kentucky. Continues with gospel music to North America on 7490 and 13595 kHz. Other U.S. religious broadcasters operating at this hour include **WWCR** on 13845 and 15685 kHz, **KTBN** on 7510 kHz, **WYFR-**

Family Radio on 6015 (or 9705) and 11830 kHz, and **WHRI-World Harvest Radio** on 9465 and 15105 kHz.

CFRX-CFRB, Toronto, Canada. Audible throughout much of the northeastern United States and southeastern Canada during the hours of daylight with a modest, but clear, signal on 6070 kHz. With programs for an Ontario audience, this pleasant, friendly station carries news, sports, weather, traffic reports—and, at times, music. Arguably most interesting are talk-show discussions concerning such topics as the status of neighboring Quebec. Call in if you'd like at +1 (514) 790-0600—comments from outside Ontario are welcomed.

14:30

Radio Nederland. Basically a repeat of the 0830 transmission, except that the arts feature *Mirror Images* replaces *No Boundaries* on Tuesdays. Beamed to South Asia (and heard well beyond) on 9890 (or 9895), 13700 (or 13770), 15150 and 17610 kHz.

Radio Tirana, Albania. Summers only at this time. *News*, press review and interviews, with interludes of delightful Albanian music. Twenty-five minutes to Europe on 7155 and 9760 kHz. One hour later during winter.

Radio Canada International. This time winters only. *News,* followed Monday through Friday by *Spectrum,* Saturday by *Innovation Canada,* and Sunday by *Arts in Canada.* Thirty minutes to Europe on 9555, 11915, 11935, 15305, 15315, 15325 and 17820 kHz. The frequencies of 15315 and 17820 kHz are not available on Sunday. One hour earlier in summer.

Radio Romania International. Fifty-five minutes of *news,* commentary, features and some enjoyable Romanian folk music. Targeted at Asia on two or more frequencies from 11775, 11810, 15335 and 17720 kHz.

RDP International—Radio Portugal. Monday through Friday, summers only, at this time. See 1800 for program details. Thirty minutes to the Mideast and South Asia on 21515 kHz. One hour later during winter.

Radio Finland. Winters only at this time. Monday through Saturday you can hear *Compass North,* a compilation of *news* and human-interest stories from and about Finland. This is replaced Sunday by *Focus* and a bulletin of news in Latin, one of the curiosities of world band radio. Thirty minutes to North America on 15400 and 17740 kHz. One hour earlier in summer.

Radio Austria International. Summers only at this time. ● *Report from Austria;* see 0730 for more details. To Europe on 6155 and 13730 kHz; to East Asia on 15450 kHz; and to West Africa (also heard in parts of Europe) on 21490 kHz.

15:00

■ **BBC World Service.** *News,* followed Saturday by *Sportsworld* and Sunday by ● *Concert Hall* (or its substitute). Weekday programming includes a documentary feature (Monday), *A Jolly Good Show* (Tuesday), comedy (Wednesday) and classical music (Thursday and Friday). Continuous to North America on 9515, 9740, 15260 and 17840 kHz; to Europe on 6195, 9410, 12095, 15070 and 17640 kHz; to the Mideast on 12095, 15070 and 21470 kHz; and to East Asia on 7180 and 9740 kHz.

■ **BBC World Service for Africa.** Monday through Friday, starts at 1515 with *Focus on Africa,* a quarter-hour of up-to-the-minute reports from all over the continent. Extended to 30 minutes (from 1500) on weekends. Saturday, it's a half hour of *Spice Taxi,* replaced Sunday by *Postmark Africa* and five minutes of African news. Targeted at Africa, but heard well beyond, on 11860, 15420, 17790 and 21490 kHz.

World Service of the Christian Science Monitor, USA. See 0100 for program details. Monday through Friday to Europe on 15665 or 17510 kHz, to western North America on 13760 kHz, and to East and Southeast Asia on 9530 and 13625 kHz. Weekend programs are devoted to the beliefs and teachings of the Christian Science Church.

Radio Sweden. Summers only at this time. *News* and features (sometimes on controversial subjects not often discussed on radio), with the accent strongly on Scandinavia. Thirty minutes to North America on 15240 and 21500 kHz, and to the Mideast on 15190 (or 15270) kHz. One hour later during winter.

Polish Radio Warsaw, Poland. This time summers only. *News,* commentary and features covering everything from politics to culture. Fifty-five minutes to Europe on 7285, 9525 and 11840 kHz. One hour later in winter.

China Radio International. See 0000 for program details, but one day earlier at this hour. To western North America winters on 7405 kHz. One hour earlier during summer.

Swiss Radio International. See 0600 for specifics. Thirty minutes to the Mideast, Asia and Australia on 13635, 15505, 17670 and 21820 kHz.

Radio Pyongyang, North Korea. See 1100 for program details. Fifty minutes of sleep-inducing propaganda to Europe, the Mideast and beyond on 9325, 9640, 9977 and 13785 kHz.

Radio Canada International. Continuation of the CBC domestic program ● *Sunday Morning.* Sunday only to North America and the Caribbean on 11955 and 17820 kHz.

■ **Deutsche Welle,** Germany. *News,* followed Monday through Friday by ● *Newsline Cologne, African News* and a feature. Weekends, the news is followed by *Development Forum* and *Science and Technology* (Saturday), and *Religion and Society* and *Through German Eyes* (Sunday).

A 50-minute broadcast aimed primarily at Africa on 9735, 11965, 13610 and 17765 kHz; but also available to the Mideast on 17735 kHz.

Radio Moscow World Service. Predominantly news-related fare for the first half-hour, then a mixed bag, depending on the day and season. Best pickings are at 1531 winter, including ● *Folk Box* (Monday), *Jazz Show* (Wednesday), ● *Music at your Request* (Friday) and *Kaleidoscope* (Saturday). Summers, try *Culture and the Arts* at 1611 Monday. Continuous to most areas, and audible on over 40 channels—try from 11670 kHz upwards, except for East Asia winters, when the 7 and 9 MHz segments are likely to provide better quality reception.

WJCR, Upton, Kentucky. Continues with gospel music to North America on 7490 and 13595 kHz. Other U.S. religious broadcasters operating at this hour include **WWCR** on 13845 and 15685 kHz, **KTBN** on 7510 kHz, and **WYFR-Family Radio** on 11705 (or 15215) and 11830 kHz.

Radio For Peace International, Costa Rica. Continuous to North America with predominantly United Nations-produced programs during the second half-hour. Earlier, there's a mixed bag of mostly New Wave and counterculture features. Not for every taste, but one of the very few world band stations to provide this type of programming. Audible in North America on 7375, 13630 and 15030 kHz. Some transmissions are in the single-sideband mode, which can be properly processed only on some radios.

Radio Jordan. A partial relay of the station's domestic broadcasts, beamed to Europe on 9560 kHz. Continuous till 1730, and one hour earlier in summer. Better heard in winters, so not exactly Amman for all seasons.

HCJB—Voice of the Andes, Ecuador. Continues with religious programming to North America on 11925 and 17890 kHz; also widely heard elsewhere on 17490 and 21455 kHz.

CFRX-CFRB, Toronto, Canada. See 1400.

15:30

Radio Nederland. A repeat of the 0730 broadcast (except for Tuesday, when the arts program *Mirror Images* is replaced by *No Boundaries*. See 0030 for specifics, with all features one day earlier. Fifty-five minutes to South Asia on 9895 (or 15150), 13700 (or 13770) and 17610 kHz, and heard widely elsewhere.

Radio Austria International. ● *Report from Austria*, a half hour of news and human interest stories. Ample coverage of national and regional issues, and a valuable source of news about Central and Eastern Europe. Winters only to Europe on 6155, 9880 and 13730 kHz; and year-round to South and Southeast Asia on 11780 kHz.

Radio Finland. Summers only at this time.

Thirty minutes of most things Finnish in *Compass North*. Targeted at Europe on 6120, 11755 and 11820 kHz; and to the Mideast on 15240 and 21550 kHz.

Radio Tirana, Albania. Winters only at this time. *News*, press review and interviews, accompanied by some enjoyable Albanian music. Twenty-five minutes to Europe on 7155 and 9760 kHz. One hour earlier in summer.

RDP International—Radio Portugal. Monday through Friday, winters only, at this time. See 1800 for program details. Thirty minutes to the Mideast and South Asia on 21515 kHz. One hour earlier in summer.

16:00

■ **BBC World Service.** *News*, followed by *News about Britain*. Feature programs that follow include sports, drama, science or music. Particularly worthwhile are *Network UK* (Thursday), ● *Science in Action* (Friday) and *Megamix* (Tuesday), depending on what your taste is. Saturday sees a continuation of *Sportsworld*, and at 1645 Sunday there's Alistair Cooke's popular ● *Letter from America*. On weekdays at the same time you can hear a news analysis program, ● *The World Today*. Continuous to North America on 9515 and 15260 kHz; to Europe on 6195, 9410, 12095 and 15070 kHz; and to the Mideast on 9410, 9740, 12095 and 15070 kHz.

World Service of the Christian Science Monitor, USA. *News*, then ● *Monitor Radio*—news analysis and news-related features with emphasis on international developments. The first part of a two-hour cyclical broadcast repeated throughout the day to different parts of the world. Available Monday through Friday to parts of Europe and the Mideast (though not beamed there) on any two frequencies from 9355, 13625, 17510 and 21640 kHz; to East and Southeast Asia on 11580 and 13625 kHz; and to Australia and the Pacific on 9355 (or 11580) and 13625 kHz. Weekends at this and other times, this news-oriented programming is replaced by religious offerings from and about the Christian Science Church, not necessarily all in English.

Radio France Internationale. Begins with world and African *news*, followed by feature programs, including *Land of France* (Tuesday), *Arts in France* (Thursday), *Club 9516* (Sunday), *Counterpoint* (Wednesday), and *Spotlight on Africa* (Saturday). Fifty-five minutes (essentially to Africa, but also audible in parts of Europe and North America) on 6175, 11705, 12015, 15530, 17620, 17795 and 17850 kHz. 15530 kHz is also available for listeners in the Mideast.

Radio Sweden. Winters only at this time. See 1500 for specifics. Thirty minutes to North America on 15240 and 21500 kHz. One hour earlier in summer.

United Arab Emirates Radio, Dubai.

Trans World Radio's Caribbean facility prepares programs heard over world band station HCJB.

Starts with a feature on Arab history or culture, then music, and a bulletin of *news* at 1630. Answers listeners' letters at weekends. Forty minutes to Europe on 11795 (or 21605), 13675, 15320 and 15395 kHz.

Radio Korea, South Korea. See 0600 for program details. To East Asia on 5975 kHz.

Polish Radio Warsaw, Poland. Winters only at this time. Fifty-five minutes of *news*, commentary and features with a distinct Polish flavor. To Europe on 7285, 9525 and 11840 kHz. One hour earlier in summer.

Radio Pakistan. Fifteen minutes of *news* from the Pakistan Broadcasting Corporation's domestic service, followed by a similar period at dictation speed. Intended for the Mideast and Africa, but heard well beyond on several channels. Choose from 7290, 11570, 13685, 15555 and 17555 kHz.

Radio Norway International. Sunday only. *Norway Now*. Repeat of the 1200 transmission. Thirty minutes of Norwegian hospitality targeted at the Mideast and Africa on any two channels from 11875, 15230 and 17825 kHz.

Radio Moscow World Service. *News*, then very much a mixed bag, depending on the day and season. Winters, there's *Focus on Asia and the Pacific* (Tuesday through Saturday) and *Culture and the Arts* (Sunday), followed on the half-hour by the daily *Africa as we See It*. Pick of the summer programming is ● *Music and Musicians* (1611 Saturday) and ● *Audio Book Club* (1631 Monday and Friday). Other options (all at 1611) include *Science and Engineering* (Tuesday), *Culture and the Arts* (Wednesday and Saturday) and the business-oriented *Newmarket* (Monday and Friday). Continuous programming, heard on an ample range of frequencies. In Europe and the Mideast try the 7, 9 and 11 MHz segments in winter; 11, 15 and 17 MHz in summer. North Americans should dial around the 11, 15 and 17 MHz segments of the spectrum, although there isn't much beamed their way at this hour.

Radio Riyadh, Saudi Arabia. The first 60 minutes of a five-hour relay of domestic programming (intended for English-speaking people within Saudi Arabia). Starts off with readings from the Holy Koran followed by a program summary, which then gives way to a 10-minute Islamic feature. What comes next is very much a mixed bag, depending on the day of the week, and can include anything from Arab literature to western pop music. Targeted at Europe on 9705 kHz.

Radio Canada International. Winters only. Final hour of CBC's ● *Sunday Morning*; Sunday only to North America and the Caribbean on 11955 and 17820 kHz.

"Rush Limbaugh Show," WRNO, New Orleans, Louisiana. Summer weekdays only at this time. The first sixty minutes of a three-hour live package from the man who has done more than anyone else since Ronald Reagan to popularize Republican conservatism. Arguably of little interest to most listeners outside North America, except those who want an inside peek at part of the American psyche. However, it commands a substantial and influential following within the United States. *Footnote:* On this WRNO airing, which has no advertisers, you can sometimes hear Limbaugh doing ad spoofs and otherwise clowning around during the slots where the ads would normally appear. To North America, the Caribbean and beyond on 15420 kHz.

Voice of America. *News*, followed Monday through Friday by *Africa World Tonight*, and replaced weekends by *Nightline Africa*—special news and features on African affairs. Heard beyond Africa—including North America—on a number of frequencies, including 11995, 13710, 15445 and 17895 kHz.

WJCR, Upton, Kentucky. Continues with gospel music to North America on 7490 and 13595 kHz. Other U.S. religious broadcasters operating at this hour include **WWCR** on 13845 and 17535 kHz, **KTBN** on 15590 kHz, and **WYFR-Family Radio** on 11705 (or 15215) and 11830 kHz.

CFRX-CFRB, Toronto, Canada. See 1400.

16:15

Radio Sweden. Summers only at this time. See 1500 for specifics. Thirty minutes to Europe on 6065 kHz. One hour later in winter.

16:30

HCJB—Voice of the Andes, Ecuador. The first half hour of a 90-minute broadcast to the Mideast. Monday through Friday, it's *Studio 9* (see 0030, except that all features are one day earlier), replaced weekends by religious programming. On 15270 (or 21480) and 17790 kHz; plus 17490 and 21455 kHz upper sideband.

Radio Finland. Winters only at this time. See 1530 for specifics. Thirty minutes of Finnish *news* and culture targeted at Europe on 6120, 9730 and 11755 kHz; and to the Mideast on 15440 and 17825 kHz. One hour earlier in summer.

17:00

■ **BBC World Service.** *News*, followed Sunday through Friday by ● *World Business Report/Review*, then a quiz show, drama, music, sports or religion. Thursday's ● *Thirty-Minute Drama* is undoubtedly the pick of the litter. There is a daily summary of world sporting news at 1745, in *Sports Roundup*. Until 1745 to North America on 9515 and 15260 kHz. Continuous to Western Europe on 6195, 9410, 12095 and 15070 kHz; and to the Mideast on 9410, 9740, 12095 and 15070 kHz.

■ **BBC World Service for Africa.** Forty-five minutes of alternative programming for and about the African continent. A bulletin of world *news* is followed by *Focus on Africa* (see 1500), with five minutes of African *news* closing the broadcast. Targeted at Africa on 3255, 6005, 6190, 9630, 15400, 15420, 17860 and 17880 kHz, but heard well beyond (especially on the higher frequencies).

■ **BBC World Service for South Asia.** *South Asia Report*, 15 minutes of in-depth analysis of political and other developments in the region. Targeted at South Asia, and audible beyond, on 5975, 7105 (or 7215), 9605 and 11705 kHz.

World Service of the Christian Science Monitor, USA. The second half of the 1600 broadcast. *News* and continuation of ● *Monitor Radio*. The final 15 minutes consist of a listener-response program and a religious article from the *Christian Science Monitor* newspaper. Available Monday through Friday to parts of Europe and the Mideast (though not beamed there) on any two channels from 9355, 13625, 17510 and 21640 kHz; and to East and Southeast Asia on 11580 and 13625 kHz. Listeners in Australia and the Pacific can try 9355 (or 11580) and 13625 kHz. Weekend programming at this and other times is of a religious nature, and may be in languages other than English.

Radio Pakistan. Opens with 15 minutes of *news* and commentary. The remainder of the broadcast is taken up by a repeat of the features from the 0800 transmission (see there for specifics). Fifty minutes to Europe on 9530 (or 15550) and 11570 kHz.

Radio Prague, Czech Republic. Summers only at this time. *News*, then a variety of short features with a distinctly Czech slant. Thirty pleasant minutes to Europe and beyond on 6055,

7345, 9490, 13600 and 15605 kHz. One hour later in winter.

Swiss Radio International. See 0500 for specifics. Thirty minutes to the Mideast on 9885, 13635, 15430 and 17635 kHz.

Polish Radio Warsaw, Poland. This time summers only. *News* and commentary, followed by a variety of features from and about Poland. Fifty-five minutes to Europe on 7270 and 9525 kHz. One hour later during winter.

Radio Riyadh, Saudi Arabia. Continues with a relay of the domestic service for English-speaking residents. *K.S.A. Today* is featured Saturday through Tuesday, on or near the half-hour, and other offerings include *Arabian Dishes* (1740 Thursday), *Music Concert* (1730 Friday) and *World of Science* (1700 Saturday). Targeted at Europe on 9705 kHz.

Radio Moscow World Service. The initial half-hour is taken up winters by *News* and features (see 1600 summer programs); summers by *News and Views*. Pick of the final 30 minutes include ● *Audio Book Club* (Monday and Friday, winter), and the summer offerings ● *Music at your Request* (Thursday) and ● *Folk Box* (Friday). In Europe, try the 7, 9 and 11 MHz segments in winter, and 11, 15 and 17 MHz in summer. For North America, best bets are in the 11, 15 and 17 MHz segments, especially in summer. Dial around to find the channel that best suits your location.

Radio Nederland staff meets to prepare programs.

Radio Almaty, Kazakhstan. Summers only at this time. See 1800 for further details. One hour later during winter.

Radio For Peace International, Costa Rica. The first daily edition of *FIRE* (Feminist International Radio Endeavor), and the start of the English portion of an eight-hour cyclical block of predominantly counterculture and New Wave programming. Audible in North America on 7375, 13630 and 15030 kHz. Some transmissions are in the single-sideband mode, which can be properly processed only on some radios.

Radio Norway International. Sunday only. *Norway Now.* Repeat of the 1200 broadcast. Thirty minutes to Europe on 9655 kHz.

HCJB—Voice of the Andes, Ecuador. The final hour of programming targeted at the Mideast. Monday through Friday, it's the second half of *Studio 9,* followed by 30 minutes of religious fare. Weekends, there's religious programming, some of it in Arabic. On 15270 (or 21480) and 17790 kHz, as well as 17490 and 21455 kHz in the upper sideband mode.

Radio Pyongyang, North Korea. See 1100 for program details. Fifty minutes of monolithic mediocrity to Europe, the Mideast and beyond on 9325, 9640, 9977 and 13785 kHz.

Voice of America. *News,* then *Newsline* (Monday through Saturday, replaced Sunday by *Critic's Choice*). Weekdays on the half-hour there's *Music U.S.A.*; Saturday features *Weekend Magazine*; and Sunday brings ● *Issues in the News.* To Europe on 6040, 9760 and 15205 kHz; and to the Mideast on 9700 kHz. For a separate service to Africa, see the next item.

Voice of America. Programs for Africa. Weekdays, identical to the service for Europe and the Mideast (see previous item), but at 1733 Saturday there's *Nightbeat Africa,* with Sunday's broadcast consisting of *Voices of Africa* and (at 1733) the lively ● *Music Time in Africa.* Audible in many parts of the world on 11995, 13710 and 15445 kHz.

"Rush Limbaugh Show," WRNO, New Orleans, Louisiana. Monday through Friday only; see 1600 for specifics. Starts at this time winters;

summers, it's already into the second hour. Continuous to North America, the Caribbean and beyond on 15420 kHz.

Kol Israel. Summers only at this time. *News* from Israel Radio's domestic network. Fifteen minutes to Western Europe on 11587 and 15640 kHz, the latter frequency also audible in parts of eastern North America.

WJCR, Upton, Kentucky. Continues with gospel music to North America on 7490 and 13595 kHz. Other U.S. religious broadcasters operating at this hour include **WWCR** on 13845 and 15685 kHz, **KTBN** on 15590 kHz, and **WHRI-World Harvest Radio** on 9590 and 13760 and 15105 kHz.

CFRX-CFRB, Toronto, Canada. See 1400.

17:15

Radio Sweden. Winters only at this time. See 1500 for specifics. Thirty minutes to Europe on 6065 kHz. One hour earlier in summer.

17:30

Radio Nederland. Targeted at Africa, but well heard in parts of North America. *News,* followed Monday through Saturday by *Newsline* and a feature. Monday's science program ● *Research File* is undoubtedly the pick of the week, but there is other interesting fare on offer—try Tuesday's documentary features, some of which are excellent. Other programs include *No Boundaries* (Tuesday), *Media Network* (Thursday), *Towards 2000* (Friday), *Airtime Africa* (Saturday), and Sunday's *Happy Station.* Monday through Saturday there is also a *Press Review.* One hour for Africa on 6020, 7120 (or 9605), 21515 and 21590 kHz. The last two frequencies are best for North America.

Radio Sweden. Summers only at this time. See 1500 for specifics. Thirty minutes to Europe and the Mideast on 6065, 9655 and 15270 kHz. One hour later in winter.

Radio Bulgaria. Summers only at this time. The first half-hour of a 90-minute look at the multiple facets of Bulgarian life and culture. Features some lively Bulgarian folk music. To Europe on 11720 and 13670 kHz.

17:45

All India Radio. The first 15 minutes of a two-hour broadcast to Europe, the Mideast and Africa, consisting of regional and international *news,* commentary, a variety of talks and features, press review and enjoyably exotic Indian music. Continuous till 1945. To Europe on 7412 and 11620 kHz; and on 9950, 11860, 11935 and 15080 to the remaining areas.

1800-2359
Europe & Mideast—Evening Prime Time
East Asia—Early Morning
Australasia—Morning
Eastern North America—Afternoon
Western North America—Midday

18:00

■ **BBC World Service.** Thirty minutes of
● *Newsdesk*, followed most days by pop music.
Notable exceptions are the quality science program ● *Discovery* (Tuesday), the consistently
informative ● *Focus on Faith* (Thursday), and
Saturday's *From Our Own Correspondent*. Continuous to Western Europe on 6195, 9410, 12095
and 15070 kHz; to the Mideast on 7160 (till
1730), 9410, 9740, 12095 and 15070 kHz; and
to Australasia on 11955 kHz.

**World Service of the Christian Science
Monitor,** USA. See 1600 for program details.
Monday through Friday to Europe and the Mid-
east on 9355 or 15665 kHz, to eastern North
America and Europe on 15665 or 17510 kHz, to
South Africa (and heard in parts of North America)
on 17612.5 or 21640 kHz, and to Oceania on
9430 or 13840 kHz. Weekends are given over to
Christian Science religious programming.

RDP International—Radio Portugal.
Monday through Friday, summers only, at this
time. *News*, followed by features: *Notebook on
Portugal* (Monday), *Musical Kaleidoscope* (Tuesday), *Challenge of the 90's* (Wednesday), *Spotlight on Portugal* (Thursday), and either *Mailbag*
or *DX Program* and *Collector's Corner* (Friday).
Thirty minutes to Europe on 9780 kHz. One hour
later in winter.

Radio Kuwait. The start of a three-hour
package of *news*, Islamic-oriented features and
western popular music. Worth a listen, even if you
don't particularly like the music. There is a full
program summary at the beginning of each transmission, to enable you to pick and choose. To
Europe and eastern North America on 13620 kHz.

Radio For Peace International, Costa Rica.
Continues to North America with mainly counterculture programming. Also heard outside North
America—try 7375, 13630 and 15030. Some
transmissions are in the single-sideband mode,
which can be properly processed only on some
radios.

Radio Riyadh, Saudi Arabia. Continues
with a relay of the domestic English service. A
mixed bag of features and music with a 15-minute
news bulletin at 1830. To Europe on 9705 kHz.

Radio Vlaanderen International, Belgium.
Summers only at this time. See 1900 for program
details. Twenty-five minutes to Europe on 5910
kHz, and to Africa and beyond (not necessarily

daily) on 13685 and 15540 kHz. One hour later
in winter.

All India Radio. Continuation of the transmission to Europe, the Mideast and beyond (see
1745). *News* and commentary, followed by programming of a more general nature. To Europe
on 7412 and 11620 kHz; and to the Mideast and
Africa on 9950, 11860, 11935 and 15080 kHz.

Radio Prague, Czech Republic. Winters
only at this time. *News* and features reflecting
Czech life and views. Thirty minutes to Europe on
5960 (or 7300), 6055, 7345 and 9490 kHz. One
hour earlier in summer.

Radio Almaty, Kazakhstan. Winters only at
this time. Thirty minutes of *news* and features,
consisting of a variety of topics, depending on
which day you listen. Offerings include programs
with an Islamic slant, readings from Kazakh literature, features on the country's history and
people, and a mailbag program. Saturdays and
Sundays are given over to recordings of the
country's music, ranging from rarely heard folk
songs to even rarer Kazakh opera. One of the
most exotic stations to be found on the world
bands, so give it a try. These broadcasts are not
targeted at any particular part of the world, since
the transmitters only use a modest 20 to 50 kilowatts, and the antennas are, in the main, omnidi-
rectional. No matter where you are, try 3955,
5035, 5260, 5960, 5970, 9505, 11825, 15215,
15250, 15270, 15315, 15360, 15385, 17605,
17715, 17730, 17765 and 21490 kHz. One hour
earlier in summer.

Radio Nacional do Brasil (Radiobras),
Brazil. A repeat of the 1200 broadcast. Eighty
minutes to Europe on 15265 kHz.

Polish Radio Warsaw, Poland. This time
winters only. *News*, commentary and features,
covering multiple aspects of Polish life and culture. Fifty-five minutes to Europe on 7270 and
9525 kHz. One hour earlier during summer.

Radio Moscow World Service. Predominantly news-related fare during the initial half-
hour, with *News and Views* the daily winter fare,
and ● *Commonwealth Update* on summer weekdays. At 1830 summers there's more of the same,
with the daily *Africa as we See It*, but winter
features are much more entertaining. Thursday
brings ● *Music at your Request*, Friday has the
eclectic and exotic ● *Folk Box*, and there's Russian jazz on Tuesday. Continuous to Europe on a
number of frequencies; winters, try the 6, 7 and 9

MHz bands, though summer channels are more likely to be found in the 9 and 11 MHz segments of the spectrum. In eastern North America winters, try the 9 and 11 MHz segments; while 15 and 17 MHz frequencies are likely to be best in summer.

Voice of America. *News,* followed by ● *Focus* (weekdays), *Newsline* and *Agriculture Today* (Saturday), and ● *Encounter* (Sunday). The second half-hour is devoted to news and features in "special English"—that is, simplified talk in the American language for those whose mother tongue is other than English. To Europe on 6040, 9760 and 15205 kHz; and to the Mideast on 9700 kHz. For a separate service to Africa, see the next item.

Voice of America. Identical to the above, except that *Africa World Tonight* replaces *Focus* at 1810 Monday through Friday. To Africa, but heard well beyond, on 11995, 13710, 15410, 15580 and 17800 kHz.

Radio Argentina al Exterior—R.A.E. Winters only at this time. See 1900 broadcast for program details. Fifty-five minutes to Europe on 15345 kHz.

Radio Bulgaria. Summers, from 1800; winters, from 1830. Part of a 90-minute transmission targeted at Europe, containing a mixture of news, features, interviews and music. Audible winters on 6235, 9560, 9700 and 11720 kHz; and summers on 11720 and 15330 kHz.

"Rush Limbaugh Show," WRNO, New Orleans, Louisiana. Monday through Friday only; see 1600 for specifics. Continuous to North America, the Caribbean and beyond on 15420 kHz.

Kol Israel. Winters only at this time. *News* from Israel Radio's domestic network. Fifteen minutes to Europe, often audible in eastern North America, on 7465 and 11587 kHz.

"For the People," WHRI, Noblesville, Indiana. Summer weekdays only; see 0200 for specifics. Two hours of live populist programming targeted at North America on 9590 (or 17830) kHz.

WJCR, Upton, Kentucky. Continues with gospel music to North America on 7490 and 13595 kHz. Other U.S. religious broadcasters operating at this time include **WWCR** on 13845 and 15685 kHz, **KTBN** on 15590 kHz, and **WHRI-World Harvest Radio** on 13760 kHz.

CFRX-CFRB, Toronto, Canada. See 1400.

18:30

Radio Nederland. Well heard in parts of North America, despite being targeted at Africa. *News,* followed Monday through Saturday by *Newsline* and a feature. These include the arts program *Mirror Images* (Tuesday), ● *Encore* (Wednesday), ● *Research File* (Thursday), *Airtime Africa* (Friday), *Sounds Interesting* (Saturday), and Sunday's *East of Edam.* One hour for Africa on 6020, 7120 (or 9605), 21515 and 21590 kHz. The last two frequencies, via the relay in the Netherlands Antilles, are best for North American listeners.

Radio Almaty, Kazakhstan. Summers only at this time. Repeat of the 1700 broadcast; see 1800 for more details. One hour later in winter.

Radio Austria International. Summers only at this time; the informative ● *Report from Austria.* A half hour to Europe, the Mideast and Africa on 5945, 6155, 9880 and 13730 kHz. One hour later during winter.

Radio Slovakia International. Summers only at this time. *News* and features dealing with multiple aspects of Slovak life and culture. Thirty minutes to Europe on 5915, 7345 and 9605 kHz. One hour later in winter.

Radio Sweden. Winters only at this time. See 1500 for specifics. Thirty minutes to Europe and the Mideast on 6065, 9655 and 15270 kHz. One hour earlier in summer.

Radio Yugoslavia. Summers only at this time. *News* and low-key reporting from one of Europe's hot spots. Thirty minutes to Europe on 6100 and 7200 kHz. One hour later during winter.

Radio Finland. Summers only at this time; see 1930 for specifics. Thirty minutes to Europe on 6120, 9730, 11755 and 15440 kHz.

■ **BBC World Service for Africa.** Monday through Friday it's *Focus on Africa* (see 1500), followed by a three-minute bulletin of African news. These are replaced Saturday by *Spice Taxi,* a somewhat offbeat look at African culture, with Sunday featuring the discussion program *African Perspective.* To the African continent (and heard elsewhere) on 6005, 6190, 9630 and 15400 kHz.

19:00

■ **BBC World Service.** Begins on weekdays with *News,* then the magazine program *Outlook.* These are followed by just about anything, depending on the day of the week, and include ● *Health Matters* (1945 Monday), *Development '93* (1930 Tuesday), and ● *Omnibus* (1930 Wednesday). For theater buffs, Sunday's ● *Play of the Week* is a listening "must" at 1901. Continuous to Europe on 3955 (winters), 6195 (not available at 1930-2000 Monday through Saturday, summers—see separate item), 9410 and 12095 kHz; to the Mideast on 7160, 9410, 9740, 12095 and 15070 kHz; and to Australasia on 11955 kHz.

World Service of the Christian Science Monitor, USA. See 1700 for program details. Monday through Friday to Europe and the Mideast on 9355 or 15665 kHz, to eastern North America and Europe on 15665 or 17510 kHz, to Africa (and audible in parts of North America) on 17612.5 or 21640 kHz, and to Australasia on 9430 or 13840 kHz. This news-oriented programming is replaced weekends by nonsecular offerings from and about Christian Scientists.

Radio Nacional do Brasil (Radiobras), Brazil. Final 20 minutes of the 1800 broadcast to Europe on 15265 kHz.

Radio Algiers, Algeria. Summers only at this time. *News*, then rock and popular music. There are occasional brief features, such as *Algiers in a Week*, which covers the main events in Algeria during the past seven days. One hour of so-so reception in Europe, where the broadcast is targeted, and occasionally audible in eastern North America. Scheduled on 7245 and 11715 kHz, and announced as being on 9535, 15205 and 17745 kHz, yet most recent observations place this station on 9535, 11715 and 17745 kHz. Other possible frequencies are 9509, 9640, 9685 and 15215 kHz, where Radio Algiers has sometimes been heard in the past. One hour later in winter.

Radio Vlaanderen International, Belgium. Winters only at this time. Weekdays, there's *News*, *Press Review* and *Belgium Today*, followed by features like *Focus on Europe* (Monday), *Around the Arts* (Tuesday and Friday), *Living in Belgium* (Wednesday) and *North-South* (Thursday). Weekends include features like *Radio World* (Saturday) and *Music from Flanders* (Sunday). Twenty-five minutes to Europe on 5900 (or 5910) kHz; also to Africa (and heard elsewhere) on 15540 kHz. One hour earlier in summer.

Radio Vilnius, Lithuania. Summers only at this time. A 30-minute window on Lithuanian life. To Europe on 9710 kHz. One hour later in winter.

Radio Kuwait. See 1800; continuous to Europe and eastern North America on 13620 kHz.

Radio Norway International. Sunday only. *Norway Now*. Repeat of the 1200 broadcast. Thirty minutes to Australasia (year-round) on 15335 or 17730 kHz; winters to Western Europe and West Africa on 15220 kHz; and summers to eastern North America on 15365 kHz.

Kol Israel. Summers only at this time. *News* and features, concentrating heavily on things Israeli. The week begins with *This Land* and *DX Corner*, then *Environment and Ecology* and *Business Update* (Monday), *Israel Mosaic* and *New from Israel* (Tuesday), *Jewish News Review* (Wednesday), *Studio Three* and *Postmark* (Thursday), *Letter from Jerusalem* and *Thank Goodness It's Friday* (on the day of the same name), and *Spotlight* (issues in the news, Saturday). A half-hour to Europe—also audible in eastern North America—on 11587, 11605, 15640 and 17575 kHz. Winters, is one hour later.

All India Radio. The final 45 minutes of a two-hour broadcast to Europe, the Mideast and Africa (see 1745). Starts off with *news*, then continues with a mixed bag of features and Indian music. To Europe on 7412 and 11620; and to the Mideast and Africa on 9950, 11860, 11935 and 15080 kHz.

Radio Bulgaria. Winters only at this time. Final hour of a 90-minute broadcast (see 1800) beamed to Europe on 6035, 9560, 9700 and 11720 kHz.

Radio Riyadh, Saudi Arabia. Predominantly musical fare, with much of it originating from western countries. Continuous to Europe on 9705 kHz.

HCJB—Voice of the Andes, Ecuador. The first evening transmission for Europe. Repeat of the 1000 broadcast to Australasia. Monday through Friday there's *Studio 9*, replaced Saturday by *DX Partyline* and Sunday by *Saludos Amigos*. Sixty minutes of popular programming on 15270 (or 21480) and 17790 kHz, plus 17490 and 21455 kHz upper sideband.

■ **Deutsche Welle,** Germany. Repeat of the 1500 broadcast. Fifty minutes to Africa and the Mideast, winters on 9765, 11765, 11785, 11905, 13790, 15350 and 17810 kHz; and summers on 9640, 11740, 11785, 11810, 13690, 13790, 15350, 15390 and 17765 kHz.

Radio Romania International. *News*, commentary, press review and features, including *Tourist News* and *Romanian Hits* (Monday), *Romanian Musicians* (Wednesday), *Listeners' Letterbox* and ● *Skylark* (Thursday), *Pages of Romanian Literature* (Saturday) and *Sunday Studio* the following day. Sixty minutes to Europe; winters on 6105, 7195, 7225 and 9690 kHz; and summers on 7145, 9690, 9750 and 11940 kHz.

Radio Moscow World Service. *News*, followed winter weekdays by ● *Commonwealth Update*. This, in turn, gives way to the daily *Africa as we See It*. Summer programming consists of a thoroughly mixed bag of features, including *Culture and the Arts* (1911 Friday), *Yours for the Asking* (1931 Tuesday), jazz (1931 Monday and Friday), ● *Music at your Request* (1931 Wednesday), *Science and Engineering* (1911 Thursday), and last but by no means least, ● *Folk Box* (1931 Thursday). To Europe winters in the 7 and 9 MHz bands; summers in the 9 and 11 MHz segments. For eastern North America, try 7, 9 and 11 MHz channels in winter, and 15 and 17 MHz frequencies in summer.

Voice of Greece. Winters only at this time, and actually starts about three minutes into the broadcast, following some Greek announcements. Approximately ten minutes of *news* from and about Greece. To Europe on 7450 and 9375 kHz.

RDP International—Radio Portugal. Monday through Friday only. See 1800 for program details. Thirty minutes to Europe (winter) on 9780 kHz, one hour earlier in summer. The same program can be heard in summer at this time, when it is beamed to Africa (and often heard elsewhere) on 17900 kHz. During winter, the African broadcast is heard one hour later on 15250 or 17900 kHz.

Radio For Peace International, Costa Rica. Part of an eight-hour cyclical block of counterculture and New Wave programming audible in Europe and North America on 7375, 13630 and 15030 kHz. Some transmissions are in the single-sideband mode, which can be properly processed only on some radios.

Spanish Foreign Radio. *News*, followed by features and a limited amount of Spanish music; see 0000 for program details. To Africa, and heard well beyond, on 15375 kHz.

Voice of America. *News* and *Newsline*, except for Africa, Saturday, when *Voices of Africa* is aired. On the half-hour, for listeners in Europe and the Mideast, there's *Magazine Show* (Monday-Friday), ● *Press Conference U.S.A.* (Saturday), and Sunday's *Music U.S.A.* For the Pacific, *Music U.S.A.* occupies the weekday slot in place of *Magazine Show*, with weekend programming identical to that for Europe. Best served of all is Africa, with ● *World of Music* (weekdays), ● *Press Conference U.S.A.* (Saturday), and Sunday's ● *Music Time in Africa*. The European transmission is on 6040, 9760 and 15205 kHz (also available for the Mideast on 9700 kHz); the broadcast to the Pacific is on 9525, 11870 and 15180 kHz; and the African service (also heard in North America) goes out on 11995, 13710, 15410, 15495, 15580 and 17800 kHz.

"Rush Limbaugh Show," WRNO, New Orleans, Louisiana. See 1600 for specifics. Winters only at this time. The final sixty minutes from the man who has created the biggest Republican media event since the Ev and Charlie Show. To North America, the Caribbean and beyond on 15420 kHz.

Radio Argentina al Exterior—R.A.E. Monday through Friday only. Lots of mini-features dealing with Argentinian life and culture, interspersed with brief examples of the country's various musical styles, from chamamé to zamba. Fifty-five minutes to Europe on 15345 kHz. Broadcast an hour earlier during summer in Argentina (winter in the Northern Hemisphere).

"For the People," WHRI, Noblesville, Indiana. See 0200 for specifics. Monday through Friday only. Starts at this time winters, but is into the final sixty minutes, summers. A two-hour populist package broadcast live to North America on 9590 (or 17830) kHz.

WJCR, Upton, Kentucky. Continues with gospel music to North America on 7490 and 13595 kHz. Other U.S. religious broadcasters operating at this time include **WWCR** on 13845 and 15685 kHz, **KTBN** on 15590 kHz, and **WHRI-World Harvest Radio** on 13760 kHz.

CFRX-CFRB, Toronto, Canada. See 1400.

19:30

■ **BBC World Service for Europe.** Summers only at this time. *Europe Today*, 30 minutes of the latest news, comment and analysis. Sunday through Friday only, on 6180 and 6195 kHz. One hour later in winter.

■ **BBC World Service for Africa.** A series of features aimed at the African continent, but worth a listen if you live farther afield and have an interest in what's going on there. The list includes *Fast Track* (Sports, Monday), *Spice Taxi* (culture, Tuesday), *Talk about Africa* (discussion, Wednesday), ● *The Jive Zone* (music and musicians, Thursday), *African Perspective* (Saturday), and *Postmark Africa* (Sunday). Best heard where it is targeted, but often reaches well beyond. On 6005, 6190 and 15400 kHz.

Polish Radio Warsaw, Poland. Summers only at this time. Fifty-five minutes of *news*, commentary and features with a heavy Polish accent. To Europe on 6135, 7270, 7285 and 9525 kHz. One hour later during winter.

Radio Slovakia International. Winters only at this time. *News* and features with a strong Slovak accent. Thirty minutes to Europe on 5915, 7345 and 9605 kHz. One hour earlier in summer.

Voice of the Islamic Republic of Iran. Sixty minutes of *news*, commentary and features with a strong Islamic slant. Not the lightest of programming fare, but reflects a point of view not often heard in western countries. To Europe on 9022 and 15260 kHz, and may be one hour earlier in summer.

Radio Yugoslavia. Winters only at this time; see 1930 for specifics. Thirty minutes to Europe on 6100 and 7200 kHz.

Radio Almaty, Kazakhstan. Winters only at

this time. Repeat of the 1800 broadcast, and on the same channels. One hour earlier in summer.

Radio Austria International. Winters only at this time. News and human-interest stories in ● *Report from Austria*. A half hour to Europe, the Mideast and Africa on 5945, 6155, 9880 and 13730 kHz. One hour earlier in winter.

Radio Nederland. Repeat of the 1730 transmission, less the press review. Fifty-five minutes to Africa, and heard well in parts of North America, on 17605 and 21590 kHz.

Radio Finland. Winters only at this time. Sunday through Friday, it's *Compass North*, from and predominantly about Finland. This is replaced Saturday by *Focus* and the scholarly curiosity of the international airwaves, *Nuntii Latini*, a bulletin of news in Latin. Thirty minutes to Europe on 6120, 9730 and 11755 kHz. One hour earlier in summer.

Radio Roma, Italy. Actually starts at 1935. Approximately 12 minutes of *news*, then music. Twenty minutes of sleep inducement targeted at unfortunate West European listeners on 7275, 9710 and 11800 kHz.

20:00

■ **BBC World Service.** *News*, then the religious *Words of Faith*. At 2015 Monday through Friday it's news analysis in *The World Today*. This is replaced Saturday by *Personal View*, while Sunday's offering is *Folk Routes*. These are followed by a quiz or feature program, and include *Meridian* (Tuesday, Thursday, Saturday), *The Vintage Chart Show* (Monday), ● *Assignment* (Wednesday), and ● *Science in Action* (Friday). Continuous to Europe on 3955 (winters only), 6180, 6195, 7325, 9410 and 12095 kHz (3955 and 6195 kHz are not available at 2030-2100 Sunday through Friday, winters); to the Mideast till 2030 on 7160, 9410, 9740, 12095 and 15070 kHz; and to Australasia on 11955 and 15340 kHz. Listeners in eastern North America can try 5975 and 15260 kHz.

World Service of the Christian Science Monitor, USA. See 1600 for program details. Monday through Friday to Europe and the Mideast on 7510, 13770 or 15665 kHz; to eastern North America and Europe on any two frequencies from 7510, 13770, 15665 and 17510 kHz; to South America (and well heard in much of North America) on 17555 kHz; to East Asia on 9455 kHz, and to Australia and the Pacific on 9430 or 13840 kHz. Replaced weekends by programs devoted to the beliefs and teachings of the Christian Science Church.

Radio Habana Cuba. One hour of *news*, features and Latin music—much of it of the lively Cuban variety. An interesting guide to where the country is headed in these rapidly changing times. To Europe winters on 15165 kHz, and summers on 17760 kHz.

Radio Damascus, Syria. Actually starts at 2005. *News*, a daily press review, and different features for each day of the week. These include *Arab Profile* and *Palestine Talk* (Monday), *Syria and the World* (Tuesday), *Selected Readings* (Wednesday), *From the World Press* (Thursday), *Arab Newsweek* and *Cultural Magazine* (Friday), *Arab Civilization* (Saturday), and *From Our Literature* (Sunday). Most of the transmission, however, is given over to Syrian and some western popular music. One hour to Europe, often audible in eastern North America, on 12085 and 15095 kHz.

Radio Vilnius, Lithuania. Winters only at this time. *News* and features reflecting events in Lithuania. Thirty minutes to Europe on 9710 (or 6100) kHz. One hour earlier in summer.

Swiss Radio International. See 0500 for specifics. Thirty minutes to the Mideast and Africa on 9885, 12035, 13635 and 15505 kHz.

Radio Algiers, Algeria. Winters only at this time; see 1900 for more details. Sixty minutes to Europe on any two (sometimes three) frequencies from 7245, 9535, 11715 and 17745 kHz. Other occasional possibilities include 9509, 9685, 15205 and 15215 kHz. One hour earlier during summer.

Radio Moscow World Service. *News*, then summers it's more of the same in *News and Views*, replaced winter by general features. These include *Science and Engineering* (Thursday and Saturday), the business-oriented *Newmarket* (Wednesday and Sunday), and Friday's *Culture*

and the Arts. The second half-hour is given over to paid programming from the Aum Shinrikyo religious movement. To Europe, eastern North America and Australasia on more than twenty channels, most of them in the 7, 9 and 11 MHz segments in winter; and 9, 11, 15 and 17 MHz in summer.

Radio Kuwait. See 1800; the final hour to Europe and eastern North America on 13620 kHz.

Radio Bulgaria. This time summers only. Sixty minutes of *news* and entertainment, including lively Bulgarian folk rhythms. To Europe (but also heard elsewhere) on 11720 and 15330 kHz. One hour later in winter.

Voice of Greece. Summers only at this time and actually starts about three minutes into the broadcast, after a little bit of Greek. Approximately ten minutes of *news* from and about Greece. To Europe on 7450 and 9375 kHz.

China Radio International. *News*, then various feature programs; see 0000 for details, although all programs are one day earlier. To Europe on 6950 (or 11500) and 9920 kHz.

Radio Riyadh, Saudi Arabia. Regular features include five minutes of *news* at 2045, followed by *Today's Diary* and the Islamic *Gems of Guidance*. At 2015 Saturday through Wednesday there's either drama or a serial, replaced Thursday by jazz and Friday by western pop music. The final sixty minutes of a five-hour package of domestic programming relayed to Europe on 9705 kHz.

Voice of Turkey. Summers only at this time. *News*, followed by *Review of the Turkish Press*, then features on Turkish history, culture and international relations, interspersed with enjoyable selections of the country's popular and classical music. Fifty minutes to Western Europe on 9445 kHz. An hour later in winter.

Radio Pyongyang, North Korea. Repeat of the 1100 broadcast. To Europe, the Mideast and beyond on 6576, 9345, 9640 and 9977 kHz.

RDP International—Radio Portugal. Winters only at this time. *News*, followed by a feature about Portugal; see 1800 for more details. A half-hour to Africa Monday through Friday on 15250 or 17900 kHz, and often heard well beyond. One hour earlier in summer.

"For the People," WHRI, Noblesville, Indiana. Winter weekdays only; see 0200 for specifics. The final sixty minutes of a two-hour populist package broadcast live to North America on 9590 (or 17830) kHz.

Kol Israel. Winters only at this time. *News*, followed by various features (see 1900). A half-hour to Europe—often also audible in eastern North America—on 7465, 9435, 11587 and 11605 kHz.

Voice of America. *News*. Listeners in Europe can then hear ● *Music U.S.A. (Jazz)*—replaced Sunday by *The Concert Hall*—on 6040, 9760 and 15205 kHz (with 9700 kHz also available for the Mideast). For African listeners there is the weekday *Africa World Tonight*, replaced weekends by *Nightline Africa*, on 13710, 15410, 15495, 15580, 17800 and 21625 kHz. Both transmissions are also audible elsewhere, including parts of North America.

Radio For Peace International, Costa Rica. Continues with mostly counterculture programming to North America and Europe on 7375, 13630 and 15030 kHz. Some transmissions are in the single-sideband mode, which can be properly processed only on some radios.

WJCR, Upton, Kentucky. Continues with gospel music to North America on 7490 and 13595 kHz. Other U.S. religious broadcasters which operate at this time include **WWCR** on 13845 and 15685 kHz, **KTBN** on 15590 kHz, and **WHRI-World Harvest Radio** on 13760 kHz.

Radio Prague, Czech Republic. This time summers only. *News* and features concentrating heavily on Czech issues. Thirty full minutes to Europe on 6055, 7300, 7345, and 9490 kHz. One hour later in winter.

CFRX-CFRB, Toronto, Canada. See 1400.

20:30

■ **BBC World Service for Europe.** This time winters only. Thirty minutes of the latest news, comment and analysis in *Europe Today*. Heard Sunday through Friday on 3955, 6180 and 6195 kHz. One hour earlier in summer.

Radio Sweden. Summers only at this time. See 1500 for specifics. Thirty minutes of *news* and features, with the accent heavily on Scandinavia. To Europe on 6065 and 9655 kHz. One hour later in winter.

Radio Canada International. Summers only at this time; see 2130 for program details. Sixty minutes to Europe on 5995, 7235, 13650, 15325 and 17875 kHz; and to Africa on 13670, 17820 and 17850 kHz. Some of these are audible in parts of North America. One hour later during winter.

Polish Radio Warsaw, Poland. Winters only at this time. Fifty-five minutes of *news*, interviews and features with a distinct Polish flavor, providing a composite picture of Poland past and present. To Europe on 6135, 7270, 7285 and 9525 kHz. One hour earlier during summer.

Radio Korea, South Korea. See 1030 for program details. Thirty minutes to Europe on 6035 kHz, to the Mideast and Africa on 9870 kHz, and to Asia on 5975 and 9640 kHz.

Radio Roma, Italy. Actually starts at 2025. Twenty soporific minutes of *news* and music targeted at the Mideast on 7235, 9575 and 11800 kHz.

20:45

All India Radio. Press review, Indian music, regional and international *news*, commentary, and a variety of talks and features of general interest. Continuous till 2230; to Western Europe on 7412, 9950 and 11620 kHz; and to Australasia on 9910, 11715 and 15265 kHz.

21:00

■ **BBC World Service.** ● *Newshour*, the standard for all in-depth news shows from international broadcasters. Sixty minutes of excellence to Europe on 3955 (winters), 6180, 6195, 9410 and (summers) 12095 kHz; to East Asia on 7180 and 11955 kHz; and to Australasia on 11955 and 15340 kHz. In eastern North America try 5975 and 15260 kHz.

World Service of the Christian Science Monitor, USA. See 1700 for program details. Monday through Friday to Europe and the Mideast on 7510, 13770 or 15665 kHz; to eastern North America and Europe on any two frequencies from 7510, 13770, 15665 and 17510 kHz; to South America (and well heard in much of North America) on 17555 kHz; to East Asia on 9455 kHz, and to Australia and the Pacific on 9430 or 13840 kHz. Weekend programming is nonsecular, and mainly of interest to Christian Scientists.

Radio Yugoslavia. Summers only at this time. *News* and short features with a strong regional slant. A valuable source of news about the area. Thirty minutes to Europe on 6100, 7200 and 9505 kHz; with 9505 kHz also well heard in eastern North America. One hour later in winter.

Spanish Foreign Radio. Repeat of the 1900 broadcast (see 0000 for program specifics). One hour to Europe on 6125 kHz.

Radio Ukraine International. Summers only at this time. *News*, commentary, reports and interviews, covering virtually every aspect of Ukrainian life. Saturdays feature a listener-response program, and most of Sunday's broadcast is a showpiece for Ukrainian music. Don't miss it. Sixty minutes to Europe on 4825, 6090, 7150, 7240, 7340, 7285, 9600, 9640, 9685, 15135, 15195 and 17725 kHz. One hour later in winter.

Radio Vlaanderen International, Belgium. Summers only at this time. Repeat of the 1800 transmission; 25 minutes daily to Europe on 5910 and 9905 kHz. One hour later in winter.

Radio Prague, Czech Republic. *News*, then a variety of features dealing with Czech life and culture. Summer features may differ from those heard at the same time in winter. A half-hour to Europe on 5960 (or 7300), 6055, 7345 and 9490 kHz.

Radio Bulgaria. This time winters only. A 60-minute look at Bulgaria past and present, including some entertaining folk music. To Europe (but also heard elsewhere) on 6235 and 9560 kHz. One hour earlier in summer.

China Radio International. Repeat of the 2000 transmission; see 0000 for details, though programs are one day earlier at this time. To Europe on 6950 (or 11500) and 9920 kHz.

Croatian Radio. Summers only at this time; actually starts at 2103. Ten minutes of on-the-spot *news* from one of Europe's most volatile regions. Best heard in Europe and eastern North America at this hour. Channel usage varies, but try 5920, 9830 and 13830 kHz. One hour later during winter.

Radio Moscow World Service. Thirty minutes of *news* and comment—*News and Views* in winter, and *Focus on Asia and the Pacific* on summer weekdays. At 2131 winters, try ● *Folk Box* (Thursday), *Jazz Show* (Monday and Friday), or Wednesday's ● *Music at your Request*. At the same time summers, choices include *Culture and the Arts* (Tuesday), *Science and Engineering* (Friday) and a listener-response program (Wednesday and Thursday). Best of the pack, however, is ● *Music and Musicians* at 2111 Saturday. Continuous to Europe, North America, East Asia and the Pacific on a wide variety of frequencies. Winters, try the 6, 7, 9 and 11 MHz segments; 15 and 17 MHz are better bets in summer.

Radio Budapest, Hungary. Summers only at this time. *News*, followed by a variety of features, including *Newsroom Magazine* (four days a week) and *The Weeklies* (Sunday and Wednesday). A number of other features are aired on a regular basis, albeit in a somewhat haphazard fashion. Sixty minutes to Europe and the Mideast on 6110, 7220, 9835 and 11910 kHz. One hour later in winter.

Radio Norway International. Sunday only. *Norway Now*. Repeat of the 1200 transmission. A pleasant half hour of *news* and human-interest stories. Winters to Australasia on 15180 kHz, and summers to North America on 15165 kHz.

■ **Deutsche Welle,** Germany. *News*, followed Sunday through Thursday by ● *European Journal* and *Asia and Pacific Report*. The remaining days' programs include *Panorama* and *Economic Notebook* (Friday), and Saturday's *Mailbag Asia*. Fifty minutes to Asia and Australasia on 6185 (winter), 9670, 9765, 11785 and (summer) 13690 and 15360 kHz.

Radio Japan. Repeat of the 0300 transmission. An hour to Europe on 11925 kHz, and to East Asia and Australasia on 6035, 9750, 11815, 11840, 15430 and 17890 kHz. As we go to press, this station is implementing a number of changes to both its program and transmission schedules, so be prepared for some adjustments.

Radio Romania International. *News*, commentary and features (see 1900), interspersed with some thoroughly enjoyable Romanian folk music. One hour to Europe; winters on 5955, 6105, 7195, 7225 and 9690 kHz; summers on 5955, 7145, 9690, 9750 and 11940 kHz.

Radio For Peace International, Costa Rica. A mix of United Nations features, counterculture programs (such as *World Citizen's Hour*, Saturday) and New Wave music (*Sound Currents of the Earth*, Sunday). Continuous to North America and Europe on 7375, 13630 and 15030 kHz. Some transmissions are in the single-sideband mode, which can be properly processed only on some radios.

Voice of Turkey. Winters only at this time. See 2000 for program details. Some rather unusual programming and friendly presentation make this station worth a listen. To Western Europe on 9445 kHz. One hour earlier in summer.

Voice of America. *News*, followed Monday through Friday by *World Report* and weekends by a variety of features, depending on the area served. Pick of the litter is the science program ● *New Horizons* (Africa, Europe and the Mideast; 2110 Sunday). Other offerings include *VOA Pacific* (Australasia, same time Sunday), ● *Issues in the News* (Africa, 2130 Sunday), *Studio One* (Europe, also 2130 Sun) and *Weekend Magazine* (Europe, Mideast and Africa, 2130 Saturday). To Europe on 6040, 9760 and 15205 kHz; to the Mideast on 9700 kHz; to Africa, and often heard elsewhere, on 13710, 15410, 15495, 15580, 17800 and 21485 kHz; and to Southeast Asia and the Pacific on 11870, 15185 and 17735 kHz.

All India Radio. Continues to Europe on 7412, 9950 and 11620 kHz; and to Australasia on 9910, 11715 and 15265 kHz. Look for some authentic Indian music from 2115 onwards. Also audible in parts of eastern North America on 11620 kHz.

CFRX-CFRB, Toronto, Canada. See 1400. Summers at this time, you can hear ● *The World Today*, 90 minutes of news, interviews, sports and commentary. On 6070 kHz.

21:15

Radio Damascus, Syria. Actually starts at 2110. *News*, a daily press review, and a variety of features (depending on the day of the week). These include *Arab Profile* (Sunday), *Palestine Talk* (Monday), *Listeners Overseas* and *Selected Readings* (Wednesday), *Arab Women in Focus* (Thursday), *From Our Literature* (Friday), and *Human Rights* (Saturday). The transmission also contains Syrian and some western popular music. Sixty minutes to North America and Australasia on 12085 and 15095 kHz.

■ **BBC World Service for the Caribbean.**
● *Caribbean Report*, although intended for listeners in the area, can also be clearly heard throughout much of eastern North America. This brief, 15-minute program provides comprehensive coverage of Caribbean economic and political affairs, both within and outside the region. Monday through Friday only, on 6110, 15390 and 17715 kHz.

Radio Cairo, Egypt. The start of a 90-minute broadcast devoted to Arab and Egyptian life and culture. The initial quarter-hour of general programming is followed by *news*, commentary and political items. This in turn is followed by a cul-

tural program until 2215, when the station again reverts to more general fare. A Middle Eastern cocktail, including exotic Arab music, beamed to Europe on 9900 kHz.

WJCR, Upton, Kentucky. Continuous gospel music to North America on 7490 and 13595 kHz. Other U.S. religious broadcasters operating at this hour include **WWCR** on 13845 and 15685 and kHz, **KTBN** on 15590 kHz, and **WHRI-World Harvest Radio** on 13760 kHz.

21:30

BBC World Service for the Falkland Islands.
▲ *Calling the Falklands* is one of the curiosities of international broadcasting. Chatty and personal, there's no other program quite like it on the international airwaves. Fifteen minutes Tuesdays and Fridays on 13660 kHz—easily heard in North America.

Radio Vilnius, Lithuania. Summers only at this time. Repeat of the 1900 broadcast. Thirty minutes to Europe on 9710 kHz. One hour later in winter.

Radio Canada International. This time winters only. *News*, followed Monday through Friday by *Spectrum*, which is replaced Saturday by *Innovation Canada* and *Earth Watch*, and Sunday by *Arts in Canada* and a listener-response program. One hour to Europe on 5995, 7260, 11945, 13650 and 15325 kHz; and to Africa on 13670, 15140 and 17820 kHz. Some of these are also audible in parts of North America. One hour earlier in summer.

Radio Yugoslavia. Summers only at this time. Repeat of the 2100 broadcast. Thirty minutes to Europe on 6100 kHz, and to Australasia on 9720 kHz. One hour later in winter.

Kol Israel. Summers only at this time. Sunday through Thursday, a repeat of the 1300 broadcast. Friday, the *news* is followed by *Studio Three* and *Letter from Jerusalem* (arts in Israel); and Saturday, it's *Spotlight* (issues in the news). A half-hour beamed to Europe and eastern North America on 11587, 11605, 15640 and 15650 kHz. One hour later during winter.

Radio Tirana, Albania. Summers only at this time. The second, and final, transmission of the day for European listeners. Approximately 10 minutes of *news* from and about Albania. Try 9760 and 11825 kHz.

Radio Finland. Summers only at this time. See 2230 for program details. Thirty minutes to Europe on 6120 and 11755 kHz, and to East Asia on 15440 kHz.

HCJB—Voice of the Andes, Ecuador. Saturday brings *Musical Mailbag*, Sunday has ● *Blues, Rags and All That Jazz*, and the rest of the week is devoted to religious offerings. Thirty minutes to Europe on 15270 (or 21480) and 17790 kHz; also available on 17490 and 21455 kHz upper sideband.

Radio Austria International. Summers only at this time. Monday through Saturday it's the informative ● *Report from Austria*, replaced Sunday by light chat and musical entertainment in *Austrian Coffeetable*. A half hour to Europe and Africa on 5945, 6155, 9880 and 13730 kHz.

Radio Sweden. Thirty minutes of predominantly Scandinavian fare. To Europe on 6065 and (summers only) 9655 kHz.

21:45

Radio Bulgaria. Summers only at this time. The first quarter-hour of a 90-minute broadcast; see 2200 for specifics. To North America on 11720 and 15330 kHz.

Radio Korea, South Korea. See 0600 for program details. One hour to Europe on 6480 and 15575 kHz.

Radio Yerevan, Armenia. Summers only at this time. Mostly *news* about Armenia, except Sunday, when a cultural feature is broadcast. Mainly of interest to Armenians abroad. To Europe (and sometimes audible in eastern North America) on 9450 and 11920 kHz. One hour later in winter.

22:00

■ **BBC World Service.** *World News* and *News about Britain*, then a wide variety of programs, depending on the day of the week: *Sports International* (Wednesday), *Jazz for the Asking* (Saturday), *Network UK* (Thursday), ● *Short Story* and ● *Letter from America* (Sunday), ●*People and Politics* (Friday) and *Megamix* (Tuesday). The hour is rounded off with fifteen minutes of *Sports Roundup*. To eastern North America on 5975, 7325 (15070, summers), 9590 and 9915 kHz; to Europe on 6195 and 7325 kHz; to East Asia on 9570 and 11955 kHz; and to Australasia on 11955 and 15340 kHz.

World Service of the Christian Science Monitor, USA. See 1600 for program details. Monday through Friday to Europe on one or more frequencies from 7510, 13770 and 15665 kHz; to North America on 9465 and 17555 kHz; to East and Southeast Asia on 13625 and 15405 kHz; and to Australia and the Pacific on 13625 kHz. Weekend programming concentrates on Christian Science beliefs and teachings.

Radio Bulgaria. Summers, continuation of 2145 broadcast; winters, does not start until 2245. Ninety minutes of *news*, interviews and features, interspersed with lively Bulgarian folk music. To North America winters on 7225, 9700 and 11720 kHz; and summers on 11720 and 15330 kHz.

Radio Cairo, Egypt. The second half of a 90-minute broadcast to Europe on 9900 kHz; see 2115 for program details.

Radio Prague, Czech Republic. This time winters only. *News* and features making up a pleasant thirty minutes to Europe on 5960 (or 7300), 6055, 7345 and 9490 kHz. One hour earlier in summer.

Swiss Radio International. See 0500 for specifics. Thirty minutes to South America (also audible in eastern North America) on 5995 (or 6030), 9810, 9885 and 12035 kHz.

Voice of America. The beginning of a three-hour block of *news*, sports, science, business, music, and features. To East and Southeast Asia and the Pacific on 9770, 11760, 15185, 15290, 15305, 17735 and 17820 kHz.

Radio Korea, South Korea. See 1030 for program details. Thirty minutes to East and South East Asia on 7275 and 9640 kHz.

Radio Moscow World Service. *News*, then Monday through Friday winters, it's *Focus on Asia and the Pacific* followed by a feature (see 2100 summer programs). Saturday's spot is given over to the interesting ● *Music and Musicians*, and Sunday has flexible programming. Summer weekdays at this time there's ● *Commonwealth Update* (replaced by features on the weekend), then ● *Audio Book Club* (Tuesday, Thursday and Sunday), *Russian by Radio* or a music program. Beamed to North America, Asia and the Pacific on more than 20 channels, most of them for Asia and Australasia. In eastern North America try the 7 and 9 MHz segments in winter, 11 and 15 MHz in summer. For western North America, best year-round bets are channels in the 17 MHz segment of the spectrum, with the area around 12050 kHz also worth a try in winter. East Asia is best served by the 7 and 9 MHz bands in winter; 9, 11 and 15 MHz in summer. Best for Southeast Asia and Australasia are frequencies in the 15 and 17 MHz segments.

Voice of Free China, Taiwan. See 0200. For Western Europe, winters on 9850 and 11915 kHz, and summers on 17750 and 21720 kHz.

Croatian Radio. Winters only at this time; actually starts at 2203. Ten minutes of on-the-spot *news* from Croatian Radio's Zagreb studio. Best heard in Europe and eastern North America. Channel usage varies, but try 5020, 5085, 5920, 6145, 6210, 9830 and 13830 kHz. One hour earlier in summer.

Radio Habana Cuba. Sixty minutes of *news* and entertainment, including some thoroughly enjoyable Cuban music. To the Caribbean (and audible in parts of North America, especially during winter) on 6180 kHz.

Radio Budapest, Hungary. Winters only at this time; see 2100 for program details. Sixty minutes to Europe and the Mideast on 6110, 9835 and 11910 kHz. One hour earlier in summer.

Voice of Turkey. Summers only at this time. See 2000 for program details. Fifty minutes to Europe on 11895 kHz, to eastern North America on 9445 kHz, and for late-night listeners in the Mideast on 7185 kHz. One hour later in winter.

Radio Yugoslavia. This time winters only. *News*, reports and features, going some way to explaining events in one of the most volatile areas of the world. To Europe on 6100, 7200 and 9505 kHz; and one hour earlier in summer. The last frequency is also well heard in eastern North America.

China Radio International. Repeat of the 2000 broadcast. To Europe winters on 7170 kHz, summers on 9740 (or 9880) kHz.

Radio Vlaanderen International, Belgium. Winters only at this time; see 1900 for program details. Twenty-five minutes to Europe on 5900

(or 5910) and 9905 kHz, with the latter frequency also being audible in parts of eastern North America. One hour earlier in summer.

Radio Canada International. Winters, for Europe and Africa, the final 30 minutes of the 2130 broadcast (see there for specifics). Summers, there's a relay of CBC domestic programming. Monday through Friday, it's *news* and news-related fare—● *World at Six* and the first half hour of ● *As It Happens*. This is replaced weekends by *Innovation Canada* (Saturday) and

---

Political Sparks from America

Time was when the left ruled the airwaves. World band programs were filled with praise for the likes of Stalin and Chairman Mao.

That's history. Most stations of the left are either gone or tamed, and in their place are conservative voices from the United States. No, not those government-funded giants, the Voice of America and RFE-RL; but, rather, private stations. Capitalism is not only the Thought of the Airwaves, but the *modus operandi*, as well. Led by pioneer station WRNO and world band maven George Jacobs, these stations now are among the financial successes of broadcasting, including FM and TV.

With advertising money avoiding world band's unfamiliar turf, stations have turned to selling air time, mainly to conservative political and religious groups. Many are interesting. Yet, some operate well off the beaten path, seeing the ills of the United States as being rooted in conspiracies of one sort or another: Jews, Freemasons, Illuminati, Skull and Bones, Bilderberg, Curia, banks. One calls for the extermination of homosexuals. Another uses bigotry to peddle investments.

Yet others air simplistic nostrums that were once the purview of the far left: Interest-free money, for example, to turn a nation into an economic paradise. However, nothing is said about those Moslem countries, such as Pakistan, that have long had interest-free money, but are prosperous only if they have oil under their feet.

Not enough? How about UFOs, or curing cancer with apricot pits?

Yet, for all the tomfoolery and nastiness, some programs focus on serious issues largely ignored by the traditional media. The Waco affair, for example. Or the case of Randy Weaver, in which a man's wife, young son and dog were shot dead by government sharpshooters in a fashion seemingly worthy of Honduran death squads.

Interestingly, the real audience grabber, Rush Limbaugh, fits none of these molds. A conservative Republican opposed to bigotry, entertainer as much as ideologue, his program is carried *gratis* by WRNO simply to attract listeners to its other programs.

Where does this leave the left? Marxism may be pretty much extinct from the airwaves, but the Sixties "new left" has a lone, low-budget voice: Radio for Peace International. Putting out a faint signal from Costa Rica, it carries the full range of feminist, liberationist, ecological and related movements that Rush Limbaugh spends his time ripping apart.

Rush Limbaugh, whom commentator George Will calls "the fourth branch of government," is now on world band. You can hear him throughout North America, the Caribbean and beyond Monday through Friday from 1700-2000 World Time (1600-1900 summer) over WRNO on 15420 kHz.

Sunday's *Arts in Canada*. Sixty minutes to Europe on 5995 and 7260 kHz; and to North America on 5960, 9755 and (till 2230) 11875 kHz. For a separate service to East Asia, see the next item.

Radio Canada International. A year-round relay of domestic programming from the Canadian Broadcasting Corporation. Thirty minutes to Southeast Asia on 11705 kHz.

Radio Roma, Italy. Approximately ten minutes of *news* followed by a quarter-hour feature (usually music). Tuesday's program of medieval and renaissance music could be a world band gem, but is ruined by the incompetence of the people in the studio. Two minutes of dead air between recordings is not unusual, so it's little wonder that people rarely bother to listen. Twenty-five exhausting minutes to East Asia on 5990 (or 15330), 9710 and 11800 kHz.

Radio Ukraine International. Winters only at this time. A potpourri of all things Ukrainian. Sixty minutes to Europe on 4825, 6010, 6020, 7195, 7240, 9710 and 15385 kHz. One hour earlier in summer.

United Arab Emirates Radio, Abu Dhabi. Begins with *Readings from the Holy Koran*, in which verses are chanted in Arabic, then translated into English. This is followed by an Arab cultural feature. The last half-hour is a relay of Capital Radio in Abu Dhabi, complete with pop music and local contests. To eastern North America winters on 9605 (or 9770), 11710 and 11815 kHz; and summers on 11885, 15305 and 15315 kHz.

Radio For Peace International, Costa Rica. Programs heavily oriented towards peace and goodwill, with Wednesday's spot being given over to New Wave music—*Sound Currents of the Earth*. Continuous to North America and Europe on 7375, 13630 and 15030 kHz. Some transmissions are in the single-sideband mode, which can be properly processed only on some radios.

All India Radio. Final half-hour of transmission to Europe and Australasia, consisting mainly of news-related fare. To Europe on 7412, 9950 and 11620 kHz; and to Australasia on 9910, 11715 and 15265 kHz. Also sometimes audible in Eastern North America on 11620 kHz.

WJCR, Upton, Kentucky. Continues with gospel music to North America on 7490 and 13595 kHz. Other U.S. religious broadcasters heard at this hour include **WWCR** on 13845 kHz, **KTBN** on 15590 kHz, and **WHRI-World Harvest Radio** on 13760 kHz.

CFRX-CFRB, Toronto, Canada. If you live in the northeastern United States or southeastern Canada, try this pleasant little local station, usually audible for hundreds of miles/kilometers during daylight hours on 6070 kHz. At this time, you can hear ● *The World Today* (summers, starts at 2100)—90 minutes of news, sport and interviews.

22:30

Radio Finland. Winters only at this time. Monday through Saturday it's *Compass North*, a window on Finland and the Finns. Saturday also features a short Finnish language lesson, while Sunday brings *Focus* and *Nuntii Latini*, a news bulletin in Latin. To Europe on 9730 kHz, and to East Asia on 9550 kHz. One hour earlier in summer.

Radio Vilnius, Lithuania. Winters only at this time. Repeat of the 2000 broadcast. Thirty minutes to Europe on 9710 (or 6100) kHz. One hour earlier during summer.

Radio Yugoslavia. Winters only at this time. Repeat of the 2200 broadcast. Thirty minutes to Europe on 6100 kHz, and to Australasia on 9720 kHz. One hour earlier in summer.

Kol Israel. Winters only at this time. *News*, followed by a variety of features, depending on which day it is (see 2130 for program details). A half-hour to eastern North America and Europe on 7465, 9435, 11587 and 11605 kHz.

Radio Tirana, Albania. Winters only at this time. Approximately 10 minutes of *news* about Albania and its neighbors. To Europe on 9760 and 11825 kHz. One hour earlier in summer.

Radio Sweden. Thirty minutes of *news* and features heavily geared to Scandinavian topics. To Europe on 6065 kHz, and to Australasia on 11910 kHz.

22:45

Vatican Radio. Twenty-five minutes of religious and secular programming to Asia and Australasia on 7310 (or 15090), 9600 and 11830 kHz.

Radio Yerevan, Armenia. See 2145 for specifics. Mainly of interest to Armenians abroad. To Europe winters on 7440 and 12060 kHz, and to South America summers on 11920 and 15365 kHz. Both transmissions are sometimes audible in eastern North America.

23:00

■ **BBC World Service.** *News*, then ● *World Business Report* (Monday-Friday), ● *World Business Review* (Sunday), or *Words of Faith* (Saturday). The remainder of the broadcast is taken up by music programs like *Multitrack* (Monday, Wednesday and Friday), Saturday's *A Jolly Good Show*, Tuesday's ● *Concert Hall* (or its substitute), and more classical music on the remaining days. Continuous to North America on 5975, 6175, 7325 (15070 in summer), 9590 and 9915 (or 12095) kHz; to East Asia on 11945, 11955 and 15370 kHz; and to Australasia, winters only, on 11955 kHz.

World Service of the Christian Science Monitor, USA. See 1700 for program details. Monday through Friday to Europe on one or more channels from 7510, 13770 and 15665 kHz; to North America on 9465 and 17555 kHz; to East and Southeast Asia on 13625 and 15405 kHz; and to the Pacific on 13625 kHz. Weekends, news-oriented fare is replaced by Christian Science religious programming.

Voice of Turkey. Winters only at this hour. See 2000 for program details. Fifty minutes to Europe on 11895 kHz, to eastern North America on 9445 kHz, and to Middle Eastern night owls on 7185 kHz. One hour earlier in summer.

Radio Vilnius, Lithuania. Summers only at this time. *News* and reports on life and events in Lithuania. Reliable, even in times of crisis. To eastern North America on 11750 or 12040 kHz. Currently Monday through Friday only, but may resume daily schedule if funds become available.

Radio Norway International. Sunday only. *Norway Today. News* and features from and about Norway, with the accent often on the lighter side of life. A pleasant thirty minutes to North America on 11795 or 11865 kHz.

Radio Japan. Similar to the 0300 broadcast, but with *Hello from Tokyo* on Sunday instead of *Media Roundup*. One hour to Europe on 6050 (or 6060), and 6125 kHz; and to East Asia on 7140, 15195, 15430 and 17810 kHz. As we go to press, this station is implementing a number of changes to both its program and transmission schedules, so be prepared for some adjustments.

Radio Bulgaria. Continuous programming to North America (see 2200); summers till 2315 on 11720 and 15330 kHz; and winters till 0015 on 7225, 9700 and 11720 kHz.

Radio Canada International. Summer weekdays, the final hour of ● *As It Happens*; winters, the first 30 minutes of the same, preceded by the up-to-the-minute *news* program ● *World at Six.* Summer weekends, look for *The Inside Track* (Saturday, sports) and *Open House* (Sunday, culture). These are replaced winter Saturdays by *Innovation Canada* and *Earth Watch* followed the next day by *Arts in Canada* and a listener-response program. To eastern North America on 5960 and 9755 kHz; and to Europe on 5995, (summer) 7195 and (winter) 7250 kHz.

Radio Pyongyang, North Korea. See 1100 for program details. Fifty minutes to the Americas on 11700 and 13650 kHz.

Radio For Peace International, Costa Rica. The final hour of a cyclical eight-hour block devoted mainly to counterculture and New Wave programming, although this spot is predominantly United Nations fare. Audible in Europe and North America on 7375, 13630 and 15030 kHz. Some transmissions are in the single-sideband mode, which can be properly processed only on some radios.

Radio Moscow World Service. *News,* then winter weekdays, try the informative ● *Commonwealth Update,* with the pick of the second half-hour being ● *Audio Book Club* (Tuesday, Thursday and Sunday). Summers,

there's *News and Views,* followed by ● *Folk Box* (Sunday and Friday), *Yours for the Asking* (Monday), *Jazz Show* (Tuesday and Thursday), *Kaleidoscope* (Saturday) and, for lovers of Russian classical music, Wednesday's ● *Music at your Request.* For eastern North America and East Asia winters, tune around the 7 and 9 MHz segments; 11 and 15 MHz are best in summer. In Southeast Asia and Australasia, try 15 and 17 MHz channels plus the year-round 21690 kHz.

United Arab Emirates Radio, Abu Dhabi. The second part of a two-hour broadcast to eastern North America. Opens with 15-20 minutes of extracts from the Arab press, then the Islamic *Studies in the Mosque,* an editorial, and an Arab cultural feature. Heard in eastern North America winters on 9605 (or 9770), 11710 and 11815 kHz, and summers on 11885, 15305 and 15315 kHz.

Voice of America. *News, Newsline* (not daily) and *VOA Morning.* Continuous programming to East Asia and the Pacific on the same frequencies as at 2200.

WJCR, Upton, Kentucky. Continuous gospel music to North America on 7490 and 13595 kHz. Other U.S. religious broadcasters heard at this time include **WWCR** on 13845 kHz, **KTBN** on 15590 kHz, and **WHRI-World Harvest Radio** on 13760 kHz.

CFRX-CFRB, Toronto, Canada. See 2200.

23:30

Radio Vlaanderen International, Belgium. Summers only at this time. See 1900 for program details. Twenty-five minutes to eastern North America on 9930 kHz; also audible on 13655 kHz, targeted at South America.

Radio Nederland. See 0830 for program specifics, except that *Towards 2000* replaces Saturday's *Airtime Africa,* and there is also a *Press Review.* One hour to North America on 6020 and 6165 kHz.

Radio Sweden. Winters only at this time. A comprehensive package of Scandinavian content. Thirty minutes to Europe on 6065 kHz.

Radio Austria International. Winters only at this time; see 2130 for program specifics. A half hour targeted at South America on 9870 and 13730 kHz, and also audible in parts of eastern North America.

23:45

Radio Yerevan, Armenia. Winters only at this time; see 2145 for specifics. Mainly of interest to Armenians abroad. To South America (and sometimes audible in eastern North America) on 9480 and 11980 kHz. One hour earlier in summer.

Prepared by Don Swampo and the staff of Passport to World Band Radio.

Worldwide Broadcasts in English

Country-by-Country Guide to Best-Heard Stations

Dozens of countries reach out to us in English over world band radio. This section of *Passport* gives you the times and frequencies (channels) where you're most likely to hear the country you want. Once you know when it's scheduled, you can also peruse the "What's On Tonight" section to see what shows are on.

No Wasted Time

Here are some tips so you don't waste your time poking through dead air:

- **Best time periods and frequency ranges:** In general, listen during the late afternoon and evening, when most programs are beamed your way. Tune between 5800-7600 kHz winters, otherwise 5800-15800 kHz. Exception for North Americans: Some Asian and Pacific stations, such as Australia, are strongest around dawn between 9300-12100 kHz. "Best Times and Frequencies for 1994" at the end of this book gives helpful specifics as to when and where to tune.
- **Best hours to listen in North America:** Shown in bold, such as **2200-0430** World Time.
- **Best hours to listen in Europe:** Underlined, such as 1900-2100 World Time.
- **Strongest frequencies:** Frequencies shown in italics—say, *6175* kHz—tend to be most powerful, as they are from transmitters that may be located near you.

World Time Simplifies Listening

Times and days of the week are in World Time, explained in the *Passport* Glossary. Midyear, many shows are an hour earlier, whereas some programs from the Southern Hemisphere are heard an hour later.

World Time—a handy concept also known as Universal Time, UTC and GMT—is used to eliminate the potential complication of so many time zones throughout the world. It treats the entire planet as a single zone and is announced regularly on the hour by many world band stations.

For example, if you're in New York and it's 6:00 AM EST, you will hear World Time announced as "11 hours." A glance at your clock shows that this is five hours ahead of your local time. You can either keep this figure in your head or use a clock. A growing number of radios come with World Time clocks built in, and separate 24-hour clocks are also widely available.

Special Times for Programs

Some stations, particularly those targeted to home audiences, shift times of transmission by one hour midyear. These are cited in *Passport*'s "Addresses PLUS" section. Stations also may extend their hours of transmission, or air special programs during national holidays.

Schedules Prepared for Entire Year

To be as helpful as possible throughout the year, *Passport's* schedules consist not just of observed activity, but also that which we have creatively opined will take place during the entire year. This latter material is original from us, and therefore, of course, will not be so exact as factual information.

Broadcasts in other than English? Turn to the next section—"Voices from Home." Also, the Blue Pages give detailed information on all broadcasts, regardless of language.

ALBANIA
RADIO TIRANA
0130-0200	9580 & 11840 (**N America**)
0230-0240	9580 & 11840 (**N America**)
1530-1600	7155 & 9760 (W Europe)
2300-2310	9760 & 11824 (W Europe)

ALGERIA
RTV ALGERIENNE
2000-2100	7245 (Europe & N Africa), 11715 (Europe)

ARGENTINA
RADIO ARGENTINA-RAE
0100-0200	Tu-Sa 11710 (**Americas**)
1800-1900	M-F 15345 (Europe & N Africa)

ARMENIA
RADIO YEREVAN
0245-0300	*11790* (**E North Am**), *15180 & 15580* (**W North Am**)
0345-0400	*9870* (**E North Am**), *17605 & 17690* (**W North Am**)
2145-2200	*9450* (Europe), 11920 (Europe & **C America**)
2245-2300	*7440* (Europe & W Africa), 9480 (Europe), 11920 (Europe & **C America**), *11920* (W Europe & **C America**)

AUSTRALIA
ABC/CAAMA RADIO—(Australasia)
2130-0830	4835, 4910

ABC/RADIO RUM JUNGLE
2130-0830	5025 (Australasia)

ARMED FORCES RADIO
0300-0400	M/F 19038 (E Africa), 23679 (SE Asia)
0900-1000	20419 (SE Asia), M/F 25323 (E Africa)
1200-1300	12071 (SE Asia)
1400-1500	M/F 13509 (E Africa)

AUSTRALIAN BROADCASTING CORP—(Australasia)
24h	9610
0900-0100	6140
1800-1300	9660
1900-1400	4920
2245-0915	15425

RADIO AUSTRALIA
0030-0600	17795 (**Pacific** & **N America**)
0030-0730	21740 (**Pacific** & **N America**)
0030-0800	11880 (**Pacific**)
0030-0900	11720 (**Pacific**), 15240 (**Pacific** & **W North Am**)
0100-0200	21525 (E Asia)
0100-0730	17715 (**Pacific**)
0200-0400	21525 (E Asia)
0400-0500	Sa/Su 17750, Sa/Su 17880 & Sa/Su 21525 (E Asia)
0400-0530	7670 & 17840 (E Asia)
0500-0530	17880 (E Asia)
0500-0700	17750 (E Asia)
0500-0730	21525 (E Asia)
0600-0900	6020 (**Pacific**)
0800-0900	6080, 7240 & 9710 (**Pacific**), 25750 (E Asia)
0800-2100	5995 (**Pacific**), 9580 (**Pacific** & **N America**)
0900-1000	13605 & 15170 (E Asia)
1100-1200	13605 & 15170 (E Asia)
1100-1230	6080 & 9710 (**Pacific**)
1100-1300	6020 (**Pacific**)
1100-2100	7240 (**Pacific**)
1300-1630	11800 (**Pacific** & **N America**)
1430-1800	7260 (S Asia & Mideast), 7260 (E Asia), 13755 (S Asia, Mideast & Europe)
1430-2100	6060 (**Pacific** & **W North Am**)
1600-2100	11695 (**Pacific**)
1700-2100	6080 (**Pacific**), 11880 (**Pacific** & **W North Am**)
1800-2100	6000 & 7260 (S Asia, Mideast & Europe), 11855 (E Asia)
1900-2400	11720 (**Pacific**)
2100-2230	9540 (E Asia), 11855 (**Pacific**)
2100-2400	11880 (**Pacific**)
2130-2300	15240 (**Pacific**), 21740 (**Pacific** & **N America**)
2200-2400	17795 (**Pacific** & **N America**)
2200-0730	15320 & 15365 (**Pacific**)
2300-2400	15240 (**Pacific** & **W North Am**), 21740 (**Pacific** & **N America**)

AUSTRIA
RADIO AUSTRIA INTERNATIONAL
0130-0200	6015 (**E North Am**), 9875 (**N America**)
0330-0400	6015 (**E North Am**), 9870 (**C America**)
0530-0600	*6015* (**N America**), 6155 & 13730 (Europe), 15410 & 17870 (Mideast)
0630-0700	*6015* (**N America**)
0730-0800	6155 & 13730 (Europe), 15410 & 17870 (Mideast)
0830-0900	6155 & 13730 (Europe), 15450 & 21490 (Australasia)
1030-1100	6155 & 13730 (Europe), 15450 & 21490 (Australasia)
1130-1200	6155 (Europe), 13730 (W Europe & **E North Am**)
1230-1300	6155 (Europe), 13730 (W Europe & **E North Am**), 15450 (E Asia)
1330-1400	15450 (E Asia)
1430-1500	6155 & 13730 (Europe), 15450 (E Asia)
1530-1600	6155 (Europe), 9880 (W Europe & W Africa), 13730 (Europe)
1830-1900	5945 & 6155 (Europe), 9880 (Mideast)
1930-2000	5945 & 6155 (Europe), 9880 (Mideast)
2130-2200	5945 & 6155 (Europe), 9880 (W Europe & W Africa)

BAHRAIN
RADIO BAHRAIN
0300-2105	6010 (Mideast)

BANGLADESH
RADIO BANGLADESH
1200-1230	13620 (Europe)
1745-1900	9565 (Europe)

BELGIUM
RADIO VLAANDEREN INTERNATIONAL
0030-0055	7370 (**E North Am**), 9930 (S America)
0630-0655	9925 (Australasia)
0730-0755	5910 & 9905 (Europe), 11695 (Europe & Australasia)
0900-0925	M-Sa 13675 (Europe)
1000-1025	M-Sa 5910 & M-Sa 9905 (Europe)
1230-1255	Su 15540 (**N America**)
1400-1425	M-Sa 15540 (**N America**)
1900-1925	5910 (Europe)
2200-2225	5910 & 9905 (Europe)
2330-2355	9930 (**E North Am**)

BHUTAN
BHUTAN BROADCASTING SERVICE
0900-1000	Su 5025 (Asia)
1415-1500	M-Sa 5025 (Asia)

BRAZIL
RADIO NACIONAL
1200-1320	15445 (**N America** & **C America**)
1800-1920	15265 (Europe & W Africa)

BULGARIA
RADIO BULGARIA
0000-0100	15330 (**E North Am**)
0100-0200	7225 (Europe & **E North Am**), 9700 & 11720 (**E North Am**)
0300-0400	9850 & 11765 (Europe)
0400-0500	7290 (Europe & **E North Am**), 9700 (Europe)
1100-1145	11765 (Europe & Mideast)
1130-1300	11720 (E Europe & Mideast), 13670, 17660 & 17825 (Mideast)
1730-1900	13670 (Europe)
1830-2000	6235, 9560, 9700 & 11720 (Europe)
2000-2100	15330 (Europe)
2100-2200	6235, 9560 & 11720 (Europe)
2145-2315	15330 (**E North Am**)
2245-0015	7225 (Europe & **E North Am**), 9700 & 11720 (**E North Am**)

CAMBODIA
NATIONAL VOICE OF CAMBODIA—(Asia)
0000-0015	11938
1200-1215	11938

CANADA
CBC NORTHERN SERVICE—(**E North Am**)
0000-0300	Su 9625
0200-0300	Tu-Sa 9625
0300-0310 &	
0330-0610	M 9625
0400-0610	Su 9625
0500-0610	Tu-Sa 9625
1200-1255	M-F 9625
1200-1505	Sa 9625
1200-1700	Su 9625
1600-1615 &	
1700-1805	Sa 9625
1800-2400	Su 9625
1945-2015,	
2200-2225 &	
2240-2330	M-F 9625

CFCX-CIQC, Montréal PQ
24h	6005 (**E North Am**)

CFRX-CFRB, Toronto ON
24h	6070 (**E North Am**)

CFVP-CFCN, Calgary AB
24h	6030 (**W North Am**)

CHNX-CHNS, Halifax NS
24h	6130 (**E North Am**)

CKZN-CBN, St. John's NF
0930-0500	6160 (**E North Am**)

CKZU-CBU, Vancouver BC
24h	6160 (**W North Am**)

RADIO CANADA INTERNATIONAL
0000-0100	5960 (**E North Am**), 5995 (Europe)
0000-0200	9755 (**E North Am**)
0100-0130	9535 (S America), 11845 (**C America**), 11940 (S America)
0100-0200	13720 (S America)
0100-0300	6120 (**W North Am**)
0130-0200	Su/M 9535 (S America), Su/M 11845 (**C America**), Su/M 11940 (S America)
0200-0300	9535 (S America), 9755 (**E North Am**), 11940 (S America)
0300-0400	6010 & 9725 (**E North Am** & **C America**), 9755 (**W North Am**)
0400-0430	6150, 9505, 9650, 9670, 11905, 11925 & 15275 (Mideast)
0500-0530	M-F 7295 (Europe), M-F 15430 & M-F 17840 (Africa)
0600-0630	M-F 6050, M-F 6150 & M-F 7155 (Europe), M-F 9740 (Africa), M-F 9760 (Europe), M-F 11905 (Mideast)
1230-1300	6150 & 9660 (E Asia), 11730 & 15195 (SE Asia)
1300-1400	M-F 11855 (**N North Am**), M-F 17820 (**E North Am** & **C America**)
1330-1400	6150 & 11795 (E Asia), 11935, 15315, 15325, M-Sa 17895, 21455 & M-Sa 21710 (Europe)
1400-1700	Su 11955 (**E North Am**), Su 17820 (**C America**)

1430-1500	9555, 11915, 11935, M-Sa 15315, 15325 & M-Sa 17820 (Europe)
1630-1700	7150 & 9550 (S Asia)
2030-2130	7235 & 13650 (Europe), 13670 (Africa), 15325 (Europe), 17850 (Africa), 17875 (Europe)
2030-2300	5995 (Europe)
2130-2230	7260 (W Europe), 11945 & 13650 (Europe), 13670 & 15140 (Africa), 15325 (Europe), 17820 (Africa)
2200-2230	11705 (SE Asia), 11730 (**C America** & S America), 11875 (**E North Am**), 15305 (**C America** & S America)
2200-2300	9755 (**E North Am**)
2200-2400	5960 (**E North Am**), **7195** (W Europe), 13670 (**C America** & S America)
2300-2330	9535 (S America), 11845 (**C America**), Sa/Su 11940, 11940 & 15235 (S America)
2300-2400	5995 (Europe), 9755 (**E North Am**)
2300-0100	7250 (W Europe)
2330-2400	Sa/Su 9535 (S America), Sa/Su 11845 (**C America**), Sa/Su 11940 & Sa/Su 15235 (S America)

CHINA (PR)
CHINA RADIO INTERNATIONAL
0000-0100	9770 & 11715 (**N America**)
0300-0400	9690 (**N America** & **C America**), 9770 & 11715 (**N America**)
0400-0500	11680 (**W North Am**)
0400-0600	11840 (**N America**)
0900-1100	11755, 15440 & 17710 (Australasia)
1200-1300	9655 (**E North Am** & **C America**), 11795 (Australasia), 15210 (**E North Am** & **C America**)
1200-1400	15440 & 15450 (**Pacific**)
1300-1500	11855 (**W North Am**)
1400-1600	7405 (**W North Am**)
1900-2000	6955 (N Africa), 11515 (Mideast & N Africa)
1900-2100	9440 (Mideast)
2000-2200	6950, 9920 & 11500 (Europe)
2200-2230	3985 (Europe)
2200-2300	7170 & 9740 (Europe)

CHINA (TAIWAN)
VOICE OF FREE CHINA
0200-0300	*5950* (**E North Am**), *11740* (**C America**)
0200-0400	*9680* (**W North Am**), 9765 (Australasia), 15345 (E Asia)
0300-0400	*5950* (**E North Am** & **C America**)
0700-0800	*5950* (**C America**)
2200-2300	*9850, 11580, 17750* & *21720* (Europe)

VOICE OF ASIA
1100-1200	7445 (Asia)

CLANDESTINE (ASIA)
"VOICE OF NATIONAL SALVATION"—(East Asia)
0030-0100	4400, 4450, 4557

"VOICE OF THE NATIONAL FRONT"—(Asia)
0100-0145	5408
1300-1330	5408

COSTA RICA
ADVENTIST WORLD RADIO—(**C America**)
Testing on 9725 and 11870
FARO DEL CARIBE
0300-0355	5055, 9645 (**C America**)

RADIO FOR PEACE INTERNATIONAL—(**C & N America**)
0100-0700	7375 USB, 7385, 13630, 15030
0700-0730	W/Th/Sa-M 7375 USB, 7385, 13630, 15030
0730-0800 &	
0900-1500	7375 USB (to 1200), 7385, 13630, 15030
1500-1530	W/Th/Sa-M 7385, 13630, 15030
1530-1600 &	
1700-2400	7385, 13630, 15030, 21465 (from 1900)

CROATIA
CROATIAN RADIO ZAGREB
0000-0015	*7315* (**E North Am**)
0500-0515	*7315* (**E North Am**), *9495* (**Americas**)
0700-0715	M-Sa 5020, M-Sa 5920, M-Sa 9830 & M-Sa 13830 (Europe)
0900-0915	M-Sa 5020, M-Sa 5920, M-Sa 9830 & M-Sa 13830 (Europe)
1300-1315	5020, 5920, 9830 & 13830 (Europe)
2200-2215	5020, 5920, 9830 & 13830 (Europe)

CUBA
RADIO HABANA CUBA
0000-0200	9815 (**E North Am**)
0000-0500	6010 (**E North Am**)
0200-0430	9655 (**N America**), 13660 (**E North Am**)
0400-0500	6180 (**C America**)
0500-0700	9510 (**W North Am**)
2100-2200	15165 (Europe), 17760 (Europe & N Africa)
2200-2300	6180 (**C America**)

CZECH REPUBLIC
RADIO PRAGUE
0000-0030	*5930* (**N America**), 7345 (**E North Am** & **C America**), 9485 (**E North Am**), *9810* & *11990* (**N America**)
0100-0130	7345 (**E North Am** & **C America**), 9485 (**E North Am**), 11990 (**N America**)
0300-0330	*5930* (**N America**), 7345 (**N America** & **C America**), 9485 (**E North Am**), *9810* (**N America**), 11990 (**Americas**)
0400-0430	*5930* (**N America**), 7345 (**N America** & **C America**), 9485 (**E North Am**), *9810* & 11990 (**N America**), 11990 (Mideast & S Asia), 13715 (Mideast & E Africa), **17535** (Mideast & S Asia)
0700-0730	*7345, 9505* & 11990 (Europe)
0700-0800	6055 (Europe)
0730-0800	11990, 13600, 17535, 17725 & *21705* (Australasia)
1130-1200	6055, *7345, 9505* & 11990 (Europe), 15355 (W Europe)
1600-1630	6055 & *7345* (Europe), *11685* (N Africa), 13600 (Mideast)
1800-1830	6055, *7300, 7345* & 9490 (Europe), *11685* (N Africa)
2100-2130	6055, *7300, 7345* & 9490 (Europe)
2200-2230	6055, *7300, 7345* & 9490 (Europe)

ECUADOR
HCJB-VOICE OF THE ANDES
0030-0430	9745 & 15155 (**N America** & **C America**), 17490 (Europe & **Pacific**)
0030-2200	21455 (Europe & **Pacific**)
0500-0700	11925 (**N America** & **C America**)
0700-0830	6205, 9600, 11835 & 15270 (Europe)
0700-0930	17490 (Europe & **Pacific**)
0715-1125	9745 & 11925 (Australasia)
1000-1030	17490 (Europe & **Pacific**)
1130-1430	15115 (**Americas**)
1130-1600	11925 & 17890 (**N America** & **C America**)
1200-1600	17490 (Europe & **Pacific**)
1630-1715	15270, 17790 & 21480 (Mideast)
1715-1745	Su-F 15270, Su-F 17790 & Su-F 21480 (Mideast)
1745-1800	M-F 15270, M-F 17790 & M-F 21480 (Mideast)
1900-2000	15270 (Europe), 17490 (Europe & **Pacific**), 17790 & 21480 (Europe)
2130-2200	11835 & 15270 (Europe), 17490 (Europe & **Pacific**), 17790 & 21480 (Europe)
2300-2400	21455 (Europe & **Pacific**)

EGYPT
RADIO CAIRO
0200-0330	9475 & 11600 (**N America**)
2115-2245	9900 (Europe)

EQUATORIAL GUINEA
RADIO AFRICA—(Africa)
1700-2300	7190

RADIO EAST AFRICA—(Africa)
0500-1600	Sa/Su 9585

ESTONIA
RADIO ESTONIA—(Europe)
1620-1630	M-F 5925
2130-2200	M-F 5925

ETHIOPIA
VOICE OF ETHIOPIA—(Africa)
1500-1600	7165, 9560

FINLAND
RADIO FINLAND
0145-0215	11755 (**Americas**), 15185 (**N America**)
0245-0315	9560 (**N America**), 11755 (**Americas**)
0430-0450	Su 6120 (Europe), Su 9665 (E Europe), 11755 (Mideast), 15440 (Mideast & E Africa)
0530-0550	Su 6120 (Europe), 11755 (Mideast)
0530-0600	9635 (Mideast & E Africa)
0645-0700	6120 & 11755 (Europe)
0745-0800	6120, 9560 & 11755 (Europe)
0800-0830	17800 & 21550 (SE Asia & Australasia)
0900-0930	15330 & 17800 (SE Asia & Australasia)
1130-1200	M-F 11900 (**N America**)
1230-1300	M-F 11735, M-F 11900 & M-F 15400 (**N America**)
1300-1330	Su 11900 (**N America**)
1330-1400	11900, M-F 15400 & M-F 17740 (**N America**)
1400-1430	Su 15400 & Su 17740 (**N America**)
1430-1500	15400 & 17740 (**N America**)
1530-1545	6120 & 11755 (Europe), 11820 (E Europe), 15240 & 21550 (Mideast)
1630-1645	6120 (Europe), 9730 (E Europe), 11755 (Europe), 15440 & 17825 (Mideast)
1830-1900	6120, 9730, 11755 & 15440 (Europe)
1930-2000	6120, 9730 & 11755 (Europe)
2130-2200	6120 & 11755 (Europe), 15440 (E Asia)
2230-2300	9550 (E Asia), 9730 (Europe)

FRANCE
RADIO FRANCE INTERNATIONALE
1230-1300	9805, 11670, 15155 & 15195 (E Europe), 15365 (**E North Am**), 17575 & 21645 (**C America**)
1400-1500	17650 (Mideast)
1600-1700	6175 (Europe & N Africa), 11705 (N Africa & W Africa), 15530 (Mideast), 17620 (Africa & **N America**)

GEORGIA
RADIO GEORGIA—(Europe)
0400-0430   9585
0600-0630   11805
1600-1630   9565

GERMANY
DEUTSCHE WELLE
0100-0150   *6040* (**N America**), 6085 (**N America &
             C America**), 6145 (**N America &
             C America**), *9515* (**N America**), 9565
             (**E North Am** & **C America**), *9700*
             (**W North Am** & **C America**), 11865
             (**N America** & **C America**), *15105* (**E North
             Am** & **C America**)
0200-0250   *6130* or *13790* (**N America**)
0300-0350   6045 (**N America** & **C America**), *6085*
             (**C America**), 6120 (**N America** & **C
             America**), 9535 or 9640 (**N America**), *9545*
             or 9700 (**N America** & **C America**), *11715*
             (**N America** & **C America**), *13790*
             (**N America** & **C America**)
0400-0450   6065 (S Europe), 7275 (Europe)
0500-0550   5960, 6045, 6120 & *9670* (**N America**)
0900-0950   *6160* (**C America** & Australasia), 17780
             (Australasia & E Asia), (E Asia), *17820*,
             21650 & 21680 (SE Asia & Australasia),
             21680 (E Asia)
2100-2150   6185 & *9670* (SE Asia & Australasia), 9765
             (Asia & Australasia), *11785* (SE Asia &
             Australasia)

GHANA
GHANA BROADCASTING CORPORATION—(Africa)
0525-0915 &
1220-0100   3366, 4915
RADIO GHANA—(Africa)
0645-0800 &
1845-2000   6130

GREECE
FONI TIS HELLADAS
0130-0140   M-Sa 9380, M-Sa 9420 & M-Sa 11645
             (**N America**)
0335-0345   M-Sa 9380, M-Sa 9420 & M-Sa 11645
             (**N America**)
0835-0845   17550 (Australasia)
0935-0950   17525 (Australasia)
1035-1050   15650 & 17525 (E Asia)
1335-1345   15630 & 17515 (**N America**)
1530-1540   15630, 15650 & 17525 (N Europe &
             N America)
1900-1915   7450 & 9375 (Europe)
2000-2015   7450 & 9375 (Europe)
2235-2250   11645 (Australasia)
2335-2350   9425 & 11595 (**C America**)

GUAM
ADVENTIST WORLD RADIO—(E Asia)
0200-0300   Sa/Su 13720
KTWR-TRANS WORLD RADIO
0750-0915   15200 (E Asia)
0855-1000   11805 (Australasia)

HOLLAND
RADIO NEDERLAND
0030-0125   *11835* (**E North Am**)
0330-0425   *6165* (**Americas**), 9590 (**W North Am**)
0730-0825   *9630* (Australasia)
0730-1025   *11895* (Australasia)
0930-1025   *9720* (Australasia)
0930-1125   *7260* (E Asia), *9860* (E Asia & SE Asia),
             12065 (E Asia), *15470* (E Asia & SE Asia)
1130-1325   5955 & 9860 (Europe)
1330-1430   *15150* (S Asia & E Asia)
1330-1625   13700 (Mideast),
2330-0125   6020 (**E North Am**), **6165** (**Americas**)

HONDURAS
LA VOZ EVANGELICA—(**C America**)
0300-0500   M 4820

RADIO COPAN INTERNATIONAL—(**E North Am**)
1400-1500   M-Sa 15675 (English & Spanish)
1745-1900   M-Sa 15675 (English & Spanish)
2100-2230   M-Sa 15675 (English & Spanish)

HUNGARY
RADIO BUDAPEST
0300-0400   6110, 9835 & 11910 (**N America**)
2200-2300   6110, 7220, 9835 & 11910 (Europe)

INDIA
ALL INDIA RADIO
1000-1100   15050 (E Asia & Australasia), 17387
             (Australasia), 17895 & 21735 (E Asia)
1745-1945   7412 (N Europe), 9950 (N Africa), 11620
             (N Europe & **N America**), 11860 (N Africa)
2045-2230   7412 (W Europe), 9910 (Australasia), 9950
             & 11620 (W Europe & **N America**), 11715 &
             15265 (Australasia)

INDONESIA
VOICE OF INDONESIA
0100-0200   9675 (Asia), 11752 (Asia & **Pacific**)
0800-0900   9675 (Asia), 11752 (Asia & **Pacific**)
2000-2100   9675 & 11752 (Europe)

IRAN
VOICE OF THE ISLAMIC REPUBLIC
0030-0130   9022 (**Americas**), 11790 & 15260 (**E North
             Am** & **C America**)
1130-1230   9525, 9685, 11715, 11745, 11930 (Mideast)
1930-2030   9022 & 15260 (Europe)

IRAQ
RADIO IRAQ INTERNATIONAL
0115-0415   15180 (**N America**)
0215-0515   11860 (**N America**)
2100-2300   11805 (Europe)
2200-2400   13680 & 15210 (Europe)

IRELAND
RADIO DUBLIN INTERNATIONAL—(**W Europe**)
0700-1900   6910

ISRAEL
KOL ISRAEL
0500-0515   9435 (W Europe & **E North Am**)

1100-1130	17545 (W Europe)
1300-1325	Su-Th 15640 (W Europe), Su-Th 15650 (SE Asia & Australasia), Su-Th 17575 (W Europe) & **E North Am**)
1400-1425	Su-Th 11587 & Su-Th 11605 (W Europe), Su-Th 15640 (W Europe & **E North Am**), Su-Th 15650 (SE Asia & Australasia), Su-Th 17575 (**E North Am**), Su-Th 17590 (E Europe)
1700-1715	15640 (W Europe & **E North Am**)
1800-1815	7465 (W Europe & **E North Am**), 11587 (W Europe), 11675 (E Europe)
1900-1930	15640 (W Europe & **E North Am**), 17575 (W Europe & **E North Am**)
2000-2030	7465, 9435 & 11587 (W Europe & **E North Am**), 11605 (**C America**), 11675 (E Europe)
2130-2200	15640 & 15650 (W Europe & **E North Am**)
2230-2300	7465 (W Europe & **E North Am**), 9435 (**C America** & S America), 11587 & 11605 (W Europe & **E North Am**), 11675 (E Europe)

ITALY

ADVENTIST WORLD RADIO—(Europe)

| 0730-0800 | 7210 |
| 1030-1100 | 7230 |

EUROPEAN CHRISTIAN RADIO—(Europe)

| 0700-0715 & | |
| 0745-0800 | Su 6220 |

ITALIAN RADIO RELAY—(English, etc.)

0300-0400	7125 (**E North Am**)
0600-0900	7125 (Europe)
0900-1700	Sa/Su 7125 (Europe)
1700-2100	7125 (Europe)
2100-2230	Sa/Su 7125 (Europe)

RADIO ROMA

0100-0120	9575 (**E North Am**), 11800 (**E North Am** & **C America**)
0425-0440	5990 & 7275 (Europe, N Africa & Mideast), 9575 (Europe, Mideast & N Africa)
1935-1955	7275, 9710 & 11800 (W Europe)
2025-2045	7235 (E Europe & Mideast), 9575 & 11800 (Mideast)
2200-2225	5990, 9710, 11800 & 15330 (E Asia)

JAPAN

RADIO JAPAN/NHK

0100-0200	5960 (**E North Am** & **C America**), 15195 & 17775 (E Asia)
0300-0330	11725 (**W North Am**), 15325 (**C America**), 21610 (**Pacific** & S America)
0300-0400	5960 (**E North Am** & **C America**), 11870 (**W North Am**), 15210 (E Asia), 15230 (**W North Am**)
0400-0600	15325 (target undetermined)
0500-0600	6085 (Europe & N Africa), 7230 (Europe), 9725 (**W North Am** & **C America**), 11725 (**W North Am**), 11870 & 15230 (**W North Am**), 15410 (E Asia), 17890 (Australasia)
0600-0700	11860 (E Asia)
0700-0800	5970 (Europe), 6025 & 6050 (Europe & N Africa), 7230 (Europe), 15170 (Europe), 15410 (E Asia), 17860 & 17890 (Australasia), 21575 (Europe & N Africa)
0900-1000	9750 (E Asia), 11890 & 11910 (E Asia), 15270, 17860 & 17890 (Australasia)
1100-1200	6120 (**N America**), 11840 & 11910 (E Asia)
1400-1500	11735 (**W North Am**)
1400-1600	9535 (**W North Am**), 9750 (E Asia), 11865 (**W North Am**)
1700-1800	7140 (E Asia), 9535 (**W North Am**), 9750 (E Asia), 11865 (**W North Am**), 17775 (Mideast)
1900-1930	5980 (Europe)
1900-2000	9535 (**W North Am**), 9640 (Australasia), 9750 (E Asia), 11865 (**W North Am**), 11875 (Australasia)
2100-2200	9640 (Australasia), 9750 (E Asia), 11925 (Europe & N Africa), 15195 (E Asia), 15280 (Australasia), 17890 (Australasia)
2300-2400	6050 & 6060 (Europe & N Africa), 6125 (Europe), 7140 & 15195 (E Asia)

JORDAN

RADIO JORDAN—(W Europe & **E North Am**)

| **1200-1300** | 9560 |
| **1500-1730** | 9560 |

KAZAKHSTAN

RADIO ALMATY—(Asia)

0100-0130	5915 & 6135
1300-1330	5915, 7255
1500-1530	5915 & 6135
1800-1830	3955, 4400, 5035, 5260, 5960, 5970, 9505, 11825, 15215, 15270, 15315, 15385, 17605, 17715, 17730, 17765, 21490
1930-2000	3955, 4400, 5035, 5260, 5960, 5970, 9505, 11825, 15215, 15270, 15315, 15360, 15385, 17605, 17715, 17730, 17765, 21490
2300-2330	5915, 7255

KENYA

KENYA BROADCASTING CORPORATION—(Africa)

| 0200-0620 | 4934, 6045 |
| 1315-2100 | 4934, 6100 |

KIRIBATI

RADIO KIRIBATI—(**Pacific**)

0600-0700	17440
1825-2000	M-Sa 17440
2000-2345	Sa 17440
2345-0130	17440

KOREA (DPR)

RADIO PYONGYANG

0000-0050	11335, 13760 & 15130 (**C America**)
0700-0750	15340 (E Asia & S Asia)
1100-1150	6576, 9977 & 11335 (**C America**)
1300-1350	9345 (Europe), 11740 (Europe)
1500-1550	9325 (Europe), 9640 (Mideast & Africa), 13785 (Europe)
1700-1750	9325 (Europe), 9640 (Mideast & Africa), 13785 (Europe)
2000-2050	6576 & 9345 (Europe), 9640 (Mideast & Africa)
2300-2350	11700 & 13650 (**C America**)

KOREA (REPUBLIC)

RADIO KOREA

0100-0200	7550 (Europe), 15575 (**E North Am**)
0600-0700	7275 (E Asia), 11945 (**E North Am**), 15155 (**W North Am**)
0800-0900	7550 & 13670 (Europe), 15575 (Mideast & Africa)
1030-1100	11715 (**N America**)
1130-1200	9650 (**N America**)
1200-1300	9640 (E Asia)
1400-1500	5975 & 6135 (E Asia)
1600-1700	5975 (E Asia)
2030-2100	5975 (E Asia), **6035** (Europe), 9870 (Mideast & Africa)
2145-2245	6480 & 15575 (Europe)

KUWAIT

RADIO KUWAIT—(Europe & **E North Am**)

| **1730-2100** | 13620 |

LAOS

LAO NATIONAL RADIO—(SE Asia)

0100-0130,	
0600-0630 &	
1330-1400	7116 (when active)

LATVIA

RADIO RIGA INTERNATIONAL—(Europe)

0700-0730	Su 5935
1830-1900	Sa 5935
2130-2140	M-F 5935

LEBANON

KING OF HOPE—(Mideast & E Europe)

0700-1100,	
1400-1700 &	
2000-0500	6280

VOICE OF LEBANON—(Mideast)

0900-0915,	
1315-1330 &	
1800-1815	6550

WINGS OF HOPE—(E Europe, Mideast & W Asia)
<u>0800-1200</u>   9895
<u>2000-0400</u>   11530 (times approx.)

LIBERIA
RADIO ELBC—(Africa)
0700-1000   7275

LITHUANIA
RADIO VILNIUS
<u>2000-2030</u>   9710 (<u>Europe</u>)
<u>2230-2300</u>   9710 (<u>Europe</u>)
2300-2330   M-F *12040* (**E North Am**)

MALAYSIA
RADIO TV MALAYSIA—(Asia)
0010-0100   7295
0100-0500   Su-Th 7295
0500-0600   7295
0600-0900   Sa-Th 7295
0910-1600 &
2200-2400   7295
VOICE OF MALAYSIA
0555-0825   6175 & 9750 (SE Asia), 15295 (Australasia)

MALTA
VOICE OF THE MEDITERRANEAN—(<u>Europe</u>, <u>N Africa</u> & Mideast)
<u>0600-0700</u>   9765
<u>1400-1500</u>   11925

MONACO
TRANS WORLD RADIO—(<u>W Europe</u>)
<u>0635-0835</u>   9480
<u>0735-0935</u>   7240
<u>0835-0850</u>   Su-F 9480
<u>0850-0915</u>   Su 9480
<u>0935-0950</u>   Su-F 7240
<u>0950-1015</u>   Su 9480

MONGOLIA
RADIO ULAANBAATAR
0910-0940   11851 & 12015 (Australasia)
1200-1230   M/Th/Sa 11851 & M/Th/Sa 12015 (E Asia)
<u>1940-2010</u>   11790 (Mideast), 11850 (<u>Europe</u> & W Asia)

MYANMAR (BURMA)
RADIO MYANMAR—(Asia)
0200-0230   7155
0700-0730   9730
1430-1600   5990

NEPAL—(Asia)
RADIO NEPAL
0215-0225,
1315-1325 &
1415-1425   5005, 7165

NEW ZEALAND
PRINT DISABLED RADIO—(Australasia)
0000-0500   M-F 7290
0500-0530   Su 3935
0530-0800   Su-F 3935
0800-0900   M-F 3935
2100-2400   Su-Th 7290
RADIO NEW ZEALAND INTERNATIONAL—(**Pacific**)
0455-1210   9730 (from Summer, 1994)
0655-1210   9700 (to Summer, 1994)
1205-1650   6035, 9510
1650-1850   M-F 6035
1650-1950   M-F 9550
1845-2140   Su-F 11735
1950-0700   Su-F 15120

NIGERIA
RADIO NIGERIA—(Africa)
0400-2305   6025
0430-2310   4770, 4990, 6050, 6090, 9570
VOICE OF NIGERIA—(Africa)
0455-0700,
1000-1100,
1500-1700 &
1900-2100   7255

NORTHERN MARIANA IS
KFBS-FAR EAST BROADCASTING—(<u>E Europe</u> & W Asia)
<u>1930-2000</u>   9465

NORWAY
RADIO NORWAY INTERNATIONAL
0000-0030   M 9675 (**W North Am**), M 9675 (**E North Am** & **C America**)
0100-0130   M 9560 (**N America**), M 9565 (**W North Am**)
0200-0230   M 9560 (**N America**), M 9565 (**W North Am**), M 11925 (**N America**)
0400-0430   M 9560, M 9565 & M 9650 (**W North Am**), M 11730 (Mideast & S Asia), M 11865 (**W North Am**), M 15175 (Mideast & S Asia)
1200-1230   Su 17860 (Australasia), Su 21705 (S Asia & Australasia)
<u>1300-1330</u>   Su 9590 & Su 15230 (<u>Europe</u>), Su 25730 (<u>Europe</u> & W Africa)
<u>1600-1630</u>   Su 11875 & Su 15230 (Mideast), Su 17825 (<u>E Europe</u> & Mideast)
<u>1700-1730</u>   Su 9655 (<u>Europe</u>)
1900-1930   Su 15355 (Australasia), Su 15365 (**E North Am** & **C America**), Su 17730 (S America & Australasia)
2100-2130   Su 15165 (**N America**), Su 15180 (S America & Australasia)
2300-2330   Su 11795 & Su 11865 (**E North Am** & **C America**)

PAKISTAN
RADIO PAKISTAN
<u>0800-0845</u>   17900 & 21520 (<u>Europe</u>)
<u>1100-1120</u>   17900 & 21520 (<u>Europe</u>)
<u>1600-1630</u>   7290 (S Asia), 11570 (Mideast & <u>N Africa</u>), 13685 (Mideast & <u>Europe</u>), 15555 (Mideast), 17555 (Mideast & <u>N Africa</u>)
<u>1700-1750</u>   9430, 11570 & 15550 (<u>Europe</u>)

PALAU
KHBN-VOICE OF HOPE—(Asia)
0900-0930   M-F 9830
1200-1400   9830
1400-1430   Sa 9830
1500-1530,
2030-2230 &
2330-0100   9830

PHILIPPINES
RADYO PILIPINAS
0230-0330   21580 (E Asia)

POLAND
POLISH RADIO—(<u>W Europe</u>)
<u>1300-1355</u>   6135, 7145, 9525, 11815
<u>1600-1655</u>   7285, 9525, 11840
<u>1800-1855</u>   7270, 9525
<u>2030-2125</u>   6135, 7270, 7285, 9525

PORTUGAL
RDP INTERNATIONAL—RADIO PORTUGAL
0230-0300   Tu-Sa 9570 (**E North Am**), Tu-Sa 9705 (**N America**)
<u>0930-0945</u>   Sa/Su 11975 (<u>Europe</u>)
1530-1600   M-F 21515 (Mideast & S Asia)
<u>1900-1930</u>   M-F 9780 (<u>Europe</u>)

ROMANIA
RADIO ROMANIA INTERNATIONAL
0200-0300   5990 (**C America**), 6155, 9510, 9570, 11830 & 11940 (**Americas**)
0400-0430   5990 (**C America**), 6155, 9510, 9570, 11830 & 11940 (**Americas**)
<u>0635-0645</u>   7225, 9510, 9570 & 11775 (<u>Europe</u>)
0645-0715   11810 & 11940 (Australasia), 15335 (Asia & Australasia), 17720, 17805 & 21665 (Australasia)
<u>1300-1400</u>   11590, 11940, 15365 & 17720 (<u>Europe</u>), 17850 (<u>W Europe</u>)
1430-1530   15335 (Mideast & S Asia)
<u>1730-1800</u>   11790 (<u>Europe</u>)
<u>1900-2000</u>   5990, 6105, 7145, 7195, 7225, 9690, 9750 & 11940 (<u>Europe</u>)
<u>2100-2200</u>   5955, 6105, 7195, 7225, 9690, 9750 & 11940 (<u>Europe</u>)

RUSSIA
ADVENTIST WORLD RADIO
<u>0430-0500</u>   15125 (<u>Europe</u>)

0530-0600 12060 (Europe)
1600-1630 15125 (Europe)
1700-1730 9640 (N Europe)

RADIO MOSCOW INTERNATIONAL

0000-0300 9700 (**N America**), 11995 (Mideast), 21530 (**W North Am**)
0000-0700 17590 (E Asia & SE Asia)
0030-0400 9530 (E Asia)
0030-0700 *17835* (E Asia), 21505 (Australasia)
0030-0800 17620 (E Asia & SE Asia), 17825 (Australasia)
0100-0300 *6110 & 7275* (Mideast)
0100-0700 11985 (Mideast)
0130-0400 17640 (Mideast & E Africa)
0130-0800 *17710* (Mideast & C Africa)
0200-0400 *11730* (E Asia)
0200-0700 7150 (N Europe & **E North Am**)
0200-0800 7130 (Mideast), 21585 (E Asia & SE Asia)
0230-0700 17720 (E Asia)
0230-1200 17735 (Mideast & E Africa)
0230-1300 *15320* (Mideast & W Asia)
0300-0400 17670 (W Europe)
0300-0600 *11790* (**E North Am**)
0300-0700 9515 (Europe), 12050 (**W North Am**), 15535 (S Asia & E Asia)
0300-1000 12070 (Europe)
0330-0400 17605 (Europe & W Africa)
0330-0700 9895 (**W North Am**)
0330-0800 7270 (**W North Am**)
0330-1600 *7305* (Mideast)
0400-0500 9580 (Europe), 17625 (Mideast & E Africa)
0400-0600 *9610* (**C America** & S America)
0400-0700 5950 & 6165 (Europe), 9665 (Mideast & E Africa), 9870 (W Europe), 15180 & 15425 (**W North Am**)
0400-1200 *15470* (Mideast)
0430-0600 21525 (Australasia)
0430-0700 17605 (**W North Am**)
0430-0800 12055 (E Asia), 15595 (S Asia & E Asia)
0430-1300 12055 & 21550 (Mideast)
0500-0700 7165 (N Europe), *7180* (**E North Am**)
0500-0800 7380 (E Asia)
0500-1000 *15320* (Mideast)
0500-1300 15540 (Mideast)
0530-0600 15545 (E Asia)
0530-0800 5905, 7175 & 9795 (**W North Am**)
0530-0900 11995 (Mideast), 21725 (SE Asia & Australasia)
0530-1400 11830 (Europe)
0600-0700 *9860* (**E North Am**), 12010 (Europe)
0600-0900 15125 (Europe)
0600-1200 15530 (Mideast)
0600-1500 15225 (N Europe & **E North Am**)
0630-0800 7345 (**W North Am**)
0630-1000 15190 (Europe)
0630-1500 17595 (Europe)
0700-0900 17680 (W Europe)
0700-1000 15540 (Europe)
0700-1200 12010 & 17660 (Europe)
0700-1300 17670 (W Europe)
0700-1330 21480 (Mideast)
0730-0900 5960 (E Asia)
0730-1000 13705 (Europe), 15525 (E Asia)
0800-0900 9580 (Europe), 15535 (S Asia & E Asia), 21505 (Australasia)
0800-1000 *15485* (Europe)
0800-1300 12020 (Europe)
0800-1500 15440 (Europe & W Africa)
0830-0900 9895, 15245 & 17720 (E Asia)
0830-1300 11920 (Europe & N Africa), 12070 (W Europe), **0830-2000 17760** (W Europe & **E North Am**)
0900-1000 15595 (S Asia & E Asia)
0900-1300 17590 (E Asia & SE Asia)
0900-1400 *15355* (**E North Am**)
0930-1000 *15495* (Europe)
0930-1200 17695 (E Asia), 17885 (N Africa & W Africa)
0930-1330 11860 (Mideast & S Asia)
1000-1100 7280 (E Asia)

1000-1200 21690 (E Asia & SE Asia)
1000-1300 15510 (Europe)
1030-1300 15130 (Australasia)
1030-1400 15320 (Mideast)
1100-1200 15420 (Europe)
1100-1300 *15220* (Mideast), 15280 (Europe), 15525 (E Asia)
1100-1400 11980 (Europe)
1100-1500 15125 (Europe)
1130-1200 17680 (N Africa & W Africa)
1130-1300 15585 (N Europe & **E North Am**)
1200-1300 4810 & 5940 (E Asia), 5950 (E Asia & **Pacific**), 5960, 7160, 7260, 7280, 7315, 9895 & 10344 (E Asia), 15480 (Mideast & W Asia)
1200-1400 13705 (Europe)
1200-1430 11710 (**W North Am**)
1200-1500 15230 (Mideast & E Africa), 17860 (Europe)
1200-1600 13705 (Europe), 15210 (E Asia & SE Asia), 15540 (Europe), 17840 (W Europe & **E North Am**)
1200-1830 7370 (Europe)
1200-1900 *15290* (W Europe & **E North Am**)
1200-2200 11850 (Mideast & E Africa)
1230-1500 15480 (E Asia & SE Asia)
1230-1600 7380 (Mideast)
1300-1400 11870 (E Asia & SE Asia)
1300-1500 7330 (E Asia & SE Asia)
1400-1500 5905 (Mideast), 5960, 7135 & 7315 (E Asia), 11830 (Europe & N Africa)
1400-1530 15425 (Mideast & W Asia)
1400-1600 9800 (Europe), 11695 (E Asia), *15320* (Mideast & W Asia), 15480 (Mideast & W Asia)
1430-1500 7280, 11980 & *12030* (Europe)
1430-1600 7160 (N Europe)
1430-1700 6055 (N Europe), 7115 (Europe)
1500-1600 5920, *7390* & 9580 (Europe), 12065 (Mideast)
1500-2000 11950 (Europe)
1500-2100 6065, 11820 (Europe)
1530-1600 5905 & *7290* (Europe), 7330 (Europe & N Africa), 7360 (Europe), 11675 (N Europe)
1530-1700 7185 (E Europe & S Europe)
1530-1800 7170 (Europe)
1530-1900 7250 (**N Pacific** & **W North Am**)
1530-2000 7260 (**W North Am**)
1530-2100 9590 (Europe)
1600-1800 9540 (**N Pacific** & **W North Am**)
1600-1900 7420 (**N Pacific** & **W North Am**)
1600-2000 15185 (Europe)
1630-1700 6000 (Europe), 6130 (E Europe & S Europe), 7150 (N Europe & **E North Am**)
1630-1800 7205 (Europe), *15385* (W Africa)
1700-1800 7330 (Europe & N Africa)
1700-1900 9625 (E Asia & Australasia), 11755 (**W North Am**)
1730-1800 7340 (Europe)
1730-2000 9685 (Australasia)
1730-2300 *9860* (**E North Am**)
1800-2100 12005 (E Asia & Australasia)
1800-2300 7245 (E Asia & SE Asia), 15590 (E Asia & Australasia)
1830-1900 6130 (E Europe & S Europe)
1900-2000 9530 (Mideast & E Africa)
1900-2200 7170, 7205 & 9640 (Europe), *15150* (W Europe & **E North Am**), 15180 (**W North Am**)
1900-2400 *15525* (E Asia)
1900-0600 7390 (E Asia)
1930-2200 7330 (Australasia), 15580 (**W North Am**)
2000-2100 7115 (Europe), 7185 (Mideast), 7250 (**N Pacific** & **W North Am**), 11675 (N Europe), 11535 (S Europe & N Africa), 15545 (E Europe)
2000-2200 6010 & 6130 (Europe), 7420 (**N Pacific** & **W North Am**), 9800 (Europe)
2000-2400 *4795* (Europe)
2000-0100 7220 (E Asia & SE Asia)
2000-0400 11970 & 15385 (E Asia)
2000-0830 7135 (E Asia)
2000-0900 7315 (E Asia)

2030-2200	7300 (<u>W Europe</u>), 9740 (<u>Europe</u>), *15355* (**E North Am**)
2030-2300	*7180* (**E North Am**), 7280 (E Asia), *15290* (<u>W Europe</u> & **E North Am**), 17605 (**W North Am**)
2030-0300	21480 (**W North Am**)
2030-0900	17655 (Australasia)
<u>2100-2200</u>	7230, 7370 & 7400 (<u>Europe</u>)
2100-2300	6030 & 7115 (<u>Europe</u>), 7150 (<u>N Europe</u> & **E North Am**)
<u>2100-2400</u>	6055 (<u>N Europe</u>), 15130 (Australasia)
2100-0400	9480 & 13775 (E Asia)
2100-0600	12050 (**W North Am**)
2130-2300	12040 (**E North Am**)
2130-0100	*9750* (**E North Am**)
2130-0330	9870 (**E North Am**)
2200-2300	5920, 5980 & 7300 (<u>Europe</u>), 9520 (**C America**), 17690 (**W North Am**)
<u>2200-2400</u>	4825 & 4860 (<u>E Europe</u> & <u>S Europe</u>)
2200-0200	*9720* (**N America**), 15265 (E Asia)
<u>2200-0300</u>	6060 (<u>Europe</u>), 9685 (Australasia)
2200-0600	11690 (**E North Am** & <u>Europe</u>)
2200-1400	17570 (Australasia)
2230-2330	21690 (E Asia & SE Asia)
2230-0200	15330 (E Asia)
2230-0300	7170 (E Asia)
2230-0700	15410 (**W North Am**)
<u>2300-2400</u>	15535 (<u>S Europe</u> & <u>N Africa</u>)
2300-0230	*11790* (**E North Am**)
2300-0400	*7115* (**E North Am**)
2300-0700	15500 (E Asia)
2330-0400	11850 (<u>N Africa</u> & Mideast), 15375 (E Asia), 15425 (**W North Am**), 17870 (E Asia)
2330-0430	21770 (Australasia)
2330-0800	9905 (E Asia), 17860 (Australasia)
2330-0900	21790 (E Asia & Australasia)
2330-1000	21690 (E Asia & SE Asia)

SAUDI ARABIA
RADIO RIYADH—(<u>W Europe</u>)
<u>1600-2100</u>	9705

SINGAPORE
SINGAPORE BROADCASTING CORPORATION—(Asia)
2200-1605	5010, 5052, 11940

SLOVAKIA
RADIO SLOVAKIA INTERNATIONAL
0100-0130	5930, 7310 & 9810 (**N America**)
0830-0900	11990, 15605, 17535 & 21705 (Australasia)
<u>1930-2000</u>	5915, 7345 & 9605 (<u>W Europe</u>)

SOLOMON ISLANDS
SOLOMON ISLANDS BROADCASTING CORP—(English, etc.)
1900-1130	5020, 9545

SOUTH AFRICA
CHANNEL AFRICA—(Africa)
0300-0455	3995 & 7270
0400-0455	7230
0400-0655	15430
0600-0655	15220
1600-1655	15220
1600-1755	15430

SPAIN
RADIO EXTERIOR DE ESPANA
0000-0200	9530 (**N America** & **C America**)
0500-0600	9530 (**N America** & **C America**)
2100-2200	6125 (<u>Europe</u>)

SRI LANKA
SRI LANKA BROADCASTING CORPORATION
1030-1130	11835 (SE Asia & Australasia), 15120 (E Asia)
2330-0030	M 15425 (**N America**)

SUDAN
RADIO NATIONAL UNITY—(<u>Europe</u>, Mideast & Africa)
1500-1530	9165

RADIO OMDURMAN—(<u>Europe</u>, Mideast & Africa)
1800-1900	9165

SWAZILAND
TRANS WORLD RADIO
0430-0500	5055 (S Africa)
0600-0820	11740 (S Africa)

SWEDEN
RADIO SWEDEN
0200-0230	9695 (**N America**), 11705 (**E North Am** & **C America**)
1330-1400	21500 (SE Asia & Australasia)
1600-1630	15240 (**N America**), 15270 (Mideast), 21500 (**E North Am** & **C America**)
<u>1715-1745</u>	6065 (<u>Europe</u>)
<u>1830-1900</u>	6065 (<u>Europe</u>), 9655 (<u>Europe</u> & <u>N Africa</u>), 15270 (Mideast)
<u>2130-2200</u>	6065 (<u>Europe</u>), 9655 (<u>Europe</u> & <u>N Africa</u>)
<u>2230-2300</u>	6065 (<u>Europe</u>), 11910 (Australasia)
<u>2330-2400</u>	6065 (<u>Europe</u>)

SWITZERLAND
RED CROSS BROADCASTING SERVICE—(<u>Europe</u> & <u>N Africa</u>)
<u>1100-1130</u>	Su 7210 (on the air as needed)
<u>1700-1730</u>	M 7210 (on the air as needed)

SWISS RADIO INTERNATIONAL
0000-0030	6135 (**N America** & **C America**), 9650 (**C America**), *17730* (**C America** & **W North Am**)
0200-0230	6135 (**N America** & **C America**), 9650 (**C America**), 9885 & 12035 (**E North Am** & **C America**)
0400-0430	6135 & 9860 (**N America** & **C America**), 9885 & 12035 (**N America**)
<u>0500-0530</u>	M-F 3985 (<u>Europe</u>), M-F 6165 & M-F 9535 (<u>Europe</u> & <u>N Africa</u>)
<u>0600-0615</u>	M-F 3985 (<u>Europe</u>), M-F 6165 & M-F 9535 (<u>Europe</u> & <u>N Africa</u>)
0600-0630	13635 (Mideast & E Africa)
<u>0700-0715</u>	3985 (<u>Europe</u>), 6165 & 9535 (<u>Europe</u> & <u>N Africa</u>)
0900-0930	9885 & 13685 (Australasia), 17670 (SE Asia & Australasia), 21820 (Australasia)
1100-1130	13635 (Australasia), 15505 (E Asia & Australasia), 17670 (SE Asia & Australasia)
<u>1100-1145</u>	6165 & 9535 (<u>Europe</u> & <u>N Africa</u>)
1300-1330	*7480* (E Asia), 13635 (E Asia)
1500-1530	13635, 15505 & 17670 (Mideast & E Africa), 21820 (Mideast)
1700-1730	9885 (Mideast), 13635 (Mideast & E Africa), 15430 (Mideast)

SYRIA
RADIO DAMASCUS
<u>2005-2105</u>	12085 & 15095 (<u>Europe</u>)
2110-2210	12085 (**N America**), 15095 (Australasia)

TANZANIA
RADIO TANZANIA—(Africa)
0330-0430	5050
1530-1915	5050

THAILAND
RADIO THAILAND—(Asia)
0500-0600,	
1130-1230 &	
2300-0430	4830 (SE Asia), 9655 (Asia)

TOGO
RADIO LOME—(Africa)
1935-1945	5047

TURKEY
VOICE OF TURKEY
0400-0450	9445 (**E North Am**)
1330-1400	9675 (Mideast & W Asia)
2100-2150	9445 (Europe)
2300-2350	7185 (Mideast), 9445 (**E North Am**), 11895 (Europe)

UGANDA
RADIO UGANDA (English, Swahili, etc. to Africa)
0300-0345	M-F 5026
0300-0600	4976
0345-0600	5026
1430-2100	4976, 5026

UKRAINE
RADIO UKRAINE
<u>0000-0100</u>	6010, 6090 & 7150 (<u>Europe</u>), 7195 (<u>W Europe</u>), 9500, 9550 (<u>Europe</u>), 9600 (<u>Europe</u>), *15180* (**W North Am**), *15580* (**W North Am**)

0030-0100 9685 (W Europe & **E North Am**), 9860 (**E North Am**)

0100-0200 4825 (N Europe), 6010 & 6020 (Europe), 6070 (E Europe), 6080 (E Europe & W Asia), 7180 (**E North Am**), 7195 (N Europe), 7240 (W Europe & W Africa), 9750 & 9860 (**E North Am**), 17605 & 17690 (**W North Am**)

2100-2200 6090 (N Europe), 7150 (Europe), 7285 (N Europe), 9600 (Europe), 9685 (Europe), 11780 (W Europe & **E North Am**)

2100-2300 4825 (N Europe)

2130-2200 11610, 11950 & 12120 (**E North Am**)

2200-2300 6010 & 6020 (Europe), 7195 (N Europe), 7240 (W Europe & W Africa), (E Europe & W Asia)

UNITED ARAB EMIRATES
UAE RADIO IN DUBAI
0330-0400 11945 & 13675 (**E North Am** & **C America**), 15400 & 17890 (**E North Am**)

0530-0600 15435 (Australasia), 17830 (E Asia), 21700 (Australasia)

1030-1110 13675 (Europe), 15320 (N Africa), 15395 & 21605 (Europe)

1330-1400 13675 (Europe), 15320 (N Africa), 15395 & 21605 (Europe)

1600-1640 11795 & 13675 (Europe), 15320 (N Africa), 15395 & 21605 (Europe)

UAE RADIO FROM ABU DHABI
2200-2400 9605, 11885, 15305 & 15315 (**E North Am**)

UNITED KINGDOM
BBC WORLD SERVICE
0000-0200 6180 (E Europe & W Asia)

0000-0330 7325 (**C America** & S America)

0000-0430 9915 (**Americas**)

0030-0145 5965 (E Europe & S Asia)

0030-0230 9590 (**C America**)

0030-0330 15310 (W Asia & S Asia)

0100-0300 Su 15280 & Su 21715 (E Asia)

0100-0330 17790 (E Asia & SE Asia)

0200-0300 7325 (E Europe & W Asia), 9410 (E Europe)

0200-0330 7135 (Mideast & W Asia), 9670 (Mideast)

0200-0815 6195 (Europe)

0300-0400 6180 (Europe), 7120 (E Europe & W Asia), 12095 (Europe), 15575 (Mideast & E Africa)

0300-0430 7230 (E Europe)

0300-0730 3955 (Europe)

0300-0815 11760 (Mideast), 15310 (Mideast & S Asia)

0300-0915 15280 (E Asia)

0300-1030 21715 (E Asia)

0300-2315 9410 (Europe)

0330-0430 6175 (**E North Am**), 12095 (**N America**)

0400-0730 6180 (Europe), 15575 (Mideast & S Asia)

0400-0900 12095 (Europe)

0430-0730 5975 (**C America**)

0500-0815 9640 (**C America** & S America)

0600-0730 15575 (Europe), 15575 (N Africa)

0600-0815 7150 (Australasia)

0600-0915 11955 (SE Asia & Australasia)

0600-1000 15360 (E Asia), 17830 (SE Asia & Australasia)

0600-2030 15070 (Europe & N Africa)

0700-0915 7325 (Europe)

0700-1200 9760 (Europe)

0730-0800 Sa/Su 9660 (Europe)

0730-0900 Sa/Su 15575 (Mideast & S Asia)

0800-0900 Sa/Su 9660 (Europe), 17705 (N Africa & W Africa)

0800-1515 17640 (Europe & N Africa)

0815-0945 Su 5975 (W Europe & N Africa)

0900-1000 11765 (E Asia)

0900-1400 11760 (Mideast)

0900-1515 9660 (Europe), 15310 & 15575 (Mideast & S Asia)

0900-1530 9750 (Europe)

0900-2315 12095 (Europe, N Africa & W Africa)

0915-0930 11680 (E Europe), 13745 (Europe), 15135, 15340 & 17750 (E Europe), 21745 (E Europe & W Asia)

0915-1000 7180 (E Asia), 11955 (E Asia & SE Asia)

0945-1400 5975 (W Europe & N Africa)

1030-1200 Su 9760 (Europe)

1030-1515 9740 (Asia & Australasia)

1100-1130 5965 (**E North Am**)

1100-1400 15220 (**E North Am** & S America)

1100-1430 6195 (**C America**)

1100-1745 9515 (**E North Am**)

1130-1200 M-Sa 5965 (**E North Am**), 9600, 9635, 11680 & **11710** (Europe), 11830 (E Europe & W Asia), 15115 (W Europe), 15115 (Europe), 15205 (E Europe & W Asia), 17695 (E Europe)

1200-1615 9760 (Europe)

1300-1500 11820 (E Asia)

1300-1615 7180 (E Asia)

1400-1615 17840 (**Americas**)

1400-1745 15260 (**N America**)

1500-2315 6195 (Europe)

1515-1830 15310 (Mideast)

1530-1615 9750 (Europe)

1700-2200 6180 (Europe)

1700-2315 3955 (Europe)

1715-1830 7160 (Mideast & W Asia)

1800-2200 11955 (SE Asia & Australasia)

1830-2030 9740 (Mideast)

1900-2030 7160 (Mideast & W Asia)

2000-2200 7325 (Europe)

2000-2315 15340 (SE Asia & Australasia)

2000-0430 5975 (**Americas**)

2030-2200 3975 (Europe)

2030-2315 15070 (W Europe & N Africa)

2100-2200 7180 (E Asia), 15070 (**E North Am** & **C America**)

2100-0030 9590 (**E North Am**)

2115-2130 M-F 6110, M-F 15140, M-F 15390 & M-F 17715 (**C America**)

2130-2145 Tu/F 13660 (**Atlantic** & S America)

2200-2400 9915 (**Americas**)

2200-0030 11955 (E Asia & Australasia), 15070 (**E North Am** & S America)

2200-0200 7325 (E Europe & W Asia)

2200-0330 12095 (**N America** & **C America**)

2200-0430 7325 (**N America** & **C America**)

2300-2400 9570 (E Asia & SE Asia)

2300-0030 11945, 15280 & 17830 (E Asia)

2300-0330 6175 (**E North Am**)

USA—Except for the VOA, American stations are generally audible throughout North America, plus the designated target zones.

CHRISTIAN SCIENCE MONITOR WORLD SERVICE
0000-0100 9850 (W Africa), Sa/Su 17865 (E Asia)

0000-0115 M 5850 (**E North Am** & **C America**), M 13760 (S America)

0000-0155 Tu-Sa 5850 (**E North Am** & **C America**), Tu-Sa 13760 (S America), M-Sa 17555 (SE Asia)

0100-0115 M 9850 (W Africa)

0100-0155 Su 5850 (**E North Am** & **C America**), Tu-F 9850 (W Africa), Su 13760 (S America), Sa 17865 (E Asia)

0200-0305 5850 (**W North Am** & **C America**), 9455 (E Africa), Sa/Su **17555** (SE Asia), Sa/Su **17865** (E Asia)

0200-0315 M 13760 (S America)

0200-0355 Tu-F 13760 (S America)

0300-0315 M 5850 (**W North Am** & **C America**)

0300-0355 Tu-F 5850 (**W North Am** & **C America**), M-F 9455 (E Africa), Sa/Su 13760 (S America), Su 17865 (E Asia)

0400-0505 5850 & 9455 (**W North Am**), 9840 (S Africa), Sa/Su 17555 (SE Asia), 17780 (E Asia)

0400-0515 M 9870 & M 13760 (**C America**)

0400-0555 Tu-F 9870 & Tu-F 13760 (**C America**)

0500-0515 M 5850 & M 9455 (**W North Am**)

0500-0555 Tu-F 5850 & Tu-F 9455 (**W North Am**), M-F 9840 (S Africa), Sa/Su 9870 & Sa/Su 13760 (**C America**), M-Sa 17780 (E Asia)

0600-0700 7395 & 9455 (**W North Am**), M-F 9840 (**C America**), 17555 (SE Asia)

0600-0755   M-F 5850, M-F 9840 & M-F 9870 (Europe), *17780* (E Asia)

0700-0755   Su 5850 (Europe), M-F 7395 & M-F 9455 (**W North Am**), 9840 (**C America**), Su 9840 & Su 9870 (Europe), Su-F *17555* (SE Asia)

0800-0900   13615 & M-F *15665* (Australasia), *17555* (E Asia)

0800-0955   M-F 9455 (S America), M-F 9840 & M-F 11705 (Europe)

0900-0955   Su 9840 & Su 11705 (Europe), M-F 13615 & *15665* (Australasia), Su-F *17555* (E Asia)

1000-1100   9495 (**E North Am**)

1000-1155   M-F 9455 (S America), *13625* (SE Asia), *17555* (E Asia)

1100-1155   Sa/Su 9455 (S America), M-F 9495 (**E North Am**)

1200-1300   M-F *9425* (Australasia), 9495 (**E North Am**), Su-F *13625* (S Asia & SE Asia), Sa/Su 15665 (Europe), M-F *15665* (Australasia), Sa/Su 17510 (Europe)

1200-1355   M-F 13760 (**C America**)

1300-1355   *9425* (Australasia), M-F 9495 (**E North Am**), *13625* (S Asia & SE Asia), Sa/Su 13760 (**C America**), *15665* (Australasia)

1400-1500   Sa/Su 13710 (**E North Am** & **C America**), M-F 13760 (**W North Am** & **C America**), Sa/Su 15665 (**E North Am** & **C America**), Sa 15665, Su 15665, Sa 17510 & Su 17510 (Europe)

1400-1555   *9530* (E Asia), *13625* (S Asia & SE Asia), M-F 15665 & M-F 17510 (Europe)

1500-1555   13760 (**W North Am** & **C America**)

1600-1700   17510 & 21640 (E Africa)

1600-1715   *9355* & *13625* (SE Asia & S Africa), Su 17555 (**W North Am** & **C America**)

1600-1755   *11580* (E Asia), Sa/Su 13710 & Sa/Su 15665 (**E North Am** & **C America**)

1700-1715   Su 17510 & Su 21640 (E Africa)

1700-1755   M-F 17510 (E Africa), Sa 17555 (**W North Am** & **C America**), M-F 21640 (E Africa)

1715-1755   M-Sa *9355* & M-Sa *13625* (SE Asia & S Africa)

1800-1900   Su-F *9430* & Su-F *13840* (Australasia), 17613 & 21640 (S Africa)

1800-1915   Su 15665 & Su 17510 (**E North Am** & Europe), Su 17555 (**W North Am** & **C America**)

1800-1955   Su-F *9355* (Europe & Mideast), M-F 15665 (**E North Am** & Europe), Su-F *15665* (Europe & Mideast), M-F 17510 (**E North Am** & Europe)

1900-1915   Su 17613 & Su 21640 (S Africa)

1900-1955   Sa *9355* (Europe & Mideast), *9430* & *13840* (Australasia), Sa 15665 (**E North Am** & Europe), Sa *15665* (Europe & Mideast), Sa 17510 (**E North Am** & Europe), Sa 17555 (**W North Am** & **C America**), M-F 17613 & M-F 21640 (S Africa)

2000-2100   Su-F *9430* & Su-F *13840* (Australasia)

2000-2115   Su 7510 (Europe & Mideast), Su 13770 (**E North Am** & Europe), Su 15665 (Europe & Mideast), Su 17510 (**E North Am** & Europe), Su 17555 (S America)

2000-2155   M-F 7510 (Europe & Mideast), *9455* (E Asia), M-F 13770 (**E North Am**), M-F 15665 (Europe & Mideast), M-F 17510 (**E North Am** & Europe), M-F 17555 (S America)

2100-2155   *9430* & *13840* (Australasia)

2200-2300   9465 (**E North Am** & **C America**)

2200-2315   Su 7510 & Su 15665 (Europe), Su 17555 (S America)

2200-2355   M-F 7510 (Europe), *13625* (SE Asia), *15405* (E Asia), M-F 15665 (Europe), M-F 17555 (S America)

2300-2315   Su 9465 (**E North Am** & **C America**)

2300-2355   Sa 17555 (S America)

KCBI—(N America)

0330-1400   9815

1430-0200   15725

KGEI-VOICE OF FRIENDSHIP

2200-2230   Su 15280 (**C America** & S America)

KJES-KING JESUS ETERNAL SAVIOR

1300-1500   11715 (**North Am**)

1800-1900   9510 (Australasia)

KNLS-NEW LIFE STATION—(E Asia)

0800-0900 &

1300-1400   7365, 9615

KTBN-TRINITY BROADCASTING NETWORK—(**E North Am**)

0000-1600   7510

1500-2400   15590

KVOH-VOICE OF HOPE—(**W North Am** & **C America**)

0000-0330   Tu-Sa 17775

0400-0800   9785

1800-1900   Su 17775

1900-2100   Sa/Su 17775

2100-2200   Su 17775

UNIVERSITY NETWORK (via Russia)

0100-1100   *12040* (S Asia)

0300-0500   *21670* (S Asia & SE Asia)

0400-0800   *21845* (S Asia & SE Asia)

1130-1600   *6070* (S Asia)

1700-0100   *6120* (S Asia)

2100-1500   *11840* (S Asia)

VOA-VOICE OF AMERICA

0000-0100   11695 (**Americas**)

0000-0200   5995, 6130, 7405, 9455, 9775, 11580, 15120 & 15205 (**Americas**)

0100-0300   *9740* (Mideast & S Asia)

0200-0230   Tu-Sa 5995, 7405, 9775, 11580, 15120 & 15205 (**Americas**)

0300-0700   7405 (W Africa & S Africa)

0400-0500   *15205* (Mideast & S Asia)

0400-0600   *7200* (Europe)

0400-0700   5995 (E Europe), *6040* & *6140* (Europe), *7170* (N Africa), *11965* (Mideast)

0500-0600   *9530* (E Europe), *9700* (N Africa & W Africa)

0500-0700   6035 (W Africa & S Africa), 9665 (W Africa), *11825* (Mideast), *12080* (Africa), *15205* (Mideast & S Asia), *15600* (C Africa & E Africa)

0600-0700   *6005* (N Africa), 6060 (E Europe), *6140* (N Africa & Mideast), 7325 (Europe), 9530 (W Africa), *11805* (N Africa & W Africa), 11925 (W Africa)

1000-1200   5985 (**Pacific** & Australasia), 7405 & 9590 (**C America**), *11720* (E Asia & Australasia), 11915 & 15120 (**C America**)

1000-1500   15425 (SE Asia & **Pacific**)

1100-1400   *15155* & *15160* (E Asia)

1100-1500   9760 (E Asia & SE Asia)

1200-1330   *11715* (E Asia & Australasia)

1400-1500   *15160* (E Asia)

1400-1800   9645 (E Asia), *15205* (Mideast & S Asia), *15255* (Mideast)

1500-2200   *9700* (Mideast & S Asia)

1530-1600   *7215* (S Asia)

1600-1730   *17785* (W Africa & S Africa), *17790* (S Africa)

1600-2100   *15320* (W Africa)

1600-2200   *15410* & *17895* (W Africa)

1630-1700   *6180, 11855, 15245* & *17735* (Europe)

1630-2200   *6040* & *9760* (Europe)

1700-1800   *7215* & *11855* (S Asia)

1800-2200   *15205* (Europe), 15580 & 17800 (W Africa)

1900-2000   9525 & *11870* (E Asia & Australasia), *15180* (**Pacific**)

2000-2200   *9575* (Europe), *15205* (Mideast & S Asia)

2100-2200   *11870* (E Asia & Australasia), *11960* (Mideast), *15290* (W Africa)

2100-0100   *15185* (**Pacific** & SE Asia), *17735* (E Asia & Australasia)

2200-2400   *15305* (E Asia & Australasia)

2200-0100   *15290* & *17820* (E Asia)

WEWN-ETERNAL WORD NETWORK (Schedule to change when additional transmitter activated)

0000-0100   15650 (S Asia)

0100-0200   9825 (S Asia)

0400-0600   7425 (**N America**)

0700-0800	7425 (**N America**), 13710 (C Africa & S Africa)
0700-0900	5825 & 9350 (Europe)
0800-0900	9430 (W Africa)
0800-1000	9370 (Europe)
0900-1000	9985 (S America)
1200-1300	15695 (Europe)
1200-1500	9350 (**N America**)
1500-1600	17510 (Mideast)
1500-1700	17535 (**N America** & **C America**), 21710 (E Africa)
1700-2200	13615 (**Americas**)
1800-1900	13740 (Europe)
1800-2000	15695 (Europe)
2000-2200	13740 (Europe)
2100-2200	11695 (Europe)
2200-2300	11820 (S America)
2300-0300	7425 (**N America**)

WINB-WORLD INTERNATIONAL BROADCASTING
0300-0330	W-M 15145 (S America)
1600-1700	15295 (Europe & N Africa)
1700-1730	M-Sa 15295 (Europe & N Africa)
1730-1800	Su-F 15295 (Europe & N Africa)
1800-2100	15295 (Europe & N Africa)
2100-2245	15185 (Europe & N Africa)
2245-2330	15145 (Europe & N Africa)
2330-2345	Th/Sa-Tu 15145 (Europe & N Africa)
2345-0300	15145 (S America)

WJCR
24h	7490 (**E North Am**), 13595 (**N America**)

WMLK-ASSEMBLIES OF YAWEH—(Europe, Mideast & **N America**)
0400-0900 &	
1700-2200	Su-F 9465

WHRI-WORLD HARVEST RADIO (Schedule in English varies, depending upon which clients purchase air time)
0000-0500	M 9495 (**Americas**)
0100-0130	Su/M 7315 (**E North Am**)
0130-0500	7315 (**E North Am**)
0600-0800	9495 (**Americas**)
0600-1300	7315 (**E North Am**)
0800-0900	Sa/Su 7355 (**C America**)
0900-1000	7355 (**C America**)
1000-1100	Su 7355 (**C America**)
1300-1500	9465 (**E North Am**)
1300-1600	15105 (**C America**)
1630-1700	9465 (**E North Am**)
1700-1800	Sa/Su 15105 (**C America**)
1700-2400	13760 (**E North Am** & W Europe)
1800-2100	17830 (**N America** & **C America**)
2100-2300	Sa/Su 17830 (**N America** & **C America**)
2300-2400	Sa/Su 9495 (**Americas**)

WRNO WORLDWIDE—(**E North Am**) (Schedule in English varies, depending on which clients purchase air time)
0300-0500	7395
1400-1600	Su 15420
1500-2300	15420
2300-0300	7355

WWCR-WORLDWIDE CHRISTIAN RADIO
0000-0800	7435 (**E North Am** & Europe)
0100-1400	5935 (**E North Am** & Europe)
1000-1100	12160 (**E North Am**) (tentative)
1000-1200	15685 (**E North Am** & Europe)
1100-1200	Su-F 12160 (**E North Am**)
1100-0200	13845 (**W North Am**)
1200-2215	15685 (**E North Am** & Europe)
2215-2245	Th-Su 15685 (**E North Am** & Europe)
2245-2400	Sa/Su 15685 (**E North Am** & Europe)

WYFR-FAMILY RADIO
0000-0045	6085 (**E North Am**)
0100-0245	15440 (**C America**)
0100-0445	6065 (**E North Am**), 9505 (**W North Am**)
0500-0600	9850 & 11580 (Europe)
0500-0700	5985 (**W North Am**)

0500-0745	11725 (Europe)
0500-0800	11580 & 13695 (W Africa)
0600-0745	7355 & 7520 (Europe)
1000-1400	5950 (**E North Am**)
1100-1200	11830 (**W North Am**)
1100-1245	7355 (**W North Am**)
1200-1345	11840 (**C America**)
1200-1445	6015 (**W North Am**)
1200-1700	11830 (**W North Am**), 17750 (**C America**)
1300-1400	13695 (**E North Am**)
1300-1445	9705 (**W North Am**)
1400-1700	17760 (**C America**)
1500-1700	11705 & 15215 (**W North Am**)
1600-1700	15355 (Europe), 21525 (C Africa & S Africa), 21615 (Europe)
1700-1900	21500 (Europe)
1900-2045	15355 (Europe)
1900-2145	21615 (Europe)
2000-2200	7355 & 15566 (Europe)
2000-2245	17613 & 17750 (W Africa), 21525 (C Africa & S Africa)
2200-2300	11915 (Europe)

UZBEKISTAN
RADIO TASHKENT
0100-0130	7190, **7265** & 9715 (Mideast)
1200-1230 &	
1330-1400	7325, 9540, 9715, 15295, 15460, 15470, **17745** & 17815 (Asia)

VANUATU
RADIO VANUATU—(Pacific)
0500-1030 &	
1800-2200	3945
2100-0600	7260

VATICAN STATE
VATICAN RADIO
0250-0315	6095 & 7305 (**E North Am**), 9605 & 11620 (**E North Am** & **C America**)
0600-0620	6245 (Europe), 7250 (W Europe)
0730-0745	M-Sa 6245 (Europe), M-Sa 7250 (Europe, Mideast & N Africa), M-Sa 9645 (Europe), M-Sa 15210 (Mideast)
1120-1130	M-Sa 6245 (Europe), M-Sa 7250 (Europe, N Africa & Mideast), M-Sa 15210 (Mideast)
1345-1415	15090 & 17525 (SE Asia & Australasia)
1600-1630	Sa 15090 & Sa 17730 (Mideast)
1715-1730	6245 & 7250 (Europe)
2050-2110	5882 (W Europe), 7250 (Europe)
2245-2315	7310 (E Asia), 9600 (Australasia), 11830 (E Asia & Australasia), 15090 (E Asia)

VIETNAM
VOICE OF VIETNAM
1230-1300	9840, 12018 & 15009 (E Asia & **Americas**)
1330-1400	9840, 12018 & 15009 (SE Asia)
1800-1830	9840, 12018 & 15009 (Europe)
1900-1930	9840, 12018 & 15009 (Europe)
2030-2100	9840, 12018 & 15009 (Europe)
2330-2400	9840, 12018 & 15009 (E Asia & **Americas**)

YUGOSLAVIA
RADIO BEOGRAD (English and other languages)
1500-1530	9505 (Europe, N Africa & Mideast)

RADIO YUGOSLAVIA
0130-0200	9580 (**E North Am**), 11870 (**W North Am**)
0230-0300	9580 (**W North Am**)
1930-2000	6100 & 7200 (Europe, N Africa & Mideast)
2200-2230	7200 (Europe, N Africa & Mideast), 9505 (W Europe & **E North Am**)
2200-2300	6100 (Europe, N Africa & Mideast)
2230-2300	9720 (Australasia)

ZAMBIA
RADIO ZAMBIA—(Africa)
0245-0600 &	
1530-2205	4910

Voices From Home

For some, the offerings in English on world band radio are merely icing on the cake. Their real interest is in listening to programs aimed at national compatriots. Voices from home.

"Home" may be a place of family origin, or perhaps it's a favorite country you once visited or lived in. Vacationers and business travelers also tune in to keep in touch. Others use world band to keep limber in a second tongue.

Schedules Prepared for Entire Year

To be as helpful as possible throughout the year, *Passport*'s schedules consist not just of observed activity, but also that which we have creatively opined will take place during the entire year. This latter material is original from us, and therefore, of course, will not be so exact as factual information.

This section gives the frequencies for stations which can be received well beyond their national borders. Some you'll hear, some you won't—depending, among other things, on your location and receiving equipment. Keep in mind that "Voices from Home" stations often come in weaker than those in English. If you're not obtaining satisfactory results, you may need better hardware.

Reception Sometimes Best Outside Prime Time

Stations in "Voices from Home," unlike those in English, sometimes come in best—or only—outside the usual prime early-evening listening hours. Choice late-afternoon and evening frequencies are usually found in the world band segments 3900-13870 kHz, although for countries to your west you might try tuning a little higher. Earlier in the day, try 11500-21785 kHz; for closer-in stations, also try 5800-10000 kHz. See "Best Times and Frequencies for 1994" at the end of this *Passport* for where and when to tune for optimum results.

Times and days of the week are given in World Time, explained in the *Passport* Glossary and "Compleat Idiot's Guide to Getting Started." Midyear, many programs are heard an hour earlier, whereas some stations from the Southern Hemisphere are heard an hour later. For transmission times and target zones, please refer to The Blue Pages.

Frequencies in *italics* tend to come in most strongly, as they are from relay transmitters close to the listening audience.

ALGERIA
"VOICE OF PALESTINE"
   Arabic 6145, 6160, 7145, 11715, 15205, 15215 kHz
RTV ALGERIENNE
   French 7245, 9509, 9685, 11910, 15160, 17745 kHz
   Arabic 6145, 6160, 7145, 7245, 9535, 11715, 15205, 15215 kHz
ARGENTINA—Spanish
RADIO ARGENTINA-RAE
   11710, 15345 kHz
RADIO NACIONAL
   6060, 9690, 11710, 15345 kHz
ARMENIA—Armenian
ARMENIAN RADIO
   7175, 17705 kHz
RADIO YEREVAN
   7390, *7440, 9450,* 9480, *9870, 11790, 11920,* 11945, *11980,* 12060, 12065, 15130, *15180,* 15385, *15580, 17605, 17690* kHz

AUSTRIA—German
RADIO AUSTRIA INTERNATIONAL
  5945, *6015*, 6155, 9870, 9875, 9880, 11780, 13730,
  15410, 15450, 17870, 21490 kHz

BAHRAIN—Arabic
RADIO BAHRAIN
  9746 kHz

BELGIUM
RADIO VLAANDEREN INTERNATIONAL
  French 5910, 7370, 9905, 9930, 13655, 13675, 13685,
  15540, 17540 kHz
  Dutch 5910, 7370, 9905, 9925, 9930, 11695, 13655,
  13675, 13685, 13710, 15540, 17540, 21815 kHz

BOSNIA HERCEGOVINA—Serbian and Croatian
RADIO BOSNIA-HERCEGOVINA
  6220 kHz (irregular)

BRAZIL—Portuguese
RADIO BRASIL CENTRAL
  4985, 11815 kHz
RADIO CLUBE DO PARA
  4885 kHz
RADIO CULTURA DO PARA
  5045 kHz
RADIODIFUSORA MARANHAO
  4755 kHz
RADIO NACIONAL DA AMAZONIA
  6180, 11780 kHz
RADIO BANDEIRANTES
  6090, 9645, 11925 kHz
RADIO CBN
  9585 kHz
RADIO CULTURA
  17815 kHz
RADIO NACIONAL
  15265, 17750 kHz

CANADA—French
CBC-CANADIAN BROADCASTING CORPORATION
  9625 kHz
RADIO CANADA INTERNATIONAL
  5960, *5995*, *6025*, *6050*, *6150*, *7155*, *7230*, *7235*, *7295*,
  9505, 9535, *9555*, 9650, *9660*, *9670*, *9740*, 9755, 9760,
  11705, *11730*, *11790*, 11845, 11855, 11875, *11905*,
  11915, *11925*, *11935*, 11940, 11945, 13650, 13670,
  15140, *15195*, 15235, 15305, *15315*, *15325*, 15390,
  15425, *15430*, 17820, *17840*, 17875, 17895, *21455*,
  21545, 21675, 21710 kHz

CHINA (PR)
CENTRAL PEOPLES BROADCASTING STATION
  Chinese 7504, 7770, 9064, 9080, 9170, 9455, 9755, 9775,
  9800, 10260, 11000, 11040, 11100, 11330, 11610, 11630,
  11740, 11935, 15390, 15500, 15550, 15710, 15880,
  17605, 17700 kHz
CHINA RADIO INTERNATIONAL
  Chinese *6165*, 7660, 9480, *9690*, *9770*, 9820, 9945,
  11445, 11650, *11680*, 11695, *11715*, *11790*, 11855,
  11945, 12015, 12055, 15100, *15110*, 15180, 15205,
  15260, 15400, 15435 kHz
  Cantonese *9770*, 9945, 11695, *11715*, 11945, 12015,
  12055, 15100, 15205, 15260 kHz
VOICE OF THE STRAIT-PLA
  Chinese 7280, 9505, 11590 kHz

CHINA (TAIWAN)
BROADCASTING CORPORATION OF CHINA
  Chinese *5950*, 9280, 9610, 9765, 11725, *11740*, *11775*,
  11845, *11855*, 11885, 15125, 15270, *15440* kHz
VOICE OF FREE CHINA
  Chinese *5950*, 7130, *9680*, 9730, 9765, 9845, 9955,
  11745, 11825, 11860, 11915, *15130*, *15215*, 15270,
  15345, 15370, 17720, *17750*, *17805*, *17845*, *21720* kHz
  Cantonese *5950*, 7130, *11740*, 11745, 11825, 11860,
  11915, 15270, 15345, 15370, 17720 kHz
VOICE OF ASIA
  Chinese 9280 kHz

CLANDESTINE (MIDDLE EAST)—Persian
"VOICE OF HUMAN RIGHTS AND FREEDOM FOR IRAN"
  9350, 11470, 15100, 15620, 15640 kHz

COLOMBIA—Spanish
CARACOL COLOMBIA
  5075 kHz
LA VOZ DEL LLANO
  6116 kHz
LV DEL CINARUCO
  4865 kHz
ONDAS DEL META
  4885 kHz
RADIO NACIONAL
  9655, 17865 kHz

CROATIA—Croatian
CROATIAN RADIO ZAGREB
  5020, 5920, *7315*, *9465*, *9495*, 9830, 13830, *15105* kHz

CUBA—Spanish
RADIO HABANA CUBA
  6060, 6180, 9550, 9655, 11760, 11875, 11970, 13660,
  15220, 15230, 15430, 17705 kHz
RADIO REBELDE
  5025 kHz (irregular)

CZECH REPUBLIC—Czech
CZECH RADIO
  5930 kHz
RADIO PRAGUE
  5930, 6055, *7300*, *7345*, 9485, 9490, *9810*, *11685*, 11990,
  12055, 13600, *15520*, *15605*, *17535*, 17725, *21705* kHz

DENMARK—Danish
DANMARKS RADIO
  5965, *7165*, *7210*, *7215*, *9560*, *9565*, *9590*, *9615*, *9640*,
  9650, *9655*, *9675*, *11730*, *11735*, *11775*, *11795*, *11805*,
  11850, *11865*, *11870*, *11875*, *11925*, *11930*, *15165*,
  15170, *15175*, *15180*, *15195*, *15220*, *15230*, *15335*,
  15355, *15365*, *17730*, *17740*, *17780*, *17785*, *17795*,
  17815, *17825*, *17845*, *17860*, *17865*, *21595*, *21705*,
  21710 kHz

DOMINICAN REPUBLIC—Spanish
RADIO CIMA
  4960 kHz (irregular)
RADIO DOMINICANA
  5980 kHz (projected)
RADIO N-103
  4800 kHz (irregular)
RADIO SANTIAGO
  9878 kHz (irregular)

ECUADOR—Spanish
HCJB-LA VOZ DE LOS ANDES
  6050, 6080, 9765, 11910, 11960, 15140, 17875 kHz
RADIO NACIONAL PROGRESO
  5062 kHz
RADIO NACIONAL
  15350 kHz
RADIO QUITO
  4920 kHz (irregular)

EGYPT—Arabic
RADIO CAIRO
  9620, 9670, 9700, 9755, 9770, 9800, 9850, 9900, 11665,
  11785, 11980, 12050, 15115, 15220, 15285, 15435,
  17670, 17745, 17770, 17800 kHz

FINLAND—Finnish and Swedish
RADIO FINLAND-YLE
  6120, 9550, 9560, 9635, 9665, 9730, 11735, 11755,
  11820, 11900, 15120, 15185, 15240, 15330, 15400,
  15440, 17740, 17800, 17825, 21550 kHz

FRANCE—French
RADIO FRANCE INTERNATIONALE
  3965, *4890*, 5910, 5915, 5920, 5945, 5990, 5995, 6040,
  6045, *6175*, 7120, 7135, *7160*, 7175, 7280, 7305, 9495,
  9550, 9605, *9650*, *9715*, 9745, *9790*, *9800*, 9805, 9830,
  9845, 11660, *11670*, *11680*, 11685, 11695, 11700, 11705,
  11790, 11845, *11850*, *11890*, 11965, 11995, *12025*, 12035,
  13625, *13660*, 15135, *15155*, 15180, 15190, 15195, *15215*,
  15285, 15300, 15315, 15360, *15365*, 15405, 15425, *15435*,
  15460, 15485, *15515*, *15530*, *17560*, *17575*, 17620, 17650,
  17690, 17695, *17710*, *17720*, 17775, 17785, 17795, 17800,
  17845, 17850, *17860*, *21520*, 21530, 21580, 21620, *21635*,
  21645, *21685*, 21765 kHz

FRENCH POLYNESIA—French and Tahitian
RFO-TAHITI
6135, 11827, 15170 kHz
GABON—French
AFRIQUE NUMERO UN
9580, 15475, 17630 kHz
GERMANY—German
BAYERISCHER RUNDFUNK
6085 kHz
DEUTSCHE WELLE
3995, *6075, 6085*, 6100, 6115, 6140, 6145, 6180, 6185,
7110, 7130, 7140, 7185, 7225, *7250, 7270,* 7275, *7315,*
7340, 9545, 9605, *9640,* 9650, 9665, *9690, 9700,* 9715,
9730, *9735,* 9755, *9885, 11655,* 11730, 11735, *11765,*
11785, *11795, 11810,* 11865, *11915,* 11950, *11965,*
11970, 13610, *13690,* 13780, 13790, 15105, 15135,
15145, *15245, 15250, 15270, 15275,* 15320, *15350,*
15390, *15410,* 15510, *15560,* 17560, 17710, *17715,*
17755, *17810,* 17820, *17830,* 17845, *17860,* 21540,
21560, 21570, 21600, *21640,* 21680 kHz
SENDER FREIES BERLIN-SFB
6190 kHz
RIAS
6005 kHz
RADIO BREMEN
6190 kHz
RADIOROPA-INFO
5980 kHz
SUDDEUTSCHER RUNDFUNK
6030 kHz
SUDWESTFUNK
7265 kHz
GREECE—Greek
FONI TIS HELLADAS
7450, 9375, 9380, 9395, 9420, 9425, 9825, 11595, 11645,
15630, 15650, 17515, 17525, 17550, 17715 kHz
RADIOFONIKOS STATHMOS MAKEDONIAS
7430, 9935, 11595 kHz
GUINEA—French
RTV GUINEENNE
4910, 6155, 7125, 9650 kHz
HOLLAND—Dutch
RADIO NEDERLAND WERELDOMROEP
5955, *6020, 6165, 7115,* 7130, *7260, 7285, 9590, 9630,*
9715, 9720, 9845, 9855, 9860, 9895, 11655, 11710,
11715, 11730, *11825, 11890, 11895,* 11935, 11950,
12005, 12065, 13700, 13770, *15120, 15155, 15210,*
15315, 15470, 15530, *15560, 17580, 17605,* 17895,
21480, 21485, 21530, 21640, 21745 kHz
HONDURAS—Spanish & English
RADIO COPAN INTERNACIONAL
15675 kHz
HUNGARY—Hungarian
RADIO BUDAPEST
6025, 7220, 9835, 11910, 13695, 15160, 15220, 17770,
21550 kHz
RADIO KOSSUTH
6025 kHz
INDIA—Hindi
ALL INDIA RADIO
7412, 9950, 11620, 11830, 15075, 15165, 17387 kHz
IRAN—Persian
VOICE OF THE ISLAMIC REPUBLIC
5995, 15084, 15365 kHz
IRAQ—Arabic
RADIO IRAQ INTERNATIONAL
11805, 11860, 13680, 15180, 15205, 15210, 17940 kHz
REPUBLIC OF IRAQ RADIO
4600 kHz
ISRAEL
KOL ISRAEL
Hebrew 11587, 11675 kHz
Yiddish 7465, 9435, 11587, 11605, 11675, 12075, 15640,
17575 kHz
RASHUTH HASHIDUR (Reshet Bet)
Hebrew 9388, 9435, 13750, 15615, 17545 kHz

ITALY—Italian
RADIO ROMA
5990, 7235, 7275, 7290, 9575, 9710, 11800, 11905,
15245, 15330, 15385, 17780, 17795, 17800, 21515,
21535, 21560, 21690, 21775 kHz
RAI-RTV ITALIANA
6060, 7175, 9515 kHz
JAPAN—Japanese
RADIO JAPAN/NHK
5960, 5970, 6005, 6025, 6030, 6050, 6060, 6120, 6125,
6185, 7140, 7210, *7230, 7255, 9535,* 9590, 9640, *9645,*
9675, 9685, 9725, 9750, 11725, *11735, 11740,* 11815,
11840, *11860,* 11865, 11870, 11875, 11910, 15190,
15195, 15210, 15230, 15240, 15280, *15325, 15350,*
15410, 15430, *17775,* 17810, *17820,* 17845, 17860,
17890, *21575,* 21610, *21640, 21700* kHz
RADIO TAMPA-NSB
3925, 3945, 6055, 6115, 9595, 9760 kHz
JORDAN—Arabic
RADIO JORDAN
7155, 9560, 9830, 11810, 11940, 11955, 15435 kHz
KOREA (DPR)—Korean
RADIO PYONGYANG
6250, 6400, 6540, 6576, 7200, 7250, 9325, 9345, 9505,
9600, 9640, 9977, 11335, 11700, 11735, 11905, 13760,
13785, 15130, 15180, 15230, 17765 kHz
KOREA (REPUBLIC)—Korean
KOREAN BROADCASTING SYSTEM
13670 kHz
RADIO KOREA
5975, 6135, *6145,* 6480, 7275, 7550, *9510,* 9515, 9570,
9640, *9650,* 9870, 11725, 11740, 11945, 13670, 15155,
15575 kHz
KUWAIT—Arabic
RADIO KUWAIT
9750, 9840, 11990, 15345, 15495, 15505, 21675 kHz
LEBANON—Arabic
KING OF HOPE
6280 kHz
VOICE OF LEBANON
6550 kHz
LIBYA—Arabic
RADIO JAMAHIRIYA
15235, 15415, 15435 kHz
LITHUANIA—Lithuanian
LITHUANIAN RADIO
9710 kHz
RADIO VILNIUS
7150, 9710, *12040* kHz
MEXICO—Spanish
RADIO EDUCACION
6185 kHz
RADIO MEXICO INTERNACIONAL
5985, 9705, 11770 kHz (irregular)
OTHERS (Sometimes audible near Mexico)
5982, 6010, 6017, 6045, 6105, 6115, 9546, 9555, 9600,
9680 kHz

MONACO—Arabic
RADIO MONTE CARLO
5960, 9755 kHz
MOROCCO
RADIO MEDI UN
French & Arabic 9575 kHz
RTV MAROCAINE
French 11920, 17595, 17815 kHz
Arabic 15105, 15330, 15335, 15345, 15360, 17815 kHz
NORWAY—Norwegian
RADIO NORWAY INTERNATIONAL
5965, 7165, 7210, 7215, 9560, 9565, 9590, 9615, 9640,
9645, 9650, 9655, 9675, 11730, 11735, 11775, 11795,
11805, 11850, 11865, 11870, 11875, 11925, 11930, 15165,
15170, 15175, 15180, 15195, 15220, 15230, 15335, 15355,
15365, 17730, 17740, 17780, 17785, 17795, 17815, 17825,
17845, 17860, 17865, 21595, 21705, 21710 kHz
OMAN—Arabic
RADIO OMAN
6085, 6120, 7230, 7270, 9735, 11890, 15375 kHz
PARAGUAY—Spanish
RADIO ENCARNACION
11940 kHz
RADIO NACIONAL
9735 kHz
PERU—Spanish
RADIO CORA
4915 kHz
RADIO UNION
6115 kHz
POLAND—Polish
POLISH RADIO
6095, 6135, 7145, 7270, 7285, 9540 kHz
PORTUGAL—Portuguese
RADIO RENASCENCA
9600 kHz
RDP INTERNATIONAL-RADIO PORTUGAL
6130, 9555, 9570, 9600, 9615, 9635, 9705, 9780, 9815,
11840, 11975, 15200, 15455, 15515, 17595, 17745,
21515, 21655, 21720 kHz
RUSSIA—Russian
GOLOS ROSSII
7120, 7300, 7310, 7440, 9450, 9470, *9510, 9650*, 9775,
9865, 9885, 9895, 11630, 11670, 11675, 11690, 11695,
11730, 11755, 11785, 12000, 12005, 12010, 12035, 12040,
12045, *12055*, 12070, *13605*, 13625, 13680, 13735 USB,
15295, 15450, 15465, 15475, 15480, 15500, 15535,
15570, 15595, 15600, 17600, 17610, 17620, 17645,
17650, *17655*, 17665, *17670*, 17700, *17840*, 21565,
21635, 21645, 21750, 21765, 21770, 21840, *21845* kHz
RADIO GALAXY (Russian and English)
9880, 11880 kHz
RADIO MOSCOW (Domestic Services)
4930, 5920, 5925, 5935, 5940, 5970 USB, 6015, 6190,
6195, 7100, 7160, 7165, 7200, 7260, 7290, 7300, 7335,
7360, 7370, 7400, 7490 USB, *9470*, 9480, 9490, 9545,
9570, 9670, 9725, 9775, 9780, 9790, 9850, 10690 USB,
11665, 11670, 11825, 11840, 11880, 11895, 11900,
12010, 12030, 12060, 12070, 13760 USB, 15255, 15460,
15490 kHz
RADIO PAMYAT
7230, 12000 kHz
RADIO RADONEZH
7230, 9865 kHz
RADIO ROSSII
5905, 5910, 6030, 7120, 7150, 7165, 7175, 7180, 7220,
7270, 7315, 7335, 7340, 7345, 7355, 7370, 9715, 9720,
9820, 11695, 11760, 11990, 12045, 15330, 15365,
15475 kHz
RADIO VEDO
7185, 9655, 11760, 13710 kHz
SAUDI ARABIA—Arabic
BROADCASTING SERVICE OF THE KINGDOM
6020, 7250, 9580, 9705, 9720, 9870, 9885, 11685, 11935,
11950, 15240, 15435, 21495, 21505, 21510, 21665,
21670 kHz

SLOVAKIA—Slovak
RADIO SLOVAKIA INTERNATIONAL
5915, 5930, 6055, 7310, 7345, 9505, 9580, 9605, 9810,
11990, 15605, 17535, 21705 kHz
SPAIN—Spanish
RADIO EXTERIOR DE ESPANA
5970, 6055, 6125, 6130, 7145, 7275, 9530, *9620, 9630*,
9650, *9745*, 9760, 9875, *11815*, 11850, 11870, *11880*,
11890, *11910*, 11920, 11945, 12035, 15110, *15125*,
15380, 17715, 17755, 17845, *17870, 17890* kHz
SWEDEN—Swedish
RADIO SWEDEN
6000, 6065, 9620, 9655, 9670, 9695, 11705, 11710,
11820, 11910, 15230, 15240, 15270, 15390, 17740,
17865, 21500 kHz
SWITZERLAND
RED CROSS BROADCASTING SERVICE
French & German 7210 kHz
SWISS RADIO INTERNATIONAL
French & German 3985, 5995, 6135, 6165, *7480*, 9535,
9650, 9810, 9860, 9885, *11690, 12035*, 13635, 13685,
15430, 15505, 17565, 17635, 17670, 21820 kHz (plus
17730 kHz German)
Italian 3985, 6135, 6165, *7480*, 9535, 9860, 9885, *12035*,
13635, 15430, 15505, 17635, 17670, *17730* kHz
SYRIA—Arabic
RADIO DAMASCUS & SYRIAN BROADCASTING SERVICE
9995, 12085, 15095 kHz
TOGO—French
RADIO LOME
5047 kHz
TUNISIA—Arabic
RTV TUNISIENNE
7475, 11550, 12005, 15450, 17500, 21535 kHz
TURKEY—Turkish
VOICE OF TURKEY
5980, 6140, 9445, 9460, 9560, 9665, 9685, 11895, 11925,
11945, 11955, 15325, 15350, 15385, 15405, 15430 kHz
UKRAINE—Ukrainian
RADIO UKRAINE
4825, 5985, 6020, 6070, 6080, 6090, 6145, *7150, 7165*,
7180, 7195, 7240, 7285, 9500, 9510, 9550, 9560, 9600,
9640, 9675, 9685, 9710, 9735, 9745, 9860, 11610, 11705,
11720, 11735, 11780, 11790, 11825, 11840, 11870,
11950, 15135, 15150, *15180*, 15195, 15260, 15375,
15385, 15525, *15580, 17605*, *17690*, 17725, 17745,
17780, 17790, 17810, 21460, 21725, 21800 kHz
UNITED ARAB EMIRATES—Arabic
UAE RADIO FROM ABU DHABI
7215, 9505, 9605, 9695, 9770, 11710, 11885, 11970,
11985, 13605, 15265, 15305, 15315, 17645, 17855,
21510, 21570, 21735 kHz
UAE RADIO IN DUBAI
11795, 11945, 13675, 15320, 15395, 15400, 15435,
17830, 17890, 21605, 21700 kHz
URUGUAY—Spanish
RADIO EL ESPECTADOR
11836 kHz
RADIO ORIENTAL
11735 kHz
VENEZUELA—Spanish
ECOS DEL TORBES
4980, 9640 kHz
RADIO NACIONAL
9540 kHz
RADIO RUMBOS
4970, 9660 kHz
RADIO TACHIRA
4830 kHz
RADIO VALERA
4840 kHz
YUGOSLAVIA—Serbian
RADIO BEOGRAD
7200, 9505 kHz
RADIO YUGOSLAVIA
6100, 9580, 9720 kHz

Addresses PLUS

Station Addresses . . . *PLUS* Local Times in Each Country, Station Personnel, Future Plans for Stations, Fax and Toll-Free Numbers, Gifts and Items for Sale

Want to sound off about a program just heard? Letters and faxes are often virtually the only link a station has with its listeners. This means that dozens—even hundreds—of broadcasters around the world are eager to hear from you . . . and, at times, be generous in return.

Or maybe you want something. What's the best hotel in La Paz, Bolivia? How to order a Central American T-shirt? Which station sells Pacific Island discs? Who will help you learn Chinese?

Unusual Items Available

Some stations give out souvenirs and tourist literature or information, as well as the usual complimentary program schedules. These goodies include brochures on national or regional history, exotic calendars (usually around year's end), offbeat magazines and newspapers, language learning aids, attractive verification postcards, costume jewelry pins, colorful pennants, stickers and decals, key chains—even, on rare occasion, recordings, weird coins and stamps. Yet other stations sell unusual items, such as native recordings and the like.

Tourist Tips Not in Your Baedeker

If you're traveling abroad, here's a little-known secret: World band stations are sometimes willing to provide helpful information to prospective visitors. When writing, especially to smaller stations, appeal to their civic pride and treat them like kindly uncles you're seeking a favor from. After all, catering to tourist inquiries is hardly a requirement of operating most radio stations. (This section mentions which stations provide tourist literature as a matter of course.)

"Applause" Correspondence Welcomed (Boos, too)

When radio was in its infancy, stations were anxious for feedback from the audience on how well their signals were being received. Listeners sent in "applause" cards not only to let stations know about reception quality, but also how much their shows were—or were not—being appreciated. By way of saying "thanks," stations would reply with a letter or postcard verifying that the station the listener reported hearing was, in fact, theirs.

Professor Simo Soininen, one of Finland's leading radio enthusiasts, poses with some of the many pennants available from world band stations.

A number of broadcasters still seek out information on reception quality, but most are chiefly interested in knowing how well you like—or don't like—their programs. Too, nearly all are interested in immediate feedback, such as by fax, when something technical has suddenly gone wrong—a transmitter drifting off frequency, for example, or poor audio quality.

But stations' biggest need, by far, is to hear what listeners think about their programs. Neighbors, friends and sophisticated

Radio Norway International analyzes listeners' letters.

rating organizations let ordinary broadcasters know in no uncertain terms exactly how they are faring. Not so with world band. Its listeners are scattered throughout the world, so in the absence of correspondence from you, most have no way of knowing what they are doing well, or not so well.

Paying the Postman

Most major stations that reply do so for free. However, many smaller organizations expect, or at least hope for, reimbursement for postage costs. Most effective, especially for Latin American and Indonesian stations, is to enclose return postage; that is, unused (mint) stamps from the *station's* country. These are available from Plum's Airmail Postage, 12 Glenn Road, Flemington NJ 08822 USA (send $1 or a self-addressed, stamped envelope for details); DX Stamp Service, 7661 Roder Parkway, Ontario NY 14519 USA (ditto); DX-QSL Associates, 434 Blair Road NW, Vienna VA 22180 USA; and some local private stamp dealers. Unused Brazilian international reply stamps (one stamp for $1 or 6 IRCs) are also available from Antonio Ribeiro da Motta, Caixa Postal 949, 12201-970 São José dos Campos—SP, Brazil.

One way to help ensure your return postage will be used for the intended purpose is to affix it onto a pre-addressed return airmail envelope (self-addressed stamped envelope, or SASE). However, if the envelope is too small the contents may have to be folded to fit in.

You can also prompt reluctant stations by donating one U.S. dollar, preferably hidden from prying eyes by a piece of foil-covered carbon paper or the like. Registration helps, too. Additionally, International Reply Coupons (IRCs), which recipients may exchange locally for air or surface stamps, are available at many post offices worldwide. Thing is, they're relatively costly, are not all that effective, and aren't accepted by postal authorities in all countries.

Writing Tips

Write to be read. When writing, remember to make your letter interesting and helpful from the recipient's point of view, and friendly without being excessively personal or forward. Well-thought-out comments on specific programs are almost always appreciated. If you must use a foreign-language form letter as the basis for your communication, individualize it for each occasion either by writing or typing it out, or by making use of a word processor.

Incorporate language courtesies. Writing in the broadcaster's tongue is always a plus—this section of *Passport* indicates when it is a requirement—but English is usually the next best bet. In addition, when writing in any language to Spanish-speaking countries, remember that what gringos think of as the "last name" is actually written as the middle name. Thus Antonio Vargas García, which also can be written as Antonio Vargas G., refers to Sr. Vargas; so your salutation should read, *Estimado Sr. Vargas.*

What's that "García" doing there, then? That's *mamita's* father's family name. Latinos more or less solved the problem of gender fairness in names long before the Anglos.

But, wait—what about Portuguese, used by all those stations in Brazil? Same concept, but in reverse. Mama's father's family name is in the middle, and the "real" last name is where we're used to it, at the end.

In Chinese the "last" name comes first. However, when writing in English, Chinese names are sometimes reversed for the benefit of *low faan*—foreigners. Use your judgment. For example, "Li" is a common Chinese last name, so if you see "Li Dan," it's "Mr. Li." But if it's "Dan Li," he's already one step ahead of you, and it's still "Mr. Li. "

Less widely known is that the same can also occur in Hungarian. For example, "Bartók Béla" for Béla Bartók.

If in doubt, fall back on the ever-safe "Dear Sir" or "Dear Madam." And be patient—replies usually take weeks, sometimes months. Slow responders, those that tend to take six months or more to reply, are cited in this section, as are erratic repliers.

Local Time Given for Every Country

Local times are given in terms of hours' difference from World Time, also known as Coordinated Universal Time (UTC), Greenwich Mean Time (GMT) and Zulu time (Z).

For example, Algeria is World Time +1; that is, one hour later than World Time. So, if World Time is 1200, the local time in Algeria is 1300 (1:00 PM). On the other hand, México City is World Time –6; that is,

six hours earlier than World Time. If World Time is 1200, in México City it's 6:00 AM. And so it goes for each country in this section. Times in (parentheses) are for the middle of the year—roughly April–October.

These nominal times are almost always the actual times, as well. Yet, there are a very few exceptions. For example, in China the actual time nationwide is World Time +8 ("Beijing Time"); yet, in one region, Xinjiang, it's officially +6 ("Urümqi Time"), even though nobody observes that time. These rare exceptions are explained in this section.

There's more information on World Time in the Glossary, "Compleat Idiot's Guide to Getting Started" and elsewhere throughout this book.

Spotted Something New?

The staff and friends of International Broadcasting Services, scattered about the globe, strive year-round to gather and prepare material for *Passport*. In addition to having unearthed and sifted through tens of thousands of items of data, they have made

UAE Radio

Ahmed Shouly, Controller-General of Foreign Programs for UAE Radio in Dubai, produces the popular "Mailbag" program.

countless judgment calls based on decades of specialized experience. Still, we don't uncover everything, we don't always call it right, and the passage of time invariably brings about a decline in the accuracy of what's on the page.

Has something changed since we went to press? A missing detail? Please let us know! Your update information, especially photocopies of material received from stations, is very much welcomed and appreciated at the IBS Editorial Office, Box 300, Penn's Park, PA 18943 USA, fax +1 (215) 598 3794. Make it to my attention: Craig Tyson, Editor, "Addresses PLUS."

Our thanks to John Herkimer, Editor-Publisher and Don Jensen, Editor Emeritus of *Número Uno*; Tetsuya Hirahara, Overseas Charge Secretary of *Radio Nuevo Mundo*; and the members of both organizations—as well as pioneering Russian editor Anatoly Klepov—for their kind cooperation in the preparation of this section.

Using Passport's Addresses PLUS Section

- All stations known to reply, or which possibly may reply, to correspondence from listeners are included. Feedback that is helpful to the station is particularly welcomed.
- Mailing addresses are given, for obvious reasons. These sometimes differ from the physical locations given in the Blue Pages.
- Private organizations that lease air time, but which possess no world band transmitters of their own, are generally not listed. However, they may be reached via the stations, which are listed, over which they were heard.
- Unless otherwise indicated, stations:
  – Reply regularly within six months to most listeners' letters in English.
  – Provide, upon request, free station schedules and souvenir verification (QSL) postcards or letters. We specify when yet other items are available for free or for purchase.
  – Do not require compensation for postage costs incurred in replying to you. Where compensation is required, details are provided as to what to send.
- Local times are given in difference from World Time (UTC). Times in (parentheses) are for the middle of the year—roughly April-October.
- **ADS** indicates the station is known to accept advertising from foreign clients.
- **AIR** indicates the station is known to sell blocks of airtime to foreign clients.

AFGHANISTAN World Time +4:30

RADIO AFGHANISTAN, External Services, P.O. Box 544, Kabul, Afghanistan. Contact: Shir Aqa Hamidy, Director of English Program; or Qasim Rarawan, Director of Information Department.

ALBANIA World Time +1

RADIO TIRANA, Radiotelevisione Shqiptar, International Service, Rrug Ismail Qemali, Tirana, Albania. Contact: Mico Dhima, Director of External Services; Gezim Guri, Correspondence Section; or Diana Koci. Free tourist literature, stickers, Albanian stamps, pins and other souvenirs. Sells Albanian audio and video cassettes.

ALGERIA World Time +1 (+2 midyear)

RADIO ALGIERS INTERNATIONAL—same details as "Radiodiffusion-Télévision Algerienne," below.

RADIODIFFUSION-TELEVISION ALGERIENNE (ENRS), 21 Boulevard el Chouhada, Algiers, Algeria. Fax: +213 (2) 605 814. Contact: (nontechnical) L. Zaghlami; or Chaabane Lounakil, Head of International Arabic Section; (technical) Direction des Services Techniques. Replies irregularly. French or Arabic preferred, but English accepted.

ANGOLA World Time +1

A VOZ DA RESISTENCIA DO GALO NEGRO (Voice of the Resistence of the Black Cockerel), Free Angola Information Service, P.O. Box 65463, Washington DC 20035 USA (physical address is 1350 Connecticut Avenue NW, Suite 907, Washington DC 20036); Contact: (Connecticut Avenue) Jaime de Azevedo Vila Santa, Director of Information; Pro-UNITA, supported by South Africa and the United States.

RADIO NACIONAL DE ANGOLA, Cx. Postal 1329, Luanda, Angola. Fax: +244 (2) 391 234. Contact: Bernardino Costa, Public Opinion Office; Sra. Luiza Fancony, Diretora de Programas; Lourdes de Almeida, Chefe de Secção; or Cesar A.B. da Silva, Diretor Geral. Replies occasionally to correspondence, preferably in Portuguese. $1, return postage or 2 IRCs most helpful.

EMISSORA PROVINCIAL DE BENGUELA, Cx. Postal 19, Benguela, Angola. Contact: Simão Martíns Cuto, Responsável Administrativo; Celestino da Silva Mota, Diretor; or José Cabral Sande. $1 or return postage required. Replies irregularly.

EMISSORA PROVINCIAL DE BIE (when operating), C.P. 33, Kuito, Bié, Angola. Contact: José Cordeiro Chimo, O Diretor. Replies occasionally to correspondence in Portuguese.

EMISSORA PROVINCIAL DE MOXICO (when operating, as destroyed in recent fighting), Cx. Postal 74, Luena, Angola. Contact: Paulo Cahilo, Diretor. $1 or return postage required. Replies to correspondence in Portuguese.

Other **EMISSORA PROVINCIAL** stations—same address, etc., as Radio Nacional, above.

ANTARCTICA World Time –2 (–3 midyear) Base Esperanza; +13 McMurdo

RADIO NACIONAL ARCANGEL SAN GABRIEL—LRA 36 (when operating), Base Antártica Esperanza (Tierra de San Martín), 9411 Territorio Antártico Argentino, Argentina. Contact: (nontechnical) Elizabeth Beltrán de Gallegos, Programación y Locución; (technical) Cristian Omar Guida, Técnica Operación. Return postage required. Replies irregularly to correspondence in Spanish. If no reply, try sending your correspondence (don't write station name on envelope) and 2 IRCs to the helpful Gabriel Iván Barrera, Casilla 2868, 1000-Buenos Aires, Argentina; fax +54 (1) 322 3351.

ANTIGUA World Time –4

BBC WORLD SERVICE—CARIBBEAN RELAY STATION, P.O. Box 1203, St. John's, Antigua. Contact: (technical) G. Hoef, Manager; Roy Fleet; or R. Pratt, Company Engineer. Nontechnical correspondence should be sent to the BBC World Service in London (see).

DEUTSCHE WELLE—ANTIGUA—same address and contact as BBC World Service, above. Nontechnical correspondence should be sent to the Deutsche Welle in Germany (see).

ARGENTINA World Time –2 (–3 midyear) Buenos Aires and most eastern provinces; –3 or –3 (–4 midyear) other provinces.

RADIODIFUSION ARGENTINA AL EXTERIOR—RAE, C.C. 555 Correo Central, 1000-Buenos Aires, Argentina. Fax: +54 (1) 325 9433. Contact: (nontechnical) Paul F. Allen, Announcer, English Team; John Anthony Middleton, Head of the English Team; Marcela G.R. Campos, Directora; María Dolores López; or Sandro Cenci, Chief, Italian Section; (technical) Gabriel Iván Barrera, DX Editor; or Patricia Menéndez. Free paper pennant and tourist literature. Return postage or $1 appreciated.

RADIO CONTINENTAL, Rivadavia 835, 1002-Buenos Aires, Argentina. Contact: Julio A. Valles. Stickers and tourist literature; $1 or return postage required. Replies to correspondence in Spanish.

RADIO MALARGÜE, Esquivel Aldao 350, 5613-Malargüé, Argentina. Contact: Eduardo V. Lucea, Jefe Técnico; or José Pandolfo, Departamento Administración. Free pennants. Return postage necessary. Prefers correspondence in Spanish.

RADIO NACIONAL, BUENOS AIRES—LRA1/LRA31, Maipú 555, 1000-Buenos Aires, Argentina.

RADIO NACIONAL, MENDOZA—LRA6/LRA34 (when operating, once transmitter parts are obtained), Emilio Civit 460, 5500-Mendoza, Argentina. Contact: Lic. Jorge Parvanoff.

ARMENIA World Time +3 (+4 midyear)

ARMENIAN RADIO—see Radio Yerevan for details.

RADIO YEREVAN, Alekmanoukyan Street 5, 375025 Yerevan, Armenia. Contact: V. Voskanian, Deputy Editor-in-Chief; R. Abalian, Editor-in-Chief; or Olga Iroshina. Replies slowly.

ASCENSION ISLAND World Time exactly

BBC WORLD SERVICE—ATLANTIC RELAY STATION, English Bay, Ascension Island. Fax: +247 6117. Contact: (technical) Andrew Marsden, Transmitter Engineer; or Dinah Fowler. Nontechnical correspondence should be sent to the BBC World Service in (see).

VOICE OF AMERICA—ASCENSION RELAY STATION—same details as "BBC World Service," above. Nontechnical correspondence should be directed to the regular VOA address (see USA).

AUSTRALIA World Time +11 (+10 midyear) Victoria (VIC), New South Wales and Tasmania; +10:30 (+9:30 midyear) South Australia; +10 Queensland (QLD); +9:30 Northern Territory (NT); +8 Western Australia (WA)

AUSTRALIAN ARMED FORCES RADIO, Department of Defense, EMU (Electronic Media Unit) ANZAC Park West, APW 1/B/07, Reid, Canberra, ACT 2600, Australia. Fax: +61 (6) 265 1099. Contact: (nontechnical) Hugh Mackenzie, Director; Lt. Carey Martin; or A. Patulny; (technical) M.A. Brown, Director of Engineering. SAE and 2 IRCs needed for a reply.

AUSTRALIAN BROADCASTING CORPORATION—ABC BRISBANE, GPO Box 9994, GPO Brisbane QLD 4001, Australia. Fax: +61 (7) 377 5442. Contact: John Kalinowski, Manager Network Services; (technical) Thomas A. Rowan, VK4BR, Transmission Manager. Free stickers, "Travellers Guide to ABC Radio." 3 IRCs or return postage helpful.

AUSTRALIAN BROADCASTING CORPORATION—ABC DARWIN, ABC Box 9994, GPO Darwin NT 0801, Australia. Fax: +61 (89) 433 235. Contact: (nontechnical) Sue Camilleri, Broadcaster and Community Liason Officer; (technical) David Stephenson. Free stickers. Free "Travellers Guide to ABC Radio." T-shirts available for US$17. Tape recordings of documentaries relating to Darwin's involvement in World War II are available for US$10. 3 IRCs or return postage helpful.

AUSTRALIAN BROADCASTING CORPORATION—ABC PERTH, ABC Box 9994, GPO Perth WA 6001, Australia. Fax: +61 (9) 220 2919. Contact: (technical) Gary Matthews, Head of Broadcast and Technical Department (Radio). Free stickers and "Travellers Guide to ABC Radio." 3 IRCs or return postage helpful.

CAAMA RADIO—ABC, Central Australian Aboriginal Media Association, Bush Radio Service, P.O. Box 2924, Alice Springs NT 0871, Australia. Fax: +61 (89) 55 219. Contact: (nontechnical or technical) Barbara Richards; or Rae Allen, Regional Programme Manager; (technical) Clint Mitchell, Receptionist. Free stickers. 2 IRCs or return postage helpful.

RADIO AUSTRALIA—ABC

Main Office: P.O. Box 755, Glen Waverley VIC 3150, Australia. Fax: (administration) +61 (3) 881 2346; (news) +61 (3) 881 2334; (technical) +61 (3) 881 2377. Contact: (nontechnical) Susan Jenkins, Correspondence Officer; Roger Broadbent, Head, English Language Programming; Judi Cooper, Businesss Development Manager; Derek White, General Manager; or Susan Kadar, Controller, News & Programmes; (technical) Nigel Holmes, Frequency Manager, Frequency Management Unit. Free literature on Australia. Books, tape recordings and T-shirts are available for sale from the Business Development Manager.

New York Bureau, Nontechnical: 1 Rockefeller Plaza, Suite 1700, New York NY 10020 USA. Fax: +1 (212) 332 2546. Contact: Maggie Jones, Manager.

London Bureau, Nontechnical: 54 Portland Place, London W1N 4DY, United Kingdom. Fax: +44 (71) 323 0059. Contact: Robert Bolton, Manager.

Bangkok Bureau, Nontechnical: 209 Soi Hutayana Off Soi Suanplu, South Sathorn Road, Bangkok 10120, Thailand. Fax: +66 (2) 287 2040. Contact: Nicholas Stuart.

RADIO RUM JUNGLE—ABC, Top Aboriginal Bush Association, P.O. Batchelor NT 0845, Australia. Fax: +61 (89) 760 270. Contact: Mae-Mae Morrison, Announcer; Andrew Joshua, Chairman; or George Butler. 3 IRCs or return postage helpful.

VNG, VNG Users Consortium, GPO Box 1090, Canberra ACT 2601, Australia. Fax: +61 (6) 249 9969. Contact: Dr. Marion Leiba, Honorary Secretary. Free promotional material available. Return postage necessary.

Alternative Address: National Standards Commission, P.O. Box 282, North Ryde, NSW 2113, Australia. Return postage helpful.

AUSTRIA World Time +1 (+2 midyear)

RADIO AUSTRIA INTERNATIONAL, A-1136 Vienna, Austria. Fax: (nontechnical) +43 (1) 87 878 3630; (technical) +43 (1) 87 878 2773. Contact: (nontechnical) Prof. Paul Lendvai, Director; Dr. Edgar Sterbenz, Deputy Director; or Vera Bock; (technical) Frequency Management Department. Free stickers, pennants and calendars. A legal case before Austria's highest court could result in the shutdown of this station's only world band facility, located in the vicinity of Vienna.

AZERBAIJAN World Time +3

AZERBAIJANI RADIO—see Radio Dada Gorud for details.

RADIO DADA GORUD, ul. M. Guzeina 1, 370011 Baku, Azerbaijan. Contact: (nontechnical) Ershad Kuliyev, Director. $1 or return postage helpful. Replies occasionally.

BAHRAIN World Time +3

RADIO BAHRAIN, Broadcasting & Television, Ministry of Information, P.O. Box 702, Al Manāmah, Bahrain. Fax: (Arabic Service) +973 681 544; or (English Service) +973 780 911. Contact: A. Suliman (for Director of Broadcasting). $1 or IRC required. Replies irregularly.

BANGLADESH World Time +6

RADIO BANGLADESH

Nontechnical correspondence: External Services, Shahbagh Post Box No. 2204, Dhaka 1000, Bangladesh. Contact: Masudul Hasan, Deputy Director; or Mobarak Hossain Khan, Director.

Technical correspondence: National Broadcasting Authority, NBA House, 121 Kazi Nazrul Islam Avenue, Dhaka 1000, Bangladesh. Contact: M.A. Haque Bhuiya, Senior Engineer in Charge; Mohammed Noor Al-Islam, Station Engineer (Research Wing); or Kazi Rafique.

BELARUS World Time +2 (+3 midyear)

BELARUSSIAN RADIO—see Radiostantsiya Belarus for details.

GRODNO RADIO—see Radiostantsiya Belarus for details.

MAHILEV RADIO—see Radiostantsiya Belarus for details.

RADIO MINSK—see Radiostantsiya Belarus for details.

RADIOSTANTSIYA BELARUS, ul. Krasnaya 4, 220807 Minsk, Belarus. Fax: +7 (0172) 366 643. Contact: Michail Tondel, Chief Editor; Jürgen Eberhardt; or Hermann A. Parli. Free Belarus stamps.

BELGIUM World Time +1 (+2 midyear)

RADIO VLAANDEREN INTERNATIONAL, Belgische Radio en Televisie, P.O. Box 26, B-1000 Brussels, Belgium. Fax: +32 (2) 732 6295 or +32 (2) 734 7804. Contact (technical): Frans Vossen, Producer, "Radio World"; or Jacques Vandersichel, Director. Free stickers and Listeners' Club magazine. Replies sometimes take a while.

BELIZE World Time –6

BELIZE RADIO ONE, Broadcasting Corporation of Belize, Albert Catouse Building, P.O. Box 89, Belize City, Belize. Fax: +501 (2) 75040. Contact: (nontechnical) Anita Chung, Traffic Department; (technical) Mike Gundy, Chief Engineer. T-shirts available for US$20. Replies to correspondence in English or Spanish.

BENIN World Time +1

OFFICE DE RADIODIFFUSION ET TELEVISION DU BENIN, La Voix de la Révolution, B.P. 366, Cotonou, Bénin; this address is for Cotonou and Parakou stations, alike. Contact: (Cotonou) Damien Zinsou Ala Hassa; Anastase Adjoko; or Leonce Goohouede; (Radio Parakou, nontechnical) J. de Matha, Le Chef de la Station, or (Radio Parakou, technical) Léon Donou, Le Chef des Services Techniques. Return postage, $1 or IRC required. Replies irregularly and slowly to correspondence in French.

BHUTAN World Time +6

BHUTAN BROADCASTING SERVICE

Station: Department of Information and Broadcasting, Ministry of Communications, P.O. Box 101, Thimphu, Bhutan. Fax: +975 23073. Contact: (nontechnical) Renchir Choden, News and Cur-

rent Affairs; (technical) C. Proden, Station Engineer. 2 IRCs, return postage or $1 required. Replies extremely irregularly; correspondence to the U.N. Mission (see following) may be more fruitful.

United Nations Mission: Permanent Mission of the Kingdom of Bhutan to the United Nations, Two United Nations Plaza, 27th Floor, New York NY 10017 USA. Fax: +1 (212) 826 2998. Contact: Mrs. Kunzang C. Namgyel, Third Secretary; Mrs. Sonam Yangchen, Attaché; Ms. Leki Wangmo, Second Secretary; or Hari K. Chhetri, Second Secretary.

BOLIVIA World Time –4

LA VOZ DEL TROPICO, "Radiodifusora CVU," Casilla 2494, Cochabamba, Bolivia. Contact: Eduardo Avila Alberdi, Director; or Carlos Pocho Hochmann, Locutor. Return postage or $1 required. Replies occasionally to correspondence in Spanish.

RADIO ABAROA, Casilla 136, Riberalta, Bení, Bolivia. Contact: René Arias Pacheco, Director. Return postage or $1 required. Replies irregularly to correspondence in Spanish.

RADIO ANIMAS, Chocaya, Animas, Potosí, Bolivia. Return postage or $1 required. Replies irregularly to correspondence in Spanish.

RADIO CENTENARIO, LA NUEVA, Casilla 818, Santa Cruz de la Sierra, Bolivia. Contact: Napoleón Ardaya Borja, Director. Return postage or $1 required. Replies to correspondence in Spanish.

RADIO COSMOS, Casilla 5303, Cochabamba, Bolivia. Contact: Laureano Rojas, Jr., Administrativo. $1 or return postage required. Replies irregularly to correspondence in Spanish.

RADIODIFUSORA MINERIA, Casilla 247, Oruro, Bolivia. Contact: Dr. José Carlos Gómez Espinoza, Gerente y Director General. Return postage or $1 required. Replies irregularly to correspondence in Spanish.

RADIO DOS DE FEBRERO (when operating), Vacadiez 400, Rurrenabaque, Bení, Bolivia. Contact: John Arce. Replies occasionally to correspondence in Spanish.

RADIO ECO, Av. Brasil, Correo Central, Reyes, Bení, Bolivia. Contact: Carlos Espinoza Gonzales Cortez, Director-Gerente; or Rolmán Medina Méndez. Free station literature. $1 or return postage required, and financial contributions solicited for the owner's physiotherapy incurred as a result of a pool accident. Replies irregularly to correspondence in Spanish.

RADIO EL MUNDO, Casilla 1984, Santa Cruz de la Sierra, Bolivia. Contact: Freddy Banegas Carrasco, Gerente. Free stickers. $1 or return postage required. Replies irregularly to correspondence in Spanish.

RADIO FIDES, Casilla 9143, La Paz, Bolivia. Fax: +591 (2) 379 030. Contact: Pedro Eduardo Pérez, Director; or Roxana Beltrán C. Replies occasionally to correspondence in Spanish.

RADIO FRONTERA, Casilla 179, Cobija, Pando, Bolivia. Contact: Lino Miahuchi von Ancken, CP9AR. Free pennants. $1 or return postage necessary. Replies to correspondence in Spanish.

RADIO GALAXIA, Guayaramerín, Bení, Bolivia. Contact: Dorián Arias, Gerente; or Jeber Hitachi Banegas, Director. Return postage or $1 required. Replies to correspondence in Spanish.

RADIO GRIGOTA, Casilla 203, Santa Cruz, Bolivia. Contact: Víctor Hugo Arteaga, Director General. $1 or return postage required. Replies occasionally to correspondence in Spanish.

RADIO HITACHI, Casilla 400, Correo Central, Guayaramerín, Bení, Bolivia; if no response, try Calle Sucre 20, Guayaramerín, Bení, Bolivia. Contact: Herbert Hitachi Valegas, Director. Return postage of $1 required. Has replied in the past to correspondence in Spanish, but as of late correspondence has sometimes been returned as "addressee unknown."

RADIO ILLIMANI, Casilla 1042, La Paz, Bolivia. Contact: Sra. Gladys de Zamora, Administradora. $1 required, and your letter should be registered and include a tourist brochure or postcard from where you live. Replies irregularly to friendly correspondence in Spanish.

RADIO INTEGRACION, Casilla 1722, La Paz, Bolivia. Contact: Juan Carlos Blanco.

RADIO JUAN XXIII, San Ignacio de Velasco, Santa Cruz, Bolivia. Contact: Fernando Manuel Picazo Torres, Director. Return postage or $1 required. Replies occasionally to correspondence in Spanish.

RADIO LA CRUZ DEL SUR, Casilla 1408, La Paz, Bolivia. Contact: Pastor Rodolfo Moya Jiménez, Director. Pennant for $1 or return postage. Replies slowly to correspondence in Spanish.

RADIO LIBERTAD, Casilla 5324, La Paz, Bolivia. Fax: +591 (2)

391 995. Contact: Carmiña Ortiz H., Jefe de Publicidad y Relaciones Públicas; or Fatimá Tamayo Muñoz, Relaciones Públicas. Free pennants and stickers. Return postage or $1 required. Replies fairly regularly to correspondence in Spanish.

RADIO LOS ANDES, Casilla 344, Tarija, Bolivia. Contact: Jaime Rollano Monje, Gerente.

RADIO MAMORE, Casilla de Correo 238, Correo Central, Guayaramerín, Bení, Bolivia. Contact: Dilson Martínez Sánchez, Director General. Free pennants. Return postage or $1 required. Replies irregularly to correspondence in Spanish or Portuguese. **ADS AIR**

RADIO MINERIA, Casilla de Correo 247, Oruro, Bolivia. Contact: Dr. José Carlos Gómez Espinoza, Gerente y Director General; or Srta. Costa Colque Flores., Responsable del programa "Minería Cultural." Free pennants. Replies to correspondence in Spanish. **ADS AIR**

RADIO MOVIMA, Calle Baptista No. 24, Santa Ana de Yacuma, Bení, Bolivia. Contact: Rubén Serrano López, Director. Return postage or $1 required. Replies irregularly to correspondence in Spanish.

RADIO NACIONAL DE HUANUNI, Casilla 681, Oruro, Bolivia. Contact: Rafael Linneo Morales, Director-General; or Alfredo Murillo, Director. Return postage or $1 required. Replies irregularly to correspondence in Spanish.

RADIO PADILLA, Padilla, Chuquisaca, Bolivia. Contact: Moisés Palma Salazar, Director. Return postage or $1 required. Replies to correspondence in Spanish.

RADIO PAITITI, Casilla 172, Guayaramerín, Bení, Bolivia. Contact: Armando Mollinedo Bacarreza, Director; Luís Carlos Santa Cruz Cuéllar, Director Gerente; or Ancir Vaca Cuellar, Gerente-Propietario. Return postage or $1 required. Replies irregularly to correspondence in Spanish.

RADIO PANAMERICANA, Casilla 5263, La Paz, Bolivia. Daniel Sánchez Rocha, Director. Replies irregularly, with correspondence in Spanish preferred. $1 or 2 IRCs helpful.

RADIO PERLA DEL ACRE, Casilla 7, Cobija, Departamento de Pando, Bolivia. Contact: Rafael Vidal, Manager. Return postage or $1 required. Replies irregularly to correspondence in Spanish.

RADIO PIO DOCE, Casilla 434, Llallagua, Potosí, Bolivia. Contact: Pbro. Roberto Durette, OMI, Director General. Return postage helpful. Replies occasionally to correspondence in Spanish.

RADIO SAN GABRIEL, Casilla 4792, La Paz, Bolivia. Contact: (nontechnical) Lic. Gary Martínez, Director Ejecutivo; (technical) Mario Mamani. $1 or return postage helpful. Free pennants, book on station, Aymara calendars and *La Voz del Pueblo Aymara* magazine. Replies fairly regularly to correspondence in Spanish.

RADIO SAN MIGUEL, Casilla 102, Riberalta, Bení, Bolivia. Contact: Felix A. Rada Q., Director. Return postage or $1 required. Replies irregularly to correspondence in Spanish.

RADIO SANTA ANA, Calle Sucre No. 250, Santa Ana de Yacuma, Bení, Bolivia. Contact: Mario Roberto Suárez, Director; or Mariano Verdugo. Return postage or $1 required. Replies irregularly to correspondence in Spanish.

RADIO SANTA CRUZ, Emisora del Instituto Radiofónico Fe y Alegría (IRFA), Casilla 672, Santa Cruz de la Sierra, Bolivia. Contact: Alvaro Puente C., S.J., Sub-Director; or Victor Blajot, S.J., Director General de INFACRUZ. Free pennants. Return postage required. Correspondence in Spanish preferred.

RADIO SANTA ROSA, Correo Central, Santa Rosa de Yacuma, Bení, Bolivia. Replies irregularly to correspondence in Spanish. $1 or 2 IRCs helpful.

RADIO TRINIDAD, Trinidad, Bení, Bolivia.

RADIO 20 DE SETIEMBRE (if operating), Bermejo, Tarija, Bolivia. Return postage or $1 required. Replies irregularly to correspondence in Spanish.

RADIO VILLAMONTES, Avenida Méndez Arcos No. 156, Villamontes, Departamento de Tarija, Bolivia. Contact: Gerardo Rocabado Galarza, Director. $1 or return postage required.

BOTSWANA World Time +2

RADIO BOTSWANA, Private Bag 0060, Gaborone, Botswana. Fax: +267 (31) 371 588; or +267 (31) 357 138. Contact: (nontechnical) Ted Makgekgenene, Director; or Monica Mphusu, Producer, "Maokaneng/Pleasure Mix"; (technical) Kingsley Reebang. Free stickers, pennants and pins. Return postage, $1 or 2 IRCs required. Replies slowly and irregularly. **ADS AIR**

VOICE OF AMERICA/VOA—BOTSWANA RELAY STATION
Transmitter Site: Voice of America, Botswana Relay Station, Moepeng Hill, Selebi-Phikwe, Botswana. Contact: William Connally, Station Manager. This address for technical correspondence only. Nontechnical correspondence should be directed to the regular VOA address (*see* USA).

Frequency and Monitoring Office:, Voice of America, 330 Independence Avenue, S.W., Washington DC 20540 USA. Fax: +1 (202) 619 1781. Contact: Daniel Ferguson, Botswana QSL Desk, VOA/EOFF:Frequency Management & Monitoring Division. The Botswana Desk is for technical correspondence only. Nontechnical correspondence should be directed to the regular VOA address (*see* USA).

BRAZIL World Time −1 (−2 midyear) Atlantic Islands; −2 (−3 midyear) Eastern, including Bras ília and Rio de Janeiro; −3 (−4 midyear) Western; −4 (−5 midyear) Acre

Note 1: Postal authorities recommend that, because of the level of theft in the Brazilian postal system, correspondence to Brazil be sent only via registered mail.

Note 2: For Brazilian return postage, see introduction to this section.

RADIO ALVORADA LONDRINA, Rua Sen. Souza Naves 9, 9 Andar, 86015 Londrina, Paraná, Brazil. Contact: Padre José Guidoreni, Diretor. Pennants for $1 or return postage. Replies to correspondence in Portuguese.

RADIO ALVORADA PARINTINS, Travessa Leopoldo Neves 503, 69150 Parintins, Amazonas, Brazil. Contact: Raimunda Ribeira da Motta, Diretora. Return postage required. Replies occasionally to correspondence in Portuguese.

RADIO ANHANGUERA, C.P. 13, 74001 Goiânia, Goiás, Brazil. Contact: Rossana F. da Silva. Return postage required. Replies to correspondence in Portuguese.

RADIO APARECIDA, C.P. 14664, 03698 São Paulo SP, Brazil. Contact: Padre Cabral; Cassiano Macedo, Producer, "Encontro DX"; or Antonio C. Moreira, Diretor-Geral. Return postage or $1 required. Replies occasionally to correspondence in Portuguese.

RADIO BANDEIRANTES, C.P. 372, Rua Radiantes 13, Morumbí, 05699 São Paulo SP, Brazil. Contact: Samir Razuk, G.M.; Carlos Newton; or Salomão Esper, Superintendente. Free stickers and canceled Brazilian stamps. $1 or return postage required.

RADIOBRAS, External Service, C.P. 08840, CEP 70912-790, Brasília DF, Brazil. Fax: +55 (61) 321 7602. Contact: Renato Geraldo de Lima, Manager; Michael Brown, Announcer; or Gaby Hertha Einstoss, Correspondence Service. Free stickers. Also, *see* Radio Nacional da Amazonia, below.

RADIO BRASIL 5000, C.P. 625, 13101 Campinas, São Paulo SP, Brazil. Contact: Wilson Roberto Correa Viana, Gerente. Return postage required. Replies to correspondence in Portuguese.

RADIO BRASIL TROPICAL, Rua Joaquim Murtinho 1456, Palácio da Rádio, 78015 Cuiabá, Mato Grosso, Brazil. Contact: K. Santos. Free stickers. $1 required. Replies to correspondence in Portuguese.

RADIO CABOCLA (when operating), Rua 4 Casa 9, Conjunto dos Secretarios, 69000 Manaus, Amazonas, Brazil. Contact: Francisco Puga, Diretor-Geral. Return postage required. Replies occasionally to correspondence in Portuguese.

RADIO CAIARI, C.P. 104, 78901 Pôrto Velho, Rondônia, Brazil. Contact: Carlos Alberto Diniz Martins, Diretor-Geral. Free stickers. Return postage helpful. Replies irregularly to correspondence in Portuguese.

RADIO CANCAO NOVA, Estrada Particular alto de Bela Vista s/n, 12630 Cachoeira Paulista, São Paulo SP, Brazil. Contact: José Cardoso de O. Neto, Diretor, Depto. Radiodifusão; or Jorge Hartmann, Diretor. Free stickers, pennants and station brochure. $1 helpful. Replies at times to correspondence in Portuguese.

RADIO CAPIXABA, C.P. 509, 29001 Vitória, Espírito Santo, Brazil. Contact: Jairo Gouvea Maia, Diretor. Replies occasionally to correspondence in Portuguese.

RADIO CBN, Rua das Palmeiras 315, 01226 São Paulo SP, Brazil. Contact: Celso A. de Freitas, Coordinad Regional de Redaçao. Return postage or $1 helpful. Replies irregularly to correspondence in Portuguese.

RADIO CLUBE DO PARA, C.P. 533, 66001 Belém, Pará, Brazil. Contact: Edyr Paiva Proença, Diretor-Geral. Return postage required. Replies irregularly to correspondence in Portuguese.

RADIO CLUBE MARILIA, C.P. 325, Marilia, 17500 São Paulo SP, Brazil. Contact: Antonio Carlos Nasser. Return postage required. Replies to correspondence in Portuguese.

RADIO CLUBE VARGINHA, C.P. 102, 37101 Varginha, Minas Gerais, Brazil. Contact: Juraci Viana. Return postage necessary. Replies slowly to correspondence in Portuguese.

RADIO CULTURA DE ARARAQUARA, Avenida de Espana 284, Araraquara 14800, São Paulo SP, Brazil.

RADIO CULTURA DO PARA, Avenida Almirante Barroso 735, 66065 Belém, Pará, Brazil. Contact: Ronald Pastor; or Augusto Proença, Diretor. Return postage required. Replies irregularly to correspondence in Portuguese.

RADIO CULTURA FOZ DO IGUACU, C.P 312, 85890 Foz do Iguaçu, Paraná, Brazil. Contact: Ennes Mendes da Rocha. Return postage necessary. Replies to correspondence in Portuguese.

RADIO CULTURA SAO PAULO, Rua Cenno Sbrighi 378, 05099 São Paulo SP, Brazil. Contact: Thais de Almeida Dias, Chefe de Produção e Programação; Sra. María Luíza Amaral Kfouri, Chefe de Produção; or José Munhoz, Coordenador. $1 or return postage required. Replies slowly to correspondence in Portuguese.

RADIO DIFUSORA AQUIDAUANA, C.P. 18, 79200 Aquidauana, Mato Grosso do Sul, Brazil. Contact: Primaz Aldo Bertoni, Diretor. Free tourist literature and used Brazilian stamps. $1 or return postage required. This station sometimes identifies during the program day as "Nova Difusora," but its sign-off announcement gives the official name as "Radio Difusora, Aquidauana."

RADIO DIFUSORA CACERES, C.P. 297, 78700 Cáceres, Mato Grosso, Brazil. Contact: Sra. Maridalva Amaral Vignardi. $1 or return postage required. Replies occasionally to correspondence in Portuguese.

RADIO DIFUSORA DE LONDRINA, C.P. 1870, 86010 Londrina, Paraná, Brazil. Contact: Walter Roberto Manganoli, Gerente. $1 or return postage helpful. Replies irregularly to correspondence in Portuguese.

RADIO DIFUSORA DO AMAZONAS, C.P. 311, 69001 Manaus, Amazonas, Brazil. Contact: J. Joaquim Marinho, Diretor.

RADIO DIFUSORA DO MARANHAO, C.P. 152, 65001 São Luíz, Maranhão, Brazil. Contact: Alonso Augusto Duque, BA, Presidente. Return postage required. Replies occasionally to correspondence in Portuguese.

RADIO DIFUSORA JATAI, C.P. 33 (or Rua José Carvalhos Bastos 542), 76801 Jataí, Goiás, Brazil. Contact: Zacarias Faleiros, Diretor.

RADIO DIFUSORA MACAPA, C.P. 2929, 68901 Macapá, Amapá, Brazil. Contact: Francisco de Paulo Silva Santos. $1 or return postage required. Replies irregularly to correspondence in Portuguese.

RADIO DIFUSORA RORAIMA, Rua Capitão Ene Garcez 830, 69300 Boa Vista, Roraima, Brazil. Contact: Geraldo França, Diretor-Geral; or Francisco Alves Vieira. Return postage required. Replies occasionally to correspondence in Portuguese.

RADIO EDUCACAO RURAL—CAMPO GRANDE, C.P. 261, 79100 Campo Grande, Mato Grosso do Sul, Brazil. Contact: Ailton Guerra, Gerente; or Diácono Tomás Schwamborn. $1 or return postage required. Replies to correspondence in Portuguese.

RADIO EDUCACAO RURAL—COARI, Praça São Sebastião 228, 69460 Coari, Amazonas, Brazil. Contact: Joaquim Florencio Coelho, Diretor Administrador da Comunidad Salgueiro; or Elijane Martins Correa. $1 or return postage helpful. Replies irregularly to correspondence in Portuguese.

RADIO EDUCADORA CARIRI, C.P. 57, 63101 Crato, Ceará, Brazil. Contact: Padre Gonçalo Farias Filho, Diretor Gerente. Return postage or $1 helpful. Replies irregularly to correspondence in Portuguese.

RADIO EDUCADORA DA BAHIA, Centro de Rádio, Rua Pedro Gama 413/E, Alto Sobradinho Federação, 40000 Salvador, Bahia, Brazil. Contact: Antonio Luís Almada, Diretor; Elza Correa Ramos; or Walter Sequieros R. Tanure. $1 or return postage required. Replies irregularly to correspondence in Portuguese.

RADIO EDUCADORA DE BRAGANCA, Rua Barão do Rio Branco 1151, 68600 Bragança, Brazil. Contact: José Rosendo de S. Neto. $1 or return postage required. Replies to correspondence in Portuguese.

RADIO 8 DE SETEMBRO, C.P. 8, 13691 Descalvado, São Paulo SP, razil. Contact: Adonias Gomes. Replies to corrrespondence in Portuguese.

RADIO EMISSORA VOZ SAO FRANCISCO, C.P. 8, 56301 Petrolina, Pernambuco, Brazil. Contact: Maria Letecia de Andrade Nunes. Return postage necessary. Replies to correspondence in Portuguese.

RADIO GAUCHA, Avenida Ipiranga 1075, Azenha, 90060 Pôrto Alegre, Rio Grande do Sul, Brazil. Contact: Alexandre Amaral de Aguiar, News Editor; or Geraldo Canali. Replies occasionally to correspondence, preferably in Portuguese.

RADIO GAZETA (when operating), Avenida Paulista 900, 01310 São Paulo SP, Brazil. Contact: Ing. Aníbal Horta Figueiredo.

RADIO GLOBO, Rua das Palmeiras 315, 01226 São Paulo SP, Brazil. Contact: Ademar Dutra, Locutor, "Programa Ademar Dutra"; or José Marques. Replies to correspondence, preferably in Portuguese.

RADIO GUARUJA, C.P. 45, 88001 Florianópolis, Santa Catarina, Brazil. Contact: Acy Cabral Tieve, Diretor; or Rosa Michels de Souza. Return postage required. Replies irregularly to correspondence in Portuguese.

RADIO INCONFIDENCIA, C.P. 1027, 30001 Belo Horizonte, Minas Gerais, Brazil. Contact: Isaias Lansky, Diretor; Manuel E. de Lima Torres, Diretor Superintendente; or Eugenio Silva. $1 or return postage helpful.

RADIO INTEGRACAO, Rua Alagoas 270, lotes 8 e 9, 69980 Cruzeiro do Sul, Acre, Brazil. Contact: Claudio Onofre Ferreiro. Return postage required. Replies to correspondence in Portuguese.

RADIO IPB AM, Rua Itajaí 433, Barrio Antonio Vendas, 79050 Campo Grande, Mato Grosso do Sul, Brazil. Contact: Pastor Laercio Paula das Neves, Dirigente Estadual; or Kelly Cristina Rodrigues da Silva, Secretária. Return postage required. Replies to correspondence in Portuguese.

RADIO ITATIAIA, Rua Itatiaia 117, 31210-170 Belo Horizonte, Minas Gerais, Brazil. Contact: Lúcia Araújo Bessa, Assistente da Directoria.

RADIO MARAJOARA, Travessa Campos Sales 370, Centro, 66015 Belém, Pará, Brazil. Contact: Elizete Ma dos Santos Pamplona, Diretora Geral; or Sra. Neide Carvalho, Secretaria da Diretoria Executiva. Return postage required. Replies irregularly to correspondence in Portuguese.

RADIO METEOROLOGIA PAULISTA, C.P. 91, 14940-970 Ibitinga, São Paulo SP, Brazil. Contact: Roque de Rosa, Diretora. Replies to correspondence in Portuguese. $1 or return postage required.

RADIO NACIONAL DA AMAZONIA, Radiobras, SCRN 702/3 Bloco B, Ed. Radiobras, Brasília DF, Brazil. Fax: +55 (61) 321 7602. Contact: Luíz Otavio de Castro Souza, Diretor; or Januario Procopio Toledo, Diretor. Free stickers. Also, see Radiobras, above.

RADIO NACIONAL SAO GABRIEL DA CACHOEIRA, Avenida Presidente Costa e Silva s/n, 69750-000 São Gabriel da Cachoeira, Amazonas, Brazil. Contact: Luiz dos Santos Franca, Gerente. Return postage necessary. Replies to correspondence in Portuguese.

RADIO NOVAS DE PAZ, C.P. 22, 80001 Curitiba, Paraná, Brazil. Contact: João Falavinha Ienze, Gerente. $1 or return postage required. Replies irregularly to correspondence in Portuguese.

RADIO PIONEIRA DE TERESINA, 24 de Janeiro 150, 64000 Teresina, Piauí, Brazil. Contact: Luíz Eduardo Bastos; or Padre Tony Batista, Diretor. $1 or return postage required. Replies slowly to correspondence in Portuguese.

RADIO PORTAL DA AMAZONIA, Rua Tenente Alcides Duarte de Souza, 533 B° Duque de Caxias, 78010 Cuiabá, Mato Grosso, Brazil; also, C.P. 277, 78001 Cuiabá, Mato Grosso, Brazil. Contact: Arnaldo Medina; or Mario Castiho, Diretor Administrativo. Return postage required. Replies occasionally to correspondence in Portuguese.

RADIO PROGRESSO, Estrada do Belmont s/n, B° Nacional, 78000 Pôrto Velho, Rondônia, Brazil. Contact: Angela Xavier, Diretora-Geral. Return postage required. Replies occasionally to correspondence in Portuguese.

RADIO PROGRESSO DO ACRE, 69900 Rio Branco, Acre, Brazil. Contact: José Alves Pereira Neto, Diretor-Presidente. Return postage or $1 required. Replies occasionally to correspondence in Portuguese.

RADIO RECORD, C.P. 7920, 04084 São Paulo SP, Brazil. Contact: Mário Luíz Catto, Diretor Geral. Free stickers. Return postage or $1 required. Replies occasionally to correspondence in Portuguese.

RADIO RIBEIRAO PRETO, C.P 814, 14001-970 Ribeirão Preto, São Paulo SP, Brazil. Contact: Lucinda de Oliveira, Secretaria; or Paulo Henríque Rocha da Silva. Replies to correspondence in Portuguese.

RADIO SENTINELA, Travessa Ruy Barbosa 142, 68250 Obidos, Pará, Brazil. Contact: Max Hamoy or Maristela Hamoy. Return postage required. Replies occasionally to correspondence in Portuguese.

RADIO TRANSAMERICA, C.P. 6084, 90031 Pôrto Alegre, Rio

Grande do Sul, Brazil; or C.P. 551, 97100 Santa María, Rio Grande do Sul, Brazil. Contact: Marlene P. Nunes, Secretária. Return postage required. Replies to correspondence in Portuguese.

RADIO TROPICAL, C.P. 214, 78601 Barra do Garças, Mato Grosso, Brazil. Contact: José Coelho da Silva, Coordenador Geral. $1 or return postage required. Replies slowly and rarely to correspondence in Portuguese.

RADIO TUPI, Rua Nadir Dias Figueiredo 1329, 02110 São Paulo SP, Brazil. Contact: Celso Rodrigues de Oliveira, Asesor Internacional da Presidencia; or Elia Soares. Return postage required. Replies occasionally to correspondence in Portuguese.

RADIO UNIVERSO, C.P. 7133, 80001 Curitiba, Paraná, Brazil. Contact: Luíz Andreu Rúbio, Diretor. Replies occasionally to correspondence in Portuguese.

RADIO VERDES FLORESTAS, C.P. 53, 69981-970 Cruzeiro do Sul, Acre, Brazil. Contact: Marlene Valente de Andrade. Return postage required. Replies occasionally to correspondence in Portuguese.

BULGARIA World Time +2 (+3 midyear)

RADIO HORIZONT, Bulgarian Radio, 4 Dragan Tsankov Blvd., 1040 Sofia, Bulgaria. Fax: (weekdays) +359 (2) 657 230. Contact: Borislav Djamdjiev, Director; or Iassen Indjev, Executive Director; (technical or nontechnical) Martin Minkov, Editor-in-Chief. **ADS**

RADIO BULGARIA, 4 Dragan Tsankov Blvd., 1040 Sofia, Bulgaria. Fax: (weekdays) +359 (2) 871 060. Contact: Mrs. Iva Delcheva, English Section; Kristina Mihailova, In Charge of Listeners' Letters, English Section; or Ms. Rayna Konstantinova, Managing Director. Free tourist literature, stickers and pennants. Gold, silver and bronze diplomas for correspondents meeting certain requirements. Free sample copies of *Bulgaria* magazine. Replies regularly, but sometimes slowly.

BURKINA FASO World Time exactly

RADIODIFFUSION-TELEVISION BURKINA, B.P. 7029, Ouagadougou, Burkina Faso. Contact: Raphael L. Onadia or Pierre Tassembedo. Replies irregularly to correspondence in French. IRC or return postage helpful.

BURMA—*see* MYANMAR.

BURUNDI World Time +2

LA VOIX DE LA REVOLUTION, B.P. 1900, Bujumbura, Burundi. Fax: +257 226 547 or +257 226 613. Contact: Gregoire Barampumba, English News Announcer; Athamase Ntiruhangura, Directeur de la Radio; Didace Baranderetse, Directeur General de la Radio; (technical) Abraham Makuza, Le Directeur Technique. $1 required. **ADS**

CAMBODIA World Time +7

RADIO PHNOM PENH

Note: Because of the unstable conditions in Cambodia, this station's actual address is not always accepted by postal authorities as being valid. Contact your local postal authorities for guidance in sending mail to Cambodia. This failing, indicate "via Hanoi, Vietnam," on the envelope.

Station Address: Overseas Service, English Section, 28 Av. Sandech Choun Nath, Phnom Penh, Cambodia. Contact: Miss Hem Bory, English Announcer; or Van Sunheng, Deputy Director General, Cambodian National Radio and Television. Free pennants and Cambodian stamps. Replies irregularly and slowly. Do not include stamps, currency, IRCs or dutiable items in envelope. Registered letters stand a much better chance of getting through.

CAMEROON World Time +1

Note: Any CRTV outlet is likely to be verified by contacting via registered mail, in English or French with $2 enclosed, James Achanyi-Fontem, Head of Programming, CRTV, B.P. 986, Douala, Cameroon.

CAMEROON RADIO TELEVISION CORPORATION (CRTV)—BAFOUSSAM, B.P. 970, Bafoussam (Ouest), Cameroon. Contact: (nontechnical) Boten Celestin; (technical) Ndam Seidou, Chef Service Technique. IRC or return postage required. Replies irregularly in French to correspondence in English or French. **ADS AIR**

CAMEROON RADIO TELEVISION CORPORATION (CRTV)—BERTOUA, B.P. 230, Bertoua (Eastern), Cameroon. Rarely replies to correspondence, preferably in French. $1 required.

CAMEROON RADIO TELEVISION CORPORATION (CRTV)—BUEA, P.M.B., Buea (Sud-Ouest), Cameroon. Contact: Ononino Oli Isidore, Chef Service Technique. 3 IRCs, $1 or return postage required.

CAMEROON RADIO TELEVISION CORPORATION (CRTV)—DOUALA, B.P. 986, Douala (Littoral), Cameroon. Contact: (tech-

nical) Emmanual Ekite, Technicien. 3 IRCs or $1 required. **ADS AIR**

CAMEROON RADIO TELEVISION CORPORATION (CRTV)—GAROUA, B.P. 103, Garoua (Nord/Adamawa), Cameroon. Contact: Kadeche Manguele. 3 IRCs or return postage required. Replies irregularly and slowly to correspondence in French.

CAMEROON RADIO TELEVISION CORPORATION (CRTV)—YAOUNDE, B.P. 1634, Yaoundé (Centre-Sud), Cameroon. Contact: Florent Etoya Eily, Le Directeur-Général; or Francis Achu Samba, Le Directeur Technique. $1 required. Replies slowly to correspondence in French.

CANADA World Time −3:30 (−2:30 midyear) Newfoundland; −4 (−3 midyear) Atlantic; −5 (−4 midyear) Eastern, including Quebec and Ontario; −6 (−5 midyear) Central; −7 (−6 midyear) Mountain; −8 (−7 midyear) Pacific, including Yukon

CANADIAN FORCES NETWORK RADIO

Studio Address: Jammstraße 9, W-7630 Lahr, Germany. Fax: +49 (7821) 21 235. Contact: Jean Choquette, VE2KL/DA1CV, Manager Technical Operations.

Transmission Offices: see Radio Canada International, below.

CBC NORTHERN QUEBEC SHORTWAVE SERVICE—same address as Radio Canada International.

CFRX-CFRB

Main Address: 2 St. Clair Avenue West, Toronto ON, M4V 1L6 Canada. Fax: +1 (416) 323 6830. Talk-show telephone: +1 (416) 872-1010. Contact: Rob Mise, Operations Manager; (technical) David Simon, Engineer. Free station history sheet. Reception reports should be sent to verification address, below.

Verification Address: ODXA, P.O. Box 161, Station A, Willowdale ON, M2N 5S8 Canada. Fax: +1 (905) 853 3169. Contact: Stephen Canney or John Grimley. Free ODXA information sheets. Reception reports are processed quickly if sent to this address and not to the station itself.

CFVP-CFCN, Broadcast House, P.O. Box 7060, Stn. E, Calgary AB, T3C 3L9 Canada. Fax: (general and technical) +1 (403) 240 5801; (news) +1 (403) 246 7099. Contact: (technical) John H. Bruins, Chief Engineer, Radio.

CHNX-CHNS, P.O. Box 400, Halifax NS, B3J 2R2 Canada. Fax: +1 (902) 422 5330. Contact: (technical) Kurt J. Arsenault, Chief Engineer. Return postage or $1 helpful. Replies irregularly.

CFCX-CIQC, Radio Montréal, Mount Royal Broadcasting, Inc., 1200 McGill College Avenue, Suite 300, Montréal PQ, H3B 4G7 Canada. Fax: +1 (514) 393 4659. Contact: André Chevalier, Program Director; or Ted Silver, Assistant Program Director; (technical) Kim Bickerdike, Technical Director.

CKFX-CKWX, 2440 Ash Street, Vancouver BC, V5Z 4J6 Canada. Fax: +1 (604) 873 0877. Contact: Vijay Chanbra, Engineer; or Jack Wiebe, Chief Engineer. Free stickers. Off the air until around 1995, when they expect to reactivate with a new 100-500W transmitter.

CKZN-CBN, CBC, P.O. Box 12010, Station "A", St. John's NF, A1B 3T8 Canada. Fax: +1 (709) 737 4280. Contact: (technical) Charles Kempf; or Shawn R. Williams, Regional Engineer. Free folder with British perspective on Newfoundland's history.

CKZU-CBU, CBC, P.O. Box 4600, Vancouver BC, V6B 4A2 Canada. Fax: +1 (604) 662 6350. Contact: Dave Newbury.

RADIO CANADA INTERNATIONAL

Main Office: P.O. Box 6000, Montréal PQ, H3C 3A8 Canada. Fax: +1 (514) 284 0891. Telephone: "As It Happens' Talkback Machine": +1 (416) 205-3331. Contact (nontechnical): Maggie Akerblom, Director of Audience Relations; Ousseynou Diop, Manager, Worldwide Programming; Terry Hargreaves, Executive Director; Bob Girolami, Producer, "The Mailbag"; or B.M. Westenhaven. Free stickers, limited supply of lapel pins, pennants and other station souvenirs. T-shirts available for $12. Canadian compact discs sold worldwide except North America, from International Sales, CBC Records, P.O. Box 500, Station "A", Toronto ON, M5W 1E6 Canada (VISA/MC), fax +1 (416) 975 3482; and within the United States from CBC/Allegro, 3434 SE Milwaukie Avenue, Portland OR 97202 USA, fax (503) 232 9504, toll-free telephone (800) 288-2007 (VISA/MC).

Transmission Office: (technical) P.O. Box 6000, Montréal PQ, H3C 3A8 Canada. Fax: +1 (514) 284 9550. Contact: Jacques Bouliane, Chief Engineer. This office only for informing about transmitter-related problems (interference, modulation quality, etc.), especially by fax. Verifications not given out at this office; requests for verification should be sent to the main office, above.

Washington Bureau, Nontechnical: CBC, Suite 500, National

Press Building, 529 14th Street NW, Washington DC 20045 USA. Fax: +1 (202) 783 9321.

London Bureau, Nontechnical: CBC, 43 Great Titchfield Street, London W1, England. Fax: +44 (71) 631 3095.

Paris Bureau, Nontechnical: CBC, 17 avenue Matignon, F-75008 Paris, France.

CENTRAL AFRICAN REPUBLIC World Time +1

RADIODIFFUSION-TELEVISION CENTRAFRICAINE, B.P. 940, Bangui, Central African Republic. Contact: (technical) Jacques Mbilo, Le Directeur des Services Techniques; or Michèl Bata, Services Techniques. Replies on rare occasion to correspondence in French; return postage required.

CHAD World Time +1

RADIODIFFUSION NATIONALE TCHADIENNE—N'DJAMENA, B.P. 892, N'Djamena, Chad. Contact: Djimadoum Ngoka Kilamian. 2 IRCs or return postage required. Replies slowly to correspondence in French.

RADIO DIFFUSION NATIONALE TCHADIENNE—RADIO ABECHE, B.P. 105, Abéché, Ouaddai, Chad. Return postage helpful. Replies rarely to correspondence in French.

RADIODIFFUSION NATIONALE TCHADIENNE—RADIO MOUNDOU, B.P. 122, Moundou, Logone, Chad. Contact: Jacques Maimos, Le Chef de la Station Régionale de Radio Moundou.

CHILE World Time −3 (−4 midyear)

RADIO ESPERANZA, Casilla 830, Temuco, Chile. Fax: +56 (45) 236 179. Contact: (nontechnical) Eleazar Jara, Dpto. de Programación; Ramón Woerner, Publicidad; (technical) Juan Luis Puentes, Dpto. Técnico. Free pennants, stickers, bookmarks and tourist information. 2 IRCs or 2 U.S. stamps appreciated. Replies, usually quite slowly, to correspondence in Spanish or English. **ADS AIR**

RADIO SANTA MARIA, Casilla 1, Coyhaique, Chile. Contact: Pedro Andrade Vera, Dpto. DX; or Rocco Martinello Avila, Director Ejecutivo. $1 or return postage required. Replies to correspondence in Spanish.

RADIO TRIUNFAL EVANGELICA, Costanera Sur 7209, Comuna de Cerro Navia, Santiago, Chile. Contact: Fernando González Segura, Obispo de la Misión Pentecostal Fundamentalista. 2 IRCs required. Replies to correspondence in Spanish.

CHINA (PR) World Time +8; still nominally +6 ("Urümqi Time") in the Xinjiang Uighur Autonomous Region, but in practice +8 is observed there, as well.

Note: China Radio International, the Central People's Broadcasting Station and certain regional outlets reply regularly to listeners' letters in a variety of languages. If a Chinese regional station does not respond to your correspondence within four months—and many will not, unless your letter is in Chinese or the regional dialect—try writing them c/o China Radio International.

CENTRAL PEOPLE'S BROADCASTING STATION (CPBS), Zhongyang Renmin Guangbo Diantai, P.O. Box 4501, Beijing, People's Republic of China. Sells T-shirts for $8 and tape recordings of music and news for $5. Free stickers. Return postage helpful. **ADS AIR**

CHINA HUAYI BROADCASTING COMPANY, P.O. Box 251, Fuzhou City, Fujian 350001, People's Republic of China. Contact: Lin Hai Chun. Replies to correspondence in English.

CHINA RADIO INTERNATIONAL

Main Office, Non-Chinese Languages Service: No. 2 Fuxingmenwai, Beijing 100866, People's Republic of China. Fax: +86 (1) 851 3174. Contact: (nontechnical or technical) Song Jianping, Head of Audience Relations; Ms. Chen Lifang, Mrs. Fan Fuquang, Ms. Qi Guilin, Audience Relations, English Department; Zhang Yuan, Producer, "Listeners' Letterbox"; or Zang Guohua, Deputy Director of English Service; (technical) Liu Yuzhou, Technical Director; or Ge Hongzhang, Frequency Manager; Free bi-monthly *The Messenger* magazine , stickers, desk calendars, pins, hair ornaments and such small souvenirs as handmade papercuts. Two-volume, 820-page set of *Day-to-Day Chinese* language-lesson books for $15, including postage worldwide; contact Li Yi, English Department. T-shirts available for $5 and CDs for $15.

Main Office, Chinese Languages Service: Box 565, Beijing, People's Republic of China. Prefers correspondence in Chinese (Mandarin), Cantonese, Hakka, Chaozhou or Amoy.

Hong Kong Office, Non-Chinese Languages Service: Box 11036, General Post office, Hong Kong.

Washington Bureau, Nontechnical: 2401 Calvert Street NW, Suite 1017, Washington DC 20008 USA. Fax: +1 (202) 387 0459, but call +1 (202) 387-6860 first so fax machine can be switched on. Contact: Wang Guoqing, Bureau Chief; or Chao Xie.

Paris Bureau, Nontechnical: 7 rue Charles Lecocq, F-75015 Paris, France. **ADS AIR**

FUJIAN PEOPLE'S BROADCASTING STATION, Fuzhou, Fujian, People's Republic of China. $1 helpful. Replies occasionally and usually slowly.

GANSU PEOPLE'S BROADCASTING STATION, Lanzhou, People's Republic of China. Contact: Li Mei. IRC helpful.

GUANGXI PEOPLE'S BROADCASTING STATION, No. 12 Min Zu Avenue, Nanning, Guangxi 530022, People's Republic of China. Contact: Song Yue, Staffer; or Li Hai Li, Staffer. Free stickers and handmade papercuts. IRC helpful. Replies irregularly.

HEILONGJIANG PEOPLE'S BROADCASTING STATION, No. 115 Zhongshan Road, Harbin City, Heilongjiang, People's Republic of China. $1 or return postage helpful.

HONGHE PEOPLE'S BROADCASTING STATION, Jianshe Donglu 32, Geji City 661400, Yunnan, People's Republic of China. Contact: Shen De-chun, Head of Station; or Mrs. Cheng Lin, Editor in Chief. Free travel brochures.

HUBEI PEOPLE'S BROADCASTING STATION, No. 563 Jie Fang Avenue, Wuhan, Hubei, People's Republic of China.

JIANGXI PEOPLE'S BROADCASTING STATION, Nanchang, Jiangxi, People's Republic of China. Contact: Tang Ji Sheng, Editor, Chief Editor's Office. Free gold/red pins. Replies irregularly; Mr. Tang enjoys music, literature and stamps, so enclosing a small memento along these lines should help assure a speedy reply.

NEI MONGGOL (INNER MONGOLIA) PEOPLE'S BROADCASTING STATION, Hohhot, Nei Monggol Zizhiqu, People's Republic of China. Contact: Zhang Xiang-Quen, Secretary. Replies irregularly.

QINGHAI PEOPLE'S BROADCASTING STATION, Xining, Qinghai, People's Republic of China. $1 helpful.

SICHUAN PEOPLE'S BROADCASTING STATION, Chengdu, Sichuan, People's Republic of China. Replies occasionally.

VOICE OF JINLING, P.O. Box 268, Nanjing, Jiangsu 210002, People's Republic of China. Fax: +86 (25) 413 235. Contact: Strong Lee, Producer/Host, "Window of Taiwan." Free stickers and calendars, plus Chinese-language color station brochure and information on the Nanjing Technology Import & Export Corporation. Replies to correspondence in Chinese and to simple correspondence in English. $1 or return postage helpful. **ADS AIR**

VOICE OF PUJIANG, P.O. Box 3064, Shanghai, People's Republic of China. Contact: Jiang Bimiao, Editor & Reporter.

VOICE OF THE STRAIT, People's Liberation Army Broadcasting Centre, P.O. Box 187, Fuzhou, Fujian, People's Republic of China. Replies very irregularly.

WENZHOU PEOPLE'S BROADCASTING STATION, Wenzhou, People's Republic of China.

XILINGOL PEOPLE'S BROADCASTING STATION, Xilinhot, Xilingol, People's Republic of China.

XINJIANG PEOPLE'S BROADCASTING STATION, Urümqi, Xinjiang, People's Republic of China. Contact: Guo Ying. Free tourist booklet.

XIZANG PEOPLE'S BROADCASTING STATION, Lhasa, Xizang (Tibet), People's Republic of China. Contact: Lobsang Chonphel, Announcer.

YUNNAN PEOPLE'S BROADCASTING STATION, No 73 Renmin Road (W), Central Building of Broadcasting & TV, Kunming, Yunnan 650031, People's Republic of China. Contact: F.K. Fan. Free Chinese-language brochure on Yunnan Province. $1 or return postage helpful. Replies occasionally. **ADS AIR**

CHINA (TAIWAN) World Time +8

CENTRAL BROADCASTING SYSTEM (CBS), 55 Pei An Road, Taipei, Taiwan, Republic of China. Contact: Lee Ming, Deputy Director. Free stickers.

VOICE OF ASIA, P.O. Box 880, Kaohsiung, Taiwan, Republic of China. Fax: +886 (2) 751 9277. Contact: (nontechnical) Vivian Pu, Co-Producer, with Isaac Guo of "Letterbox"; or Ms. Chao Mei-Yi, Deputy Chief; (technical) Engineering Department. Free shopping bags, inflatable globes, coasters, calendars, stickers and booklets. T-shirts for $5.

VOICE OF FREE CHINA, P.O. Box 24-38, Taipei, Taiwan, Republic of China. Fax: +886 (2) 751 9277. Contact: (nontechnical) Daniel Dong, Chief, Listeners' Service Section; James Tsung-Kwei Lee, Deputy Director; John C.T. Feng, Director;

or Jade Lim, Producer, "Mailbag Time"; (technical) Wen-Bin Tsai, Engineer, Engineering Department; Tai-Lau Ying, Engineering Department; or Huang Shuh-shyun, Director, Engineering Department. Free stickers, caps, shopping bags, *Voice of Free China Journal*, annual diary, "Let's Learn Chinese" language-learning course materials, booklets and other publications, and Taiwanese stamps. Station offers listeners a free Frisbee-type saucer if they return the "Request Card" sent to them by the station. T-shirts available for $5.

San Francisco Bureau, Nontechnical: P.O. Box 192793, San Francisco CA 94119-2793 USA.

CLANDESTINE—see DISESTABLISHMENTARIAN AND CLANDESTINE.

COLOMBIA   World Time −5 (−4 irregularly)

Note: Colombia, the country, is always spelled with two o's. It is never written as "Columbia."

CARACOL COLOMBIA

Nontechnical: Radio Reloj, Apartado Aéreo 8700, Santa Fé de Bogotá, Colombia. Contact: Ruth Vásquez; or Ricardo Alarcón G., Director-General. Free stickers. Return postage or $1 required. Replies infrequently and slowly to correspondence in Spanish.

Technical: DX Caracol, Apartado Aéreo 9291, Santa Fé de Bogotá, Colombia. Fax: +57 (1) 268 1582. Replies to correspondence in Spanish.

ECOS CELESTIALES, Apartado Aéreo 8447, Medellín, Colombia. Contact: Arnulfo Villalba, Director. Return postage or $1 required. Replies occasionally to correspondence in Spanish. This station does not appear to be licensed by the Colombian authorities.

ECOS DEL ATRATO, Apartado Aéreo 278, Quibdó, Chocó, Colombia. Contact: Alvaro Pérez García, Director; Oswaldo Moreno Blandon, Locutor; or Julia Ma Cuesta L. Return postage or $1 required. Replies rarely to correspondence in Spanish.

ECOS DEL COMBEIMA, Parque Murillo Toro No. 3-29, piso 3°, Ibagué, Tolima, Colombia. Contact: Jesús Erney Torres, Cronista. Return postage or $1 helpful. Replies irregularly to correspondence in Spanish.

EMISORA ARMONIAS DEL CAQUETA, Florencia, Caquetá, Colombia. Contact: P. Alvaro Serna Alzate, Director. Replies rarely to correspondence in Spanish. Return postage required.

LA VOZ DE LA SELVA, Apartado Aéreo 465, Florencia, Caquetá, Colombia. Contact: Alonso Orozco, Gerente. Replies occaisonally to correspondence in Spanish. Return postage helpful.

LA VOZ DE LOS CENTAUROS, Apartado Aéreo 2472, Villavicencio, Meta, Colombia. Contact: Carlos Torres Leyva, Gerencia; or Cielo de Corredor, Administradora. Return postage required. Replies to correspondence in Spanish.

LA VOZ DEL CINARUCO, Calle 19 No. 19-62, Arauca, Colombia. Contact: Efrahim Valera, Director. Pennants for return postage. Replies rarely to correspondence in Spanish; return postage required.

LA VOZ DEL GUAINIA, Calle 6 con Carretera 3, Puerto Inírida, Guainía, Colombia. Contact: Ancizar Gómez Arzimendi, Director. Return postage or $1 required. Replies occasionally to correspondence in Spanish.

LA VOZ DEL LLANO, Carrera 31 No. 38-07, piso 2, Villavicencio, Meta, Colombia. Contact: Alcides Antonio Jauregui B., Director. Replies occasionally to correspondence in Spanish. $1 or return postage necessary.

LA VOZ DEL RIO ARAUCA, Apartado Aéreo 16555, Santa Fé de Bogotá, Colombia. Contact: Guillermo Pulido, Gerente; or Alvaro Perez Garcia. Free stickers. $1 or return postage required; return postage on a preaddressed airmail envelope even better. Replies occasionally to correspondence in Spanish; persist.

LA VOZ DEL YOPAL, Calle 9 No. 22-63, Yopal, Casanare, Colombia. Contact: Pedro Antonio Socha Pérez, Gerente; or Marta Cecilia Socha Pérez, Subgerente. Return postage necessary. Replies to correspondence in Spanish.

ONDAS DEL META, Apartado Aéreo 2196, Villavicencio, Meta, Colombia. Contact: Yolanda Plazas de Lozada, Administradora. Return postage required. Replies irregularly and slowly to correspondence in Spanish.

ONDAS DEL ORTEGUAZA, Calle 16, No. 12-48, piso 2, Florencia, Caquetá, Colombia. Contact: Sra. Dani Yasmín Anturi Durán, Secretaria; Jorge Daniel Santos Calderon, Gerente; or C.P. Norberto Plaza Vargas, Subgerente. Free stickers. IRC, return postage or $1 required. Replies occasionally to correspondence in Spanish.

RADIO BUENAVENTURA, Calle 1 #2-39, piso 2, Buenaventura, Valle de Cauca, Colombia. Contact: Mauricio Castaño Angulo, Gerente. Return postage or $1 required. Replies to correspondence in Spanish.

RADIODIFUSORA NACIONAL DE COLOMBIA, CAN, Apartado Aéreo 94321, Santa Fé de Bogotá, Colombia. Contact: Javier Mora Sánchez, Director, English Section; Juan Carlos Pardo, Director, Spanish Section; Jaime Molina Uribe, Producer, "Colombia DX"; or Adriana Giraldo Cifuentes, Directora. Tends to reply a bit slowly.

RADIO MELODIA, Calle 61, No. 3B-05, Santa Fé de Bogotá, Colombia. Contact: Gerardo Páez Mejía, Vicepresidente; Elvira Mejía de Páez, Gerente General; or Gracilla Rodriguez, Assistente Gerente. Stickers and pennants for $1 or return postage. Replies, rarely, to correspondence in Spanish.

RADIO MIRA, Apartado Aéreo 165, Tumaco, Nariño, Colombia. Contact: Julio Cortes Benavides. $1 or return postage required.

RADIO NUEVA VIDA, Apatado Aéreo 3068, Bucaramanga, Santander, Colombia. Contact: (nontechnical) Marco Antonio Caicedo, Director; (technical) Christian Caicedo Aguiar, Locutor. Free stickers. Cassettes with Biblical studies for $3 each. Return postage. Replies slowly to correspondence in Spanish. **ADS AIR**

RADIO SANTA FE, Calle 57, No. 17-48, Santa Fé de Bogotá, Colombia. Fax: (certain working hours only) +57 (1) 249 60 95. Contact: María Luisa Bernal Mahe, Gerente. Free stickers. IRC, $1 or return postage required. Replies to correspondence in Spanish.

RADIO SUPER, Apartado Aéreo 23316, Santa Fé de Bogotá, Colombia. Contact: Néstor Molina Ramírez, Director; or Juan Carlos Pava Camelo, Gerente. Free stickers and pennants. Return postage required. Replies, very rarely, to correspondence in Spanish.

COMOROS   World Time +4

RADIO COMORO, B.P. 250, Moroni, Grande Comore, Comoros. Contact: Ali Hamoi Hissani; or Antufi Mohamed Bacar, Le Directeur de Programme. Return postage required. Replies very rarely to correspondence in French.

CONGO   World Time +1

RADIO CONGO, Radiodiffusion-Télévision Congolaise, B.P. 2241, Brazzaville, Congo. Contact: Antoine Ngongo, Rédacteur en chef; or Albert Fayette Mikano, Directeur. $1 required. Replies irregularly to letters in French sent via registered mail.

COOK ISLANDS   World Time −10

RADIO COOK ISLANDS, P.O. Box 126, Avarua, Rarotonga. Fax: +686 21907. Contact: (nontechnical) Tauraki Rongo Raea; (technical) Orango Tango, Assistant Chief Engineer. Has replied extremely irregularly since 1985. Station's shortwave transmitter was destroyed by fire in 1992 and is currently off the air. This station appears to have no interest in responding to listeners letters or follow up reports. It appears unlikely that the shortwave service will be back on the air in the foreseeable future.

COSTA RICA   World Time −6

ADVENTIST WORLD RADIO, THE VOICE OF HOPE, TIAWR, Radio Lira Internacional, Radiodifusora Adventista, Apartado 1177, 4050 Alajuela, Costa Rica. Fax +506 (41) 1282. Contact: David L. Gregory, General Manager; Juan Ochoa, Senior Administrator; or William Gómez, Producer, "Su Correo Amigo." Free stickers, calendars, Costa Rican stamps, pennants and religious printed matter. $1, IRC or return postage helpful, with $0.50 in unused U.S. stamps being acceptable. Also, see USA.

FARO DEL CARIBE

Main Office: TIFC, Apartado 2710, 1000 San José, Costa Rica. Fax: +506 (27) 1725. Contact: Juan Francisco Ochoa, Director; or Jacinto Ochoa A., Administrador. Free stickers. $1 or IRCs helpful.

U.S. Office, Nontechnical: P.O. Box 620485, Orlando FL 32862 USA. Contact: Lim Ortiz.

RADIO CASINO, Apartado 287, 7301 Puerto Limón, Costa Rica. Contact: (technical) Ing. Jorge Pardo, Director Técnico.

RADIO FOR PEACE INTERNATIONAL

Main Office: University for Peace, Apartado 88, Santa Ana, Costa Rica. Fax (weekdays): +506 (49) 1929, Att'n. James Latham. Contact: (nontechnical) Debra Latham, General Manager; (nontechnical or technical) James L. Latham, Station Manager; Helga Müller-Farenholz, Director, German Department; Willie Barrantes, Director, Spanish Department; María Suarez, Director, Women's Programming; or Producer, "RFPI's Mailbag"; (technical) Bentley Born, Broadcast Engineer. Replies sometimes slow in coming because of the mail. Audio cassette presentations, in English or Spanish, from women's perspectives welcomed for replay over "FIRE" program. Free *SEE Energy Saving Products* catalog (resource-conserving insulation, doormats, reusable menstral pads, deodorant stones, composting bins, etc.), stickers, sample *Vista* newsletter and sociopolitical literature; quarterly *Vista* newsletter for $35 annual membership; station commemorative T-shirts and rainforest T-shirts $15 (VISA/MC). Actively solicits listener contributions, directly and through MCI's "PeaceCOM" long distance telephone service, for operating expenses and to help replace transmitting equipment destroyed in a recent earthquake and hurricane. $1, 3 IRCs or return postage required.

U.S. Office, Nontechnical: World Peace University, P.O. Box 10869, Eugene OR 97440 USA. Fax: +1 (503) 741 1279. Contact: Dr. F. Richard Schneider, Chancellor CEO. Newsletter, T-shirts and so forth as above.

Willie Nelson's Farm Aid, American Office, via RFPI: Outlaw for Peace, 805 Paisley #6, Spicewood TX 78669 USA. Fax: +1 (512) 264 2926. Contact: Bob Wishoff or Gloria Castillo. Free souvenir reception cards, usually signed by singer Willie Nelson, but small donation appreciated. T-shirts US$15.95; *Best of the West* annual magazine US$5.50. Contributions actively solicited.

Willie Nelson's Farm Aid, European Office, via RFPI: Outlaw for Peace, The Poplars, Weston Green, Thames Ditton, Surrey KT7 0JP, United Kingdom. Fax: +44 (81) 398 7564. Contact: Peter Wilson. T-shirts US$15.95; *Best of the West* annual magazine US$5.50 (VISA/MC). Contributions actively solicited.

Willie Nelson's Farm Aid, Australian Office, via RFPI: Outlaw for Peace, P.O. Box 42504, Casuarina NT 0810, Australia. Fax: +61 (89) 854 440. Contact: Christoper Wardle. T-shirts US$15.95; *Best of the West* annual magazine US$5.50. Contributions actively solicited.

RADIO RELOJ, Sistema Radiofónico H.B., Apartado 341, 1000 San José, Costa Rica. Contact: Roger Barahona, Gerente; or Francisco Barahona Gómez. $1 required.

RADIO UNIVERSIDAD DE COSTA RICA, Ciudad Universitaria Rodrigo Facio, 1000 San José, Costa Rica. Contact: Marco González; or Nora Garita B., Directora.

COTE D'IVOIRE World Time exactly

AFRIQUE NUMERO UN—see GABON for details of this station, which hopes to add transmissions, reportedly at 500 kW, from Côte d'Ivoire in early 1993.

CROATIA World Time +1 (+2 midyear)

CROATIAN RADIO, STUDIO ZAGREB

Main Office: Hrvatska Radio-Televizija (HRT), Studio Zagreb, P.O. Box 1000 (or Odasiljaci i veze, Radnicka c. 22) (or Jurišićeva 4), 41000 Zagreb, Croatia. Fax: +38 (41) 451 145 or +38 (41) 451 060. Free Croatian stamps. Sells subscriptions to *Croatian Voice.* $1 helpful. Replies regularly, although sometimes slowly.

Washington Bureau, Nontechnical: Croatian-American Association, 1912 Sunderland Place NW, Washington DC 20036 USA. Fax: +1 (202) 429 5545. Contact: Bob Schneider, Director.

HRVATSKA RADIO TELEVIZIJA—see Croatian Radio, Studio Zagreb, above, for details.

"RADIO FREE CROATIA"—see DISESTABLISHMENTARIAN AND CLANDESTINE for address.

CUBA World Time −5 (−4 midyear)

RADIO HABANA CUBA, (nontechnical) P.O. Box 7026, Havana, Cuba; (technical) P.O. Box 6240, Havana, Cuba. Fax: +53 (7) 795 007 (direct dialing not available from the United States). Contact: (nontechnical) Rolando Peláez, Head of Correspondence; Mike La Guardia, Senior Editor; or Ms. Milagro Hernández Cuba, General Director; (technical) Arnie Coro, Director of DX Programming; or Luis Pruna Amer, Director Técnico. Free wallet and wall calendars, pennants, stickers, keychains and pins. DX Listeners' Club. Replies slowly to correspondence from the United States, which has no diplomatic relations with Cuba, because of circuitous mail service, usually via Canada.

RADIO REBELDE, Apartado 6277, Havana 6, Cuba. Contact: Noemí Cairo Marín, Secretaria, Relaciones Públicas; or Jorge Luis Mas Zabala, Director, Relaciones Públicas. Replies slowly, with correspondence in Spanish preferred.

CYPRUS World Time +2

Greek Sector

BBC WORLD SERVICE—EAST MEDITERRANEAN RELAY, P.O. Box 219, Limassol, Cyprus. Nontechnical correspondence should be sent to the BBC World Service in London (see).

CYPRUS BROADCASTING CORPORATION, Broadcasting House, P.O. Box 4824, Nicosia, Cyprus. Fax: +357 (2) 314 050. Contact: Dimitris Kiprianou, Director General. Replies occasionally, sometimes slowly. IRC or $1 helpful.

Turkish Sector

RADIO BAYRAK, Bayrak Radio & T.V. Corporation, P.O. Box 417, Lefkoşa, Mersin 10, Turkey. Fax: +90 (5) 208 1991. Contact: (technical) A. Ziya Dincer, Technical Director; or D. Ozer Berkam, Director General. Replies occasionally.

RADIO MONTE-CARLO MIDDLE EAST (Somera) - see Monaco.

CZECH REPUBLIC World Time +1 (+2 midyear)

RADIO PRAGUE, Czech Radio, Vinohradská 12, 120 99 Prague 2, Czech Republic. Fax: (External Programs) +42 (2) 235 4760 or (Domestic Programs) +42 (2) 232 1020. Contact: Markéta Albrechtová or Lenka Adamová, "Mailbag"; Zdenek Dohnal; Dr. Richard Seeman, Director, Foreign Broadcasts; L. Kubik; or Jan Valeška, Head of English Section. Free stickers, pennants and calendars; free Radio Prague Monitor Club "DX Diploma" for regular correspondents. Free books available for Czech-language course called "Check out Czech." Samples of *Welcome to the Czech Republic* and *Czech Life* available upon request from Orbis, Vinohradská 46, 120 41 Prague 2, Czech Republic.

RADIO ROPA INFO, Technic Park, Postfach 549, W-5568 Daun, Germany. Fax: +49 (6592) 203 537. Contact: Sabine K. Thome. Free stickers and booklets. Transmits via the facilities of Radio Prague.

DENMARK World Time +1 (+2 midyear)

DANMARKS RADIO

Main Office, Nontechnical: Radiohuset, DK-1999 Frederiksberg C, Denmark. Danish-language 24-hour telephone tape recording for schedule information +45 (35) 363-270 (Americas, Europe, Africa), +45 (35) 363-090 (elsewhere). Fax: + 45 (35) 205 781. Contact: Lulu Vittrup, Audience Communications; or Jorgan T. Madsen, Head of External Service. $1-2 required, and enclosing local souvenirs helpful. Free stickers. Replies occasionally to friendly correspondence in English, particularly to those who point out they are of Danish ancestry, but regularly to correspondence in Danish. As of June 1, 1989, has not issued verifications from this office.

Norwegian Office, Technical: Details of reception quality are best sent to the Engineering Department of Radio Norway International (see), which operates the transmitters used for Radio Denmark.

Washington News Bureau, Nontechnical: 3001 Q Street NW, Washington DC 20007 USA. Fax: +1 (202) 342 2463.

DISESTABLISHMENTARIAN AND CLANDESTINE (via unlicensed transmitters or as programs by disestablishmentarian groups over licensed stations).

Note: Disestablishmentarian and clandestine organizational activities, including addresses and broadcasting schedules, are unusually subject to abrupt change or termination. Being operated by anti-establishment political and/or military organizations, these groups tend to be suspicious of outsiders' motives. Thus, they are most likely to reply to correspondence from those who write in the station's native tongue, and who are perceived to be at least somewhat favorably disposed to their cause. Most will provide, upon request, printed matter in their native tongue on their cause.

"AL KUDS RADIO", Palestinian Arab Broadcasting, P.O. Box 10412, Tripoli, Libya; or P.O. Box 5092, Damascus, Syria. Pro-Palestinian, anti-Israeli government. Broadcasts on behalf of Ahmad Jibril's Popular Front for the Liberation of Palestine-General Command. ("Al Kuds ash Sherif" is an Arab name for Jerusalem). Rarely replies except to correspondence in Arabic.

"ALTERNATIVA"—see Radio Miami Internacional, USA, for address. Contact: Orlando Gutiérrez, Executive Producer. Anti-Castro, anti-communist; privately supported by the Directorio Revolucionario Democrático Cubano.

A VOZ DA RESISTENCIA DO GALO NEGRO (Voice of the Resistence of the Black Cockerel)—see Angola.

"CCC RADIO", Conservative Consolidated Confederacy, P.O. Box 5635, Longview TX 75608 USA. Contact: Tim Harper. Free Ku Klux Klan printed matter.

"DEMOCRATIC VOICE OF BURMA" ("Democratic Myanmar a-Than"), P.O. Box 6720, St. Olavs Plass, 0130 Oslo, Norway. Fax: +47 (2) 114 988. Contact: Maung Maung Myint or Khin Maung Win. Programs produced by four expatriate Burmese students belonging to a jungle based revolutionary student organization called "All Burma Students' Democratic Front." Anti-Myanmar government. Transmits via the facilities of Radio Norway International.

"ESPERANZA"—see Radio Miami Internacional, USA, for address. Contact: Julio Esterino, Program Director. Anti-Castro, anti-communist; privately supported by Los Municipios de Cuba en el Exilio.

"FOR THE PEOPLE"—see WHRI, USA, for address.

"FORUM REVOLUCIONARIO"—see Radio Miami Internacional, USA, for address. Anti-Castro, anti-communist; privately supported by the Forum Revolucionario Democratico Cubano.

"IRAN'S FLAG OF FREEDOM RADIO", P.O. Box 19740, Irving CA 92714 USA; Postfach 05559B, W-2000 Hamburg, Germany; Post Boks 103, DK-2670 Greve Strand, Denmark; or 20 rue de Concorcet, F-75009 Paris, France. Five-minute news in Farsi from station's organizers may be heard by telephone: (USA) +1 (818) 792-4726; (U.K.) +44(71)376-1611. Contact: (USA) Reza Farhadi; (elsewhere) Sazeman Darferesh Kaviani; M. Ganji, Secretary General; or M.K. Fathi. Anti-Iranian government, pro-monarchist station of the Suzmani Darashta Kaviane group; supported by CIA and Egyptian government.

"LA VOZ DE ALPHA 66"—see Radio Miami Internacional, USA, for address. Contact: Diego Medina, Producer. Anti-Castro, anti-communist; privately supported by the Alpha 66 organization.

"LA VOZ DE LA FUNDACION", P.O. Box 440069, Miami FL 33144 USA. Contact: Ninoska Pérez Castellón, Executive Producer; (technical) Mariela Ferretti. Free stickers. Anti-Castro, anti-communist; privately supported by the Cuban American National Foundation.

"LA VOZ DEL CID", 10021 SW 37th Terrace, Miami FL 33165 USA; if no result, try Apartado de Correo 8130, 1000 San José, Costa Rica; or Apartado Postal 51403, Sabana Grande 1050, Caracas, Venezuela. Fax: +1 (305) 559 9365. Contact: Alfredo Aspitia, Assistente de Prensa e Información; or Francisco Fernández. Anti-Castro, anti-communist; privately supported by Cuba Independiente y Democrática. Free political literature.

AIR

"LA VOZ DEL MOVIMIENTO 30 DE NOVIEMBRE"—see Radio Miami Internacional, USA, for address. Anti-Castro, anti-communist; privately supported by the Movimiento 30 de Noviembre.

"LA VOZ DE LOS MEDICOS CUBANOS LIBRES"—see Radio Miami Internacional, USA, for address. Anti-Castro, anti-communist; privately supported by the PACHA organization.

"LA VOZ DE TRIBUNA LIBRE"—see Radio Miami Internacional, USA, for address. Contact: José Pérez Linares, Director. Anti-Castro, anti-communist; privately supported by the Alianza Cubana.

"LA VOZ POPULAR", Arcoios, P.O. Box 835, Seattle WA 98111 USA; Apartado 19619, México City D.F. 03910, Mexico; or Network in Solidarity with the People of Guatemala, 930 "F" Street NW, Suite 720, Washington DC 20004 USA.

"NATIONAL VANGUARD RADIO", P.O. Box 90, Hillsboro WV 24946 USA; or P.O. Box 596, Boring OR 97009, USA. Contact: Kevin Alfred Strom, Producer, "American Dissident Voices." $1 for catalog of books and tapes. Free bumper stickers and sample copies of *Patriot Review* newsletter. Program, possibly replacing "Voice of To-Morrow," of the neo-Nazi National Alliance. Via facilities of WRNO.

"PUEBLO LIBRE"—see Radio Miami Internacional, USA, for address. Anti-Castro, anti-communist; privately supported by the Junta Patriótica Cubana.

"RADIO CONCIENCIA"—see Radio Miami Internacional, USA, for address. Contact: Ramón Sánchez, Director. Anti-Castro, anti-communist; privately supported by the Comisión Nacional Cubana.

"RADIO FREE AMERICA"
Network: Sun Radio Network, 2857 Executive Drive, Clearwater FL 34622 USA. Contact: Tom Valentine, Host. Sells tapes of past broadcasts for $9. Aired via WWCR, succeeds *Liberty Lobby* program aired two decades ago.
Sponsoring Organization: Liberty Lobby, 300 Independence Avenue SE, Washington DC 20003 USA. Fax: +1 (202) 546 3626. Contact: Don Markey, Public Affairs Associate. *Spotlight* newspaper nominally $36/year, but often offered over the air for much less; sells books at various prices. Anti-Bilderberg/Trilateralist organization described by itself as populist; described by PBS' *Frontline* as "the largest anti-semitic group in the country."

"RADIO FREE BOUGAINVILLE"
Main Address: 2 Griffith Avenue, Roseville NSW 2069, Australia.

Fax: +61 (2) 417 1066. Contact: Sam Voron, Australian Director. $5, AUS$5 or 5 IRCs required.
Alternative Address: P.O. Box 1203, Honiara, Solomon Islands. Contact: Martin R. Miriori, Humanitarian Aid Coordinator. $1, AUS$2 or 3 IRCs required.

"RADIO FREE CROATIA", P.O. Box 25481, Chicago IL 60625 USA; or 3611 Wood Street, Chicago IL 60609 USA. Contact: Ivica Metzger, Chicago Media Workshop. Supportive of Croatian independence. This address for nontechnical correspondence only; technical correspondence should be sent to "Croatian Radio—Studio Zagreb" (see Croatia).

"RADIO HYVONG" ("Radio Nadejda")
Main Office: Box 174, Moscow International Post Office, Moscow, Russia. Contact: Daniel J. Kaszeta, N5SIA, Assistant Director; or Irina Zisman, Director. Transmits via the facilities of Radio Moscow International; yet, their programs, which are opposed to the Vietnamese government, are independent of RMI and are privately funded. Replies to correspondence in Russian, English, or Vietnamese.
Virginia Office: 6433 Northana Drive, Springfield, VA 22150 USA. Contact: Dao Thi Hoi, Ed.D.

"RADIO LIBERTY OF IRAN"—see "Radio Azadi Iran," above.

"RADIO MOJAHEDIN OF AFGHANISTAN" (if operating), P.O. Box 204, Peshawar, Pakistan; or MIFF—MB, Box 9720, London WC1N 3XX, United Kingdom. Contact: Barak Amani. Pro-Islamic fighters.

"RADIO NEG MAWON", P.O. Box 557, Warwick, NY 10990 USA; or P.O. Box 271, Nyack, NY 10960 USA. Fax: +1 (201) 489 9604. Contact: Jean Jean-Pierre, Producer; or Molly Graver. A small radio collective made up of Haitians & North Americans committed to the restoration of democracy in Haiti.
Station Address: See Radio For Peace International, Costa Rica.

"RADIO OF THE IRAQI REPUBLIC FROM BAGHDAD, VOICE OF THE IRAQI PEOPLE" ("Idha'at al-Jamahiriya al-Iraqiya min Baghdad, Saut al-Sha'b al-Iraqi"), Broadcasting Service of the Kingdom of Saudi Arabia, P.O. Box 61718, Riyadh 11575, Saudi Arabia. Contact: Suliman A. Al-Samnan, Director of Frequency Management. Anti-Saddam Hussein "black" clandestine supported by CIA, British intelligence and, surprisingly openly, Saudi Arabia. The name of this station has changed periodically since its inception during the Gulf crisis.

"RADIO PERIODICO PANAMERICANO"—see Radio Miami Internacional, USA for address. Contact: René L. Díaz, Program Director. Moderately anti-Castro and anti-communist; privately supported by Caribe Infopress and allied with the Plataforma Democrática Cubana.

"RADIO PERIODICO SEMANAL DE LOS COORDINADORES SOCIAL DEMOCRATA DE CUBA"—see "Un Solo Pueblo," below.

"RADIO 16TH DECEMBER" ("RADIO 16 DE SANM"), Chancery of Haiti, 2311 Massachusetts Av. NW, Washington DC 20008 USA. Contact: Patrick Elie or Louki Yves Cal. Return postage helpful. Wants to restore the former Aristide government back to power in Haiti.

"RADIO VOLUNTAD DEMOCRATICA"—see Radio Miami Internacional, USA, for address. Contact: Dr. Antonio de Varona, Jefe. Anti-Castro, anti-communist; privately supported by the Partido Revolucionario Cubano Auténtico.

"RUMBO A LA LIBERTAD"—see Radio Miami Internacional, USA, for address. Contact: Rafael Cabezas, Brigade President. Anti-Castro, anti-communist; privately supported by the Brigada 2506, consisting of veterans of the Bay of Pigs.

"RUSH LIMBAUGH SHOW"—see WRNO, USA, for address.

"UN SOLO PUEBLO"—see Radio Miami Internacional, USA, for address. Anti-Castro, anti-communist; privately supported by the Coordinadora Social Democrata.

"VOICE OF CHINA", Democratization of China, P.O. Box 11663, Berkeley CA 94701 USA; Foundation for China in the 21st Century, P.O. Box 11696, Berkeley CA 94701 USA; or P.O. Box 79218, Monkok, Hong Kong. Fax: +1 (510) 843 4370. Contact: Bang Tai Xu, Director. Mainly "overseas Chinese students" interested in the democratisation of China. Financial support from the Foundation for China in the 21st Century. Have "picked up the mission" of the earlier Voice of June 4th, but have no organizational relationship with it. Transmits via the facilities of the Central Broadcasting System, Taiwan (see), which also may be contacted.

"VOICE of ETHIOPIAN PATRIOTISM" ("Admas Ethiopia Yeager Fikir Dimts"), P.O. Box 5077, 163 05 Spanga, Stockholm, Sweden;

or Coalition of Ethiopian Democratic Forces, P.O. Box 21307, Washington DC 20009 USA. Pro-Coalition of Ethiopian Democratic Forces. Anti-Transitional Government of Ethiopia. Transmits via the facilities of Radio Moscow.

"VOICE OF KASHMIR FREEDOM", P.O. Box 102, Muzaffarabad, Azad Kashmir, Pakistan. Favors Azad Kashmiri independence from India; pro-Moslem.

"VOICE OF NATIONAL SALVATION" ("Gugugui Sori Pangsong"), Front for National Salvation, Kankoku Minzoku Minshu Tensen, Amatsu Building, 2-1 Hirakawa 1-chome, Chiyoda-ku, Tokyo, Japan. Free newspaper. Pro-North Korea, pro-Korean unification; supported by North Korean government. On the air since 1967, but not under the same name.

"VOICE OF PALESTINE" ("Saut ath-Filistine"), Office of the Permanent Observer for Palestine to the United Nations, 115 East 65th Street, New York NY 10021 USA. Contact: Dr. Nasser Al-Kidwa, Permanent Observer to the United Nations. Fax: +1 (212) 517 2377. Radio organ of the main, pro-Arafat, faction of the Palestine Liberation Organization (PLO). This is the oldest disestablishmentarian/clandestine operation on the air using the same name, having been heard via the facilities of RTV Algerienne and other stations since at least 1972.

"VOICE OF REBELLIOUS IRAQ", P.O. Box 1959/14155, Tehran, Iran. Anti-Iraqi regime.

"VOICE OF TO-MORROW" (when and if operating), P.O. Box 314, Clackamas OR 97015 USA. Contact: Michael Rosetti. Return postage helpful. Replies irregular and sometimes slow in coming. Neo-Nazi National Alliance. May have been replaced by "National Vanguard Radio" (see above).

"VOICE OF THE COMMUNIST PARTY OF IRAN"—see "Voice of the Iranian Revolution," below, for details.

"VOICE OF THE FREE SAHARA" ("La Voz del Sahara Libre, La Vox del Pueblo Sahel"), Sahara Libre, Frente Polisario, B.P. 10, El Mouradia, Algiers, Algeria; or Sahara Libre, Ambassade de la République Arabe Saraoui Démocratique, 1 Av. Franklin Roosevelt, 16000 Algiers, Algeria; or B.P. 10, Al-Mouradia, Algiers, Algeria. Fax: +213 747 933. Contact: Mohamed Lamin Abdesalem; Mahafud Zein; or Sneiba Lehbib. Free stickers, booklets, cards, maps, paper flags and calendars. 2 IRCs helpful. Pro-Polisario Front; supported by Algerian government.

"VOICE OF THE GREAT NATIONAL UNION FRONT OF CAMBODIA", 212 E. 47th Street #24G, New York NY 10017 USA; or Permanent Mission of Democratic Kampuchea to the United Nations, 747 3rd Avenue, 8th Floor, New York NY 10017 USA. Contact: Phobel Cheng, First Secretary, Permanent Mission of Cambodia to the United Nations. Khmer Rouge station.

"VOICE OF THE IRAQI PEOPLE"—see "Radio of the Iraqi Republic from Baghdad, Voice of the Iraqi People," above.

"VOICE OF THE KHMER" ("Samleng Khmer"), P.O. Box 22-25, Ramindra Post Office, Bangkok 10220, Thailand. Contact: Pol Ham, Chief Editor. Return postage required. Replies irregularly. Station of the Khmer Nationalist Forces, which consist of two groups: the Khmer People's National Liberation Front, and the National United Front for an Independent, Neutral, Peaceful and Cooperative Cambodia; nominally non-communist and anti-Vietnamese.

DJIBOUTI World Time +3

RADIODIFFUSION-TELEVISION DE DJIBOUTI, B.P. 97, Djibouti. Return postage helpful. Correspondence in French preferred.

DOMINICAN REPUBLIC World Time −4

LA N-103/RADIO NORTE, Apartado Postal 320, Santiago, Dominican Republic. Contact: Héctor Castillo, Gerente.

RADIO AMANECER INTERNACIONAL, Apartado Postal 1500, Santo Domingo, Dominican Republic. Contact: (nontechnical) Pastor Alexis Muñoz D., Director; or Rosa O. Alcantara, Secretaria; (technical) Ing. Sócrates Domínguez. $1 or return postage required. Replies slowly to correspondence in Spanish.

RADIO BARAHONA, Apartado 201, Barahona, Dominican Republic; or Gustavo Mejía Ricart No. 293, Apto. 2-B, Ens. Quisqueya, Santo Domingo, Dominican Republic. Contact: (nontechnical) Rodolfo Z. Lama Jaar, Administrador; (technical) Ing. Roberto Lama Sajour, Administrador General. Free stickers. Letters should be sent via registered mail. $1 or return postage helpful. Replies to correspondence in Spanish.

RADIO CIMA, Apartado 804, Santo Domingo, Dominican Republic. Fax: +1 (809) 541 1088. Contact: Roberto Vargas, Director. Free pennants, postcards, coins and taped music.

RADIO QUISQUEYA, Apartado Postal 135-2, Santo Domingo,

Dominican Republic. Contact: Lic. Gregory Castellanos Ruano, Director. Replies occasionally to correspondence in Spanish.

RADIO SANTIAGO, Apartado 282, Santiago, Dominican Republic.
Contact: Luís Felipe Moscos Finke, Gerente; Luís Felipe Moscos Cordero, Jefe Ingeniero; or Carlos Benoit, Announcer & Program Manager.

ECUADOR World Time −5 (−4 in times of drought); −6 Galapagos

Note: According to HCJB's "DX Party Line," during periods of drought, such as caused by "El Niño," electricity rationing causes periods in which transmitters cannot operate, as well as spikes which occasionally damage transmitters. Accordingly, Ecuadorian stations tend to be somewhat irregular during drought conditions.

ECOS DEL ORIENTE, 11 de Febrero y Mariscal Sucre, Lago Agrio, Sucumbios, Ecuador. Contact: Elsa Irene Velástegui, Secretaria. Sometimes includes free 20 sucre note (Ecuadorian currency) with reply. $1 or return postage required. Replies, often slowly, to correspondence in Spanish.

EMISORA ATALAYA, Casilla 204, Guayaquil, Guayas, Ecuador. Contact: Miss Mendejer Beledinez, Secretaria. $1 or return postage necessary. Replies to correspondence in Spanish.

EMISORAS GRAN COLOMBIA (when operating), Casilla 17 01-2246, Quito, Pichincha, Ecuador. Fax: +593 (2) 580 442. Contact: (nontechnical) Nancy Cevallos Castro, Asistente General. Return postage or $1 required. Replies to correspondence in Spanish. **ADS**

ESCUELAS RADIOFONICAS POPULARES DEL ECUADOR, Casilla 06-01-693, Riobamba, Ecuador. Fax: +593 (2) 961 625. Contact: Juan Pérez Sarmiento, Director Ejecutivo; or Patricio Muñoz Jacome, Director Ejecutivo de ERPE. Return postage helpful. Replies to correspondence in Spanish.

HCJB, VOICE OF THE ANDES

Main Office: Casilla 17-17-691, Quito, Pichincha, Ecuador. Fax: +593 (2) 447 263. Contact: (nontechnical or technical) Ken MacHarg, Host, Saludos Amigos (letterbox); (technical) Glen Volkhardt, Director of Broadcasting; Wolfgang Brinkmann, Frequency Manager; or Karen Schmidt. Free religious brochures, calendars and pennants. ANDEX International listeners' club bulletin. *Catch the Vision* book for $8, postpaid. IRC or unused U.S., Canadian or Ecuadorian stamps required for airmail reply.

U.S. Main Office: International Headquarters, World Radio Missionary Fellowship, Inc., P.O. Box 39800, Colorado Springs CO 80949 USA. Fax: +1 (719) 590 9801. Contact: Richard D. Jacquin, Manager; or Marie Stevens. Various items sold via U.S. address—catalog available.

U.S. Engineering Center: 1718 W. Mishawaka Road, Elkhart IN 46517 USA. Fax: +1 (219) 294 8329. Contact: Dave Pasechnik, Project Manager; or Bob Moore, Engineering. This address concerned only with the design and manufacture of transmitter and antenna equipment.

Canadian Office: 6981 Millcreek Drive, Unit 23, Mississauga ON, L5N 6B8 Canada.

U.K. Office: HCJB-Europa, 131 Grattan Road, Bradford, West Yorkshire BD1 2HS, United Kingdom. Fax: +44 (274) 741 302. Contact: Andrew Steele, Director; or Bill Rapley, Producer.

Australian Office: G.P.O. Box 691, Melbourne, VIC 3001, Australia. Fax: +61 (3) 870 6597. Contact: David C. Maindonald, Australian Director; or Greg Pretty, Studio Director. **AIR**

LA VOZ DE LOS CARAS (when not off during drought), Casilla 628, Bahía de Caráquez, Manabi, Ecuador. Contact: Prof. Eduardo Rodríguez Coll, Director de Programación. $1 or return postage required. Replies occasionally and slowly to correspondence in Spanish.

LA VOZ DE SAQUISILI—RADIO LIBERTADOR (when not off during drought), Casilla 669, Saquisilí, Ecuador. Contact: Srta. Carmen Mena Corrales. Return postage required. Replies irregularly and slowly to correspondence in Spanish.

LA VOZ DEL NAPO, Misión Josefina, Tena, Napo, Ecuador. Contact: Ramiro Cubrero, Director. Free pennants and stickers. $1 or return postage required. Replies occasionally to correspondence in Spanish.

LA VOZ DEL UPANO, Vicariato Apostólico de Méndez, Misión Salesiana, 10 de Agosto s/n, Macas, Ecuador. Contact: Sor Luz Benigna Torres, Directora; or Ramiro Cabrera. Free stickers, pennants and calendars. On one occasion, not necessarily to be repeated, sent tape of Ecuadorian folk music for $2. Otherwise, $1 required. Replies to correspondence in Spanish.

ONDAS QUEVEDENAS, 12ma. Calle 207, Quevedo, Ecuador. Contact: Sra. Maruja Jaramillo, Gerente; or Humberto Alvarado P., Director-Dueño. Return postage required. Replies irregularly to correspondence in Spanish.

RADIO BAHA'I, Instituto Baha'í, Calle Quito 7-12, Otavalo, Ecuador. Contact: Sra. Nooshin Burwell, Coordinadora; or Maricela Bermeo, Secretario. Return postage helpful. This station of the Baha'í faith replies irregularly.

RADIO CATOLICA, Apartado Postal 17-24-00006, Santo Domingo de los Colorados, Pichincha, Ecuador. Contact: Nancy Moncada, Secretaria RCSD; or Padre Cesareo Tiestos L.,Sch.P, Director. Free pennants. Return postage or $1 helpful. Replies to correspondence in Spanish.

RADIO CATOLICA NACIONAL, Av. América 1830 y Mercadillo, Apartado 540A, Quito, Pichincha, Ecuador. Contact: Sra. Yolanda de Suquitana, Secretaria. Free stickers. Return postage required. Replies to correspondence in Spanish.

RADIO CENTRO (when not off during drought), Casilla 18-01-0574, Ambato, Tungurahua, Ecuador. Contact: (nontechnical) Luis A. Gamboa T., Director-Gerente; (technical) Sócrates Domínguez, Ingeniero. Free stickers and sometimes free newspaper. Return postage or $1 required. Replies occasionally to correspondence in Spanish.

RADIO CENTINELA DEL SUR, Casilla 196, Loja, Ecuador. Return postage of $1 helpful, as are canceled non-Ecuadorian stamps. Replies occasionally to correspondence in Spanish.

RADIODIFUSORA CULTURAL, LA VOZ DEL NAPO—see La Voz del Napo, above.

RADIODIFUSORA NACIONAL DEL ECUADOR, c/o DX Party Line, HCJB, Casilla 691, Quito, Pichincha, Ecuador. Contact: Gustavo Cevallos, Director; or Eduardo Rodríguez, Productor, "Cartas para los Ecuatorianos Ausentes." IRC or $1 required.

RADIO FEDERACION, Casilla 1422, Quito, Pichincha, Ecuador. Contact: Prof. Albino M. Utitiaj P., Director de Medios. Return postage or $1 required. Replies irregularly to correspondence in Spanish.

RADIO INTEROCEANICA, Santa Rosa de Quijos, Cantón El Chaco, Provincia de Napo, Ecuador. Contact: Byron Medina, Gerente; or Ing. Olaf Hegmuir. $1 or return postage required, and donations appreciated (station owned by Swedish Covenant Church). Replies slowly to correspondence in Spanish or Swedish.

RADIO JESUS DEL GRAN PODER, Casilla de Correo 133, Quito, Pichincha, Ecuador. Contact: Padre Jorge Enríquez. Free pennants and religious material. Return postage required. Replies irregularly to correspondence in Spanish.

RADIO LUZ Y VIDA, Casilla 222, Loja, Ecuador. Contact: Srta. Jolly Pardo. Replies irregularly to correspondence in Spanish.

RADIO NACIONAL ESPEJO (when not off during drought), Casilla 352, Quito, Pichincha, Ecuador. Contact: Marco Caceido, Gerente; or Mercedes B. de Caceido, Secretaria. Replies to correspondence in Spanish.

RADIO NACIONAL PROGRESO (when not off during drought), Sistema de Emisoras Progreso, Casilla V, Loja, Ecuador. Contact: José Guaman Guajala, Director del programa Círculo Dominical. Replies irregularly to correspondence in Spanish, particularly for feedback on "Círculo Dominical" program aired Sundays between 1100-1300. Free pennants.

RADIO PASTAZA (if shortwave transmitter repaired and relicensed), Casilla 728, El Puyo, Pastaza, Ecuador. Contact: Galo Amores, Gerente. Return postage or $1 required. Replies irregularly to correspondence in Spanish. As the station manager is also head of the local taxi drivers' union, printed matter, photos or discussion of this topic may help elicit a response.

RADIO PAZ Y BIEN, Casilla 94, Ambato, Tungurahua, Ecuador. Contact: P. Luís Florencio León E, OFM, Gerente-Director.

RADIO POPULAR INDEPENDIENTE, Av. Loja 2408, Cuenca, Azuay, Ecuador. Contact: Sra. Manena de Villavicencio, Secretaria. Return postage or $1 required. Replies occasionally to correspondence in Spanish.

RADIO QUITO, "El Comercio," Casilla 57, Quito, Pichincha, Ecuador. Contact: Fernando Fegan, Gerente; or José Almeida, Subgerente. Pennants. Return postage required. Replies slowly, but regularly.

RADIO RIO TARQUI, Casilla 877, Cuenca, Azuay, Ecuador. Contact: Boris Cornejo or Manuel Peña F. Replies irregularly to correspondence in Spanish.

RADIO ZARACAY, Casilla 31, Santo Domingo de los Colorados, Pinchincha, Ecuador.

EGYPT   World Time +2 (UTC +3 midyear)

RADIO CAIRO

Nontechnical: P.O. Box 566, Cairo, Egypt. Contact: Mrs. Sahar Khalil, Director of English Service to North America & Producer, "Questions and Answers"; or Mrs. Magda Hamman, Secretary. Free stickers, stamps, maps, papyrus souvenirs, calendars and *External Services of Radio Cairo* book. Free individually tutored Arabic-language lessons with loaned textbooks from Arabic by Radio, Radio Cairo, P.O. Box 325, Cairo, Egypt. Arabic-language religious, cultural and language-learning audio and video tapes from the Egyptian Radio and Television Union sold via Sono Cairo Audio-Video, P.O. Box 2017, Cairo, Egypt; when ordering video tapes, inquire to ensure they function on the television standard (NTSC, PAL or SECAM) in your country. Replies regularly, but sometimes slowly.

Technical: P.O. Box 1186, Cairo, Egypt. Contact: Nivene W. Laurence, Engineer; Hamdy Abdel Hallem, Director of Propagation; or Fathi El Bayoumi, Chief Engineer. Comments and suggestions on audio quality and level welcomed.

EL SALVADOR   World Time -6

RADIO VENCEREMOS

Main Office: Casilla de Correo 05-209, Metrocentro, San Salvador, El Salvador. Contact: (nontechnical) Carlos Henríquez Gonsalves ("Camarada Santiago"), Publicidad; or Carlos Latino, Director; (technical) "El Cieguito." Free posters. Two books (*Las Mil y Una Historias de Radio Venceremos*, $8, and *La Terquedad del Izote*, $12) sold. $1 helpful.

North American Office: El Salvador Media Project, 335 West 38th Street, New York NY 10018 USA. Contact: Anita Ocampo; or Gustavo Acosta, Director. $1 required.

German Office: SRV Pres Bureau, Scharnhorstr. 6, D(W) 5000 Cologne 60, Germany. Contact: A. Albararo. $1 or DM2.00 required. **ADS AIR**

ENGLAND—see UNITED KINGDOM.

EQUATORIAL GUINEA   World Time +1

RADIO AFRICA 2000, Embajada de España, Cooperación Española, Malabo, Isla Bioko, Equatorial Guinea. Contact: Concha Chamorro; or Teodora Silochi Thompson, Secretaría, who likes to correspond with people in other countries. Replies to correspondence in Spanish.

RADIO AFRICA

Transmission Office: Same details as "Radio Nacional Bata," below.

U.S. Office: Pierce International Communications, 10201 Torre Avenue, Suite 320, Cupertino CA 95014 USA. Fax: +1 (408) 252 6855. Contact: Carmen Jung or James Manero. $1 or return postage required.

RADIO EAST AFRICA—same details as "Radio Africa," above.

RADIO NACIONAL BATA, Apartado 749, Bata, Río Muni, Equatorial Guinea. Contact: José Mba Obama, Director. Spanish preferred. Also, see U.S. Office under "Radio Africa," above.

RADIO NACIONAL MALABO, Apartado 195, Malabo, Isla Bioko, Equatorial Guinea. Contact: (nontechnical) Román Manuel Mané-Abaga, Jefe de Programación; or Manuel Chema Lobede; (technical) Hermenegildo Moliko Chele, Jefe Servicios Técnicos de Radio y Televisión. $1 or return postage required. Replies irregularly to correspondence in Spanish.

ERITREA   World Time +3

VOICE OF THE BROAD MASSES OF ERITREA (Dimisi Hafash), EPLF National Guidance, Information Department, Radio Branch, P.O. Box 872, Asmera, Eritrea; EPLF National Guidance, Information Department, Radio Branch, P.O. Box 2571, Addis Ababa, Ethiopia; Eritrean Relief Committee, 475 Riverside Drive, Suite 907, New York NY 10015 USA; or EPLF National Guidance, Information Department, Radio Branch, Sahel Eritrea, P.O. Box 891, Port Sudan, Sudan; or EPLF Desk for Nordic Countries, Torsplan 3, 1 tr, S-113 64 Stockholm, Sweden. Fax (Stockholm) +46 (8) 322 337. Contact: (Eritrea) Ghebreab Ghebremedhin; (Ethiopia and Sudan) Mehreteab Tesfa Giorgis. Return postage or $1 helpful. Free information on history of station, Ethiopian People's Liberation Front and Eritrea.

ESTONIA   World Time +2 (+3 midyear)

ESTONIAN RADIO (Eesti Raadio)—same details as "Radio Estonia," below, except replace "External Service, The Estonian Broadcasting Company" with "Eesti Raadio."

RADIO ESTONIA, External Service, The Estonian Broadcasting Company, 21 Gonsier Street, EE-0100 Tallinn, Estonia. Fax: +372 (2) 43 44 57. Contact: Silja Orusalu, Editor, I.C.A. Department;

Harry Tiido; Kusta Reinsoo, Deputy Head of External Service; Mrs. Tiina Sillam, Head of English Service; Mrs. Kai Siidiratsep, Head of German Service; Enno Turmen, Head of Swedish Service; Juri Vilosius, Head of Finnish Service; or Elena Rogova. Free pennants. $1 required. Replies occasionally.

ETHIOPIA World Time +3
VOICE OF ETHIOPIA: P.O. Box 654 (External Service), or P.O. Box 1020 (Domestic Service)—both in Addis Ababa, Ethiopia. Contact: (External Service) Mr Kasa Miliko, Head of Station; Kahsai Tewoldemedhin, Program Director; or Yohness Kufael, Producer, "Contact"; (technical) Technical Director. A very poor replier to correspondence in recent years, but with the new political structure this could change.

FINLAND World Time +2 (+3 midyear)
YLE/RADIO FINLAND
Main Office: Radio and TV Centre, P.O. Box 10, SF-00241 Helsinki, Finland. Fax: +358 (0) 14 80 11 69; (International Information) +358 (0) 14 80 33 90; or (technical Affairs) +358 (0) 14 80 35 88. Contact: Mrs. Riitta Raukko, International Information; Juhani Niinist, Head of External Broadcasting; Ms. Salli Korpela, International Relations/Radio; or Kate Moore, Producer, "Airmail." (technical) Mr. Kari Llmonen, Technical Affairs. Free stickers, tourist and other magazines. Finnish by Radio and Nuntii Latini textbooks available. Replies to correspondence, but doesn't provide verification data.
U.S. Office: P.O. Box 462, Windsor CT 06095 USA. 24-hour toll-free telephone for schedule: (toll-free, U.S. only) (800) 221-9539.

FRANCE World Time +1 (+2 midyear)
RADIO FRANCE INTERNATIONALE (RFI)
Main Office: B.P. 9516, F-75016 Paris Cedex 16, France. Fax: +33 (1) 45 24 39 13; +33 (1) 42 30 44 81; or +33 (1) 42 30 30 71. Three minutes of tape-delayed RFI news in English audible 24 hours by telephoning the Washington (USA) number of +1 (202) 944-6075. Fax: (general information and English programs) +33 (1) 45 24 39 13; (non-English programs) +33 (1) 42 30 44 81. Contact: (English programs) Simson Najovits, Chief, English Department; (other programs) Daniel Ollivier, Directeur du développement et de la communication; André Larquié, Président; or J.P. Charbonnier, Producer, "Lettres des Auditeurs"; (technical) M. Raymond Pincon, Producer, "Le Courrier Technique." Free souvenir keychains, pins, pencils, T-shirts and stickers have been received by some—especially when visiting the headquarters at 116 avenue du Président Kennedy, in the chichi 16th Arrondissement. Can provide supplementary materials for "Dites-moi tout" French-language course; write to the attention of Mme. Chantal de Grandpre, "Dites-moi tout."
Transmission Office, Technical: Télédiffusion de France, Ondes Décamétriques, 21-27 rue Barbès, F-92120 Montrouge, France. Fax: +33 (1) 49 65 19 11. Contact: Daniel Bochent, Chef du service ondes décamétriques; or, for the most significant matters only, Xavier Gouyou Beauchamps, Président. This office only for informing about transmitter-related problems (interference, modulation quality, etc.), especially by fax. Verifications not given out at this office; requests for verification should be sent to the main office, above. Station plans to set up a shortwave broadcasting center in Jibuti which may be operational in two or three years time.
New York News Bureau, Nontechnical: 1290 Avenue of the Americas, New York New York NY 10019. Fax: +1 (212) 541 4309. Contact: Bruno Albin, reporter.
San Francisco Office, Schedules: 2654 17th Avenue, San Francisco CA 94116 USA. Contact: George Poppin. This address only provides RFI schedules to listeners. All other correspondence should be sent directly to Paris.

FRENCH GUIANA World Time –3
SOCIETE NATIONALE DE RADIO TELEVISION FRANCAISE D'OUTRE-MER—RFO GUYANE, Cayenne, French Guiana. Free stickers. Replies occasionally and sometimes slowly; correspondence in French preferred, but English often okay.

FRENCH POLYNESIA World Time –10 Tahiti
SOCIETE NATIONALE DE RADIO TELEVISION FRANCAISE D'OUTRE-MER—RFO TAHITI, B.P. 125, Papeete, Tahiti, French Polynesia. Fax: +689 413 155. Contact: (technical or nontechnical) León Siquin, Services Techniques. Free stickers, tourist brochures and broadcast-coverage map. 3 IRCs, return postage, 5 francs or $1 helpful, but not mandatory. M. Siquin and his teenage sons Xavier and Philippe, all friendly and fluent in English, collect pins from radio/TV stations, memorabilia from the Chicago Bulls basketball team and other souvenirs of American pop culture;

these make more appropriate enclosures than the usual postage-reimbursement items. Station hopes to obtain new studios and transmitters.

GABON World Time +1
AFRIQUE NUMERO UN, B.P. 1, Libreville, Gabon. Fax: +241 742 133. Contact: (nontechnical) Gaston Didace Singangoye; or A. Letamba, Le Directeur des Programmes; (technical) Mme. Marguerite Bayimbi, Le Directeur [sic] Technique. Free calendars and bumper stickers. $1, 2 IRCs or return postage helpful. Replies very slowly.
RTV GABONAISE, B.P. 10150, Libreville, Gabon. Free stickers. $1 required. Replies occasionally, but slowly, to correspondence in French.

GEORGIA World Time +4
GEORGIAN RADIO, TV-Radio Tbilisi, ul. M. Kostava 68, 380071 Tbilisi, Republic of Georgia. Contact: (External Service) Helena Apkhadze, Foreign Editor; Tamar Shengelia; or Maya Chihradze; (Domestic Service) Lia Uumlaelsa, Manager; or V. Khundadze, Acting Director of Television and Radio Department. Replies occasionally and slowly.

GERMANY World Time +1 (+2 midyear)
ADVENTIST WORLD RADIO, THE VOICE OF HOPE, P.O. Box 13 02 08, 64 242 Darmstadt 13, Germany. Fax: +49 (6151) 537 639. Contact: Mrs. Andrea Steele, PR Director. Free religious printed matter, pennants, stickers and other small souvenirs. Transmitters are located in Costa Rica, Guam, Guatemala, Italy, Perú and Russia. Additionally, drop-mailing address are:
African Office: AWR, B.P. 1751, Abidjan 08, Côte d'Ivoire. Fax: +225 442 341 or +225 445 118. Contact: Daniel B. Grisier, Director; Julien M. Thiombiano, Program Director; or "Listener Mailbox."
Hong Kong Office: AWR-Asia, P.O. Box 310, Hong Kong. Free quarterly *AWR-Asiawaves* newsletter, religious printed matter, stickers, pennants and other small souvenirs.
BAYERISCHER RUNDFUNK, Rundfunkplatz 1, W-8000 Munich, Germany. Fax: +49 (89) 590 001. Contact: Dr. Gualtiero Guidi. Free stickers and 250-page program schedule book.
CANADIAN FORCES NETWORK RADIO—*see* CANADA.
DEUTSCHE WELLE, THE VOICE OF GERMANY
Main Office: Postfach 10 04 44, 50588 Cologne 1, Germany. Fax: (general) +49 (221) 389 4155 or +49 (221) 389 3000; (English Service) +49 (221) 389 4599; or (Public Relations) +49 (221) 389 2047. Toll-free telephone (U.S. and parts of Canada only): (800) 392-3248. Contact: (nontechnical, general Ernst Peterssen, Head of Audience Research and Listeners' Mail; Dr. Wilhelm Nobel, Director of Public Relations; or Dr. Burkhard Nowotny, Director of Media Department; (nontechnical, "German by Radio" language course) Herrad Meese; (technical) Peter Senger, Head, Radio Frequency Department. Free pennants, stickers, key chains, pens, *Deutsch-warum nicht?* language-course book, *Germany—A European Country and its People* book, and the excellent *tune-in* magazine. Local Deutsche Welle Listeners' Clubs in selected countries.
Brussels News Bureau: International Press Center, 1 Boulevard Charlemagne, B-1040 Brussels, Belgium.
Washington News Bureau: P.O. Box 14163, Washington DC 20004 USA. Fax: +1 (202) 526 2255. Contact: Adnan Al-Katib, Correspondent.
Tokyo Bureau: C.P.O. Box 132, Tokyo 100-91, Japan.
RADIO IN THE AMERICAN SECTOR (RIAS), Kufsteinerstr. 69, W-1000 Berlin 62, Germany. Fax: +49 (30) 850 3390. Contact: Janina Penkel or Lydia Duive. $1 or return postage required. Free stickers, postcards and *RIAS Yearbook.*
RADIO BREMEN, Bürgemeister-Spittaallee 45, W-2800 Bremen 33, Germany. Fax: +49 (421) 246 1010. Contact: Jim Senberg. Free stickers and shortwave guidebook.
SENDER FREIES BERLIN, Nordostdeutscher Rundfunk, Masurenallee 14, W-1000 Berlin 19, Germany. Fax: +49 (30) 301 5062. Free stickers and frequency publication.
SÜDDEUTSCHER RUNDFUNK, Postfach 106040, W-7000 Stuttgart 1, Germany. Fax: +49 (711) 288 2600 or +49 (711) 929 2600. Free stickers.
SÜDWESTFUNK, Postfach 820, W-7570 Baden-Baden, Germany. Fax: +49 (7221) 922 010. Contact: (technical) Prof. Dr. Krank, Technical Director; or Hans Krankl, Chief Engineer.
GHANA World Time exactly
RADIO GHANA, Ghana Broadcasting Corporation, P.O. Box 1633, Accra, Ghana. Fax: +233 (21) 773 227. Contact: (nontech-

nical) Maud Blankson-Mills, Head, Audience Research; Robinson Aryee, Head, English Section; Emmanuel Felli, Head, French Section; Mrs. Anna Sai, Assistant Director of Radio; or Victor Markin, Producer, English Section. (Mr. Markin is interested in reception reports as well as feedback on the program he produces, "Health Update"); (technical) E. Heneath, Propagation Department. IRC, return postage or $1 helpful.

GREECE World Time +2 (+3 midyear)

FONI TIS HELLADAS
Nontechnical: ERT A.E., ERA-E Program, Voice of Greece, Mesogion 432 Str., Aghia Paraskevi, GR-153 42 Athens, Greece. Fax: (specify "5th Program" on cover sheet) +30 (1) 655 0943 or +30 (1) 686 8305. Contact: Kosta Valetas, Director, Programs for Abroad; or Demetri Vafaas. Free tourist literature.

Technical: ERT 5th Program, Direction of Engineering, P.O. Box 60019, GR-153 10 Aghia Paraskevi Attikis, Athens, Greece. Fax: +30 (1) 639 0652 or +30 (1) 600 9608.

RADIOPHONIKOS STATHMOS MAKEDONIAS
Nontechnical: Odos Yeorghikis Scholis 129, GR-546 39 Thessaloniki, Greece.

Technical: ERT S.A., Subdirection of Technical Support, P.O. Box 11312, GR-541 10 Thessaloniki, Greece. Contact: Tassos A. Glias, Telecommunications Engineer.

VOICE OF AMERICA—Does not welcome direct correspondence at its Greek facilities in Kaválla and Rhodes. *See* USA for acceptable VOA address and related information.

GUAM World Time +10

ADVENTIST WORLD RADIO, THE VOICE OF HOPE—KSDA
Main Office, General Programs: P.O. Box 7500, Agat, Guam 96928 USA. Fax: +671 565 2983. Contact: (nontechnical) Chris Carey, Assistant Program Director & Producer, "Listener Mailbox"; Gregory Scott, Program Director; or Max Torkelsen, General Manager; (technical) Elvin Vence, Engineer. Free pennants, stickers, postcards, quarterly *AWR-Asiawaves* newsletter and religious printed matter. Also, *see* USA.

"DX-Asiawaves" Program: ARDXC, Box 227, Box Hill 3128 VIC, Australia.

Hong Kong Office: AWR-Asia, P.O. Box 310, Hong Kong. Free religious printed matter, pennants, stickers and other small souvenirs.

TRANS WORLD RADIO—KTWR
Main Office: P.O. Box CC, Agana, Guam 96910 USA. Fax: +671 477 2838. Contact: (nontechnical, general) Mrs. Shelley Frost; ("Friends in Focus" listeners-questions program) Wayne T. Frost, Producer; (technical) Kevin Mayer. Also, *see* USA. Free stickers.

Australian Office: G.P.O. Box 602D, Melbourne 3001, Australia. Fax: +61 (3) 874 8890. Contact: (nontechnical or technical) John Reeder, Director.

Singapore Bureau, Nontechnical: 134-136 Braddel Road, Singapore. **AIR**

India Office: P.O. Box 4310, New Delhi-110 019, India. Contact: N. Emil Jebasingh, Vishwa Vani.

GUATEMALA World Time –6 (–5 midyear)

ADVENTIST WORLD RADIO, THE VOICE OF HOPE—UNION RADIO, Radiodifusora Adventista, Apartado de Correo 35-C, Guatemala City, Guatemala. Contact: Lizbeth de Morán; Nora Lissette Vásquez R.; or M.J. Castaneda, Sec. Free tourist and religious literature, and Guatemalan stamps. Return postage, 3 IRCs or $1 helpful. Correspondence in Spanish preferred. Also, *see* USA.

RADIO CULTURAL—TGNA, Apartado de Correo 601, Guatemala City, Guatemala. Contact: Mariella Posadas, QSL Secretary; or Wayne Berger, Chief Engineer. Free religious printed matter. Return postage or $1 appreciated.

LA VOZ DE ATITLAN—TGDS, Santiago Atitlán, Guatemala. Contact: Juan Ajtzip Alvarado, Director. Free 25th anniversary (1992) pennants, while they last. Return postage required. Replies to correspondence in Spanish.

LA VOZ DE NAHUALA, Nahualá, Sololá, Guatemala. Contact: (technical) Juan Fidel Lepe Juárez, Técnico Auxiliar. Return postage required. Correspondence in Spanish preferred.

RADIO BUENAS NUEVAS, 13020 San Sebastián, Huehuetenango, Guatemala. Contact: Israel Rodas Mérida, Gerente; Roberto Rice, Technician; or Andres Maldonado López, Julian Pérez Megía, and Israel Maldonado, Locutores. $1 or return postage helpful. Free religious and station information in Spanish. Replies to correspondence in Spanish.

RADIO CHORTIS, Centro Social, 20004 Jocotán, Chiquimula,

Guatemala. Contact: Padre Juan María Boxus, Director. $1 or return postage required. Replies irregularly to correspondence in Spanish.

RADIO K'EKCHI—TGVC, K'ekchi Baptist Association, 16015 Fray Bartolomé de las Casas, Alta Verapaz, Guatemala. Contact: Gilberto Sun Xicol, Gerente; Carlos Díaz Araújo, Director; or David Daniel, Media Consultant. Free paper pennant. $1 or return postage required. Replies to correspondence in Spanish.

RADIO MAM, Acu'Mam, Cabricán, Quetzaltenango, Guatemala. Contact: José Benito Escalante Ramos, Director. Free stickers and pennants. $1 or return postage required. Replies irregularly to correspondence in Spanish. Donations permitting (the station is religious), they would like to get a new transmitter to replace the current unit, which is failing. **ADS AIR**

RADIO MAYA DE BARILLAS—TGBA, 13026 Villa de Barillas, Huehuetenango, Guatemala. Contact: José Castaneda, Gerente. Free pennants and pins. $1 or return postage required. Replies occasionally to correspondence in Spanish and Indian languages.

RADIO TEZULUTLAN, Apartado de Correo 19, 16901 Cobán, Guatemala. Contact: Alberto P.A. Macz, Director; or Hno. Antonio Jacobs, Director Ejecutivo. $1 or return postage required. Replies to correspondence in Spanish.

GUINEA World Time exactly

RADIODIFFUSION-TELEVISION GUINEENNE, B.P. 391, Conakry, Guinea. Contact: (nontechnical) Yaoussou Diaby, Journaliste Sportif; (technical) Mbaye Gagne, Chef de Studio; Alpha Sylla, Directeur, Sofoniya I Centre de Transmission; or Direction des Services Techniques. Return postage or $1 required. Replies very irregularly to correspondence in French.

GUYANA World Time –3

VOICE OF GUYANA, Guyana Broadcasting Corporation, P.O. Box 10760, Georgetown, Guyana. Contact: (technical) Roy Marshall, Senior Technician; or S. Goodman, Chief Engineer. $1 or IRC helpful. Sending a spare sticker from another station helps assure a reply.

HAITI World Time –5 (–4 midyear)

RADIO 4VEH
Main Office: B.P. 1, Cap-Haïtien, Haiti. Contact: (nontechnical) Gaudin Charles, Director; (technical) Mardy Picazo, Development Engineer, or Jean Van Dervort, Verification Secretary. Return postage, IRC or $1 required.

U.S. Office, Nontechnical: Oriental Missionary Society International, Inc., Box A, Greenwood IN 46142 USA. Contact: Robert Erny, Vice President of Field Operations.

HOLLAND (THE NETHERLANDS) World Time +1 (+2 midyear)

RADIO NEDERLAND WERELDOMROEP
Main Office: Postbus 222, NL-1200 JG Hilversum, Holland. Fax: +31 (35) 72 43 52 or +31 (35) 181 12 (indicate destination department on fax cover sheet). Contact (RNW): (nontechnical) Hans Veltcamp Helbach, Director of Public Relations; Jonathan Marks, Head, English World Service; Frank Suasso, Director of Programs; Mrs. Lupita Kingma; or Robert Chesal, Host, "Sounds Interesting" (include your telephone number); (technical) ing. Hans Bakhuizen, Frequency Bureau; Martine Jolly; or Jan Willern Drexhage, Head, Frequency Bureau. Free RNW stickers, semiannual *On Target* newsletter and booklets. Free "Happy Station" (Sunday program) calendars and stickers.

Latin American Office: Apartado 880-1007, Ventro Colón, Costa Rica.

HONDURAS World Time –6

LA VOZ DE LA MOSQUITIA, Puerto Lempira, Región Mosquitia, Honduras. Contact: Sammy Simpson, Director; Sra. Wilkinson; or Larry Sexton.

LA VOZ EVANGELICA—HRVC
Main Office: Apartado Postal 3252, Tegucigalpa, D.C., Honduras. Fax: +504 33 3933. Contact: Srta. Orfa Esther Durón Mendoza, Secretaria; Saúl Berrios, Dpto. de Producción; Hermann Lagos Naira; or Uelsen Raul Acosta Castillo. Free stickers. 3 IRCs or $1 required.

Regional Office: Apartado 2336, San Pedro Sula, Honduras. Considering replacing the existing transmitter, which is very old.

U.S. Office: Conservative Baptist Home Mission Society, Box 828, Wheaton IL 60187 USA. Fax: +1 (708) 653 4936. Contact: Jill W. Smith. **ADS AIR**

RADIO COPAN INTERNATIONAL
Station: Apartado 955, Tegucigalpa, D.C., Honduras.

Miami Office: P.O. Box 526852, Miami FL 33152 USA. Fax: +1 (305) 267 9253. Contact: Jeff White.

RADIO LUZ Y VIDA—HRPC, Apartado 303, San Pedro Sula, Honduras. Fax: +504 57 0394. Contact: C. Paul Easley, Director; or, to have your letter read over the air, "English Friendship Program." Return postage or $1 appreciated.

SANI RADIO, Apartado 113, La Ceiba, Honduras. Contact: Jacinto Molina G., Director ; or Mario S. Corzo. Return postage or $1 required.

HONG KONG   World Time +8

BBC WORLD SERVICE—HONG KONG RELAY, Flat B, 24 Beacon Hill Road, Kowloon Tong, Kowloon, Hong Kong. Contact: (technical) Phillip Sandell, Resident Engineer. Nontechnical correspondence should be sent to the BBC World Service in London (see).

RADIO TELEVISION HONG KONG, C.P.O. Box 70200, Kowloon, Hong Kong. Fax: +852 (3) 380 279. Contact: (technical) W.K. Li, for Director of Broadcasting. May broadcast weather reports every even two years, usually around late April, on 3940 kHz for the South China Yacht Sea Race.

HUNGARY   World Time +1 (+2 midyear)

RADIO BUDAPEST, Bródy Sándor utca 5-7, H-1800 Budapest, Hungary. Fax: (Administrative) +36 (1) 801 3175; or (Editorial) +36 (1) 138 8838. Contact: Charles Taylor Coutts, Len Scott, Ilona Kiss or Anton Réger. Free Budapest International station newsletter, pennants, stickers and T-shirts, while they last.

ICELAND   World Time exactly

RIKISUTVARPID, Efstaleiti 1, 150 Reykjavík, Iceland. Fax: +354 (1) 693 010. Free stickers.

INDIA   World Time +5:30

ALL INDIA RADIO—AIZAWL, Radio Tila, Tuikhuahtlang, Aizawl-796 001, Mizoram, India.

ALL INDIA RADIO—BANGALORE
Headquarters: See All India Radio—External Services Division.
AIR Office near Transmitter: P.O. Box 5096, Bangalore-560 001, Karnataka, India.

ALL INDIA RADIO—BHOPAL, Akashvani Bhawan, Shamla Hills, Bhopal-462 002, Madhya Pradesh, India.

ALL INDIA RADIO—BOMBAY
External Services: See All India Radio—External Services Division.
Domestic Service: P.O. Box 13034, Bombay-400 020, India. Contact: Sarla Mirchandani, Programme Executive, for Station Director. Return postage helpful.

ALL INDIA RADIO—CALCUTTA, G.P.O. Box 696, Calcutta-700 001, West Bengal, India.

ALL INDIA RADIO—DELHI, P.O. Box 70, New Delhi-110 011, India. $1 helpful.

ALL INDIA RADIO—EXTERNAL SERVICES DIVISION, Parliament Street, P.O. Box 500, New Delhi-110 001, India. Contact: (nontechnical) P. M. Iyer, Director of External Services; or Audience Relations Officer; (technical) S.A.S. Abidi, Assistant Director Engineering (F.A.). Free monthly India Calling magazine and stickers. Except for stations listed below, correspondence to domestic stations is more likely to be responded to if it is sent via the External Services Division; request that your letter be forwarded to the appropriate domestic station.

ALL INDIA RADIO—GANGTOK, Old MLA hostel, Gangtok-737 101, Sikkim, India.

ALL INDIA RADIO—GORAKHPUR
Nepalese External Service: See All India Radio—External Services Division.
Domestic Service: Post Bag 26, Town Hall, Gorakhpur-273 001, Uttar Pradesh, India. Contact: (technical) V.K. Sharma, Superintendent Engineer.

ALL INDIA RADIO—GUWAHATI, P.O. Box 28, Chandmari, Guwahati-781 003, Assam, India. N.C. Jain, Assistant Station Engineer.

ALL INDIA RADIO—HYDERABAD, Rocklands, Saifabad, Hyderabad-500 004, Andhra Pradesh, India.

ALL INDIA RADIO—IMPHAL, Palau Road, Imphal-795 001, Manipur, India.

ALL INDIA RADIO—ITANAGAR, Naharlagun, Itanagar-791 110, Arunachal Pradesh, India.

ALL INDIA RADIO—JAIPUR, 5 Park House, Mirza Ismail Road, Jaipur-302 001, Rajasthan, India. Contact: S.C. Sharma, Station Engineer.

ALL INDIA RADIO—JAMMU—see Radio Kashmir—Jammu.

ALL INDIA RADIO—KOHIMA, Kohima-797 001, Nagaland, India. Contact: (technical) G.C. Tyagi, Superintending Engineer. Return postage, $1 or IRC helpful.

ALL INDIA RADIO—KURSEONG, Mehta Club Building, Kurseong-734 203, Darjeeling, West Bengal, India. Contact: Madan Lei, Assistant Director of Engineering.

ALL INDIA RADIO—LEH—see Radio Kashmir—Leh.

ALL INDIA RADIO—LUCKNOW, 18 Vidhan Sabha Marg, Lucknow-226 001, Uttar Pradesh, India.

ALL INDIA RADIO—MADRAS
External Services: see All India Radio—External Services Division.
Domestic Service: Kamrajar Salai, Mylapore, Madras-600 004, Tamil Nadu, India.

ALL INDIA RADIO—NEW DELHI—see All India Radio—Delhi.

ALL INDIA RADIO—PANAJI
Headquarters: See All India Radio—External Services Division, above.
AIR Office near Transmitter: P.O. Box 220, Altinho, Pajaji-403 001, Goa, India.

ALL INDIA RADIO—PORT BLAIR, Dilanipur, Port Blair-744 102, South Andaman, Andaman & Nicobar Islands, Union Territory, India. Contact: (nontechnical) P.L. Thakur; (technical) Yuvraj Bajaj, Station Engineer; B. Sekhar Reddy, Assistant Station Engineer; or K. Muraleedharan, Assistant Engineer. Registering letter appears to be useful.

ALL INDIA RADIO—RANCHI, 6 Ratu Road, Ranchi-834 001, Bihar, India.

ALL INDIA RADIO—SHILLONG, P.O. Box 14, Shillong-793 001, Meghalaya, India. Contact: C. Lalrosanga, Director.

ALL INDIA RADIO—SHIMLA, Choura Maidan, Shimla-171 004, Himachal Pradesh, India.

ALL INDIA RADIO—SRINAGAR—See Radio Kashmir—Srinagar.

ALL INDIA RADIO—THIRUVANANTHAPURAM, P.O. Box 403, Bhakti Vilas, Vazuthacaud, Thiruvananthapuram-695 014, Kerala, India.

RADIO KASHMIR—JAMMU
Nontechnical: AIR, Begum Haveli, Old Palace Road, Jammu-180 001, Jammu & Kashmir, India.
Technical: See All India Radio—External Services Division, above. Contact: S.A.S. Abidi, Assistant Director Engineering (F.A.).

RADIO KASHMIR—LEH, AIR, Leh-194 101, Ladakh District, Jammu & Kashmir, India.

RADIO KASHMIR—SRINAGAR, AIR, Sherwani Road, Srinagar-190 001, Jammu & Kashmir, India.

RADIO TILA—See All India Radio—Aizawl.
see All India Radio in Jammu, Leh and Srinagar.

INDONESIA   World Time +7 Western: Waktu Indonesia Bagian Barat (Jawa, Sumatera); +8 Central: Waktu Indonesia Bagian Tengal (Bali, Kalimantan, Sulawesi, Nusa Tenggara); +9 Eastern: Waktu Indonesia Bagian Timur (Irian Jaya, Maluku).

Note: Except where otherwise indicated, Indonesian stations, especially those of the Radio Republik Indonesia (RRI) network, will reply to at least some correspondence in English. However, correspondence in Indonesian is more likely to ensure a reply.

ELKIRA RADIO, Kotak Pos No. 199, JAT, Jakarta 13001, Indonesia. This "amatir" station is unlicensed.

RADIO ARISTA, Jalan Timbangan No. 25., Rt. 005/RW01, Kelurahan Kembangan, Jakarta Barat 10610, Indonesia. This "amatir" station is unlicensed.

RADIO GEMA PESONA MUDA, c/o Wisma Pondok Gede, Jakarta Selatan, Indonesia. This "amatir" station is unlicensed.

RADIO KHUSUS PEMERINTAH DAERAH TK II—RKPD BIMA, Jalan A. Yani Atau, Sukarno Hatta No. 2, Nusa Tenggara Barat (NTB), Kode Pos 84116, Indonesia. Fax: +62 (374) 2812. Contact: (nontechnical) Baya Asmara Dhana, Publik Relations; or Lalu Suherman; (technical) Mr. Chairil, Technisi RKPD Dati II; or Lara Kawirna, Tehnik Manager. Free stickers. Replies slowly and irregularly to correspondence in Indonesian; return postage required.

RADIO PEMERINTAH DAERAH TK II—RPD BENGKALIS, Kotak Pos 0123, Bengkalis, Riau, Indonesia. Contact: Meiriqal, SMHK. Return postage required. Replies occasionally to correspondence in Indonesian. Return postage required.

RADIO PEMERINTAH DAERAH TK II—RPD POSO, Jalan Jendral Sudirman 7, Poso, Sulawesi Tengah, Indonesia. Contact: Joseph Tinagari, Kepala Stasiun. Return postage necessary. Replies occasionally to correspondence in Indonesian.

RADIO PEMERINTAH DAERAH KABUPATEN TK II—RPDK BERAU, Jalan SA Maulana, Tanjungredeb, Kalimantan Timur, Indonesia. Contact: Kus Syariman. Return postage necessary.

RADIO PEMERINTAH DAERAH KABUPATEN TK II—RPDK BIMA, Jalan Achmad Yani No. 1, Bima (Raba), Sumbawa, Nusa Tenggara Barat, Indonesia. Free stickers. Return postage required. Replies irregularly to correspondence in Indonesian.

RADIO PEMERINTAH DAERAH KABUPATEN—RPDK BOLAANG MONGONDOW, Jalan S. Parman 192, Kotamobagu, Sulawesi Utara, Indonesia. Replies occasionally to correspondence in Indonesian.

RADIO PEMERINTAH DAERAH KABUPATEN TK II—RPDK BUOL-TOLITOLI, Jalan Mohamed Ismail Bantilan No. 4, Tolitoli 94511, Sulawesi Tengah, Indonesia. Contact: Said Rasjid, Kepala Studio; Wiraswasta, Operator/Penyiar; or Muh. Yasin, SM. Return postage required. Replies extremely irregularly to correspondence in Indonesian.

RADIO PEMERINTAH DAERAH KABUPATEN TK II—RPDK ENDE, Jalan Panglima Sudirman, Ende, Flores, Nusa Tenggara Timor, Indonesia. Contact: (technical) Thomas Keropong, YC9LHD. Return postage required.

RADIO PEMERINTAH DAERAH KABUPATEN TK II—RPDK LUWU, Kantor Deppen Kabupaten Luwu, Jalan Diponegoro 5, Palopo, Sulawesi Selatan, Indonesia. Contact: Arman Mailangkay.

RADIO PEMERINTAH DAERAH KABUPATEN TK II—RPDK MANGGARAI, Ruteng, Flores, Nusa Tenggara Timur, Indonesia. Contact: Simon Saleh, B.A. Return postage required.

RADIO PEMERINTAH DAERAH KABUPATEN TK II—RPDK SAMBAS, Jalan M. Sushawary, Sambas, Kalimantan Barat, Indonesia.

RADIO PEMERINTAH DAERAH KABUPATEN TK II—RPDK TAPANULI SELATAN, Kotak Pos No. 9, Padang-Sidempuan, Sumatera Utara, Indonesia. Return postage required.

RADIO PEMERINTAH KABUPATEN DAERAH TK II—RPKD BELITUNG, Jalan A. Yani, Tanjungpandan 33412, Belitung, Indonesia. Contact: Drs. H. Fadjri Nashir B., Kepala Stasiun. Free tourist brochure. 1 IRC helpful.

RADIO PRIMADONA, Jalan Bintaro Permai Raya No. 5, Jakarta Selatan, Indonesia. This "amatir" station is unlicensed.

RADIO REPUBLIK INDONESIA—RRI AMBON, Jalan Jendral Akhmad Yani 1, Ambon, Maluku, Indonesia. Contact: Drs. H. Ali Amran or C. Noija. A very poor replier to correspondence in recent years. Correspondence in Indonesian and return postage essential.

RADIO REPUBLIK INDONESIA—RRI BANDA ACEH, Kotak Pos No. 112, Banda Aceh, Aceh, Indonesia. Contact: S.H. Rosa Kim. Return postage helpful.

RADIO REPUBLIK INDONESIA—RRI BANDUNG, Stasiun Regional 1, Kotak Pos No. 1055, Bandung 40010, Jawa Barat, Indonesia. Contact: Beni Koesbani, Kepala; or Eem Suhaemi, Kepala Seksi Siaran. Return postage or IRC helpful.

RADIO REPUBLIK INDONESIA—RRI BANJARMASIN, Stasiun Nusantara 111, Kotak Pos No. 117, Banjarmasin 70234, Kalimantan Selatan, Indonesia. Contact: Jul Chaidir, Stasiun Kepala. Return postage or IRCs helpful.

RADIO REPUBLIK INDONESIA—RRI BENGKULU, Stasiun Regional 1, Kotak Pos No. 13 Kawat, Kotamadya Bengkulu, Indonesia. Contact: Drs. H. Hamdan Syahbeni, Head of RRI Bengkulu. Free picture postcards, decals and tourist literature. Return postage or 2 IRCs helpful.

RADIO REPUBLIK INDONESIA—RRI BUKITTINGGI, Stasiun Regional 1 Bukittinggi, Jalan Prof. Muhammad Yamin No. 199, Aurkuning, Bukittinggi 26131, Propinsi Sumatera Barat, Indonesia. Fax: +62 (752) 367 132. Contact: Mr. Effendi, Sekretaris; Zul Arifin Mukhtar, SH; or Samirwan Sarjana Hukum, Producer, "Phone in Program." Replies to correspondence in Indonesian or English. Return postage helpful.

RADIO REPUBLIK INDONESIA—RRI CIREBON, Jalan Brigjen. Dharsono/By Pass, Cirebon, Jawa Barat, Indonesia. Contact: Ahmad Sugiarto, Kepala Seksi Siaran; Darmadi, Produsennya, "Kantong Surat"; Nasuko, Sub Seksi Periklanan dan Jasa; or Bagus Giarto, B.Sc. Return postage helpful.

RADIO REPUBLIK INDONESIA—RRI Denpasar, P.O. Box 31, Denpasar, Bali, Indonesia. Replies slowly to correspondence in Indonesian. Return postage or IRCs helpful.

RADIO REPUBLIK INDONESIA—RRI DILI, Stasiun Regional 1 Dili, Jalan Kaikoli, Kotak Pos 103, Dili 88000, Timor-Timur, Indonesia. Contact: Harry A. Silalahi, Kepala Stasiun; or Paul J. Amalo, BA. Return postage or $1 helpful. Replies occasionally to correspondence in Indonesian.

RADIO REPUBLIK INDONESIA—RRI FAK FAK, Jalan Kapten P. Tendean, Kotak Pos No. 54, Fak-Fak 98601, Irian Jaya, Indonesia. Contact: A. Rachman Syukur, Kepala Stasiun; Bahrum Siregar; Aloys Ngotra, Kepala Seksi Siaran; or Richart Tan. Return postage required. Replies occasionally.

RADIO REPUBLIK INDONESIA—RRI GORONTALO, Jalan Jendral Sudirman, Gorontalo, Sulawesi Utara, Indonesia. Contact: Emod. Iskander, Kepala; or Saleh S. Thalib. Return postage helpful. Replies occasionally, preferably to correspondence in Indonesian.

RADIO REPUBLIK INDONESIA—RRI JAKARTA, Stasiun Nasional Jakarta, Kotak Pos No. 356, Jakarta, Jawa Barat, Indonesia. Contact: Drs R. Baskara, Stasiun Kepala. Return postage helpful. Replies irregularly.

RADIO REPUBLIK INDONESIA—RRI JAMBI, Jalan Jendral A. Yani No. 5, Telanaipura, Jambi 36122, Propinsi Jambi, Indonesia. Contact: Marlis Ramali, Manager; M. Yazid, Kepala Siaran; or A. Tjang Abbas. Return postage helpful.

RADIO REPUBLIK INDONESIA—RRI JAYAPURA, Jalan Tasangkapura No. 23, Jayapura, Irian Jaya, Indonesia. Contact: Harry Liborang, Direktorat Radio. Return postage helpful.

RADIO REPUBLIK INDONESIA—RRI KENDARI, Kotak Pos No. 7, Kendari, Sulawesi Tenggara, Indonesia. Contact: H. Sjahbuddin, BA. Return postage required. Replies slowly to correspondence in Indonesian.

RADIO REPUBLIK INDONESIA—RRI KUPANG, Jalan Tompello No. 8, Kupang, Timor, Indonesia. Contact: Qustigap Bagang, Kepala Seksi Siaran; or Alfonsus Soetarno, BA, Kepala Stasiun. Return postage helpful. Correspondence in Indonesian preferred.

RADIO REPUBLIK INDONESIA—RRI MADIUN, Jalan Mayor Jendral Panjaitan No. 10, Madiun, Jawa Timur, Indonesia. Fax: +62 (351) 4964. Contact: Imam Soeprapto, Kepala Seksi Siaran. Replies to correspondence in English or Indonesian. Return postage helpful.

RADIO REPUBLIK INDONESIA—RRI MALANG, Kotak Pos No. 78, Malang 65112, Jawa Timur, Indonesia. Contact: Ml. Mawahib, Kepala Seksi Siaran; or Dra Hartati Soekemi, Mengetahui. Return postage necessary. Replies to correspondence in Indonesian.

RADIO REPUBLIK INDONESIA—RRI MANADO, Kotak Pos No. 1110, Manado 95124 Propinsi Sulawesi Utara, Indonesia. Fax: +62 (431) 63492. Contact: Costher H. Gulton, Kepala Stasiun. Free postcards. Return postage or $1 required. Replies occasionally to correspondence in Indonesian.

RADIO REPUBLIK INDONESIA—RRI MANOKWARI, Regional II, Jalan Merdeka No. 68, Manokwari, Irian Jaya, Indonesia. Contact: Nurdin Mokoginta, P.J, Kepala Stasiun. Return postage helpful.

RADIO REPUBLIK INDONESIA—RRI MATARAM, Stasiun Regional I Mataram, Jalan Langko No. 83, Mataram 83114, Nusa Tenggara Barat, Indonesia. Contact: Mr. Soekino, Kepala, Direktorat Radio; or Ketua Dewan, Pimpinan Harian. Return postage required. With sufficient return postage or small token gift, sometimes sends tourist information and Batik print. Replies to correspondence in Indonesian.

RADIO REPUBLIK INDONESIA—RRI MEDAN, Jalan Letkol Martinus Lubis No. 5, Medan 20232, Sumatera, Indonesia. Contact: Kepala Stasiun, Ujamalul Abidin Ass; or Suprapto. Free stickers. Return postage required. Replies to correspondence in Indonesian.

RADIO REPUBLIK INDONESIA—RRI MERAUKE, Stasiun Regional 1, Kotak Pos No. 11, Merauke, Irian Jaya, Indonesia. Contact: (nontechnical) Achmad Ruskaya B.A., Kepala Stasiun, or John Manuputty, Kepala Subseksi Pemancar; (technical) Daf'an Kubangun, Kepala Seksi Tehnik. Return postage helpful.

RADIO REPUBLIK INDONESIA—RRI NABIRE, Kotak Pos No. 11, Nabire 98801, Irian Jaya, Indonesia. Contact: Muchtar Yushaputra, Kepala Stasiun. Free stickers and occasional free picture postcards. Return postage or IRCs helpful.

RADIO REPUBLIK INDONESIA—RRI PADANG, Kotak Pos No. 77, Padang, Sumatera Barat, Indonesia. Contact: Syair Siak, Kepala Stasiun. Return postage helpful.

RADIO REPUBLIK INDONESIA—RRI PALANGKARAYA, Jalan Husni Thamrin No. 1, Palangkaraya, Kalimantan Tengah, Indonesia. Contact: Drs Amiruddin; Gumer Kamis; or Soedarsono, Kepala Stasiun. Return postage helpful. Correspondence in Indonesian preferred.

RADIO REPUBLIK INDONESIA—RRI PALEMBANG, Jalan Radio No. 2, Km. 4, Palembang, Sumatera Selatan, Indonesia.

Contact: H.A. Syukri Ahkab. Return postage helpful. Replies slowly and occasionally.

RADIO REPUBLIK INDONESIA—RRI PALU, Jalan R.A. Kartini, Palu, Sulawesi (Tg. Karang), Indonesia. Contact: Akson Boole; Elrick Johannes, Kepala Seksi Siaran; or M. Hasjim, Head of Programming. Return postage required. Replies slowly to correspondence in Indonesian.

RADIO REPUBLIK INDONESIA—RRI PEKANBARU, Jalan Jendral Sudirman No. 440, Tromolpos 51, Pekanbaru, Riau, Indonesia. Contact: Drs. Mukidi, Kepala Stasiun; or Zainal Abbas. Return postage helpful.

RADIO REPUBLIK INDONESIA—RRI PONTIANAK, Kotak Pos No. 6, Pontianak 78111, Kalimantan Barat, Indonesia. Contact: Daud Hamzah, Kepala Seksi Siaran; Achmad Ruskaya; Drs. Effendi Afati, Producer, "Dalam Acara Kantong Surat"; Subagio, Kepala Sub Bagian Tata Usaha; Daud Hamzah; or Muchlis Marzuki B.A. Return postage or $1 helpful. Replies to correspondence in Indonesian or English.

RADIO REPUBLIK INDONESIA—RRI PURWOKERTO, Stasiun Regional II, Kotak Pos No. 5, Purwokerto 53116, Propinsi Jawa Tengah, Indonesia. Fax: +62 (281) 21999. Contact: Yon Maryono, Stasiun Kepala; or A.R. Imam Soepardi, Produsennya, "Kontak Pendengar." Return postage helpful. Replies to correspondence in Indonesian or English.

RADIO REPUBLIK INDONESIA—RRI SAMARINDA, Kotak Pos No. 45, Samarinda, Kalimantan Timur 75001, Indonesia. Contact: Siti Thomah, Kepala Seksi Siaran; or Sunendra, Kepala Stasiun. May send tourist brochures and maps. Return postage helpful. Replies to correspondence in Indonesian.

RADIO REPUBLIK INDONESIA—RRI SEMARANG, Kotak Pos No. 74, Semarang Jateng, Jawa Tengah, Indonesia. Contact: Djarwanto, SH; Drs. Purwadi, Program Director; or Mardanon, Kepala Teknik. Return postage helpful.

RADIO REPUBLIK INDONESIA—RRI SERUI, Jalan Pattimura, Serui, Irian Jaya, Indonesia. Contact: Agus Raunsai, Kepala Stasiun; or Drs. Jasran Abubakar. Replies occasionally to correspondence in Indonesian. IRC or return postage helpful.

RADIO REPUBLIK INDONESIA—RRI SIBOLGA, Jalan Ade Irma Suryani, Nasution No. 5, Sibolga, Sumatera Utara, Indonesia. Contact: Mrs. Laiya, Mrs. S. Sitoupul or B.A. Tanjung. Return postage required. Replies occasionally to correspondence in Indonesian.

RADIO REPUBLIK INDONESIA—RRI SORONG, Jalan Jendral Achmad Yani, Klademak II, Sorong, Irian Jaya, Indonesia. Contact: Tetty Rumbay S., Kasubsi Siaran Kata; Mrs. Tien Widarsanto; Ressa Molle; or Linda Rumbay. Return postage helpful.

RADIO REPUBLIK INDONESIA—RRI SUMENEP, Jalan Urip Sumoharjo No. 26, Sumenep, Madura, Jawa Timur, Indonesia. Return postage helpful.

RADIO REPUBLIK INDONESIA—RRI SURABAYA, Stasiun Regional 1, Kotak Pos No. 239, Surabaya 60271, Jawa Timur, Indonesia. Fax: +62 (31) 42351. Contact: Zainal Abbas, Kepala Stasiun; Drs Agus Widjaja, Kepala Subseksi Programa Siaran; Usmany Johozua, Kepala Seksi Siaran; or Ny Koen Tarjadi. Return postage or IRCs helpful.

RADIO REPUBLIK INDONESIA—RRI SURAKARTA, Kotak Pos No. 40, Surakarta 57133, Jawa Tengah, Indonesia. Contact: Ton Martono, Head of Broadcasting. Return postage helpful.

RADIO REPUBLIK INDONESIA—RRI TANJUNGKARANG, Kotak Pos No. 24, Pahoman 35213, Bandar Lampung, Indonesia. Contact: Hi Hanafie Umar; Djarot Nursinggih, Tech. Transmission; Drs. Zulhaqqi Hafiz, Kepala Sub Seksi Periklanan; or Sutakno, S.E., Kepala Stasiun. Return postage helpful. Replies in Indonesian to correspondence in English or Indonesian.

RADIO REPUBLIK INDONESIA—RRI TANJUNG PINANG, Stasiun RRI Regional II Tanjung Pinang, Kotak Pos No. 8, Tanjung Pinang 29123, Riau, Indonesia. Contact: M. Yazid, Kepala Stasiun. Return postage helpful. Replies occasionally to correspondence in Indonesian or English.

RADIO REPUBLIK INDONESIA—RRI TERNATE, Jalan Kedaton, Ternate (Ternate), Maluku, Indonesia. Contact: (technical) Rusdy Bachmid, Head of Engineering; or Abubakar Alhadar. Return postage helpful.

RADIO REPUBLIK INDONESIA—RRI UJUNG PANDANG, RRI Nusantara IV, Kotak Pos No. 103, Ujung Pandang, Sulawesi Selatan, Indonesia. Contact: Drs. H. Harmyn Husein, Kepala Stasiun; H. Kamaruddin Alkaf, Head of Broadcasting Department;

or Drs. Bambang Pudjono. Return postage, $1 or IRCs helpful. Replies irregularly and sometimes slowly.

RADIO REPUBLIK INDONESIA—RRI WAMENA, RRI Regional II, Kotak Pos No. 10, Wamena, Irian Jaya 99501, Indonesia. Contact: Yoswa Kumurawak, Penjab Subseksi Pemancar. Return postage helpful.

RADIO REPUBLIK INDONESIA—RRI YOGYAKARTA, Jalan Amat Jazuli 4, Tromol Pos 18, Yogyakarta, Jawa Tengah, Indonesia. Contact: Phoenix Sudomo Sudaryo. IRC, return postage or $1 helpful. Replies occasionally to correspondence in Indonesian or English.

RADIO RIBUBUNG SUBANG, Komplek AURI, Subang, Jawa Barat, Indonesia.

RADIO SUARA KASIH AGUNG, Jalan Trikora No. 30, Dok V, Jayapura, Irian Jaya 99114, Indonesia. Contact: Ny. Setiyono Hadi, Pimpinan Studio. Return postage or $1 helpful. This "amatir" station is unlicensed.

RADIO SUARA KENCANA BROADCASTING SYSTEM, Jalan Yos Sudarso Timur, Gombong, Jawa Tengah, Indonesia. This "amatir" station is unlicensed.

RADIO SUARA MITRA, Jalan Haji Lut, Gang Kresem No. 15, Cigudak, Tangerang, Jawa Barat, Indonesia. This "amatir" station is unlicensed.

VOICE OF INDONESIA, Kotak Pos No. 157, Jakarta 10001, Indonesia. Contact: Anastasia Yasmine, Head of Foreign Affairs Section.

IRAN World Time +3:30 (+4:30 midyear)

VOICE OF THE ISLAMIC REPUBLIC OF IRAN

Main Office: IRIB External Services, P.O. Box 3333, Tehran, Iran. Fax: +98 (21) 295 056 or +98 (21) 291 095. Contact: Hamid Yasamin, Public Affairs; or Hameed Barimani, Producer, "Listeners Special." Free seven-volume set of books on Islam, magazines, calendars, book markers, tourist literature and postcards.

Mashhad Regional Radio: P.O. Box 555, Mashhad Center, Jomhoriye Eslame, Iran. Contact: J. Ghanbari, General Director.

IRAQ World Time +3 (+4 midyear)

RADIO IRAQ INTERNATIONAL (Idha'at al-Iraq al-Duwaliyah)

Main Office: P.O. Box 8145, Baghdad, Iraq. Contact: Muzaffar 'Abd-al'-Al, Director.

India Address: P.O. Box 3044, New Delhi 110003, India.

RADIO OF IRAQ, CALL OF THE KINFOLK (Idha'at al-Iraq, Nida' al-Ahl)—same details as "Radio Iraq International," above.

IRELAND World Time exactly (+1 midyear)

Community Radio, Radio Dublin International, P.O. Box 2077, 4 St. Vincent Street West, Dublin 8, Ireland. Contact: (non technical) Jane Cooke; (technical) Eamon Cooke, Director; or Joe Doyle, Producer, "DX Show." 12-page station history $2 postpaid. Free stickers and calendar. $1 required. Replies irregularly. This station is as yet unlicensed, but those wishing to support Community Radio and other potential world band shortwave broadcasts from Ireland may write the Minister for Communications, Dublin 2, Ireland.

ISRAEL World Time +2 (+3 midyear)

KOL ISRAEL, ISRAEL RADIO, THE VOICE OF ISRAEL

Main Office: P.O. Box 1082, 91 010 Jerusalem, Israel. Fax: +972 (2) 253 282 or +972 (2) 248 392. Contact: (nontechnical) Sara Manobla, Head of English Service; Yishai Eldar, Senior Editor, English Service & Producer, "Calling All Listeners"; (technical) Ben Dalfen, Editor, "DX Corner." Quarterly *Kol Israel* magazine, for 4 IRCs, *Israel and the Arab States* booklet of maps, station booklets, "Ulpan of the Air" Hebrew-language lesson scripts, pennants and other small souvenirs, and various political, religious, tourist, immigration and language publications. IRC required for reply. Programs sometimes disrupted by work stoppages.

Transmission Office: (technical) Engineering & Planning Division, TV & Radio Broadcasting Section, Bezeq, P.O. Box 29555, 61 290 Tel Aviv, Israel. Fax: +972 (3) 510 0696 or +972 (3) 515 1232. Contact: Marian Kaminski, Head of AM Radio Broadcasting. This address only for pointing out transmitter-related problems (interference, modulation quality, network mixups, etc.), especially by fax. Verifications not given out at this office; requests for verification should be sent to English Department at the main office, above.

San Francisco Office, Schedules: 2654 17th Avenue, San Francisco CA 94116 USA. Contact: George Poppin. This address only provides Kol Israel schedules to listeners. All other correspondence should be sent directly to the main office in Jerusalem.

ITALY World Time +1 (+2 midyear)

ADVENTIST WORLD RADIO, THE VOICE OF HOPE, C.P. 383, I-47100 Forlì, Italy. Fax: +39 (543) 768 198. Contact: Paolo Benini, Director; Lina Lega, Secretary; Roger Graves, Producer, "Update"; or Stefano Losio, Producer, "DX News" in Italian. Free home study Bible guides and other religious material, envelope openers, stickers, pennants, *AWR Current* newsletter every month, pocket calendar and other small souvenirs. 2 IRCs, $1 or return postage required. Also, see USA.

EUROPEAN CHRISTIAN RADIO, Postfach 500, A-2345 Brunn, Austria. Fax: +39 (2) 29 51 74 63. Contact: John Adams, Director; or C.R. Coleman, Station Manager. $1 or 2 IRCs required.

IDEA RADIO, C.P. 38, I-16030 Gattorna (GE), Italy. Fax: +39 (10) 653 0836. Contact: Dott. Mandini Pietro; or Andrea Laudicina. $1 or return postage necessary.

ITALIAN RADIO RELAY SERVICE, IRRS-Shortwave, Nexus IBA, P.O. Box 10980, I-20110 Milan MI, Italy. Fax: +39 (2) 7063 81 51. Contact: (nontechnical) Alfredo E. Cotroneo, President & Producer of "Hello There"; (technical) Ms. Anna S. Boschetti, Verification Manager. Free station literature. 2 IRCs or $1 helpful.

RADIO EUROPA INTERNATIONAL, via Turati 40, I-20121 Milano, Italy. Contact: Mariarosa Zahella. Return postage helpful.

RADIO EUROPE, via Davanzati 8, I-20158 Milan MI, Italy. Fax: +39 (2) 670 4900. Contact: Dario Monferini, Director; or Alex Bertini, General Manager. $30 for a lifetime membership to Radio Europe's Listeners' Club. Membership includes T-shirt, poster, stickers, flags, gadgets, etc. with a monthly drawing for prizes. Application forms available from station.

RADIO IDEA—see Idea Radio.

RADIO ITALIA INTERNAZIONALE, Vicolo Volusio 1, I-06049 Spoleto, Italy. Fax: +37 (743) 223 310. Contact: Nicola Mastoro, Owner. Free stickers. Return postage helpful.

RADIO ROMA-RAI

Main Office, Nontechnical: Direzione Servizi Giornalistici e Programmi per L'Estero (DPA), Casella Postale 320, Centro Corrispondenza, I-00100 Rome, Italy. Contact: Giorgio Brovelli, Director; Gabriella Tambroni, Assistant Director; Rosaria Vassallo, Correspondence Sector; or Augusto Milana, Editor-in-Chief, Short Wave Programs in Foreign Languages. Free stickers, banners and *RAI Calling from Rome* magazine. Can provide supplementary materials for Italian-language course aired over RAI's Italian-language (sic) external service. Hopes to obtain approval for a new world band transmitter complex in Tuscany; if this comes to pass, then they plan to expand news, cultural items and music in various language services—including Spanish, Portuguese, Italian, Chinese and Japanese.

Technical Office: Supporto Técnico, Progettazione Alta Frequenza, Onda Corta (PAOC), Viale Mazzini 14, I-00195 Rome, Italy. Contact: Maria Luisa I. This office is scheduled to be replaced shortly by new facilities in Saxa Rubra, north of Rome.

New York Office, Nontechnical: RAI/Radio Division, 21st floor, 1350 Avenue of the Americas, New York NY 10019 USA. Fax: +1 (212) 765 1956. RAI caps, aprons and tote bags for sale at Boutique RAI, c/o the New York address.

RTV ITALIANA-RAI, Radio Uno (Caltanissetta), Via Cerda 19, I-90139 Palermo, Sicily, Italy. $1 required.

VOICE OF EUROPE, P.O. Box 26, I-33170 Pordenone, Italy. IRC or $1 helpful. Fax: +39 (6) 488 0196.

JAPAN World Time +9

NHK OSAKA, 3-43 Bamba-cho, Higashi-ku, Osaka 540, Japan. Fax: +81 (6) 941 0612. Contact: (technical) Technical Bureau; or Mr. Hideo Ishida, Radio Engineer. IRC or $1 helpful.

NHK SAPPORO, 1 Ohdori Nisha, Chuo-ku, Sapporo 060, Japan. Fax: +81 (11) 232 5951.

NHK TOKYO/SHOBU-KUKI, JOAK, 3047-1 Sanga Shoubu-Machi, Saitama, Japan. Fax: +81 (480) 85 1508. Contact: Hisao Kakinuma, Transmission Technical Center; or H. Ota. IRC or $1 helpful. Replies occasionally. Letters should be sent via registered mail.

RADIO JAPAN/NHK

Main Office: 2-2-1 Jinnan, Shibuya-ku, Tokyo 150-01, Japan. Fax: +81 (3) 3481 1350 or +81 (3) 3481 1413 Contact: (nontechnical) Mr. Ohnishi, Producer, "Hello from Tokyo"; Yojiro Kume, Researcher; Takao Kiyohara, Director, Public Relations; or Takeshi Sakurai, Director, English Service; (technical) Mark Robinson, Producer, "Media Roundup"; or Verification Secretary. Free *Radio Japan News* publication, sundry other small souvenirs and "Let's

Learn/Practice Japanese" language-course materials. Quizzes with prizes, including beautiful wall calendars, over "Media Roundup."

Washington Bureau, Nontechnical: NHK, 2030 M Street NW, Suite 706, Washington DC 20036 USA. Fax: +1 (202) 828 4571. Contact: Ms. Izumi Okubo, Assistant Director.

London Bureau: NHK General Bureau for Europe, 66-67 Newman Street, London W1P 3LA, United Kingdom.

Sydney Bureau, Nontechnical: c/o Broad Production Unit 14, 175 Gibbes Street, Chatswood NSW 2067, Australia.

Singapore Office, Nontechnical: NHK, 1 Scotts Road #15-06, Shaw Centre, Singapore 0922, Singapore. Fax: +65 737 5251.

RADIO TAMPA/NSB

Main Office: 9-15 Akasaka 1-chome, Minato-ku, Tokyo 107, Japan. Fax: +81 (3) 3583 9062. Contact: H. Nagao, Public Relations; M. Teshima; or H. Ono. Free stickers and Japanese stamps. $1 or IRC helpful. Once scheduled to terminate shortwave broadcasting around 1997, Radio Tampa now plans to stay on shortwave until the year 2000 and possibly indefinitely.

New York News Bureau, Nontechnical: 1325 Avenue of the Americas #2403, New York NY 10019 USA. Fax: +1 (212) 261 6449. Contact: Noboru Fukui, reporter.

JORDAN World Time +2 (+3 midyear)

RADIO JORDAN, Radio of the Hashemite Kingdom of Jordan, P.O. Box 909, Amman, Jordan. Fax: +962 (6) 744 662. Contact: Jawad Zada, Director of English Service & Producer of "Mailbag"; Muwaffaq al-Rahaiyfah, Director of Shortwave Services; Qasral Mushatta; or Radi Alkhas, General Director; (technical) Yousef Arini. Free stickers. Replies irregularly and slowly, but does not verify reception reports. **ADS**

KAZAKHSTAN World Time +6 (+7 midyear)

KAZAKH RADIO, Kazakh Broadcasting Company, Zheltoksan Str. 175A, 480013 Almaty, Kazakhstan. Contact: B. Shalakhmentov, Chairman; or S.D. Primbetov, Deputy Chairman.

RADIO ALMATY WORLD SERVICE, Zheltoksan Str. 175A, 480013 Almaty, Kazakhstan. Fax: +7 (3272) 631 207. Contact: Mr. Gulnar.

KENYA World Time +3

KENYA BROADCASTING CORPORATION, P.O. Box 30456, Nairobi, Kenya. Fax: +254 (2) 220 675. Contact: (nontechnical) Managing Director; (technical) Augustine Kenyanjier Gochui; Lawrence Holnati, Engineering Division; or Manager Technical Services. IRC required. Replies irregularly.

KIRIBATI World Time +13

RADIO KIRIBATI, P.O. Box 78, Bairiki, Tarawa Atoll, Republic of Kiribati. Fax: +686 21096. Contact: Teraku Tekanene, Managing Director; Atiota Bauro, Program Organiser; Mrs. Otiri Laboia; or Moia Tetoa, Producer, "Kaoti Ami Iango," a program devoted to listeners views; (technical) Trakaogo, Engineer-in-Charge; or T. Fakaofo, Technical Staff. Cassettes of local songs available for purchase. $1 or return postage required for a reply. (IRCs not accepted).

KOREA (DPR) World Time +9

RADIO PYONGYANG, External Service, Pyongyang Broadcasting Station, Ministry of Posts and Telecommunications, Pyongyang, Democratic People's Republic of Korea (not "North Korea"). Fax: +850 (2) 814 418. Free Great Leader book, book for German speakers to learn Korean, sundry other publications, pennants, calendars, artistic prints and pins. Do not include dutiable items in your envelope. Replies are irregular, as mail from countries not having diplomatic relations with North Korea is sent via circuitous routes and apparently does not always arrive. Indeed, some listeners who have not obtained replies have received, instead, what appears to be bogus ("black propaganda") correspondence from alleged North Korean dissidents at Radio Pyongyang. This correspondence, mailed from Japan, appears to originate from South Korean sources, which tends to verify that at least some correspondence to Radio Pyongyang is not getting to North Korea. Nevertheless, this station appears to be replying increasingly often to mail sent from the United States and other countries with which North Korea has no diplomatic relations.

Regional Korean Central Broadcasting Stations—Not known to reply, but a long-shot possibility is to try writing in Korean to: Korean Central Broadcasting Station, Ministry of Posts and Telecommunications, Pyongyang, Democratic People's Republic of Korea. Contact: Chong Ha-chol, Chairman, Radio and Television Broadcasting Committee.

KOREA (REPUBLIC) World Time +9
RADIO KOREA
Main Office: Overseas Service, Korean Broadcasting System, 18 Yoido-dong, Youngdungpo-gu, Seoul 150-790, Republic of Korea. Fax: +82 (2) 781 2477. Contact: Che Hong-Pyo, Director of English Section; or Choi Jang-Hoon, Director. Free stickers, calendars, *Let's Learn Korean* book and a wide variety of other small souvenirs.
Washington Bureau, Nontechnical: National Press Building, Suite 1076, 529 14th Street NW, Washington DC 20045 USA. Fax: +1 (202) 662 7347.
KUWAIT World Time +3 (+4 midyear)
RADIO KUWAIT, P.O. Box 397, 13004 Safat, Kuwait. Fax: +965 241 5946 or +965 245 6660. Contact: Manager, External Service; (technical) Ali N. Jaffar, Chief of Frequency Management Section.
KYRGYZSTAN World Time +5 (+6 midyear)
KYRGYZ RADIO, Kyrgyz TV and Radio Center, Prospekt Moloday Gvardil 63, Bishkek 720 300, Kyrgyzstan. Fax: +7 (3312) 257 930. Contact: A.I. Vitshkov or E.M. Abdukarimov.
LAOS World Time +7
LAO NATIONAL RADIO, LUANG PRABANG ("Sathani Withayu Kachaisiang Khueng Luang Prabang"), Luang Prabang, Laos; or B.P. Box 310, Vientiane, Laos. Return postage required (IRCs not accepted). Replies slowly and very rarely. Best bet is to write in Laotian or French directly to Luang Prabang, where the transmitter is located.
LAO NATIONAL RADIO, VIENTIANE, Laotian National Radio and Television, B.P. 310, Vientiane, Laos. Contact: Bounthan Inthasai, Deputy Managing Director.
LATVIA World Time +2 (+3 midyear)
LATVIAN RADIO, Latvijas Radio, 8 Doma Laukums, LV 1505 Riga, Latvia. Fax: +7 (0132) 206 709. Contact: (nontechnical) Arnolds Klotins, Director General; Alvars Ginters, International Relations; Gunars Treimanis, Producer; or Darija Juškevica; (technical) Aigars Semevics. Replies to nontechnical correspondence in Latvian. Does not issue verification replies. **ADS**
RADIO RIGA INTERNATIONAL, P.O. Box 266, LV-1098 Riga, Latvia. Contact: R. Visnere, Mailbag Editor, English Department. Free stickers and pennants. Unlike Latvian Radio, preceding, Radio Riga International verifies regularly.
LEBANON World Time +2 (+3 midyear)
HCJB (via King/Wings of Hope)—see Ecuador for details.
KING OF HOPE, WINGS OF HOPE, P.O. Box 77, 10292 Metulla, Israel; or P.O. Box 3379, Limassol, Cyprus. Contact: Isaac Gronberg, Director; Mark Christian; or Pete Reilly. Free stickers. Also, see KVOH—High Adventure Radio, USA.
VOICE OF LEBANON (when operating), P.O. Box 165271, Al-Ashrafiyah, Beirut, Lebanon. $1 required. Replies extremely irregularly to correspondence in Arabic.
LESOTHO World Time +2
Radio Lesotho, P.O. Box 552, Maseru 100, Lesotho. Fax: +266 310 003. Contact: (nontechnical) Mrs. Florence Lesenya, Controller of Programs; Sekhonyana Motlohi, Producer, "What Do Listeners Say?"; or Ms. Mpine Tente, Director; (technical) B. Moeti, Chief Engineer. Return postage necessary. **ADS** **AIR**
LIBERIA World Time exactly
ELBC, Liberian Broadcasting System, P.O. Box 594, 1000 Monrovia, Liberia. Contact: Noah A. Bordolo, Sr., Deputy Director General, Broadcasting. Station has requested that listeners outside Liberia should send their reception reports to LBS, Box 242, Danane, La Cote d'Ivoire, West Africa. Those in Liberia should contact LBS, Box 16, Gbarnga, Liberia. Note that there is another world band station that calls itself "ELBC."
ELWA
Main Office: (when operating), P.O. Box 192, 1000 Monrovia, Liberia. Contact: (technical) Dwight, EL2W. Also, see Northern Mariana Islands.
U.S. Office: SIM, P.O. Box 7900, Charlotte NC 28241 USA. Donations to replace destroyed transmitters welcomed.
VOICE OF AMERICA—Facility in Monrovia has been destroyed by civil unrest and is not expected to be reactivated for some time.
LIBYA World Time +1
RADIO JAMAHIRIYA
Main Office: P.O. Box 4677 (or P.O. Box 4396), Tripoli, Libya. Contact: R. Cachia. Arabic preferred.
Malta Office: European Branch Office, P.O. Box 17, Hamrun, Malta. This office replies more consistently than does the main office.

LITHUANIA World Time +2 (+3 midyear)
Warning—Mail theft: Lithuanian officials warn that money or other items of any value whatsoever are routinely being stolen within the Lithuanian postal system. Authorities are taking steps to alleviate this problem, but for the time being nothing of value should be entrusted to the postal system. To help ensure your letter from abroad won't disappear—these are often stolen on the assumption they might contain money—either correspond by postcard or fax, or don't seal your envelope tightly.
Warning—Fake "Charities": An alleged charity, "Informacinis Klubas" (IK) of Vilnius, has been soliciting funds from American and European world band listeners and others for "sick children." Informed sources report that this solicitation is a scam, and other such scams may be in the works. Should you wish to aid needy Lithuanian children, there are at least two legitimate charities very much in need of your assistance: Lithuanian Catholic Religious Aid, 351 Highland Boulevard, Brooklyn NY 11207 USA, fax +1 (718) 827 6696 (newsletter available to contributors); or SOS Children, P.O. Box 497, South Boston MA 02127 USA.
LITHUANIAN RADIO, Lietuvos Radijas, Konarskio 49, LT-2674 Vilnius, Lithuania. Fax: +7 (0122) 66 05 26. Contact: Nerijus Maliukevicius, Director.
RADIOCENTRAS, Spauda, P.O. Box 1792, LT-2019 Vilnius, Lithuania. Fax: +370 (2) 22 01 72. Contact: (nontechnical or technical) Sigitas Žilionis; Rimantas Pleikys, Editor-in-chief; or Gintautas Babravičius, Chief Executive. Cassette recordings of Lithuanian Folk Music available for $6. 2 IRCs or return postage required. **ADS** **AIR**
RADIO GIMTINES SVYTURYS, P.O. Box 512, 5802 Klaipeda, Lithuania. (program aired via Lithuanian Radio).
RADIO VILNIUS, Lietuvos Radijas, Konarskio 49, LT-2674 Vilnius, Lithuania. Fax: +370 (2) 66 05 26. Contact: Rasa Lukaite, "Letterbox"; Edvinas Butkus, Editor-in-Chief; Ilonia Rukiene, Head of English Department; or Virginijus Razmantas, Acting Editor. Free stickers, pennants, Lithuanian stamps and other souvenirs. Radio Vilnius' Listeners' Club may be reached by writing Mary Sabatini, 24 Sherman Terrace #4, Madison WI 53704 USA.
LUXEMBOURG World Time +1 (+2 midyear)
RADIO LUXEMBOURG
Main Office: 45 Boulevard Pierre Frieden, L-2850 Kirchberg, Luxembourg. Fax: +352 421 422 756. Free T-shirts and a wide variety of different stickers.
London Bureau, Nontechnical: 38 Hertford Street, London W1Y 8BA, United Kingdom.
Paris Bureau, Nontechnical: 22 rue Bayard, F-75008 Paris, France. Fax: +33 (1) 40 70 42 72 or +33 (1) 40 70 44 11.
MADAGASCAR World Time +3
RADIO MADAGASIKARA, B.P. 1202, Antananarivo, Madagascar. Contact: Mlle. Rakotoniaina Soa Herimanitia, Secrétaire de Direction, a young lady who collects stamps. $1 required, and enclosing used stamps from various countries may help. Replies very rarely and slowly, preferably to friendly philatelist gentlemen who correspond in French.
RADIO NEDERLAND WERELDOMREOP—MADAGASCAR RELAY, B.P. 404, Antananarivo, Madagascar. Contact: (technical) J.A. Ratobimiarana, Chief Engineer. Nontechnical correspondence should be sent to Radio Nederland Wereldomreop in Holland (see).
MALAWI World Time +2
MALAWI BROADCASTING CORPORATION, P.O. Box 30133, Chichiri, Blantyre 3, Malawi. Fax: +265 671 353 or +265 671 257. Contact: Henry R. Chirwa, Head of Production; P. Chinseu; or T.J. Sineta. Return postage or $1 helpful.
MALAYSIA World Time +8
RADIO MALAYSIA, KAJANG, RTM, Angkasapuri, Bukit Putra, 50614 Kuala Lumpur, Peninsular Malaysia, Malaysia. Contact (Radio 4): Santokh Sing Gill, Controller, Radio 4. Return postage required.
RADIO MALAYSIA, KOTA KINABALU, RTM, 88614 Kota Kinabalu, Sabah, Malaysia. Contact: Benedict Janil, Director of Broadcasting; or Hasbullah Latiff. Return postage required.
RADIO MALAYSIA, SARAWAK (KUCHING), RTM, Broadcasting House, Jalan Satok, Kuching, Sarawak, Malaysia. Contact: Kho Kwang Khoon, Deputy Director of Engineering. Return postage helpful.
RADIO MALAYSIA, SARAWAK (MIRI), RTM, Miri, Sarawak, Malaysia. Contact: Mohammed Nasir B. Mohammed. $1 or return postage helpful.

RADIO MALAYSIA, SARAWAK (SIBU), RTM, Jabatan Penyiaran, Bangunan Penyiaran, 96009 Sibu, Sarawak, Malaysia. Contact: Clement Stia, Divisional Controller, Broadcasting Department. $1 or return postage required. Replies irregularly and slowly.

VOICE OF MALAYSIA, Suara Malaysia, Wisma Radio, P.O. Box 11272-KL, 50740 Angkasapuri, Kuala Lumpur, Malaysia. Fax: +60 (3) 282 4735. Contact: (nontechnical) Mrs. Mahani bte Ujang, Supervisor, English Service; Mrs. Adilan bte Omar, Assistant Director; or Santokh Singh Gill, Director; (technical) Lin Chew, Director of Engineering. 2 IRCs or return postage helpful. Replies slowly and irregularly.

MALI World Time exactly

RADIODIFFUSION TELEVISION MALIENNE, B.P. 171, Bamako, Mali. $1 or IRC helpful. Replies slowly and irregularly to correspondence in French.

MALTA World Time +1 (+2 midyear)

VOICE OF THE MEDITERRANEAN, P.O. Box 143, Valletta, CMR 01, Malta. Fax: +356 241 501. Contact: Richard Vella Laurenti, Managing Director; or Charles A. Micallef, Deputy Head of News and Programs. IRC helpful. Sometimes replies slowly. Station is a joint venture of the Libyan and Maltese governments.

MAURITANIA World Time exactly

OFFICE DE RADIODIFFUSION-TELEVISION DE MAURITANIE, B.P. 200, Nouakchott, Mauritania. Contact: Madame Amir Feu; Lemrabott Boukhary; or Mr. Hane Abou. Return postage or $1 required. Rarely replies.

MEXICO World Time –6 Central, including México; –7 Mountain; –8 (–7 midyear) Pacific

LA HORA EXACTA—XEQK, IMER, Margaritas 18, Col. Florida, México, D.F. 01030, Mexico. Contact: Gerardo Romero.

LA VOZ DE VERACRUZ—XEFT, Apartado Postal 21, 91700-4H. Veracruz, Ver., Mexico. Contact: C.P. Miguel Rodríguez Sáez, Sub-Director; or Lic. Juan de Dios Rodríguez Díaz, Director-Gerente. Likely to reply to correspondence in Spanish. Free tourist guide to Vera Cruz. Return postage, IRC or $1 probably helpful.

RADIO EDUCACION—XEPPM, SPE-333/92, Dirección de Producción y Planeación, Dirección General de Radio Educación, Angel Urraza 662, Col. del Valle, México, D.F. 03100, Mexico. Contact: (nontechnical or technical) Lic. Luis Ernesto Pi Orozco, Director General; (technical) Ing. Gustavo Carreño López, Subdirector, Dpto. Técnico; Replies slowly to correspondence in Spanish. Free station photo. Return postage or $1 required.

RADIO HUAYACOCOTLA—XEJN, Apartado Postal No. 13, 92600 Huayacocotla, Veracruz, Mexico. Return postage or $1 helpful. Replies irregularly to correspondence in Spanish.

RADIO MIL—XEOI, NRM, Insurgentes Sur 1870, Col. Florida, México, D.F. 01030, Mexico. Fax: +52 (5) 662 0974. Contact: Guillermo Salas Vargas, Presidente; or Zoila Quintanar Flores. Free stickers. $1 or return postage required.

RADIO UNIVERSIDAD/UNAM—XEUDS, Apartado Postal No. 1817, Hermosillo, Sonora 83000, Mexico. Contact: A. Merino M., Director. Free tourist literature. $1 or return postage required. Replies irregularly to correspondence in Spanish.

RADIO XEQQ, LA VOZ DE LA AMERICA LATINA, Sistema Radiópolis, Ayuntamiento 52, México D.F. 06070, Mexico; or Ejército Nacional No. 579 (6to piso), 11520 México, D.F., Mexico. Contact: (nontechnical) Sra. Martha Aguilar Sandoval; (technical) Ing. Miguel Angel Barrientos, Director Técnico de Plantas Transmisoras. Free pennants. $1, IRC or return postage required. Replies fairly regularly to correspondence in Spanish.

RADIO XEUJ, Apartado Postal No. 62, Linares, Nuevo León, Mexico. Contact: Marielo Becerra Gonzáles, Director General. Replies very irregularly to correspondence in Spanish.

RADIO XEUW, Ocampo 119, 91700 Veracruz, Mexico. Contact: Ing. Baltazar Pazos de la Torre, Director General. Free pennants. Return postage required. Replies occasionally to correspondence in Spanish.

TUS PANTERAS—XEQM, Apartado Postal No. 217, 97000 Mérida, Yucatán, Mexico. Fax: +52 (99) 28 06 80. Contact: Arturo Iglesias Villalobos; or Ylmar Pacheco Gomez, Locutor. Replies irregularly to correspondence in Spanish.

MOLDOVA World Time +2 (+3 midyear)

Note: A Radio Moldova International Service on world band—in English, French, Spanish and possibly other languages—is being considered.

MONACO World Time +1 (+2 midyear)

RADIO MONTE-CARLO

Main Office: 16 Boulevard Princesse Charlotte, MC-98080 Monaco Cedex, Monaco. Fax: +33 (93) 15 16 30 or +33 (93) 15 94 48. Contact: Jacques Louret; Bernard Poizat, Service Diffusion; or Caroline Wilson, Director of Communication. Free stickers.

Main Paris Office, Nontechnical: 12 rue Magellan, F-75008 Paris, France. Fax: +33 (1) 40 69 88 55 or +33 (1) 45 00 92 45.

Paris Office (Arabic Service): RMC Somera, 78 Avenue Raymond Poincaré, F-75008 Paris, France.

Cyprus Office (Arabic Service): RMC Somera, B.P. 2026, Nicosia, Cyprus. Contact: M. Pavlides, Chef de Station.

TRANS WORLD RADIO

Station: B.P. 349, MC-98007 Monte-Carlo, Monaco. Fax: +33 (92) 16 56 01. Contact: Mrs. Jeanne Olson; or Richard Olson, Station Manager. Free paper pennant. IRC or $1 helpful. Also, *see* USA.

European Office: P.O. Box 2020, NL-1200 CA Hilversum, Holland. Fax: (nontechnical) +31 (35) 23 48 61. Contact: Beate Kiebel, Manager Broadcast Department; or Felix Widmer. **AIR**

MONGOLIA World Time +8

RADIO ULAANBAATAR, External Services, C.P.O. Box 365, Ulaanbaatar, Mongolia. Contact: (non-technical) Mr. Bayasa, Mail Editor, English Department; N. Tuya, Head of English Department; or Ch. Surenjav, Director; (technical) Ganhuu, Chief of Technical Department. Free pennants, newspapers and Mongolian stamps.

MOROCCO World Time exactly

RADIO MEDI UN

Main Office: B.P. 2055, Tangier, Morocco. 2 IRCs helpful. Contact: J. Dryk, Responsable Haute Frequence; or C. Thuret. Free stickers. Correspondence in French preferred.

Paris Bureau, Nontechnical: 78 avenue Raymond Poincaré, F-75016 Paris, France. Correspondence in French preferred.

RTV MAROCAINE, 1 rue al-Brihi, Rabat, Morocco. Fax +212 (7) 70 32 08. Contact: Mohammed Jamal Eddine Tanane, Technical Director; Hammouda Mohamed, Engineer; or N. Read.

VOICE OF AMERICA—Does not welcome direct correspondence at its Moroccan facilities. *See* USA for acceptable VOA address and related information. Ten 500 kW transmitters, currently being installed at a second site in Morocco—Tangier is the initial site—are expected to be on the air sometime in the future.

MOZAMBIQUE World Time +2

RADIO MOCAMBIQUE, C.P. 2000, Maputo, Mozambique. Fax: +258 (1) 42 18 16 . Contact: (nontechnical) Teodosio Mbanze, Program Diretor; Manuel Tomé, Diretor-Geral; Antonio Alves da Fonseca, Comercial Diretor; or Iain P. Christie, Head of External Service; (technical) Rufino de Matos, Technical Diretor. Free medallions and pens. Cassettes featuring local music are available for $15. Return postage, $1 or 2 IRCs required. Replies to correspondence in Portuguese.

MYANMAR (BURMA) World Time +6:30

RADIO MYANMAR

Station: GPO Box 1432, Yangon, Myanmar. Fax: +95 (1) 30211. Currently does not reply directly to correspondence, but this could change as political events evolve. See following.

Washington Embassy: Embassy of the Union of Myanmar, 2300 S Street NW, Washington DC 20008 USA. Fax: +1 (202) 332 9046. Contact: Daw Kyi Kyi Sein, Third Secretary. This address currently replies on behalf of Radio Myanmar.

NAMIBIA World Time +2

RADIO NAMIBIA/NBC, P.O. Box 321, Windhoek 9000, Namibia. Fax: +264 (61) 217 760. Contact: P. Schachtschneider, Manager, Transmitter Maintenance. Free stickers.

NEPAL World Time +5:45

RADIO NEPAL, P.O. Box 634, Singha Durbar, Kathmandu, Nepal. Fax: +977 (1) 221 952. Contact: (nontechnical) B. P. Shivakoti; or S. K. Pant, Producer, "Question Answer"; (technical) Ram S. Karki, Executive Engineer. **ADS AIR**

NEW ZEALAND World Time +13 (+12 midyear)

KIWI RADIO (unlicensed, but left alone by the government), P.O. Box 1437, Hastings, New Zealand. Contact: Graham J. Barclay. Free stickers.

RADIO NEW ZEALAND INTERNATIONAL, P.O. Box 2092, Wellington, New Zealand. Fax: +64 (4) 474 1433. Contact: Linden Clark, Manager; Ian V. Morrison, News Editor; Tony King, Listener Services; Myra Oh, Producer, "Mailbox"; or Adrian

Sainsbury, Frequency Manager. Free schedule/flyer about station, map of New Zealand and tourist literature. English/Maori T-shirts for US$20; an interesting variety of CD recordings and a large range of music cassettes/spoken programs in Domestic "Replay Radio" catalog (VISA/MC). Three IRCs for verification, one IRC for schedule/catalog.

PRINT DISABLED RADIO—ZLXA, P.O. Box 360, Levin 5500, New Zealand. Fax: +64 (6) 368 0151. Contact: Allen J. Little, Station Director; Ron Harper; Ash Bell; or Jim Meecham ZLZ BHF, Producer, "CQ Pacific, Radio about Radio." Free brochure. $1, return postage or 3 IRCs appreciated.

NICARAGUA World Time −6

RADIO MISKUT, Correo Central (Bragman's Bluff), Puerto Cabezas, Nicaragua. Contact: Evaristo Mercado Pérez, Director. $1 helpful. Replies slowly and irregularly to correspondence in Spanish.

RADIO NICARAGUA (when operating), Apartado Postal No. 3170, Managua, Nicaragua. Contact: Frank Arana, Gerente.

RADIO RICA, Apartado Postal No. 38, Sucursal 14 de Septiembre, Managua, Nicaragua. Contact: Digna Bendaña B., Directora. Free black T-shirts. $1 required. Correspondence in Spanish preferred.

NIGER World Time +1

LA VOIX DU SAHEL, O.R.T.N., B.P. 361, Niamey, Niger. Fax: +227 72 35 48. Contact: Yacouba Alwali; (nontechnical) Oumar Tiello, Directeur; or Mounkaïla Inazadan, Producer, "Inter Jeunes Variétés"; (technical) Afo Sourou Victor. $1 helpful. Correspondence in French preferred. Correspondence by males with this station may result in requests for certain unusual types of magazines. **ADS AIR**

NIGERIA World Time +1

Warning—Mail Theft: For the time being, correspondence from abroad to Nigerian addresses has a relatively high probability of being stolen. Consequently, some governments are considering suspension of postal services to Nigeria.

Warning—Confidence Artists: Correspondence with Nigerian stations may result in requests from skilled confidence artists for money, free electronic or other products, publications or immigration sponsorship.

RADIO NIGERIA—ENUGU, P.M.B. 1051, Enugu (Anambra), Nigeria. Contact: Louis Nnamuchi, Assistant Director Technical Services. 2 IRCs, return postage or $1 required. Replies slowly.

RADIO NIGERIA—IBADAN, P.M.B. 5003, Ibadan, Oyo State, Nigeria. Contact: V.A. Kalejaiye, Technical Services Department. $1 or return postage required. Replies slowly.

RADIO NIGERIA—KADUNA, P.O. Box 250, Kaduna (Kaduna), Nigeria. Contact: Yusuf Garba or Johnson D. Allen. $1 or return postage required. Replies slowly.

RADIO NIGERIA—LAGOS, P.M.B. 12504, Ikoyi, Lagos, Nigeria. Contact: Babatunde Olalekan Raji, Monitoring Unit. 2 IRCs or return postage helpful. Replies slowly and irregularly.

VOICE OF NIGERIA, P.M.B. 40003 Falomo, Ikoyi, Lagos, Nigeria. Fax: +234 (1) 269 1944. Contact: (nontechnical) Alhaji Lawal Y. Saulawa, Director of Programmes; Mrs. Stella Bassey, Deputy Director of Programs; Alhaji Mohammed Okoridion, Deputy Director of News; or Alhaji Yahaya Abubakar, Director General; (technical) J.O. Kroni, Deputy Director of Engineering Services; or G.C. Uzi, Director of Engineering. 2 IRCs or return postage helpful.

NORTHERN MARIANA ISLANDS World Time +10

CHRISTIAN SCIENCE MONITOR WORLD SERVICE—KHBI, P.O. Box 1387, Saipan, MP 96950 USA; or write to Boston address (see USA"). Fax: +670 234 6515. Contact: A. Hgisaio, Staff Member; or Doming Villar, Station Manager. Free stickers. Return postage appreciated if writing to Saipan; no return postage when writing to Boston.

ELWA—see KFBS Saipan, below, and ELWA, Liberia for details.

KFBS SAIPAN

Main Office: P.O. Box 209, Saipan, Mariana Islands CM 96950 USA. Fax: +670 322 9088 or +670 322 3060. Contact: Doug Campbell, Field Director; or Robert Springer or Ana I. Kapilec. Replies sometimes take months.

NORWAY World Time +1 (+2 midyear)

RADIO NORWAY INTERNATIONAL

Main Office: Utgitt av Utenlandssendingen/NRK, N-0340 Oslo, Norway. Norwegian-language 24-hour telephone tape recording for schedule information +47 (22) 45-80-08 (Americas, Europe, Africa), +47 (22) 45-80-09 (elsewhere). Fax: (general) +47 (22)

45 71 34 or +47 (22) 60 57 19; ("Listener's Corner") +47 (22) 45 72 29. Contact: (nontechnical) Kirsten Ruud Salomonsen, Head of External Broadcasting; or Gundel Krauss Dahl, Head of Radio projects, Producer, "Listeners Corner"; (technical) Olav Grimdalen, Frequency Manager. Free stickers and flags.

Singapore Bureau, Nontechnical: NRK, 325 River Valley Road #01-04, Singapore. **AIR**

OMAN World Time +4

BBC WORLD SERVICE—EASTERN RELAY STATION, P.O. Box 6898 (or 3716), Ruwi Post Office, Muscat, Oman. Contact: (technical) David P. Bones, Senior Transmitter Engineer; or Dave Plater, G4MZY, Senior Transmitter Engineer. Nontechnical correspondence should be sent to the BBC World Service in London (see).

RADIO OMAN, P.O. Box 600, Muscat, Oman. Fax: +968 602 055 or +968 602 831. Contact: (nontechnical) Director General, Radio; (technical) Rashid Haroon or A. Al-Sawafi. Replies irregularly, and responses can take anywhere from two weeks to two years; but $1, return postage or 3 IRCs helpful.

PAKISTAN World Time +5

AZAD KASHMIR RADIO, Muzaffarabad, Azad Kashmir, Pakistan. Contact: (technical) M. Sajjad Ali Siddiqui, Director of Engineering; or Liaquatullah Khan, Engineering Manager. Registered mail helpful. Rarely replies to correspondence.

PAKISTAN BROADCASTING CORPORATION—same address, fax and contact as "Radio Pakistan," below.

RADIO PAKISTAN, External Services, Pakistan Broadcasting Corporation Headquarters, Broadcasting House, Constitution Avenue, Islamabad, Pakistan. Fax: +92 (51) 811 861. Contact: (technical) Anwer Inayet Khan, Senior Broadcast Engineer, Room No. 324, Frequency Management Cell; Syed Abrar Hussain, Senior Broadcast Engineer; or Nasirahmad Bajwa, Frequency Management. Free stickers, pennants and "Pakistan Calling" magazine.

PALAU World Time +9

VOICE OF HOPE/KHBN, High Adventure Radio—Asia, P.O. Box 66, Koror, Palau PW 96940, Pacific Islands (USA). Fax: +1 (680) 488 2163. Contact: Ben Cabral; (technical) Paul Swartzendruber, Chief Engineer. Solicits funds for transmitter roof repair. Also, see USA. Return postage in the form of IRCs is requested.

PAPUA NEW GUINEA World Time +10

NATIONAL BROADCASTING COMMISSION OF PAPUA NEW GUINEA (when operating), P.O. Box 1359, Boroko, Papua New Guinea. Contact: Bob Kabewa, Sr. Technical Officer; G. Nakau; Iga Kila, Manager, Karai Service; Moses Ngihal; or Downey Fova, Producer, "What Do You Think?" 2 IRCs or return postage helpful. Replies irregularly.

RADIO CENTRAL, P.O. Box 1359, Boroko, NCD, Papua New Guinea. Contact: Steven Gamini, Station Manager; or Amos Langit, Technician. $1, 2 IRCs or return postage helpful. Replies irregularly.

RADIO EASTERN HIGHLANDS, "Karai Bilong Kumul," P.O. Box 311, Goroka, EHP, Papua New Guinea. Fax: +675 72 2841. Contact: Ignas Yanam, Technical Officer; or Kiri Nige, Engineering Division. $1 or return postage required. Replies irregularly.

RADIO EAST NEW BRITAIN, P.O. Box 393, Rabaul, ENBP, Papua New Guinea. Fax: +675 92 3254. Contact: Esekia Mael, Station Manager. Return postage required. Replies slowly.

RADIO EAST SEPIK, P.O. Box 65, Wewak, E.S.P., Papua New Guinea. Fax: +675 86 2405. Contact: Luke Umbo, Station Manager.

RADIO ENGA, P.O. Box 196, Wabag, Enga, Papua New Guinea. Fax: +675 57 1069. Contact: (technical) Felix Tumun K., Station Technician; (nontechnical or technical) John Lyein Kur, Station Manager.

RADIO GULF (when operating), P.O. Box 36, Kerema, Gulf, Papua New Guinea. Contact: Robin Wainetta, Station Manager.

RADIO MADANG, P.O. Box 2138, Yomba, Madang, Papua New Guinea. Fax: +675 82 2360. Contact: Simon Tiori, Station Manager; D. Boaging, Assistant Manager; James S. Valakvi, Assistant Provincial Program Manager; or Lloyd Guvil, Technician.

RADIO MANUS, P.O. Box 505, Lorengau, Manus, Papua New Guinea. Fax: +675 40 9079. Contact: Eliun Sereman, Provincial Programme Manager.

RADIO MILNE BAY, P.O. Box 111, Alotau, Milne Bay, Papua New Guinea. Contact: Trevor Webumo, Assistant Manager; Simon Muraga, Station Manager; or Philip Maik, Technician.

RADIO MOROBE, P.O. Box 1262, Lae, Morobe, Papua New

Guinea. Fax: +675 42 6423. Contact: Ken L. Tropu, Assistant Program Manager; or Aloysius R. Nase, Station Manager.

RADIO NEW IRELAND, P.O. Box 140, Kavieng, New Ireland, Papua New Guinea. Fax: +675 94 1489. Contact: Otto A. Malatana, Station Manager; or Ruben Bale, Program Manager. Return postage or $1 helpful.

RADIO NORTHERN, Voice of Oro, P.O. Box 137, Popondetta, Oro, Papua New Guinea. Contact: Eustace Ero, Assistant Provincial Programme Manager; or Misael Pendaia, Station Manager. Return postage required.

RADIO NORTH SOLOMONS, P.O. Box 393, Rabaul, ENBP, Papua New Guinea. Fax: +675 92 3254. Contact: Aloysius L. Rumina, Station Manager. Replies irregularly.

RADIO SANDAUN, P.O. Box 37, Vanimo, West Sepik, Papua New Guinea. Fax: +675 87 1305. Contact: Gabriel Deckwalen, Station Manager; Elias Rathley, Provincial Program Manager; or Miss Norryne Pate, Secretary. $1 helpful.

RADIO SIMBU, P.O. Box 228, Kundiawa, Chimbu, Papua New Guinea. Fax: +675 75 1012. Contact: (technical) Gabriel Paiao, Station Technician. Free two-Kina banknote.

RADIO SOUTHERN HIGHLANDS, P.O. Box 104, Mendi, SHP, Papua New Guinea. Fax: +675 59 1017. Contact: Andrew Meles, Station Manager; or Jay Emma, Producer, "Listeners Choice - Thinking of You." $1 or return postage helpful; or donate a wall poster of a rock band, singer or American landscape.

RADIO WESTERN, P.O. Box 23, Daru, Western Province, Papua New Guinea. Contact: Geo Gedabing, Provincial Programme Manager; or Samson Tobel, Technician. $1 or return postage required. Replies irregularly.

RADIO WESTERN HIGHLANDS, P.O. Box 311, Mount Hagen, WHP, Papua New Guinea. Fax: +675 52 1279. Contact: Esau Okole, Technician. $1 or return postage helpful. Replies occasionally.

RADIO WEST NEW BRITAIN, P.O. Box 412, Kimbe, WNBP, Papua New Guinea. Fax: +675 93 5600. Contact: Valuka Lowa, Provincial Station Manager; or Esekia Mael, Provincial Program Manager. Return postage required.

PARAGUAY World Time –3 (–4 midyear)

RADIO NACIONAL, Calle Montevideo. esq. Estrella, Asunción, Paraguay. Contact: (technical) Carlos Montaner, Director Técnico; or Filemón G. Argüello M, Jefe del Departamento de Recursos Humanos. $1 or return postage required. Replies, sometimes slowly, to correspondence in Spanish. Registration of correspondence helps assure receipt.

PERU World Time –5 year-round in Loreto, Cusco and Puno. Other departments sometimes move to World Time –4 for a few weeks of the year.

Note: Internal unrest and terrorism, widespread cholera, a tottering economy, and devastating earthquakes all combine to make Peruvian broadcasting a perilous affair. Obtaining replies from Peruvian stations thus calls for creativity, tact, patience—and the proper use of Spanish, not form letters and the like. There are nearly 150 world band stations operating from Perú on any given day. While virtually all of these may be reached simply by using as the address the station's city, as given in the Blue Pages, the following are the only stations known to be replying—even if only occasionally—to correspondence from abroad.

LA VOZ DE ALTO MAYO—see Radio La Voz de Alto Mayo.

LA VOZ DE LA SELVA—see Radio La Voz de la Selva.

LA VOZ DE CELENDIN—see Radio La Voz de Celendín.

ONDAS DEL SUR ORIENTE, Correo Central, Quillabamba, Cusco, Perú. Contact: Roberto Challco Cusi Huallpa, Periodista. $1 helpful. Replies occasionally to correspondence in Spanish.

RADIO ADVENTISTA MUNDIAL, Jirón 2 de Mayo 218, Celendín, Cajamarca, Perú.

RADIO ALTURA, Casilla de Correo 140, Cerro de Pasco, Pasco, Perú. Contact: Oswaldo de la Cruz Vásquez, Gerente-General. Replies to correspondence in Spanish.

RADIO ANCASH, Casilla de Correo 210, Huáraz. Perú. Contact: Armando Moreno Romero, Gerente-General; or Dante Moreno Neglia, Gerente de Programación. $1 required. Replies to correspondence in Spanish.

RADIO ANDAHUAYLAS S.A., Jr. Ayacucho No. 248, Andahuaylas, Apurímac, Perú. Contact: Sr. Daniel Andréu C., Gerente. $1 required. Replies irregularly to correspondence in Spanish.

RADIO ATALAYA, Teniente Mejía y Calle Iquitos s/n, Atalaya,

Depto. de Ucayali, Perú. Replies irregularly to correspondence in Spanish.

RADIO ATLANTIDA, Casilla de Correo 786, Iquitos, Loreto, Perú. Contact: Pablo Rojas Bardales. $1 or return postage required. Replies irregularly to correspondence in Spanish.

RADIO CHOTA, Apartado 3, Chota, Cajamarca, Perú. Contact: Aladino Gavidia Huaman, Administrador. $1 or return postage required. Replies slowly to correspondence in Spanish.

RADIO CORA, Compañía Radiofónica Lima, S.A., Paseo de la República 144, Centro Cívico, Oficina 5, Lima 1, Perú. Fax: +51 (14) 336 134. Contact: (nontechnical and technical) Juan Ramírez Lazo, Director Gerente; (technical) Ing. Roger Antonio Roldán Mercedes. Free stickers. 2 IRCs or $1 required. Replies slowly to most correspondence in Spanish.

RADIO CUZCO, Casilla de Correo 251, Cusco, Perú. Contact: Raúl Siú Almonte, Gerente. $1 or return postage required. Replies irregularly to correspondence in Spanish. Note that station name continues to be spelled with a "z", even though the city and provincial names have been changed by decree to be spelled with an "s".

RADIO DEL PACIFICO, Casilla de Correo 4236, Lima 1, Perú. Contact: J. Petronio Allauca, Secretario, Depto. de Relaciones Públicas. $1 or return postage required. Replies occasionally to correspondence in Spanish.

RADIO ESTACION "C", Casilla de Correo 210, Moyobamba, San Martín, Perú.

RADIO FRECUENCIA LIDER, Jirón Jorge Chávez 416, Bambamarca, Hualgayoc, Cajamarca, Perú. Contact: (nontechnical) Valentín Peralta Díaz, Gerente; or Carlos Antonio Peralta Rojas; (technical) Oscar Lino Peralta Rojas. Free station photos. La Historia de Bambamarca book for 5 Soles; cassettes of Peruvian and Latin American folk music for 4 Soles each; T-shirts for 10 Soles each (sending US$1 per Sol should suffice and cover foreign postage costs, as well). Replies occasionally to correspondence in Spanish. Considering replacing their transmitter to improve reception. **ADS AIR**

RADIO GRAN PAJATEN, Jirón Amazonas 710, Celendín, Cajamarca, Perú. Replies occasionally to correspondence in Spanish.

RADIO HORIZONTE, Apartado 12, Chachapoyas, Amazonas, Perú. Contact: Juan Vargas Rojas, Director de Publicidad; Rafael Alberto Vela Pinedo, Gerente; or José Garcia Castenado. Replies occasionally to correspondence in Spanish. $1 required.

RADIO IMAGEN, Casilla de Correo 42, Tarapoto, San Martín, Perú. Contact: Jaime Ríos Tapullima, Gerente General. Replies irregularly to correspondence in Spanish. $1 or return postage helpful.

RADIO INCA, Jirón Manco Cápac 275, Baños del Inca, Cajamarca, Perú. Contact: Enrique Ocas Sánchez, Director. May reply to correspondence in Spanish.

RADIO INTERNACIONAL DEL PERU, Jirón Bolognesi 532, San Pablo, Cajamarca, Perú.

RADIO JUANJI, Juanjuí, San Martín, Perú. Replies occasionally to correspondence in Spanish.

RADIO LA HORA, Casilla de Correo 540, Cusco, Perú. Contact: Edmundo Montesinos Gallo, Gerente General. Free stickers, pins, pennants and postcards of Cusco. Return postage required. Replies occasionally to correspondence in Spanish. Hopes to increase transmitter power if and when the economic situation improves. **ADS AIR**

RADIO LA MERCED, (Tongod) Congoyo, San Miguel, Cajamarca, Perú. Contact: Roberto Ramos Chanas, Director Gerente. $1 or return postage required. Replies irregularly to correspondence in Spanish.

RADIO LA VOZ DE ALTO MAYO, Nuevo Cajamarca, Rioja, San Martín, Peru.

RADIO LA VOZ DE CELENDIN, Jirón Unión 311 y Plaza de Armas, Celendín, Cajamarca, Perú. Contact: Fernando Vásquez Castro, Gerente. Replies occasionally to correspondence in Spanish.

RADIO LA VOZ DE LA SELVA, Casilla de Correo 207, Iquitos, Loreto, Perú. Contact: Julia Jauregui Rengifo, Directora; or Mery Blas Rojas. May reply occasionally to correspondence in Spanish.

RADIO LA VOZ DE SAN ANTONIO, Mariscal Sucre 731, Bambamarca, Cajamarca, Perú. Contact: Valentin Mejia Vasquez, Director; or Hilaria Vasquez Campos, Encargado Administracion. $1 or return postage required. Replies to correspondence in Spanish.

RADIO LIRCAY, Jirón Libertad 188, Lircay, Angaraes, Huancavelica, Perú. Contact: Gilmar Zorilla Llancari, DJ; or Valentin Mejia Vasquez, Director. Replies rarely to correspondence in Spanish.

RADIO LOS ANDES, Pasaje Damián Nicolau s/n, Huamachuco, Perú. Contact: Pasio J. Cárdenas Valverde, Gerente-General. Return postage required. Replies occasionally to correspondence in Spanish.

RADIO MADRE DE DIOS, Apartado 37, Puerto Maldonado, Madre de Dios, Perú. Contact: Javier Aniz, Administración. Replies to correspondence in Spanish. $1 or return postage necessary.

RADIO MARANON, Apartado 50, Jaén, Cajamarca, Perú. Contact: P. Ubaldo Ramos Cisneros S.J., Director. Return postage necessary. Replies slowly to correspondence in Spanish.

RADIO NAYLAMP, Avenida Huamachuco 1080, 2do Piso, Lambayeque, Perú. Contact: Dr. Juan José Grandez Vargas, Director Gerente.

RADIO NORANDINA, Jirón Pardo 579, Celendín, Cajamarca, Perú. Contact: (nontechnical) Misail Elcántara Guevara, Gerente y Jefe de Contabilidad; (technical) Roberto Alcántara G. Free calendar. $1 required. Donations (registered mail best) sought for the Committee for Good Health for Children, headed by Sr. Alcántara, which is active in saving the lives of hungry youngsters in poverty-stricken Cajamarca Province. Replies irregularly to casual or technical correspondence in Spanish, but regularly to Children's Committee donors and helpful correspondence in Spanish.

RADIO NUEVO CONTINENTE, Jirón Amazonas 660, Cajamarca, Perú. Contact: Eduardo Cabrera Urteaga, Gerente. May reply to correspondence in Spanish.

RADIO ONDAS DEL HUALLAGA, Apartado 343, Jirón Leoncio Prado 723, Huánuco, Perú. Contact: Flaviano Llanos M. $1 or return postage required. Replies to correspondence in Spanish.

RADIO ONDAS DEL MAYO, Jirón Huallaga 350, Nuevo Cajamarca, San Martín, Perú. Contact: Edilberto Lucio Peralta Lozada, Gerente; or Víctor Huaras Rojas, Locutor. Free pennants. Return postage helpful. Replies slowly to correspondence in Spanish.

RADIO ORIENTE, Av. Progreso 112, Yurimaguas, Loreto, Perú. Contact: (non-technical or technical) Prof. Ricardo Arevaldo Flores, Director-Gerente; or Juan Antonio López-Manzanares Mascunana, Director de Redacción y Programación; (technical) Pedro Capo Moragues, Gerente Técnico. $1 or return postage required. Replies occasionally to correspondence in Spanish.

RADIO ORIGENES, Avenida Augusto B. Leguía 126, Huancavelica, Perú. Contact: Jesús Acuna Quispe, Jefe de Programaciónes. $1 or return postage required. Replies occasionally to correspondence in Spanish.

RADIO OYON, Av. Huánuco 144, Oyón, Lima, Perú. Contact: Aurelio Liberato A., Director. Return postage necessary. Replies slowly to correspondence in Spanish.

RADIO PAUCARTAMBO, Jirón Conde de las Lagunas, 2 do piso, Frente al Hostal San José, Paucartambo, Pasco, Peru. Contact: Irwin Junio Berrios Pariona, Gerente General. Replies occasionally to correspondence in Spanish.

RADIO POMABAMBA, Jirón Huamachuco 400, Piso 2, Pomabamba, Región Chavín, Ancash, Perú. Contact: Juan Raúl Montero Jiménez, Director-Productor. Free pennants. $1 or return postage required. Replies occasionally to correspondence in Spanish. **ADS AIR**

RADIO QUILLABAMBA, Centro de los Medios de la Comunicación Social, Quillabamba, La Convención, Cusco, Perú. Contact: P. Francisco Panera, Director. Replies very irregularly to correspondence in Spanish.

RADIO SAN ANTONIO DE PADUA, Difusora Mariana, Arequipa, Arequipa, Perú. $1 or return postage required. Replies irregularly to correspondence in Spanish.

RADIO SAN JUAN, Jirón Pumacahua 528, Caraz, Ancash, Perú. Contact: Víctor Morales. $1 or return postage helpful. Replies occasionally to correspondence in Spanish.

RADIO SAN MARTIN, Jirón Progreso 225, Tarapoto, San Martín, Perú. Contact: José Roberto Chong, Gerente-General. Return postage required. Replies occasionally to correspondence in Spanish.

RADIO SAN MIGUEL, Av. Huayna Cápac 146, Huánchac, Cusco, Perú. Replies to correspondence in Spanish.

RADIO SAN NICOLAS, Correo Central, San Nicolás, Rodríguez de Mendoza, Amazonas, Perú. Contact: Juan José Gróndez

Santillán, Director Gerente. Free pamphlets. $1 required. Replies to correspondence in Spanish. **ADS AIR**

RADIO SANTA MONICA, Calle Mariscal Cáceres No. 453, Santa Mónica, Santiago de Chuco, La Libertad, Perú. Contact: Faustino Leonidas Rodríguez Rebaza, Gerente. Free pennants and music cassettes. $1 required. Replies occasionally to correspondence in Spanish.

RADIO SATELITE E.U.C., Jirón Cutervo No. 543, Cajamarca, Santa Cruz, Perú. Contact: Sabino Llamas Chávez, Gerente. Free tourist brochure. $1 or return postage required. Replies irregularly to correspondence in Spanish.

RADIO TACNA, Casilla de Correo 370, Tacna, Perú. Contact: Yolanda Vda. de Cáceres C., Directora Gerente; or Alfonso Cáceres C., Director Técnico. Free small pennants. $1 or return postage required. Replies irregularly to correspondence in Spanish.

RADIO TARAPOTO, Jirón Federico Sánchez 720, Tarapoto, Perú. Contact: Luis Humberto Hidalgo Sanchez, Gerente General. Replies occasionally to correspondence in Spanish.

RADIO TARMA, Casilla de Correo 167, Tarma, Perú. Contact: Mario Monteverde Pomareda, Gerente General. Sometimes sends 100 Inti banknote in return when $1 enclosed. $1 or return postage required. Replies irregularly to correspondence in Spanish.

RADIO TINGO MARIA, Av. Raymondi 592, Casilla de Correo 25, Tingo María, Huánuco, Perú. Contact: Gina A. de la Cruz Ricalde, Administradora; or Ricardo Abad Vásquez, Gerente. Free brochures. $1 required. Replies irregularly to correspondence in Spanish.

RADIO TROPICAL S.A., Casilla de Correo 31, Tarapoto, Perú. Contact: Luis F. Mori Roatogui, Gerente. Free pennant and station history booklet. Return postage required. Replies occasionally to correspondence in Spanish.

RADIO UNION, Apartado 6205, Lima 1, Perú. Contact: Juan Carlos Sologuren, Dpto. de Administración, who collects stamps. Free satin pennants and stickers. IRC required, and enclosing used or new stamps from various countries is especially appreciated. Replies irregularly to correspondence and tape recordings, especially from young women, with Spanish preferred.

RADIO VILLA RICA
Nontechnical Correspondence: Jirón Virrey Toledo 544, Huancavelica, Perú. Srta. Maritza Pozo Manrique. Free informative pamphlets. Local storybooks and poems from Huancavelica for $15; cassettes of Peruvian and Andean regional music for $20; also sells cloth and wooden folk articles. $3 reportedly required, which is excessive. Replies occasionally to correspondence in Spanish.
Technical Correspondence: Casilla de Correos 92, Huancavelica, Perú. Contact: Augusto Mendoza; or Fidel Hilario Huamani, Director. **ADS AIR**

RADIO VISION 2000, Radiodifusora Comercial Visión 2000, Jirón Mariscal Sucre, Bambamarca, Perú; or Jiron F. Bolognesi 738, Bambamarca, Perú.

PHILIPPINES World Time +8

Note: Philippine stations sometimes send publications with lists of Philippine young ladies seeking "pen pal" courtships.

FAR EAST BROADCASTING COMPANY—FEBC RADIO INTERNATIONAL
Main Office: P.O. Box 1, Valenzuela, Metro Manila 0560, Philippines; or O/EARS, Box 2041, Valenzuela, Metro Manila 0560, Philippines. Fax: +63 (2) 359 490. Contact: (nontechnical) Jane J. Colley; Peter McIntyre, Manager, International Operations Division; Christine D. Johnson, Program Supervisor, Overseas English Department; or Efren M. Pallorina, Managing Director; (technical) Martin Lind, Verification Secretary; or Romualdo Lintag, Chief Engineer. Free stickers and "QSL Team" membership. 3 IRCs required for airmail reply.
Bangalore Bureau, Nontechnical: FEBA, Box 2526, Bangalore-560 025, India. Fax: +91 (812) 343 432.
New Delhi Bureau, Nontechnical: FEBA, Box 6, New Delhi-110 001, India.
Tokyo Bureau, Nontechnical: CPO Box 1055, Tokyo, Japan.
Singapore Bureau, Nontechnical: 20 Maxwell Road #03-01, Singapore. Fax: +65 222 1805.

RADYO PILIPINAS, Philippine Broadcasting Service, P/A Building Visayas Avenue, 1103 Quezon City, Metro Manila, Philippines. Fax: +63 (2) 924 2745. Contact: (nontechnical) Evelyn Salvador Agato, Producer, Office of the Press Secretary; or Elvie Catacutan, Co-Producer, with Evelyn S. Agato of "Kumusta ka,

Kaibigan and Listeners and Friends"; (technical) Mike Pangilinan, Engineer. Free postcards.

RADIO VERITAS ASIA, P.O. Box 2642, Manila, Quezon City, Philippines. Fax: +63 (2) 907 436. Contact: Ms. Cleofe R. Labindao, Audience Relations Officer; (technical) Ing. Floremundo L. Kiguchi, Technical Director. Free station brochure.

VOICE OF AMERICA—Does not welcome direct correspondence at its Philippines facilities in Poro or Tinang. *See* USA for acceptable VOA address and related information.

PIRATE

Pirate radio stations are usually one-person operations airing home-brew entertainment and/or iconoclastic viewpoints. In order to avoid detection by the authorities, they tend to appear irregularly, with little concern for the niceties of conventional program scheduling.

Most are found just above 6200 kHz, chiefly in Europe on Sundays; and just above 7375 kHz (notably 7415 kHz, although with the Voice of America sometime here this usage may diminish), mainly evenings in North America. These *sub rosa* stations and their addresses are subject to unusually abrupt change or termination, sometimes as a result of forays by radio authorities.

Two worthy sources of current addresses and other information on American pirate radio activity are: *The Pirate Radio Directory* (George Zeller, Tiare Publications), an excellent annual reference available from radio specialty stores; and A*C*E, Box 11201, Shawnee Mission KS 66207 USA, a club which publishes a periodical for serious pirate radio enthusiasts.

For Europirate DX news, try: *Pirate Connection*, Kämnärsvägen 13D:220, S-226 46 Lund, Sweden (six issues annually for about $23); *Pirate Chat*, 21 Green Park, Bath, Avon, BA1 1HZ, United Kingdom; *FRS Goes DX*, P.O. Box 2727, 6049 ZG Herten, Holland; *Free-DX*, 3 Greenway, Harold Park, Romford, Essex, RM3 OHH, United Kingdom; *FRC-Finland*, P.O. Box 82, SF-40101 Jyvaskyla, Finland; *Pirate Express*, P.O. Box 220342, Wuppertal, Germany.

POLAND World Time +1 (+2 midyear)

POLISH RADIO WARSAW, External Service, P.O. Box 46, 00-950 Warsaw, Poland. Fax: +48 (22) 445 280; +48 (22) 447 307 or +48 (22) 444 123.

Contact: Jacek Detco, Editor of English Section; María Goc, Editor of English Section; Miroslaw Lubo, Deputy Director; or Jerzy Jagodzinski, Director and Editor-in-Chief. Free stickers. DX Listeners' Club. A new Swiss 250 kW transmitter is being installed in Poland, possibly for a new station. Polish Radio Warsaw might have at least some access to this to improve reception.

PORTUGAL World Time +1 (+2 midyear); Azores World Time −1 (World Time midyear)

IBRA RADIO

Swedish Office: International Broadcasting Association, Box 396, S-105 36 Stockholm, Sweden. Fax: +46 (8) 579 029. Free pennants and stickers, plus green-on-white IBRA T-shirt available. IBRA Radio is heard as a program over various radio stations, including Radio Trans Europe, Portugal; the Voice of Hope, Lebanon; and Trans World Radio, Monaco.

Canadian Office: P.O. Box 444, Niagara Falls ON, L2E 6T8 Canada.

RDP INTERNATIONAL—RADIO PORTUGAL, Box 1011, Lisbon 1011, Portugal. Fax: +351 (1) 347 44 75. Contact: (nontechnical) English Service; Carminda Días da Silva; Carlo Pinto Coelho, Assistant to Head; or João Louro, Chairman; (technical) Winnie Almeida, DX Producer/Host, English Section. Free stickers, paper pennants and calendars. May send literature from the Portuguese National Tourist Office.

RADIO RENASCENCA, Rua Capelo 5, 1294 Lisbon, Portugal. Fax: +351 (1) 342 2658. Contact: C. Pabil, Director-Manager.

RADIO TRANS EUROPE, 6th Floor, Rua Braamcamp 84, 1200 Lisbon, Portugal.

VOICE OF ORTHODOXY (program via Radio Trans Europe), B.P. 416-08, F-75366 Paris Cedex 08, France. Contact: Valentin Korelsky, General Secretary.

QATAR World Time +3

QATAR BROADCASTING SERVICE, P.O. Box 3939, Doha, Qatar. Contact: Jassem Mohamed Al-Qattan, Head of Public Relations. Rarely replies, but return postage helpful.

ROMANIA World Time +2 (+3 midyear)

RADIO ROMANIA INTERNATIONAL, 60-62 General Berthelot Street, P.O. Box 111, 70756 Bucharest, Romania; or Romanian embassies worldwide. Fax: +40 (1) 312 1057 or +40 (1) 617

2856. Contact: (English, Romanian or German) Frederica Dochinoiu, Producer, "Listeners' Letterbox" and "DX Mailbag," English Department; (French or Romanian) Doru Vasile Ionescu, Director. Free booklets, stickers, pennants and Romanian stamps. Can provide supplementary materials for "Romanian by Radio" course. Listeners' Club. Replies slowly but regularly.

RUSSIA (Times given for republics, oblasts and krays):

• World Time +2 (+3 midyear) Kaliningradskaya;
• World Time +3 (+4 midyear) Arkhangel'skaya (incl. Nenetskiy), Astrakhanskaya, Belgorodskaya, Bryanskaya, Ivanovskaya, Kaluzhskaya, Karelia, Kirovskaya, Komi, Kostromskaya, Kurskaya, Lipetskaya, Moscovskaya, Murmanskaya, Nizhegorodskaya, Novgorodskaya, Orlovskaya, Penzenskaya, Pskovskaya, Riazanskaya, Samarskaya, Sankt-Peterburgskaya, Smolenskaya, Tambovskaya, Tulskaya, Tverskaya, Vladimirskaya, Vologodskaya, Volgogradskaya, Voronezhskaya, Yaroslavskaya;
• World Time +4 (+5 midyear) Checheno-Ingushia, Chuvashia, Dagestan, Kabardino-Balkaria, Kalmykia, Krasnodarskiy, Mari-Yel, Mordovia, Severnaya Osetia, Stavropolskiy, Tatarstan, Udmurtia;
• World Time +5 (+6 midyear) Bashkortostan, Chelyabinskaya, Kurganskaya, Orenburgskaya, Permskaya, Yekaterinburgskaya, Tyumenskaya;
• World Time +6 (+7 midyear) Omskaya;
• World Time +7 (+8 midyear) Altayskiy, Kemerovskaya, Krasnoyarskiy (incl. Evenkiyskiy), Novosibirskaya, Tomskaya, Tuva;
• World Time +8 (+9 midyear) Buryatia, Irkutskaya;
• World Time +9 (+10 midyear) Amurskaya, Chitinskaya, Sakha (West);
• World Time +10 (+11 midyear) Khabarovskiy, Primorskiy, Sakha (Center), Yevreyskaya;
• World Time +11 (+12 midyear) Magadanskaya (exc. Chukotskiy), Sakha (East), Sakhalinskaya;
• World Time +12 (+13 midyear) Chukotskiy, Kamchatskaya;
• World Time +13 (+14 midyear) all points east of longtitude 172.30 E.

Warning—Mail Theft: For the time being, airmail correspondence, especially containing funds or IRCs, from North America and Japan to Russian stations is unlikely to arrive safely even if sent by registered air mail, as such mail enters via the Moscow Airport, gateway to the world's most notorious nest of mail thieves. However, funds sent from Europe, North America and Japan via surface mail enter via St. Petersburg, and thus stand a decent chance of arriving safely.

Translation Service: Your correspondence and reception reports in English may be translated into Russian and forwarded to the appropriate Russian station, with a guaranteed return reply from the station, by sending your material plus $3 or its equivalent in Deutsche Marks by registered surface mail (*see* preceding warning) to Anatoly Klepov, ul. Tvardovskogo, d. 23, kv. 365, Moscow 123 458, Russia.

ADVENTIST WORLD RADIO, THE VOICE OF HOPE

Main Office: AWR-Russia Media Centre, P.O. Box 170, 300000 Tula-Centre, Tulskaya Oblast, Russia. Contact: Esther Hanselmann, Administrative Secretary. Free home study Bible guides and other religious material, envelope openers, pennants, stickers, calendars and other small souvenirs. However, most letters to the Russian Media Centre wind up being answered by the AWR European Office (*see* "Adventist World Radio, Germany"), so correspondence is best directed there.

ARKHANGEL'SK RADIO, Dom Radio, ul. Popova 2, 163000 Arkhangel'sk, Arkhangel'skaya Oblast, Russia; or U1PR, Valentin G. Kalasnikov, ul. Suvorov 2, kv. 16, Arkhangel'sk, Arkhangel'skaya Oblast, Russia. Replies irregularly to correspondence in Russian.

BURYAT RADIO, Dom Radio, ul. Erbanova 7, 670000 Ulan-Ude, Republic of Buryatia, Russia. Contact: Z.A. Telin or L.S. Shikhanova.

CHITA RADIO, Box 45, 672090 Chita, Chitinskaya Oblast, Russia. Contact: (technical) V.A. Klimov, Chief Engineer; or A.A. Anufriyev.

CHRISTIAN RADIO STATION ALPHA AND OMEGA, Izdatelstvo "Protestant," Mukomolsky proezd, d.1, kor.2, 123290 Moscow, Russia. Contact: Elena Yasnova, Manager.

FAR EAST CHRISTIAN BROADCASTING

Main Office: FEBC-Russia, Box 2128, 680020 Khabarovsk, Khavarovskiy Kray, Russia.

California Office: Far East broadcasting Company, Inc., Box 1, 15700 Imperial Highway, La Mirada CA 90637 USA. Fax: +1 (213) 943 0160. Contact: Jim Bowman or Viktor Akhterov, FEBC Russian Ministries. Free stickers.

GOLOS ROSSII (Voice of Russia), ul. Pyatnitskaya 25, 113326 Moscow, Russia. Fax: +7 (095) 233 6449 or +7 (095) 973 2000. Contact: Oleg Maksimovich Poptsov, Chairman of All-Russian State Teleradio Broadcasting Company. Correspondence in Russian preferred.

KABARDINO-BALKAR RADIO, ul. Nogmova 38, Nalchik 360000, Russia.

KAMCHATKA RADIO, RTV Center, Dom Radio, ul. Sovietskaya 62-G, 683000 Petropavlovsk-Kamchatskiy, Kamchatskaya Oblast, Russia. Contact: A. Borodin, Chief OTK; or V.I. Aibabin. $1 required. Replies in Russian to correspondence in Russian or English.

KHABAROVSK RADIO, RTV Center, ul. Lenina 71, 680013 Khabarovsk, Khabarovskiy Kray, Russia; or Dom Radio, pl. Slavy, 682632 Khabarovsk, Khabarovskiy Kray, Russia. Contact: (technical) V.N. Kononov, Glavnyy Inzhener.

KHANTY-MANSIYSK RADIO, Dom Radio, ul. Lenina 21, 626200 Khanty-Mansiysk, Tyumenskaya Oblast, Russia. Contact: (technical) Vladimir Sokolov, Engineer.

KRASNOYARSK RADIO, RTV Center, Sovietskaya 128, 660017 Krasnoyarsk, Krasnoyarskiy Kray, Russia. Contact: Valeriy Korotchenko; or Anatoliy A. Potehin, RA0AKE. Replies in Russian to correspondence in English or Russian. Return postage helpful.

MAGADAN RADIO, RTV Center, ul. Komuny 8/12, 685013 Magadan, Magadanskaya Oblast, Russia. Contact: Viktor Loktionov or V.G. Kuznetsov. Return postage helpful. May reply to correspondence in Russian.

MARIY RADIO, ul. Krasnoarmejskaya 76-a, Yoshkar-Ola 424031, Russia.

MURMANSK RADIO, per. Rusanova 7, 183767 Murmansk, Murmanskaya Oblast, Russia; or RTV Center, Sopka Varnichaya, 183042 Murmansk, Murmanskaya Oblast, Russia.

NEW WAVE RADIO STATION (Radiostantsiya Novaya Volna) (independent program aired via Radio Moscow's First Program and Golos Rossii), ul. Akademika Koroleva 19, 127427 Moscow, Russia. Fax: +7 (095) 215 0847. Contact: Vladimir Razin, Editor-in-Chief.

PRIMORSK RADIO, RTV Center, ul. Uborevieha 20A, 690000 Vladivostok, Primorskiy Kray, Russia. Contact: A.G. Giryuk. Return postage helpful.

RADIO ALEF (joint project of Radio Moscow and Yiddish Child's Organization.), P.O. Box 72, 123154 Moscow, Russia.

RADIO ART, ul. Tverskaya 29, str.1, 103050 Moscow, Russia. Fax: +7 (095) 299 2449. Contact: Mr. E.A. Sotnikov, President.

RADIO AUM SHINRIKYO ("Evangelion tis Vasilias," Gospel of the Kingdom), 3-8-11 Miyamae, Suginami-ku, Tokyo 168, Japan. Fax: +81 (3) 5370 1604. Contact: Shoko Ashara. Replies to listener technical and other correspondence in Japanese and English. Free *The Teaching of the Truth* and other books by Shoko Ashara. Transmitted via facilities of Radio Moscow International. *U.S. Branch Address:* Aum Supreme Truth, 8 East 48th St. #2E, New York NY 10017 USA.

RADIO CENTER, ul. Nikolskaya d.7, 103012 Moscow, Russia. Contact: Andrey Nekrasov.

RADIO DIAPAZON—see Krasnoyarsk Radio.

RADIO GALAXY (Radiostantsiya Galaktika), P.O. Box 7, 117418 Moscow, Russia. Fax: +7 (095) 128 2822. Contact: Edward I. Kozlov, Director General.

RADIO MOSCOW (domestic service), ul. Akademika Koroleva 19, 127427 Moscow, Russia. Fax: +7 (095) 215 0847. Correspondence in Russian preferred, but English increasingly accepted.

RADIO MOSCOW INTERNATIONAL (typically identifies simply as "Radio Moscow"), TV & Radio Agency "Astra," ul. Pyatnitskaya 25, 113326 Moscow, Russia. Fax: +7 (095) 230 2828. Contact (World Service in English): (Listeners' questions to be answered on the air) Joe Adamov; (all other listener correspondence) Valentina Knjasewa; or Ms. Olga Troshina; (letters of business) Eugene Nikitenko, Consultant/Moderator; (administrative correspondence) Youri Minayev, Director; (problems with frequency management) Mr. Titov, Director of C.I.S. Frequency Planning. Free stickers, key holders, wooden toys, calendars, "Russian by Radio" supplementary materials, booklets and cookbooks on request.

Warning-Mail Fraud: Radio Moscow International advertises that its souvenirs may be purchased via a company in Nova Scotia, Canada. This Canadian firm has been noted for a number of financial irregularities in recent years, including taking money from Radio Moscow International listeners and not providing anything in return. **ADS** **AIR**

RADIO NADEZHDA (Radio Hope), ul. Pyatnitskaya 25, 113326 Moscow, Russia. Fax: +7 (095) 230 2828. Contact: Tatyana Zeleranskaya, Editor-in-Chief.

RADIO NIKA-M4, Z. Kosmodemyanskoy Str. 16-35, 183008 Murmansk, Russia. Contact: V.Yefremov, Director.

RADIO NOVAYA VOLNA 2 (Radio New Wave 2), Vorovskogo Str. 6, 454091 Chelyabinsk 91, Russia.

RADIO ROSSII—see Russia's Radio, below.

RADIO RUKHI MEROC (Radio Spiritual Heritage), Vypolzov per., d.7, 129090 Moscow, Russia.

RADIO SAMARA, ul. Sovietscoj Army 205, Samara, Samarskaya Oblast, Russia.

RADIO SEVEN, ul. Gagarina 6A, 443079 Samara, Samarskaya Oblast, Russia. Contact: A.P. Nenashjev; or Mrs. A.S. Shamsutdinova.

RADIO SHARK

Ufa Office: Prospekt Oktyabrya 56/1, 450054 Ufa, Bashkortostan, Russia. Contact: Gergey Anatsky; or Anatskiy Sergey, Director.

Moscow Office: Rukhi Miras, Islamic Center of Moscow Region, Moscow Jami Mosque, Vipolzov by-str. 7, 129090 Moscow, Russia. Fax: +7 (095) 284 7908. Contact: Sheik Ravil Gainutdin.

RADIO TITAN KOMPANI (programs aired via Radio Shark), ul. Sovietskaya 14, kabinet 9, 450008 Ufa, Bashkortostan, Russia.

RADIOSTANTSIYA ATLANTIKA (program of Radio Riga and Murmansk Radio, aired via Golo Rossii), per. Rusanova 7 "A", 183767 Murmansk, Russia.

RADIOSTANTSIYA PAMYAT (Memory Radio Station), P.O. Box 23, 113535 Moscow, Russia; or Mirolyubov, ul. Valovaya, d.32, kv.4, 113054 Moscow, Russia. Contact: (nontechnical) Dimitrly Vasilyev, Leader; (technical) Yuri Mirolyukov, Radio Operator. Audio cassettes of broadcasts available for five rubles or $2. Correspondence in Russian preferred.

RADIOSTANTSIYA RADONEZH (Radonezh Orthodox Radio Station), Studio 58, ul. Pyatnitskaya 25, 113326 Moscow, Russia. Contact: Anton Parshin, Announcer.

RADIOSTANTSIYA SOFIYA, Moscow Patriarchy's Department for Religious Education and the Teaching of the Catechism, ul. Kachalova 24, 113326 Moscow, Russia.

RADIOSTANTSIYA VEDO, P.O. Box 1940, 400123 Volgograd, Volgogradskaya Oblast, Russia. Contact: Andrei Bogdanov. Correspondence in Russian preferred, but French and English also acceptable.

RADIOSTANTSIYA YAKUTSK, ul. Semena Dezhneva, 75/2, Radiocenter, 677000 Yakutsk, Russia.

RADIOSTANTSIYA YUNOST (Radio 2), ul. Pyatnitskaya 25, 113326 Moscow, Russia. Fax: +7 (095) 233 6244.

RADIO TIKHIY OKEAN (program of Primorsk Radio aired via Golos Rossii), RTV Center, ul. Uborevieha 20A, 690000 Vladivostok, Primorskiy Kray, Russia.

RUSSIA'S RADIO (Radio Rossii), Room 121, 5-R Ulitsa, 19/21 Yamskogo Polya, Moscow 125124, Russia. Fax: +7 (095) 250 0105. Contact: Sergei Yerofeyev, Director of International Operations; or Sergei Davidov, Director. Free English-language information sheet.

SAKHALIN RADIO, Dom Radio, ul. Komsomolskaya 209, 693000 Yuzhno-Sakhalinsk, Sakhalin Is., Sakhalinskaya Oblast, Russia. Contact: V. Belyaev, Chairman of Sakhalinsk RTV Committee.

TATAR RADIO, RTV Center, ul. M. Gorkova 15, 420015 Kazan', Republic of Tatarstan, Russia. May reply to correspondence in Russian. Return postage helpful.

TYUMEN' RADIO, RTV Center, ul. Permyakova 6, 625013 Tyumen', Tyumenskaya Oblast, Russia. Contact: (technical) V.D. Kizerov, Engineer, Technical Center. May reply to correspondence in Russian. Return postage helpful.

VOICE OF RUSSIA—see Golos Rossii.

VOICE OF THE ASSYRIANS—see Radio Moscow International.

YAKUT RADIO, Dom Radio, 48 Ordzhonikdze Street, 677892 Yakutsk, Sakha (Yakutia) Republic, Russia. Fax: +7 (095) 230 2919. Contact: (nontechnical) Alexandra Borisova; Lia Sharoborina, Advertising Editor; or Albina Danilova, Producer, "Your Letters"; (technical) Sergei Bobnev, Technical Director. Russian books available for $15. C60 audio cassettes available for $10. Free station stickers and original Yakutian souvenirs. Replies to correspondence in English.

RWANDA World Time +2

RADIO RWANDA, B.P. 83, Kigali, Rwanda. Fax: +250 (7) 6185. Contact: Alfred Mukezamfura, Chef de Section Programmes; Marcel Singirankabo, Chef de Section Documentation et Censure; Kassim Zayana, Producer, "Musique et Réflexion"; or Etienne Ntirugirisonu. $1 required. Rarely replies, slowly, with correspondence in French being preferred. **ADS** **AIR**

SAO TOME E PRINCIPE   World Time exactly

VOICE OF AMERICA—future new site, post-1993, for the Voice of America, using 100 kW transmitters. *See* USA for address and other details.

SAUDI ARABIA   World Time +3

BROADCASTING SERVICE OF THE KINGDOM OF SAUDI ARABIA, P.O. Box 61718, Riyadh 11575, Saudi Arabia. Fax: +966 (1) 404 1692. Contact: (technical) Sulaiman Samnan, Director of Frequency Management; or A. Shah. Free travel information and book on Saudi history. Sometimes replies slowly.

RADIO ISLAM FROM HOLY MECCA (Idha'at Islam min Mecca al-Mukarama)—same details as "Broadcasting Service of the Kingdom of Saudi Arabia," above.

RADIO RIYADH, P.O. Box 60059, Riyadh 11545, Saudi Arabia. Fax: +966 (1) 402 8177. Contact: (nontechnical) Mutlaq A. Albegami, European Service Manager; or Producer, "K.S.A. Today"; (technical) Technical Department. Free stickers and publications.

SENEGAL   World Time exactly

OFFICE DE RADIODIFFUSION-TELEVISION DU SENEGAL, B.P. 1765, Dakar, Senegal. Contact: Joseph Nesseim. Free stickers and Senegalese stamps. Return postage, $1 or 2 IRCs required; as Mr. Nesseim collects stamps, unusual stamps may be even more appreciated. Replies to correspondence in French.

SEYCHELLES   World Time +4

BBC WORLD SERVICE—INDIAN OCEAN RELAY STATION, P.O. Box 448, Victoria, Mahé, Seychelles; or Grand Anse, Mahé, Seychelles. Fax: +248 78500. Contact: (technical) Peter Lee, Resident Engineer; Steve Welch, Assistant Resident Engineer; or Peter J. Loveday, Station Manager. Nontechnical correspondence should be sent to the BBC World Service in London (see).

FAR EAST BROADCASTING ASSOCIATION—FEBA RADIO
Main Office: P.O. Box 234, Mahé, Seychelles. Fax: +248 25171. Contact: (nontechnical) Roger Foyle, Audience Relations Counsellor; or Jonathan Hargreaves, English Program Coordinator; (technical) Mary Asba, Verification Secretary; or Peter Williams, Chief Engineer. Free stickers and station information sheet. $1 or one IRC helpful.
Canadian Office: Box 2233, Vancouver BC, Canada.

SIERRA LEONE   World Time exactly

SIERRA LEONE BROADCASTING SERVICE, New England, Freetown, Sierra Leone. Contact: Joshua Nicol, Special Assistant to the Director of Broadcasting; (technical) Emmanuel B. Ehirim, Project Engineer.

SINGAPORE   World Time +8

BBC WORLD SERVICE—FAR EASTERN RELAY STATION, P.O. Box 434, 26 Olive Road, Singapore. Fax: +65 669 0834. Contact: (technical) Far East Resident Engineer. Nontechnical correspondence should be sent to the BBC World Service in London (see).

SINGAPORE BROADCASTING CORPORATION, P.O. Box 60, Singapore 1129, Singapore. Fax: +65 253 8119. Contact: (nontechnical) Lillian Tan, Public Relations Division; Lim Heng Tow, Manager, International & Community Relations; Lucy Leong; Sakuntala Gupta, Program Manager; or Karamjit Kaur, Senior Controller. (technical) Lee Wai Meng. Free stickers and lapel pins. Do not include currency in envelope. **ADS** **AIR**

SLOVAKIA World Time +1 (+2 midyear)
Slovak Radio, External Services, Mýtna 1, 81290 Bratislava, Slovakia. Contact: PhDr. Karol Palkovic, Chief Editor; or Richard Guga, Director of English Broadcasting. Free stickers.

SOLOMON ISLANDS   World Time +11

SOLOMON ISLANDS BROADCASTING CORPORATION, P.O. Box 654, Honiara, Solomon Islands. Fax: +677 23159. Contact: (nontechnical) James Kilua, Secretary; Julian Maka'a, Producer, "Listeners From Far Away"; Alison Ofotalau, Voice Performer; or Programme Director; (technical) George Tora, Chief Engineer. IRC or $1 helpful.

SOMALIA   World Time +3

RADIO MOGADISHU, Ministry of Information, Private Postbag, Mogadishu, Somalia. Contact: (nontechnical) Abdel-Rahman Umar Ma"Alim Dhagah, Acting Director; or Dr. Abdel-Qadir Muhammad Mursal, Director, Media Department; (technical) Yusuf Dahir Siyad, Chief Engineer. Replies irregularly. Letters should be via registered mail.

"Somaliland"
Note: "Somaliland," claimed as a independent nation, is diplomatically recognized only as part of Somalia.

RADIO HARGEISA, P.O. Box 14, Hargeisa, Somaliland, Somalia. Sulayman Abdel-Rahman, announcer. Most likely to respond to correspondence in Somali or Arabic.

SOUTH AFRICA   World Time +2

CHANNEL AFRICA, P.O. Box 91313, Auckland Park 2006, Republic of South Africa. Fax: (nontechnical) +27 (11) 714 4956 or +27 (11) 714 6377; (technical) +27 (11) 714 5812. Contact: (nontechnical) G.A. Wynne, Manager of English Service; Robert Michel, Head of Research; or Lionel Williams, Executive Editor; (technical) Lucienne Libotte, Technology Operations. Free stickers. **ADS** **AIR**

SOUTH AFRICAN BROADCASTING CORPORATION, P.O. Box 91312, Auckland Park 2006, South Africa. Fax: (nontechnical) +27 (11) 714 5055; (technical) +27 (11) 714 3106. Contact: *Radio Five*: Helena Boshoff, Public Relations Officer; *Radio Oranje*: Hennie Klopper, Announcer; or Christo Olivier; *Radio Orion*: Public Relations Officer; or Kathy Otto, Shortwave Section. *All networks*: Karel van der Merwe, Head of Radio. Free stickers.

SPAIN   World Time +1 (+2 midyear)

RADIO EXTERIOR DE ESPANA
Main Office: Apartado 156.202, E-28080 Madrid, Spain. Fax: +34 (1) 346 1097. Contact: Pilar Salvador M., Relaciones con la Audiencia; Nuria Alonso Veiga, Head of Information Service; or Penelope Eades, Foreign Language Programmer. Free stickers, calendars and pennants.
Washington News Bureau, Nontechnical: National Press Building, 529 14th Street NW, Washington DC 20045 USA.

SRI LANKA   World Time +5:30

DEUTSCHE WELLE—SRI LANKA, 92/2 Rt. Hon. D.S. Senanayake Mwts, Colombo 8, Sri Lanka. Nontechnical correspondence should be sent to the Deutsche Welle in Germany (see).

RADIO JAPAN/NHK, c/o SLBC, P.O. Box 574, Torrington Square, Colombo 7, Sri Lanka. Nontechnical listener correspondence should be sent to the Radio Japan address in Japan; news-orientated correspondence may also be sent to the NHK Bangkok Bureau, 6F MOT Building (Thai TV CH9), 222 Rama 9 Road, Bangkok 10310, Thailand.

SRI LANKA BROADCASTING CORPORATION, P.O. Box 574, Colombo 7, Sri Lanka. Fax: +94 (1) 695 488. Contact: H. Jerando, Director of Audience Research; Lal Herath, Deputy Director General of Broadcasting; or Icumar Ratnayake, Controller, "Mailbag Program." Color magazine available celebrating 25 years of broadcasting for US$20, while they last. Has tended to reply irregularly, but this seems to have improved as of late. **ADS** **AIR**

TRANS WORLD RADIO
Transmitter: P.O. Box 364, 91 Wijerama Mawatha, Colombo 7, Sri Lanka. Fax: +94 (1) 685 245. Contact: Roger Halliday, South Asia Monitor Coordinator; (technical) Robert Schultz.
Studio: P.O. Box 4407, L-15, Green Park, New Delhi-110 016, India. Fax: +91 (11) 686 8049. Contact: N. Emil Jebasingh, Director. **AIR**

VOICE OF AMERICA—COLOMBO RELAY STATION, 228/1 Galle Road, Colombo 4, Sri Lanka. Fax: +94 (1) 502 675. Contact: David M. Sites, Relay Station Manager. This address, which verifies correct reception reports, is for technical correspondence only. Nontechnical correspondence should be directed to the regular VOA address (see "USA").

ST. HELENA   World Time exactly

ST. HELENA GOVERNMENT BROADCASTING SERVICE, The Castle, Jamestown, St. Helena, South Atlantic Ocean. Fax: +290 4669. Contact: Tony Leo, Station Manager. $1, return postage or 2 IRCs required

SUDAN   World Time +2

NATIONAL UNITY RADIO—see Sudan National Broadcasting Corporation, below, for details.

SUDAN NATIONAL BROADCASTING CORPORATION, P.O. Box 572, Omdurman, Sudan. Contact: (nontechnical) Mohammed Elmahdi Khalil or Mohammed Elfatih El Sumoal; (technical) Abbas Sidig, Director General, Engineering and Technical Affairs; or Adil Didahammed, Engineering Department. Replies irregularly. Return postage necessary.

SURINAME   World Time –3

RADIO APINTIE, Postbus 595, Paramaribo, Suriname. Contact:

Ch. E. Vervuurt, Director. Free pennant. Return postage or $1 required.

SWAZILAND World Time +2

SWAZILAND COMMERCIAL RADIO
Nontechnical Correspondence: P.O. Box 23114, Joubert Park 2044, South Africa. Contact: Rob Vickers, Manager Religion. IRC helpful. Replies irregularly.
Technical Correspondence: P.O. Box 99, Amsterdam 2375, South Africa. Contact: Guy Doult, Chief Engineer.

TRANS WORLD RADIO
Main Office: P.O. Box 64, Manzini, Swaziland. Fax: +268 55333. Contact: (nontechnical) Dawn-Lynn Prediger, Propagation Secretary; L. Stavropoulos; or Mrs. Carol J. Tatlow; (technical or nontechnical) Rev. Tom Tatlow. Free stickers and calendars. $1, return postage or IRC required. Also, *see* USA. **AIR**
South African Office: P.O. Box 36000, Menlo Park 0102, Republic of South Africa.
Zimbabwe Office: P.O. Box H-74, Hatfield, Harare, Zimbabwe.

SWEDEN World Time +1 (+2 midyear)

RADIO SWEDEN
Main Office: S-105 10 Stockholm, Sweden. Fax: (general) +46 (8) 667 62 83; (polling to receive schedule) +46 8 667 37 01. Contact: (nontechnical) Alan Prix, Host, "In Touch with Stockholm" (include your telephone number); Sarah Roxtröm, Editor, English Service; Marta Rose Ugirst; Lilian von Arnold; Inga Holmberg, Assistant to the Director; or Hans Wachholz, Director; (technical) Rolf Beckman, Head, Technical Department. Free stickers. "Moose Gustafsson" T-shirts for $17 or £10.
New York News Bureau, Nontechnical: 12 W. 37th Street, 7th Floor, New York NY 10018 USA. Fax: +1 (212) 594 6413. Contact: Elizabeth Johansson or Ann Hedengren.

SWITZERLAND World Time +1 (+2 midyear)

RED CROSS BROADCASTING SERVICE, Département de la Communication, CICR/ICRC, 19 Avenue de la Paix, CH-1202 Geneva, Switzerland. Fax: +41 (22) 734 8280. Contact: Elisabeth Copson or Patrick Piper, "Red Crossroads"; or Carlos Bauverd, Chef, Division de la Presse. Free stickers, wall calendar and station information. IRC appreciated.

SWISS RADIO INTERNATIONAL
Main Office: SSR, Giacomettistrasse 1, CH-3000 Berne 15, Switzerland. Fax: +41 (31) 350 9544 (Public Relations and Marketing); or (Programme Department) +41 (31) 350 9569. Contact: Bob Zanotti, Planning Manager; Ulrich Küendig, Directeur; Walter Fankhauser, Press and Public Relations Officer; Gillian Zbinden, Secretary, English Programs; or Thérèse Schafter, Secrétaire Programmes en langue Française; Free station flyers, posters, stickers and pennants. SRI compact discs of Swiss music available for sale. Station also offers listeners a line of articles for sale that bear the station's SRI logo. These include watches, clocks, microphone lighters, letter openers and army knives. For more details contact SRI Merchandising, c/o the above address. Plans future use of the RFI relay station in Montsinery, French Guiana.
Washington News Bureau, Nontechnical: 2030 M Street NW, Washington DC 20554 USA. Contact: Christophe Erbea, reporter. **AIR**

SYRIA World Time +2 (+3 midyear)

RADIO DAMASCUS, Syrian Radio & Television, Ommayad Square, Damascus, Syria. Contact: AFAF, Director General; Lisa Arslanian; or Mrs. Wafa Ghawi. Free stickers, paper pennants and *The Syria Times* newspaper. Replies can be highly erratic, but as of late have been more regular, if sometimes slow.

TAHITI—*see* FRENCH POLYNESIA.

TAJIKISTAN World Time +6

RADIO DUSHANBE, Radio House, 31 Chapayev Street, Dushanbe 735 025, Tajikistan. Correspondence in Russian, Farsi, Dari, Tajik or Uzbek preferred.

RADIO PAY-I 'AJAM—*see* Radio Dushanbe for details.

TAJIK RADIO, Radio House, 31 Chapayev Street, Dushanbe 735025, Tajikstan. Contact: Mirbobo Mirrakhimov, Chairman of State Television and Radio Corporation. Correspondence in Russian, Tajik or Uzbek preferred.

TANZANIA World Time +3

RADIO TANZANIA, Director of Broadcasting, P.O. Box 9191, Dar es Salaam, Tanzania. Fax: +255 (51) 29416. Contact: (nontechnical) Mrs. Deborah Mwenda; Acting Head of External Service; Abdul Ngarawa, Acting Controller of Programs; B.M. Kapings, Director of Broadcasting; or Ahmed Jongo, Producer, "Your Answer"; (technical) Head of Research & Planning. Replies to correspondence in English.

VOICE OF TANZANIA ZANZIBAR, P.O. Box 1178, Zanzibar, Tanzania. Contact: (nontechnical) Yusuf Omar Chunda, Director Department of Information and Broadcasting; (technical) Nassor M. Suleiman, Maintenance Engineer. Return postage helpful.

THAILAND World Time +7

RADIO THAILAND, External Service, Rajchadamnern Klang Road, Phra Nakhon Region, Bangkok 10200, Thailand. Contact: Mrs. Bupha Laemluang, Chief of External Services; or Patra Lamjiack. Free pennants. Replies irregularly, especially to those who persist.

VOICE OF AMERICA, (technical) Thailand QSL Desk, Voice of America, Room G-759, Washington DC 20547 USA.

TOGO World Time exactly

RADIO LOME, Lomé, Togo. Return postage, $1 or 2 IRCs helpful.

TONGA World Time +13

TONGA BROADCASTING COMMISSION (when facilities, damaged by a cyclone, are repaired), A3Z, P.O. Box 36, Nuku'alofa, Tonga. Fax: +676 22670 or +676 24417. Contact: (nontechnical) Mateaki Heimuli, Controller of Programs; or Tavake Fusimalohi, General Manager; (technical) M. Indiran, Chief Engineer; or Kifitoni Sikulu, Controller, Technical Services. **ADS** **AIR**

TUNISIA World Time +1

RADIODIFFUSION TELEVISION TUNISIENNE, Radio Sfax, 71 Avenue de la Liberté, Tunis, Tunisia. Contact: Mongai Caffai, Director General; Mohamed Abdelkafi, Director; or Smaoui Sadok, Chief Engineer. Replies irregularly and slowly to correspondence in French or Arabic.

TURKEY World Time +2 (+3 midyear)

TURKISH POLICE RADIO, T.C. Içişleri Bakanligi, Emniyet Genel Müdürlügü, Ankara, Turkey. Contact: Station Director. Tourist literature for return postage. Replies irregularly.

TURKISH RADIO-TELEVISION CORPORATION—VOICE OF TURKEY
Main Office, Nontechnical: P.K. 333, 06.443 Yenisehir Ankara, Turkey. Fax: +90 (4) 435 3816 or +90 (4) 431 0322. Contact: (English) Osman Erkan, Host, "Letterbox"; or Ms. Semra Eren, Head of English Department; (other foreign languages) Rafet Esit, Foreign Languages Section Chief; (all languages) A. Akad Gukuriva, Deputy Director General; or Savas Kiratli, Managing Director; (technical) Mete Coşkun. Free key holders, framed sultan seals, stickers, pennants and tourist literature.
Main Office, Technical: P.K. 333, 06.443 Yenisehir Ankara, Turkey. Fax: +90 (4) 490 1733. Contact: A. Akad Cukurova, Deputy Director General, Engineering.
San Francisco Office, Schedules: 2654 17th Avenue, San Francisco CA 94116 USA. Contact: George Poppin. This address only provides TRT schedules to listeners. All other correspondence should be sent directly to Ankara.

VOICE OF METEOROLOGY, T.C. Tarim Bakanligi, Devlet Meteoroloji Isleri, Genel Müdürlügü, P.K. 401, Ankara, Turkey. Contact: Mehmet Ormeci, Director General. Free tourist literature. Return postage helpful.

TURKMENISTAN World Time +5

TURKMEN RADIO, Kurortnaya III, 744024 Ashkhabad, Turkmenistan. Contact: K. Karayev; Yu M. Pashev, Deputy Chairman of State Television and Radio Company.

UGANDA World Time +3

RADIO UGANDA, P.O. Box 7142, Kampala, Uganda. Fax: +256 (41) 256 888. Contact: Kikulwe Rashid Harolin or A.K. Mlamizo. $1 or return postage required. Replies infrequently and slowly.

UKRAINE World Time +2 (+3 midyear)

Warning—Mail Theft: For the time being, letters to Ukrainian stations, especially containing funds or IRCs, are most likely to arrive safely if sent by registered mail.

RADIO UKRAINE INTERNATIONAL, ul. Kreshchatik 26, 252001 Kiev, Ukraine. Free stickers and Ukrainian stamps. Replies slowly and, as of late, irregularly, perhaps because of deteriorating mail service.

RADIO LUGANSK, ul. Dem'ochina 25, 348000 Lugansk, Ukraine. Contact: A.N.Mospanova.

RADIO NEZALEZHNIST (Radio Independence), ul. Vatutina 6, 290005 Lvov, Ukraine.

UKRAINIAN RADIO, ul. Kreshchatik 26, 252001 Kiev, Ukraine. Contact: Vasyl Yurychek, Vice President of State Television and Radio Company.

UNITED ARAB EMIRATES World Time +4
CAPITAL RADIO—see UAE Radio from Abu Dhabi, below, for details.
UAE RADIO IN DUBAI, P.O. Box 1695, Dubai, United Arab Emirates. Fax: +971 (4) 374 111 or +971 (4) 370 975. Contact: (technical) K.F. Fenner, Chief Engineer—Radio; or Ahmed Al Muhaideb. Free pennants.
UAE RADIO FROM ABU DHABI, Ministry of Information & Culture, P.O. Box 63, Abu Dhabi, United Arab Emirates. Fax: +971 (2) 451 155. Contact: (nontechnical) Ahmed A. Shouly, Controller General & Producer, "Mailbag"; Aïda Hamza, Director; or Abdul Hadi Mubarak, Producer, "Live Program"; (technical) Ibrahim Rashid, Technical Department; or Fauzi Saleh, Chief Engineer. Free stickers, postcards and stamps.
UNITED KINGDOM World Time exactly (+1 midyear)
BBC WORLD SERVICE
Main Office, Nontechnical: P.O. Box 76, Bush House, Strand, London WC2B 4PH, United Kingdom. Fax: ("Write On" listeners' letters program) +44 (71) 497 0287; (general information, World Service) +44 (71) 240 8760; (general information, World Service in English) +44 (71) 379 6785; (World Service Shop) +44 (71) 379 6640; Contact: ("Write On") Paddy Feeny, Presenter; Ernest Warburton, Editor, World Service in English. Superb monthly *BBC Worldwide* magazine, which may be subscribed to for $40 or £24 per year. Numerous audio/video (PAL/VHS only for video) recordings, publications (including *Passport to World Band Radio*), portable world band radios, T-shirts, sweatshirts and other BBC souvenirs available by mail from BBC World Service Shop, at the above London address (VISA/MC/AX/Access). Tapes of BBC programs from BBC Topical Tapes, also at the above London address. *BBC English* magazine, to aid in learning English, from BBC English, P.O. Box 96, Cambridge, United Kingdom. Also, *see* Antigua, Ascension Island, Oman, Seychelles and Singapore, which are where technical correspondence concerning these BBC relay transmissions should be sent if you seek a reply with full verification data, as no such data are provided via the London address.
Main Office, Technical: BBC Coverage Department, Reception Analysis Unit, Room 703, N.E. Wing, BBC World Service, P.O. Box 76, Bush House, Strand, London WC2B 4PH, United Kingdom. Fax: +44 (71) 240 8926. Contact: James Chilton, Engineer. This address only for technical reception reports from those interested in regular monitoring.
Foreign Broadcasts Monitoring: BBC Monitoring, Caversham Park, Reading RG4 8TZ, United Kingdom. Fax: +44 (734) 461 993. Contact: (sales) Ann Dubina, Marketing Department; (monitoring) Richard Measham, Manager. World Broadcasting Information. World band schedules and weekly *WBI* newsletter for £350 plus air postage per year; audio and teletype feeds for news agencies and others; and world broadcasting program summaries for researchers.
New York Office: 630 Fifth Avenue, New York NY 10020 USA. Fax: +1 (212) 245 0565. Contact: (nontechnical) Heather Maclean, World Service Affairs.
Ottawa Office: P.O. Box 1555, Station "B", Ottawa ON, K1P 5R5 Canada.
Paris Office: 155 rue du Faubourg St. Honoré, F-75008 Paris, France. Fax: +33 (1) 45 63 67 12.
Berlin Office: Savingnyplatz 6, W-1000 Berlin 12, Germany.
Tokyo Office: P.O. Box 29, Kopjimachi, Tokyo, Japan.
Singapore Office: P.O. Box 434, Maxwell Road Post Office, Singapore 9008, Singapore. Fax: +65 253 8131.
Australian Office: Suite 101, 80 William Street, East Sydney, NSW 2011, Australia. Fax: 61 (2) 361 0853. Contact: (nontechnical) Michelle Rowland; or Marilyn Eccles, Information Desk.
BRITISH FORCES BROADCASTING SERVICE, Bridge House, North Wharf Road, London W2 1LA, United Kingdom. Fax: +44 (71) 706 1582. Contact: Richard Astbury, Station Manager. Free station brochure.
UNITED NATIONS World Time –5 (–4 midyear)
UNITED NATIONS RADIO, R/S-850, United Nations, UN Plaza, New York NY 10017 USA; or write the station over which UN Radio was heard (Radio Myanmar, Radio Cairo, China Radio International Sierra Leone Broadcasting Service, Radio Zambia, Radio Tanzania, Polish Radio Warsaw, Voice of the OAS, HCJB/Ecuador, IRRS/Italy, All India Radio or RFPI/Costa Rica). Fax: +1 (212) 963 0765. Contact: Sylvester E. Rowe, Chief, Electronic Magazine

and Features Service; Ayman El-Amir, Chief, Radio Section, Department of Public Information; Carmen Blandon, Secretary. Free UN stickers, T-shirts, pennants, stamps and *UN Frequency* publication.
Paris Office: UNESCO Radio, 7 Pl.de Fontenoy, 75018 Paris, France. Fax: +33 (1) 45 67 30 72. Contact: Erin Faherty, Executive Radio Producer.
URUGUAY World Time –2 (–3 midyear)
EL ESPECTADOR, Río Branco 1483, 11100 Montevideo, Uruguay.
LA VOZ DE ARTIGAS, Av. Lecueder 483, 55000 Artigas, Uruguay.
RADIO INTEGRACION AMERICANA, Soriano 1287, 11100 Montevideo, Uruguay. Contact: Andrea Cruz. $1 or return postage required. Replies irregularly to correspondence in Spanish.
RADIO MONTE CARLO, Av. 18 de Julio 1224, 11100 Montevideo, Uruguay. Contact: Ana Ferreira de Errázquin, Secretaria, Departamento de Prensa de la Cooperativa de Radioemisoras; or Ulises Graceras. Correspondence in Spanish preferred.
RADIO ORIENTAL—Same as Radio Monte Carlo, above.
SODRE
Publicity: Casilla 1412, 11000 Montevideo, Uruguay. Contact: Daniel Ayala González, Publicidad.
Other: "Radioactividades," Casilla 801 (or Casilla 6541), 11000 Montevideo, Uruguay. Fax: +598 (2) 48 71 27. Contact: Daniel Muñoz Faccioli.
USA World Time –4 Atlantic, including Puerto Rico and Virgin Islands; –5 (–4 midyear) Eastern, excluding Indiana; –5 Indiana, except northwest and southwest portions; –6 (–5 midyear) Central, including northwest and southwest Indiana; –7 (–6 midyear) Mountain, except Arizona; –7 Arizona; –8 (–7 midyear) Pacific; –9 (–10 midyear) Alaska, except Aleutian Islands; –10 (–11 3midyear) Aleutian Islands; –10 Hawaii; –11 Samoa
ADVENTIST WORLD RADIO, THE VOICE OF HOPE
World Headquarters: 12501 Old Columbia Pike, Silver Spring MD 20904 USA. Fax: +1 (301) 680 6303 and +1 (301) 680 6390. Contact: (nontechnical) Walter R.L. Scragg, President; or Greg Hodgson; (technical) Technical Director. Free religious printed matter, pennants, stickers and other small souvenirs. IRC or $1 appreciated. Technical correspondence is best sent to the country where the transmitter is located—Costa Rica, Guam, Guatemala, Italy, Perú or Russia. Provides aid to the poor via the Adventist Development and Relief Agency.
Indiana Headquarters: 15250 N. Meridian Street, Carmel IN 46032 USA. Contact: (technical or nontechnical) Dr. Adrian M. Peterson, Special Projects Coordinator. Provides DX Clubs with regular news releases and technical information.
German Headquarters: P.O. Box 13 02 08, D-64242 Darmstadt 13, Germany. Fax: +49 (6151) 537 639. Contact: Mrs. Andrea Steele, PR Director. Free religious printed matter, pennants, stickers and other small souvenirs.
Hong Kong Office: AWR-Asia, P.O. Box 310, Hong Kong. Free religious printed matter, stickers, pennants and other small souvenirs.
CHRISTIAN SCIENCE MONITOR, SHORTWAVE WORLD SERVICE, WCNS/WSHB/KHBI, P.O. Box 860, Boston MA 02123 USA. Toll-free telephone (U.S. only) (800) 288-7090 [+1 (617) 450-2929 outside U.S.], extension 2060 (24-hour for schedules) or 2929 (Shortwave Helpline). Telephone: "Monitor Radio Listener Line" +1 (617) 450-7777. Contact: Catherine Aitken-Smith, Director of International Broadcasting, Herald Broadcasting Syndicate; Bill Badger, Host, "Letterbox"; or Dave Casanave, Producer, "Letterbox." Free stickers and information on Christian Science religion. *Christian Science Monitor* newspaper and full line of Christian Science books available from 1 Norway Street, Boston MA 02115 USA. *Science and Health with Key to the Scriptures* available in English for $14.95 ($16.95 in French, German, Portuguese or Spanish) from Science and Health, P.O. Box 1875, Boston MA 02117 USA. Also, *see* Northern Mariana Islands.
CHRISTIAN SCIENCE MONITOR, SHORTWAVE WORLD SERVICE/WCSN, P.O. Box 130, Costigan ME 04423 USA. Fax: +1 (207) 732 4741. Contact: (technical) Ken Fox, Engineer; or Robert Stessel, Station Manager. This address for technical feedback on Maine transmissions only; other inquiries should be directed to the usual Boston address.
CHRISTIAN SCIENCE MONITOR, SHORTWAVE WORLD SERVICE/WSHB, Rt. 2, Box 107A, Pineland SC 29934 USA. Fax: +1 (803) 625 5559. Contact: (technical) Tony Kobatake, Chief Transmitter Engineer; C. Ed Evans, Senior Station Manager; or Judy P.

Cooke. This address for technical feedback on South Carolina transmissions only; other inquiries should be directed to the usual Boston address.

C-SPAN, 400 N. Capitol Street NW, Suite 650, Washington DC 20001 USA. Fax: +1 (202) 737 3323. Contact: Thomas Patton, Audio Network; or Rayne Pollack, Manager, Press Relations. Relays selected world band broadcasts over U.S. cable systems.

KGEI—VOICE OF FRIENDSHIP, 1406 Radio Road, Redwood City CA 94065 USA. Fax: +1 (415) 591 0233. Contact: (nontechnical) Dean Brubaker, General Manager; or José Holowaty, Producer, "Contestamos"; (technical) Lewis Entz, Chief Engineer. Free religious literature.

KJES—KING JESUS ETERNAL SAVIOR

Station: The Lord's Ranch, Star Route Box 300, Mesquite NM 88048 USA. Fax: +1 (505) 233 3019. Contact: (nontechnical or technical) Michael Reuter. $1 or return postage required.

Sponsoring Organization: Our Lady's Youth Center, P.O. Box 1422, El Paso TX 79948 USA.

KNLS—NEW LIFE STATION

Operations Center: World Christian Broadcasting Corporation, P.O. Box 681706, Franklin TN 37068 USA (letters sent to the Alaska transmitter site are usually forwarded to Franklin). Fax: +1 (615) 371 8791. Contact: Wesley Jones, Manager, Follow-Up Department; Mrs. Beverly Jones, Follow-Up Department; or Michael Osborne, Production Manager. Free pennants, stickers, Russian language religious tapes and literature, and English-language learning course materials for Russian speakers. Swaps cancelled stamps from different countries to help listeners round out their stamp collections. Return postage helpful.

Transmitter Site: P.O. Box 473, Anchor Point AK 99556 USA. Contact: (technical) Kevin Chambers, Engineer.

Administrative Office: P.O. Box 3857, Abilene TX 79604 USA. Fax: +1 (915) 676 5663.

Tokyo Office: P.O. Box 27, Tachikawa, Tokyo 190, Japan. Fax: +81 (425) 34 0062.

KTBN—TRINITY BROADCASTING NETWORK:

General Correspondence: P.O. Box A, Santa Ana CA 92711 USA. Fax: +1 (714) 731 4196 or +1 (714) 730 0661. Contact: Alice Fields. Monthly TBN newsletter. Religious merchandise sold. Return postage helpful.

Technical Correspondence: Engineering/QSL Department, 2442 Michelle Drive, Tustin CA 92680 USA. Contact: Ben Miller, WB5TLZ, Director of Engineering.

KVOH—HIGH ADVENTURE RADIO

Main Office: P.O. Box 93937, Los Angeles CA 90093 USA. Fax: +1 (805) 520 7823. Contact: (nontechnical) Mark Gallardo, General Manager; John Tayloe, International Program Director; David E. Laufer, Public Relations; or Pat Kowalick, Producer, "Music of Hope"; (technical) Dr. Don Myers, Chief Engineer. Free stickers, *Voice of Hope* book, "High Adventure Ministries" pamphlet and sample "Voice of Hope" broadcast tape. Also, *see* Lebanon. Replies as time permits. **ADS AIR**

Canadian Office, Nontechnical: Box 425, Station "E", Toronto, M6H 4E3 Canada. Contact: Don McLaughlin, Director. **ADS AIR**

London Office, Nontechnical: BM Box 2575, London WC1N 3XX, United Kingdom. Contact: Paul Ogle, Director. **ADS AIR**

Singapore Office: Orchard Point, P.O. Box 796, 9123 Singapore. **ADS AIR**

KWHR, WHRI/KWHR, P.O. Box 12, South Bend IN 46624 USA. Fax: +1 (219) 291 9043. Contact: (nontechnical) Joe Hill, World Band Manager; or Peter Sumrall, Vice President. KWHR expects to be on the air from Hawaii by the end of 1993. Free stickers. **AIR**

RADIO FREE AFGHANISTAN—see RFE-RL, below, for details.

RADIO MARTI—see Voice of America, below, for details, but contact: Mike Pallone; or Bruce Sherman, Deputy Director.

RFE-RL

Main Office: Oettingenstrasse. 67 AM Englischen Garten, D-80538 Munich 22, Germany. Fax: (general) +49 (89) 228 5188; (Public Affairs) +49 (89) 2102 3322. Contact: (nontechnical) Terry B. Shroeder, Director, Public Affairs, Mail Box 5; or Melissa Fleming, Public Affairs Specialist, Mail Box 5.

Washington Office, Nontechnical: 1201 Connecticut Avenue NW, 11th floor, Washington DC 20036 USA. Contact: Patricia Gates Lynch. Fax: +1 (202) 457 6998.

New York Office: 1775 Broadway, New York NY 10019 USA. Fax: +1 (212) 397 5380. Contact: (*RFE Research Report*) Irina Klionsky;

(technical) David Walcutt, Engineering. Annual subscription to *RFE Research Report* $150, $75 for students.

Governing Organization: Board for International Broadcasting, 1201 Connecticut Avenue, N.W., Suite 400, Washington DC 20036 USA. Fax: +1 (202) 254 3929. Contact: Malcolm S. Forbes, Jr., Chairman; Bianca McHugh; or Gregory Garland.

TRANS WORLD RADIO, International Headquarters, P.O. Box 700, Cary NC 27512 USA. Fax: +1 (919) 460 3702. Contact: (nontechnical) Donna Moss, Public Affairs; Rosemarie Jaszka, Director, Public Relations; or Mark Christensen. Free "Towers to Eternity" publication. Technical correspondence should be sent directly to the country where the transmitter is located—Guam, Monaco, Netherlands Antilles, Sri Lanka or Swaziland. **AIR**

VOICE OF AMERICA/VOA—ALL TRANSMITTER LOCATIONS

Main Office: 330 Independence Avenue SW, Washington DC 20547 USA. If contacting the VOA directly is impractical, write c/o the American Embassy or USIS Center in your country. Fax: (general information) +1 (202) 376 1066; (Public Liaison) +1 (202) 485 1241; (Office of External Affairs) +1 (202) 205 0634; or (Africa Division) +1 (202) 619 1664. Contact: (listeners outside the United States) Irene Greene, Audience Mail, Room G-759. (listeners within the United States) Janice Davis, In Charge of Correspondence, Room 3323. Free key rings, *The Constitution of the United States* book, sundry booklets on the United States, stickers, posters, pens, plastic tote bags, tie tack pins and other items to listeners with addresses *outside* the United States. Free "Music Time in Africa" calendar, to non-U.S. addresses only, from Mrs. Rita Rochelle, Africa Division, Room 1602. If you're an American and miffed because you can't receive these goodies from the VOA, don't blame the station—they're only following the law.

Main Office, Technical: 330 Independence Avenue SW, Washington DC 20547 USA. Contact: Irene Green, Verification Officer.

Frequency and Monitoring Office, Technical: VOA:EOFF: Frequency Management & Monitoring Division, 330 Independence Avenue SW, Washington DC 20547 USA. Fax: +1 (202) 619 1781. Contact: Dan Ferguson. Enclosing pre-addressed labels will help with reply. Also, *see* Ascension Island, Botswana and Sri Lanka.

Portuguese Office: Apartado 4258, Lisbon 1700, Portugal.

VOICE OF AMERICA/VOA CINCINNATI—BETHANY RELAY STATION, P.O. Box 227, Mason OH 45040 USA. Fax: +1 (513) 777 4736. Contact: (technical) John Vodenik, WB9AUJ, Engineer. Nontechnical correspondence should be sent to the appropriate contact person at the VOA address in Washington.

VOICE OF AMERICA/VOA—DELANO RELAY STATION, Rt. 1, Box 1350, Delano CA 93215 USA. Fax: +1 (805) 725 6511. Contact: (technical) Jim O'Neill, Engineer. Nontechnical correspondence should be sent to the VOA address in Washington.

VOICE OF AMERICA/VOA—GREENVILLE RELAY STATION, P.O. Box 1826, Greenville NC 27834 USA. Fax: +1 (919) 752 5959. Contact: (technical) Dennis Brewer, Deputy Manager. Nontechnical correspondence should be sent to the VOA address in Washington.

VOICE OF THE OAS, Organization of American States, 17th St. & Constitution Avenue NW, Washington DC 20006 USA. Fax: +1 (202) 458 3930. Contact: Mario Martínez, Co-director; or Carlos Flores, Co-director.

WCSN—see Christian Science Monitor, above.

WEWN SHORTWAVE RADIO, Eternal Word Radio Network (ETWN), Catholic Radio Service, P.O. Box 100234, Birmingham AL 35210 USA. Fax: (Engineering) +1 (205) 672 9988; (all others) +1 (205) 951 0340. Contact: (nontechnical) William Steltemeier, President; or W. Glen Tapley, Director of Network Radio Operations; (technical) Matt Cadak, Chief Engineer. Sells religious publications, as well as possibly T-shirts, world band radios and related items. IRC or return postage requested. Their order may be reached at Our Lady of Angels Monastery, 5817 Old Leeds Road, Birmingham AL 35210 USA.

WHRI—WORLD HARVEST RADIO, WHRI/KWHR, P.O. Box 12, South Bend IN 46624 USA. Fax: +1 (219) 291 9043. Contact: (nontechnical) Joe Hill, World Band Manager; Peter Sumrall, Vice President; or Robert Willinger; (technical) Joe Hill, Operations Manager; (technical) Douglas Garlinger, Chief Engineer. Free stickers. Return postage appreciated. Carries programs from various expatriate political organizations, such as Cuban nationalist groups; these may be contacted via WHRI. "For the People" may be contacted direct at the Telford Hotel, 3 River Street, White

Springs FL 32096 USA; fax: +1 (904) 397 4149; toll-free telephone (U.S.only) (800) 888-9999. **ADS AIR**

WINB, P.O. Box 88, Red Lion PA 17356 USA. Fax: +1 (717) 244 9316. Contact: John Thomas; or John W. Norris, Jr., Manager. Return postage helpful outside United States. **AIR**

WJCR, P.O. Box 91, Upton KY 42784 USA. Contact: Pastor Don Powell, President; Gerri Powell; or Trish Powell. Free religious printed matter. Return postage appreciated. Actively solicits listener contributions.

WMLK—ASSEMBLIES OF YAHWEH, P.O. Box C, Bethel PA 19507 USA. Contact: Elder Jacob O. Mayer, Manager & Producer of "The Open Door to the Living World." Free *Yahweh* magazine, stickers and religious material. Bibles and religious paperback books offered for sale. Replies slowly, but enclosing return postage or IRCs helps speed things up.

WRMI—RADIO MIAMI INTERNACIONAL
Main Office: P.O. Box 526852, Miami FL 33152 USA. Fax: +1 (305) 267 9253. Contact: (nontechnical or technical) Jeff White, Producer, "Miami en Vivo"; (technical) Indalecio "Kiko" Espinosa, Chief Engineer. Free station stickers. Radio Miami Internacional also acts as a broker for anti-Castro programs aired via U.S. stations WHRI and WRNO. Technical correspondence may be sent either to WRMI or to the station over which the program was heard. **ADS AIR**
Venezuelan Office: Apartado 485, Valencia 2001, Venezuela. Contact: Yoslen Silva. **ADS AIR**

WRNO, Box 100, New Orleans LA 70181 USA; or 4539 I-10 Service Road North, Metairie LA 70006 USA. Fax: +1 (504) 889 0602. Contact: Joseph Mark Costello III, General Manager; David Schneider; Joe Pollett; or Jack Bruce. Free stickers. T-shirts available for $10. Reception reports to the Rush Limbaugh Show should be sent directly to WRNO, but program-orientated correspondence or calls should be directed to: Rush Limbaugh, EIB World Band, WABC, #2 Pennsylvania Avenue, New York NY 10121 USA; telephone (toll-free, USA only) (800) 282-2882; fax (during working hours) +1 (212) 563 9166. **ADS AIR**

WSHB—*see* Christian Science Monitor, above.

WWCR—WORLD WIDE CHRISTIAN RADIO, F.W. Robbert Broadcasting Co., 1300 WWCR Avenue, Nashville TN 37218 USA. Contact: (nontechnical) Adam W. Lock, Sr., WA2JAL, International Program Director; George McClintock, K4BTY, General Manager; or Joseph Brashier, National Program Director; (technical) Watt Hariston, Chief Engineer. Free program guide, updated monthly. Return postage helpful. Replies as time permits. Has fully returned to the air after having been destroyed by a fire of undetermined origin in April, 1993. **ADS AIR**

WWV, Frequency-Time Broadcast Services Section, Time and Frequency Division, NIST, Mail Station 847, 2000 East County Road #58, Boulder CO 80524 USA. Fax: +1 (303) 497 3371. Contact: (technical) James C. Maxton, Engineer-in-Charge; or John B. Milton. Free Special Publication 432 "NIST Time & Frequency Services" pamphlet.

WWVH, NIST, P.O. Box 417, Kekaha, Kauai HI 96752 USA. Fax: +1 (808) 335 4747. Contact: (technical) Dean T. Yokohama, Engineer-in-Charge. Free Special Publication 432 "NIST Time & Frequency Services" pamphlet.

WYFR—FAMILY RADIO
Nontechnical: Family Stations, Inc., 290 Hegenberger Road, Oakland CA 94621 USA. Toll-free telephone (U.S. only) (800) 534-1495. Fax: +1 (415) 562 1023 or +1 (415) 430 0893. Contact: Producer, "Mailbag"; Producer, "Open Forum"; or Thomas A. Schaff, Shortwave Program Manager. Free stickers, bookmarks, pocket diaries (sometimes), religious books and booklets, and quarterly *Family Radio News* magazine. **ADS**
Technical: WYFR/Family Radio, 10400 NW 240th Street, Okeechobee FL 34972 USA. Fax: +1 (813) 763 8867. Contact: Dan Elyea, Engineering Manager.

UZBEKISTAN World Time +5
RADIO TASHKENT, 49 Khorezm Street, 740047 Tashkent, Uzbekistan. Contact: V. Danchev, Correspondence Section; Zulfiya Ibragimova; Mrs. G. Babadjanova, Chief Director of Programmes; or Mrs. Florida Perevertailo, Producer, "At Listeners' Request and Others." Free pennants, badges, wallet calendars and postcards. Books in English by Uzbek writers are apparently available for purchase.
UZBEK RADIO—*see* Radio Tashkent for details.

VANUATU World Time +12 (+11 midyear)
RADIO VANUATU, Information & Public Relations, P.M.B. 049,

Port Vila, Vanuatu. Fax: +678 22026 (no direct dial as yet). Contact: (technical) K.J. Page, Principal Engineer.

VATICAN CITY STATE World Time +1 (+2 midyear)
RADIO VATICANA, 00120 Città del Vaticano, Vatican State (via Italy). Fax: (Direction General) +39 (6) 6988 3237; (Technical Direction) +39 (6) 6988 5125. Contact: Fr. Federico Lombardi, S.J., Program Manager; Fr. Pasquale Borgomeo, S.I., Direttore Generale; S. de Maillardoz, International Relations; or Umberto Tolaini. Correspondence sought on religious and programming matters, rather than the technical minutiae of radio. Free station stickers. Compact disc musical recordings for $13 each from Ufficio Promozione e Sviluppo, Radio Vaticana, 00120 Città del Vaticano, Vatican State.

VENEZUELA World Time –4
ECOS DEL TORBES, Apartado 152, San Cristóbal 5001, Táchira, Venezuela. Contact: (nontechnical) Eleázer Silva Malave, Director; or Gregorio González Lovera, Presidente; (technical) Ing. Iván Escobar S., Jefe Técnico.

RADIO CONTINENTAL, Apartado 202, Barinas 5201, Venezuela. Contact: (nontechnical) Angel M. Pérez, Director; (technical) Ing. Santiago San Gil G. $1, return postage or 2 IRCs required. Free small souvenirs. Replies occasionally to correspondence in Spanish.

RADIO CONTINENTE, Apartado Postal 866, Caracas 1010-A, Venezuela. Replies occasionally to correspondence in Spanish.

RADIO FRONTERA, Edificio Radio, San Antonio del Táchira, Táchira, Venezuela. Contact: N. Marchena, Director. May reply to correspondence in Spanish. $1 or return postage suggested. If no reply, try with $1 via Sr. Contín at Radio Mara, below.

RADIO LOS ANDES, Apartado 40, Mérida, Venezuela. May reply to correspondence in Spanish. $1 or return postage suggested.

RADIO MARA, Calle Los Lirios No. 1219, Urbanización Miraflores, Cabimas 4013, Zulia, Venezuela. Contact: Antonio J. Contín E. $1 required. Replies occasionally.

RADIO MARACAIBO, Calle 67 No. 24-88, Maracaibo, Venezuela. Contact: Máximo Flores Velázquez, Director-Gerente. $1 or return postage required. Replies to correspondence in Spanish. If no reply, try with $1 via Sr. Contín at Radio Mara, above.

RADIO NACIONAL DE VENEZUELA, RNV
Main Office: Apartado 3979, Caracas 1050, Venezuela. Contact: Martin G. Delfin, English News Director; Jaime Alsina, Director; or Sra. Haydee Briceno, Gerente. Free 50th anniversary stickers, while they last, and other small souvenirs. Lone Star exile Marty Delfin, a former TV newscaster, hails from San Antonio and UT/Austin, Texas. If no response, try Apartado 50700, Caracas 1050, Venezuela.
Miami Postal Address: Jet Cargo International, M-7, P.O. Box 020010, Miami FL 33102 USA. Contact: Martin G. Delfin, English News Director.

RADIO RUMBOS
Main Address: Apartado 2618, Caracas 1010A, Venezuela. Fax: +58 (2) 33 51 64. Contact: (nontechnical) Andrés Felipe Serrano, Vice-Presidente; (technical) Ing. José Corrales. Free pamphlets, keychains and stickers. $1 or IRC required. Replies occasionally to correspondence in Spanish.
Miami Address: P.O. Box 020010, Miami FL 33102 USA. **ADS AIR**

RADIO TACHIRA, Apartado 152, San Cristóbal 5001, Táchira, Venezuela. Contact: Desire González Zerpe, Director; or Eleázar Silva M., Gerente.

RADIO TURISMO (when operating), Apartado 12, Valera, Trujillo, Venezuela. Contact: Pedro José Fajardo, President. Rarely replies to correspondence in Spanish. If no reply, try with $1 via Sr. Contín at Radio Mara, above.

RADIO VALERA, Av. 10 No. 9-31, Valera, Trujillo, Venezuela. If no reply, try with $1 via Sr. Contín at Radio Mara, above.

VIETNAM World Time +7
BAC THAI BROADCASTING SERVICE—contact via "Voice of Vietnam, Overseas Service," below.
LAI CHAU BROADCASTING SERVICE—contact via "Voice of Vietnam, Overseas Service," below.
LAM DONG BROADCASTING SERVICE, Da Lat, Vietnam. Contact: Hoang Van Trung. Replies slowly to correspondence in Vietnamese, but French may also suffice.
SON LA BROADCASTING SERVICE, Son La, Vietnam. Contact: Nguyen Hang, Director. Replies slowly to correspondence in Vietnamese, but French may also suffice.

RCI

Where it all comes from: Radio Canada's mighty transmitting facilities at Sackville, New Brunswick. These not only beam RCI's programs, but also those of the BBC World Service, Deutsche Welle, Radio Korea, China Radio International, Radio Monte Carlo, Radio Austria International and Radio Japan.

VOICE OF VIETNAM, Domestic Service - see Voice of Vietnam, Overseas Service, below. Contact: Phan Quang, Director General.
VOICE OF VIETNAM, Overseas Service, 58 Quan Su Street, Hanoi, Vietnam; or (technical) Office of Radio Reception Quality, Central Department of Radio and Television Broadcast Engineering, Vietnam General Corporation of Posts and Telecommunications, Hanoi, Vietnam. Contact: Dao Dinh Tuan, Director of External Broadcasting. Free pennant and Vietnamese stamps. $1 helpful, but IRCs apparently of no use. Replies slowly.
YEN BAI BROADCASTING STATION—contact via "Voice of Vietnam, Overseas Service," above.
YEMEN World Time +3
REPUBLIC OF YEMEN RADIO—ADEN, Program 2, P.O. Box 1222, Tawahi, Aden, Yemen. Contact: Ahmed Abdulla Fadaq, Director of Oriented and Foreign Programs. Free station pamphlet in English and Arabic. Replies occasionally and slowly.
REPUBLIC OF YEMEN RADIO—SAN'A, Ministry of Information, San'a, Yemen. Contact: (nontechnical correspondence in English) English Service; (technical) Abdullah Farhan, Technical Director.
YUGOSLAVIA World Time +1 (+2 midyear)
RADIO BEOGRAD, Hilendarska 2/IV, YU-11000 Belgrade, Serbia, Yugoslavia. Fax: +38 (11) 332 014. Contact: (technical) B. Miletic, Operations Manager of HF Broadcasting.
RADIO YUGOSLAVIA, P.O. Box 200, Hilendarska 2/IV, YU-11000 Belgrade, Serbia, Yugoslavia. Fax: +38 (11) 332 014. Contact: (nontechnical) Aleksandar Georgiev; Aleksandar Popovic, Head of Public Relations; Pance Zafirovski, Head of Programs; or Slobodan Topović, Producer, "Post Office Box 200/Radio Hams' Corner." (technical) B. Miletic, Operations Manager of HF Broadcasting, Technical Department; or Rodoljub Medan, Chief Engineer. Free pennants and pins. $1 helpful. Responses are now relatively fast, friendly and reliable.
ZAIRE World Time +1 Western, including Kinshasa; +2 Eastern
LA VOIX DU ZAIRE—BUKAVU, B.P. 475, Bukavu, Zaïre. Contact: Jacques Nyembo-Kibeya; or Baruti Lusongela, Directeur Sez. $1 or return postage required. Replies slowly. Correspondence in French preferred.

LA VOIX DU ZAIRE—KINSHASA, B.P. 3171, Kinshasa-Gombe, Zaïre. Contact: Ayimpam Mwan-a-ngo, Directeur des Programmes, Radio; or Faustin Mbula, Ingenieur Technicien. Letters should be sent via registered mail. $1 or 3 IRCs helpful. Correspondence in French preferred.
LA VOIX DU ZAIRE—KISANGANI, B.P. 1745, Kisangani, Zaïre. Contact: (nontechnical) Lumeto lue Lumeto, Le Directeur Regional de l'O.Z.R.T.; (technical) Lukusa Kowumayi Branly, Technician. $1 or 2 IRCs required. Correspondence in French preferred. Replies to North American listeners sometimes are mailed via the Oakland, California, post office.
RADIO LUBUMBASHI, LA VOIX DU ZAIRE, B.P. 7296, Lubumbashi, Zaïre. Contact: Senga Lokavu, Le Chef du Service de l'Audiovisuel; Bébé Beshelemu, Le Directeur Regional de l'O.Z.R.T; or Mulenga Kanso, Le Chef du Service Logistique. Letters should be sent via registered mail. $1 or 3 IRCs helpful. Correspondence in French preferred.
ZAMBIA World Time +2
RADIO ZAMBIA, Broadcasting House, P.O. Box 50015, Lusaka, Zambia. Fax: +260 (1) 254013. Contact: (nontechnical) Emmanuel Chayi, Acting Director-General; (technical) W. Lukozu, Project Engineer. $1 required, and postal correspondence should be sent via registered mail. Replies slowly and irregularly.

Credits: Craig Tyson; also Tony Jones, Lawrence Magne, Número Uno *and* Radio Nuevo Mundo, *with special thanks to Abdelkader Abbadi,* DX Moscow/*Anatoly Klepov, Gabriel Iván Barrera, Antonio Ribeiro da Motta, Gordon Darling, Marie Lamb, Gigi Lytle, Toshimichi Ohtake, George Poppin, Thomas Risher and Harlan Seyfer.*

Blue Pages

Channel-by-Channel Guide to World Band Schedules

Hard to believe, but there are *hundreds* of channels of news, music and entertainment packed into world band radio. Most are actually shared by several stations!

With so many choices, it's no wonder it takes some doing just to figure out what's on, when.

Schedules at a Glance

With *Passport*'s Blue Pages, everything—stations, times, languages, targets and more—shows up at a glance. If an abbreviation or something else isn't clear, the Glossary at the back of the book tells what's what. There is even a key to languages and symbols at the bottom of the pages.

Say you're in North America, listening to 6175 kHz at 2300 World Time. Look there, and it shows that the BBC World Service is broadcast in English to where you are, and at that time. The transmitter is located in Canada and operates at a power of 250 kW.

To help you hear as much as possible throughout the year, *Passport*'s schedules consist not just of observed activity, but also that which we have creatively opined will take place during the entire year. This latter information is original from us, and therefore will not be so exact as factual information.

When to Listen?

The best way to find stations is to tune in during the late afternoon and evening from 5800-13870 kHz summers, 4750-10000 kHz winters; outside North America, also try 3900-4000 kHz. For really helpful information on when and where to tune, see "Best Times and Frequencies for 1994" at the end of this book.

Stations Heard Beyond Designated Target

With several hundred stations on the air at the same time, many on the same channels, you can't begin to hear all—or even most. Yet, you can hear some fascinating stations even though they're not targeted to your part of the world.

Tune around, using the Blue Pages, and you'll discover more variety than if you just listened to stations aimed your way.

World Time

Times are given in World Time, with days of the week in World Day—all explained in the Glossary. Midyear, some programs are heard an hour earlier, but certain stations from the Southern Hemisphere buck the trend by being heard an hour later.

Guide to Blue Pages Format

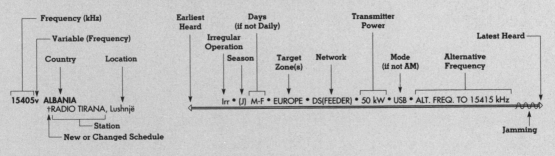

FREQUENCY   COUNTRY, STATION, LOCATION   TARGET • NETWORK • POWER (kW)   World Time

Freq	Country / Station / Location	Details
2310	**AUSTRALIA** ABC/CAAMA RADIO, Alice Springs	ENGLISH, ETC • Australasia • DS • 50 kW
2325	**AUSTRALIA** ABC/CAAMA RADIO, Tennant Creek	ENGLISH, ETC • Australasia • DS • 50 kW
2340	**CHINA (PR)** †FUJIAN PEOPLES BS, Fuzhou	DS-1 • 10 kW / TAIWAN SVC • 10 kW
2349.8	**INDONESIA** RRI, Yogyakarta, Jawa	DS-TEMP INACTIVE • 1 kW
2360	**GUATEMALA** R MAYA DE BARILLAS, Huehuetenango	DS • 0.5 kW
2377	**INDONESIA** RRI, Surabaya, Jawa	Irr • DS • 0.5/1 kW
2380	**BRAZIL** RADIO EDUCADORA, Limeira	PORTUGUESE • DS-TEMP INACTIVE • 0.25 kW
2390	**GUATEMALA** †LA VOZ DE ATITLAN, Santiago Atitlán	SPANISH, ETC • DS • 1 kW / Su • SPANISH, ETC • DS • 1 kW
	INDONESIA RRI, Cirebon, Jawa	DS • 1 kW / DS-TEMP INACTIVE • 1 kW
	MEXICO RADIO HUAYACOCOTLA, Huayacocotla	Tu-Su • DS • 0.5 kW / M-Sa • DS • 0.5 kW
2410	**BRAZIL** R TRANSAMAZONICA, Sen'r Guiomard	PORTUGUESE • DS • 1 kW • ALT. FREQ. TO 3255 kHz
	PAPUA NEW GUINEA RADIO ENGA, Wabag	DS • 10 kW
2415	**CHINA (PR)** WENZHOU PEOPLES BS, Wenzhou	DS
2420	**BRAZIL** RADIO SAO CARLOS, São Carlos	Irr • PORTUGUESE • DS • 0.5 kW
2432.5	**INDONESIA** RRI, Banda Aceh	DS-TEMP INACTIVE • 1 kW
	RRI, Purwokerto, Jawa	DS-TEMP INACTIVE • 1 kW
2445	**CHINA (PR)** JIANGXI PEOPLES BS, Nanchang	DS-1 • 10 kW / Su • DS-1 • 10 kW
2460	**CHINA (PR)** YUNNAN PEOPLES BS, Kunming	DS-1 • 15 kW
2475	**CHINA (PR)** ZHEJIANG PBS, Hangzhou	DS-1 • 10 kW
2485	**AUSTRALIA** ABC/R RUM JUNGLE, Katherine	Australasia • DS • 50 kW
2490	**INDONESIA** RRI, Ujung Pandang	DS
2490.7	**BRAZIL** †RADIO 8 SETEMBRO, Descalvado	PORTUGUESE • DS • 0.25 kW
2495v	**MADAGASCAR** RTV MALAGASY, Antananarivo	Irr • DS-1 • 30/100 kW / Irr • M-F • DS-1 • 30/100 kW
2500	**AUSTRALIA** †VNG, Llandilo	WORLD TIME • 1 kW
	USA WWV, Ft Collins, Colorado	WEATHER/WORLD TIME • 2.5 kW
	WWVH, Kekaha, Hawaii	WEATHER/WORLD TIME • 5 kW
2560	**CHINA (PR)** †XINJIANG PBS, Urümqi	DS • 15 kW
2584.6	**INDONESIA** †RPD TENGAH SELATAN, Soë, Timur	DS • 0.3 kW / Irr • DS • 0.3 kW
2694v	**INDONESIA** RPD ENDE, Ende, Flores	DS-TEMP INACTIVE • 0.5 kW
2850v	**KOREA (DPR)** KOREAN CENTRAL BS, Pyongyang	KOREAN • DS • 100 kW
2904.8	**INDONESIA** †RPD NGADA, Bajawa, N Tenggara	DS • 0.5 kW / Irr • DS • 0.5 kW
2960.2	**INDONESIA** RPD MANGGARAI, Ruteng, Flores	DS • 0.3 kW
3000v	**INDONESIA** †RPD BENGKALIS, Bengkalis, Sumatera	DS • 0.25 kW
3000.5	**KOREA (DPR)** †YOUNG SOLDIERS BC	KOREAN • DS
3025.4	**KOREA (DPR)** †YOUNG SOLDIERS BC	KOREAN • DS
3143	**INDONESIA** †RPD BELITUNG, Tanjung Pandan, Sum	DS • 0.3 kW
3160	**INDONESIA** †RPHDI IND HILIR, Tembilahan, Sum	DS • 0.03 kW
3200	**SWAZILAND** †TRANS WORLD RADIO, Manzini	S Africa • 25 kW / (J) • S Africa • 25 kW / (J) • Su • S Africa • 25 kW
3200.4	**BOLIVIA** †RADIO 9 DE ABRIL, Pulacayo	DS / Tu-Su • DS
3204.4	**INDONESIA** RRI, Bandung, Jawa	DS • 10 kW
3205 (con'd)	**BRAZIL** R RIBEIRAO PRETO, Ribeirão Prêto	PORTUGUESE • DS • 1 kW

0 1 2 3 4 5 6 7 8 9 10 11 12 13 14 15 16 17 18 19 20 21 22 23 24

SUMMER ONLY (J)   WINTER ONLY (D)   JAMMING / OR ∧   EARLIEST HEARD ◁   LATEST HEARD ▷   NEW OR CHANGED FOR 1994 †

FREQUENCY   COUNTRY, STATION, LOCATION

TARGET • NETWORK • POWER (kW)

World Time

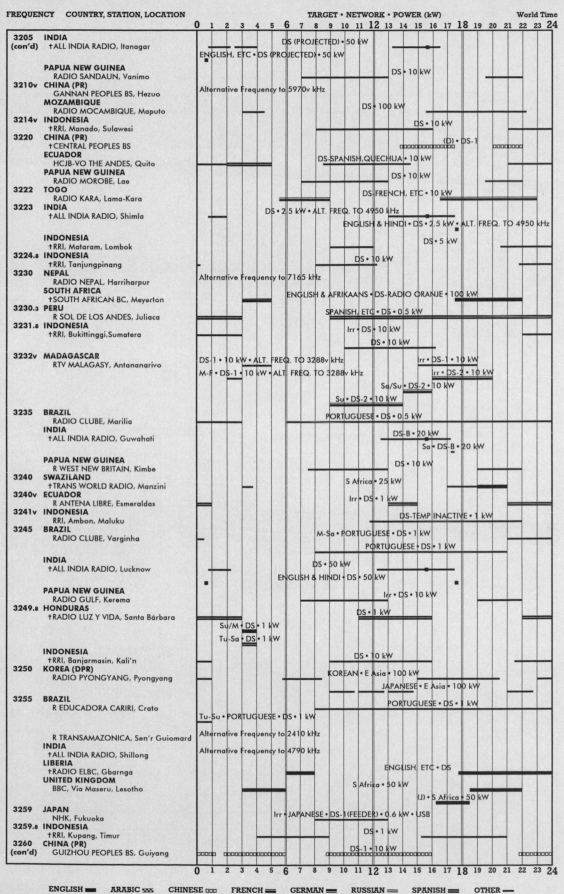

3205 (con'd)	**INDIA** †ALL INDIA RADIO, Itanagar	DS (PROJECTED) • 50 kW / ENGLISH, ETC • DS (PROJECTED) • 50 kW
	PAPUA NEW GUINEA RADIO SANDAUN, Vanimo	DS • 10 kW
3210v	**CHINA (PR)** GANNAN PEOPLES BS, Hezuo	Alternative Frequency to 5970v kHz
	MOZAMBIQUE RADIO MOCAMBIQUE, Maputo	DS • 100 kW
3214v	**INDONESIA** †RRI, Manado, Sulawesi	DS • 10 kW
3220	**CHINA (PR)** †CENTRAL PEOPLES BS	(D) • DS-1
	ECUADOR HCJB-VO THE ANDES, Quito	DS-SPANISH, QUECHUA • 10 kW
	PAPUA NEW GUINEA RADIO MOROBE, Lae	DS • 10 kW
3222	**TOGO** RADIO KARA, Lama-Kara	DS-FRENCH, ETC • 10 kW
3223	**INDIA** †ALL INDIA RADIO, Shimla	DS • 2.5 kW • ALT. FREQ. TO 4950 kHz / ENGLISH & HINDI • DS • 2.5 kW • ALT. FREQ. TO 4950 kHz
	INDONESIA †RRI, Mataram, Lombok	DS • 5 kW
3224.8	**INDONESIA** †RRI, Tanjungpinang	DS • 10 kW
3230	**NEPAL** RADIO NEPAL, Harriharpur	Alternative Frequency to 7165 kHz
	SOUTH AFRICA †SOUTH AFRICAN BC, Meyerton	ENGLISH & AFRIKAANS • DS-RADIO ORANJE • 100 kW
3230.3	**PERU** R SOL DE LOS ANDES, Juliaca	SPANISH, ETC • DS • 0.5 kW
3231.8	**INDONESIA** †RRI, Bukittinggi, Sumatera	Irr • DS • 10 kW / DS • 10 kW
3232v	**MADAGASCAR** RTV MALAGASY, Antananarivo	DS-1 • 10 kW • ALT. FREQ. TO 3288v kHz / M-F • DS-1 • 10 kW • ALT. FREQ. TO 3288v kHz / Irr • DS-1 • 10 kW / Irr • DS-2 • 10 kW / Sa/Su • DS-2 • 10 kW / Su • DS-2 • 10 kW
3235	**BRAZIL** RADIO CLUBE, Marilia	PORTUGUESE • DS • 0.5 kW
	INDIA †ALL INDIA RADIO, Guwahati	DS-B • 20 kW / Sa • DS-B • 20 kW
	PAPUA NEW GUINEA R WEST NEW BRITAIN, Kimbe	DS • 10 kW
3240	**SWAZILAND** †TRANS WORLD RADIO, Manzini	S Africa • 25 kW
3240v	**ECUADOR** R ANTENA LIBRE, Esmeraldas	Irr • DS • 1 kW
3241v	**INDONESIA** RRI, Ambon, Maluku	DS-TEMP INACTIVE • 1 kW
3245	**BRAZIL** RADIO CLUBE, Varginha	M-Sa • PORTUGUESE • DS • 1 kW / PORTUGUESE • DS • 1 kW
	INDIA †ALL INDIA RADIO, Lucknow	DS • 50 kW / ENGLISH & HINDI • DS • 50 kW
	PAPUA NEW GUINEA RADIO GULF, Kerema	Irr • DS • 10 kW
3249.8	**HONDURAS** †RADIO LUZ Y VIDA, Santa Bárbara	DS • 1 kW / Su/M • DS • 1 kW / Tu-Sa • DS • 1 kW
	INDONESIA †RRI, Banjarmasin, Kali'n	DS • 10 kW
3250	**KOREA (DPR)** RADIO PYONGYANG, Pyongyang	KOREAN • E Asia • 100 kW / JAPANESE • E Asia • 100 kW
3255	**BRAZIL** R EDUCADORA CARIRI, Crato	PORTUGUESE • DS • 1 kW / Tu-Su • PORTUGUESE • DS • 1 kW
	R TRANSAMAZONICA, Sen'r Guiomard	Alternative Frequency to 2410 kHz
	INDIA †ALL INDIA RADIO, Shillong	Alternative Frequency to 4790 kHz
	LIBERIA †RADIO ELBC, Gbarnga	ENGLISH, ETC • DS
	UNITED KINGDOM BBC, Via Maseru, Lesotho	S Africa • 50 kW / (J) • S Africa • 50 kW
3259	**JAPAN** NHK, Fukuoka	Irr • JAPANESE • DS-1 (FEEDER) • 0.6 kW • USB
3259.8	**INDONESIA** †RRI, Kupang, Timur	DS • 1 kW
3260 (con'd)	**CHINA (PR)** GUIZHOU PEOPLES BS, Guiyang	DS-1 • 10 kW

ENGLISH ▬   ARABIC ⬚⬚⬚   CHINESE ⬚⬚⬚   FRENCH ▬▬   GERMAN ▬▬   RUSSIAN ══   SPANISH ▬▬   OTHER ▬

FREQUENCY	COUNTRY, STATION, LOCATION	TARGET • NETWORK • POWER (kW) / World Time

3260 **NIGER**
(con'd) †LA VOIX DU SAHEL, Niamey — FRENCH, ETC • DS • 4 kW / Sa • FRENCH, ETC • DS • 4 kW

PAPUA NEW GUINEA
RADIO MADANG, Madang — DS • 10 kW

PERU
LA VOZ DE OXAPAMPA, Oxapampa — SPANISH, ETC • DS • 2.5 kW

3264.8 **INDONESIA**
†RRI, Bengkulu, Sumatera — DS • 10 kW

3265 **CONGO**
†RTV CONGOLAISE, Brazzaville — Alternative Frequency to 5985 kHz

3266.4 **INDONESIA**
†RRI, Gorontalo, Sulawesi — DS • 10 kW

3268 **INDIA**
†ALL INDIA RADIO, Kohima — DS-A • 50 kW • ALT. FREQ. TO 3277 kHz

†RADIO KASHMIR, Srinagar — Alternative Frequency to 3277 kHz

3269.3 **ECUADOR**
ECOS DEL ORIENTE, Lago Agrio — DS • 1 kW

3270 **NAMIBIA**
NAMIBIAN BC CORP, Windhoek — ENGLISH, GERMAN, ETC • DS • 100 kW

3275 **PAPUA NEW GUINEA**
R SOUTH HIGHLANDS, Mendi — DS • 10 kW

SWAZILAND
TRANS WORLD RADIO, Manzini — S Africa • 25 kW

VENEZUELA
RADIO MARA, Maracaibo — DS-VERY IRREGULAR • 1 kW

3277 **INDIA**
†ALL INDIA RADIO, Kohima — Alternative Frequency to 3268 kHz

†RADIO KASHMIR, Srinagar — DS-B • 50 kW • ALT. FREQ. TO 3268 kHz / ENGLISH, ETC • DS-B • 50 kW • ALT. FREQ. TO 3268 kHz

3277v **INDONESIA**
†RRI, Jakarta, Jawa — DS-TEMP INACTIVE • 1 kW

3279.8 **ECUADOR**
LA VOZ DEL NAPO, Tena — DS-SPANISH, ETC • 2.5 kW / Su • DS-SPANISH, ETC • 2.5 kW

3280 **CHINA (PR)**
VOICE OF PUJIANG, Shanghai — (D) • E Asia • ALT. FREQ. TO 3990 kHz

PERU
†ESTACION WARI — DS • 1 kW

3280v **MOZAMBIQUE**
EP DE SOFALA, Beira — DS-2 • 100 kW

3285 **BELIZE**
RADIO BELIZE, Belmopan — DS-ENGLISH, SPANISH • 1 kW

BRAZIL
RTV SENTINELA, Obidos — PORTUGUESE • DS • 1 kW

3285v **ECUADOR**
RADIO RIO TARQUI, Cuenca — DS • 0.36 kW / Irr • DS • 0.36 kW

3286 **INDONESIA**
†RRI, Madiun — DS • 10 kW

3288v **MADAGASCAR**
RTV MALAGASY, Antananarivo — Alternative Frequency to 3232v kHz

3289.8 **ECUADOR**
RADIO CENTRO, Ambato — SPANISH, ETC • DS • 0.5 kW

3290 **NAMIBIA**
NAMIBIAN BC CORP, Windhoek — DS • 100 kW

PAPUA NEW GUINEA
RADIO CENTRAL, Port Moresby — ENGLISH, ETC • DS • 10 kW

3296 **RUSSIA**
†RADIO MOSCOW — (D) • DS-MAYAK

3300 **GUATEMALA**
RADIO CULTURAL, Guatemala City — DS • 10 kW / M • DS • 10 kW / M-Sa • DS • 10 kW / Tu-Su • DS • 10 kW / Su • DS • 10 kW

3304.5 **INDIA**
†ALL INDIA RADIO, Ranchi — DS • 2 kW / ENGLISH & HINDI • DS • 2 kW

3305 **INDIA**
†ALL INDIA RADIO, Bhopal — Alternative Frequency to 3315 kHz

†ALL INDIA RADIO, Imphal — DS (PROJECTED) • 50 kW

PAPUA NEW GUINEA
RADIO WESTERN, Daru — ENGLISH, ETC • DS • 10 kW

3306.4 **INDONESIA**
†RRI, Dili, Timur — DS • 10 kW

3310 **CHINA (PR)**
JILIN PEOPLES BS, Changchun — Irr • DS • 10 kW

3315 **INDIA**
†ALL INDIA RADIO, Bhopal — DS-A • 10 kW • ALT. FREQ. TO 3305 kHz / ENGLISH & HINDI • DS-A • 10 kW • ALT. FREQ. TO 3305 kHz

PAPUA NEW GUINEA
RADIO MANUS, Lorengau — ENGLISH, ETC • DS • 10 kW

3316 **SIERRA LEONE**
SIERRA LEONE BS, Goderich — ENGLISH, ETC • DS • 10 kW

3320 **KOREA (DPR)**
RADIO PYONGYANG, Pyongyang — KOREAN • E Asia

PIRATE (EUROPE)
(con'd) "BLACK SEA RADIO, Ukraine — Sa • E Europe • USB

World Time: 0 1 2 3 4 5 6 7 8 9 10 11 12 13 14 15 16 17 18 19 20 21 22 23 24

FREQUENCY   COUNTRY, STATION, LOCATION   TARGET • NETWORK • POWER (kW)   World Time

Frequency	Country, Station, Location	Target • Network • Power
3320 (con'd)	SOUTH AFRICA †SOUTH AFRICAN BC, Meyerton	AFRIKAANS STEREO • 100 kW
3324.8	GUATEMALA R MAYA DE BARILLAS, Huehuetenango	DS • 1 kW
3325	BRAZIL RADIO LIBERAL, Belém	PORTUGUESE • DS • 5 kW
	RADIO TUPI, São Paulo	PORTUGUESE • DS • 2.5 kW
	INDONESIA †RRI, Palangkaráya, Kali'n	DS • 10 kW
	PAPUA NEW GUINEA R NORTH SOLOMONS, Rabaul	ENGLISH, ETC • DS • 8 kW
3325v	ECUADOR ONDAS QUEVEDENAS, Quevedo	Irr • DS • 1.5 kW
3326	NIGERIA RADIO NIGERIA, Lagos	ENGLISH, ETC • DS-1 • 50 kW
3329.8	PHILIPPINES †FAR EAST BC CO, Baco, Mindoro	DS
3330	COMOROS RADIO COMORO, Moroni	Irr • DS-TEMP INACTIVE • 4/60 kW
	RWANDA †RADIO RWANDA, Kigali	C Africa & E Africa • 20 kW / FRENCH, ENGLISH, ETC • C Africa & E Africa • 20 kW
3330.4	PERU ONDAS DEL HUALLAGA, Huánuco	DS • 0.5 kW • ALT. FREQ. TO 3331.2 kHz / Su • DS • 0.5 kW • ALT. FREQ. TO 3331.2 kHz
3331.2	PERU ONDAS DEL HUALLAGA, Huánuco	Alternative Frequency to 3330.4 kHz
3335	BRAZIL RADIO ALVORADA, Londrina	PORTUGUESE • DS • 5 kW • ALT. FREQ. TO 4865 kHz / Tu–Su • PORTUGUESE • DS • 5 kW • ALT. FREQ. TO 4865 kHz
	CHINA (TAIWAN) CENTRAL BC SYSTEM, T'ai-pei	PRC-5 (HAKKA) • 10 kW
	PAPUA NEW GUINEA RADIO EAST SEPIK, Wewak	DS • 10 kW
3338v	MOZAMBIQUE RADIO MOCAMBIQUE, Maputo	DS • 10 kW
3340	PERU RADIO ALTURA, Cerro de Pasco	DS • 1 kW
3340.2	BOLIVIA †RADIO VILOCO, Viloco	SPANISH, ETC • DS • 1 kW
3345	INDIA †ALL INDIA RADIO, Jaipur	Alternative Frequency to 4910 kHz / DS-A • 50 kW / ENGLISH & HINDI • DS-A • 50 kW
	†RADIO KASHMIR, Jammu	Alternative Frequency to 4950 kHz / DS-A • 2 kW / ENGLISH & HINDI • DS-A • 2 kW
	INDONESIA †RRI, Ternate, Maluku	DS • 10 kW
	PAPUA NEW GUINEA †RADIO NORTHERN, Popondetta	ENGLISH, ETC • DS • 10 kW / Irr • ENGLISH, ETC • DS • 10 kW
3346	ZAMBIA RADIO ZAMBIA-ZBS, Lusaka	DS-TEMP INACTIVE • 50 kW
3350	BOLIVIA †R 27 DE DICIEMBRE, Villamontes	DS • 1 kW
	KOREA (DPR) SOUTH PYONGYANG PS, Pyŏngsong	KOREAN • DS
3351	ECUADOR RADIO CUMANDA, El Coca	DS • 0.5 kW
3354v	ANGOLA RADIO NACIONAL, Luanda	DS-1 / S Africa / DS-2
3355	INDIA ALL INDIA RADIO, Kurseong	DS • 20 kW / ENGLISH & HINDI • DS • 20 kW
	PAPUA NEW GUINEA RADIO SIMBU, Kundiawa	DS • 10 kW
3355v	CLANDESTINE (M EAST) "VO THE MOJAHED", Iraq	PERSIAN • Mideast
3355.2	INDONESIA †RRI, Sumenep, Jawa	DS • 1 kW
3356	BOTSWANA †RADIO BOTSWANA, Gaborone	ENGLISH, ETC • DS • 50 kW
3359	MADAGASCAR †RTV MALAGASY, Antananarivo	DS-1 • 30/100 kW
3360.5	GUATEMALA †LA VOZ DE NAHUALA, Nahualá	SPANISH, ETC • DS • 0.5/1 kW / Su • SPANISH, ETC • DS • 0.5/1 kW
3365	BRAZIL RADIO CULTURA, Araraquara	PORTUGUESE • DS • 1 kW
	INDIA ALL INDIA RADIO, Delhi	Irr • DS • 20 kW / Irr • ENGLISH & HINDI • DS • 20 kW
(con'd)	PAPUA NEW GUINEA RADIO MILNE BAY, Alotau	ENGLISH, ETC • DS • 10 kW

0 1 2 3 4 5 6 7 8 9 10 11 12 13 14 15 16 17 18 19 20 21 22 23 24

ENGLISH ▬▬   ARABIC ﹋﹋   CHINESE ▫▫▫   FRENCH ══   GERMAN ▬▬   RUSSIAN ══   SPANISH ▬▬   OTHER ▬

FREQUENCY	COUNTRY, STATION, LOCATION	TARGET • NETWORK • POWER (kW)	World Time

Frequency	Country, Station, Location	Schedule / Notes
3365 (con'd)	**SWAZILAND** — TRANS WORLD RADIO, Manzini	S Africa • 25 kW
3366	**GHANA** — †GHANA BC CORP, Accra	DS-2 • 50 kW
3366v	**CUBA** — RADIO REBELDE, Havana	Irr • DS • 0.5 kW
3370	**GUATEMALA** — †RADIO TEZULUTLAN, Cobán	SPANISH, ETC • DS • 1 kW
3370v	**MOZAMBIQUE** — EP DE SOFALA, Beira	DS-1 • 10 kW
3370.5	**BOLIVIA** — †RADIO FLORIDA, Samaipata	DS • 1 kW
3375	**BRAZIL** — R NACIONAL, S Gabriel Cachoeira	PORTUGUESE • DS • 5 kW
	RADIO CLUBE, Dourados	PORTUGUESE • DS • 5 kW / M-Sa • PORTUGUESE • DS • 5 kW
	RADIO EDUCADORA, Guajará Mirim	PORTUGUESE • DS • 5 kW
	RADIO EQUATORIAL, Macapá	PORTUGUESE • DS-TEMP INACTIVE • 1 kW
	INDIA — ALL INDIA RADIO, Guwahati	DS-A • 50 kW / ENGLISH & HINDI • DS-A • 50 kW
	PAPUA NEW GUINEA — R WEST HIGHLANDS, Mount Hagen	DS • 10 kW
3376v	**INDONESIA** — †RRI, Medan, Sumatera	DS • 7.5 kW
3377v	**ANGOLA** — RADIO NACIONAL, Luanda	DS-A • 10 kW
3377.5	**JAPAN** — NHK, Osaka	Irr • JAPANESE • DS-2 (FEEDER) • 0.5 kW
3380	**GUATEMALA** — †RADIO CHORTIS, Jocotán	DS-SPANISH, CHORTI • 1 kW / Tu-Su • DS • 1 kW / M-Sa • DS-SPANISH, CHORTI • 1 kW
3380.5	**INDONESIA** — †RRI, Malang, Jawa	DS • 1 kW
3380.7	**MALAWI** — MALAWI BC CORP, Limbe	ENGLISH, ETC • DS • 100 kW
3384	**RUSSIA** — †RADIO MOSCOW	(D) • DS-MAYAK • USB / (D) • DS-MAYAK
3385	**BRAZIL** — R EDUCACAO RURAL, Tefé	PORTUGUESE • DS • 1 kW
	FRENCH GUIANA — RFO-GUYANE, Cayenne	DS • 4 kW
	INDONESIA — RRI, Kupang, Timur	DS • 10 kW
	MALAYSIA — RTM-SARAWAK, Miri	DS-IBAN • 10 kW
	PAPUA NEW GUINEA — R EAST NEW BRITAIN, Rabaul	DS • 10 kW
3390	**INDIA** — †ALL INDIA RADIO, Gangtok	Alternative Frequency to 4775 kHz
3390v	**ZAIRE** — RADIO CANDIP, Bunia	FRENCH, ETC • DS • 1 kW / Su • FRENCH, ETC • DS • 1 kW
3390.7	**BOLIVIA** — †RADIO CAMARGO, Camargo	DS • 1 kW / Irr • DS • 1 kW
3394.8	**ECUADOR** — RADIO CATOLICA, Santo Domingo	DS • 5 kW
3395	**INDONESIA** — †RRI, Tanjungkarang, Sum	DS • 10 kW
	PAPUA NEW GUINEA — R EAST HIGHLANDS, Goroka	DS • 10 kW
3396v	**PERU** — †R INTL DEL PERU, San Pablo	DS
3401v	**BRAZIL** — RADIO 6 DE AGOSTO, Xapuri	PORTUGUESE • DS • 2 kW / Tu-Su • PORTUGUESE • DS • 2 kW
3460v	**INDONESIA** — †RPD ACEH TIMUR, Langsa, Sumatera	DS
3475v	**BOLIVIA** — †RADIO PADILLA, Padilla	DS • 0.5 kW
3481v	**CLANDESTINE (ASIA)** — "VO NAT SALVATION", Haeju, N Korea	KOREAN • TO SOUTH KOREA • 100 kW / TO SOUTH KOREA • 100 kW
3541	**INDONESIA** — †RSPD MAUJAWA, Maujawa, Sumba	DS
3569v	**BRAZIL** — RADIO 3 DE JULHO, Brasiléia	PORTUGUESE • DS • 1.5 kW
3581v	**INDONESIA** — †RPD POSO, Poso, Sulawesi	DS • 0.35 kW
3607.5	**JAPAN** — NHK, Tokyo-Shobu	Irr • JAPANESE • DS-1 (FEEDER) • 0.9 kW • USB
3644v	**INDONESIA** — †RRI, Fak Fak, Irian Jaya	DS • 0.5 kW
3654	**INDONESIA** — †RKP BUOL, Tolitoli, Sulawesi	Irr • DS • 0.2 kW
3664v	**PAKISTAN (AZAD K)** — AZAD KASHMIR RADIO, Muzaffarabad	DS • 1 kW

World Time scale: 0 1 2 3 4 5 6 7 8 9 10 11 12 13 14 15 16 17 18 19 20 21 22 23 24

FREQUENCY   COUNTRY, STATION, LOCATION

TARGET • NETWORK • POWER (kW)   World Time

0 1 2 3 4 5 6 7 8 9 10 11 12 13 14 15 16 17 18 19 20 21 22 23 24

Frequency	Country, Station, Location	Notes
3740v	BOLIVIA †R 20 DE DICIEMBRE, Culpina	DS-VERY IRREGULAR
3778v	IRAN VO THE ISLAMIC REP, Tehrān	Irr • PERSIAN • Mideast • DS • 50 kW
3780v	CLANDESTINE (M EAST) "VO THE MOJAHED", Iraq	PERSIAN • Mideast
3800.3	PERU RADIO OYON, Oyón	DS-SPANISH, QUECHUA • 1 kW / Tu-Su • DS • 1 kW
3815	CHINA (PR) CENTRAL PEOPLES BS, Beijing	(D) • CHINESE, ETC • TAIWAN-1 • 10/50 kW
3870	CLANDESTINE (PAC) †"FREE BOUGAINVILLE, Arawa, B'ville	Alternative Frequency to 3875 kHz
3870v	PERU †LV DE LA ESPERANZA, Celendin	DS
3875	CLANDESTINE (PAC) †"FREE BOUGAINVILLE, Arawa, B'ville	Irr • ENGLISH, ETC • Pacific & Australasia • PRO-REBEL • 0.3 kW • ALT. FREQ TO 3870 kHz
3875v	CLANDESTINE (M EAST) "VO IRANIAN KURDS"	Mideast • ANTI-IRANIAN GOVT / PERSIAN • Mideast • ANTI-IRANIAN GOVT
3900	CHINA (PR) HULUNBEI'ER PBS, Hailar	DS
3905	INDIA †ALL INDIA RADIO, Delhi	DS • 100 kW / Irr • DS • 100 kW / ENGLISH & HINDI • DS • 100 kW
	PAPUA NEW GUINEA RADIO NEW IRELAND, Kavieng	DS • 10 kW
3905v	INDONESIA †RRI, Banda Aceh	DS-TEMP INACTIVE
	†RRI, Merauke, Irian Jaya	DS • 1 kW
3910	PIRATE (EUROPE) †REFLECTIONS EUROPE, Ireland	Irr • Su • W Europe • 0.23 kW
3910v	PIRATE (EUROPE) †"LIVE WIRE RADIO", England	Irr • Su • W Europe • 0.15 kW / Irr • Sa • W Europe • 0.15 kW
	†"WEEKEND MUSIC R", England	Irr • Su • W Europe • 0.1 kW / Irr • Sa • W Europe • 0.1 kW
3912	CLANDESTINE (ASIA) †"VO THE PEOPLE", Seoul, S Korea	KOREAN • E Asia
3912v	PIRATE (EUROPE) †"RADIO FUSION INTL, Scandinavia	Irr • Su • Europe • 0.04 kW / Irr • Sa • Europe • 0.04 kW
3915	UNITED KINGDOM BBC, Via Singapore	S Asia & SE Asia • 100 kW
3915v	PIRATE (EUROPE) †"RADIO PIRANA INTL	Irr • Su • W Europe • 0.1 kW
3917v	PIRATE (EUROPE) †"R WITHOUT BORDERS, Russia	Irr • Su • RUSSIAN, ETC • Europe • 0.03 kW / Irr • Sa • RUSSIAN, ETC • Europe • 0.03 kW
3920	KOREA (DPR) NORTH PYONGYANG PS, Sinuiju	KOREAN • DS
3925	INDIA †ALL INDIA RADIO, Delhi	DS • 20 kW / ENGLISH & HINDI • DS • 20 kW
	JAPAN RADIO TAMPA, Multiple Locations	JAPANESE • DS-1 • 10/50 kW
	RADIO TAMPA, Tokyo-Nagara	JAPANESE • DS-1 • 50 kW
3926v	PERU †R SAN NICOLAS, San Nicolás	DS
3927.4	SOUTH AFRICA CAPITAL RADIO, Umtata	DS • 20 kW
3930	KOREA (REPUBLIC) KOREAN BC SYSTEM, Hwasung	KOREAN • DS-1 • 5 kW
3932	PIRATE (EUROPE) †"RADIO PLUTO", Holland	Irr • Su • W Europe • 0.008 kW
3934.2	INDONESIA †RRI, Semarang, Jawa	DS • 5/10 kW
3935	NEW ZEALAND PRINT DISABLED R, Levin	M-F • DS • 1 kW / Su • DS • 1 kW / Su-F • DS • 1 kW
3940	CHINA (PR) HUBEI PEOPLES BS, Wuhan	DS-1
	ERITREA †VO BROAD MASSES, Asmera	M-Sa • DS-1 / E Africa / W, F • E Africa
3945	INDIA †ALL INDIA RADIO, Gorakhpur	S Asia • 50 kW / DS • 50 kW / ENGLISH, ETC • DS • 50 kW
	INDONESIA RRI, Denpasar, Bali	DS-TEMP INACTIVE • 1/10 kW
	JAPAN RADIO TAMPA, Tokyo-Nagara	JAPANESE • DS-2 • 10 kW
	VANUATU RADIO VANUATU, Vila, Efate Island	ENGLISH, FRENCH, ETC • DS • 10 kW
3946	INDONESIA †RRI, Tanjungkarang	DS • 2.5 kW

0 1 2 3 4 5 6 7 8 9 10 11 12 13 14 15 16 17 18 19 20 21 22 23 24

ENGLISH ▬   ARABIC ≈≈≈   CHINESE □□□   FRENCH ══   GERMAN ▬▬   RUSSIAN ══   SPANISH ▬▬   OTHER ▬

FREQUENCY　　COUNTRY, STATION, LOCATION　　　　　TARGET • NETWORK • POWER (kW)　　　World Time

0　1　2　3　4　5　6　7　8　9　10　11　12　13　14　15　16　17　18　19　20　21　22　23　24

Frequency	Country / Station / Location	Notes
3950	**CHINA (PR)** †QINGHAI PEOPLES BS, Xining	DS-1 • 10 kW
3952v	**VIETNAM** †LAI CHAU BC STN, Lai Chau	DS
3955	**HUNGARY** †RADIO BUDAPEST	Europe
	KAZAKHSTAN †KAZAKH RADIO, Via N'sibirsk,Russia	DS-2
	†RADIO ALMATY, Via N'sibirsk,Russia	
	SOUTH AFRICA †CHANNEL AFRICA, Meyerton	(J) • S Africa • 100 kW
	UNITED KINGDOM †BBC, Skelton, Cumbria	Europe • 250 kW / (D) • Europe • 250 kW
3959.6	**INDONESIA** †RRI, Palu, Sulawesi	DS • 10 kW
3959.8	**KOREA (DPR)** CHAGONG PROVINCIAL, Kanggye	KOREAN • DS
3960	**CHINA (PR)** XINJIANG PBS, Ürümqi	(D) • DS-CHINESE • 50 kW
	INDONESIA †RRI, Padang, Sumatera	DS • 1 kW
	MONGOLIA †RADIO ULAANBAATAR, Dalandzadgad	DS-1 • 12 kW
	USA †RFE-RL, Via Germany	(D) • E Europe • 100 kW
3965	**FRANCE** R FRANCE INTL, Issoudun-Allouis	Europe • 4 kW
3970	**CAMEROON** CAMEROON RTV CORP, Buea	FRENCH, ENGLISH, ETC • DS • 4 kW
	CHINA (PR) NEI MONGGOL PBS, Hohhot	DS
	JAPAN NHK, Sapporo	Irr • JAPANESE • DS-1(FEEDER) • 0.6 kW
	KOREA (DPR) KANGWONG PS, Wonsan	DS
	USA RFE-RL, Via Germany	(D) • M-Sa • E Europe • 100 kW / (D) • E Europe • 100 kW
3970.2	**JAPAN** †NHK, Nagoya	Irr • JAPANESE • DS-1(FEEDER) • 0.3 kW • USB
3975	**UNITED KINGDOM** BBC, Skelton, Cumbria	(D) • Europe • 250 kW / (J) • Europe • 250 kW
3976	**INDONESIA** †RRI, Surabaya, Jawa	DS • 10 kW
3980	**KOREA (DPR)** NORTH HAMGYONG PS, Ch'ŏngjin	KOREAN • DS
	USA †VOA, Via Germany	Europe • 100 kW / (D) • Europe • 100 kW / (J) • Europe • 100 kW
3985	**CHINA (PR)** CHINA RADIO INTL, Via Switzerland	Europe • 250 kW
	CLANDESTINE (ASIA) †"ECHO OF HOPE", Seoul, South Korea	KOREAN • E Asia • 50 kW / (D) • KOREAN • E Asia • 50 kW
	SWITZERLAND †SWISS RADIO INTL, Beromünster	Europe • 250 kW / ITALIAN • Europe • 250 kW / M-F • Europe • 250 kW / GERMAN, FRENCH & ITALIAN • Europe • 250 kW / M-F • ITALIAN • Europe • 250 kW / M-F • GERMAN, FRENCH & ITALIAN • Europe • 250 kW
3987.4	**INDONESIA** †RRI, Manokwari,Irian Jaya	DS • 1 kW
3990	**CHINA (PR)** †VOICE OF PUJIANG, Shanghai	Alternative Frequency to 3280 kHz
	†XINJIANG PBS, Ürümqi	(D) • DS-UIGHUR • 50 kW
	UNITED KINGDOM †BBC, Via Zyyi, Cyprus	(D) • E Europe & Mideast • 250 kW / (D) M-Sa • E Europe & Mideast • 250 kW
	USA †RFE-RL, Via Germany	(D) • E Europe • 100 kW
3995	**GERMANY** †DEUTSCHE WELLE, Jülich	Europe • 100 kW / (D) • Europe • 100 kW
	INDONESIA †RRI, Pontianak,Kalimantan	DS • 1 kW
	RUSSIA RADIO MOSCOW, Khabarovsk	(D) • DS-MAYAK • 50 kW
	TUVIN RADIO, Kyzyl	RUSSIAN, ETC • DS • 15 kW
	SOUTH AFRICA †CHANNEL AFRICA, Meyerton	(J) • S Africa • 250 kW / (D) • S Africa • 100 kW
3996	**INDONESIA** RRI, Kendari, Sulawesi	DS • 5 kW
4000v	**CAMEROON** CAMEROON RTV CORP, Bafoussam	FRENCH, ENGLISH, ETC • DS • 20 kW

0　1　2　3　4　5　6　7　8　9　10　11　12　13　14　15　16　17　18　19　20　21　22　23　24

SUMMER ONLY (J)　　WINTER ONLY (D)　　JAMMING / OR ∧　　EARLIEST HEARD ◁　　LATEST HEARD ▷　　NEW OR CHANGED FOR 1994 †

FREQUENCY   COUNTRY, STATION, LOCATION   TARGET • NETWORK • POWER (kW)   World Time

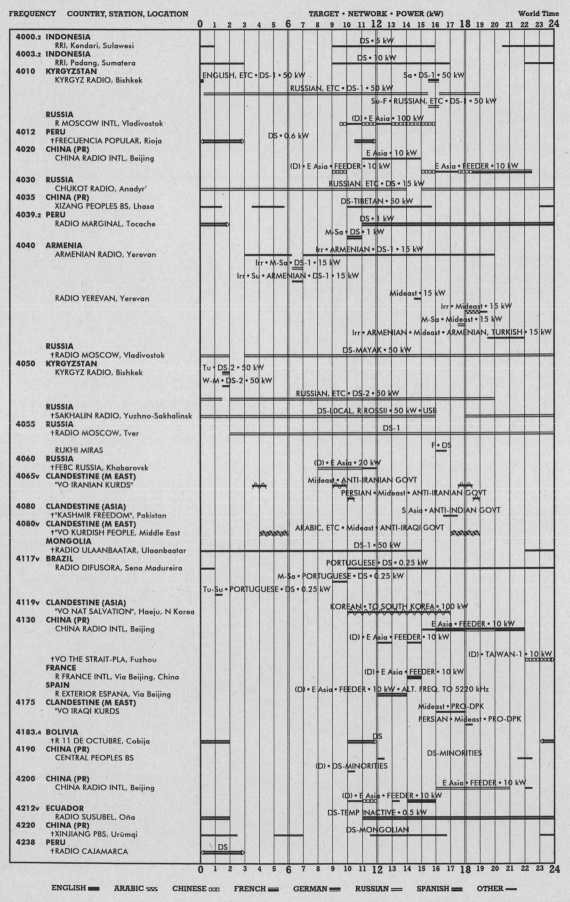

FREQUENCY	COUNTRY, STATION, LOCATION	Schedule
4000.2	**INDONESIA** RRI, Kendari, Sulawesi	DS • 5 kW
4003.2	**INDONESIA** RRI, Padang, Sumatera	DS • 10 kW
4010	**KYRGYZSTAN** KYRGYZ RADIO, Bishkek	ENGLISH, ETC • DS-1 • 50 kW / Sa • DS-1 • 50 kW / RUSSIAN, ETC • DS-1 • 50 kW / Su-F • RUSSIAN, ETC • DS-1 • 50 kW
	RUSSIA R MOSCOW INTL, Vladivostok	(D) • E Asia • 100 kW
4012	**PERU** †FRECUENCIA POPULAR, Rioja	DS • 0.6 kW
4020	**CHINA (PR)** CHINA RADIO INTL, Beijing	E Asia • 10 kW / (D) • E Asia • FEEDER • 10 kW / E Asia • FEEDER • 10 kW
4030	**RUSSIA** CHUKOT RADIO, Anadyr'	RUSSIAN, ETC • DS • 15 kW
4035	**CHINA (PR)** XIZANG PEOPLES BS, Lhasa	DS-TIBETAN • 50 kW
4039.2	**PERU** RADIO MARGINAL, Tocache	DS • 1 kW / M-Sa • DS • 1 kW
4040	**ARMENIA** ARMENIAN RADIO, Yerevan	Irr • ARMENIAN • DS-1 • 15 kW / Irr • M-Sa • DS-1 • 15 kW / Irr • Su • ARMENIAN • DS-1 • 15 kW
	RADIO YEREVAN, Yerevan	Mideast • 15 kW / Irr • Mideast • 15 kW / M-Sa • Mideast • 15 kW / Irr • ARMENIAN • Mideast • ARMENIAN, TURKISH • 15 kW
	RUSSIA †RADIO MOSCOW, Vladivostok	DS-MAYAK • 50 kW
4050	**KYRGYZSTAN** KYRGYZ RADIO, Bishkek	Tu • DS-2 • 50 kW / W-M • DS-2 • 50 kW / RUSSIAN, ETC • DS-2 • 50 kW
	RUSSIA †SAKHALIN RADIO, Yuzhno-Sakhalinsk	DS-LOCAL, R ROSSII • 50 kW • USB
4055	**RUSSIA** †RADIO MOSCOW, Tver	DS-1
	RUKHI MIRAS	F • DS
4060	**RUSSIA** †FEBC RUSSIA, Khabarovsk	(D) • E Asia • 20 kW
4065v	**CLANDESTINE (M EAST)** "VO IRANIAN KURDS"	Mideast • ANTI-IRANIAN GOVT / PERSIAN • Mideast • ANTI-IRANIAN GOVT
4080	**CLANDESTINE (ASIA)** †"KASHMIR FREEDOM", Pakistan	S Asia • ANTI-INDIAN GOVT
4080v	**CLANDESTINE (M EAST)** †"VO KURDISH PEOPLE, Middle East	ARABIC, ETC • Mideast • ANTI-IRAQI GOVT
	MONGOLIA †RADIO ULAANBAATAR, Ulaanbaatar	DS-1 • 50 kW
4117v	**BRAZIL** RADIO DIFUSORA, Sena Madureira	PORTUGUESE • DS • 0.25 kW / M-Sa • PORTUGUESE • DS • 0.25 kW / Tu-Su • PORTUGUESE • DS • 0.25 kW
4119v	**CLANDESTINE (ASIA)** "VO NAT SALVATION", Haeju, N Korea	KOREAN • TO SOUTH KOREA • 100 kW
4130	**CHINA (PR)** CHINA RADIO INTL, Beijing	E Asia • FEEDER • 10 kW / (D) • E Asia • FEEDER • 10 kW / (D) • TAIWAN-1 • 10 kW
	†VO THE STRAIT-PLA, Fuzhou	
	FRANCE R FRANCE INTL, Via Beijing, China	(D) • E Asia • FEEDER • 10 kW
	SPAIN R EXTERIOR ESPANA, Via Beijing	(D) • E Asia • FEEDER • 10 kW • ALT. FREQ. TO 5220 kHz
4175	**CLANDESTINE (M EAST)** "VO IRAQI KURDS	Mideast • PRO-DPK / PERSIAN • Mideast • PRO-DPK
4183.4	**BOLIVIA** †R 11 DE OCTUBRE, Cobija	DS
4190	**CHINA (PR)** CENTRAL PEOPLES BS	DS-MINORITIES / (D) • DS-MINORITIES
4200	**CHINA (PR)** CHINA RADIO INTL, Beijing	E Asia • FEEDER • 10 kW / (D) • E Asia • FEEDER • 10 kW
4212v	**ECUADOR** RADIO SUSUBEL, Oña	DS-TEMP INACTIVE • 0.5 kW
4220	**CHINA (PR)** †XINJIANG PBS, Urümqi	DS-MONGOLIAN
4238	**PERU** †RADIO CAJAMARCA	DS

FREQUENCY	COUNTRY, STATION, LOCATION	TARGET • NETWORK • POWER (kW)

World Time: 0 1 2 3 4 5 6 7 8 9 10 11 12 13 14 15 16 17 18 19 20 21 22 23 24

4271v	ECUADOR	
	RADIO GONZANAMA, Gonzanamá	Irr • DS • 1 kW
4299.8	PERU	
	†RADIO NAYLAMP, Lambayeque	DS • 0.5 kW
4330	CHINA (PR)	
	XINJIANG PBS, Urümqi	DS-KAZAKH • 50 kW
4395	KAZAKHSTAN	
	†KAZAKH RADIO, Almaty	Alternative Frequency to 4400 kHz
	†RADIO ALMATY, Almaty	Alternative Frequency to 4400 kHz
	RUSSIA	
	RADIO ROSSII, Yakutsk	DS • 100 kW
4400	KAZAKHSTAN	
	†KAZAKH RADIO, Almaty	DS-2 • ALT. FREQ. TO 4395 kHz
	†RADIO ALMATY, Almaty	ALT. FREQ. TO 4395 kHz
4400v	CLANDESTINE (ASIA)	
	"VO NAT SALVATION", Haeju, N Korea	KOREAN • TO SOUTH KOREA • 100 kW / TO SOUTH KOREA • 100 kW
4409.2	BOLIVIA	
	RADIO ECO, Reyes	DS • 1 kW
4419v	PERU	
	†FRECUENCIA LIDER, Bambamarca	DS • 0.85 kW
4420v	BOLIVIA	
	R SANTA ROSA, Sta Rosa de Yacuma	Irr • DS • 1 kW
4433	INDONESIA	
	RRI, Bukittingi, Sumatera	DS
4450	BOLIVIA	
	RADIO FRONTERA, Cobija	DS
4450v	CLANDESTINE (ASIA)	
	"VO NAT SALVATION", Haeju, N Korea	KOREAN • TO SOUTH KOREA • 100 kW / TO SOUTH KOREA • 100 kW
4451.3	BOLIVIA	
	†R ECOLOGIA INTL, San Matias	Irr • DS DS
4460	CHINA (PR)	
	†CENTRAL PEOPLES BS, Beijing	DS-1 • 10/15 kW
4461.8	PERU	
	RADIO NORANDINA, Celendin	DS
4470v	CLANDESTINE (M EAST)	
	"VO THE MOJAHED", Iraq	PERSIAN • Mideast
4472v	BOLIVIA	
	†RADIO MOVIMA, Santa Ana	DS • 0.25 kW / Irr • DS • 0.25 kW
4485	PERU	
	LA VOZ DE CELENDIN, Celendin	DS
	RUSSIA	
	BASHKIR RADIO, Ufa	DS-RUSSIAN, BASHKIR • 50 kW
	R PETROPAVLOVSK, Petropavlovsk-Kam	DS/TIKHIY OKEAN • 50 kW
4501.3	CHINA (PR)	
	XINJIANG PBS, Urümqi	DS-CHINESE • 50 kW
4505v	PERU	
	†RADIO HORIZONTE, Chiclayo	DS
4510	UZBEKISTAN	
	FERGANA RADIO, Fergana	M-F • DS • 15 kW
4510v	PERU	
	†R PAUCARTAMBO, Paucartambo	DS
4520	RUSSIA	
	KORYASK RADIO, Palana	Sa/Su • DS • 15 kW / Su • DS • 15 kW / Irr • W/F • DS • 15 kW
	RADIO MOSCOW, Khanty-Mansiysk	DS-MAYAK • 50 kW
4525	CHINA (PR)	
	NEI MONGGOL PBS, Dongsheng	Irr • DS-MONGOLIAN • 10 kW
4530.2	BOLIVIA	
	RADIO HITACHI, Guayaramerin	Irr • DS DS
4545	KAZAKHSTAN	
	†KAZAKH RADIO, Almaty	RUSSIAN, GERMAN, ETC • DS-1 • 50 kW
4552.4	BOLIVIA	
	†RADIO TROPICO, Trinidad	Tu-Sa • DS • 0.75 kW / DS • 0.75 kW / M-Sa • DS • 0.75 kW
4557v	CLANDESTINE (ASIA)	
	"VO NAT SALVATION", Haeju, N Korea	KOREAN • TO SOUTH KOREA • 100 kW / TO SOUTH KOREA • 100 kW
4593v	PERU	
	†ESTACION X, Yurimaguas	DS
4599.7	BOLIVIA	
	†RADIO VILLA MONTES, Villa Montes	DS • 1 kW / M-Sa • DS • 1 kW
4600	BOLIVIA	
	†R PERLA DEL ACRE, Cobija	DS
		Tu-Su • DS M-Sa • DS
4600v	IRAQ	
	†REP OF IRAQ RADIO	DS-1
4606.4	INDONESIA	
	†RRI, Serui, Irian Jaya	DS • 0.5 kW / Irr • DS • 0.5 kW
4606.6	PERU	
	RADIO AYAVIRI, Ayaviri	DS • 1 kW • ALT. FREQ. TO 5035 kHz

0 1 2 3 4 5 6 7 8 9 10 11 12 13 14 15 16 17 18 19 20 21 22 23 24

FREQUENCY   COUNTRY, STATION, LOCATION   TARGET • NETWORK • POWER (kW)   World Time

		0 ... 12 ... 24

4610 RUSSIA
   KHABAROVSK RADIO, Khabarovsk — DS-1/DS-2 • 50 kW
4620 CHINA (PR)
   CHINA RADIO INTL, Beijing — E Asia • 10 kW
4625.7 BOLIVIA
   †RADIO MACHUPO, San Ramón — DS
4635 TAJIKISTAN
   TAJIK RADIO, Dushanbe — RUSSIAN, ETC • DS-1 • 50 kW
4649 BOLIVIA
   †RADIO SANTA ANA, Santa Ana — DS • 1 kW
      Irr • DS • 1 kW
      M-Sa • DS • 1 kW
      Tu-Su • DS • 1 kW
4665v VIETNAM
   †SON LA BC STATION, Son La — DS
4682v BOLIVIA
   †RADIO PAITITI, Guayaramerin — DS • 0.75 kW
      Tu-Su • DS • 0.75 kW
4697.3 INDONESIA
   †RK INFORMASI PER'N, Surabaya, Jawa — DS • 2 kW
4700v CLANDESTINE (M EAST)
   "VO THE MOJAHED", Iraq — PERSIAN • Mideast
4704v PERU
   †ESTACION LASER, Rioja — Irr • DS
4712.6 BOLIVIA
   †RADIO ABAROA, Riberalta — DS • 0.5 kW
      Irr • DS • 0.5 kW
4719 INDONESIA
   †RRI, Ujung Pandang — Alternative Frequency to 4753.4 kHz
4725 MYANMAR (BURMA)
   RADIO MYANMAR, Yangon — DS-MINORITIES • 50 kW
4735 CHINA (PR)
   †XINJIANG PBS, Urümqi — DS-UIGHUR • 50 kW
4739v BOLIVIA
   †RADIO MAMORE, Guayaramerín — Irr • Tu-Su • DS • 0.5 kW   Irr • DS • 0.5 kW
4740 RUSSIA
   R MOSCOW INTL, Via Tajikistan — (D) • W Asia & S Asia • 100 kW
   RADIO MOSCOW, Via Tajikistan — (J) • DS-2 • 100 kW
4747v PERU
   †RADIO HUANTA 2000, Huanta — DS • 0.5 kW
      DS • 1 kW
4750 CHINA (PR)
   HULUNBEI'ER PBS, Hailar — DS-MONGOLIAN • 15 kW
   XIZANG PEOPLES BS, Lhasa — DS • 50 kW
MONGOLIA
   †RADIO ULAANBAATAR, Olgiy — DS-1 • 12 kW
4750v CAMEROON
   CAMEROON RTV CORP, Bertoua — Irr • FRENCH, ENGLISH, ETC • DS • 20 kW
4753.4 INDONESIA
   †RRI, Ujung Pandang — DS • 50 kW • ALT. FREQ. TO 4719 kHz
4755 BRAZIL
   R DIF MARANHAO, São Luíz — Irr • PORTUGUESE • DS • 5 kW
   R EDUCACAO RURAL, Campo Grande — PORTUGUESE • DS • 10 kW
      M-Sa • PORTUGUESE • DS • 10 kW
      Tu-Su • PORTUGUESE • DS • 10 kW
4759v PERU
   RADIO TINGO MARIA, Tinga Maria — Irr • DS • 1 kW
4760 AZERBAIJAN
   †AZERBAIJANI RADIO, Baku — Alternative Frequency to 4785 kHz
CHINA (PR)
   †YUNNAN PEOPLES BS, Kunming — DS-1 • 50 kW
      W-M • DS-1 • 50 kW
INDIA
   †ALL INDIA RADIO, Imphal — DS (PROJECTED) • 50 kW
      ENGLISH, ETC • DS (PROJECTED) • 50 kW
   †ALL INDIA RADIO, Port Blair — DS • 10 kW • ALT. FREQ. TO 4950 kHz
      Irr • DS • 10 kW • ALT. FREQ. TO 4950 kHz
      ENGLISH & HINDI • DS • 10 kW • ALT. FREQ. TO 4950 kHz
   †RADIO KASHMIR, Leh — DS • 10 kW
      ENGLISH & HINDI • DS • 10 kW
RUSSIA
   RADIO MOSCOW, Various Locations — DS-MAYAK
SWAZILAND
   TRANS WORLD RADIO, Manzini — S Africa • 25 kW
      Sa/Su • S Africa • 25 kW
4760.2 ECUADOR
   EMISORA ATALAYA, Guayaquil — DS • 5 kW
      Irr • Sa/Su • DS • 5 kW
      Tu-Su • DS • 5 kW
4760.8 VENEZUELA
   RADIO FRONTERA, San Antonio — Irr • DS • 1 kW
4765 BRAZIL
(con'd) RADIO INTEGRACAO, Cruzeiro do Sul — PORTUGUESE • DS • 10 kW

ENGLISH ▬▬   ARABIC ꠲꠲꠲   CHINESE □□□   FRENCH ══   GERMAN ▬▬   RUSSIAN ══   SPANISH ▬▬   OTHER ▬▬

FREQUENCY	COUNTRY, STATION, LOCATION	TARGET • NETWORK • POWER (kW)	World Time

Time scale: 0 1 2 3 4 5 6 7 8 9 10 11 12 13 14 15 16 17 18 19 20 21 22 23 24

Frequency	Country / Station / Location	Notes
4765 (con'd)	**BRAZIL** RADIO INTEGRACAO, Cruzeiro do Sul	Tu-Su • PORTUGUESE • DS • 10 kW
	RADIO RURAL, Santarém	PORTUGUESE • DS • 10 kW
	CONGO †RTV CONGOLAISE, Brazzaville	Irr • Sa • DS • 50 kW / FRENCH, ETC • DS • 50 kW
4766	**INDONESIA** †RRI, Medan, Sumatera	DS
4770	**NIGERIA** RADIO NIGERIA, Kaduna	ENGLISH, ETC • DS-2 • 50 kW
4770v	**ECUADOR** †CENTINELA DEL SUR, Loja	DS • 2 kW • ALT. FREQ. TO 4890v kHz / Irr • DS • 5 kW • ALT. FREQ. TO 4890v kHz / DS • 5 kW • ALT. FREQ. TO 4890v kHz
4775	**AFGHANISTAN** RADIO AFGHANISTAN, Kabul	Irr • DS-1 • 100 kW
	BRAZIL PORTAL DA AMAZONIA, Cuiabá	PORTUGUESE • DS • 1 kW
	†RADIO AMARELA, Rolim do Moura	PORTUGUESE • DS • 5 kW
	RADIO CONGONHAS, Congonhas	PORTUGUESE • DS • 1 kW
	INDIA †ALL INDIA RADIO, Gangtok	DS • 10 kW • ALT. FREQ. TO 3390 kHz / ENGLISH, ETC • DS • 10 kW • ALT. FREQ. TO 3390 kHz
	PERU RADIO TARMA, Tarma	DS • 1 kW
4775.3	**BOLIVIA** †RADIO LOS ANDES, Tarija	DS • 3 kW / M-Sa • DS • 3 kW
	INDIA †ALL INDIA RADIO, Guwahati	DS-B • 10/20 kW • ALT. FREQ. TO 4990 kHz / ENGLISH & HINDI • DS-B • 10/20 kW • ALT. FREQ. TO 4990 kHz
4777	**GABON** RTV GABONAISE, Libreville	DS • 100 kW / M-Sa • DS • 100 kW / Irr • DS • 100 kW
4777.3	**INDONESIA** †RRI, Jakarta, Jawa	DS • 50 kW
4780	**DJIBOUTI (JIBUTI)** †RTV DE DJIBOUTI, Djibouti	DS • 20 kW / Irr • DS-RAMADAN • 20 kW
	KOREA (DPR) †RADIO PYONGYANG, Pyongyang	KOREAN • E Asia • 100 kW
4783v	**MALI** RTV MALIENNE, Bamako	Su • DS • 18 kW / FRENCH, ETC • DS • 18 kW / M-Sa • FRENCH, ETC • DS • 18 kW
4785	**AZERBAIJAN** †AZERBAIJANI RADIO, Baku	DS-1/RUSSIAN, AZERI • 50 kW • ALT. FREQ. TO 4760 kHz
	BRAZIL RADIO BRASIL 5000, Campinas	Irr • PORTUGUESE • DS • 1 kW
	RADIO CAIARI, Pôrto Velho	PORTUGUESE • DS • 1 kW
	CHINA (PR) †ZHEJIANG PBS, Qu Xian	DS-1 • 10 kW
4785v	**COLOMBIA** ECOS DEL COMBEIMA, Ibagué	Irr • DS-SUPER • 5 kW
4785.7	**PERU** RADIO COSAT, Satipo	DS • 1 kW
4788v	**VIETNAM** †RTV GIA LAI, Pleiku	DS / Irr • DS
4789.8	**INDONESIA** †RRI, Fak Fak, Irian Jaya	DS • 1 kW
4790	**INDIA** †ALL INDIA RADIO, Shillong	DS • 50 kW / DS • 50 kW • ALT. FREQ. TO 3255 kHz / ENGLISH & HINDI • DS • 50 kW • ALT. FREQ. TO 3255 kHz
	PAKISTAN (AZAD K) †AZAD KASHMIR RADIO, Via Islamabad	DS • 100 kW
	PERU RADIO ATLANTIDA, Iquitos	DS • 1/3 kW
	SAUDI ARABIA †BS OF THE KINGDOM, Jiddah	DS-2 (0.5X9580 KHZ) • SPR
	SWAZILAND TRANS WORLD RADIO, Manzini	S Africa • 25 kW
4795	**BRAZIL** RADIO AQUIDAUANA, Aquidauana	PORTUGUESE • DS • 1 kW
	CAMEROON CAMEROON RTV CORP, Douala	FRENCH, ENGLISH, ETC • DS • 100 kW
	RUSSIA BURYAT RADIO, Ulan-Ude	DS-RUSSIAN, BURYAT • 50 kW • ALT. FREQ. TO 4860 kHz
	†R MOSCOW INTL, Via Ukraine	(D) • Europe • 100 kW
4795.3	**ECUADOR** LV DE LOS CARAS, Bahía de Caráquez	DS • 5 kW
4799.8 (con'd)	**DOMINICAN REPUBLIC** RADIO N-103, Santiago	Irr • DS • 1 kW

FREQUENCY   COUNTRY, STATION, LOCATION   TARGET · NETWORK · POWER (kW)   World Time

0 1 2 3 4 5 6 7 8 9 10 11 12 13 14 15 16 17 18 19 20 21 22 23 24

Frequency	Country, Station, Location	Target · Network · Power (kW)
4799.8 (con'd)	GUATEMALA — R BUENAS NUEVAS, San Sebastián	DS · 1 kW
4800	CHINA (PR) — CENTRAL PEOPLES BS, Shijiazhuang	DS-2 · 10/50 kW · DS-MINORITIES · 10/50 kW
	ECUADOR — †RADIO POPULAR, Cuenca	DS · 5 kW
	INDIA — †ALL INDIA RADIO, Hyderabad	DS · 50 kW · ENGLISH, ETC · DS · 50 kW
	KAZAKHSTAN — KAZAKH RADIO	RUSSIAN, GERMAN, ETC · DS-1
	LESOTHO — †RADIO LESOTHO, Maseru	DS-ENGLISH, SESOTHO · 100 kW
	RUSSIA — YAKUT RADIO, Yakutsk	DS-RUSSIAN, YAKUT · 50 kW
4801v	PERU — RADIO ONDA AZUL, Puno	SPANISH, ETC · DS · 1.5 kW
4804v	PERU — †RADIO VILLA RICA, Huancavelica	DS · 1 kW · M-Sa · DS · 1 kW · Su · DS · 1 kW
4805	BRAZIL — DIFUSORA AMAZONAS, Manaus	PORTUGUESE · DS · 5 kW
	RADIO ITATIAIA, Belo Horizonte	PORTUGUESE · DS · 0.5 kW
4805.4	INDONESIA — †RRI, Kupang, Timor	DS · 0.3 kW
4808.8	BOLIVIA — †RADIO LIBERTAD, Dist. Santa Fe	Irr · Tu-Su · DS · 1 kW · Irr · DS · 1 kW · Irr · M-Sa · DS · 1 kW · Irr · Su · DS · 1 kW
4809v	VIETNAM — †HA GIANG BC STN, Ha Giang	DS
4810	ARMENIA — ARMENIAN RADIO, Yerevan	Irr · ARMENIAN · DS-1 · 50 kW · Irr · M-Sa · DS-1 · 50 kW · Irr · Su · ARMENIAN · DS-1 · 50 kW
	RADIO YEREVAN, Yerevan	Mideast · 50 kW · ARMENIAN · Mideast · 50 kW · Irr · Mideast · 50 kW · M-Sa · Mideast · 50 kW · Irr · ARMENIAN · Mideast · ARMENIAN, TURKISH · 50 kW
	RUSSIA — R MOSCOW INTL	(D) · JAPANESE · E Asia · (D) · E Asia
	SOUTH AFRICA — †SOUTH AFRICAN BC, Meyerton	AFRIKAANS STEREO · 100 kW
4810.2	PERU — †RADIO SAN MARTIN, Tarapoto	DS · 3 kW · M-Sa · DS · 3 kW
4815	BRAZIL — RADIO CABOCLA, Benjamim Constant	PORTUGUESE · DS · 10 kW
	RADIO DIFUSORA, Londrina	PORTUGUESE · DS · 10 kW
	BURKINA FASO — RTV BURKINA, Ouagadougou	FRENCH, ETC · DS · 50 kW · M-F · FRENCH, ETC · DS · 50 kW
	CHINA (PR) — CHINA RADIO INTL, Togtoh	E Asia · RUSSIAN, MONGOLIAN · 10 kW
	PERU — RADIO AMAZONAS, Iquitos	DS · 1 kW
4815v	PAKISTAN — PAKISTAN BC CORP, Karachi	(D) · DS-ENGLISH, ETC · 10 kW
4819.6	ECUADOR — †RADIO PAZ Y BIEN, Ambato	DS · 1.5 kW
4820	CHINA (PR) — †XIZANG PEOPLES BS, Lhasa	DS-TIBETAN · 50 kW
	INDIA — †ALL INDIA RADIO, Calcutta	DS-A · 50 kW
	RUSSIA — KHANTY-MANSIYSK R, Khanty-Mansiysk	DS · 50 kW
4820.2	ANGOLA — EP DA HUILA, Lubango	DS · 25 kW
	HONDURAS — †LA VOZ EVANGELICA, Tegucigalpa	DS · 5 kW · M · DS · 5 kW · Tu-Su · DS · 5 kW
4820.8	PERU — RADIO ATAHUALPA, Cajamarca	DS · 1 kW
4824.5	PERU — LV DE LA SELVA, Iquitos	DS · 10 kW · Irr · DS · 10 kW
4825 (con'd)	BRAZIL — R CANCAO NOVA, Cachoeira Paulista	PORTUGUESE · DS · 10 kW

0 1 2 3 4 5 6 7 8 9 10 11 12 13 14 15 16 17 18 19 20 21 22 23 24

ENGLISH ▬   ARABIC ∿∿∿   CHINESE □□□   FRENCH ═   GERMAN ▬▬   RUSSIAN ═══   SPANISH ▬▬   OTHER ▬

FREQUENCY   COUNTRY, STATION, LOCATION   TARGET • NETWORK • POWER (kW)   World Time

0 1 2 3 4 5 6 7 8 9 10 11 12 13 14 15 16 17 18 19 20 21 22 23 24

Frequency	Country, Station, Location	Target • Network • Power
4825 (con'd)	**BRAZIL** RADIO EDUCADORA, Bragança	PORTUGUESE • DS • 10 kW
	GUATEMALA †RADIO MAM, Cabricán	M-F • SPANISH, ETC • DS • 1 kW
		M-Sa • SPANISH, ETC • DS • 1 kW
		Su-F • SPANISH, ETC • DS • 1 kW
	RUSSIA †R MOSCOW INTL	(D) • E Europe & S Europe
	YAKUT RADIO, Yakutsk	(D) • RUSSIAN, ETC • DS-LOCAL, ROSSII • 50 kW
	UKRAINE †RADIO UKRAINE, Star'obel'sk	(D) • N Europe • 100 kW
		(D) • UKRAINIAN • N Europe • 100 kW
		(J) • UKRAINIAN • N Europe • 100 kW
		(J) • N Europe • 100 kW
4826.3	**PERU** RADIO SICUANI, Sicuani	DS-SPANISH, QUECHUA • 0.35 kW
4828v	**MONGOLIA** †RADIO ULAANBAATAR, Altai	DS-1 • 12 kW
4830	**BOLIVIA** †RADIO GRIGOTA, Santa Cruz	Irr • Tu-Su • DS • 1 kW
		DS • 1 kW
	BOTSWANA RADIO BOTSWANA, Gaborone	ENGLISH, ETC • DS • 50 kW
	CHINA (PR) CHINA HUAYI BC CO, Fuzhou	DS-TEMP INACTIVE
	THAILAND †RADIO THAILAND, Pathum Thani	SE Asia • 10 kW
		JAPANESE • SE Asia • 10 kW
	VENEZUELA †RADIO TACHIRA, San Cristóbal	DS • 10 kW
4832v	**COSTA RICA** RADIO RELOJ, San José	Irr • DS • 3 kW
4835	**AUSTRALIA** ABC/CAAMA RADIO, Alice Springs	ENGLISH, ETC • Australasia • DS • 50 kW
	GUATEMALA †RADIO TEZULUTLAN, Cobán	SPANISH, ETC • DS • 5 kW
	MALAYSIA RTM-SARAWAK, Kuching-Stapok	DS-MALAY, MELANAU • 10 kW
	PERU RADIO MARANON, Jaén	DS • 1 kW
4835v	**MALI** RTV MALIENNE, Bamako	Su • DS • 18 kW
		FRENCH, ETC • DS • 18 kW
		M-Sa • FRENCH, ETC • DS • 18 kW
	PAKISTAN PAKISTAN BC CORP, Islamabad	(D) • DS • 100 kW
4836v	**COLOMBIA** †RADIO BUENAVENTURA, Buenaventura	Irr • DS • 1 kW
4840	**CHINA (PR)** HEILONGJIANG PBS, Harbin	DS-1 • 50 kW
	ECUADOR R INTEROCEANICA, Sta Rosa De Quijos	DS • 1 kW
	R INTEROCEANICA, Sta Rosa de Quijos	DS • 1 kW
	INDIA ALL INDIA RADIO, Bombay	DS-B • 10 kW
		ENGLISH, ETC • DS-B • 10 kW
	PERU RADIO ANDAHUAYLAS, Andahuaylas	DS-SPANISH, QUECHUA • 2 kW
4840v	**VENEZUELA** RADIO VALERA, Valera	DS • 1 kW
		Tu-Su • DS • 1 kW
4844.4	**GUATEMALA** RADIO K'EKCHI, San Cristóbal V	SPANISH, ETC • DS • 1.2/5 kW
		M-Sa • SPANISH, ETC • DS • 1.2/5 kW
		Tu-Su • SPANISH, ETC • DS • 1.2/5 kW
		Su • SPANISH, ETC • DS • 1.2/5 kW
4845	**BOLIVIA** †RADIO FIDES, La Paz	Sa/Su • DS • 5 kW
		DS • 5 kW
		Tu-Su • DS • 5 kW
		Irr • DS • 5 kW
	BRAZIL R METEOROLOGIA, Ibitinga	PORTUGUESE • DS • 1 kW
	RADIO CABOCLA, Manaus	PORTUGUESE • DS • 250 kW
	MALAYSIA RADIO TV MALAYSIA, Kajang	DS-6 (TAMIL) • 50 kW
		Sa/Su • DS-6 (TAMIL) • 50 kW
		Su • DS-6 (TAMIL) • 50 kW
	MAURITANIA †ORT DE MAURITANIE, Nouakchott	ARABIC, FRENCH, ETC • DS • 100 kW
		Irr • ARABIC & FRENCH • DS-RAMADAN • 100 kW
4845v	**COLOMBIA** CARACOL, Bucaramanga	DS-VERY IRREGULAR • 1 kW
4850	**CAMEROON** CAMEROON RTV CORP, Yaoundé	FRENCH & ENGLISH • DS • 100 kW
(con'd)	**INDIA** ALL INDIA RADIO, Kohima	DS-A • 50 kW

0 1 2 3 4 5 6 7 8 9 10 11 12 13 14 15 16 17 18 19 20 21 22 23 24

SUMMER ONLY (J)   WINTER ONLY (D)   JAMMING / OR ∧   EARLIEST HEARD ◁   LATEST HEARD ▷   NEW OR CHANGED FOR 1994 †

FREQUENCY   COUNTRY, STATION, LOCATION

TARGET • NETWORK • POWER (kW)

World Time

Frequency	Country, Station, Location	Schedule
4850 (con'd)	**INDIA** ALL INDIA RADIO, Kohima	ENGLISH, ETC • DS-A • 50 kW
	MONGOLIA †RADIO ULAANBAATAR, Ulaanbaatar	DS-1 • 50 kW
	UZBEKISTAN †UZBEK RADIO, Tashkent	DS-2 • 50 kW
4851v	**ECUADOR** RADIO LUZ Y VIDA, Loja	DS • 5 kW / Irr • DS • 5 kW
4853	**YEMEN (REPUBLIC)** REP YEMEN RADIO, San'ā	DS • 50 kW
4855	**BOLIVIA** †RADIO CENTENARIO, Santa Cruz	Tu-Sa • DS • 1 kW / DS • 1 kW / M-F • DS • 1 kW
	BRAZIL R MUNDO MELHOR, Gov Valadares	PORTUGUESE • DS-TEMP INACTIVE • 1 kW
	†RADIO TROPICAL, Barra do Garças	M-Sa • PORTUGUESE • DS-TEMP INACTIVE • 1 kW / PORTUGUESE • DS • 1 kW
4855v	**MOZAMBIQUE** RADIO MOCAMBIQUE, Maputo	DS • 20 kW
4855.8	**INDONESIA** †RRI, Palembang, Sumatera	DS • 10 kW
4856v	**PERU** †RADIO LA HORA, Cusco	Alternative Frequency to 4899v kHz
4860	**INDIA** †ALL INDIA RADIO, Delhi	DS • 20 kW / S Asia • 50 kW / ENGLISH & HINDI • DS • 20 kW / S Asia & W Asia • 50 kW / DS • 50 kW / ENGLISH & HINDI • DS • 50 kW
	RUSSIA BURYAT RADIO, Ulan-Ude	Alternative Frequency to 4795 kHz
	CHITA RADIO, Chita	DS • 15 kW
	†R MOSCOW INTL, Tver	(D) • FEEDER • 100 kW
	VENEZUELA RADIO MARACAIBO, Maracaibo	Irr • DS • 10 kW
4863.8	**INDONESIA** †RRI, Ambon, Maluku	DS • 10 kW
4864v	**BOLIVIA** RADIO 16 DE MARZO, Oruro	Tu-Su • DS / DS
4865	**BRAZIL** R VERDES FLORESTAS, Cruzeiro do Sul	PORTUGUESE • DS • 5 kW
	RADIO ALVORADA, Londrina	Alternative Frequency to 3335 kHz
	RADIO SOCIEDADE, Feira de Santana	PORTUGUESE • DS-TEMP INACTIVE • 1 kW
	CHINA (PR) GANSU PEOPLES BS, Lanzhou	DS-1 • 50 kW
	COLOMBIA LV DEL CINARUCO, Arauca	DS-CARACOL • 5 kW
	MONGOLIA †RADIO ULAANBAATAR, Saynshand	DS-1 • 12 kW
4866v	**MOZAMBIQUE** RADIO MOCAMBIQUE, Maputo	DS • 20 kW
4867.8	**INDONESIA** †RRI, Wamena, Irian Jaya	Alternative Frequency to 4871.2 kHz
4870	**BENIN** ORT DU BENIN, Cotonou	FRENCH, ETC • DS • 30 kW / M-F • FRENCH, ETC • DS • 30 kW / Sa/Su • FRENCH, ETC • DS • 30 kW
	SRI LANKA SRI LANKA BC CORP, Colombo-Ekala	DS-SINHALA 2 • 10 kW
4871.2	**INDONESIA** †RRI, Wamena, Irian Jaya	DS • 0.5 kW • ALT. FREQ. TO 4867.8 kHz
4874.6	**INDONESIA** RRI, Sorong, Irian Jaya	DS • 10 kW
4875	**BOLIVIA** R LA CRUZ DEL SUR, La Paz	Tu-Sa • DS • 10 kW / DS • 10 kW / M-F • DS • 10 kW
	BRAZIL R DIFUSORA RORAIMA, Boa Vista	PORTUGUESE • DS • 10 kW / Irr • PORTUGUESE • DS • 10 kW
	CHINA (PR) VOICE OF JINLING, Nanjing	E Asia • 50 kW
	GEORGIA GEORGIAN RADIO, Tbilisi	DS-2 • 200 kW
	SOUTH AFRICA †SOUTH AFRICAN BC, Meyerton	ENGLISH & AFRIKAANS • DS-RADIO ORANJE • 100 kW
4877.5	**MOZAMBIQUE** EP DE CABO DELGADO, Pemba	DS
4880	**ANGOLA** AV DO GALO NEGRO, Jamba	S Africa • UNITA
	BANGLADESH †RADIO BANGLADESH, Dhaka	BANGLA • DS • 100 kW / ENGLISH & BANGLA • DS • 100 kW / DS • 100 kW
	INDIA †ALL INDIA RADIO, Lucknow	DS-B • 50 kW
4880v	**ECUADOR** †R NACIONAL ESPEJO, Quito	DS • 5 kW

ENGLISH ▬▬   ARABIC ⋙   CHINESE ▫▫▫   FRENCH ▬▬   GERMAN ▬▬   RUSSIAN ▭▭   SPANISH ▬▬   OTHER ▬▬

FREQUENCY	COUNTRY, STATION, LOCATION	TARGET • NETWORK • POWER (kW)

World Time
0 1 2 3 4 5 6 7 8 9 10 11 12 13 14 15 16 17 18 19 20 21 22 23 24

4881.2 INDONESIA
   †SUARA KASIH AGUNG, Jayapura, Jawa — DS

4881.7 PERU
   RADIO NUEVO MUNDO, Pucallpa — DS • 0.25/1 kW

4883 CHINA (PR)
   CHINA RADIO INTL, Hohhot — E Asia • RUSSIAN, MONGOLIAN • 50 kW

4884.8 BOLIVIA
   †RADIO SARARENDA, Camiri — Irr • DS • 1 kW
   Irr • M-Sa • DS • 1 kW

4885 BRAZIL
   R CLUBE DO PARA, Belém — PORTUGUESE • DS • 5 kW
   R DIF ACREANA, Rio Branco — PORTUGUESE • DS • 5 kW
   Irr • PORTUGUESE • DS • 5 kW
   RADIO CARAJA, Anápolis — PORTUGUESE • DS • 0.5 kW

COLOMBIA
   ONDAS DEL META, Villavicencio — Irr • DS-SUPER • 5 kW

KENYA
   KENYA BC CORP, Nairobi — M-F • DS-EASTERN • 10 kW

4890 FRANCE
   R FRANCE INTL, Via Moyabi, Gabon — C Africa • 250 kW

PAPUA NEW GUINEA
   NBC, Port Moresby — ENGLISH, ETC • DS • 2 kW

4890v ECUADOR
   †CENTINELA DEL SUR, Loja — Alternative Frequency to 4770v kHz

SENEGAL
   ORT DU SENEGAL, Dakar — FRENCH, ETC • DS • 100 kW

4890.2 PERU
   RADIO CHOTA, Chota — DS

4895 BRAZIL
   RADIO BARE, Manaus — PORTUGUESE • DS • 1 kW
   RADIO IPB AM, Campo Grande — PORTUGUESE • DS • 5 kW

COLOMBIA
   LV DEL RIO ARAUCA, Arauca — DS-RCN • 10 kW
   M-Sa • DS-RCN • 10 kW

INDIA
   †ALL INDIA RADIO, Kurseong — DS • 20 kW

MALAYSIA
   RTM-SARAWAK, Kuching-Stapok — DS-IBAN • 10 kW

RUSSIA
   TYUMEN RADIO, Tyumen — DS • 15 kW

4895v PAKISTAN
   †PAKISTAN BC CORP, Islamabad — DS

VIETNAM
   VOICE OF VIETNAM, Hanoi — VIETNAMESE • DS

4897v MONGOLIA
   †RADIO ULAANBAATAR, Murun — DS-1 • 12 kW

4899 ECUADOR
   CENTINELA DEL SUR, Loja — Alternative Frequency to 4899 kHz
   M-Sa • DS • 2 kW • ALT. FREQ. TO 4899 kHz
   Tu-Su • DS • 2 kW • ALT. FREQ. TO 4899 kHz

4899v PERU
   †RADIO LA HORA, Cusco — Tu-Su • DS • 1 kW • ALT. FREQ. TO 4856v kHz
   DS-SPANISH, QUECHUA • 1 kW • ALT. FREQ. TO 4856v kHz

4900v ECUADOR
   RADIO LIBERTADOR, Saquisilí — Irr • DS • 0.45 kW

INDONESIA
   †RRI, Surakarta, Jawa — DS • 0.5 kW

4902 SRI LANKA
   SRI LANKA BC CORP, Colombo-Ekala — DS-SINHALA 1 • 10 kW

4904v BOLIVIA
   †RADIO LA PALABRA, S Ignacio de Moxos — Irr • DS

4904.5 CHAD
   †RADIODIF NATIONALE, N'Djamena — FRENCH, ETC • DS • 100 kW • ALT. FREQ. TO 6165 kHz

4905 BRAZIL
   R RELOGIO FEDERAL, Rio de Janeiro — PORTUGUESE • DS • 5 kW
   RADIO ANHANGUERA, Araguaína — PORTUGUESE • DS • 1 kW

CHINA (PR)
   †CENTRAL PEOPLES BS — DS-2

4908v PERU
   RADIO TAWANTINSUYO, Cusco — DS-SPANISH, QUECHUA • 5 kW
   Irr • DS • 5 kW

4910 AUSTRALIA
   ABC/CAAMA RADIO, Tennant Creek — ENGLISH, ETC • Australasia • DS • 50 kW

GUINEA
   RTV GUINEENNE, Conakry-Kipe — M-Sa • FRENCH, ETC • DS • 100 kW
   DS • 100 kW
   FRENCH, ETC • DS • 100 kW
   Su • FRENCH, ETC • DS • 100 kW

INDIA
   †ALL INDIA RADIO, Jaipur — DS-A • 50 kW • ALT. FREQ. TO 3345 kHz

4910v CAMBODIA
   RADIO PHNOM PENH, Phnom Penh — DS • 50 kW
   Su • DS • 50 kW

HONDURAS
   †LV DE LA MOSQUITIA, Puerto Lempira — Irr • DS • 0.1/0.5 kW

ZAMBIA
   RADIO ZAMBIA-ZBS, Lusaka — ENGLISH, ETC • DS-1 • 50 kW

0 1 2 3 4 5 6 7 8 9 10 11 12 13 14 15 16 17 18 19 20 21 22 23 24

SUMMER ONLY (J)   WINTER ONLY (D)   JAMMING / OR ∧   EARLIEST HEARD ◁   LATEST HEARD ▷   NEW OR CHANGED FOR 1994 †

FREQUENCY   COUNTRY, STATION, LOCATION

TARGET • NETWORK • POWER (kW)   World Time

0 1 2 3 4 5 6 7 8 9 10 11 12 13 14 15 16 17 18 19 20 21 22 23 24

Frequency	Country, Station, Location	Schedule
4911	ECUADOR	
	†EM GRAN COLOMBIA, Quito	DS-VERY IRREGULAR • 5 kW
4914.5	PERU	
	RADIO CORA, Lima-Puente Piedra	DS • 10 kW / M-Sa • DS • 10 kW
4915	BRAZIL	
	RADIO ANHANGUERA, Goiânia	PORTUGUESE • DS • 10 kW / Irr • PORTUGUESE • DS • 10 kW
	RADIO NACIONAL, Macapá	PORTUGUESE • DS • 10 kW
	CHINA (PR)	
	GUANGXI PEOPLES BS, Nanning	CHINESE, ETC • DS-1 • 10 kW
	GHANA	
	†GHANA BC CORP, Accra	ENGLISH, ETC • DS-1 • 50 kW / Sa/Su • ENGLISH, ETC • DS-1 • 50 kW
	KENYA	
	KENYA BC CORP, Nairobi	M-F • DS-CENTRAL • 100 kW
	PAKISTAN	
	†PAKISTAN BC CORP, Islamabad	DS • 10 kW
4915v	COLOMBIA	
	ARMONIAS CAQUETA, Florencia	DS • 3 kW / Tu-Su • DS • 3 kW / M-Sa • DS • 3 kW
4920	AUSTRALIA	
	AUSTRALIAN BC CORP, Brisbane	Australasia • DS • 10 kW
	ECUADOR	
	RADIO QUITO, Quito	DS • 5 kW / Tu-Su • DS • 5 kW / M-Sa • DS • 5 kW
	INDIA	
	†ALL INDIA RADIO, Madras	DS-A • 50 kW / ENGLISH, ETC • DS-A • 50 kW
	RUSSIA	
	YAKUT RADIO, Yakutsk	DS-RUSSIAN, YAKUT • 50 kW
4922v	PERU	
	ONDAS DEL TITICACA, Puno	SPANISH, ETC • DS • 1 kW / Tu-Su • DS • 1 kW
4924.6	PERU	
	†ONDA VERDE, Pichanaqui	Alternative Frequency to 4944.6 kHz
4925	BRAZIL	
	RADIO DIFUSORA, Taubaté	PORTUGUESE • DS • 1 kW
	CHINA (PR)	
	HEILONGJIANG PBS, Harbin	DS-CHINESE, KOREAN • 50 kW
	COLOMBIA	
	EM MERIDIANO 70, Arauca	DS • 2.5 kW
	INDONESIA	
	†RRI, Jambi, Sumatera	DS • 7.5 kW / Sa • DS • 7.5 kW
4925v	BOLIVIA	
	†RADIO SAN MIGUEL, Riberalta	DS • 1 kW
4925.6	EQUATORIAL GUINEA	
	RADIO NACIONAL, Bata	DS-SPANISH, ETC • 100 kW • ALT. FREQ. TO 5004v kHz
4926v	MOZAMBIQUE	
	RADIO MOCAMBIQUE, Maputo	DS • 10 kW / DS • 7.5 kW
4930	DOMINICAN REPUBLIC	
	RADIO BARAHONA, Barahona	DS-TEMP INACTIVE • 1 kW
	RUSSIA	
	RADIO MOSCOW, Various Locations	DS-MAYAK • 50 kW
4931.7	INDONESIA	
	†RRI, Surakarta, Jawa	DS • 10 kW
4932v	CHINA (PR)	
	HONGHE PEOPLES BS, Honghe	DS
4934	KENYA	
	KENYA BC CORP, Nairobi	DS-GENERAL • 100 kW
4935	BRAZIL	
	RADIO DIFUSORA, Jataí	PORTUGUESE • DS • 2.5 kW
4935v	BRAZIL	
	RADIO CAPIXABA, Vitória	PORTUGUESE • DS • 1 kW
	PERU	
	RADIO TROPICAL, Tarapoto	DS • 3 kW
4939.3	BOLIVIA	
	†RADIO NORTE, Montero	Tu-Sa • DS • 1 kW / DS • 1 kW / M-Sa • DS • 1 kW / Su • DS • 1 kW
4939.6	VENEZUELA	
	RADIO CONTINENTAL, Barinas	Irr • DS • 1 kW / Irr • M-Sa • DS • 1 kW
4940	CHINA (PR)	
	QINGHAI PEOPLES BS, Xining	Irr • DS-1 • 10 kW
	†VO THE STRAIT-PLA, Fuzhou	TAIWAN-1 • 10 kW
	COTE D'IVOIRE	
	R COTE D'IVOIRE, Abidjan	DS-1 • 25 kW
	INDIA	
	ALL INDIA RADIO, Guwahati	DS-A • 50 kW
	RUSSIA	
	†R MOSCOW INTL, Via Tajikistan	(D) • W Asia & S Asia • 100 kW
	YAKUT RADIO, Yakutsk	(D) • DS-RUSSIAN, YAKUT • 50 kW
	SRI LANKA	
(con'd)	SRI LANKA BC CORP, Colombo-Ekala	DS • 10 kW

0 1 2 3 4 5 6 7 8 9 10 11 12 13 14 15 16 17 18 19 20 21 22 23 24

ENGLISH ▬   ARABIC ⧌⧌⧌   CHINESE □□□   FRENCH ▬▬   GERMAN ▬   RUSSIAN ═   SPANISH ▬   OTHER ▬

FREQUENCY   COUNTRY, STATION, LOCATION

TARGET • NETWORK • POWER (kW)

World Time

0 1 2 3 4 5 6 7 8 9 10 11 12 13 14 15 16 17 18 19 20 21 22 23 24

FREQUENCY	COUNTRY, STATION, LOCATION	TARGET • NETWORK • POWER (kW)
4940 (con'd)	UKRAINE — UKRAINIAN R, Kiev	RUSSIAN & UKRAINIAN • DS-3 • 50 kW
4944.6	PERU — †ONDA VERDE, Pichanaqui	DS • ALT. FREQ. TO 4924.6 kHz
4945	BOLIVIA — †RADIO ILLIMANI, La Paz	Irr • DS • 10 kW / Irr • Tu-Su • DS • 10 kW / Irr • M-Sa • DS • 10 kW
	BRAZIL — RADIO DIFUSORA, Poços de Caldas	PORTUGUESE • DS • 1 kW / Tu-Su • PORTUGUESE • DS • 1 kW
	RADIO NACIONAL, Pôrto Velho	PORTUGUESE • DS • 50 kW / Irr • PORTUGUESE • DS • 50 kW
	VOZ SAO FRANCISCO, Petrolina	PORTUGUESE • DS • 2 kW
	SOUTH AFRICA — †CHANNEL AFRICA, Meyerton	(J) • E Africa & S Africa • 250 kW
4950	CHINA (PR) — VOICE OF PUJIANG, Shanghai	E Asia
	XILINGOL PBS, Abagnar Qi	DS-MONGOLIAN
	ECUADOR — RADIO BAHA'I, Otavalo	DS • 1 kW
	INDIA — †ALL INDIA RADIO, Port Blair	Alternative Frequency to 4760 kHz
	†ALL INDIA RADIO, Shimla	Alternative Frequency to 3223 kHz
	†RADIO KASHMIR, Jammu	DS-A • 2 kW • ALT. FREQ. TO 3345 kHz
	MALAYSIA — RTM-SARAWAK, Kuching-Stapok	DS • 10 kW
	PERU — R MADRE DE DIOS, Puerto Maldonado	DS • 5 kW / Irr • DS • 5 kW
4951v	ANGOLA — RADIO NACIONAL, Luanda	Irr • DS
4955	BRAZIL — RADIO CLUBE, Rondonópolis	PORTUGUESE • DS-TEMP INACTIVE • 2.5 kW / M-Sa • PORTUGUESE • DS-TEMP INACTIVE • 2.5 kW
	RADIO CULTURA, Campos	PORTUGUESE • DS • 2.5 kW
	PERU — RADIO AMAUTA, Huanta	DS-SPANISH, QUECHUA • 1 kW
4955v	BRAZIL — RADIO MARAJOARA, Belém	PORTUGUESE • DS • 10 kW
4957.5	AZERBAIJAN — AZERBAIJANI RADIO, Baku	DS-2 • 50 kW
4959.8	DOMINICAN REPUBLIC — †RADIO CIMA, Santo Domingo	Irr • DS • 1 kW
4960	CHINA (PR) — CHINA RADIO INTL, Kunming	JAPANESE • E Asia • 50 kW
	INDIA — †ALL INDIA RADIO, Delhi	DS • 10/50 kW / ENGLISH, ETC • DS • 10/50 kW
	VIETNAM — †VOICE OF VIETNAM, Hanoi	DS-TESTS • 50 kW
4960.3	PERU — RADIO LA MERCED, La Merced	Tu-Su • DS • 0.5 kW / DS • 0.5 kW / M-Sa • DS • 0.5 kW
4961v	ECUADOR — RADIO FEDERACION, Sucúa	DS • 5 kW
4965	BRAZIL — RADIO ALVORADA, Parintins	PORTUGUESE • DS • 5 kW
	RADIO POTI, Natal	PORTUGUESE • DS • 1 kW
4965v	BOLIVIA — †RADIO JUAN XXIII, San Ignacio Velasco	DS • 3 kW / M-Sa • DS • 3 kW / Irr • M-Sa • DS • 3 kW / Su • DS • 3 kW
4965.2	COLOMBIA — RADIO SANTA FE, Santa Fé de Bogotá	Irr • DS • 5 kW
4966	PERU — RADIO SAN MIGUEL, Cusco	DS-SPANISH, QUECHUA • 5 kW / Tu-Su • DS • 5 kW
4970	CHINA (PR) — XINJIANG PBS, Urümqi	DS-KAZAKH • 50 kW
	MALAYSIA — †RTM-KOTA KINABALU, Kota Kinabalu	DS-MALAY • 10 kW / Irr • DS-MALAY • 10 kW
4970v	VENEZUELA — RADIO RUMBOS, Villa de Cura	DS • 10 kW
4970.3	PERU — RADIO IMAGEN, Tarapoto	DS • 1 kW / Su • DS • 1 kW / Tu-Su • DS • 1 kW
4975	BRAZIL — RADIO TIMBIRA, São Luís	PORTUGUESE • DS • 2.5 kW
(con'd)	RADIO TUPI, São Paulo	PORTUGUESE • DS • 1 kW

0 1 2 3 4 5 6 7 8 9 10 11 12 13 14 15 16 17 18 19 20 21 22 23 24

SUMMER ONLY (J)   WINTER ONLY (D)   JAMMING / OR ∧   EARLIEST HEARD ◁   LATEST HEARD ▷   NEW OR CHANGED FOR 1994 †

FREQUENCY   COUNTRY, STATION, LOCATION   TARGET • NETWORK • POWER (kW)   World Time

0 1 2 3 4 5 6 7 8 9 10 11 12 13 14 15 16 17 18 19 20 21 22 23 24

Frequency	Country, Station, Location	Schedule details
4975 (con'd)	CHINA (PR) †FUJIAN PEOPLES BS, Jianyang	DS-1 • 10 kW; TAIWAN SVC • 10 kW
	PERU RADIO DEL PACIFICO, Lima	DS • 4 kW; Su/M • DS • 4 kW; Tu-Sa • DS • 4 kW; DS • 4 kW • ALT. FREQ. TO 9675 kHz
	RUSSIA †R MOSCOW INTL, Via Tajikistan	(D) • W Asia & S Asia • 100 kW
4976	UGANDA RADIO UGANDA, Kampala	DS-ENGLISH, ETC • 50 kW; M-F • DS-ENGLISH, ETC • 50 kW; M-Sa • DS-ENGLISH, ETC • 50 kW
4976v	COLOMBIA ONDAS ORTEGUAZA, Florencia	Irr • DS-TODELAR • 1 kW; DS-TODELAR • 1 kW
4977v	ECUADOR RADIO TARQUI, Quito	Irr • DS • 3 kW
4980	CHINA (PR) †XINJIANG PBS, Urümqi	DS-MONGOLIAN • 50 kW
	VENEZUELA ECOS DEL TORBES, San Cristóbal	DS • 10 kW
4981v	BOLIVIA †RADIO MINERIA, Oruro	DS • 1 kW
4985	BRAZIL R BRASIL CENTRAL, Goiânia	PORTUGUESE • DS • 10 kW; Irr • PORTUGUESE • DS • 10 kW
	IRAN VO THE ISLAMIC REP, Tehrān	Irr • PERSIAN • Mideast • ALT. FREQ. TO 4990 kHz
4988	INDONESIA †RRI, Gorontalo, Sulawesi	DS • 10 kW
4990	ARMENIA RADIO YEREVAN, Yerevan	Irr • Mideast • 50 kW; Irr • ARMENIAN • Mideast • 50 kW; Mideast • 50 kW; M-Sa • Mideast • 50 kW; ARMENIAN • Mideast • ARMENIAN, TURKISH • 50 kW
	CHINA (PR) †HUNAN PEOPLES BS, Changsha	DS-1 • 10 kW
	INDIA †ALL INDIA RADIO, Bhopal	DS (PROJECTED); ENGLISH, ETC • DS (PROJECTED)
	†ALL INDIA RADIO, Guwahati	Alternative Frequency to 4775.3 kHz
	ALL INDIA RADIO, Madras	SE Asia • 100 kW
	IRAN VO THE ISLAMIC REP, Tehrān	Alternative Frequency to 4985 kHz
	NIGERIA RADIO NIGERIA, Lagos	ENGLISH, ETC • DS-1 • 50 kW
4990.7	PERU RADIO ANCASH, Huáraz	DS • 5/10 kW
4991	BOLIVIA †RADIO ANIMAS, Animas	Tu-Su • DS • 1 kW; DS • 1 kW; M-Sa • DS • 1 kW
	SURINAME †RADIO APINTIE, Paramaribo	DS • 0.05/0.35 kW • ALT. FREQ. TO 5005.7 kHz; Tu-Su • DS • 0.05/0.35 kW • ALT. FREQ. TO 5005.7 kHz
4994	SUDAN †REP OF SUDAN RADIO, Omdurman	Irr • DS • 20 kW; Irr • DS-RAMADAN • 20 kW
4995	MONGOLIA †RADIO ULAANBAATAR, Choybalsan	DS-1 • 12 kW
4995.8	PERU RADIO ANDINA, Huancayo	DS • 1 kW; Tu-Su • DS • 1 kW
5000	AUSTRALIA †VNG, Llandilo	WORLD TIME • 10 kW
	CLANDESTINE (ASIA) †"KASHMIR FREEDOM"	S Asia • ANTI-INDIAN GOVT
	ERITREA †VO BROAD MASSES, Asmera	E Africa; Sa/Su • E Africa
	USA WWV, Ft Collins, Colorado	WEATHER/WORLD TIME • 10 kW
	WWVH, Kekaha, Hawaii	WEATHER/WORLD TIME • 5 kW
	VENEZUELA OBSERVATORIO NAVAL, Caracas	DS • 1 kW
5004v	EQUATORIAL GUINEA RADIO NACIONAL, Bata	Alternative Frequency to 4925.6 kHz
5004.8	BOLIVIA RADIO LIBERTAD, La Paz	Tu-Sa • DS • 1/5 kW; DS • 1/5 kW; Tu-Su • DS • 1/5 kW; M-F • DS • 1/5 kW; M-Sa • DS • 1/5 kW
5005 (con'd)	MALAYSIA RTM-SARAWAK, Sibu	DS-IBAN • 10 kW

0 1 2 3 4 5 6 7 8 9 10 11 12 13 14 15 16 17 18 19 20 21 22 23 24

ENGLISH ■■   ARABIC ☒☒☒   CHINESE ▫▫▫   FRENCH ≡≡   GERMAN ▬▬   RUSSIAN ══   SPANISH ▦▦   OTHER ▬

FREQUENCY	COUNTRY, STATION, LOCATION	TARGET • NETWORK • POWER (kW)	World Time

5005 **NEPAL**
(con'd) †RADIO NEPAL, Harriharpur — DS • 100 kW
5005.7 **SURINAME**
   †RADIO APINTIE, Paramaribo — Alternative Frequency to 4991 kHz
5008.8 **PERU**
   RADIO HORIZONTE, Chachapoyas — DS • 5 kW
5009v **MADAGASCAR**
   RTV MALAGASY, Antananarivo — DS-1 • 30/100 kW
   M-Sa • DS-1 • 30/100 kW

5010 **CAMEROON**
   CAMEROON RTV CORP, Garoua — FRENCH, ENGLISH, ETC • DS • 100 kW
   CHINA (PR)
   GUANGXI PEOPLES BS, Nanning — DS-2/CHINESE, ETC • 10 kW
   INDIA
   †ALL INDIA RADIO, Thiruvananthapuram — DS (PROJECTED) • 50 kW
   ENGLISH, ETC • DS (PROJECTED) • 50 kW
   SINGAPORE
   SINGAPORE BC CORP, Jurong — DS-1 • 50 kW
5010v **ECUADOR**
   †ESCUELAS R'FONICAS, Riobamba — DS • 10 kW
   M-Sa • DS • 10 kW

5014.6 **BRAZIL**
   RADIO PIONEIRA, Teresina — PORTUGUESE • DS • 1 kW
5015 **BRAZIL**
   R BRASIL TROPICAL, Cuiabá — PORTUGUESE • DS • 5 kW
   RUSSIA
   ARKHANGELSK RADIO, Arkhangelsk — DS • 50 kW
   †PRIMORSK RADIO, Vladivostok — DS/TIKHIY OKEAN • 50 kW
   RADIO MOSCOW, Via Turkmenistan — DS-1 • 50 kW
   TURKMENISTAN
   †TURKMEN RADIO, Ashkhabad — RUSSIAN, ETC • DS-1 • 50 kW
5015v **PERU**
   RADIO TARAPOTO, Tarapoto — DS • 0.7 kW
5020 **CHINA (PR)**
   JIANGXI PEOPLES BS, Nanchang — DS-1 • 10 kW
   Su • DS-1 • 10 kW
   CROATIA
   †CROATIAN RADIO, Zagreb — Irr • Europe • DS-1 • 10 kW
   Irr • M-Sa • Europe • DS-1 • 10 kW
   Irr • Su • Europe • DS-1 • 10 kW
   ECUADOR
   LA VOZ DEL UPANO, Macas — DS • 10 kW
   SOLOMON ISLANDS
   †SOLOMON ISLANDS BC, Honiara — Su • DS-ENGLISH, PIDGIN • 10 kW
   Sa • DS-ENGLISH, PIDGIN • 10 kW
   M-F • DS-ENGLISH, PIDGIN • 10 kW
   SRI LANKA
   SRI LANKA BC CORP, Colombo-Ekala — DS-TAMIL • 10 kW
5020v **COLOMBIA**
   ECOS DEL ATRATO, Quibdó — Irr • DS-CARACOL • 2 kW
   NIGER
   †LA VOIX DU SAHEL, Niamey — FRENCH, ETC • DS • 20/100 kW
   Irr • FRENCH, ETC • DS • 20/100 kW
   Sa • FRENCH, ETC • DS • 20/100 kW
5021v **CHINA (PR)**
   †XIZANG PEOPLES BS, Lhasa — DS-TIBETAN • 50 kW
5025 **AUSTRALIA**
   ABC/R RUM JUNGLE, Katherine — Australasia • DS • 50 kW
   BENIN
   †RADIO PARAKOU, Parakou — FRENCH, ETC • DS • 20 kW • ALT. FREQ. TO 7190 kHz
   M-F • FRENCH, ETC • DS • 20 kW
   FRENCH, ETC • DS • 20 kW
   Sa/Su • FRENCH, ETC • DS • 20 kW • ALT. FREQ. TO 7190 kHz
   BHUTAN
   BHUTAN BC SERVICE, Thimbu — Su • DS • 50 kW
   M-Sa • DS • 50 kW
   BRAZIL
   R TRANSAMAZONICA, Altamira — PORTUGUESE • DS • 5 kW
   RADIO BORBOREMA, Campina Grande — PORTUGUESE • DS-TEMP INACTIVE • 1 kW
   RADIO MORIMOTO, Ji-Paraná — PORTUGUESE • DS-TEMP INACTIVE • 5 kW
   PERU
   RADIO QUILLABAMBA, Quillabamba — DS-SPANISH, ETC • 5 kW
   Tu-Su • DS • 5 kW
   M-Sa • DS-SPANISH, ETC • 5 kW
5025v **CUBA**
   RADIO REBELDE, Havana — Irr • DS • 10 kW
   PAKISTAN
   †PAKISTAN BC CORP, Islamabad — DS • 100 kW
5026 **UGANDA**
   RADIO UGANDA, Kampala — DS-ENGLISH, SWAHILI • 50/250 kW
   M-F • DS-ENGLISH, SWAHILI • 50/250 kW
   M-Sa • DS-ENGLISH, SWAHILI • 50/250 kW
5030 **COSTA RICA**
   †ADVENTIST WORLD R, Cahuita — C America • TESTS • 20 kW
   ECUADOR
(con'd) R CATOLICA NAC, Quito — DS • 9 kW

SUMMER ONLY (J)   WINTER ONLY (D)   JAMMING / OR ∧   EARLIEST HEARD ◁   LATEST HEARD ▷   NEW OR CHANGED FOR 1994 †

FREQUENCY   COUNTRY, STATION, LOCATION   TARGET • NETWORK • POWER (kW)   World Time

Frequency	Country, Station, Location	Schedule
5030 (con'd)	**ECUADOR** R CATOLICA NAC, Quito	M-Sa • DS • 9 kW
	MALAYSIA RTM-SARAWAK, Kuching-Stapok	DS-BIDAYUTH • 10 kW
	TONGA TONGA BC COMMISS'N, Nuku'alofa	Irr • Tu-Su • DS-ENGLISH, TONGAN • 1 kW Irr • M-Sa • DS-ENGLISH, TONGAN • 1 kW
5030.6	**PERU** RADIO LOS ANDES, Huamachuco	DS • 1 kW
5031v	**VIETNAM** †VOICE OF VIETNAM, Hanoi	DS
5034v	**CENTRAL AFRICAN REP** RTV CENTRAFRICAINE, Bangui	FRENCH, ETC • DS • 100 kW
5035	**BRAZIL** R EDUCACAO RURAL, Coari	PORTUGUESE • DS • 1 kW
	RADIO APARECIDA, Aparecida	PORTUGUESE • DS • 10 kW
	KAZAKHSTAN †KAZAKH RADIO, Almaty	DS-2 • 50 kW
	†RADIO ALMATY, Almaty	50 kW
	PERU RADIO AYAVIRI, Ayaviri	Alternative Frequency to 4606.6 kHz
5039.2	**PERU** RADIO LIBERTAD, Junín	DS • 1 kW
5039.8	**CHINA (PR)** †FUJIAN PEOPLES BS, Fuzhou	DS-1 • 10 kW
5040	**ECUADOR** LA VOZ DEL UPANO, Macas	DS • 10 kW
	GEORGIA GEORGIAN RADIO, Tbilisi	RUSSIAN, ETC • DS-1 • 100 kW
5040v	**VENEZUELA** RADIO MATURIN, Maturín	DS-VERY IRREGULAR • 10 kW
5040.7	**GUATEMALA** †LA VOZ DE NAHUALA, Nahualá	SPANISH, ETC • DS
5041v	**ANGOLA** EP DE BENGUELA, Benguela	DS • 1 kW
5045	**BOLIVIA** RADIO ALTIPLANO, La Paz	M-Sa • DS-TEMP INACTIVE • 5 kW
	BRAZIL R CULTURA DO PARA, Belém	PORTUGUESE • DS • 10 kW
	RADIO DIFUSORA, Presidente Prudente	PORTUGUESE • DS • 0.5 kW Tu-Su • PORTUGUESE • DS • 0.5 kW
5046.2	**PERU** †RADIO YURIMAGUAS, Yurimaguas	DS
5046.7	**INDONESIA** RRI, Yogyakarta, Jawa	DS-TEMP INACTIVE • 20 kW
5047	**TOGO** RADIO LOME, Lomé-Togblekope	FRENCH, ETC • DS • 100 kW DS • 100 kW
5049.8	**ECUADOR** R JESUS GRAN PODER, Quito	DS • 5 kW
5050	**CHINA (PR)** GUANGXI BC STATION, Nanning	SE Asia • 50 kW
	INDIA ALL INDIA RADIO, Aizawl	DS • 50 kW ENGLISH, ETC • DS • 50 kW Sa • DS • 50 kW Sa • ENGLISH, ETC • DS • 50 kW
	†RADIO KASHMIR, Srinagar	DS-B (PROJECTED) • 50 kW Su • DS-B (PROJECTED) • 50 kW ENGLISH, ETC • DS-B (PROJECTED) • 50 kW
	TANZANIA †RADIO TANZANIA, Dar es Salaam	E Africa • 10/50 kW Sa/Su • E Africa • 10/50 kW
5050.3	**COLOMBIA** †LA VOZ DE YOPAL, Yopal	DS-CARACOL • 1 kW Irr • DS-CARACOL • 1 kW
5050.4	**PERU** RADIO MUNICIPAL, Cangallo	DS • 0.5 kW
5051.8	**SINGAPORE** SINGAPORE BC CORP, Jurong	DS-1 • 50 kW
5055	**BRAZIL** RADIO DIFUSORA, Cáceres	PORTUGUESE • DS • 1 kW M-Sa • PORTUGUESE • DS • 1 kW
	COSTA RICA FARO DEL CARIBE, San José	DS • 5 kW
	SWAZILAND TRANS WORLD RADIO, Manzini	S Africa • 25 kW
5055.2	**INDONESIA** RRI, Nabire, Irian Jaya	DS-TEMP INACTIVE • 1 kW
5056	**FRENCH GUIANA** RFO-GUYANE, Cayenne	DS • 10 kW
5057v	**VIETNAM** †RTV KONTUM, Kontum	DS Irr • DS
5060	**CHINA (PR)** †XINJIANG PBS, Changji	DS-MONGOLIAN • 10 kW
5060.5	**ECUADOR** R NAC PROGRESO, Loja	DS • 5 kW

0 1 2 3 4 5 6 7 8 9 10 11 12 13 14 15 16 17 18 19 20 21 22 23 24

ENGLISH ▬   ARABIC ⌇⌇⌇   CHINESE ▯▯▯   FRENCH ▭▭▭   GERMAN ▬   RUSSIAN ═══   SPANISH ▬   OTHER ▬

FREQUENCY   COUNTRY, STATION, LOCATION   TARGET • NETWORK • POWER (kW)   World Time

World Time scale: 0 1 2 3 4 5 6 7 8 9 10 11 12 13 14 15 16 17 18 19 20 21 22 23 24

Frequency	Country / Station / Location	Notes
5066v	ZAIRE — RADIO CANDIP, Bunia	FRENCH, ETC • DS • 1 kW; Sa • FRENCH, ETC • DS • 1 kW
5068.6	PERU — †ONDAS SUR ORIENTE, Quillabamba	DS
5068.7	PERU — ONDAS SUR ORIENTE, Quillabamba	DS • 1.5 kW
5070	RUSSIA — †RADIO BERYOZOVO, Beryozovo	Su • RUSSIAN, ETC • DS
5075	COLOMBIA — †CARACOL COLOMBIA, Bogotá	DS • 10 kW
5083v	PERU — RADIO MUNDO, Cusco	SPANISH, ETC • DS • 1 kW
5090	CHINA (PR) — CENTRAL PEOPLES BS, Beijing	(D) • CHINESE, ETC • TAIWAN-2 • 10 kW
5097.3	PERU — RADIO ECO, Iquitos	DS • 1 kW
5125	CHINA (PR) — CENTRAL PEOPLES BS, Beijing	(D) • CHINESE, ETC • TAIWAN-1 • 10 kW
5131v	PERU — †RADIO VISION 2000, Bambamarca	DS
5145	CHINA (PR) — CHINA RADIO INTL, Beijing	E Asia • RUSSIAN, MONGOLIAN • 120 kW
5145v	PERU — RADIO RQ, Tingo Maria	DS
5156.2	BOLIVIA — RADIO GALAXIA, Guayaramerin	Tu-Su • DS • 0.2 kW; M-Sa • DS • 0.2 kW
5163	CHINA (PR) — CENTRAL PEOPLES BS, Xi'an	DS-2 • 50 kW
5220	CHINA (PR) — CHINA RADIO INTL, Beijing	E Asia • FEEDER • 10 kW; (J) • E Asia • FEEDER • 10 kW
	SPAIN — R EXTERIOR ESPANA, Via Beijing	Alternative Frequency to 4130 kHz
5230v	CLANDESTINE (M EAST) — "VO THE MOJAHED", Iraq	PERSIAN • Mideast
5245v	PERU — †RADIO TAYABAMBA, Tayabamba	Alternative Frequency to 5390v kHz
5250	CHINA (PR) — CHINA RADIO INTL, Beijing	Irr • E Asia • FEEDER • 10 kW
	SPAIN — R EXTERIOR ESPANA, Via Beijing	(D) • E Asia • FEEDER • 10 kW
5256v	INDONESIA — RRI, Sibolga, Sumatera	DS-TEMP INACTIVE • 1 kW
5260	KAZAKHSTAN — †KAZAKH RADIO, Almaty	DS-2 • 50 kW
	†RADIO ALMATY, Almaty	50 kW
5260v	PERU — R NORORIENTAL, S Rosa Huayabamba	DS • 0.5 kW
5275	USA — FAMILY RADIO, Via Taiwan	E Asia • 250 kW
5287v	CHAD — RADIODIF NATIONALE, Moundou	FRENCH, ARABIC, ETC • DS • 5 kW
5290	RUSSIA — KRASNOYARSK RADIO, Krasnoyarsk	DS • 100 kW
5320	CHINA (PR) — †CENTRAL PEOPLES BS, Beijing	DS-1 • 10/15 kW
5323.5	PERU — †RADIO ORIGENES, Huancavelica	DS • 0.5 kW
5338	PERU — †RADIO LIDER, Cajamarca	DS
5344	PERU — †RADIO POMABAMBA, Pomabamba	DS • 0.5 kW
5388v	PERU — †RADIO SONORAMA, Saposoa	DS
5390v	PERU — †RADIO TAYABAMBA, Tayabamba	DS • 1 kW • ALT. FREQ. TO 5245v kHz
5408v	CLANDESTINE (ASIA) — †"VO NATIONAL FRONT, Southern Laos	SE Asia
5420	CHINA (PR) — CENTRAL PEOPLES BS, Beijing	DS-MINORITIES • 10 kW; (D) • DS-MINORITIES • 10 kW
5430	BYELARUS — RADIO MAHILEU	RUSSIAN & BYELORUSSIAN • DS
5440	CHINA (PR) — XINJIANG PBS, Urümqi	DS-KAZAKH • 50 kW
5445	PERU — R ALTO HUALLAGA, Uchiza	DS
5450	RUSSIA — †RADIO NOVAYA VOLNA, Chelyabinsk	DS
5486.5	PERU — †REINA DE LA SELVA, Chachapoyas	Irr • DS
5505.3	BOLIVIA — RADIO 2 DE FEBRERO, Rurrenabaque	Irr • DS • 0.5 kW; Irr • Tu-Su • DS • 0.5 kW; Irr • M-Sa • DS • 0.5 kW
5535	COLOMBIA — ECOS CELESTIALES, Medellin	DS
5569v	COLOMBIA — RADIO NUEVA VIDA, Tibú	DS • 0.1 kW
5580.2	BOLIVIA — †RADIO SAN JOSE, San José Chiquitos	Irr • DS • 0.5 kW; DS • 0.5 kW

Bottom time scale: 0 1 2 3 4 5 6 7 8 9 10 11 12 13 14 15 16 17 18 19 20 21 22 23 24

FREQUENCY   COUNTRY, STATION, LOCATION   TARGET • NETWORK • POWER (kW)   World Time

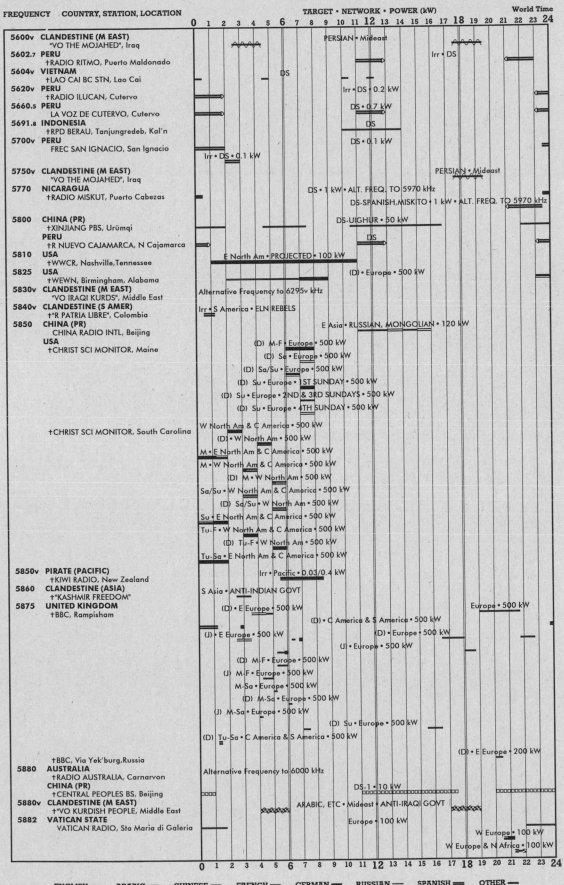

Frequency	Country, Station, Location	Schedule
5600v	CLANDESTINE (M EAST) "VO THE MOJAHED", Iraq	PERSIAN • Mideast
5602.7	PERU †RADIO RITMO, Puerto Maldonado	Irr • DS
5604v	VIETNAM †LAO CAI BC STN, Lao Cai	DS
5620v	PERU †RADIO ILUCAN, Cutervo	Irr • DS • 0.2 kW
5660.5	PERU LA VOZ DE CUTERVO, Cutervo	DS • 0.7 kW
5691.8	INDONESIA †RPD BERAU, Tanjungredeb, Kal'n	DS
5700v	PERU FREC SAN IGNACIO, San Ignacio	DS • 0.1 kW; Irr • DS • 0.1 kW
5750v	CLANDESTINE (M EAST) "VO THE MOJAHED", Iraq	PERSIAN • Mideast
5770	NICARAGUA †RADIO MISKUT, Puerto Cabezas	DS • 1 kW • ALT. FREQ. TO 5970 kHz; DS-SPANISH, MISKITO • 1 kW • ALT. FREQ. TO 5970 kHz
5800	CHINA (PR) †XINJIANG PBS, Urümqi	DS-UIGHUR • 50 kW
	PERU †R NUEVO CAJAMARCA, N Cajamarca	DS
5810	USA †WWCR, Nashville, Tennessee	E North Am • PROJECTED • 100 kW
5825	USA †WEWN, Birmingham, Alabama	(D) • Europe • 500 kW
5830v	CLANDESTINE (M EAST) "VO IRAQI KURDS", Middle East	Alternative Frequency to 6295v kHz
5840v	CLANDESTINE (S AMER) †"R PATRIA LIBRE", Colombia	Irr • S America • ELN REBELS
5850	CHINA (PR) CHINA RADIO INTL, Beijing	E Asia • RUSSIAN, MONGOLIAN • 120 kW
	USA †CHRIST SCI MONITOR, Maine	(D) M-F • Europe • 500 kW; (D) Sa • Europe • 500 kW; (D) Sa/Su • Europe • 500 kW; (D) Su • Europe • 1ST SUNDAY • 500 kW; (D) Su • Europe • 2ND & 3RD SUNDAYS • 500 kW; (D) Su • Europe • 4TH SUNDAY • 500 kW
	†CHRIST SCI MONITOR, South Carolina	W North Am & C America • 500 kW; (D) • W North Am • 500 kW; M • E North Am & C America • 500 kW; M • W North Am & C America • 500 kW; (D) M • W North Am • 500 kW; Sa/Su • W North Am & C America • 500 kW; (D) Sa/Su • W North Am • 500 kW; Su • E North Am & C America • 500 kW; Tu-F • W North Am & C America • 500 kW; (D) Tu-F • W North Am • 500 kW; Tu-Sa • E North Am & C America • 500 kW
5850v	PIRATE (PACIFIC) †KIWI RADIO, New Zealand	Irr • Pacific • 0.03/0.4 kW
5860	CLANDESTINE (ASIA) †"KASHMIR FREEDOM"	S Asia • ANTI-INDIAN GOVT
5875	UNITED KINGDOM †BBC, Rampisham	(D) • E Europe • 500 kW; Europe • 500 kW; (D) • C America & S America • 500 kW; (J) • E Europe • 500 kW; (D) • Europe • 500 kW; (J) • Europe • 500 kW; (D) M-F • Europe • 500 kW; (J) M-F • Europe • 500 kW; M-Sa • Europe • 500 kW; (D) M-Sa • Europe • 500 kW; (J) M-Sa • Europe • 500 kW; (D) Su • Europe • 500 kW; (D) Tu-Sa • C America & S America • 500 kW
	†BBC, Via Yek'burg, Russia	(D) • E Europe • 200 kW
5880	AUSTRALIA †RADIO AUSTRALIA, Carnarvon	Alternative Frequency to 6000 kHz
	CHINA (PR) †CENTRAL PEOPLES BS, Beijing	DS-1 • 10 kW
5880v	CLANDESTINE (M EAST) †"VO KURDISH PEOPLE, Middle East	ARABIC, ETC • Mideast • ANTI-IRAQI GOVT
5882	VATICAN STATE VATICAN RADIO, Sta Maria di Galeria	Europe • 100 kW; W Europe • 100 kW; W Europe & N Africa • 100 kW

ENGLISH ▬ ARABIC ⬚⬚⬚ CHINESE □□□ FRENCH ▬ GERMAN ▬ RUSSIAN ═ SPANISH ▬ OTHER ▬

FREQUENCY   COUNTRY, STATION, LOCATION

TARGET • NETWORK • POWER (kW)   World Time

0 1 2 3 4 5 6 7 8 9 10 11 12 13 14 15 16 17 18 19 20 21 22 23 24

5885	MONACO
	†TRANS WORLD RADIO, Monte Carlo	(D) • E Europe • 100 kW
		(D) • M-F • E Europe • 100 kW
5895	BULGARIA
	†RADIO BULGARIA, Plovdiv	E Europe • 250 kW
5900	BELGIUM
	†R VLAANDEREN INTL, Wavre	Alternative Frequency to 5910 kHz
	ISRAEL
	KOL ISRAEL, Tel Aviv	Mideast • DS-D • 20/50 kW
	RUSSIA
	†U RADIO, Moscow	Tu-F • DS • 20 kW
5900v	CHINA (PR)
	SICHUAN PEOPLES BS, Chengdu	CHINESE, ETC • DS-2 • 15 kW
5902v	CHAD
	RADIO TCHAD LIBRE, Abéché	FRENCH, ARABIC, ETC • DS • 1 kW
5905	RUSSIA
	ADYGEY RADIO, Armavir	(D) • F • DS • 100 kW • ALT. FREQ. TO 7130 kHz
	KABARDINO-BALKAR R, Armavir	(D) • Su • DS • 100 kW • ALT. FREQ. TO 7130 kHz
	†R MOSCOW INTL, Armavir	(D) • Mideast • 100 kW
		(D) • M/W/F/Sa • Mideast • 100 kW
	†R MOSCOW INTL, Petropavlovsk-K	(D) • W North Am • NORTH AMERICAN SVC • 100 kW
	†R MOSCOW INTL, St Petersburg	(D) • Europe • 240 kW
	†R TIKHIY OKEAN, Petropavlovsk-K	(D) • Pacific & W North Am • MARINERS • 100 kW
	†RADIO ALEF, Armavir	(D) • Su/Tu/Th • DS • 100 kW • ALT. FREQ. TO 7130 kHz
	†RADIO NADEZHDA	(D) • DS
	†RADIO ROSSII, Kazan'	(D) • DS • 100 kW
5910	BELGIUM
	†R VLAANDEREN INTL, Wavre	DUTCH • Europe • 250 kW • ALT. FREQ. TO 5900 kHz
		Europe • 250 kW • ALT. FREQ. TO 5900 kHz
		M-Sa • DUTCH • Europe • 250 kW • ALT. FREQ. TO 5900 kHz
		M-Sa • Europe • 250 kW • ALT. FREQ. TO 5900 kHz
		Su • Europe • 250 kW • ALT. FREQ. TO 5900 kHz
		Su • DUTCH • Europe • 250 kW • ALT. FREQ. TO 5900 kHz
	CLANDESTINE (M EAST)
	"AL-QUDS RADIO", Syria	Irr • Mideast • ALT. FREQ. TO 5990 kHz
	FRANCE
	†R FRANCE INTL, Issoudun-Allouis	(D) • E Europe • 100 kW
	RUSSIA
	†RADIO ROSSII, Tula	(D) • DS • 100 kW
5915	BULGARIA
	†RADIO BULGARIA, Sofia	(D) • E Europe & Mideast • 100 kW
		(D) • M-Sa • E Europe & Mideast • 100 kW
		(D) • Su • E Europe & Mideast • 100 kW
	CHINA (PR)
	†CENTRAL PEOPLES BS, Beijing	DS-1 • 50 kW
	FRANCE
	†R FRANCE INTL, Issoudun-Allouis	(J) • E Europe • 100 kW
	ISRAEL
	KOL ISRAEL, Tel Aviv	Mideast • DS-D • 20/50 kW
	KAZAKHSTAN
	†RADIO ALMATY, Almaty	(D) • Asia • 100 kW
		(J) • Asia • 100 kW
	RUSSIA
	†RADIO VEDO, Volgograd	Sa/Su • DS • 20 kW
	SLOVAKIA
	†R SLOVAKIA INTL, Rimavská Sobota	E Europe • 250 kW • ALT. FREQ. TO 5960 kHz
		W Europe • 250 kW • ALT. FREQ. TO 5960 kHz
	USA
	†VOA, Via Irkutsk, Russia	(D) • E Asia • 1000 kW
	†VOA, Via N'sibirsk, Russia	(D) • E Asia • 200 kW
	UZBEKISTAN
	†RADIO TASHKENT, Via Kazakhstan	(D) • Asia • 100 kW
		(J) • Asia • 100 kW
5919v	CHINA (PR)
	GUANGXI PEOPLES BS, Nanning	CHINESE, ETC • DS-3 • 10 kW
5920	CROATIA
	†CROATIAN RADIO, Zagreb	Europe • DS-1
		M-Sa • Europe • DS-1
		Su • Europe • DS-1
	FRANCE
	†R FRANCE INTL, Issoudun-Allouis	(D) • C America • 100 kW
	RUSSIA
	†R MOSCOW INTL, St Petersburg	(D) • Europe • 500 kW
	†RADIO MOSCOW, Various Locations	(D) • DS-2 • 20/100 kW
	USA
	†WWCR, Nashville, Tennessee	Alternative Frequency to 5935 kHz
5924v	VIETNAM
	VOICE OF VIETNAM, Hanoi	VIETNAMESE • DS

0 1 2 3 4 5 6 7 8 9 10 11 12 13 14 15 16 17 18 19 20 21 22 23 24

SUMMER ONLY (J)   WINTER ONLY (D)   JAMMING / OR /\   EARLIEST HEARD ◁   LATEST HEARD ▷   NEW OR CHANGED FOR 1994 †

FREQUENCY   COUNTRY, STATION, LOCATION   TARGET • NETWORK • POWER (kW)   World Time

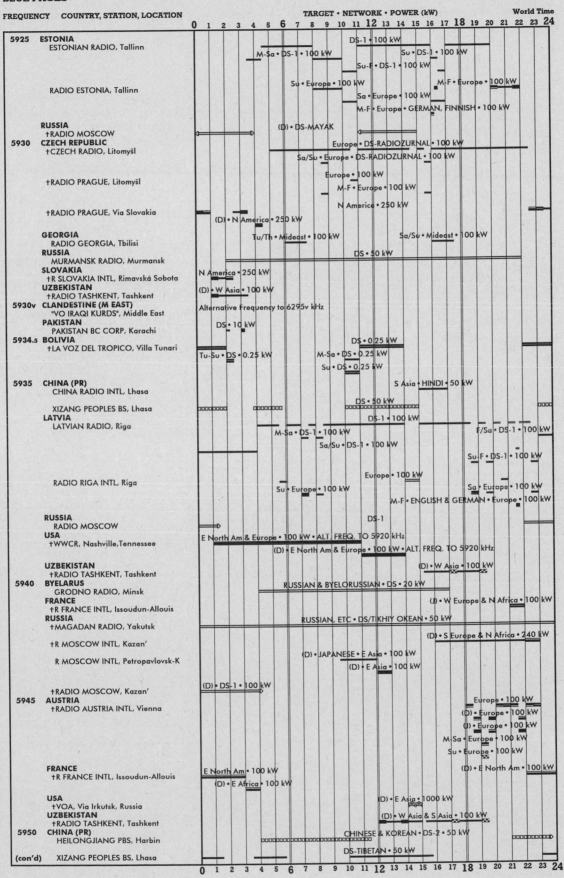

ENGLISH ▬▬   ARABIC ⌇⌇⌇   CHINESE ▫▫▫   FRENCH ══   GERMAN ▬▬   RUSSIAN ══   SPANISH ▬▬   OTHER ▬▬

FREQUENCY   COUNTRY, STATION, LOCATION

TARGET • NETWORK • POWER (kW)   World Time

0 1 2 3 4 5 6 7 8 9 10 11 12 13 14 15 16 17 18 19 20 21 22 23 24

5950 **CHINA (TAIWAN)**
(con'd)   BC CORP CHINA, Via Okeechobee, USA — E North Am • 100 kW

    VO FREE CHINA, Via Okeechobee, USA — CANTONESE • E North Am • 100 kW
    E North Am • 100 kW C America • 100 kW
    E North Am & C America • 100 kW
    CANTONESE • E North Am & C America • 100 kW
    CANTONESE • C America • 100 kW

RUSSIA
    R MOSCOW INTL, Petropavlovsk-K — (D) • JAPANESE • E Asia & Pacific • 100 kW
    (D) • E Asia & Pacific • 100 kW

    †R MOSCOW INTL, Samara — (D) • Europe • 240 kW

    †R MOSCOW INTL, Tula — (D) • Europe • 240 kW

    †RADIO ROSSII — (D) • DS
USA
    WYFR-FAMILY RADIO, Okeechobee, Fl — E North Am • 100 kW
YEMEN (REPUBLIC)
    "VO PALESTINE", Via Rep Yemen Radio — PLO • 300 kW

    REP YEMEN RADIO, San'ā — DS • 300 kW
    F • DS • 300 kW   Irr • DS-RAMADAN • 300 kW

5950.3 GUYANA
    VOICE OF GUYANA, Georgetown — Irr • DS • 10 kW
5952v BOLIVIA
    †RADIO PIO DOCE, Llallagua-Siglo XX — Tu-Su • SPANISH, ETC • DS • 1 kW
    SPANISH, ETC • DS • 1 kW
    M-Sa • SPANISH, ETC • DS • 1 kW
    Su • SPANISH, ETC • DS • 1 kW

5954v COSTA RICA
    RADIO CASINO, Limón — Irr • DS • 0.7 kW
    Irr • M • DS • 0.7 kW
    Irr • Tu-Su • DS • 0.7 kW

5955 **BOTSWANA**
    †RADIO BOTSWANA, Gaborone — Alternative Frequency to 9595 kHz
BRAZIL
    RADIO GAZETA, São Paulo — PORTUGUESE • DS • 7.5 kW
CAMEROON
    CAMEROON RTV CORP, Bafoussam — FRENCH, ENGLISH, ETC • DS • 20 kW
CANADA
    †R CANADA INTL, Via Tokyo, Japan — (D) • E Asia • 300 kW
CHINA (PR)
    †CENTRAL PEOPLES BS — DS-1
GUATEMALA
    RADIO CULTURAL, Guatemala City — Irr • DS • 0.25/10 kW
    Irr • M • DS • 0.25/10 kW   Irr • M-Sa • DS • 0.25/10 kW
    Irr • Tu-Su • DS • 0.25/10 kW   Irr • Su • DS • 0.25/10 kW

HOLLAND
    †RADIO NEDERLAND, Flevoland — DUTCH • Europe • 500 kW
    Europe • 500 kW

ROMANIA
    RADIO ROMANIA INTL, Bucharest — (J) • Europe • 250 kW
SOUTH AFRICA
    †SOUTH AFRICAN BC, Meyerton — AFRIKAANS STEREO • 100 kW
UNITED KINGDOM
    †BBC, Rampisham — (D) • Africa • 500 kW
USA
    †RFE-RL, Various Locations — E Europe • 100/500 kW
    E Europe • 100/250 kW

    †RFE-RL, Via Germany — (D) • W Asia • 100 kW
    (J) • E Europe • 100/250 kW

    †RFE-RL, Via Portugal — (D) • E Europe • 500 kW   (D) • E Europe • 250 kW

    VOA, Via Kaválla, Greece — (D) • E Europe • 250 kW
UZBEKISTAN
    RADIO TASHKENT, Tashkent — (D) • S Asia • 100 kW
5955.3 COLOMBIA
    CARACOL, Villavicencio — DS-CARACOL • 5 kW
PERU
    RADIO HUANCAYO, Huancayo — DS • 0.5 kW
5958v CHINA (PR)
    †YUNNAN PEOPLES BS, Kunming — DS-EDUCATIONAL • 50 kW
    DS-EDUCATIONAL • 50 kW
    M-Sa • DS-EDUCATIONAL • 50 kW

5960 **CANADA**
    †R CANADA INTL, Sackville, NB — E North Am • 250 kW
    (D) • E North Am • 250 kW
    (J) • E North Am • 250 kW

CZECH REPUBLIC
    †RADIO PRAGUE, Via Slovakia — Alternative Frequency to 7300 kHz
GERMANY
(con'd)   DEUTSCHE WELLE, Multiple Locations — N America • 100/500 kW

0 1 2 3 4 5 6 7 8 9 10 11 12 13 14 15 16 17 18 19 20 21 22 23 24

SUMMER ONLY (J)   WINTER ONLY (D)   JAMMING / OR ∧   EARLIEST HEARD ◁   LATEST HEARD ▷   NEW OR CHANGED FOR 1994 †

FREQUENCY	COUNTRY, STATION, LOCATION	TARGET • NETWORK • POWER (kW)	World Time

World Time scale: 0 1 2 3 4 5 6 7 8 9 10 11 12 13 14 15 16 17 18 19 20 21 22 23 24

5960
(con'd) **GERMANY**
　†DEUTSCHE WELLE, Via Sines, Portugal — (D) • W Africa • 250 kW
　INDIA
　†RADIO KASHMIR, Jammu — DS-A • 2 kW / Su • DS-A • 2 kW
　JAPAN
　　RADIO JAPAN/NHK, Via Sackville, Can — JAPANESE • E North Am & C America • GENERAL • 250 kW / (D) • E North Am & C America • GENERAL • 250 kW / (J) • E North Am & C America • GENERAL • 250 kW
　†RADIO JAPAN/NHK, Via Skelton, UK — JAPANESE • Europe & N Africa • GENERAL • 250 kW
　KAZAKHSTAN
　†KAZAKH RADIO, Almaty — DS-2 • 100 kW
　†RADIO ALMATY, Almaty — 100 kW
　MONACO
　　R MONTE CARLO, Via Sackville, Canada — (D) • N America • 250 kW / (J) • N America • 250 kW
　RUSSIA
　†R MOSCOW INTL, Vladivostok — (D) • E Asia • 100 kW / (D) • JAPANESE • E Asia • 100 kW
　SLOVAKIA
　†R SLOVAKIA INTL, Rimavská Sobota — Alternative Frequency to 5915 kHz
　SOUTH AFRICA
　†CHANNEL AFRICA, Meyerton — (J) • E Africa • 250 kW / (D) • E Africa & S Africa • 250 kW / (J) • W Africa & S Africa • 250 kW

5964.7 BOLIVIA
　†RADIO NACIONAL, Huanuni — Tu-Su • DS • 2 kW / DS • 2 kW / M-Sa • DS • 2 kW

5965 CHINA (PR)
　　CHINA RADIO INTL, Shijiazhuang — E Asia • 50 kW
　DENMARK
　　DANMARKS RADIO, Via Norway — (D) • Europe • 500 kW
　ECUADOR
　　LA VOZ DEL UPANO, Macas — DS • 10 kW
　GERMANY
　†DEUTSCHE WELLE, Jülich — (D) • E Europe • 100 kW
　†DEUTSCHE WELLE, Via Sines, Portugal — (D) • E Europe • 250 kW
　MALAYSIA
　　RADIO TV MALAYSIA, Kajang — DS-1 (MALAY) • 100 kW
　NIGERIA
　　RADIO PLATEAU, Jos — ENGLISH, ETC • DS • 10 kW
　NORWAY
　　RADIO NORWAY INTL, Kvitsøy — (D) • Europe • 500 kW
　RUSSIA
　　KHABAROVSK R, Komsomol'sk 'Amure — DS-1/DS-2 • 20 kW
　SOUTH AFRICA
　†SOUTH AFRICAN BC, Meyerton — ENGLISH & AFRIKAANS • DS-RADIO ORANJE • 100 kW
　UKRAINE
　†UKRAINIAN R, Star'obel'sk — (D) • UKRAINIAN • E Europe • DS-2 • 20 kW
　UNITED KINGDOM
　†BBC, Via Hong Kong — (D) • E Asia • 250 kW
　†BBC, Via Maşirah, Oman — (D) • S Asia • 100 kW
　　BBC, Via Sackville, Can — E North Am • 250 kW / M-Sa • E North Am • 250 kW
　†BBC, Via Zyyi, Cyprus — (D) • E Europe & W Asia • 100/250 kW / (D) • W Asia • 250 kW
　USA
　†VOA, Via Germany — E Europe • 500 kW / (J) • E Europe • 500 kW / (D) • E Europe • 100/500 kW
　†VOA, Via Morocco
　†VOA, Via Rhodes, Greece — Mideast • 50 kW
　†VOA, Via Woofferton, UK — (D) • E Europe • 300 kW

5965v BRAZIL
　　RADIO TRANSAMERICA, Santa Maria — PORTUGUESE • DS • 10 kW
5969v INDONESIA
　　RRI, Banjarmasin, Kali'n — DS-TEMP INACTIVE • 10 kW
5969.7 PERU
　　RADIO EL SOL, Lima — DS • 2 kW
5970 BRAZIL
　†RADIO ITATIAIA, Belo Horizonte — PORTUGUESE • DS • 10 kW
　HUNGARY
　†RADIO BUDAPEST, Jászberény — Europe • 250 kW
　JAPAN
　　RADIO JAPAN/NHK, Via Skelton, UK — (D) • JAPANESE • Europe • GENERAL • 250 kW / (D) • Europe • GENERAL • 250 kW
　KAZAKHSTAN
　†KAZAKH RADIO, Almaty — DS-2 • 50 kW
　†RADIO ALMATY, Almaty — 50 kW
　NICARAGUA
(con'd) †RADIO MISKUT, Puerto Cabezas — Alternative Frequency to 5770 kHz

World Time scale: 0 1 2 3 4 5 6 7 8 9 10 11 12 13 14 15 16 17 18 19 20 21 22 23 24

ENGLISH ▬ ARABIC � CHINESE □□□ FRENCH ═ GERMAN ▬ RUSSIAN ═ SPANISH ▬ OTHER —

FREQUENCY   COUNTRY, STATION, LOCATION

TARGET • NETWORK • POWER (kW)   World Time

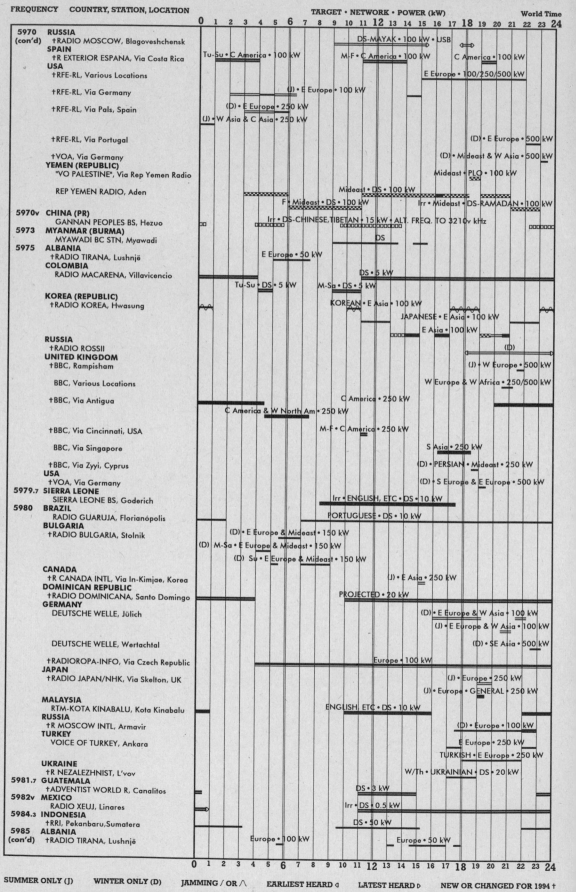

FREQUENCY   COUNTRY, STATION, LOCATION

TARGET • NETWORK • POWER (kW)   World Time

0 1 2 3 4 5 6 7 8 9 10 11 12 13 14 15 16 17 18 19 20 21 22 23 24

5985	CONGO	
(con'd)	†RTV CONGOLAISE, Brazzaville	Irr • Sa • DS • 50 kW • ALT. FREQ. TO 3265 kHz
		FRENCH, ETC • DS • 50 kW • ALT. FREQ. TO 3265 kHz
	ECUADOR	
	†RADIO FEDERACION, Sucúa	DS • 5 kW
	KAZAKHSTAN	
	†KAZAKH RADIO, Via Uzbekistan	DS-2 • 100 kW
	MEXICO	
	†RADIO MEXICO INTL, México City	Irr • W North Am & C America • 10 kW
	RUSSIA	
	†R MOSCOW INTL, Via Tajikistan	(D) • S Asia & SE Asia • 50 kW
	UKRAINE	
	†RADIO UKRAINE, Kiev	(D) • UKRAINIAN • Europe & Atlantic • 200 kW
		(D) • Europe & Atlantic • 200 kW
	USA	
	†RFE-RL, Via Germany	(J) • E Europe • 100 kW
		E Europe • 100 kW (D) • E Europe • 100 kW
		(D) • W Asia & C Asia • 100 kW
		(D) M-Sa • E Europe • 100 kW
		(J) M-Sa • E Europe • 100 kW
		(D) • E Europe • 500 kW
	†RFE-RL, Via Portugal	Pacific & Australasia • 250 kW
	VOA, Delano, California	(D) • C Asia • 250 kW
	†VOA, Via Kaválla, Greece	(D) • E Europe • 100/500 kW
	†VOA, Via Morocco	C America • 50 kW
	†WYFR-FAMILY RADIO, Okeechobee, Fl	W North Am • 100 kW
		(J) • C America • 50 kW
5990	CLANDESTINE (M EAST)	
	"AL-QUDS RADIO", Syria	Alternative Frequency to 5910 kHz
	ETHIOPIA	DS • 100 kW
	VOICE OF ETHIOPIA, Gedja	M-Sa • DS • 100 kW M-F • DS • 100 kW
		Su • DS • 100 kW Sa/Su • DS • 100 kW
	FRANCE	
	R FRANCE INTL, Issoudun-Allouis	E Europe • 100/500 kW
		(D) • E Europe • 500 kW
		(J) • E Europe • 100/500 kW
	INDIA	
	†ALL INDIA RADIO, Aligarh	W Asia & S Asia • 250 kW
	†ALL INDIA RADIO, Bhopal	DS • 10 kW
		Su • DS • 10 kW
	ITALY	
	†RADIO ROMA, Rome	(D) • E Europe • 100 kW E Europe • 100 kW
		(D) • ITALIAN • Europe, N Africa & Mideast • 100 kW ITALIAN • Europe • 100 kW
		(D) • Europe, N Africa & Mideast • 100 kW Europe • 100 kW
		(D) • ITALIAN • N Africa • 100 kW
		(D) • Europe • 100 kW
		(D) • E Asia • 100 kW
	MYANMAR (BURMA)	
	RADIO MYANMAR, Yangon	DS-ENGLISH, BURMESE • 50 kW
	ROMANIA	
	RADIO ROMANIA INTL, Bucharest	C America • 250 kW (D) • Europe • 250 kW
		(D) • C America • 250 kW
	RUSSIA	
	RADIO MOSCOW, Yakutsk	DS-MAYAK • 100 kW
	UNITED KINGDOM	
	BBC, Rampisham	(D) • E Europe • 500 kW
5995	AUSTRALIA	
	†RADIO AUSTRALIA, Shepparton	Pacific • 100 kW
	CANADA	
	†R CANADA INTL, Via Skelton, UK	Europe • 300 kW
		(D) • Europe • 300 kW
		(J) • Europe • 300 kW
	CHINA (PR)	
	XIZANG PEOPLES BS, Lhasa	DS-TIBETAN • 50 kW
	FRANCE	
	R FRANCE INTL, Issoudun-Allouis	(D) • W Europe • 100 kW
	GERMANY	
	DEUTSCHE WELLE, Wertachtal	(D) • E Europe • 500 kW
		(J) • E Europe • 500 kW
	IRAN	
	†VO THE ISLAMIC REP, Tehrān	PERSIAN • Mideast & W Asia • DS • 500 kW
	MALAWI	
	MALAWI BC CORP, Limbe	ENGLISH, ETC • DS • 20/100 kW
	MALI	
	RTV MALIENNE, Bamako	Su • DS • 50 kW
		FRENCH, ETC • DS • 50 kW
(con'd)		

0 1 2 3 4 5 6 7 8 9 10 11 12 13 14 15 16 17 18 19 20 21 22 23 24

ENGLISH ▬▬   ARABIC ≋≋≋   CHINESE □□□   FRENCH ═══   GERMAN ▬▬   RUSSIAN ═══   SPANISH ▬▬   OTHER ▬▬

FREQUENCY   COUNTRY, STATION, LOCATION

TARGET • NETWORK • POWER (kW)   World Time

| 0 1 2 3 4 5 6 7 8 9 10 11 12 13 14 15 16 17 18 19 20 21 22 23 24 |

5995 **MALI**
(con'd)   RTV MALIENNE, Bamako — M-Sa • FRENCH, ETC • DS • 50 kW

POLAND
    †POLISH RADIO, Warsaw — E Europe • 100 kW

ROMANIA
    RADIO ROMANIA INTL, Bucharest — (D) • Europe • 250 kW

RUSSIA
    †RADIO MOSCOW, Kenga — (D) • DS-2 • 50 kW

    †RADIO ROSSII, Tula — DS • 100 kW

SWITZERLAND
    †SWISS RADIO INTL, Schwarzenburg — S America • 100/250 kW • ALT. FREQ. TO 6030 kHz

USA
    VOA, Greenville, NC — C America & S America • 250 kW
    Tu-Sa • C America & S America • 250 kW

    VOA, Via Germany — E Europe • 500 kW
    (J) • E Europe • 500 kW

UZBEKISTAN
    †UZBEK RADIO, Tashkent — DS-1/RUSSIAN, UZBEK • 100 kW

5995.3 PERU
    RADIO MELODIA, Arequipa — DS • 5 kW

5999v ECUADOR
    LA VOZ DEL UPANO, Macas — DS • 10 kW

6000 **AUSTRALIA**
    †RADIO AUSTRALIA, Carnarvon — S Asia, Mideast & Europe • 250 kW • ALT. FREQ. TO 5880 kHz

BRAZIL
    RADIO GUAIBA, Pôrto Alegre — PORTUGUESE • DS • 7.5 kW

CHINA (PR)
    †VO THE STRAIT-PLA, Fuzhou — TAIWAN-2 • 50 kW

GERMANY
    †DEUTSCHE WELLE, Jülich — (D) • Mideast • 100 kW

    †DEUTSCHE WELLE, Wertachtal — (D) • W Europe • 500 kW
    (D) • E Europe & W Asia • 500 kW

INDIA
    RADIO KASHMIR, Leh — DS • 10 kW
    ENGLISH & HINDI • DS • 10 kW

RUSSIA
    †R MOSCOW INTL, Yekaterinburg — (D) • Europe • 240 kW

    †RADIO MOSCOW, Yekaterinburg — (D) • DS-1 • 240 kW

SINGAPORE
    SINGAPORE BC CORP, Jurong — DS • 50 kW

SWEDEN
    †RADIO SWEDEN, Hörby — E Europe • 500 kW
    SWEDISH • E Europe • 500 kW
    Sa/Su • E Europe • 500 kW

6005 **CAMEROON**
    CAMEROON RTV CORP, Buea — FRENCH, ENGLISH ETC • DS • 4 kW

CANADA
    CFCX-CIQC, Montréal, Québec — E North Am • DS • 0.5 kW

CHINA (PR)
    †GANSU PEOPLES BS, Lanzhou — DS-1 • 15 kW

GERMANY
    R AMERICAN SECTOR, Berlin — Europe • RIAS-1 • 100 kW

IRAN
    †VO THE ISLAMIC REP, Zāhedān — W Asia & S Asia • 500 kW

JAPAN
    NHK, Nagoya — Irr • JAPANESE • DS-1 (FEEDER) • 0.3 kW • USB

    NHK, Sapporo — Irr • JAPANESE • DS-1 (FEEDER) • 0.6 kW

    †RADIO JAPAN/NHK, Via Skelton, UK — (D) • Europe • 250 kW
    (D) • JAPANESE • Europe • GENERAL • 250 kW

RUSSIA
    †FEBC RUSSIA, Khabarovsk — E Asia • 20 kW

SRI LANKA
    SRI LANKA BC CORP, Colombo-Ekala — S Asia • 10 kW

UNITED KINGDOM
    BBC, Via Ascension — W Africa • 250 kW
    (D) • W Africa • 250 kW

    †BBC, Via Meyerton, S Af — (J) • S Africa • 250 kW

    †BBC, Via Seychelles — E Africa • 250 kW

    †BBC, Via Zyyi, Cyprus — (D) • E Europa • 250 kW

USA
    †VOA, Via Morocco — (J) • N Africa • 100 kW

YUGOSLAVIA
    †RADIO YUGOSLAVIA, Belgrade — E Europe • 500 kW

6005.5 COSTA RICA
    RADIO RELOJ, San José — Irr • DS • 3 kW

6010 **BAHRAIN**
    RADIO BAHRAIN, Abu Hayan — DS • 60 kW

BRAZIL
    R INCONFIDENCIA, Belo Horizonte — PORTUGUESE • DS • 25 kW

BYELARUS
    †RS BYELARUS, Via Ukraine — (D) • BYELORUSSIAN • Europe • 100 kW
    (D) • M/Tu/Th/F • BYELORUSSIAN • Europe • 100 kW

(con'd)

| 0 1 2 3 4 5 6 7 8 9 10 11 12 13 14 15 16 17 18 19 20 21 22 23 24 |

SUMMER ONLY (J)   WINTER ONLY (D)   JAMMING / OR ∧   EARLIEST HEARD ◁   LATEST HEARD ▷   NEW OR CHANGED FOR 1994 †

FREQUENCY   COUNTRY, STATION, LOCATION

TARGET • NETWORK • POWER (kW)

World Time

0 1 2 3 4 5 6 7 8 9 10 11 12 13 14 15 16 17 18 19 20 21 22 23 24

Frequency	Country, Station, Location	Schedule
6010 (con'd)	BYELARUS	
	†RS BYELARUS, Via Ukraine	(D) • W Sa • Europe • 100 kW
	CANADA	
	†R CANADA INTL, Sackville, NB	(D) • E North Am & C America • 100 kW
	CHINA (PR)	
	CHINA RADIO INTL, Kunming	SE Asia • 50 kW • ALT. FREQ. TO 6025 kHz
	CUBA	
	†RADIO HABANA, Havana	E North Am • 100 kW
	GERMANY	
	†DEUTSCHE WELLE, Multiple Locations	(D) • E Europe & W Asia • 100/500 kW; (D) • Asia • 100/500 kW
	INDIA	
	ALL INDIA RADIO, Calcutta	DS • 10/50 kW; ENGLISH & HINDI • DS • 10/50 kW
	ITALY	
	RADIO ROMA, Rome	(D) • Europe • 100 kW
	LITHUANIA	
	LITHUANIAN R, Via Moscow, Russia	LITHUANIAN • DS-1 • 20 kW; DS-1 • 20 kW
	MEXICO	
	RADIO MIL, México City	DS • 1 kW
	PAKISTAN	
	RADIO PAKISTAN, Islamabad	S Asia • 100 kW
	RUSSIA	
	†R MOSCOW INTL, Moscow	(J) • Europe • 250 kW
	SWITZERLAND	
	†"DIE ANTWORT", Via RS Byelarus	(D) • Su • Europe • 100 kW
	UKRAINE	
	†RADIO UKRAINE, Kiev	(J) • Europe • 100 kW; (D) • UKRAINIAN • Europe • 100 kW; (J) • UKRAINIAN • Europe • 100 kW
	UNITED KINGDOM	
	†BBC, Skelton, Cumbria	(D) • E Europe • 300 kW; (J) • W Europe • 250 kW; (J) • N Africa • 250 kW
	†BBC, Via Zyyi, Cyprus	(D) • E Europe • 250 kW
	USA	
	VOA, Via Kaválla, Greece	S Asia • 250 kW
	†VOA, Via Woofferton, UK	(D) • E Europe • 300 kW
6010v	CLANDESTINE (ASIA)	
	"VO NAT SALVATION", Haeju, N Korea	KOREAN • TO SOUTH KOREA • 100 kW
6011v	VENEZUELA	
	RADIO LOS ANDES, Mérida	Irr • DS • 1 kW
6012	ANTARCTICA	
	AFAN-US MILITARY, McMurdo Base	DS-TEMP INACTIVE • 1 kW
	ITALY	
	†TELE RADIO STEREO, Rome	ITALIAN • Europe • 2 kW
6015	AUSTRIA	
	RADIO AUSTRIA INTL, Via Sackville, Can	N America • 250 kW
	†RADIO AUSTRIA INTL, Vienna	E North Am • 100 kW
	GERMANY	
	†DEUTSCHE WELLE, Nauen	(J) • E Europe • 500 kW; (J) • E Europe • 100 kW
	†DEUTSCHE WELLE, Via Kigali, Rwanda	C Africa & E Africa • 250 kW
	†DEUTSCHE WELLE, Via Sines, Portugal	(D) • Europe • 250 kW
	†DEUTSCHE WELLE, Wertachtal	(D) • E Europe • 500 kW; (J) • E Europe • 500 kW
	HOLLAND	
	†RADIO NEDERLAND, Flevoland	Alternative Frequency to 6020 kHz
	KOREA (REPUBLIC)	
	KOREAN BC SYSTEM, Hwasung	KOREAN • E Asia • LIBERTY-1 • 100 kW
	RUSSIA	
	RADIO MOSCOW, Various Locations	DS-MAYAK • 100/150 kW
	UNITED KINGDOM	
	†BBC, Rampisham	(D) • W Europe • 500 kW
	†BBC, Via Zyyi, Cyprus	Su • Mideast • 250 kW; (J) • E Europe & Mideast • 250 kW; M-F • Mideast • 250 kW
	USA	
	VOA, Via Kaválla, Greece	(D) • W Asia & S Asia • 250 kW
	†VOA, Via Portugal	(D) • Europe • 250 kW
	†VOA, Via Woofferton, UK	(D) • E Europe • 300 kW
	WYFR-FAMILY RADIO, Okeechobee, Fl	(J) • W North Am • 100 kW
6015v	TANZANIA	
	VOICE OF TANZANIA, Dole, Zanzibar	DS-SWAHILI • 50 kW
6016v	BOLIVIA	
	RADIO EL MUNDO, Santa Cruz	Su • DS • 10 kW; DS • 10 kW; Irr • Tu-Sa • DS • 10 kW; Tu-Su • DS • 10 kW

0 1 2 3 4 5 6 7 8 9 10 11 12 13 14 15 16 17 18 19 20 21 22 23 24

ENGLISH ▬   ARABIC ⌇⌇⌇   CHINESE □□□   FRENCH ▬   GERMAN ═   RUSSIAN ═   SPANISH ▬   OTHER —

FREQUENCY   COUNTRY, STATION, LOCATION

TARGET • NETWORK • POWER (kW)   World Time

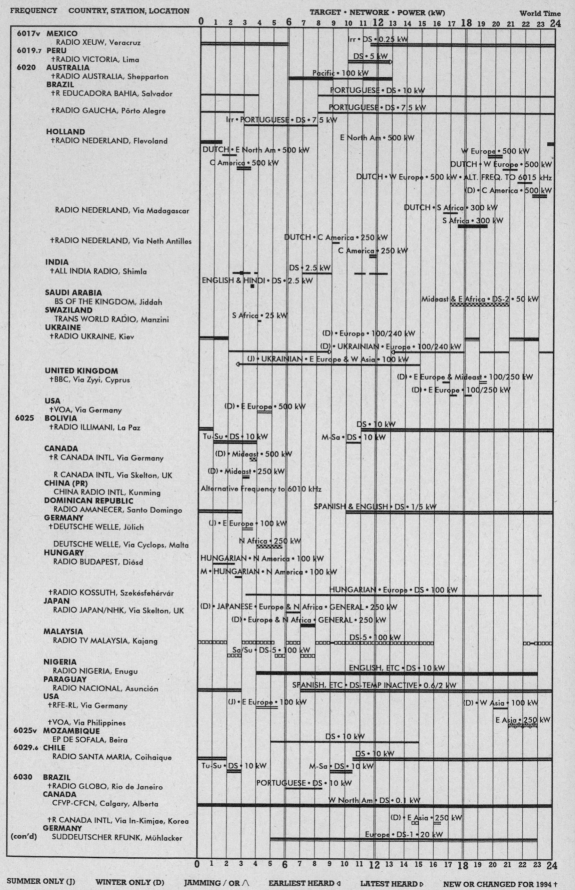

FREQUENCY	COUNTRY, STATION, LOCATION	TARGET • NETWORK • POWER (kW)
6017v	**MEXICO** RADIO XEUW, Veracruz	Irr • DS • 0.25 kW
6019.7	**PERU** †RADIO VICTORIA, Lima	DS • 5 kW
6020	**AUSTRALIA** †RADIO AUSTRALIA, Shepparton	Pacific • 100 kW
	BRAZIL †R EDUCADORA BAHIA, Salvador	PORTUGUESE • DS • 10 kW
	†RADIO GAUCHA, Pôrto Alegre	PORTUGUESE • DS • 7.5 kW / Irr • PORTUGUESE • DS • 7.5 kW
	HOLLAND †RADIO NEDERLAND, Flevoland	E North Am • 500 kW / DUTCH • E North Am • 500 kW / C America • 500 kW / W Europe • 500 kW / DUTCH • W Europe • 500 kW / DUTCH • W Europe • 500 kW • ALT. FREQ. TO 6015 kHz / (D) • C America • 500 kW
	RADIO NEDERLAND, Via Madagascar	DUTCH • S Africa • 300 kW / S Africa • 300 kW
	†RADIO NEDERLAND, Via Neth Antilles	DUTCH • C America • 250 kW / C America • 250 kW
	INDIA †ALL INDIA RADIO, Shimla	DS • 2.5 kW / ENGLISH & HINDI • DS • 2.5 kW
	SAUDI ARABIA BS OF THE KINGDOM, Jiddah	Mideast & E Africa • DS-2 • 50 kW
	SWAZILAND TRANS WORLD RADIO, Manzini	S Africa • 25 kW
	UKRAINE †RADIO UKRAINE, Kiev	(D) • Europe • 100/240 kW / (D) • UKRAINIAN • Europe • 100/240 kW / (J) • UKRAINIAN • E Europe & W Asia • 100 kW
	UNITED KINGDOM †BBC, Via Zyyi, Cyprus	(D) • E Europe & Mideast • 100/250 kW / (D) • E Europe • 100/250 kW
	USA †VOA, Via Germany	(D) • E Europe • 500 kW
6025	**BOLIVIA** †RADIO ILLIMANI, La Paz	DS • 10 kW / Tu-Su • DS • 10 kW / M-Sa • DS • 10 kW
	CANADA †R CANADA INTL, Via Germany	(D) • Mideast • 500 kW
	R CANADA INTL, Via Skelton, UK	(D) • Mideast • 250 kW
	CHINA (PR) CHINA RADIO INTL, Kunming	Alternative Frequency to 6010 kHz
	DOMINICAN REPUBLIC RADIO AMANECER, Santo Domingo	SPANISH & ENGLISH • DS • 1/5 kW
	GERMANY †DEUTSCHE WELLE, Jülich	(J) • E Europe • 100 kW
	DEUTSCHE WELLE, Via Cyclops, Malta	N Africa • 250 kW
	HUNGARY RADIO BUDAPEST, Diósd	HUNGARIAN • N America • 100 kW / M • HUNGARIAN • N America • 100 kW
	†RADIO KOSSUTH, Szekésfehérvár	HUNGARIAN • Europe • DS • 100 kW
	JAPAN RADIO JAPAN/NHK, Via Skelton, UK	(D) • JAPANESE • Europe & N Africa • GENERAL • 250 kW / (D) • Europe & N Africa • GENERAL • 250 kW
	MALAYSIA RADIO TV MALAYSIA, Kajang	DS-5 • 100 kW / Sa/Su • DS-5 • 100 kW
	NIGERIA RADIO NIGERIA, Enugu	ENGLISH, ETC • DS • 10 kW
	PARAGUAY RADIO NACIONAL, Asunción	SPANISH, ETC • DS-TEMP INACTIVE • 0.6/2 kW
	USA †RFE-RL, Via Germany	(J) • E Europe • 100 kW / (D) • W Asia • 100 kW
	†VOA, Via Philippines	E Asia • 250 kW
6025v	**MOZAMBIQUE** EP DE SOFALA, Beira	DS • 10 kW
6029.6	**CHILE** RADIO SANTA MARIA, Coihaique	DS • 10 kW / Tu-Su • DS • 10 kW / M-Sa • DS • 10 kW
6030	**BRAZIL** †RADIO GLOBO, Rio de Janeiro	PORTUGUESE • DS • 10 kW
	CANADA CFVP-CFCN, Calgary, Alberta	W North Am • DS • 0.1 kW
	†R CANADA INTL, Via In-Kimjae, Korea	(D) • E Asia • 250 kW
(con'd)	**GERMANY** SUDDEUTSCHER RFUNK, Mühlacker	Europe • DS-1 • 20 kW

FREQUENCY   COUNTRY, STATION, LOCATION

TARGET • NETWORK • POWER (kW)   World Time

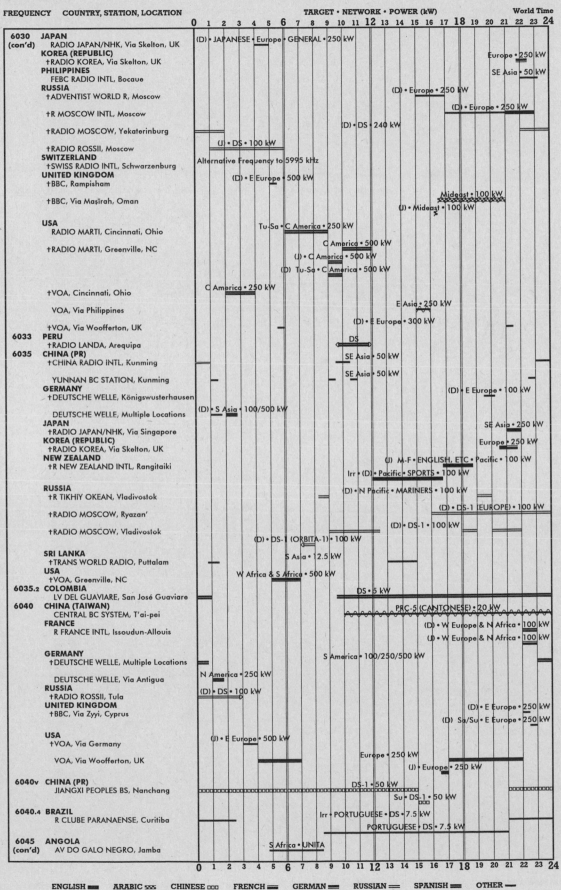

6030 (con'd)	**JAPAN**
	RADIO JAPAN/NHK, Via Skelton, UK
	KOREA (REPUBLIC)
	†RADIO KOREA, Via Skelton, UK
	PHILIPPINES
	FEBC RADIO INTL, Bocaue
	RUSSIA
	†ADVENTIST WORLD R, Moscow
	†R MOSCOW INTL, Moscow
	†RADIO MOSCOW, Yekaterinburg
	†RADIO ROSSII, Moscow
	SWITZERLAND
	†SWISS RADIO INTL, Schwarzenburg
	UNITED KINGDOM
	†BBC, Rampisham
	†BBC, Via Maşīrah, Oman
	USA
	RADIO MARTI, Cincinnati, Ohio
	†RADIO MARTI, Greenville, NC
	†VOA, Cincinnati, Ohio
	VOA, Via Philippines
	†VOA, Via Woofferton, UK
6033	**PERU**
	†RADIO LANDA, Arequipa
6035	**CHINA (PR)**
	†CHINA RADIO INTL, Kunming
	YUNNAN BC STATION, Kunming
	GERMANY
	†DEUTSCHE WELLE, Königswusterhausen
	DEUTSCHE WELLE, Multiple Locations
	JAPAN
	†RADIO JAPAN/NHK, Via Singapore
	KOREA (REPUBLIC)
	†RADIO KOREA, Via Skelton, UK
	NEW ZEALAND
	†R NEW ZEALAND INTL, Rangitaiki
	RUSSIA
	†R TIKHIY OKEAN, Vladivostok
	†RADIO MOSCOW, Ryazan'
	†RADIO MOSCOW, Vladivostok
	SRI LANKA
	†TRANS WORLD RADIO, Puttalam
	USA
	†VOA, Greenville, NC
6035.2	**COLOMBIA**
	LV DEL GUAVIARE, San José Guaviare
6040	**CHINA (TAIWAN)**
	CENTRAL BC SYSTEM, T'ai-pei
	FRANCE
	R FRANCE INTL, Issoudun-Allouis
	GERMANY
	†DEUTSCHE WELLE, Multiple Locations
	DEUTSCHE WELLE, Via Antigua
	RUSSIA
	†RADIO ROSSII, Tula
	UNITED KINGDOM
	†BBC, Via Zyyi, Cyprus
	USA
	†VOA, Via Germany
	VOA, Via Woofferton, UK
6040v	**CHINA (PR)**
	JIANGXI PEOPLES BS, Nanchang
6040.4	**BRAZIL**
	R CLUBE PARANAENSE, Curitiba
6045 (con'd)	**ANGOLA**
	AV DO GALO NEGRO, Jamba

Chart annotations (left to right by row):

- (D) • JAPANESE • Europe • GENERAL • 250 kW
- Europe • 250 kW
- SE Asia • 50 kW
- (D) • Europe • 250 kW
- (D) • Europe • 250 kW
- (D) • DS • 240 kW
- (J) • DS • 100 kW
- Alternative Frequency to 5995 kHz
- (D) • E Europe • 500 kW
- Mideast • 100 kW
- (J) • Mideast • 100 kW
- Tu-Sa • C America • 250 kW
- C America • 500 kW
- (J) • C America • 500 kW
- (D) Tu-Sa • C America • 500 kW
- C America • 250 kW
- E Asia • 250 kW
- (D) • E Europe • 300 kW
- DS
- SE Asia • 50 kW
- SE Asia • 50 kW
- (D) • E Europe • 100 kW
- (D) • S Asia • 100/500 kW
- SE Asia • 250 kW
- Europe • 250 kW
- (J) M-F • ENGLISH, ETC • Pacific • 100 kW
- Irr • (D) • Pacific • SPORTS • 100 kW
- (D) • N Pacific • MARINERS • 100 kW
- (D) • DS-1 (EUROPE) • 100 kW
- (D) • DS-1 • 100 kW
- (D) • DS-1 (ORBITA-1) • 100 kW
- S Asia • 12.5 kW
- W Africa & S Africa • 500 kW
- DS • 5 kW
- PRC-5 (CANTONESE) • 20 kW
- (D) • W Europe & N Africa • 100 kW
- (J) • W Europe & N Africa • 100 kW
- S America • 100/250/500 kW
- N America • 250 kW
- (D) • DS • 100 kW
- (D) • E Europe • 250 kW
- (D) Sa/Su • E Europe • 250 kW
- (J) • E Europe • 500 kW
- Europe • 250 kW
- (J) • Europe • 250 kW
- DS-1 • 50 kW
- Su • DS-1 • 50 kW
- Irr • PORTUGUESE • DS • 7.5 kW
- PORTUGUESE • DS • 7.5 kW
- S Africa • UNITA

FREQUENCY	COUNTRY, STATION, LOCATION	TARGET • NETWORK • POWER (kW)	World Time

6045
(con'd) FRANCE
†R FRANCE INTL, Issoudun-Allouis
- E Europe • 100/500 kW
- (D) • E Europe • 100/500 kW
- (J) • E Europe • 100/500 kW

GERMANY
†DEUTSCHE WELLE, Multiple Locations
- (D) • C America • 500 kW
- (D) • N America & C America • 100/250 kW
- (D) • N America • 100/500 kW

INDIA
†ALL INDIA RADIO, Delhi
- S Asia • 20/50 kW
- S Asia • 50 kW
- (J) • DS • 20 kW
- (D) • S Asia & W Asia • 250 kW
- (D) • DS • 250 kW

KENYA
KENYA BC CORP, Koma Rock
- DS-GENERAL • 250 kW

MEXICO
RADIO UNIVERSIDAD, San Luis Potosí
- Irr • DS • 0.25 kW

RUSSIA
†GOLOS ROSSII, Moscow
- (D) • Europe & Atlantic • 240 kW

UNITED KINGDOM
†BBC, Skelton, Cumbria
- (D) • Europe • 300 kW

URUGUAY
R INTEGRACION AMER, Montevideo
- S America • 1 kW

USA
†VOA, Via Thailand
- (D) • E Asia • 250 kW
- E Asia • 250/500 kW

6045v PERU
†RADIO SANTA ROSA, Lima
- Irr • DS • 3 kW

6045.5 COLOMBIA
RADIO MELODIA, Santa Fé de Bogotá
- Irr • DS • 5 kW

6050 BRAZIL
RADIO GUARANI, Belo Horizonte
- PORTUGUESE • DS • 10 kW

CANADA
†R CANADA INTL, Via Skelton, UK
- M-F • Europe • 300 kW

ECUADOR
HCJB-VO THE ANDES, Quito
- S America • DS-SPANISH,QUECHUA • 100 kW
- Pacific & Australasia • 100 kW

JAPAN
†RADIO JAPAN/NHK, Via Skelton, UK
- (J) • Europe & N Africa • 250 kW • ALT. FREQ. TO 6170 kHz   (D) • Europe & N Africa • 250 kW
- (D) • JAPANESE • Europe & N Africa • GENERAL • 250 kW
- (D) • Europe & N Africa • GENERAL • 250 kW
- (J) • JAPANESE • Europe & N Africa • GENERAL • 250 kW • ALT. FREQ. TO 6170 kHz
- (J) • Europe & N Africa • GENERAL • 250 kW • ALT. FREQ. TO 6170 kHz

MALAYSIA
RTM-SARAWAK, Sibu
- DS-IBAN • 10 kW

NIGERIA
†RADIO NIGERIA, Ibadan
- ENGLISH, ETC • DS • 50 kW

RUSSIA
†RADIO MOSCOW, Various Locations
- (D) • DS-MAYAK • 100/150 kW

UNITED KINGDOM
†BBC, Rampisham
- (D) • E Europe • 500 kW
- (D) M-F • E Europe • 500 kW
- (D) M-Sa • E Europe & Mideast • 500 kW

†BBC, Via Zyyi, Cyprus
- (J) • E Europe & Mideast • 250 kW
- E Europe • 250 kW
- (D) • E Europe • 250 kW
- (J) • E Europe • 250 kW
- (J) M-Sa • E Europe & Mideast • 250 kW   (D) M-F • E Europe • 250 kW
- (J) M-F • E Europe • 250 kW   (D) Sa/Su • E Europe • 250 kW
- (J) Sa/Su • E Europe • 250 kW

USA
†RFE-RL, Various Locations
- (J) • E Europe & W Asia • 100/500 kW

†RFE-RL, Via Germany
- (D) • W Asia & C Asia • 100 kW

6055 CZECH REPUBLIC
†RADIO PRAGUE, Litomyšl
- Europe • 100/200/300 kW
- (J) • Europe • 100/300 kW   M-F • Europe • 300 kW

GERMANY
†DEUTSCHE WELLE, Multiple Locations
- (D) • E Europe • 100/500 kW

JAPAN
RADIO TAMPA, Tokyo-Nagara
- JAPANESE • DS-1 • 50 kW

KUWAIT
†RADIO KUWAIT, Kabd
- Alternative Frequency to 9750 kHz

RUSSIA
†R MOSCOW INTL, Kazan'
- (D) • N Europe • 100 kW

RWANDA
†RADIO RWANDA, Kigali
- DS • 100 kW
- Su • DS • 100 kW

SLOVAKIA
†R SLOVAKIA INTL, Vel'ké Kostolany
- W Europe • 100 kW

SPAIN
†R EXTERIOR ESPANA, Noblejas
- N America & C America • 350 kW

UKRAINE
†UKRAINIAN R, Star'obel'sk
- (D) • UKRAINIAN • W Asia • DS-2 • 100 kW

6055.3 PERU
RADIO CONTINENTAL, Arequipa
- DS • 2 kW

FREQUENCY   COUNTRY, STATION, LOCATION

TARGET • NETWORK • POWER (kW)   World Time

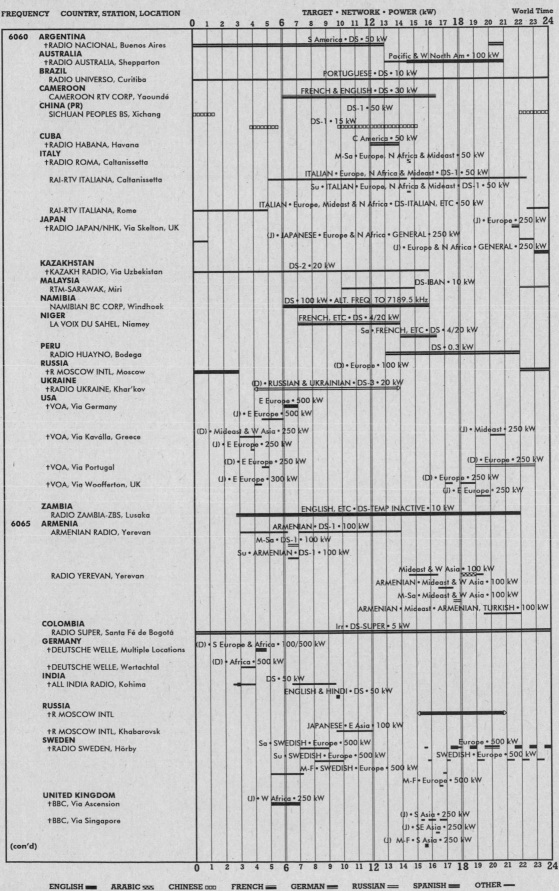

6060	**ARGENTINA**
	†RADIO NACIONAL, Buenos Aires	S America • DS • 50 kW
	AUSTRALIA
	†RADIO AUSTRALIA, Shepparton	Pacific & W North Am • 100 kW
	BRAZIL
	RADIO UNIVERSO, Curitiba	PORTUGUESE • DS • 10 kW
	CAMEROON
	CAMEROON RTV CORP, Yaoundé	FRENCH & ENGLISH • DS • 30 kW
	CHINA (PR)
	SICHUAN PEOPLES BS, Xichang	DS-1 • 50 kW / DS-1 • 15 kW
	CUBA
	†RADIO HABANA, Havana	C America • 50 kW
	ITALY
	†RADIO ROMA, Caltanissetta	M-Sa • Europe, N Africa & Mideast • 50 kW
	RAI-RTV ITALIANA, Caltanissetta	ITALIAN • Europe, N Africa & Mideast • DS-1 • 50 kW / Su • ITALIAN • Europe, N Africa & Mideast • DS-1 • 50 kW
	RAI-RTV ITALIANA, Rome	ITALIAN • Europe, Mideast & N Africa • DS-ITALIAN, ETC • 50 kW
	JAPAN
	†RADIO JAPAN/NHK, Via Skelton, UK	(J) • Europe • 250 kW / (J) • JAPANESE • Europe & N Africa • GENERAL • 250 kW / (J) • Europe & N Africa • GENERAL • 250 kW
	KAZAKHSTAN
	†KAZAKH RADIO, Via Uzbekistan	DS-2 • 20 kW
	MALAYSIA
	RTM-SARAWAK, Miri	DS-IBAN • 10 kW
	NAMIBIA
	NAMIBIAN BC CORP, Windhoek	DS • 100 kW • ALT. FREQ TO 7189.5 kHz
	NIGER
	LA VOIX DU SAHEL, Niamey	FRENCH, ETC • DS • 4/20 kW / Sa • FRENCH, ETC • DS • 4/20 kW
	PERU
	RADIO HUAYNO, Bodega	DS • 0.3 kW
	RUSSIA
	†R MOSCOW INTL, Moscow	(D) • Europe • 100 kW
	UKRAINE
	†RADIO UKRAINE, Khar'kov	(D) • RUSSIAN & UKRAINIAN • DS-3 • 20 kW
	USA
	†VOA, Via Germany	E Europe • 500 kW / (J) • E Europe • 500 kW
	†VOA, Via Kaválla, Greece	(D) • Mideast & W Asia • 250 kW / (J) • E Europe • 250 kW / (J) • Mideast • 250 kW
	†VOA, Via Portugal	(D) • E Europe • 250 kW / (D) • Europe • 250 kW
	†VOA, Via Woofferton, UK	(J) • E Europe • 300 kW / (D) • Europe • 250 kW / (J) • E Europe • 250 kW
	ZAMBIA
	RADIO ZAMBIA-ZBS, Lusaka	ENGLISH, ETC • DS-TEMP INACTIVE • 10 kW
6065	**ARMENIA**
	ARMENIAN RADIO, Yerevan	ARMENIAN • DS-1 • 100 kW / M-Sa • DS-1 • 100 kW / Su • ARMENIAN • DS-1 • 100 kW
	RADIO YEREVAN, Yerevan	Mideast & W Asia • 100 kW / ARMENIAN • Mideast & W Asia • 100 kW / M-Sa • Mideast & W Asia • 100 kW / ARMENIAN • Mideast • ARMENIAN, TURKISH • 100 kW
	COLOMBIA
	RADIO SUPER, Santa Fé de Bogotá	Irr • DS-SUPER • 5 kW
	GERMANY
	†DEUTSCHE WELLE, Multiple Locations	(D) • S Europe & Africa • 100/500 kW
	†DEUTSCHE WELLE, Wertachtal	(D) • Africa • 500 kW
	INDIA
	†ALL INDIA RADIO, Kohima	DS • 50 kW / ENGLISH & HINDI • DS • 50 kW
	RUSSIA
	†R MOSCOW INTL	
	†R MOSCOW INTL, Khabarovsk	JAPANESE • E Asia • 100 kW
	SWEDEN
	†RADIO SWEDEN, Hörby	Sa • SWEDISH • Europe • 500 kW / Su • SWEDISH • Europe • 500 kW / M-F • SWEDISH • Europe • 500 kW / Europe • 500 kW / SWEDISH • Europe • 500 kW / M-F • Europe • 500 kW
	UNITED KINGDOM
	†BBC, Via Ascension	(J) • W Africa • 250 kW
	†BBC, Via Singapore	(J) • S Asia • 250 kW / (J) • SE Asia • 250 kW / (J) M-F • S Asia • 250 kW

(con'd)

FREQUENCY   COUNTRY, STATION, LOCATION

TARGET • NETWORK • POWER (kW)   World Time

0   1   2   3   4   5   6   7   8   9   10 11 12 13 14 15 16 17 18 19 20 21 22 23 24

6065 **UNITED KINGDOM**
(con'd)   †BBC, Via Singapore — (J) Sa/Su • S Asia • 250 kW
          USA
          †VOA, Via Botswana — (J) • Africa • 100 kW

          †VOA, Via Woofferton, UK — (D) • C Asia • 250 kW

          †WYFR-FAMILY RADIO, Okeechobee, Fl — (D) • E North Am • 100 kW
6068v **PAKISTAN (AZAD K)**
          AZAD KASHMIR RADIO, Via Islamabad — DS • 10/100 kW
6069.8 **INDONESIA**
          †RRI, Jayapura, Irian Jaya — DS • 20 kW
6070 **BULGARIA**
          †RADIO BULGARIA, Plovdiv — (D) • Europe • 250 kW
          CANADA
          CFRX-CFRB, Toronto, Ontario — E North Am • DS • 1 kW
          PAKISTAN
          PAKISTAN BC CORP, Islamabad — DS • 100 kW
          RUSSIA
          RADIO MOSCOW, Novosibirsk — (D) • DS-1 • 100 kW
          THAILAND
          †RADIO THAILAND, Pathum Thani — DS-1 • 10 kW
          UKRAINE
          †RADIO UKRAINE, Simferopol' — (D) • E Europe • 50 kW
                                         (D) • UKRAINIAN • E Europe • 50 kW

          †UKRAINIAN R, Simferopol' — UKRAINIAN • E Europe • DS-2 • 50 kW
                                      (D) • UKRAINIAN • E Europe • DS-2 • 50 kW
                                      (J) • UKRAINIAN • E Europe • DS-2 • 50 kW

          UNITED KINGDOM
          †BBC, Via Meyerton, S Af — S Africa • 100 kW
          USA
          †RFE-RL, Via Germany — E Europe • 100 kW

          †UNIVERSITY NET'K, Via N'sibirsk, Russia — (D) • S Asia

          †VOA, Via Thailand — (D) • S Asia & SE Asia • 500 kW
6073.3 **URUGUAY**
          LA VOZ DE ARTIGAS, Artigas — DS • 2.5 kW

          R INTEGRACION AMER, Artigas — S America • 2.5 kW
6075 **ECUADOR**
          †HCJB-VO THE ANDES, Quito — (D) • JAPANESE • E Asia • 500 kW
          GERMANY
          DEUTSCHE WELLE, Jülich — (D) • N America • 100 kW

          †DEUTSCHE WELLE, Multiple Locations — Europe • 100/250/500 kW
                                                Africa • 250/500 kW

          DEUTSCHE WELLE, Via Antigua — N America • 250 kW

          DEUTSCHE WELLE, Via Brasília, Brazil — S America • 250 kW
          KAZAKHSTAN
          KAZAKH RADIO, Almaty — DS-2 • 20 kW
          KENYA
          KENYA BC CORP, Koma Rock — DS-NATIONAL • 250 kW
          SRI LANKA
          SRI LANKA BC CORP, Colombo-Ekala — S Asia • 10 kW
          USA
          RADIO MARTI, Cincinnati, Ohio — C America • 250 kW
6075v **HONDURAS**
          LA VOZ DEL JUNCO, Santa Barbara — DS • 3 kW
6080 **ALBANIA**
          †RADIO TIRANA, Lushnjë — Europe • 50/100 kW
          AUSTRALIA
          †RADIO AUSTRALIA, Shepparton — Pacific • 100 kW
                                         (D) • Pacific • 100 kW

          BRAZIL
          RADIO ANHANGUERA, Goiânia — Irr • PORTUGUESE • DS • 10 kW   PORTUGUESE • DS • 10 kW

          †RADIO NOVAS DE PAZ, Curitiba — PORTUGUESE • DS • 10 kW
                                          Sa/Su • PORTUGUESE • DS • 10 kW

          BYELARUS
          †BYELARUSSIAN R, Minsk — BYELORUSSIAN • E Europe • DS • 20 kW
          CANADA
          CKFX-CKWX, Vancouver, BC — W North Am • DS • 0.01/0.1 kW
          CHILE
          †RADIO PATAGONIA, Coihaique — DS • 1 kW

          M-Sa • DS • 1 kW
          ECUADOR
          HCJB-VO THE ANDES, Quito — DS-SPANISH, QUECHUA • 10 kW
          KYRGYZSTAN
          †KYRGYZ RADIO, Bishkek — ENGLISH, ETC • DS-1 • 50 kW
                                   RUSSIAN, ETC • DS-1 • 50 kW

          RUSSIA
          †RADIO MOSCOW, Komsomol'sk 'Amure — (D) • DS-1 • 100 kW   (J) • DS-1 • 100 kW

          †RADIO MOSCOW, Zhigulevsk — (D) • DS-1 • 20 kW
          SOUTH AFRICA
(con'd)   †CHANNEL AFRICA, Meyerton — (J) • S Africa • 250 kW

0   1   2   3   4   5   6   7   8   9   10 11 12 13 14 15 16 17 18 19 20 21 22 23 24

SUMMER ONLY (J)   WINTER ONLY (D)   JAMMING / OR ∧   EARLIEST HEARD ◁   LATEST HEARD ▷   NEW OR CHANGED FOR 1994 †

FREQUENCY	COUNTRY, STATION, LOCATION	TARGET • NETWORK • POWER (kW)	World Time

0 1 2 3 4 5 6 7 8 9 10 11 12 13 14 15 16 17 18 19 20 21 22 23 24

6080 (con'd)	**UKRAINE** †RADIO UKRAINE, Kiev	(D) • E Europe & W Asia • 20 kW (D) • UKRAINIAN • E Europe & W Asia • 20 kW
	UNITED KINGDOM BBC, Via Singapore	SE Asia • 100 kW
6081v	**PAKISTAN** †PAKISTAN BC CORP, Islamabad	DS • 10 kW
6085	**BOLIVIA** †RADIO SAN GABRIEL, La Paz	DS • 5 kW Tu-Sa • DS • 5 kW M-Sa • DS • 5 kW Sa • DS • 5 kW Tu-Su • DS • 5 kW
	BULGARIA RADIO BULGARIA, Sofia	(D) • Europe • 100 kW
	GERMANY BAYERISCHER RFUNK, Ismaning	DS-1, ARD-NACHT • 100 kW
	†DEUTSCHE WELLE, Multiple Locations	(D) • N America & C America • 100/250/500 kW
	DEUTSCHE WELLE, Nauen	(J) • S America • 500 kW
	†DEUTSCHE WELLE, Via Cyclops, Malta	(D) • C America • 250 kW
	DEUTSCHE WELLE, Via Sackville, Can	N America & C America • 250 kW
	INDIA †ALL INDIA RADIO, Delhi	DS • 100 kW
	JAPAN RADIO JAPAN/NHK, Via Skelton, UK	Europe & N Africa • 250 kW
	OMAN †RADIO OMAN, Sīb	Mideast • DS • 100 kW Irr • Mideast • DS-RAMADAN • 100 kW
	†RADIO OMAN, Thamarīt	E Africa • DS • 100 kW
	USA VOA, Via Kaválla, Greece	(D) • E Europe • 250 kW
	†WYFR-FAMILY RADIO, Okeechobee, Fl	(D) • C America • 50 kW C America • 100 kW (J) • E North Am • 100 kW
6087	**CHINA (TAIWAN)** CENTRAL BC SYSTEM, T'ai-pei	PRC-4 • 50/100 kW
6090	**BRAZIL** †RADIO BANDEIRANTES, São Paulo	PORTUGUESE • DS • 10 kW
	CAMBODIA RADIO PHNOM PENH, Phnom Penh	DS • 50 kW Su • DS • 50 kW
	CHILE †RADIO ESPERANZA, Temuco	DS • 10 kW Sa/Su • DS • 10 kW F/Sa • DS • 10 kW
	LIBERIA †RADIO ELBC, Gbarnga	ENGLISH, ETC • DS
	LUXEMBOURG †RADIO LUXEMBOURG, Junglinster	Europe
	NIGERIA †RADIO NIGERIA, Kaduna	ENGLISH, ETC • DS-1 • 50/250 kW
	RUSSIA †RADIO ROSSII	(D) • DS
	UKRAINE †RADIO UKRAINE, Khar'kov	(J) • Europe • 100 kW (J) • UKRAINIAN • Europe • 100 kW
	†RADIO UKRAINE, Kiev	(J) • N Europe • 100 kW (J) • UKRAINIAN • N Europe • 100 kW
	USA †VOA, Via Germany	E Asia • 500 kW (J) • E Europe • 500 kW
	†VOA, Via Kaválla, Greece	(D) • E Europe • 250 kW
6093v	**PERU** RADIO UNIVERSAL, Cusco	Irr • DS
6095	**BOLIVIA** RADIO COSMOS, Cochabamba	Irr • DS • 1 kW
	CHINA (PR) CENTRAL PEOPLES BS, Nanchang	CHINESE, ETC • TAIWAN-2 • 50 kW W-M • CHINESE, ETC • TAIWAN-2 • 50 kW
	GERMANY †DEUTSCHE WELLE, Via Cyclops, Malta	(D) • W Asia • 250 kW
	POLAND †POLISH RADIO, Warsaw	E Europe • 100 kW W Europe • 100 kW POLISH • W Europe • 100 kW POLISH • E Europe • 100 kW
	RUSSIA †RADIO MOSCOW, Serpuhkov	(D) • DS-2 • 100 kW
	RADIO MOSCOW, Serpukhov	(D) • DS-MAYAK • 100 kW
(con'd)	**USA** RFE-RL, Via Portugal	(D) • E Europe • 500 kW

0 1 2 3 4 5 6 7 8 9 10 11 12 13 14 15 16 17 18 19 20 21 22 23 24

ENGLISH ▬ ARABIC ⌇⌇⌇ CHINESE ▭▭▭ FRENCH ▬ GERMAN ▬ RUSSIAN ═══ SPANISH ▬ OTHER ▬

FREQUENCY	COUNTRY, STATION, LOCATION	TARGET • NETWORK • POWER (kW)	World Time

World Time scale: 0 1 2 3 4 5 6 7 8 9 10 11 12 13 14 15 16 17 18 19 20 21 22 23 24

6095 USA
(con'd)   VOA, Greenville, NC — Alternative Frequency to 15120 kHz
- †VOA, Via Philippines — SE Asia • 100 kW
- VOA, Via Portugal — (D) • Europe • 250 kW
- VOA, Via Rhodes, Greece — (J) • Mideast • 50 kW
- †VOA, Via Woofferton, UK — (D) • E Europe • 300 kW

VATICAN STATE
- VATICAN RADIO, Sta Maria di Galeria — (D) • E North Am • 500 kW / (D) • C America • 500 kW

6100 AFGHANISTAN
- RADIO AFGHANISTAN, Kabul — DS-2 • 100 kW

CHINA (PR)
- XINJIANG PBS, Urümqi — DS-CHINESE • 50 kW

GERMANY
- †DEUTSCHE WELLE, Multiple Locations — N America & C America • 100/500 kW
- †DEUTSCHE WELLE, Wertachtal — N America • 500 kW

KENYA
- KENYA BC CORP, Koma Rock — DS-GENERAL • 250 kW

KOREA (DPR)
- KOREAN CENTRAL BS, Kanggye — KOREAN • DS 200 kW

LITHUANIA
- LITHUANIAN R, Sitkunai — Alternative Frequency to 9710 kHz
- †RADIO VILNIUS, Sitkunai — Alternative Frequency to 9710 kHz

MALAYSIA
- VOICE OF MALAYSIA, Kajang — SE Asia • 100 kW

PORTUGAL
- RADIO RENASCENCA, Muge — M-F • Europe • 100 kW

RUSSIA
- †R MOSCOW INTL, Kenga — (D) • E Asia • 100 kW

YUGOSLAVIA
- †RADIO YUGOSLAVIA, Belgrade — Europe, N Africa & Mideast • 250 kW

6100v ALBANIA
- †RTV SHQIPTAR, Lushnjë — Europe • DS • 25 kW

CENTRAL AFRICAN REP
- RTV CENTRAFRICAINE, Bangui — Alternative Frequency to 7220v kHz

6105 BRAZIL
- R CANCAO NOVA, Cachoeira Paulista — PORTUGUESE • DS • 5 kW
- RADIO CULTURA, Foz do Iguaçú — Irr • PORTUGUESE • DS • 5 kW

MEXICO
- RADIO XEQM, Mérida — Irr • DS • 0.25 kW

ROMANIA
- RADIO ROMANIA INTL, Bucharest — (D) • Europe • 250 kW

RUSSIA
- †RADIO MOSCOW, Tver' — (D) • DS-2 • 100 kW

TANZANIA
- †RADIO TANZANIA, Dar es Salaam — E Africa • DS-NATIONAL • 50 kW

USA
- RFE-RL, Various Locations — E Europe • 100/250/500 kW
- WYFR-FAMILY RADIO, Okeechobee, Fl — (D) • S America • 100 kW

6105.5 BOLIVIA
- †RADIO PANAMERICANA, La Paz — Irr • Tu-Sa • DS • 10 kW / DS • 10 kW / Tu-Su • DS • 10 kW / M-F • DS • 10 kW / M-Sa • DS • 10 kW

6110 AZERBAIJAN
- RADIO BAKU, Baku — Mideast • 200 kW

CHINA (PR)
- †CENTRAL PEOPLES BS, Beijing — DS-MINORITIES • 50 kW

ECUADOR
- †HCJB-VO THE ANDES, Quito — S America • 100 kW

HUNGARY
- †RADIO BUDAPEST, Diósd — (D) • N America • 100 kW / Europe • 100 kW

INDIA
- †RADIO KASHMIR, Srinagar — DS-B • 50 kW / Su • DS-B • 50 kW / ENGLISH, ETC • DS-B • 50 kW

RUSSIA
- †R MOSCOW INTL, Via Azerbaijan — Mideast • 200 kW
- †RADIO MOSCOW, Via Azerbaijan — Mideast • 200 kW
- †RADIO NADEZHDA — (D) • DS

UNITED KINGDOM
- BBC, Multiple Locations — C America & S America • 125/250 kW / Tu-Sa • C America & S America • 125/250 kW
- †BBC, Various Locations — N Africa • 300/500 kW
- †BBC, Via Antigua — C America & S America • 125 kW / Tu-Sa • C America & S America • 125 kW / (D) • S America • 250 kW / (J) • S America • 250 kW / M-F • C America • 250 kW

USA
- †VOA, Via Philippines — SE Asia • 250 kW / S Asia & SE Asia • 250 kW

World Time scale: 0 1 2 3 4 5 6 7 8 9 10 11 12 13 14 15 16 17 18 19 20 21 22 23 24

FREQUENCY	COUNTRY, STATION, LOCATION	TARGET • NETWORK • POWER (kW) — World Time

Time scale: 0 1 2 3 4 5 6 7 8 9 10 11 12 13 14 15 16 17 18 19 20 21 22 23 24

Frequency	Country / Station / Location	Target • Network • Power
6112v	**MOZAMBIQUE**	
	RADIO MOCAMBIQUE, Maputo	Irr • DS • 100 kW
6115	**CHINA (PR)**	
	†VO THE STRAIT-PLA, Fuzhou	TAIWAN-1 • 50 kW
	GERMANY	
	†DEUTSCHE WELLE, Königswusterhausen	Europe • 100 kW
		(J) • Europe • 100 kW
	†DEUTSCHE WELLE, Nauen	(D) • Europe • 100 kW
		(D) • E Europe • 100 kW
	INDIA	
	ALL INDIA RADIO, Madras	DS • 100 kW
	JAPAN	
	RADIO TAMPA, Tokyo-Nagara	JAPANESE • DS-2 • 50 kW
	MEXICO	
	RADIO UNIVERSIDAD, Hermosillo	DS • 1 kW
	PERU	
	RADIO UNION, Lima	DS • 10 kW
		M-Sa • DS • 10 kW
		Su • DS • 10 kW
	RUSSIA	
	†RADIO SEVEN, Zhigulevsk	RUSSIAN, GERMAN, ETC • DS • 5 kW
		Sa/Su • RUSSIAN, ETC • DS • 5 kW
	†TATAR RADIO, Zhigulevsk	M-F • DS • 5 kW
		RUSSIAN, ETC • DS • 5 kW
	USA	
	†RFE-RL, Via Germany	E Europe • 100 kW
		(D) • E Europe • 100 kW
		(J) • E Europe • 100 kW
6116v	**COLOMBIA**	
	LA VOZ DEL LLANO, Villavicencio	DS • 2/10 kW
6120	**BRAZIL**	
	RADIO GLOBO, São Paulo	Irr • PORTUGUESE • DS • 7.5 kW
		PORTUGUESE • DS • 7.5 kW
	CANADA	
	†R CANADA INTL, Sackville, NB	W North Am • 250 kW
		(J) • W North Am • 250 kW
	FINLAND	
	†RADIO FINLAND, Pori	(D) • Europe • 100/250/500 kW
		(J) • Europe • 100/500 kW
		(D) M-Sa • Europe • 100/250 kW
		(J) M-Sa • Europe • 100 kW
		(D) Su • Europe • 100/250 kW
		(J) Su • Europe • 100 kW
	GERMANY	
	†DEUTSCHE WELLE, Multiple Locations	(D) • N America & C America • 100/500 kW
	†DEUTSCHE WELLE, Nauen	(D) • S America • 100 kW
	†DEUTSCHE WELLE, Wertachtal	(D) • N America • 500 kW
	INDIA	
	†ALL INDIA RADIO, Hyderabad	DS • 10 kW
		Su • DS • 10 kW
	JAPAN	
	RADIO JAPAN/NHK, Via Sackville, Can	N America • GENERAL • 250 kW
		(D) • JAPANESE • N America • GENERAL • 250 kW
		(J) • JAPANESE • N America • GENERAL • 250 kW
	OMAN	
	†RADIO OMAN, Sib	(D) • Mideast • DS • 100 kW
	SOUTH AFRICA	
	†CHANNEL AFRICA, Meyerton	(J) • S Africa • 250 kW
	SWAZILAND	
	†TRANS WORLD RADIO, Manzini	S Africa • 25 kW
	USA	
	†UNIVERSITY NET'K, Via N'sibirsk,Russia	(D) • S Asia • ALT. FREQ. TO 7355 kHz
6121v	**ALBANIA**	
	†RADIO TIRANA, Krujë	S America • 100 kW
6122.8	**BOLIVIA**	
	†RADIO INTEGRACION, La Paz	SPANISH, ETC • DS • 5 kW
		Tu-Su • DS • 5 kW
		M-Sa • SPANISH, ETC • DS • 5 kW
6125	**CHINA (PR)**	
	CENTRAL PEOPLES BS, Shijiazhuang	DS-1 • 50 kW
	ECUADOR	
	†HCJB-VO THE ANDES, Quito	S America • 100 kW
	JAPAN	
	†RADIO JAPAN/NHK, Via Skelton, UK	JAPANESE • Europe • GENERAL • 250 kW
		Europe • GENERAL • 250 kW
	KAZAKHSTAN	
	KAZAKH RADIO, Almaty	DS-2 • 20 kW
	KOREA (DPR)	
	RADIO PYONGYANG, Pyongyang	E Asia • 200 kW
		KOREAN • E Asia • 200 kW
	RUSSIA	
(con'd)	MARIY RADIO, Yoshkar Ola	DS • 20 kW

Time scale: 0 1 2 3 4 5 6 7 8 9 10 11 12 13 14 15 16 17 18 19 20 21 22 23 24

ENGLISH ▬　ARABIC ⋙　CHINESE ☐☐☐　FRENCH ▬　GERMAN ▬　RUSSIAN ═　SPANISH ▬　OTHER ▬

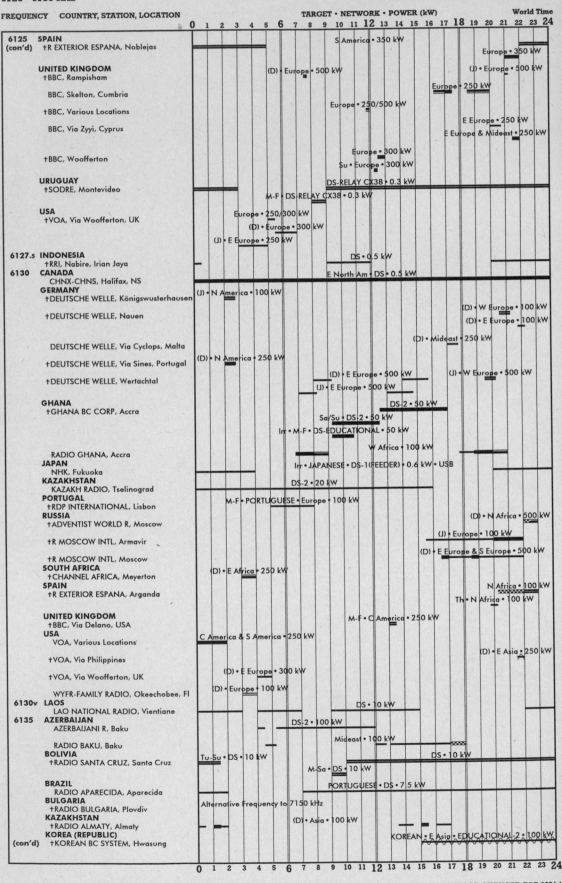

FREQUENCY   COUNTRY, STATION, LOCATION

TARGET • NETWORK • POWER (kW)   World Time

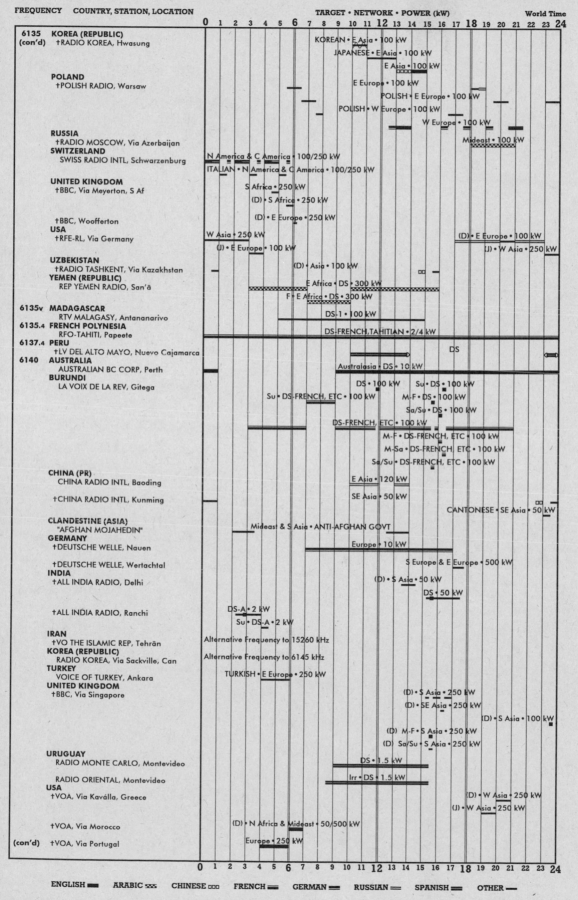

Frequency	Country, Station, Location	Target • Network • Power
6135 (con'd)	**KOREA (REPUBLIC)** †RADIO KOREA, Hwasung	KOREAN • E Asia • 100 kW / JAPANESE • E Asia • 100 kW / E Asia • 100 kW
	POLAND †POLISH RADIO, Warsaw	E Europe • 100 kW / POLISH • E Europe • 100 kW / POLISH • W Europe • 100 kW / W Europe • 100 kW
	RUSSIA †RADIO MOSCOW, Via Azerbaijan	Mideast • 100 kW
	SWITZERLAND SWISS RADIO INTL, Schwarzenburg	N America & C America • 100/250 kW / ITALIAN • N America & C America • 100/250 kW
	UNITED KINGDOM †BBC, Via Meyerton, S Af	S Africa • 250 kW / (D) • S Africa • 250 kW
	†BBC, Woofferton	(D) • E Europe • 250 kW
	USA †RFE-RL, Via Germany	W Asia • 250 kW / (D) • E Europe • 100 kW / (J) • E Europe • 100 kW / (J) • W Asia • 250 kW
	UZBEKISTAN †RADIO TASHKENT, Via Kazakhstan	(D) • Asia • 100 kW
	YEMEN (REPUBLIC) REP YEMEN RADIO, San'ā	E Africa • DS • 300 kW / F • E Africa • DS • 300 kW
6135v	**MADAGASCAR** RTV MALAGASY, Antananarivo	DS-1 • 100 kW
6135.4	**FRENCH POLYNESIA** RFO-TAHITI, Papeete	DS-FRENCH, TAHITIAN • 2/4 kW
6137.4	**PERU** †LV DEL ALTO MAYO, Nuevo Cajamarca	DS
6140	**AUSTRALIA** AUSTRALIAN BC CORP, Perth	Australasia • DS • 10 kW
	BURUNDI LA VOIX DE LA REV, Gitega	DS • 100 kW / Su • DS • 100 kW / Su • DS-FRENCH, ETC • 100 kW / M-F • DS • 100 kW / Sa/Su • DS • 100 kW / DS-FRENCH, ETC • 100 kW / M-F • DS-FRENCH, ETC • 100 kW / M-Sa • DS-FRENCH, ETC • 100 kW / Sa/Su • DS-FRENCH, ETC • 100 kW
	CHINA (PR) CHINA RADIO INTL, Baoding	E Asia • 120 kW
	†CHINA RADIO INTL, Kunming	SE Asia • 50 kW / CANTONESE • SE Asia • 50 kW
	CLANDESTINE (ASIA) "AFGHAN MOJAHEDIN"	Mideast & S Asia • ANTI-AFGHAN GOVT
	GERMANY †DEUTSCHE WELLE, Nauen	Europe • 10 kW
	†DEUTSCHE WELLE, Wertachtal	S Europe & E Europe • 500 kW
	INDIA †ALL INDIA RADIO, Delhi	(D) • S Asia • 50 kW / DS • 50 kW
	†ALL INDIA RADIO, Ranchi	DS-A • 2 kW / Su • DS-A • 2 kW
	IRAN †VO THE ISLAMIC REP, Tehrān	Alternative Frequency to 15260 kHz
	KOREA (REPUBLIC) RADIO KOREA, Via Sackville, Can	Alternative Frequency to 6145 kHz
	TURKEY VOICE OF TURKEY, Ankara	TURKISH • E Europe • 250 kW
	UNITED KINGDOM †BBC, Via Singapore	(D) • S Asia • 250 kW / (D) • SE Asia • 250 kW / (D) • S Asia • 100 kW / (D) • M-F • S Asia • 250 kW / (D) • Sa/Su • S Asia • 250 kW
	URUGUAY RADIO MONTE CARLO, Montevideo	DS • 1.5 kW
	RADIO ORIENTAL, Montevideo	Irr • DS • 1.5 kW
	USA †VOA, Via Kaválla, Greece	(D) • W Asia • 250 kW / (J) • W Asia • 250 kW
	†VOA, Via Morocco	(D) • N Africa & Mideast • 50/500 kW
(con'd)	†VOA, Via Portugal	Europe • 250 kW

ENGLISH ▬▬   ARABIC ⋙   CHINESE ▫▫▫   FRENCH ▭▭   GERMAN ▬▬   RUSSIAN ══   SPANISH ▬▬   OTHER ▬

FREQUENCY   COUNTRY, STATION, LOCATION   TARGET • NETWORK • POWER (kW)   World Time

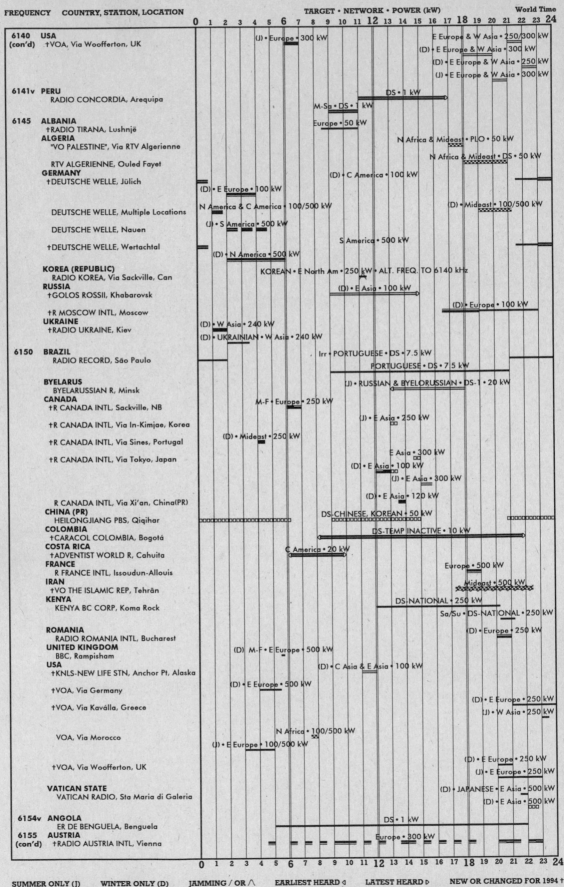

6140 **USA**	
(con'd) †VOA, Via Woofferton, UK	(J) • Europe • 300 kW
	E Europe & W Asia • 250/300 kW
	(D) • E Europe & W Asia • 300 kW
	(D) • E Europe & W Asia • 250 kW
	(J) • E Europe & W Asia • 300 kW
6141v **PERU**	
RADIO CONCORDIA, Arequipa	DS • 1 kW
	M-Sa • DS • 1 kW
6145 **ALBANIA**	
†RADIO TIRANA, Lushnjë	Europe • 50 kW
ALGERIA	
"VO PALESTINE", Via RTV Algerienne	N Africa & Mideast • PLO • 50 kW
RTV ALGERIENNE, Ouled Fayet	N Africa & Mideast • DS • 50 kW
GERMANY	
†DEUTSCHE WELLE, Jülich	(D) • C America • 100 kW
	(D) • E Europe • 100 kW
DEUTSCHE WELLE, Multiple Locations	N America & C America • 100/500 kW
	(D) • Mideast • 100/500 kW
DEUTSCHE WELLE, Nauen	(J) • S America • 500 kW
	S America • 500 kW
†DEUTSCHE WELLE, Wertachtal	(D) • N America • 500 kW
KOREA (REPUBLIC)	
RADIO KOREA, Via Sackville, Can	KOREAN • E North Am • 250 kW • ALT. FREQ. TO 6140 kHz
RUSSIA	
†GOLOS ROSSII, Khabarovsk	(D) • E Asia • 100 kW
†R MOSCOW INTL, Moscow	(D) • Europe • 100 kW
UKRAINE	
†RADIO UKRAINE, Kiev	(D) • W Asia • 240 kW
	(D) • UKRAINIAN • W Asia • 240 kW
6150 **BRAZIL**	
RADIO RECORD, São Paulo	Irr • PORTUGUESE • DS • 7.5 kW
	PORTUGUESE • DS • 7.5 kW
BYELARUS	
BYELARUSSIAN R, Minsk	(J) • RUSSIAN & BYELORUSSIAN • DS-1 • 20 kW
CANADA	
†R CANADA INTL, Sackville, NB	M-F • Europe • 250 kW
†R CANADA INTL, Via In-Kimjae, Korea	(J) • E Asia • 250 kW
†R CANADA INTL, Via Sines, Portugal	(D) • Mideast • 250 kW
†R CANADA INTL, Via Tokyo, Japan	E Asia • 300 kW
	(D) • E Asia • 100 kW
	(J) • E Asia • 300 kW
R CANADA INTL, Via Xi'an, China(PR)	(D) • E Asia • 120 kW
CHINA (PR)	
HEILONGJIANG PBS, Qiqihar	DS • CHINESE, KOREAN • 50 kW
COLOMBIA	
†CARACOL COLOMBIA, Bogotá	DS-TEMP INACTIVE • 10 kW
COSTA RICA	
†ADVENTIST WORLD R, Cahuita	C America • 20 kW
FRANCE	
R FRANCE INTL, Issoudun-Allouis	Europe • 500 kW
IRAN	
†VO THE ISLAMIC REP, Tehrān	Mideast • 500 kW
KENYA	
KENYA BC CORP, Koma Rock	DS-NATIONAL • 250 kW
	Sa/Su • DS-NATIONAL • 250 kW
ROMANIA	
RADIO ROMANIA INTL, Bucharest	(D) • Europe • 250 kW
UNITED KINGDOM	
BBC, Rampisham	(D) • M-F • E Europe • 500 kW
USA	
†KNLS-NEW LIFE STN, Anchor Pt, Alaska	(D) • C Asia & E Asia • 100 kW
†VOA, Via Germany	(D) • E Europe • 500 kW
†VOA, Via Kaválla, Greece	(D) • E Europe • 250 kW
	(J) • W Asia • 250 kW
VOA, Via Morocco	N Africa • 100/500 kW
	(J) • E Europe • 100/500 kW
†VOA, Via Woofferton, UK	(D) • E Europe • 250 kW
	(J) • E Europe • 250 kW
VATICAN STATE	
VATICAN RADIO, Sta Maria di Galeria	(D) • JAPANESE • E Asia • 500 kW
	(D) • E Asia • 500 kW
6154v **ANGOLA**	
ER DE BENGUELA, Benguela	DS • 1 kW
6155 **AUSTRIA**	
(con'd) †RADIO AUSTRIA INTL, Vienna	Europe • 300 kW

FREQUENCY   COUNTRY, STATION, LOCATION

TARGET • NETWORK • POWER (kW)

World Time

6155 **AUSTRIA**	
(con'd) †RADIO AUSTRIA INTL, Vienna	(D) • Europe • 300 kW
	(J) • Europe • 300 kW
	M-Sa • Europe • 300 kW
	Su • Europe • 300 kW
BOLIVIA	
†RADIO FIDES, La Paz	Sa/Su • DS • 10 kW
	DS • 10 kW
	Tu-Su • DS • 10 kW
	Irr • DS • 10 kW
CHINA (PR)	
GANSU PEOPLES BS, Lanzhou	DS-1 • 15 kW
GUINEA	
RTV GUINEENNE, Conakry-Sofoniya	M-Sa • FRENCH, ETC • DS • 100 kW
	DS • 100 kW
	FRENCH, ETC • DS • 100 kW
	Su • FRENCH, ETC • DS • 100 kW
INDIA	
†ALL INDIA RADIO, Delhi	S Asia & W Asia • 100 kW
ROMANIA	
RADIO ROMANIA INTL, Bucharest	Americas • 250 kW
	(D) • Americas • 250 kW
RUSSIA	
†RADIO MOSCOW	(D) • DS-MAYAK
	DS-MAYAK • 50 kW
†RADIO MOSCOW, Nikolayevsk 'Amure	
SINGAPORE	DS-MALAY • 50 kW
SINGAPORE BC CORP, Jurong	
SWAZILAND	
†SWAZI RADIO, Sandlane	M-Sa • S Africa • RADIO CIDADE • 50 kW
	S Africa • 50 kW
	Su • S Africa • 50 kW
	Sa • S Africa • RADIO CIDADE • 50 kW
	Su-F • S Africa • 50 kW
	Sa/Su • S Africa • RADIO CIDADE • 50 kW
	Su • S Africa • RADIO CIDADE • 50 kW
	Sa • ENGLISH & PORTUGUESE • S Africa • RADIO CIDADE • 50 kW
TOGO	
RADIO KARA, Lama-Kara	FRENCH, ETC • DS • 10 kW
	Sa/Su • FRENCH, ETC • DS • 10 kW
UNITED KINGDOM	
†BBC, Via Ascension	(D) • W Africa • 250 kW
	(J) • C Africa • 250 kW
†BBC, Via Maṣīrah, Oman	(D) • W Asia & S Asia • 100 kW
	(D) • W Asia • 100 kW
USA	
†VOA, Via Ascension	E Africa • 250 kW
6160 **ALGERIA**	
"VO PALESTINE", Via RTV Algerienne	Irr • N Africa • PLO • 50 kW
RTV ALGERIENNE, Ouled Fayet	Irr • N Africa • 50 kW
BRAZIL	
RADIO RIO MAR, Manaus	PORTUGUESE • DS • 10 kW
	Sa • DS • 10 kW
	Su-F • DS • 10 kW
CANADA	
CKZN-CBN, St John's, Nfld	E North Am • DS • 0.3 kW
CKZU-CBU, Vancouver, BC	W North Am • DS • 0.5 kW
COLOMBIA	
†R CADENA NACIONAL, Bogotá	DS (PROJECTED) • 50 kW
GERMANY	
DEUTSCHE WELLE, Via Antigua	C America & Australasia • 250 kW
UKRAINE	
†UKRAINIAN R	(D) • RUSSIAN & UKRAINIAN • DS-3
UNITED KINGDOM	
†BBC, Via Zyyi, Cyprus	(J) • W Asia • 100 kW
USA	
†RFE-RL, Via Germany	(J) • E Europe • 100 kW
†RFE-RL, Via Portugal	(D) • E Europe • 500 kW
†VOA, Various Locations	N Africa & W Africa • 250/500 kW
VOA, Via Germany	Mideast • 50/500 kW
VOA, Via Kaválla, Greece	(D) • S Asia • 250 kW
	(D) • W Asia • 250 kW
†VOA, Via Philippines	(J) • E Asia • 250 kW
†VOA, Via Portugal	(D) • Europe • 250 kW
†VOA, Via Woofferton, UK	(D) • E Europe • 250 kW
	(J) • E Europe • 250 kW
6160.7 **ARGENTINA**	
RADIO MALARGUE, Malargüe	DS • 0.3/1 kW
6161v **VIETNAM**	
†VOICE OF VIETNAM, Hanoi	DS

FREQUENCY   COUNTRY, STATION, LOCATION   TARGET • NETWORK • POWER (kW)   World Time

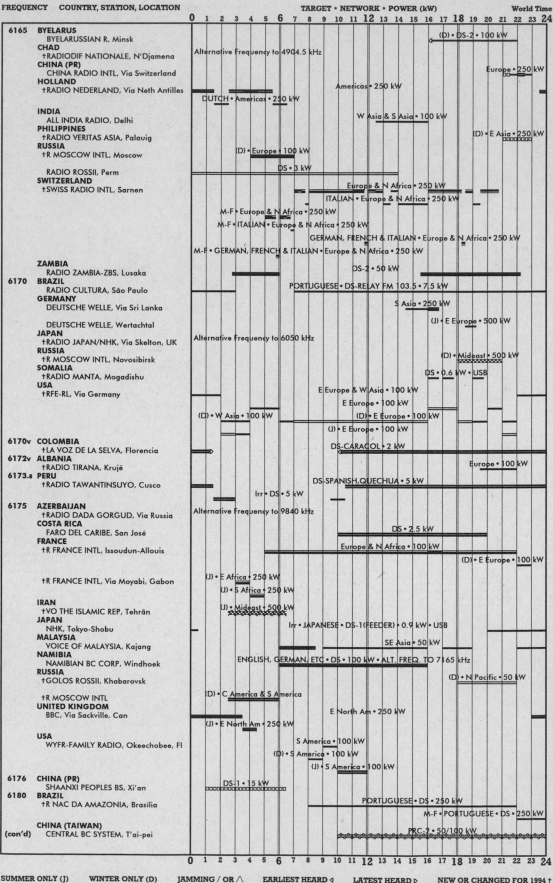

6165	**BYELARUS**
	BYELARUSSIAN R, Minsk
	CHAD
	†RADIODIF NATIONALE, N'Djamena
	CHINA (PR)
	CHINA RADIO INTL, Via Switzerland
	HOLLAND
	†RADIO NEDERLAND, Via Neth Antilles
	INDIA
	ALL INDIA RADIO, Delhi
	PHILIPPINES
	†RADIO VERITAS ASIA, Palauig
	RUSSIA
	†R MOSCOW INTL, Moscow
	RADIO ROSSII, Perm
	SWITZERLAND
	†SWISS RADIO INTL, Sarnen
	ZAMBIA
	RADIO ZAMBIA-ZBS, Lusaka
6170	**BRAZIL**
	RADIO CULTURA, São Paulo
	GERMANY
	DEUTSCHE WELLE, Via Sri Lanka
	DEUTSCHE WELLE, Wertachtal
	JAPAN
	†RADIO JAPAN/NHK, Via Skelton, UK
	RUSSIA
	†R MOSCOW INTL, Novosibirsk
	SOMALIA
	†RADIO MANTA, Mogadishu
	USA
	†RFE-RL, Via Germany
6170v	**COLOMBIA**
	†LA VOZ DE LA SELVA, Florencia
6172v	**ALBANIA**
	†RADIO TIRANA, Krujë
6173.8	**PERU**
	†RADIO TAWANTINSUYO, Cusco
6175	**AZERBAIJAN**
	†RADIO DADA GORGUD, Via Russia
	COSTA RICA
	FARO DEL CARIBE, San José
	FRANCE
	†R FRANCE INTL, Issoudun-Allouis
	†R FRANCE INTL, Via Moyabi, Gabon
	IRAN
	†VO THE ISLAMIC REP, Tehrān
	JAPAN
	NHK, Tokyo-Shobu
	MALAYSIA
	VOICE OF MALAYSIA, Kajang
	NAMIBIA
	NAMIBIAN BC CORP, Windhoek
	RUSSIA
	†GOLOS ROSSII, Khabarovsk
	†R MOSCOW INTL
	UNITED KINGDOM
	BBC, Via Sackville, Can
	USA
	WYFR-FAMILY RADIO, Okeechobee, Fl
6176	**CHINA (PR)**
	SHAANXI PEOPLES BS, Xi'an
6180	**BRAZIL**
	†R NAC DA AMAZONIA, Brasilia
	CHINA (TAIWAN)
(con'd)	CENTRAL BC SYSTEM, T'ai-pei

Chart entries (target • network • power):

- BYELARUSSIAN R, Minsk: (D) • DS-2 • 100 kW
- RADIODIF NATIONALE: Alternative Frequency to 4904.5 kHz
- CHINA RADIO INTL, Via Switzerland: Europe • 250 kW
- RADIO NEDERLAND: Americas • 250 kW; DUTCH • Americas • 250 kW
- ALL INDIA RADIO: W Asia & S Asia • 100 kW
- RADIO VERITAS ASIA: (D) • E Asia • 250 kW
- R MOSCOW INTL, Moscow: (D) • Europe • 100 kW
- RADIO ROSSII, Perm: DS • 3 kW
- SWISS RADIO INTL: Europe & N Africa • 250 kW; ITALIAN • Europe & N Africa • 250 kW; M-F • Europe & N Africa • 250 kW; M-F • ITALIAN • Europe & N Africa • 250 kW; GERMAN, FRENCH & ITALIAN • Europe & N Africa • 250 kW; M-F • GERMAN, FRENCH & ITALIAN • Europe & N Africa • 250 kW
- RADIO ZAMBIA-ZBS: DS-2 • 50 kW
- RADIO CULTURA: PORTUGUESE • DS-RELAY FM 103.5 • 7.5 kW
- DEUTSCHE WELLE, Via Sri Lanka: S Asia • 250 kW
- DEUTSCHE WELLE, Wertachtal: (J) • E Europe • 500 kW
- RADIO JAPAN/NHK: Alternative Frequency to 6050 kHz
- R MOSCOW INTL, Novosibirsk: (D) • Mideast • 500 kW
- RADIO MANTA: DS • 0.6 kW • USB
- RFE-RL, Via Germany: E Europe & W Asia • 100 kW; E Europe • 100 kW; (D) • W Asia • 100 kW; (D) • E Europe • 100 kW; (J) • E Europe • 100 kW
- LA VOZ DE LA SELVA: DS-CARACOL • 2 kW
- RADIO TIRANA: Europe • 100 kW
- RADIO TAWANTINSUYO: DS-SPANISH,QUECHUA • 5 kW; Irr • DS • 5 kW
- RADIO DADA GORGUD: Alternative Frequency to 9840 kHz
- FARO DEL CARIBE: DS • 2.5 kW
- R FRANCE INTL, Issoudun-Alouis: Europe & N Africa • 100 kW; (D) • E Europe • 100 kW
- R FRANCE INTL, Via Moyabi, Gabon: (J) • E Africa • 250 kW; (J) • S Africa • 250 kW
- VO THE ISLAMIC REP: (J) • Mideast • 500 kW
- NHK, Tokyo-Shobu: Irr • JAPANESE • DS-1 (FEEDER) • 0.9 kW • USB
- VOICE OF MALAYSIA: SE Asia • 50 kW
- NAMIBIAN BC CORP: ENGLISH, GERMAN, ETC • DS • 100 kW • ALT. FREQ. TO 7165 kHz
- GOLOS ROSSII: (D) • N Pacific • 50 kW
- R MOSCOW INTL: (D) • C America & S America
- BBC, Via Sackville: E North Am • 250 kW; (J) • E North Am • 250 kW
- WYFR-FAMILY RADIO: S America • 100 kW; (D) • S America • 100 kW; (J) • S America • 100 kW
- SHAANXI PEOPLES BS: DS-1 • 15 kW
- R NAC DA AMAZONIA: PORTUGUESE • DS • 250 kW; M-F • PORTUGUESE • DS • 250 kW
- CENTRAL BC SYSTEM: PRC-2 • 50/100 kW

FREQUENCY   COUNTRY, STATION, LOCATION

TARGET • NETWORK • POWER (kW)

World Time

0 1 2 3 4 5 6 7 8 9 10 11 12 13 14 15 16 17 18 19 20 21 22 23 24

Frequency	Country, Station, Location	Schedule
6180 (con'd)	CUBA †RADIO HABANA, Havana	C America • 50 kW / (D) • C America • 50 kW
	CYPRUS †CYPRUS BC CORP, Zyyi	F-Su • Europe • 250 kW
	GERMANY DEUTSCHE WELLE, Jülich	(D) • S Asia • 100 kW
	KAZAKHSTAN KAZAKH RADIO, Almaty	RUSSIAN, GERMAN, ETC • DS-1 • 100 kW
	UNITED KINGDOM †BBC, Via Zyyi, Cyprus	Europe • 100/250 kW / (J) • E Europe & W Asia • 100 kW / (D) • Europe • 250 kW / (J) • Europe • 250 kW
	USA VOA, Via Woofferton, UK	(D) • E Europe • 250 kW
6185	CHINA (PR) †CHINA HUAYI BC CO, Fuzhou	E Asia • DS • 15 kW
	GERMANY DEUTSCHE WELLE, Jülich	(D) • SE Asia & Australasia • 100 kW
	JAPAN †RADIO JAPAN/NHK, Tokyo-Yamata	(D) • E Asia • 100 kW / (D) • JAPANESE • E Asia • GENERAL • 100 kW
	MEXICO †RADIO EDUCACION, México City	SPANISH & ENGLISH • DS • 5 kW
	RUSSIA †R MOSCOW INTL, Armavir	(D) • C America & S America • 500 kW
	†RADIO SHARK, Ufa	DS • 15 kW / Su/M/W • DS • 15 kW / M/F • DS • 15 kW / Tu/Th/F/Sa • DS • 15 kW / Su/Tu/Th • DS • 15 kW / W/Sa • DS • 15 kW
	†RADIO TITAN, Ufa	DS • 15 kW / Sa • DS • 15 kW
	SWEDEN †RADIO SWEDEN, Hörby	E Europe • 500 kW
	VATICAN STATE †VATICAN RADIO, Sta Maria di Galeria	E Europe & W Asia • 250 kW / (D) • E Europe & W Asia • 250 kW / E Europe • 250 kW / Europe • 250 kW / (D) • E Europe • 250 kW / N Europe • 250 kW / M/Tu/Th/Sa • E Europe • 250 kW / (D) • E Europe • 100 kW / Th • N Europe • 250 kW / (D) Su/M/W/F • E Europe • 250 kW
6188.8	INDONESIA †RRI, Manokwari,Irian Jaya	DS • 1 kW
6190	GERMANY FREIES BERLIN-SFB, Bremen	Europe • DS • 10 kW / Sa • Europe • DS • 10 kW / Su-F • Europe • DS • 10 kW
	RADIO BREMEN, Bremen	Sa • Europe • DS • 10 kW / Su-F • Europe • DS • 10 kW
	INDIA ALL INDIA RADIO, Delhi	DS • 10 kW / ENGLISH & HINDI • DS • 10 kW
	JAPAN NHK, Osaka	Irr • JAPANESE • DS-2(FEEDER) • 0.5 kW
	PERU †RADIO ORIENTE, Yurimaguas	DS • 1.5 kW / M-Sa • DS • 1.5 kW
	ROMANIA RADIO ROMANIA INTL, Bucharest	(D) • Europe • 250 kW / (J) • Europe • 250 kW
	RUSSIA †R MOSCOW INTL, Via Uzbekistan	(D) • Mideast • 100 kW
	†RADIO MOSCOW, Omsk	DS-MAYAK • 100 kW
	UNITED KINGDOM †BBC, Rampisham	(D) • C America • 500 kW / (D) Tu-Sa • C America • 500 kW
	BBC, Via Maseru, Lesotho	S Africa • 100 kW / Sa/Su • S Africa • 100 kW
	USA †VOA, Greenville, NC	C America & S America • 500 kW
6190.8	INDONESIA †RRI, Padang, Sumatera	DS • 10 kW
6194.5	BOLIVIA †R METROPOLITANA, La Paz	Tu-Su • DS • 10 kW / DS • 10 kW / M-Sa • DS • 10 kW
	PERU †RADIO CUZCO, Cusco	Alternative Frequency to 6203.7 kHz
6195	RUSSIA †RADIO MOSCOW	(D) • DS-MAYAK
(con'd)	†RADIO MOSCOW, Zhigulevsk	(D) • DS-1 • 100 kW

0 1 2 3 4 5 6 7 8 9 10 11 12 13 14 15 16 17 18 19 20 21 22 23 24

ENGLISH ▬▬   ARABIC ⁓⁓⁓   CHINESE ▭▭▭   FRENCH ══   GERMAN ▬▬   RUSSIAN ══   SPANISH ▬▬   OTHER ──

FREQUENCY   COUNTRY, STATION, LOCATION   TARGET • NETWORK • POWER (kW)   World Time

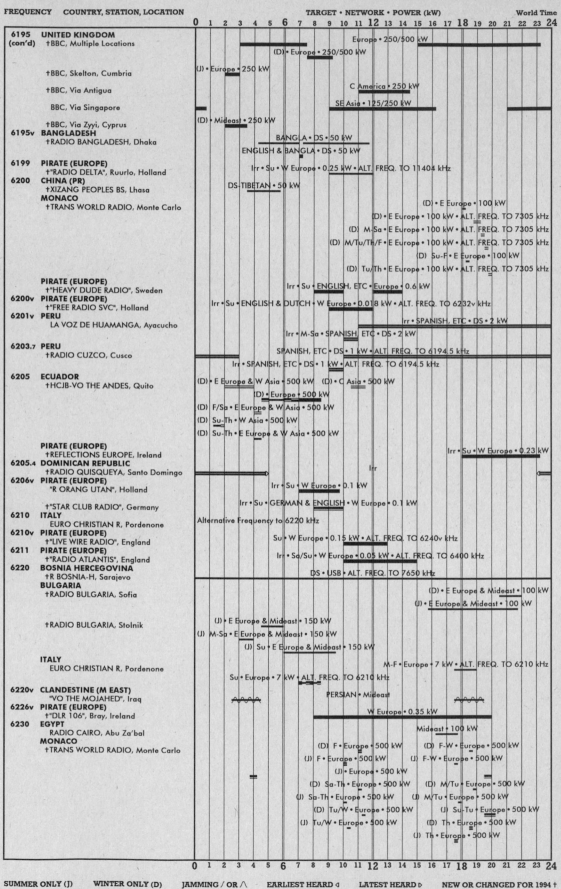

6195 UNITED KINGDOM
(con'd) †BBC, Multiple Locations — Europe • 250/500 kW
— (D) • Europe • 250/500 kW
†BBC, Skelton, Cumbria — (J) • Europe • 250 kW
†BBC, Via Antigua — C America • 250 kW
BBC, Via Singapore — SE Asia • 125/250 kW
†BBC, Via Zyyi, Cyprus — (D) • Mideast • 250 kW

6195v BANGLADESH
†RADIO BANGLADESH, Dhaka — BANGLA • DS • 50 kW
— ENGLISH & BANGLA • DS • 50 kW

6199 PIRATE (EUROPE)
†"RADIO DELTA", Ruurlo, Holland — Irr • Su • W Europe • 0.25 kW • ALT. FREQ. TO 11404 kHz

6200 CHINA (PR)
†XIZANG PEOPLES BS, Lhasa — DS-TIBETAN • 50 kW
MONACO
†TRANS WORLD RADIO, Monte Carlo — (D) • E Europe • 100 kW
— (D) • E Europe • 100 kW • ALT. FREQ. TO 7305 kHz
— (D) M-Sa • E Europe • 100 kW • ALT. FREQ. TO 7305 kHz
— (D) M/Tu/Th/F • E Europe • 100 kW • ALT. FREQ. TO 7305 kHz
— (D) Su-F • E Europe • 100 kW
— (D) Tu/Th • E Europe • 100 kW • ALT. FREQ. TO 7305 kHz

PIRATE (EUROPE)
†"HEAVY DUDE RADIO", Sweden — Irr • Su • ENGLISH, ETC • Europe • 0.6 kW
6200v PIRATE (EUROPE)
†"FREE RADIO SVC", Holland — Irr • Su • ENGLISH & DUTCH • W Europe • 0.018 kW • ALT. FREQ. TO 6232v kHz
6201v PERU
LA VOZ DE HUAMANGA, Ayacucho — Irr • SPANISH, ETC • DS • 2 kW
— Irr • M-Sa • SPANISH, ETC • DS • 2 kW

6203.7 PERU
†RADIO CUZCO, Cusco — SPANISH, ETC • DS • 1 kW • ALT. FREQ. TO 6194.5 kHz
— Irr • SPANISH, ETC • DS • 1 kW • ALT. FREQ. TO 6194.5 kHz

6205 ECUADOR
†HCJB-VO THE ANDES, Quito — (D) • E Europe & W Asia • 500 kW   (D) • C Asia • 500 kW
— (D) • Europe • 500 kW
— (D) F/Sa • E Europe & W Asia • 500 kW
— (D) Su-Th • W Asia • 500 kW
— (D) Su-Th • E Europe & W Asia • 500 kW

PIRATE (EUROPE)
†REFLECTIONS EUROPE, Ireland — Irr • Su • W Europe • 0.23 kW
6205.4 DOMINICAN REPUBLIC
†RADIO QUISQUEYA, Santo Domingo — Irr
6206v PIRATE (EUROPE)
"R ORANG UTAN", Holland — Irr • Su • W Europe • 0.1 kW
†"STAR CLUB RADIO", Germany — Irr • Su • GERMAN & ENGLISH • W Europe • 0.1 kW
6210 ITALY
EURO CHRISTIAN R, Pordenone — Alternative Frequency to 6220 kHz
6210v PIRATE (EUROPE)
†"LIVE WIRE RADIO", England — Su • W Europe • 0.15 kW • ALT. FREQ. TO 6240v kHz
6211 PIRATE (EUROPE)
†"RADIO ATLANTIS", England — Irr • Sa/Su • W Europe • 0.05 kW • ALT. FREQ. TO 6400 kHz
6220 BOSNIA HERCEGOVINA
†R BOSNIA-H, Sarajevo — DS • USB • ALT. FREQ. TO 7650 kHz
BULGARIA
†RADIO BULGARIA, Sofia — (D) • E Europe & Mideast • 100 kW
— (J) • E Europe & Mideast • 100 kW
†RADIO BULGARIA, Stolnik — (J) • E Europe & Mideast • 150 kW
— (J) M-Sa • E Europe & Mideast • 150 kW
— (J) Su • E Europe & Mideast • 150 kW

ITALY
EURO CHRISTIAN R, Pordenone — M-F • Europe • 7 kW • ALT. FREQ. TO 6210 kHz
— Su • Europe • 7 kW • ALT. FREQ. TO 6210 kHz

6220v CLANDESTINE (M EAST)
"VO THE MOJAHED", Iraq — PERSIAN • Mideast
6226v PIRATE (EUROPE)
†"DLR 106", Bray, Ireland — W Europe • 0.35 kW
6230 EGYPT
RADIO CAIRO, Abu Za'bal — Mideast • 100 kW
MONACO
†TRANS WORLD RADIO, Monte Carlo — (D) F • Europe • 500 kW   (D) F-W • Europe • 500 kW
— (J) F • Europe • 500 kW   (J) F-W • Europe • 500 kW
— (J) • Europe • 500 kW
— (D) Sa-Th • Europe • 500 kW   (D) M/Tu • Europe • 500 kW
— (J) Sa-Th • Europe • 500 kW   (J) M/Tu • Europe • 500 kW
— (D) Tu/W • Europe • 500 kW   (J) Su-Tu • Europe • 500 kW
— (J) Tu/W • Europe • 500 kW   (D) Th • Europe • 500 kW
— (J) Th • Europe • 500 kW

FREQUENCY • COUNTRY, STATION, LOCATION — **TARGET • NETWORK • POWER (kW)** — **World Time** (0 1 2 3 4 5 6 7 8 9 10 11 12 13 14 15 16 17 18 19 20 21 22 23 24)

Frequency	Country, Station, Location	Target • Network • Power
6230v	PIRATE (EUROPE) "BRITAIN R INTL", Germany	Irr • Su • ENGLISH & GERMAN • W Europe • 0.05 kW
	"JOLLY ROGER R", Ireland	Sa/Su • W Europe
6232v	PIRATE (EUROPE) †"FREE RADIO SVC", Holland	Alternative Frequency to 6200v kHz
6234v	PIRATE (EUROPE) †"RADIO MARABU", Germany	Irr • Su • GERMAN & ENGLISH • W Europe • ALT. FREQ. TO 7470v kHz
6235	BULGARIA †RADIO BULGARIA, Plovdiv	(D) • Europe • 250 kW
6235v	PIRATE (EUROPE) "RADIO GEMINI", England	Irr • Su • W Europe • 0.15 kW
6240	PIRATE (EUROPE) "WEEKEND MUSIC R", Scotland	Alternative Frequency to 6296v kHz
	†BELGIAN INTL RELAY, Essex, England	Irr • Sa/Su • W Europe • 0.05 kW
6240v	PERU RADIO MUNICIPAL, Calca	DS • 0.12 kW
	PIRATE (EUROPE) †"LIVE WIRE RADIO", England	Alternative Frequency to 6210v kHz
6245	VATICAN STATE †VATICAN RADIO, Sta Maria di Galeria	E Europe • 100 kW M-Sa • Europe • 100 kW
		Europe • 100 kW
		Su • Europe • 100 kW
6250v	EQUATORIAL GUINEA RADIO NACIONAL, Malabo	SPANISH, ETC • DS • 10 kW
	KOREA (DPR) RADIO PYONGYANG, Pyongyang	KOREAN • E Asia • 50/100 kW
6255v	PIRATE (EUROPE) †"R EAST COAST COMM", England	Irr • Su • W Europe
6260	CHINA (PR) †QINGHAI PEOPLES BS, Xining	DS-1 • 10 kW
6270v	CLANDESTINE (S AMER) †"R PATRIA LIBRE", Colombia	Irr • S America • ELN REBELS • ALT. FREQ. TO 15050v kHz
6280	PIRATE (EUROPE) "OZONE RADIO INTL", Ireland	Su • W Europe • 0.08 kW
6280.2	LEBANON KING OF HOPE, Marjayoûn	Mideast & E Europe • 12 kW
6281v	PERU RADIO HUANCABAMBA, Huancabamba	DS • 1.5 kW
6285v	PIRATE (EUROPE) †"PIRATE FREAKS BC", Germany	Irr • Su • ENGLISH & GERMAN • W Europe • ALT. FREQ. TO 9985v kHz
6294v	PIRATE (EUROPE) †"RADIO CAROLINE", Ireland	Sa/Su • W Europe • 0.5/1 kW
6295	PAKISTAN PAKISTAN BC CORP, Islamabad	(D) • DS • 100 kW
6295v	CLANDESTINE (M EAST) "VO IRAQI KURDS", Middle East	Mideast • ANTI-IRAQI GOVT • ALT. FREQ. TO 5930v kHz
		Mideast • ANTI-IRAQI GOVT • ALT. FREQ. TO 5830v kHz
		Irr • Mideast • ANTI-IRAQI GOVT • ALT. FREQ. TO 5830v kHz
6296v	PIRATE (EUROPE) "WEEKEND MUSIC R", Scotland	Irr • Su • W Europe • 0.1 kW • ALT. FREQ. TO 6240 kHz
6298.2	PIRATE (EUROPE) †"R IRELAND INTL", Ireland	Irr • Su • W Europe • 0.012 kW
6299.3	HONDURAS SANI RADIO, Puerto Lempira	SPANISH, ETC • DS-TEMP INACTIVE • 10 kW
6300	CLANDESTINE (ASIA) †"KASHMIR FREEDOM", Pakistan	S Asia • ANTI-INDIAN GOVT
	USA FAMILY RADIO, Via Taiwan	E Asia • 250 kW
6305	CLANDESTINE (C AMER) "LA VOZ DEL CID", Guatemala	C America • ANTI-CASTRO
6320v	EL SALVADOR RADIO VENCEREMOS, Perquin	C America • TEMP INACTIVE • ALT. FREQ. TO 6750v kHz
		M-Sa • C America • TEMP INACTIVE • ALT. FREQ. TO 6750v kHz
		Su • C America • TEMP INACTIVE • ALT. FREQ. TO 6750v kHz
6325.8	PERU RADIO ABANCAY, Abancay	DS-SPANISH, QUECHUA • 1 kW
		M-Sa • DS-SPANISH, QUECHUA • 1 kW
6330v	PERU †ESTACION C, Moyobamba	Alternative Frequency to 6499v kHz
	VIETNAM †SON LA BC STATION, Son La	DS
6339	PERU RADIO SAN MIGUEL, San Miguel	DS
		Tu-Su • DS
6340	CLANDESTINE (AFRICA) †"RADIO MUHABURA"	E Africa • RWANDA REBELS
6348	CLANDESTINE (ASIA) †"ECHO OF HOPE", Seoul, South Korea	KOREAN • E Asia • 50 kW
		(J) • KOREAN • E Asia • 50 kW
6390	RUSSIA RADIO MOSCOW	(D) • DS-1 (FEEDER) • ISU
		(D) • DS-1 (FEEDER) • ISL
6390v	VIETNAM LAM DONG BC STN, Da Lat	DS
6392v	VIETNAM †YEN BAI BC STN, Yen Bai	DS
6400 (con'd)	CLANDESTINE (AFRICA) †"RADIO MUHABURA"	E Africa • RWANDA REBELS

ENGLISH ■■■   ARABIC ≈≈≈   CHINESE □□□   FRENCH ══   GERMAN ▬▬   RUSSIAN ══   SPANISH ▬▬   OTHER ──

FREQUENCY   COUNTRY, STATION, LOCATION

TARGET • NETWORK • POWER (kW)

World Time

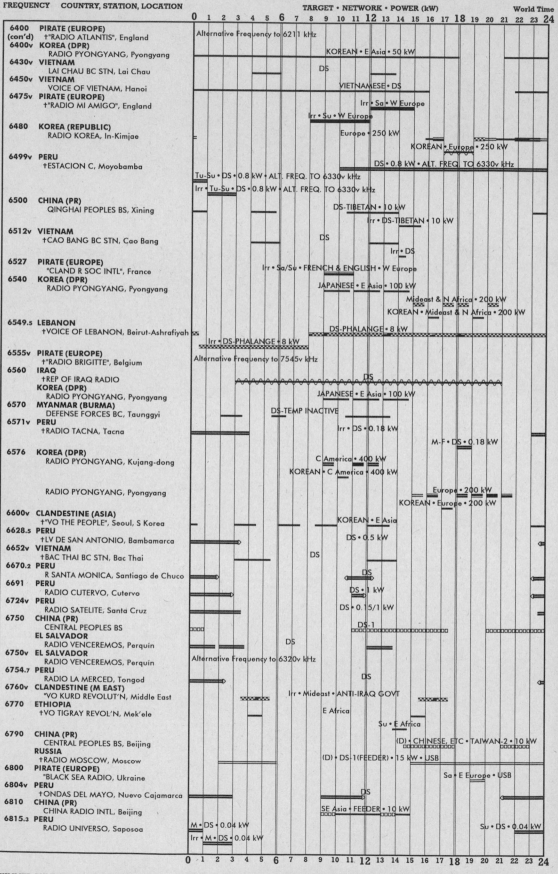

6400	**PIRATE (EUROPE)**
(con'd)	†"RADIO ATLANTIS", England
6400v	**KOREA (DPR)**
	RADIO PYONGYANG, Pyongyang
6430v	**VIETNAM**
	LAI CHAU BC STN, Lai Chau
6450v	**VIETNAM**
	VOICE OF VIETNAM, Hanoi
6475v	**PIRATE (EUROPE)**
	†"RADIO MI AMIGO", England
6480	**KOREA (REPUBLIC)**
	RADIO KOREA, In-Kimjae
6499v	**PERU**
	†ESTACION C, Moyobamba
6500	**CHINA (PR)**
	QINGHAI PEOPLES BS, Xining
6512v	**VIETNAM**
	†CAO BANG BC STN, Cao Bang
6527	**PIRATE (EUROPE)**
	"CLAND R SOC INTL", France
6540	**KOREA (DPR)**
	RADIO PYONGYANG, Pyongyang
6549.5	**LEBANON**
	†VOICE OF LEBANON, Beirut-Ashrafiyah
6555v	**PIRATE (EUROPE)**
	†"RADIO BRIGITTE", Belgium
6560	**IRAQ**
	†REP OF IRAQ RADIO
	KOREA (DPR)
	RADIO PYONGYANG, Pyongyang
6570	**MYANMAR (BURMA)**
	DEFENSE FORCES BC, Taunggyi
6571v	**PERU**
	†RADIO TACNA, Tacna
6576	**KOREA (DPR)**
	RADIO PYONGYANG, Kujang-dong
	RADIO PYONGYANG, Pyongyang
6600v	**CLANDESTINE (ASIA)**
	†"VO THE PEOPLE", Seoul, S Korea
6628.5	**PERU**
	†LV DE SAN ANTONIO, Bambamarca
6652v	**VIETNAM**
	†BAC THAI BC STN, Bac Thai
6670.2	**PERU**
	R SANTA MONICA, Santiago de Chuco
6691	**PERU**
	RADIO CUTERVO, Cutervo
6724v	**PERU**
	RADIO SATELITE, Santa Cruz
6750	**CHINA (PR)**
	CENTRAL PEOPLES BS
	EL SALVADOR
	RADIO VENCEREMOS, Perquin
6750v	**EL SALVADOR**
	RADIO VENCEREMOS, Perquin
6754.7	**PERU**
	RADIO LA MERCED, Tongod
6760v	**CLANDESTINE (M EAST)**
	"VO KURD REVOLUT'N, Middle East
6770	**ETHIOPIA**
	†VO TIGRAY REVOL'N, Mek'ele
6790	**CHINA (PR)**
	CENTRAL PEOPLES BS, Beijing
	RUSSIA
	†RADIO MOSCOW, Moscow
6800	**PIRATE (EUROPE)**
	"BLACK SEA RADIO, Ukraine
6804v	**PERU**
	†ONDAS DEL MAYO, Nuevo Cajamarca
6810	**CHINA (PR)**
	CHINA RADIO INTL, Beijing
6815.3	**PERU**
	RADIO UNIVERSO, Saposoa

Chart annotations:
- Alternative Frequency to 6211 kHz
- KOREAN • E Asia • 50 kW
- DS
- VIETNAMESE • DS
- Irr • Sa • W Europe
- Irr • Su • W Europe
- Europe • 250 kW
- KOREAN • Europe • 250 kW
- DS • 0.8 kW • ALT. FREQ. TO 6330v kHz
- Tu-Su • DS • 0.8 kW • ALT. FREQ. TO 6330v kHz
- Irr • Tu-Su • DS • 0.8 kW • ALT. FREQ. TO 6330v kHz
- DS-TIBETAN • 10 kW
- Irr • DS-TIBETAN • 10 kW
- DS
- Irr • DS
- Irr • Sa/Su • FRENCH & ENGLISH • W Europe
- JAPANESE • E Asia • 100 kW
- Mideast & N Africa • 200 kW
- KOREAN • Mideast & N Africa • 200 kW
- DS-PHALANGE • 8 kW
- Irr • DS-PHALANGE • 8 kW
- Alternative Frequency to 7545v kHz
- DS
- JAPANESE • E Asia • 100 kW
- DS-TEMP INACTIVE
- Irr • DS • 0.18 kW
- M-F • DS • 0.18 kW
- C America • 400 kW
- KOREAN • C America • 400 kW
- Europe • 200 kW
- KOREAN • Europe • 200 kW
- KOREAN • E Asia
- DS • 0.5 kW
- DS
- DS
- DS • 1 kW
- DS • 0.15/1 kW
- DS-1
- DS
- Alternative Frequency to 6320v kHz
- DS
- Irr • Mideast • ANTI-IRAQ GOVT
- E Africa
- Su • E Africa
- (D) • CHINESE, ETC • TAIWAN-2 • 10 kW
- (D) • DS-1(FEEDER) • 15 kW • USB
- Sa • E Europe • USB
- DS
- SE Asia • FEEDER • 10 kW
- M • DS • 0.04 kW
- Su • DS • 0.04 kW
- Irr • M • DS • 0.04 kW

| FREQUENCY | COUNTRY, STATION, LOCATION | TARGET • NETWORK • POWER (kW) | World Time |

0 1 2 3 4 5 6 7 8 9 10 11 12 13 14 15 16 17 18 19 20 21 22 23 24

6825 **CHINA (PR)**
CHINA RADIO INTL, Beijing — E Asia • FEEDER • 10 kW
(J) • E Asia • FEEDER • 10 kW

6840 **CHINA (PR)**
CENTRAL PEOPLES BS, Hohhot — DS-1 • 50 kW
W-M • DS-1 • 50 kW

6870 **SOMALIA**
†RADIO MOGADISHU, Mogadishu — E Africa • USB

6873 **USA**
†VOA, Greenville, NC — N Africa • (FEEDER) • 40 kW • ISU
N Africa • (FEEDER) • 40 kW • ISL
(D) • N Africa • (FEEDER) • 40 kW • ISU
(J) • N Africa • (FEEDER) • 40 kW • ISU

6875 **PIRATE (EUROPE)**
†"EMERALD RADIO", Ireland — Irr • Su • W Europe • 0.1 kW

6890 **CHINA (PR)**
CENTRAL PEOPLES BS, Beijing — DS-2 • 10 kW

6895.2 **PERU**
RADIO SENSACION, Huancabamba — Irr • DS / DS

6900 **TURKEY**
VO METEOROLOGY, Ankara — TURKISH • DS • 5 kW
Su • TURKISH • DS • 5 kW

6910 **IRELAND**
RADIO DUBLIN INTL, Dublin — Irr • DS • 0.3 kW

6910v **EQUATORIAL GUINEA**
RADIO AFRICA 2000, Malabo — W Africa • 10 kW
Sa/Su • W Africa

6933 **CHINA (PR)**
CHINA RADIO INTL, Beijing — Europe & N Africa • 120 kW

6937v **CHINA (PR)**
†YUNNAN PEOPLES BS, Kunming — DS-MINORITIES • 50 kW

6940 **ETHIOPIA**
VO OROMO MASSES, Addis Ababa — E Africa

VOICE OF THE EPPDF, Addis Ababa — E Africa
Su • E Africa

6950 **CHINA (PR)**
†CHINA RADIO INTL, Xi'an — (D) • Europe • 120 kW

6955 **CHINA (PR)**
CHINA RADIO INTL, Beijing — E Asia • 120 kW
(D) • N Africa • 120 kW
(D) • Mideast • 120 kW

6962.2 **CLANDESTINE (ASIA)**
"VO NAT SALVATION", Haeju, N Korea — KOREAN • TO SOUTH KOREA • 100 kW

6974v **CHINA (PR)**
CHINA RADIO INTL, Kunming — (D) • E Europe & N Africa • 50 kW

NEI MONGGOL PBS, Hohhot — DS • 50 kW

6995 **CHINA (PR)**
†CHINA RADIO INTL, Beijing — SE Asia

7020 **ERITREA**
†VO BROAD MASSES, Asmera — E Africa
Sa/Su • E Africa

7030v **CLANDESTINE (M EAST)**
†"VO INDEP'NT KURDS, Iraq — Mideast • ANTI-TURKISH GOVT

7060v **CLANDESTINE (M EAST)**
†"VO REBEL IRAQ", Middle East — ARABIC, ETC • Mideast • ANTI-SADDAM

PERU
†RADIO AZANGARO, Azángaro — Irr • DS

7070v **CLANDESTINE (M EAST)**
"VO THE MOJAHED", Iraq — PERSIAN • Mideast

7079v **BANGLADESH**
†RADIO BANGLADESH, Dhaka — DS • 7.5 kW

7090v **CLANDESTINE (ASIA)**
"R FREEDOM MESSAGE — S Asia • ANTI-AFGHAN GOVT

7100 **ANGOLA**
AV DO GALO NEGRO, Jamba — S Africa • UNITA

RUSSIA
†RADIO MOSCOW — DS-2

7103.5 **TURKEY**
†RADIO IZMIR, Izmir — TURKISH • DS • 0.25 kW

7105 **ALBANIA**
†RADIO TIRANA, Lushnjë — Europe • 100 kW

CHINA (TAIWAN)
CENTRAL BC SYSTEM, T'ai-pei — PRC-2 • 10/50 kW

CONGO
†RTV CONGOLAISE, Brazzaville — FRENCH, ETC • DS • 50 kW

GERMANY
†DEUTSCHE WELLE, Jülich — (D) • Mideast • 100 kW
(J) • E Europe • 100 kW

†DEUTSCHE WELLE, Via Sri Lanka — (J) • SE Asia • 250 kW

INDIA
†ALL INDIA RADIO, Lucknow — DS-B • 50 kW
Su • DS-B • 50 kW
ENGLISH, ETC • DS-B • 50 kW

ROMANIA
RADIO ROMANIA INTL, Bucharest — (D) • E Europe • 250 kW

RUSSIA
(con'd) RADIO MOSCOW, Simferopol' — (D) • DS-MAYAK • 250 kW

0 1 2 3 4 5 6 7 8 9 10 11 12 13 14 15 16 17 18 19 20 21 22 23 24

ENGLISH ■■■ ARABIC ⋙ CHINESE ▭▭▭ FRENCH ▬ GERMAN ══ RUSSIAN ══ SPANISH ▬▬ OTHER ▬

FREQUENCY   COUNTRY, STATION, LOCATION   TARGET • NETWORK • POWER (kW)   World Time

0 1 2 3 4 5 6 7 8 9 10 11 12 13 14 15 16 17 18 19 20 21 22 23 24

7105 **UNITED KINGDOM**
(con'd)   †BBC, Rampisham
(D) • E Europe • 500 kW
(D) • Europe • 500 kW
(J) • Europe • 500 kW
(D) • Sa/Su • E Europe • 500 kW

   †BBC, Via Ascension
C Africa • 250 kW
W Africa • 250 kW

   †BBC, Via Singapore
S Asia • 100 kW
SE Asia • 100 kW
(J) • S Asia • 100 kW
M-F • S Asia • 100 kW
Sa/Su • S Asia • 100 kW

   USA
   †VOA, Via Germany
S Asia • 500 kW
   †VOA, Via Kaválla, Greece
(J) • S Asia • 250 kW
(J) • Mideast • 250 kW
   VOA, Via Woofferton, UK
(J) • E Europe • 300 kW
(J) • Europe • 300 kW
   UZBEKISTAN
   †UZBEK RADIO, Tashkent
DS-2 • 100 kW

7108v **CHINA (PR)**
   NEI MONGGOL PBS, Hohhot
DS • 15 kW

7110 **ALBANIA**
   †RADIO TIRANA, Lushnjë
Europe • 50 kW
   CHINA (PR)
   CHINA RADIO INTL, Hohhot
E Asia • 50 kW

   XIZANG PEOPLES BS, Lhasa
DS-TIBETAN • 50 kW
   ETHIOPIA
   VOICE OF ETHIOPIA, Gedja
DS • 100 kW
M-Sa • DS • 100 kW   M-F • DS • 100 kW
Su • DS • 100 kW   Sa/Su • DS • 100 kW

   INDIA
   †ALL INDIA RADIO, Delhi
DS • 20 kW
ENGLISH, ETC • DS • 20 kW

   MALI
   RTV MALIENNE, Bamako
FRENCH, ETC • DS • 50 kW
Su • FRENCH, ETC • DS • 50 kW

   PAKISTAN
   †PAKISTAN BC CORP, Peshawar
DS • 10 kW   (J) • DS • 10 kW
   RUSSIA
   †R MOSCOW INTL, Samara
(D) • W Asia & S Asia • 100 kW
   TURKEY
   VOICE OF TURKEY, Ankara
E Europe • 250 kW
   UGANDA
   RADIO UGANDA, Kampala
ENGLISH, ETC • DS • 50 kW
Sa/Su • ENGLISH, ETC • DS • 50 kW
Su • ENGLISH, ETC • DS • 50 kW

   USA
   VOA, Via Kaválla, Greece
(J) • Mideast • 250 kW
   †VOA, Via Morocco
(D) • E Europe • 100/500 kW
   †VOA, Via Philippines
(D) • E Asia • 250 kW
7113v **MOZAMBIQUE**
   RADIO MOCAMBIQUE, Maputo
Irr • DS • 25 kW
7115 **BULGARIA**
   †RADIO BULGARIA, Plovdiv
(D) • Europe • 500 kW
(D) M-Sa • Europe • 500 kW
(D) Su • Europe • 500 kW

   CHINA (PR)
   VOICE OF PUJIANG, Shanghai
(J) • E Asia
   HOLLAND
   †RADIO NEDERLAND, Via Chita, Russia
(D) • DUTCH • S Asia • 500 kW
   IRAN
   †VO THE ISLAMIC REP, Tehrān
(D) • Mideast • 500 kW
   KAZAKHSTAN
   KAZAKH RADIO, Multiple Locations
DS-2 • 20 kW
   RUSSIA
   †R MOSCOW INTL, Via Plovdiv, Bulgaria
(D) • E North Am • 500 kW

   †R MOSCOW INTL, Zhigulevsk
Europe • 100 kW
(D) • Europe • 100 kW
(J) • Europe • 100 kW

   †R TIKHIY OKEAN
(D) • N Pacific
   THAILAND
   †RADIO THAILAND, Pathum Thani
DS-1 • 10 kW
   USA
   †RFE-RL, Via Germany
E Europe • 100 kW
(D) • E Europe • 100 kW
(J) • E Europe • 100 kW

(con'd)

0 1 2 3 4 5 6 7 8 9 10 11 12 13 14 15 16 17 18 19 20 21 22 23 24

SUMMER ONLY (J)   WINTER ONLY (D)   JAMMING / OR ∧   EARLIEST HEARD ◁   LATEST HEARD ▷   NEW OR CHANGED FOR 1994 †

FREQUENCY   COUNTRY, STATION, LOCATION   TARGET • NETWORK • POWER (kW)   World Time

7115 **(con'd)**	**USA** †RFE-RL, Via Portugal	(D) • E Europe • 250 kW (J) • E Europe • 500 kW
	†VOA, Via Germany	E Europe • 500 kW (J) • E Europe • 500 kW
	VOA, Via Sri Lanka	S Asia • 10 kW
7115v	**BANGLADESH** RADIO BANGLADESH, Dhaka	S Asia • 100 kW
7116v	**LAOS** LAO NATIONAL RADIO, Vientiane	SE Asia • TEMP INACTIVE • 25 kW
7120	**BULGARIA** †RADIO BULGARIA, Sofia	(D) • Europe • 100 kW
	CHAD RADIODIF NATIONALE, N'Djamena	FRENCH, ETC • DS • 100 kW Sa/Su • FRENCH, ETC • DS • 100 kW
	CHINA (PR) CHINA RADIO INTL, Via France	Alternative Frequency to 9845 kHz
	FRANCE R FRANCE INTL, Issoudun-Allouis	S Asia & SE Asia • 500 kW
	GERMANY †DEUTSCHE WELLE, Jülich	(D) • W Asia • 100 kW (D) • E Europe & W Asia • 100 kW
	HOLLAND †RADIO NEDERLAND, Via Madagascar	(J) • E Africa • 300 kW
	KENYA KENYA BC CORP, Koma Rock	M-F • DS-EASTERN • 250 kW
	RUSSIA †GOLOS ROSSII, Via Turkmenistan	(D) • N Africa & W Africa • 1000 kW
	†R MOSCOW INTL, Kazan'	(D) • W Asia • 150 kW
	†RADIO ROSSII, Tula	(J) • DS • 150 kW
	UNITED KINGDOM BBC, Rampisham	(D) • E Europe & W Asia • 500 kW
	USA †VOA, Via Kaválla, Greece	(D) • N Africa & Mideast • 250 kW
7125	**CYPRUS** CYPRUS BC CORP, Zyyi	(D) F-Su • Europe • 250 kW
	FRANCE R FRANCE INTL, Via Xi'an, China	Alternative Frequency to 11910 kHz
	GUINEA RTV GUINEENNE, Conakry-Sofoniya	M-Sa • FRENCH, ETC • DS • 100 kW DS • 100 kW FRENCH, ETC • DS • 100 kW Su • FRENCH, ETC • DS • 100 kW
	INDIA †ALL INDIA RADIO, Bangalore	S Asia & W Asia • 500 kW
	ALL INDIA RADIO, Ranchi	DS • 2 kW ENGLISH & HINDI • DS • 2 kW
	ITALY †ITALIAN R RELAY, Milan	E North Am • 8.5 kW Sa/Su • ENGLISH, ETC • Europe • 8.5 kW ENGLISH, ETC • Europe • 8.5 kW
	RUSSIA †RADIO VEDO, Volgograd	Sa/Su • DS • 20 kW
	SOUTH AFRICA †SOUTH AFRICAN BC, Meyerton	ENGLISH & AFRIKAANS • DS-RADIO ORANJE • 100 kW • ALT. FREQ. TO 9630 kHz
	USA †VOA, Via Kaválla, Greece	(D) • S Asia • 250 kW
	†VOA, Via Philippines	(J) • SE Asia • 50 kW
	VOA, Via Portugal	(J) • Europe • 250 kW
	VOA, Via Sri Lanka	S Asia • 10 kW
	VOA, Via Woofferton, UK	(J) • E Europe • 300 kW
7130	**CHINA (PR)** CHINA RADIO INTL, Via Russia	(D) • Mideast • 500 kW
	CHINA (TAIWAN) VO FREE CHINA, T'ai-pei	SE Asia • 50/100 kW E Asia • 50/100 kW CANTONESE • SE Asia • 50/100 kW JAPANESE • E Asia • 50/100 kW
	GERMANY †DEUTSCHE WELLE, Jülich	(D) • E Europe • 100 kW (D) • W Europe • 100 kW (J) • E Europe • 100 kW (J) • W Europe • 100 kW
	DEUTSCHE WELLE, Königswusterhausen	(D) • E Europe • 100 kW
	†DEUTSCHE WELLE, Nauen	(D) • E Europe • 500 kW
	DEUTSCHE WELLE, Wertachtal	S Europe & N Africa • 500 kW (D) • SE Asia • 500 kW
	HOLLAND †RADIO NEDERLAND, Flevoland	DUTCH • Europe • 500 kW (D) • DUTCH • Europe • 500 kW
(con'd)		(J) • DUTCH • Europe • 500 kW

ENGLISH ▬▬   ARABIC ≋≋   CHINESE ▫▫▫   FRENCH ▭▭   GERMAN ▬▬   RUSSIAN ══   SPANISH ▬▬   OTHER ▬

FREQUENCY	COUNTRY, STATION, LOCATION	TARGET • NETWORK • POWER (kW)	World Time

TARGET • NETWORK • POWER (kW) scale: 0 1 2 3 4 5 6 7 8 9 10 11 12 13 14 15 16 17 18 19 20 21 22 23 24

7130 (con'd)	**RUSSIA**	
	ADYGEY RADIO, Armavir	Alternative Frequency to 5905 kHz
	KABARDINO-BALKAR R, Armavir	Alternative Frequency to 5905 kHz
	†R MOSCOW INTL, Armavir	(D) • Mideast • 100 kW
	†RADIO ALEF, Armavir	Alternative Frequency to 5905 kHz
	USA	
	†VOA, Via Kaválla, Greece	(D) • E Europe • 250 kW / (J) • E Europe • 250 kW
	†VOA, Via Woofferton, UK	(D) • W Asia & C Asia • 300 kW
7135	**FRANCE**	
	†R FRANCE INTL, Issoudun-Allouis	(D) • E Europe & Mideast • 500 kW ; E Europe • 100 kW ; E Europe • 500 kW ; (D) • E Europe • 500 kW ; (J) • E Europe • 100/500 kW
	†R FRANCE INTL, Multiple Locations	Africa • 100/250/500 kW
	GERMANY	
	†DEUTSCHE WELLE, Jülich	(J) • E Europe • 100 kW
	RUSSIA	
	†R MOSCOW INTL, Irkutsk	(D) • E Asia • 250 kW ; (D) • JAPANESE • E Asia • 250 kW
	†R MOSCOW INTL, Komsomol'sk 'Amure	(D) • E Asia • 100/1000 kW
	†RADIO MOSCOW, Novosibirsk	(J) • DS-MAYAK • 50 kW
	UNITED KINGDOM	
	BBC, Via Zyyi, Cyprus	W Asia • 100 kW
	USA	
	†RFE-RL, Via Germany	(D) • W Asia • 100 kW
7140	**BYELARUS**	
	GRODNO RADIO, Minsk	RUSSIAN & BYELORUSSIAN • DS • 20 kW
	GERMANY	
	†DEUTSCHE WELLE, Jülich	(J) • E Europe • 100 kW
	†DEUTSCHE WELLE, Nauen	(D) • S Europe & N Africa • 500 kW
	INDIA	
	†ALL INDIA RADIO, Delhi	S Asia • 100 kW
	†ALL INDIA RADIO, Hyderabad	DS • 50 kW ; Irr • DS • 50 kW ; Sa/Su • DS • 50 kW ; Su • DS • 50 kW
	JAPAN	
	†RADIO JAPAN/NHK, Tokyo-Yamata	JAPANESE • E Asia • GENERAL • 300 kW ; E Asia • GENERAL • 300 kW ; (D) • JAPANESE • E Asia • GENERAL • 300 kW ; (D) • E Asia • GENERAL • 300 kW
	KENYA	
	KENYA BC CORP, Nairobi	DS-NATIONAL • 100 kW
	RUSSIA	
	†ADVENTIST WORLD R, Yekaterinburg	(D) • Europe • 200 kW
	†R MOSCOW INTL, Moscow	(D) • Europe • 250 kW
	UNITED KINGDOM	
	†BBC, Via Zyyi, Cyprus	Mideast & E Africa • 100 kW ; M-Sa • Mideast & E Africa • 100 kW
	USA	
	†VOA, Via Germany	(D) • N Africa • 500 kW
	†VOA, Via Irkutsk, Russia	(J) • E Asia • 1000 kW
7140.7	**ITALY**	
	†RADIO ITALIA INTL, Spoleto	Irr • DS • 1 kW
7140.8	**INDONESIA**	
	RRI, Ambon, Maluku	DS-TEMP INACTIVE • 10 kW
7145	**FRANCE**	
	R FRANCE INTL, Issoudun-Allouis	Europe • 500 kW
	GERMANY	
	DEUTSCHE WELLE, Leipzig	(J) • E Europe • 100 kW
	†DEUTSCHE WELLE, Multiple Locations	(D) • E Europe & W Asia • 100/500 kW
	MALAYSIA	
	RTM-SARAWAK, Kuching-Stapok	DS-MALAY, MELANAU • 10 kW
	POLAND	
	†POLISH RADIO, Warsaw	W Europe • 100 kW ; Europe • 100 kW ; E Europe • 100 kW ; N Europe • 100 kW ; POLISH • E Europe • 100 kW
	ROMANIA	
	RADIO ROMANIA INTL, Bucharest	Europe • 250 kW
	RUSSIA	
	†R MOSCOW INTL, Via Uzbekistan	(D) • SE Asia • 100 kW
(con'd)	†RADIO MOSCOW, Via Byelarus	(D) • DS-MAYAK • 20 kW

World Time scale (bottom): 0 1 2 3 4 5 6 7 8 9 10 11 12 13 14 15 16 17 18 19 20 21 22 23 24

SUMMER ONLY (J)   WINTER ONLY (D)   JAMMING / OR ∧   EARLIEST HEARD ◁   LATEST HEARD ▷   NEW OR CHANGED FOR 1994 †

FREQUENCY　　COUNTRY, STATION, LOCATION　　　　TARGET • NETWORK • POWER (kW)　　World Time

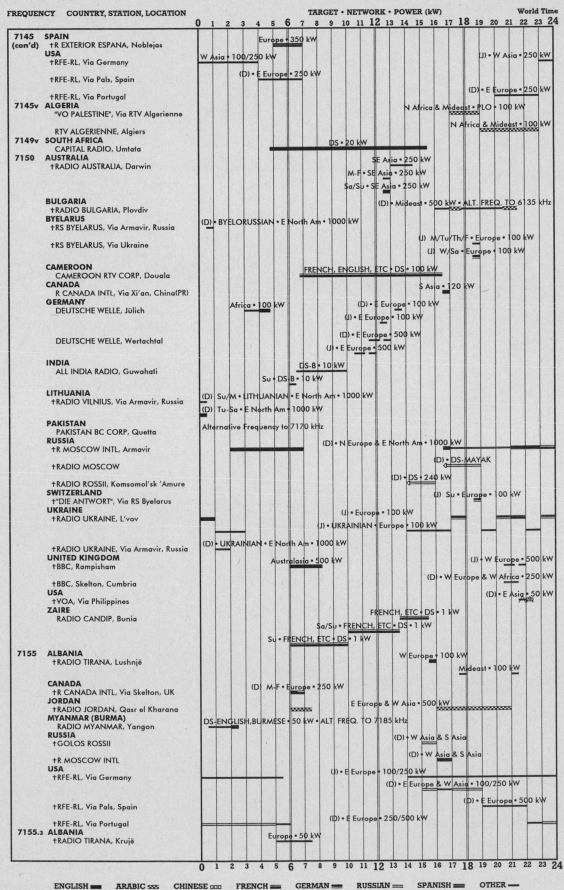

FREQUENCY	COUNTRY, STATION, LOCATION	TARGET • NETWORK • POWER (kW)
7145 (con'd)	SPAIN †R EXTERIOR ESPANA, Noblejas	Europe • 350 kW
	USA †RFE-RL, Via Germany	W Asia • 100/250 kW / (J) • W Asia • 250 kW
	†RFE-RL, Via Pals, Spain	(D) • E Europe • 250 kW
	†RFE-RL, Via Portugal	(D) • E Europe • 250 kW
7145v	ALGERIA "VO PALESTINE", Via RTV Algerienne	N Africa & Mideast • PLO • 100 kW
	RTV ALGERIENNE, Algiers	N Africa & Mideast • 100 kW
7149v	SOUTH AFRICA CAPITAL RADIO, Umtata	DS • 20 kW
7150	AUSTRALIA †RADIO AUSTRALIA, Darwin	SE Asia • 250 kW / M-F • SE Asia • 250 kW / Sa/Su • SE Asia • 250 kW
	BULGARIA †RADIO BULGARIA, Plovdiv	(D) • Mideast • 500 kW • ALT. FREQ. TO 6135 kHz
	BYELARUS †RS BYELARUS, Via Armavir, Russia	(D) • BYELORUSSIAN • E North Am • 1000 kW
	†RS BYELARUS, Via Ukraine	(J) M/Tu/Th/F • Europe • 100 kW / (J) W/Sa • Europe • 100 kW
	CAMEROON CAMEROON RTV CORP., Douala	FRENCH, ENGLISH, ETC • DS • 100 kW
	CANADA R CANADA INTL, Via Xi'an, China(PR)	S Asia • 120 kW
	GERMANY DEUTSCHE WELLE, Jülich	Africa • 100 kW / (D) • E Europe • 100 kW / (J) • E Europe • 100 kW
	DEUTSCHE WELLE, Wertachtal	(D) • E Europe • 500 kW / (J) • E Europe • 500 kW
	INDIA ALL INDIA RADIO, Guwahati	DS-B • 10 kW / Su • DS-B • 10 kW
	LITHUANIA †RADIO VILNIUS, Via Armavir, Russia	(D) Su/M • LITHUANIAN • E North Am • 1000 kW / (D) Tu-Sa • E North Am • 1000 kW
	PAKISTAN PAKISTAN BC CORP, Quetta	Alternative Frequency to 7170 kHz
	RUSSIA †R MOSCOW INTL, Armavir	(D) • N Europe & E North Am • 1000 kW
	†RADIO MOSCOW	(D) • DS-MAYAK
	†RADIO ROSSII, Komsomol'sk 'Amure	(D) • DS • 240 kW
	SWITZERLAND †"DIE ANTWORT", Via RS Byelarus	(J) Su • Europe • 100 kW
	UKRAINE †RADIO UKRAINE, L'vov	(J) • Europe • 100 kW / (J) • UKRAINIAN • Europe • 100 kW
	†RADIO UKRAINE, Via Armavir, Russia	(D) • UKRAINIAN • E North Am • 1000 kW
	UNITED KINGDOM †BBC, Rampisham	Australasia • 500 kW / (J) • W Europe • 500 kW
	†BBC, Skelton, Cumbria	(D) • W Europe & W Africa • 250 kW
	USA †VOA, Via Philippines	(D) • E Asia • 50 kW
	ZAIRE RADIO CANDIP, Bunia	FRENCH, ETC • DS • 1 kW / Sa/Su • FRENCH, ETC • DS • 1 kW / Su • FRENCH, ETC • DS • 1 kW
7155	ALBANIA †RADIO TIRANA, Lushnjë	W Europe • 100 kW / Mideast • 100 kW
	CANADA †R CANADA INTL, Via Skelton, UK	(D) M-F • Europe • 250 kW
	JORDAN †RADIO JORDAN, Qasr el Kharana	E Europe & W Asia • 500 kW
	MYANMAR (BURMA) RADIO MYANMAR, Yangon	DS-ENGLISH, BURMESE • 50 kW • ALT. FREQ. TO 7185 kHz
	RUSSIA †GOLOS ROSSII	(D) • W Asia & S Asia
	†R MOSCOW INTL	(D) • W Asia & S Asia
	USA †RFE-RL, Via Germany	(J) • E Europe • 100/250 kW / (D) • E Europe & W Asia • 100/250 kW
	†RFE-RL, Via Pals, Spain	(D) • E Europe • 500 kW
	†RFE-RL, Via Portugal	(D) • E Europe • 250/500 kW
7155.3	ALBANIA †RADIO TIRANA, Krujë	Europe • 50 kW

ENGLISH ▬▬　ARABIC ⬚⬚⬚　CHINESE ▫▫▫　FRENCH ══　GERMAN ▭▭　RUSSIAN ══　SPANISH ══　OTHER ──

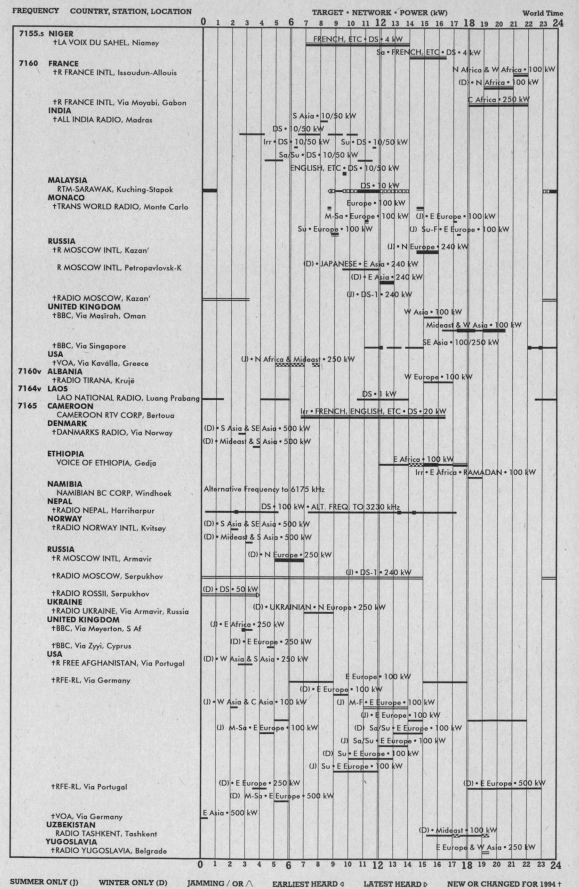

FREQUENCY   COUNTRY, STATION, LOCATION

TARGET • NETWORK • POWER (kW)   World Time

0 1 2 3 4 5 6 7 8 9 10 11 12 13 14 15 16 17 18 19 20 21 22 23 24

Frequency	Country, Station, Location	Schedule
7170	ALBANIA †RADIO TIRANA, Lushnjë	Europe • 100 kW / Europe • 50 kW
	BULGARIA †RADIO BULGARIA, Sofia	(D) • E Europe & Mideast • 100 kW
		(D) M-Sa • E Europe & Mideast • 100 kW
		(D) Su • E Europe & Mideast • 100 kW
	CHINA (PR) CHINA RADIO INTL, Via Russia	(D) • Europe • 250 kW
		DS • 50 kW
	XIZANG PEOPLES BS, Lhasa	▯▯▯▯▯▯▯▯ ▯▯▯▯▯▯▯ ▯▯▯▯▯▯▯▯▯▯▯▯▯▯ ▯▯▯▯
	GERMANY †DEUTSCHE WELLE, Via Kigali, Rwanda	(J) • C Africa & E Africa • 250 kW
	PAKISTAN PAKISTAN BC CORP, Quetta	DS • 10 kW
		DS • 10 kW • ALT. FREQ. TO 7150 kHz
	RUSSIA †GOLOS ROSSII, Komsomol'sk 'Amure	(D) • E Asia & SE Asia • 250 kW
	†R MOSCOW INTL, Moscow	(D) • Europe • 240 kW
	†R MOSCOW INTL, Novosibirsk	(D) • E Asia • 500 kW
	SINGAPORE SINGAPORE BC CORP, Jurong	DS-TAMIL • 10 kW
		Irr • DS-TAMIL • 10 kW
	USA VOA, Via Germany	(D) • E Europe • 500 kW
	VOA, Via Kaválla, Greece	(D) • E Europe • 250 kW
		(D) • Mideast • 250 kW
		(J) • SE Asia • 250 kW
	†VOA, Via Philippines	N Africa • 300 kW
	†VOA, Via Woofferton, UK	(J) • E Europe & W Asia • 300 kW
7170v	SENEGAL †ORT DU SENEGAL, Dakar	FRENCH, ETC • DS • 100 kW
		M-Sa • FRENCH, ETC • DS • 100 kW
7173	INDONESIA †RRI, Serui, Irian Jaya	DS • 0.5 kW
7175	ARMENIA ARMENIAN RADIO, Via Moscow, Russia	ARMENIAN • DS-1 • 20 kW
		M-Sa • DS-1 • 20 kW
		Su • ARMENIAN • DS-1 • 20 kW
	RADIO YEREVAN, Via Moscow, Russia	M-Sa • 20 kW
	FRANCE R FRANCE INTL, Issoudun-Allouis	(D) • Africa • 500 kW
	GERMANY †DEUTSCHE WELLE, Via Kigali, Rwanda	(D) • Africa • 250 kW
	DEUTSCHE WELLE, Wertachtal	(D) • E Europe • 500 kW
		(J) • E Europe • 500 kW
	ITALY RAI-RTV ITALIANA, Rome	ITALIAN • Europe, Mideast & N Africa • DS-2 • 50 kW
	ROMANIA RADIO ROMANIA INTL, Bucharest	(D) • E Europe • 250 kW
	RUSSIA †R MOSCOW INTL, Khabarovsk	(D) • W North Am • NORTH AMERICAN SVC • 100 kW
	†R MOSCOW INTL, Novosibirsk	(D) • W Africa • 500 kW
	†R TIKHIY OKEAN, Khabarovsk	(D) • W North Am • MARINERS • 100 kW
	†RADIO ROSSII, St Petersburg	(D) • DS • 240 kW
	UNITED KINGDOM †BBC, Rampisham	(D) • W Europe • 500 kW
	†BBC, Skelton, Cumbria	(D) • E Europe • 300 kW
7180	INDIA ALL INDIA RADIO, Bhopal	DS-A • 10 kW
		Su • DS-A • 10 kW
		ENGLISH, ETC • DS-A • 10 kW
	ALL INDIA RADIO, Port Blair	DS • 10 kW
		ENGLISH & HINDI • DS • 10 kW
	IRAQ †REP OF IRAQ RADIO, Baghdad	DS-1
	JAPAN RADIO JAPAN/NHK, Via Moyabi, Gabon	E Africa • 500 kW
	RUSSIA †R MOSCOW INTL, Via Kazakhstan	(D) • E Asia • 100 kW
	†R MOSCOW INTL, Via Ukraine	(D) • E North Am
	†RADIO ROSSII, Kazan'	(J) • DS • 150 kW
	†RADIO ROSSII, Moscow	(J) • DS • 200 kW
		(D) • DS • 200 kW
(con'd)		DS • 200 kW

0 1 2 3 4 5 6 7 8 9 10 11 12 13 14 15 16 17 18 19 20 21 22 23 24

ENGLISH ▬   ARABIC ≷≷≷   CHINESE ▭▭▭   FRENCH ═══   GERMAN ═══   RUSSIAN ═══   SPANISH ═══   OTHER ───

FREQUENCY   COUNTRY, STATION, LOCATION

TARGET • NETWORK • POWER (kW)   World Time

0 1 2 3 4 5 6 7 8 9 10 11 12 13 14 15 16 17 18 19 20 21 22 23 24

FREQUENCY	COUNTRY, STATION, LOCATION	TARGET • NETWORK • POWER (kW)
7180 (con'd)	TURKEY VOICE OF TURKEY, Ankara	E Europe • 250 kW
	UKRAINE †RADIO UKRAINE	(D) • E North Am
		(D) • UKRAINIAN • E North Am
	UNITED KINGDOM BBC, Via Hong Kong	E Asia • 250 kW
	†BBC, Via Singapore	(J) • E Asia • 100 kW
	†BBC, Via Zyyi, Cyprus	(D) • W Asia • 100 kW
	USA †RFE-RL, Various Locations	W Asia • 100/250 kW
	†RFE-RL, Via Germany	(D) • E Europe & W Asia • 100 kW
		(J) • E Europe • 100 kW
	†VOA, Via Germany	(D) • E Europe • 500 kW
	†VOA, Via Woofferton, UK	E Europe • 300 kW
		(D) • E Europe • 300 kW
		(J) • E Europe • 300 kW
7185	GERMANY †DEUTSCHE WELLE, Nauen	(D) • E Europe • 100 kW
	†DEUTSCHE WELLE, Via Kigali, Rwanda	C Africa & E Africa • 250 kW
	MYANMAR (BURMA) RADIO MYANMAR, Yangon	Alternative Frequency to 7155 kHz
	RUSSIA †GOLOS ROSSII, Blagoveshchensk	(D) • E Asia & SE Asia • 500 kW
	†R MOSCOW INTL, Moscow	(J) • Mideast • 100 kW
	†R MOSCOW INTL, Novosibirsk	(D) • E Europe & S Europe • 240 kW
	†R TIKHIY OKEAN, Blagoveshchensk	(D) • E Asia & SE Asia • 500 kW
	†RADIO VEDO, Volgograd	Sa/Su • DS • 20 kW DS • 20 kW
	TATAR RADIO, Perm	RUSSIAN, ETC • DS • 3 kW
	SOUTH AFRICA †CHANNEL AFRICA, Meyerton	(J) • C Africa • 250 kW
	TURKEY VOICE OF TURKEY, Ankara	Mideast • 250 kW
7189	INDONESIA †RRI, Yogyakarta, Jawa	DS • 50 kW
7189.5	NAMIBIA NAMIBIAN BC CORP, Windhoek	Alternative Frequency to 6060 kHz
7190	BENIN RADIO PARAKOU, Parakou	Alternative Frequency to 5025 kHz
	CHINA (PR) †CHINA RADIO INTL, Kunming	SE Asia • 50 kW
		CANTONESE • SE Asia • 50 kW
	INDIA †ALL INDIA RADIO, Shillong	DS • 50 kW
		ENGLISH & HINDI • DS • 50 kW
		ENGLISH, ETC • DS • 50 kW
	IRAN †VO THE ISLAMIC REP, Tehrān	(J) • Mideast • 500 kW
	SRI LANKA SRI LANKA BC CORP, Colombo-Ekala	S Asia • 10 kW
		Su • S Asia • 10 kW
	USA †RFE-RL, Via Germany	W Asia & C Asia • 100 kW E Europe • 100 kW
		(J) • W Asia & C Asia • 100 kW (D) • E Europe • 100 kW
		(J) • E Europe • 100 kW
	†RFE-RL, Via Portugal	E Europe • 250/500 kW (D) • E Europe • 500 kW
		(D) • E Europe & W Asia • 500 kW
		(D) • E Europe • 250 kW
		(J) • E Europe • 500 kW
	†VOA, Various Locations	C Asia • 250/500 kW
	UZBEKISTAN †RADIO TASHKENT, Tashkent	(D) • Mideast • 240 kW
	YEMEN (REPUBLIC) "VO PALESTINE", Via Rep Yemen Radio	Mideast • PLO • 100 kW
	REP YEMEN RADIO, Aden	Mideast • DS • 100 kW
		F • Mideast • DS • 100 kW Irr • Mideast • DS-RAMADAN • 100 kW
7190v	EQUATORIAL GUINEA RADIO AFRICA, Bata	W Africa • 50 kW • ALT. FREQ. TO 7203v kHz
7195	CANADA †R CANADA INTL, Via Skelton, UK	(J) • W Europe • 300 kW
	CHINA (PR) †XINJIANG PBS, Urümqi	(J) • DS-UIGHUR • 15 kW
	GERMANY (con'd) †DEUTSCHE WELLE, Jülich	(D) • W Asia • 100 kW

0 1 2 3 4 5 6 7 8 9 10 11 12 13 14 15 16 17 18 19 20 21 22 23 24

SUMMER ONLY (J)   WINTER ONLY (D)   JAMMING / OR ∧   EARLIEST HEARD ◁   LATEST HEARD ▷   NEW OR CHANGED FOR 1994 †

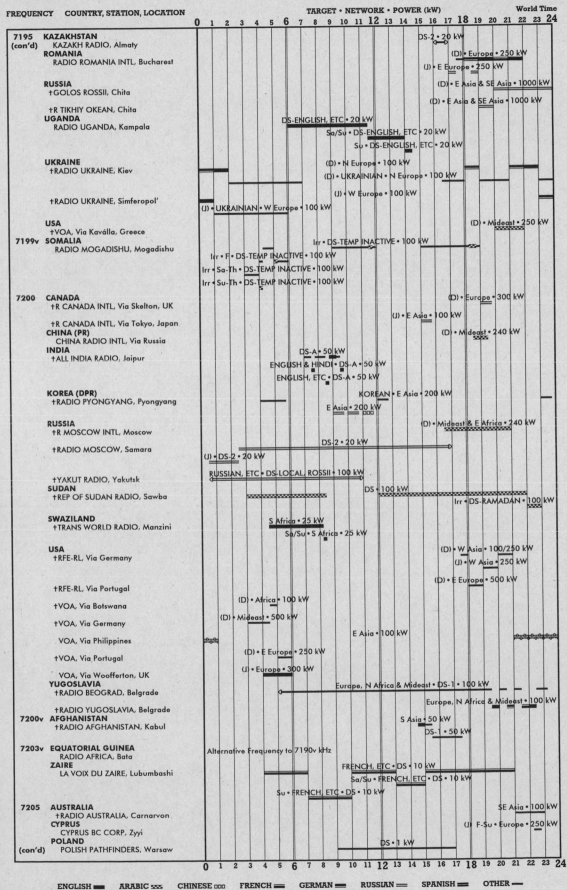

FREQUENCY   COUNTRY, STATION, LOCATION

TARGET • NETWORK • POWER (kW)   World Time

7195	KAZAKHSTAN	
(con'd)	KAZAKH RADIO, Almaty	DS-2 • 20 kW
	ROMANIA	
	RADIO ROMANIA INTL, Bucharest	(D) • Europe • 250 kW
		(J) • E Europe • 250 kW
	RUSSIA	
	†GOLOS ROSSII, Chita	(D) • E Asia & SE Asia • 1000 kW
	†R TIKHIY OKEAN, Chita	(D) • E Asia & SE Asia • 1000 kW
	UGANDA	
	RADIO UGANDA, Kampala	DS-ENGLISH, ETC • 20 kW
		Sa/Su • DS-ENGLISH, ETC • 20 kW
		Su • DS-ENGLISH, ETC • 20 kW
	UKRAINE	
	†RADIO UKRAINE, Kiev	(D) • N Europe • 100 kW
		(D) • UKRAINIAN • N Europe • 100 kW
	†RADIO UKRAINE, Simferopol'	(J) • W Europe • 100 kW
		(J) • UKRAINIAN • W Europe • 100 kW
	USA	
	†VOA, Via Kaválla, Greece	(D) • Mideast • 250 kW
7199v	SOMALIA	
	RADIO MOGADISHU, Mogadishu	Irr • DS-TEMP INACTIVE • 100 kW
		Irr • F • DS-TEMP INACTIVE • 100 kW
		Irr • Sa-Th • DS-TEMP INACTIVE • 100 kW
		Irr • Su-Th • DS-TEMP INACTIVE • 100 kW
7200	CANADA	
	†R CANADA INTL, Via Skelton, UK	(D) • Europe • 300 kW
	†R CANADA INTL, Via Tokyo, Japan	(J) • E Asia • 100 kW
	CHINA (PR)	
	CHINA RADIO INTL, Via Russia	(D) • Mideast • 240 kW
	INDIA	
	†ALL INDIA RADIO, Jaipur	DS-A • 50 kW
		ENGLISH & HINDI • DS-A • 50 kW
		ENGLISH, ETC • DS-A • 50 kW
	KOREA (DPR)	
	†RADIO PYONGYANG, Pyongyang	KOREAN • E Asia • 200 kW
		E Asia • 200 kW
	RUSSIA	
	†R MOSCOW INTL, Moscow	(D) • Mideast & E Africa • 240 kW
	†RADIO MOSCOW, Samara	DS-2 • 20 kW
		(J) • DS-2 • 20 kW
	†YAKUT RADIO, Yakutsk	RUSSIAN, ETC • DS-LOCAL, ROSSII • 100 kW
	SUDAN	
	†REP OF SUDAN RADIO, Sawba	DS • 100 kW
		Irr • DS-RAMADAN • 100 kW
	SWAZILAND	
	†TRANS WORLD RADIO, Manzini	S Africa • 25 kW
		Sa/Su • S Africa • 25 kW
	USA	
	†RFE-RL, Via Germany	(D) • W Asia • 100/250 kW
		(J) • W Asia • 250 kW
		(D) • E Europe • 500 kW
	†RFE-RL, Via Portugal	
	†VOA, Via Botswana	(D) • Africa • 100 kW
	†VOA, Via Germany	(D) • Mideast • 500 kW
	VOA, Via Philippines	E Asia • 100 kW
	†VOA, Via Portugal	(D) • E Europe • 250 kW
	VOA, Via Woofferton, UK	(J) • Europe • 300 kW
	YUGOSLAVIA	
	†RADIO BEOGRAD, Belgrade	Europe, N Africa & Mideast • DS-1 • 100 kW
	†RADIO YUGOSLAVIA, Belgrade	Europe, N Africa & Mideast • 100 kW
7200v	AFGHANISTAN	
	†RADIO AFGHANISTAN, Kabul	S Asia • 50 kW
		DS-1 • 50 kW
7203v	EQUATORIAL GUINEA	
	RADIO AFRICA, Bata	Alternative Frequency to 7190v kHz
	ZAIRE	
	LA VOIX DU ZAIRE, Lubumbashi	FRENCH, ETC • DS • 10 kW
		Sa/Su • FRENCH, ETC • DS • 10 kW
		Su • FRENCH, ETC • DS • 10 kW
7205	AUSTRALIA	
	†RADIO AUSTRALIA, Carnarvon	SE Asia • 100 kW
	CYPRUS	
	CYPRUS BC CORP, Zyyi	(J) F-Su • Europe • 250 kW
	POLAND	
(con'd)	POLISH PATHFINDERS, Warsaw	DS • 1 kW

0 1 2 3 4 5 6 7 8 9 10 11 12 13 14 15 16 17 18 19 20 21 22 23 24

ENGLISH ▬ ARABIC ▨ CHINESE ▯▯▯ FRENCH ▭ GERMAN ▬ RUSSIAN ═ SPANISH ▭ OTHER ▬

FREQUENCY   COUNTRY, STATION, LOCATION

TARGET • NETWORK • POWER (kW)   World Time

0 1 2 3 4 5 6 7 8 9 10 11 12 13 14 15 16 17 18 19 20 21 22 23 24

Frequency	Country / Station / Location	Schedule details
7205 (con'd)	**RUSSIA**	
	†R MOSCOW INTL, Various Locations	(D) • Europe • 100 kW
	USA	
	VOA, Via Kaválla, Greece	S Asia • 250 kW / (J) • W Asia • 250 kW
		(D) • S Asia • 250 kW
	VOA, Via Rhodes, Greece	(D) • Mideast • 50 kW
7210	**BYELARUS**	
	BYELARUSSIAN R, Minsk	DS-2 • 50 kW
	†RS BYELARUS, Minsk	Europe • 50 kW
		M/Tu/Th/F • Europe • 50 kW
		W/Sa • Europe • 50 kW
	CANADA	
	R CANADA INTL, Via Sines, Portugal	(D) • Mideast • 250 kW
	DENMARK	
	DANMARKS RADIO, Via Norway	(D) • Mideast • 500 kW
	INDIA	
	†ALL INDIA RADIO, Calcutta	DS • 50 kW
		Irr • DS • 50 kW
		ENGLISH & HINDI • DS • 50 kW
		ENGLISH, ETC • DS • 50 kW
	†ALL INDIA RADIO, Delhi	S Asia • 20/100 kW
		DS • 100 kW
	ITALY	
	†ADVENTIST WORLD R, Forlì	Europe • 10 kW
	JAPAN	
	†RADIO JAPAN/NHK, Tokyo-Yamata	E Asia • 100 kW
		(D) • E Asia • 100 kW
		(D) • JAPANESE • SE Asia • GENERAL • 100 kW
		(J) • JAPANESE • E Asia • GENERAL • 100 kW
	NORWAY	
	RADIO NORWAY INTL, Kvitsøy	(D) • Mideast • 500 kW
	RUSSIA	
	KHABAROVSK RADIO, Khabarovsk	DS/TIKHIY OKEAN • 100 kW
	†R MOSCOW INTL, Kazan'	(D) • Mideast & E Africa • 240 kW
	†RADIO MOSCOW, Yekaterinburg	Irr • DS-1 • 200 kW
	SWITZERLAND	
	†"DIE ANTWORT", Via RS Byelarus	Su • Europe • 50 kW
	RED CROSS BC SVC, Beromünster	Irr • M • Europe & N Africa • 1ST OR LAST MONDAY • 250 kW
		Irr • Su • Europe & N Africa • 1ST OR LAST SUNDAY • 250 kW
	UNITED KINGDOM	
	†BBC, Rampisham	(D) • E Europe • 500 kW
		Europe • 500 kW
		(J) • E Europe • 500 kW
		(D) • Europe • 500 kW
		(J) M-F • E Europe • 500 kW
		(J) • Europe • 500 kW
		(J) M-Sa • E Europe & Mideast • 500 kW
	†BBC, Skelton, Cumbria	(J) • Europe • 300 kW
	†BBC, Via Zyyi, Cyprus	(D) M-F • E Europe • 250 kW
		(J) • Europe • 250 kW
	USA	
	†VOA, Via Kaválla, Greece	(D) • E Europe • 250 kW
	†VOA, Via Morocco	(D) • E Europe • 500 kW
		(D) • E Europe • 100/500 kW
	†VOA, Via Portugal	(D) • E Europe • 250 kW
	†VOA, Via Woofferton, UK	(J) • E Europe • 300 kW
7210v	**CHINA (PR)**	
	†YUNNAN PEOPLES BS, Kunming	DS-1 • 50 kW
		W-M • DS-1 • 50 kW
7215	**CHINA (PR)**	
	VOICE OF JINLING, Nanjing	E Asia • 50 kW
	CLANDESTINE (M EAST)	
	†"VO ISLAMIC REV'N", Tehran, Iran	Mideast • ANTI-SADDAM • 500 kW
	COTE D'IVOIRE	
	R COTE D'IVOIRE, Abidjan	DS-1 • 20 kW
	DENMARK	
	DANMARKS RADIO, Via Norway	Europe • 350 kW
	IRAN	
	†VO THE ISLAMIC REP, Tehrän	(D) • N Africa • 500 kW / N Africa • 500 kW
	NORWAY	
	RADIO NORWAY INTL, Fredrikstad	Europe • 350 kW
	PAKISTAN	
	RADIO PAKISTAN, Islamabad	S Asia • 100 kW
	PHILIPPINES	
	†RADIO VERITAS ASIA, Palauig	(D) • E Asia • 100 kW
	RUSSIA	
	†R MOSCOW INTL, Tula	(D) • Europe • 240 kW
	SEYCHELLES	
	†FAR EAST BC ASS'N, North Pt, Mahé Is	S Asia • 100 kW
	SWAZILAND	
(con'd)	†TRANS WORLD RADIO, Manzini	S Africa • 25 kW

0 1 2 3 4 5 6 7 8 9 10 11 12 13 14 15 16 17 18 19 20 21 22 23 24

FREQUENCY   COUNTRY, STATION, LOCATION

TARGET • NETWORK • POWER (kW)

World Time

Frequency	Country, Station, Location	Schedule
7215 (con'd)	UNITED ARAB EMIRATES UAE RADIO, Abu Dhabi	(D) • N Africa & Mideast • 500 kW / (D) • E North Am • 500 kW / (J) • N Africa & Mideast • 500 kW
	UNITED KINGDOM †BBC, Via Maşīrah, Oman	(D) • S Asia • 100 kW / (D) • W Asia & S Asia • 100 kW / (J) • S Asia • 100 kW / (D) • S Asia • 100 kW
	†BBC, Via Singapore	
	USA †VOA, Via Philippines	SE Asia • 50 kW
	†VOA, Via Thailand	(J) • E Asia • 250 kW / (J) • S Asia • 250 kW
7215v	ANGOLA RADIO NACIONAL, Luanda	DS-2 • 10 kW
7220	HUNGARY †RADIO BUDAPEST, Diósd	HUNGARIAN • Europe • 100 kW / Europe • 100 kW
	RADIO BUDAPEST, Jászberény	Su • HUNGARIAN • Europe • 250 kW / Su • Europe • 250 kW
	†RADIO BUDAPEST, Szekésfehérvár	Europe • 20 kW / M-Sa • Europe • 20/100 kW
	†RADIO BUDAPEST, Various Locations	
	RUSSIA †GOLOS ROSSII, Chita	(D) • E Asia & SE Asia • 1000 kW
	†R MOSCOW INTL, Chita	(D) • E Asia & SE Asia • 1000 kW
	†RADIO ROSSII, Yekaterinburg	DS • 150/240 kW
	USA RFE-RL, Various Locations	E Europe & W Asia • 100/250/500 kW
	YUGOSLAVIA †RADIO YUGOSLAVIA, Belgrade	W Europe • 250 kW
7220v	CENTRAL AFRICAN REP RTV CENTRAFRICAINE, Bangui	FRENCH, ETC • DS • 20 kW • ALT FREQ. TO 6100v kHz
	ZAMBIA RADIO ZAMBIA-ZBS, Lusaka	ENGLISH, ETC • DS-1 • 50 kW
7225	BULGARIA †RADIO BULGARIA, Sofia	(D) • Europe & E North Am • 100 kW
	CHINA (PR) SICHUAN PEOPLES BS, Chengdu	DS-1 • 15 kW
	GERMANY DEUTSCHE WELLE, Jülich	(D) • S Asia • 100 kW
	DEUTSCHE WELLE, Via Cyclops, Malta	(D) • Mideast • 250 kW
	DEUTSCHE WELLE, Via Kigali, Rwanda	C Africa & S Africa • 250 kW
	DEUTSCHE WELLE, Via Sri Lanka	S Asia • 250 kW
	†DEUTSCHE WELLE, Wertachtal	(D) • E Europe • 500 kW
	INDIA †ALL INDIA RADIO, Delhi	S Asia • 100 kW
	ROMANIA †RADIO ROMANIA, Bucharest	Europe • DS-1 (ACTUALITATI) • 125 kW
	RADIO ROMANIA INTL, Bucharest	Europe • 250 kW / E Europe • 250 kW / (D) • Europe • 250 kW / (J) • E Europe • 250 kW
	UNITED KINGDOM †BBC, Skelton, Cumbria	(D) • E Europe • 300 kW
	UZBEKISTAN RADIO TASHKENT, Tashkent	Alternative Frequency to 7335 kHz
7230	BURKINA FASO RTV BURKINA, Ouagadougou	FRENCH, ETC • DS • 50 kW / Th/Sa/Su • FRENCH, ETC • DS • 50 kW
	CANADA †R CANADA INTL, Via Skelton, UK	(D) • Europe • 300 kW
	INDIA ALL INDIA RADIO, Kurseong	S Asia • 20 kW / DS • 20 kW / ENGLISH, ETC • DS • 20 kW
	ITALY †ADVENTIST WORLD R, Forlì	Europe • 10 kW / Sa/Su • Europe • 10 kW
	JAPAN †RADIO JAPAN/NHK, Via Skelton, UK	(J) • Europe • 250 kW / Europe • GENERAL • 250 kW / (J) • JAPANESE • Europe • GENERAL • 250 kW / (J) • Europe • GENERAL • 250 kW
	KOREA (DPR) RADIO PYONGYANG, Pyongyang	SE Asia • 200 kW
(con'd)	OMAN †RADIO OMAN, Sib	Mideast & N Africa • DS • 100 kW

ENGLISH ▬   ARABIC ▨▨▨   CHINESE □□□   FRENCH ══   GERMAN ▬▬   RUSSIAN ═══   SPANISH ══   OTHER ──

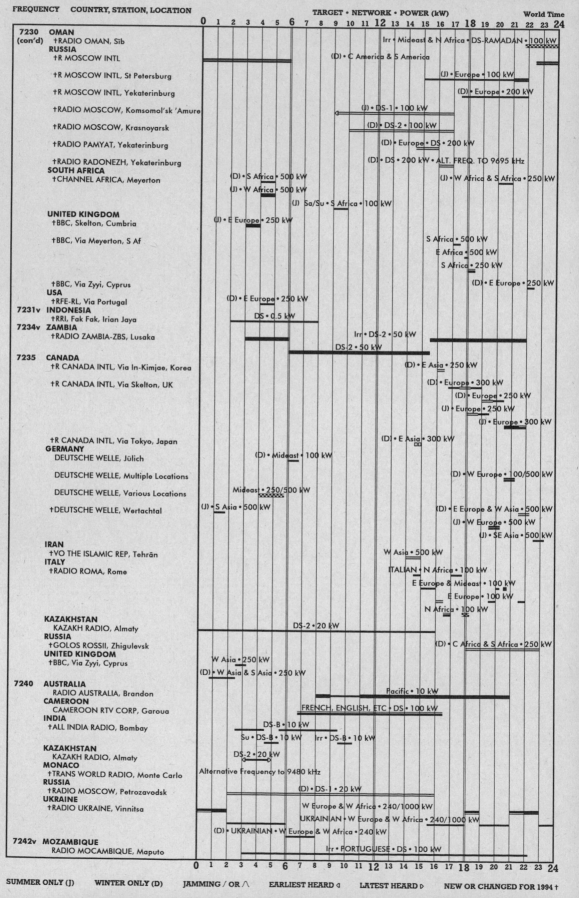

FREQUENCY   COUNTRY, STATION, LOCATION

TARGET • NETWORK • POWER (kW)

World Time

0 1 2 3 4 5 6 7 8 9 10 11 12 13 14 15 16 17 18 19 20 21 22 23 24

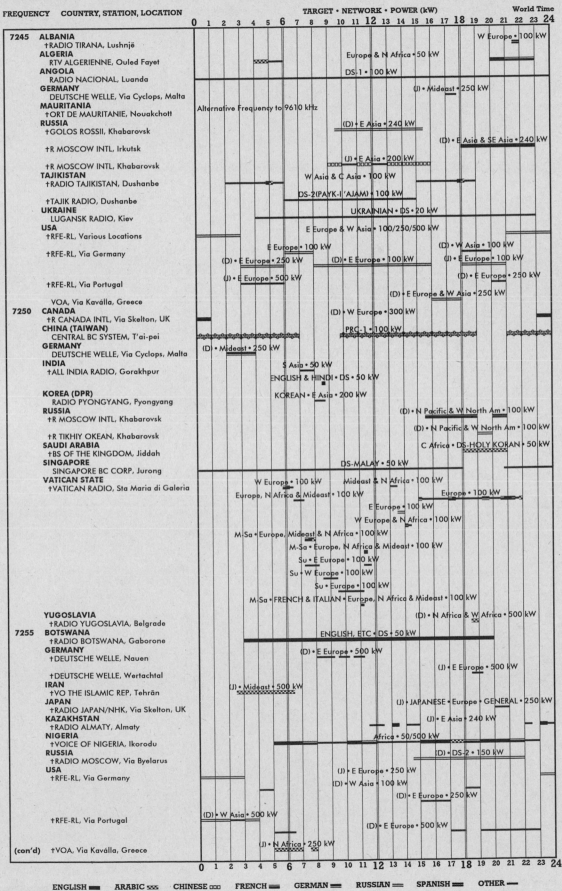

7245	ALBANIA	
	†RADIO TIRANA, Lushnjë	W Europe • 100 kW
	ALGERIA	
	RTV ALGERIENNE, Ouled Fayet	Europe & N Africa • 50 kW
	ANGOLA	
	RADIO NACIONAL, Luanda	DS-1 • 100 kW
	GERMANY	
	DEUTSCHE WELLE, Via Cyclops, Malta	(J) • Mideast • 250 kW
	MAURITANIA	
	†ORT DE MAURITANIE, Nouakchott	Alternative Frequency to 9610 kHz
	RUSSIA	
	†GOLOS ROSSII, Khabarovsk	(D) • E Asia • 240 kW
	†R MOSCOW INTL, Irkutsk	(D) • E Asia & SE Asia • 240 kW
	†R MOSCOW INTL, Khabarovsk	(J) • E Asia • 200 kW
	TAJIKISTAN	
	†RADIO TAJIKISTAN, Dushanbe	W Asia & C Asia • 100 kW
	†TAJIK RADIO, Dushanbe	DS-2(PAYK-I 'AJAM) • 100 kW
	UKRAINE	
	LUGANSK RADIO, Kiev	UKRAINIAN • DS • 20 kW
	USA	
	†RFE-RL, Various Locations	E Europe & W Asia • 100/250/500 kW
		E Europe • 100 kW (D) • W Asia • 100 kW
	†RFE-RL, Via Germany	(D) • E Europe • 250 kW (D) • E Europe • 100 kW (J) • E Europe • 100 kW
	†RFE-RL, Via Portugal	(J) • E Europe • 500 kW (D) • E Europe • 250 kW
		(D) • E Europe & W Asia • 250 kW
	VOA, Via Kaválla, Greece	(D) • W Europe • 300 kW
7250	CANADA	
	†R CANADA INTL, Via Skelton, UK	PRC-1 • 100 kW
	CHINA (TAIWAN)	
	CENTRAL BC SYSTEM, T'ai-pei	
	GERMANY	
	DEUTSCHE WELLE, Via Cyclops, Malta	(D) • Mideast • 250 kW
	INDIA	
	†ALL INDIA RADIO, Gorakhpur	S Asia • 50 kW
		ENGLISH & HINDI • DS • 50 kW
	KOREA (DPR)	
	RADIO PYONGYANG, Pyongyang	KOREAN • E Asia • 200 kW
	RUSSIA	
	†R MOSCOW INTL, Khabarovsk	(D) • N Pacific & W North Am • 100 kW
	†R TIKHIY OKEAN, Khabarovsk	(D) • N Pacific & W North Am • 100 kW
	SAUDI ARABIA	
	†BS OF THE KINGDOM, Jiddah	C Africa • DS-HOLY KORAN • 50 kW
	SINGAPORE	
	SINGAPORE BC CORP, Jurong	DS-MALAY • 50 kW
	VATICAN STATE	
	†VATICAN RADIO, Sta Maria di Galeria	W Europe • 100 kW Mideast & N Africa • 100 kW
		Europe, N Africa & Mideast • 100 kW Europe • 100 kW
		E Europe • 100 kW
		W Europe & N Africa • 100 kW
		M-Sa • Europe, Mideast & N Africa • 100 kW
		M-Sa • Europe, N Africa & Mideast • 100 kW
		Su • E Europe • 100 kW
		Su • W Europe • 100 kW
		Su • Europe • 100 kW
		M-Sa • FRENCH & ITALIAN • Europe, N Africa & Mideast • 100 kW
	YUGOSLAVIA	
	†RADIO YUGOSLAVIA, Belgrade	(D) • N Africa & W Africa • 500 kW
7255	BOTSWANA	
	†RADIO BOTSWANA, Gaborone	ENGLISH, ETC • DS • 50 kW
	GERMANY	
	†DEUTSCHE WELLE, Nauen	(D) • E Europe • 500 kW
	†DEUTSCHE WELLE, Wertachtal	(J) • E Europe • 500 kW
	IRAN	
	†VO THE ISLAMIC REP, Tehrān	(J) • Mideast • 500 kW
	JAPAN	
	†RADIO JAPAN/NHK, Via Skelton, UK	(J) • JAPANESE • Europe • GENERAL • 250 kW
	KAZAKHSTAN	
	†RADIO ALMATY, Almaty	(J) • E Asia • 240 kW
	NIGERIA	
	†VOICE OF NIGERIA, Ikorodu	Africa • 50/500 kW
	RUSSIA	
	†RADIO MOSCOW, Via Byelarus	(D) • DS-2 • 150 kW
	USA	
	†RFE-RL, Via Germany	(J) • E Europe • 250 kW
		(D) • W Asia • 100 kW
		(D) • E Europe • 250 kW
	†RFE-RL, Via Portugal	(D) • W Asia • 500 kW
		(D) • E Europe • 500 kW
(con'd)	†VOA, Via Kaválla, Greece	(J) • N Africa • 250 kW

0 1 2 3 4 5 6 7 8 9 10 11 12 13 14 15 16 17 18 19 20 21 22 23 24

ENGLISH ▬   ARABIC ░   CHINESE ▫▫▫   FRENCH ▭   GERMAN ▬   RUSSIAN ═   SPANISH ▬   OTHER ▬

FREQUENCY	COUNTRY, STATION, LOCATION	TARGET • NETWORK • POWER (kW)

World Time
0 1 2 3 4 5 6 7 8 9 10 11 12 13 14 15 16 17 18 19 20 21 22 23 24

7255 **USA**
(con'd) †VOA, Via Morocco — (J) • E Europe • 100 kW

VOA, Via Portugal — (J) • E Europe • 250 kW
UZBEKISTAN
†RADIO TASHKENT, Via Kazakhstan — (J) • E Asia • 240 kW
7260 **AUSTRALIA**
†RADIO AUSTRALIA, Carnarvon — S Asia, Mideast & Europe • 300 kW
(D) • E Asia • 100 kW
(J) • S Asia & Mideast • 300 kW

CANADA
†R CANADA INTL, Via In-Kimjae, Korea — (D) • E Asia • 250 kW

†R CANADA INTL, Via Skelton, UK — (D) • W Europe • 300 kW
CHINA (PR)
CHINA RADIO INTL, Baoding — S Asia • 120 kW
S Asia & E Africa • 120 kW

COMOROS
†RADIO COMORO, Moroni — FRENCH, ETC • DS-TEMP INACTIVE • 4/60 kW
HOLLAND
†RADIO NEDERLAND, Via Petro-K, Russia — (D) • E Asia • 240 kW
(D) • DUTCH • E Asia • 240 kW

INDIA
ALL INDIA RADIO, Bombay — DS • 100 kW
RUSSIA
†GOLOS ROSSII, Petropavlovsk-K — (D) • W North Am • 100 kW • USB

(D) • W North Am • 100 kW

†R MOSCOW INTL, Petropavlovsk-K — (D) • JAPANESE • E Asia • 240 kW
(D) • E Asia • 240 kW
(D) • W North Am • 240 kW

R TIKHIY OKEAN, Petropavlovsk-K — (D) • W North Am • MARINERS • 100 kW

†RADIO MOSCOW, Yekaterinburg — (J) • DS-MAYAK • 200 kW
UNITED KINGDOM
†BBC, Rampisham — (D) • Europe • 500 kW
(J) • Europe • 500 kW
(D) M-F • Europe • 500 kW
(J) M-F • Europe • 500 kW
(D) M-Sa • Europe • 500 kW
(J) M-Sa • Europe • 500 kW
(D) Su • Europe • 500 kW

†BBC, Via Zyyi, Cyprus — (D) M-F • Europe • 250 kW
(D) M-Sa • Europe • 250 kW

USA
†VOA, Via Philippines — SE Asia • 250 kW
(D) • SE Asia • 250 kW

VANUATU
RADIO VANUATU, Vila, Efate Island — ENGLISH, FRENCH, ETC • DS • 10 kW
7260v **ALBANIA**
†RADIO TIRANA, Krujë — W Europe • 100 kW

†RADIO TIRANA, Lushnjë — W Europe • 100 kW
MONGOLIA
†RADIO ULAANBAATAR, Ulaanbaatar — (D) • S Asia • 50 kW
(D) Tu/F • E Europe & W Asia • 50 kW

7265 **GERMANY**
DEUTSCHE WELLE, Via Cyclops, Malta — Mideast • 250 kW

†DEUTSCHE WELLE, Via Kigali, Rwanda — W Africa • 250 kW

SUDWESTFUNK, Rohrdorf — Europe • DS-3, ARD-NACHT • 20 kW
INDIA
ALL INDIA RADIO, Delhi — W Asia & Mideast • 100 kW
PHILIPPINES
†RADIO VERITAS ASIA, Palauig — (D) • C Asia • 250 kW
RUSSIA
†R MOSCOW INTL, Chita — (D) • S Asia • 250 kW

YAKUT RADIO, Yakutsk — RUSSIAN, ETC • DS-LOCAL, ROSSII • 100 kW
TOGO
RADIO LOME, Lomé-Togblekope — DS • 100 kW
FRENCH, ETC • DS • 100 kW

USA
VOA, Via Botswana — Africa • 100 kW
UZBEKISTAN
†RADIO TASHKENT, Via Turkmenistan — (D) • Mideast • 100 kW
7267v **PAKISTAN (AZAD K)**
AZAD KASHMIR RADIO, Via Islamabad — DS • 100 kW
7270 **ALBANIA**
†RADIO TIRANA, Lushnjë — Europe • 50/100 kW
GABON
RTV GABONAISE, Libreville — DS • 100 kW
GERMANY
(con'd) DEUTSCHE WELLE, Via Cyclops, Malta — (D) • N Africa • 250 kW

0 1 2 3 4 5 6 7 8 9 10 11 12 13 14 15 16 17 18 19 20 21 22 23 24

SUMMER ONLY (J)   WINTER ONLY (D)   JAMMING / OR ∧   EARLIEST HEARD ◁   LATEST HEARD ▷   NEW OR CHANGED FOR 1994 †

FREQUENCY   COUNTRY, STATION, LOCATION

TARGET • NETWORK • POWER (kW)

World Time

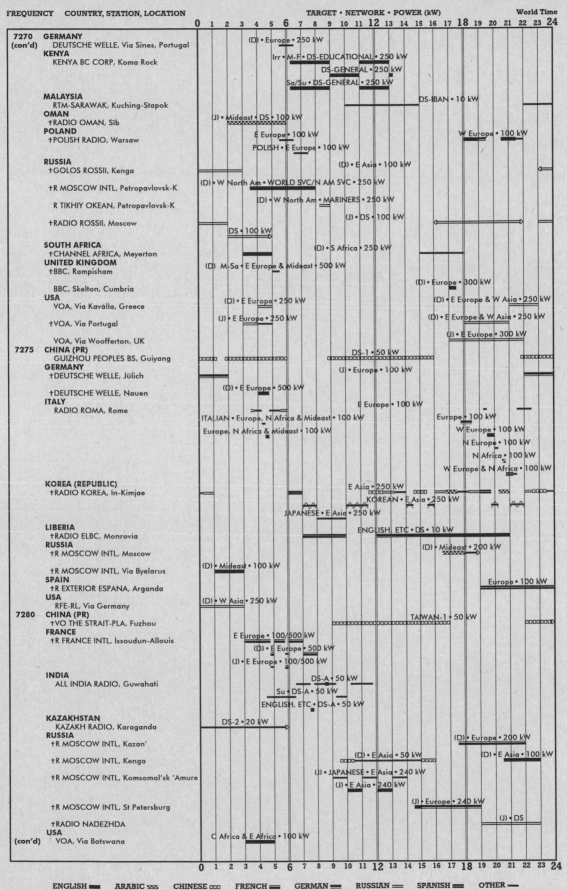

Frequency	Country, Station, Location
7270 (con'd)	**GERMANY** — DEUTSCHE WELLE, Via Sines, Portugal — (D) • Europe • 250 kW
	KENYA — KENYA BC CORP, Koma Rock — Irr • M-F • DS-EDUCATIONAL • 250 kW; DS-GENERAL • 250 kW; Sa/Su • DS-GENERAL • 250 kW
	MALAYSIA — RTM-SARAWAK, Kuching-Stapok — DS-IBAN • 10 kW
	OMAN — †RADIO OMAN, Sīb — (J) • Mideast • DS • 100 kW
	POLAND — †POLISH RADIO, Warsaw — E Europe • 100 kW; W Europe • 100 kW; POLISH • E Europe • 100 kW
	RUSSIA — †GOLOS ROSSII, Kenga — (D) • E Asia • 100 kW
	†R MOSCOW INTL, Petropavlovsk-K — (D) • W North Am • WORLD SVC/N AM SVC • 250 kW
	R TIKHIY OKEAN, Petropavlovsk-K — (D) • W North Am • MARINERS • 250 kW
	†RADIO ROSSII, Moscow — (J) • DS • 100 kW; DS • 100 kW
	SOUTH AFRICA — †CHANNEL AFRICA, Meyerton — (D) • S Africa • 250 kW
	UNITED KINGDOM — †BBC, Rampisham — (D) • M-Sa • E Europe & Mideast • 500 kW
	BBC, Skelton, Cumbria — (D) • Europe • 300 kW
	USA — VOA, Via Kavála, Greece — (D) • E Europe • 250 kW; (D) • E Europe & W Asia • 250 kW
	†VOA, Via Portugal — (J) • E Europe • 250 kW; (D) • E Europe & W Asia • 250 kW
	VOA, Via Woofferton, UK — (J) • E Europe • 300 kW
7275	**CHINA (PR)** — GUIZHOU PEOPLES BS, Guiyang — DS-1 • 50 kW
	GERMANY — †DEUTSCHE WELLE, Jülich — (J) • Europe • 100 kW
	†DEUTSCHE WELLE, Nauen — (D) • E Europe • 500 kW
	ITALY — RADIO ROMA, Rome — E Europe • 100 kW; ITALIAN • Europe, N Africa & Mideast • 100 kW; Europe, N Africa & Mideast • 100 kW; Europe • 100 kW; W Europe • 100 kW; N Europe • 100 kW; N Africa • 100 kW; W Europe & N Africa • 100 kW
	KOREA (REPUBLIC) — †RADIO KOREA, In-Kimjae — E Asia • 250 kW; KOREAN • E Asia • 250 kW; JAPANESE • E Asia • 250 kW
	LIBERIA — †RADIO ELBC, Monrovia — ENGLISH, ETC • DS • 10 kW
	RUSSIA — †R MOSCOW INTL, Moscow — (D) • Mideast • 200 kW
	†R MOSCOW INTL, Via Byelarus — (D) • Mideast • 100 kW
	SPAIN — †R EXTERIOR ESPANA, Arganda — Europe • 100 kW
	USA — RFE-RL, Via Germany — (D) • W Asia • 250 kW
7280	**CHINA (PR)** — †VO THE STRAIT-PLA, Fuzhou — TAIWAN-1 • 50 kW
	FRANCE — †R FRANCE INTL, Issoudun-Allouis — E Europe • 100/500 kW; (D) • E Europe • 500 kW; (J) • E Europe • 100/500 kW
	INDIA — ALL INDIA RADIO, Guwahati — DS-A • 50 kW; Su • DS-A • 50 kW; ENGLISH, ETC • DS-A • 50 kW
	KAZAKHSTAN — KAZAKH RADIO, Karaganda — DS-2 • 20 kW
	RUSSIA — †R MOSCOW INTL, Kazan' — (D) • Europe • 200 kW
	†R MOSCOW INTL, Kenga — (D) • E Asia • 50 kW; (D) • E Asia • 100 kW
	†R MOSCOW INTL, Komsomol'sk 'Amure — (J) • JAPANESE • E Asia • 240 kW; (J) • E Asia • 240 kW
	†R MOSCOW INTL, St Petersburg — (J) • Europe • 240 kW
	†RADIO NADEZHDA — (J) • DS
USA (con'd)	VOA, Via Botswana — C Africa & E Africa • 100 kW

FREQUENCY   COUNTRY, STATION, LOCATION

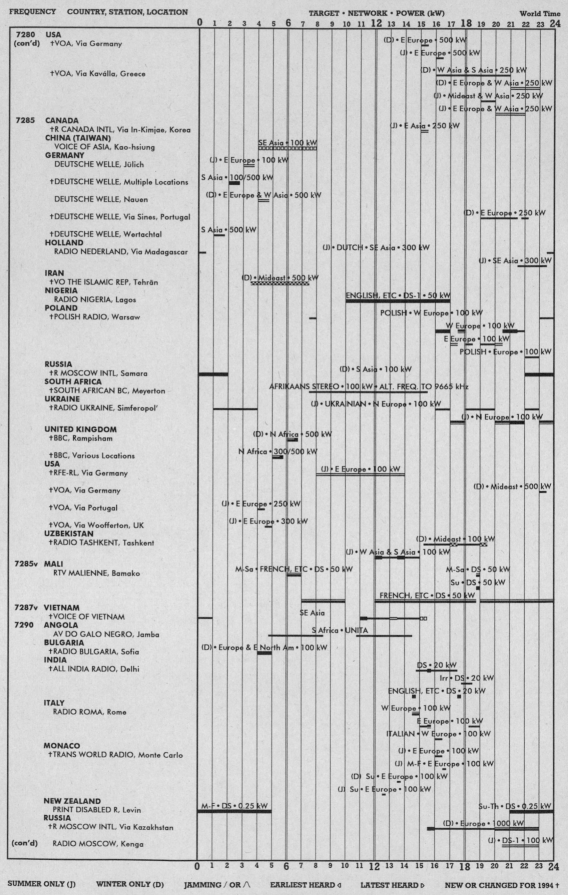

7280	**USA**	
(con'd)	†VOA, Via Germany	(D) • E Europe • 500 kW / (J) • E Europe • 500 kW
	†VOA, Via Kaválla, Greece	(D) • W Asia & S Asia • 250 kW / (D) • E Europe & W Asia • 250 kW / (J) • Mideast & W Asia • 250 kW / (J) • E Europe & W Asia • 250 kW
7285	**CANADA**	
	†R CANADA INTL, Via In-Kimjae, Korea	(J) • E Asia • 250 kW
	CHINA (TAIWAN)	
	VOICE OF ASIA, Kao-hsiung	SE Asia • 100 kW
	GERMANY	
	DEUTSCHE WELLE, Jülich	(J) • E Europe • 100 kW
	†DEUTSCHE WELLE, Multiple Locations	S Asia • 100/500 kW
	DEUTSCHE WELLE, Nauen	(D) • E Europe & W Asia • 500 kW
	†DEUTSCHE WELLE, Via Sines, Portugal	(D) • E Europe • 250 kW
	†DEUTSCHE WELLE, Wertachtal	S Asia • 500 kW
	HOLLAND	
	RADIO NEDERLAND, Via Madagascar	(J) • DUTCH • SE Asia • 300 kW / (J) • SE Asia • 300 kW
	IRAN	
	†VO THE ISLAMIC REP, Tehrän	(D) • Mideast • 500 kW
	NIGERIA	
	RADIO NIGERIA, Lagos	ENGLISH, ETC • DS-1 • 50 kW
	POLAND	
	†POLISH RADIO, Warsaw	POLISH • W Europe • 100 kW / W Europe • 100 kW / E Europe • 100 kW / POLISH • Europe • 100 kW
	RUSSIA	
	†R MOSCOW INTL, Samara	(D) • S Asia • 100 kW
	SOUTH AFRICA	
	†SOUTH AFRICAN BC, Meyerton	AFRIKAANS STEREO • 100 kW • ALT. FREQ. TO 9665 kHz
	UKRAINE	
	†RADIO UKRAINE, Simferopol'	(J) • UKRAINIAN • N Europe • 100 kW / (J) • N Europe • 100 kW
	UNITED KINGDOM	
	†BBC, Rampisham	(D) • N Africa • 500 kW
	†BBC, Various Locations	N Africa • 300/500 kW
	USA	
	†RFE-RL, Via Germany	(J) • E Europe • 100 kW
	†VOA, Via Germany	(D) • Mideast • 500 kW
	†VOA, Via Portugal	(J) • E Europe • 250 kW
	†VOA, Via Woofferton, UK	(J) • E Europe • 300 kW
	UZBEKISTAN	
	†RADIO TASHKENT, Tashkent	(D) • Mideast • 100 kW / (J) • W Asia & S Asia • 100 kW
7285v	**MALI**	
	RTV MALIENNE, Bamako	M-Sa • FRENCH, ETC • DS • 50 kW / M-Sa • DS • 50 kW / Su • DS • 50 kW / FRENCH, ETC • DS • 50 kW
7287v	**VIETNAM**	
	†VOICE OF VIETNAM	SE Asia
7290	**ANGOLA**	
	AV DO GALO NEGRO, Jamba	S Africa • UNITA
	BULGARIA	
	†RADIO BULGARIA, Sofia	(D) • Europe & E North Am • 100 kW
	INDIA	
	†ALL INDIA RADIO, Delhi	DS • 20 kW / Irr • DS • 20 kW / ENGLISH, ETC • DS • 20 kW
	ITALY	
	RADIO ROMA, Rome	W Europe • 100 kW / E Europe • 100 kW / ITALIAN • W Europe • 100 kW
	MONACO	
	†TRANS WORLD RADIO, Monte Carlo	(J) • E Europe • 100 kW / (J) • M-F • E Europe • 100 kW / (D) • Su • E Europe • 100 kW / (J) • Su • E Europe • 100 kW
	NEW ZEALAND	
	PRINT DISABLED R, Levin	M-F • DS • 0.25 kW / Su-Th • DS • 0.25 kW
	RUSSIA	
	†R MOSCOW INTL, Via Kazakhstan	(D) • Europe • 1000 kW
(con'd)	RADIO MOSCOW, Kenga	(J) • DS-1 • 100 kW

FREQUENCY   COUNTRY, STATION, LOCATION   TARGET • NETWORK • POWER (kW)   World Time

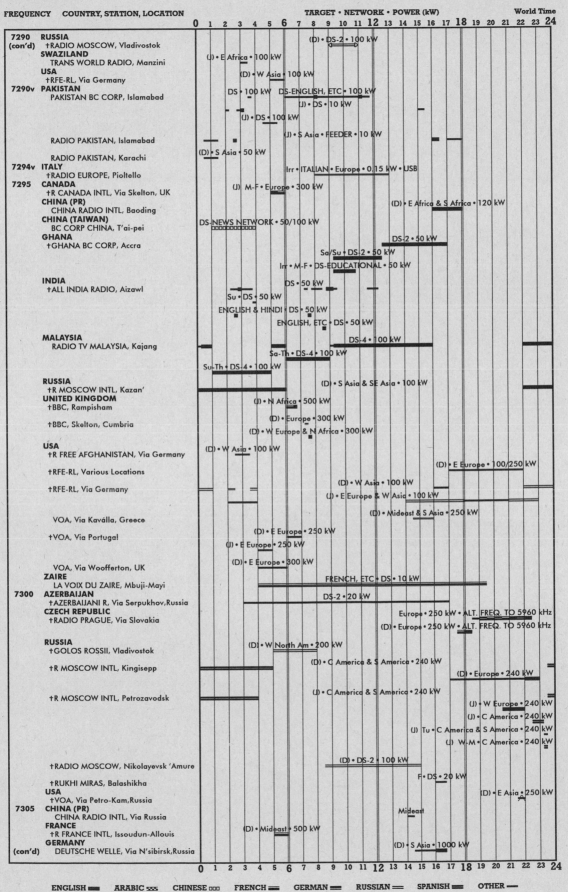

Frequency	Country, Station, Location	Details
7290 (con'd)	RUSSIA †RADIO MOSCOW, Vladivostok	(D) • DS-2 • 100 kW
	SWAZILAND TRANS WORLD RADIO, Manzini	(J) • E Africa • 100 kW
	USA †RFE-RL, Via Germany	(D) • W Asia • 100 kW
7290v	PAKISTAN PAKISTAN BC CORP, Islamabad	DS • 100 kW DS-ENGLISH, ETC • 100 kW / (J) • DS • 10 kW / (J) • DS • 100 kW
	RADIO PAKISTAN, Islamabad	(J) • S Asia • FEEDER • 10 kW
	RADIO PAKISTAN, Karachi	(D) • S Asia • 50 kW
7294v	ITALY †RADIO EUROPE, Pioltello	Irr • ITALIAN • Europe • 0.15 kW • USB
7295	CANADA †R CANADA INTL, Via Skelton, UK	(J) • M-F • Europe • 300 kW
	CHINA (PR) CHINA RADIO INTL, Baoding	(D) • E Africa & S Africa • 120 kW
	CHINA (TAIWAN) BC CORP CHINA, T'ai-pei	DS-NEWS NETWORK • 50/100 kW
	GHANA †GHANA BC CORP, Accra	DS-2 • 50 kW / Sa/Su • DS-2 • 50 kW / Irr • M-F • DS-EDUCATIONAL • 50 kW
	INDIA †ALL INDIA RADIO, Aizawl	DS • 50 kW / Su • DS • 50 kW / ENGLISH & HINDI • DS • 50 kW / ENGLISH, ETC • DS • 50 kW
	MALAYSIA RADIO TV MALAYSIA, Kajang	DS-4 • 100 kW / Sa-Th • DS-4 • 100 kW / Su-Th • DS-4 • 100 kW
	RUSSIA †R MOSCOW INTL, Kazan'	(D) • S Asia & SE Asia • 100 kW
	UNITED KINGDOM †BBC, Rampisham	(J) • N Africa • 500 kW
	†BBC, Skelton, Cumbria	(D) • Europe • 300 kW / (D) • W Europe & N Africa • 300 kW
	USA †R FREE AFGHANISTAN, Via Germany	(D) • W Asia • 100 kW
	†RFE-RL, Various Locations	(D) • E Europe • 100/250 kW
	†RFE-RL, Via Germany	(D) • W Asia • 100 kW / (J) • E Europe & W Asia • 100 kW
	VOA, Via Kaválla, Greece	(D) • Mideast & S Asia • 250 kW
	†VOA, Via Portugal	(D) • E Europe • 250 kW / (J) • E Europe • 250 kW
	VOA, Via Woofferton, UK	(D) • E Europe • 300 kW
	ZAIRE LA VOIX DU ZAIRE, Mbuji-Mayi	FRENCH, ETC • DS • 10 kW
7300	AZERBAIJAN †AZERBAIJANI R, Via Serpukhov, Russia	DS-2 • 20 kW
	CZECH REPUBLIC †RADIO PRAGUE, Via Slovakia	Europe • 250 kW • ALT. FREQ. TO 5960 kHz / (D) • Europe • 250 kW • ALT. FREQ. TO 5960 kHz
	RUSSIA †GOLOS ROSSII, Vladivostok	(D) • W North Am • 200 kW
	†R MOSCOW INTL, Kingisepp	(D) • C America & S America • 240 kW / (D) • Europe • 240 kW
	†R MOSCOW INTL, Petrozavodsk	(J) • C America & S America • 240 kW / (J) • W Europe • 240 kW / (J) • C America • 240 kW / (J) Tu • C America & S America • 240 kW / (J) W-M • C America • 240 kW
	†RADIO MOSCOW, Nikolayevsk 'Amure	(D) • DS-2 • 100 kW
	†RUKHI MIRAS, Balashikha	F • DS • 20 kW
	USA †VOA, Via Petro-Kam, Russia	(D) • E Asia • 250 kW
7305	CHINA (PR) CHINA RADIO INTL, Via Russia	Mideast
	FRANCE †R FRANCE INTL, Issoudun-Allouis	(D) • Mideast • 500 kW
(con'd)	GERMANY DEUTSCHE WELLE, Via N'sibirsk, Russia	(D) • S Asia • 1000 kW

FREQUENCY　　COUNTRY, STATION, LOCATION

TARGET • NETWORK • POWER (kW)　　　　　World Time

0　1　2　3　4　5　6　7　8　9　10　11　12　13　14　15　16　17　18　19　20　21　22　23　24

7305　HOLLAND
(con'd)　†RADIO NEDERLAND, Via Kazakhstan — (D) • S Asia • 500 kW
　　　　MONACO
　　　　†TRANS WORLD RADIO, Monte Carlo — Alternative Frequency to 6200 kHz
　　　　RUSSIA
　　　　　ADYGEY RADIO — (J) F
　　　　　KABARDINO-BALKAR R — (J) F
　　　　　†R MOSCOW INTL, Tula — (D) • W Asia & S Asia • 100 kW
　　　　　†R MOSCOW INTL, Via Ukraine — (J) • Mideast • 100 kW
　　　　VATICAN STATE
　　　　†VATICAN RADIO, Sta Maria di Galeria — S America • 100/500 kW
　　　　　(D) • S America • 100 kW
　　　　　(D) • E North Am • 100 kW

7310　RUSSIA
　　　　　ADVENTIST WORLD R, Yekaterinburg — (J) • Europe • 200 kW
　　　　　†AUM SHINRIKYO, Novosibirsk — (D) • JAPANESE • E Asia • 200 kW
　　　　　†GOLOS ROSSII, Armavir — (D) • Europe • 240 kW
　　　　　†R MOSCOW INTL, Moscow — (D) • Europe, W Africa & S America • 1000 kW
　　　　　†R MOSCOW INTL, Yekaterinburg — (J) • Europe • 200 kW
　　　　SLOVAKIA
　　　　†R SLOVAKIA INTL, Vel'ké Kostolany — N America • 100 kW
　　　　VATICAN STATE
　　　　†VATICAN RADIO, Sta Maria di Galeria — (D) • JAPANESE • E Asia • 500 kW
　　　　　(D) • E Asia • 500 kW
　　　　　(D) • SE Asia • 500 kW

7315　CROATIA
　　　　　CROATIAN RADIO, Via WHRI, USA — E North Am • 100 kW
　　　　GERMANY
　　　　　DEUTSCHE WELLE, Via N'sibirsk, Russia — (D) • SE Asia • 1000 kW
　　　　　†DEUTSCHE WELLE, Via Samara, Russia — S Asia • 250 kW
　　　　RUSSIA
　　　　†R MOSCOW INTL, Komsomol'sk 'Amure — (J) • E Asia • 100 kW
　　　　　(J) • JAPANESE • E Asia • 100 kW
　　　　　†RADIO ROSSII, Ryazan' — (J) • DS • 100 kW
　　　　　†RADIO ROSSII, St Petersburg — (D) • DS • 500 kW
　　　　UNITED KINGDOM
　　　　†BBC, Via Uzbekistan — (D) • S Asia • 200 kW
　　　　USA
　　　　†WORLD HARVEST R, Noblesville,Indiana — E North Am • 100 kW
　　　　　Su/M • E North Am • 100 kW
　　　　　Tu-Sa • E North Am • 100 kW

7320　KAZAKHSTAN
　　　　　KAZAKH RADIO, Almaty — DS-2 • 20 kW
　　　　RUSSIA
　　　　　MAGADAN RADIO, Yakutsk — RUSSIAN, ETC • DS/TIKHIY OKEAN • 100 kW
　　　　　†R MOSCOW INTL, Various Locations — (D) • Europe • 1000 kW
　　　　　†RADIO MOSCOW, Volgograd — (J) • DS-MAYAK • 20 kW
　　　　UNITED KINGDOM
　　　　†BBC, Rampisham — (D) • E Europe • 500 kW
　　　　　(J) • E Europe • 500 kW

7325　MONACO
　　　　†TRANS WORLD RADIO, Monte Carlo — (D) • E Europe • 100 kW • ALT. FREQ. TO 7355 kHz
　　　　　(D) W-Su • E Europe • 100 kW • ALT. FREQ. TO 7355 kHz
　　　　UNITED KINGDOM
　　　　†BBC, Multiple Locations — (D) • N America & C America • 250/300/500 kW
　　　　　E Europe • 250/300 kW
　　　　　N Africa • 300/500 kW
　　　　　Europe • 250/300/500 kW
　　　　　(J) • C America & S America • 300/500 kW
　　　　　BBC, Rampisham — (J) • E Europe • 500 kW
　　　　　†BBC, Via Uzbekistan — (D) • S Asia • 200 kW
　　　　　BBC, Woofferton — (D) • E Europe • 300 kW
　　　　USA
　　　　　VOA, Via Woofferton, UK — Europe • 300 kW
　　　　UZBEKISTAN
　　　　　RADIO TASHKENT, Tashkent — (J) • S Asia • 100 kW
　　　　　(J) • Mideast • 100 kW

7330　RUSSIA
　　　　†R MOSCOW INTL, Komsomol'sk 'Amure — (D) • E Asia & SE Asia • 240 kW — (D) • Australasia • 200 kW
　　　　†R MOSCOW INTL, Serpukhov — (D) • W Africa & S America • 240 kW — (D) • Europe & N Africa • 240 kW
(con'd)　†RADIO MOSCOW, Petrozavodsk — DS-MAYAK • 20 kW

0　1　2　3　4　5　6　7　8　9　10　11　12　13　14　15　16　17　18　19　20　21　22　23　24

FREQUENCY	COUNTRY, STATION, LOCATION	TARGET • NETWORK • POWER (kW)	World Time

(Time scale: 0 1 2 3 4 5 6 7 8 9 10 11 12 13 14 15 16 17 18 19 20 21 22 23 24)

Frequency	Country / Station / Location	Target • Network • Power
7330 (con'd)	**UNITED KINGDOM** †BBC, Via Chita, Russia	(D) • E Asia • 500 kW
7335	**CHINA (PR)** CHINA RADIO INTL, Xi'an	Africa • 150 kW
		(D) • E Africa & S Africa • 150 kW
		(D) • Europe & N Africa • 150 kW
	RUSSIA †R MOSCOW INTL, Kazan'	(D) • W Asia & S Asia • 250 kW
	†RADIO MOSCOW, Khabarovsk	(J) • DS-1 • 100 kW
	†RADIO ROSSII, Khabarovsk	(D) • DS • 100 kW
	UZBEKISTAN RADIO TASHKENT, Tashkent	(J) • S Asia • 100 kW • ALT. FREQ. TO 7225 kHz
	VATICAN STATE †VATICAN RADIO, Sta Maria di Galeria	(D) • S Asia • 500 kW
7340	**CHINA (PR)** CHINA RADIO INTL, Xi'an	(D) • Europe • 120 kW
	GERMANY DEUTSCHE WELLE, Via N'sibirsk, Russia	E Asia • 1000 kW (D) • E Asia • 1000 kW
	INDIA †ALL INDIA RADIO, Madras	S Asia • 100 kW
	RUSSIA †R MOSCOW INTL, Kazan'	(D) • W Asia & S Asia • 100 kW
	†R MOSCOW INTL, Serpukhov	(D) • Europe • 500 kW
	†RADIO MOSCOW, Yekaterinburg	(J) • DS-1 • 200 kW
	†RADIO ROSSII, St Petersburg	(D) • DS • 500 kW
	USA †VOA, Via Botswana	Africa • 100 kW
		M-F • Africa • 100 kW
		Sa/Su • Africa • 100 kW
7340v	**CLANDESTINE (C AMER)** "LA VOZ DEL CID", Guatemala City	C America • ANTI-CASTRO
7345	**CZECH REPUBLIC** †RADIO PRAGUE, Litomyšl	E North Am & C America • 200 kW
		C America & S America • 200 kW S America • 200 kW
		N America & C America • 200 kW E North Am & S America • 200 kW
		Europe • 100 kW
	†RADIO PRAGUE, Via Slovakia	Europe • 250 kW Europe • 100 kW
		M-F • Europe • 100 kW
	RUSSIA †R MOSCOW INTL, Petropavlovsk-K	(D) • W North Am • NORTH AMERICAN SVC • 100 kW
	†R TIKHIY OKEAN, Petropavlovsk-K	(D) • N Pacific & W North Am • MARINERS • 100 kW
	†RADIO ROSSII, Moscow	(D) • DS • 100 kW
	†RADIO ROSSII, Yakutsk	DS • 50 kW
	SLOVAKIA †R SLOVAKIA INTL, Rimavská Sobota	W Europe • 250 kW
	†R SLOVAKIA INTL, Vel'ké Kostolany	E Europe • 100 kW
		W Europe • 100 kW
7350	**CHINA (PR)** CHINA RADIO INTL, Kunming	SE Asia • 50 kW
	CHINA RADIO INTL, Xi'an	(D) • Europe & N Africa • 120 kW
		(D) • Europe • 120 kW
	HEILONGJIANG PBS, Harbin	DS • 50 kW
	CLANDESTINE (M EAST) "VO THE MOJAHED", Via R Baghdad	PERSIAN • Mideast • ANTI-IRAN GOVT
	RUSSIA †R MOSCOW INTL	(D) • S Europe
7355	**BULGARIA** †RADIO BULGARIA, Plovdiv	(J) • Europe • 250 kW
	†RADIO BULGARIA, Sofia	(J) M-Sa • E Europe & Mideast • 100 kW
	MONACO †TRANS WORLD RADIO, Monte Carlo	Alternative Frequency to 7325 kHz
	RUSSIA †R MOSCOW INTL	(D)
	†RADIO ROSSII, Novosibirsk	(D) • DS • 100 kW
	†RADIO ROSSII, Samara	(J) • DS • 100 kW
	USA †KNLS-NEW LIFE STN, Anchor Pt, Alaska	E Asia • 100 kW
		(D) • C Asia • 100 kW
		(D) • ENGLISH & JAPANESE • E Asia • 100 kW
	†UNIVERSITY NET'K, Via N'sibirsk, Russia	Alternative Frequency to 6120 kHz
	WORLD HARVEST R, Noblesville, Indiana	C America • 100 kW
		M-F • C America • 100 kW
(con'd)		

(Time scale: 0 1 2 3 4 5 6 7 8 9 10 11 12 13 14 15 16 17 18 19 20 21 22 23 24)

ENGLISH ▬　ARABIC ⠶⠶⠶　CHINESE □□□　FRENCH ▭▭　GERMAN ▬▬　RUSSIAN ══　SPANISH ▬▬　OTHER ──

FREQUENCY   COUNTRY, STATION, LOCATION   TARGET • NETWORK • POWER (kW)   World Time

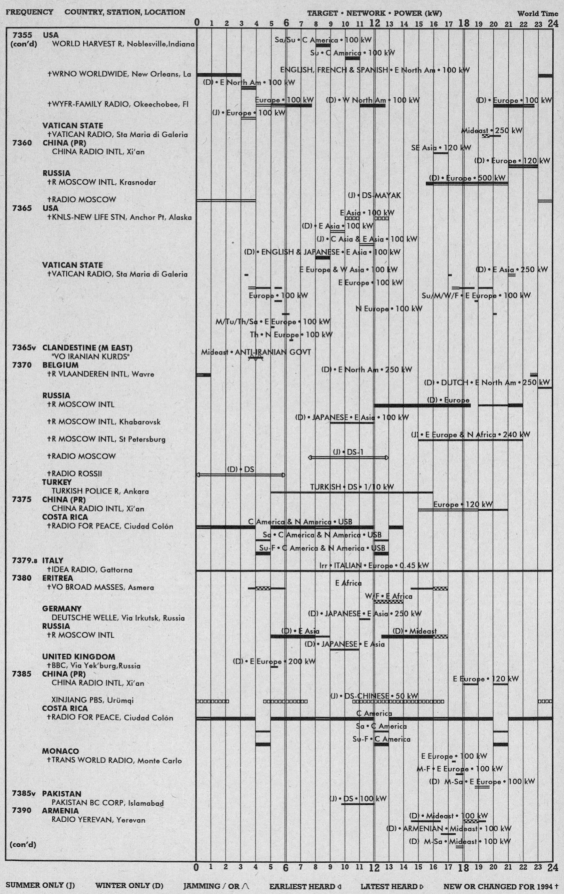

Frequency	Country, Station, Location	Target • Network • Power
7355 (con'd)	**USA**	
	WORLD HARVEST R, Noblesville, Indiana	Sa/Su • C America • 100 kW
		Su • C America • 100 kW
	†WRNO WORLDWIDE, New Orleans, La	ENGLISH, FRENCH & SPANISH • E North Am • 100 kW
		(D) • E North Am • 100 kW
	†WYFR-FAMILY RADIO, Okeechobee, Fl	Europe • 100 kW (D) • W North Am • 100 kW (D) • Europe • 100 kW
		(J) • Europe • 100 kW
	VATICAN STATE	
	†VATICAN RADIO, Sta Maria di Galeria	Mideast • 250 kW
7360	**CHINA (PR)**	
	CHINA RADIO INTL, Xi'an	SE Asia • 120 kW
		(D) • Europe • 120 kW
	RUSSIA	
	†R MOSCOW INTL, Krasnodar	(D) • Europe • 500 kW
	†RADIO MOSCOW	(J) • DS-MAYAK
7365	**USA**	
	†KNLS-NEW LIFE STN, Anchor Pt, Alaska	E Asia • 100 kW
		(D) • E Asia • 100 kW
		(J) • C Asia & E Asia • 100 kW
		(D) • ENGLISH & JAPANESE • E Asia • 100 kW
	VATICAN STATE	
	†VATICAN RADIO, Sta Maria di Galeria	E Europe & W Asia • 100 kW (D) • E Asia • 250 kW
		E Europe • 100 kW
		Europe • 100 kW Su/M/W/F • E Europe • 100 kW
		N Europe • 100 kW
		M/Tu/Th/Sa • E Europe • 100 kW
		Th • N Europe • 100 kW
7365v	**CLANDESTINE (M EAST)**	
	"VO IRANIAN KURDS"	Mideast • ANTI-IRANIAN GOVT
7370	**BELGIUM**	
	†R VLAANDEREN INTL, Wavre	(D) • E North Am • 250 kW
		(D) • DUTCH • E North Am • 250 kW
	RUSSIA	
	†R MOSCOW INTL	(D) • Europe
	†R MOSCOW INTL, Khabarovsk	(D) • JAPANESE • E Asia • 100 kW
	†R MOSCOW INTL, St Petersburg	(J) • E Europe & N Africa • 240 kW
	†RADIO MOSCOW	(J) • DS-1
	†RADIO ROSSII	(D) • DS
	TURKEY	
	TURKISH POLICE R, Ankara	TURKISH • DS • 1/10 kW
7375	**CHINA (PR)**	
	CHINA RADIO INTL, Xi'an	Europe • 120 kW
	COSTA RICA	
	†RADIO FOR PEACE, Ciudad Colón	C America & N America • USB
		Sa • C America & N America • USB
		Su-F • C America & N America • USB
7379.8	**ITALY**	
	†IDEA RADIO, Gattorna	Irr • ITALIAN • Europe • 0.45 kW
7380	**ERITREA**	
	†VO BROAD MASSES, Asmera	E Africa
		W/F • E Africa
	GERMANY	
	DEUTSCHE WELLE, Via Irkutsk, Russia	(D) • JAPANESE • E Asia • 250 kW
	RUSSIA	
	†R MOSCOW INTL	(D) • E Asia (D) • Mideast
		(D) • JAPANESE • E Asia
	UNITED KINGDOM	
	†BBC, Via Yek'burg, Russia	(D) • E Europe • 200 kW
7385	**CHINA (PR)**	
	CHINA RADIO INTL, Xi'an	E Europe • 120 kW
	XINJIANG PBS, Urümqi	(J) • DS-CHINESE • 50 kW
	COSTA RICA	
	†RADIO FOR PEACE, Ciudad Colón	C America
		Sa • C America
		Su-F • C America
	MONACO	
	†TRANS WORLD RADIO, Monte Carlo	E Europe • 100 kW
		M-F • E Europe • 100 kW
		(D) M-Sa • E Europe • 100 kW
7385v	**PAKISTAN**	
	PAKISTAN BC CORP, Islamabad	(J) • DS • 100 kW
7390	**ARMENIA**	
	RADIO YEREVAN, Yerevan	(D) • Mideast • 100 kW
		(D) • ARMENIAN • Mideast • 100 kW
		(D) M-Sa • Mideast • 100 kW
(con'd)		

FREQUENCY   COUNTRY, STATION, LOCATION

TARGET • NETWORK • POWER (kW)   World Time

0 1 2 3 4 5 6 7 8 9 10 11 12 13 14 15 16 17 18 19 20 21 22 23 24

Frequency	Country, Station, Location	Target • Network • Power
7390 (con'd)	**ARMENIA** RADIO YEREVAN, Yerevan	(D) • ARMENIAN • Mideast • ARMENIAN, TURKISH • 100 kW
	CLANDESTINE (ASIA) †"KASHMIR FREEDOM"	S Asia • ANTI-INDIAN GOVT
	GERMANY DEUTSCHE WELLE, Via N'sibirsk, Russia	(D) • E Asia • 200 kW
	RUSSIA †R MOSCOW INTL	(D) • E Asia
	†R MOSCOW INTL, Via Ukraine	(D) • C America & S America
		(D) • Europe
7395	**PAKISTAN** †RADIO PAKISTAN, Islamabad	(D) • Mideast • 100 kW
	USA †CHRIST SCI MONITOR, South Carolina	(D) • W North Am • 500 kW
		(D) M-F • W North Am • 500 kW
		(D) Sa/Su • W North Am • 500 kW
	†WRNO WORLDWIDE, New Orleans, La	(J) • E North Am • 100 kW
7400	**RUSSIA** †R MOSCOW INTL	(D) • W Europe & C America
	R MOSCOW INTL, Moscow	(J) • Europe • 120 kW
	RADIO MOSCOW, Moscow	(D) • DS-1 • 100 kW
	†RADIO MOSCOW, Volgograd	(J) • DS-MAYAK • 50 kW
	USA †VOA, Via Irkutsk, Russia	(J) • Africa • 1000 kW
7405	**CHINA (PR)** CHINA RADIO INTL, Jinhua	(D) • W North Am • 500 kW
	CHINA RADIO INTL, Xi'an	(D) • Africa • 240 kW
		(D) • Europe • 120 kW
	USA †VOA, Cincinnati, Ohio	C America • 250 kW
		Tu-Sa • C America • 250 kW
	†VOA, Greenville, NC	W Africa & S Africa • 250/500 kW
7410	**ITALY** †RADIO EUROPE, Pioltello	Irr • ITALIAN • Europe • 0.15 kW • USB
7412	**INDIA** †ALL INDIA RADIO, Aligarh	S Asia & E Asia • 250 kW
		HINDI • Mideast • 250 kW
		DS • 250 kW
	†ALL INDIA RADIO, Delhi	N Europe • 250 kW
		HINDI • W Europe • 250 kW
		W Europe • 250 kW
7415	**USA** †VOA, Via Botswana	Africa • 100 kW
7416v	**PIRATE (EUROPE)** †"RADIO PIRANA INTL"	Irr • Su • W Europe • 0.2 kW
7420	**BYELARUS** †RS BYELARUS, Osipovichi	(D) • Europe • 100 kW
		(D) M/Tu/Th/F • Europe • 100 kW
		(D) W/Sa • Europe • 100 kW
	CHINA (PR) †CHINA RADIO INTL, Xi'an	(D) • E Europe & N Africa • 120 kW
	RUSSIA †R MOSCOW INTL	(D) • N Pacific & W North Am
	†R MOSCOW INTL, Via Byelarus	(D) • Europe • 100 kW
	†R TIKHIY OKEAN	(D) • N Pacific & W North Am
	SWITZERLAND †"DIE ANTWORT", Via RS Byelarus	(D) • Su • Europe • 100 kW
	UNITED KINGDOM †BBC, Via Irkutsk, Russia	(D) • E Asia • 250 kW
7420v	**IRAQ** †REP OF IRAQ RADIO, Baghdad	DS-1
7425	**USA** †WEWN, Birmingham, Alabama	N America • 500 kW
		(D) • Europe • 500 kW
7430	**GREECE** RS MAKEDONIAS, Thessaloniki	GREEK • Mideast • DS • 35 kW
		M-F • GREEK • Mideast • DS • 35 kW
7435	**CHINA (PR)** †CHINA RADIO INTL, Xi'an	(D) • S America • 120 kW
	USA †WWCR, Nashville, Tennessee	E North Am & Europe • 100 kW
7435v	**CLANDESTINE (M EAST)** "VO KURD STRUGGLE", Middle East	Mideast • ANTI-IRANIAN GOVT
7440	**ARMENIA** RADIO YEREVAN, Via Russia	(D) • ARMENIAN • Europe & W Africa • 240 kW
		(D) • Europe & W Africa • 240 kW
(con'd)	**CHINA (PR)** CENTRAL PEOPLES BS, Xi'an	DS-2 • 120 kW

0 1 2 3 4 5 6 7 8 9 10 11 12 13 14 15 16 17 18 19 20 21 22 23 24

ENGLISH ▬   ARABIC ⟋⟍⟍   CHINESE □□□   FRENCH ═══   GERMAN ▭▭   RUSSIAN ══   SPANISH ▭▭   OTHER ▬▬

FREQUENCY   COUNTRY, STATION, LOCATION

TARGET • NETWORK • POWER (kW)   World Time

0 1 2 3 4 5 6 7 8 9 10 11 12 13 14 15 16 17 18 19 20 21 22 23 24

7440   **RUSSIA**
(con'd)   †GOLOS ROSSII, Moscow — (D) • Europe & W Africa • 240 kW

7445   **CHINA (TAIWAN)**
     VO FREE CHINA, T'ai-pei — E Asia • 50 kW
     CANTONESE • E Asia • 50 kW
     VOICE OF ASIA, Kao-hsiung — SE Asia • 100 kW

7445v   **PIRATE (PACIFIC)**
     †KIWI RADIO, New Zealand — Irr • Pacific • 0.03/0.4 kW

7446   **PIRATE (EUROPE)**
     †"RADIO STELLA", Scotland — Irr • Su • W Europe • 0.09 kW • ALT. FREQ. TO 11413 kHz

7450   **GREECE**
     †FONI TIS HELLADAS, Athens
     GREEK • Mideast • 100 kW   GREEK • Australasia • 100 kW
     Mideast • 100 kW   (D) • Europe • 100 kW
     GREEK • Europe • 100 kW   (D) • E Europe • 100 kW
     Europe • 100 kW   (J) • E Europe • 100 kW
     (J) • Europe • 100 kW
     (D) W-M • GREEK • Europe • 100 kW
     (D) W-M • Europe • 100 kW

7455   **ETHIOPIA**
     †VO TIGRAY REVOL'N, Mek'ele — E Africa
     Su • E Africa

     GUAM
     †ADVENTIST WORLD R, Agat — (D) • E Asia • 100 kW
     (D) • S Asia • 100 kW

7465   **ISRAEL**
     †KOL ISRAEL, Tel Aviv — (D) • E Europe • 100/300 kW
     (D) • YIDDISH • E Europe • 100/300 kW
     (D) • W Europe & E North Am • 300 kW
     (J) • E Europe • 300 kW

     USA
     †WEWN, Birmingham, Alabama — (D) • Europe • 500 kW

7470   **CHINA (PR)**
     CHINA RADIO INTL, Xi'an — Europe & N Africa • 500 kW

7470v   **PIRATE (EUROPE)**
     †"RADIO MARABU", Germany — Alternative Frequency to 6234v kHz

7473   **PIRATE (EUROPE)**
     "RADIO WAVES INTL", France — Irr • Su • ENGLISH & FRENCH • W Europe • 0.015 kW

7475   **TUNISIA**
     RTV TUNISIENNE, Sfax — Irr • DS-RAMADAN • 100 kW
     DS • 100 kW

7480   **CHINA (PR)**
     CHINA RADIO INTL, Jinhua — Mideast • 500 kW
     SWITZERLAND
     SWISS RADIO INTL, Via Beijing, China — E Asia • 120 kW
     ITALIAN • E Asia • 120 kW

7480v   **PIRATE (EUROPE)**
     "RADIO BENELUX", Germany — Irr • Su • GERMAN & ENGLISH • W Europe

7490   **RUSSIA**
     RADIO MOSCOW, Khabarovsk — DS-2 (FEEDER) • 15 kW • USB
     USA
     WJCR, Upton, Kentucky — E North Am • 50 kW

7504   **CHINA (PR)**
     CENTRAL PEOPLES BS, Xi'an — DS-1 • 120 kW
     W-M • DS-1 • 120 kW

7510   **USA**
     †CHRIST SCI MONITOR, Maine
     (D) M-F • Europe & Mideast • 500 kW
     (D) M-F • Europe • 500 kW
     (D) Sa • Europe & Mideast • 500 kW
     (D) Sa • Europe • 500 kW
     (D) Su • Europe & Mideast • 500 kW
     (D) Su • Europe • 500 kW

     †KTBN, Salt Lake City, Utah — E North Am • 100 kW
     (D) • E North Am • 100 kW

7516   **CHINA (PR)**
     CENTRAL PEOPLES BS, Beijing — DS-2 • 50 kW

7520   **USA**
     †WEWN, Birmingham, Alabama — (D) • Europe • 500 kW
     †WYFR-FAMILY RADIO, Okeechobee, Fl — (D) • Europe • 100 kW

7545v   **PIRATE (EUROPE)**
     †"RADIO BRIGITTE", Belgium — Irr • Su • W Europe • ALT. FREQ. TO 6555v kHz

7550   **KOREA (REPUBLIC)**
     †RADIO KOREA, In-Kimjae — Europe • 250 kW   Mideast & Africa • 250 kW
     KOREAN • Europe • 250 kW   KOREAN • Mideast & Africa • 250 kW

7580   **KOREA (DPR)**
     †RADIO PYONGYANG, Pyongyang — JAPANESE • E Asia • 100 kW

7590   **CHINA (PR)**
     CHINA RADIO INTL, Beijing — S Asia • 120 kW
     CHINA RADIO INTL, Kunming — SE Asia • 120 kW
     (J) • S Asia • 120 kW
     (J) • SE Asia • 120 kW

0 1 2 3 4 5 6 7 8 9 10 11 12 13 14 15 16 17 18 19 20 21 22 23 24

SUMMER ONLY (J)   WINTER ONLY (D)   JAMMING / OR ∧   EARLIEST HEARD ◁   LATEST HEARD ▷   NEW OR CHANGED FOR 1994 †

FREQUENCY   COUNTRY, STATION, LOCATION   TARGET • NETWORK • POWER (kW)   World Time

0 1 2 3 4 5 6 7 8 9 10 11 12 13 14 15 16 17 18 19 20 21 22 23 24

Freq	Country, Station, Location	Target • Network • Power
7620	CHINA (PR) CENTRAL PEOPLES BS	(D) • CHINESE, ETC • TAIWAN-1
7650	BOSNIA HERCEGOVINA †R BOSNIA-H, Sarajevo	Alternative Frequency to 6220 kHz
7651	USA †VOA, Greenville, NC	Europe • (FEEDER) • 40 kW • ISL Europe • (FEEDER) • 40 kW • ISU (D) • Europe • (FEEDER) • 40 kW • ISU (D) • Europe • (FEEDER) • 40 kW • ISL (J) • Europe • (FEEDER) • 40 kW • ISU (J) • Europe • (FEEDER) • 40 kW • ISL
7660	CHINA (PR) CHINA RADIO INTL, Xi'an	E Europe • 120 kW
7670	BULGARIA BULGARIAN RADIO, Stolnik	DS-1 • 15 kW
7700	CHINA (PR) CHINA RADIO INTL, Kunming	N Africa & W Africa • 50 kW
7705	ITALY †RAI-RTV ITALIANA, Rome	ITALIAN • DS-ITALIAN, ETC(FEEDER) • USB ITALIAN • DS-1(FEEDER) • USB
7768.5	USA VOA, Greenville, NC	(J) • N Africa • 40 kW • LSB
7770	CHINA (PR) †CENTRAL PEOPLES BS, Kunming	DS-2 • 50 kW
7800	CHINA (PR) CHINA RADIO INTL, Beijing CHINA RADIO INTL, Kunming	(J) • C Asia • 120 kW (D) • Europe & N Africa • 50 kW
7820	CHINA (PR) CHINA RADIO INTL, Beijing ETHIOPIA †VO TIGRAY REVOL'N, Mek'ele	C Asia • 120 kW E Africa Su • E Africa
7870	ICELAND †RIKISUTVARPID, Reykjavik	Atlantic & Europe • DS-1 • 10 kW • USB
7935	CHINA (PR) †CENTRAL PEOPLES BS, Beijing	DS-1 • 15 kW (D) • DS-1 • 15 kW
8000	ETHIOPIA VO OROMO MASSES, Addis Ababa VOICE OF THE EPPDF, Addis Ababa	E Africa E Africa Su • E Africa
8005	RUSSIA †RADIO ROSSII, Moscow	(D) • DS • 20 kW • USB
8040	RUSSIA †RADIO ROSSII, Moscow	(D) • DS(FEEDER) • USB
8260	CHINA (PR) CHINA RADIO INTL, Beijing	E Asia • FEEDER • 10 kW (D) • E Asia • FEEDER • 10 kW
8345	CHINA (PR) CHINA RADIO INTL, Beijing	(J) • E Asia • FEEDER • 10 kW
8425	CHINA (PR) CHINA RADIO INTL, Beijing FRANCE R FRANCE INTL, Via Beijing, China	E Asia • FEEDER • 100 kW (D) • E Asia • FEEDER • 100 kW E Asia • FEEDER • 100 kW
8450	CHINA (PR) CHINA RADIO INTL, Beijing	E Asia • FEEDER • 100 kW (J) • E Asia • FEEDER • 100 kW
8514.2	PERU RADIO AMISTAD, Soritor	DS • 0.2 kW
8566	CHINA (PR) CENTRAL PEOPLES BS, Beijing	DS-MINORITIES (J) • DS-MINORITIES
8660	CHINA (PR) CHINA RADIO INTL, Beijing	E Asia • FEEDER • 10 kW
9022	IRAN †VO THE ISLAMIC REP, Tehrān	Americas • 500 kW Europe • 500 kW Europe & Mideast • 500 kW E Europe & W Asia • 500 kW
9064	CHINA (PR) CENTRAL PEOPLES BS, Beijing	DS-2 • 15 kW Th/Sa-Tu • DS-2 • 15 kW
9080	CHINA (PR) †CENTRAL PEOPLES BS, Beijing	(D) • DS-1 • 50 kW DS-1 • 50 kW
9165v	CLANDESTINE (AFRICA) †RADIO SPLA SUDAN †R NATIONAL UNITY, Omdurman †RADIO OMDURMAN, Omdurman †REP OF SUDAN RADIO, Omdurman	Irr • ARABIC, ETC • E Africa • ANTI-SUDAN GOVT • ALT. FREQ. TO 9190v kHz 100 kW • ALT. FREQ. TO 9190v kHz Europe, Mideast & Africa • 100 kW • ALT. FREQ. TO 9190v kHz DS • 100 kW • ALT. FREQ. TO 9190v kHz Irr • DS-RAMADAN • 100 kW • ALT. FREQ. TO 9190v kHz
9170	CHINA (PR) CENTRAL PEOPLES BS, Beijing	CHINESE, ETC • TAIWAN-2 • 10 kW (D) • CHINESE, ETC • TAIWAN-2 • 10 kW (J) • CHINESE, ETC • TAIWAN-2 • 10 kW

0 1 2 3 4 5 6 7 8 9 10 11 12 13 14 15 16 17 18 19 20 21 22 23 24

ENGLISH ▬▬ ARABIC ▨▨ CHINESE □□□ FRENCH ▬▬ GERMAN ▬▬ RUSSIAN ▬▬ SPANISH ▬▬ OTHER ▬

FREQUENCY   COUNTRY, STATION, LOCATION

TARGET • NETWORK • POWER (kW)   World Time

0 1 2 3 4 5 6 7 8 9 10 11 12 13 14 15 16 17 18 19 20 21 22 23 24

Frequency	Country, Station, Location	Schedule details
9180	**RUSSIA** †RADIO MOSCOW	Irr • DS-MAYAK(FEEDER) • USB
9190v	**CLANDESTINE (AFRICA)** †RADIO SPLA	Alternative Frequency to 9165v kHz
	SUDAN †R NATIONAL UNITY, Omdurman	Alternative Frequency to 9165v kHz
	†RADIO OMDURMAN, Omdurman	Alternative Frequency to 9165v kHz
	†REP OF SUDAN RADIO, Omdurman	Alternative Frequency to 9165v kHz
9275	**ICELAND** †RIKISUTVARPID, Reykjavik	Atlantic & E North Am • DS-1 • 10 kW • USB
9280	**CHINA (TAIWAN)** †BC CORP CHINA, Kao-hsiung	E Asia • DS(FM-1) • 100 kW
	†VOICE OF ASIA, Kao-hsiung	E Asia • 100 kW
	USA FAMILY RADIO, Via Taiwan	E Asia • 250 kW
9290	**CHINA (PR)** CENTRAL PEOPLES BS, Beijing	DS-1 • 50 kW
		W-M • DS-1 • 50 kW
9325	**KOREA (DPR)** †RADIO PYONGYANG, Pyongyang	Europe & W Asia • 200 kW Europe • 200 kW KOREAN • Europe • 200 kW
9345	**KOREA (DPR)** †RADIO PYONGYANG, Pyongyang	KOREAN • E Asia • 200 kW Europe • 200 kW Asia • 200 kW KOREAN • Asia • 200 kW KOREAN • Europe • 200 kW
9350	**CLANDESTINE (M EAST)** †"VO HUMAN RIGHTS", Egypt	PERSIAN • Mideast • ANTI-IRANIAN GOVT • 100 kW (D) • PERSIAN • Mideast • ANTI-IRANIAN GOVT • 100 kW
	USA †CHRIST SCI MONITOR, Maine	Alternative Frequency to 9455 kHz
	†WEWN, Birmingham, Alabama	(J) • Europe • 500 kW (J) • N America • 500 kW
9355	**USA** †CHRIST SCI MONITOR, Via Saipan	(J) • SE Asia & S Africa • 100 kW (J) M-Sa • SE Asia & S Africa • 100 kW Sa • Europe & Mideast • 100 kW Su-F • Europe & Mideast • 100 kW (J) Su • SE Asia & S Africa • 100 kW
9365	**CHINA (PR)** CHINA RADIO INTL, Xi'an	Europe • 120 kW
9369.3	**PAKISTAN** RADIO PAKISTAN, Karachi	S Asia • 50 kW
9370	**GUAM** †ADVENTIST WORLD R, Agat	(D) • S Asia • 100 kW
	USA †WEWN, Birmingham, Alabama	(D) • Europe • 500 kW (J) • Europe • 500 kW (D) • E Asia • 500 kW
9375	**GREECE** †FONI TIS HELLADAS, Athens	GREEK • Europe • 100 kW • ALT. FREQ. TO 9395 kHz (D) • Europe • 100 kW Europe • 100 kW • ALT. FREQ. TO 9395 kHz (D) • E Europe • 100 kW (J) • E Europe • 100 kW (J) • Europe • 100 kW
9380	**CHINA (PR)** CENTRAL PEOPLES BS, Beijing	(J) • CHINESE, ETC • TAIWAN-1 • 10 kW (D) • CHINESE, ETC • TAIWAN-1 • 10 kW
	GREECE †FONI TIS HELLADAS, Athens	GREEK • N America • 100 kW • ALT. FREQ. TO 9395 kHz M-Sa • N America • 100 kW • ALT. FREQ. TO 9395 kHz Su • GREEK • N America • 100 kW • ALT. FREQ. TO 9395 kHz
9388	**ISRAEL** †RASHUTH HASHIDUR, Tel Aviv	HEBREW • Europe • DS-B • 50/100 kW (J) • HEBREW • Europe • DS-B • 50 kW (D) • HEBREW • Europe • DS-B • 50/100 kW (D) Su-F • HEBREW • Europe • DS-B • 50/100 kW (J) Su-F • HEBREW • Europe • DS-B • 50 kW
9395	**GREECE** †FONI TIS HELLADAS, Athens	Alternative Frequency to 9375 kHz Alternative Frequency to 9380 kHz W-M • GREEK • Europe • 100 kW W-M • Europe • 100 kW
9400v	**PAKISTAN** †RADIO PAKISTAN, Islamabad	(D) • Mideast • 100 kW
9410	**UNITED KINGDOM** BBC, Multiple Locations	Europe • 250/300/500 kW
	BBC, Rampisham	(J) • N Europe • 500 kW
	USA †WEWN, Birmingham, Alabama	(D) • Europe • 500 kW (J) • Europe • 500 kW
9418	**PAKISTAN** †RADIO PAKISTAN, Islamabad	Alternative Frequency to 9430 kHz

0 1 2 3 4 5 6 7 8 9 10 11 12 13 14 15 16 17 18 19 20 21 22 23 24

SUMMER ONLY (J)   WINTER ONLY (D)   JAMMING / OR ∧   EARLIEST HEARD ◁   LATEST HEARD ▷   NEW OR CHANGED FOR 1994 †

FREQUENCY   COUNTRY, STATION, LOCATION   TARGET • NETWORK • POWER (kW)   World Time

0 1 2 3 4 5 6 7 8 9 10 11 12 13 14 15 16 17 18 19 20 21 22 23 24

9420 GREECE
　　†FONI TIS HELLADAS, Athens
　　　　GREEK • N America • 100 kW
　　　　M-Sa • N America • 100 kW
　　　　Su • GREEK • N America • 100 kW

　　PHILIPPINES
　　†FEBC RADIO INTL, Bocaue
　　　　Alternative Frequency to 9815 kHz

9425 GREECE
　　†FONI TIS HELLADAS, Athens
　　　　GREEK • Mideast • 100 kW
　　　　Mideast • 100 kW
　　　　GREEK • Europe • 100 kW
　　　　Europe • 100 kW
　　　　GREEK • Australasia • 100 kW
　　　　GREEK • C America • 100 kW
　　　　C America • 100 kW

　　FONI TIS HELLADAS, Kaválla
　　　　GREEK • E Europe • 250 kW
　　　　E Europe • 250 kW

　　FONI TIS HELLADAS, Various Locations
　　　　GREEK • E Europe • 100/250 kW
　　　　E Europe • 100/250 kW

　　USA
　　CHRIST SCI MONITOR, Via Saipan
　　　　(J) • Australasia • 100 kW
　　　　(J) M-F • Australasia • 100 kW
　　　　(J) Sa/Su • Australasia • 100 kW

9430 PAKISTAN
　　†RADIO PAKISTAN, Islamabad
　　　　(D) • Europe • 250 kW • ALT. FREQ. TO 9418 kHz
　　USA
　　†CHRIST SCI MONITOR, Via Saipan
　　　　(J) • Australasia • 100 kW
　　　　(J) Sa • Australasia • 100 kW
　　　　(J) Su-F • Australasia • 100 kW

　　†WEWN, Birmingham, Alabama
　　　　(D) • W Africa • 500 kW
9435 ISRAEL
　　†KOL ISRAEL, Tel Aviv
　　　　W Europe & E North Am • 300 kW
　　　　(D) • Europe • 300 kW
　　　　(D) • YIDDISH • Europe • 300 kW
　　　　(D) • W Europe & E North Am • 300 kW
　　　　(D) • E Europe • 300 kW
　　　　(D) • C America & S America • 300 kW
　　　　(J) • E Europe • 300 kW

　　†RASHUTH HASHIDUR, Tel Aviv
　　　　HEBREW • W Europe & E North Am • DS-B • 300 kW
　　　　Su-F • HEBREW • W Europe & E North Am • DS-B • 300 kW

　　MONACO
　　†TRANS WORLD RADIO, Monte Carlo
　　　　(D) • E Europe • 100 kW
　　　　(D) F-W • E Europe • 100 kW
　　　　(J) • E Europe • 100 kW
　　　　(D) M-F • E Europe • 100 kW
　　　　(J) W-Su • E Europe • 100 kW

9440 CHINA (PR)
　　†CHINA RADIO INTL, Beijing
　　　　SE Asia • 120 kW
　　　　Mideast • 120 kW
　　　　CANTONESE • SE Asia • 120 kW

　　CHINA RADIO INTL, Xi'an
　　　　SE Asia • 120 kW
9445 TURKEY
　　VOICE OF TURKEY, Ankara
　　　　TURKISH • E North Am • 500 kW
　　　　Europe • 250 kW
　　　　E North Am • 500 kW

9450 ARMENIA
　　†RADIO YEREVAN, Via Moscow, Russia
　　　　(J) • ARMENIAN • Europe • 240 kW
　　　　(J) • Europe • 240 kW

　　RUSSIA
　　†GOLOS ROSSII
　　　　(D) • E Asia

　　†GOLOS ROSSII, Moscow
　　　　(J) • Europe • 240 kW

　　†R MOSCOW INTL, Novosibirsk
　　　　(D) • E Asia • 250 kW

　　†RADIO MOSCOW, Novosibirsk
　　　　DS-1 • 100 kW
　　　　(J) • DS-1 • 100 kW

9455 CHINA (PR)
　　CENTRAL PEOPLES BS, Kunming
　　　　(J) • CHINESE, ETC • TAIWAN-1 • 50 kW
　　　　CHINESE, ETC • TAIWAN-1 • 50 kW

　　USA
　　†CHRIST SCI MONITOR, Maine
　　　　E Africa • 500 kW • ALT. FREQ. TO 9350 kHz
　　　　M-F • E Africa • 500 kW • ALT. FREQ. TO 9350 kHz
　　　　Sa/Su • E Africa • 500 kW • ALT. FREQ. TO 9350 kHz

　　†CHRIST SCI MONITOR, South Carolina
　　　　(J) • W North Am • 500 kW
　　　　M-F • S America • 500 kW
　　　　(J) M-F • W North Am • 500 kW
　　　　(J) M • W North Am • 500 kW
　　　　Sa/Su • S America • 500 kW

(con'd)

0 1 2 3 4 5 6 7 8 9 10 11 12 13 14 15 16 17 18 19 20 21 22 23 24

ENGLISH ▬   ARABIC ⌇⌇⌇   CHINESE □□□   FRENCH ▬   GERMAN ▭   RUSSIAN ▭   SPANISH ▭   OTHER ▬

FREQUENCY	COUNTRY, STATION, LOCATION	TARGET • NETWORK • POWER (kW)

World Time
0 1 2 3 4 5 6 7 8 9 10 11 12 13 14 15 16 17 18 19 20 21 22 23 24

9455 (con'd)	USA
	†CHRIST SCI MONITOR, South Carolina	(J) Sa/Su • W North Am • 500 kW
		(J) Tu-F • W North Am • 500 kW
	CHRIST SCI MONITOR, Via Saipan	E Asia • 100 kW
	VOA, Greenville, NC	C America & S America • 500 kW
		(D) • C America & S America • 250 kW
		(J) • C America & S America • 250 kW
9460	TURKEY
	†VOICE OF TURKEY, Ankara	TURKISH • Europe & E North Am • 500 kW
9465	CROATIA
	CROATIAN RADIO, Via WHRI, USA	E North Am • 100 kW
	NORTHERN MARIANA IS	E Europe & W Asia • 100 kW
	†KFBS-FAR EAST BC, Saipan Island	F-Tu • E Europe & W Asia • 100 kW
		M-Sa • E Europe & W Asia • 100 kW
		Su • E Europe & W Asia • 100 kW
		W/Th • E Europe & W Asia • 100 kW
	USA
	CHRIST SCI MONITOR, South Carolina	E North Am & C America • 500 kW
		Sa • E North Am & C America • 500 kW
		Su • E North Am & C America • 500 kW
	FAMILY RADIO, Via Taiwan	E Asia • 250 kW
	†VOA, Delano, California	C America & S America • 250 kW
	WMLK, Bethel, Pa	Su-F • Europe, Mideast & N America • 50 kW
	WORLD HARVEST R, Noblesville,Indiana	E North Am • 100 kW
9470	RUSSIA
	†GOLOS ROSSII	(D)
	†R MOSCOW INTL, Armavir	(D) • C America & S America • 1000 kW
	†R MOSCOW INTL, Moscow	(J) • Europe • 500 kW
	†RADIO MOSCOW, Novosibirsk	(D) • DS-MAYAK • 100 kW
	†RADIO MOSCOW, Via Byelarus	(J) • DS-MAYAK • 100 kW
9475	EGYPT
	RADIO CAIRO, Kafr Silim-Abis	N America • 250 kW
	NORTHERN MARIANA IS
	KFBS-FAR EAST BC, Saipan Island	W Africa • RELAY ELWA • 100 kW
	PHILIPPINES
	†FEBC RADIO INTL, Bocaue	E Asia • 100 kW
9475v	CLANDESTINE (AFRICA)
	"RADIO MOGADISHU", Somalia	Irr • E Africa • USB
9480	ARMENIA
	RADIO YEREVAN	(D) • ARMENIAN • Europe
		(D) • Europe
	RADIO YEREVAN, Yerevan	(D) • ARMENIAN • S America • 240 kW
		(D) • S America • 240 kW
	CHINA (PR)
	CHINA RADIO INTL, Beijing	E Asia • 120 kW
	CHINA RADIO INTL, Xi'an	Mideast • 120 kW S America • 120 kW
	MONACO
	†TRANS WORLD RADIO, Monte Carlo	(J) • W Europe • 100 kW • ALT. FREQ. TO 7240 kHz
		Su • W Europe • 100 kW • ALT. FREQ. TO 7240 kHz
	RUSSIA
	†R MOSCOW INTL	(D) • Europe
	†R MOSCOW INTL, Novosibirsk	(D) • E Asia • 100 kW
		E Asia • 100 kW
		(J) • E Asia • 100 kW
	R MOSCOW INTL, Via Armenia	(D) • S America • 240 kW
	†RADIO MOSCOW, Kaliningrad	(J) • DS-MAYAK • 100 kW
9485	CZECH REPUBLIC
	†RADIO PRAGUE, Litomyšl	E North Am • 100 kW
		S America • 100 kW
	PAKISTAN
	†RADIO PAKISTAN, Islamabad	Mideast & N Africa • 100 kW
9486	PERU
	RADIO TACNA, Tacna	Su • DS • 0.18 kW
9490	CZECH REPUBLIC
	†RADIO PRAGUE, Litomyšl	Europe • 100 kW
	MONACO
	†TRANS WORLD RADIO, Monte Carlo	E Europe • 100 kW
		M-Sa • E Europe • 100 kW
		Sa • E Europe • 100 kW
		Sa/Su • E Europe • 100 kW
		Th-M • E Europe • 100 kW

(con'd)

0 1 2 3 4 5 6 7 8 9 10 11 12 13 14 15 16 17 18 19 20 21 22 23 24

FREQUENCY	COUNTRY, STATION, LOCATION	TARGET • NETWORK • POWER (kW)	World Time

9490 **RUSSIA**
(con'd) †R MOSCOW INTL — (D) • W Africa & S America

†RADIO MOSCOW, Samara — DS-1 • 100 kW

†RADIO NADEZHDA, Samara — DS • 100 kW

9490.2 **CHINA (PR)**
XIZANG PEOPLES BS, Lhasa — DS • 50 kW

9495 **CROATIA**
CROATIAN RADIO, Via WHRI, USA — Americas • 100 kW

FRANCE
†R FRANCE INTL, Issoudun-Allouis — (J) • E Europe • 500 kW

GUAM
†ADVENTIST WORLD R, Agat — E Asia • 100 kW
Sa/Su • E Asia • 100 kW

MONACO
†TRANS WORLD RADIO, Monte Carlo — (J) • E Europe • 100 kW
(J) M-Sa • E Europe • 100 kW
(J) M/Tu/Th/F • E Europe • 100 kW
(J) Tu/Th • E Europe • 100 kW

NORTHERN MARIANA IS
†KFBS-FAR EAST BC, Saipan Island — E Asia • 100 kW
C Asia & W Asia • 100 kW

PHILIPPINES
†FEBC RADIO INTL, Bocaue — SE Asia • 100 kW

USA
CHRIST SCI MONITOR, South Carolina — E North Am • 500 kW
M-F • E North Am • 500 kW
Sa/Su • E North Am • 500 kW

WORLD HARVEST R, Noblesville, Indiana — Americas • 100 kW
M-F • Americas • 100 kW
M • Americas • 100 kW
Sa/Su • Americas • 100 kW
Tu-Su • Americas • 100 kW

9500 **RUSSIA**
†AMUR RADIO, Blagoveshchensk — DS • 50 kW

SWAZILAND
TRANS WORLD RADIO, Manzini — Alternative Frequency to 9620 kHz

UKRAINE
†RADIO UKRAINE — (J)
(J) • UKRAINIAN

VATICAN STATE
†VATICAN RADIO, Sta Maria di Galeria — E Asia • 100 kW

9504.8 **PERU**
†RADIO TACNA, Tacna — Su • DS • 0.18 kW
M-Sa • DS • 0.18 kW
Tu-Su • DS • 0.18 kW

9505 **BRAZIL**
RADIO RECORD, São Paulo — Irr • PORTUGUESE • DS • 7.5 kW
PORTUGUESE • DS • 7.5 kW

CANADA
R CANADA INTL, Via Germany — (D) • Mideast • 500 kW

†R CANADA INTL, Via Vienna, Austria — (D) • Mideast • 300 kW

CHINA (PR)
†VO THE STRAIT-PLA, Fuzhou — TAIWAN-2 • 50 kW

CZECH REPUBLIC
†RADIO PRAGUE, Via Slovakia — Europe • 100 kW

KAZAKHSTAN
†KAZAKH RADIO, Almaty — DS-2 • 100 kW

†RADIO ALMATY, Almaty — 100 kW

KOREA (DPR)
†RADIO PYONGYANG, Pyongyang — JAPANESE • E Asia • 200 kW
KOREAN • E Asia • 200 kW

RUSSIA
†R MOSCOW INTL — (J)

SLOVAKIA
†R SLOVAKIA INTL, Vel'ké Kostolany — W Europe • 100 kW

UNITED ARAB EMIRATES
†UAE RADIO, Abu Dhabi — (D) • N America • 500 kW

USA
RFE-RL, Various Locations — E Europe • 100/500 kW

†RFE-RL, Via Pals, Spain — (D) • W Asia & C Asia • 250 kW

†RFE-RL, Via Portugal — E Europe • 250/500 kW

VOA, Via Morocco — (J) • E Europe • 100 kW

†VOA, Via Philippines — (D) • SE Asia • 100 kW

†WYFR-FAMILY RADIO, Okeechobee, Fl — W North Am • 100 kW

YUGOSLAVIA
†RADIO BEOGRAD, Belgrade — Europe, N Africa & Mideast • DS-JU RADIO • 100 kW
ENGLISH, GERMAN, FRENCH, ETC • Europe, N Africa & Mideast • DS-JU RADIO • 100 kW

†RADIO YUGOSLAVIA, Belgrade — W Europe • 250 kW
W Europe & E North Am • 500 kW

(con'd)

ENGLISH ▬▬ ARABIC ≋≋ CHINESE ▫▫▫ FRENCH ▬ GERMAN ▬ RUSSIAN ═ SPANISH ▬ OTHER ▬

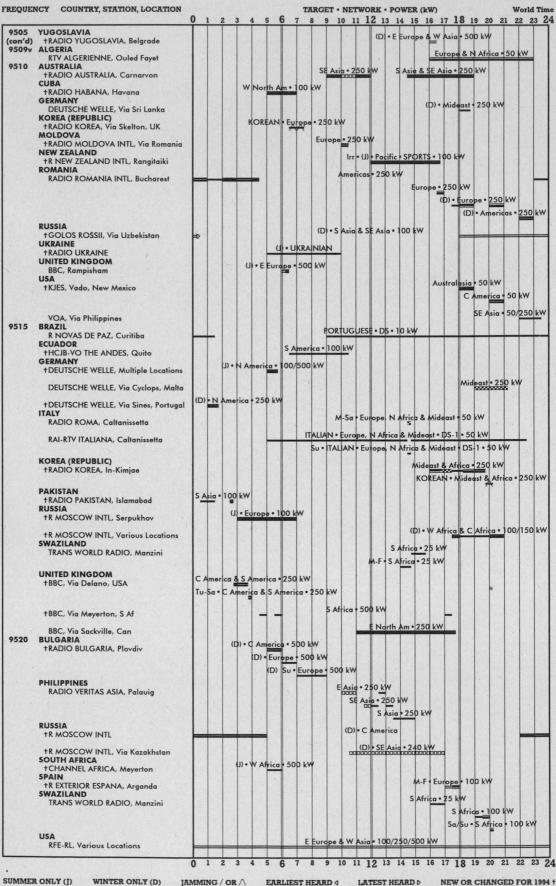

FREQUENCY   COUNTRY, STATION, LOCATION

FREQUENCY   COUNTRY, STATION, LOCATION

TARGET • NETWORK • POWER (kW)

World Time

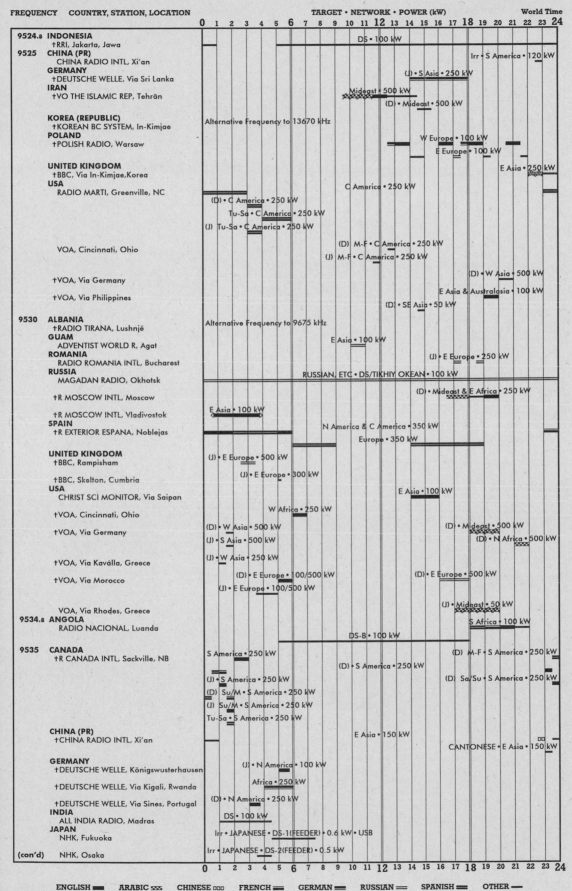

FREQUENCY	COUNTRY, STATION, LOCATION	Target • Network • Power
9524.8	**INDONESIA** †RRI, Jakarta, Jawa	DS • 100 kW
9525	**CHINA (PR)** CHINA RADIO INTL, Xi'an	Irr • S America • 120 kW
	GERMANY †DEUTSCHE WELLE, Via Sri Lanka	(J) • S Asia • 250 kW
	IRAN †VO THE ISLAMIC REP, Tehrän	Mideast • 500 kW / (D) • Mideast • 500 kW
	KOREA (REPUBLIC) †KOREAN BC SYSTEM, In-Kimjae	Alternative Frequency to 13670 kHz
	POLAND †POLISH RADIO, Warsaw	W Europe • 100 kW / E Europe • 100 kW
	UNITED KINGDOM †BBC, Via In-Kimjae, Korea	E Asia • 250 kW
	USA RADIO MARTI, Greenville, NC	C America • 250 kW / (D) • C America • 250 kW / Tu-Sa • C America • 250 kW / (J) Tu-Sa • C America • 250 kW
	VOA, Cincinnati, Ohio	(D) M-F • C America • 250 kW / (J) M-F • C America • 250 kW
	†VOA, Via Germany	(D) • W Asia • 500 kW
	†VOA, Via Philippines	E Asia & Australasia • 100 kW / (D) • SE Asia • 50 kW
9530	**ALBANIA** †RADIO TIRANA, Lushnjë	Alternative Frequency to 9675 kHz
	GUAM ADVENTIST WORLD R, Agat	E Asia • 100 kW
	ROMANIA RADIO ROMANIA INTL, Bucharest	(J) • E Europe • 250 kW
	RUSSIA MAGADAN RADIO, Okhotsk	RUSSIAN, ETC • DS/TIKHIY OKEAN • 100 kW
	†R MOSCOW INTL, Moscow	(D) • Mideast & E Africa • 250 kW
	†R MOSCOW INTL, Vladivostok	E Asia • 100 kW
	SPAIN †R EXTERIOR ESPANA, Noblejas	N America & C America • 350 kW / Europe • 350 kW
	UNITED KINGDOM †BBC, Rampisham	(J) • E Europe • 500 kW
	†BBC, Skelton, Cumbria	(J) • E Europe • 300 kW
	USA CHRIST SCI MONITOR, Via Saipan	E Asia • 100 kW
	†VOA, Cincinnati, Ohio	W Africa • 250 kW
	†VOA, Via Germany	(D) • W Asia • 500 kW / (D) • Mideast • 500 kW / (J) • S Asia • 500 kW / (D) • N Africa • 500 kW
	†VOA, Via Kaválla, Greece	(J) • W Asia • 250 kW
	†VOA, Via Morocco	(D) • E Europe • 100/500 kW / (D) • E Europe • 500 kW / (J) • E Europe • 100/500 kW
	VOA, Via Rhodes, Greece	(J) • Mideast • 50 kW
9534.8	**ANGOLA** RADIO NACIONAL, Luanda	S Africa • 100 kW / DS-B • 100 kW
9535	**CANADA** †R CANADA INTL, Sackville, NB	S America • 250 kW / (D) M-F • S America • 250 kW / (D) • S America • 250 kW / (D) Sa/Su • S America • 250 kW / (J) • S America • 250 kW / (D) Su/M • S America • 250 kW / (J) Su/M • S America • 250 kW / Tu-Sa • S America • 250 kW
	CHINA (PR) †CHINA RADIO INTL, Xi'an	E Asia • 150 kW / CANTONESE • E Asia • 150 kW
	GERMANY †DEUTSCHE WELLE, Königswusterhausen	(J) • N America • 100 kW
	†DEUTSCHE WELLE, Via Kigali, Rwanda	Africa • 250 kW
	†DEUTSCHE WELLE, Via Sines, Portugal	(D) • N America • 250 kW
	INDIA ALL INDIA RADIO, Madras	DS • 100 kW
	JAPAN NHK, Fukuoka	Irr • JAPANESE • DS-1 (FEEDER) • 0.6 kW • USB
(con'd)	NHK, Osaka	Irr • JAPANESE • DS-2 (FEEDER) • 0.5 kW

ENGLISH ■■ ARABIC ▩▩ CHINESE □□□ FRENCH ══ GERMAN ▬▬ RUSSIAN ══ SPANISH ══ OTHER ──

FREQUENCY   COUNTRY, STATION, LOCATION   TARGET • NETWORK • POWER (kW)   World Time

World Time scale: 0 1 2 3 4 5 6 7 8 9 10 11 12 13 14 15 16 17 18 19 20 21 22 23 24

Frequency	Country / Station / Location	Target • Network • Power
9535 (con'd)	**JAPAN** — NHK, Sapporo	Irr • JAPANESE • DS-1 (FEEDER) • 0.6 kW
	†RADIO JAPAN/NHK, Tokyo-Yamata	(D) • JAPANESE • W North Am • GENERAL • 300 kW
		(D) • W North Am • GENERAL • 300 kW
		(J) • JAPANESE • S Asia • GENERAL • 300 kW
	RADIO JAPAN/NHK, Via Sri Lanka	S Asia • 300 kW
		JAPANESE • S Asia • GENERAL • 300 kW
		S Asia • GENERAL • 300 kW
	PHILIPPINES — †RADIO VERITAS ASIA, Palauig	(D) • SE Asia • 250 kW
	SWITZERLAND — †SWISS RADIO INTL, Lenk	Europe & N Africa • 250 kW
		ITALIAN • Europe & N Africa • 250 kW
		M-F • Europe & N Africa • 250 kW
		M-F • ITALIAN • Europe & N Africa • 250 kW
		GERMAN, FRENCH & ITALIAN • Europe & N Africa • 250 kW
		M-F • GERMAN, FRENCH & ITALIAN • Europe & N Africa • 250 kW
	USA — †RFE-RL, Via Germany	(J) • E Europe & W Asia • 100 kW
	VOA, Via Kaválla, Greece	(J) • E Europe & W Asia • 250 kW
	†VOA, Via Morocco	(D) • E Europe • 100/500 kW
	†VOA, Via Philippines	(J) • SE Asia • 100 kW
9535v	**ALGERIA** — RTV ALGERIENNE, Bouchaoui	E Africa • 100 kW
9540	**AUSTRALIA** — †RADIO AUSTRALIA, Carnarvon	SE Asia • 250 kW
	†RADIO AUSTRALIA, Shepparton	(D) • E Asia • 100 kW
	BRAZIL — R EDUCADORA BAHIA, Salvador	PORTUGUESE • DS • 10 kW
	CLANDESTINE (AFRICA) — "VO OROMO LIBER'N", Sudan	E Africa • ALT. FREQ. TO 11705 kHz
	POLAND — †POLISH RADIO, Warsaw	W Europe • 100 kW
		N Europe • 100 kW
		POLISH • W Europe • 100 kW
	RUSSIA — †R MOSCOW INTL, Petropavlovsk-K	(D) • N Pacific & W North Am • 250 kW
	†R TIKHIY OKEAN, Petropavlovsk-K	(D) • N Pacific & W North Am • 250 kW
	†RADIO MOSCOW, Moscow	(D) • DS-1 • 100 kW
	SOMALIA — †RADIO MANTA, Mogadishu	DS • 0.6 kW • USB
	USA — †RFE-RL, Via Germany	(D) • W Asia • 100/250 kW
	VOA, Via Kaválla, Greece	(J) • W Asia & S Asia • 250 kW
	UZBEKISTAN — RADIO TASHKENT, Tashkent	(D) • S Asia • 100 kW
	†UZBEK RADIO, Tashkent	Mideast • DS-2 • 100 kW
	VENEZUELA — †RADIO NACIONAL, Caracas	M-Sa • SPANISH, ENGLISH & FRENCH • C America • 50 kW
		Tu-Su • SPANISH, ENGLISH & FRENCH • C America • 50 kW
9545	**GERMANY** — †DEUTSCHE WELLE, Jülich	(D) • S America • 100 kW
		(D) • E North Am • 100 kW
	†DEUTSCHE WELLE, Multiple Locations	C America & S America • 100/500 kW
		Europe • 100/250/500 kW
		Europe & Mideast • 100/250/500 kW
		(D) • Africa • 100/500 kW
	†DEUTSCHE WELLE, Nauen	(J) • E Europe • 500 kW
	†DEUTSCHE WELLE, Via Antigua	(D) • N America & C America • 250 kW
	DEUTSCHE WELLE, Via Sackville, Can	(D) • N America • 250 kW
	RUSSIA — †RADIO MOSCOW, Khabarovsk	DS-MAYAK • 50 kW
	SOLOMON ISLANDS — †SOLOMON ISLANDS BC, Honiara	Su • DS-ENGLISH, PIDGIN • 10 kW
		Sa • DS-ENGLISH, PIDGIN • 10 kW
		M-F • DS-ENGLISH, PIDGIN • 10 kW
	USA — VOA, Via Philippines	E Asia • 250 kW
	UZBEKISTAN — †UZBEK RADIO, Tashkent	(D) • DS-2 • 100 kW
9545v	**PAKISTAN** — PAKISTAN BC CORP, Islamabad	DS • 10 kW
9546v	**MEXICO** — LV DE VERACRUZ, Veracruz	Irr • DS • 0.25 kW

World Time scale: 0 1 2 3 4 5 6 7 8 9 10 11 12 13 14 15 16 17 18 19 20 21 22 23 24

FREQUENCY   COUNTRY, STATION, LOCATION   TARGET • NETWORK • POWER (kW)   World Time

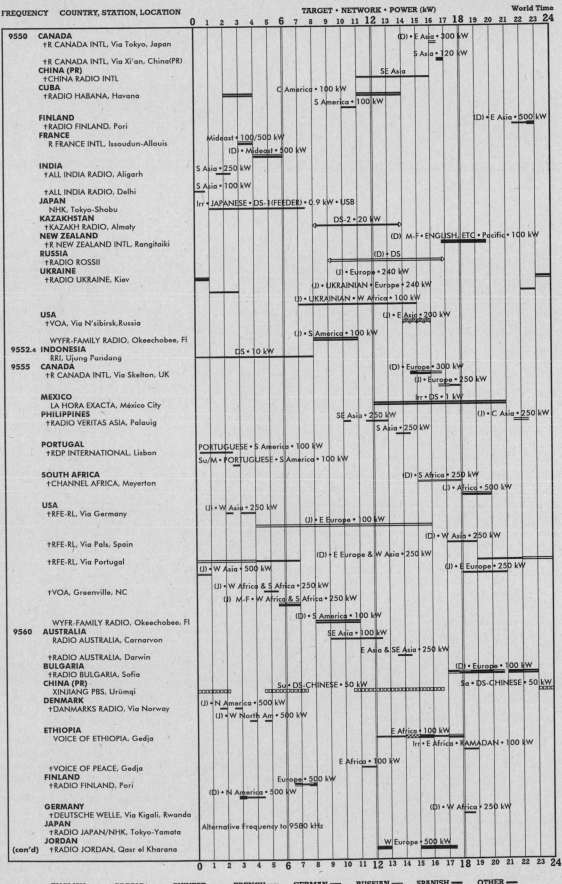

FREQUENCY	COUNTRY, STATION, LOCATION	TARGET • NETWORK • POWER (kW)
9550	CANADA	
	†R CANADA INTL, Via Tokyo, Japan	(D) • E Asia • 300 kW
	†R CANADA INTL, Via Xi'an, China(PR)	S Asia • 120 kW
	CHINA (PR)	
	†CHINA RADIO INTL	SE Asia
	CUBA	
	†RADIO HABANA, Havana	C America • 100 kW
		S America • 100 kW
	FINLAND	
	†RADIO FINLAND, Pori	(D) • E Asia • 500 kW
	FRANCE	
	R FRANCE INTL, Issoudun-Allouis	Mideast • 100/500 kW
		(D) • Mideast • 500 kW
	INDIA	
	†ALL INDIA RADIO, Aligarh	S Asia • 250 kW
	†ALL INDIA RADIO, Delhi	S Asia • 100 kW
	JAPAN	
	NHK, Tokyo-Shobu	Irr • JAPANESE • DS-1 (FEEDER) • 0.9 kW • USB
	KAZAKHSTAN	
	†KAZAKH RADIO, Almaty	DS-2 • 20 kW
	NEW ZEALAND	
	†R NEW ZEALAND INTL, Rangitaiki	(D) • M-F • ENGLISH, ETC • Pacific • 100 kW
	RUSSIA	
	†RADIO ROSSII	(D) • DS
	UKRAINE	
	†RADIO UKRAINE, Kiev	(J) • Europe • 240 kW
		(J) • UKRAINIAN • Europe • 240 kW
		(J) • UKRAINIAN • W Africa • 100 kW
	USA	
	†VOA, Via N'sibirsk, Russia	(J) • E Asia • 200 kW
	WYFR-FAMILY RADIO, Okeechobee, Fl	(J) • S America • 100 kW
9552.4	INDONESIA	
	RRI, Ujung Pandang	DS • 10 kW
9555	CANADA	
	†R CANADA INTL, Via Skelton, UK	(D) • Europe • 300 kW
		(J) • Europe • 250 kW
	MEXICO	
	LA HORA EXACTA, México City	Irr • DS • 1 kW
	PHILIPPINES	
	†RADIO VERITAS ASIA, Palauig	SE Asia • 250 kW
		(J) • C Asia • 250 kW
		S Asia • 250 kW
	PORTUGAL	
	†RDP INTERNATIONAL, Lisbon	PORTUGUESE • S America • 100 kW
		Su/M • PORTUGUESE • S America • 100 kW
	SOUTH AFRICA	
	†CHANNEL AFRICA, Meyerton	(D) • S Africa • 250 kW
		(J) • Africa • 500 kW
	USA	
	†RFE-RL, Via Germany	(J) • W Asia • 250 kW
		(J) • E Europe • 100 kW
	†RFE-RL, Via Pals, Spain	(D) • W Asia • 250 kW
	†RFE-RL, Via Portugal	(D) • E Europe & W Asia • 250 kW
		(J) • W Asia • 500 kW
		(J) • E Europe • 250 kW
	†VOA, Greenville, NC	(J) • W Africa & S Africa • 250 kW
		(J) • M-F • W Africa & S Africa • 250 kW
	WYFR-FAMILY RADIO, Okeechobee, Fl	(D) • S America • 100 kW
9560	AUSTRALIA	
	RADIO AUSTRALIA, Carnarvon	SE Asia • 100 kW
		E Asia & SE Asia • 250 kW
	†RADIO AUSTRALIA, Darwin	
	BULGARIA	
	†RADIO BULGARIA, Sofia	(D) • Europe • 100 kW
	CHINA (PR)	
	XINJIANG PBS, Urümqi	Su • DS-CHINESE • 50 kW Sa • DS-CHINESE • 50 kW
	DENMARK	
	†DANMARKS RADIO, Via Norway	(J) • N America • 500 kW
		(J) • W North Am • 500 kW
	ETHIOPIA	
	VOICE OF ETHIOPIA, Gedja	E Africa • 100 kW
		Irr • E Africa • RAMADAN • 100 kW
	†VOICE OF PEACE, Gedja	E Africa • 100 kW
	FINLAND	
	†RADIO FINLAND, Pori	Europe • 500 kW
		(D) • N America • 500 kW
	GERMANY	
	†DEUTSCHE WELLE, Via Kigali, Rwanda	(D) • W Africa • 250 kW
	JAPAN	
	†RADIO JAPAN/NHK, Tokyo-Yamata	Alternative Frequency to 9580 kHz
	JORDAN	
(con'd)	†RADIO JORDAN, Qasr el Kharana	W Europe • 500 kW

FREQUENCY   COUNTRY, STATION, LOCATION

TARGET • NETWORK • POWER (kW)   World Time

0 1 2 3 4 5 6 7 8 9 10 11 12 13 14 15 16 17 18 19 20 21 22 23 24

9560 **JORDAN**
(con'd)   †RADIO JORDAN, Qasr el Kharana — (D) • W Europe & E North Am • 500 kW
NORWAY
†RADIO NORWAY INTL, Sveio — (J) • W North Am • 500 kW
(J) M • N America • 500 kW
(J) M • W North Am • 500 kW
(J) Tu-Su • N America • 500 kW
(J) Tu/Su • W North Am • 500 kW

PHILIPPINES
†RADIO VERITAS ASIA, Palauig — (D) • S Asia • 250 kW   SE Asia • 250 kW
(D) • S Asia & SE Asia • 250 kW   (D) • SE Asia • 250 kW

RUSSIA
†FEBC RUSSIA, Khabarovsk — (J) • E Asia • 20 kW

†GOLOS ROSSII, Kazan' — (D) • S Africa • 240 kW
SWITZERLAND
†SWISS RADIO INTL, Schwarzenburg — Alternative Frequency to 9885 kHz
TURKEY
†VOICE OF TURKEY, Ankara — TURKISH • Australasia • 500 kW
UKRAINE
†RADIO UKRAINE, L'vov — UKRAINIAN • W Asia • 240 kW
(J) • W Asia • 240 kW   (D) • UKRAINIAN • W Asia • 240 kW
(J) • UKRAINIAN • W Asia • 240 kW

UNITED KINGDOM
BBC, Via Ascension — (D) • S America • 250 kW
(J) • S America • 250 kW

†BBC, Via Zyyi, Cyprus — (D) • E Europe • 250 kW
(J) • E Europe • 250 kW

USA
†VOA, Via Thailand — (D) • SE Asia • 500 kW
(D) • S Asia • 500 kW

9565 **BANGLADESH**
†RADIO BANGLADESH, Dhaka — Europe • 250 kW • ALT. FREQ. TO 9570 kHz
BANGLA • Europe • 250 kW • ALT. FREQ. TO 9570 kHz

BRAZIL
RADIO UNIVERSO, Curitiba — PORTUGUESE • DS • 7.5 kW
DENMARK
†DANMARKS RADIO, Via Norway — (D) • W North Am • 500 kW
(D) • N America • 500 kW

GERMANY
†DEUTSCHE WELLE, Jülich — (D) • Americas • 100 kW

†DEUTSCHE WELLE, Multiple Locations — (D) • Americas • 100/250 kW

DEUTSCHE WELLE, Via Kigali, Rwanda — S Africa • 250 kW
C Africa & E Africa • 250 kW

†DEUTSCHE WELLE, Via Sines, Portugal — (D) • N Africa • 250 kW
(J) • Mideast • 250 kW

INDIA
†ALL INDIA RADIO, Delhi — S Asia & E Asia • 50 kW   Irr • DS • 50 kW
DS • 50 kW
ENGLISH, ETC • DS • 50 kW

NORWAY
†RADIO NORWAY INTL, Sveio — (D) • N America • 500 kW
(D) M • W North Am • 500 kW
(D) Tu-Su • W North Am • 500 kW

RUSSIA
†R MOSCOW INTL, Irkutsk — (D) • W Asia & S Asia • 240 kW
SEYCHELLES
FAR EAST BC ASS'N, North Pt, Mahé Is — C Africa & S Africa • 100 kW
Th-M • C Africa & S Africa • 100 kW

USA
†RFE-RL, Via Germany — (D) • E Europe & W Asia • 100/250 kW
(J) • E Europe • 100 kW
(J) Sa/Su • E Europe • 100 kW

†RFE-RL, Via Portugal — (D) • E Europe • 500 kW
(D) • W Asia • 250 kW
(J) • E Europe • 500 kW

VOICE OF THE OAS, Cincinnati, Ohio — C America & S America • 250 kW
M-Sa • C America & S America • 250 kW
Su • C America & S America • 250 kW

9565.3 **GEORGIA**
†RADIO GEORGIA, Tbilisi — (D) • E Europe & N Europe • 100 kW
9570 **BANGLADESH**
†RADIO BANGLADESH, Dhaka — Alternative Frequency to 9565 kHz
CHINA (PR)
CHINA RADIO INTL, Xi'an — E Africa & S Africa • 300 kW
CLANDESTINE (M EAST)
(con'd)   "VO IRAQI PEOPLE", Saudi Arabia — Mideast • ANTI-SADDAM • ALT. FREQ. TO 9575 kHz

0 1 2 3 4 5 6 7 8 9 10 11 12 13 14 15 16 17 18 19 20 21 22 23 24

SUMMER ONLY (J)   WINTER ONLY (D)   JAMMING / OR ⋀   EARLIEST HEARD ◁   LATEST HEARD ▷   NEW OR CHANGED FOR 1994 †

FREQUENCY   COUNTRY, STATION, LOCATION

TARGET • NETWORK • POWER (kW)

World Time

0 1 2 3 4 5 6 7 8 9 10 11 12 13 14 15 16 17 18 19 20 21 22 23 24

9570 (con'd)	GERMANY	
	DEUTSCHE WELLE, Nauen	(D) • E Asia • 500 kW
	KOREA (REPUBLIC)	
	†RADIO KOREA, In-Kimjae	KOREAN • S America • 250 kW
		S America • 250 kW
		SE Asia • 250 kW
		KOREAN • SE Asia • 250 kW
	NIGERIA	
	RADIO NIGERIA, Kaduna	ENGLISH, ETC • DS-2 • 50 kW
	PORTUGAL	
	RDP INTERNATIONAL, Lisbon	PORTUGUESE • E North Am • 100 kW
		Su/M • PORTUGUESE • E North Am • 100 kW
		Tu-Sa • E North Am • 100 kW
	ROMANIA	
	RADIO ROMANIA INTL, Bucharest	Americas • 250 kW
		Su • Atlantic • MARINERS • 250 kW
		(D) • E Europe • 250 kW
		(D) • Europe • 250 kW
		(J) • Mideast • 120 kW (D) • Americas • 250 kW
	RUSSIA	
	†RADIO MOSCOW, Via Byelarus	DS-2 • 150/240 kW
		(J) • DS-2 • 150 kW
	UNITED KINGDOM	
	BBC, Via Singapore	SE Asia • 100/250 kW
	USA	
	†VOA, Via Portugal	(D) • E Europe • 250 kW
9575	CLANDESTINE (M EAST)	
	"VO IRAQI PEOPLE", Saudi Arabia	Alternative Frequency to 9570 kHz
	ITALY	
	†RADIO ROMA, Rome	ITALIAN • E North Am • 100 kW
		E North Am • 100 kW W Europe • 100 kW Mideast • 100 kW
		ITALIAN • S America • 100 kW E Europe • 100 kW
		S America • 100 kW ITALIAN • Europe • 100 kW
		(J) • ITALIAN • Europe, N Africa & Mideast • 100 kW Europe • 100 kW
		(J) • E Europe • 100 kW
		(J) • Europe, Mideast & N Africa • 100 kW (J) • W Europe & N Africa • 100 kW
	MOROCCO	
	†RADIO MEDI UN, Nador	FRENCH & ARABIC • Europe & N Africa • 250 kW
	PORTUGAL	
	RADIO RENASCENCA, Muge	Su • Europe • 100 kW
	RUSSIA	
	†R MOSCOW INTL, Via Kazakhstan	(D) • E Africa & S Africa • 1000 kW
	USA	
	†R FREE AFGHANISTAN, Via Germany	(J) • W Asia & S Asia • 100 kW
	†RFE-RL, Via Germany	(D) • W Asia & C Asia • 100 kW
	†RFE-RL, Via Pals, Spain	(J) • W Asia • 250 kW
	†VOA, Cincinnati, Ohio	N Africa • 250 kW
	†VOA, Via Morocco	(D) • Europe • 500 kW
	†VOA, Via Philippines	SE Asia • 50 kW
		E Asia • 250 kW
		(D) • S Asia • 250 kW
	†WYFR-FAMILY RADIO, Okeechobee, Fl	(D) • S America • 100 kW
9580	ALBANIA	
	†RADIO TIRANA, Lushnjë	N America • 100 kW
		C America • 100 kW
	AUSTRALIA	
	†RADIO AUSTRALIA, Shepparton	Pacific & N America • 100 kW
	GABON	
	AFRIQUE NUMERO UN, Moyabi	C Africa • 250 kW
	GERMANY	
	†DEUTSCHE WELLE, Via Sines, Portugal	(J) • S America • 250 kW
	JAPAN	
	†RADIO JAPAN/NHK, Tokyo-Yamata	Mideast • 300 kW • ALT. FREQ. TO 9560 kHz
		(D) • E Asia • 100 kW
		(J) • E Asia • 100 kW
	RUSSIA	
	†GOLOS ROSSII, Kazan'	(D) • Europe & Atlantic • 250 kW
	†R MOSCOW INTL, Kaliningrad	(J) • W Africa • 150 kW
	†R MOSCOW INTL, Kazan'	(J) • Europe • 250 kW
	†R MOSCOW INTL, Tula	(D) • Europe • 250 kW
	SAUDI ARABIA	
	BS OF THE KINGDOM, Jiddah	Mideast & E Africa • DS-2 • 50 kW
	SLOVAKIA	
	†R SLOVAKIA INTL, Rimavská Sobota	S America • 250 kW
	UNITED KINGDOM	
(con'd)	†BBC, Via Hong Kong	E Asia • 250 kW

0 1 2 3 4 5 6 7 8 9 10 11 12 13 14 15 16 17 18 19 20 21 22 23 24

ENGLISH ▬▬   ARABIC ⧖⧖⧖   CHINESE □□□   FRENCH ══   GERMAN ▬▬   RUSSIAN ══   SPANISH ▬▬   OTHER —

FREQUENCY   COUNTRY, STATION, LOCATION — TARGET • NETWORK • POWER (kW) — World Time

9580 **UNITED KINGDOM**	
(con'd) †BBC, Via Maṣīrah, Oman	S Asia • 100 kW
	(D) • W Asia & S Asia • 100 kW
†BBC, Via Singapore	(J) • SE Asia • 100 kW
USA	
VOA, Via Woofferton, UK	N Africa • 300 kW
YUGOSLAVIA	
†RADIO YUGOSLAVIA, Belgrade	E North Am • 500 kW
	W North Am • 500 kW
9585 **BRAZIL**	
RADIO CBN, São Paulo	Irr • PORTUGUESE • DS • 10 kW
	PORTUGUESE • DS • 10 kW
EQUATORIAL GUINEA	
RADIO EAST AFRICA, Bata	Sa/Su • E Africa • 50 kW
GERMANY	
†DEUTSCHE WELLE, Multiple Locations	(D) • S Asia • 100/500 kW
RUSSIA	
†RADIO MOSCOW, Moscow	DS-2 • 150 kW
SOUTH AFRICA	
†CHANNEL AFRICA, Meyerton	(D) Sa/Su • S Africa • 100 kW
UNITED KINGDOM	
BBC, Rampisham	(D) • E Europe & W Asia • 500 kW
†BBC, Via Maṣīrah, Oman	(D) • E Europe & W Asia • 100 kW
†BBC, Via Zyyi, Cyprus	(D) • E Europe • 250 kW
	(J) • E Europe & W Asia • 250 kW
USA	
†VOA, Via Germany	(J) • Mideast • 500 kW
†VOA, Via Kaválla, Greece	(J) • W Asia • 250 kW
	(J) • E Europe • 250 kW
†VOA, Via Morocco	(J) • E Europe • 100 kW
†VOA, Via Portugal	(D) • E Europe • 250 kW
	(J) • E Europe • 250 kW
†VOA, Via Woofferton, UK	(D) • Europe • 300 kW
	(J) • Europe • 250 kW
9585.3 GEORGIA	
†RADIO GEORGIA, Tbilisi	(D) • E Europe & N Europe • 100 kW
9590 **DENMARK**	
†DANMARKS RADIO, Via Norway	Europe • 500 kW
	Europe • 350 kW
GUAM	
†KTWR-TRANS WORLD R, Merizo	E Asia • 100 kW
HOLLAND	
†RADIO NEDERLAND, Flevoland	Sa • DUTCH • Europe • 500 kW
RADIO NEDERLAND, Via Madagascar	DUTCH • SE Asia • 300 kW
	SE Asia • 300 kW
RADIO NEDERLAND, Via Neth Antilles	W North Am • 250 kW
JAPAN	
†RADIO JAPAN/NHK, Tokyo-Yamata	E Africa • 300 kW
	(D) • JAPANESE • S Asia • GENERAL • 300 kW
NORWAY	
†RADIO NORWAY INTL, Fredrikstad	Europe • 350 kW
RADIO NORWAY INTL, Kvitsøy	M-Sa • Europe • 500 kW
	Su • Europe • 500 kW
†RADIO NORWAY INTL, Sveio	Europe • 500 kW
ROMANIA	
RADIO ROMANIA INTL, Bucharest	(D) • Mideast • 120 kW
	Su • W Europe & Atlantic • MARINERS • 250 kW
RUSSIA	
†R MOSCOW INTL, Moscow	(D) • Europe • 100 kW
TURKEY	
VOICE OF TURKEY, Ankara	W Asia • 250 kW
UNITED KINGDOM	
BBC, Via Delano, USA	C America • 250 kW
†BBC, Via Maṣīrah, Oman	Mideast & W Asia • 100 kW
BBC, Via Sackville, Can	E North Am • 250 kW
†BBC, Via Zyyi, Cyprus	W Asia • 100/250 kW
USA	
RADIO MARTI, Cincinnati, Ohio	C America • 250 kW
VOA, Greenville, NC	C America • 250 kW
†VOA, Via Philippines	(J) • S Asia & SE Asia • 250 kW
(con'd) †VOA, Via Thailand	(J) • E Asia • 250 kW

FREQUENCY   COUNTRY, STATION, LOCATION

TARGET • NETWORK • POWER (kW)   World Time

0 1 2 3 4 5 6 7 8 9 10 11 12 13 14 15 16 17 18 19 20 21 22 23 24

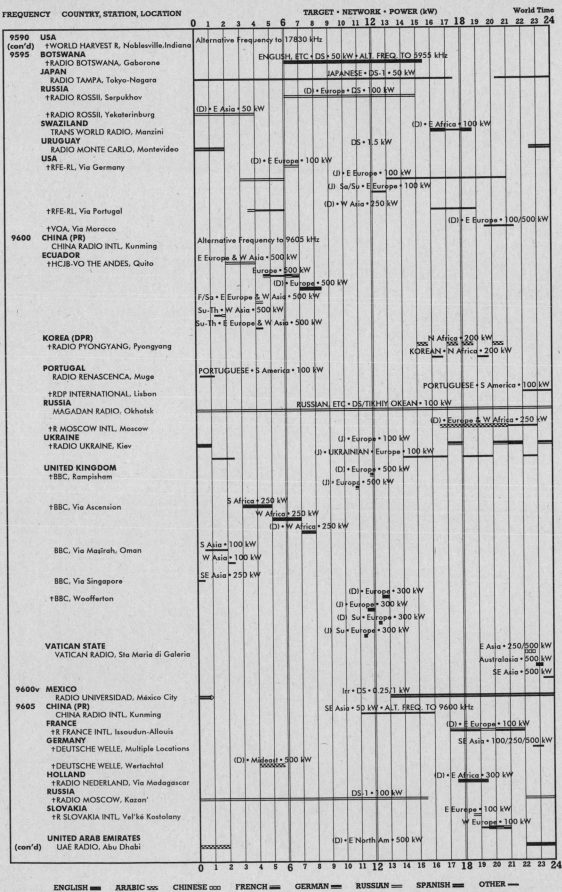

Frequency	Country, Station, Location	Details
9590 (con'd)	USA †WORLD HARVEST R, Noblesville, Indiana	Alternative Frequency to 17830 kHz
9595	BOTSWANA †RADIO BOTSWANA, Gaborone	ENGLISH, ETC • DS • 50 kW • ALT. FREQ. TO 5955 kHz
	JAPAN RADIO TAMPA, Tokyo-Nagara	JAPANESE • DS-1 • 50 kW
	RUSSIA †RADIO ROSSII, Serpukhov	(D) • Europe • DS • 100 kW
	†RADIO ROSSII, Yekaterinburg	(D) • E Asia • 50 kW
	SWAZILAND TRANS WORLD RADIO, Manzini	(D) • E Africa • 100 kW
	URUGUAY RADIO MONTE CARLO, Montevideo	DS • 1.5 kW
	USA †RFE-RL, Via Germany	(D) • E Europe • 100 kW
		(J) • E Europe • 100 kW
		(J) • Sa/Su • E Europe • 100 kW
		(D) • W Asia • 250 kW
	†RFE-RL, Via Portugal	(D) • E Europe • 100/500 kW
	†VOA, Via Morocco	
9600	CHINA (PR) CHINA RADIO INTL, Kunming	Alternative Frequency to 9605 kHz
	ECUADOR †HCJB-VO THE ANDES, Quito	E Europe & W Asia • 500 kW
		Europe • 500 kW
		(D) • Europe • 500 kW
		F/Sa • E Europe & W Asia • 500 kW
		Su-Th • W Asia • 500 kW
		Su-Th • E Europe & W Asia • 500 kW
	KOREA (DPR) †RADIO PYONGYANG, Pyongyang	N Africa • 200 kW
		KOREAN • N Africa • 200 kW
	PORTUGAL RADIO RENASCENCA, Muge	PORTUGUESE • S America • 100 kW
	†RDP INTERNATIONAL, Lisbon	PORTUGUESE • S America • 100 kW
	RUSSIA MAGADAN RADIO, Okhotsk	RUSSIAN, ETC • DS/TIKHIY OKEAN • 100 kW
	†R MOSCOW INTL, Moscow	(D) • Europe & W Africa • 250 kW
	UKRAINE †RADIO UKRAINE, Kiev	(J) • Europe • 100 kW
		(J) • UKRAINIAN • Europe • 100 kW
	UNITED KINGDOM †BBC, Rampisham	(D) • Europe • 500 kW
		(J) • Europe • 500 kW
	†BBC, Via Ascension	S Africa • 250 kW
		W Africa • 250 kW
		(D) • W Africa • 250 kW
	BBC, Via Maṣīrah, Oman	S Asia • 100 kW
		W Asia • 100 kW
	BBC, Via Singapore	SE Asia • 250 kW
	†BBC, Woofferton	(D) • Europe • 300 kW
		(J) • Europe • 300 kW
		(D) Su • Europe • 300 kW
		(J) Su • Europe • 300 kW
	VATICAN STATE VATICAN RADIO, Sta Maria di Galeria	E Asia • 250/500 kW
		Australasia • 500 kW
		SE Asia • 500 kW
9600v	MEXICO RADIO UNIVERSIDAD, México City	Irr • DS • 0.25/1 kW
9605	CHINA (PR) CHINA RADIO INTL, Kunming	SE Asia • 50 kW • ALT. FREQ. TO 9600 kHz
	FRANCE †R FRANCE INTL, Issoudun-Allouis	(D) • E Europe • 100 kW
	GERMANY †DEUTSCHE WELLE, Multiple Locations	SE Asia • 100/250/500 kW
	†DEUTSCHE WELLE, Wertachtal	(D) • Mideast • 500 kW
	HOLLAND †RADIO NEDERLAND, Via Madagascar	(D) • E Africa • 300 kW
	RUSSIA †RADIO MOSCOW, Kazan'	DS-1 • 100 kW
	SLOVAKIA †R SLOVAKIA INTL, Vel'ké Kostolany	E Europe • 100 kW
		W Europe • 100 kW
(con'd)	UNITED ARAB EMIRATES UAE RADIO, Abu Dhabi	(D) • E North Am • 500 kW

0 1 2 3 4 5 6 7 8 9 10 11 12 13 14 15 16 17 18 19 20 21 22 23 24

ENGLISH ▬   ARABIC ▧   CHINESE ▭▭▭   FRENCH ▬   GERMAN ▬   RUSSIAN ═   SPANISH ▬   OTHER ▬

FREQUENCY   COUNTRY, STATION, LOCATION

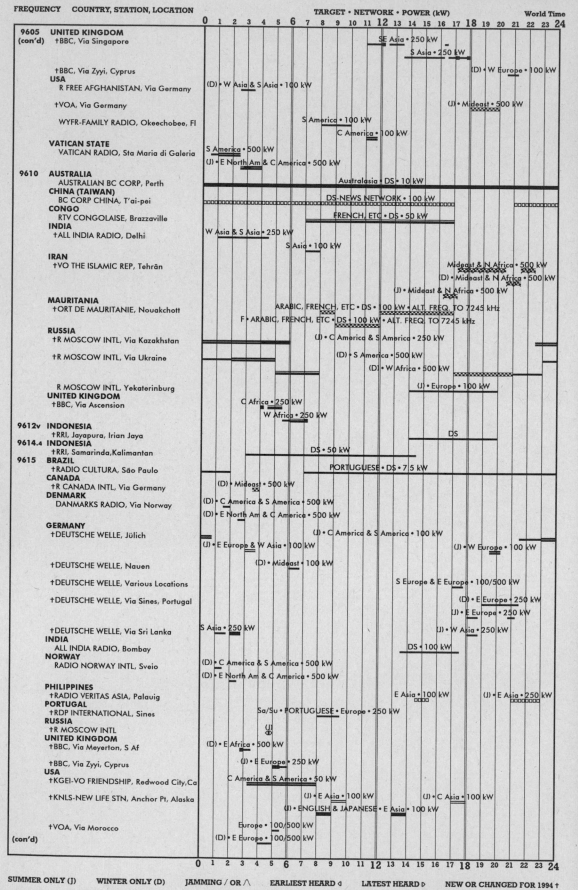

FREQUENCY   COUNTRY, STATION, LOCATION

TARGET • NETWORK • POWER (kW)

World Time

Frequency	Country, Station, Location	Schedule details
9615 (con'd)	USA †VOA, Via Morocco	(D) • Europe • 100/500 kW
	†VOA, Via Thailand	E Asia • 250 kW
	†VOA, Via Woofferton, UK	(D) • Europe • 300 kW
9616	MONGOLIA †RADIO ULAANBAATAR, Ulaanbaatar	Alternative Frequency to 11851v kHz
9618v	MOZAMBIQUE RADIO MOCAMBIQUE, Maputo	DS • 100 kW
	PHILIPPINES DZFM, Marulas	Irr • DS • 2.5 kW
9620	EGYPT RADIO CAIRO, Abu Za'bal	N Africa • DS-GENERAL • 100 kW
	GERMANY †DEUTSCHE WELLE, Via Sri Lanka	(D) • S Asia • 250 kW
	SPAIN †R EXTERIOR ESPANA, Arganda	Europe • 100 kW; M-Sa • Europe • 100 kW; Su • Europe • 100 kW; Sa • Europe • 100 kW; S America • 350 kW
	†R EXTERIOR ESPANA, Noblejas	Sa-Th • S America • 350 kW; F • S America • LADINO • 350 kW
	R EXTERIOR ESPANA, Via Beijing	E Asia • 120 kW
	SWAZILAND TRANS WORLD RADIO, Manzini	(J) • E Africa • 100 kW • ALT. FREQ. TO 9500 kHz
	SWEDEN †RADIO SWEDEN, Hörby	SWEDISH • Europe • 500 kW; Sa • SWEDISH • Europe • 500 kW; Sa/Su • Europe • 500 kW; Sa/Su • SWEDISH • Europe • 500 kW; Su • SWEDISH • Europe • 500 kW
	UKRAINE †UKRAINIAN R, Star'obel'sk	UKRAINIAN • W Asia • DS-2 • 100 kW; (D) • UKRAINIAN • W Asia • DS-2 • 100 kW
	USA VOA, Via Philippines	SE Asia • 50 kW; SE Asia • 250 kW
	YUGOSLAVIA †RADIO YUGOSLAVIA, Belgrade	W Europe • 250 kW
9620.2	URUGUAY SODRE, Montevideo	DS-TEMP INACTIVE • 0.3 kW
9625	BOLIVIA †RADIO FIDES, La Paz	Sa/Su • DS • 15 kW; DS • 15 kW; Tu-Su • DS • 15 kW; Irr • DS • 15 kW
	CANADA CANADIAN BC CORP, Sackville, NB	M • E North Am • DS-NORTHERN • 100 kW; M-F • E North Am • DS-NORTHERN • 100 kW; Tu-Sa • E North Am • DS-NORTHERN • 100 kW; Sa • E North Am • DS-NORTHERN • 100 kW; Su • E North Am • DS-NORTHERN • 100 kW; Sa • ENGLISH & FRENCH • E North Am • DS-NORTHERN • 100 kW; M-F • ENGLISH, FRENCH, ETC • E North Am • DS-NORTHERN • 100 kW
	CHINA (PR) CHINA RADIO INTL, Kunming	S Asia • 120 kW; E Africa & S Africa • 120 kW
	GERMANY DEUTSCHE WELLE, Multiple Locations	(D) • Mideast • 100/250 kW
	ROMANIA †RADIO ROMANIA, Bucharest	Europe • DS-1 (ACTUALITATI) • 125 kW
	RADIO ROMANIA INTL, Bucharest	Europe • 250 kW; E Europe • 250 kW; (D) • Europe • 250 kW; (J) • E Europe • 250 kW
	RUSSIA †GOLOS ROSSII, Kazan'	(D) • Mideast & E Africa • 200 kW
	†GOLOS ROSSII, Omsk	(D) • E Asia & Australasia • 100 kW
	†R MOSCOW INTL, Omsk	(D) • E Asia & Australasia • 100 kW
	†R TIKHIY OKEAN, Omsk	(D) • E Asia & Australasia • 100 kW
	USA †RFE-RL, Via Germany	E Europe • 100 kW; (D) • W Asia • 100 kW; (D) • E Europe • 100 kW; (J) • E Europe • 100 kW
	†RFE-RL, Via Pals, Spain	(J) • W Asia • 250 kW; (J) • E Europe • 250 kW; (J) • E Europe • 250/500 kW
	WYFR-FAMILY RADIO, Okeechobee, Fl	(J) • S America • 100 kW
9630	ALBANIA †RADIO TIRANA, Lushnjë	W Africa • 100 kW; Mideast • 100 kW
(con'd)		

ENGLISH ▬   ARABIC ⌇⌇   CHINESE ▭▭▭   FRENCH ═══   GERMAN ▬▬   RUSSIAN ═══   SPANISH ▬▬   OTHER ——

FREQUENCY   COUNTRY, STATION, LOCATION

TARGET • NETWORK • POWER (kW)

World Time

0 1 2 3 4 5 6 7 8 9 10 11 12 13 14 15 16 17 18 19 20 21 22 23 24

9630 **CHINA (TAIWAN)**
(con'd)   CENTRAL BC SYSTEM, T'ai-pei — E Asia • PRC-4
HOLLAND
    RADIO NEDERLAND, Via Neth Antilles — DUTCH • Australasia • 250 kW
    — Australasia • 250 kW
PORTUGAL
    RDP INTERNATIONAL, Sines — M-F • Europe • 250 kW
RUSSIA
    †R MOSCOW INTL, Serpukhov — (D) • W Africa • 250 kW
    †R MOSCOW INTL, Via Uzbekistan — (D) • C America & S America • 1000 kW
SOUTH AFRICA
    †SOUTH AFRICAN BC, Meyerton — Alternative Frequency to 7125 kHz
SPAIN
    †R EXTERIOR ESPANA, Via Costa Rica — Tu-Su • N America & C America • 100 kW
UNITED KINGDOM
    †BBC, Via Seychelles — (D) • E Africa • 250 kW   E Africa • 250 kW
    — S Africa • 250 kW

9630v **BRAZIL**
    RADIO APARECIDA, Aparecida — PORTUGUESE • DS • 10 kW
CLANDESTINE (M EAST)
    "HOLY MEDINA RADIO, Iraq — Alternative Frequency to 11860v kHz
9634v **ALBANIA**
    †RADIO TIRANA, Lushnjë — Alternative Frequency to 9725v kHz
9634.7 **SINGAPORE**
    SINGAPORE BC CORP, Jurong — DS • 50 kW
9635 **AFGHANISTAN**
    †RADIO AFGHANISTAN, Kabul — DS-TEMP INACTIVE • 100 kW
    — S Asia • TEMP INACTIVE • 100 kW
FINLAND
    †RADIO FINLAND, Pori — (D) • Mideast & E Africa • 500 kW
PORTUGAL
    RDP INTERNATIONAL, Lisbon — PORTUGUESE • C America & S America • 100 kW
    — Su/M • PORTUGUESE • C America & S America • 100 kW
RUSSIA
    †RADIO NADEZHDA — (J) • DS
UNITED KINGDOM
    †BBC, Rampisham — (D) • E Europe • 500 kW
    — (D) M-Sa • E Europe • 500 kW   (D) Sa/Su • E Europe • 500 kW
    — (D) Su • E Europe & Mideast • 500 kW   (J) Sa/Su • E Europe • 500 kW
    — (D) Su • Europe • 500 kW
    — (J) Su • E Europe & Mideast • 500 kW
    — (J) Su • Europe • 500 kW
    †BBC, Via Zyyi, Cyprus — (D) M-F • Europe • 500 kW   E Europe • 250 kW
    — (D) • E Europe • 250 kW
    — (J) M-F • E Europe • 250 kW   (J) • E Europe • 250 kW
    BBC, Woofferton — (J) • Europe • 250 kW
    — (J) Su • Europe • 250 kW
USA
    RFE-RL, Via Germany — (J) • W Asia • 250 kW
    †VOA, Via Kaválla, Greece — (D) • W Asia & S Asia • 250 kW
    — (J) • S Asia • 250 kW
    †VOA, Via Morocco — (D) • Africa • 500 kW
    — (D) M-F • Africa • 500 kW
    VOA, Via Portugal — (J) • E Europe • 250 kW
9635v **MALI**
    RTV MALIENNE, Bamako — FRENCH, ETC • DS • 50 kW
    — Su • FRENCH, ETC • DS • 50 kW
9638v **MOZAMBIQUE**
    EP DE SOFALA, Beira — DS-2 • 100 kW
9640 **DENMARK**
    DANMARKS RADIO, Via Norway — (D) • S Asia & SE Asia • 500 kW
GERMANY
    †DEUTSCHE WELLE, Jülich — (D) • S America • 100 kW
    — (J) • N America & C America • 100 kW
    †DEUTSCHE WELLE, Nauen — (D) • C America • 500 kW
    — (J) • E Europe • 500 kW
    †DEUTSCHE WELLE, Via Antigua — (D) • S America • 250 kW
    †DEUTSCHE WELLE, Via Brasilia, Brazil — S America & C America • 250 kW
    †DEUTSCHE WELLE, Via Cyclops, Malta — Mideast • 250 kW
    — (D) • W Asia • 250 kW
    †DEUTSCHE WELLE, Via Kigali, Rwanda — (J) • W Africa • 250 kW
    — (J) • C Africa & E Africa • 250 kW
(con'd)   †DEUTSCHE WELLE, Wertachtal — (J) • Mideast • 500 kW   (D) • Mideast • 500 kW

0 1 2 3 4 5 6 7 8 9 10 11 12 13 14 15 16 17 18 19 20 21 22 23 24

FREQUENCY   COUNTRY, STATION, LOCATION

TARGET • NETWORK • POWER (kW)

World Time

0 1 2 3 4 5 6 7 8 9 10 11 12 13 14 15 16 17 18 19 20 21 22 23 24

9640 **IRAN**
(con'd) †VO THE ISLAMIC REP, Zāhedān — W Asia & S Asia • 500 kW
JAPAN
  †RADIO JAPAN/NHK, Tokyo-Yamata — JAPANESE • Australasia • GENERAL • 100 kW
  — (J) • Australasia • GENERAL • 100 kW
  — (J) • JAPANESE • Australasia • GENERAL • 100 kW

KOREA (DPR)
  RADIO PYONGYANG, Pyongyang — S Asia • 200 kW
  — KOREAN • S Asia • 200 kW
  — Mideast & Africa • 200 kW
  — KOREAN • Mideast & Africa • 200 kW

KOREA (REPUBLIC)
  †RADIO KOREA, In-Kimjae — SE Asia • 250 kW
  — E Asia • 100 kW
  — KOREAN • SE Asia • 250 kW

NORWAY
  RADIO NORWAY INTL, Kvitsøy — (D) • S Asia & SE Asia • 500 kW
RUSSIA
  †ADVENTIST WORLD R, Samara — (D) • N Europe • 250 kW
  †R MOSCOW INTL, St Petersburg — (J) • Europe • 200 kW
  †R MOSCOW INTL, Via Uzbekistan — (D) • Europe • 1000 kW
SWAZILAND
  TRANS WORLD RADIO, Manzini — (D) • E Africa • 100 kW
UKRAINE
  †RADIO UKRAINE, Star'obel'sk — UKRAINIAN • W Asia • 100/200 kW
  — (D) • UKRAINIAN • W Asia • 100 kW
  — (J) • W Asia • 200 kW
  — (J) • UKRAINIAN • W Asia • 200 kW

UNITED KINGDOM
  BBC, Via Antigua — S America • 125 kW
  †BBC, Via In-Kimjae,Korea — (D) • E Asia • 250 kW
VENEZUELA
  ECOS DEL TORBES, San Cristóbal — DS • 1 kW
  — Su • DS • 1 kW

9640v **ALGERIA**
  "VO FREE SAHARA", Via RTV Algerienne — SPANISH, ETC • W Africa & S America • POLISARIO FRONT • 50 kW
  — W Africa & S America • 50 kW
  RTV ALGERIENNE, Bouchaoui — SE Asia • 300 kW
9645 **AUSTRALIA**
  †RADIO AUSTRALIA, Carnarvon
BRAZIL
  †RADIO BANDEIRANTES, São Paulo — PORTUGUESE • DS • 10 kW
COSTA RICA
  FARO DEL CARIBE, San José — DS • 0.5 kW
DENMARK
  DANMARKS RADIO, Via Norway — (D) • Mideast & E Africa • 500 kW
JAPAN
  RADIO JAPAN/NHK, Via Moyabi, Gabon — (D) • JAPANESE • S Africa • GENERAL • 500 kW
NORWAY
  RADIO NORWAY INTL, Kvitsøy — (D) • Mideast & E Africa • 500 kW
USA
  †RFE-RL, Via Germany — (D) • E Europe & W Asia • 100/250 kW
  †VOA, Via Kaválla, Greece — (J) • C Asia • 250 kW
  †VOA, Via Morocco — (D) • Africa • 500 kW
  VOA, Via Philippines — SE Asia • 50 kW
  VOA, Via Sri Lanka — E Asia • 35 kW
VATICAN STATE
  †VATICAN RADIO, Sta Maria di Galeria — Europe • 100 kW — E Europe • 100 kW — Africa • 100 kW
  — M-Sa • Europe • 100 kW — W Europe • 100 kW
  — (D) • N Africa • 100 kW
  — M-Sa • N Africa • 100 kW — (D) • W Africa • 100 kW
  — Su • E Europe • 100 kW — (D) • W Africa • 500 kW
  — (J) • Mideast • 100 kW
  — (J) • C Africa & S Africa • 100 kW
  — Su • W Europe • 100 kW

9645v **PAKISTAN**
  PAKISTAN BC CORP, Islamabad — (J) • DS • 10 kW
  RADIO PAKISTAN, Islamabad — S Asia • FEEDER • 10 kW
9650 **CANADA**
  R CANADA INTL, Sackville, NB — M-F • E North Am • 250 kW
  †R CANADA INTL, Via Sines, Portugal — (J) • Mideast • 250 kW
DENMARK
  †DANMARKS RADIO, Via Norway — (D) • W North Am • 350 kW
  — (D) • W North Am • 500 kW
FRANCE
  †R FRANCE INTL, Via Tokyo, Japan — E Asia • 300 kW
  — (D) • SE Asia • 300 kW

(con'd)

0 1 2 3 4 5 6 7 8 9 10 11 12 13 14 15 16 17 18 19 20 21 22 23 24

ENGLISH ▬ ARABIC ⧑⧑ CHINESE ▯▯▯ FRENCH ═ GERMAN ▬ RUSSIAN ═ SPANISH ▬ OTHER ▬

FREQUENCY   COUNTRY, STATION, LOCATION

TARGET • NETWORK • POWER (kW)   World Time

0 1 2 3 4 5 6 7 8 9 10 11 12 13 14 15 16 17 18 19 20 21 22 23 24

9650
(con'd)   **GERMANY**
             †DEUTSCHE WELLE, Nauen   (D) • C Africa & E Africa • 500 kW   (J) • E Europe • 500 kW
                                                   (J) • E Europe • 100 kW

             DEUTSCHE WELLE, Via Cyclops, Malta   (J) • Mideast • 250 kW

             †DEUTSCHE WELLE, Via Kigali, Rwanda   S America • 250 kW
                                                   (J) • S America • 250 kW

             †DEUTSCHE WELLE, Via Sines, Portugal (J) • Europe • 250 kW

             †DEUTSCHE WELLE, Wertachtal   E Europe • 500 kW   (D) • Mideast • 500 kW
                                                   (D) • E Europe • 500 kW
                                                              (J) • E Europe • 500 kW

             GUAM
             †ADVENTIST WORLD R, Agat   E Asia • 100 kW
                                                   (D) • JAPANESE • E Asia • 100 kW
             GUINEA
             RTV GUINEENNE, Conakry-Sofoniya   M-Sa • FRENCH, ETC • DS • 100 kW   DS • 100 kW
                                                              FRENCH, ETC • DS • 100 kW
                                                   Su • FRENCH, ETC • DS • 100 kW

             HOLLAND
             †RADIO NEDERLAND, Flevoland   Alternative Frequency to 9860 kHz
             KOREA (DPR)
             RADIO PYONGYANG, Pyongyang   JAPANESE • E Asia • 200 kW
             KOREA (REPUBLIC)
             RADIO KOREA, Via Sackville, Can   KOREAN • E North Am • 250 kW
                                                   (D) • N America • 250 kW

             MONACO
             TRANS WORLD RADIO, Monte Carlo   Europe • 100 kW
             NORWAY
             †RADIO NORWAY INTL, Fredrikstad   (D) • W North Am • 350 kW

             RADIO NORWAY INTL, Sveio   (D) M • W North Am • 500 kW
                                              (D) Tu-Su • W North Am • 500 kW

             RUSSIA
             †GOLOS ROSSII, Moscow   (D) • C Africa & S Africa • 240 kW

             †GOLOS ROSSII, Via Kyrgyzstan   (D) • W Africa & S America • 250 kW
             SOUTH AFRICA
             †CHANNEL AFRICA, Meyerton   (J) • W Africa & S America • 250 kW
                                                   (J) M-F • S Africa • 100 kW

             SPAIN
             R EXTERIOR ESPANA, Noblejas   Australasia • 350 kW
             SWAZILAND
             TRANS WORLD RADIO, Manzini   S Africa • 25 kW
             SWITZERLAND
             SWISS RADIO INTL, Sottens   C America • 500 kW
             USA
             †RFE-RL, Via Germany   (J) • W Asia • 100 kW

             †VOA, Via Kavála, Greece   (D) • E Africa • 250 kW

             †VOA, Via Morocco   (D) • E Europe • 100/500 kW

             †VOA, Via Rhodes, Greece   (D) • Mideast • 50 kW

             †VOA, Via Woofferton, UK   (J) • E Europe • 300 kW
             VATICAN STATE
             VATICAN RADIO, Sta Maria di Galeria (D) • S Asia • 250 kW
9655   **BYELARUS**
             BYELARUS RADIO, Orcha   RUSSIAN, ETC • DS-1 • 20 kW
             CHINA (PR)
             †CHINA RADIO INTL, Shijiazhuang   (D) • E North Am & C America • 500 kW
             COLOMBIA
             †RADIO NACIONAL, El Rosal   DS • 20 kW • ALT. FREQ. TO 9685 kHz
             CUBA
             †RADIO HABANA, Havana   (D) • N America • 100 kW
             DENMARK
             †DANMARKS RADIO, Via Norway   Europe • 500 kW
                                                              W North Am • 350 kW
             GERMANY
             †DEUTSCHE WELLE, Via Sri Lanka   (J) • S Asia • 250 kW
             NORWAY
             †RADIO NORWAY INTL, Fredrikstad   W North Am • 350 kW

             †RADIO NORWAY INTL, Sveio   M-Sa • Europe • 500 kW
                                                        Su • Europe • 500 kW

             PERU
             †RADIO NORPERUANA, Chachapoyas   DS • 1 kW
             RUSSIA
             †RADIO VEDO, Volgograd   DS • 20 kW
             SWAZILAND
             TRANS WORLD RADIO, Manzini   S Africa • 25 kW
                                             Sa • S Africa • 25 kW
                                             Sa/Su • S Africa • 25 kW

             SWEDEN
(con'd) †RADIO SWEDEN, Hörby   Europe & N Africa • 500 kW

0 1 2 3 4 5 6 7 8 9 10 11 12 13 14 15 16 17 18 19 20 21 22 23 24

FREQUENCY   COUNTRY, STATION, LOCATION   TARGET • NETWORK • POWER (kW)   World Time

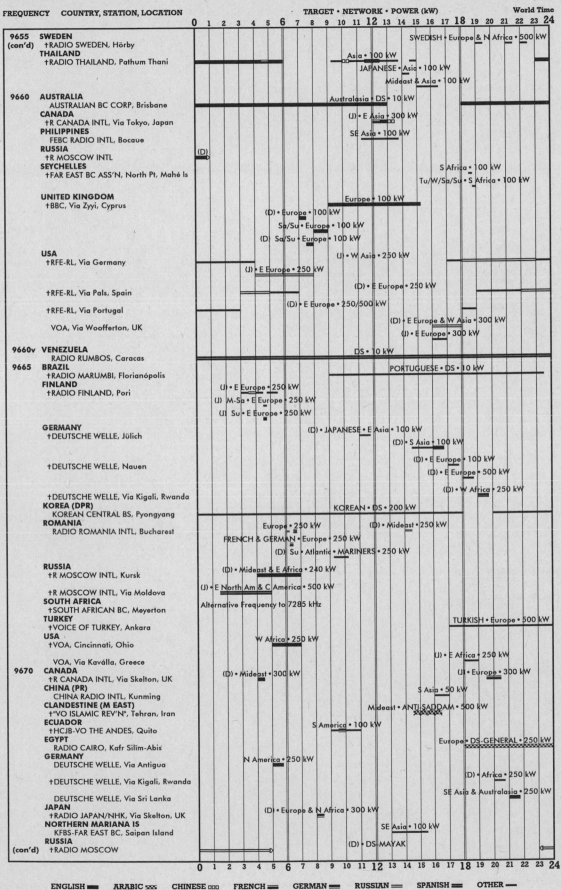

9655 **SWEDEN**		
(con'd) †RADIO SWEDEN, Hörby		SWEDISH • Europe & N Africa • 500 kW
THAILAND		
†RADIO THAILAND, Pathum Thani		Asia • 100 kW
		JAPANESE • Asia • 100 kW
		Mideast & Asia • 100 kW
9660 **AUSTRALIA**		
AUSTRALIAN BC CORP, Brisbane		Australasia • DS • 10 kW
CANADA		
†R CANADA INTL, Via Tokyo, Japan		(J) • E Asia • 300 kW
PHILIPPINES		
FEBC RADIO INTL, Bocaue		SE Asia • 100 kW
RUSSIA		
†R MOSCOW INTL	(D)	
SEYCHELLES		
†FAR EAST BC ASS'N, North Pt, Mahé Is		S Africa • 100 kW
		Tu/W/Sa/Su • S Africa • 100 kW
UNITED KINGDOM		
†BBC, Via Zyyi, Cyprus		Europe • 100 kW
		(D) • Europe • 100 kW
		Sa/Su • Europe • 100 kW
		(D) Sa/Su • Europe • 100 kW
USA		
†RFE-RL, Via Germany		(J) • W Asia • 250 kW
		(J) • E Europe • 250 kW
†RFE-RL, Via Pals, Spain		(D) • E Europe • 250 kW
†RFE-RL, Via Portugal		(D) • E Europe • 250/500 kW
VOA, Via Woofferton, UK		(D) • E Europe & W Asia • 300 kW
		(J) • E Europe • 300 kW
9660v **VENEZUELA**		
RADIO RUMBOS, Caracas		DS • 10 kW
9665 **BRAZIL**		
†RADIO MARUMBI, Florianópolis		PORTUGUESE • DS • 10 kW
FINLAND		
†RADIO FINLAND, Pori		(J) • E Europe • 250 kW
		(J) • M-Sa • E Europe • 250 kW
		(J) • Su • E Europe • 250 kW
GERMANY		
†DEUTSCHE WELLE, Jülich		(D) • JAPANESE • E Asia • 100 kW
		(D) • S Asia • 100 kW
†DEUTSCHE WELLE, Nauen		(D) • E Europe • 100 kW
		(D) • E Europe • 500 kW
†DEUTSCHE WELLE, Via Kigali, Rwanda		(D) • W Africa • 250 kW
KOREA (DPR)		
KOREAN CENTRAL BS, Pyongyang		KOREAN • DS • 200 kW
ROMANIA		
RADIO ROMANIA INTL, Bucharest		Europe • 250 kW
		(D) • Mideast • 250 kW
		FRENCH & GERMAN • Europe • 250 kW
		(D) Su • Atlantic • MARINERS • 250 kW
RUSSIA		
†R MOSCOW INTL, Kursk		(D) • Mideast & E Africa • 240 kW
†R MOSCOW INTL, Via Moldova		(J) • E North Am & C America • 500 kW
SOUTH AFRICA		
†SOUTH AFRICAN BC, Meyerton	Alternative Frequency to 7285 kHz	
TURKEY		
†VOICE OF TURKEY, Ankara		TURKISH • Europe • 500 kW
USA		
†VOA, Cincinnati, Ohio		W Africa • 250 kW
VOA, Via Kaválla, Greece		(J) • E Africa • 250 kW
9670 **CANADA**		
†R CANADA INTL, Via Skelton, UK		(D) • Mideast • 300 kW
		(J) • Europe • 300 kW
CHINA (PR)		
CHINA RADIO INTL, Kunming		S Asia • 50 kW
CLANDESTINE (M EAST)		
†"VO ISLAMIC REV'N", Tehran, Iran		Mideast • ANTI-SADDAM • 500 kW
ECUADOR		
†HCJB-VO THE ANDES, Quito		S America • 100 kW
EGYPT		
RADIO CAIRO, Kafr Silim-Abis		Europe • DS-GENERAL • 250 kW
GERMANY		
DEUTSCHE WELLE, Via Antigua		N America • 250 kW
†DEUTSCHE WELLE, Via Kigali, Rwanda		(D) • Africa • 250 kW
DEUTSCHE WELLE, Via Sri Lanka		SE Asia & Australasia • 250 kW
JAPAN		
†RADIO JAPAN/NHK, Via Skelton, UK		(D) • Europe & N Africa • 300 kW
NORTHERN MARIANA IS		
KFBS-FAR EAST BC, Saipan Island		SE Asia • 100 kW
RUSSIA		
(con'd) †RADIO MOSCOW		(D) • DS-MAYAK

ENGLISH ▬▬ ARABIC ≋≋ CHINESE ▫▫▫ FRENCH ══ GERMAN ▬▬ RUSSIAN ═══ SPANISH ▬▬ OTHER ──

FREQUENCY   COUNTRY, STATION, LOCATION

TARGET • NETWORK • POWER (kW)   World Time

0 1 2 3 4 5 6 7 8 9 10 11 12 13 14 15 16 17 18 19 20 21 22 23 24

9670 **RUSSIA**
(con'd)   †RADIO MOSCOW
- (J) • DS-2
- (D) • DS-2
- (J) • DS-MAYAK

SWEDEN
†RADIO SWEDEN, Hörby
- SWEDISH • Europe & N Africa • 500 kW
- M-F • Europe & N Africa • 500 kW
- M-F • SWEDISH • Europe & N Africa • 500 kW

UNITED KINGDOM
†BBC, Via Cincinnati, USA
- M-F • C America • 250 kW

†BBC, Via Zyyi, Cyprus
- (D) • E Africa • 250 kW

USA
†RFE-RL, Via Germany
- (D) • W Asia • 100 kW

†VOA, Delano, California
- (D) M-F • C America • 250 kW

†VOA, Greenville, NC
- C America & S America • 500 kW
- (D) • C America • 250 kW
- (J) • C America • 250 kW

†VOA, Via Germany
- (J) • N Africa & Mideast • 500 kW

VOA, Via Kaválla, Greece
- (J) • W Asia • 250 kW

†VOA, Via Morocco
- (D) • N Africa & Mideast • 35/500 kW
- (J) • E Europe • 100 kW

9675 **ALBANIA**
†RADIO TIRANA, Lushnjë
- Europe • 100 kW • ALT. FREQ. TO 9530 kHz

BRAZIL
R CANCAO NOVA, Cachoeira Paulista
- PORTUGUESE • DS • 10 kW

DENMARK
†DANMARKS RADIO, Via Norway
- (D) • W North Am • 500 kW
- (J) • E North Am & C America • 500 kW

ECUADOR
†HCJB-VO THE ANDES, Quito
- (D) • Europe • 500 kW

INDIA
†ALL INDIA RADIO, Delhi
- S Asia & W Asia • 100 kW
- DS • 100 kW
- ENGLISH & HINDI • DS • 100 kW

INDONESIA
†VOICE OF INDONESIA, Padang Cermin
- Asia • 250 kW
- Europe • 250 kW
- JAPANESE • Asia • 250 kW

JAPAN
RADIO JAPAN/NHK, Via French Guiana
- S America • 500 kW
- JAPANESE • S America • GENERAL • 500 kW

NORWAY
†RADIO NORWAY INTL, Fredrikstad
- (J) M • E North Am & C America • 350 kW
- (J) Tu-Su • E North Am & C America • 350 kW

†RADIO NORWAY INTL, Sveio
- (D) M • W North Am • 500 kW
- (D) Tu-Su • W North Am • 500 kW

PERU
RADIO DEL PACIFICO, Lima
- Alternative Frequency to 4975 kHz

RUSSIA
†GOLOS ROSSII, Komsomol'sk 'Amure
- (D) • E Asia & SE Asia • 100 kW

†R MOSCOW INTL, Via Uzbekistan
- (D) • Mideast • 1000 kW

TURKEY
VOICE OF TURKEY, Ankara
- Mideast & W Asia • 250 kW

UKRAINE
†RADIO UKRAINE
- (J) • UKRAINIAN
- (J)

UNITED KINGDOM
†BBC, Via Singapore
- (D) • SE Asia • 250 kW

USA
VOA, Via Kaválla, Greece
- (D) • S Asia • 250 kW

†VOA, Via Philippines
- E Asia • 35 kW

9680 **CANADA**
R CANADA INTL, Via Tokyo, Japan
- (J) • E Asia • 300 kW

CHINA (TAIWAN)
VO FREE CHINA, Via Okeechobee, USA
- W North Am • 100 kW

GERMANY
†DEUTSCHE WELLE, Jülich
- (J) • S Asia • 100 kW

†DEUTSCHE WELLE, Nauen
- (J) • E Europe • 500 kW

†DEUTSCHE WELLE, Wertachtal
- (D) • JAPANESE • E Asia • 500 kW

INDONESIA
†RRI, Jakarta, Jawa
- DS • 50/100 kW

PORTUGAL
RADIO RENASCENCA, Muge
- Europe • 100 kW
- Sa/Su • Europe • 100 kW

USA
†R FREE AFGHANISTAN, Via Portugal
- (D) • W Asia & S Asia • 500 kW

†RFE-RL, Via Germany
- (D) • W Asia • 100 kW
- W Asia • 100 kW
- (J) • W Asia • 100 kW

(con'd)

0 1 2 3 4 5 6 7 8 9 10 11 12 13 14 15 16 17 18 19 20 21 22 23 24

SUMMER ONLY (J)   WINTER ONLY (D)   JAMMING / OR ∧   EARLIEST HEARD ◁   LATEST HEARD ▷   NEW OR CHANGED FOR 1994 †

FREQUENCY	COUNTRY, STATION, LOCATION	TARGET • NETWORK • POWER (kW) — World Time

9680 USA
(con'd) †RFE-RL, Via Portugal — (D) • W Asia • 500 kW

†VOA, Delano, California — (J) M-F • C America • 250 kW

VOA, Via Kaválla, Greece — Mideast & S Asia • 250 kW / (D) • Mideast & S Asia • 250 kW / (J) • Mideast & S Asia • 250 kW

†VOA, Via Morocco — (D) • E Europe • 100 kW

†VOA, Via Thailand — (D) • E Asia • 500 kW

†WYFR-FAMILY RADIO, Okeechobee, Fl — (D) • S America • 100 kW

9680v MEXICO
RADIO XEQQ, México City — Irr • DS 0.5 kW

9685 ALGERIA
RTV ALGERIENNE, Algiers — W Europe • 100 kW

BYELARUS
†RS BYELARUS, Via Ukraine — (J) • Europe • 240 kW / (J) M/Tu/Th/F • Europe • 240 kW / (J) W/Sa • Europe • 240 kW

CHINA (PR)
†CHINA RADIO INTL, Kunming — Europe & N Africa • 120 kW

COLOMBIA
†RADIO NACIONAL, El Rosal — Alternative Frequency to 9655 kHz

IRAN
†VO THE ISLAMIC REP, Tehrān — (D) • S Asia • 500 kW / (D) • Mideast • 500 kW

JAPAN
RADIO JAPAN/NHK, Via French Guiana — JAPANESE • S America • GENERAL • 500 kW

RUSSIA
†R MOSCOW INTL, Irkutsk — (D) • SE Asia • 500 kW

†R MOSCOW INTL, Kenga — (D) • Australasia • 500 kW

SWITZERLAND
†"DIE ANTWORT", Via RS Byelarus — (J) • Su • Europe • 240 kW

TURKEY
VOICE OF TURKEY, Ankara — TURKISH • Europe • 500 kW

UKRAINE
†RADIO UKRAINE, L'vov — (J) • W Europe & E North Am • 500 kW / (J) • UKRAINIAN • Europe • 240 kW / (J) • UKRAINIAN • W Europe & E North Am • 500 kW / (J) • Europe • 240 kW

USA
†RFE-RL, Via Pals, Spain — (D) • W Asia • 250 kW

9685.2 BRAZIL
RADIO GAZETA, São Paulo — PORTUGUESE • DS-TEMP INACTIVE • 7.5 kW

9689v MADAGASCAR
RTV MALAGASY, Antananarivo — Irr • DS-1 • 10 kW

9690 ARGENTINA
†R ARGENTINA-RAE, Buenos Aires — M-F • S America • 25 kW

†RADIO NACIONAL, Buenos Aires — Sa/Su • S America • DS • 25 kW

CHINA (PR)
CHINA RADIO INTL, Via Noblejas, Spain — N America & C America • 350 kW

CHINA (TAIWAN)
CENTRAL BC SYSTEM, T'ai-pei — E Asia • PRC-5 (CANTONESE) • 10 kW

GERMANY
DEUTSCHE WELLE, Jülich — (D) • E Europe • 100 kW

†DEUTSCHE WELLE, Multiple Locations — S Asia • 100/500 kW / (J) • Mideast • 100/500 kW

†DEUTSCHE WELLE, Nauen — (D) • W Africa • 500 kW

DEUTSCHE WELLE, Via Antigua — Australasia • 250 kW

DEUTSCHE WELLE, Via Cyclops, Malta — (J) • Mideast • 250 kW

†DEUTSCHE WELLE, Wertachtal — S Asia • 500 kW / W Asia • 500 kW

KAZAKHSTAN
KAZAKH RADIO, Various Locations — DS-2 • 20 kW

ROMANIA
RADIO ROMANIA INTL, Bucharest — Europe • 250 kW / (D) • Mideast • 250 kW / (D) • E Europe • 250 kW / (D) • Europe • 250 kW / (J) • Europe • 250 kW

RUSSIA
RADIO MOSCOW, Igark'a — DS-1 • 20 kW

SPAIN
R EXTERIOR ESPANA, Noblejas — F • N America & C America • LADINO • 350 kW

SWEDEN
†RADIO SWEDEN, Hörby — Alternative Frequency to 9695 kHz

UNITED KINGDOM
†BBC, Via Delano, USA — M-F • C America • 250 kW / (D) M-F • C America • 250 kW

USA
†VOA, Via Thailand — (J) • S Asia • 250 kW

†VOA, Via Woofferton, UK — (D) • E Europe & W Asia • 300 kW

0 1 2 3 4 5 6 7 8 9 10 11 12 13 14 15 16 17 18 19 20 21 22 23 24

ENGLISH ▬ ARABIC ⫶⫶⫶ CHINESE ▫▫▫ FRENCH ▭ GERMAN ▬ RUSSIAN ═ SPANISH ▭ OTHER —

FREQUENCY   COUNTRY, STATION, LOCATION   TARGET • NETWORK • POWER (kW)   World Time

World Time scale: 0 1 2 3 4 5 6 7 8 9 10 11 12 13 14 15 16 17 18 19 20 21 22 23 24

9695 BRAZIL
†RADIO RIO MAR, Manaus — PORTUGUESE • DS • 7.5 kW
RUSSIA
†R ALPHA & OMEGA, Yekaterinburg — Alternative Frequency to 9795 kHz
†RADIO RADONEZH, Yekaterinburg — Alternative Frequency to 7230 kHz
SOUTH AFRICA
†CHANNEL AFRICA, Meyerton — (J) • W Africa • 500 kW
SWEDEN
†RADIO SWEDEN, Hörby
- S America • 500 kW
- SWEDISH • S America • 500 kW
- SWEDISH • S Asia • 500 kW
- Sa/Su • E Europe • 500 kW
- S Asia • 500 kW
- SWEDISH • N America • 500 kW
- N America • 500 kW
- M-F • SWEDISH • N America & C America • 500 kW • ALT. FREQ. TO 9690 kHz

UNITED ARAB EMIRATES
UAE RADIO, Abu Dhabi — Mideast & S Asia • 120 kW
USA
†R FREE AFGHANISTAN, Via Germany — (D) • W Asia & C Asia • 250 kW
†RFE-RL, Via Germany
- (D) • E Europe & W Asia • 100 kW
- W Asia • 100 kW
- (D) • W Asia & C Asia • 250 kW
RFE-RL, Via Portugal
- E Europe • 250/500 kW
- (D) • E Europe • 250 kW
- (J) • E Europe • 500 kW
VATICAN STATE
†VATICAN RADIO, Sta Maria di Galeria
- E Africa • 500 kW
- (D) • E Africa • 500 kW
- (D) • S Africa • 500 kW

9700 ANGOLA
AV DO GALO NEGRO, Jamba — S Africa • UNITA
BULGARIA
†RADIO BULGARIA, Plovdiv
- (D) • E North Am • 250 kW
- (D) • Europe • 250 kW
- (J) • Europe • 250 kW
- (J) • Su • Europe • 250 kW
RADIO BULGARIA, Stolnik
- (D) • E Europe & Mideast • 150 kW
- (D) • Su • E Europe & Mideast • 150 kW
CANADA
R CANADA INTL, Via In-Kimjae, Korea — (J) • E Asia • 250 kW
CHINA (PR)
CHINA RADIO INTL, Xi'an — Mideast & S Asia • 150 kW
EGYPT
RADIO CAIRO, Abu Za'bal — N Africa • DS-VO THE ARABS • 100 kW
GERMANY
†DEUTSCHE WELLE, Multiple Locations — (D) • Americas • 250/500 kW
DEUTSCHE WELLE, Via Antigua — (J) • N America & C America • 250 kW
DEUTSCHE WELLE, Via Sackville, Can — (J) • N America • 250 kW
†DEUTSCHE WELLE, Wertachtal
- (J) • S America • 500 kW
- C America & S America • 500 kW
- (J) • N America & C America • 500 kW
INDIA
ALL INDIA RADIO, Aligarh — S Asia • 250 kW
NEW ZEALAND
†R NEW ZEALAND INTL, Rangitaiki — (D) • ENGLISH, ETC • Pacific • 100 kW
RUSSIA
R MOSCOW INTL — (D) • N America
RADIO MOSCOW, Kenga — (J) • DS-1 • 100 kW
USA
†VOA, Via Kaválla, Greece
- (D) • Mideast & S Asia • 250 kW
- Mideast & S Asia • 250 kW
- (D) • N Africa & W Africa • 250 kW
- (J) • Mideast & S Asia • 250 kW

9705 BRAZIL
RADIO NACIONAL, Rio de Janeiro — PORTUGUESE • DS • 10 kW
ETHIOPIA
†VOICE OF ETHIOPIA, Gedja
- DS • 100 kW
- M-Sa • DS • 100 kW
- M-F • DS • 100 kW
- Su • DS • 100 kW
- Sa/Su • DS • 100 kW
INDONESIA
†RRI, Pontianak, Kalimantan — DS • 50 kW
KAZAKHSTAN
KAZAKH RADIO, Almaty — DS-2 • 20 kW
MEXICO
†RADIO MEXICO INTL, México City — Irr • W North Am & C America • 10 kW
NIGER
LA VOIX DU SAHEL, Niamey — FRENCH, ETC • DS • 100 kW
— Sa • FRENCH, ETC • DS • 100 kW
PORTUGAL
RDP INTERNATIONAL, Lisbon
- PORTUGUESE • N America • 100 kW
- Su/M • PORTUGUESE • N America • 100 kW

(con'd)

Time scale: 0 1 2 3 4 5 6 7 8 9 10 11 12 13 14 15 16 17 18 19 20 21 22 23 24

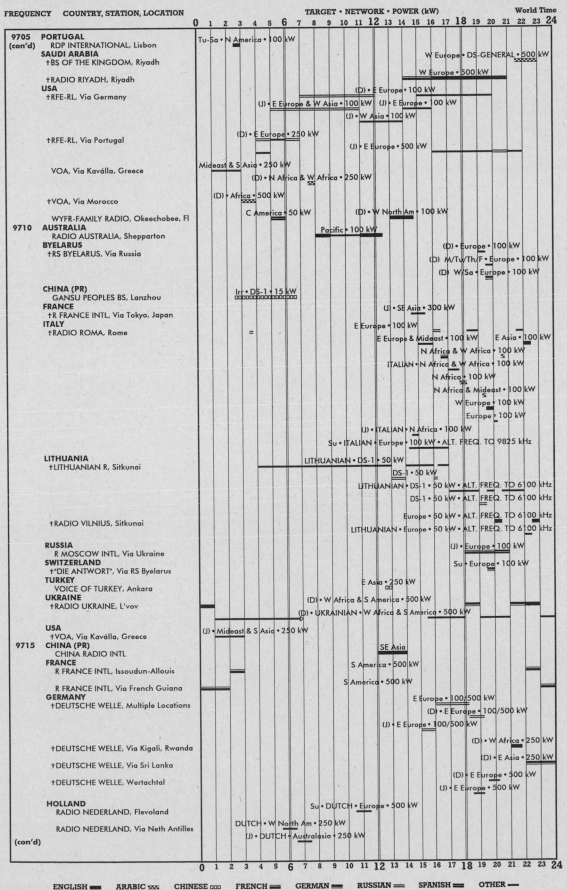

FREQUENCY COUNTRY, STATION, LOCATION — TARGET • NETWORK • POWER (kW) — World Time

9705 (con'd)	PORTUGAL RDP INTERNATIONAL, Lisbon	Tu-Sa • N America • 100 kW
	SAUDI ARABIA †BS OF THE KINGDOM, Riyadh	W Europe • DS-GENERAL • 500 kW
	†RADIO RIYADH, Riyadh	W Europe • 500 kW
	USA †RFE-RL, Via Germany	(D) • E Europe • 100 kW; (J) E Europe & W Asia • 100 kW; (J) • E Europe • 100 kW; (J) • W Asia • 100 kW
	†RFE-RL, Via Portugal	(D) • E Europe • 250 kW; (J) • E Europe • 500 kW
	VOA, Via Kaválla, Greece	Mideast & S Asia • 250 kW; (D) • N Africa & W Africa • 250 kW
	†VOA, Via Morocco	(D) • Africa • 500 kW
	WYFR-FAMILY RADIO, Okeechobee, Fl	C America • 50 kW; (D) • W North Am • 100 kW
9710	AUSTRALIA RADIO AUSTRALIA, Shepparton	Pacific • 100 kW
	BYELARUS †RS BYELARUS, Via Russia	(D) • Europe • 100 kW; (D) M/Tu/Th/F • Europe • 100 kW; (D) W/Sa • Europe • 100 kW
	CHINA (PR) GANSU PEOPLES BS, Lanzhou	Irr • DS-1 • 15 kW
	FRANCE †R FRANCE INTL, Via Tokyo, Japan	(J) • SE Asia • 300 kW
	ITALY †RADIO ROMA, Rome	E Europe • 100 kW; E Europe & Mideast • 100 kW; E Asia • 100 kW; N Africa & W Africa • 100 kW; ITALIAN • N Africa & W Africa • 100 kW; N Africa • 100 kW; N Africa & Mideast • 100 kW; W Europe • 100 kW; Europe • 100 kW; (J) • ITALIAN • N Africa • 100 kW; Su • ITALIAN • Europe • 100 kW • ALT. FREQ. TO 9825 kHz
	LITHUANIA †LITHUANIAN R, Sitkunai	LITHUANIAN • DS-1 • 50 kW; DS-1 • 50 kW; LITHUANIAN • DS-1 • 50 kW • ALT. FREQ. TO 6100 kHz; DS-1 • 50 kW • ALT. FREQ. TO 6100 kHz
	†RADIO VILNIUS, Sitkunai	Europe • 50 kW • ALT. FREQ. TO 6100 kHz; LITHUANIAN • Europe • 50 kW • ALT. FREQ. TO 6100 kHz
	RUSSIA R MOSCOW INTL, Via Ukraine	(J) • Europe • 100 kW
	SWITZERLAND †"DIE ANTWORT", Via RS Byelarus	Su • Europe • 100 kW
	TURKEY VOICE OF TURKEY, Ankara	E Asia • 250 kW
	UKRAINE †RADIO UKRAINE, L'vov	(D) • W Africa & S America • 500 kW; (D) • UKRAINIAN • W Africa & S America • 500 kW
	USA †VOA, Via Kaválla, Greece	(J) • Mideast & S Asia • 250 kW
9715	CHINA (PR) CHINA RADIO INTL	SE Asia
	FRANCE R FRANCE INTL, Issoudun-Allouis	S America • 500 kW
	R FRANCE INTL, Via French Guiana	S America • 500 kW
	GERMANY †DEUTSCHE WELLE, Multiple Locations	E Europe • 100/500 kW; (D) • E Europe • 100/500 kW; (J) • E Europe • 100/500 kW
	†DEUTSCHE WELLE, Via Kigali, Rwanda	(D) • W Africa • 250 kW
	†DEUTSCHE WELLE, Via Sri Lanka	(D) • E Asia • 250 kW
	†DEUTSCHE WELLE, Wertachtal	(D) • E Europe • 500 kW; (J) • E Europe • 500 kW
	HOLLAND RADIO NEDERLAND, Flevoland	Su • DUTCH • Europe • 500 kW
	RADIO NEDERLAND, Via Neth Antilles	DUTCH • W North Am • 250 kW; (J) • DUTCH • Australasia • 250 kW
(con'd)		

FREQUENCY	COUNTRY, STATION, LOCATION	TARGET • NETWORK • POWER (kW)	World Time

World Time scale: 0 1 2 3 4 5 6 7 8 9 10 11 12 13 14 15 16 17 18 19 20 21 22 23 24

9715 (con'd)	RUSSIA	
	†RADIO ROSSII, Kingisepp	(J) • DS • 200 kW
	USA	
	RFE-RL, Via Portugal	(D) • W Asia • 250 kW
	†VOA, Various Locations	(D) • E Europe • 250/500 kW
	†VOA, Via Kaválla, Greece	(J) • N Africa • 250 kW / (J) • Mideast • 250 kW
	†VOA, Via Philippines	(J) • SE Asia • 50 kW
	†VOA, Via Portugal	(D) • E Europe • 250 kW
	†VOA, Via Rhodes, Greece	(J) • Mideast • 50 kW
	†VOA, Via Thailand	(D) • E Asia • 500 kW
	†VOA, Via Woofferton, UK	(D) • E Europe • 300 kW
	WYFR-FAMILY RADIO, Okeechobee, Fl	C America • 50 kW
	UZBEKISTAN	
	†RADIO TASHKENT, Tashkent	(D) • Mideast • 100 kW / (J) • S Asia • 50 kW
9715.3	QATAR	
	†QATAR BC SERVICE, Doha	Mideast • 250 kW
9717v	BOLIVIA	
	RADIO LA PLATA, Sucre	DS • 1 kW / Su • DS • 1 kW
9720	GERMANY	
	†DEUTSCHE WELLE, Via Sri Lanka	(D) • E Asia • 250 kW
	HOLLAND	
	†RADIO NEDERLAND, Via Neth Antilles	Australasia • 250 kW / DUTCH • Australasia • 250 kW / C America • 250 kW / (J) • C America • 250 kW
	IRAN	
	†VO THE ISLAMIC REP, Tehrān	N Africa • 500 kW / W Asia • 500 kW / (D) • W Asia • 500 kW / (D) • Mideast • 500 kW
	RUSSIA	
	GOLOS ROSSII, Ryazan'	(J) • Europe • 240 kW
	R MOSCOW INTL, Moscow	(D) • W Europe & W Africa • 120 kW
	R MOSCOW INTL, Ryazan'	(J) • Europe • 240 kW
	R MOSCOW INTL, Via Ukraine	(D) • N America • 240 kW
	†RADIO ROSSII, Volgograd	(J) • DS • 20 kW
	SAUDI ARABIA	
	†BS OF THE KINGDOM, Ad Dir'iyah	Mideast & E Africa • DS-GENERAL • 50 kW
	SRI LANKA	
	SRI LANKA BC CORP, Colombo-Ekala	S Asia • 100 kW / E Asia • 100 kW / W North Am • 100 kW
	YUGOSLAVIA	
	†RADIO YUGOSLAVIA, Belgrade	C America & S America • 500 kW / Australasia • 500 kW
9720.3	ANGOLA	
	†RADIO NACIONAL, Luanda	DS-1 • 100 kW
9722.5	COSTA RICA	
	†ADVENTIST WORLD R, Cahuita	Alternative Frequency to 9725 kHz
9725	CANADA	
	†R CANADA INTL, Sackville, NB	(D) • E North Am & C America • 250 kW
	CHINA (PR)	
	CHINA RADIO INTL, Hohhot	Irr • E Asia • 50 kW
	COSTA RICA	
	†ADVENTIST WORLD R, Cahuita	SPANISH & ENGLISH • C America • TESTS • 50 kW • ALT. FREQ. TO 9722.5 kHz
	JAPAN	
	†RADIO JAPAN/NHK, Via Sackville, Can	(J) • JAPANESE • W North Am & C America • GENERAL • 250 kW / (J) • W North Am & C America • GENERAL • 250 kW
	RUSSIA	
	†RADIO MOSCOW, Serpukhov	(J) • DS-2 • 100 kW
	USA	
	†RFE-RL, Via Germany	E Europe • 100 kW / (J) • E Europe • 100 kW / (D) • E Europe • 100 kW / (D) Sa/Su • E Europe • 100 kW / (D) Su • E Europe • 100 kW / (J) Su • E Europe • 100 kW
	†RFE-RL, Via Portugal	W Asia & C Asia • 500 kW / (D) • E Europe • 250 kW / E Europe • 500 kW / (D) • E Europe & W Asia • 500 kW / (J) • E Europe • 500 kW / (D) M-Sa • E Europe • 500 kW / (J) M-Sa • E Europe • 500 kW
9725v	ALBANIA	
	†RADIO TIRANA, Lushnjë	W Europe • 100 kW • ALT. FREQ. TO 9634v kHz
	BRAZIL	
(con'd)	†R CLUBE PARANAENSE, Curitiba	PORTUGUESE • DS • 7.5 kW

Bottom scale: 0 1 2 3 4 5 6 7 8 9 10 11 12 13 14 15 16 17 18 19 20 21 22 23 24

FREQUENCY   COUNTRY, STATION, LOCATION

TARGET • NETWORK • POWER (kW)   World Time

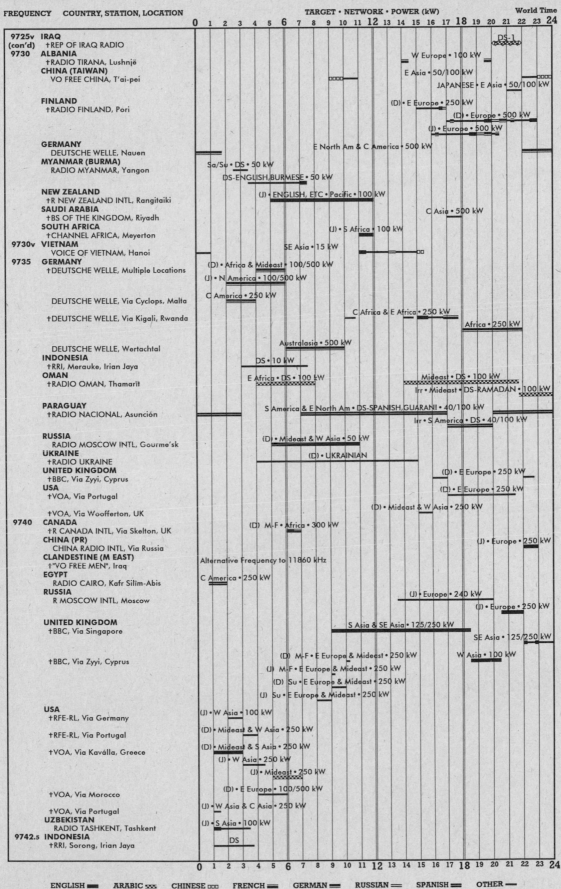

Freq	Country, Station, Location	Details
9725v	**IRAQ** †REP OF IRAQ RADIO	DS-1
9730	**ALBANIA** †RADIO TIRANA, Lushnjë	W Europe • 100 kW
	CHINA (TAIWAN) VO FREE CHINA, T'ai-pei	E Asia • 50/100 kW; JAPANESE • E Asia • 50/100 kW
	FINLAND †RADIO FINLAND, Pori	(D) • E Europe • 250 kW; (D) • Europe • 500 kW; (J) • Europe • 500 kW
	GERMANY DEUTSCHE WELLE, Nauen	E North Am & C America • 500 kW
	MYANMAR (BURMA) RADIO MYANMAR, Yangon	Sa/Su • DS • 50 kW; DS-ENGLISH, BURMESE • 50 kW
	NEW ZEALAND †R NEW ZEALAND INTL, Rangitaiki	(J) • ENGLISH, ETC • Pacific • 100 kW
	SAUDI ARABIA †BS OF THE KINGDOM, Riyadh	C Asia • 500 kW
	SOUTH AFRICA †CHANNEL AFRICA, Meyerton	(J) • S Africa • 100 kW
9730v	**VIETNAM** VOICE OF VIETNAM, Hanoi	SE Asia • 15 kW
9735	**GERMANY** †DEUTSCHE WELLE, Multiple Locations	(D) • Africa & Mideast • 100/500 kW; (J) • N America • 100/500 kW
	DEUTSCHE WELLE, Via Cyclops, Malta	C America • 250 kW
	†DEUTSCHE WELLE, Via Kigali, Rwanda	C Africa & E Africa • 250 kW; Africa • 250 kW
	DEUTSCHE WELLE, Wertachtal	Australasia • 500 kW
	INDONESIA †RRI, Merauke, Irian Jaya	DS • 10 kW
	OMAN †RADIO OMAN, Thamarīt	E Africa • DS • 100 kW; Mideast • DS • 100 kW; Irr • Mideast • DS-RAMADAN • 100 kW
	PARAGUAY †RADIO NACIONAL, Asunción	S America & E North Am • DS-SPANISH, GUARANI • 40/100 kW; Irr • S America • DS • 40/100 kW
	RUSSIA RADIO MOSCOW INTL, Gourme'sk	(D) • Mideast & W Asia • 50 kW
	UKRAINE †RADIO UKRAINE	(D) • UKRAINIAN
	UNITED KINGDOM †BBC, Via Zyyi, Cyprus	(D) • E Europe • 250 kW
	USA †VOA, Via Portugal	(D) • E Europe • 250 kW
	†VOA, Via Woofferton, UK	(D) • Mideast & W Asia • 250 kW
9740	**CANADA** †R CANADA INTL, Via Skelton, UK	(D) • M-F • Africa • 300 kW
	CHINA (PR) CHINA RADIO INTL, Via Russia	(J) • Europe • 250 kW
	CLANDESTINE (M EAST) †"VO FREE MEN", Iraq	Alternative Frequency to 11860 kHz
	EGYPT RADIO CAIRO, Kafr Silîm-Abis	C America • 250 kW
	RUSSIA R MOSCOW INTL, Moscow	(J) • Europe • 240 kW; (J) • Europe • 250 kW
	UNITED KINGDOM †BBC, Via Singapore	S Asia & SE Asia • 125/250 kW; SE Asia • 125/250 kW; W Asia • 100 kW
	†BBC, Via Zyyi, Cyprus	(D) • M-F • E Europa & Mideast • 250 kW; (J) • M-F • E Europa & Mideast • 250 kW; (D) • Su • E Europe & Mideast • 250 kW; (J) • Su • E Europe & Mideast • 250 kW
	USA †RFE-RL, Via Germany	(J) • W Asia • 100 kW
	†RFE-RL, Via Portugal	(D) • Mideast & W Asia • 250 kW
	†VOA, Via Kaválla, Greece	(D) • Mideast & S Asia • 250 kW; (J) • W Asia • 250 kW; (J) • Mideast • 250 kW
	†VOA, Via Morocco	(D) • E Europe • 100/500 kW
	†VOA, Via Portugal	(J) • W Asia & C Asia • 250 kW
	UZBEKISTAN RADIO TASHKENT, Tashkent	(J) • S Asia • 100 kW
9742.5	**INDONESIA** †RRI, Sorong, Irian Jaya	DS

ENGLISH ▬   ARABIC ▒   CHINESE □□□   FRENCH ▬   GERMAN ▬   RUSSIAN ═   SPANISH ▬   OTHER ▬

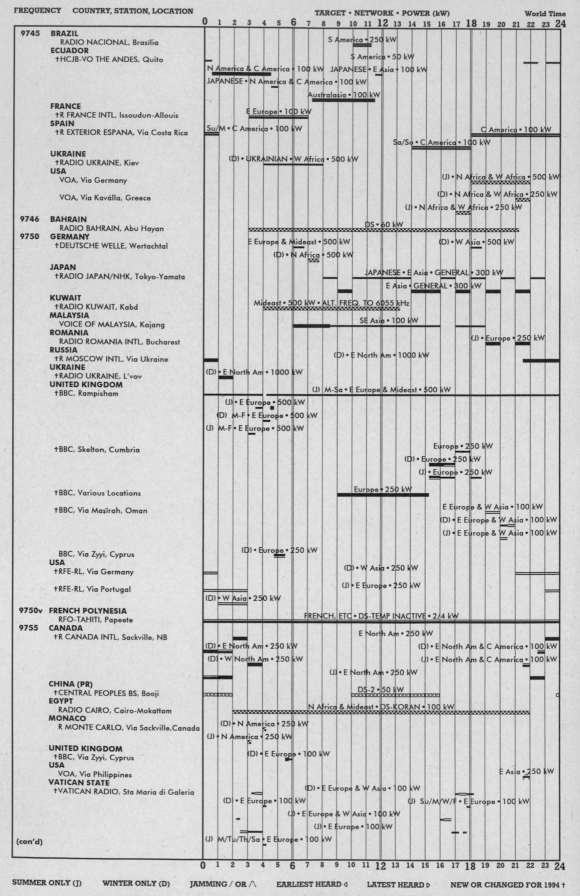

9745 BRAZIL
RADIO NACIONAL, Brasília
ECUADOR
†HCJB-VO THE ANDES, Quito

FRANCE
†R FRANCE INTL, Issoudun-Allouis
SPAIN
†R EXTERIOR ESPANA, Via Costa Rica

UKRAINE
†RADIO UKRAINE, Kiev
USA
VOA, Via Germany

VOA, Via Kaválla, Greece

9746 BAHRAIN
RADIO BAHRAIN, Abu Hayan
9750 GERMANY
†DEUTSCHE WELLE, Wertachtal

JAPAN
†RADIO JAPAN/NHK, Tokyo-Yamata

KUWAIT
†RADIO KUWAIT, Kabd
MALAYSIA
VOICE OF MALAYSIA, Kajang
ROMANIA
RADIO ROMANIA INTL, Bucharest
RUSSIA
†R MOSCOW INTL, Via Ukraine
UKRAINE
†RADIO UKRAINE, L'vov
UNITED KINGDOM
†BBC, Rampisham

†BBC, Skelton, Cumbria

†BBC, Various Locations

†BBC, Via Maṣīrah, Oman

BBC, Via Zyyi, Cyprus
USA
†RFE-RL, Via Germany

†RFE-RL, Via Portugal

9750v FRENCH POLYNESIA
RFO-TAHITI, Papeete
9755 CANADA
†R CANADA INTL, Sackville, NB

CHINA (PR)
†CENTRAL PEOPLES BS, Baoji
EGYPT
RADIO CAIRO, Cairo-Mokattam
MONACO
R MONTE CARLO, Via Sackville, Canada

UNITED KINGDOM
†BBC, Via Zyyi, Cyprus
USA
VOA, Via Philippines
VATICAN STATE
†VATICAN RADIO, Sta Maria di Galeria

(con'd)

FREQUENCY   COUNTRY, STATION, LOCATION

TARGET • NETWORK • POWER (kW)   World Time

Frequency	Country, Station, Location	Target • Network • Power
9755 (con'd)	VATICAN STATE	
	†VATICAN RADIO, Sta Maria di Galeria	(D) Su • E Europe • 100 kW
		(J) Su • E Europe • 100 kW
9760	ALBANIA	
	†RADIO TIRANA, Lushnjë	N America • 100 kW · W Europe • 100 kW
	CANADA	
	†R CANADA INTL, Sackville, NB	(D) M-F • Europe • 250 kW
	JAPAN	
	RADIO TAMPA, Tokyo-Nagara	JAPANESE • DS-2 • 50 kW
	RUSSIA	
	†RADIO MOSCOW, Kenga	(J) • DS-1 • 100 kW
	SPAIN	
	†R EXTERIOR ESPANA, Noblejas	Europe • 350 kW
	UNITED KINGDOM	
	†BBC, Skelton, Cumbria	(J) • Mideast • 300 kW · (D) • Europe • 250 kW
		(J) • Europe • 250 kW
	†BBC, Various Locations	Europe • 250/500 kW
	†BBC, Via Zyyi, Cyprus	(D) • Mideast • 100 kW
	USA	
	VOA, Via Philippines	E Asia & SE Asia • 250 kW
		SE Asia • 250 kW
	†VOA, Via Portugal	E Europe • 250 kW
		(D) • E Europe • 250 kW
	†VOA, Via Woofferton, UK	E Europe • 300 kW
9765	CHINA (PR)	
	CHINA RADIO INTL, Beijing	(J) • E Europe • 500 kW
	CHINA (TAIWAN)	
	BC CORP CHINA, T'ai-pei	DS-NEWS NETWORK • 50/100 kW
	VO FREE CHINA, T'ai-pei	Australasia • 50/100 kW
	ECUADOR	
	†HCJB-VO THE ANDES, Quito	S Africa • 100 kW · N America & C America • 100 kW
		M-F • S Africa • 100 kW
	GERMANY	
	†DEUTSCHE WELLE, Jülich	W Africa • 100 kW · (D) • E Asia • 100 kW
		(D) • W Africa • 100 kW
	†DEUTSCHE WELLE, Multiple Locations	Africa • 100/500 kW · (D) • W Africa • 100/500 kW
		(D) • Africa • 100/500 kW
	†DEUTSCHE WELLE, Via Kigali, Rwanda	(D) • S America • 250 kW
	†DEUTSCHE WELLE, Wertachtal	(D) • Africa • 500 kW · SE Asia & Australasia • 500 kW
		(D) • W Africa • 500 kW
	MALTA	
	VO MEDITERRANEAN, Cyclops	Europe, N Africa & Mideast • 250 kW
9770	AUSTRALIA	
	†RADIO AUSTRALIA, Darwin	(D) • SE Asia • 250 kW
	†RADIO AUSTRALIA, Shepparton	SE Asia • 100 kW
		M-F • SE Asia • 100 kW
		Sa/Su • SE Asia • 100 kW
	CHINA (PR)	
	CHINA RADIO INTL, Via Bamako, Mali	N America • 50 kW
		CANTONESE • N America • 50 kW
	CYPRUS	
	CYPRUS BC CORP, Zyyi	F-Su • Europe • 250 kW
	EGYPT	
	RADIO CAIRO, Kafr Silim-Abis	N Africa • DS-GENERAL • 250 kW
	GERMANY	
	DEUTSCHE WELLE, Jülich	(D) • E Europe • 100 kW
		(J) • E Europe • 100 kW
	DEUTSCHE WELLE, Wertachtal	(D) • E Europe • 500 kW
		(J) • E Europe • 500 kW
	IRAN	
	†VO THE ISLAMIC REP, Tehrān	(D) • N Africa & Mideast • 500 kW
	JAPAN	
	†RADIO JAPAN/NHK, Via Skelton, UK	(D) • Europe • 250 kW
	SEYCHELLES	
	†FAR EAST BC ASS'N, North Pt, Mahé Is	S Asia • 100 kW · E Africa • 100 kW
	UNITED ARAB EMIRATES	
	†UAE RADIO, Abu Dhabi	Irr • Europe • DS-RAMADAN • 500 kW
		(D) • N Africa & Mideast • 500 kW · Europe • 500 kW
	UNITED KINGDOM	
	†BBC, Rampisham	E Europe • 500 kW
		(D) • E Europe • 500 kW
		(J) • E Europe • 500 kW
		(D) Sa/Su • E Europe • 500 kW
		(J) Sa/Su • E Europe • 500 kW
(con'd)	†BBC, Via Zyyi, Cyprus	(J) • E Europe • 250 kW · (D) • Europe • 250 kW

ENGLISH ▬   ARABIC ⨯⨯⨯   CHINESE ▫▫▫   FRENCH ═   GERMAN ▬   RUSSIAN ═   SPANISH ▬   OTHER ▬

FREQUENCY	COUNTRY, STATION, LOCATION	TARGET • NETWORK • POWER (kW)	World Time

0 1 2 3 4 5 6 7 8 9 10 11 12 13 14 15 16 17 18 19 20 21 22 23 24

9770 **USA**
(con'd) †R FREE AFGHANISTAN, Via Portugal — (J) • W Asia & C Asia • 250 kW

†RFE-RL, Via Germany — (D) • W Asia • 100 kW

VOA, Via Philippines — SE Asia • 250 kW

WYFR-FAMILY RADIO, Okeechobee, Fl — (D) • Europe • 100 kW

9775 **CHINA (PR)**
CENTRAL PEOPLES BS, Baoji — DS-2 • 50 kW
DS-MINORITIES • 50 kW

RUSSIA
ADVENTIST WORLD R, Tula — (J) • Europe • 240 kW

GOLOS ROSSII, Tula — (D) • E Africa • 100 kW
E Africa • 100 kW

R MOSCOW INTL, Tula — (D) • E Africa • 100 kW

†RADIO MOSCOW, Kazan' — (D) • DS-1 • 200 kW

USA
†VOA, Greenville, NC — C America & S America • 250 kW
E Africa • 500 kW
W Africa & S Africa • 500 kW
M-F • W Africa & S Africa • 500 kW
Tu-Sa • C America & S America • 250 kW

9780 **CHINA (PR)**
QINGHAI PEOPLES BS, Xining — Irr • DS-1 • 10 kW
KAZAKHSTAN
KAZAKH RADIO, Almaty — RUSSIAN, GERMAN, ETC • DS-1 • 50 kW
PHILIPPINES
†FEBC RADIO INTL, Bocaue — SE Asia • 100 kW
PORTUGAL
†RDP INTERNATIONAL, Lisbon — PORTUGUESE • Europe • 100 kW
M-F • Europe • 100 kW
Sa/Su • PORTUGUESE • Europe • 100 kW

RUSSIA
†RADIO MOSCOW, Nikolayevsk 'Amure — DS-1 • 50 kW
(D) • DS-1 • 50 kW
(J) • DS-1 • 50 kW

9780v **YEMEN (REPUBLIC)**
"VO PALESTINE", Via Rep Yemen Radio — PLO • 50 kW

REP YEMEN RADIO, San'ā — DS • 50 kW
F • DS • 50 kW
Irr • DS-RAMADAN • 50 kW

9785 **GUAM**
†KTWR-TRANS WORLD R, Merizo — E Asia • 100 kW
C Asia & E Asia • 100 kW
M-F • C Asia & E Asia • 100 kW

USA
KVOH-VO HOPE, Rancho Simi, Ca — W North Am & C America • 50 kW
9790 **FRANCE**
†R FRANCE INTL, Issoudun-Allouis — E North Am & C America • 100/500 kW
Mideast • 500 kW
(D) • S Asia & SE Asia • 500 kW

R FRANCE INTL, Multiple Locations — Africa • 100/250/500 kW

†R FRANCE INTL, Via French Guiana — (D) • C America • 500 kW
(J) • C America & S America • 500 kW
(J) • C America • 500 kW

R FRANCE INTL, Via Moyabi, Gabon — C Africa • 250 kW
RUSSIA
RADIO MOSCOW, Yekaterinburg — DS-2
UZBEKISTAN
RADIO TASHKENT, Tashkent — (J) • Mideast • 50 kW
9795 **MONACO**
TRANS WORLD RADIO, Monte Carlo — Europe • 100 kW
M-Sa • Europe • 100 kW
Su • Europe • 100 kW

RUSSIA
†R ALPHA & OMEGA, Yekaterinburg — (D) • DS • 200 kW • ALT. FREQ. TO 9695 kHz

R MOSCOW INTL, Komsomol'sk 'Amure — (D) • W North Am • NORTH AMERICAN SVC • 100 kW
TURKEY
VOICE OF TURKEY, Ankara — Europe • 250 kW
9800 **CHINA (PR)**
CENTRAL PEOPLES BS — DS-1
EGYPT
RADIO CAIRO, Abu Za'bal — Mideast • DS-GENERAL • 100 kW
FRANCE
†R FRANCE INTL, Issoudun-Allouis — E North Am & C America • 100/500 kW
(D) • S America • 500 kW

(con'd) R FRANCE INTL, Via French Guiana — C America • 500 kW

0 1 2 3 4 5 6 7 8 9 10 11 12 13 14 15 16 17 18 19 20 21 22 23 24

FREQUENCY   COUNTRY, STATION, LOCATION   TARGET • NETWORK • POWER (kW)   World Time

FREQUENCY	COUNTRY, STATION, LOCATION	TARGET • NETWORK • POWER (kW)
9800 (con'd)	RUSSIA / R MOSCOW INTL	(J) • Europe
9805	FRANCE / †R FRANCE INTL, Issoudun-Allouis	S Asia & SE Asia • 500 kW
		E Europe • 100/500 kW
		(D) • N Africa & E Africa • 100 kW
		(D) • E Europe • 100/500 kW
		(J) • E Europe • 100/500 kW
	†R FRANCE INTL, Multiple Locations	N Africa & E Africa • 100/250/500 kW
9810	CZECH REPUBLIC / †RADIO PRAGUE, Via Slovakia	N America • 100 kW
	RUSSIA / R MOSCOW INTL, Via Ukraine	(D) • S America • 500 kW
		(D) • W Africa • 500 kW
	RADIO MOSCOW, Khabarovsk	(J) • DS-2
	SEYCHELLES / †FAR EAST BC ASS'N, North Pt, Mahé Is	S Asia • 100 kW
		W Asia & S Asia • 100 kW
		E Africa • 100 kW
		M-Sa • W Asia & S Asia • 100 kW
		Sa • W Asia & S Asia • 100 kW
	SLOVAKIA / †R SLOVAKIA INTL, Vel'ké Kostolany	N America • 100 kW
	SWITZERLAND / SWISS RADIO INTL, Schwarzenburg	S America • 100/250 kW
9815	CUBA / †RADIO HABANA, Havana	(D) • E North Am • 30 kW • USB
	GERMANY / †DEUTSCHE WELLE, Via N'sibirsk, Russia	(D) • S Asia • 1000 kW
	ISRAEL / KOL ISRAEL, Tel Aviv	Mideast • DS-D • 20/50 kW • USB
	PHILIPPINES / †FEBC RADIO INTL, Bocaue	SE Asia • 100 kW • ALT. FREQ. TO 9850 kHz
		SE Asia • 100 kW • ALT. FREQ. TO 9420 kHz
	PORTUGAL / †RDP INTERNATIONAL, Lisbon	PORTUGUESE • Europe • 100 kW
		Sa/Su • PORTUGUESE • Europe • 100 kW
	USA / †KCBI, Dallas, Texas	N America • 100 kW
9820	CHINA (PR) / CHINA RADIO INTL, Xi'an	(J) • Europe & N Africa • 120 kW
	RUSSIA / R MOSCOW INTL, Kalinin	(J) • Europe • 100 kW
	†RADIO ROSSII, Irkutsk	Irr • DS • 100 kW
9825	GREECE / †FONI TIS HELLADAS, Athens	GREEK • Mideast • 100 kW
		Mideast • 100 kW
	HOLLAND / †RADIO NEDERLAND, Via Kazakhstan	(J) • S Asia • 500 kW
	ITALY / †RADIO ROMA, Rome	Alternative Frequency to 9710 kHz
	UNITED KINGDOM / †BBC, Multiple Locations	(J) • C America & S America • 300/500 kW
		(J) Tu-Sa • C America & S America • 300/500 kW
	†BBC, Rampisham	N Africa • 500 kW
		(D) • S America • 500 kW
		(J) • C America & S America • 500 kW
		(J) • Europe • 500 kW
		(J) • S America • 500 kW
		(D) • Su • Europe • 500 kW
		(J) • Su • Europe • 500 kW
		(J) Tu-Sa • C America & S America • 500 kW
	BBC, Skelton, Cumbria	(D) • Mideast • 300 kW
	†BBC, Woofferton	E Europe • 250 kW
		(D) • E Europe • 250 kW
		(J) • E Europe • 250 kW
	USA / †WEWN, Birmingham, Alabama	(D) • S Asia • 500 kW
		(D) • Mideast • 500 kW
9830	CROATIA / CROATIAN RADIO, Zagreb	Europe • DS-1 • 10 kW
		M-Sa • Europe • DS-1 • 10 kW
		Su • Europe • DS-1 • 10 kW
	FRANCE / †R FRANCE INTL, Issoudun-Allouis	(D) • E Europe • 100 kW
	JORDAN / †RADIO JORDAN, Qasr el Kharana	W Europe • 500 kW
	PALAU / †KHBN-VO HOPE, Koror	Asia • 100 kW
		M-F • Asia • 100 kW
		Sa • Asia • 100 kW
(con'd)		

ENGLISH ▬ ARABIC ⋙ CHINESE ▯▯▯ FRENCH ═ GERMAN ▬▬ RUSSIAN ══ SPANISH ▭▭ OTHER ▬

FREQUENCY   COUNTRY, STATION, LOCATION

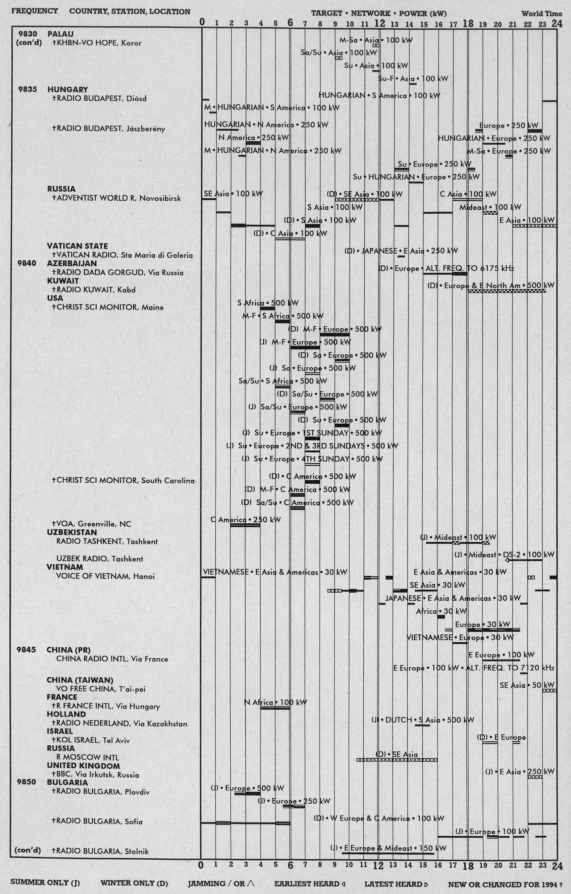

TARGET • NETWORK • POWER (kW)   World Time

9830	**PALAU**
(con'd)	†KHBN-VO HOPE, Koror
9835	**HUNGARY**
	†RADIO BUDAPEST, Diósd
	†RADIO BUDAPEST, Jászberény
	RUSSIA
	†ADVENTIST WORLD R, Novosibirsk
	VATICAN STATE
	†VATICAN RADIO, Sta Maria di Galeria
9840	**AZERBAIJAN**
	†RADIO DADA GORGUD, Via Russia
	KUWAIT
	†RADIO KUWAIT, Kabd
	USA
	†CHRIST SCI MONITOR, Maine
	†CHRIST SCI MONITOR, South Carolina
	†VOA, Greenville, NC
	UZBEKISTAN
	RADIO TASHKENT, Tashkent
	UZBEK RADIO, Tashkent
	VIETNAM
	VOICE OF VIETNAM, Hanoi
9845	**CHINA (PR)**
	CHINA RADIO INTL, Via France
	CHINA (TAIWAN)
	VO FREE CHINA, T'ai-pei
	FRANCE
	†R FRANCE INTL, Via Hungary
	HOLLAND
	†RADIO NEDERLAND, Via Kazakhstan
	ISRAEL
	†KOL ISRAEL, Tel Aviv
	RUSSIA
	R MOSCOW INTL
	UNITED KINGDOM
	†BBC, Via Irkutsk, Russia
9850	**BULGARIA**
	†RADIO BULGARIA, Plovdiv
	†RADIO BULGARIA, Sofia
(con'd)	†RADIO BULGARIA, Stolnik

SUMMER ONLY (J)   WINTER ONLY (D)   JAMMING / OR ∧   EARLIEST HEARD ◁   LATEST HEARD ▷   NEW OR CHANGED FOR 1994 †

FREQUENCY | COUNTRY, STATION, LOCATION | TARGET • NETWORK • POWER (kW) | World Time

World Time scale: 0 1 2 3 4 5 6 7 8 9 10 11 12 13 14 15 16 17 18 19 20 21 22 23 24

Freq	Country / Station / Location	Entry
9850 (con'd)	**CHINA (TAIWAN)** VO FREE CHINA, Via Okeechobee, USA	(D) • Europe • 100 kW
	EGYPT	N Africa • DS-GENERAL • 250 kW
	RADIO CAIRO, Kafr Silim-Abis	N Africa & Mideast • DS-VO THE ARABS • 250 kW
	PHILIPPINES †FEBC RADIO INTL, Bocaue	Alternative Frequency to 9815 kHz
	RUSSIA †RADIO MOSCOW, Samara	(D) • DS-1 • 200 kW
	USA CHRIST SCI MONITOR, Maine	W Africa • 500 kW
		M • W Africa • 500 kW
		Sa/Su • W Africa • 500 kW
		Tu-F • W Africa • 500 kW
	†WORLD HARVEST R, Noblesville, Indiana	M-Sa • C America • 100 kW
		Su • C America • 100 kW
	†WYFR-FAMILY RADIO, Okeechobee, Fl	Europe • 100 kW
		(D) • Europe • 100 kW
		(J) • Europe • 100 kW
9855	**CHINA (PR)** CHINA RADIO INTL	JAPANESE • E Asia
	HOLLAND RADIO NEDERLAND, Flevoland	(D) • DUTCH • Mideast • 500 kW
	†RADIO NEDERLAND, Via Uzbekistan	(D) • DUTCH • SE Asia • 240 kW
		(D) • SE Asia • 240 kW
9860	**HOLLAND** †RADIO NEDERLAND, Flevoland	Europe • 500 kW • ALT. FREQ. TO 9650 kHz
		DUTCH • W Europe • 500 kW
		N Africa & W Africa • 500 kW
	†RADIO NEDERLAND, Via Irkutsk, Russia	(D) • E Asia & SE Asia • 250 kW
		(D) • DUTCH • E Asia & SE Asia • 250 kW
	RADIO NEDERLAND, Via Madagascar	S Asia • 300 kW
		W Africa & C Africa • 300 kW
	PHILIPPINES †RADIO VERITAS ASIA, Palauig	(J) • E Asia • 100 kW
	RUSSIA †R MOSCOW INTL, Via Ukraine	(D) • E North Am • 500 kW
	SWITZERLAND †SWISS RADIO INTL, Schwarzenburg	(D) • W Africa • 100/250 kW
		(D) • ITALIAN • W Africa • 100/250 kW
	†SWISS RADIO INTL, Sottens	N America & C America • 500 kW
		ITALIAN • N America & C America • 500 kW
	UKRAINE †RADIO UKRAINE, Simferopol'	UKRAINIAN • E North Am • 500/1000 kW
		(D) • UKRAINIAN • E North Am • 500 kW
		(D) • E North Am • 500 kW
		(J) • E North Am • 1000 kW
		(J) • UKRAINIAN • E North Am • 1000 kW
9865	**RUSSIA** GOLOS ROSSII	(D) • Atlantic
		(D) • E Asia & Pacific
	†R ALPHA & OMEGA, Yekaterinburg	(J) • DS • 200 kW
	RADIO MOSCOW	(J) • DS-MAYAK
	†RADIO RADONEZH, Yekaterinburg	(J) • DS • 200 kW
9870	**ARMENIA** †RADIO YEREVAN, Via Armavir, Russia	(D) • ARMENIAN • E North Am • 1000 kW
		(D) • E North Am • 1000 kW
	AUSTRIA †RADIO AUSTRIA INTL, Vienna	S America • 300 kW
		S America • 500 kW
		C America • 300 kW
		(D) • S America • 500 kW
		(J) • S America • 500 kW
	GUAM †KTWR-TRANS WORLD R, Merizo	JAPANESE • E Asia • 100 kW
		E Asia • 100 kW
	KOREA (REPUBLIC) †RADIO KOREA, In-Kimjae	KOREAN • Mideast & Africa • 250 kW
		Mideast & Africa • 250 kW
	RUSSIA †R MOSCOW INTL, Armavir	(D) • E North Am • 1000 kW
		(D) • W Europe • 1000 kW
	SAUDI ARABIA †BS OF THE KINGDOM, Riyadh	W Europe • DS-GENERAL • 500 kW
	USA †CHRIST SCI MONITOR, South Carolina	(J) M-F • Europe • 500 kW
		(D) M • C America • 500 kW
(con'd)		(D) Sa/Su • C America • 500 kW

World Time scale: 0 1 2 3 4 5 6 7 8 9 10 11 12 13 14 15 16 17 18 19 20 21 22 23 24

ENGLISH ▬ ARABIC ⨯⨯⨯ CHINESE ▭▭▭ FRENCH ▬ GERMAN ▬ RUSSIAN ═ SPANISH ▬ OTHER ▬

FREQUENCY   COUNTRY, STATION, LOCATION   TARGET • NETWORK • POWER (kW)   World Time

9870 **USA**
(con'd) †CHRIST SCI MONITOR, South Carolina
(J) Sa/Su • Europe • 500 kW
(D) Tu-F • C America • 500 kW
(J) Su • Europe • 1ST SUNDAY • 500 kW
(J) Su • Europe • 2ND & 3RD SUNDAYS • 500 kW
(J) Su • Europe • 4TH SUNDAY • 500 kW

WYFR-FAMILY RADIO, Okeechobee, Fl
(J) • Europe • 100 kW

9875 **AUSTRIA**
RADIO AUSTRIA INTL, Vienna
N America • 500 kW

GERMANY
†DEUTSCHE WELLE, Via N'sibirsk, Russia
(J) • S Asia • 1000 kW

PHILIPPINES
FEBC RADIO INTL, Bocaue
SE Asia • 100 kW
F/Sa • SE Asia • 50 kW

SPAIN
†R EXTERIOR ESPANA, Arganda
N Africa • 100 kW

†R EXTERIOR ESPANA, Noblejas
Europe • 350 kW
M-Sa • Europe • 350 kW

9878v DOMINICAN REPUBLIC
RADIO SANTIAGO, Santiago
Irr • DS • 1 kW

9880 AUSTRIA
†RADIO AUSTRIA INTL, Vienna
W Europe & W Africa • 100 kW
Mideast • 100 kW
(D) • W Europe & W Africa • 100 kW
(D) • Mideast • 100 kW
(J) • W Europe & W Africa • 100 kW
(J) • Mideast • 100 kW
M-Sa • Mideast • 100 kW
Su • Mideast • 100 kW

CHINA (PR)
CHINA RADIO INTL, Beijing
SE Asia • 120 kW

RUSSIA
†RADIO GALAXY
(D) • RUSSIAN & ENGLISH • Europe

9885 RUSSIA
GOLOS ROSSII
(J) • E Asia & Pacific

SAUDI ARABIA
†BS OF THE KINGDOM, Riyadh
Europe • DS-GENERAL • 500 kW

SWITZERLAND
†SWISS RADIO INTL, Schwarzenburg
E North Am & C America • 100/250 kW
Mideast • 100/250 kW
ITALIAN • E North Am & C America • 100/250 kW
Africa • 100/250 kW
N America • 100/250 kW
Australasia • 100/250 kW • ALT. FREQ. TO 9560 kHz
ITALIAN • Australasia • 100/250 kW • ALT. FREQ. TO 9560 kHz

SWISS RADIO INTL, Sottens
S America • 500 kW
ITALIAN • S America • 500 kW

USA
†VOA, Via Botswana
C Africa & E Africa • 100 kW

UZBEKISTAN
RADIO TASHKENT, Tashkent
(D) • Europe & Mideast • 240 kW
(J) • Mideast • 100 kW

9890 HOLLAND
†RADIO NEDERLAND, Via Madagascar
(J) • S Asia • 300 kW

USA
†VOA, Via Philippines
SE Asia • 50 kW
(D) • E Africa • 250 kW
(D) M-F • E Africa • 250 kW

9895 ARMENIA
RADIO YEREVAN, Yerevan
(J) • Mideast • 100 kW

HOLLAND
†RADIO NEDERLAND, Flevoland
C America • 500 kW
N Africa & W Africa • 500 kW
S America • 500 kW
DUTCH • E North Am • 500 kW
(D) • DUTCH • Mideast • 500 kW
S America • 300 kW
(D) • DUTCH • E North Am • 500 kW
DUTCH • Europe • 500 kW

†RADIO NEDERLAND, Via Madagascar
DUTCH • Mideast • 300 kW
(D) • S Asia • 300 kW

LEBANON
†WINGS OF HOPE, Marjayoûn
E Europe, Mideast & W Asia • 25 kW

RUSSIA
GOLOS ROSSII, Petropavlovsk-K
(J) • E Asia • 100 kW

R MOSCOW INTL
(D) • W North Am

R MOSCOW INTL, Petropavlovsk-K
JAPANESE • E Asia • 100 kW
(D) • E Asia • 100 kW
(J) • E Asia • 100 kW
(J) • JAPANESE • E Asia • 100 kW

(con'd)

SUMMER ONLY (J)   WINTER ONLY (D)   JAMMING / OR /\   EARLIEST HEARD ◁   LATEST HEARD ▷   NEW OR CHANGED FOR 1994 †

FREQUENCY   COUNTRY, STATION, LOCATION

TARGET • NETWORK • POWER (kW)   World Time

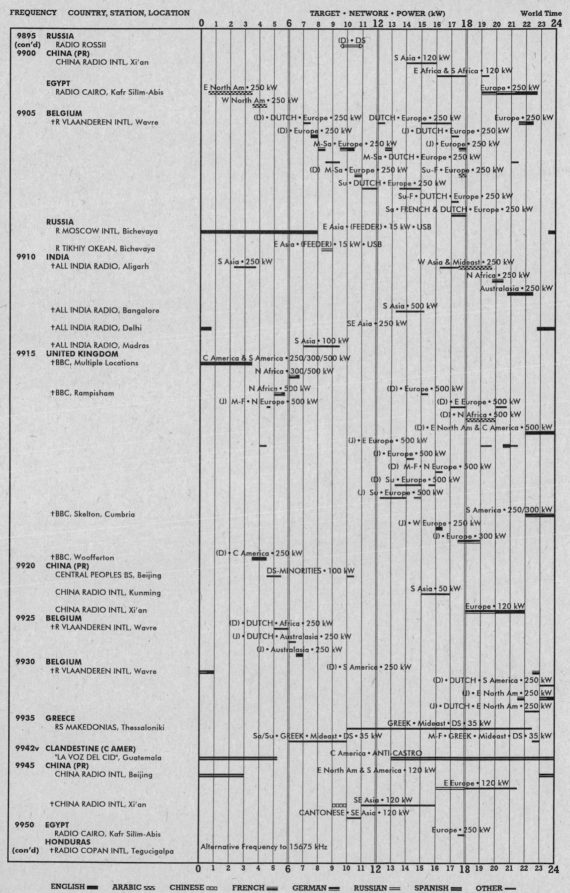

Frequency	Country, Station, Location
9895 (con'd)	**RUSSIA** — RADIO ROSSII
9900	**CHINA (PR)** — CHINA RADIO INTL, Xi'an
	EGYPT — RADIO CAIRO, Kafr Silīm-Abis
9905	**BELGIUM** — †R VLAANDEREN INTL, Wavre
	RUSSIA — R MOSCOW INTL, Bichevaya
	R TIKHIY OKEAN, Bichevaya
9910	**INDIA** — †ALL INDIA RADIO, Aligarh
	†ALL INDIA RADIO, Bangalore
	†ALL INDIA RADIO, Delhi
	†ALL INDIA RADIO, Madras
9915	**UNITED KINGDOM** — †BBC, Multiple Locations
	†BBC, Rampisham
	†BBC, Skelton, Cumbria
	†BBC, Woofferton
9920	**CHINA (PR)** — CENTRAL PEOPLES BS, Beijing
	CHINA RADIO INTL, Kunming
	CHINA RADIO INTL, Xi'an
9925	**BELGIUM** — †R VLAANDEREN INTL, Wavre
9930	**BELGIUM** — †R VLAANDEREN INTL, Wavre
9935	**GREECE** — RS MAKEDONIAS, Thessaloniki
9942v	**CLANDESTINE (C AMER)** — "LA VOZ DEL CID", Guatemala
9945	**CHINA (PR)** — CHINA RADIO INTL, Beijing
	†CHINA RADIO INTL, Xi'an
9950	**EGYPT** — RADIO CAIRO, Kafr Silīm-Abis
(con'd)	**HONDURAS** — †RADIO COPAN INTL, Tegucigalpa

Timeline annotations:

- RADIO ROSSII: (D) • DS
- CHINA RADIO INTL, Xi'an: S Asia • 120 kW; E Africa & S Africa • 120 kW
- RADIO CAIRO: E North Am • 250 kW; W North Am • 250 kW; Europe • 250 kW
- R VLAANDEREN INTL, Wavre: (D) • DUTCH • Europe • 250 kW; DUTCH • Europe • 250 kW; Europe • 250 kW; (D) • Europe • 250 kW; (J) • DUTCH • Europe • 250 kW; M-Sa • Europe • 250 kW; (J) • Europe • 250 kW; M-Sa • DUTCH • Europe • 250 kW; (D) M-Sa • Europe • 250 kW; Su-F • Europe • 250 kW; Su • DUTCH • Europe • 250 kW; Su-F • DUTCH • Europe • 250 kW; Sa • FRENCH & DUTCH • Europe • 250 kW
- R MOSCOW INTL, Bichevaya: E Asia • (FEEDER) • 15 kW • USB
- R TIKHIY OKEAN, Bichevaya: E Asia • (FEEDER) • 15 kW • USB
- ALL INDIA RADIO, Aligarh: S Asia • 250 kW; W Asia & Mideast • 250 kW; N Africa • 250 kW; Australasia • 250 kW
- ALL INDIA RADIO, Bangalore: S Asia • 500 kW
- ALL INDIA RADIO, Delhi: SE Asia • 250 kW
- ALL INDIA RADIO, Madras: S Asia • 100 kW
- BBC, Multiple Locations: C America & S America • 250/300/500 kW; N Africa • 300/500 kW
- BBC, Rampisham: N Africa • 500 kW; (J) M-F • N Europe • 500 kW; (D) • Europe • 500 kW; (D) • E Europe • 500 kW; (D) • N Africa • 500 kW; (D) • E North Am & C America • 500 kW; (J) • E Europe • 500 kW; (J) • Europe • 500 kW; (D) M-F • N Europe • 500 kW; (D) Su • Europe • 500 kW; (J) Su • Europe • 500 kW
- BBC, Skelton, Cumbria: S America • 250/300 kW; (J) • W Europe • 250 kW; (J) • Europe • 300 kW
- BBC, Woofferton: (D) • C America • 250 kW
- CENTRAL PEOPLES BS, Beijing: DS-MINORITIES • 100 kW
- CHINA RADIO INTL, Kunming: S Asia • 50 kW
- CHINA RADIO INTL, Xi'an: Europe • 120 kW
- R VLAANDEREN INTL, Wavre (9925): (D) • DUTCH • Africa • 250 kW; (J) • DUTCH • Australasia • 250 kW; (J) • Australasia • 250 kW
- R VLAANDEREN INTL, Wavre (9930): (D) • S America • 250 kW; (D) • DUTCH • S America • 250 kW; (J) • E North Am • 250 kW; (J) • DUTCH • E North Am • 250 kW
- RS MAKEDONIAS, Thessaloniki: GREEK • Mideast • DS • 35 kW; Sa/Su • GREEK • Mideast • DS • 35 kW; M-F • GREEK • Mideast • DS • 35 kW
- "LA VOZ DEL CID", Guatemala: C America • ANTI-CASTRO
- CHINA RADIO INTL, Beijing: E North Am & S America • 120 kW; E Europe • 120 kW
- CHINA RADIO INTL, Xi'an: SE Asia • 120 kW; CANTONESE • SE Asia • 120 kW
- RADIO CAIRO (9950): Europe • 250 kW
- RADIO COPAN INTL: Alternative Frequency to 15675 kHz

ENGLISH ▬ ARABIC ≋ CHINESE □□□ FRENCH ═ GERMAN ▬ RUSSIAN ═ SPANISH ▬ OTHER ▬

FREQUENCY   COUNTRY, STATION, LOCATION   TARGET • NETWORK • POWER (kW)   World Time

0 1 2 3 4 5 6 7 8 9 10 11 12 13 14 15 16 17 18 19 20 21 22 23 24

9950 INDIA
(con'd) †ALL INDIA RADIO, Aligarh
- SE Asia • 250 kW
- N Africa • 250 kW
- HINDI • SE Asia • 250 kW
- (J) • E Africa • 250 kW
- (J) • HINDI • E Africa • 250 kW

†ALL INDIA RADIO, Delhi
- SE Asia • 100 kW
- S Asia & E Asia • 100 kW
- DS • 50 kW
- HINDI • W Europe • 250 kW
- (D) • DS • 50 kW
- W Europe • 250 kW
- ENGLISH, ETC • DS • 50 kW
- (D) • ENGLISH, ETC • DS • 50 kW

SYRIA
†SYRIAN BC SERVICE, Adhra
- DS • 500 kW • ALT. FREQ. TO 9955 kHz

9955 CHINA (TAIWAN)
VO FREE CHINA, T'ai-pei
- Mideast & N Africa • 50/100 kW

SYRIA
†SYRIAN BC SERVICE, Adhra
- Alternative Frequency to 9950 kHz

USA
FAMILY RADIO, Via Taiwan
- Europe & Asia • 250 kW
- E Asia • 250 kW

WRMI-R MIAMI INTL, Miami
- C America • PROJECTED • 50 kW

9965 CHINA (PR)
CHINA RADIO INTL, Beijing
- Europe, Mideast & N Africa • 120 kW
- (D) • E Europe • 120 kW

CLANDESTINE (C AMER)
†"RADIO CAIMAN", Guatemala City
- C America • ANTI-CASTRO
- M-Sa • C America • ANTI-CASTRO
- Sa/Su • C America • ANTI-CASTRO
- Su • C America • ANTI-CASTRO

9977 KOREA (DPR)
RADIO PYONGYANG, Pyongyang
- C America • 400 kW
- Africa • 200 kW
- KOREAN • C America • 400 kW
- KOREAN • Africa • 200 kW
- SE Asia • 200 kW
- KOREAN • SE Asia • 200 kW

9980 CLANDESTINE (M EAST)
"VO IRAQI PEOPLE", Saudi Arabia
- Mideast • ANTI-SADDAM • ALT. FREQ. TO 9985 kHz

9985 CHINA (PR)
CHINA RADIO INTL
- E Europe

CLANDESTINE (M EAST)
"VO IRAQI PEOPLE", Saudi Arabia
- Alternative Frequency to 9980 kHz

USA
†WEWN, Birmingham, Alabama
- (D) • S America • 500 kW

9985v PIRATE (EUROPE)
†"PIRATE FREAKS BC", Germany
- Alternative Frequency to 6285v kHz

9990 EGYPT
†RADIO CAIRO, Kafr Silim-Abis
- Europe • 250 kW

9995 SYRIA
†RADIO DAMASCUS, Adhra
- E Europe & Mideast • 500 kW
- Mideast • "VOICE OF IRAQ" • 500 kW

10000 USA
WWV, Ft Collins, Colorado
- WEATHER/WORLD TIME • 10 kW

WWVH, Kekaha, Hawaii
- WEATHER/WORLD TIME • 10 kW

10010v VIETNAM
VOICE OF VIETNAM, Hanoi
- E Asia • 30 kW
- SE Asia • 30 kW

10059v VIETNAM
VOICE OF VIETNAM, Hanoi
- VIETNAMESE • DS • 30 kW

10100 MOZAMBIQUE
†A VOZ DA RENAMO, Marinque
- S Africa

10200v CLANDESTINE (ASIA)
"R LAO LIBERATION", Northern Laos
- SE Asia • ANTI-LAO GOVT • 0.1 kW

10233.5 ITALY
†RAI-RTV ITALIANA, Rome
- ITALIAN • DS-ITALIAN, ETC(FEEDER) • USB
- ITALIAN • DS-1 (FEEDER) • USB

10235 USA
†VOA, Greenville, NC
- (D) • N Africa • (FEEDER) • 40 kW • ISU
- (D) • N Africa • (FEEDER) • 40 kW • ISL

10260 CHINA (PR)
CENTRAL PEOPLES BS, Beijing
- DS-2 • 15 kW
- DS-MINORITIES • 15 kW

10330 INDIA
†ALL INDIA RADIO, Delhi
- Sa/Su • DS • 50 kW
- SE Asia • 100 kW
- DS • 50 kW

10344 ARMENIA
RADIO YEREVAN, Via Russia
- ARMENIAN • E Asia • (FEEDER) • USB
- E Asia • (FEEDER) • USB

BYELARUS
RS BYELARUS, Via Russia
- E Asia • (FEEDER) • USB

LITHUANIA
RADIO VILNIUS, Via Russia
- E Asia • (FEEDER) • USB

RUSSIA
†R MOSCOW INTL
- JAPANESE • E Asia • (FEEDER) • USB
- E Asia • (FEEDER) • USB

UKRAINE
(con'd) RADIO UKRAINE, Via Russia
- E Asia • (FEEDER) • USB

0 1 2 3 4 5 6 7 8 9 10 11 12 13 14 15 16 17 18 19 20 21 22 23 24

SUMMER ONLY (J)   WINTER ONLY (D)   JAMMING / OR ∧   EARLIEST HEARD ◁   LATEST HEARD ▷   NEW OR CHANGED FOR 1994 †

FREQUENCY   COUNTRY, STATION, LOCATION   TARGET • NETWORK • POWER (kW)   World Time

Time scale: 0 1 2 3 4 5 6 7 8 9 10 11 12 13 14 15 16 17 18 19 20 21 22 23 24

Frequency	Country, Station, Location	Schedule notes
10344 (con'd)	UKRAINE — RADIO UKRAINE, Via Russia	UKRAINIAN • E Asia • (FEEDER) • USB
10690	RUSSIA — †RADIO MOSCOW, Novosibirsk	(J) • DS-2(FEEDER) • 15 kW • USB; DS-2(FEEDER) • 15 kW • USB
10855	RUSSIA — RADIO MOSCOW, Yekaterinburg	DS-MAYAK(FEEDER) • 15 kW • ISU; DS-1(FEEDER) • 15 kW • ISL
10869	USA — †VOA, Cincinnati, Ohio	N Africa • (FEEDER) • 50 kW • USB
11000	CHINA (PR) — CENTRAL PEOPLES BS	CHINESE, ETC • TAIWAN-2; W-M • CHINESE, ETC • TAIWAN-2; (J) • CHINESE, ETC • TAIWAN-2
11020	RUSSIA — †RADIO ROSSII, Moscow	(D) • DS • USB
11040	CHINA (PR) — CENTRAL PEOPLES BS	DS-2; Th/Sa-Tu • DS-2
11092.5	ST HELENA — †RADIO ST HELENA, Jamestown	Irr • SPECIAL EVENTS • 1.5 kW • USB
11100	CHINA (PR) — CENTRAL PEOPLES BS, Beijing	(J) • CHINESE, ETC • TAIWAN-1 • 120 kW; CHINESE, ETC • TAIWAN-1 • 120 kW
11330	CHINA (PR) — †CENTRAL PEOPLES BS	DS-1; W-M • DS-1; (J) • DS-1
11335	KOREA (DPR) — †RADIO PYONGYANG, Kujang-dong	C America • 400 kW; KOREAN • C America • 400 kW
	RADIO PYONGYANG, Pyongyang	Asia • 200 kW
11375	CHINA (PR) — CENTRAL PEOPLES BS	DS-MINORITIES
11390	ITALY — †MARCONI RADIO INTL, Taranto	Irr • ITALIAN • Europe • 0.5 kW
11400v	PIRATE (PACIFIC) — "RADIO G'DAY", Australia	Irr • Australasia • 0.016 kW
11401v	PIRATE (EUROPE) — "RADIO WAVES INTL", France	Irr • Su • ENGLISH & FRENCH • W Europe • 0.015 kW
11402	ICELAND — †RIKISUTVARPID, Reykjavik	Atlantic & Europe • DS-1 • 10 kW • USB; Atlantic & E North Am • DS-1 • 10 kW • USB
11404	PIRATE (EUROPE) — †"RADIO DELTA", Ruurlo, Holland	Alternative Frequency to 6199 kHz
11413	PIRATE (EUROPE) — †"RADIO STELLA", Scotland	Alternative Frequency to 7446 kHz
11419v	PIRATE (EUROPE) — †"RADIO PIRANA INTL	Irr • Su • W Europe • 0.02 kW
11445	CHINA (PR) — CHINA RADIO INTL, Kunming	S America • 240 kW; SE Asia • 50 kW; Africa • 120 kW; S Asia • 120 kW
11455	CHINA (PR) — CHINA RADIO INTL, Beijing	SE Asia
11470	CLANDESTINE (M EAST) — †"VO HUMAN RIGHTS", Egypt	PERSIAN • Mideast • ANTI-IRANIAN GOVT • 100 kW
11500	CHINA (PR) — CHINA RADIO INTL, Beijing	E Europe & W Asia • 120 kW
	†CHINA RADIO INTL, Kunming	(J) • S America • 120 kW; S America • 120 kW
	†CHINA RADIO INTL, Xi'an	(J) • Europe • 120 kW
11515	CHINA (PR) — CHINA RADIO INTL, Beijing	E Europe • 120 kW; JAPANESE • E Asia • 120 kW; S America • 120 kW; Mideast & N Africa • 120 kW
11530	LEBANON — †WINGS OF HOPE, Marjayoûn	E Europe, Mideast & W Asia • 25 kW
11550	TUNISIA — †RTV TUNISIENNE, Sfax	DS • 100 kW
	USA — FAMILY RADIO, Via Taiwan	S Asia • ENGLISH, HINDI • 250 kW; E Asia • 250 kW
11560	EGYPT — RADIO CAIRO, Kafr Silim-Abis	Mideast • 250 kW
11570	PAKISTAN — †RADIO PAKISTAN, Islamabad	Mideast & N Africa • 100 kW; Europe • 250 kW; (D) • Mideast • 250 kW
11575	CHINA (PR) — CHINA RADIO INTL, Xi'an	Mideast & S Asia • 120 kW; E Africa & S Africa • 120 kW
11580	CHINA (TAIWAN) — VO FREE CHINA, Via Okeechobee, USA	(D) • Europe • 100 kW
	GUAM — †KTWR-TRANS WORLD R, Merizo	E Asia • 100 kW
	USA — CHRIST SCI MONITOR, Via Saipan	E Asia • 100 kW
(con'd)	VOA, Greenville, NC	C America & S America • 250 kW

Time scale: 0 1 2 3 4 5 6 7 8 9 10 11 12 13 14 15 16 17 18 19 20 21 22 23 24

ENGLISH ▬▬   ARABIC ∽∽∽   CHINESE □□□   FRENCH ═══   GERMAN ▬▬   RUSSIAN ═══   SPANISH ▬▬   OTHER ──

FREQUENCY   COUNTRY, STATION, LOCATION

TARGET • NETWORK • POWER (kW)   World Time

0 1 2 3 4 5 6 7 8 9 10 11 12 13 14 15 16 17 18 19 20 21 22 23 24

FREQUENCY	COUNTRY, STATION, LOCATION	Transmission details
11580 (con'd)	USA — VOA, Greenville, NC	Tu-Sa • C America & S America • 250 kW
	†WEWN, Birmingham, Alabama	(J) • Europe • 500 kW
	†WYFR-FAMILY RADIO, Okeechobee, Fl	(D) • W Africa • 100 kW; (D) • Europe • 100 kW; (J) • Europe • 100 kW
11587	ISRAEL — KOL ISRAEL, Tel Aviv	W Europe • 100/300 kW; YIDDISH • W Europe • 100/300 kW; HEBREW • W Europe • 100/300 kW; W Europe & E North Am • 100/300 kW; F/Sa • W Europe • 100/300 kW; Su-Th • W Europe • 100/300 kW
11590	CHINA (PR) — †VO THE STRAIT-PLA, Fuzhou	TAIWAN-1 • 50 kW
11595	GREECE — †FONI TIS HELLADAS, Athens	(J) • GREEK • C America • 100 kW; (J) • C America • 100 kW
	RS MAKEDONIAS, Thessaloniki	GREEK • Europe • DS 35 kW; Sa/Su • GREEK • Europe • DS • 35 kW; M-F • GREEK • Europe • DS • 35 kW
11600	CHINA (PR) — CHINA RADIO INTL, Kunming	S Asia • 120 kW; S Asia & E Africa • 120 kW
	EGYPT — †RADIO CAIRO, Kafr Silim-Abis	N America • 250 kW
11605	ISRAEL — †KOL ISRAEL, Tel Aviv	(D) • W Asia • 300 kW; C America • 300 kW; (J) • W Europe • 300 kW; E Europe • 300 kW; W Europe & E North Am • 300 kW; (D) • W Europe • 300 kW; (D) • YIDDISH • W Europe • 300 kW; F/Sa • E Europe & W Asia • 300 kW; (J) • E Europe • 300 kW; (J) • YIDDISH • E Europe • 300 kW; Su-Th • W Europe • 300 kW; (D) Su-Th • PERSIAN • W Asia • 300 kW; (J) Su-Th • PERSIAN • W Europe • 300 kW
11610	CHINA (PR) — CENTRAL PEOPLES BS, Beijing	DS-2 • 10/50 kW; Th/Sa-Tu • DS-2 • 10/50 kW
	UKRAINE — †RADIO UKRAINE, Simferopol'	(J) • E North Am • 2X11780-11950 KHZ • SPR; (J) • UKRAINIAN • E North Am • 2X11780-11950 KHZ • SPR
11620	INDIA — ALL INDIA RADIO, Bangalore	S Asia & W Asia • 500 kW; W Europe • 500 kW; HINDI • S Asia & W Asia • 500 kW; N Europe • 500 kW; HINDI • W Europe • 500 kW
	†ALL INDIA RADIO, Delhi	SE Asia • 250 kW; S Asia & W Asia • 250 kW; HINDI • SE Asia • 250 kW
	VATICAN STATE — †VATICAN RADIO, Sta Maria di Galeria	S America • 100 kW; (J) • S America • 100 kW; (J) • E North Am & C America • 500 kW
11625	MONACO — †TRANS WORLD RADIO, Monte Carlo	E Europe & W Asia • 100/500 kW; M-Sa • E Europe & W Asia • 100/500 kW
	VATICAN STATE — †VATICAN RADIO, Sta Maria di Galeria	E Africa • 100 kW; C Africa & S Africa • 100 kW; (D) • C Africa & S Africa • 100 kW; W Africa • 100 kW; (J) • W Africa • 100 kW; (J) • W Africa • 250 kW
11630	CHINA (PR) — †CENTRAL PEOPLES BS, Beijing	DS-2 • 50 kW; DS-MINORITIES • 50 kW
	RUSSIA — †GOLOS ROSSII	(D)
	†GOLOS ROSSII, Moscow	(J) • Europe & S America • 250 kW
	†R MOSCOW INTL, Moscow	(J) • Europe • 250 kW
	†RADIO ROSSII	(D) • DS
	†RUKHI MIRAS, Balashikha	F • DS • 20 kW

0 1 2 3 4 5 6 7 8 9 10 11 12 13 14 15 16 17 18 19 20 21 22 23 24

FREQUENCY   COUNTRY, STATION, LOCATION   TARGET • NETWORK • POWER (kW)   World Time

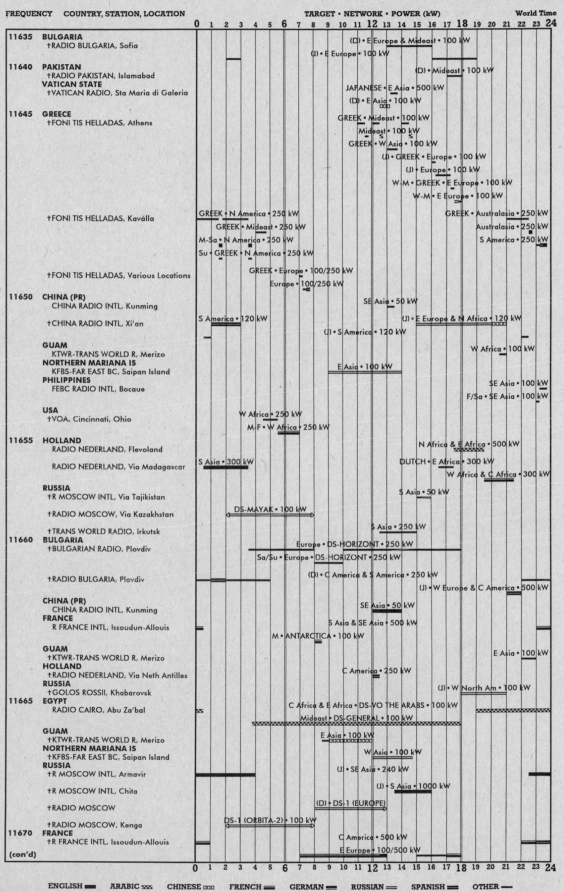

Frequency	Country, Station, Location	Target • Network • Power
11635	**BULGARIA** †RADIO BULGARIA, Sofia	(D) • E Europe & Mideast • 100 kW; (J) • E Europe • 100 kW
11640	**PAKISTAN** †RADIO PAKISTAN, Islamabad	(D) • Mideast • 100 kW
	VATICAN STATE †VATICAN RADIO, Sta Maria di Galeria	JAPANESE • E Asia • 500 kW; (D) • E Asia • 100 kW
11645	**GREECE** †FONI TIS HELLADAS, Athens	GREEK • Mideast • 100 kW; Mideast • 100 kW; GREEK • W Asia • 100 kW; (J) • GREEK • Europe • 100 kW; (J) • Europe • 100 kW; W-M • GREEK • E Europe • 100 kW; W-M • E Europe • 100 kW
	†FONI TIS HELLADAS, Kaválla	GREEK • N America • 250 kW; GREEK • Mideast • 250 kW; M-Sa • N America • 250 kW; Su • GREEK • N America • 250 kW; GREEK • Australasia • 250 kW; Australasia • 250 kW; S America • 250 kW
	†FONI TIS HELLADAS, Various Locations	GREEK • Europe • 100/250 kW; Europe • 100/250 kW
11650	**CHINA (PR)** CHINA RADIO INTL, Kunming	SE Asia • 50 kW
	†CHINA RADIO INTL, Xi'an	S America • 120 kW; (J) • E Europe & N Africa • 120 kW; (J) • S America • 120 kW
	GUAM KTWR-TRANS WORLD R, Merizo	W Africa • 100 kW
	NORTHERN MARIANA IS KFBS-FAR EAST BC, Saipan Island	E Asia • 100 kW
	PHILIPPINES FEBC RADIO INTL, Bocaue	SE Asia • 100 kW; F/Sa • SE Asia • 100 kW
	USA †VOA, Cincinnati, Ohio	W Africa • 250 kW; M-F • W Africa • 250 kW
11655	**HOLLAND** RADIO NEDERLAND, Flevoland	N Africa & E Africa • 500 kW
	RADIO NEDERLAND, Via Madagascar	S Asia • 300 kW; DUTCH • E Africa • 300 kW; W Africa & C Africa • 300 kW
	RUSSIA †R MOSCOW INTL, Via Tajikistan	S Asia • 50 kW
	†RADIO MOSCOW, Via Kazakhstan	DS-MAYAK • 100 kW
	†TRANS WORLD RADIO, Irkutsk	S Asia • 250 kW
11660	**BULGARIA** †BULGARIAN RADIO, Plovdiv	Europe • DS-HORIZONT • 250 kW; Sa/Su • Europe • DS-HORIZONT • 250 kW
	†RADIO BULGARIA, Plovdiv	(D) • C America & S America • 250 kW; (J) • W Europe & C America • 500 kW
	CHINA (PR) CHINA RADIO INTL, Kunming	SE Asia • 50 kW
	FRANCE R FRANCE INTL, Issoudun-Allouis	S Asia & SE Asia • 500 kW; M • ANTARCTICA • 100 kW
	GUAM †KTWR-TRANS WORLD R, Merizo	E Asia • 100 kW
	HOLLAND †RADIO NEDERLAND, Via Neth Antilles	C America • 250 kW
	RUSSIA †GOLOS ROSSII, Khabarovsk	(J) • W North Am • 100 kW
11665	**EGYPT** RADIO CAIRO, Abu Za'bal	C Africa & E Africa • DS-VO THE ARABS • 100 kW; Mideast • DS-GENERAL • 100 kW
	GUAM †KTWR-TRANS WORLD R, Merizo	E Asia • 100 kW
	NORTHERN MARIANA IS †KFBS-FAR EAST BC, Saipan Island	W Asia • 100 kW
	RUSSIA †R MOSCOW INTL, Armavir	(J) • SE Asia • 240 kW
	†R MOSCOW INTL, Chita	(J) • S Asia • 1000 kW
	†RADIO MOSCOW	(D) • DS-1 (EUROPE)
	†RADIO MOSCOW, Kenga	DS-1 (ORBITA-2) • 100 kW
11670	**FRANCE** †R FRANCE INTL, Issoudun-Allouis	C America • 500 kW; E Europe • 100/500 kW
(con'd)		

ENGLISH ▬   ARABIC ▨   CHINESE ▭▭▭   FRENCH ▬   GERMAN ▬   RUSSIAN ═   SPANISH ▬   OTHER ▬

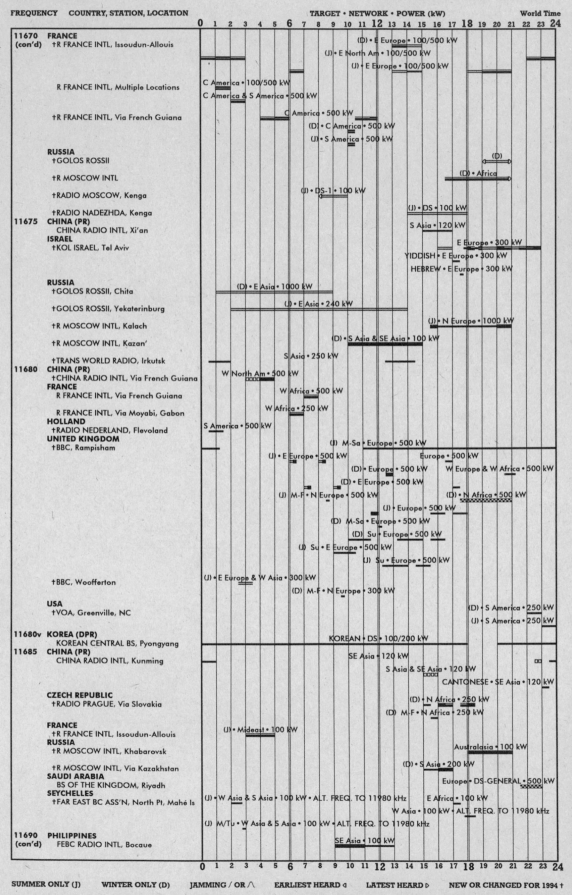

FREQUENCY   COUNTRY, STATION, LOCATION   TARGET • NETWORK • POWER (kW)   World Time

11670 FRANCE
(con'd) †R FRANCE INTL, Issoudun-Allouis   (D) • E Europe • 100/500 kW
                                                     (J) • E North Am • 100/500 kW
                                                     (J) • E Europe • 100/500 kW

         R FRANCE INTL, Multiple Locations   C America • 100/500 kW
                                              C America & S America • 500 kW

         †R FRANCE INTL, Via French Guiana   C America • 500 kW
                                                   (D) • C America • 500 kW
                                                   (J) • S America • 500 kW

         RUSSIA
         †GOLOS ROSSII   (D)

         †R MOSCOW INTL   (D) • Africa

         †RADIO MOSCOW, Kenga   (J) • DS-1 • 100 kW

         †RADIO NADEZHDA, Kenga   (J) • DS • 100 kW
11675 CHINA (PR)
         CHINA RADIO INTL, Xi'an   S Asia • 120 kW
         ISRAEL
         †KOL ISRAEL, Tel Aviv   E Europe • 300 kW
                                                    YIDDISH • E Europe • 300 kW
                                                    HEBREW • E Europe • 300 kW

         RUSSIA
         †GOLOS ROSSII, Chita   (D) • E Asia • 1000 kW

         †GOLOS ROSSII, Yekaterinburg   (J) • E Asia • 240 kW

         †R MOSCOW INTL, Kalach   (J) • N Europe • 1000 kW

         †R MOSCOW INTL, Kazan'   (D) • S Asia & SE Asia • 100 kW

         †TRANS WORLD RADIO, Irkutsk   S Asia • 250 kW
11680 CHINA (PR)
         †CHINA RADIO INTL, Via French Guiana W North Am • 500 kW
         FRANCE
         R FRANCE INTL, Via French Guiana   W Africa • 500 kW

         R FRANCE INTL, Via Moyabi, Gabon   W Africa • 250 kW
         HOLLAND
         †RADIO NEDERLAND, Flevoland   S America • 500 kW
         UNITED KINGDOM
         †BBC, Rampisham   (J) • M-Sa • Europe • 500 kW
                                                             Europe • 500 kW
                                                    (D) • Europe • 500 kW   W Europe & W Africa • 500 kW
                                                    (D) • E Europe • 500 kW
                                              (J) M-F • N Europe • 500 kW   (D) • N Africa • 500 kW
                                                        (J) • Europe • 500 kW
                                                    (D) M-Sa • Europe • 500 kW
                                                    (D) Su • Europe • 500 kW
                                              (J) Su • E Europe • 500 kW
                                                        (J) • Su • Europe • 500 kW

         †BBC, Woofferton   (J) • E Europe & W Asia • 300 kW
                                                    (D) M-F • N Europe • 300 kW

         USA
         †VOA, Greenville, NC   (D) • S America • 250 kW
                                                                   (J) • S America • 250 kW
11680v KOREA (DPR)
         KOREAN CENTRAL BS, Pyongyang   KOREAN • DS • 100/200 kW
11685 CHINA (PR)
         CHINA RADIO INTL, Kunming   SE Asia • 120 kW
                                                        S Asia & SE Asia • 120 kW
                                                            CANTONESE • SE Asia • 120 kW

         CZECH REPUBLIC
         †RADIO PRAGUE, Via Slovakia   (D) • N Africa • 250 kW
                                                          (D) M-F • N Africa • 250 kW

         FRANCE
         †R FRANCE INTL, Issoudun-Allouis   (J) • Mideast • 100 kW
         RUSSIA
         †R MOSCOW INTL, Khabarovsk   Australasia • 100 kW

         †R MOSCOW INTL, Via Kazakhstan   (D) • S Asia • 200 kW
         SAUDI ARABIA
         BS OF THE KINGDOM, Riyadh   Europe • DS-GENERAL • 500 kW
         SEYCHELLES
         †FAR EAST BC ASS'N, North Pt, Mahé Is (J) • W Asia & S Asia • 100 kW • ALT. FREQ. TO 11980 kHz   E Africa • 100 kW
                                                                   W Asia • 100 kW • ALT. FREQ. TO 11980 kHz
                                              (J) M/Tu • W Asia & S Asia • 100 kW • ALT. FREQ. TO 11980 kHz

11690 PHILIPPINES
(con'd) FEBC RADIO INTL, Bocaue   SE Asia • 100 kW

FREQUENCY　　COUNTRY, STATION, LOCATION　　　　　TARGET • NETWORK • POWER (kW)　　　World Time

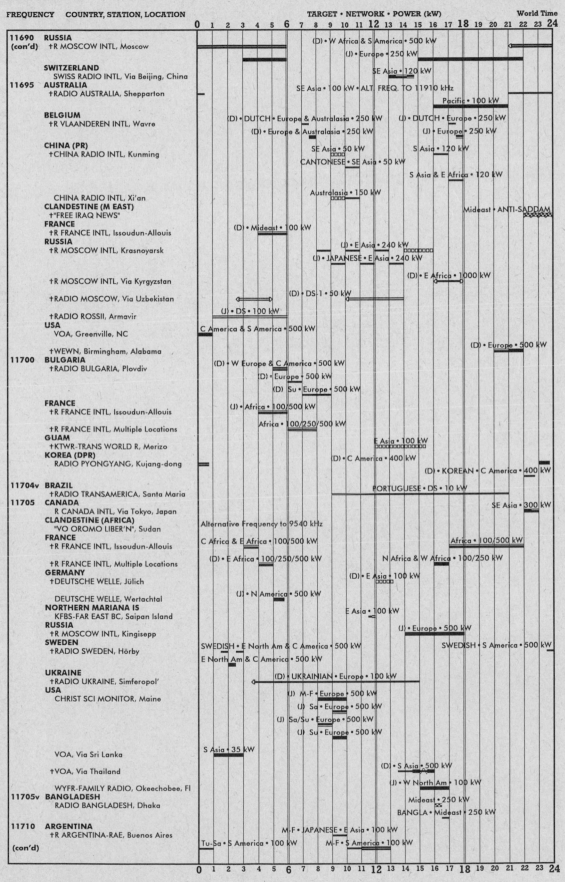

Frequency	Country, Station, Location	Target • Network • Power
11690 (con'd)	**RUSSIA** †R MOSCOW INTL, Moscow	(D) • W Africa & S America • 500 kW; (J) • Europe • 250 kW
	SWITZERLAND SWISS RADIO INTL, Via Beijing, China	SE Asia • 120 kW
11695	**AUSTRALIA** †RADIO AUSTRALIA, Shepparton	SE Asia • 100 kW • ALT. FREQ. TO 11910 kHz; Pacific • 100 kW
	BELGIUM †R VLAANDEREN INTL, Wavre	(D) • DUTCH • Europe & Australasia • 250 kW; (J) • DUTCH • Europe • 250 kW; (D) • Europe & Australasia • 250 kW; (J) • Europe • 250 kW
	CHINA (PR) †CHINA RADIO INTL, Kunming	SE Asia • 50 kW; S Asia • 120 kW; CANTONESE • SE Asia • 50 kW; S Asia & E Africa • 120 kW
	CHINA RADIO INTL, Xi'an	Australasia • 150 kW
	CLANDESTINE (M EAST) †"FREE IRAQ NEWS"	Mideast • ANTI-SADDAM
	FRANCE †R FRANCE INTL, Issoudun-Allouis	(D) • Mideast • 100 kW
	RUSSIA †R MOSCOW INTL, Krasnoyarsk	(J) • E Asia • 240 kW; (J) • JAPANESE • E Asia • 240 kW
	†R MOSCOW INTL, Via Kyrgyzstan	(D) • E Africa • 1000 kW
	†RADIO MOSCOW, Via Uzbekistan	(D) • DS-1 • 50 kW
	†RADIO ROSSII, Armavir	(J) • DS • 100 kW
	USA VOA, Greenville, NC	C America & S America • 500 kW
	†WEWN, Birmingham, Alabama	(D) • Europe • 500 kW
11700	**BULGARIA** †RADIO BULGARIA, Plovdiv	(D) • W Europe & C America • 500 kW; (D) • Europe • 500 kW; (D) • Su • Europe • 500 kW
	FRANCE †R FRANCE INTL, Issoudun-Allouis	(J) • Africa • 100/500 kW
	†R FRANCE INTL, Multiple Locations	Africa • 100/250/500 kW
	GUAM †KTWR-TRANS WORLD R, Merizo	E Asia • 100 kW
	KOREA (DPR) RADIO PYONGYANG, Kujang-dong	(D) • C America • 400 kW; (D) • KOREAN • C America • 400 kW
11704v	**BRAZIL** †RADIO TRANSAMERICA, Santa Maria	PORTUGUESE • DS • 10 kW
11705	**CANADA** R CANADA INTL, Via Tokyo, Japan	SE Asia • 300 kW
	CLANDESTINE (AFRICA) "VO OROMO LIBER'N", Sudan	Alternative Frequency to 9540 kHz
	FRANCE †R FRANCE INTL, Issoudun-Allouis	C Africa & E Africa • 100/500 kW; Africa • 100/500 kW
	†R FRANCE INTL, Multiple Locations	(D) • E Africa • 100/250/500 kW; N Africa & W Africa • 100/250 kW
	GERMANY †DEUTSCHE WELLE, Jülich	(D) • E Asia • 100 kW
	DEUTSCHE WELLE, Wertachtal	(J) • N America • 500 kW
	NORTHERN MARIANA IS KFBS-FAR EAST BC, Saipan Island	E Asia • 100 kW
	RUSSIA †R MOSCOW INTL, Kingisepp	(J) • Europe • 500 kW
	SWEDEN †RADIO SWEDEN, Hörby	SWEDISH • E North Am & C America • 500 kW; E North Am & C America • 500 kW; SWEDISH • S America • 500 kW
	UKRAINE †RADIO UKRAINE, Simferopol'	(D) • UKRAINIAN • Europe • 100 kW
	USA CHRIST SCI MONITOR, Maine	(J) • M-F • Europe • 500 kW; (J) • Sa • Europe • 500 kW; (J) • Sa/Su • Europe • 500 kW; (J) • Su • Europe • 500 kW
	VOA, Via Sri Lanka	S Asia • 35 kW
	†VOA, Via Thailand	(D) • S Asia • 500 kW; (J) • W North Am • 100 kW
	WYFR-FAMILY RADIO, Okeechobee, Fl	
11705v	**BANGLADESH** RADIO BANGLADESH, Dhaka	Mideast • 250 kW; BANGLA • Mideast • 250 kW
11710	**ARGENTINA** †R ARGENTINA-RAE, Buenos Aires	M-F • JAPANESE • E Asia • 100 kW; Tu-Sa • S America • 100 kW; M-F • S America • 100 kW
(con'd)		

ENGLISH ▬▬　ARABIC ※※※　CHINESE □□□　FRENCH ══　GERMAN ▬▬　RUSSIAN ＝＝　SPANISH ▬▬　OTHER ──

| FREQUENCY | COUNTRY, STATION, LOCATION | TARGET • NETWORK • POWER (kW) | World Time |

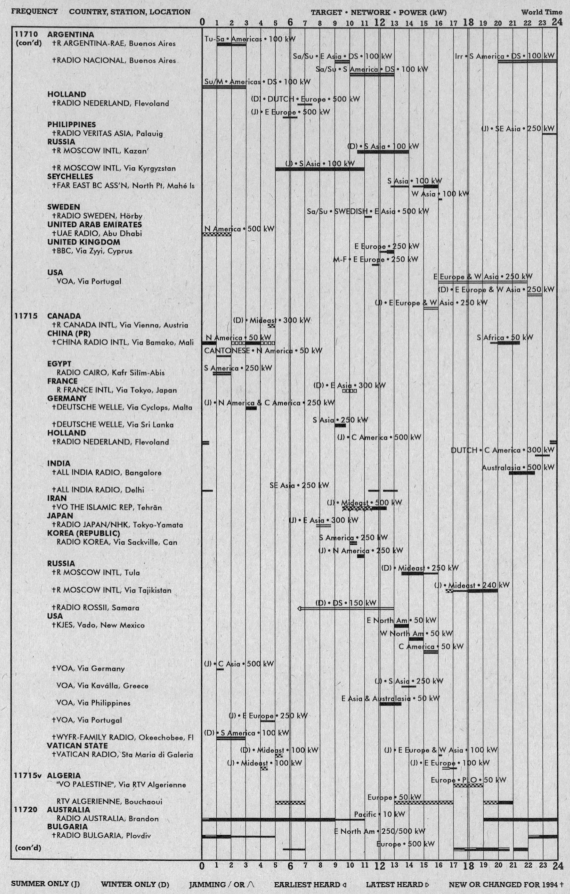

11710 **ARGENTINA**
(con'd) †R ARGENTINA-RAE, Buenos Aires — Tu-Sa • Americas • 100 kW

†RADIO NACIONAL, Buenos Aires — Sa/Su • E Asia • DS • 100 kW / Irr • S America • DS • 100 kW

Sa/Su • S America • DS • 100 kW

Su/M • Americas • DS • 100 kW

HOLLAND
†RADIO NEDERLAND, Flevoland — (D) • DUTCH • Europe • 500 kW

(J) • E Europe • 500 kW

PHILIPPINES
†RADIO VERITAS ASIA, Palauig — (J) • SE Asia • 250 kW

RUSSIA
†R MOSCOW INTL, Kazan' — (D) • S Asia • 100 kW

†R MOSCOW INTL, Via Kyrgyzstan — (J) • S Asia • 100 kW

SEYCHELLES
†FAR EAST BC ASS'N, North Pt, Mahé Is — S Asia • 100 kW

W Asia • 100 kW

SWEDEN
†RADIO SWEDEN, Hörby — Sa/Su • SWEDISH • E Asia • 500 kW

UNITED ARAB EMIRATES
†UAE RADIO, Abu Dhabi — N America • 500 kW

UNITED KINGDOM
†BBC, Via Zyyi, Cyprus — E Europe • 250 kW

M-F • E Europe • 250 kW

USA
VOA, Via Portugal — E Europe & W Asia • 250 kW

(D) • E Europe & W Asia • 250 kW

(J) • E Europe & W Asia • 250 kW

11715 **CANADA**
†R CANADA INTL, Via Vienna, Austria — (D) • Mideast • 300 kW

CHINA (PR)
†CHINA RADIO INTL, Via Bamako, Mali — N America • 50 kW / S Africa • 50 kW

CANTONESE • N America • 50 kW

EGYPT
RADIO CAIRO, Kafr Silim-Abis — S America • 250 kW

FRANCE
R FRANCE INTL, Via Tokyo, Japan — (D) • E Asia • 300 kW

GERMANY
†DEUTSCHE WELLE, Via Cyclops, Malta — (J) • N America & C America • 250 kW

†DEUTSCHE WELLE, Via Sri Lanka — S Asia • 250 kW

HOLLAND
†RADIO NEDERLAND, Flevoland — (J) • C America • 500 kW

DUTCH • C America • 300 kW

Australasia • 500 kW

INDIA
†ALL INDIA RADIO, Bangalore — SE Asia • 250 kW

†ALL INDIA RADIO, Delhi

IRAN
†VO THE ISLAMIC REP, Tehrān — (J) • Mideast • 500 kW

JAPAN
†RADIO JAPAN/NHK, Tokyo-Yamata — (J) • E Asia • 300 kW

KOREA (REPUBLIC)
RADIO KOREA, Via Sackville, Can — S America • 250 kW

(J) • N America • 250 kW

RUSSIA
†R MOSCOW INTL, Tula — (D) • Mideast • 250 kW

†R MOSCOW INTL, Via Tajikistan — (J) • Mideast • 240 kW

†RADIO ROSSII, Samara — (D) • DS • 150 kW

USA
†KJES, Vado, New Mexico — E North Am • 50 kW

W North Am • 50 kW

C America • 50 kW

†VOA, Via Germany — (J) • C Asia • 500 kW

VOA, Via Kaválla, Greece — (J) • S Asia • 250 kW

VOA, Via Philippines — E Asia & Australasia • 50 kW

†VOA, Via Portugal — (J) • E Europe • 250 kW

†WYFR-FAMILY RADIO, Okeechobee, Fl — (D) • S America • 100 kW

VATICAN STATE
†VATICAN RADIO, Sta Maria di Galeria — (D) • Mideast • 100 kW / (J) • E Europe & W Asia • 100 kW

(J) • Mideast • 100 kW / (J) • E Europe • 100 kW

11715v **ALGERIA**
"VO PALESTINE", Via RTV Algerienne — Europe • PLO • 50 kW

RTV ALGERIENNE, Bouchaoui — Europe • 50 kW

11720 **AUSTRALIA**
RADIO AUSTRALIA, Brandon — Pacific • 10 kW

BULGARIA
†RADIO BULGARIA, Plovdiv — E North Am • 250/500 kW

(con'd) — Europe • 500 kW

FREQUENCY   COUNTRY, STATION, LOCATION

TARGET • NETWORK • POWER (kW)

World Time

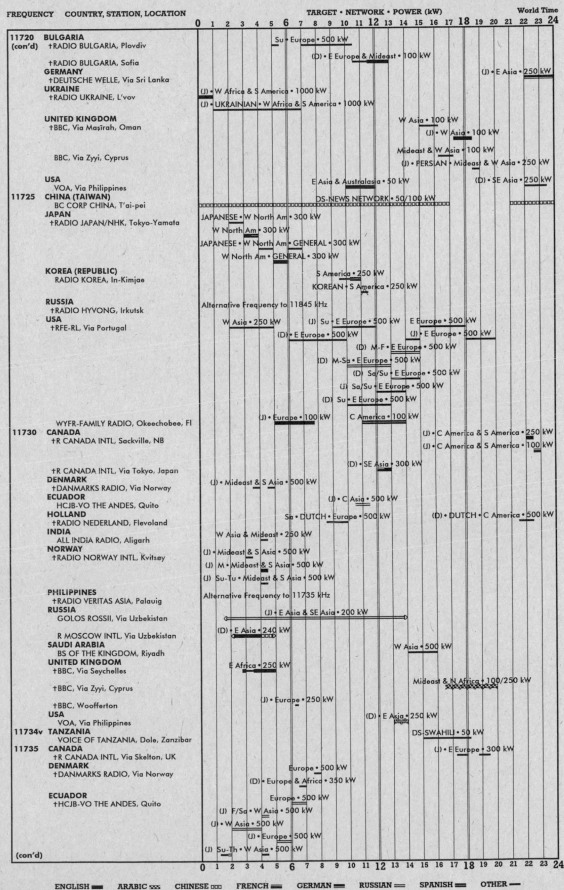

FREQUENCY	COUNTRY, STATION, LOCATION	Details
11720 (con'd)	BULGARIA	
	†RADIO BULGARIA, Plovdiv	Su • Europe • 500 kW
	†RADIO BULGARIA, Sofia	(D) • E Europe & Mideast • 100 kW
	GERMANY	
	†DEUTSCHE WELLE, Via Sri Lanka	(J) • E Asia • 250 kW
	UKRAINE	
	†RADIO UKRAINE, L'vov	(J) • W Africa & S America • 1000 kW
		(J) • UKRAINIAN • W Africa & S America • 1000 kW
	UNITED KINGDOM	
	†BBC, Via Maṣīrah, Oman	W Asia • 100 kW
		(J) • W Asia • 100 kW
	BBC, Via Zyyi, Cyprus	Mideast & W Asia • 100 kW
		(J) • PERSIAN • Mideast & W Asia • 250 kW
	USA	
	VOA, Via Philippines	E Asia & Australasia • 50 kW
		(D) • SE Asia • 250 kW
11725	CHINA (TAIWAN)	
	BC CORP CHINA, T'ai-pei	DS-NEWS NETWORK • 50/100 kW
	JAPAN	
	†RADIO JAPAN/NHK, Tokyo-Yamata	JAPANESE • W North Am • 300 kW
		W North Am • 300 kW
		JAPANESE • W North Am • GENERAL • 300 kW
		W North Am • GENERAL • 300 kW
	KOREA (REPUBLIC)	
	RADIO KOREA, In-Kimjae	S America • 250 kW
		KOREAN • S America • 250 kW
	RUSSIA	
	†RADIO HYVONG, Irkutsk	Alternative Frequency to 11845 kHz
	USA	
	†RFE-RL, Via Portugal	W Asia • 250 kW
		(J) Su • E Europe • 500 kW
		E Europe • 500 kW
		(D) • E Europe • 500 kW
		(J) • E Europe • 500 kW
		(D) • M-F • E Europe • 500 kW
		(D) M-Sa • E Europe • 500 kW
		(D) • Sa/Su • E Europe • 500 kW
		(J) • Sa/Su • E Europe • 500 kW
		(D) • Su • E Europe • 500 kW
	WYFR-FAMILY RADIO, Okeechobee, Fl	(J) • Europe • 100 kW
		C America • 100 kW
11730	CANADA	
	†R CANADA INTL, Sackville, NB	(J) • C America & S America • 250 kW
		(J) • C America & S America • 100 kW
	†R CANADA INTL, Via Tokyo, Japan	(D) • SE Asia • 300 kW
	DENMARK	
	†DANMARKS RADIO, Via Norway	(J) • Mideast & S Asia • 500 kW
	ECUADOR	
	HCJB-VO THE ANDES, Quito	(J) • C Asia • 500 kW
	HOLLAND	
	†RADIO NEDERLAND, Flevoland	Sa • DUTCH • Europe • 500 kW
		(D) • DUTCH • C America • 500 kW
	INDIA	
	ALL INDIA RADIO, Aligarh	W Asia & Mideast • 250 kW
	NORWAY	
	†RADIO NORWAY INTL, Kvitsøy	(J) • Mideast & S Asia • 500 kW
		(J) • M • Mideast & S Asia • 500 kW
		(J) • Su-Tu • Mideast & S Asia • 500 kW
	PHILIPPINES	
	†RADIO VERITAS ASIA, Palauig	Alternative Frequency to 11735 kHz
	RUSSIA	
	GOLOS ROSSII, Via Uzbekistan	(J) • E Asia & SE Asia • 200 kW
	R MOSCOW INTL, Via Uzbekistan	(D) • E Asia • 240 kW
	SAUDI ARABIA	
	BS OF THE KINGDOM, Riyadh	W Asia • 500 kW
	UNITED KINGDOM	
	†BBC, Via Seychelles	E Africa • 250 kW
	†BBC, Via Zyyi, Cyprus	Mideast & N Africa • 100/250 kW
	†BBC, Woofferton	(J) • Europe • 250 kW
	USA	
	VOA, Via Philippines	(D) • E Asia • 250 kW
11734v	TANZANIA	
	VOICE OF TANZANIA, Dole, Zanzibar	DS-SWAHILI • 50 kW
11735	CANADA	
	†R CANADA INTL, Via Skelton, UK	(J) • E Europe • 300 kW
	DENMARK	
	†DANMARKS RADIO, Via Norway	Europe • 500 kW
		(D) • Europe & Africa • 350 kW
	ECUADOR	
	†HCJB-VO THE ANDES, Quito	Europe • 500 kW
		(J) • F/Sa • W Asia • 500 kW
		(J) • W Asia • 500 kW
		(J) • Europe • 500 kW
(con'd)		(J) Su-Th • W Asia • 500 kW

ENGLISH ▬▬ ARABIC ⌇⌇⌇ CHINESE □□□ FRENCH ══ GERMAN ▬▬ RUSSIAN ══ SPANISH ══ OTHER ──

FREQUENCY   COUNTRY, STATION, LOCATION   TARGET • NETWORK • POWER (kW)   World Time

0 1 2 3 4 5 6 7 8 9 10 11 12 13 14 15 16 17 18 19 20 21 22 23 24

Frequency	Country, Station, Location	Target • Network • Power (kW)
11735 (con'd)	**FINLAND** †RADIO FINLAND, Pori	(D) • N America • 500 kW
		(D) M-F • N America • 500 kW
		(D) Sa/Su • N America • 500 kW
	GERMANY †DEUTSCHE WELLE, Jülich	(J) • E Europe • 100 kW
	†DEUTSCHE WELLE, Via Cyclops, Malta	(D) • JAPANESE • E Asia • 250 kW
	†DEUTSCHE WELLE, Via Sri Lanka	S Asia • 250 kW (D) • SE Asia • 250 kW
	INDIA ALL INDIA RADIO, Delhi	S Asia • 100 kW E Asia • 250 kW
	JAPAN †RADIO JAPAN/NHK, Via Sackville, Can	JAPANESE • W North Am • GENERAL • 250 kW
		W North Am • GENERAL • 250 kW
	KOREA (DPR) †RADIO PYONGYANG, Kujang-dong	KOREAN • E Asia • 200 kW S Asia • 200 kW
	NEW ZEALAND R NEW ZEALAND INTL, Rangitaiki	(J) Su-F • ENGLISH, ETC • Pacific • DS • 100 kW
	NORWAY †RADIO NORWAY INTL, Fredrikstad	(D) • Europe & Africa • 350 kW
	†RADIO NORWAY INTL, Kvitsøy	Europe • 500 kW
	PHILIPPINES †RADIO VERITAS ASIA, Palauig	(J) • S Asia • 250 kW • ALT. FREQ. TO 11730 kHz
	RUSSIA R MOSCOW INTL, Serpukhov	(J) • E Europe & W Africa • 240 kW
	TURKEY VOICE OF TURKEY, Ankara	W Asia • 250 kW
	UKRAINE †RADIO UKRAINE	(J) • UKRAINIAN
	UNITED KINGDOM †BBC, Via Zyyi, Cyprus	(D) • E Europe • 250 kW
	URUGUAY RADIO ORIENTAL, Montevideo	Irr • DS • 1.5 kW
		DS • 1.5 kW
	USA †VOA, Via Philippines	(J) • E Asia • 250 kW
		(J) • S Asia • 100 kW
	†WEWN, Birmingham, Alabama	(D) • C America • 500 kW
		(J) • C America & W North Am • 500 kW
	YUGOSLAVIA †RADIO YUGOSLAVIA, Belgrade	Mideast • 500 kW
11740	**CHINA (PR)** †CENTRAL PEOPLES BS, Beijing	DS-2 • 50 kW
	CHINA (TAIWAN) BC CORP CHINA, Via Okeechobee, USA	(J) • C America • 100 kW
	VO FREE CHINA, Via Okeechobee, USA	C America • 100 kW
		CANTONESE • C America • 100 kW
	GERMANY †DEUTSCHE WELLE, Via Kigali, Rwanda	W Africa • 250 kW
	†DEUTSCHE WELLE, Via Sri Lanka	(J) • SE Asia • 250 kW
	HOLLAND †RADIO NEDERLAND, Via Madagascar	(J) • SE Asia • 300 kW
	JAPAN †RADIO JAPAN/NHK, Via Singapore	SE Asia • GENERAL • 250 kW
		JAPANESE • SE Asia • GENERAL • 250 kW
	KOREA (DPR) †RADIO PYONGYANG, Pyongyang	W Asia • 200 kW
		Europe • 200 kW
	KOREA (REPUBLIC) RADIO KOREA, In-Kimjae	KOREAN • E Asia • 100 kW
		E Asia • 100 kW
	ROMANIA RADIO ROMANIA INTL, Bucharest	(D) • Mideast • 250 kW
	RUSSIA RADIO MOSCOW, Novosibirsk	DS-1 • 50 kW
	SWAZILAND †TRANS WORLD RADIO, Manzini	S Africa • 25 kW
		Sa/Su • S Africa • 25 kW
	UNITED KINGDOM †BBC, Rampisham	(J) • E Europe • 500 kW
		(J) M-F • N Europe • 500 kW
	†BBC, Via Masirah, Oman	(J) • W Asia • 100 kW
	†BBC, Via Zyyi, Cyprus	(J) • Mideast • 100 kW
	USA †VOA, Via Germany	(D) • Mideast • 500 kW
	VOA, Via Kavála, Greece	E Africa • 250 kW
		(D) • E Europe & W Asia • 250 kW
	†VOA, Via Morocco	(D) • Mideast • 100/500 kW
(con'd)	VOA, Via Philippines	(D) • E Asia • 250 kW

0 1 2 3 4 5 6 7 8 9 10 11 12 13 14 15 16 17 18 19 20 21 22 23 24

FREQUENCY　　COUNTRY, STATION, LOCATION　　　　　TARGET • NETWORK • POWER (kW)　　　World Time

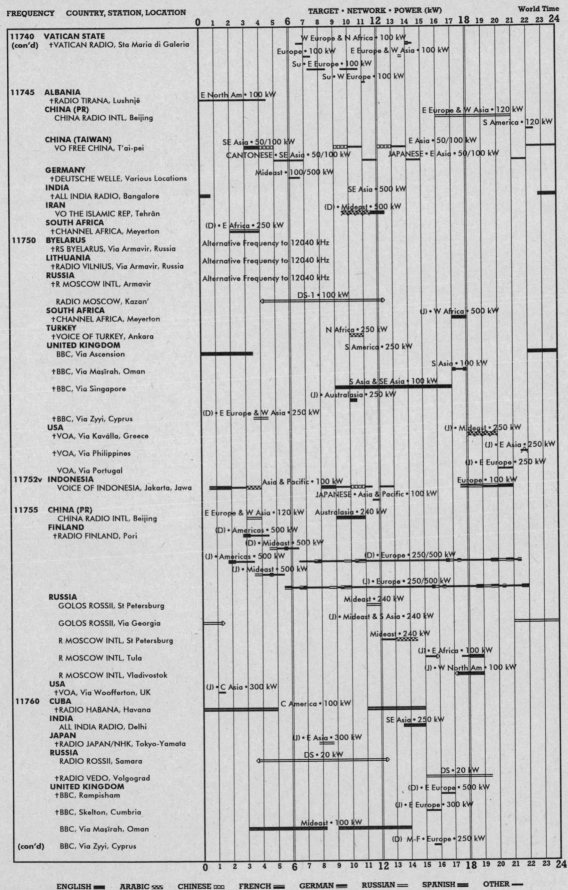

11740	**VATICAN STATE**
(con'd)	†VATICAN RADIO, Sta Maria di Galeria
	W Europe & N Africa • 100 kW
	Europe • 100 kW　　E Europe & W Asia • 100 kW
	Su • E Europe • 100 kW
	Su • W Europe • 100 kW
11745	**ALBANIA**
	†RADIO TIRANA, Lushnjë — E North Am • 100 kW
	CHINA (PR)
	CHINA RADIO INTL, Beijing — E Europe & W Asia • 120 kW / S America • 120 kW
	CHINA (TAIWAN)
	VO FREE CHINA, T'ai-pei — SE Asia • 50/100 kW / E Asia • 50/100 kW
	CANTONESE • SE Asia • 50/100 kW / JAPANESE • E Asia • 50/100 kW
	GERMANY
	†DEUTSCHE WELLE, Various Locations — Mideast • 100/500 kW
	INDIA
	†ALL INDIA RADIO, Bangalore — SE Asia • 500 kW
	IRAN
	VO THE ISLAMIC REP, Tehrān — (D) • Mideast • 500 kW
	SOUTH AFRICA
	†CHANNEL AFRICA, Meyerton — (D) • E Africa • 250 kW
11750	**BYELARUS**
	†RS BYELARUS, Via Armavir, Russia — Alternative Frequency to 12040 kHz
	LITHUANIA
	†RADIO VILNIUS, Via Armavir, Russia — Alternative Frequency to 12040 kHz
	RUSSIA
	†R MOSCOW INTL, Armavir — Alternative Frequency to 12040 kHz
	RADIO MOSCOW, Kazan' — DS-1 • 100 kW
	SOUTH AFRICA
	†CHANNEL AFRICA, Meyerton — (J) • W Africa • 500 kW
	TURKEY
	†VOICE OF TURKEY, Ankara — N Africa • 250 kW
	UNITED KINGDOM
	BBC, Via Ascension — S America • 250 kW
	†BBC, Via Maṣīrah, Oman — S Asia • 100 kW
	†BBC, Via Singapore — S Asia & SE Asia • 100 kW
	(J) • Australasia • 250 kW
	†BBC, Via Zyyi, Cyprus — (D) • E Europe & W Asia • 250 kW
	USA
	†VOA, Via Kaválla, Greece — (J) • Mideast • 250 kW
	†VOA, Via Philippines — (J) • E Asia • 250 kW
	VOA, Via Portugal — (J) • E Europe • 250 kW
11752v	**INDONESIA**
	VOICE OF INDONESIA, Jakarta, Jawa — Asia & Pacific • 100 kW / Europe • 100 kW
	JAPANESE • Asia & Pacific • 100 kW
11755	**CHINA (PR)**
	CHINA RADIO INTL, Beijing — E Europe & W Asia • 120 kW / Australasia • 240 kW
	FINLAND
	†RADIO FINLAND, Pori — (D) • Americas • 500 kW
	(D) • Mideast • 500 kW
	(J) • Americas • 500 kW / (D) • Europe • 250/500 kW
	(J) • Mideast • 500 kW
	(J) • Europe • 250/500 kW
	RUSSIA
	GOLOS ROSSII, St Petersburg — Mideast • 240 kW
	GOLOS ROSSII, Via Georgia — (J) • Mideast & S Asia • 240 kW
	R MOSCOW INTL, St Petersburg — Mideast • 240 kW
	R MOSCOW INTL, Tula — (J) • E Africa • 100 kW
	R MOSCOW INTL, Vladivostok — (J) • W North Am • 100 kW
	USA
	†VOA, Via Woofferton, UK — (J) • C Asia • 300 kW
11760	**CUBA**
	†RADIO HABANA, Havana — C America • 100 kW
	INDIA
	ALL INDIA RADIO, Delhi — SE Asia • 250 kW
	JAPAN
	†RADIO JAPAN/NHK, Tokyo-Yamata — (J) • E Asia • 300 kW
	RUSSIA
	RADIO ROSSII, Samara — DS • 20 kW
	†RADIO VEDO, Volgograd — DS • 20 kW
	UNITED KINGDOM
	†BBC, Rampisham — (D) • E Europe • 500 kW
	†BBC, Skelton, Cumbria — (J) • E Europe • 300 kW
	BBC, Via Maṣīrah, Oman — Mideast • 100 kW
(con'd)	BBC, Via Zyyi, Cyprus — (D) M-F • Europe • 250 kW

ENGLISH ▬　ARABIC ⁓⁓⁓　CHINESE ▫▫▫　FRENCH ═══　GERMAN ▭▭　RUSSIAN ══　SPANISH ▭▭　OTHER ──

FREQUENCY   COUNTRY, STATION, LOCATION

TARGET • NETWORK • POWER (kW)   World Time

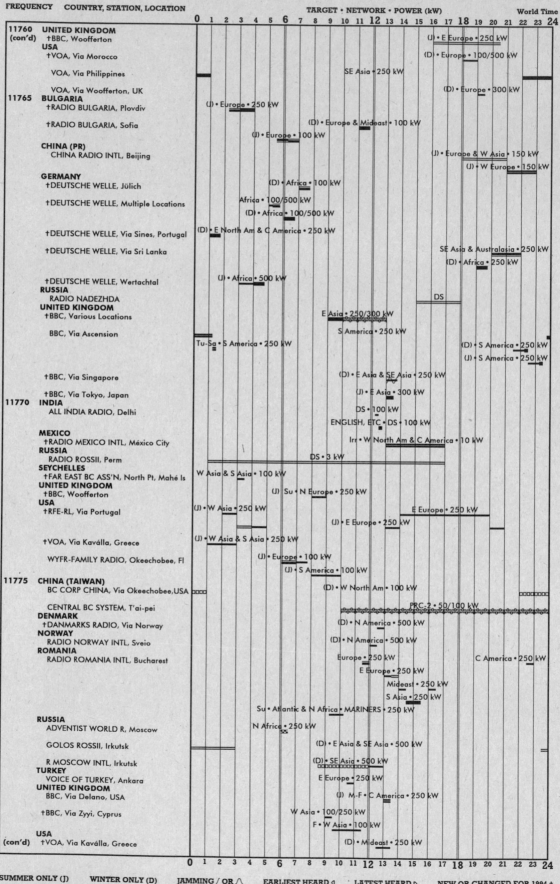

FREQUENCY	COUNTRY, STATION, LOCATION	Notes
11760 (con'd)	UNITED KINGDOM †BBC, Woofferton	(J) • E Europe • 250 kW
	USA †VOA, Via Morocco	(D) • Europe • 100/500 kW
	VOA, Via Philippines	SE Asia • 250 kW
	VOA, Via Woofferton, UK	(D) • Europe • 300 kW
11765	BULGARIA †RADIO BULGARIA, Plovdiv	(J) • Europe • 250 kW
	†RADIO BULGARIA, Sofia	(D) • Europe & Mideast • 100 kW; (J) • Europe • 100 kW
	CHINA (PR) CHINA RADIO INTL, Beijing	(J) • Europe & W Asia • 150 kW; (J) • W Europe • 150 kW
	GERMANY †DEUTSCHE WELLE, Jülich	(D) • Africa • 100 kW
	†DEUTSCHE WELLE, Multiple Locations	Africa • 100/500 kW; (D) • Africa • 100/500 kW
	†DEUTSCHE WELLE, Via Sines, Portugal	(D) • E North Am & C America • 250 kW
	†DEUTSCHE WELLE, Via Sri Lanka	SE Asia & Australasia • 250 kW; (D) • Africa • 250 kW
	†DEUTSCHE WELLE, Wertachtal	(J) • Africa • 500 kW
	RUSSIA RADIO NADEZHDA	DS
	UNITED KINGDOM †BBC, Various Locations	E Asia • 250/300 kW
	BBC, Via Ascension	S America • 250 kW; Tu-Sa • S America • 250 kW; (D) • S America • 250 kW; (J) • S America • 250 kW
	†BBC, Via Singapore	(D) • E Asia & SE Asia • 250 kW
	†BBC, Via Tokyo, Japan	(J) • E Asia • 300 kW
11770	INDIA ALL INDIA RADIO, Delhi	DS • 100 kW; ENGLISH, ETC • DS • 100 kW
	MEXICO †RADIO MEXICO INTL, México City	Irr • W North Am & C America • 10 kW
	RUSSIA RADIO ROSSII, Perm	DS • 3 kW
	SEYCHELLES †FAR EAST BC ASS'N, North Pt, Mahé Is	W Asia & S Asia • 100 kW
	UNITED KINGDOM †BBC, Woofferton	(J) • Su • N Europe • 250 kW
	USA †RFE-RL, Via Portugal	(J) • W Asia • 250 kW; E Europe • 250 kW; (J) • E Europe • 250 kW
	†VOA, Via Kaválla, Greece	(J) • W Asia & S Asia • 250 kW
	WYFR-FAMILY RADIO, Okeechobee, Fl	(J) • Europe • 100 kW; (J) • S America • 100 kW
11775	CHINA (TAIWAN) BC CORP CHINA, Via Okeechobee, USA	(D) • W North Am • 100 kW
	CENTRAL BC SYSTEM, T'ai-pei	PRC-2 • 5D/100 kW
	DENMARK †DANMARKS RADIO, Via Norway	(D) • N America • 500 kW
	NORWAY RADIO NORWAY INTL, Sveio	(D) • N America • 500 kW
	ROMANIA RADIO ROMANIA INTL, Bucharest	Europe • 250 kW; C America • 250 kW; E Europe • 250 kW; Mideast • 250 kW; S Asia • 250 kW; Su • Atlantic & N Africa • MARINERS • 250 kW
	RUSSIA ADVENTIST WORLD R, Moscow	N Africa • 250 kW
	GOLOS ROSSII, Irkutsk	(D) • E Asia & SE Asia • 500 kW
	R MOSCOW INTL, Irkutsk	(D) • SE Asia • 500 kW
	TURKEY VOICE OF TURKEY, Ankara	E Europe • 250 kW
	UNITED KINGDOM BBC, Via Delano, USA	(J) • M-F • C America • 250 kW
	†BBC, Via Zyyi, Cyprus	W Asia • 100/250 kW; F • W Asia • 100 kW
(con'd)	USA †VOA, Via Kaválla, Greece	(D) • Mideast • 250 kW

FREQUENCY   COUNTRY, STATION, LOCATION

TARGET • NETWORK • POWER (kW)   World Time

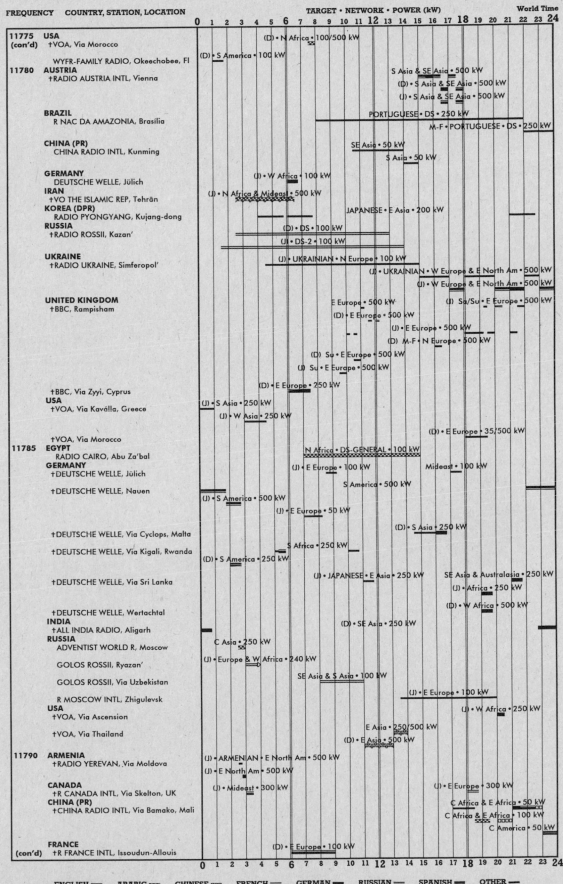

11775 USA
(con'd) †VOA, Via Morocco — (D) • N Africa • 100/500 kW

WYFR-FAMILY RADIO, Okeechobee, Fl — (D) • S America • 100 kW

11780 AUSTRIA
†RADIO AUSTRIA INTL, Vienna — S Asia & SE Asia • 500 kW
(D) • S Asia & SE Asia • 500 kW
(J) • S Asia & SE Asia • 500 kW

BRAZIL
R NAC DA AMAZONIA, Brasília — PORTUGUESE • DS • 250 kW
M-F • PORTUGUESE • DS • 250 kW

CHINA (PR)
CHINA RADIO INTL, Kunming — SE Asia • 50 kW
S Asia • 50 kW

GERMANY
DEUTSCHE WELLE, Jülich — (J) • W Africa • 100 kW

IRAN
†VO THE ISLAMIC REP, Tehrān — (J) • N Africa & Mideast • 500 kW

KOREA (DPR)
RADIO PYONGYANG, Kujang-dong — JAPANESE • E Asia • 200 kW

RUSSIA
†RADIO ROSSII, Kazan' — (D) • DS • 100 kW
(J) • DS-2 • 100 kW

UKRAINE
†RADIO UKRAINE, Simferopol' — (J) • UKRAINIAN • N Europe • 100 kW
(J) • UKRAINIAN • W Europe & E North Am • 500 kW
(J) • W Europe & E North Am • 500 kW

UNITED KINGDOM
†BBC, Rampisham — E Europe • 500 kW
(J) Sa/Su • E Europe • 500 kW
(D) • E Europe • 500 kW
(J) • E Europe • 500 kW
(D) M-F • N Europe • 500 kW
(D) Su • E Europe • 500 kW
(J) Su • E Europe • 500 kW

†BBC, Via Zyyi, Cyprus — (D) • E Europe • 250 kW

USA
†VOA, Via Kaválla, Greece — (J) • S Asia • 250 kW
(J) • W Asia • 250 kW

†VOA, Via Morocco — (D) • E Europe • 35/500 kW

11785 EGYPT
RADIO CAIRO, Abu Za'bal — N Africa • DS-GENERAL • 100 kW

GERMANY
†DEUTSCHE WELLE, Jülich — (J) • E Europe • 100 kW
Mideast • 100 kW

†DEUTSCHE WELLE, Nauen — S America • 500 kW
(J) • S America • 500 kW
(J) • E Europe • 50 kW

†DEUTSCHE WELLE, Via Cyclops, Malta — (D) • S Asia • 250 kW

†DEUTSCHE WELLE, Via Kigali, Rwanda — S Africa • 250 kW
(D) • S America • 250 kW

†DEUTSCHE WELLE, Via Sri Lanka — (J) • JAPANESE • E Asia • 250 kW
SE Asia & Australasia • 250 kW
(J) • Africa • 250 kW

†DEUTSCHE WELLE, Wertachtal — (D) • W Africa • 500 kW

INDIA
†ALL INDIA RADIO, Aligarh — (D) • SE Asia • 250 kW

RUSSIA
ADVENTIST WORLD R, Moscow — C Asia • 250 kW

GOLOS ROSSII, Ryazan' — (J) • Europe & W Africa • 240 kW

GOLOS ROSSII, Via Uzbekistan — SE Asia & S Asia • 100 kW

R MOSCOW INTL, Zhigulevsk — (J) • E Europe • 100 kW

USA
†VOA, Via Ascension — (J) • W Africa • 250 kW

†VOA, Via Thailand — E Asia • 250/500 kW
(D) • E Asia • 500 kW

11790 ARMENIA
†RADIO YEREVAN, Via Moldova — (J) • ARMENIAN • E North Am • 500 kW
(J) • E North Am • 500 kW

CANADA
†R CANADA INTL, Via Skelton, UK — (J) • Mideast • 300 kW
(J) • E Europe • 300 kW

CHINA (PR)
†CHINA RADIO INTL, Via Bamako, Mali — C Africa & E Africa • 50 kW
C Africa & E Africa • 100 kW
C America • 50 kW

FRANCE
(con'd) †R FRANCE INTL, Issoudun-Allouis — (D) • E Europe • 100 kW

FREQUENCY COUNTRY, STATION, LOCATION

TARGET • NETWORK • POWER (kW)

World Time

11790 FRANCE	
(con'd) †R FRANCE INTL, Issoudun-Allouis	(J) • E Europe • 100 kW
IRAN	
†VO THE ISLAMIC REP, Tehrān	E North Am & C America • 500 kW
	S Asia & SE Asia • 500 kW
	Europe • 500 kW
	W Asia • 500 kW
	E Europe • 500 kW
PHILIPPINES	
†RADIO VERITAS ASIA, Palauig	(J) • SE Asia • 250 kW
	SE Asia • 250 kW
ROMANIA	
RADIO ROMANIA INTL, Bucharest	Europe • 250 kW
	(D) • Europe • 250 kW
	(J) • Europe • 250 kW
RUSSIA	
†R MOSCOW INTL, Via Moldova	(J) • E North Am • 500 kW
SEYCHELLES	
†FAR EAST BC ASS'N, North Pt, Mahé Is	E Africa • 100 kW
UKRAINE	
†RADIO UKRAINE	(J) • UKRAINIAN
USA	
†WORLD HARVEST R, Noblesville, Indiana	Alternative Frequency to 15105 kHz
11790v MONGOLIA	
†RADIO ULAANBAATAR, Ulaanbaatar	Mideast • 50 kW
	Tu/F • W Asia • 50 kW
11795 CANADA	
R CANADA INTL, Via Xi'an, China(PR)	(J) • E Asia • 120 kW
CHINA (PR)	
†CHINA RADIO INTL	Australasia
CYPRUS	
CYPRUS BC CORP, Zyyi	(J) F-Su • Europe • 250 kW
DENMARK	
†DANMARKS RADIO, Via Norway	(J) • E North Am & C America • 500 kW
GERMANY	
†DEUTSCHE WELLE, Jülich	(J) • S Asia • 100 kW Australasia • 100 kW Africa • 100 kW
	(D) • E Asia • 100 kW
	(D) • S Asia • 100 kW
	(J) • E Europe • 100 kW
†DEUTSCHE WELLE, Nauen	(D) • S Asia & SE Asia • 500 kW
	(D) • JAPANESE • E Asia • 500 kW
DEUTSCHE WELLE, Via Antigua	S America • 250 kW
†DEUTSCHE WELLE, Via Kigali, Rwanda	W Africa & S America • 250 kW (D) • W Africa & S America • 250 kW
DEUTSCHE WELLE, Via N'sibirsk, Russia	(J) • E Asia • 1000 kW
†DEUTSCHE WELLE, Via Sines, Portugal	(J) • E Europe • 250 kW
NORWAY	
RADIO NORWAY INTL, Sveio	(J) M-Sa • E North Am & C America • 500 kW
	(J) Su • E North Am & C America • 500 kW
RUSSIA	
†RADIO MOSCOW, Armavir	DS-1 • 100 kW
UNITED ARAB EMIRATES	
UAE RADIO, Dubai	Europe • 300 kW
	(D) • Europe • 300 kW
UNITED KINGDOM	
BBC, Via Zyyi, Cyprus	(J) M-F • E Europe • 250 kW
11800 AUSTRALIA	
†RADIO AUSTRALIA, Shepparton	Pacific & N America • 100 kW
ETHIOPIA	
†VOICE OF PEACE, Gedja	E Africa • 100 kW
ITALY	
RADIO ROMA, Rome	ITALIAN • E North Am & C America • 100 kW
	E North Am & C America • 100 kW W Europe • 100 kW
	Mideast • 100 kW
	(D) • E Europe • 100 kW N Europe • 100 kW
	E Asia • 100 kW
RUSSIA	
RADIO NADEZHDA	DS
SOUTH AFRICA	
†CHANNEL AFRICA, Meyerton	(D) • E Africa • 500 kW
	(D) • E Africa • 250 kW
SRI LANKA	
SRI LANKA BC CORP, Colombo-Ekala	S Asia • 100 kW
	Su • S Asia • 100 kW Mideast • 100 kW
11805 DENMARK	
†DANMARKS RADIO, Via Norway	(J) • SE Asia • 500 kW
GUAM	
†KTWR-TRANS WORLD R, Merizo	Australasia • 100 kW
	E Asia • 100 kW
INDIA	
(con'd) †ALL INDIA RADIO, Delhi	E Africa • 100 kW

SUMMER ONLY (J)   WINTER ONLY (D)   JAMMING / OR ∧   EARLIEST HEARD ◁   LATEST HEARD ▷   NEW OR CHANGED FOR 1994 †

FREQUENCY	COUNTRY, STATION, LOCATION	TARGET • NETWORK • POWER (kW) — World Time

Frequency	Country, Station, Location	Schedule
11805 (con'd)	**IRAQ** †RADIO IRAQ INTL	Europe • ALT. FREQ. TO 11810 kHz
	NORWAY †RADIO NORWAY INTL, Kvitsøy	(J) • SE Asia • 500 kW
	RUSSIA RADIO MOSCOW, Kazan'	(D) • DS-1 • 50 kW
	SEYCHELLES †FAR EAST BC ASS'N, North Pt, Mahé Is	E Africa • 100 kW
	SWAZILAND TRANS WORLD RADIO, Manzini	S Africa • 25 kW
	USA VOA, Via Germany	(D) • E Europe & W Asia • 500 kW
		(J) • Mideast • 500 kW
	†VOA, Via Kaválla, Greece	N Africa & W Africa • 250 kW
		(J) • N Africa & W Africa • 250 kW
		(D) • W Asia • 250 kW
		(J) • E Africa • 250 kW
	†VOA, Via Morocco	(J) • E Europe • 100 kW
	VOA, Via Philippines	SE Asia • 250 kW
	†VOA, Via Portugal	(J) • E Europe • 250 kW
		E Europe & W Asia • 250 kW
		(D) • E Europe • 250 kW
		(J) • E Europe & W Asia • 250 kW
	†VOA, Via Thailand	(J) • SE Asia • 250 kW
	†VOA, Via Woofferton, UK	Europe • 250/300 kW
	YUGOSLAVIA †RADIO YUGOSLAVIA, Belgrade	E Europe & W Asia • 500 kW
11805v	**BRAZIL** †RADIO GLOBO, Rio de Janeiro	PORTUGUESE • DS • 10 kW
11805.3	**GEORGIA** †RADIO GEORGIA, Tbilisi	(D) • E Europe & N Europe • 100 kW
11810	**GERMANY** DEUTSCHE WELLE, Jülich	C Africa & S Africa • 100 kW
	†DEUTSCHE WELLE, Nauen	(J) • N America • 500 kW
		(J) • W Africa • 500 kW
	†DEUTSCHE WELLE, Various Locations	(J) • W Africa • 500 kW
	DEUTSCHE WELLE, Via Antigua	C America • 250 kW
		(J) • Australasia & C America • 250 kW
	DEUTSCHE WELLE, Via Brasília, Brazil	C America & S America • 250 kW
	DEUTSCHE WELLE, Via Kigali, Rwanda	C Africa & E Africa • 250 kW
	†DEUTSCHE WELLE, Via Sines, Portugal	(D) • W Africa • 250 kW
	†DEUTSCHE WELLE, Wertachtal	(J) • Africa • 500 kW
	INDIA †ALL INDIA RADIO, Aligarh	(D) • E Europe • 100 kW
	IRAQ †RADIO IRAQ INTL	Alternative Frequency to 11805 kHz
	JORDAN †RADIO JORDAN, Qasr el Kharana	Mideast & S Asia • 500 kW
	ROMANIA RADIO ROMANIA INTL, Bucharest	Australasia • 250 kW
		Europe • 250 kW
		(D) Su • W Europe & Atlantic • MARINERS • 250 kW
		(D) • Australasia • 250 kW
	RUSSIA R MOSCOW INTL, Yuzhno-Sakhalinsk	(D) • E Asia • 100 kW
	SEYCHELLES FAR EAST BC ASS'N, North Pt, Mahé Is	E Africa • 100 kW
11815	**BRAZIL** R BRASIL CENTRAL, Goiânia	PORTUGUESE • DS • 7.5 kW
	CHINA (PR) CHINA RADIO INTL	S Asia
		(D) • S America • 120 kW
	†CHINA RADIO INTL, Xi'an	
	JAPAN †RADIO JAPAN/NHK, Tokyo-Yamata	SE Asia • 300 kW
		SE Asia • GENERAL • 300 kW
		JAPANESE • SE Asia • GENERAL • 300 kW
		SE Asia • GENERAL • 100 kW
	POLAND †POLISH RADIO, Warsaw	W Europe • 100 kW — E Europe • 100 kW
	RUSSIA RADIO MOSCOW, Khabarovsk	(J) • DS-1 • 100 kW
	†RADIO MOSCOW, Via Georgia	(D) • DS-1 • 100 kW
	SPAIN †R EXTERIOR ESPANA, Via Costa Rica	Tu-Su • C America • 100 kW
	UNITED ARAB EMIRATES †UAE RADIO, Abu Dhabi	Alternative Frequency to 11885 kHz
	UNITED KINGDOM BBC, Rampisham	E Europe • 500 kW
		Su • E Europe • 500 kW
(con'd)	†BBC, Various Locations	M-F • N Europe • 300/500 kW

ENGLISH ▬ ARABIC ▨ CHINESE ▭▭▭ FRENCH ▬ GERMAN ▬ RUSSIAN ═ SPANISH ▬ OTHER ▬

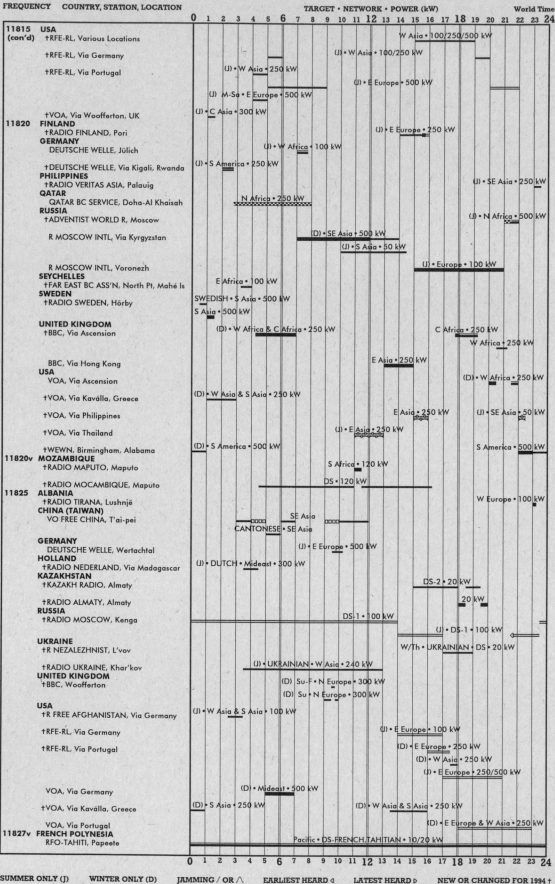

FREQUENCY   COUNTRY, STATION, LOCATION

FREQUENCY	COUNTRY, STATION, LOCATION
11815 (con'd)	USA †RFE-RL, Various Locations
	†RFE-RL, Via Germany
	†RFE-RL, Via Portugal
	†VOA, Via Woofferton, UK
11820	FINLAND †RADIO FINLAND, Pori
	GERMANY DEUTSCHE WELLE, Jülich
	†DEUTSCHE WELLE, Via Kigali, Rwanda
	PHILIPPINES †RADIO VERITAS ASIA, Palauig
	QATAR QATAR BC SERVICE, Doha-Al Khaisah
	RUSSIA †ADVENTIST WORLD R, Moscow
	R MOSCOW INTL, Via Kyrgyzstan
	R MOSCOW INTL, Voronezh
	SEYCHELLES †FAR EAST BC ASS'N, North Pt, Mahé Is
	SWEDEN †RADIO SWEDEN, Hörby
	UNITED KINGDOM †BBC, Via Ascension
	BBC, Via Hong Kong
	USA VOA, Via Ascension
	†VOA, Via Kaválla, Greece
	†VOA, Via Philippines
	†VOA, Via Thailand
	†WEWN, Birmingham, Alabama
11820v	MOZAMBIQUE †RADIO MAPUTO, Maputo
	†RADIO MOCAMBIQUE, Maputo
11825	ALBANIA †RADIO TIRANA, Lushnjë
	CHINA (TAIWAN) VO FREE CHINA, T'ai-pei
	GERMANY DEUTSCHE WELLE, Wertachtal
	HOLLAND †RADIO NEDERLAND, Via Madagascar
	KAZAKHSTAN †KAZAKH RADIO, Almaty
	†RADIO ALMATY, Almaty
	RUSSIA †RADIO MOSCOW, Kenga
	UKRAINE †R NEZALEZHNIST, L'vov
	†RADIO UKRAINE, Khar'kov
	UNITED KINGDOM †BBC, Woofferton
	USA †R FREE AFGHANISTAN, Via Germany
	†RFE-RL, Via Germany
	†RFE-RL, Via Portugal
	VOA, Via Germany
	†VOA, Via Kaválla, Greece
	VOA, Via Portugal
11827v	FRENCH POLYNESIA RFO-TAHITI, Papeete

TARGET • NETWORK • POWER (kW)   World Time

W Asia • 100/250/500 kW
(J) • W Asia • 100/250 kW
(J) • W Asia • 250 kW
(J) • E Europe • 500 kW
(J) M-Sa • E Europe • 500 kW
(J) • C Asia • 300 kW
(J) • E Europe • 250 kW
(J) • W Africa • 100 kW
(J) • S America • 250 kW
(J) • SE Asia • 250 kW
N Africa • 250 kW
(J) • N Africa • 500 kW
(D) • SE Asia • 500 kW
(J) • S Asia • 50 kW
(J) • Europe • 100 kW
E Africa • 100 kW
SWEDISH • S Asia • 500 kW
S Asia • 500 kW
(D) • W Africa & C Africa • 250 kW
C Africa • 250 kW
W Africa • 250 kW
E Asia • 250 kW
(D) • W Africa • 250 kW
(D) • W Asia & S Asia • 250 kW
E Asia • 250 kW
(J) • SE Asia • 50 kW
(J) • E Asia • 250 kW
(D) • S America • 500 kW
S America • 500 kW
S Africa • 120 kW
DS • 120 kW
W Europe • 100 kW
SE Asia
CANTONESE • SE Asia
(J) • E Europe • 500 kW
(J) • DUTCH • Mideast • 300 kW
DS-2 • 20 kW
20 kW
DS-1 • 100 kW
(J) • DS-1 • 100 kW
W/Th • UKRAINIAN • DS • 20 kW
(J) • UKRAINIAN • W Asia • 240 kW
(D) Su-F • N Europe • 300 kW
(D) Su • N Europe • 300 kW
(J) • W Asia & S Asia • 100 kW
(J) • E Europe • 100 kW
(D) • E Europe • 250 kW
(D) • W Asia • 250 kW
(D) • E Europe • 250/500 kW
(D) • Mideast • 500 kW
(D) • S Asia • 250 kW
(D) • W Asia & S Asia • 250 kW
(D) • E Europe & W Asia • 250 kW
Pacific • DS-FRENCH, TAHITIAN • 10/20 kW

FREQUENCY   COUNTRY, STATION, LOCATION

TARGET • NETWORK • POWER (kW)

World Time

0 1 2 3 4 5 6 7 8 9 10 11 12 13 14 15 16 17 18 19 20 21 22 23 24

Frequency	Country, Station, Location	Schedule
11830	**ANGOLA**	
	AV DO GALO NEGRO, Jamba	S Africa • UNITA
	BRAZIL	
	RADIO ANHANGUERA, Goiânia	Irr • PORTUGUESE • DS • 1 kW / PORTUGUESE • DS • 1 kW
	INDIA	
	†ALL INDIA RADIO, Aligarh	(D) • E Africa • 250 kW / (D) • HINDI • E Africa • 250 kW / (J) • E Europe • 250 kW
	†ALL INDIA RADIO, Bombay	DS • 100 kW / Sa/Su • DS • 100 kW
	†ALL INDIA RADIO, Delhi	(D) • DS • 100 kW
	ROMANIA	
	RADIO ROMANIA INTL, Bucharest	Americas • 250 kW / (D) • Africa • 250 kW / (D) • S America • 250 kW
	RUSSIA	
	GOLOS ROSSII, Moscow	(D) • Europe & N Africa • 500 kW
	R MOSCOW INTL, Moscow	(D) • Europe & N Africa • 500 kW / (J) • Europe • 240 kW
	†RADIO MOSCOW, Petrozavodsk	(D) • DS-1 • 20 kW
	UNITED KINGDOM	
	BBC, Via Zyyi, Cyprus	(J) • W Asia • 250 kW
	USA	
	†VOICE OF THE OAS, Cincinnati, Ohio	C America & S America • 250 kW • ALT. FREQ. TO 11835 kHz / M-Sa • C America & S America • 250 kW • ALT. FREQ. TO 11835 kHz / Su • C America & S America • 250 kW • ALT. FREQ. TO 11835 kHz
	†WYFR-FAMILY RADIO, Okeechobee, Fl	W North Am • 100 kW / (J) • W North Am • 100 kW
	VATICAN STATE	
	†VATICAN RADIO, Sta Maria di Galeria	JAPANESE • E Asia • 500 kW / E Asia & SE Asia • 250/500 kW / E Asia & Australasia • 100/250/500 kW / (J) • E Asia • 500 kW
11835	**ALBANIA**	
	RADIO TIRANA, Lushnjë	S Africa • 100 kW
	ECUADOR	
	†HCJB-VO THE ANDES, Quito	(J) • Europe • 500 kW / (D) • Europe • 500 kW
	GERMANY	
	†DEUTSCHE WELLE, Jülich	E Europe • 100 kW / (D) • E Europe • 100 kW
	HOLLAND	
	RADIO NEDERLAND, Via Neth Antilles	E North Am • 250 kW • USB
	RUSSIA	
	R MOSCOW INTL, Kenga	(D) • E Asia & SE Asia • 100 kW / (J) • S Asia • 100 kW
	SRI LANKA	
	SRI LANKA BC CORP, Colombo-Ekala	SE Asia & Australasia • 35 kW
	USA	
	†RFE-RL, Via Portugal	(D) • E Europe & W Asia • 500 kW
	VOA, Greenville, NC	W Africa & S Africa • 500 kW / M-F • W Africa & S Africa • 500 kW
	†VOA, Via Germany	(J) • S Asia • 500 kW
	†VOA, Via Kaválla, Greece	W Asia • 250 kW / (J) • W Asia & S Asia • 250 kW
	VOA, Via Morocco	(D) • C Asia • 35/500 kW
	VOA, Via Philippines	SE Asia • 250 kW / (D) • SE Asia • 250 kW
	†VOA, Via Woofferton, UK	(J) • Europe • 300 kW
	†VOICE OF THE OAS, Cincinnati, Ohio	Alternative Frequency to 11830 kHz
	YUGOSLAVIA	
	†RADIO YUGOSLAVIA, Belgrade	S America • 500 kW / W Europe • 250 kW
11835v	**MOZAMBIQUE**	
	†RADIO MAPUTO, Maputo	S Africa • 25/120 kW
11835.7	**URUGUAY**	
	R EL ESPECTADOR, Montevideo	Irr • DS • 5 kW / DS • 5 kW
11840	**ALBANIA**	
	†RADIO TIRANA, Lushnjë	N America • 100 kW / C America • 100 kW
	CHINA (PR)	
	CHINA RADIO INTL, Via Sackville, Can	S America • 250 kW / (D) • N America • 250 kW / (J) • N America • 250 kW
(con'd)		

0 1 2 3 4 5 6 7 8 9 10 11 12 13 14 15 16 17 18 19 20 21 22 23 24

ENGLISH ▬ ARABIC ▨ CHINESE ▫▫▫ FRENCH ═ GERMAN ▭ RUSSIAN ═ SPANISH ▬ OTHER ▬

FREQUENCY	COUNTRY, STATION, LOCATION	TARGET • NETWORK • POWER (kW) / World Time

TARGET • NETWORK • POWER (kW) — World Time
0 1 2 3 4 5 6 7 8 9 10 11 12 13 14 15 16 17 18 19 20 21 22 23 24

11840 (con'd) **JAPAN**
†RADIO JAPAN/NHK, Tokyo-Yamata
- (D) • E Asia • 300 kW
- E Asia • 100 kW
- SE Asia • 100 kW
- (J) • E Asia • 300 kW
- (D) • SE Asia • GENERAL • 100 kW
- (D) • JAPANESE • E Asia • GENERAL • 300 kW
- (D) • E Asia • GENERAL • 300 kW
- (D) • JAPANESE • SE Asia • GENERAL • 100 kW

RADIO JAPAN/NHK, Via Sri Lanka
- S Asia • 300 kW
- S Asia • GENERAL • 300 kW

POLAND
†POLISH RADIO, Warsaw
- E Europe • 100 kW
- W Europe • 100 kW

PORTUGAL
RDP INTERNATIONAL, Lisbon
- PORTUGUESE • S America • 100 kW
- Su/M • PORTUGUESE • S America • 100 kW

RUSSIA
RADIO MOSCOW, Kenga
- DS-1 • 50 kW

†SAKHALIN RADIO, Yuzhno-Sakhalinsk
- DS-LOCAL, R ROSSII • 50 kW • USB

SEYCHELLES
†FAR EAST BC ASS'N, North Pt, Mahé Is
- E Africa • 100 kW
- Mideast • 100 kW
- Su/F • Mideast • 100 kW

UKRAINE
†RADIO UKRAINE, Vinnitsa
- UKRAINIAN • E Europe • 100 kW
- (D) • UKRAINIAN • E Europe • 100 kW

UNITED KINGDOM
BBC, Via Zyyi, Cyprus
- (J) • E Europe • 250 kW

USA
†UNIVERSITY NET'K, Via N'sibirsk, Russia
- (J) • S Asia

VOA, Via Germany
- N Africa • 500 kW

†VOA, Via Philippines
- SE Asia • 250 kW

†WYFR-FAMILY RADIO, Okeechobee, Fl
- (D) • C America • 100 kW

11845 **CANADA**
†R CANADA INTL, Sackville, NB
- C America • 100 kW
- (D) • C America • 100 kW
- Su/M • C America • 100 kW
- (D) M-F • C America • 100 kW
- Tu-Sa • C America • 100 kW
- (D) Sa/Su • C America • 100 kW
- (J) Tu-Sa • C America • 100 kW

CHINA (TAIWAN)
BC CORP CHINA, T'ai-pei
- DS-NEWS NETWORK • 50/100 kW

ECUADOR
†HCJB-VO THE ANDES, Quito
- Alternative Frequency to 11885 kHz
- (J) • JAPANESE • E Asia • 500 kW

FRANCE
R FRANCE INTL, Issoudun-Allouis
- N Africa • 100 kW

GERMANY
DEUTSCHE WELLE, Wertachtal
- (J) • SE Asia • 500 kW

KOREA (DPR)
†RADIO PYONGYANG, Kujang-dong
- SE Asia • 200 kW
- N Africa • 200 kW

RUSSIA
GOLOS ROSSII, Kazan'
- (J) • S Asia & SE Asia • 100 kW

R MOSCOW INTL, Kazan'
- S Asia & SE Asia • 100 kW
- (J) • S Asia & SE Asia • 100 kW

†RADIO HYVONG, Irkutsk
- (J) Th-Tu • SE Asia • ANTI-VIET GOVT • 500 kW • ALT. FREQ. TO 11725 kHz
- (J) W • SE Asia • ANTI-VIET GOVT • 500 kW • ALT. FREQ. TO 11725 kHz

UNITED KINGDOM
†BBC, Rampisham
- (J) • E Europe • 500 kW
- (J) Su • E Europe • 500 kW

BBC, Via Maşīrah, Oman
- (D) • E Europe & W Asia • 100 kW

†BBC, Via Zyyi, Cyprus
- (D) • E Europe • 250 kW
- E Europe • 100/250 kW
- (J) M-F • N Europe • 250 kW
- (D) • E Europe & W Asia • 250 kW
- (J) • E Europe • 250 kW
- (D) M-F • N Europe • 250 kW
- (J) Su • E Europe • 250 kW

USA
†VOA, Via Portugal
- (J) • Europe • 250 kW

†VOA, Via Woofferton, UK
- (J) • Europe • 300 kW

11850 **DENMARK**
†DANMARKS RADIO, Via Norway
- (D) • S America • 500 kW
- (D) • W North Am • 500 kW

FRANCE
†R FRANCE INTL, Via Hungary
- N Africa • 250 kW

GERMANY
DEUTSCHE WELLE, Nauen
- (D) • N Africa • 500 kW

(con'd) DEUTSCHE WELLE, Wertachtal
- (D) • E Europe • 500 kW

0 1 2 3 4 5 6 7 8 9 10 11 12 13 14 15 16 17 18 19 20 21 22 23 24

FREQUENCY   COUNTRY, STATION, LOCATION

TARGET • NETWORK • POWER (kW)   World Time

0 1 2 3 4 5 6 7 8 9 10 11 12 13 14 15 16 17 18 19 20 21 22 23 24

11850 (con'd)	JAPAN †RADIO JAPAN/NHK, Tokyo-Yamata	Alternative Frequency to 11875 kHz
	MONGOLIA †RADIO ULAANBAATAR, Ulaanbaatar	Europe & W Asia • 250 kW / Tu/F • Europe & W Asia • 250 kW
	NORWAY †RADIO NORWAY INTL, Kvitsøy	(D) • S America • 500 kW
	†RADIO NORWAY INTL, Sveio	(D) • W North Am • 500 kW / (D) • S America • 500 kW
	RUSSIA GOLOS ROSSII, Konevo	(D) • Europe • 240 kW / (J) • N Africa & Mideast • 240 kW
	R MOSCOW INTL, Ryazan'	Mideast & E Africa • 200 kW / (J) • Mideast & E Africa • 240 kW
	RADIO MOSCOW, Khabarovsk	(J) • DS-2 • 100 kW
	SPAIN †R EXTERIOR ESPANA, Noblejas	E North Am & C America • 350 kW
	UNITED KINGDOM †BBC, Various Locations	S Asia • 100/250 kW / N Africa • 300/500 kW / W Asia • 100 kW
	†BBC, Via Maşīrah, Oman	(J) • S Asia • 100 kW / (J) • W Asia • 100 kW
	†BBC, Via Singapore	SE Asia • 100/250 kW / (D) • SE Asia • 250 kW / Sa/Su • SE Asia • 250 kW
11851v	MONGOLIA †RADIO ULAANBAATAR, Ulaanbaatar	Australasia • 50 kW / (J) • S Asia • 50 kW / E Asia • 50 kW • ALT. FREQ. TO 9616 kHz / M/Th/Sa • E Asia • 50 kW / M/Tu/Th-Sa • E Asia • 50 kW • ALT. FREQ. TO 9616 kHz / W/Su • E Asia • 50 kW • ALT. FREQ. TO 9616 kHz
11854.5	BRAZIL †RADIO APARECIDA, Aparecida	PORTUGUESE • DS • 7.5 kW
11855	AUSTRALIA †RADIO AUSTRALIA, Carnarvon	SE Asia • 250 kW / (D) • SE Asia • 100 kW / (J) • E Asia • 100 kW
	†RADIO AUSTRALIA, Shepparton	S Asia & SE Asia • 100 kW / (D) • Pacific • 100 kW
	CANADA R CANADA INTL, Sackville, NB	M-F • E North Am • 250 kW / Su • E North Am • 100 kW
	CHINA (PR) †CHINA RADIO INTL, Jinhua	(J) • W North Am • 500 kW / (J) • Mideast • 500 kW / (J) • Mideast & N Africa • 500 kW
	CHINA (TAIWAN) BC CORP CHINA, Via Okeechobee, USA	(J) • W North Am • 100 kW / (D) • C America • 100 kW
	RUSSIA †ADVENTIST WORLD R, Novosibirsk	(J) • S Asia • 100 kW / (J) • C Asia • 100 kW / (J) • SE Asia • 100 kW
	USA †RFE-RL, Via Germany	(D) • E Europe & W Asia • 100 kW
	†RFE-RL, Via Portugal	(D) • Mideast & W Asia • 100 kW / (J) • E Europe • 250 kW
	†VOA, Via Germany	Mideast & W Asia • 500 kW
	VOA, Via Portugal	(D) • E Europe • 250 kW / (J) • E Europe & W Asia • 250 kW
	†VOA, Via Thailand	(D) • S Asia • 500 kW
	†VOA, Via Woofferton, UK	(D) • Europe • 250 kW / (J) • Europe • 300 kW
	WYFR-FAMILY RADIO, Okeechobee, Fl	C America • 100 kW / (J) • S America • 100 kW
11860	BULGARIA †RADIO BULGARIA, Sofia	(D) • Su • Europe • 100 kW
	BYELARUS RS BYELARUS, Via Russia	(J) • M/Tu/Th/F • Europe • 240 kW / (J) • W/Sa/Su • Europe • 240 kW
	CHINA (TAIWAN) VO FREE CHINA, T'ai-pei	SE Asia • 50 kW / CANTONESE • SE Asia • 50 kW
(con'd)		

0 1 2 3 4 5 6 7 8 9 10 11 12 13 14 15 16 17 18 19 20 21 22 23 24

ENGLISH ■■   ARABIC ≋   CHINESE □□□   FRENCH ══   GERMAN ▬▬   RUSSIAN ══   SPANISH ══   OTHER ──

FREQUENCY   COUNTRY, STATION, LOCATION

TARGET • NETWORK • POWER (kW)   World Time

Frequency / Station	Schedule notes
11860 (con'd) **CLANDESTINE (M EAST)** †"VO FREE MEN", Iraq	Mideast • ANTI-SAUDI GOVT • ALT. FREQ. TO 9740 kHz
DENMARK †DANMARKS RADIO, Via Norway	Alternative Frequency to 11865 kHz
INDIA ALL INDIA RADIO, Aligarh	N Africa • 250 kW
IRAQ †RADIO IRAQ INTL	N Africa / Mideast / (D) • ENGLISH & ARABIC • N America
JAPAN †RADIO JAPAN/NHK, Tokyo-Yamata	(J) • E Asia • GENERAL • 300 kW
†RADIO JAPAN/NHK, Via Singapore	SE Asia • GENERAL • 250 kW / JAPANESE • SE Asia • GENERAL • 250 kW
NORWAY †RADIO NORWAY INTL, Kvitsøy	Alternative Frequency to 11865 kHz
RUSSIA R MOSCOW INTL, Nizhniy Novgorod	(J) • Mideast & S Asia • 240 kW / (J) • Europe • 240 kW
R MOSCOW INTL, Tver'	(D) • Mideast & S Asia • 240 kW
SEYCHELLES FAR EAST BC ASS'N, North Pt, Mahé Is	E Africa • 100 kW / W-Su • E Africa • 100 kW
SOUTH AFRICA †CHANNEL AFRICA, Meyerton	(D) M-F • S Africa • 100 kW
UNITED KINGDOM †BBC, Via Ascension	W Africa & C Africa • 250 kW / C Africa • 250 kW / (J) • C Africa • 250 kW / (J) • W Africa • 250 kW
BBC, Via Seychelles	E Africa • 250 kW / M-F • E Africa • 250 kW / Sa/Su • E Africa • 250 kW
USA †VOA, Via Philippines	E Asia • 250 kW
11860v CLANDESTINE (M EAST) "HOLY MEDINA RADIO, Iraq	Mideast • ANTI-SAUDI GOVT • 500 kW • ALT. FREQ. TO 9630v kHz
11865 DENMARK †DANMARKS RADIO, Via Norway	(D) • Africa • 350 kW / (D) • S America • 500 kW • ALT. FREQ. TO 11860 kHz
GERMANY †DEUTSCHE WELLE, Jülich	(J) • W North Am • 500 kW / (D) • E North Am & C America • 500 kW / (J) • Mideast • 100 kW / (J) • E Europe • 100 kW
†DEUTSCHE WELLE, Multiple Locations	S America • 100/250 kW / (D) • E Asia • 250/500 kW
	(J) • E North Am & C America • 100/250 kW / (J) • C America & S America • 100/250 kW
DEUTSCHE WELLE, Nauen	Europe • 500 kW
DEUTSCHE WELLE, Via Antigua	(J) • C America • 250 kW
DEUTSCHE WELLE, Via Sines, Portugal	(D) • E Europe • 250 kW
†DEUTSCHE WELLE, Via Sri Lanka	(D) • JAPANESE • E Asia • 250 kW
DEUTSCHE WELLE, Wertachtal	(D) • W Asia • 500 kW / (J) • E Europe • 500 kW
HOLLAND RADIO NEDERLAND, Flevoland	(J) • W Europe • 500 kW
JAPAN †RADIO JAPAN/NHK, Tokyo-Yamata	JAPANESE • W North Am • GENERAL • 100/300 kW / (J) • JAPANESE • W North Am • GENERAL • 300 kW / (J) • W North Am • GENERAL • 300 kW
NORWAY RADIO NORWAY INTL, Fredrikstad	(D) • Africa • 350 kW
†RADIO NORWAY INTL, Kvitsøy	(D) • S America • 500 kW • ALT. FREQ. TO 11860 kHz
†RADIO NORWAY INTL, Sveio	(J) • W North Am • 500 kW / (D) M-Sa • E North Am & C America • 500 kW / (J) M • W North Am • 500 kW / (D) Su • E North Am & C America • 500 kW / (J) Tu-Su • W North Am • 500 kW
UNITED KINGDOM †BBC, Via Singapore	(J) • E Asia • 250 kW / E Asia • 100 kW
USA †RFE-RL, Via Germany	(J) • W Asia • 250 kW
†VOA, Via Philippines	(D) • E Asia • 250 kW
†VOA, Via Portugal	(D) • E Europe • 250 kW / (J) • E Europe • 250 kW
†VOA, Via Woofferton, UK	(J) • Mideast & W Asia • 250 kW

FREQUENCY   COUNTRY, STATION, LOCATION

TARGET • NETWORK • POWER (kW)   World Time

0 1 2 3 4 5 6 7 8 9 10 11 12 13 14 15 16 17 18 19 20 21 22 23 24

Frequency	Country, Station, Location	Schedule
11869.8	COSTA RICA	
	ADVENTIST WORLD R, Alajuela	C America • 5 kW
		Sa • C America • 5 kW
		Su-F • C America • 5 kW
11870	BULGARIA	
	†RADIO BULGARIA, Plovdiv	(D) • Mideast • 500 kW — Mideast • 500 kW
	DENMARK	
	†DANMARKS RADIO, Via Norway	(J) • S Asia & SE Asia • 500 kW
	JAPAN	
	RADIO JAPAN/NHK, Tokyo-Yamata	(D) • JAPANESE • W North Am • GENERAL • 100 kW
		(D) • W North Am • GENERAL • 100 kW
	NORWAY	
	†RADIO NORWAY INTL, Kvitsøy	(J) • S Asia & SE Asia • 500 kW
	RUSSIA	
	GOLOS ROSSII, Serpukhov	(D) • Europe • 240 kW
	R MOSCOW INTL, Khabarovsk	(J) • E Asia & SE Asia • 240 kW
	RADIO MOSCOW	DS-1
	SPAIN	
	†R EXTERIOR ESPANA, Noblejas	N Africa & Mideast • 350 kW
	UKRAINE	
	†RADIO UKRAINE	(J) • UKRAINIAN
	†RADIO UKRAINE, Simferopol'	(D) • UKRAINIAN • E North Am & W Europe • 500 kW
	USA	
	VOA, Via Philippines	E Asia & Australasia • 250 kW
		(D) • S Asia • 250 kW
	YUGOSLAVIA	
	†RADIO YUGOSLAVIA, Belgrade	W North Am • 500 kW
11875	CANADA	
	†R CANADA INTL, Sackville, NB	(J) • E North Am • 250 kW
	CUBA	
	†RADIO HABANA, Havana	S America • 250 kW
	DENMARK	
	DANMARKS RADIO, Via Norway	(D) • Mideast • 500 kW
	EGYPT	
	RADIO CAIRO, Kafr Silim-Abis	S Africa • 250 kW
	GERMANY	
	†DEUTSCHE WELLE, Via Kigali, Rwanda	S Asia & SE Asia • 250 kW
	†DEUTSCHE WELLE, Wertachtal	(J) • E Asia • 500 kW
	JAPAN	
	†RADIO JAPAN/NHK, Tokyo-Yamata	S America • 300 kW
		SE Asia • 300 kW
		JAPANESE • S America • GENERAL • 300 kW
		JAPANESE • Australasia • GENERAL • 300 kW • ALT. FREQ. TO 11850 kHz
		Australasia • GENERAL • 300 kW • ALT. FREQ. TO 11850 kHz
	NORWAY	
	RADIO NORWAY INTL, Kvitsøy	(D) • M-Sa • Mideast • 500 kW
		(D) • Su • Mideast • 500 kW
	TURKEY	
	VOICE OF TURKEY, Ankara	E Europe • 250 kW
	USA	
	†RFE-RL, Various Locations	W Asia • 100/250 kW
	†RFE-RL, Via Germany	W Asia • 100/250 kW
		(D) • W Asia • 100/250 kW
		(J) • W Asia • 100/250 kW
	VOA, Via Kaválla, Greece	M-F • N Africa • 250 kW
	VOA, Via Woofferton, UK	(J) • N Africa • 300 kW
11880	AUSTRALIA	
	RADIO AUSTRALIA, Brandon	Pacific • 10 kW
	†RADIO AUSTRALIA, Shepparton	Pacific & W North Am • 100 kW
	BULGARIA	
	†RADIO BULGARIA, Plovdiv	(J) • Europe • 500 kW
	INDIA	
	†ALL INDIA RADIO, Delhi	SE Asia • 250 kW
		S Asia & E Asia • 100 kW
	JAPAN	
	†RADIO JAPAN/NHK, Tokyo-Yamata	S Asia • 100 kW
	RUSSIA	
	R MOSCOW INTL, Moscow	(J) • S Asia • 240 kW
		(J) • Europe • 240 kW
		(J) • RUSSIAN & ENGLISH • Europe
	†RADIO GALAXY	
	RADIO MOSCOW	(D) • DS-2
	RADIO MOSCOW, Yekaterinburg	(J) • DS-2 • 240 kW
	SPAIN	
	†R EXTERIOR ESPANA, Via Costa Rica	M-F • C America • 100 kW
	UNITED KINGDOM	
	BBC, Via Ascension	W Africa & C Africa • 250 kW
11885 (con'd)	CHINA (TAIWAN)	DS(FM-1)
	BC CORP CHINA	

0 1 2 3 4 5 6 7 8 9 10 11 12 13 14 15 16 17 18 19 20 21 22 23 24

ENGLISH ▬   ARABIC ⌇⌇⌇   CHINESE ▫▫▫   FRENCH ▬   GERMAN ▬   RUSSIAN ═   SPANISH ▬   OTHER ▬

FREQUENCY   COUNTRY, STATION, LOCATION

TARGET • NETWORK • POWER (kW)   World Time

0 1 2 3 4 5 6 7 8 9 10 11 12 13 14 15 16 17 18 19 20 21 22 23 24

11885 ECUADOR
(con'd)   †HCJB-VO THE ANDES, Quito — S America • 100 kW • ALT. FREQ. TO 11845 kHz
       MALAYSIA
          VOICE OF MALAYSIA, Kajang — E Asia • 500 kW
       ROMANIA
          RADIO ROMANIA INTL, Bucharest — (D) • Africa • 250 kW
       UNITED ARAB EMIRATES
          †UAE RADIO, Abu Dhabi — (J) • Mideast • 500 kW / E North Am • 500 kW • ALT. FREQ. TO 11815 kHz
       USA
          †RFE-RL, Various Locations — E Europe • 100/250/500 kW
          †RFE-RL, Via Portugal — (J) • W Asia • 250 kW / (J) • E Europe • 250 kW

11890 FRANCE
          R FRANCE INTL, Via Beijing, China — SE Asia • 120 kW
       HOLLAND
          RADIO NEDERLAND, Via Madagascar — (D) • DUTCH • SE Asia • 300 kW / (D) • SE Asia • 300 kW
       JAPAN
          †RADIO JAPAN/NHK, Tokyo-Yamata — (D) • E Asia • GENERAL • 100 kW
       OMAN
          †RADIO OMAN, Sīb — Mideast • DS • 100 kW / (J) • Mideast • DS • 100 kW
       RUSSIA
          GOLOS ROSSII, Kingisepp — (J) • S Asia • 240 kW
          GOLOS ROSSII, Ryazan' — (D) • Europe & W Africa • 240 kW
          R MOSCOW INTL, Kingisepp — (J) • S Asia • 240 kW
          R MOSCOW INTL, Ryazan' — (D) • SE Asia • 240 kW / (J) • E Europe • 240 kW
       SPAIN
          †R EXTERIOR ESPANA, Noblejas — N Africa & Mideast • 350 kW
       USA
          †VOA, Greenville, NC — C America • 230/500 kW / (D) • C America • 250 kW
                                  Sa/Su • C America • 250/500 kW / (J) • C America • 250 kW
                                  M-F • C America • 250 kW
          †VOA, Via Philippines — (J) • SE Asia • 50 kW

11895 HOLLAND
          RADIO NEDERLAND, Via Neth Antilles — Australasia • 250 kW / DUTCH • Australasia • 250 kW
       IRAN
          †VO THE ISLAMIC REP, Tehrān — (J) • Mideast • 500 kW / (J) • W Asia • 500 kW
       RUSSIA
          RADIO MOSCOW, Yekaterinburg — (J) • DS-2 • 240 kW
       TURKEY
          VOICE OF TURKEY, Ankara — TURKISH • Europe • 250 kW / Europe • 250 kW
       USA
          †R FREE AFGHANISTAN, Via Germany — (D) • W Asia & S Asia • 100 kW
          †RFE-RL, Via Germany — E Europe & W Asia • 100/250 kW / (D) • W Asia • 100 kW
                                  (D) • E Europe & W Asia • 250 kW / (D) • E Europe • 100 kW
                                  (J) • E Europe & W Asia • 100/250 kW
          †RFE-RL, Via Portugal — (D) • W Asia & C Asia • 250 kW / (J) • E Europe • 500 kW
          †VOA, Greenville, NC — C America & S America • 500 kW
          VOA, Via Germany — (D) • Mideast • 100 kW
          †VOA, Via Philippines — E Asia • 250 kW / SE Asia • 250 kW
                                  (J) • SE Asia • 250 kW / (J) • E Asia • 250 kW

11900 FINLAND
          †RADIO FINLAND, Pori — (J) • N America • 500 kW
                                  (J) M-F • N America • 500 kW
                                  (J) M-Sa • N America • 500 kW
                                  (J) Sa/Su • N America • 500 kW
                                  (J) • Su • N America • 500 kW
                                  (D) • W Europe • 500 kW
       HOLLAND
          †RADIO NEDERLAND, Flevoland
       RUSSIA
          ADVENTIST WORLD R, Yekaterinburg — (J) • E Europe • 200 kW
          GOLOS ROSSII, Komsomol'sk 'Amure — (D) • Pacific • 100 kW
          R MOSCOW INTL, Armavir — (D) • S America • 500 kW / (D) • W Africa • 500 kW
          R MOSCOW INTL, Via Tajikistan — (J) • N Africa & Mideast • 500 kW
(con'd)   RADIO MOSCOW — (J) • DS-MAYAK

0 1 2 3 4 5 6 7 8 9 10 11 12 13 14 15 16 17 18 19 20 21 22 23 24

SUMMER ONLY (J)   WINTER ONLY (D)   JAMMING / OR ∧   EARLIEST HEARD ◁   LATEST HEARD ▷   NEW OR CHANGED FOR 1994 †

FREQUENCY   COUNTRY, STATION, LOCATION

TARGET • NETWORK • POWER (kW)

World Time

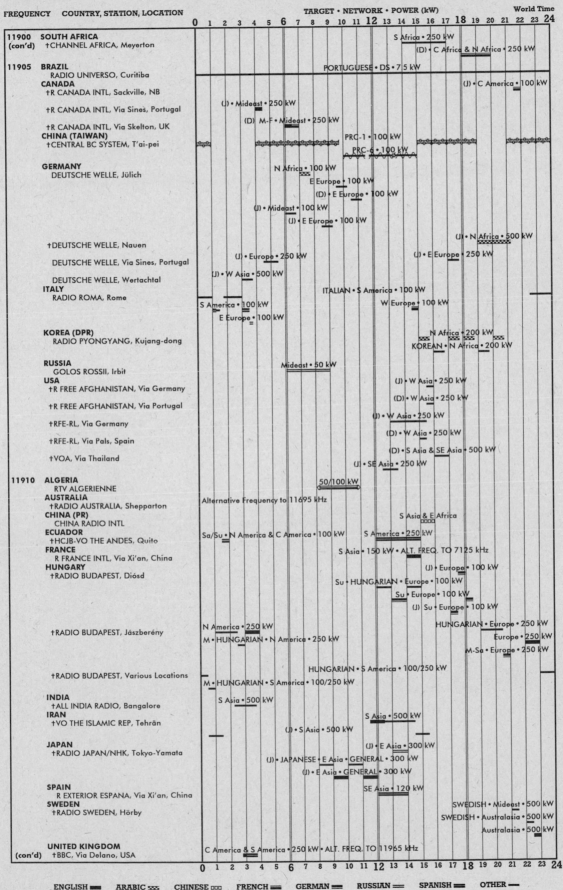

11900	SOUTH AFRICA	
(con'd)	†CHANNEL AFRICA, Meyerton	S Africa • 250 kW
		(D) • C Africa & N Africa • 250 kW
11905	BRAZIL	
	RADIO UNIVERSO, Curitiba	PORTUGUESE • DS • 7.5 kW
	CANADA	
	†R CANADA INTL, Sackville, NB	(J) • C America • 100 kW
		(J) • Mideast • 250 kW
	†R CANADA INTL, Via Sines, Portugal	(D) • M-F • Mideast • 250 kW
	†R CANADA INTL, Via Skelton, UK	
	CHINA (TAIWAN)	PRC-1 • 100 kW
	†CENTRAL BC SYSTEM, T'ai-pei	PRC-6 • 100 kW
	GERMANY	
	DEUTSCHE WELLE, Jülich	N Africa • 100 kW
		E Europe • 100 kW
		(D) • E Europe • 100 kW
		(J) • Mideast • 100 kW
		(J) • E Europe • 100 kW
		(J) • N Africa • 500 kW
	†DEUTSCHE WELLE, Nauen	(J) • Europe • 250 kW (J) • E Europe • 250 kW
	DEUTSCHE WELLE, Via Sines, Portugal	(J) • W Asia • 500 kW
	DEUTSCHE WELLE, Wertachtal	
	ITALY	ITALIAN • S America • 100 kW
	RADIO ROMA, Rome	S America • 100 kW W Europe • 100 kW
		E Europe • 100 kW
	KOREA (DPR)	N Africa • 200 kW
	RADIO PYONGYANG, Kujang-dong	KOREAN • N Africa • 200 kW
	RUSSIA	
	GOLOS ROSSII, Irbit	Mideast • 50 kW
	USA	
	†R FREE AFGHANISTAN, Via Germany	(J) • W Asia • 250 kW
	†R FREE AFGHANISTAN, Via Portugal	(D) • W Asia • 250 kW
	†RFE-RL, Via Germany	(J) • W Asia • 250 kW
	†RFE-RL, Via Pals, Spain	(D) • W Asia • 250 kW
	†VOA, Via Thailand	(D) • S Asia & SE Asia • 500 kW
		(J) • SE Asia • 250 kW
11910	ALGERIA	
	RTV ALGERIENNE	50/100 kW
	AUSTRALIA	
	†RADIO AUSTRALIA, Shepparton	Alternative Frequency to 11695 kHz
	CHINA (PR)	
	CHINA RADIO INTL	S Asia & E Africa
	ECUADOR	
	†HCJB-VO THE ANDES, Quito	Sa/Su • N America & C America • 100 kW S America • 250 kW
	FRANCE	
	R FRANCE INTL, Via Xi'an, China	S Asia • 150 kW • ALT. FREQ. TO 7125 kHz
	HUNGARY	(J) • Europe • 100 kW
	†RADIO BUDAPEST, Diósd	Su • HUNGARIAN • Europe • 100 kW
		Su • Europe • 100 kW
		(J) • Su • Europe • 100 kW
		HUNGARIAN • Europe • 250 kW
	†RADIO BUDAPEST, Jászberény	N America • 250 kW Europe • 250 kW
		M • HUNGARIAN • N America • 250 kW
		M-Sa • Europe • 250 kW
	†RADIO BUDAPEST, Various Locations	HUNGARIAN • S America • 100/250 kW
		M • HUNGARIAN • S America • 100/250 kW
	INDIA	
	†ALL INDIA RADIO, Bangalore	S Asia • 500 kW
	IRAN	
	†VO THE ISLAMIC REP, Tehrān	S Asia • 500 kW
		(J) • S Asia • 500 kW
	JAPAN	
	†RADIO JAPAN/NHK, Tokyo-Yamata	(J) • E Asia • 300 kW
		(J) • JAPANESE • E Asia • GENERAL • 300 kW
		(J) • E Asia • GENERAL • 300 kW
	SPAIN	
	R EXTERIOR ESPANA, Via Xi'an, China	SE Asia • 120 kW
	SWEDEN	SWEDISH • Mideast • 500 kW
	†RADIO SWEDEN, Hörby	SWEDISH • Australasia • 500 kW
		Australasia • 500 kW
	UNITED KINGDOM	
(con'd)	†BBC, Via Delano, USA	C America & S America • 250 kW • ALT. FREQ. TO 11965 kHz

FREQUENCY	COUNTRY, STATION, LOCATION	TARGET • NETWORK • POWER (kW) ... World Time

0 1 2 3 4 5 6 7 8 9 10 11 12 13 14 15 16 17 18 19 20 21 22 23 24

11910 **UNITED KINGDOM**
(con'd) †BBC, Via Delano, USA — Tu-Sa • C America & S America • 250 kW • ALT. FREQ. TO 11965 kHz

†BBC, Woofferton — (D) • Sa/Su • N Europe • 300 kW

11915 **BRAZIL**
†RADIO GAUCHA, Pôrto Alegre — PORTUGUESE • DS • 7.5 kW
Irr • PORTUGUESE • DS • 7.5 kW

CANADA
†R CANADA INTL, Via Sines, Portugal — (D) • Europe • 250 kW
(D) • E Europe • 250 kW

CHINA (TAIWAN)
VO FREE CHINA, T'ai-pei — SE Asia • 50/100 kW
CANTONESE • SE Asia • 50/100 kW

GERMANY
†DEUTSCHE WELLE, Jülich — (J) • E Europe • 100 kW

†DEUTSCHE WELLE, Multiple Locations — (J) • E Europe & W Asia • 100/500 kW

DEUTSCHE WELLE, Via Cyclops, Malta — (D) • C America • 250 kW

USA
†RFE-RL, Via Pals, Spain — (J) • W Asia • 250 kW   (D) • W Asia • 250 kW
(J) • E Europe & W Asia • 250 kW

VOA, Greenville, NC — C America • 250 kW

†VOA, Via Morocco — (J) • W Africa • 500 kW
(J) • M-F • W Africa • 500 kW
(J) • Sa/Su • W Africa • 500 kW

†VOA, Via Woofferton, UK — Europe • 300 kW
(J) • Europe • 300 kW

†WYFR-FAMILY RADIO, Okeechobee, Fl — (D) • Europe • 100 kW

11920 **ARMENIA**
RADIO YEREVAN — (J) • Europe & C America
(J) • ARMENIAN • Europe & C America

†RADIO YEREVAN, Via Armavir, Russia — (J) • ARMENIAN • W Europe & C America • 1000 kW
(J) • W Europe & C America • 1000 kW

COTE D'IVOIRE
R COTE D'IVOIRE, Abidjan — DS-2 • 25 kW
MOROCCO
RTV MAROCAINE, Tangier — Europe & W Africa • 50 kW
M-Sa • Europe & W Africa • 50 kW
Su • Europe & W Africa • 50 kW

RUSSIA
†R MOSCOW INTL, Armavir — (J) • W Europe & C America • 1000 kW

R MOSCOW INTL, Moscow — (D) • Europe & N Africa • 250 kW
SPAIN
†R EXTERIOR ESPANA, Noblejas — Australasia • 350 kW
UNITED KINGDOM
†BBC, Via Singapore — SE Asia • 100 kW
S Asia • 100 kW
M-F • S Asia • 100 kW
Sa/Su • S Asia • 100 kW

USA
†VOA, Via Philippines — E Africa • 250 kW
11925 **BRAZIL**
†RADIO BANDEIRANTES, São Paulo — PORTUGUESE • DS • 10 kW
CANADA
†R CANADA INTL, Via Skelton, UK — (J) • Mideast • 300 kW

†R CANADA INTL, Via Vienna, Austria — (J) • Mideast • 300 kW
DENMARK
†DANMARKS RADIO, Via Norway — (J) • E North Am & C America • 350 kW
(J) • N America • 350 kW

ECUADOR
†HCJB-VO THE ANDES, Quito — N America & C America • 100 kW
Australasia • 100 kW   S America • 100 kW

JAPAN
†RADIO JAPAN/NHK, Via Moyabi, Gabon — Europe & N Africa • GENERAL • 500 kW
MALTA
VO MEDITERRANEAN, Cyclops — Europe, N Africa & Mideast • 250 kW
NORWAY
†RADIO NORWAY INTL, Fredrikstad — (J) • E North Am & C America • 350 kW
(J) • M • N America • 350 kW
(J) • Tu-Su • N America • 350 kW

RUSSIA
R MOSCOW INTL, Krasnoyarsk — (D) • E Asia & SE Asia • 500 kW
TURKEY
VOICE OF TURKEY, Ankara — TURKISH • W Asia • 250 kW   W Asia • 250 kW
UNITED KINGDOM
†BBC, Rampisham — (D) • E Europe & Mideast • 500 kW
USA
(con'd) †RFE-RL, Via Germany — (J) • E Europe & W Asia • 100 kW

0 1 2 3 4 5 6 7 8 9 10 11 12 13 14 15 16 17 18 19 20 21 22 23 24

FREQUENCY   COUNTRY, STATION, LOCATION   TARGET • NETWORK • POWER (kW)   World Time

Frequency	Country, Station, Location	Target • Network • Power
11925 (con'd)	**USA** †RFE-RL, Via Portugal	(D) • E Europe • 250 kW
		(J) • E Europe & W Asia • 250 kW
	†VOA, Cincinnati, Ohio	(D) • W Africa • 250 kW
	VOA, Via Morocco	(J) • E Europe • 35/500 kW
	VOA, Via Philippines	E Asia • 250 kW
11930	**DENMARK** DANMARKS RADIO, Via Norway	(D) • Atlantic & E North Am • 350 kW
	IRAN †RADIO ZAHEDAN, Zāhedān	W Asia • 500 kW
	†VO THE ISLAMIC REP, Zāhedān	Mideast • 500 kW
	MALAYSIA RADIO MALAYSIA, Kajang	DS-1 (MALAY) • 100 kW
	NORWAY RADIO NORWAY INTL, Fredrikstad	(D) • Atlantic & E North Am • 350 kW
	RUSSIA RADIO MOSCOW, Armavir	(D) • DS-1 • 100 kW
	SEYCHELLES FAR EAST BC ASS'N, North Pt, Mahé Is	S Africa • 100 kW
	USA RADIO MARTI, Greenville, NC	C America • 250 kW
	†VOA, Via Philippines	E Asia • 250 kW SE Asia • 50 kW
		SE Asia • 250 kW
		(D) • E Asia • 250 kW
		(J) • E Asia • 250 kW
11935	**CANADA** †R CANADA INTL, Via Skelton, UK	(D) • Europe • 300 kW
		(J) • Europe • 300 kW
	CHINA (PR) CENTRAL PEOPLES BS, Beijing	(J) • CHINESE, ETC • TAIWAN-1 • 50 kW
		CHINESE, ETC • TAIWAN-1 • 50 kW
	HOLLAND RADIO NEDERLAND, Flevoland	DUTCH • W Europe • 500 kW
		(J) • DUTCH • Europe • 500 kW
	INDIA †ALL INDIA RADIO, Bombay	E Africa • 100 kW
	†ALL INDIA RADIO, Delhi	W Asia & Mideast • 100 kW
	SAUDI ARABIA †BS OF THE KINGDOM, Riyadh	N Africa • DS-HOLY KORAN • 500 kW
	USA †RFE-RL, Via Pals, Spain	(J) • W Asia • 250 kW
		(J) • E Europe • 250 kW
	†RFE-RL, Via Portugal	(D) • E Europe • 250 kW
		(J) • E Europe • 250 kW
	VOA, Greenville, NC	(D) • M-F • C America • 500 kW
		(J) M-F • C America • 500 kW
	†VOA, Via Portugal	(D) • E Europe • 250 kW
	VATICAN STATE VATICAN RADIO, Sta Maria di Galeria	(J) • S Asia • 250 kW
11938v	**CAMBODIA** †NATIONAL VOICE, Phnom Penh	SE Asia • 50 kW
11939.5	**PARAGUAY** RADIO ENCARNACION, Encarnación	DS • 0.5 kW
11940	**CANADA** †R CANADA INTL, Sackville, NB	S America • 250 kW M-F • S America • 250 kW
		(D) • S America • 250 kW
		(J) • S America • 250 kW Sa/Su • S America • 250 kW
		Su/M • S America • 250 kW (J) Sa/Su • S America • 250 kW
		(D) Su/M • S America • 250 kW
		(J) Su/M • S America • 250 kW
		Tu-Sa • S America • 250 kW
		(J) Tu-Sa • S America • 250 kW
	JORDAN †RADIO JORDAN, Qasr el Kharana	N America & W Europe • 500 kW (J) • W Europe & E North Am • 500 kW
	ROMANIA †RADIO ROMANIA, Bucharest	Europe • DS-1 (ACTUALITATI) • 125 kW
	RADIO ROMANIA INTL, Bucharest	Americas • 250 kW
		Europe • 250 kW
		Australasia • 250 kW Mideast • 250 kW
		FRENCH & GERMAN • Europe • 250 kW (D) • Europe • 250 kW
		Su • W Europe & Atlantic • MARINERS • 120 kW (J) • Europe • 250 kW
	RUSSIA GOLOS ROSSII, Yekaterinburg	(D) • E Asia • 100 kW
(con'd)	R MOSCOW INTL, Yekaterinburg	(D) • E Asia • 100 kW

ENGLISH ▬ ARABIC ⋙ CHINESE ▭▭▭ FRENCH ═ GERMAN ▬ RUSSIAN ⹀ SPANISH ▬ OTHER ▬

FREQUENCY   COUNTRY, STATION, LOCATION

TARGET • NETWORK • POWER (kW)

World Time

0 1 2 3 4 5 6 7 8 9 10 11 12 13 14 15 16 17 18 19 20 21 22 23 24

Frequency	Country, Station, Location	Target • Network • Power
11940 (con'd)	RUSSIA	
	R MOSCOW INTL, Yekaterinburg	(J) • E Asia • 100 kW
	SINGAPORE	
	SINGAPORE BC CORP, Jurong	DS-1 • 50 kW
	UNITED KINGDOM	
	BBC, Via Maseru, Lesotho	S Africa • 100 kW
		Sa/Su • S Africa • 100 kW (D) • S Africa • 100 kW
	†BBC, Via Meyerton, S Af	S Africa • 500 kW
11940v	CLANDESTINE (C AMER)	
	"LA VOZ DEL CID", Guatemala City	C America • ANTI-CASTRO
11945	ARMENIA	
	†RADIO YEREVAN, Yerevan	(J) • ARMENIAN • S America • 1000 kW
		(J) • S America • 1000 kW
	CANADA	
	†R CANADA INTL, Sackville, NB	(D) • Europe • 250 kW
	CHINA (PR)	
	†CHINA RADIO INTL, Xi'an	SE Asia • 150 kW
		CANTONESE • SE Asia • 150 kW
	CLANDESTINE (M EAST)	
	"NEWS OF FREE IRAQ, Saudi Arabia	Mideast • ANTI-SADDAM
	GERMANY	
	DEUTSCHE WELLE, Various Locations	S Asia • 250/500 kW
	†DEUTSCHE WELLE, Via Antigua	(D) • C America • 250 kW
	HOLLAND	
	†RADIO NEDERLAND, Flevoland	(J) • W Africa • 500 kW
	KOREA (REPUBLIC)	
	†RADIO KOREA, In-Kimjae	E North Am • 250 kW
		KOREAN • E North Am • 250 kW
	RUSSIA	
	†R MOSCOW INTL, Via Armenia	(J) • S America • 1000 kW
	SPAIN	
	†R EXTERIOR ESPANA, Noblejas	S America • 350 kW
	TURKEY	
	†VOICE OF TURKEY, Ankara	TURKISH • N Africa • 250 kW
	UNITED ARAB EMIRATES	
	UAE RADIO, Dubai	E North Am & C America • 300 kW
	UNITED KINGDOM	
	†BBC, Rampisham	(J) • E Europe • 500 kW
		(J) Su • E Europe • 500 kW
	†BBC, Via Hong Kong	E Asia • 250 kW
		(J) • E Asia • 250 kW
	†BBC, Via Zyyi, Cyprus	(J) • E Europe • 250 kW
	USA	
	†RFE-RL, Via Portugal	(J) • E Europe • 250 kW
	†VOA, Delano, California	C America • 250 kW
		Sa/Su • C America • 250 kW
	†VOA, Via Kaválla, Greece	(D) • C Asia • 250 kW
		(D) • S Asia • 250 kW
		(J) • E Europe • 250 kW
	VOA, Via Portugal	
11950	GERMANY	
	DEUTSCHE WELLE, Via Cyclops, Malta	(J) • N Africa • 250 kW
	DEUTSCHE WELLE, Via Sines, Portugal	(D) • E Europe • 250 kW
	DEUTSCHE WELLE, Via Sri Lanka	Mideast • 250 kW
	†DEUTSCHE WELLE, Wertachtal	(J) • Africa • 500 kW
	HOLLAND	
	RADIO NEDERLAND, Flevoland	DUTCH • C America • 500 kW
	KAZAKHSTAN	
	KAZAKH RADIO, Almaty	RUSSIAN, GERMAN, ETC • DS-1 • 100 kW
	MOLDOVA	
	†RADIO MOLDOVA INTL, Via Romania	Europe • 250 kW
	RUSSIA	
	GOLOS ROSSII, Tula	(J) • Mideast & E Africa • 250 kW
	R MOSCOW INTL	(D) • Europe • 240/500 kW
	R MOSCOW INTL, Tula	(J) • Mideast & E Africa • 250 kW
	SAUDI ARABIA	
	†BS OF THE KINGDOM, Ad Dir'iyah	Mideast & E Africa • DS-CALL OF ISLAM • 50 kW
		Mideast & E Africa • DS-GENERAL • 50 kW
	UKRAINE	
	†RADIO UKRAINE, Khar'kov	(J) • UKRAINIAN • Europe • 100 kW
	†RADIO UKRAINE, Simferopol'	(J) • E North Am • 500 kW
		(J) • UKRAINIAN • E North Am • 500 kW
	UNITED KINGDOM	
	†BBC, Via Zyyi, Cyprus	(J) • E Europe • 100 kW
11954.8	ANGOLA	
	RADIO NACIONAL, Luanda	S Africa • DS-1 • 100 kW
11955 (con'd)	CANADA	
	R CANADA INTL, Sackville, NB	Su • E North Am • 100 kW

0 1 2 3 4 5 6 7 8 9 10 11 12 13 14 15 16 17 18 19 20 21 22 23 24

FREQUENCY	COUNTRY, STATION, LOCATION	TARGET • NETWORK • POWER (kW)	World Time

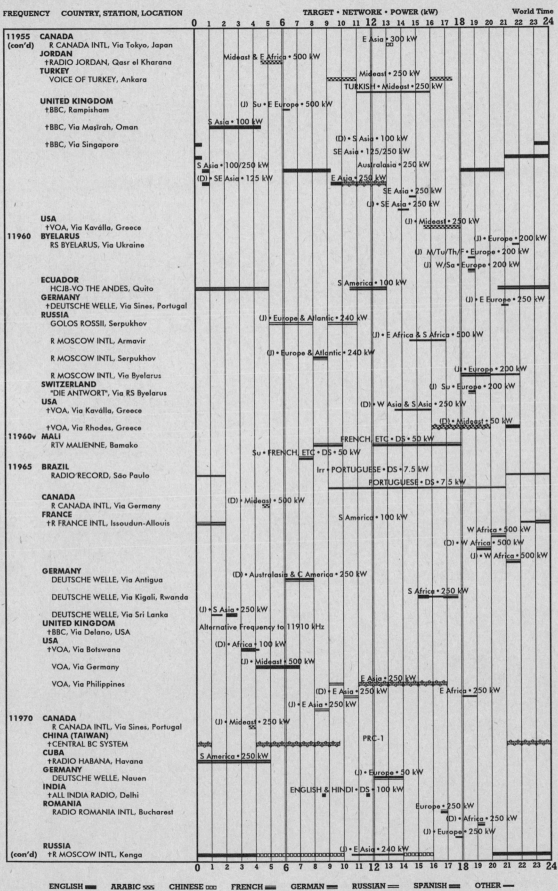

11955 **CANADA**
(con'd) R CANADA INTL, Via Tokyo, Japan — E Asia • 300 kW
JORDAN
 †RADIO JORDAN, Qasr el Kharana — Mideast & E Africa • 500 kW
TURKEY
 VOICE OF TURKEY, Ankara — Mideast • 250 kW / TURKISH • Mideast • 250 kW

UNITED KINGDOM
 †BBC, Rampisham — (J) Su • E Europe • 500 kW
 †BBC, Via Maṣīrah, Oman — S Asia • 100 kW / (D) • S Asia • 100 kW
 †BBC, Via Singapore — SE Asia • 125/250 kW / S Asia • 100/250 kW / Australasia • 250 kW / (D) SE Asia • 125 kW / E Asia • 250 kW / SE Asia • 250 kW / (J) • SE Asia • 250 kW

USA
 †VOA, Via Kaválla, Greece — (J) • Mideast • 250 kW
11960 **BYELARUS**
 RS BYELARUS, Via Ukraine — (J) • Europe • 200 kW / (J) M/Tu/Th/F Europe • 200 kW / (J) W/Sa • Europe • 200 kW

ECUADOR
 HCJB-VO THE ANDES, Quito — S America • 100 kW
GERMANY
 †DEUTSCHE WELLE, Via Sines, Portugal — (J) • E Europe • 250 kW
RUSSIA
 GOLOS ROSSII, Serpukhov — (J) • Europe & Atlantic • 240 kW
 R MOSCOW INTL, Armavir — (J) • E Africa & S Africa • 500 kW
 R MOSCOW INTL, Serpukhov — (J) • Europe & Atlantic • 240 kW
 R MOSCOW INTL, Via Byelarus — (J) • Europe • 200 kW
SWITZERLAND
 "DIE ANTWORT", Via RS Byelarus — (J) Su • Europe • 200 kW
USA
 †VOA, Via Kaválla, Greece — (D) • W Asia & S Asia • 250 kW
 †VOA, Via Rhodes, Greece — (D) • Mideast • 50 kW
11960v **MALI**
 RTV MALIENNE, Bamako — FRENCH, ETC • DS • 50 kW / Su • FRENCH, ETC • DS • 50 kW
11965 **BRAZIL**
 RADIO RECORD, São Paulo — Irr • PORTUGUESE • DS • 7.5 kW / PORTUGUESE • DS • 7.5 kW

CANADA
 R CANADA INTL, Via Germany — (D) • Mideast • 500 kW
FRANCE
 †R FRANCE INTL, Issoudun-Allouis — S America • 100 kW / W Africa • 500 kW / (D) • W Africa • 500 kW / (J) • W Africa • 500 kW

GERMANY
 DEUTSCHE WELLE, Via Antigua — (D) • Australasia & C America • 250 kW
 DEUTSCHE WELLE, Via Kigali, Rwanda — S Africa • 250 kW
 DEUTSCHE WELLE, Via Sri Lanka — (J) • S Asia • 250 kW
UNITED KINGDOM
 †BBC, Via Delano, USA — Alternative Frequency to 11910 kHz
USA
 †VOA, Via Botswana — (D) • Africa • 100 kW
 VOA, Via Germany — (J) • Mideast • 500 kW
 VOA, Via Philippines — E Asia • 250 kW / (D) • E Asia • 250 kW / E Africa • 250 kW / (J) • E Asia • 250 kW

11970 **CANADA**
 R CANADA INTL, Via Sines, Portugal — (J) • Mideast • 250 kW
CHINA (TAIWAN)
 †CENTRAL BC SYSTEM — PRC-1
CUBA
 †RADIO HABANA, Havana — S America • 250 kW
GERMANY
 DEUTSCHE WELLE, Nauen — (J) • Europe • 50 kW
INDIA
 †ALL INDIA RADIO, Delhi — ENGLISH & HINDI • DS • 100 kW
ROMANIA
 RADIO ROMANIA INTL, Bucharest — Europe • 250 kW / (D) • Africa • 250 kW / (J) • Europe • 250 kW

RUSSIA
(con'd) †R MOSCOW INTL, Kenga — (J) • E Asia • 240 kW

ENGLISH ▬ ARABIC ✕✕✕ CHINESE ▫▫▫ FRENCH ══ GERMAN ▬ RUSSIAN ══ SPANISH ══ OTHER ──

FREQUENCY   COUNTRY, STATION, LOCATION   TARGET • NETWORK • POWER (kW)   World Time

0 1 2 3 4 5 6 7 8 9 10 11 12 13 14 15 16 17 18 19 20 21 22 23 24

11970   **UNITED ARAB EMIRATES**
(con'd)   †UAE RADIO, Abu Dhabi   Europe • 500 kW
           UNITED KINGDOM
             BBC, Via Zyyi, Cyprus   (D) • E Europe • 250 kW
                                    (D) • Su • E Europe • 250 kW
           USA
             †R FREE AFGHANISTAN, Via Portugal   (J) • W Asia & C Asia • 500 kW
             †RFE-RL, Via Germany   (D) • W Asia • 250 kW
             †RFE-RL, Via Pals, Spain   (J) • E Europe • 250 kW
                                    (J) • W Asia • 250 kW
             †RFE-RL, Via Portugal   (D) • E Europe & W Asia • 500 kW   (D) • E Europe • 500 kW
                                (J) • E Europe • 500 kW
             WYFR-FAMILY RADIO, Okeechobee, Fl   (J) • S America • 100 kW
11975   **CHINA (PR)**
             CHINA RADIO INTL   S Asia
           EGYPT
             RADIO CAIRO, Abu Za'bal   E Africa & S Africa • 100 kW
           FRANCE
             R FRANCE INTL, Issoudun-Allouis   (D) • Mideast • 500 kW
           PORTUGAL
             †RDP INTERNATIONAL, Lisbon   PORTUGUESE • Europe • 100/250 kW
                                M-F • PORTUGUESE • Europe • 100 kW
                                Sa/Su • PORTUGUESE • Europe • 100/250 kW
                          Sa/Su • ENGLISH, FRENCH & ITALIAN • Europe • 100/250 kW
           RUSSIA
             †R MOSCOW INTL, Kazan'   (J) • S Asia • 100 kW
             †R MOSCOW INTL, Via Uzbekistan   (D) • S Asia • 100 kW
11980   **ARMENIA**
             †RADIO YEREVAN, Via Armavir, Russia   (D) • ARMENIAN • S America • 1000 kW
                                    (D) • S America • 1000 kW
           CHINA (PR)
             CHINA RADIO INTL, Beijing   (D) • W Asia • 120 kW
           GUAM
             †ADVENTIST WORLD R, Agat   E Asia • 100 kW   (J) • S Asia • 100 kW
                                (J) • JAPANESE • E Asia • 100 kW
                                (J) • E Asia • 100 kW
           RUSSIA
             †R MOSCOW INTL, Armavir   (D) • S America • 1000 kW
                                    (J) • Europe • 240 kW
             †R MOSCOW INTL, Kingisepp   (D) • Europe • 500 kW
           SEYCHELLES
             †FAR EAST BC ASS'N, North Pt, Mahé Is   Alternative Frequency to 11685 kHz
11980v   **EGYPT**
             RADIO CAIRO, Abu Za'bal   N Africa & Mideast • DS-VO THE ARABS • 100 kW
11985   **RUSSIA**
             †R MOSCOW INTL, St Petersburg   (J) • Mideast • 500 kW
             †R MOSCOW INTL, Via Ukraine   (D) • S Asia • 100 kW
           UNITED ARAB EMIRATES
             UAE RADIO, Abu Dhabi   Europe • 500 kW
11990   **CZECH REPUBLIC**
             †RADIO PRAGUE, Litomyšl   N America • 100 kW
                     Americas • 100 kW   Europe • 100 kW
                          Australasia • 100 kW
                   (D) • Mideast & S Asia • 100 kW
                   (J) • N America • 100 kW
           KUWAIT
             RADIO KUWAIT, Kabd   Mideast • 500 kW
           RUSSIA
             †R MOSCOW INTL, Kenga   (J) • W Africa • 500 kW
             †RADIO MOSCOW   (J) • DS-1
             †RADIO ROSSII, Kazan'   (D) • DS • 100 kW
           SLOVAKIA
             †R SLOVAKIA INTL, Rimavská Sobota   W Europe • 250 kW
             †R SLOVAKIA INTL, Vel'ké Kostolany   Australasia • 100 kW
11995   **FRANCE**
             †R FRANCE INTL, Issoudun-Allouis   (J) • E Africa • 100 kW   E Europe • 100 kW
                                    E Africa • 100 kW
                            (D) • E Africa • 100 kW
                                    (J) • E Europe • 100 kW
             †R FRANCE INTL, Multiple Locations   (J) • Mideast & E Africa • 100/250 kW
             †R FRANCE INTL, Via French Guiana   S America • 500 kW
                             Irr • S America • 500 kW
           PHILIPPINES
(con'd)   †FEBC RADIO INTL, Bocaue   SE Asia • 100 kW

0 1 2 3 4 5 6 7 8 9 10 11 12 13 14 15 16 17 18 19 20 21 22 23 24

SUMMER ONLY (J)   WINTER ONLY (D)   JAMMING / OR ∧   EARLIEST HEARD ◁   LATEST HEARD ▷   NEW OR CHANGED FOR 1994 †

FREQUENCY   COUNTRY, STATION, LOCATION

TARGET • NETWORK • POWER (kW)   World Time

0 1 2 3 4 5 6 7 8 9 10 11 12 13 14 15 16 17 18 19 20 21 22 23 24

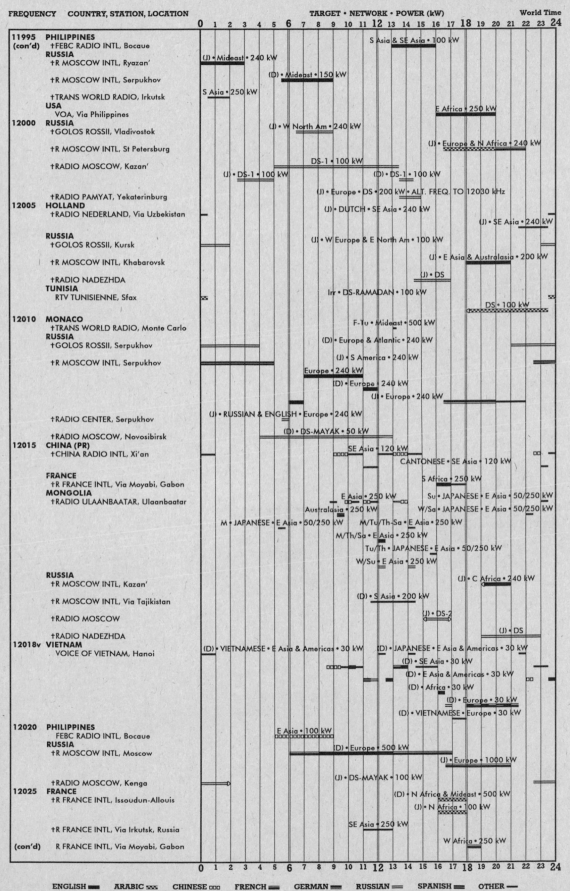

Frequency	Country, Station, Location	Details
11995 (con'd)	**PHILIPPINES** †FEBC RADIO INTL, Bocaue	S Asia & SE Asia • 100 kW
	RUSSIA †R MOSCOW INTL, Ryazan'	(J) • Mideast • 240 kW
	†R MOSCOW INTL, Serpukhov	(D) • Mideast • 150 kW
	†TRANS WORLD RADIO, Irkutsk	S Asia • 250 kW
	USA VOA, Via Philippines	E Africa • 250 kW
12000	**RUSSIA** †GOLOS ROSSII, Vladivostok	(J) • W North Am • 240 kW
	†R MOSCOW INTL, St Petersburg	(J) • Europe & N Africa • 240 kW
	†RADIO MOSCOW, Kazan'	DS-1 • 100 kW; (J) • DS-1 • 100 kW; (D) • DS-1 • 100 kW
	†RADIO PAMYAT, Yekaterinburg	(J) • Europe • DS • 200 kW • ALT. FREQ. TO 12030 kHz
12005	**HOLLAND** †RADIO NEDERLAND, Via Uzbekistan	(J) • DUTCH • SE Asia • 240 kW; (J) • SE Asia • 240 kW
	RUSSIA †GOLOS ROSSII, Kursk	(J) • W Europe & E North Am • 100 kW
	†R MOSCOW INTL, Khabarovsk	(J) • E Asia & Australasia • 200 kW
	†RADIO NADEZHDA	(J) • DS
	TUNISIA RTV TUNISIENNE, Sfax	Irr • DS-RAMADAN • 100 kW; DS • 100 kW
12010	**MONACO** †TRANS WORLD RADIO, Monte Carlo	F-Tu • Mideast • 500 kW
	RUSSIA †GOLOS ROSSII, Serpukhov	(D) • Europe & Atlantic • 240 kW
	†R MOSCOW INTL, Serpukhov	(J) • S America • 240 kW; Europe • 240 kW; (D) • Europe • 240 kW; (J) • Europe • 240 kW
	†RADIO CENTER, Serpukhov	(J) • RUSSIAN & ENGLISH • Europe • 240 kW
	†RADIO MOSCOW, Novosibirsk	(D) • DS-MAYAK • 50 kW
12015	**CHINA (PR)** †CHINA RADIO INTL, Xi'an	SE Asia • 120 kW; CANTONESE • SE Asia • 120 kW
	FRANCE †R FRANCE INTL, Via Moyabi, Gabon	S Africa • 250 kW
	MONGOLIA †RADIO ULAANBAATAR, Ulaanbaatar	E Asia • 250 kW; Su • JAPANESE • E Asia • 50/250 kW; Australasia • 250 kW; W/Sa • JAPANESE • E Asia • 50/250 kW; M • JAPANESE • E Asia • 50/250 kW; M/Tu/Th-Sa • E Asia • 250 kW; M/Th/Sa • E Asia • 250 kW; Tu/Th • JAPANESE • E Asia • 50/250 kW; W/Su • E Asia • 250 kW
	RUSSIA †R MOSCOW INTL, Kazan'	(J) • C Africa • 240 kW
	†R MOSCOW INTL, Via Tajikistan	(D) • S Asia • 200 kW
	†RADIO MOSCOW	(J) • DS-2
	†RADIO NADEZHDA	(J) • DS
12018v	**VIETNAM** VOICE OF VIETNAM, Hanoi	(D) • VIETNAMESE • E Asia & Americas • 30 kW; (D) • JAPANESE • E Asia & Americas • 30 kW; (D) • SE Asia • 30 kW; (D) • E Asia & Americas • 30 kW; (D) • Africa • 30 kW; (D) • Europe • 30 kW; (D) • VIETNAMESE • Europe • 30 kW
12020	**PHILIPPINES** FEBC RADIO INTL, Bocaue	E Asia • 100 kW
	RUSSIA †R MOSCOW INTL, Moscow	(D) • Europe • 500 kW; (J) • Europe • 1000 kW
	†RADIO MOSCOW, Kenga	(J) • DS-MAYAK • 100 kW
12025	**FRANCE** †R FRANCE INTL, Issoudun-Allouis	(D) • N Africa & Mideast • 500 kW; (J) • N Africa • 100 kW
	†R FRANCE INTL, Via Irkutsk, Russia	SE Asia • 250 kW
(con'd)	R FRANCE INTL, Via Moyabi, Gabon	W Africa • 250 kW

0 1 2 3 4 5 6 7 8 9 10 11 12 13 14 15 16 17 18 19 20 21 22 23 24

ENGLISH ▬▬   ARABIC ⋙   CHINESE □□□   FRENCH ═══   GERMAN ▬▬   RUSSIAN ══   SPANISH ▬▬   OTHER ──

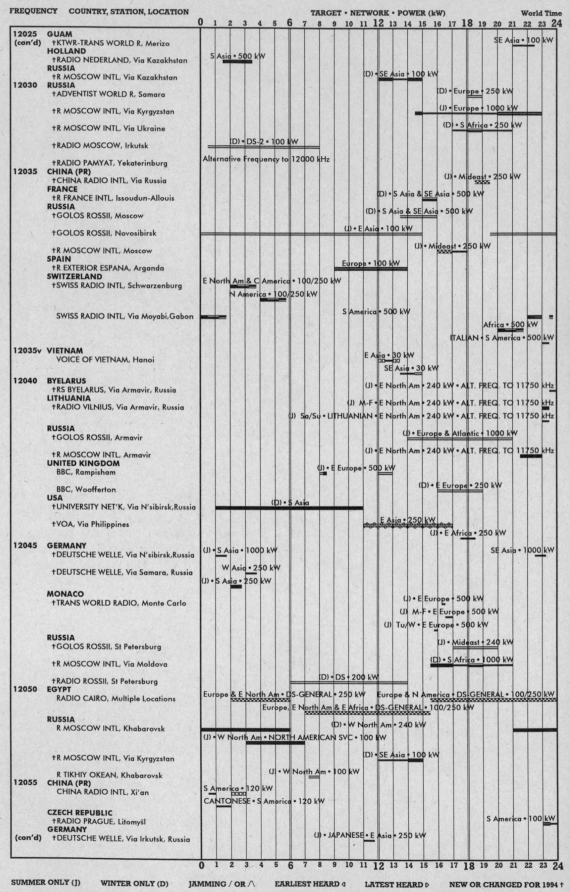

FREQUENCY   COUNTRY, STATION, LOCATION

TARGET • NETWORK • POWER (kW)   World Time

12025	GUAM	
(con'd)	†KTWR-TRANS WORLD R, Merizo	SE Asia • 100 kW
	HOLLAND	
	†RADIO NEDERLAND, Via Kazakhstan	S Asia • 500 kW
	RUSSIA	
	†R MOSCOW INTL, Via Kazakhstan	(D) • SE Asia • 100 kW
12030	**RUSSIA**	
	†ADVENTIST WORLD R, Samara	(D) • Europe • 250 kW
	†R MOSCOW INTL, Via Kyrgyzstan	(J) • Europe • 1000 kW
	†R MOSCOW INTL, Via Ukraine	(D) • S Africa • 250 kW
	†RADIO MOSCOW, Irkutsk	(D) • DS-2 • 100 kW
	†RADIO PAMYAT, Yekaterinburg	Alternative Frequency to 12000 kHz
12035	**CHINA (PR)**	
	†CHINA RADIO INTL, Via Russia	(J) • Mideast • 250 kW
	FRANCE	
	†R FRANCE INTL, Issoudun-Allouis	(D) • S Asia & SE Asia • 500 kW
	RUSSIA	
	†GOLOS ROSSII, Moscow	(D) • S Asia & SE Asia • 500 kW
	†GOLOS ROSSII, Novosibirsk	(J) • E Asia • 100 kW
	†R MOSCOW INTL, Moscow	(J) • Mideast • 250 kW
	SPAIN	
	†R EXTERIOR ESPANA, Arganda	Europe • 100 kW
	SWITZERLAND	
	†SWISS RADIO INTL, Schwarzenburg	E North Am & C America • 100/250 kW
		N America • 100/250 kW
	SWISS RADIO INTL, Via Moyabi,Gabon	S America • 500 kW
		Africa • 500 kW
		ITALIAN • S America • 500 kW
12035v	**VIETNAM**	
	VOICE OF VIETNAM, Hanoi	E Asia • 30 kW
		SE Asia • 30 kW
12040	**BYELARUS**	
	†RS BYELARUS, Via Armavir, Russia	(J) • E North Am • 240 kW • ALT. FREQ. TO 11750 kHz
	LITHUANIA	
	†RADIO VILNIUS, Via Armavir, Russia	(J) M-F • E North Am • 240 kW • ALT. FREQ. TO 11750 kHz
		(J) Sa/Su • LITHUANIAN • E North Am • 240 kW • ALT. FREQ. TO 11750 kHz
	RUSSIA	
	†GOLOS ROSSII, Armavir	(J) • Europe & Atlantic • 1000 kW
	†R MOSCOW INTL, Armavir	(J) • E North Am • 240 kW • ALT. FREQ. TO 11750 kHz
	UNITED KINGDOM	
	BBC, Rampisham	(J) • E Europe • 500 kW
	BBC, Woofferton	(D) • E Europe • 250 kW
	USA	
	†UNIVERSITY NET'K, Via N'sibirsk,Russia	(D) • S Asia
	†VOA, Via Philippines	E Asia • 250 kW
		(J) • E Africa • 250 kW
12045	**GERMANY**	
	†DEUTSCHE WELLE, Via N'sibirsk,Russia	(J) • S Asia • 1000 kW
		SE Asia • 1000 kW
		W Asia • 250 kW
	†DEUTSCHE WELLE, Via Samara, Russia	(J) • S Asia • 250 kW
	MONACO	
	†TRANS WORLD RADIO, Monte Carlo	(J) • E Europe • 500 kW
		(J) M-F • E Europe • 500 kW
		(J) Tu/W • E Europe • 500 kW
	RUSSIA	
	†GOLOS ROSSII, St Petersburg	(J) • Mideast • 240 kW
	†R MOSCOW INTL, Via Moldova	(D) • S Africa • 1000 kW
	†RADIO ROSSII, St Petersburg	(D) • DS • 200 kW
12050	**EGYPT**	
	RADIO CAIRO, Multiple Locations	Europe & E North Am • DS-GENERAL • 250 kW Europe & N America • DS-GENERAL • 100/250 kW
		Europe, E North Am & E Africa • DS-GENERAL • 100/250 kW
	RUSSIA	
	R MOSCOW INTL, Khabarovsk	(D) • W North Am • 240 kW
		(J) • W North Am • NORTH AMERICAN SVC • 100 kW
	†R MOSCOW INTL, Via Kyrgyzstan	(D) • SE Asia • 100 kW
	R TIKHIY OKEAN, Khabarovsk	(J) • W North Am • 100 kW
12055	**CHINA (PR)**	
	CHINA RADIO INTL, Xi'an	S America • 120 kW
		CANTONESE • S America • 120 kW
	CZECH REPUBLIC	
	†RADIO PRAGUE, Litomyšl	S America • 100 kW
	GERMANY	
(con'd)	†DEUTSCHE WELLE, Via Irkutsk, Russia	(J) • JAPANESE • E Asia • 250 kW

| FREQUENCY | COUNTRY, STATION, LOCATION | TARGET • NETWORK • POWER (kW) | World Time |

12055 **RUSSIA**
(con'd) †GOLOS ROSSII, Via Uzbekistan — (D) • S Asia & SE Asia • 240 kW

†R MOSCOW INTL, Armavir — (D) • Mideast • 120 kW

†R MOSCOW INTL, Komsomol'sk 'Amure — (J) • E Asia • 200 kW
— (J) • JAPANESE • E Asia • 200 kW

UNITED KINGDOM
†BBC, Via Chita, Russia — (J) • E Asia • 500 kW

†BBC, Via Uzbekistan — (J) • S Asia • 200 kW

12060 **ARMENIA**
†RADIO YEREVAN, Yerevan — (D) • ARMENIAN • W Africa & S America • 1000 kW
— (D) • W Africa & S America • 1000 kW

RUSSIA
ADVENTIST WORLD R, Samara — (D) • Europe • 250 kW

†R MOSCOW INTL, Via Armenia — (D) • W Africa & S America • 1000 kW
— (D) • W Africa • 1000 kW

†R MOSCOW INTL, Via Kazakhstan — (J) • Europe • 1000 kW

†RADIO MOSCOW, Chita — (J) • DS-1 • 50 kW

†RADIO MOSCOW, Volgograd — DS-MAYAK • 100 kW

12065 **ARMENIA**
RADIO YEREVAN, Yerevan — (J) • Mideast • 100 kW
— (J) • ARMENIAN • Mideast • 100 kW
— (J) • M-Sa • Mideast • 100 kW
— (J) • ARMENIAN • Mideast • ARMENIAN, TURKISH • 100 kW

CHINA (PR)
†CHINA RADIO INTL, Via Russia — (J) • Mideast

HOLLAND
†RADIO NEDERLAND, Via Petro-K, Russia — (J) • E Asia • 240 kW
— (J) • DUTCH • E Asia • 240 kW

RUSSIA
†R MOSCOW INTL, Kingisepp — (D) • Mideast • 240 kW

12070 **RUSSIA**
†GOLOS ROSSII, Khabarovsk — W North Am • 100 kW
— (D) • W North Am • 100 kW

†R MOSCOW INTL, Moscow — (J) • Europe • 240 kW

†R MOSCOW INTL, Serpukhov — (D) • W Africa • 250 kW

†R MOSCOW INTL, St Petersburg — (D) • W Europe • 250 kW

R TIKHIY OKEAN, Khabarovsk — (J) • Pacific & W North Am • 100 kW

†RADIO MOSCOW, Khabarovsk — DS-1 • 100 kW
— (J) • DS-1 • 100 kW

12070.5 **AUSTRALIA**
†ARMED FORCES RADIO, Belconnen — SE Asia • 40 kW • USB

12075 **ISRAEL**
†KOL ISRAEL, Tel Aviv — (J) F/Sa • E Europe • 300 kW
— (J) • E Europe • 300 kW
— (J) • W Europe • 300 kW
— (J) • YIDDISH • W Europe • 300 kW
— (J) Su-Th • PERSIAN • E Europe • 300 kW

MONACO
†TRANS WORLD RADIO, Monte Carlo — Alternative Frequency to 12080 kHz

RUSSIA
R MOSCOW INTL, Balashikha — (J) • 20 kW
— (J) M/W/F/Sa • 20 kW

†RADIO ALEF, Balashikha — (J) Su/Tu/Th • DS • 20 kW

RUKHI MIRAS, Balashikha — F • DS • 20 kW

12080 **MONACO**
†TRANS WORLD RADIO, Monte Carlo — Mideast • 500 kW • ALT. FREQ. TO 12075 kHz
— M-F • Mideast • 500 kW • ALT. FREQ. TO 12075 kHz

USA
†VOA, Via Botswana — Africa • 100 kW
— M-F • Africa • 100 kW
— Sa/Su • Africa • 100 kW

12085 **SYRIA**
†RADIO DAMASCUS, Adhra — S America • 500 kW
— E Europe • 500 kW
— Europe • 500 kW
— N America • 500 kW

†SYRIAN BC SERVICE, Adhra — DS • 500 kW
— (J) • DS • 500 kW — (D) • DS • 500 kW

12095 **UNITED KINGDOM**
(con'd) BBC, Multiple Locations — Europe • 250/300/500 kW

ENGLISH ▬ ARABIC ⋙ CHINESE □□□ FRENCH ══ GERMAN ▬▬ RUSSIAN ══ SPANISH ▬▬ OTHER ──

FREQUENCY	COUNTRY, STATION, LOCATION	TARGET • NETWORK • POWER (kW) / World Time

World Time scale: 0 1 2 3 4 5 6 7 8 9 10 11 12 13 14 15 16 17 18 19 20 21 22 23 24

12095
(con'd) UNITED KINGDOM
BBC, Multiple Locations — (J) • Europe • 250 kW; Europe, N Africa & W Africa • 250/300/500 kW

BBC, Woofferton — (J) • N America & C America • 250 kW
(J) • N America • 250 kW

12110 CHINA (PR)
CHINA RADIO INTL, Kunming — SE Asia • 50 kW
12120 CHINA (PR)
CENTRAL PEOPLES BS — DS-1
W-M • DS-1

RUSSIA
†RADIO MOSCOW — (J) • DS-MAYAK
UKRAINE
†RADIO UKRAINE, Simferopol' — (J) • E North Am • 2X11950–11780 • SPR
(J) • UKRAINIAN • E North Am • 2X11950–11780 • SPR

12160 USA
†WEWN, Birmingham, Alabama — (J) • Europe • 500 kW
12175 RUSSIA
†RADIO ROSSII, Moscow — (D) • DS(FEEDER) • 100 kW • USB
12250 RUSSIA
RADIO ROSSII, Moscow — (J) • DS(FEEDER) • 100 kW • USB
12450 CHINA (PR)
CHINA RADIO INTL — SE Asia
13365 RUSSIA
†RADIO MOSCOW — (D) • DS-MAYAK(FEEDER) • LSB
13430 RUSSIA
†RADIO ROSSII, Moscow — (J) • DS(FEEDER) • 50/100 kW • USB
13508.5 AUSTRALIA
†ARMED FORCES RADIO, Exmouth — M/F • E Africa • 40 kW • USB
13595 USA
†WJCR, Upton, Kentucky — N America • 50 kW
13600 CZECH REPUBLIC
†RADIO PRAGUE, Litomyšl — Australasia • 100 kW; Mideast • 100 kW
W Africa • 100 kW
M-F • Mideast • 100 kW

13605 AUSTRALIA
†RADIO AUSTRALIA, Carnarvon — (D) • SE Asia • 100 kW

†RADIO AUSTRALIA, Darwin — E Asia • 250 kW
BULGARIA
†RADIO BULGARIA, Sofia — (D) • S America • 100 kW
RUSSIA
†GOLOS ROSSII, Via Kazakhstan — (D) • SE Asia • 240 kW

†R TIKHIY OKEAN, Via Kazakhstan — (J) • SE Asia • 240 kW
UNITED ARAB EMIRATES
†UAE RADIO, Abu Dhabi — (D) • Europe • 500 kW; (D) • E Asia • 500 kW
13610 GERMANY
DEUTSCHE WELLE, Nauen — Australasia • 500 kW

DEUTSCHE WELLE, Various Locations — Africa • 500 kW

†DEUTSCHE WELLE, Wertachtal — (D) • SE Asia • 500 kW
13615 BANGLADESH
†RADIO BANGLADESH, Dhaka — Alternative Frequency to 13620 kHz
RUSSIA
†R MOSCOW INTL, Via Kazakhstan — (D) • E Asia & SE Asia • 100 kW
USA
CHRIST SCI MONITOR, South Carolina — Australasia • 500 kW
M-F • Australasia • 500 kW
Sa • Australasia • 500 kW
Su • Australasia • 500 kW

†WEWN, Birmingham, Alabama — Americas • 500 kW
(J) • Europe • 500 kW

13620 BANGLADESH
†RADIO BANGLADESH, Dhaka — Europe • 250 kW • ALT. FREQ. TO 13615 kHz
Mideast • 250 kW • ALT. FREQ. TO 13615 kHz
BANGLA • Mideast • 250 kW • ALT. FREQ. TO 13615 kHz

KUWAIT
†RADIO KUWAIT, Kabd — Europe & E North Am • 500 kW
13625 FRANCE
†R FRANCE INTL, Via French Guiana — (J) • S America • 500 kW
RUSSIA
†GOLOS ROSSII, Novosibirsk — (J) • E Asia • 100 kW
E Asia • 100 kW

USA
†CHRIST SCI MONITOR, Via Saipan — SE Asia • 100 kW
S Asia & SE Asia • 100 kW
(D) • SE Asia & S Africa • 100 kW
(D) • M-Sa • SE Asia & S Africa • 100 kW
Sa • S Asia & SE Asia • 100 kW
Su-F • S Asia & SE Asia • 100 kW
(D) • Su • SE Asia & S Africa • 100 kW

13630v COSTA RICA
(con'd) †RADIO FOR PEACE, Ciudad Colón — N America • USB

World Time scale: 0 1 2 3 4 5 6 7 8 9 10 11 12 13 14 15 16 17 18 19 20 21 22 23 24

SUMMER ONLY (J)   WINTER ONLY (D)   JAMMING / OR ∧   EARLIEST HEARD ◁   LATEST HEARD ▷   NEW OR CHANGED FOR 1994 †

FREQUENCY   COUNTRY, STATION, LOCATION   TARGET • NETWORK • POWER (kW)   World Time

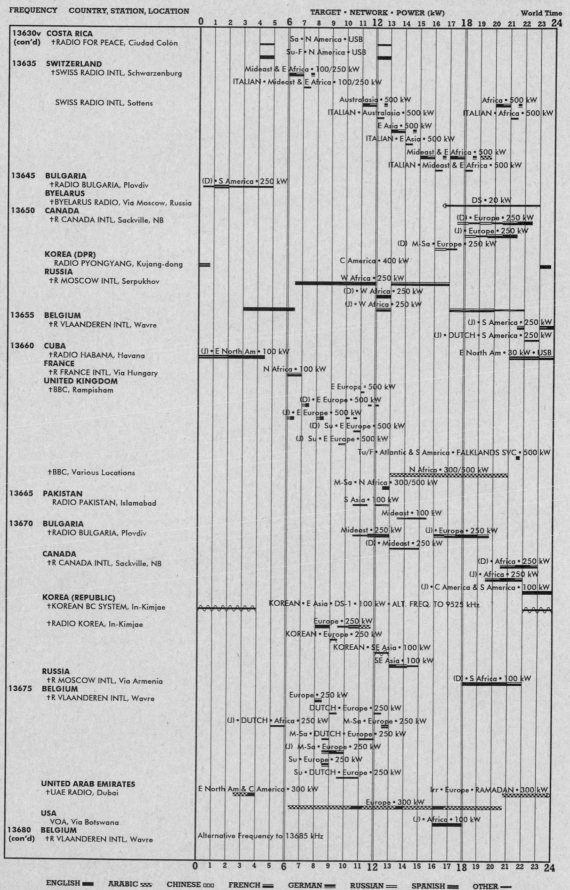

Frequency	Country, Station, Location	Schedule detail
13630v (con'd)	**COSTA RICA** †RADIO FOR PEACE, Ciudad Colón	Sa • N America • USB; Su-F • N America • USB
13635	**SWITZERLAND** †SWISS RADIO INTL, Schwarzenburg	Mideast & E Africa • 100/250 kW; ITALIAN • Mideast & E Africa • 100/250 kW
	SWISS RADIO INTL, Sottens	Australasia • 500 kW; Africa • 500 kW; ITALIAN • Australasia • 500 kW; ITALIAN • Africa • 500 kW; E Asia • 500 kW; ITALIAN • E Asia • 500 kW; Mideast & E Africa • 500 kW; ITALIAN • Mideast & E Africa • 500 kW
13645	**BULGARIA** †RADIO BULGARIA, Plovdiv	(D) • S America • 250 kW
	BYELARUS †BYELARUS RADIO, Via Moscow, Russia	DS • 20 kW
13650	**CANADA** †R CANADA INTL, Sackville, NB	(D) • Europe • 250 kW; (J) • Europe • 250 kW; (D) M-Sa • Europe • 250 kW
	KOREA (DPR) RADIO PYONGYANG, Kujang-dong	C America • 400 kW
	RUSSIA †R MOSCOW INTL, Serpukhov	W Africa • 250 kW; (D) • W Africa • 250 kW; (J) • W Africa • 250 kW
13655	**BELGIUM** †R VLAANDEREN INTL, Wavre	(J) • S America • 250 kW; (J) • DUTCH • S America • 250 kW
13660	**CUBA** †RADIO HABANA, Havana	(J) • E North Am • 100 kW; E North Am • 30 kW • USB
	FRANCE †R FRANCE INTL, Via Hungary	N Africa • 100 kW
	UNITED KINGDOM †BBC, Rampisham	E Europe • 500 kW; (D) • E Europe • 500 kW; (J) • E Europe • 500 kW; (D) Su • E Europe • 500 kW; (J) Su • E Europe • 500 kW; Tu/F • Atlantic & S America • FALKLANDS SVC • 500 kW
	†BBC, Various Locations	N Africa • 300/500 kW; M-Sa • N Africa • 300/500 kW
13665	**PAKISTAN** RADIO PAKISTAN, Islamabad	S Asia • 100 kW; Mideast • 100 kW
13670	**BULGARIA** †RADIO BULGARIA, Plovdiv	Mideast • 250 kW; (J) • Europe • 250 kW; (D) • Mideast • 250 kW
	CANADA †R CANADA INTL, Sackville, NB	(D) • Africa • 250 kW; (J) • Africa • 250 kW; (J) • C America & S America • 100 kW
	KOREA (REPUBLIC) †KOREAN BC SYSTEM, In-Kimjae	KOREAN • E Asia • DS-1 • 100 kW • ALT. FREQ. TO 9525 kHz
	†RADIO KOREA, In-Kimjae	Europe • 250 kW; KOREAN • Europe • 250 kW; KOREAN • SE Asia • 100 kW; SE Asia • 100 kW
	RUSSIA †R MOSCOW INTL, Via Armenia	(D) • S Africa • 100 kW
13675	**BELGIUM** †R VLAANDEREN INTL, Wavre	Europe • 250 kW; DUTCH • Europe • 250 kW; (J) • DUTCH • Africa • 250 kW; M-Sa • Europe • 250 kW; M-Sa • DUTCH • Europe • 250 kW; (J) M-Sa • Europe • 250 kW; Su • Europe • 250 kW; Su • DUTCH • Europe • 250 kW
	UNITED ARAB EMIRATES †UAE RADIO, Dubai	E North Am & C America • 300 kW; Irr • Europe • RAMADAN • 300 kW
	USA VOA, Via Botswana	Europe • 300 kW; (J) • Africa • 100 kW
13680 (con'd)	**BELGIUM** †R VLAANDEREN INTL, Wavre	Alternative Frequency to 13685 kHz

0 1 2 3 4 5 6 7 8 9 10 11 12 13 14 15 16 17 18 19 20 21 22 23 24

ENGLISH ▬   ARABIC ▨   CHINESE ▢▢▢   FRENCH ═   GERMAN ▭   RUSSIAN ═   SPANISH ▭   OTHER ▬

FREQUENCY	COUNTRY, STATION, LOCATION	TARGET • NETWORK • POWER (kW) — World Time

13680 (con'd) IRAQ †RADIO IRAQ INTL — N Africa / Europe

RUSSIA †GOLOS ROSSII, St Petersburg — W Europe & Atlantic • 240/500 kW — (J) • W Europe & Atlantic • 240 kW

13685 BELGIUM †R VLAANDEREN INTL, Wavre
- (J) • M/Tu/Th/F • DUTCH • Africa • 250 kW
- (J) • Su-Tu/Th/F • Africa • 250 kW
- (D) • W/Sa • DUTCH • Africa • 250 kW • ALT. FREQ. TO 13680 kHz
- (J) • W/Sa • DUTCH • Africa • 250 kW
- (D) • Su • FRENCH & DUTCH • Africa • 250 kW • ALT. FREQ. TO 13680 kHz

CHINA (PR) CHINA RADIO INTL, Via French Guiana — S America • 500 kW

PAKISTAN †RADIO PAKISTAN, Islamabad
- (D) • Mideast & Europe • 100 kW
- (J) • Mideast • 100 kW

SWITZERLAND SWISS RADIO INTL, Sottens — Australasia • 500 kW

13690 GERMANY †DEUTSCHE WELLE, Jülich
- Mideast • 100 kW
- (J) • W Africa • 100 kW
- (J) • E Asia • 100 kW

†DEUTSCHE WELLE, Königswusterhausen — (J) • Mideast • 100 kW

†DEUTSCHE WELLE, Nauen
- (J) • S America • 100 kW
- Europe • 500 kW
- (D) • Europe • 500 kW

†DEUTSCHE WELLE, Wertachtal — (D) • W Asia • 500 kW

13695 HUNGARY †RADIO BUDAPEST
- HUNGARIAN • S America
- M • HUNGARIAN • S America

USA †WYFR-FAMILY RADIO, Okeechobee, Fl
- (D) • S America • 100 kW
- (D) • C Africa & S Africa • 100 kW   E North Am • 100 kW
- (J) • W Africa • 100 kW

13700 HOLLAND †RADIO NEDERLAND, Flevoland
- (D) • DUTCH • Mideast • 500 kW   DUTCH • S Europe • 500 kW
- (J) • S Asia • 500 kW   DUTCH • Mideast • 500 kW
- (J) • DUTCH • W Europe • 500 kW   C Africa • 500 kW
- (D) • DUTCH • S America • 500 kW
- (J) • Mideast • 500 kW   (J) • S America • 500 kW
- (J) • DUTCH • C America • 500 kW

†RADIO NEDERLAND, Via Madagascar
- DUTCH • Mideast • 300 kW   SE Asia • 300 kW
- (D) • DUTCH • SE Asia • 300 kW

13705 RUSSIA R MOSCOW INTL — (D) • Europe • ALT. FREQ. TO 13710 kHz

†R MOSCOW INTL, Moscow — (D) • Europe • 250 kW • ALT. FREQ. TO 13710 kHz

13710 BELGIUM †R VLAANDEREN INTL, Wavre — Su • DUTCH • Europe • 250 kW

RUSSIA R MOSCOW INTL — Alternative Frequency to 13705 kHz

†R MOSCOW INTL, Moscow — Alternative Frequency to 13705 kHz

†RADIO VEDO, Volgograd — DS • 20 kW

USA CHRIST SCI MONITOR, South Carolina — (J) • Sa/Su • E North Am & C America • 500 kW

VOA, Via Botswana — Africa • 100 kW

†WEWN, Birmingham, Alabama
- (D) • C Africa & S Africa • 500 kW
- (J) • Mideast • 500 kW   (J) • E Asia • 500 kW

13715 CZECH REPUBLIC †RADIO PRAGUE, Litomyšl — Mideast & E Africa • 100 kW

13720 CANADA †R CANADA INTL, Sackville, NB
- (D) • S America • 250 kW
- (D) • Tu-Sa • S America • 250 kW

GUAM †ADVENTIST WORLD R, Agat
- E Asia • 100 kW   (D) • SE Asia • 100 kW
- Sa/Su • E Asia • 100 kW   SE Asia • 100 kW
- (J) • S Asia • 100 kW
- Sa/Su • S Asia & E Africa • 100 kW

13725 RUSSIA †R MOSCOW INTL, Serpukhov — (J) • S Asia & SE Asia • 240 kW

13730 AUSTRIA †RADIO AUSTRIA INTL, Vienna
- Europe • 100 kW   S America • 100 kW
- W Europe & E North Am • 100 kW   S Africa • 500 kW
- (D) • Europe • 100 kW   (D) • S Africa • 500 kW
- (D) • W Europe & E North Am • 100 kW   (D) • S America • 100 kW

(con'd)

World Time scale: 0 1 2 3 4 5 6 7 8 9 10 11 12 13 14 15 16 17 18 19 20 21 22 23 24

SUMMER ONLY (J)   WINTER ONLY (D)   JAMMING / OR ∧   EARLIEST HEARD ◁   LATEST HEARD ▷   NEW OR CHANGED FOR 1994 †

FREQUENCY   COUNTRY, STATION, LOCATION   TARGET • NETWORK • POWER (kW)   World Time

0 1 2 3 4 5 6 7 8 9 10 11 12 13 14 15 16 17 18 19 20 21 22 23 24

13730 AUSTRIA
(con'd) †RADIO AUSTRIA INTL, Vienna
(J) • Europe • 100 kW
(J) • S Africa • 500 kW
(J) • W Europe & E North Am • 100 kW
(J) • S America • 100 kW
M-Sa • Europe • 100 kW
M-Sa • S Africa • 500 kW
Su • Europe • 100 kW
Su • S Africa • 500 kW

13735 RUSSIA
†GOLOS ROSSII, Zhigulevsk
W Europe & Atlantic • 100 kW • USB • ALT. FREQ. TO 13751.8 kHz
(J) • W Europe & Atlantic • 100 kW • USB • ALT. FREQ. TO 13751.8 kHz

13740 USA
†KCBI, Dallas, Texas
Alternative Frequency to 15725 kHz

†VOA, Cincinnati, Ohio
S America • 250 kW
(D) • C America • 250 kW
(J) • C America • 250 kW

†WEWN, Birmingham, Alabama
(D) • ENGLISH, ETC • Europe • PROJECTED • 500 kW

13745 UNITED KINGDOM
†BBC, Rampisham
(D) • Europe • 500 kW
(D) • E Europe • 500 kW
(J) • Europe • 500 kW
(D) M-Sa • Europe • 500 kW
(J) M-Sa • Europe • 500 kW
(D) Su • Europe • 500 kW
(J) Su • Europe • 500 kW

†BBC, Skelton, Cumbria
(J) Su • Europe • 300 kW

13750 COSTA RICA
†ADVENTIST WORLD R, Cahuita
C America & N America • TESTS • 20 kW
ISRAEL
†RASHUTH HASHIDUR, Tel Aviv
HEBREW • N Europe & E Europe • DS-B • 20/50 kW
Su-F • HEBREW • N Europe & E Europe • DS-B • 20/50 kW

13751.8 RUSSIA
†GOLOS ROSSII, Zhigulevsk
Alternative Frequency to 13735 kHz
13755 AUSTRALIA
†RADIO AUSTRALIA, Carnarvon
SE Asia • 100 kW
S Asia, Mideast & Europe • 100/300 kW
M-F • SE Asia • 100 kW
Sa/Su • SE Asia • 100 kW

13760 GERMANY
†DEUTSCHE WELLE, Jülich
(D) • Mideast • 100 kW
KOREA (DPR)
RADIO PYONGYANG, Kujang-dong
C America • 400 kW
KOREAN • C America • 400 kW
RUSSIA
†RADIO MOSCOW, Moscow
DS-1(FEEDER) • 50 kW • USB
(J) • DS-1(FEEDER) • 50 kW • USB
USA
CHRIST SCI MONITOR, South Carolina
M • S America • 500 kW
W North Am & C America • 500 kW
(J) M • C America • 500 kW
M-F • C America • 500 kW
Sa/Su • S America • 500 kW
M-F • W North Am & C America • 500 kW
(J) Sa/Su • C America • 500 kW
Sa/Su • C America • 500 kW
Su • S America • 500 kW
Sa/Su • W North Am & C America • 500 kW
Tu-F • S America • 500 kW
(J) Tu-F • C America • 500 kW
Tu-Sa • S America • 500 kW

WORLD HARVEST R, Noblesville, Indiana
ENGLISH, ETC • E North Am & W Europe • 100 kW
13770 GERMANY
†DEUTSCHE WELLE, Jülich
(J) • Mideast • 100 kW
HOLLAND
†RADIO NEDERLAND, Flevoland
(J) • DUTCH • E Europe & Mideast • 500 kW
Mideast • 500 kW
(D) • S Asia • 500 kW
USA
CHRIST SCI MONITOR, Maine
Sa/Su • Europe • 500 kW

†CHRIST SCI MONITOR, South Carolina
(D) M-F • E North Am • 500 kW
(D) Sa • E North Am & Europe • 500 kW
(D) Su • E North Am & Europe • 500 kW

13775 RUSSIA
†R MOSCOW INTL, Kenga
(J) • E Asia • 100 kW
USA
†VOA, Greenville, NC
C America • 250 kW
Sa/Su • C America • 250 kW

13780 GERMANY
†DEUTSCHE WELLE, Jülich
(J) • E North Am & C America • 100 kW
S Europe • 100 kW
(J) • S Asia • 100 kW
(D) • S Europe • 100 kW
(D) • W Africa • 100 kW
(J) • Mideast • 100 kW
(J) • C Africa & E Africa • 100 kW

(con'd) †DEUTSCHE WELLE, Via Sines, Portugal
S America • 250 kW

0 1 2 3 4 5 6 7 8 9 10 11 12 13 14 15 16 17 18 19 20 21 22 23 24

ENGLISH ▬   ARABIC ⌇⌇⌇   CHINESE ▫▫▫   FRENCH ▭   GERMAN ▬   RUSSIAN ═   SPANISH ▭   OTHER ▬

FREQUENCY   COUNTRY, STATION, LOCATION

TARGET • NETWORK • POWER (kW)   World Time

0 1 2 3 4 5 6 7 8 9 10 11 12 13 14 15 16 17 18 19 20 21 22 23 24

Frequency	Country, Station, Location	Schedule Details
13780 (con'd)	GERMANY †DEUTSCHE WELLE, Wertachtal	(D) • E Asia • 500 kW
13780v	MONGOLIA †RADIO ULAANBAATAR, Ulaanbaatar	S Asia • 50 kW
13785	KOREA (DPR) †RADIO PYONGYANG, Kujang-dong	Europe • 200 kW / KOREAN • Europe • 200 kW
13790	GERMANY †DEUTSCHE WELLE, Jülich	(J) • S Asia • 100 kW / (J) • Mideast • 100 kW / W Africa • 100 kW
	†DEUTSCHE WELLE, Leipzig	(J) • W Asia • 100 kW
	†DEUTSCHE WELLE, Multiple Locations	(J) • S America • 100/250 kW
	†DEUTSCHE WELLE, Via Sackville, Can	N America • 250 kW
	†DEUTSCHE WELLE, Via Sines, Portugal	(J) • E North Am & C America • 250 kW
	†DEUTSCHE WELLE, Wertachtal	(D) • JAPANESE • E Asia • 500 kW / Africa • 500 kW / (D) • E Asia • 500 kW
13795	RUSSIA RADIO MOSCOW	DS-MAYAK
	UKRAINE †RADIO UKRAINE, Multiple Locations	E Europe • 20 kW
	†UKRAINIAN R, Multiple Locations	Irr • UKRAINIAN • DS-2 • 20 kW / Irr • UKRAINIAN • DS-3 • 20 kW
13820	RUSSIA †RADIO MOSCOW, Moscow	DS-1 (FEEDER) • 15 kW • ISU / DS-MAYAK (FEEDER) • 15 kW • ISL
13830	CROATIA CROATIAN RADIO, Zagreb	Irr • Europe • DS-1 / Irr • M-Sa • Europe • DS-1 / Irr • Su • Europe • DS-1
13835	ICELAND †RIKISUTVARPID, Reykjavik	Atlantic & Europe • DS-1 • 10 kW • USB
13840	USA †CHRIST SCI MONITOR, Via Saipan	(D) • Australasia • 100 kW / (D) Sa • Australasia • 100 kW / (D) Su-F • Australasia • 100 kW
13845	USA †WWCR, Nashville, Tennessee	W North Am • 100 kW / (J) • W North Am • 100 kW
13855	ICELAND RIKISUTVARPID, Reykjavik	Atlantic & E North Am • DS-1 • 10 kW • USB
14526	USA †VOA, Greenville, NC	Europe • (FEEDER) • 40 kW • ISL / Europe • (FEEDER) • 40 kW • ISU / (D) • Europe • (FEEDER) • 40 kW • ISU / (D) • Europe • (FEEDER) • 40 kW • ISL / (J) • Europa • (FEEDER) • 40 kW • ISL / (J) • Europe • (FEEDER) • 40 kW • ISU
14917.7	KIRIBATI †RADIO KIRIBATI, Betio	Alternative Frequency to 17440 kHz
15000	USA WWV, Ft Collins, Colorado	WEATHER/WORLD TIME • 10 kW
	WWVH, Kekaha, Hawaii	WEATHER/WORLD TIME • 10 kW
15009v	VIETNAM VOICE OF VIETNAM, Ha Son Binh	(J) • VIETNAMESE • E Asia & Americas • 30 kW / (J) • JAPANESE • E Asia & Americas • 30 kW / (J) • SE Asia • 30 kW / (J) • E Asia & Americas • 30 kW / (J) • Africa • 30 kW / (J) • Europe • 30 kW / (J) • VIETNAMESE • Europe • 30 kW
15020	INDIA ALL INDIA RADIO, Aligarh	S Asia • 250 kW
15030v	COSTA RICA †RADIO FOR PEACE, Ciudad Colón	N America • 0.4/0.5 kW / Sa • N America • 0.4/0.5 kW / Su-F • N America • 0.4/0.5 kW
15040v	PIRATE (PACIFIC) "RADIO G'DAY", Australia	Irr • Australasia • 0.016 kW
15045v	PIRATE (EUROPE) "WEEKEND MUSIC R", Scotland	Irr • Su • W Europe • 0.1 kW
15050	INDIA †ALL INDIA RADIO, Aligarh	W Asia & Mideast • 250 kW / E Asia • 250 kW / SE Asia • 250 kW / E Asia & Australasia • 250 kW / Irr • W Asia & Mideast • HAJJ • 250 kW
15050v	CLANDESTINE (S AMER) †"R PATRIA LIBRE", Colombia	Alternative Frequency to 6270v kHz

0 1 2 3 4 5 6 7 8 9 10 11 12 13 14 15 16 17 18 19 20 21 22 23 24

SUMMER ONLY (J)   WINTER ONLY (D)   JAMMING / OR ⋀   EARLIEST HEARD ◁   LATEST HEARD ▷   NEW OR CHANGED FOR 1994 †

FREQUENCY   COUNTRY, STATION, LOCATION   TARGET • NETWORK • POWER (kW)   World Time

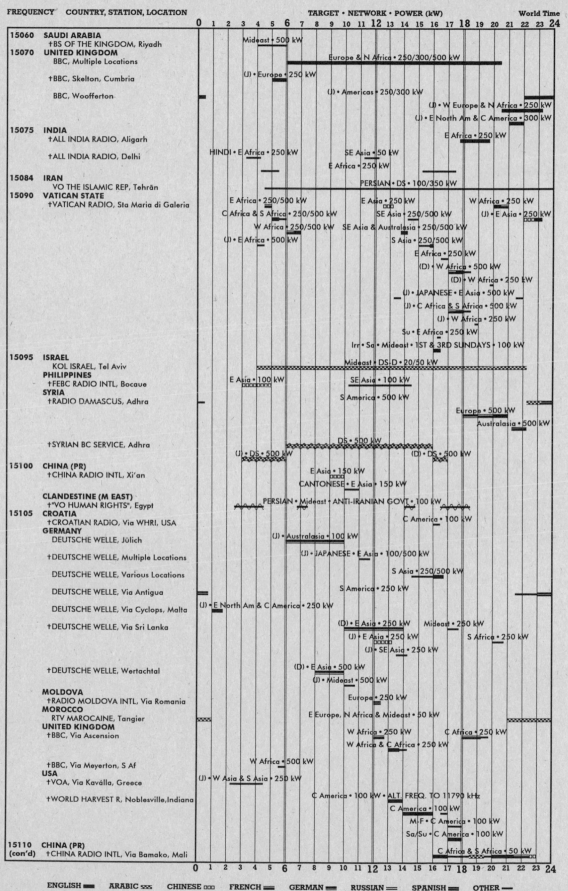

15060	**SAUDI ARABIA**	
	†BS OF THE KINGDOM, Riyadh	Mideast • 500 kW
15070	**UNITED KINGDOM**	
	BBC, Multiple Locations	Europe & N Africa • 250/300/500 kW
	†BBC, Skelton, Cumbria	(J) • Europe • 250 kW
	BBC, Woofferton	(J) • Americas • 250/300 kW
		(J) • W Europe & N Africa • 250 kW
		(J) • E North Am & C America • 300 kW
15075	**INDIA**	
	†ALL INDIA RADIO, Aligarh	E Africa • 250 kW
	†ALL INDIA RADIO, Delhi	HINDI • E Africa • 250 kW SE Asia • 50 kW
		E Africa • 250 kW
15084	**IRAN**	
	VO THE ISLAMIC REP, Tehrān	PERSIAN • DS • 100/350 kW
15090	**VATICAN STATE**	
	†VATICAN RADIO, Sta Maria di Galeria	E Africa • 250/500 kW E Asia • 250 kW W Africa • 250 kW
		C Africa & S Africa • 250/500 kW SE Asia • 250/500 kW (J) • E Asia • 250 kW
		W Africa • 250/500 kW SE Asia & Australasia • 250/500 kW
		(J) • E Africa • 500 kW S Asia • 250/500 kW
		E Africa • 250 kW
		(D) • W Africa • 500 kW
		(D) • W Africa • 250 kW
		(J) • JAPANESE • E Asia • 500 kW
		(J) • C Africa & S Africa • 500 kW
		(J) • W Africa • 250 kW
		Su • E Africa • 250 kW
		Irr • Sa • Mideast • 1ST & 3RD SUNDAYS • 100 kW
15095	**ISRAEL**	
	KOL ISRAEL, Tel Aviv	Mideast • DS-D • 20/50 kW
	PHILIPPINES	
	†FEBC RADIO INTL, Bocaue	E Asia • 100 kW SE Asia • 100 kW
	SYRIA	
	†RADIO DAMASCUS, Adhra	S America • 500 kW
		Europe • 500 kW
		Australasia • 500 kW
	†SYRIAN BC SERVICE, Adhra	DS • 500 kW
		(J) • DS • 500 kW (D) • DS • 500 kW
15100	**CHINA (PR)**	
	†CHINA RADIO INTL, Xi'an	E Asia • 150 kW
		CANTONESE • E Asia • 150 kW
	CLANDESTINE (M EAST)	
	†"VO HUMAN RIGHTS", Egypt	PERSIAN • Mideast • ANTI-IRANIAN GOVT • 100 kW
15105	**CROATIA**	
	†CROATIAN RADIO, Via WHRI, USA	C America • 100 kW
	GERMANY	
	DEUTSCHE WELLE, Jülich	(J) • Australasia • 100 kW
	†DEUTSCHE WELLE, Multiple Locations	(J) • JAPANESE • E Asia • 100/500 kW
	DEUTSCHE WELLE, Various Locations	S Asia • 250/500 kW
	DEUTSCHE WELLE, Via Antigua	S America • 250 kW
	DEUTSCHE WELLE, Via Cyclops, Malta	(J) • E North Am & C America • 250 kW
	†DEUTSCHE WELLE, Via Sri Lanka	(D) • E Asia • 250 kW Mideast • 250 kW
		(J) • E Asia • 250 kW S Africa • 250 kW
		(J) • SE Asia • 250 kW
	†DEUTSCHE WELLE, Wertachtal	(D) • E Asia • 500 kW
		(J) • Mideast • 500 kW
	MOLDOVA	
	†RADIO MOLDOVA INTL, Via Romania	Europe • 250 kW
	MOROCCO	
	RTV MAROCAINE, Tangier	E Europe, N Africa & Mideast • 50 kW
	UNITED KINGDOM	
	†BBC, Via Ascension	W Africa • 250 kW C Africa • 250 kW
		W Africa & C Africa • 250 kW
	†BBC, Via Meyerton, S Af	W Africa • 500 kW
	USA	
	†VOA, Via Kaválla, Greece	(J) • W Asia & S Asia • 250 kW
	†WORLD HARVEST R, Noblesville, Indiana	C America • 100 kW • ALT. FREQ. TO 11790 kHz
		C America • 100 kW
		M-F • C America • 100 kW
		Sa/Su • C America • 100 kW
15110	**CHINA (PR)**	
(con'd)	†CHINA RADIO INTL, Via Bamako, Mali	C Africa & S Africa • 50 kW

ENGLISH ▬▬   ARABIC ▨▨   CHINESE ▢▢▢   FRENCH ══   GERMAN ▬▬   RUSSIAN ══   SPANISH ▬   OTHER ▬

FREQUENCY   COUNTRY, STATION, LOCATION

TARGET • NETWORK • POWER (kW)   World Time

0 1 2 3 4 5 6 7 8 9 10 11 12 13 14 15 16 17 18 19 20 21 22 23 24

Frequency	Country, Station, Location	Target • Network • Power
15110 (con'd)	**INDIA** †ALL INDIA RADIO, Aligarh	SE Asia • 250 kW
	PHILIPPINES RADIO VERITAS ASIA, Palauig	C Asia • 250 kW
	RUSSIA †GOLOS ROSSII, Moscow	(J) • W Africa & S America • 500 kW
	†GOLOS ROSSII, Yekaterinburg	(D) • Mideast & E Africa • 240 kW
	†R MOSCOW INTL, Kazan'	(J) • S Asia • 240 kW
	SPAIN †R EXTERIOR ESPANA, Noblejas	N Africa & Mideast • 350 kW E North Am & C America • 350 kW
15114.3	**PAKISTAN** RADIO PAKISTAN, Karachi	(D) • S Asia & SE Asia • 50 kW
15115	**ECUADOR** HCJB-VO THE ANDES, Quito	Americas • 100 kW
	EGYPT RADIO CAIRO, Abu Za'bal	W Africa • DS-GENERAL • 100 kW
	UNITED KINGDOM †BBC, Rampisham	Europe • 500 kW
	†BBC, Skelton, Cumbria	W Europe • 250 kW Su • W Europe • 250 kW
	USA †RFE-RL, Via Portugal	E Europe • 250 kW (J) • E Europe • 250 kW
15120	**FINLAND** †RADIO FINLAND, Pori	Europe • 500 kW (J) • E Asia • 500 kW
	HOLLAND RADIO NEDERLAND, Via Neth Antilles	Su • DUTCH • C America • 250 kW
	INDIA †ALL INDIA RADIO, Aligarh	SE Asia • 250 kW E Africa • 250 kW
	†ALL INDIA RADIO, Delhi	DS • 100 kW ENGLISH, ETC • DS • 100 kW
	NEW ZEALAND †R NEW ZEALAND INTL, Rangitaiki	Su-F • ENGLISH, ETC • Pacific • DS • 100 kW (D) Su-F • ENGLISH, ETC • Pacific • DS • 100 kW
	RUSSIA †RADIO MOSCOW, Novosibirsk	(J) • DS-1 • 100 kW
	SRI LANKA SRI LANKA BC CORP, Colombo-Ekala	E Asia • 35 kW Mideast • 35 kW
	USA VOA, Delano, California	C America & S America • 250 kW Tu-Sa • C America & S America • 250 kW
	VOA, Greenville, NC	C America • 250/500 kW • ALT. FREQ. TO 6095 kHz (D) • C America • 250 kW (J) • C America • 250 kW M-F • C America & S America • 250 kW
	VATICAN STATE †VATICAN RADIO, Sta Maria di Galeria	Su • E Europe • 100 kW
15125	**CHINA (PR)** CHINA RADIO INTL, Beijing	S Asia • 120 kW
	CHINA (TAIWAN) BC CORP CHINA	DS(FM-1)
	INDIA †ALL INDIA RADIO, Madras	DS • 100 kW Sa/Su • DS • 100 kW
	RUSSIA ADVENTIST WORLD R, Samara	(J) • Europe • 250 kW
	†R MOSCOW INTL, Samara	(J) • Europe • 250 kW
	SEYCHELLES FAR EAST BC ASS'N, North Pt, Mahé Is	Mideast • 100 kW
	SPAIN †R EXTERIOR ESPANA, Via Costa Rica	M-F • C America • 100 kW
	UNITED KINGDOM †BBC, Via Maşîrah, Oman	(J) • SE Asia • 100 kW
	†BBC, Via Zyyi, Cyprus	(D) • W Asia • 250 kW (D) Su • W Asia • 250 kW
	USA VOA, Via Kaválla, Greece	(J) • W Asia & S Asia • 250 kW
	†VOA, Via Morocco	(D) • E Europe • 35/500 kW
	VOA, Via Philippines	SE Asia • 250 kW
15130	**ARMENIA** RADIO YEREVAN, Yerevan	(J) • Mideast • 100 kW (J) • ARMENIAN • Mideast • 100 kW (J) M-Sa • Mideast • 100 kW (J) • Mideast • ARMENIAN, TURKISH • 100 kW
	CHINA (PR) CHINA RADIO INTL, Via Bamako, Mali	S Africa • 50 kW C America • 50 kW
(con'd)	**CHINA (TAIWAN)** VO FREE CHINA, Via Okeechobee, USA	S America • 100 kW

0 1 2 3 4 5 6 7 8 9 10 11 12 13 14 15 16 17 18 19 20 21 22 23 24

SUMMER ONLY (J)   WINTER ONLY (D)   JAMMING / OR ∧   EARLIEST HEARD ◁   LATEST HEARD ▷   NEW OR CHANGED FOR 1994 †

FREQUENCY   COUNTRY, STATION, LOCATION

TARGET • NETWORK • POWER (kW)   World Time

```
0   1   2   3   4   5   6   7   8   9  10  11  12  13  14  15  16  17  18  19  20  21  22  23  24
```

15130 KOREA (DPR)
(con'd) †RADIO PYONGYANG, Kujang-dong — C America • 400 kW
KOREAN • C America • 400 kW

RUSSIA
†GOLOS ROSSII, Serpukhov — (J) • Mideast • 240 kW

†GOLOS ROSSII, Vladivostok — (D) • Australasia • 240 kW

†R MOSCOW INTL, Chita — (D) • Australasia • 1000 kW

†R MOSCOW INTL, Vladivostok — (J) • Australasia • 240 kW
USA
†RFE-RL, Via Portugal — W Asia • 500 kW
(D) • W Asia • 500 kW
(J) • W Asia • 500 kW
(J) • E Europe • 250/500 kW

†VOA, Via Kaválla, Greece — (J) • W Asia & S Asia • 250 kW

†VOA, Via Morocco — (J) • Europe • 100/500 kW

†VOA, Via Portugal — (D) • Europe • 250 kW

WYFR-FAMILY RADIO, Okeechobee, Fl — S America • 100 kW
C America • 50 kW
(D) • S America • 100 kW

15135 CHINA (PR)
CHINA RADIO INTL, Kunming — SE Asia • 120 kW
FRANCE
†R FRANCE INTL, Issoudun-Allouis — (D) • E Africa • 100 kW
(J) • E Africa • 100 kW

GERMANY
†DEUTSCHE WELLE, Jülich — (D) • C Africa & E Africa • 100 kW

†DEUTSCHE WELLE, Via Kigali, Rwanda — (J) • W Africa • 250 kW

†DEUTSCHE WELLE, Via Sri Lanka — (J) • Africa • 250 kW
MOLDOVA
†RADIO MOLDOVA INTL, Via Romania — S America • 250 kW
UKRAINE
†RADIO UKRAINE, Vinnitsa — (J) • UKRAINIAN • E North Am • 500 kW
(J) • E North Am • 500 kW

UNITED KINGDOM
†BBC, Skelton, Cumbria — (J) • E Europe • 300 kW

BBC, Via Zyyi, Cyprus — (D) • E Europe • 250 kW

†BBC, Woofferton — (D) • E Europe • 300 kW   (J) • E Europe & Mideast • 300 kW
15140 CANADA
†R CANADA INTL, Sackville, NB — (D) • Africa • 100 kW
CLANDESTINE (ASIA)
†"DEMOCTC VO BURMA", Via Norway — Alternative Frequency to 15180 kHz
ECUADOR
HCJB-VO THE ANDES, Quito — N America & C America • 100 kW
INDIA
ALL INDIA RADIO, Bangalore — W Asia • 500 kW
PHILIPPINES
†RADIO VERITAS ASIA, Palauig — Mideast • 250 kW
Sa-M • Mideast • 250 kW

PORTUGAL
†RDP INTERNATIONAL, Lisbon — Alternative Frequency to 17745 kHz
RUSSIA
†GOLOS ROSSII, St Petersburg — (J) • W Africa • 500 kW

†R MOSCOW INTL, Via Kyrgyzstan — (J) • SE Asia • 250 kW
15145 BULGARIA
†RADIO BULGARIA, Plovdiv — (D) • S America • 250 kW
GERMANY
DEUTSCHE WELLE, Jülich — (J) • Europe • 100 kW

†DEUTSCHE WELLE, Wertachtal — (D) • W Asia • 500 kW   (D) • S Africa • 500 kW
INDIA
†ALL INDIA RADIO, Delhi — SE Asia • 50 kW
SEYCHELLES
†FAR EAST BC ASS'N, North Pt, Mahé Is — Sa-M • E Africa • 100 kW
W-Su • E Africa • 100 kW

SOUTH AFRICA
†CHANNEL AFRICA, Meyerton — (D) • W Africa & S Africa • 250 kW
M-F • S Africa • 250 kW • ALT. FREQ. TO 15155 kHz

SWEDEN
†RADIO SWEDEN, Hörby — W Asia • 500 kW • ALT. FREQ. TO 15170 kHz
UNITED KINGDOM
†BBC, Via Zyyi, Cyprus — (J) • E Europe & W Asia • 250 kW
USA
†VOA, Via Kaválla, Greece — (D) • Mideast • 250 kW   (J) • Mideast • 250 kW
(D) • W Asia & S Asia • 250 kW

(con'd)   VOA, Via Philippines — (D) • SE Asia • 50 kW

```
0   1   2   3   4   5   6   7   8   9  10  11  12  13  14  15  16  17  18  19  20  21  22  23  24
```

ENGLISH ▬ ARABIC ⋝⋝⋝ CHINESE ▫▫▫ FRENCH ▭ GERMAN ▦ RUSSIAN ═ SPANISH ▭ OTHER ▬

FREQUENCY   COUNTRY, STATION, LOCATION

TARGET • NETWORK • POWER (kW)   World Time

0 1 2 3 4 5 6 7 8 9 10 11 12 13 14 15 16 17 18 19 20 21 22 23 24

15145 USA
(con'd)   WINB-WORLD INTL BC, Red Lion, Pa

Tu • S America • 50 kW
W-M • S America • 50 kW
S America • 50 kW
Europe & N Africa • 50 kW
F • Europe & N Africa • 50 kW
Th/Sa-Tu • Europe & N Africa • 50 kW
W • Europe & N Africa • 50 kW

WYFR-FAMILY RADIO, Okeechobee, Fl
(J) • C America • 100 kW

15150 HOLLAND
†RADIO NEDERLAND, Via Madagascar
S Asia • 300 kW
(J) • S Asia & E Asia • 300 kW

RUSSIA
†R MOSCOW INTL, Moscow
(D) • SE Asia • 240 kW

†R MOSCOW INTL, Via Moldova
(J) • W Europe & E North Am • 500 kW

SOUTH AFRICA
†CHANNEL AFRICA, Meyerton
(J) M-F • S Africa • 100/250 kW

UKRAINE
†RADIO UKRAINE, Kiev
UKRAINIAN • E North Am & W Europe • 240 kW
(D) • UKRAINIAN • E North Am & W Europe • 240 kW
(J) • UKRAINIAN • E North Am & W Europe • 240 kW

USA
VOA, Via Philippines
E Asia • 250 kW
E Africa • 250 kW
(D) • E Asia • 250 kW
(D) • E Africa • 250 kW
(J) • E Asia • 250 kW
M-F • E Africa • 250 kW

15154.5 INDONESIA
†RRI, Jakarta, Jawa
DS • 250 kW

15155 ECUADOR
HCJB-VO THE ANDES, Quito
N America & C America • 100 kW
JAPANESE • N America & C America • 100 kW

EGYPT
RADIO CAIRO, Abu Za'bal
E Africa • 100 kW

FRANCE
†R FRANCE INTL, Issoudun-Allouis
E Africa • 100 kW
E Europe • 100 kW
(D) • E Africa • 100 kW
(D) • E Europe • 100 kW
(J) • E Africa • 100 kW
(J) • E Europe • 100 kW

†R FRANCE INTL, Via Moyabi, Gabon
W Africa • 250 kW
(D) • E Africa & S Africa • 250 kW

GERMANY
DEUTSCHE WELLE, Via Sines, Portugal
(J) • E Europe • 250 kW

HOLLAND
†RADIO NEDERLAND, Via Neth Antilles
(J) • DUTCH • E North Am • 250 kW

KOREA (REPUBLIC)
†RADIO KOREA, In-Kimjae
W North Am • 250 kW
KOREAN • W North Am • 250 kW

RUSSIA
†GOLOS ROSSII, Kazan'
(J) • S Asia • 250 kW

†R MOSCOW INTL, Kazan'
(J) • S Asia • 250 kW

SOUTH AFRICA
†CHANNEL AFRICA, Meyerton
Alternative Frequency to 15145 kHz

USA
VOA, Via Germany
(D) • Mideast • 500 kW

VOA, Via Kaválla, Greece
(D) • Mideast • 250 kW

†VOA, Via Philippines
(D) • E Asia • 250 kW

†VOA, Via Portugal
(J) • Europe • 250 kW

15160 BULGARIA
†RADIO BULGARIA, Plovdiv
Europe • 250 kW

HUNGARY
†RADIO BUDAPEST
HUNGARIAN • Asia

†RADIO BUDAPEST, Diósd
HUNGARIAN • W Europe • 100 kW
(J) • Europe • 100 kW
(J) M-Sa • Europe • 100 kW
(J) Su • Europe • 100 kW

RADIO BUDAPEST, Jászberény
S America • 250 kW
M • S America • 250 kW

RUSSIA
†GOLOS ROSSII, Nikolayevsk 'Amure
(D) • E Asia • 1000 kW

TURKEY
†VOICE OF TURKEY, Ankara
Alternative Frequency to 15430 kHz

UNITED KINGDOM
BBC, Via Ascension
S Africa • 250 kW

USA
VOA, Via Ascension
S Africa • 250 kW

†VOA, Via Kaválla, Greece
Mideast • 250 kW
(J) • S Asia • 250 kW

(con'd)   †VOA, Via Philippines
E Asia • 250 kW

0 1 2 3 4 5 6 7 8 9 10 11 12 13 14 15 16 17 18 19 20 21 22 23 24

SUMMER ONLY (J)   WINTER ONLY (D)   JAMMING / OR /\   EARLIEST HEARD ◁   LATEST HEARD ▷   NEW OR CHANGED FOR 1994 †

FREQUENCY	COUNTRY, STATION, LOCATION	TARGET • NETWORK • POWER (kW) / World Time

TARGET • NETWORK • POWER (kW) — World Time scale 0–24

15160 USA
(con'd) †VOA, Via Philippines — (J) • E Asia • 250 kW
VOICE OF THE OAS, Greenville, NC — C America & S America • 500 kW
  M-Sa • C America & S America • 500 kW
  Su • C America & S America • 500 kW

15160v ALGERIA
  RTV ALGERIENNE, Bouchaoui — Europe • 100 kW
15165 CHINA (PR)
  CHINA RADIO INTL, Xi'an — S Asia & E Africa • 150 kW
CUBA
  †RADIO HABANA, Havana — (D) • Europe • 100 kW
DENMARK
  †DANMARKS RADIO, Via Norway — (D) • Atlantic • 350 kW   (J) • N America • 350 kW
    (J) • S America • 500 kW
    (J) • W Africa • 500 kW
    (J) • Australasia • 500 kW
    (J) • Atlantic • 350 kW

INDIA
  †ALL INDIA RADIO, Bangalore — SE Asia • 500 kW   HINDI • SE Asia • 500 kW
    HINDI • E Africa • 500 kW

NORWAY
  †RADIO NORWAY INTL, Fredrikstad — (D) • Atlantic • 350 kW   (J) M-Sa • N America • 350 kW
    (J) • C America • 350 kW   (J) Su • N America • 350 kW
  †RADIO NORWAY INTL, Kvitsøy — (J) • W Africa • 500 kW   (J) • S America • 500 kW
    (J) • Australasia • 500 kW
    (J) M • S America • 500 kW
    (J) Tu-Su • S America • 500 kW

  RADIO NORWAY INTL, Sveio — (J) • Atlantic • 500 kW
RUSSIA
  †R MOSCOW INTL, Via Ukraine — (J) • W Africa & S America • 500 kW
UNITED KINGDOM
  †BBC, Rampisham — (D) Su • N Europe • 500 kW
  †BBC, Skelton, Cumbria — (J) Su • N Europe • 250 kW
  BBC, Via Zyyi, Cyprus — (D) • E Europe & W Asia • 250 kW
USA
  †VOA, Via Botswana — (J) • Africa • 100 kW
    (J) M-F • Africa • 100 kW
    E Africa • 250 kW
  VOA, Via Philippines
  †VOA, Via Portugal — (D) • Europe • 250 kW
UZBEKISTAN
  †UZBEK RADIO, Tashkent — DS-2 • 50 kW
    (J) • DS-2 • 50 kW

15170 AUSTRALIA
  †RADIO AUSTRALIA, Carnarvon — E Asia • 300 kW
BULGARIA
  †RADIO BULGARIA, Sofia — (J) • Europe • 100 kW
DENMARK
  †DANMARKS RADIO, Via Norway — (J) • E Europe & Mideast • 500 kW
JAPAN
  †RADIO JAPAN/NHK, Tokyo-Yamata — Europe • 300 kW
    (D) • Europe • 300 kW
    Europe • GENERAL • 300 kW
NORWAY
  †RADIO NORWAY INTL, Kvitsøy — (J) • E Europe & Mideast • 500 kW
RUSSIA
  †R MOSCOW INTL, Moscow — (J) • S Asia & SE Asia • 100 kW
SWEDEN
  †RADIO SWEDEN, Hörby — Alternative Frequency to 15145 kHz
USA
  †RFE-RL, Via Portugal — W Asia • 250 kW
  †VOA, Via Morocco — (J) • E Europe • 100/500 kW
    E Africa • 250 kW
  †VOA, Via Philippines
  †WYFR-FAMILY RADIO, Okeechobee, Fl — (J) • S America • 100 kW
    (D) • S America • 100 kW
    S America • 100 kW
    (J) • C Africa & S Africa • 100 kW

YUGOSLAVIA
  †RADIO YUGOSLAVIA, Belgrade — (J) • N Africa & W Africa • 500 kW
15170v FRENCH POLYNESIA
  RFO-TAHITI, Papeete — Pacific • DS-FRENCH, TAHITIAN • 10/20 kW
15175 AZERBAIJAN
  AZERBAIJANI R, Via Russia — DS-2 • 20 kW
BYELARUS
  BYELARUS RADIO, Minsk — RUSSIAN, ETC • DS-1 • 20 kW
DENMARK
(con'd) †DANMARKS RADIO, Via Norway — (D) • Africa • 500 kW   (J) • Australasia • 500 kW

ENGLISH ▬   ARABIC ⋙   CHINESE ▫▫▫   FRENCH ═   GERMAN ▬   RUSSIAN ══   SPANISH ▬   OTHER ▬

FREQUENCY   COUNTRY, STATION, LOCATION

TARGET • NETWORK • POWER (kW)   World Time

0 1 2 3 4 5 6 7 8 9 10 11 12 13 14 15 16 17 18 19 20 21 22 23 24

Frequency	Country, Station, Location	Target • Network • Power
15175 (con'd)	**DENMARK** †DANMARKS RADIO, Via Norway	(D) • E Asia & Australasia • 500 kW
		(J) • Mideast & S Asia • 500 kW
	NORWAY †RADIO NORWAY INTL, Kvitsøy	(D) • Africa • 500 kW
		(J) • Australasia • 500 kW
		(J) • M • Mideast & S Asia • 500 kW
		(J) • Tu-Su • Mideast & S Asia • 500 kW
	RADIO NORWAY INTL, Sveio	(D) • E Asia & Australasia • 500 kW
	PHILIPPINES †RADIO VERITAS ASIA, Palauig	S Asia • 250 kW
	RUSSIA †R MOSCOW INTL, Orenburg	(J) • Europe • 240 kW
	†R MOSCOW INTL, Tver'	(D) • S Asia • 500 kW
	†R MOSCOW INTL, Via Kyrgyzstan	(J) • S America • 500 kW
	SWAZILAND †TRANS WORLD RADIO, Manzini	W Asia & S Asia • 100 kW
	USA †VOA, Via Kaválla, Greece	(J) • Mideast • 250 kW
	YUGOSLAVIA †RADIO YUGOSLAVIA, Belgrade	(D) • N Africa & W Africa • 500 kW
		(J) • E Europe & W Asia • 500 kW
		(J) • N Africa & W Africa • 500 kW
15180	**ARMENIA** †RADIO YEREVAN, Via Russia	(J) • ARMENIAN • W North Am • 100 kW
		(J) • W North Am • 100 kW
	BYELARUS †RS BYELARUS, Via Russia	(J) • BYELORUSSIAN • W North Am • 100 kW
	CHINA (PR) †CHINA RADIO INTL, Xi'an	E Asia • 150 kW
	CLANDESTINE (ASIA) †"DEMOCTC VO BURMA", Via Norway	(D) • SE Asia • ANTI-MYANMAR GOVT • 500 kW • ALT. FREQ TO 15140 kHz
	DENMARK DANMARKS RADIO, Via Norway	(D) • S America & Australasia • 500 kW
	FRANCE R FRANCE INTL, Issoudun-Allouis	E Europe • 100 kW
		(J) • E Europe • 100 kW
	IRAQ †RADIO IRAQ INTL	(J) • ENGLISH & ARABIC • N America
		(D) • ARABIC & ENGLISH • C America & S America
	KOREA (DPR) RADIO PYONGYANG, Kujang-dong	SE Asia • 200 kW
		KOREAN • SE Asia • 200 kW
	NORWAY RADIO NORWAY INTL, Kvitsøy	(D) • M-Sa • S America & Australasia • 500 kW
		(D) • Su • S America & Australasia • 500 kW
	RUSSIA †R MOSCOW INTL, Komsomol'sk 'Amure	(J) • W North Am • N AMERICAN SVC • 100 kW
		(J) • W North Am • 100 kW
	†R TIKHIY OKEAN, Komsomol'sk 'Amure	(J) • N Pacific & W North Am • 100 kW
	UKRAINE †RADIO UKRAINE, Via Russia	(J) • W North Am • 100 kW
		(J) • UKRAINIAN • W North Am • 100 kW
	UNITED KINGDOM †BBC, Rampisham	(J) • N Africa • 500 kW
	†BBC, Various Locations	N Africa • 300/500 kW
	USA VOA, Via Philippines	Pacific • 50 kW
15185	**FINLAND** †RADIO FINLAND, Pori	(J) • N America • 500 kW
	GERMANY †DEUTSCHE WELLE, Nauen	(J) • JAPANESE • E Asia • 500 kW
	†DEUTSCHE WELLE, Via Kigali, Rwanda	(J) • S Asia • 250 kW
	DEUTSCHE WELLE, Via Sri Lanka	(D) • E Asia • 250 kW
	DEUTSCHE WELLE, Wertachtal	W Africa • 500 kW
		W Asia • 500 kW
	INDIA ALL INDIA RADIO, Bangalore	Mideast & N Africa • 500 kW
	RUSSIA †R MOSCOW INTL, Serpukhov	(J) • Europe • 240 kW
	†RADIO CENTER, Serpukhov	(J) • RUSSIAN & ENGLISH • Europe • 240 kW
	†RADIO MOSCOW, Zhigulevsk	DS-1 • 240 kW
		(J) • DS-1 • 240 kW
	USA VOA, Greenville, NC	M-F • C America • 500 kW
	VOA, Via Kaválla, Greece	(J) • S Asia • 250 kW
	VOA, Via Philippines	Pacific & SE Asia • 50 kW
(con'd)		S Asia • 250 kW

0 1 2 3 4 5 6 7 8 9 10 11 12 13 14 15 16 17 18 19 20 21 22 23 24

FREQUENCY   COUNTRY, STATION, LOCATION

TARGET • NETWORK • POWER (kW)   World Time

15185 **USA**	
(con'd) VOA, Via Portugal	(J) • Mideast & W Asia • 250 kW
VOA, Via Woofferton, UK	(D) • C Asia • 250 kW
WINB-WORLD INTL BC, Red Lion, Pa	Europe & N Africa • 50 kW
15190 **BRAZIL**	
R INCONFIDENCIA, Belo Horizonte	PORTUGUESE • DS • 5 kW
CONGO	
†RTV CONGOLAISE, Brazzaville	FRENCH, ETC • DS • 50 kW
FRANCE	
†R FRANCE INTL, Issoudun-Allouis	(J) • S America • 100 kW
JAPAN	
†RADIO JAPAN/NHK, Tokyo-Yamata	JAPANESE • SE Asia • GENERAL • 100 kW
	SE Asia • GENERAL • 100 kW
PAKISTAN	
RADIO PAKISTAN, Islamabad	S Asia & SE Asia • 100 kW
PHILIPPINES	
RADYO PILIPINAS, Tinang	Mideast • 250 kW
RUSSIA	
†R MOSCOW INTL, Tula	(D) • Europe • 240 kW
SWEDEN	
†RADIO SWEDEN, Hörby	Alternative Frequency to 15270 kHz
UNITED KINGDOM	
BBC, Via Ascension	S America • 250 kW
	M-F • S America • 250 kW
15195 **CANADA**	
†R CANADA INTL, Via Tokyo, Japan	(J) • SE Asia • 300 kW
DENMARK	
DANMARKS RADIO, Via Norway	SE Asia • 500 kW
FRANCE	
R FRANCE INTL, Issoudun-Allouis	E Europe • 100 kW
	(D) • E Europe • 100 kW
	(J) • E Europe • 100 kW
JAPAN	
†RADIO JAPAN/NHK, Tokyo-Yamata	E Asia • GENERAL • 100 kW (D) • E Asia • GENERAL • 100 kW
	(D) • JAPANESE • E Asia • GENERAL • 100 kW
NORWAY	
RADIO NORWAY INTL, Kvitsøy	SE Asia • 500 kW
UKRAINE	
†RADIO UKRAINE, Simferopol'	(J) • W Africa & S America • 1000 kW
	(J) • UKRAINIAN • W Africa & S America • 1000 kW
USA	
†VOA, Via Germany	Mideast • 100 kW (D) • Mideast & W Asia • 500 kW
VOA, Via Morocco	(D) • E Europe • 100/500 kW
VOA, Via Philippines	E Asia • 250 kW
VOA, Via Portugal	(J) • E Europe & W Asia • 250 kW
15200 **FRANCE**	
R FRANCE INTL, Via French Guiana	S America • 500 kW
	C America • 500 kW
GUAM	
†KTWR-TRANS WORLD R, Merizo	E Asia • 100 kW
	SE Asia • 100 kW
PORTUGAL	
†RDP INTERNATIONAL, Lisbon	Sa/Su • PORTUGUESE • E North Am • 100 kW
RUSSIA	
TATAR RADIO, Perm	DS • 3 kW
SOUTH AFRICA	
†CHANNEL AFRICA, Meyerton	(J) • W Africa • 500 kW
USA	
†VOA, Via Philippines	(D) • E Asia • 250 kW
UZBEKISTAN	
†UZBEK RADIO, Tashkent	(J) • Mideast • DS-2 • 100 kW
15205 **CHINA (PR)**	
†CHINA RADIO INTL	SE Asia
	CANTONESE • SE Asia
GERMANY	
†DEUTSCHE WELLE, Multiple Locations	(J) • W Africa • 100/250 kW
DEUTSCHE WELLE, Via Antigua	S America • 250 kW
IRAQ	
†RADIO IRAQ INTL	(J) • S Asia
USA	
VOA, Greenville, NC	C America & S America • 250 kW
	Tu-Sa • C America & S America • 250 kW
†VOA, Via Germany	Mideast • 500 kW
†VOA, Via Kaválla, Greece	Mideast & S Asia • 250 kW (D) • Mideast & S Asia • 35/100 kW
	(D) • Mideast & S Asia • 250 kW
	(J) • Mideast & S Asia • 250 kW
†VOA, Via Morocco	Europe • 35/100/500 kW
	(J) • Europe • 100/500 kW
(con'd) †VOA, Via Philippines	SE Asia • 50 kW

ENGLISH ▬▬ ARABIC ⬚⬚⬚ CHINESE □□□ FRENCH ▬▬ GERMAN ▬▬ RUSSIAN ══ SPANISH ▬▬ OTHER ▬▬

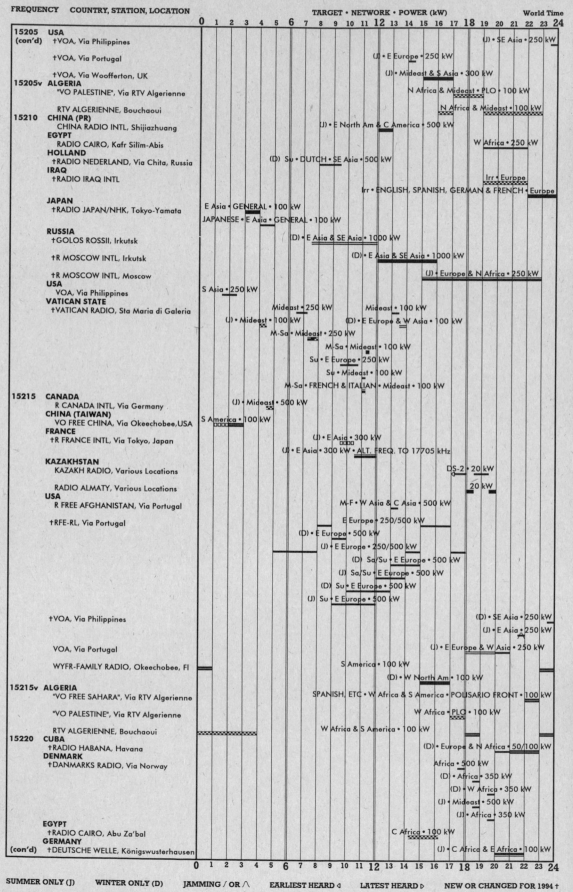

FREQUENCY   COUNTRY, STATION, LOCATION

TARGET • NETWORK • POWER (kW)   World Time

15205 (con'd)	**USA**	
	†VOA, Via Philippines	(J) • SE Asia • 250 kW
	†VOA, Via Portugal	(J) • E Europe • 250 kW
	†VOA, Via Woofferton, UK	(J) • Mideast & S Asia • 300 kW
15205v	**ALGERIA**	
	"VO PALESTINE", Via RTV Algerienne	N Africa & Mideast • PLO • 100 kW
	RTV ALGERIENNE, Bouchaoui	N Africa & Mideast • 100 kW
15210	**CHINA (PR)**	
	CHINA RADIO INTL, Shijiazhuang	(J) • E North Am & C America • 500 kW
	EGYPT	
	RADIO CAIRO, Kafr Silim-Abis	W Africa • 250 kW
	HOLLAND	
	†RADIO NEDERLAND, Via Chita, Russia	(D) Su • DUTCH • SE Asia • 500 kW
	IRAQ	
	†RADIO IRAQ INTL	Irr • Europe
		Irr • ENGLISH, SPANISH, GERMAN & FRENCH • Europe
	JAPAN	
	†RADIO JAPAN/NHK, Tokyo-Yamata	E Asia • GENERAL • 100 kW
		JAPANESE • E Asia • GENERAL • 100 kW
	RUSSIA	
	†GOLOS ROSSII, Irkutsk	(D) • E Asia & SE Asia • 1000 kW
	†R MOSCOW INTL, Irkutsk	(D) • E Asia & SE Asia • 1000 kW
	†R MOSCOW INTL, Moscow	(J) • Europe & N Africa • 250 kW
	USA	
	VOA, Via Philippines	S Asia • 250 kW
	VATICAN STATE	
	†VATICAN RADIO, Sta Maria di Galeria	Mideast • 250 kW / Mideast • 100 kW
		(J) • Mideast • 100 kW / (D) • E Europe & W Asia • 100 kW
		M-Sa • Mideast • 250 kW
		M-Sa • Mideast • 100 kW
		Su • E Europe • 250 kW
		Su • Mideast • 100 kW
		M-Sa • FRENCH & ITALIAN • Mideast • 100 kW
15215	**CANADA**	
	R CANADA INTL, Via Germany	(J) • Mideast • 500 kW
	CHINA (TAIWAN)	
	VO FREE CHINA, Via Okeechobee,USA	S America • 100 kW
	FRANCE	
	†R FRANCE INTL, Via Tokyo, Japan	(J) • E Asia • 300 kW
		(J) • E Asia • 300 kW • ALT. FREQ. TO 17705 kHz
	KAZAKHSTAN	
	KAZAKH RADIO, Various Locations	DS-2 • 20 kW
	RADIO ALMATY, Various Locations	20 kW
	USA	
	R FREE AFGHANISTAN, Via Portugal	M-F • W Asia & C Asia • 500 kW
	†RFE-RL, Via Portugal	E Europe • 250/500 kW
		(D) • E Europe • 500 kW
		(J) • E Europe • 250/500 kW
		(D) Sa/Su • E Europe • 500 kW
		(J) Sa/Su • E Europe • 500 kW
		(D) Su • E Europe • 500 kW
		(J) Su • E Europe • 500 kW
	†VOA, Via Philippines	(D) • SE Asia • 250 kW
		(J) • E Asia • 250 kW
	VOA, Via Portugal	(J) • E Europe & W Asia • 250 kW
	WYFR-FAMILY RADIO, Okeechobee, Fl	S America • 100 kW
		(D) • W North Am • 100 kW
15215v	**ALGERIA**	
	"VO FREE SAHARA", Via RTV Algerienne	SPANISH, ETC • W Africa & S America • POLISARIO FRONT • 100 kW
	"VO PALESTINE", Via RTV Algerienne	W Africa • PLO • 100 kW
	RTV ALGERIENNE, Bouchaoui	W Africa & S America • 100 kW
15220	**CUBA**	
	†RADIO HABANA, Havana	(D) • Europe & N Africa • 50/100 kW
	DENMARK	
	†DANMARKS RADIO, Via Norway	Africa • 500 kW
		(D) • Africa • 350 kW
		(D) • W Africa • 350 kW
		(J) • Mideast • 500 kW
		(J) • Africa • 350 kW
	EGYPT	
	†RADIO CAIRO, Abu Za'bal	C Africa • 100 kW
(con'd)	**GERMANY**	
	†DEUTSCHE WELLE, Königswusterhausen	(J) • C Africa & E Africa • 100 kW

FREQUENCY	COUNTRY, STATION, LOCATION	TARGET • NETWORK • POWER (kW)	World Time

15220 **HUNGARY**
(con'd) †RADIO BUDAPEST, Diósd
- (J) • HUNGARIAN • N America • 100 kW
- (J) • N America • 100 kW
- (J) M • HUNGARIAN • N America • 100 kW

INDIA
†ALL INDIA RADIO, Delhi
- DS • 50 kW
- ENGLISH, ETC • DS • 50 kW

MOLDOVA
†RADIO MOLDOVA INTL, Via Romania
- S America • 250 kW
- Europe • 250 kW

NORWAY
RADIO NORWAY INTL, Fredrikstad
- (D) M-Sa • W Africa • 350 kW
- (D) Su • W Africa • 350 kW

†RADIO NORWAY INTL, Kvitsøy
- Africa • 500 kW
- (D) • Africa • 500 kW
- (J) • Mideast • 500 kW
- (J) • Africa • 500 kW

RUSSIA
†GOLOS ROSSII, Zhigulevsk
- (D) • S Asia • 240 kW

†R MOSCOW INTL, Via Tajikistan
- (J) • SE Asia • 150 kW
- (J) • Mideast • 150 kW

†R MOSCOW INTL, Zhigulevsk
- (D) • S Asia • 240 kW

SOUTH AFRICA
†CHANNEL AFRICA, Meyerton
- (J) • W Africa • 500 kW

UNITED KINGDOM
BBC, Via Antigua
- E North Am & S America • 125 kW

15220v **EGYPT**
†RADIO CAIRO, Kafr Silim-Abis
- C America & S America • 250 kW

15225 **GUAM**
ADVENTIST WORLD R, Agat
- E Asia • 100 kW
- Sa/Su • E Asia • 100 kW

RUSSIA
†R MOSCOW INTL, Armavir
- (J) • N Europe & E North Am • 500 kW

UNITED KINGDOM
BBC, Rampisham
- (J) • E Europe • 500 kW

USA
VOA, Via Ascension
- (J) • S Africa • 250 kW

VOA, Via Kaválla, Greece
- (D) • W Asia & S Asia • 250 kW
- (D) • Mideast • 250 kW
- (D) • Europe • 250 kW

†VOA, Via Portugal
- (J) • Mideast & W Asia • 250 kW

15230 **CUBA**
†RADIO HABANA, Havana
- S America • 100/250 kW
- S America • 50/100 kW

DENMARK
†DANMARKS RADIO, Via Norway
- Mideast & S Asia • 350 kW
- (D) • Africa • 500 kW
- (J) • Europe • 350 kW
- (J) • Mideast • 500 kW

JAPAN
†RADIO JAPAN/NHK, Tokyo-Yamata
- JAPANESE • W North Am • GENERAL • 100 kW
- W North Am • GENERAL • 100 kW

KOREA (DPR)
RADIO PYONGYANG, Kujang-dong
- SE Asia • 200 kW
- KOREAN • SE Asia • 200 kW

NORWAY
†RADIO NORWAY INTL, Fredrikstad
- Mideast & S Asia • 350 kW
- (J) M-Sa • Europe • 350 kW
- (J) Su • Europe • 350 kW

RADIO NORWAY INTL, Kvitsøy
- (D) M-Sa • Africa • 500 kW
- (J) M-Sa • Mideast • 500 kW
- (D) Su • Africa • 500 kW
- (J) Su • Mideast • 500 kW

RUSSIA
†R MOSCOW INTL, Moscow
- (J) • Mideast & E Africa • 250 kW

†R MOSCOW INTL, Via Kazakhstan
- (D) • SE Asia • 240 kW

SWEDEN
†RADIO SWEDEN, Hörby
- SWEDISH • Europe & N Africa • 500 kW

USA
†VOA, Via Philippines
- (D) • SE Asia • 250 kW

15235 **CANADA**
R CANADA INTL, Sackville, NB
- (J) • S America • 250 kW
- (J) Su/M • S America • 250 kW
- (J) Tu-Sa • S America • 250 kW
- (J) M-F • S America • 250 kW
- (J) Sa/Su • S America • 250 kW

GERMANY
(con'd) †DEUTSCHE WELLE, Jülich
- (D) • W Asia • 100 kW

ENGLISH ▬ ARABIC ▨ CHINESE ▦ FRENCH ▬ GERMAN ▬ RUSSIAN ═ SPANISH ▬ OTHER ▬

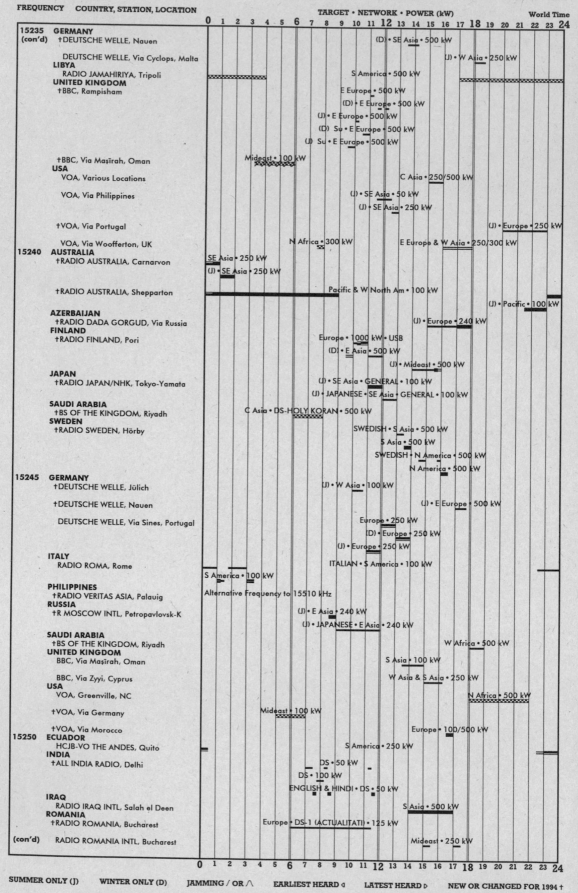

FREQUENCY   COUNTRY, STATION, LOCATION

TARGET • NETWORK • POWER (kW)   World Time

15235	**GERMANY**
(con'd)	†DEUTSCHE WELLE, Nauen — (D) • SE Asia • 500 kW
	DEUTSCHE WELLE, Via Cyclops, Malta — (J) • W Asia • 250 kW
	LIBYA
	RADIO JAMAHIRIYA, Tripoli — S America • 500 kW
	UNITED KINGDOM
	†BBC, Rampisham — E Europe • 500 kW
	(D) • E Europe • 500 kW
	(J) • E Europe • 500 kW
	(D) Su • E Europe • 500 kW
	(J) Su • E Europe • 500 kW
	†BBC, Via Maşīrah, Oman — Mideast • 100 kW
	USA
	VOA, Various Locations — C Asia • 250/500 kW
	VOA, Via Philippines — (J) • SE Asia • 50 kW
	(J) • SE Asia • 250 kW
	†VOA, Via Portugal — (J) • Europe • 250 kW
	VOA, Via Woofferton, UK — N Africa • 300 kW E Europe & W Asia • 250/300 kW
15240	**AUSTRALIA**
	†RADIO AUSTRALIA, Carnarvon — SE Asia • 250 kW
	(J) • SE Asia • 250 kW
	†RADIO AUSTRALIA, Shepparton — Pacific & W North Am • 100 kW (J) • Pacific • 100 kW
	AZERBAIJAN
	†RADIO DADA GORGUD, Via Russia — (J) • Europe • 240 kW
	FINLAND
	†RADIO FINLAND, Pori — Europe • 1000 kW • USB
	(D) • E Asia • 500 kW
	(J) • Mideast • 500 kW
	JAPAN
	†RADIO JAPAN/NHK, Tokyo-Yamata — (J) • SE Asia • GENERAL • 100 kW
	(J) • JAPANESE • SE Asia • GENERAL • 100 kW
	SAUDI ARABIA
	†BS OF THE KINGDOM, Riyadh — C Asia • DS-HOLY KORAN • 500 kW
	SWEDEN
	†RADIO SWEDEN, Hörby — SWEDISH • S Asia • 500 kW
	S Asia • 500 kW
	SWEDISH • N America • 500 kW
	N America • 500 kW
15245	**GERMANY**
	†DEUTSCHE WELLE, Jülich — (J) • W Asia • 100 kW
	†DEUTSCHE WELLE, Nauen — (J) • E Europe • 500 kW
	DEUTSCHE WELLE, Via Sines, Portugal — Europe • 250 kW
	(D) • Europe • 250 kW
	(J) • Europe • 250 kW
	ITALY
	RADIO ROMA, Rome — ITALIAN • S America • 100 kW
	S America • 100 kW
	PHILIPPINES
	†RADIO VERITAS ASIA, Palauig — Alternative Frequency to 15510 kHz
	RUSSIA
	†R MOSCOW INTL, Petropavlovsk-K — (J) • E Asia • 240 kW
	(J) • JAPANESE • E Asia • 240 kW
	SAUDI ARABIA
	†BS OF THE KINGDOM, Riyadh — W Africa • 500 kW
	UNITED KINGDOM
	BBC, Via Maşīrah, Oman — S Asia • 100 kW
	BBC, Via Zyyi, Cyprus — W Asia & S Asia • 250 kW
	USA
	VOA, Greenville, NC — N Africa • 500 kW
	†VOA, Via Germany — Mideast • 100 kW
	†VOA, Via Morocco — Europe • 100/500 kW
15250	**ECUADOR**
	HCJB-VO THE ANDES, Quito — S America • 250 kW
	INDIA
	†ALL INDIA RADIO, Delhi — DS • 50 kW
	DS • 100 kW
	ENGLISH & HINDI • DS • 50 kW
	IRAQ
	RADIO IRAQ INTL, Salah el Deen — S Asia • 500 kW
	ROMANIA
	†RADIO ROMANIA, Bucharest — Europe • DS-1 (ACTUALITATI) • 125 kW
(con'd)	RADIO ROMANIA INTL, Bucharest — Mideast • 250 kW

FREQUENCY   COUNTRY, STATION, LOCATION

TARGET • NETWORK • POWER (kW)

World Time

0 1 2 3 4 5 6 7 8 9 10 11 12 13 14 15 16 17 18 19 20 21 22 23 24

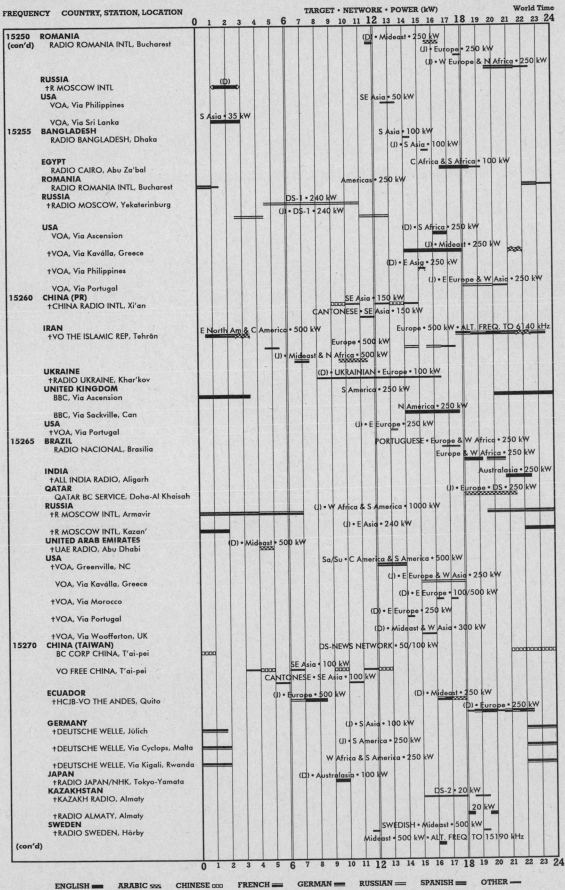

Frequency	Country, Station, Location	Schedule
15250 (con'd)	**ROMANIA** RADIO ROMANIA INTL, Bucharest	(D) • Mideast • 250 kW; (J) • Europe • 250 kW; (J) • W Europe & N Africa • 250 kW
	RUSSIA †R MOSCOW INTL	(D)
	USA VOA, Via Philippines	SE Asia • 50 kW
	VOA, Via Sri Lanka	S Asia • 35 kW
15255	**BANGLADESH** RADIO BANGLADESH, Dhaka	S Asia • 100 kW; (J) • S Asia • 100 kW
	EGYPT RADIO CAIRO, Abu Za'bal	C Africa & S Africa • 100 kW
	ROMANIA RADIO ROMANIA INTL, Bucharest	Americas • 250 kW
	RUSSIA †RADIO MOSCOW, Yekaterinburg	DS-1 • 240 kW; (J) • DS-1 • 240 kW
	USA VOA, Via Ascension	(D) • S Africa • 250 kW
	†VOA, Via Kaválla, Greece	(J) • Mideast • 250 kW
	†VOA, Via Philippines	(D) • E Asia • 250 kW
	VOA, Via Portugal	(J) • E Europe & W Asia • 250 kW
15260	**CHINA (PR)** †CHINA RADIO INTL, Xi'an	SE Asia • 150 kW; CANTONESE • SE Asia • 150 kW
	IRAN †VO THE ISLAMIC REP, Tehrān	E North Am & C America • 500 kW; Europe • 500 kW • ALT. FREQ. TO 6140 kHz; Europe • 500 kW; (J) • Mideast & N Africa • 500 kW
	UKRAINE †RADIO UKRAINE, Khar'kov	(D) • UKRAINIAN • Europe • 100 kW
	UNITED KINGDOM BBC, Via Ascension	S America • 250 kW
	BBC, Via Sackville, Can	N America • 250 kW
	USA †VOA, Via Portugal	(J) • E Europe • 250 kW
15265	**BRAZIL** RADIO NACIONAL, Brasília	PORTUGUESE • Europe & W Africa • 250 kW; Europe & W Africa • 250 kW
	INDIA †ALL INDIA RADIO, Aligarh	Australasia • 250 kW
	QATAR QATAR BC SERVICE, Doha-Al Khaisah	(J) • Europe • DS • 250 kW
	RUSSIA †R MOSCOW INTL, Armavir	(J) • W Africa & S America • 1000 kW
	†R MOSCOW INTL, Kazan'	(J) • E Asia • 240 kW
	UNITED ARAB EMIRATES †UAE RADIO, Abu Dhabi	(D) • Mideast • 500 kW
	USA †VOA, Greenville, NC	Sa/Su • C America & S America • 500 kW
	VOA, Via Kaválla, Greece	(J) • E Europe & W Asia • 250 kW
	†VOA, Via Morocco	(D) • E Europe • 100/500 kW
	†VOA, Via Portugal	(D) • E Europe • 250 kW
	†VOA, Via Woofferton, UK	(D) • Mideast & W Asia • 300 kW
15270	**CHINA (TAIWAN)** BC CORP CHINA, T'ai-pei	DS-NEWS NETWORK • 50/100 kW
	VO FREE CHINA, T'ai-pei	SE Asia • 100 kW; CANTONESE • SE Asia • 100 kW
	ECUADOR †HCJB-VO THE ANDES, Quito	(J) • Europe • 500 kW; (D) • Mideast • 250 kW; (D) • Europe • 250 kW
	GERMANY †DEUTSCHE WELLE, Jülich	(J) • S Asia • 100 kW
	†DEUTSCHE WELLE, Via Cyclops, Malta	(J) • S America • 250 kW
	†DEUTSCHE WELLE, Via Kigali, Rwanda	W Africa & S America • 250 kW
	JAPAN †RADIO JAPAN/NHK, Tokyo-Yamata	(D) • Australasia • 100 kW
	KAZAKHSTAN †KAZAKH RADIO, Almaty	DS-2 • 20 kW
	†RADIO ALMATY, Almaty	20 kW
	SWEDEN †RADIO SWEDEN, Hörby	SWEDISH • Mideast • 500 kW; Mideast • 500 kW • ALT. FREQ TO 15190 kHz

(con'd)

0 1 2 3 4 5 6 7 8 9 10 11 12 13 14 15 16 17 18 19 20 21 22 23 24

ENGLISH ▬▬ ARABIC ░░ CHINESE □□□ FRENCH ▭▭ GERMAN ▭▭ RUSSIAN ═══ SPANISH ▭▭ OTHER ▬▬

FREQUENCY   COUNTRY, STATION, LOCATION

TARGET • NETWORK • POWER (kW)   World Time

0 1 2 3 4 5 6 7 8 9 10 11 12 13 14 15 16 17 18 19 20 21 22 23 24

15270 SWEDEN
(con'd)   †RADIO SWEDEN, Hörby
- SWEDISH • Mideast • 500 kW • ALT. FREQ. TO 15190 kHz
- Mideast • 500 kW
- M-F • Mideast • 500 kW • ALT. FREQ. TO 15190 kHz
- M-F • SWEDISH • Mideast • 500 kW • ALT. FREQ. TO 15190 kHz

USA
  VOA, Via Woofferton, UK
- (J) • E Europe • 300 kW

15275 CANADA
  R CANADA INTL, Via Vienna, Austria
- (J) • Mideast • 300 kW

FRANCE
  †R FRANCE INTL, Via Beijing, China
- Alternative Frequency to 17710 kHz

GERMANY
  †DEUTSCHE WELLE, Jülich
- Mideast • 100 kW
- (D) • Africa • 100 kW
- (J) • E Europe • 100 kW

  †DEUTSCHE WELLE, Multiple Locations
- (J) • Africa • 100/500 kW
- Mideast & S Asia • 100/500 kW
- (J) • W Africa • 100/250 kW
- W Africa • 100/500 kW

  DEUTSCHE WELLE, Via Antigua
- (D) • N America • 250 kW

  †DEUTSCHE WELLE, Wertachtal
- (J) • Mideast & S Asia • 500 kW
- (J) • Mideast • 500 kW

15280 JAPAN
  †RADIO JAPAN/NHK, Tokyo-Yamata
- (D) • JAPANESE • Australasia • GENERAL • 100 kW
- (D) • Australasia • GENERAL • 100 kW

RUSSIA
  †R MOSCOW INTL, Serpukhov
- (J) • Europe • 240 kW

  †R MOSCOW INTL, Zhigulevsk
- S Asia & SE Asia • 240 kW
- (D) • S Asia & SE Asia • 240 kW
- (J) • S Asia & SE Asia • 240 kW

UNITED KINGDOM
  †BBC, Rampisham
- (J) • M-F • N Europe • 500 kW

  †BBC, Via Hong Kong
- E Asia • 250 kW
- Su • E Asia • 250 kW
- (J) • E Asia • 250 kW

  †BBC, Via Maşīrah, Oman
- (D) • SE Asia • 100 kW

  BBC, Via Singapore
- E Asia • 100 kW

USA
  KGEI-VO FRIENDSHIP, Redwood City, Ca
- C America & S America • 50 kW
- M • C America & S America • 50 kW
- M-Sa • C America & S America • 50 kW
- Tu-Su • C America & S America • 50 kW
- Su • C America & S America • 50 kW

  †VOA, Via Morocco
- (J) • E Europe • 100/500 kW

15280v CLANDESTINE (ASIA)
  "VOICE OF CHINA", Taiwan
- E Asia • 100 kW

15285 EGYPT
  RADIO CAIRO, Abu Za'bal
- Mideast • DS-VO THE ARABS • 100 kW

FRANCE
  R FRANCE INTL, Via Beijing, China
- Australasia & Pacific • 120 kW

USA
  VOA, Via Philippines
- SE Asia • 250 kW

15290 RUSSIA
  †R MOSCOW INTL, Via Moldova
- (J) • W Europe & E North Am • 500 kW

  †R MOSCOW INTL, Via Ukraine
- (J) • W Europe & E North Am • 1000 kW

USA
  †RFE-RL, Various Locations
- E Europe & W Asia • 250 kW

  RFE-RL, Via Germany
- (J) • E Europe & W Asia • 250 kW

  †RFE-RL, Via Portugal
- (J) • E Europe & W Asia • 250 kW

  †VOA, Via Morocco
- (D) • W Africa • 35/500 kW

  VOA, Via Philippines
- E Asia • 250 kW

15295 ECUADOR
  †HCJB-VO THE ANDES, Quito
- S America • 100 kW
- JAPANESE • S America • 100 kW

MALAYSIA
  VOICE OF MALAYSIA, Kajang
- Australasia • 500 kW
- Mideast • 500 kW

MOZAMBIQUE
  RADIO MOCAMBIQUE, Maputo
- DS • 100 kW

PAKISTAN
  RADIO PAKISTAN, Islamabad
- S Asia & SE Asia • 100 kW

RUSSIA
  †GOLOS ROSSII, Kazan'
- (J) • S Asia • 250 kW

  †GOLOS ROSSII, Via Uzbekistan
- (D) • S Asia & SE Asia • 240 kW

USA
  †VOA, Via Philippines
- (J) • E Asia • 250 kW

  WINB-WORLD INTL BC, Red Lion, Pa
- Europe & N Africa • 50 kW
- M-Sa • Europe & N Africa • 50 kW

(con'd)

0 1 2 3 4 5 6 7 8 9 10 11 12 13 14 15 16 17 18 19 20 21 22 23 24

SUMMER ONLY (J)   WINTER ONLY (D)   JAMMING / OR /\   EARLIEST HEARD ◁   LATEST HEARD ▷   NEW OR CHANGED FOR 1994 †

FREQUENCY   COUNTRY, STATION, LOCATION

TARGET • NETWORK • POWER (kW)

World Time

0　1　2　3　4　5　6　7　8　9　10　11　12　13　14　15　16　17　18　19　20　21　22　23　24

Frequency	Country, Station, Location	Target • Network • Power
15295 (con'd)	**USA** WINB-WORLD INTL BC, Red Lion, Pa	Sa • Europe & N Africa • 50 kW / Su • Europe & N Africa • 50 kW / Su-F • Europe & N Africa • 50 kW
	UZBEKISTAN †RADIO TASHKENT, Tashkent	(J) • W Asia • 100 kW
15300	**FRANCE** †R FRANCE INTL, Issoudun-Allouis	Africa • 100/500 kW / (J) • Mideast • 100 kW / N Africa & W Africa • 100/500 kW
	†R FRANCE INTL, Multiple Locations	Mideast & Africa • 250/500 kW / Africa • 100/500 kW
	PHILIPPINES †RADIO VERITAS ASIA, Palauig	S Asia • 250 kW / (J) • S Asia & SE Asia • 250 kW
	USA †VOA, Via Philippines	(J) • E Asia • 250 kW
15305	**BULGARIA** †RADIO BULGARIA, Sofia	(J) • S America • 100 kW / (J) • C America & S America • 250 kW
	CANADA †R CANADA INTL, Sackville, NB	(J) • M-Sa • Europe • 100 kW
	RUSSIA †GOLOS ROSSII, Armavir	(D) • Europe & Atlantic • 1000 kW
	UNITED ARAB EMIRATES UAE RADIO, Abu Dhabi	(J) • E North Am • 500 kW
	USA †VOA, Via Germany	(D) • Mideast • 500 kW / (J) • Mideast • 500 kW / E Asia & Australasia • 35 kW
	VOA, Via Philippines	
15310	**GUAM** ADVENTIST WORLD R, Agat	(J) • E Asia • 100 kW / (J) • JAPANESE • E Asia • 100 kW
	UNITED KINGDOM †BBC, Via Maṣīrah, Oman	W Asia & S Asia • 100 kW / S Asia • 100 kW / (D) • S Asia • 100 kW / (J) • W Asia • 100 kW
	†BBC, Via Zyyi, Cyprus	(J) • W Asia • 250 kW / (J) • Africa • 100 kW
15315	**CANADA** †R CANADA INTL, Sackville, NB	(D) • M-Sa • Europe • 100 kW / (J) • Europe • 250 kW
	†R CANADA INTL, Via Sines, Portugal	N Africa • 100 kW
	FRANCE †R FRANCE INTL, Issoudun-Allouis	W Africa • 500 kW / N Africa • 100/500 kW / (J) • W Africa • 500 kW
	HOLLAND †RADIO NEDERLAND, Via Neth Antilles	S America • 250 kW / DUTCH • S America • 250 kW / DUTCH • W Africa • 250 kW
	KAZAKHSTAN †KAZAKH RADIO, Tselinograd	DS-2 • 20 kW
	†RADIO ALMATY, Tselinograd	20 kW
	RUSSIA †GOLOS ROSSII, Krasnoyarsk	(D) • E Asia • 100 kW
	†R MOSCOW INTL, Krasnoyarsk	(D) • E Asia • 100 kW
	†R MOSCOW INTL, Via Kazakhstan	(J) • E Asia & SE Asia • 1000 kW
	UNITED ARAB EMIRATES †UAE RADIO, Abu Dhabi	(D) • E Asia • 500 kW / (J) • Europe • 500 kW / (J) • E North Am • 500 kW
	UNITED KINGDOM BBC, Via Cincinnati, USA	M-F • C America & S America • 250 kW
	USA †RFE-RL, Via Germany	(J) • E Europe & W Asia • 100 kW
15320	**AUSTRALIA** RADIO AUSTRALIA, Shepparton	Pacific • 100 kW
	CHINA (TAIWAN) †CENTRAL BC SYSTEM, T'ai-pei	PRC-1 • 100 kW / PRC-6 • 100 kW
	RUSSIA †R MOSCOW INTL, Via Byelarus	(J) • Mideast & W Asia • 100 kW
	UNITED ARAB EMIRATES UAE RADIO, Dubai	N Africa • 300 kW
	USA VOA, Via Morocco	(D) • W Africa • 35/500 kW
15325	**CANADA** †R CANADA INTL, Sackville, NB	(D) • Europe • 100 kW / (D) • Europe • 250 kW / (J) • Europe • 250 kW
(con'd)		

0　1　2　3　4　5　6　7　8　9　10　11　12　13　14　15　16　17　18　19　20　21　22　23　24

ENGLISH ▬　ARABIC ▨　CHINESE ▫▫▫　FRENCH ═　GERMAN ▭　RUSSIAN ＝　SPANISH ▭　OTHER ▬

FREQUENCY   COUNTRY, STATION, LOCATION

TARGET • NETWORK • POWER (kW)   World Time

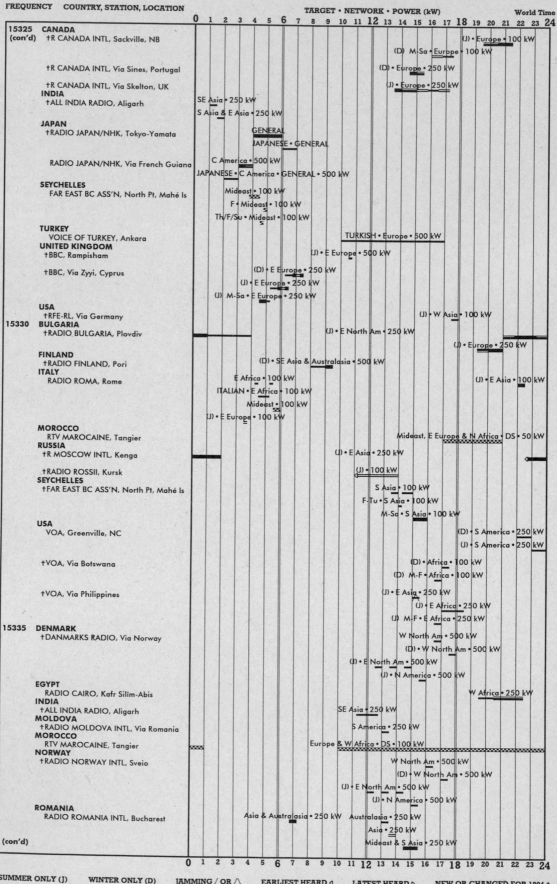

FREQUENCY	COUNTRY, STATION, LOCATION	TARGET • NETWORK • POWER (kW)
15325 (con'd)	CANADA †R CANADA INTL, Sackville, NB	(J) • Europe • 100 kW (D) M-Sa • Europe • 100 kW
	†R CANADA INTL, Via Sines, Portugal	(D) • Europe • 250 kW
	†R CANADA INTL, Via Skelton, UK	(J) • Europe • 250 kW
	INDIA †ALL INDIA RADIO, Aligarh	SE Asia • 250 kW S Asia & E Asia • 250 kW
	JAPAN †RADIO JAPAN/NHK, Tokyo-Yamata	GENERAL JAPANESE • GENERAL
	RADIO JAPAN/NHK, Via French Guiana	C America • 500 kW JAPANESE • C America • GENERAL • 500 kW
	SEYCHELLES FAR EAST BC ASS'N, North Pt, Mahé Is	Mideast • 100 kW F • Mideast • 100 kW Th/F/Su • Mideast • 100 kW
	TURKEY VOICE OF TURKEY, Ankara	TURKISH • Europe • 500 kW
	UNITED KINGDOM †BBC, Rampisham	(J) • E Europe • 500 kW
	†BBC, Via Zyyi, Cyprus	(D) • E Europe • 250 kW (J) • E Europe • 250 kW (J) M-Sa • E Europe • 250 kW
	USA †RFE-RL, Via Germany	(J) • W Asia • 100 kW
15330	BULGARIA †RADIO BULGARIA, Plovdiv	(J) • E North Am • 250 kW (J) • Europe • 250 kW
	FINLAND †RADIO FINLAND, Pori	(D) • SE Asia & Australasia • 500 kW
	ITALY RADIO ROMA, Rome	E Africa • 100 kW ITALIAN • E Africa • 100 kW Mideast • 100 kW (J) • E Europe • 100 kW (J) • E Asia • 100 kW
	MOROCCO RTV MAROCAINE, Tangier	Mideast, E Europe & N Africa • DS • 50 kW
	RUSSIA †R MOSCOW INTL, Kenga	(J) • E Asia • 250 kW
	†RADIO ROSSII, Kursk	(J) • 100 kW
	SEYCHELLES †FAR EAST BC ASS'N, North Pt, Mahé Is	S Asia • 100 kW F-Tu • S Asia • 100 kW M-Sa • S Asia • 100 kW
	USA VOA, Greenville, NC	(D) • S America • 250 kW (J) • S America • 250 kW
	†VOA, Via Botswana	(D) • Africa • 100 kW (D) M-F • Africa • 100 kW
	†VOA, Via Philippines	(J) • E Asia • 250 kW (J) • E Africa • 250 kW (J) M-F • E Africa • 250 kW
15335	DENMARK †DANMARKS RADIO, Via Norway	W North Am • 500 kW (D) • W North Am • 500 kW (J) • E North Am • 500 kW (J) • N America • 500 kW
	EGYPT RADIO CAIRO, Kafr Silim-Abis	W Africa • 250 kW
	INDIA †ALL INDIA RADIO, Aligarh	SE Asia • 250 kW
	MOLDOVA †RADIO MOLDOVA INTL, Via Romania	S America • 250 kW
	MOROCCO RTV MAROCAINE, Tangier	Europe & W Africa • DS • 100 kW
	NORWAY †RADIO NORWAY INTL, Sveio	W North Am • 500 kW (D) • W North Am • 500 kW (J) • E North Am • 500 kW (J) • N America • 500 kW
	ROMANIA RADIO ROMANIA INTL, Bucharest	Asia & Australasia • 250 kW Australasia • 250 kW Asia • 250 kW Mideast & S Asia • 250 kW
(con'd)		

FREQUENCY	COUNTRY, STATION, LOCATION	TARGET • NETWORK • POWER (kW)

TARGET • NETWORK • POWER (kW) — World Time scale: 0 1 2 3 4 5 6 7 8 9 10 11 12 13 14 15 16 17 18 19 20 21 22 23 24

15335 ROMANIA (con'd) — RADIO ROMANIA INTL, Bucharest
- (J) • W Africa • 250 kW
- Su • S Asia & SE Asia • MARINERS • 250 kW   (J) • Mideast • 250 kW
- Su • W Africa & Atlantic • MARINERS • 250 kW

15340 CUBA — RADIO HABANA, Havana
- S America • 50 kW

ITALY — RADIO ROMA, Rome
- Mideast • 100 kW

JAPAN — †RADIO JAPAN/NHK, Via Moyabi, Gabon
- Alternative Frequency to 15380 kHz

KOREA (DPR) — RADIO PYONGYANG, Kujang-dong
- E Asia & S Asia • 200 kW

ROMANIA — RADIO ROMANIA INTL, Bucharest
- (J) • Africa • 250 kW
- W Africa • 250 kW
- (D) • W Africa • 250 kW   Africa • 250 kW
- (D) • Africa • 250 kW

RUSSIA — †R MOSCOW INTL, Via Moldova
- (J) • W Africa & S America • 500 kW

UNITED KINGDOM — †BBC, Rampisham
- (J) • N Europe • 500 kW
- (D) • E Europe • 500 kW
- (D) • M-F • N Europe • 500 kW
- (D) • Su • E Europe • 500 kW

†BBC, Skelton, Cumbria
- (D) • E Europe • 250 kW
- (D) • E Europe • 500 kW
- (D) • M-F • N Europe • 250 kW

†BBC, Via Singapore
- E Asia • 100 kW
- Australasia • 100 kW
- (D) • Australasia • 100 kW

†BBC, Via Zyyi, Cyprus
- (J) • E Europe & W Asia • 250 kW
- (J) Su • E Europe & W Asia • 250 kW

USA — †RFE-RL, Via Germany
- W Asia • 100 kW
- (J) • W Asia • 100 kW   (D) • W Asia • 100 kW

†RFE-RL, Via Portugal
- (D) • Mideast & W Asia • 250 kW
- (J) • Mideast & W Asia • 250 kW

15345 ARGENTINA — †R ARGENTINA-RAE, Buenos Aires
- M-F • S America • 50/100 kW
- Tu-Sa • Mideast & N Africa • 50/100 kW   M-F • Europe & N Africa • 50/100 kW
- M-F • Mideast & N Africa • 50/100 kW

†RADIO NACIONAL, Buenos Aires
- Sa/Su • S America • DS • 50/100 kW
- Su/M • Mideast & N Africa • DS • 50/100 kW   Sa/Su • Europe & N Africa • DS • 50/100 kW
- Sa/Su • Mideast & N Africa • DS • 50/100 kW

CHINA (TAIWAN) — VO FREE CHINA, T'ai-pei
- E Asia • 100 kW   SE Asia • 50/100 kW
- CANTONESE • E Asia • 100 kW

JAPAN — †RADIO JAPAN/NHK, Via Sri Lanka
- Alternative Frequency to 17775 kHz

KUWAIT — RADIO KUWAIT, Kabd
- S Asia & SE Asia • 500 kW

MOROCCO — RTV MAROCAINE, Tangier
- N Africa • 50 kW

SAUDI ARABIA — †BS OF THE KINGDOM, Riyadh
- S Asia • 500 kW

15350 ECUADOR — RADIO NACIONAL, Via HCJB
- N America • 50 kW

GERMANY — †DEUTSCHE WELLE, Jülich
- (J) • W Africa • 100 kW

†DEUTSCHE WELLE, Multiple Locations
- (J) • W Africa • 100/500 kW

†DEUTSCHE WELLE, Nauen
- (J) • N Africa • 500 kW   W Africa • 500 kW
- (J) • W Africa • 500 kW

†DEUTSCHE WELLE, Various Locations
- W Africa • 250/500 kW

DEUTSCHE WELLE, Via Cyclops, Malta
- (J) • S Asia • 250 kW

JAPAN — RADIO JAPAN/NHK, Via French Guiana
- S America • 500 kW
- JAPANESE • S America • GENERAL • 500 kW

LUXEMBOURG — †RADIO LUXEMBOURG, Junglinster
- E North Am • 10 kW

RUSSIA — †R MOSCOW INTL, Via Tajikistan
- (D) • S Asia • 240 kW
- (J) • SE Asia • 1000 kW

TURKEY — VOICE OF TURKEY, Ankara
- TURKISH • Europe • 500 kW

UNITED KINGDOM — †BBC, Skelton, Cumbria
- (D) • Sa/Su • N Europe • 250 kW

15355 CZECH REPUBLIC (con'd) — †RADIO PRAGUE, Litomyšl
- W Europe • 100 kW

World Time scale: 0 1 2 3 4 5 6 7 8 9 10 11 12 13 14 15 16 17 18 19 20 21 22 23 24

ENGLISH ▬ ARABIC ⚬⚬⚬ CHINESE □□□ FRENCH ═ GERMAN ▬ RUSSIAN ═ SPANISH ▬ OTHER ▬

FREQUENCY   COUNTRY, STATION, LOCATION

TARGET • NETWORK • POWER (kW)   World Time

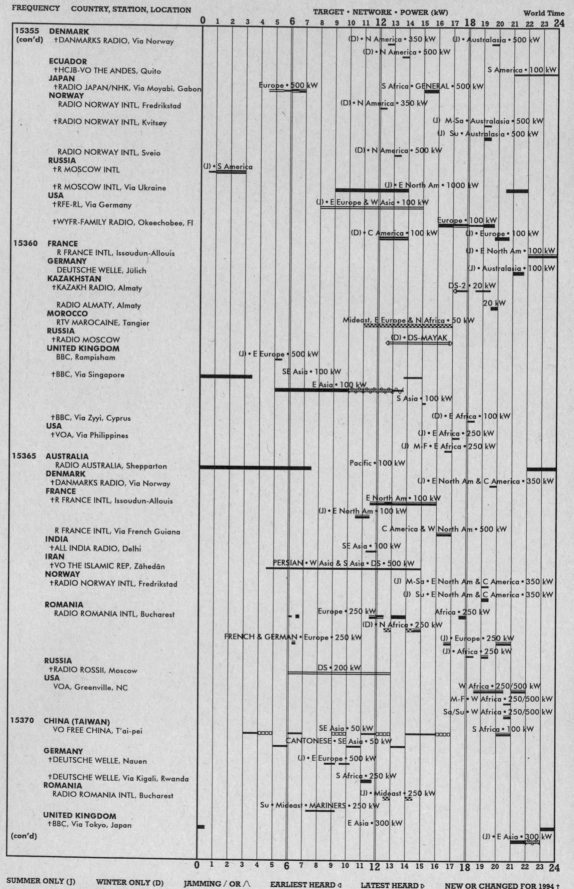

Frequency	Country, Station, Location	Schedule details
15355 (con'd)	**DENMARK** †DANMARKS RADIO, Via Norway	(D) • N America • 350 kW; (J) • Australasia • 500 kW; (D) • N America • 500 kW
	ECUADOR †HCJB-VO THE ANDES, Quito	S America • 100 kW
	JAPAN †RADIO JAPAN/NHK, Via Moyabi, Gabon	Europe • 500 kW; S Africa • GENERAL • 500 kW
	NORWAY RADIO NORWAY INTL, Fredrikstad	(D) • N America • 350 kW
	†RADIO NORWAY INTL, Kvitsøy	(J) • M-Sa • Australasia • 500 kW; (J) • Su • Australasia • 500 kW
	RADIO NORWAY INTL, Sveio	(D) • N America • 500 kW
	RUSSIA †R MOSCOW INTL	(J) • S America
	†R MOSCOW INTL, Via Ukraine	(J) • E North Am • 1000 kW
	USA †RFE-RL, Via Germany	(J) • E Europe & W Asia • 100 kW
	†WYFR-FAMILY RADIO, Okeechobee, Fl	Europe • 100 kW; (D) • C America • 100 kW; (J) • Europe • 100 kW
15360	**FRANCE** R FRANCE INTL, Issoudun-Allouis	(J) • E North Am • 100 kW
	GERMANY DEUTSCHE WELLE, Jülich	(J) • Australasia • 100 kW
	KAZAKHSTAN †KAZAKH RADIO, Almaty	DS-2 • 20 kW
	RADIO ALMATY, Almaty	20 kW
	MOROCCO RTV MAROCAINE, Tangier	Mideast, E Europe & N Africa • 50 kW
	RUSSIA †RADIO MOSCOW	(D) • DS-MAYAK
	UNITED KINGDOM BBC, Rampisham	(J) • E Europe • 500 kW
	†BBC, Via Singapore	SE Asia • 100 kW; E Asia • 100 kW; S Asia • 100 kW
	†BBC, Via Zyyi, Cyprus	(D) • E Africa • 100 kW
	USA †VOA, Via Philippines	(J) • E Africa • 250 kW; (J) M-F • E Africa • 250 kW
15365	**AUSTRALIA** RADIO AUSTRALIA, Shepparton	Pacific • 100 kW
	DENMARK †DANMARKS RADIO, Via Norway	(J) • E North Am & C America • 350 kW
	FRANCE †R FRANCE INTL, Issoudun-Allouis	E North Am • 100 kW; (J) • E North Am • 100 kW
	R FRANCE INTL, Via French Guiana	C America & W North Am • 500 kW
	INDIA †ALL INDIA RADIO, Delhi	SE Asia • 100 kW
	IRAN †VO THE ISLAMIC REP, Zāhedān	PERSIAN • W Asia & S Asia • DS • 500 kW
	NORWAY †RADIO NORWAY INTL, Fredrikstad	(J) M-Sa • E North Am & C America • 350 kW; (J) Su • E North Am & C America • 350 kW
	ROMANIA RADIO ROMANIA INTL, Bucharest	Europe • 250 kW; Africa • 250 kW; (D) • N Africa • 250 kW; FRENCH & GERMAN • Europe • 250 kW; (J) • Europe • 250 kW; (J) • Africa • 250 kW
	RUSSIA †RADIO ROSSII, Moscow	DS • 200 kW
	USA VOA, Greenville, NC	W Africa • 250/500 kW; M-F • W Africa • 250/500 kW; Sa/Su • W Africa • 250/500 kW
15370	**CHINA (TAIWAN)** VO FREE CHINA, T'ai-pei	SE Asia • 50 kW; S Africa • 100 kW; CANTONESE • SE Asia • 50 kW
	GERMANY †DEUTSCHE WELLE, Nauen	(J) • E Europe • 500 kW
	†DEUTSCHE WELLE, Via Kigali, Rwanda	S Africa • 250 kW
	ROMANIA RADIO ROMANIA INTL, Bucharest	(J) • Mideast • 250 kW; Su • Mideast • MARINERS • 250 kW
	UNITED KINGDOM †BBC, Via Tokyo, Japan	E Asia • 300 kW; (J) • E Asia • 300 kW
(con'd)		

SUMMER ONLY (J)   WINTER ONLY (D)   JAMMING / OR ∧   EARLIEST HEARD ◁   LATEST HEARD ▷   NEW OR CHANGED FOR 1994 †

FREQUENCY   COUNTRY, STATION, LOCATION

TARGET • NETWORK • POWER (kW)   World Time

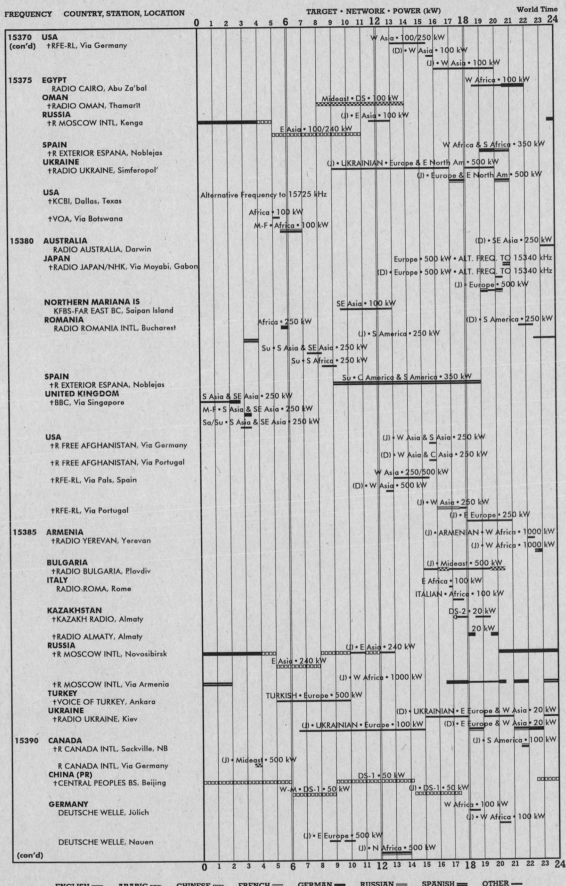

FREQUENCY	COUNTRY, STATION, LOCATION	TARGET • NETWORK • POWER (kW)
15370 (con'd)	**USA**	
	†RFE-RL, Via Germany	W Asia • 100/250 kW
		(D) • W Asia • 100 kW
		(J) • W Asia • 100 kW
15375	**EGYPT**	
	RADIO CAIRO, Abu Za'bal	W Africa • 100 kW
	OMAN	
	†RADIO OMAN, Thamarīt	Mideast • DS • 100 kW
	RUSSIA	
	†R MOSCOW INTL, Kenga	(J) • E Asia • 100 kW
		E Asia • 100/240 kW
	SPAIN	
	†R EXTERIOR ESPANA, Noblejas	W Africa & S Africa • 350 kW
	UKRAINE	
	†RADIO UKRAINE, Simferopol'	(J) • UKRAINIAN • Eurape & E North Am • 500 kW
		(J) • Europe & E North Am • 500 kW
	USA	
	†KCBI, Dallas, Texas	Alternative Frequency to 15725 kHz
	†VOA, Via Botswana	Africa • 100 kW
		M-F • Africa • 100 kW
15380	**AUSTRALIA**	
	RADIO AUSTRALIA, Darwin	(D) • SE Asia • 250 kW
	JAPAN	
	†RADIO JAPAN/NHK, Via Moyabi, Gabon	Europe • 500 kW • ALT. FREQ. TO 15340 kHz
		(D) • Europe • 500 kW • ALT. FREQ. TO 15340 kHz
		(J) • Europe • 500 kW
	NORTHERN MARIANA IS	
	KFBS-FAR EAST BC, Saipan Island	SE Asia • 100 kW
	ROMANIA	
	RADIO ROMANIA INTL, Bucharest	Africa • 250 kW
		(D) • S America • 250 kW
		(J) • S America • 250 kW
		Su • S Asia & SE Asia • 250 kW
		Su • S Africa • 250 kW
	SPAIN	
	†R EXTERIOR ESPANA, Noblejas	Su • C America & S America • 350 kW
	UNITED KINGDOM	
	†BBC, Via Singapore	S Asia & SE Asia • 250 kW
		M-F • S Asia & SE Asia • 250 kW
		Sa/Su • S Asia & SE Asia • 250 kW
	USA	
	†R FREE AFGHANISTAN, Via Germany	(J) • W Asia & S Asia • 250 kW
	†R FREE AFGHANISTAN, Via Portugal	(D) • W Asia & C Asia • 250 kW
	†RFE-RL, Via Pals, Spain	W Asia • 250/500 kW
		(D) • W Asia • 500 kW
	†RFE-RL, Via Portugal	(J) • W Asia • 250 kW
		(J) • E Europe • 250 kW
15385	**ARMENIA**	
	†RADIO YEREVAN, Yerevan	(J) • ARMENIAN • W Africa • 1000 kW
		(J) • W Africa • 1000 kW
	BULGARIA	
	†RADIO BULGARIA, Plovdiv	(J) • Mideast • 500 kW
	ITALY	
	RADIO ROMA, Rome	E Africa • 100 kW
		ITALIAN • Africa • 100 kW
	KAZAKHSTAN	
	†KAZAKH RADIO, Almaty	DS-2 • 20 kW
	†RADIO ALMATY, Almaty	20 kW
	RUSSIA	
	†R MOSCOW INTL, Novosibirsk	(J) • E Asia • 240 kW
		E Asia • 240 kW
	†R MOSCOW INTL, Via Armenia	(J) • W Africa • 1000 kW
	TURKEY	
	†VOICE OF TURKEY, Ankara	TURKISH • Europe • 500 kW
	UKRAINE	
	†RADIO UKRAINE, Kiev	(D) • UKRAINIAN • E Europe & W Asia • 20 kW
		(J) • UKRAINIAN • Europe • 100 kW	(D) • E Europe & W Asia • 20 kW
15390	**CANADA**	
	†R CANADA INTL, Sackville, NB	(J) • S America • 100 kW
	R CANADA INTL, Via Germany	(J) • Mideast • 500 kW
	CHINA (PR)	
	†CENTRAL PEOPLES BS, Beijing	DS-1 • 50 kW
		W-M • DS-1 • 50 kW	(J) • DS-1 • 50 kW
	GERMANY	
	DEUTSCHE WELLE, Jülich	W Africa • 100 kW
		(J) • W Africa • 100 kW
	DEUTSCHE WELLE, Nauen	(J) • E Europe • 500 kW
		(J) • N Africa • 500 kW
(con'd)		

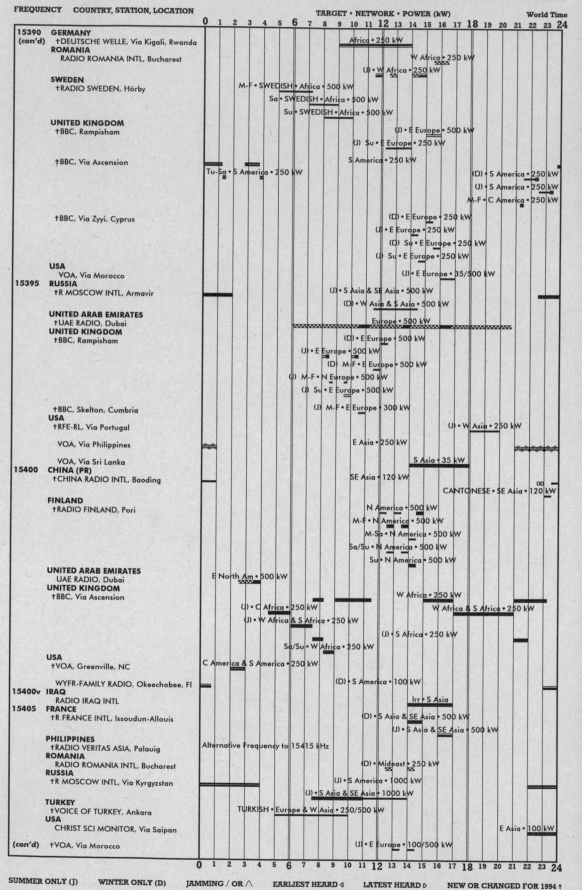

FREQUENCY   COUNTRY, STATION, LOCATION

TARGET • NETWORK • POWER (kW)   World Time

15390   GERMANY
(con'd)   †DEUTSCHE WELLE, Via Kigali, Rwanda
         ROMANIA
            RADIO ROMANIA INTL, Bucharest

         SWEDEN
            †RADIO SWEDEN, Hörby

         UNITED KINGDOM
            †BBC, Rampisham

            †BBC, Via Ascension

            †BBC, Via Zyyi, Cyprus

         USA
            VOA, Via Morocco
15395   RUSSIA
            †R MOSCOW INTL, Armavir

         UNITED ARAB EMIRATES
            †UAE RADIO, Dubai
         UNITED KINGDOM
            †BBC, Rampisham

            †BBC, Skelton, Cumbria
         USA
            †RFE-RL, Via Portugal

            VOA, Via Philippines

            VOA, Via Sri Lanka
15400   CHINA (PR)
            †CHINA RADIO INTL, Baoding

         FINLAND
            †RADIO FINLAND, Pori

         UNITED ARAB EMIRATES
            UAE RADIO, Dubai
         UNITED KINGDOM
            †BBC, Via Ascension

         USA
            †VOA, Greenville, NC

            WYFR-FAMILY RADIO, Okeechobee, Fl
15400v   IRAQ
            RADIO IRAQ INTL
15405   FRANCE
            †R FRANCE INTL, Issoudun-Allouis

         PHILIPPINES
            †RADIO VERITAS ASIA, Palauig
         ROMANIA
            RADIO ROMANIA INTL, Bucharest
         RUSSIA
            †R MOSCOW INTL, Via Kyrgyzstan

         TURKEY
            †VOICE OF TURKEY, Ankara
         USA
            CHRIST SCI MONITOR, Via Saipan

(con'd)   †VOA, Via Morocco

FREQUENCY   COUNTRY, STATION, LOCATION

TARGET • NETWORK • POWER (kW)   World Time

15405 (con'd)	**USA** †VOA, Via Philippines — E Asia • 250 kW
15410	**AUSTRIA** RADIO AUSTRIA INTL, Vienna — Mideast • 100 kW; (D) • Mideast • 100 kW; (J) • Mideast • 100 kW; M-Sa • Mideast • 100 kW; Su • Mideast • 100 kW
	GERMANY DEUTSCHE WELLE, Via Antigua — S America • 250 kW
	†DEUTSCHE WELLE, Via Kigali, Rwanda — S Africa • 250 kW; W Africa • 250 kW; C Africa & E Africa • 250 kW
	DEUTSCHE WELLE, Via Sri Lanka — Mideast & S Asia • 250 kW
	JAPAN †RADIO JAPAN/NHK, Tokyo-Yamata — E Asia • 300 kW; E Asia • GENERAL • 300 kW; JAPANESE • E Asia • GENERAL • 300 kW
	RUSSIA †R MOSCOW INTL, Petropavlovsk-K — (J) • W North Am • 100 kW
	USA †VOA, Via Morocco — W Africa • 500 kW
	VOA, Via Philippines — E Asia • 250 kW; (D) • E Asia • 250 kW; (J) • E Asia • 250 kW
15415	**GERMANY** †DEUTSCHE WELLE, Various Locations — SE Asia • 250/500 kW
	LIBYA RADIO JAMAHIRIYA, Tripoli — Europe • 500 kW; ARABIC, RUSSIAN, ETC • Europe • 500 kW
	PHILIPPINES †RADIO VERITAS ASIA, Palauig — S Asia • 250 kW • ALT. FREQ. TO 15405 kHz
	RUSSIA †R MOSCOW INTL, Kenga — (J) • S Asia • 1000 kW
	†R MOSCOW INTL, Via Kazakhstan — (J) • Africa • 1000 kW
	USA †RFE-RL, Via Portugal — (J) • W Asia • 250 kW
15420	**EGYPT** RADIO CAIRO, Abu Za'bal — S America • 100 kW
	RUSSIA †GOLOS ROSSII, Serpukhov — (J) • Europe • 250 kW
	†R MOSCOW INTL, Serpukhov — (D) • SE Asia • 240 kW; (J) • Europe • 250 kW
	UNITED KINGDOM †BBC, Via Meyerton, S Af — E Africa • 250 kW
	†BBC, Via Seychelles — (J) • E Africa • 250 kW; E Africa • 250 kW; S Africa • 250 kW; M-Sa • E Africa • 250 kW; Sa/Su • E Africa • 250 kW
	USA WRNO WORLDWIDE, New Orleans, La — (J) • E North Am • 100 kW; Su • E North Am • 100 kW; (D) Su • E North Am • 100 kW; ENGLISH, FRENCH & GERMAN • E North Am • 100 kW
15425	**AUSTRALIA** AUSTRALIAN BC CORP, Perth — Australasia • DS • 50 kW
	CANADA R CANADA INTL, Sackville, NB — M-F • C America • 250 kW
	FRANCE R FRANCE INTL, Issoudun-Allouis — E Europe • 100 kW; (J) • E Europe & Mideast • 100 kW
	GERMANY DEUTSCHE WELLE, Jülich — (D) • W Africa • 100 kW; (D) • W Africa • 250 kW
	†DEUTSCHE WELLE, Via Kigali, Rwanda — (J) • S America • 250 kW
	†DEUTSCHE WELLE, Via Sines, Portugal — (J) • E Europe • 500 kW
	DEUTSCHE WELLE, Wertachtal — (J) • N Africa • 500 kW
	RUSSIA †R MOSCOW INTL, Kenga — (J) • Mideast & W Asia • 1000 kW
	†R MOSCOW INTL, Petropavlovsk-K — (D) • W North Am • 240 kW; (J) • W North Am • NORTH AMERICAN SVC • 240 kW
	†R TIKHIY OKEAN, Petropavlovsk-K — (J) • W North Am • 240 kW
	SRI LANKA SRI LANKA BC CORP, Colombo-Ekala — S Asia • 35 kW; M • N America • 300 kW
(con'd)	

ENGLISH ▬   ARABIC ⧉   CHINESE ▫▫▫   FRENCH ▬   GERMAN ▬   RUSSIAN ═   SPANISH ▬   OTHER ▬

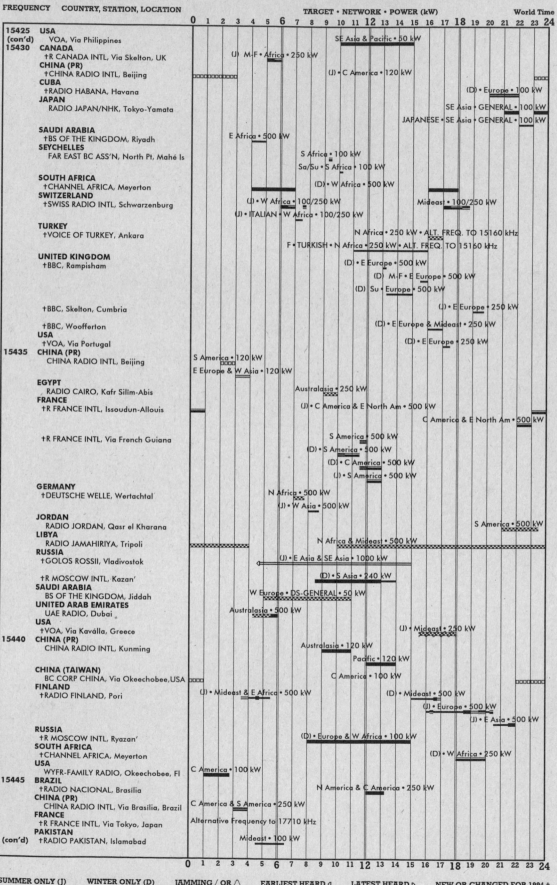

FREQUENCY   COUNTRY, STATION, LOCATION

15425	**USA**
(con'd)	VOA, Via Philippines — SE Asia & Pacific • 50 kW
15430	**CANADA**
	†R CANADA INTL, Via Skelton, UK — (J) • M-F • Africa • 250 kW
	CHINA (PR)
	†CHINA RADIO INTL, Beijing — (J) • C America • 120 kW
	CUBA
	†RADIO HABANA, Havana — (D) • Europe • 100 kW
	JAPAN
	RADIO JAPAN/NHK, Tokyo-Yamata — SE Asia • GENERAL • 100 kW / JAPANESE • SE Asia • GENERAL • 100 kW
	SAUDI ARABIA
	†BS OF THE KINGDOM, Riyadh — E Africa • 500 kW
	SEYCHELLES
	FAR EAST BC ASS'N, North Pt, Mahé Is — S Africa • 100 kW / Sa/Su • S Africa • 100 kW
	SOUTH AFRICA
	†CHANNEL AFRICA, Meyerton — (D) • W Africa • 500 kW
	SWITZERLAND
	†SWISS RADIO INTL, Schwarzenburg — (J) • W Africa • 100/250 kW / Mideast • 100/250 kW / (J) • ITALIAN • W Africa • 100/250 kW
	TURKEY
	†VOICE OF TURKEY, Ankara — N Africa • 250 kW • ALT. FREQ. TO 15160 kHz / F • TURKISH • N Africa • 250 kW • ALT. FREQ. TO 15160 kHz
	UNITED KINGDOM
	†BBC, Rampisham — (D) • E Europe • 500 kW / (D) • M-F • E Europe • 500 kW / (D) • Su • Europe • 500 kW
	†BBC, Skelton, Cumbria — (J) • E Europe • 250 kW
	†BBC, Woofferton — (D) • E Europe & Mideast • 250 kW
	USA
	†VOA, Via Portugal — (D) • E Europe • 250 kW
15435	**CHINA (PR)**
	CHINA RADIO INTL, Beijing — S America • 120 kW / E Europe & W Asia • 120 kW
	EGYPT
	RADIO CAIRO, Kafr Silim-Abis — Australasia • 250 kW
	FRANCE
	†R FRANCE INTL, Issoudun-Allouis — (J) • C America & E North Am • 500 kW / C America & E North Am • 500 kW
	†R FRANCE INTL, Via French Guiana — S America • 500 kW / (D) • S America • 500 kW / (D) • C America • 500 kW / (J) • S America • 500 kW
	GERMANY
	†DEUTSCHE WELLE, Wertachtal — N Africa • 500 kW / (J) • W Asia • 500 kW
	JORDAN
	RADIO JORDAN, Qasr el Kharana — S America • 500 kW
	LIBYA
	RADIO JAMAHIRIYA, Tripoli — N Africa & Mideast • 500 kW
	RUSSIA
	†GOLOS ROSSII, Vladivostok — (J) • E Asia & SE Asia • 1000 kW
	†R MOSCOW INTL, 'Kazan' — (D) • S Asia • 240 kW
	SAUDI ARABIA
	BS OF THE KINGDOM, Jiddah — W Europe • DS-GENERAL • 50 kW
	UNITED ARAB EMIRATES
	UAE RADIO, Dubai — Australasia • 500 kW
	USA
	†VOA, Via Kaválla, Greece — (J) • Mideast • 250 kW
15440	**CHINA (PR)**
	CHINA RADIO INTL, Kunming — Australasia • 120 kW / Pacific • 120 kW
	CHINA (TAIWAN)
	BC CORP CHINA, Via Okeechobee, USA — C America • 100 kW
	FINLAND
	†RADIO FINLAND, Pori — (J) • Mideast & E Africa • 500 kW / (D) • Mideast • 500 kW / (J) • Europe • 500 kW / (J) • E Asia • 500 kW
	RUSSIA
	†R MOSCOW INTL, Ryazan' — (D) • Europe & W Africa • 100 kW
	SOUTH AFRICA
	†CHANNEL AFRICA, Meyerton — (D) • W Africa • 250 kW
	USA
	WYFR-FAMILY RADIO, Okeechobee, Fl — C America • 100 kW
15445	**BRAZIL**
	†RADIO NACIONAL, Brasília — N America & C America • 250 kW
	CHINA (PR)
	CHINA RADIO INTL, Via Brasília, Brazil — C America & S America • 250 kW
	FRANCE
	†R FRANCE INTL, Via Tokyo, Japan — Alternative Frequency to 17710 kHz
	PAKISTAN
(con'd)	†RADIO PAKISTAN, Islamabad — Mideast • 100 kW

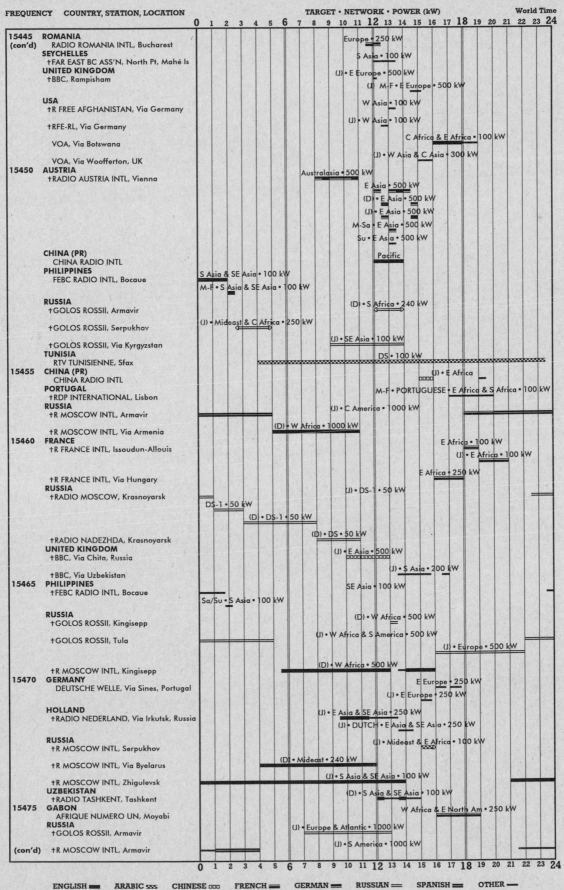

FREQUENCY   COUNTRY, STATION, LOCATION

TARGET • NETWORK • POWER (kW)   World Time

15445	ROMANIA	
(con'd)	RADIO ROMANIA INTL, Bucharest	Europe • 250 kW
	SEYCHELLES	
	†FAR EAST BC ASS'N, North Pt, Mahé Is	S Asia • 100 kW
	UNITED KINGDOM	
	†BBC, Rampisham	(J) • E Europe • 500 kW
		(J) • M-F • E Europe • 500 kW
	USA	
	†R FREE AFGHANISTAN, Via Germany	W Asia • 100 kW
	†RFE-RL, Via Germany	(J) • W Asia • 100 kW
	VOA, Via Botswana	C Africa & E Africa • 100 kW
	VOA, Via Woofferton, UK	(J) • W Asia & C Asia • 300 kW
15450	AUSTRIA	
	†RADIO AUSTRIA INTL, Vienna	Australasia • 500 kW
		E Asia • 500 kW
		(D) • E Asia • 500 kW
		(J) • E Asia • 500 kW
		M-Sa • E Asia • 500 kW
		Su • E Asia • 500 kW
	CHINA (PR)	
	CHINA RADIO INTL	Pacific
	PHILIPPINES	
	FEBC RADIO INTL, Bocaue	S Asia & SE Asia • 100 kW
		M-F • S Asia & SE Asia • 100 kW
	RUSSIA	
	†GOLOS ROSSII, Armavir	(D) • S Africa • 240 kW
	†GOLOS ROSSII, Serpukhov	(J) • Mideast & C Africa • 250 kW
	†GOLOS ROSSII, Via Kyrgyzstan	(J) • SE Asia • 100 kW
	TUNISIA	
	RTV TUNISIENNE, Sfax	DS • 100 kW
15455	CHINA (PR)	
	CHINA RADIO INTL	(J) • E Africa
	PORTUGAL	
	†RDP INTERNATIONAL, Lisbon	M-F • PORTUGUESE • E Africa & S Africa • 100 kW
	RUSSIA	
	†R MOSCOW INTL, Armavir	(J) • C America • 1000 kW
	†R MOSCOW INTL, Via Armenia	(D) • W Africa • 1000 kW
15460	FRANCE	
	†R FRANCE INTL, Issoudun-Allouis	E Africa • 100 kW
		(J) • E Africa • 100 kW
	†R FRANCE INTL, Via Hungary	E Africa • 250 kW
	RUSSIA	
	†RADIO MOSCOW, Krasnoyarsk	(J) • DS-1 • 50 kW
		DS-1 • 50 kW
		(D) • DS-1 • 50 kW
	†RADIO NADEZHDA, Krasnoyarsk	(D) • DS • 50 kW
	UNITED KINGDOM	
	†BBC, Via Chita, Russia	(J) • E Asia • 500 kW
	†BBC, Via Uzbekistan	(J) • S Asia • 200 kW
15465	PHILIPPINES	
	†FEBC RADIO INTL, Bocaue	SE Asia • 100 kW
		Sa/Su • S Asia • 100 kW
	RUSSIA	
	†GOLOS ROSSII, Kingisepp	(D) • W Africa • 500 kW
	†GOLOS ROSSII, Tula	(J) • W Africa & S America • 500 kW
		(J) • Europe • 500 kW
	†R MOSCOW INTL, Kingisepp	(D) • W Africa • 500 kW
15470	GERMANY	
	DEUTSCHE WELLE, Via Sines, Portugal	E Europe • 250 kW
		(J) • E Europe • 250 kW
	HOLLAND	
	†RADIO NEDERLAND, Via Irkutsk, Russia	(J) • E Asia & SE Asia • 250 kW
		(J) • DUTCH • E Asia & SE Asia • 250 kW
	RUSSIA	
	†R MOSCOW INTL, Serpukhov	(J) • Mideast & E Africa • 100 kW
	†R MOSCOW INTL, Via Byelarus	(D) • Mideast • 240 kW
	†R MOSCOW INTL, Zhigulevsk	(J) • S Asia & SE Asia • 100 kW
	UZBEKISTAN	
	†RADIO TASHKENT, Tashkent	(D) • S Asia & SE Asia • 100 kW
15475	GABON	
	AFRIQUE NUMERO UN, Moyabi	W Africa & E North Am • 250 kW
	RUSSIA	
	†GOLOS ROSSII, Armavir	(J) • Europe & Atlantic • 1000 kW
		(J) • S America • 1000 kW
(con'd)	†R MOSCOW INTL, Armavir	

FREQUENCY   COUNTRY, STATION, LOCATION

TARGET • NETWORK • POWER (kW)   World Time

FREQUENCY	COUNTRY, STATION, LOCATION	TARGET • NETWORK • POWER (kW)
15475 (con'd)	RUSSIA †R MOSCOW INTL, Armavir	(D) • E Africa & S Africa • 240 kW
	†RADIO ROSSII, Irkutsk	DS • 100 kW
15476v	ANTARCTICA R NACIONAL-LRA36, Base Esperanza	M-F • DS-TEMP INACTIVE • 1 kW
15480	ISRAEL KOL ISRAEL, Tel Aviv	Mideast • DS-D • 20/50 kW
	RUSSIA †GOLOS ROSSII, St Petersburg	(D) • Mideast & W Asia • 500 kW
	†R MOSCOW INTL, Serpukhov	(J) • S Asia & SE Asia • 500 kW
	†R MOSCOW INTL, St Petersburg	(D) • Mideast & W Asia • 500 kW
	†R MOSCOW INTL, Vladivostok	(J) • E Asia & SE Asia • 1000 kW
15485	FRANCE †R FRANCE INTL, Issoudun-Allouis	Mideast • 100 kW / (J) • Mideast • 100 kW
	GUAM KTWR-TRANS WORLD R, Merizo	JAPANESE • E Asia • 100 kW
	RUSSIA †R MOSCOW INTL, Via Armenia	(D) • Europe • 500 kW / (J) • Europe • 1000 kW
15490	RUSSIA †R MOSCOW INTL, Irkutsk	(J) • SE Asia • 1000 kW
	†R MOSCOW INTL, Tula	(J) • S America • 240 kW
	†R MOSCOW INTL, Via Kyrgyzstan	(D) • S Asia & SE Asia • 1000 kW
	†R TIKHIY OKEAN, Irkutsk	(J) • SE Asia • 1000 kW
	†RADIO MOSCOW, Kenga	DS-2 • 50 kW
15495	FRANCE R FRANCE INTL, Issoudun-Allouis	(J) • Mideast • 500 kW
	KUWAIT RADIO KUWAIT, Kabd	Mideast • 500 kW
	RUSSIA †R MOSCOW INTL, Via Ukraine	(D) • Europe • 240 kW
15500	CHINA (PR) †CENTRAL PEOPLES BS, Beijing	DS-2 • 120 kW / Th/Sa-Tu • DS-2 • 120 kW / (J) • DS-2 • 120 kW
	RUSSIA †GOLOS ROSSII, Moscow	(D) • Mideast • 250 kW
	†R MOSCOW INTL, Armavir	(D) • C Africa • 100 kW
	†R MOSCOW INTL, Yekaterinburg	(J) • E Asia • 200 kW
15505	KUWAIT †RADIO KUWAIT, Kabd	(J) • Europe & E North Am • 500 kW
	SWITZERLAND †SWISS RADIO INTL, Schwarzenburg	E Asia & Australasia • 100/250 kW Africa • 100/250 kW / ITALIAN • E Asia & Australasia • 100/250 kW W Africa • 100/250 kW / S Asia & SE Asia • 100/250 kW / Mideast & E Africa • 100/250 kW / ITALIAN • W Africa • 100/250 kW
15510	AUSTRALIA †RADIO AUSTRALIA, Darwin	(J) • S Asia & SE Asia • 250 kW
	PHILIPPINES †RADIO VERITAS ASIA, Palauig	SE Asia • 250 kW • ALT. FREQ. TO 15245 kHz
	RUSSIA †R MOSCOW INTL, Moscow	(D) • Europe • 100 kW
	†R MOSCOW INTL, Omsk	(J) • S Asia • 500 kW
15514v	PAKISTAN RADIO PAKISTAN, Karachi	S Asia • 50 kW
15515	FRANCE †R FRANCE INTL, Via French Guiana	(J) • C America • 500 kW / (J) • M-Sa • C America • 500 kW / (J) • Su • C America • 500 kW
	PAKISTAN †RADIO PAKISTAN, Islamabad	Mideast • 100 kW
	PHILIPPINES FEBC RADIO INTL, Bocaue	SE Asia • 100 kW
	PORTUGAL †RDP INTERNATIONAL, Lisbon	PORTUGUESE • E Africa & S Africa • 100 kW • ALT. FREQ. TO 17900 kHz / M-F • E Africa & S Africa • 100 kW • ALT. FREQ. TO 17900 kHz / Sa/Su • PORTUGUESE • E Africa & S Africa • 100 kW • ALT. FREQ. TO 17900 kHz
15520	CZECH REPUBLIC †RADIO PRAGUE, Via Slovakia	(D) • E Africa • 250 kW / (D) M-F • E Africa • 250 kW
	RUSSIA †R MOSCOW INTL, Armavir	(J) • S Africa • 1000 kW
	†R MOSCOW INTL, Moscow	(J) • S America • 500 kW
	†R MOSCOW INTL, Serpukhov	(D) • SE Asia • 120 kW
15520v (con'd)	BANGLADESH †RADIO BANGLADESH, Dhaka	Irr • BANGLA • DS • 50 kW

SUMMER ONLY (J)   WINTER ONLY (D)   JAMMING / OR ∧   EARLIEST HEARD ◁   LATEST HEARD ▷   NEW OR CHANGED FOR 1994 †

FREQUENCY   COUNTRY, STATION, LOCATION   TARGET • NETWORK • POWER (kW)   World Time

`0  1  2  3  4  5  6  7  8  9  10  11  12  13  14  15  16  17  18  19  20  21  22  23  24`

15520v BANGLADESH
(con'd)   †RADIO BANGLADESH, Dhaka
- BANGLA • DS • 50 kW
- DS • 50 kW
- Irr • ENGLISH & BANGLA • DS • 50 kW
- ENGLISH & BANGLA • DS • 50 kW

15525 GERMANY
   †DEUTSCHE WELLE, Via N'sibirsk, Russia
- (J) • E Asia • 200 kW

   †DEUTSCHE WELLE, Via Samara, Russia
RUSSIA
   †R MOSCOW INTL, Kenga
- W Asia • 200 kW
- (J) • E Asia • 240 kW

   †R MOSCOW INTL, Via Kazakhstan
- (J) • E Asia • 240 kW
UKRAINE
   †RADIO UKRAINE, Kiev
- (D) • UKRAINIAN • Europe • 100 kW

15530 AUSTRALIA
   †RADIO AUSTRALIA, Darwin
- (J) • SE Asia • 250 kW
- SE Asia • 250 kW

FRANCE
   R FRANCE INTL, Issoudun-Allouis
- Mideast • 100 kW
- W Africa • 500 kW

   †R FRANCE INTL, Via Hungary
- N Africa • 250 kW
HOLLAND
   †RADIO NEDERLAND, Flevoland
- (J) • DUTCH • SE Asia • 500 kW
- (J) • DUTCH • S Asia • 500 kW

RUSSIA
   †R MOSCOW INTL, St Petersburg
- (D) • Mideast • 500 kW

15535 GERMANY
   DEUTSCHE WELLE, Via N'sibirsk, Russia
- (J) • S Asia • 1000 kW
RUSSIA
   †GOLOS ROSSII, Komsomol'sk 'Amure
- (D) • N Pacific • 100 kW

   †R MOSCOW INTL, Chita
- (J) • SE Asia • 1000 kW

   †R MOSCOW INTL, Kazan'
- (J) • S Europe & N Africa • 240 kW

   †R MOSCOW INTL, Kenga
- (J) • S Asia & E Asia • 500 kW

   †R MOSCOW INTL, Via Kyrgyzstan
- (D) • SE Asia • 240 kW

   †R TIKHIY OKEAN, Kenga
- (J) • S Asia & E Asia • 500 kW

   †R TIKHIY OKEAN, Komsomol'sk 'Amure
- (D) • N Pacific • 100 kW

15540 BELGIUM
   †R VLAANDEREN INTL, Wavre
- DUTCH • Africa • 250 kW
- (D) • DUTCH • Africa • 250 kW
- (D) • Africa • 250 kW
- (J) • Mideast & E Africa • 250 kW • ALT. FREQ. TO 15545 kHz
- M-Sa • DUTCH • N America • 250 kW • ALT. FREQ. TO 21810 kHz
- M-Sa • N America • 250 kW • ALT. FREQ. TO 21810 kHz
- M-Sa • Africa • 250 kW
- (J) M-Sa • DUTCH • Mideast & E Africa • 250 kW • ALT. FREQ. TO 15545 kHz
- Su • N America • 250 kW • ALT. FREQ. TO 21810 kHz
- Su • DUTCH • N America • 250 kW • ALT. FREQ. TO 21810 kHz
- Su • DUTCH • Africa • 250 kW
- (J) Su • FRENCH & DUTCH • Africa • 250 kW

RUSSIA
   †R MOSCOW INTL, St Petersburg
- (J) • Mideast • 500 kW

   †R MOSCOW INTL, Zhigulevsk
- (D) • Europe • 250 kW

15545 BELGIUM
   †R VLAANDEREN INTL, Wavre
- Alternative Frequency to 15540 kHz
GERMANY
   DEUTSCHE WELLE, Wertachtal
- E Europe • 500 kW
- (D) • E Europe • 500 kW
- (J) • E Europe • 500 kW

RUSSIA
   †R MOSCOW INTL, Krasnoyarsk
- E Asia • 100 kW
- (D) • E Asia • 100 kW
- (J) • E Asia • 100 kW

   †R MOSCOW INTL, Serpukhov
- (J) • S America • 240 kW

   †R MOSCOW INTL, Yekaterinburg
- (J) • E Europe • 240 kW

15550 CHINA (PR)
   †CENTRAL PEOPLES BS, Beijing
- DS-1 • 15 kW
- W-M • DS-1 • 15 kW

PAKISTAN
   †RADIO PAKISTAN, Islamabad
- (J) • Europe • 250 kW
RUSSIA
   †R MOSCOW INTL, Tula
- (D) • S Asia & SE Asia • 500 kW

(con'd)
- (J) • W Asia & S Asia • 500 kW

`0  1  2  3  4  5  6  7  8  9  10  11  12  13  14  15  16  17  18  19  20  21  22  23  24`

ENGLISH ▄▄▄   ARABIC ⋙   CHINESE ▫▫▫   FRENCH ▬▬   GERMAN ▬▬   RUSSIAN ══   SPANISH ▬▬   OTHER ▬▬

FREQUENCY   COUNTRY, STATION, LOCATION   TARGET • NETWORK • POWER (kW)   World Time

	0 1 2 3 4 5 6 7 8 9 10 11 12 13 14 15 16 17 18 19 20 21 22 23 24
15550 USA (con'd) †VOA, Via Petro-Kam, Russia	(J) • E Asia • 250 kW
15555 PAKISTAN †RADIO PAKISTAN, Islamabad	Mideast • 250 kW
15560 HOLLAND †RADIO NEDERLAND, Flevoland	Mideast • 500 kW
	(J) • DUTCH • Mideast • 500 kW
†RADIO NEDERLAND, Via Neth Antilles	(D) • DUTCH • Australasia • 250 kW S America • 250 kW
RUSSIA †R MOSCOW INTL, Moscow	(D) • S Asia & SE Asia • 500 kW
15566 USA WYFR-FAMILY RADIO, Okeechobee, Fl	Europe • 100 kW
	(D) • Europe • 100 kW
	(J) • Europe • 100 kW
15570 HOLLAND †RADIO NEDERLAND, Flevoland	(D) • W Africa & C Africa • 500 kW
PHILIPPINES †RADIO VERITAS ASIA, Palauig	S Asia • 250 kW
RUSSIA †GOLOS ROSSII, Vladivostok	(J) • E Asia & SE Asia • 240 kW
†R TIKHIY OKEAN, Vladivostok	(J) • E Asia & SE Asia • 240 kW
UZBEKISTAN †UZBEK RADIO, Tashkent	(D) • Mideast • DS-2 • 100 kW
15575 AUSTRALIA RADIO AUSTRALIA, Carnarvon	SE Asia • 100 kW
†RADIO AUSTRALIA, Darwin	E Asia • 250 kW
KOREA (REPUBLIC) †RADIO KOREA, In-Kimjae	Europe • 250 kW
	KOREAN • E North Am • 250 kW
	E North Am • 250 kW KOREAN • Mideast & Africa • 250 kW
	Mideast & Africa • 250 kW
UNITED KINGDOM †BBC, Via Zyyi, Cyprus	W Asia • 100/250 kW (J) • E Africa • 250 kW
	(J) • W Asia & S Asia • 250 kW Mideast & W Asia • 100/250 kW
	(D) • N Africa • 100 kW
	(J) • W Asia • 100 kW
	(J) • E Europe • 100 kW
	Sa/Su • Mideast & S Asia • 100/250 kW
15580 ARMENIA †RADIO YEREVAN, Via Petro-K, Russia	(J) • ARMENIAN • W North Am • 240 kW
	(J) • W North Am • 240 kW
BYELARUS †RS BYELARUS, Via Petro-K, Russia	(J) • W North Am • 240 kW
RUSSIA †GOLOS ROSSII, Chita	(J) • SE Asia • 1000 kW
†R MOSCOW INTL, Armavir	(J) • SE Asia • 240 kW
†R MOSCOW INTL, Petropavlovsk-K	(J) • W North Am • 240 kW
UKRAINE †RADIO UKRAINE, Via Petro-K, Russia	(J) • W North Am • 240 kW
	(J) • UKRAINIAN • W North Am • 240 kW
USA VOA, Greenville, NC	W Africa • 250 kW
15585 RUSSIA †R MOSCOW INTL, Armavir	(D) • N Europe & E North Am • 500 kW
†R MOSCOW INTL, Moscow	(J) • W Africa & S America • 500 kW
15590 RUSSIA †R MOSCOW INTL, Irkutsk	(J) • E Asia & Australasia • 250 kW
†R MOSCOW INTL, Serpukhov	(J) • S Asia & SE Asia • 500 kW
UNITED KINGDOM †BBC, Via Zyyi, Cyprus	Mideast • 100/250 kW
	W Asia • 100/250 kW
	F • W Asia • 100 kW
	M-Sa • Mideast • 100 kW
USA †KTBN, Salt Lake City, Utah	E North Am • 100 kW
	(J) • E North Am • 100 kW
15595 GERMANY †DEUTSCHE WELLE, Jülich	(J) • W Asia • 100 kW
†DEUTSCHE WELLE, Multiple Locations	E Asia • 100/250/500 kW
	(J) • SE Asia • 100/500 kW
†DEUTSCHE WELLE, Via Cyclops, Malta	(D) • JAPANESE • E Asia • 250 kW
†DEUTSCHE WELLE, Wertachtal	(J) • S Asia • 500 kW
RUSSIA †GOLOS ROSSII, Vladivostok	(J) • W North Am • 240 kW
(con'd) †R MOSCOW INTL, Kenga	(D) • S Asia & E Asia • 500 kW

0 1 2 3 4 5 6 7 8 9 10 11 12 13 14 15 16 17 18 19 20 21 22 23 24

SUMMER ONLY (J)   WINTER ONLY (D)   JAMMING / OR ∧   EARLIEST HEARD ⊲   LATEST HEARD ⊳   NEW OR CHANGED FOR 1994 †

FREQUENCY   COUNTRY, STATION, LOCATION   TARGET • NETWORK • POWER (kW)   World Time

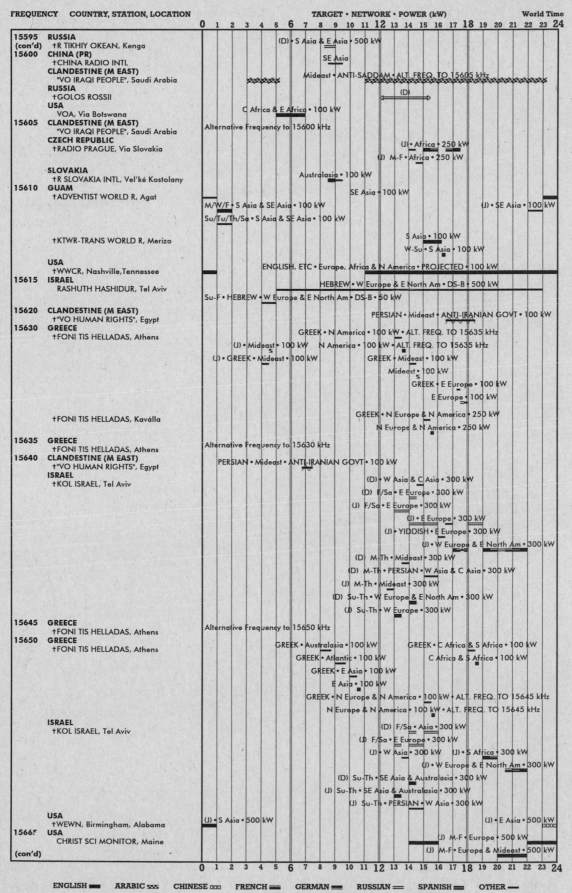

15595	RUSSIA
(con'd)	†R TIKHIY OKEAN, Kenga
15600	CHINA (PR)
	†CHINA RADIO INTL
	CLANDESTINE (M EAST)
	"VO IRAQI PEOPLE", Saudi Arabia
	RUSSIA
	†GOLOS ROSSII
	USA
	VOA, Via Botswana
15605	CLANDESTINE (M EAST)
	"VO IRAQI PEOPLE", Saudi Arabia
	CZECH REPUBLIC
	†RADIO PRAGUE, Via Slovakia
	SLOVAKIA
	†R SLOVAKIA INTL, Vel'ké Kostolany
15610	GUAM
	†ADVENTIST WORLD R, Agat
	†KTWR-TRANS WORLD R, Merizo
	USA
	†WWCR, Nashville,Tennessee
15615	ISRAEL
	RASHUTH HASHIDUR, Tel Aviv
15620	CLANDESTINE (M EAST)
	†"VO HUMAN RIGHTS", Egypt
15630	GREECE
	†FONI TIS HELLADAS, Athens
	†FONI TIS HELLADAS, Kaválla
15635	GREECE
	†FONI TIS HELLADAS, Athens
15640	CLANDESTINE (M EAST)
	†"VO HUMAN RIGHTS", Egypt
	ISRAEL
	†KOL ISRAEL, Tel Aviv
15645	GREECE
	†FONI TIS HELLADAS, Athens
15650	GREECE
	†FONI TIS HELLADAS, Athens
	ISRAEL
	†KOL ISRAEL, Tel Aviv
	USA
	†WEWN, Birmingham, Alabama
15665	USA
	CHRIST SCI MONITOR, Maine
(con'd)	

FREQUENCY COUNTRY, STATION, LOCATION

TARGET • NETWORK • POWER (kW)   World Time

0 1 2 3 4 5 6 7 8 9 10 11 12 13 14 15 16 17 18 19 20 21 22 23 24

15665	USA	
(con'd)	CHRIST SCI MONITOR, Maine	(J) • Sa • Europe • 500 kW
		(J) • Sa • Europe & Mideast • 500 kW
		(J) • Sa/Su • Europe • 500 kW
		(J) • Su • Europe • 500 kW
		(J) • Su • Europe & Mideast • 500 kW
		(J) • Sa • Europe • 1ST & 3RD SATURDAY • 500 kW
		(J) • Sa • Europe • 2ND SATURDAY • 500 kW
		(J) • Sa • Europe • 4TH SATURDAY • 500 kW
	CHRIST SCI MONITOR, South Carolina	(D) • M-F • E North Am & Europe • 500 kW
		(D) • Sa • E North Am & Europe • 500 kW
		(D) • Sa/Su • E North Am & C America • 500 kW
		(D) • Su • E North Am & Europe • 500 kW
	CHRIST SCI MONITOR, Via Saipan	Australasia • 100 kW (J) • Sa • Europe & Mideast • 100 kW
		(D) • Australasia • 100 kW
		M-F • Australasia • 100 kW (J) • Su-F • Europe & Mideast • 100 kW
		(D) • M-F • Australasia • 100 kW
		Sa/Su • Australasia • 100 kW
		(D) • Sa/Su • Australasia • 100 kW
15670	CHINA (PR)	
	CENTRAL PEOPLES BS, Kunming	DS-MINORITIES • 50 kW
15675	DENMARK	
	†WORLD MUSIC RADIO, Via Bulgaria	Alternative Frequency to 15720 kHz
	HONDURAS	
	†RADIO COPAN INTL, Tegucigalpa	M-Sa • ENGLISH & SPANISH • E North Am • 0.1 kW • ALT. FREQ. TO 9950 kHz
15685	USA	
	†WWCR, Nashville, Tennessee	E North Am & Europe • 100 kW
		(J) • E North Am & Europe • 100 kW
		M-F • E North Am & Europe • 100 kW
		M-W • E North Am & Europe • 100 kW
		Sa/Su • E North Am & Europe • 100 kW
		Th-Su • E North Am & Europe • 100 kW
15690	GUAM	
	†KTWR-TRANS WORLD R, Merizo	S Asia • 100 kW
15695	USA	
	†WEWN, Birmingham, Alabama	(D) • E Asia • 500 kW (D) • S America • 500 kW
		(J) • Europe • 500 kW
15710	CHINA (PR)	
	CENTRAL PEOPLES BS, Beijing	(J) • CHINESE, ETC • TAIWAN-1 • 10 kW
		CHINESE, ETC • TAIWAN-1 • 10 kW
15720	DENMARK	
	†WORLD MUSIC RADIO, Via Bulgaria	Su • Europe • PROJECTED • 50 kW • ALT. FREQ. TO 15675 kHz
15725	USA	
	†KCBI, Dallas, Texas	N America • 100 kW • ALT. FREQ. TO 13740 kHz
		N America • 100 kW • ALT. FREQ. TO 15375 kHz
15750	DENMARK	
	†WORLD MUSIC RADIO, Via Bulgaria	Su • Europe • PROJECTED • 50 kW
15770	ICELAND	
	†RIKISUTVARPID, Reykjavik	Atlantic & Europe • DS-1 • 10 kW • USB
		Atlantic & E North Am • DS-1 • 10 kW • USB
15880	CHINA (PR)	
	CENTRAL PEOPLES BS, Beijing	CHINESE, ETC • TAIWAN-2 • 15 kW
		(J) • CHINESE, ETC • TAIWAN-2 • 15 kW
		W-M • CHINESE, ETC • TAIWAN-2 • 15 kW
16000	AUSTRALIA	
	†VNG, Llandilo	WORLD TIME • 5 kW
17387	INDIA	
	†ALL INDIA RADIO, Aligarh	HINDI • Mideast & E Africa • 250 kW
		E Africa • 250 kW
		SE Asia • 250 kW
	†ALL INDIA RADIO, Bangalore	Australasia • 500 kW
		SE Asia • 500 kW
17440	KIRIBATI	
	†RADIO KIRIBATI, Betio	Irr • ENGLISH, ETC • DS(FEEDER) • 0.5 kW • USB • ALT. FREQ. TO 14917.7 kHz
		Irr • DS(FEEDER) • 0.5 kW • USB • ALT. FREQ. TO 14917.7 kHz
		M-Sa • ENGLISH, ETC • DS(FEEDER) • 0.5 kW • USB • ALT. FREQ. TO 14917.7 kHz
		Sa • ENGLISH, ETC • DS(FEEDER) • 0.5 kW • USB • ALT. FREQ. TO 14917.7 kHz
17490	ECUADOR	
	†HCJB-VO THE ANDES, Quito	Europe & Pacific • 10 kW • USB
		JAPANESE • Europe & Pacific • 10 kW • USB
17500	TUNISIA	
	RTV TUNISIENNE, Sfax	DS • 100 kW
17510	USA	
	CHRIST SCI MONITOR, Maine	(J) • E Africa • 500 kW
(con'd)		(D) • M-F • Europe • 500 kW

0 1 2 3 4 5 6 7 8 9 10 11 12 13 14 15 16 17 18 19 20 21 22 23 24

SUMMER ONLY (J)   WINTER ONLY (D)   JAMMING / OR ∧   EARLIEST HEARD ◁   LATEST HEARD ▷   NEW OR CHANGED FOR 1994 †

| FREQUENCY | COUNTRY, STATION, LOCATION | TARGET • NETWORK • POWER (kW) | World Time |

Time scale: 0 1 2 3 4 5 6 7 8 9 10 11 12 13 14 15 16 17 18 19 20 21 22 23 24

17510 USA
(con'd) CHRIST SCI MONITOR, Maine
- (J) • M-F • E Africa • 500 kW
- (D) • Sa • Europe • 500 kW
- (J) • Sa • E Africa • 500 kW
- (D) • Sa/Su • Europe • 500 kW
- (D) • Su • Europe • 500 kW
- (J) • Su • E Africa • 500 kW
- (D) • Sa • Europe • 1ST & 3RD SATURDAY • 500 kW
- (D) • Sa • Europe • 2ND SATURDAY • 500 kW
- (D) • Sa • Europe • 4TH SATURDAY • 500 kW

CHRIST SCI MONITOR, South Carolina
- (J) • M-F • E North Am & Europe • 500 kW
- (J) • Sa • E North Am & Europe • 500 kW
- (J) • Su • E North Am & Europe • 500 kW

†WEWN, Birmingham, Alabama
- (J) • Mideast • 500 kW
- (J) • E Asia • 500 kW

17515 BELGIUM
†R VLAANDEREN INTL, Wavre — Alternative Frequency to 17540 kHz
GREECE
†FONI TIS HELLADAS, Athens
- GREEK • N America • 100 kW
- N America • 100 kW

17525 GREECE
†FONI TIS HELLADAS, Athens
- GREEK • Australasia • 100 kW
- GREEK • C Africa & S Africa • 100 kW
- Australasia • 100 kW
- C Africa & S Africa • 100 kW
- GREEK • E Asia • 100 kW
- E Asia • 100 kW
- GREEK • N Europe & N America • 100 kW
- N Europe & N America • 100 kW

VATICAN STATE
†VATICAN RADIO, Sta Maria di Galeria
- E Asia • 500 kW
- SE Asia & Australasia • 100/500 kW
- SE Asia • 500 kW
- (J) • JAPANESE • E Asia • 500 kW

17535 CZECH REPUBLIC
†RADIO PRAGUE, Litomyšl
- Australasia • 100 kW
- (J) • W Africa • 100 kW
- (J) • Mideast & S Asia • 250 kW
- (J) • M-F • E Africa • 250 kW

†RADIO PRAGUE, Via Slovakia
SLOVAKIA
†R SLOVAKIA INTL, Rimavská Sobota
- Australasia • 250 kW
USA
†WEWN, Birmingham, Alabama
- (J) • N America & C America • 500 kW

17540 BELGIUM
†R VLAANDEREN INTL, Wavre
- DUTCH • Africa • 250 kW • ALT. FREQ. TO 17515 kHz
- DUTCH • SE Asia • 250 kW • ALT. FREQ. TO 17550 kHz
- Africa • 250 kW • ALT. FREQ. TO 17515 kHz
- M-Sa • DUTCH • SE Asia • 250 kW • ALT. FREQ. TO 17550 kHz
- M-Sa • SE Asia • 250 kW • ALT. FREQ. TO 17550 kHz
- Su • Africa • 250 kW • ALT. FREQ. TO 17515 kHz
- Su • DUTCH • Africa • 250 kW • ALT. FREQ. TO 17515 kHz
- Su • SE Asia • 250 kW • ALT. FREQ. TO 17550 kHz

17540v PAKISTAN
†RADIO PAKISTAN, Karachi
- Mideast • 50 kW

17545 ISRAEL
†KOL ISRAEL, Tel Aviv
- W Europe • 50/300 kW

†RASHUTH HASHIDUR, Tel Aviv
- HEBREW • W Europe • DS-B • 50/300 kW
- (J) • HEBREW • W Europe & E North Am • DS-B • 50/300 kW

17550 BELGIUM
†R VLAANDEREN INTL, Wavre — Alternative Frequency to 17540 kHz
GREECE
FONI TIS HELLADAS, Athens
- (D) • GREEK • Australasia • 100 kW
- (D) • Australasia • 100 kW

VATICAN STATE
†VATICAN RADIO, Sta Maria di Galeria
- (J) • E Europe & W Asia • 100 kW
- (J) • W Europe • 100 kW

17555 USA
CHRIST SCI MONITOR, South Carolina
- M-F • S America • 500 kW
- Sa • W North Am & C America • 500 kW
- Sa • S America • 500 kW
- Su • W North Am & C America • 500 kW
- Su • S America • 500 kW

CHRIST SCI MONITOR, Via Saipan
- SE Asia • 100 kW
- M-Sa • SE Asia • 100 kW
- E Asia • 100 kW
- Sa • SE Asia • 100 kW
- Su • SE Asia • 100 kW
- Sa • E Asia • 100 kW
- Sa/Su • SE Asia • 100 kW

(con'd)

Time scale: 0 1 2 3 4 5 6 7 8 9 10 11 12 13 14 15 16 17 18 19 20 21 22 23 24

ENGLISH ▬   ARABIC ≋   CHINESE ▭▭▭   FRENCH ▬   GERMAN ▬   RUSSIAN ══   SPANISH ▬   OTHER —

FREQUENCY   COUNTRY, STATION, LOCATION

TARGET • NETWORK • POWER (kW)   World Time

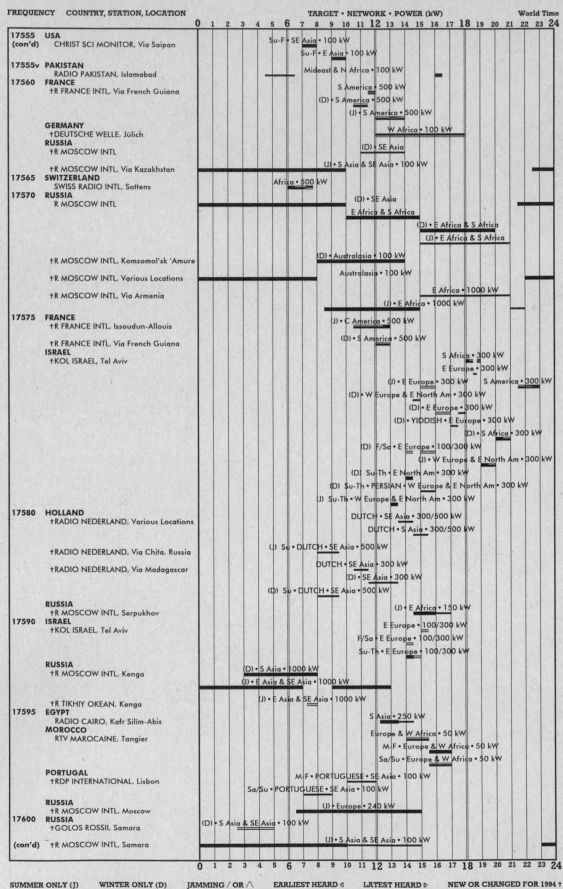

Frequency	Country, Station, Location	Target • Network • Power
17555 (con'd)	**USA** CHRIST SCI MONITOR, Via Saipan	Su-F • SE Asia • 100 kW / Su-F • E Asia • 100 kW
17555v	**PAKISTAN** RADIO PAKISTAN, Islamabad	Mideast & N Africa • 100 kW
17560	**FRANCE** †R FRANCE INTL, Via French Guiana	S America • 500 kW / (D) S America • 500 kW / (J) S America • 500 kW
	GERMANY †DEUTSCHE WELLE, Jülich	W Africa • 100 kW
	RUSSIA †R MOSCOW INTL	(D) • SE Asia
	†R MOSCOW INTL, Via Kazakhstan	(J) • S Asia & SE Asia • 100 kW
17565	**SWITZERLAND** SWISS RADIO INTL, Sottens	Africa • 500 kW
17570	**RUSSIA** R MOSCOW INTL	(D) • SE Asia / E Africa & S Africa / (D) • E Africa & S Africa / (J) • E Africa & S Africa
	†R MOSCOW INTL, Komsomol'sk 'Amure	(D) • Australasia • 100 kW
	†R MOSCOW INTL, Various Locations	Australasia • 100 kW
	†R MOSCOW INTL, Via Armenia	E Africa • 1000 kW / (J) • E Africa • 1000 kW
17575	**FRANCE** †R FRANCE INTL, Issoudun-Allouis	(J) • C America • 500 kW
	†R FRANCE INTL, Via French Guiana	(D) • S America • 500 kW
	ISRAEL †KOL ISRAEL, Tel Aviv	S Africa • 300 kW / E Europe • 300 kW / (J) • E Europe • 300 kW S America • 300 kW / (D) • W Europe & E North Am • 300 kW / (D) • E Europe • 300 kW / (D) • YIDDISH • E Europe • 300 kW / (D) • S Africa • 300 kW / (D) F/Sa • E Europe • 100/300 kW / (J) • W Europe & E North Am • 300 kW / (D) Su-Th • E North Am • 300 kW / (D) Su-Th • PERSIAN • W Europe & E North Am • 300 kW / (J) Su-Th • W Europe & E North Am • 300 kW
17580	**HOLLAND** †RADIO NEDERLAND, Various Locations	DUTCH • SE Asia • 300/500 kW / DUTCH • S Asia • 300/500 kW
	†RADIO NEDERLAND, Via Chita, Russia	(J) Su • DUTCH • SE Asia • 500 kW
	†RADIO NEDERLAND, Via Madagascar	DUTCH • SE Asia • 300 kW / (D) • SE Asia • 300 kW / (D) Su • DUTCH • SE Asia • 500 kW
	RUSSIA †R MOSCOW INTL, Serpukhov	(J) • E Africa • 150 kW
17590	**ISRAEL** †KOL ISRAEL, Tel Aviv	E Europe • 100/300 kW / F/Sa • E Europe • 100/300 kW / Su-Th • E Europe • 100/300 kW
	RUSSIA †R MOSCOW INTL, Kenga	(D) • S Asia • 1000 kW / (J) • E Asia & SE Asia • 1000 kW
	†R TIKHIY OKEAN, Kenga	(J) • E Asia & SE Asia • 1000 kW
17595	**EGYPT** RADIO CAIRO, Kafr Silim-Abis	S Asia • 250 kW
	MOROCCO RTV MAROCAINE, Tangier	Europe & W Africa • 50 kW / M-F • Europe & W Africa • 50 kW / Sa/Su • Europe & W Africa • 50 kW
	PORTUGAL †RDP INTERNATIONAL, Lisbon	M-F • PORTUGUESE • SE Asia • 100 kW / Sa/Su • PORTUGUESE • SE Asia • 100 kW
	RUSSIA †R MOSCOW INTL, Moscow	(J) • Europe • 240 kW
17600	**RUSSIA** †GOLOS ROSSII, Samara	(D) • S Asia & SE Asia • 100 kW
(con'd)	†R MOSCOW INTL, Samara	(J) • S Asia & SE Asia • 100 kW

FREQUENCY	COUNTRY, STATION, LOCATION	TARGET • NETWORK • POWER (kW)

World Time
0 1 2 3 4 5 6 7 8 9 10 11 12 13 14 15 16 17 18 19 20 21 22 23 24

17600 **RUSSIA**
(con'd) †R MOSCOW INTL, Samara — (D) • S Asia & SE Asia • 100 kW

17605 **ARMENIA**
†RADIO YEREVAN, Via Petro-K, Russia — (D) • ARMENIAN • W North Am • 100 kW
(D) • W North Am • 100 kW

BYELARUS
†RS BYELARUS, Via Petro-K, Russia — (D) • W North Am • 100 kW

CHINA (PR)
†CENTRAL PEOPLES BS, Beijing — DS-1 • 15 kW
W-M • DS-1 • 15 kW

HOLLAND
†RADIO NEDERLAND, Via Neth Antilles — W Africa • 250 kW
DUTCH • W Africa • 250 kW
Su • DUTCH • E North Am • 250 kW

KAZAKHSTAN
†KAZAKH RADIO, Almaty — DS-2 • 20 kW
†RADIO ALMATY, Almaty — 20 kW

RUSSIA
†R MOSCOW INTL, Petropavlovsk-K — (J) • W North Am • NORTH AMERICAN SVC • 240 kW   (D) • W North Am • 240 kW
†R MOSCOW INTL, Serpukhov — (J) • Europe & W Africa • 500 kW
†R TIKHIY OKEAN, Petropavlovsk-K — (J) • W North Am • 240 kW

UKRAINE
†RADIO UKRAINE, Via Petro-K, Russia — (D) • W North Am • 100 kW
(D) • UKRAINIAN • W North Am • 100 kW

17610 **HOLLAND**
†RADIO NEDERLAND, Flevoland — SE Asia • 500 kW
S Asia • 500 kW

RUSSIA
†GOLOS ROSSII, Chita — (J) • E Asia • 1000 kW
†R MOSCOW INTL, Moscow — (D) • S Asia & SE Asia • 100 kW

17612.5 **USA**
†CHRIST SCI MONITOR, Maine — (J) • S Africa • 500 kW
(J) • M-F • S Africa • 500 kW
(J) • Sa • S Africa • 500 kW
(J) • Su • S Africa • 500 kW
(J) • W Africa • 100 kW
WYFR-FAMILY RADIO, Okeechobee, Fl

17615 **RUSSIA**
†R MOSCOW INTL, Serpukhov — (D) • N Africa & W Africa • 50 kW

17620 **FRANCE**
†R FRANCE INTL, Issoudun-Allouis — Africa • 100/500 kW
(J) • E Africa • 100 kW
R FRANCE INTL, Multiple Locations — W Africa • 500 kW
R FRANCE INTL, Via French Guiana — S America • 500 kW
C America • 500 kW

GERMANY
†DEUTSCHE WELLE, Via Samara, Russia — (J) • S Asia • 250 kW
(J) • W Asia • 250 kW

RUSSIA
†GOLOS ROSSII, Nizhniy Novgorod — (J) • S Asia • 240 kW
†R MOSCOW INTL, Novosibirsk — (D) • E Asia & SE Asia • 500 kW
†R TIKHIY OKEAN, Novosibirsk — (D) • E Asia & SE Asia • 500 kW

17625 **RUSSIA**
†R MOSCOW INTL, Armavir — (D) • Mideast & E Africa • 100 kW   (J) • Mideast & E Africa • 100 kW
†R MOSCOW INTL, Via Moldova — (D) • S Africa • 500 kW

17630 **GABON**
AFRIQUE NUMERO UN, Moyabi — W Africa • 250 kW

17635 **RUSSIA**
†R MOSCOW INTL, Tula — S Asia & SE Asia • 250/500 kW
(D) • S Asia & SE Asia • 500 kW
(J) • S Asia & SE Asia • 250 kW

SWITZERLAND
SWISS RADIO INTL, Schwarzenburg — E Africa • 100/250 kW
ITALIAN • E Africa • 100/250 kW

17640 **RUSSIA**
†R MOSCOW INTL, Zhigulevsk — (J) • Mideast & E Africa • 250 kW

UNITED KINGDOM
†BBC, Multiple Locations — Europe & N Africa • 250/300/500 kW
†BBC, Skelton, Cumbria — (J) • E Europe & Mideast • 300 kW
†BBC, Woofferton — (J) • Europe • 250 kW

USA
VOA, Greenville, NC — W Africa • 500 kW
M-F • W Africa • 500 kW
Sa/Su • W Africa • 500 kW

17645 **RUSSIA**
(con'd) †GOLOS ROSSII, Armavir — (D) • SE Asia • 250 kW

0 1 2 3 4 5 6 7 8 9 10 11 12 13 14 15 16 17 18 19 20 21 22 23 24

ENGLISH ▬▬ ARABIC ✕✕✕ CHINESE □□□ FRENCH ═══ GERMAN ▬▬ RUSSIAN ══ SPANISH ▬▬ OTHER ▬▬

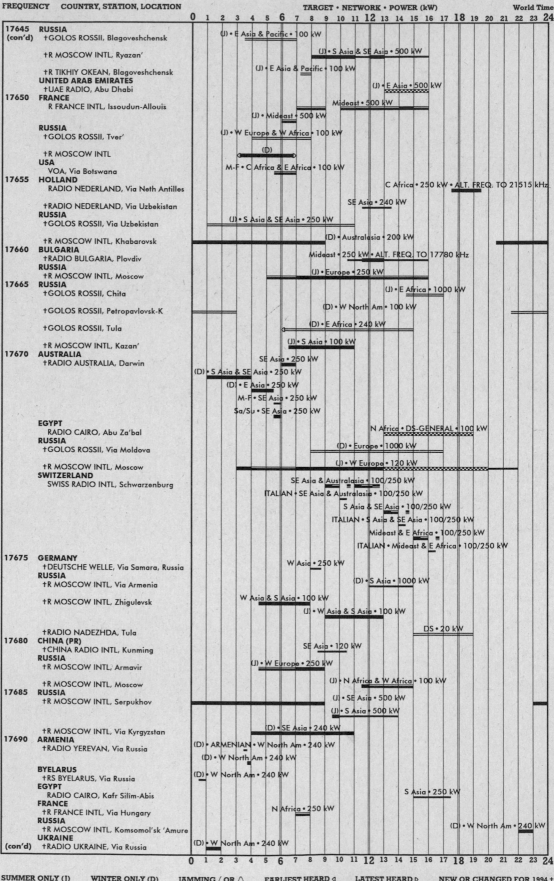

FREQUENCY   COUNTRY, STATION, LOCATION

TARGET • NETWORK • POWER (kW)   World Time

17645	RUSSIA	
(con'd)	†GOLOS ROSSII, Blagoveshchensk	(J) • E Asia & Pacific • 100 kW
	†R MOSCOW INTL, Ryazan'	(J) • S Asia & SE Asia • 500 kW
	†R TIKHIY OKEAN, Blagoveshchensk	(J) • E Asia & Pacific • 100 kW
	UNITED ARAB EMIRATES	
	†UAE RADIO, Abu Dhabi	(J) • E Asia • 500 kW
17650	FRANCE	
	R FRANCE INTL, Issoudun-Allouis	Mideast • 500 kW
		(J) • Mideast • 500 kW
	RUSSIA	
	†GOLOS ROSSII, Tver'	(J) • W Europe & W Africa • 100 kW
	†R MOSCOW INTL	(D)
	USA	
	VOA, Via Botswana	M-F • C Africa & E Africa • 100 kW
17655	HOLLAND	
	RADIO NEDERLAND, Via Neth Antilles	C Africa • 250 kW • ALT. FREQ. TO 21515 kHz
	†RADIO NEDERLAND, Via Uzbekistan	SE Asia • 240 kW
	RUSSIA	
	†GOLOS ROSSII, Via Uzbekistan	(J) • S Asia & SE Asia • 250 kW
	†R MOSCOW INTL, Khabarovsk	(D) • Australasia • 200 kW
17660	BULGARIA	
	†RADIO BULGARIA, Plovdiv	Mideast • 250 kW • ALT. FREQ. TO 17780 kHz
	RUSSIA	
	†R MOSCOW INTL, Moscow	(J) • Europe • 250 kW
17665	RUSSIA	
	†GOLOS ROSSII, Chita	(J) • E Africa • 1000 kW
	†GOLOS ROSSII, Petropavlovsk-K	(D) • W North Am • 100 kW
	†GOLOS ROSSII, Tula	(D) • E Africa • 240 kW
	†R MOSCOW INTL, Kazan'	(J) • S Asia • 100 kW
17670	AUSTRALIA	
	†RADIO AUSTRALIA, Darwin	SE Asia • 250 kW
		(D) • S Asia & SE Asia • 250 kW
		(D) • E Asia • 250 kW
		M-F • SE Asia • 250 kW
		Sa/Su • SE Asia • 250 kW
	EGYPT	
	RADIO CAIRO, Abu Za'bal	N Africa • DS-GENERAL • 100 kW
	RUSSIA	
	†GOLOS ROSSII, Via Moldova	(D) • Europe • 1000 kW
	†R MOSCOW INTL, Moscow	(J) • W Europe • 120 kW
	SWITZERLAND	
	SWISS RADIO INTL, Schwarzenburg	SE Asia & Australasia • 100/250 kW
		ITALIAN • SE Asia & Australasia • 100/250 kW
		S Asia & SE Asia • 100/250 kW
		ITALIAN • S Asia & SE Asia • 100/250 kW
		Mideast & E Africa • 100/250 kW
		ITALIAN • Mideast & E Africa • 100/250 kW
17675	GERMANY	
	†DEUTSCHE WELLE, Via Samara, Russia	W Asia • 250 kW
	RUSSIA	
	†R MOSCOW INTL, Via Armenia	(D) • S Asia • 1000 kW
	†R MOSCOW INTL, Zhigulevsk	W Asia & S Asia • 100 kW
		(J) • W Asia & S Asia • 100 kW
	†RADIO NADEZHDA, Tula	DS • 20 kW
17680	CHINA (PR)	
	†CHINA RADIO INTL, Kunming	SE Asia • 120 kW
	RUSSIA	
	†R MOSCOW INTL, Armavir	(J) • W Europe • 250 kW
	†R MOSCOW INTL, Moscow	(J) • N Africa & W Africa • 100 kW
17685	RUSSIA	
	†R MOSCOW INTL, Serpukhov	(J) • SE Asia • 500 kW
		(J) • S Asia • 500 kW
	†R MOSCOW INTL, Via Kyrgyzstan	(D) • SE Asia • 240 kW
17690	ARMENIA	
	†RADIO YEREVAN, Via Russia	(D) • ARMENIAN • W North Am • 240 kW
		(D) • W North Am • 240 kW
	BYELARUS	
	†RS BYELARUS, Via Russia	(D) • W North Am • 240 kW
	EGYPT	
	RADIO CAIRO, Kafr Silim-Abis	S Asia • 250 kW
	FRANCE	
	†R FRANCE INTL, Via Hungary	N Africa • 250 kW
	RUSSIA	
	†R MOSCOW INTL, Komsomol'sk 'Amure	(D) • W North Am • 240 kW
	UKRAINE	
(con'd)	†RADIO UKRAINE, Via Russia	(D) • W North Am • 240 kW

FREQUENCY   COUNTRY, STATION, LOCATION   TARGET • NETWORK • POWER (kW)   World Time

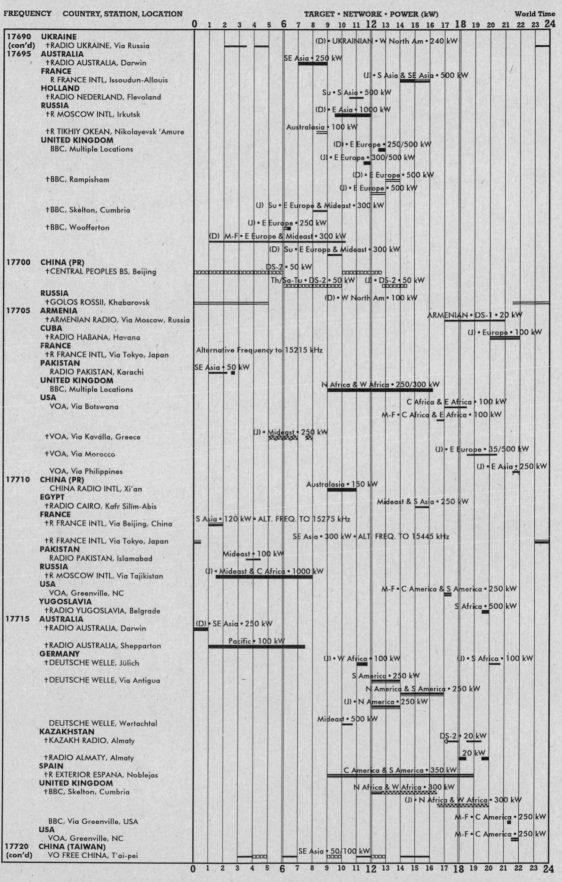

Frequency	Country, Station, Location	Target • Network • Power (kW)
17690 (con'd)	**UKRAINE** †RADIO UKRAINE, Via Russia	(D) • UKRAINIAN • W North Am • 240 kW
17695	**AUSTRALIA** †RADIO AUSTRALIA, Darwin	SE Asia • 250 kW
	FRANCE R FRANCE INTL, Issoudun-Allouis	(J) • S Asia & SE Asia • 500 kW
	HOLLAND †RADIO NEDERLAND, Flevoland	Su • S Asia • 500 kW
	RUSSIA †R MOSCOW INTL, Irkutsk	(D) • E Asia • 1000 kW
	†R TIKHIY OKEAN, Nikolayevsk 'Amure	Australasia • 100 kW
	UNITED KINGDOM BBC, Multiple Locations	(D) • E Europe • 250/500 kW (J) • E Europe • 300/500 kW
	†BBC, Rampisham	(D) • E Europe • 500 kW (J) • E Europe • 500 kW
	†BBC, Skelton, Cumbria	(J) Su • E Europe & Mideast • 300 kW
	†BBC, Woofferton	(J) • E Europe • 250 kW (D) M-F • E Europe & Mideast • 300 kW (D) Su • E Europe & Mideast • 300 kW
17700	**CHINA (PR)** †CENTRAL PEOPLES BS, Beijing	DS-2 • 50 kW Th/Sa-Tu • DS-2 • 50 kW (J) • DS-2 • 50 kW
	RUSSIA †GOLOS ROSSII, Khabarovsk	(D) • W North Am • 100 kW
17705	**ARMENIA** †ARMENIAN RADIO, Via Moscow, Russia	ARMENIAN • DS-1 • 20 kW
	CUBA †RADIO HABANA, Havana	(J) • Europe • 100 kW
	FRANCE †R FRANCE INTL, Via Tokyo, Japan	Alternative Frequency to 15215 kHz
	PAKISTAN RADIO PAKISTAN, Karachi	SE Asia • 50 kW
	UNITED KINGDOM BBC, Multiple Locations	N Africa & W Africa • 250/300 kW
	USA VOA, Via Botswana	C Africa & E Africa • 100 kW M-F • C Africa & E Africa • 100 kW
	†VOA, Via Kaválla, Greece	(J) • Mideast • 250 kW
	†VOA, Via Morocco	(J) • E Europe • 35/500 kW
	VOA, Via Philippines	(J) • E Asia • 250 kW
17710	**CHINA (PR)** CHINA RADIO INTL, Xi'an	Australasia • 150 kW
	EGYPT †RADIO CAIRO, Kafr Silim-Abis	Mideast & S Asia • 250 kW
	FRANCE †R FRANCE INTL, Via Beijing, China	S Asia • 120 kW • ALT. FREQ. TO 15275 kHz
	†R FRANCE INTL, Via Tokyo, Japan	SE Asia • 300 kW • ALT. FREQ. TO 15445 kHz
	PAKISTAN RADIO PAKISTAN, Islamabad	Mideast • 100 kW
	RUSSIA †R MOSCOW INTL, Via Tajikistan	(J) • Mideast & C Africa • 1000 kW
	USA VOA, Greenville, NC	M-F • C America & S America • 250 kW
	YUGOSLAVIA †RADIO YUGOSLAVIA, Belgrade	S Africa • 500 kW
17715	**AUSTRALIA** †RADIO AUSTRALIA, Darwin	(D) • SE Asia • 250 kW
	†RADIO AUSTRALIA, Shepparton	Pacific • 100 kW
	GERMANY †DEUTSCHE WELLE, Jülich	(J) • W Africa • 100 kW (J) • S Africa • 100 kW
	†DEUTSCHE WELLE, Via Antigua	S America • 250 kW N America & S America • 250 kW (J) • N America • 250 kW
	DEUTSCHE WELLE, Wertachtal	Mideast • 500 kW
	KAZAKHSTAN †KAZAKH RADIO, Almaty	DS-2 • 20 kW
	†RADIO ALMATY, Almaty	20 kW
	SPAIN †R EXTERIOR ESPANA, Noblejas	C America & S America • 350 kW
	UNITED KINGDOM †BBC, Skelton, Cumbria	N Africa & W Africa • 300 kW (J) • N Africa & W Africa • 300 kW
	BBC, Via Greenville, USA	M-F • C America • 250 kW
	USA VOA, Greenville, NC	M-F • C America • 250 kW
17720 (con'd)	**CHINA (TAIWAN)** VO FREE CHINA, T'ai-pei	SE Asia • 50/100 kW

ENGLISH ▬▬   ARABIC ⨯⨯⨯   CHINESE ▭▭▭   FRENCH ═══   GERMAN ▬▬   RUSSIAN ══   SPANISH ▭▭   OTHER ▬▬

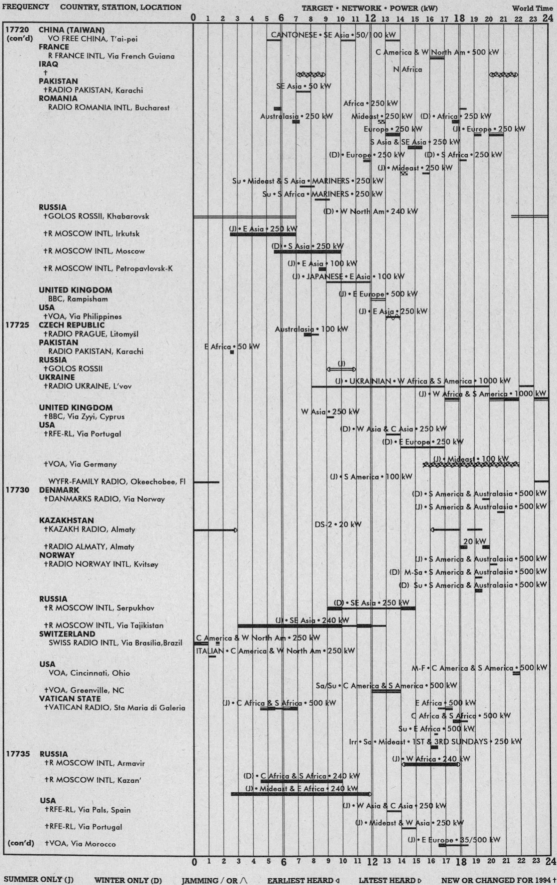

FREQUENCY   COUNTRY, STATION, LOCATION

TARGET • NETWORK • POWER (kW)

World Time

17720 CHINA (TAIWAN)
(con'd)   VO FREE CHINA, T'ai-pei — CANTONESE • SE Asia • 50/100 kW
         FRANCE
         R FRANCE INTL, Via French Guiana — C America & W North Am • 500 kW
         IRAQ
         † — N Africa
         PAKISTAN
         †RADIO PAKISTAN, Karachi — SE Asia • 50 kW
         ROMANIA
         RADIO ROMANIA INTL, Bucharest — Africa • 250 kW
            Australasia • 250 kW   Mideast • 250 kW   (D) • Africa • 250 kW
            Europe • 250 kW   (J) • Europe • 250 kW
            S Asia & SE Asia • 250 kW
            (D) • Europe • 250 kW   (D) • S Africa • 250 kW
            (J) • Mideast • 250 kW
            Su • Mideast & S Asia • MARINERS • 250 kW
            Su • S Africa • MARINERS • 250 kW

         RUSSIA
         †GOLOS ROSSII, Khabarovsk — (D) • W North Am • 240 kW
         †R MOSCOW INTL, Irkutsk — (J) • E Asia • 250 kW
         †R MOSCOW INTL, Moscow — (D) • S Asia • 250 kW
         †R MOSCOW INTL, Petropavlovsk-K — (J) • E Asia • 100 kW
            (J) • JAPANESE • E Asia • 100 kW
         UNITED KINGDOM
         BBC, Rampisham — (J) • E Europe • 500 kW
         USA
         †VOA, Via Philippines — (J) • E Asia • 250 kW
17725 CZECH REPUBLIC
         †RADIO PRAGUE, Litomyšl — Australasia • 100 kW
         PAKISTAN
         RADIO PAKISTAN, Karachi — E Africa • 50 kW
         RUSSIA
         †GOLOS ROSSII — (J)
         UKRAINE
         †RADIO UKRAINE, L'vov — (J) • UKRAINIAN • W Africa & S America • 1000 kW
            (J) • W Africa & S America • 1000 kW
         UNITED KINGDOM
         †BBC, Via Zyyi, Cyprus — W Asia • 250 kW
         USA
         †RFE-RL, Via Portugal — (D) • W Asia & C Asia • 250 kW
            (D) • E Europe • 250 kW
         †VOA, Via Germany — (J) • Mideast • 100 kW
         WYFR-FAMILY RADIO, Okeechobee, Fl — (J) • S America • 100 kW
17730 DENMARK
         †DANMARKS RADIO, Via Norway — (D) • S America & Australasia • 500 kW
            (J) • S America & Australasia • 500 kW
         KAZAKHSTAN
         †KAZAKH RADIO, Almaty — DS-2 • 20 kW
         †RADIO ALMATY, Almaty — 20 kW
         NORWAY
         RADIO NORWAY INTL, Kvitsøy — (J) • S America & Australasia • 500 kW
            (D) • M-Sa • S America & Australasia • 500 kW
            (D) • Su • S America & Australasia • 500 kW
         RUSSIA
         †R MOSCOW INTL, Serpukhov — (D) • SE Asia • 250 kW
         †R MOSCOW INTL, Via Tajikistan — (J) • SE Asia • 240 kW
         SWITZERLAND
         SWISS RADIO INTL, Via Brasilia, Brazil — C America & W North Am • 250 kW
            ITALIAN • C America & W North Am • 250 kW
         USA
         VOA, Cincinnati, Ohio — M-F • C America & S America • 500 kW
         †VOA, Greenville, NC — Sa/Su • C America & S America • 500 kW
         VATICAN STATE
         †VATICAN RADIO, Sta Maria di Galeria — (J) • C Africa & S Africa • 500 kW
            E Africa • 500 kW
            C Africa & S Africa • 500 kW
            Su • E Africa • 500 kW
            Irr • Sa • Mideast • 1ST & 3RD SUNDAYS • 250 kW
17735 RUSSIA
         †R MOSCOW INTL, Armavir — (J) • W Africa • 240 kW
         †R MOSCOW INTL, Kazan' — (D) • C Africa & S Africa • 240 kW
            (J) • Mideast & E Africa • 240 kW
         USA
         †RFE-RL, Via Pals, Spain — (J) • W Asia & C Asia • 250 kW
         †RFE-RL, Via Portugal — (J) • Mideast & W Asia • 250 kW
(con'd)   †VOA, Via Morocco — (J) • E Europe • 35/500 kW

SUMMER ONLY (J)   WINTER ONLY (D)   JAMMING / OR ∧   EARLIEST HEARD ◁   LATEST HEARD ▷   NEW OR CHANGED FOR 1994 †

FREQUENCY   COUNTRY, STATION, LOCATION

TARGET • NETWORK • POWER (kW)

World Time

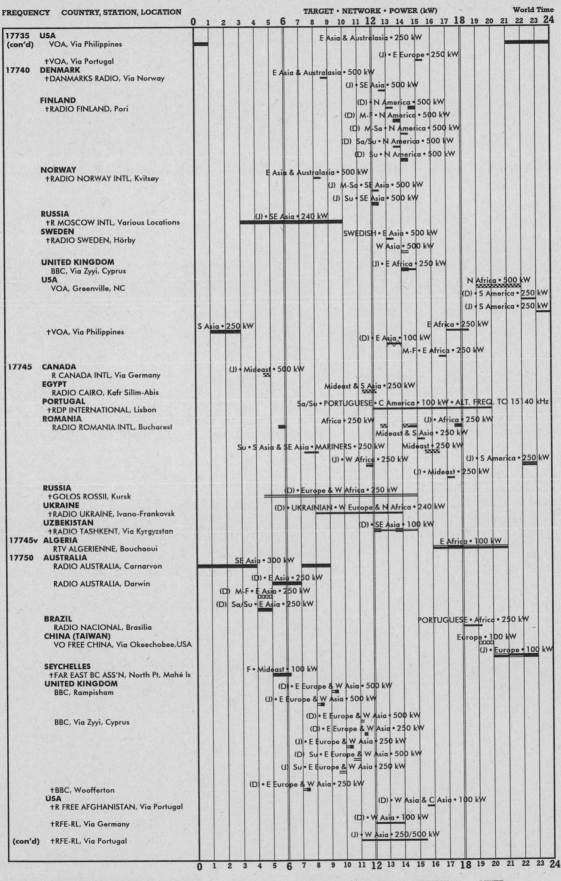

Frequency	Country, Station, Location	Network/Target/Power
17735 (con'd)	USA · VOA, Via Philippines	E Asia & Australasia • 250 kW
	†VOA, Via Portugal	(J) • E Europe • 250 kW
17740	DENMARK · †DANMARKS RADIO, Via Norway	E Asia & Australasia • 500 kW / (J) • SE Asia • 500 kW
	FINLAND · †RADIO FINLAND, Pori	(D) • N America • 500 kW / (D) M-F • N America • 500 kW / (D) M-Sa • N America • 500 kW / (D) Sa/Su • N America • 500 kW / (D) Su • N America • 500 kW
	NORWAY · †RADIO NORWAY INTL, Kvitsøy	E Asia & Australasia • 500 kW / (J) M-Sa • SE Asia • 500 kW / (J) Su • SE Asia • 500 kW
	RUSSIA · †R MOSCOW INTL, Various Locations	(J) • SE Asia • 240 kW
	SWEDEN · †RADIO SWEDEN, Hörby	SWEDISH • E Asia • 500 kW / W Asia • 500 kW
	UNITED KINGDOM · BBC, Via Zyyi, Cyprus	(J) • E Africa • 250 kW
	USA · VOA, Greenville, NC	N Africa • 500 kW / (D) • S America • 250 kW / (J) • S America • 250 kW
	†VOA, Via Philippines	S Asia • 250 kW / E Africa • 250 kW / (D) • E Asia • 100 kW / M-F • E Africa • 250 kW
17745	CANADA · R CANADA INTL, Via Germany	(J) • Mideast • 500 kW
	EGYPT · RADIO CAIRO, Kafr Silim-Abis	Mideast & S Asia • 250 kW
	PORTUGAL · †RDP INTERNATIONAL, Lisbon	Sa/Su • PORTUGUESE • C America • 100 kW • ALT. FREQ. TO 15140 kHz
	ROMANIA · RADIO ROMANIA INTL, Bucharest	Africa • 250 kW / (J) • Africa • 250 kW / Mideast & S Asia • 250 kW / Su • S Asia & SE Asia • MARINERS • 250 kW / Mideast • 250 kW / (J) • W Africa • 250 kW / (J) • S America • 250 kW / (J) • Mideast • 250 kW
	RUSSIA · †GOLOS ROSSII, Kursk	(D) • Europe & W Africa • 250 kW
	UKRAINE · †RADIO UKRAINE, Ivano-Frankovsk	(D) • UKRAINIAN • W Europe & N Africa • 240 kW
	UZBEKISTAN · †RADIO TASHKENT, Via Kyrgyzstan	(D) • SE Asia • 100 kW
17745v	ALGERIA · RTV ALGERIENNE, Bouchaoui	E Africa • 100 kW
17750	AUSTRALIA · RADIO AUSTRALIA, Carnarvon	SE Asia • 300 kW / (D) • E Asia • 250 kW
	RADIO AUSTRALIA, Darwin	(D) M-F • E Asia • 250 kW / (D) Sa/Su • E Asia • 250 kW
	BRAZIL · RADIO NACIONAL, Brasília	PORTUGUESE • Africa • 250 kW
	CHINA (TAIWAN) · VO FREE CHINA, Via Okeechobee, USA	Europe • 100 kW / (J) • Europe • 100 kW
	SEYCHELLES · †FAR EAST BC ASS'N, North Pt, Mahé Is	F • Mideast • 100 kW
	UNITED KINGDOM · BBC, Rampisham	(D) • E Europe & W Asia • 500 kW / (J) • E Europe & W Asia • 500 kW
	BBC, Via Zyyi, Cyprus	(D) • E Europe & W Asia • 500 kW / (D) • E Europe & W Asia • 250 kW / (J) • E Europe & W Asia • 250 kW / (D) Su • E Europe & W Asia • 500 kW / (J) Su • E Europe & W Asia • 250 kW
	†BBC, Woofferton	(D) • E Europe & W Asia • 250 kW
	USA · †R FREE AFGHANISTAN, Via Portugal	(D) • W Asia & C Asia • 100 kW
	†RFE-RL, Via Germany	(D) • W Asia • 100 kW
(con'd)	†RFE-RL, Via Portugal	(J) • W Asia • 250/500 kW

ENGLISH ▬▬   ARABIC ⋙   CHINESE □□□   FRENCH ══   GERMAN ▭▭   RUSSIAN ══   SPANISH ══   OTHER ──

FREQUENCY   COUNTRY, STATION, LOCATION

TARGET • NETWORK • POWER (kW)   World Time

0 1 2 3 4 5 6 7 8 9 10 11 12 13 14 15 16 17 18 19 20 21 22 23 24

17750	USA	
(con'd)	WYFR-FAMILY RADIO, Okeechobee, Fl	(J) • S America • 100 kW
		Europe • 100 kW
		(J) • C America • 100 kW (D) • W Africa • 100 kW
17755	CHINA (PR)	C America & S America • 250 kW
	CHINA RADIO INTL, Via Brasília, Brazil	
	RUSSIA	(D) • SE Asia • 240 kW
	†R MOSCOW INTL, Via Uzbekistan	(J) • S Asia & SE Asia • 100 kW
	SAUDI ARABIA	(J) • E Africa & S Africa • 500 kW
	†BS OF THE KINGDOM, Riyadh	
	SPAIN	W Africa & S Africa • 350 kW • ALT. FREQ. TO 21555 kHz
	†R EXTERIOR ESPANA, Noblejas	F-W • W Africa & S Africa • 350 kW • ALT. FREQ. TO 21555 kHz
	USA	(D) • S Africa • 250 kW
	†VOA, Via Ascension	(J) • W Africa • 250 kW
		(D) M-F • S Africa • 250 kW
		(J) M-F • W Africa • 250 kW
		(J) Sa/Su • W Africa • 250 kW
17760	CUBA	(J) • Europe & N Africa • 100 kW
	†RADIO HABANA, Havana	
	PHILIPPINES	S Asia • 250 kW
	RADYO PILIPINAS, Tinang	
	RUSSIA	(J) • W Europe & E North Am • 500 kW
	†R MOSCOW INTL, Via Moldova	
	SAUDI ARABIA	(D) • E Africa & S Africa • 500 kW
	†BS OF THE KINGDOM, Riyadh	
	UNITED KINGDOM	E Africa • 100/250 kW
	†BBC, Via Zyyi, Cyprus	
	USA	(J) • Mideast & W Asia • 250 kW
	†RFE-RL, Via Portugal	
	†VOA, Via Kaválla, Greece	(J) • Mideast • 250 kW
	†WYFR-FAMILY RADIO, Okeechobee, Fl	(D) • C America • 100 kW
17765	GERMANY	Africa • 250 kW
	†DEUTSCHE WELLE, Via Sri Lanka	(J) • Africa • 250 kW
	†DEUTSCHE WELLE, Wertachtal	W Africa • 500 kW (J) • W Africa • 500 kW
		E Africa • 500 kW
		Africa • 500 kW
	KAZAKHSTAN	DS-2 • 20 kW
	†KAZAKH RADIO, Almaty	
	†RADIO ALMATY, Almaty	20 kW
	KOREA (DPR)	SE Asia • 200 kW
	†RADIO PYONGYANG, Kujang-dong	KOREAN • SE Asia • 200 kW
	RUSSIA	(D) • S Asia & SE Asia • 1000 kW
	†R MOSCOW INTL, Armavir	
	USA	E Asia • 250 kW
	†VOA, Via Philippines	
17770	EGYPT	SE Asia • 250 kW
	RADIO CAIRO, Kafr Silim-Abis	
	HUNGARY	HUNGARIAN • Asia
	†RADIO BUDAPEST	
	QATAR	(J) • Europe • 100/250 kW
	QATAR BC SERVICE, Doha-Al Khaisah	
	USA	(J) • Mideast & W Asia • 500 kW
	VOA, Via Germany	
	VOA, Via Morocco	(J) • E Europe • 35/500 kW
17770v	EGYPT	S America • 250 kW
	RADIO CAIRO, Kafr Silim-Abis	
17775	FRANCE	E Africa • MEDIAS FRANCE • 100 kW
	R FRANCE INTL, Issoudun-Allouis	
	JAPAN	E Asia • 300 kW • ALT. FREQ. TO 17835 kHz
	†RADIO JAPAN/NHK, Tokyo-Yamata	E Asia • GENERAL • 300 kW • ALT FREQ. TO 17835 kHz
		JAPANESE • E Asia • GENERAL • 300 kW • ALT. FREQ. TO 17835 kHz
	†RADIO JAPAN/NHK, Via Sri Lanka	(J) • Mideast • 300 kW • ALT. FREQ. TO 15345 kHz
		(J) • Mideast • GENERAL • 300 kW • ALT. FREQ. TO 15345 kHz
		(J) • JAPANESE • Mideast • GENERAL • 300 kW • ALT. FREQ. TO 15345 kHz
	ROMANIA	(D) • W Africa • 250 kW
	RADIO ROMANIA INTL, Bucharest	
	RUSSIA	(D) • S Asia & SE Asia • 100 kW
	†R MOSCOW INTL, Via Kyrgyzstan	
	†R MOSCOW INTL, Via Uzbekistan	(J) • S Asia & SE Asia • 240 kW
	USA	Su/M • W North Am & C America • 50 kW W North Am & C America • 50 kW
	KVOH-VO HOPE, Rancho Simi, Ca	Tu-Sa • W North Am & C America • 50 kW M-F • W North Am & C America • 50 kW
		M-Sa • W North Am & C America • 50 kW
(con'd)		

0 1 2 3 4 5 6 7 8 9 10 11 12 13 14 15 16 17 18 19 20 21 22 23 24

SUMMER ONLY (J)   WINTER ONLY (D)   JAMMING / OR ⋀   EARLIEST HEARD ◁   LATEST HEARD ▷   NEW OR CHANGED FOR 1994 †

FREQUENCY   COUNTRY, STATION, LOCATION

TARGET • NETWORK • POWER (kW)

World Time

0 1 2 3 4 5 6 7 8 9 10 11 12 13 14 15 16 17 18 19 20 21 22 23 24

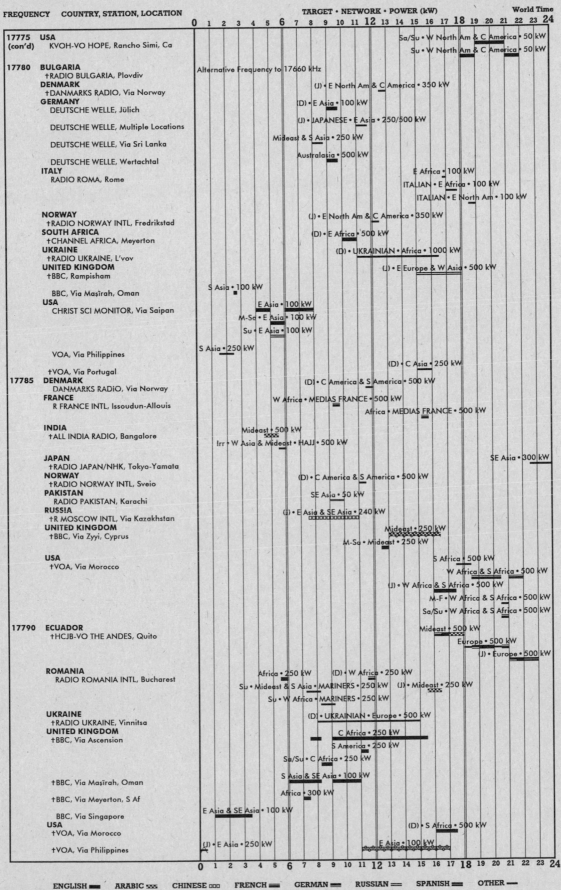

| 17775 (con'd) | USA |
| | KVOH-VO HOPE, Rancho Simi, Ca |

Sa/Su • W North Am & C America • 50 kW
Su • W North Am & C America • 50 kW

| 17780 | BULGARIA |
| | †RADIO BULGARIA, Plovdiv |

Alternative Frequency to 17660 kHz

DENMARK
†DANMARKS RADIO, Via Norway

(J) • E North Am & C America • 350 kW

GERMANY
DEUTSCHE WELLE, Jülich

(D) • E Asia • 100 kW

DEUTSCHE WELLE, Multiple Locations

(J) • JAPANESE • E Asia • 250/500 kW

DEUTSCHE WELLE, Via Sri Lanka

Mideast & S Asia • 250 kW

DEUTSCHE WELLE, Wertachtal

Australasia • 500 kW

ITALY
RADIO ROMA, Rome

E Africa • 100 kW
ITALIAN • E Africa • 100 kW
ITALIAN • E North Am • 100 kW

NORWAY
†RADIO NORWAY INTL, Fredrikstad

(J) • E North Am & C America • 350 kW

SOUTH AFRICA
†CHANNEL AFRICA, Meyerton

(D) • E Africa • 500 kW

UKRAINE
†RADIO UKRAINE, L'vov

(D) • UKRAINIAN • Africa • 1000 kW

UNITED KINGDOM
†BBC, Rampisham

(J) • E Europe & W Asia • 500 kW

BBC, Via Maşīrah, Oman

S Asia • 100 kW

USA
CHRIST SCI MONITOR, Via Saipan

E Asia • 100 kW
M-Sa • E Asia • 100 kW
Su • E Asia • 100 kW

VOA, Via Philippines

S Asia • 250 kW

†VOA, Via Portugal

(D) • C Asia • 250 kW

| 17785 | DENMARK |
| | DANMARKS RADIO, Via Norway |

(D) • C America & S America • 500 kW

FRANCE
R FRANCE INTL, Issoudun-Allouis

W Africa • MEDIAS FRANCE • 500 kW
Africa • MEDIAS FRANCE • 500 kW

INDIA
†ALL INDIA RADIO, Bangalore

Mideast • 500 kW
Irr • W Asia & Mideast • HAJJ • 500 kW

JAPAN
†RADIO JAPAN/NHK, Tokyo-Yamata

SE Asia • 300 kW

NORWAY
†RADIO NORWAY INTL, Sveio

(D) • C America & S America • 500 kW

PAKISTAN
RADIO PAKISTAN, Karachi

SE Asia • 50 kW

RUSSIA
†R MOSCOW INTL, Via Kazakhstan

(J) • E Asia & SE Asia • 240 kW

UNITED KINGDOM
†BBC, Via Zyyi, Cyprus

Mideast • 250 kW
M-Sa • Mideast • 250 kW

USA
†VOA, Via Morocco

S Africa • 500 kW
W Africa & S Africa • 500 kW
(J) • W Africa & S Africa • 500 kW
M-F • W Africa & S Africa • 500 kW
Sa/Su • W Africa & S Africa • 500 kW

| 17790 | ECUADOR |
| | †HCJB-VO THE ANDES, Quito |

Mideast • 500 kW
Europe • 500 kW
(J) • Europe • 500 kW

ROMANIA
RADIO ROMANIA INTL, Bucharest

Africa • 250 kW
(D) • W Africa • 250 kW
Su • Mideast & S Asia • MARINERS • 250 kW
(J) • Mideast • 250 kW
Su • W Africa • MARINERS • 250 kW

UKRAINE
†RADIO UKRAINE, Vinnitsa

(D) • UKRAINIAN • Europe • 500 kW

UNITED KINGDOM
†BBC, Via Ascension

C Africa • 250 kW
S America • 250 kW
Sa/Su • C Africa • 250 kW

†BBC, Via Maşīrah, Oman

S Asia & SE Asia • 100 kW

†BBC, Via Meyerton, S Af

Africa • 300 kW

BBC, Via Singapore

E Asia & SE Asia • 100 kW

USA
†VOA, Via Morocco

(D) • S Africa • 500 kW

†VOA, Via Philippines

(J) • E Asia • 250 kW
E Asia • 100 kW

0 1 2 3 4 5 6 7 8 9 10 11 12 13 14 15 16 17 18 19 20 21 22 23 24

ENGLISH ▬▬   ARABIC ⌗⌗⌗   CHINESE ▭▭▭   FRENCH ══   GERMAN ▬▬   RUSSIAN ═══   SPANISH ▬▬   OTHER ──

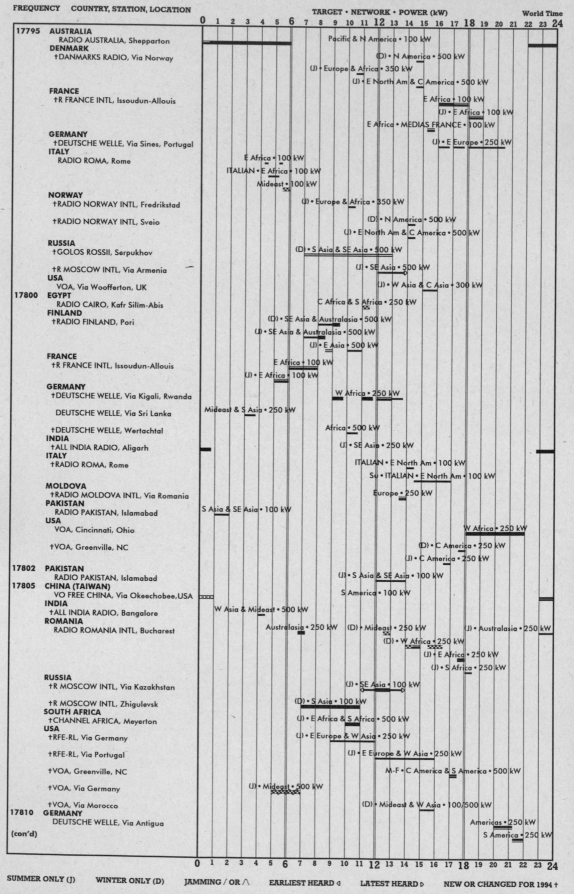

FREQUENCY   COUNTRY, STATION, LOCATION

TARGET • NETWORK • POWER (kW)

World Time

17795	**AUSTRALIA**
	RADIO AUSTRALIA, Shepparton — Pacific & N America • 100 kW
	DENMARK
	†DANMARKS RADIO, Via Norway — (D) • N America • 500 kW
	(J) • Europe & Africa • 350 kW
	(J) • E North Am & C America • 500 kW
	FRANCE
	†R FRANCE INTL, Issoudun-Allouis — E Africa • 100 kW
	(J) • E Africa • 100 kW
	E Africa • MEDIAS FRANCE • 100 kW
	GERMANY
	†DEUTSCHE WELLE, Via Sines, Portugal — (J) • E Europe • 250 kW
	ITALY
	RADIO ROMA, Rome — E Africa • 100 kW
	ITALIAN • E Africa • 100 kW
	Mideast • 100 kW
	NORWAY
	†RADIO NORWAY INTL, Fredrikstad — (J) • Europe & Africa • 350 kW
	†RADIO NORWAY INTL, Sveio — (D) • N America • 500 kW
	(J) • E North Am & C America • 500 kW
	RUSSIA
	†GOLOS ROSSII, Serpukhov — (D) • S Asia & SE Asia • 500 kW
	†R MOSCOW INTL, Via Armenia — (J) • SE Asia • 500 kW
	USA
	VOA, Via Woofferton, UK — (J) • W Asia & C Asia • 300 kW
17800	**EGYPT**
	RADIO CAIRO, Kafr Silim-Abis — C Africa & S Africa • 250 kW
	FINLAND
	†RADIO FINLAND, Pori — (D) • SE Asia & Australasia • 500 kW
	(J) • SE Asia & Australasia • 500 kW
	(J) • E Asia • 500 kW
	FRANCE
	†R FRANCE INTL, Issoudun-Allouis — E Africa • 100 kW
	(J) • E Africa • 100 kW
	GERMANY
	†DEUTSCHE WELLE, Via Kigali, Rwanda — W Africa • 250 kW
	DEUTSCHE WELLE, Via Sri Lanka — Mideast & S Asia • 250 kW
	†DEUTSCHE WELLE, Wertachtal — Africa • 500 kW
	INDIA
	†ALL INDIA RADIO, Aligarh — (J) • SE Asia • 250 kW
	ITALY
	†RADIO ROMA, Rome — ITALIAN • E North Am • 100 kW
	Su • ITALIAN • E North Am • 100 kW
	MOLDOVA
	†RADIO MOLDOVA INTL, Via Romania — Europe • 250 kW
	PAKISTAN
	RADIO PAKISTAN, Islamabad — S Asia & SE Asia • 100 kW
	USA
	VOA, Cincinnati, Ohio — W Africa • 250 kW
	†VOA, Greenville, NC — (D) • C America • 250 kW
	(J) • C America • 250 kW
17802	**PAKISTAN**
	RADIO PAKISTAN, Islamabad — (J) • S Asia & SE Asia • 100 kW
17805	**CHINA (TAIWAN)**
	VO FREE CHINA, Via Okeechobee, USA — S America • 100 kW
	INDIA
	†ALL INDIA RADIO, Bangalore — W Asia & Mideast • 500 kW
	ROMANIA
	RADIO ROMANIA INTL, Bucharest — Australasia • 250 kW (D) • Mideast • 250 kW (J) • Australasia • 250 kW
	(D) • W Africa • 250 kW
	(J) • E Africa • 250 kW
	(J) • S Africa • 250 kW
	RUSSIA
	†R MOSCOW INTL, Via Kazakhstan — (J) • SE Asia • 100 kW
	†R MOSCOW INTL, Zhigulevsk — (D) • S Asia • 100 kW
	SOUTH AFRICA
	†CHANNEL AFRICA, Meyerton — (J) • E Africa & S Africa • 500 kW
	USA
	†RFE-RL, Via Germany — (J) • E Europe & W Asia • 250 kW
	†RFE-RL, Via Portugal — (J) • E Europe & W Asia • 250 kW
	†VOA, Greenville, NC — M-F • C America & S America • 500 kW
	†VOA, Via Germany — (J) • Mideast • 500 kW
	†VOA, Via Morocco — (D) • Mideast & W Asia • 100/500 kW
17810	**GERMANY**
	DEUTSCHE WELLE, Via Antigua — Americas • 250 kW
	S America • 250 kW
(con'd)	

FREQUENCY   COUNTRY, STATION, LOCATION

TARGET • NETWORK • POWER (kW)   World Time

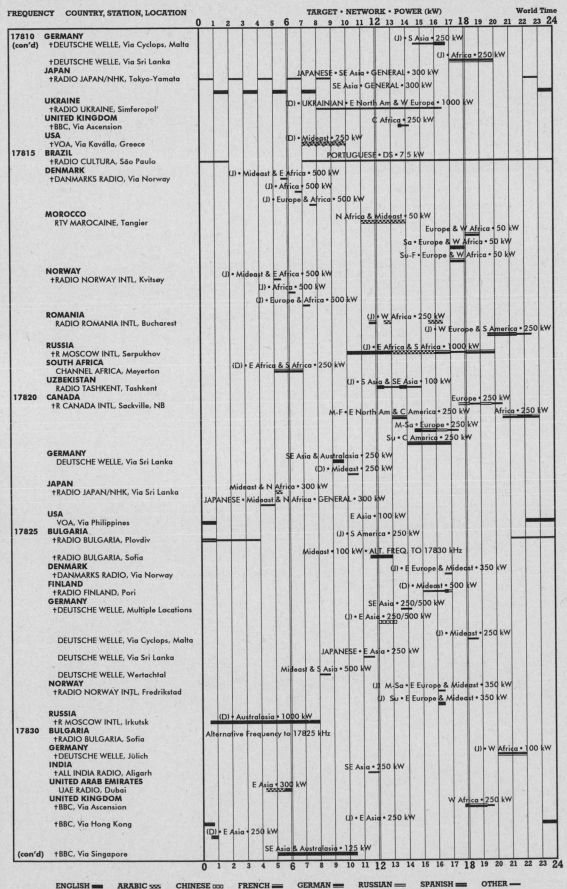

Frequency	Country, Station, Location	Details
17810 (con'd)	**GERMANY** †DEUTSCHE WELLE, Via Cyclops, Malta	(J) • S Asia • 250 kW
	†DEUTSCHE WELLE, Via Sri Lanka	(J) • Africa • 250 kW
	JAPAN †RADIO JAPAN/NHK, Tokyo-Yamata	JAPANESE • SE Asia • GENERAL • 300 kW; SE Asia • GENERAL • 300 kW
	UKRAINE †RADIO UKRAINE, Simferopol'	(D) • UKRAINIAN • E North Am & W Europe • 1000 kW
	UNITED KINGDOM †BBC, Via Ascension	C Africa • 250 kW
	USA †VOA, Via Kaválla, Greece	(D) • Mideast • 250 kW
17815	**BRAZIL** †RADIO CULTURA, São Paulo	PORTUGUESE • DS • 7.5 kW
	DENMARK †DANMARKS RADIO, Via Norway	(J) • Mideast & E Africa • 500 kW; (J) • Africa • 500 kW; (J) • Europe & Africa • 500 kW
	MOROCCO RTV MAROCAINE, Tangier	N Africa & Mideast • 50 kW; Europe & W Africa • 50 kW; Sa • Europe & W Africa • 50 kW; Su-F • Europe & W Africa • 50 kW
	NORWAY †RADIO NORWAY INTL, Kvitsøy	(J) • Mideast & E Africa • 500 kW; (J) • Africa • 500 kW; (J) • Europe & Africa • 500 kW
	ROMANIA RADIO ROMANIA INTL, Bucharest	(J) • W Africa • 250 kW; (J) • W Europe & S America • 250 kW
	RUSSIA †R MOSCOW INTL, Serpukhov	(J) • E Africa & S Africa • 1000 kW
	SOUTH AFRICA CHANNEL AFRICA, Meyerton	(D) • E Africa & S Africa • 250 kW
	UZBEKISTAN RADIO TASHKENT, Tashkent	(J) • S Asia & SE Asia • 100 kW
17820	**CANADA** †R CANADA INTL, Sackville, NB	Europe • 250 kW; Africa • 250 kW; M-F • E North Am & C America • 250 kW; M-Sa • Europe • 250 kW; Su • C America • 250 kW
	GERMANY DEUTSCHE WELLE, Via Sri Lanka	SE Asia & Australasia • 250 kW; (D) • Mideast • 250 kW
	JAPAN †RADIO JAPAN/NHK, Via Sri Lanka	Mideast & N Africa • 300 kW; JAPANESE • Mideast & N Africa • GENERAL • 300 kW
	USA VOA, Via Philippines	E Asia • 100 kW
17825	**BULGARIA** †RADIO BULGARIA, Plovdiv	(J) • S America • 250 kW
	†RADIO BULGARIA, Sofia	Mideast • 100 kW • ALT. FREQ. TO 17830 kHz
	DENMARK †DANMARKS RADIO, Via Norway	(J) • E Europe & Mideast • 350 kW
	FINLAND †RADIO FINLAND, Pori	(D) • Mideast • 500 kW
	GERMANY †DEUTSCHE WELLE, Multiple Locations	SE Asia • 250/500 kW; (J) • E Asia • 250/500 kW
	DEUTSCHE WELLE, Via Cyclops, Malta	(J) • Mideast • 250 kW
	DEUTSCHE WELLE, Via Sri Lanka	JAPANESE • E Asia • 250 kW
	DEUTSCHE WELLE, Wertachtal	Mideast & S Asia • 500 kW
	NORWAY †RADIO NORWAY INTL, Fredrikstad	(J) M-Sa • E Europe & Mideast • 350 kW; (J) Su • E Europe & Mideast • 350 kW
	RUSSIA †R MOSCOW INTL, Irkutsk	(D) • Australasia • 1000 kW
17830	**BULGARIA** †RADIO BULGARIA, Sofia	Alternative Frequency to 17825 kHz
	GERMANY †DEUTSCHE WELLE, Jülich	(J) • W Africa • 100 kW
	INDIA †ALL INDIA RADIO, Aligarh	SE Asia • 250 kW
	UNITED ARAB EMIRATES UAE RADIO, Dubai	E Asia • 300 kW
	UNITED KINGDOM †BBC, Via Ascension	W Africa • 250 kW
	†BBC, Via Hong Kong	(J) • E Asia • 250 kW; (D) • E Asia • 250 kW
(con'd)	†BBC, Via Singapore	SE Asia & Australasia • 125 kW

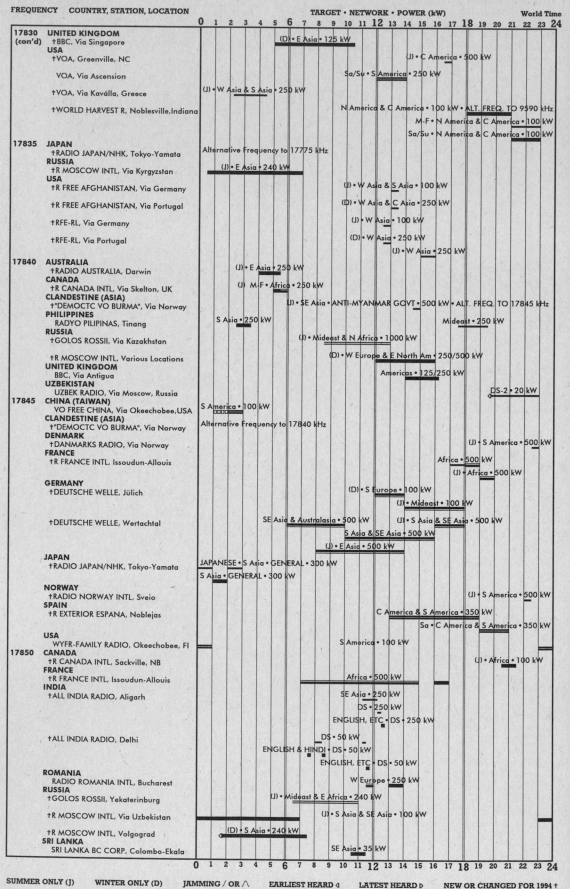

FREQUENCY   COUNTRY, STATION, LOCATION

FREQUENCY   COUNTRY, STATION, LOCATION   TARGET • NETWORK • POWER (kW)   World Time

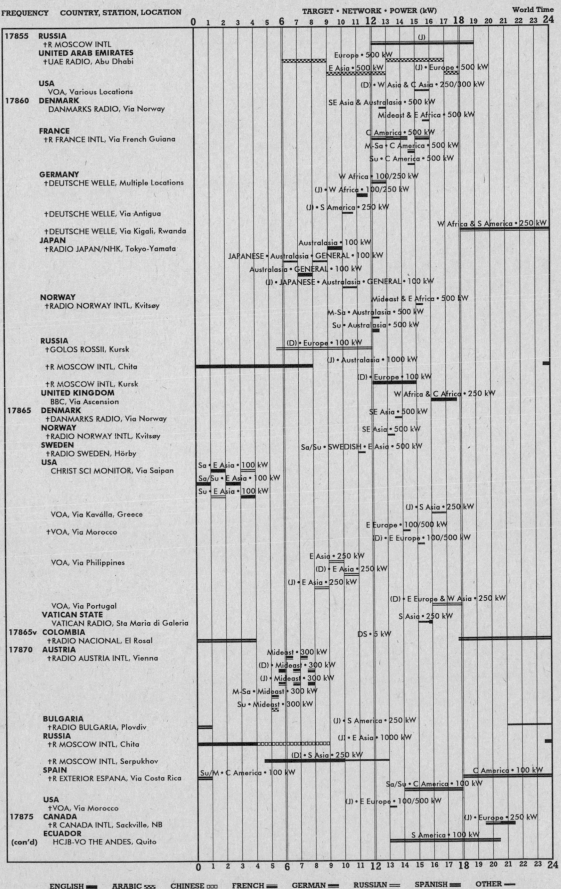

17855	**RUSSIA**	
	†R MOSCOW INTL	(J)
	UNITED ARAB EMIRATES	
	†UAE RADIO, Abu Dhabi	Europe • 500 kW
		E Asia • 500 kW (J) • Europe • 500 kW
	USA	
	VOA, Various Locations	(D) • W Asia & C Asia • 250/300 kW
17860	**DENMARK**	
	DANMARKS RADIO, Via Norway	SE Asia & Australasia • 500 kW
		Mideast & E Africa • 500 kW
	FRANCE	
	†R FRANCE INTL, Via French Guiana	C America • 500 kW
		M-Sa • C America • 500 kW
		Su • C America • 500 kW
	GERMANY	
	†DEUTSCHE WELLE, Multiple Locations	W Africa • 100/250 kW
		(J) • W Africa • 100/250 kW
	†DEUTSCHE WELLE, Via Antigua	(J) • S America • 250 kW
	†DEUTSCHE WELLE, Via Kigali, Rwanda	W Africa & S America • 250 kW
	JAPAN	
	†RADIO JAPAN/NHK, Tokyo-Yamata	Australasia • 100 kW
		JAPANESE • Australasia • GENERAL • 100 kW
		Australasia • GENERAL • 100 kW
		(J) • JAPANESE • Australasia • GENERAL • 100 kW
	NORWAY	
	†RADIO NORWAY INTL, Kvitsøy	Mideast & E Africa • 500 kW
		M-Sa • Australasia • 500 kW
		Su • Australasia • 500 kW
	RUSSIA	
	†GOLOS ROSSII, Kursk	(D) • Europe • 100 kW
	†R MOSCOW INTL, Chita	(J) • Australasia • 1000 kW
	†R MOSCOW INTL, Kursk	(D) • Europe • 100 kW
	UNITED KINGDOM	
	BBC, Via Ascension	W Africa & C Africa • 250 kW
17865	**DENMARK**	
	†DANMARKS RADIO, Via Norway	SE Asia • 500 kW
	NORWAY	
	†RADIO NORWAY INTL, Kvitsøy	SE Asia • 500 kW
	SWEDEN	
	†RADIO SWEDEN, Hörby	Sa/Su • SWEDISH • E Asia • 500 kW
	USA	
	CHRIST SCI MONITOR, Via Saipan	Sa • E Asia • 100 kW
		Sa/Su • E Asia • 100 kW
		Su • E Asia • 100 kW
	VOA, Via Kaválla, Greece	(J) • S Asia • 250 kW
	†VOA, Via Morocco	E Europe • 100/500 kW
		(D) • E Europe • 100/500 kW
	VOA, Via Philippines	E Asia • 250 kW
		(D) • E Asia • 250 kW
		(J) • E Asia • 250 kW
	VOA, Via Portugal	(D) • E Europe & W Asia • 250 kW
	VATICAN STATE	
	VATICAN RADIO, Sta Maria di Galeria	S Asia • 250 kW
17865v	**COLOMBIA**	
	†RADIO NACIONAL, El Rosal	DS • 5 kW
17870	**AUSTRIA**	
	†RADIO AUSTRIA INTL, Vienna	Mideast • 300 kW
		(D) • Mideast • 300 kW
		(J) • Mideast • 300 kW
		M-Sa • Mideast • 300 kW
		Su • Mideast • 300 kW
	BULGARIA	
	†RADIO BULGARIA, Plovdiv	(J) • S America • 250 kW
	RUSSIA	
	†R MOSCOW INTL, Chita	(J) • E Asia • 1000 kW
	†R MOSCOW INTL, Serpukhov	(D) • S Asia • 250 kW
	SPAIN	
	†R EXTERIOR ESPANA, Via Costa Rica	Su/M • C America • 100 kW C America • 100 kW
		Sa/Su • C America • 100 kW
	USA	
	†VOA, Via Morocco	(J) • E Europe • 100/500 kW
17875	**CANADA**	
	†R CANADA INTL, Sackville, NB	(J) • Europe • 250 kW
	ECUADOR	
(con'd)	HCJB-VO THE ANDES, Quito	S America • 100 kW

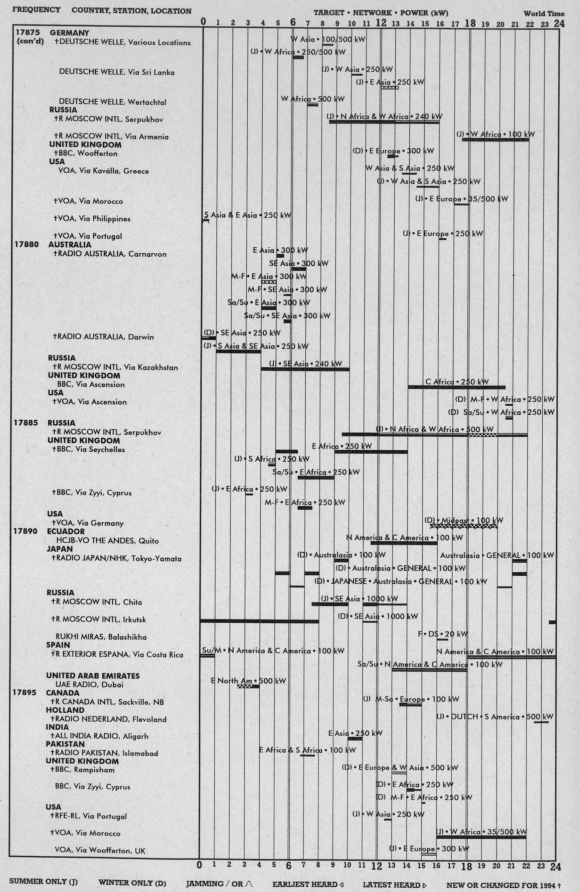

FREQUENCY   COUNTRY, STATION, LOCATION

TARGET • NETWORK • POWER (kW)   World Time

17875	GERMANY	
(con'd)	†DEUTSCHE WELLE, Various Locations	W Asia • 100/500 kW
		(J) • W Africa • 250/500 kW
	DEUTSCHE WELLE, Via Sri Lanka	(J) • W Asia • 250 kW
		(J) • E Asia • 250 kW
	DEUTSCHE WELLE, Wertachtal	W Africa • 500 kW
	RUSSIA	
	†R MOSCOW INTL, Serpukhov	(J) • N Africa & W Africa • 240 kW
	†R MOSCOW INTL, Via Armenia	(J) • W Africa • 100 kW
	UNITED KINGDOM	
	†BBC, Woofferton	(D) • E Europe • 300 kW
	USA	
	VOA, Via Kaválla, Greece	W Asia & S Asia • 250 kW
		(J) • W Asia & S Asia • 250 kW
	†VOA, Via Morocco	(J) • E Europe • 35/500 kW
	†VOA, Via Philippines	S Asia & E Asia • 250 kW
	†VOA, Via Portugal	(J) • E Europe • 250 kW
17880	AUSTRALIA	
	†RADIO AUSTRALIA, Carnarvon	E Asia • 300 kW
		SE Asia • 300 kW
		M-F • E Asia • 300 kW
		M-F • SE Asia • 300 kW
		Sa/Su • E Asia • 300 kW
		Sa/Su • SE Asia • 300 kW
	†RADIO AUSTRALIA, Darwin	(D) • SE Asia • 250 kW
		(J) • S Asia & SE Asia • 250 kW
	RUSSIA	
	†R MOSCOW INTL, Via Kazakhstan	(J) • SE Asia • 240 kW
	UNITED KINGDOM	
	BBC, Via Ascension	C Africa • 250 kW
	USA	
	†VOA, Via Ascension	(D) M-F • W Africa • 250 kW
		(D) Sa/Su • W Africa • 250 kW
17885	RUSSIA	
	†R MOSCOW INTL, Serpukhov	(J) • N Africa & W Africa • 500 kW
	UNITED KINGDOM	
	†BBC, Via Seychelles	E Africa • 250 kW
		(J) • S Africa • 250 kW
		Sa/Su • E Africa • 250 kW
	†BBC, Via Zyyi, Cyprus	(J) • E Africa • 250 kW
		M-F • E Africa • 250 kW
	USA	
	†VOA, Via Germany	(D) • Mideast • 100 kW
17890	ECUADOR	
	HCJB-VO THE ANDES, Quito	N America & C America • 100 kW
	JAPAN	
	†RADIO JAPAN/NHK, Tokyo-Yamata	(D) • Australasia • 100 kW
		Australasia • GENERAL • 100 kW
		(D) • Australasia • GENERAL • 100 kW
		(D) • JAPANESE • Australasia • GENERAL • 100 kW
	RUSSIA	
	†R MOSCOW INTL, Chita	(J) • SE Asia • 1000 kW
	†R MOSCOW INTL, Irkutsk	(D) • SE Asia • 1000 kW
	RUKHI MIRAS, Balashikha	F • DS • 20 kW
	SPAIN	
	†R EXTERIOR ESPANA, Via Costa Rica	Su/M • N America & C America • 100 kW
		N America & C America • 100 kW
		Sa/Su • N America & C America • 100 kW
	UNITED ARAB EMIRATES	
	UAE RADIO, Dubai	E North Am • 500 kW
17895	CANADA	
	†R CANADA INTL, Sackville, NB	(J) M-Sa • Europe • 100 kW
	HOLLAND	
	†RADIO NEDERLAND, Flevoland	(J) • DUTCH • S America • 500 kW
	INDIA	
	†ALL INDIA RADIO, Aligarh	E Asia • 250 kW
	PAKISTAN	
	†RADIO PAKISTAN, Islamabad	E Africa & S Africa • 100 kW
	UNITED KINGDOM	
	†BBC, Rampisham	(D) • E Europe & W Asia • 500 kW
	BBC, Via Zyyi, Cyprus	(D) • E Africa • 250 kW
		(D) M-F • E Africa • 250 kW
	USA	
	†RFE-RL, Via Portugal	(J) • W Asia • 250 kW
	†VOA, Via Morocco	(J) • W Africa • 35/500 kW
	VOA, Via Woofferton, UK	(J) • E Europe • 300 kW

FREQUENCY	COUNTRY, STATION, LOCATION	TARGET • NETWORK • POWER (kW) / World Time
17900	**PORTUGAL** †RDP INTERNATIONAL, Lisbon	Alternative Frequency to 15515 kHz
17900v	**PAKISTAN** RADIO PAKISTAN, Islamabad	Europe • 250 kW
17940	**IRAQ** †RADIO IRAQ INTL, Salah el Deen	(J) • ARABIC & ENGLISH • E North Am • 500 kW
17950v	**CLANDESTINE (M EAST)** "VO IRAQI PEOPLE", Saudi Arabia	Mideast • ANTI-SADDAM
18195	**RUSSIA** †RADIO ROSSII, Moscow	DS(FEEDER) • 20 kW • USB / (J) • DS(FEEDER) • 20 kW • USB
18275	**USA** †VOA, Greenville, NC	N Africa • (FEEDER) • 50 kW • ISL / (D) • N Africa • (FEEDER) • 50 kW • ISU / (D) • N Africa • (FEEDER) • 50 kW • ISL / (J) • N Africa • (FEEDER) • 50 kW • ISU
18730	**RUSSIA** †RADIO MOSCOW	DS-MAYAK(FEEDER) • USB
18870	**RUSSIA** †RADIO ROSSII	DS(FEEDER) • 15/100 kW • USB
18930	**USA** †WEWN, Birmingham, Alabama	S America • 500 kW / (J) • S America • 500 kW
19037.5	**AUSTRALIA** †ARMED FORCES RADIO, Exmouth	M/F • E Africa • 40 kW • USB
19379	**USA** †VOA, Greenville, NC	Europe • (FEEDER) • 40 kW • ISL / Europe • (FEEDER) • 40 kW • ISU / (D) • Europe • (FEEDER) • 40 kW • ISU
20000	**USA** WWV, Ft Collins, Colorado	WEATHER/WORLD TIME • 2.5 kW
20418.5	**AUSTRALIA** †ARMED FORCES RADIO, Belconnen	SE Asia • 40 kW • USB
21450	**RUSSIA** †R MOSCOW INTL, Armavir	(J) • C Africa • 100 kW / (D) • S Asia • 240 kW
	†R MOSCOW INTL, Moscow	
21455	**CANADA** †R CANADA INTL, Via Sines, Portugal	(J) • Europe • 250 kW
	ECUADOR †HCJB-VO THE ANDES, Quito	Europe & Pacific • 10 kW • USB / JAPANESE • Europe & Pacific • 10 kW • USB
	PHILIPPINES RADYO PILIPINAS, Tinang	Mideast • 250 kW
21460	**UKRAINE** †RADIO UKRAINE, Simferopol'	(D) • UKRAINIAN • W Europe & E North Am • 500 kW • ALT. FREQ. TO 21765 kHz
21465	**GERMANY** †DEUTSCHE WELLE, Jülich	(D) • SE Asia • 100 kW
	RUSSIA †R MOSCOW INTL, Via Ukraine	(J) • W Africa • 500 kW
21465v	**COSTA RICA** †RADIO FOR PEACE, Ciudad Colón	N America • USB / Sa • N America • USB / Su-F • N America • USB
21468v	**PAKISTAN** †RADIO PAKISTAN, Karachi	SE Asia • 50 kW
21470	**UNITED KINGDOM** BBC, Via Zyyi, Cyprus	E Africa • 250 kW / Sa/Su • E Africa • 250 kW
21474v	**PAKISTAN** †RADIO PAKISTAN, Karachi	SE Asia • 50 kW
21475	**USA** VOA, Via Philippines	S Asia • 250 kW
21480	**ECUADOR** †HCJB-VO THE ANDES, Quito	(J) • Mideast • 250 kW / (J) • Europe • 250 kW
	GERMANY †DEUTSCHE WELLE, Via Kigali, Rwanda	(J) • W Africa • 250 kW
	HOLLAND †RADIO NEDERLAND, Flevoland	(D) • SE Asia • 500 kW / (D) • DUTCH • SE Asia • 500 kW
	†RADIO NEDERLAND, Via Madagascar	DUTCH • E Asia • 300 kW / (D) • DUTCH • S Asia • 300 kW
	RUSSIA †R MOSCOW INTL, Petropavlovsk-K	(D) • W North Am • 100 kW
	†R MOSCOW INTL, St Petersburg	(J) • Mideast • 240 kW
21485	**HOLLAND** †RADIO NEDERLAND, Via Madagascar	Su • DUTCH • SE Asia • 300 kW
	RUSSIA †R MOSCOW INTL	(J)
	USA †VOA, Greenville, NC	W Africa & S Africa • 250 kW / (D) • S Africa • 250 kW / (D) • M-F • S Africa • 250 kW

ENGLISH ▬ ARABIC ∞ CHINESE □□□ FRENCH ▬ GERMAN ▬ RUSSIAN ═ SPANISH ▬ OTHER ▬

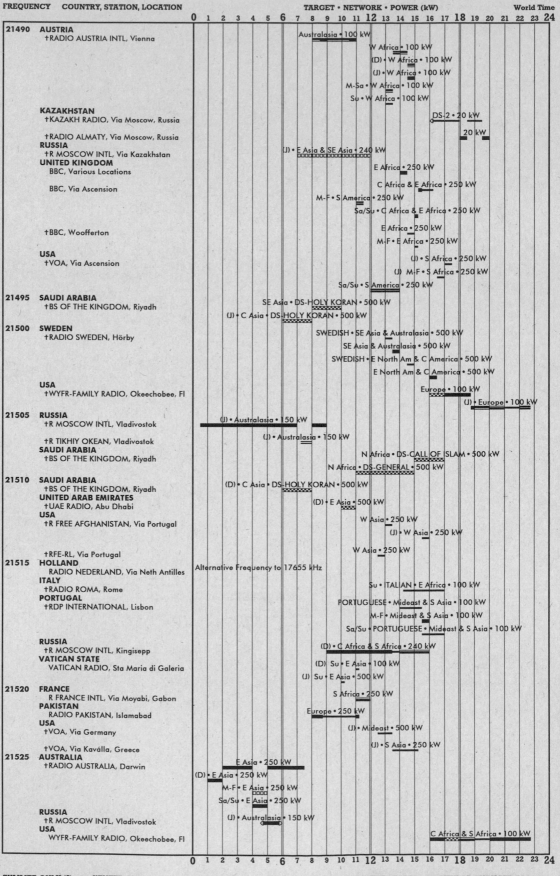

FREQUENCY   COUNTRY, STATION, LOCATION

TARGET • NETWORK • POWER (kW)   World Time

21490 AUSTRIA
   †RADIO AUSTRIA INTL, Vienna
      Australasia • 100 kW
      W Africa • 100 kW
      (D) • W Africa • 100 kW
      (J) • W Africa • 100 kW
      M-Sa • W Africa • 100 kW
      Su • W Africa • 100 kW

   KAZAKHSTAN
      †KAZAKH RADIO, Via Moscow, Russia
         DS-2 • 20 kW
      †RADIO ALMATY, Via Moscow, Russia
         20 kW
   RUSSIA
      †R MOSCOW INTL, Via Kazakhstan
         (J) • E Asia & SE Asia • 240 kW
   UNITED KINGDOM
      BBC, Various Locations
         E Africa • 250 kW
      BBC, Via Ascension
         C Africa & E Africa • 250 kW
         M-F • S America • 250 kW
         Sa/Su • C Africa & E Africa • 250 kW
      †BBC, Woofferton
         E Africa • 250 kW
         M-F • E Africa • 250 kW
   USA
      †VOA, Via Ascension
         (J) • S Africa • 250 kW
         (J) M-F • S Africa • 250 kW
         Sa/Su • S America • 250 kW

21495 SAUDI ARABIA
   †BS OF THE KINGDOM, Riyadh
      SE Asia • DS-HOLY KORAN • 500 kW
      (J) • C Asia • DS-HOLY KORAN • 500 kW

21500 SWEDEN
   †RADIO SWEDEN, Hörby
      SWEDISH • SE Asia & Australasia • 500 kW
      SE Asia & Australasia • 500 kW
      SWEDISH • E North Am & C America • 500 kW
      E North Am & C America • 500 kW
   USA
      †WYFR-FAMILY RADIO, Okeechobee, Fl
         Europe • 100 kW
         (J) • Europe • 100 kW

21505 RUSSIA
   †R MOSCOW INTL, Vladivostok
      (J) • Australasia • 150 kW
   †R TIKHIY OKEAN, Vladivostok
      (J) • Australasia • 150 kW
   SAUDI ARABIA
      †BS OF THE KINGDOM, Riyadh
         N Africa • DS-CALL OF ISLAM • 500 kW
         N Africa • DS-GENERAL • 500 kW

21510 SAUDI ARABIA
   †BS OF THE KINGDOM, Riyadh
      (D) • C Asia • DS-HOLY KORAN • 500 kW
   UNITED ARAB EMIRATES
      †UAE RADIO, Abu Dhabi
         (D) • E Asia • 500 kW
   USA
      †R FREE AFGHANISTAN, Via Portugal
         W Asia • 250 kW
         (J) • W Asia • 250 kW
      †RFE-RL, Via Portugal
         W Asia • 250 kW
21515 HOLLAND
      RADIO NEDERLAND, Via Neth Antilles
         Alternative Frequency to 17655 kHz
   ITALY
      †RADIO ROMA, Rome
         Su • ITALIAN • E Africa • 100 kW
   PORTUGAL
      †RDP INTERNATIONAL, Lisbon
         PORTUGUESE • Mideast & S Asia • 100 kW
         M-F • Mideast & S Asia • 100 kW
         Sa/Su • PORTUGUESE • Mideast & S Asia • 100 kW
   RUSSIA
      †R MOSCOW INTL, Kingisepp
         (D) • C Africa & S Africa • 240 kW
   VATICAN STATE
      VATICAN RADIO, Sta Maria di Galeria
         (D) Su • E Asia • 100 kW
         (J) Su • E Asia • 500 kW

21520 FRANCE
      R FRANCE INTL, Via Moyabi, Gabon
         S Africa • 250 kW
   PAKISTAN
      RADIO PAKISTAN, Islamabad
         Europe • 250 kW
   USA
      †VOA, Via Germany
         (J) • Mideast • 500 kW
      †VOA, Via Kaválla, Greece
         (J) • S Asia • 250 kW
21525 AUSTRALIA
   †RADIO AUSTRALIA, Darwin
      E Asia • 250 kW
      (D) • E Asia • 250 kW
      M-F • E Asia • 250 kW
      Sa/Su • E Asia • 250 kW
   RUSSIA
      †R MOSCOW INTL, Vladivostok
         (J) • Australasia • 150 kW
   USA
      WYFR-FAMILY RADIO, Okeechobee, Fl
         C Africa & S Africa • 100 kW

SUMMER ONLY (J)   WINTER ONLY (D)   JAMMING / OR ∧   EARLIEST HEARD ◁   LATEST HEARD ▷   NEW OR CHANGED FOR 1994 †

FREQUENCY	COUNTRY, STATION, LOCATION	TARGET • NETWORK • POWER (kW)

World Time: 0 1 2 3 4 5 6 7 8 9 10 11 12 13 14 15 16 17 18 19 20 21 22 23 24

21530 FRANCE
†R FRANCE INTL, Issoudun-Allouis — (D) • Mideast • 500 kW
HOLLAND
RADIO NEDERLAND, Flevoland — (J) Su • DUTCH • W Africa, C Africa & Asia • 500 kW
RUSSIA
†R MOSCOW INTL, Petropavlovsk-K — (D) • W North Am • 100 kW

21535 ITALY
†RADIO ROMA, Rome — Su • ITALIAN • S America • 100 kW
TUNISIA
RTV TUNISIENNE, Sfax — Mideast & N Africa • DS • 100 kW

21540 GERMANY
†DEUTSCHE WELLE, Nauen — (D) • E Asia • 500 kW / (J) • E Africa • 500 kW

21545 CANADA
†R CANADA INTL, Sackville, NB — (D) • Europe • 250 kW / (J) • Europe • 250 kW / (J) M-Sa • Europe • 250 kW
RUSSIA
†R MOSCOW INTL, Moscow — (J) • C Africa & S Africa • 200 kW

21550 FINLAND
†RADIO FINLAND, Pori — (J) • SE Asia & Australasia • 500 kW / (J) • Mideast • 500 kW
HUNGARY
†RADIO BUDAPEST — HUNGARIAN • Asia
RUSSIA
†R MOSCOW INTL, St Petersburg — (D) • Mideast • 500 kW
USA
VOA, Via Philippines — S Asia • 50 kW

21555 SPAIN
†R EXTERIOR ESPANA, Noblejas — Alternative Frequency to 17755 kHz

21560 GERMANY
†DEUTSCHE WELLE, Jülich — Mideast • 100 kW
†DEUTSCHE WELLE, Via Kigali, Rwanda — Africa • 250 kW
ITALY
RADIO ROMA, Rome — E Africa • 100 kW / ITALIAN • E North Am • 100 kW / ITALIAN • E Africa • 100 kW

21565 RUSSIA
†GOLOS ROSSII, St Petersburg — (J) • W Africa • 240 kW
†R MOSCOW INTL, Irkutsk — (D) • S Asia & S Africa • 500 kW

21570 UNITED ARAB EMIRATES
†UAE RADIO, Abu Dhabi — Europe • 500 kW • ALT. FREQ. TO 21630 kHz
USA
†VOA, Via Kavála, Greece — (D) • Mideast • 250 kW

21575 JAPAN
RADIO JAPAN/NHK, Via Moyabi, Gabon — Europe & N Africa • GENERAL • 500 kW / JAPANESE • Europe & N Africa • GENERAL • 500 kW
RUSSIA
†R MOSCOW INTL, Moscow — (J) • SE Asia • 500 kW

21580 FRANCE
†R FRANCE INTL, Issoudun-Allouis — C Africa & S Africa • 500 kW / (D) • C Africa & S Africa • 500 kW
GERMANY
DEUTSCHE WELLE, Via Sri Lanka — (D) • Mideast • 250 kW
PAKISTAN
RADIO PAKISTAN, Islamabad — Mideast & N Africa • 250 kW
PHILIPPINES
RADYO PILIPINAS, Tinang — E Asia • 250 kW
USA
†VOA, Greenville, NC — C America & S America • 250 kW / Sa/Su • C America & S America • 250 kW

21585 RUSSIA
†R MOSCOW INTL, Armavir — (J) • S Asia & SE Asia • 500 kW
†R MOSCOW INTL, Chita — (D) • E Asia & SE Asia • 500 kW
†R TIKHIY OKEAN, Chita — (D) • E Asia & SE Asia • 500 kW
USA
†VOA, Via Philippines — (D) • E Asia • 250 kW

21590 AUSTRALIA
†RADIO AUSTRALIA, Carnarvon — Alternative Frequency to 21595 kHz
HOLLAND
RADIO NEDERLAND, Via Neth Antilles — W Africa • 250 kW
RUSSIA
†R MOSCOW INTL, Petrozavodsk — (J) • W Africa • 240 kW
UNITED KINGDOM
†BBC, Woofferton — SE Asia • 250 kW

21595 AUSTRALIA
†RADIO AUSTRALIA, Carnarvon — S Asia • 250 kW • ALT. FREQ. TO 21590 kHz / (D) • S Asia • 250 kW • ALT. FREQ. TO 21590 kHz
DENMARK
†DANMARKS RADIO, Via Norway — (D) • W Africa • 500 kW / (J) • Australasia • 500 kW
NORWAY
†RADIO NORWAY INTL, Kvitsøy — (D) • W Africa • 500 kW / (J) • Australasia • 500 kW

21600 GERMANY
†DEUTSCHE WELLE, Jülich — Africa • 100 kW / (J) • Africa • 100 kW / E Africa • 100 kW

(con'd)

World Time: 0 1 2 3 4 5 6 7 8 9 10 11 12 13 14 15 16 17 18 19 20 21 22 23 24

ENGLISH ▬▬   ARABIC ⋙   CHINESE ▯▯▯   FRENCH ▭▭   GERMAN ▬▬   RUSSIAN ══   SPANISH ▬▬   OTHER ▬

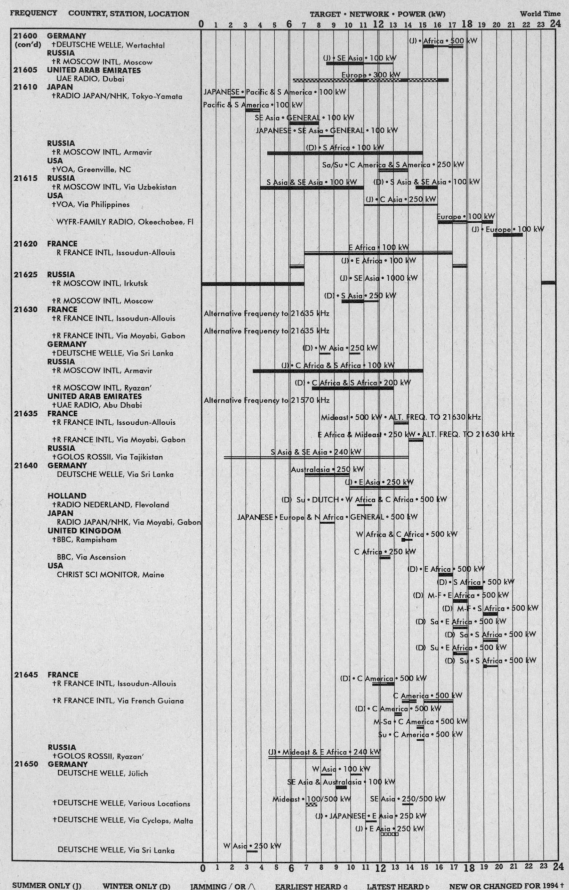

FREQUENCY   COUNTRY, STATION, LOCATION   TARGET • NETWORK • POWER (kW)   World Time

0 1 2 3 4 5 6 7 8 9 10 11 12 13 14 15 16 17 18 19 20 21 22 23 24

Frequency	Country, Station, Location	Target • Network • Power
21655	**PORTUGAL** †RDP INTERNATIONAL, Lisbon	PORTUGUESE • W Africa & S America • 100 kW
		Irr • PORTUGUESE • W Africa & S America • 100 kW
		Sa/Su • PORTUGUESE • W Africa & S America • 100 kW
	RUSSIA †R MOSCOW INTL, Armavir	(D) • S Asia • 240 kW
		(D) • S Asia & SE Asia • 240 kW
21660	**UNITED KINGDOM** †BBC, Via Ascension	S Africa • 250 kW
		Sa/Su • S Africa • 250 kW
21665	**ROMANIA** RADIO ROMANIA INTL, Bucharest	Africa • 250 kW
		Australasia • 250 kW
	SAUDI ARABIA †BS OF THE KINGDOM, Riyadh	(J) • SE Asia • DS-HOLY KORAN • 500 kW
	VATICAN STATE †VATICAN RADIO, Sta Maria di Galeria	Alternative Frequency to 21670 kHz
21670	**RUSSIA** †R MOSCOW INTL, Armavir	(J) • S Asia & SE Asia • 240 kW
		(J) • C Africa & S Africa • 100 kW
	†RADIO MOSCOW, Armavir	Irr • (J) • S Asia & SE Asia • DS-MAYAK • 240 kW
	SAUDI ARABIA †BS OF THE KINGDOM, Riyadh	(D) • SE Asia • 500 kW
		(D) • SE Asia • DS-HOLY KORAN • 500 kW
	USA †UNIVERSITY NET'K, Via Armavir, Russia	(J) • S Asia & SE Asia • 240 kW
	VATICAN STATE †VATICAN RADIO, Sta Maria di Galeria	E Africa & S Africa • 100 kW
		Su • E Africa & S Africa • 100/250 kW • ALT. FREQ. TO 21665 kHz
21675	**CANADA** †R CANADA INTL, Sackville, NB	(J) • Europe • 250 kW
	KUWAIT RADIO KUWAIT, Kabd	Europe & E North Am • 500 kW
21680	**GERMANY** †DEUTSCHE WELLE, Jülich	W Asia • 100 kW
		(D) • S Asia & SE Asia • 100 kW
		(J) • E Asia • 100 kW
	DEUTSCHE WELLE, Via Cyclops, Malta	(J) • S Asia • 250 kW
	†DEUTSCHE WELLE, Via Sines, Portugal	(J) • S Asia • 250 kW
	DEUTSCHE WELLE, Via Sri Lanka	(J) • Mideast • 250 kW
	DEUTSCHE WELLE, Wertachtal	SE Asia & Australasia • 500 kW
21685	**FRANCE** †R FRANCE INTL, Issoudun-Allouis	W Africa • 500 kW
		W Africa • MEDIAS FRANCE • 500 kW
	†R FRANCE INTL, Via French Guiana	W Africa • 500 kW
		(J) • W Africa • 500 kW
21690	**ITALY** RADIO ROMA, Rome	E Africa • 100 kW
		ITALIAN • Africa • 100 kW
		Su • ITALIAN • Africa • 50 kW
	RUSSIA †R MOSCOW INTL, Vladivostok	E Asia & SE Asia • 500/1000 kW
		(J) • E Asia & SE Asia • 1000 kW
21695	**GERMANY** DEUTSCHE WELLE, Via Sri Lanka	(J) • W Asia • 250 kW
21700	**JAPAN** RADIO JAPAN/NHK, Via Moyabi, Gabon	JAPANESE • Europe • GENERAL • 500 kW
	PORTUGAL †RDP INTERNATIONAL, Lisbon	Alternative Frequency to 21720 kHz
	UNITED ARAB EMIRATES UAE RADIO, Dubai	Australasia • 300 kW
21705	**CZECH REPUBLIC** †RADIO PRAGUE, Via Slovakia	Australasia • 250 kW
	DENMARK †DANMARKS RADIO, Via Norway	Mideast & E Africa • 350 kW
		(J) • Africa • 350 kW
		(D) • W Africa • 350 kW
		(D) • S Asia & Australasia • 500 kW
		(J) • E Asia • 500 kW
		(J) • S America • 350 kW
	GERMANY †DEUTSCHE WELLE, Via Kigali, Rwanda	(D) • W Africa • 250 kW
	NORWAY †RADIO NORWAY INTL, Fredrikstad	Mideast & E Africa • 350 kW
		(J) • Africa • 350 kW
		(D) • W Africa • 350 kW
		(J) • S America • 350 kW
	†RADIO NORWAY INTL, Kvitsøy	(J) • E Asia • 500 kW
		(D) • M-Sa • S Asia & Australasia • 500 kW
		(D) • Su • S Asia & Australasia • 500 kW

(con'd)

0 1 2 3 4 5 6 7 8 9 10 11 12 13 14 15 16 17 18 19 20 21 22 23 24

ENGLISH ▬   ARABIC ≋   CHINESE □□□   FRENCH ═   GERMAN ▬   RUSSIAN ═   SPANISH ▬   OTHER ▬

FREQUENCY	COUNTRY, STATION, LOCATION	TARGET • NETWORK • POWER (kW)	World Time

0 1 2 3 4 5 6 7 8 9 10 11 12 13 14 15 16 17 18 19 20 21 22 23 24

21705	**SAUDI ARABIA**	
(con'd)	†BS OF THE KINGDOM, Riyadh	(J) • SE Asia • 500 kW
	SLOVAKIA	
	†R SLOVAKIA INTL, Rimavská Sobota	Australasia • 250 kW
21710	**CANADA**	
	†R CANADA INTL, Sackville, NB	(J) M-Sa • Europe • 250 kW
	DENMARK	
	DANMARKS RADIO, Via Norway	(D) • E North Am & C America • 350 kW
	NORWAY	
	RADIO NORWAY INTL, Fredrikstad	(D) • E North Am & C America • 350 kW
	USA	
	†WEWN, Birmingham, Alabama	(D) • ENGLISH, ETC • E Africa • PROJECTED • 500 kW
	VATICAN STATE	
	VATICAN RADIO, Sta Maria di Galeria	S America • 250 kW
21715	**UNITED KINGDOM**	
	†BBC, Via Hong Kong	E Asia • 250 kW
		Sa/Su • E Asia • 250 kW
	BBC, Via Singapore	E Asia • 100 kW
21720	**CHINA (TAIWAN)**	
	†VO FREE CHINA, Via Okeechobee,USA	(J) • Europe • 100 kW
	PORTUGAL	
	†RDP INTERNATIONAL, Lisbon	PORTUGUESE • E Africa & S Africa • 100 kW • ALT. FREQ. TO 21700 kHz
		Sa/Su • PORTUGUESE • E Africa & S Africa • 100 kW • ALT. FREQ. TO 21700 kHz
	USA	
	†WYFR-FAMILY RADIO, Okeechobee, Fl	Europe • 100 kW
21725	**AUSTRALIA**	
	†RADIO AUSTRALIA, Darwin	Alternative Frequency to 21745 kHz
	RUSSIA	
	†R MOSCOW INTL, Armavir	(J) • SE Asia & Australasia • 1000 kW
	UKRAINE	
	†RADIO UKRAINE, Vinnitsa	(J) • UKRAINIAN • S America • 1000 kW
21730	**PAKISTAN**	
	RADIO PAKISTAN, Islamabad	S Asia & SE Asia • 100 kW
	RUSSIA	
	R MOSCOW INTL, Armavir	(J) • S Asia • 250 kW
21735	**INDIA**	
	†ALL INDIA RADIO, Bangalore	E Asia • 500 kW
	UNITED ARAB EMIRATES	
	†UAE RADIO, Abu Dhabi	Europe • 500 kW
		(J) • Europe • 500 kW
		E Asia • 500 kW
21740	**AUSTRALIA**	
	†RADIO AUSTRALIA, Shepparton	Pacific & N America • 100 kW
		(J) • Pacific & N America • 100 kW
	RUSSIA	
	†R MOSCOW INTL, Via Armenia	(J) • E Africa & S Africa • 100 kW
21745	**AUSTRALIA**	
	†RADIO AUSTRALIA, Darwin	S Asia • 250 kW • ALT. FREQ. TO 21725 kHz
	HOLLAND	
	†RADIO NEDERLAND, Flevoland	(D) • DUTCH • SE Asia • 500 kW
	UNITED KINGDOM	
	†BBC, Rampisham	(D) • E Europe & W Asia • 500 kW
		(D) • Su • E Europe & W Asia • 500 kW
	USA	
	RFE-RL, Via Portugal	(J) • E Europe • 250 kW
	VOA, Cincinnati, Ohio	M-F • C America & S America • 250 kW
21750	**RUSSIA**	
	†GOLOS ROSSII, Various Locations	Mideast & S Asia • 100/240/1000 kW
		(D) • S Asia • 100/240 kW
21755	**RUSSIA**	
	†R MOSCOW INTL, Via Ukraine	(D) • W Africa • 240 kW
21765	**FRANCE**	
	R FRANCE INTL, Via French Guiana	(D) • S America • 500 kW
	RUSSIA	
	†GOLOS ROSSII, St Petersburg	(D) • N Africa & W Africa • 500 kW
	UKRAINE	
	†RADIO UKRAINE, Simferopol'	Alternative Frequency to 21460 kHz
21770	**RUSSIA**	
	†GOLOS ROSSII, Kenga	(J) • E Asia & Australasia • 250 kW
	†R MOSCOW INTL, Irkutsk	(D) • Australasia • 250 kW
21775	**ITALY**	
	†RADIO ROMA, Rome	ITALIAN • Australasia • DS-2 • 100 kW
21785	**RUSSIA**	
	†R MOSCOW INTL, Armavir	E Africa • 1000 kW
		(J) • E Africa • 1000 kW
21790	**RUSSIA**	
	†R MOSCOW INTL, Irkutsk	E Asia & Australasia • 250 kW
21800	**UKRAINE**	
	†RADIO UKRAINE, Simferopol'	UKRAINIAN • Africa • 1000 kW
21810	**BELGIUM**	
	†R VLAANDEREN INTL, Wavre	Alternative Frequency to 15540 kHz
21815	**BELGIUM**	
	†R VLAANDEREN INTL, Wavre	(J) Su • DUTCH • Africa • 250 kW
21820	**RUSSIA**	
	†R MOSCOW INTL, Via Tajikistan	(J) • S Asia • 100 kW
	SWITZERLAND	
	±SWISS RADIO INTL, Schwarzenburg	Australasia • 100/250 kW
		SE Asia • 100/250 kW
		S Asia & SE Asia • 100/250 kW
(con'd)		

0 1 2 3 4 5 6 7 8 9 10 11 12 13 14 15 16 17 18 19 20 21 22 23 24

SUMMER ONLY (J)   WINTER ONLY (D)   JAMMING / OR ∧   EARLIEST HEARD ◁   LATEST HEARD ▷   NEW OR CHANGED FOR 1994 †

FREQUENCY   COUNTRY, STATION, LOCATION

TARGET • NETWORK • POWER (kW)

World Time

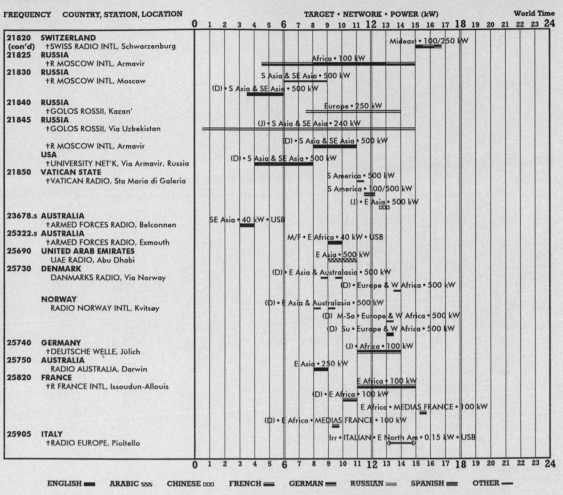

Frequency	Country, Station, Location	Target • Network • Power
21820 (con'd)	SWITZERLAND †SWISS RADIO INTL, Schwarzenburg	Mideas • 100/250 kW
21825	RUSSIA †R MOSCOW INTL, Armavir	Africa • 100 kW
21830	RUSSIA †R MOSCOW INTL, Moscow	S Asia & SE Asia • 500 kW / (D) • S Asia & SE Asia • 500 kW
21840	RUSSIA †GOLOS ROSSII, Kazan'	Europe • 250 kW
21845	RUSSIA †GOLOS ROSSII, Via Uzbekistan	(J) • S Asia & SE Asia • 240 kW
	†R MOSCOW INTL, Armavir	(D) • S Asia & SE Asia • 500 kW
	USA †UNIVERSITY NET'K, Via Armavir, Russia	(D) • S Asia & SE Asia • 500 kW
21850	VATICAN STATE †VATICAN RADIO, Sta Maria di Galeria	S America • 500 kW / S America • 100/500 kW / (J) • E Asia • 500 kW
23678.5	AUSTRALIA †ARMED FORCES RADIO, Belconnen	SE Asia • 40 kW • USB
25322.5	AUSTRALIA †ARMED FORCES RADIO, Exmouth	M/F • E Africa • 40 kW • USB
25690	UNITED ARAB EMIRATES UAE RADIO, Abu Dhabi	E Asia • 500 kW
25730	DENMARK DANMARKS RADIO, Via Norway	(D) • E Asia & Australasia • 500 kW / (D) • Europe & W Africa • 500 kW
	NORWAY RADIO NORWAY INTL, Kvitsøy	(D) • E Asia & Australasia • 500 kW / (D) M-Sa • Europe & W Africa • 500 kW / (D) Su • Europe & W Africa • 500 kW
25740	GERMANY †DEUTSCHE WELLE, Jülich	(J) • Africa • 100 kW
25750	AUSTRALIA RADIO AUSTRALIA, Darwin	E Asia • 250 kW
25820	FRANCE †R FRANCE INTL, Issoudun-Allouis	E Africa • 100 kW / (D) • E Africa • 100 kW / E Africa • MEDIAS FRANCE • 100 kW / (D) • E Africa • MEDIAS FRANCE • 100 kW
25905	ITALY †RADIO EUROPE, Pioltello	Irr • ITALIAN • E North Am • 0.15 kW • USB

ENGLISH ▬   ARABIC ⋙   CHINESE ☐☐☐   FRENCH ▬   GERMAN ▬   RUSSIAN ═   SPANISH ▬   OTHER ▬

Directory of Advertisers

Glossary

Terms and Abbreviations Used in World Band Radio

A wide variety of terms and abbreviations are used in world band radio. Some are specialized and may need explanation; several are foreign words that benefit from translation; and yet others are simply adaptations of common usage.

Here, then, is *Passport's* guide to what's what in world band buzzwords—including what each one means. For a thorough writeup on what determines how well a world band radio performs, please read the RDI White Paper, *How to Interpret Receiver Specifications and Lab Tests*.

Adjacent-Channel Rejection. *See* Selectivity.
AGC. *See* Automatic Gain Control.
Alt. Alternative frequency or channel. Frequency or channel that may be used unexpectedly in place of the regularly scheduled one.
Amateur Radio. *See* Hams.
AM Band. The local radio band, which currently runs from 520 to 1611 kHz (530–1705 kHz in the Western Hemisphere), within the Medium Frequency (MF) range of the radio spectrum. In many countries it is called the mediumwave (MW) band.
Analog Frequency Readout. Needle-and-dial tuning, greatly inferior to synthesized tuning for world band use. *See* Synthesizer.
Audio Quality, Audio Fidelity. *See* High Fidelity.
Automatic Gain Control (AGC). Smoothes out fluctuations in signal strength brought about by fading, a regular occurrence with world band signals.
AV. A Voz—Portuguese for "Voice of."
Bandwidth. The main variable to determine selectivity (*see*), bandwidth is the amount of radio signal at –6 dB a radio will let pass through, and thus be heard. With world band channel spacing at 5 kHz, the best single bandwidths are usually in the vicinity of 3 to 6 kHz. Better radios offer two or more selectable bandwidths: one of 5 to 7 kHz or so for when a station is in the clear, and one or more others between 2 to 4 kHz for when a station is hemmed in by other stations next to it. Proper selectivity is a key determinant of the aural quality of what you hear.
Baud. Rate by which radioteletype (*see*) is transmitted.
BC. Broadcasting, Broadcasting Company, Broadcasting Corporation.
Broadcast. A radio or TV transmission meant for the general public. *Compare* Utility Stations, Hams.
BS. Broadcasting Station, Broadcasting Service.
Cd. Ciudad—Spanish for "City."
Channel. An everyday term to indicate where a station is supposed to be located on the dial. World band channels are spaced exactly 5 kHz apart. Stations operating outside this norm are "off channel" (for these, *Passport* provides resolution to better than 1 kHz to aid in station identification).

Chugging. The sound made by some synthesized tuning systems when the tuning knob is turned. Called "chugging," as it is suggestive of the rhythmic "chug, chug" sound of a steam engine or chugalugging.
Cl. Club, Clube.
Cult. Cultura, Cultural.
(D). December. Heard winters only; not heard midyear.
Default. The setting a radio normally operates at, and to which it will eventually return.
Digital Frequency Display, Digital Tuning. *See* Synthesizer.
Domestic Service. *See* DS.
DS. Domestic Service—Broadcasting intended primarily for audiences in the broadcaster's home country. However, some domestic programs are relayed on world band to expatriates and other kinfolk abroad. *Compare* ES.
DXers. From an old telegraph term "to DX"; that is, to communicate over a great distance. Thus, DXers are those who specialize in finding distant or exotic stations. Few are considered to be regular DXers, but many others seek out DX stations every now and then, usually by bandscanning, which is facilitated by *Passport's* Blue Pages.
Dynamic Range. The ability of a receiver to handle weak signals in the presence of strong competing signals within the same world band segment (see World Band Spectrum). Sets with inferior dynamic range sometimes "overload," causing a mishmash of false signals mixed together up and down—and even beyond—the band segment being received.
Earliest Heard (or Latest Heard). See key at the bottom of each "Blue Page." If the *Passport* monitoring team cannot establish the definite sign-on (or sign-off) time of a station, the earliest (or latest) time that station could be traced is indicated, instead, by a triangular "flag." This means that the station almost certainly operates beyond the time shown by that "flag." It also means that, unless you live relatively close to the station, you're unlikely to be able to hear it beyond that "flagged" time.
ECSS. Exalted-carrier selectable sideband. *See* Synchronous Detector.
Ed, Educ. Educational , Educação, Educadora.
Em. Emissora, Emisora, Emissor, Emetteur—in effect, station in various languages.

Enhanced Fidelity. See High Fidelity.

EP. Emissor Provincial—Portuguese for "Provincial Station."

ER. Emissor Regional—Portuguese for "Regional Station."

Ergonomics. How handy and comfortable a set is to operate, especially hour after hour.

ES. External Service—Broadcasting intended primarily for audiences abroad. Compare DS.

External Service. See ES.

F. Friday.

Fax. See Radiofax.

Feeder. A utility station that transmits programs from the broadcaster's home country to a relay site some distance away. Although these specialized stations carry world band programming, they are not intended to be received by the general public. Many world band radios can process these quasi-broadcasts anyway. Feeders operate in lower sideband (LSB), upper sideband (USB) or independent sideband (termed ISL if heard on the lower side, ISU if heard on the upper side) modes. See Single Sideband, Utility Stations.

Frequency. The standard term to indicate where a station is located on the dial—regardless of whether it's "on-channel" or "off-channel" (see Channel). Measured in kilohertz (kHz) or Megahertz (MHz). Either measurement is equally valid, but to minimize confusion Passport designates frequencies only in kHz.

GMT. Greenwich Mean Time—See UTC.

Hams. Government-licensed amateur radio hobbyists who transmit to each other by radio, often by single sideband (see), for pleasure within special amateur bands. Many of these bands are within the shortwave spectrum (see). This is the same spectrum used by world band radio, but world band and ham radio are two very separate entities.

High Fidelity, Enhanced Fidelity. Radios with good audio performance and certain high-tech circuits can improve on the fidelity of world band reception. Among the newer fidelity-enhancing techniques is Synchronous Detection (see).

Image Rejection. A type of spurious-signal rejection (see).

Independent Sideband. See Single Sideband.

Interference. Sounds from other stations that are disturbing the one you're trying to hear. Worthy radios reduce interference by having good selectivity (see).

International Telecommunication Union (ITU). The regulatory body, headquartered in Geneva, for all international telecommunications, including world band radio.

Ionosphere. See Propagation.

Irr. Irregular operation or hours of operation; i.e., schedule tends to be unpredictable.

ISB. Independent sideband. See Single Sideband.

ISL. Independent sideband, lower. See Feeder.

ISU. Independent sideband, upper. See Feeder.

ITU. See International Telecommunication Union.

(J). June. Heard midyear only; not heard winters.

Jamming. Deliberate interference to a transmission with the intent of discouraging listening.

kHz. Kilohertz, the most common unit for measuring where a station is on the world band dial. Formerly known as "kilocycles/second." 1,000 kilohertz equals one Megahertz.

kW. Kilowatt(s), the most common unit of measurement for transmitter power (see).

LCD. Liquid-crystal display. LCDs, if properly designed, are fairly easily seen in bright light, but require sidelighting under darker conditions. LCDs, being gray on gray, also tend to have mediocre contrast, and sometimes can be seen from only a certain angle or angles, but they consume nearly no battery power.

LED. Light-emitting diode. LEDs are very easily seen in the dark or in normal room light, but consume battery power and are hard to see in bright light.

Loc. Local.

Location. The physical location of a station's transmitter, which may be different from the studio location. Transmitter location is useful as a guide to reception quality. For example, if you're in Eastern North America and wish to listen to Radio Moscow International, a transmitter located in St. Petersburg will almost certainly provide better reception than one located in Siberia.

Longwave Band. The 148.5–283.5 kHz portion of the low-frequency (LF) radio spectrum used in Europe, the Near East, North Africa, Russia and Mongolia for domestic broadcasting. In general, these longwave signals, which have nothing to do with world band or shortwave signals, are not audible in other parts of the world.

LSB. Lower Sideband. See Feeder, Single Sideband.

LV. La Voix, La Voz—French and Spanish for "The Voice."

M. Monday.

Mediumwave Band, Mediumwave AM Band. See AM Band.

Memory(ies). See Preset.

Meters. An outdated unit of measurement used for individual world band segments of the shortwave spectrum. The frequency range covered by a given meters designation—also known as "wavelength"—can be gleaned from the following formula: frequency (kHz) = 299,792/meters. Thus, 49 meters comes out to a frequency of 6118 kHz—well within the range of frequencies included in that segment (see World Band Spectrum). Inversely, meters can be derived from the following: meters = 299,792/frequency (kHz).

MHz. Megahertz, a common unit to measure where a station is on the dial. Formerly known as "Megacycles/second." One Megahertz equals 1,000 kilohertz.

Mode. Method of transmission of radio signals. World band radio broadcasts are almost always in the AM mode, the same that's also used in the mediumwave AM band. The AM mode consists of three components: two "sidebands" and one "carrier." Each sideband contains the same programming as the other, and the carrier carries no programming, so a few stations are experimenting with the single-sideband (SSB) mode. SSB contains only one sideband, either the lower sideband (LSB) or upper sideband (USB), and no carrier. It requires special radio circuitry to be demodulated, or made intelligible. There are yet other modes used on shortwave, but usually not for world band. These include CW (Morse-type code), radiofax, RTTY (radioteletype) and narrow-band FM used by utility and ham stations. Narrow-band FM is not used for music, and is different from usual FM. See Single Sideband, ISB, ISL, ISU, LSB and USB.

N. New, Nueva, Nuevo, Nouvelle, Nacional, National, Nationale.

Nac. Spanish and Portuguese for "Nacional."

Nat. Natl. National, Nationale.

Other. Programs are in a language other than one of the world's primary languages.

Overloading. See Dynamic Range.

PBS. People's Broadcasting Station.

Power. Transmitter power before amplification by the antenna, expressed in kilowatts (kW). The present range of world band powers is 0.01 to 1,000 kW.

PR. People's Republic.

Preset. Allows you to select a station pre-stored in a radio's memory. The handiest presets require only one push of a button, as on a car radio.

Propagation. World band signals travel, like a basketball, up and down from the station to your radio. The "floor" below is the earth's surface, whereas the "player's hand" on high is the ionosphere, a gaseous layer that envelops the earth. While the earth's surface remains pretty much the same from day to day, the ionosphere—nature's own passive "satellite"—varies in how it propagates radio signals, depending on how much sunlight hits the "bounce points."

Thus, some world band segments do well mainly by day, whereas others are best by night. During winter there's less sunlight, so the "night bands" become unusually active, whereas the "day bands" become correspondingly less useful (see World Band Spectrum). Day-to-day changes in the sun's weather also cause short-term changes in world band radio reception; this explains why some days you can hear rare signals.

Additionally, the 11-year sunspot cycle has a long-term effect on propagation. Currently, the sunspot cycle is moving into its trough. This means that while the upper world band segments will be less active than usual over the next few years, the lower segments will be even more active and strong.

PS. Provincial Station, Pangsong.

Pto. Puerto, Porto.

QSL. See Verification.

R. Radio, Radiodiffusion, Radiodifusora, Radiodifusão, Radiofonikos, Radiostantsiya, Radyo, Radyosu, and so forth.

Radiofax. Like ordinary fax-by-telephone, but by radio.

Radioteletype. Characters, but not illustrations, transmitted by radio. "Radio modem." See Baud.

Receiver. Synonym for a radio.

Reduced Carrier. See Single Sideband.

Reg. Regional.

Relay. A retransmission facility, shown in bold in "Worldwide Broadcasts in English" and "Voices from Home" in Passport's Worldscan section. Relay facilities are considered to be located outside the broadcaster's country. Being closer to the target audience, they usually provide superior reception. See Feeder.

Rep. Republic, République, República.

RN. See R and N.

RS. Radio Station, Radiostantsiya, Radiostudiya, Radiofonikos Stathmos.

RT, RTV. Radiodiffusion Télévision, Radio Télévision, and so forth.

RTTY. See Radioteletype.

S. San, Santa, Santo, São, Saint, Sainte. Also, South.

Sa. Saturday.

Scan, Scanning. Circuitry within a radio that allows it to band-scan or memory-scan automatically.

Selectivity. The ability of a radio to reject interference from signals on adjacent channels. Thus, also known as adjacent-channel rejection. A key variable in radio quality.

Sensitivity. The ability of a radio to receive weak signals. Also known as weak-signal sensitivity. Of special importance if you listening during the day, or if you're located in such parts of the world as Western North America and Australasia, where signals tend to be relatively weak.

Shortwave Spectrum. The shortwave spectrum—also known as the High Frequency (HF) spectrum—is, strictly speaking, that portion of the radio spectrum from 3-30 MHz (3,000-30,000 kHz). However, common usage places it from 2.3-30 MHz (2,000-30,000 kHz). World band operates on shortwave, but most of the shortwave spectrum is occupied by Hams (see) and Utility Stations (see)—not world band. Also, see World Band Spectrum.

Single Sideband, Independent Sideband. Spectrum- and power-conserving modes of transmission commonly used by utility stations and hams. Few broadcasters use these modes, but this may change early in the 21st century. Many world band radios are already capable of demodulating single-sideband transmissions, and some can even process independent-sideband transmissions. Certain single-sideband signals operate with reduced carrier, which allows them to be listened to, albeit with some distortion, on ordinary radios not equipped to demodulate single sideband. Properly designed synchronous detectors (see) prevent such distortion. See Feeder, Mode.

Site. See Location.

Slew Controls. Elevator-button-type up and down controls to tune a radio. On some radios with synthesized tuning, slewing is used in lieu of tuning by knob. Better is when slew controls are complemented by a tuning knob, which is more versatile.

SPR. Spurious (false) extra signal from a transmitter actually operating on another frequency.

Spurious-Signal Rejection. The ability of a radio receiver not to produce false, or "ghost," signals that might otherwise interfere with the clarity of the station you're trying to hear.

St, Sta, Sto. Abbreviations for words that mean "Saint."

Su. Sunday.

Synchronous Detector. World band radios are increasingly coming equipped with this high-tech circuit that greatly reduces fading distortion. Better synchronous detectors also allow for selectable sideband; that is, the ability to select the clearer of the two sidebands of a world band or other AM-mode signal. See Mode.

Synthesizer. Simple radios usually use archaic needle-and-dial tuning that makes it difficult to find a desired channel or to tell which station you are hearing, except by ear. Advanced models utilize a digital frequency synthesizer to tune in signals without your having to hunt and peck. Among other things, synthesizers allow for push-button tuning and presets, and display the exact frequency digitally—pluses that make tuning in the world considerably easier. Nearly a "must" feature.

Target. Where a transmission is beamed.

Th. Thursday.

Travel Power Lock. Control to disable the on/off switch to prevent a radio from switching on accidentally.

Transmitter Power. See Power.

Tu. Tuesday.

Universal Day. See UTC.

Universal Time. See UTC.

USB. Upper Sideband. See Feeder, Single Sideband.

UTC. Coordinated Universal Time, also known as World Time, Greenwich Mean Time and Zulu time. With nearly 170 countries on world band radio, if each announced its own local time you would need a calculator to figure it all out. To get around this, a single international time—UTC—is used. The difference between UTC and local time is detailed in the "Addresses PLUS" section of this Passport, or determined simply by listening to UTC announcements given on the hour by world band stations—or minute by minute by WWV and WWVH in the United States on such frequencies as 5000, 10000, 15000 and 20000 kHz. A 24-hour clock format is used, so "1800 UTC" means 6:00 PM UTC. If you're in, say, North America, Eastern Time is five hours behind UTC winters and four hours behind UTC summers, so 1800 UTC would be 1:00 PM EST or 2:00 PM EDT. The easiest solution is to use a 24-hour clock set to UTC. Many radios already have these built in, and UTC clocks are also available as accessories.

UTC also applies to the days of the week. So if it's 9:00 PM (21:00) Wednesday in New York during the winter, it's 0200 UTC Thursday World Day or Universal Day.

Utility Stations. Most signals within the shortwave spectrum are not world band stations. Rather, they are utility stations—radio telephones, ships at sea, aircraft and the like—that transmit strange sounds (growls, gurgles, dih-dah sounds and the like) point-to-point and are not intended to be heard by the general public. Compare Broadcast, Hams and Feeders.

v. Variable frequency; i.e., one that is unstable or drifting because of a transmitter malfunction.

Verification. A card or letter from a station verifying that a listener indeed heard that particular station. In order to stand a chance of qualifying for a verification card or letter, you need to provide the station heard with the following information in a three-number "SIO" code, in which "SIO 555" is best and "SIO 111" is worst:

- Signal strength, with 5 being of excellent quality, comparable to that of a local mediumwave AM station, and 1 being inaudible or at least so weak as to be virtually unintelligible. 2 (faint, but somewhat intelligible), 3 (moderate strength) and 4 (good strength) represent the signal-strength levels usually encountered with world band stations.
- Interference from other stations, with 5 indicating no interference whatsoever, and 1 indicating such extreme interference that the desired signal is virtually drowned out. 2 (heavy interference), 3 (moderate interference) and 4 (slight interference) represent the differing degrees of interference more typically encountered with world band signals. If possible, indicate the names of the interfering signal(s) and the channel(s) they are on. Otherwise, at least describe what the interference sounds like.
- Overall quality of the signal, with 5 being best, 1 worst.
- In addition to the SIO code, providing details of the programs heard, as well as comments on how you liked or disliked those programs, are especially welcomed. Refer to the "Addresses PLUS" section of this book for information on where and to whom your report should be sent, and whether return postage should be included.

Vo. Voice of.

W. Wednesday.

Wavelength. See Meters.

World Band Radio. Similar to regular mediumwave AM band and FM band radio, except that world band broadcasters can be heard over enormous distances and thus often carry news, music and entertainment programs created especially for audiences abroad. Some world band stations have audiences of over 100 million worldwide each day.

World Band Spectrum. See Best Times and Frequencies" box on last page.

World Day. See UTC.

World Time. See UTC.

WS. World Service.

Printed in USA

Best Times and Frequencies for 1994

With world band, if you dial around just any old place, you're almost as likely to get dead air as you are a favorite program. For one thing, a number of world band segments are alive and kicking by day, while others are nocturnal. For another, some fare better at specific times of the year.

Official and "Outside" Segments

Segments of the shortwave spectrum are set aside for world band radio by the International Telecommunication Union (*see*), headquartered in Geneva. However, the ITU also countenances some world band broadcasts outside these parameters. Stations operating within these "outside" portions tend to encounter less interference from competing broadcasters. However, as these portions are also shared with utility stations (*see*), they sometimes suffer from other forms of interference.

"Real-world" segments—those actually being used, regardless of official status—are shown in bold (e.g., **5800-6300 kHz**). These are where you should tune to hear world band programs. For the record, official ITU world band segments are shown in ordinary small type (e.g., 5950-6200 kHz).

What you'll actually hear will vary. It depends on your location, where the station is, the time of year, your radio, and so on (e.g., *see* Propagation). Although stations come in 24 hours a day, signals are usually best from around sunset until sometime after midnight. Too, try a couple of hours on either side of dawn.

Here, then, are the most attractive times and frequencies for world band listening, based on reception conditions forecast for the coming year.

Rare Reception

2 MHz (120 meters) **2300-2500 kHz**[1,2]
> ITU: 2300–2498 kHz[3] (Tropical domestic transmissions only)

Limited Reception Winter Nights

3 MHz (90 meters) **3200-3400 kHz**[1]
> ITU: 3200–3400 kHz (Tropical domestic transmissions only)

Good-to-Fair During Winter Nights in Europe and Asia

4 MHz (75 meters) **3900-4000 kHz**[4]
> ITU: 3900-3950 kHz (Asian & Pacific transmissions only)
> 3950-4000 kHz (European, African, Asian & Pacific transmissions only)

(continued on next page)

---

[1] Entire segment shared with utility stations for the time being.
[2] 2498-2505, 4995-5005, 9995-10005 and 14990-15005 kHz are reserved for standard time and frequency signals, such as WWV/WWVH.
[3] 2300-2495 kHz within Central and South America and the Caribbean.
[4] Shared with American ham stations.
[5] Expansion portions—5900-5950, 7300-7350, 9400-9500, 9775-9900, 11600-11700, 11975-12100, 15450-15800, 17480-17700 and 21750-21850 kHz—will continue to be shared with utility stations until these portions are made official for broadcasting.
[6] 7100-7300 kHz shared with American ham stations; 7300-7600 kHz shared with utility stations.
[7] Certain portions of the expanded segments may be implemented before April 2007, provided an appropriate frequency-planning procedure can be agreed upon and implemented by the ITU.

Best Times and Frequencies for 1994, Continued

Some Reception During Nights Except Spring

5 MHz (60 meters) **4700-5100 kHz**[1,2]
ITU: 4750–4995/5005-5060 kHz[2] (Tropical domestic transmissions only)

Excellent During Winter Nights
Good During Summer Nights
Regional Reception Daytime

6 MHz (49 meters) **5800-6300 kHz**
ITU: 5950–6200 kHz now, 5900-6200 kHz[5] from April 2007

Good During Nights Except Mid-Winter
Variable During Mid-Winter Nights
Regional Reception Daytime

7 MHz (41 meters) **7100-7600 kHz**[6]
ITU: 7100–7300 kHz now, 7100-7350 kHz[5] from April 2007
(No American-based transmissions below 7300 kHz)

Good During Summer Nights
Some Reception Daytime and Winter Nights
Good Asian and Pacific Reception Mornings in America

9 MHz (31 meters) **9020-9080 kHz/9250-10000 kHz**[2]
ITU: 9500–9775 kHz now, 9400-9900 kHz[5] from April 2007[7]

11 MHz (25 meters) **11500-12160 kHz**
ITU: 11700–11975 kHz now, 11600-12100 kHz[5] from April 2007[7]

Good During Daytime
Generally Good During Summer Nights

13 MHz (22 meters) **13570-13870 kHz**[1]
ITU: 13570-13870 kHz in full official use from April 2007[7]

15 MHz (19 meters) **15000-15800 kHz**[2]
ITU: 15100–15450 kHz now, 15100-15800 kHz[5] from April 2007[7]

17 MHz (16 meters) **17480-17900 kHz**
ITU: 17700–17900 kHz now, 17480-17900 kHz[5] from April 2007[7]

19 MHz (15 meters) **18900-19020 kHz**[1] (few stations for now)
ITU: 18900-19020 kHz in official use from April 2007

21 MHz (13 meters) **21450-21850 kHz**
ITU: 21450–21750 kHz now, 21450-21850 kHz[5] eventually

Variable, Limited Reception Daytime

25 MHz (11 meters) **25670-26100 kHz**
ITU: 25600–26100 kHz now, 25670-26100 kHz eventually

---

[1] Entire segment shared with utility stations for the time being.
[2] 2498-2505, 4995-5005, 9995-10005 and 14990-15005 kHz are reserved for standard time and frequency signals, such as WWV/WWVH.
[3] 2300-2495 kHz within Central and South America and the Caribbean.
[4] Shared with American ham stations.
[5] Expansion portions—5900-5950, 7300-7350, 9400-9500, 9775-9900, 11600-11700, 11975-12100, 15450-15800, 17480-17700 and 21750-21850 kHz—will continue to be shared with utility stations until these portions are made official for broadcasting.
[6] 7100-7300 kHz shared with American ham stations; 7300-7600 kHz shared with utility stations.
[7] Certain portions of the expanded segments may be implemented before April 2007, provided an appropriate frequency-planning procedure can be agreed upon and implemented by the ITU.